MW00787891

Introducing Ethics

A Critical Thinking Approach with Readings

Justin P. McBrayer

Peter J. Markie

New York   Oxford
OXFORD UNIVERSITY PRESS

Oxford University Press is a department of the University of Oxford.
It furthers the University's objective of excellence in research,
scholarship, and education by publishing worldwide.

Oxford   New York
Auckland   Cape Town   Dar es Salaam   Hong Kong   Karachi
Kuala Lumpur   Madrid   Melbourne   Mexico City   Nairobi
New Delhi   Shanghai   Taipei   Toronto

With offices in
Argentina   Austria   Brazil   Chile   Czech Republic   France   Greece
Guatemala   Hungary   Italy   Japan   Poland   Portugal   Singapore
South Korea   Switzerland   Thailand   Turkey   Ukraine   Vietnam

For titles covered by Section 112 of the US Higher Education
Opportunity Act, please visit www.oup.com/us/he for the latest
information about pricing and alternate formats.

Published by Oxford University Press
198 Madison Avenue, New York, New York 10016
www.oup.com

Oxford is a registered trademark of Oxford University Press.

Library of Congress Cataloging-in-Publication Data

McBrayer, Justin P.
Introducing ethics : a critical thinking approach with readings / Justin P. McBrayer, Peter J. Markie.
pages cm
ISBN 978-0-19-979378-5
1. Ethics. 2. Critical thinking. I. Title.
BJ1012.M27 2013
170--dc23
2013036372

Printing Number: 9 8 7 6 5 4 3 2 1

Printed in the United States of America
on acid-free paper

This book is dedicated to our respective children: Patrick and Aeneas; Elizabeth and Robert.

BRIEF CONTENTS

CONTENTS

The guiding premise of this book is that students should be taught to think critically about ethics for themselves. Many current ethics texts fail to cultivate critical thinking in this way. Commentaries carefully lay out and critique various ethical positions, leaving no work for a student to do. Anthologies contain difficult readings that the average student cannot digest.

This book is neither a commentary nor an anthology but a hybrid of both. The commentary portion of the text provides students with the tools and conceptual background to understand and critique an ethical position. The anthology portion of the text consists of new and classical readings in ethics that have been heavily edited to improve accessibility for students. Together these components arm students with the tools to do ethics for themselves. In particular, this text includes the following features:

- *Diverse Content*. This text includes units on metaethics, normative ethics, and applied ethics, making it suitable for a wide range of courses and flexible enough to meet a variety of course outcomes.
- *Logic and Moral Reasoning Primer*. The first unit of the text includes a short primer on logic that introduces the basic concepts of deductive and inductive reasoning as well as a short introduction to moral reasoning and moral epistemology.
- *How to Write and Read Philosophy*. The first unit of the text also includes a primer on how to write a philosophy paper and how to read philosophy.
- *Unit and Chapter Introductions*. Each new unit and chapter open with an accessibly written commentary that introduces the main themes and issues of the chapter without attempting to summarize or evaluate any of the readings that follow. The result is that students can see the "landscape" and understand

the importance of an issue by the time they approach the readings themselves.
- *Reading and Discussion Questions*. Each reading is preceded by a list of reading questions that are designed to guide the student's reading of the material. These questions are suitable for reading quizzes, etc. Each reading is also followed by a list of discussion questions that are designed to move the student into the evaluation phase of philosophy. These questions are suitable for opening class discussion, essay prompts, etc.
- *Edited Readings*. The reading selections have been heavily edited to include boldfaced terms, italics marking key arguments or moves, subheadings, etc. The result is a classic piece of philosophy that has been "partially digested" for students' consumption.
- *Argument Reconstruction Exercises*. Each anthologized reading is followed by a set of related argument reconstruction exercises in which the student is asked to identify the premises and conclusion of the inferential passage. Suggested reconstructions are provided in the answer key in the back of the book.
- *Glossary*. The text includes a glossary of key terms that are highlighted in bold throughout the text.

The textbook includes a number of ancillary materials, including an instructor's manual and a website. The instructor's manual includes sample syllabi, extended summaries of each reading, lecture outlines in PowerPoint, and a testbank with sample questions for each reading. The website includes flashcards for key terms, reading questions, web links to other media resources, etc.

We want this to be the very best textbook available for teaching students how to do ethics for themselves. We welcome feedback and criticism about how to improve the book. Please contact us at *jpmcbrayer@fortlewis.edu.*

This text has benefitted from the insight and wisdom of a number of philosophers, including Michael Bradley at Georgia Perimeter College, Sarah Conrad at the University of North Texas, Peter Cvek at St. Peter's College, Robert D'Amico at the University of Florida, Janet Davis at Marist College, Daniel Deen at Florida State University, Steven Duncan at Bellevue College, Joan Forry at Vanderbilt University, Dimitria Gatzia at the University of Akron, David Hammond at High Point University, Nathan Jun at Midwestern State University, Richard McGowan at Baylor University, Richard Musselwhite at North Carolina Central University, Marcella Norling at Orange Coast College, Dugald Owen at Fort Lewis College, David Przekupowski at San Antonio College, Sarah Roberts-Cady at Fort Lewis College, Brandon Schmidly at Evangel College, Ted Stryk at Roane State Community College, and Jerry Wallulis at the University of South Carolina. Thanks to all of you.

Thanks to Caleb Ontiveros Gabrielle Roman and Margaret Renault-Varian for assistance with the manuscript and Joel Kirkpatrick for administrative assistance. Finally, thanks to our editor, Robert Miller, and Emily Krupin at OUP. This project would have been impossible without their guidance, sage advice, and flexibility.

UNIT

Philosophy and
Methodology

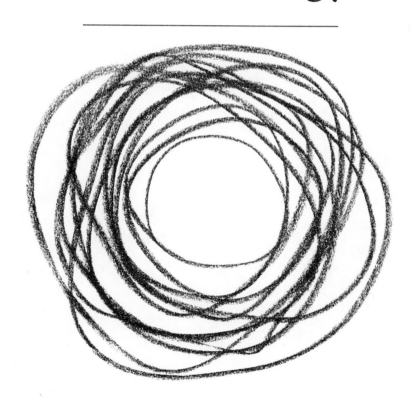

CHAPTER 1

Introductions

[T]he really important thing is not to live, but to live well... and to live well means the same thing as to live honorably or rightly..."

—SOCRATES, PLATO'S *CRITO*

INTRODUCTION

What is it to live honorably or rightly? We'll consider lots more questions before our study of ethics is done, but they will all be rooted in Socrates' basic concern.

Ethics is one branch of philosophy. There are others. In epistemology, philosophers investigate issues about the nature and extent of human knowledge and rational belief. Do we know anything at all? What is it to know, rather than merely believe, that something is true? How and to what extent can we gain knowledge? In metaphysics, philosophers investigate the fundamental nature of reality. Does reality contain non-physical or spiritual things as well as physical ones? Is there a God? Do we have non-physical minds that might survive the destruction of our bodies? Does the world, in addition to containing objective facts about what *is* the case, also contain objective facts about what *ought* to be the case? In logic, philosophers investigate the nature of reasoning and, in particular, how the truth of some claims can support or fail to support that of others. Consider these claims:

1. There is a finite distance between the tip of the arrow and the target.
2. To cross that finite distance, the tip of the arrow first has to cross half of it, and before crossing that half, it has to cross

half of it, and so on and so on an infinite number of times.

Does the obvious truth of these two claims support the truth of this one?

3. The arrow will never reach the target, as it will always have another distance to cross before getting there.

If (1) and (2) are true but (3) is false, where does the reasoning go wrong and why? That's the purview of logic.

So philosophy covers a lot of intellectual ground. In fact, the word "philosophy" comes from the Greek for "lover of wisdom." Philosophy is the search for *reasoned* answers to *important, non-empirical* questions about the nature and meaning of life. Each of these qualifiers is important. Philosophers don't value opinions or mere guesses. They want answers based on good reasons. And philosophers try not to waste time on questions that aren't of fundamental importance. Finally, philosophers are not trained to answer empirical questions—that's the job of scientists, psychologists, etc. Instead, philosophers focus on questions that can't be answered by science or any other empirical discipline.

Our concern here is not with philosophy in general but with ethics and Socrates' question. What is it to live rightly? Philosophers have responded to this question in three different ways. Some philosophers have focused on the various assumptions behind the question. For example, Socrates seems to assume both that his question has a correct answer and that we're capable of discovering it. Yet, perhaps there is no special way or set of ways in which we *ought* to live; there are just lots of different ways to live, each one of which is just as good, just as appropriate, as any other. And even if there is one particular way in which we ought to live our lives, how are we to discover it? Is it revealed to us by God, taught to us by others (How then are *they* to know it?), found through our own experiences of the world?

Socrates' concern also rests on a further assumption: we have some control over our lives. After all, there is no point to asking how the moon *should* orbit the earth—it has no choice in the matter. What makes Socrates think that we have a choice in how we live our lives? Perhaps our lives are already determined, as the philosopher Baron von Holbach puts it:

> Man's life is a line that nature commands him to describe upon the surface of the earth, without his ever being able to swerve from it, even for an instant.

Like so much of philosophy, answering Socrates' question leads to other background questions, and many philosophers working in ethics are concerned with these foundational issues.

Other philosophers respond to Socrates' question by implicitly accepting his background assumptions and proceeding to develop general theories of the right way to live. These theories are composed of fundamental principles that explain why some ways of living are better than others. Their suggestions are many and varied: we should live so as to best promote our own interest; we should live so as to best promote the good of all; we should live so as to develop and display certain virtues, such as courage, justice, honesty, and charity. The list goes on.

Still other philosophers take Socrates' question to heart with regard to particular areas of activity. Instead of attempting to formulate an answer that generalizes over all cases, these philosophers focus on particular issues. How should we live when it comes to the environment? Or when it comes to caring for the seriously ill, might euthanasia ever be appropriate? How should we live when it comes to meeting threats to our safety? Does the sort of life for which Socrates is searching have any room in it for torture, if it's necessary to save innocent lives?

We'll examine some of the best and most challenging proposals that philosophers have made in all three of these areas of ethics. We'll consider debates over the foundational assumptions behind Socrates' question. We'll examine some of the general theories that try to answer it. And we'll see how philosophers have answered Socrates' question with regard to such particular topics as the environment, abortion, famine relief, and torture.

Philosophy is personal. We all answer Socrates' question somewhat differently. Yet, there is more here to unite than divide us. We are bound together by the question itself. None of us gets out of this life without answering it—even refusing to consider the question is a way of answering it! Socrates' challenge, to his audience in ancient Greece and to us today, is to answer it on the basis of our common humanity, our common ability to reason, using a process of argument to sift through the different options and find the ones we've the best reasons to think are true. The readings here are a chance to do just that. Engage with the philosophers in this text. Read their essays carefully, evaluate their proposals, looking for good reasons to accept or reject them, and form your own view out of your evaluation of theirs. This process of rational discussion and argument in response to questions like Socrates' is how we develop ourselves as human beings.

CHAPTER 2

The Method of Philosophy

It is not enough to have a good mind; the main thing is to use it well.
—RENÉ DESCARTES (*DISCOURSE ON THE METHOD*)

INTRODUCTION

We saw in the last section that philosophy is a non-empirical discipline. Philosophy asks questions like the following:

1. Are we free?
2. Is there a God?
3. Do we know anything?
4. How ought we to act?
5. Do we have souls?

Look again at this list. How would you go about answering any of these questions? Are they the kinds of questions that you could answer by thinking hard about each question or do you have to do some research of some kind? If research would help, what kind of research would it be? Digging around in the dirt? Surveying people? Using litmus paper and test tubes?

The fact that none of these procedures would help to answer the questions shows that philosophy is a *non-empirical* discipline. Something is empirical if it is open to physical observation or testing. Philosophical claims are only indirectly related to anything that is observable or testable in this sense, and in this way it differs from other important disciplines. To answer a historical question, we read historical texts or do an archeological dig. To answer a social science question, we might conduct a survey to find out what people think. To answer a question in chemistry, we might set up an experiment in a lab. But notice that none of these options would help us answer the questions above. It's not as if we could use Bunsen burners and litmus paper to find out whether or not God exists. And it's not as if we could dig in the dirt, read ancient texts, or weigh ourselves to find out whether or not we have souls!

But if none of this sort of evidence is available, how can we ever make any progress in answering philosophical questions? Though philosophers cannot avail themselves of empirical tools when answering philosophical questions, there is a tool that is quite helpful in making headway in answering such questions, and that is the tool of logic. Philosophers use logic to sort good arguments from bad arguments and to construct careful lines of reasoning that give us reason to accept or reject competing answers to philosophical questions. So if you're going to learn how to do philosophy, you've got to learn some logic first.

2.1 ARGUMENTS AND LOGIC

Philosophers are preoccupied with arguments. This sounds strange at first because we normally think of an argument as a nasty altercation between two people, as in "I went home last weekend, and my mom and I had a big argument." But that's not how the term "argument" is used in philosophy. Instead, an argument is any set of statements in which some of the statements are used as assumptions in a case for some further statement. The assumptions are called 'premises.' The further statement is called the 'conclusion.' So an argument is a set of premises that are supposed to provide a reason to believe the conclusion.

Here's how arguments are connected with the philosophical questions we started with: when we're trying to answer philosophical questions, the answer that we should accept is the one that is supported by the best arguments. But saying that there can be a *best* argument indicates that arguments can be *better* or *worse*. What makes an argument a good one? This is where the tool of logic comes in handy. An argument is good any time it has both of the following features[1]:

1. All of the premises are true
2. The premises strongly support the conclusion

If all of the premises of a given argument are true and the premises strongly support the conclusion, then the argument is a good one.

We all have a pretty good handle on what it means for a statement to be true. A statement is true when it corresponds to the way the world really is. For example, the statement "Colin is wearing a sweater" is true just in case Colin is wearing a sweater. Of course, we'd have to specify which Colin we were talking about, but after we made the sentence precise, we'd see that the statement would be true just in case it accurately described the way the world happened to be at that time. So an argument meets the first condition of a good argument just in case all of its premises accurately describe the way the world really is.

But what does it mean for the premises to "strongly support" the conclusion? This relation between the premises and the conclusion is often described in various ways: the premises "lead" to the conclusion, the premises imply the conclusion, the premises provide a reason for the conclusion, etc. We may describe the relationship in a conditional way: If the premises are true, will they provide us with a good reason for thinking that the conclusion is true? If so, then the premises strongly support the conclusion. If not, they don't.

Now it should be obvious why there are two conditions for a good argument. If an argument meets the second condition, then we know that *if* the premises are true that we'll have a reason for thinking the conclusion is true. And if the argument also meets the first condition, then we know that all the premises *are* true. Thus the argument provides us with a reason for thinking the conclusion is true. It is a good argument.

The remainder of this chapter will explain the various ways that a set of premises can support a conclusion. The premises can guarantee that the conclusion is true (deductive arguments), make the conclusion likely without guaranteeing it (inductive arguments), or not make the conclusion any more likely at all (fallacious arguments). Thus, all arguments can be divided up in the following way:

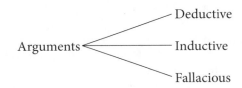

We'll take a closer look at all three types of argument below.

2.2 DEDUCTIVE ARGUMENTS

An argument is **deductive** when the premises support the conclusion in the following way: If all the premises are true, the conclusion must be true. The form of a deductive argument guarantees that if you start with truth, you end up with truth. Philosophers call this kind of guarantee *validity*.

An argument is **valid** just in case *if* all of its premises are true, *then* its conclusion must also be true.

Given this definition, it's easy to see that every argument is either valid or invalid. There are no other options. Two things are important to notice. First, validity is a concept that applies to arguments as a whole, not to individual premises. It doesn't make any sense to say that a premise is valid (or invalid). Similarly, it doesn't make any sense to say that an argument as a whole is true (or false).

Second, validity does not require that the premises be actually true. One could have a valid argument with false premises. Instead, validity refers to the logical relationship between the premises and the conclusion. Is it at least *possible* for all of the premises to be true while the conclusion is false? If so, the argument is invalid. Consider the following example:

1. If the moon is made of green cheese, then it smells bad.
2. The moon is made of green cheese.
3. Therefore, the moon smells bad.

Is this argument valid? Yes. If (1) and (2) are true, (3) has to be true, too. And this fact is compatible with the fact that (2) is actually false. The moon is not made of green cheese. In this case the conclusion is false, too: the moon doesn't actually smell bad. But the argument is valid nonetheless.

Consider another example:

1. If a city is in Kentucky, then it is in the USA.
2. Paris is not in Kentucky.
3. Therefore, Paris is not in the USA.

Unlike the previous argument, each of these premises is true and the conclusion is true as well. Is it valid? No. It's not valid because the truth of (1) and (2) wouldn't guarantee that (3) is true. Think of it this way: if someone were trying to convince you that a particular city is not in the USA, would it help to be told both that if that city is in Kentucky, then it's in the USA

and that the particular city is not in Kentucky? No way! That's because even if both of those claims are true, they give you no good reason to conclude that the city is not in the USA—perhaps, for example, it's in a part of the USA that is outside of Kentucky.

How do we apply the two conditions of a good argument to deductive arguments? First, any argument that is valid will meet condition two. The premises support the conclusion. So if all of the premises are true, the argument will meet condition one as well. If this happens, the argument is *sound*.

An argument is **sound** just in case it is valid and has all true premises.

If you find out that an argument is sound, you thereby know that it is a good argument.

Philosophers have used logic to identify particular patterns of argument that are always valid. Let's look at two of these forms that will play a big part of the arguments in this book. First is a pattern called **modus ponens**. *Modus ponens* is Latin for something like "in the mode of affirming." As such, *modus ponens* arguments affirm that something is the case. Here is an example:

1. If Adam graduated, then Adam took a biology course.
2. Adam graduated.
3. Therefore, Adam took a biology course.

This is a *modus ponens* argument. Notice that the second premise of this argument affirms that something is the case (namely, that Adam graduated). If we symbolize the statement "Adam graduated" as A and "Adam took a biology course" as B, we can symbolize the entire argument as follows:

1. If A, then B.
2. A.
3. Therefore, B.

Every *modus ponens* argument follows this same form. If you find that an argument can be symbolized in this same form, it is a valid instance of a *modus ponens*.

But not every argument with an if–then state-ment and an affirmation is a *modus ponens*. Consider the following argument:

1. If Adam graduated, then Adam took a biology course.
2. Adam took a biology course.
3. Therefore, Adam graduated.

This argument is invalid, and thus is not a *modus ponens* despite the fact that it contains an if–then statement and the fact that the second premise affirms that something is the case. The argument can be symbolized as follows:

1. If A, then B.
2. B.
3. Therefore, A.

This argument is a fallacy. It affirms the wrong thing. Logicians call this the fallacy of affirm-ing the consequent because instead of affirm-ing the *antecedent* of the if–then statement, this argument affirms the *consequent* of the if–then statement. Even if it were true that if Adam grad-uated, then he took a biology course and that he took a biology course, we can't yet conclude that he actually graduated. Perhaps he took biology but failed some other requirement for gradua-tion. Keep in mind that a *modus ponens* argu-ment supports its conclusion by affirming the first part of the if–then statement (the antecedent) and not the second part (the consequent).

The second pattern that is important to learn is a pattern called **modus tollens**. *Modus tollens* is Latin for something like "in the mode of deny-ing." As such, *modus tollens* arguments deny that something is the case. Here is an example:

1. If Adam graduated, then Adam took a biology course.
2. It is not the case that Adam took a biology course.
3. Therefore, it is not the case that Adam graduated.

This is a *modus tollens* argument. Notice that the second premise of this argument denies that something is the case (namely, that Adam took

a biology course). If we symbolize the statement "Adam graduated" as A and "Adam took a biol-ogy course" as B, we can symbolize the entire argument as follows:

1. If A, then B.
2. It is not the case that B.
3. Therefore, it is not the case that A.

Every *modus tollens* argument follows this same form. If you find that an argument can be sym-bolized to this same form, it is a valid instance of a *modus tollens*.

But not every argument with an if–then state-ment and a denial is a *modus tollens*. Consider the following argument:

1. If Adam graduated, then Adam took a biology course.
2. It is not the case that Adam graduated.
3. Therefore, it is not the case that Adam took a biology course.

This argument is invalid, and thus is not a *modus tollens* despite the fact that it contains an if–then statement and the fact that the second premise denies that something is the case. The argument can be symbolized as follows:

1. If A, then B.
2. It is not the case that A.
3. Therefore, it is not the case that B.

This argument is a fallacy. It denies the wrong thing. Logicians call this the fallacy of denying the antecedent because instead of denying the *consequent* of the if–then statement, this argu-ment denies the *antecedent* of the if–then state-ment. Even if it were true that if Adam graduated, then he took a biology course and that he didn't graduate, we can't yet conclude that he hasn't had a biology course. Perhaps he took biology but failed some other requirement for graduation. Keep in mind that a *modus tollens* argument sup-ports its conclusion by denying the second part of the if–then statement (the consequent) and not the first part (the antecedent).

There are literally an infinite number of valid argument forms besides *modus ponens* and *modus tollens*. Obviously you can't memorize all of them. However, here's a handy tool that often helps to determine whether or not an argument is valid. The tool is called a **counterexample**, and a counterexample is an instance of an argument form in which all of the premises are true but the conclusion is false. If you can successfully construct a counterexample to any argument, then you can conclude that any argument with that same form is invalid. Here's an example:

1. No Democrats are Christians.
2. All Christians are moral.
3. Therefore, no Democrats are moral.

Don't focus on whether or not the premises are true. The question at present is whether or not the argument is valid. If (1) and (2) were true, would that give us a reason for thinking that (3) is true? In other words, is the argument valid? Suppose it were true that no Democrats are Christians and that all Christians are moral. Could we safely conclude that no Democrats are moral? It's hard to tell since this argument is not in the form of either a *modus ponens* or a *modus tollens*. Let's try to construct a counterexample. First, let's symbolize the argument so that we can see its form. Let D stand for Democrat, C for Christian and M for moral. The argument's form is as follows:

1. No D are C.
2. All C are M.
3. So, no D are M.

How can we tell whether or not this argument form is valid? Well, if we can construct a case in which both (1) and (2) are true but (3) is false, then we've constructed a counterexample. And a counterexample shows that any argument of this form—including the one we started with—is invalid. Here's a simple counterexample: let D stand for dog, C for cat, and M for mammal. The new argument would go as follows:

1. No dogs are cats.
2. All cats are mammals.
3. So, no dogs are mammals.

In this case, both (1) and (2) are true. No dog is a cat, and all cats are mammals. But (3) is false because dogs are mammals. Thus we have a counterexample to our original argument: it is possible for all of the premises to be true but the conclusion false. The original argument is invalid—it provides us with no reason for thinking that no Democrats are moral.

2.3 INDUCTIVE ARGUMENTS

An argument is **inductive** when its premises support its conclusion in the following way: If all the premises are true, then it is more likely (though not guaranteed) that the conclusion is true. Inductive arguments are weaker than deductive arguments in the following respect: deductive arguments are such that true premises *guarantee* a true conclusion, whereas inductive arguments are such that true premises merely make the conclusion more likely. Though not as strong as deductive arguments, inductive arguments can still be good arguments.

Recall that for deductive arguments, the relationship between the premises and the conclusion had a particular name: validity. There is also a terminology that describes the relationship between the premises and the conclusion for inductive arguments. However, unlike with deductive arguments, the relationship for inductive arguments is of two sorts: weak and strong.

An argument is **weak** just in case the truth of the premises makes the conclusion more likely (but not more likely than not) but without guaranteeing it.

An argument is **strong** just in case the truth of the premises makes the conclusion more likely than not but without guaranteeing it.

With a weak argument, finding out that all of the premises are true gives one some reason to accept the conclusion, but not very much reason. Here is an example of a weak argument:

1. The weather forecast calls for a 30% chance of rain tomorrow.
2. Therefore, it will rain tomorrow.

Even if it were true that the weather forecast called for a 30% chance of rain tomorrow, that would not give you very good reason for thinking that it will rain tomorrow. However, it does provide a slight reason to think that it will rain tomorrow. For this reason, the argument is weak. How about this one:

1. Both of the GM cars that I've owned were lemons.
2. Therefore, all GM cars are lemons.

This argument is also very weak. The fact that two out of several million cars were lemons provides only a very, very slight reason to think that all such cars are lemons.

But inductive arguments can be stronger than this. Consider this one:

1. 90% of people are right-handed.
2. Christy is a person.
3. Therefore, Christy is right-handed.

This argument is strong. If both (1) and (2) are true, then you have powerful reason for accepting (3) as true as well. Note, however, that the truth of (1) and (2) don't guarantee the truth of (3). Perhaps Christy is in the lucky 10% who are left-handed. In other words, it's possible that (1) and (2) are true while (3) is false. For this reason, the argument is invalid (though strong).

How do we apply the two conditions of a good argument to inductive arguments? First, any inductive argument will support the conclusion at least slightly. That's because all inductive arguments are either weak or strong, and even weak arguments support their conclusions weakly. This is why in our criteria for a good argument we specified that the premises need to *strongly* support the conclusion. And only valid or strong arguments will provide that kind of support. Thus, if an inductive argument is strong, it will meet the second condition of a good argument: the premises will strongly support the conclusion. So if all of the premises of a strong argument are true, the argument will meet the first condition as well. If this happens, the argument is *cogent*.

An argument is **cogent** just in case it is strong and has all true premises.

If an argument is cogent, then it is a good argument. It has all true premises and the relation between the premises and the conclusion is such that if all the premises are true, it is more likely than not that the conclusion is true.

If you're concerned that inductive arguments might not be good enough for philosophy, note that most everything done in both the sciences and everyday life is the result of inductive inferences. Scientists notice that doing A results in B, and they naturally conclude that A causes B. Inferences in everyday life are much the same: the last 10 times you ate mushrooms you had an allergic reaction, so you naturally conclude that you're allergic to mushrooms. Notice that your reasoning doesn't guarantee that you're allergic to the mushrooms—perhaps it was something else you ate along with them—but it sure gives you a good reason to think that you're allergic to mushrooms.

One form of inductive argument in particular deserves to be mentioned. It is called an inference to the best explanation. Suppose you were a detective working at a crime scene. You find Jones' fingerprints at the scene as well as his DNA. You have good reason to believe that he would benefit from the crime. When questioned, Jones has no reliable alibi. He also has a criminal record of doing precisely what was done in this scenario. Furthermore, you have no other leads or ideas of who could have committed the crime. You naturally come to believe that Jones is guilty.

This is an example of inductive reasoning. In this case, we have a host of data and only one plausible way of explaining the data. Thus we conclude that our explanation is correct. We could make the argument more formal in the following way:

1. The data: Jones' fingerprints were at the scene, Jones' DNA was at the scene, Jones would have benefitted from the crime, Jones has no reliable alibi, Jones has a criminal record, etc.

2. The best explanation for the data: Jones committed the crime.
3. Therefore, Jones committed the crime.

The facts of the case constitute the data that we are trying to explain. The best way that we know how to explain the data is by assuming that Jones committed the crime. And it is quite reasonable to believe the best explanation for a set of data. Therefore, it is reasonable to think that Jones committed the crime. Of course, it is at least possible that both of these premises are true and that Jones is actually innocent. Inductive arguments are risky in that way. However, the facts of the case do make it more likely than not that Jones committed the crime.

Thinking carefully about inferences to the best explanation naturally prompts two questions:

1. What makes an explanation the best?
2. Why is it reasonable to think that the best explanation is true?

Philosophers have spilled a great deal of ink answering both questions. While there is much to say, for our purposes we may note two things. First, there are a variety of factors that affect the quality of an explanation. For example, a simpler explanation that posited the existence of only one criminal would be better than a more complex one that posited the existence of two dozen criminals. And while there will certainly be hard cases, we can all tell when an explanation is better than another in a great range of cases. Second, most of us already think that it is reasonable to accept the best explanation in other walks of life (e.g., in criminal work, science, etc.), and if we do, then we should be willing to accept arguments from the best explanation in ethics, too.

You are now at a point where you can see how deductive and inductive arguments relate to one another. Consider the following analogy:

Validity :: Strength

Soundness :: Cogency

Validity describes the logical relationship between the premises and the conclusion of a deductive argument. Strength describes the logical relationship between the premises and the conclusion of a strong inductive argument. Validity is required for a deductive argument to be sound. Strength is required for an inductive argument to be cogent. And all good arguments are either sound or cogent.

2.4 FALLACIOUS ARGUMENTS

An argument is fallacious when its premises do *not* support its conclusion. In other words, fallacious arguments fail the second condition on a good argument. If you find out that a particular argument is a fallacy, you can conclude that it is a bad argument. We saw a couple of examples of fallacies in the section on deductive arguments. Here's one with a different structure:

1. There is a lot of disagreement over whether or not the Earth's atmosphere is slowly getting warmer.
2. Therefore, there is no global warming.

This argument is a fallacy because the premise doesn't support the conclusion. To see this, suppose that the premise is true. Would that guarantee the truth of the conclusion? No. Would it even make the conclusion more likely? No. At best, if the premise is true we ought to be agnostic about the conclusion (i.e., neither affirm nor deny that there is global warming). But the mere fact that people disagree about a claim does not give us a reason to deny the claim. Thus the argument is a fallacy.

Here's another:

1. You can get into the club only if you're 21 years old or older.
2. Amanda is 21 years old.
3. Therefore, Amanda can get into the club.

At first glance, this argument looks like a deductive argument rather than a fallacy. But it's not. Suppose it's true that you have to be 21 to get into the club. And suppose that it's true that Amanda is 21. Does it follow from these two facts *alone* that Amanda can get into the club? No. Suppose, for example, that the club required a cover charge but that Amanda doesn't have enough money. In that case, both premises would be true but the conclusion would be false. The argument is thus an instance of a counterexample and is fallacious. Even if both premises were true, they don't, all by themselves, give you a reason for endorsing the conclusion.

So when evaluating an argument, it's important to examine the structure of the argument and not just the truth value of its assumptions. As shown above, an argument might have premises that are true and yet still offer no reason to believe the conclusion. Keep this in mind for the readings to come—just because you agree with the author's assumptions or premises doesn't mean that you should agree with his conclusion as well!

2.5 CONDITIONS AND ANALYSIS

In the final argument from the last section, premise (1) asserts that being 21 years old is a *necessary* condition for getting into the club, but the conclusion follows only if being 21 years old is a *sufficient* condition. In order to be mindful of fallacious arguments such as this, it is helpful to get clear on the difference between these two sorts of conditions.

Have you ever been presented with a hypothetical situation? Suppose you come home and your roommate says the following: "Hypothetically speaking, if your roommate accidentally crashed your computer, would you be mad?" What your roommate is asking is this: "if it were the case that I crashed your computer, would you be mad?" She puts it this way to avoid actually claiming to have crashed your computer. Instead, she phrases her question as a hypothetical.

In English, hypotheticals are expressed as conditional statements. A conditional statement often uses an 'if' and a 'then' as in the following:

If you are in Paris, then you are in France.

This statement is true even if you aren't currently in France. That's because it doesn't assert that you are in France. It says only that *if* you are in

Paris, *then* you're also in France. In other words, you are in France conditional on your being in Paris. And that is true regardless of where you actually happen to be at present. The *if* portion of the conditional statement ('you are in Paris') is called the antecedent because it comes first. The *then* portion of the conditional statement ('you are in France') is called the consequent because it comes after the antecedent.

Here is why this terminology is important: the **antecedent** is always a **sufficient** condition for the consequent, and the **consequent** is always a **necessary** condition for the antecedent. In the example above, being in Paris is a sufficient condition for being in France. Any time you're in Paris, you're in France. And being in France is a necessary condition for being in Paris. You can't be in Paris without also being in France. See if you can correctly identify the following types of conditions:

Being at least 35 years old is a _____ condition for being president of the USA.

Stealing a test is a _____ condition for being a cheater.

Chewing with your mouth open is a _____ condition for being rude.

Buying a lottery ticket is a _____ condition for winning the lottery.

Is being at least 35 years old a necessary or sufficient condition for being president? It's a necessary condition. If it were a sufficient condition, then everyone who is at least 35 would be president! Translated as a conditional statement, this claim would look like this: "If a person is president, then that person is at least 35 years old." How about stealing a test? This is sufficient for being a cheater, but it's not necessary. You could, for example, sneak answers into an exam period and qualify as a cheater. Similarly, chewing with your mouth open is a sufficient condition for being rude, but it's not necessary—there are lots of things you could do that would count as being rude! Lastly, buying a lottery ticket is necessary for winning the lottery but (alas) it isn't sufficient.

Be cautious about how you translate English statements into conditional form. In the if–then form, it's easy to identify the antecedent and consequent. But while it's true that the antecedent is always the sufficient condition for the consequent, in other translations it's not always obvious which clause is the antecedent clause. Where P and Q stand for independent clauses, here are some tips to keep translations straight:

P only if Q.	translated: If P, then Q.
P if Q.	translated: If Q, then P.
P unless Q	translated: If it's not the case that Q, then P.
P if and only if Q.	translated: If P, then Q AND if Q, then P.
P just in case Q	translated: If P, then Q AND if Q, then P.

One final point will be helpful going forward. At many places in our discussion we will be looking for an **analysis** of a concept. In particular, various authors will try to analyze some of the concepts that play central roles in ethics. Concepts are our way of carving up the world into understandable pieces. For example, we have the concepts of a table, a molecule, and a bachelor. Suppose we wanted to analyze the concept of a bachelor. To do so, we would want to know all and only the conditions something has to meet to be properly classified as a bachelor. We would want to fill in the following blank:

> A person is a bachelor if and only if _____.

As noted above, the English construction 'if and only if' serves as shorthand for two conditional statements:

> If a person is a bachelor, then that person is _____.
>
> and
>
> If a person is _____, then that person is a bachelor.

So to analyze a concept is to provide both the necessary AND sufficient conditions for the proper application of that concept. In the case of the concept 'bachelor,' a successful analysis would give us the necessary and sufficient conditions for someone's being a bachelor. Here is a full analysis of bachelor:

> A person is a bachelor if and only if that person is an unmarried male.

Now obviously we won't worry too much with bachelorhood in this text. But we will deal closely with a number of important ethical concepts. For example, a central question in the second part of the book will be the following analysis:

> An act is morally wrong if and only if _____.

Here the analysis is of the concept 'morally wrong.' Filling in this blank—and hence providing an analysis—requires that we identify the necessary and sufficient conditions for an action's being morally wrong. If we can do so successfully, then we have successfully analyzed the concept. Unit 3 of this text will entertain different ways of filling in this blank.

2.6 MORAL REASONING

Our study of ethics is motivated by more than idle curiosity. This unit opened with Socrates' famous dictum from the *Crito* we are concerned with living honourably and rightly. As rational agents, we strive to act on good reasons, and our reasons sometimes include our moral beliefs. We act one way rather than another because we believe that the one way is morally required and the other is morally wrong. Yet our moral beliefs provide us with good reasons for our actions only if they too are rational. Mere guesses or unthinking prejudices hardly support rational action. How then do we go about forming moral beliefs that are rational? There's a quick answer: Base your moral beliefs on good reasons, and they will be rational. But what counts as a good reason for a moral belief?

The question is difficult and even controversial in itself, for, as we'll see in the readings to follow, some philosophers question the very existence of rational moral beliefs. For now though, let's put that controversy on the back burner. Assume that we can have rational moral beliefs and need them to act rationally. How do we best form them?

Consider a simple case of moral reasoning, based on an example given by the philosopher James Rachels (*The Right Thing to Do*). Suppose some students take a test. The test is so poorly designed that no one, not even the most excellent student, could possibly complete it in the time allowed, yet the test must be completed for a passing grade. The questions on the test do not concern the assigned material covered in the class lectures and readings. They deal with matters barely related to the course material. Most of the questions are so poorly written as to make it impossible to determine what is being asked. Given all this, the students complain to the professor that the test is unfair. They back up their complaint by citing the points just listed. They form a moral belief—that the test was unfair—and their belief is quite rational, for it is based on established and obviously good reasons. The points about the exam that they cite in presenting their complaint are both known to be true and good reasons for them, and anyone else, to believe that the exam is unfair.

This is, of course, an easy case. The exam's defects are known, and the concept of an unfair exam is clear enough to make it obvious that those defects are good reasons to think it is unfair. The exam also lacks any counterbalancing features that count in favor of its being fair, so the students don't face the task of balancing competing reasons against one another. Other cases are not so easy. Is it morally right for the state to execute someone who has been correctly convicted of a horrific murder? In this case, our concept of a morally right or permissible punishment is not so clear as to make it obvious what counts as a good reason to believe one way or the other. Suppose that, before she died, the victim forgave

the murderer and asked that he not be executed. Is this a good reason to believe that execution is wrong? If the death penalty were shown to be a strong deterrent against violent crimes, would that fact then be a good reason to believe that this execution is right? Are considerations about the murderer's age and abusive upbringing good reasons on one side or the other? Moreover, even if we can identify the various good reasons for or against the belief that the execution is right, can we then establish that the belief is true? Assuming that the deterrent value of the death penalty is a relevant reason, can we establish what that deterrent value is? Finally, once we establish the good reasons for and against the moral permissibility of the execution, how are we to weigh them to form a rational belief on the matter? In short, the task of forming a rational moral belief is not so easy in this case. Our concept of a morally permissible punishment is not so clear as to make it obvious what the relevant considerations are. It is hard to know whether some of the *apparently* relevant considerations are *genuinely* relevant. The proper balance between competing considerations eludes us. All of this is, of course, why the issue of capital punishment remains controversial.

It is helpful at this point to separate some of the issues at hand. Three different questions apply to both the exam and the capital punishment cases:

First, what are the considerations that, if true, count for or against a particular moral belief in the case (e.g., that the exam is unfair; that the execution is right)?

Second, how are the considerations for and against the belief to be weighed?

Third, how are we to establish the non-moral facts of the case that might be relevant (e.g., that the exam did not cover the course material; that capital punishment deters violent crimes)?

The third issue is an issue about how we come to know about the world in general. We can set this issue aside to be dealt with by the best theory, whatever it is, of how we can gain non-moral knowledge of the world. But what about the first two? How, in seeking to form a rational moral belief, can we determine the morally relevant considerations and their relative weights?

Moral reasons are generalizable. If the fact that this exam did not cover the course material is a good reason to think it was unfair, then the same is true of any other exam. If the fact that this murderer is less than sixteen years old is a good reason to believe that his execution is morally wrong, the same holds for any other murderer. Similarly, if, in this particular case, a combination of reasons to think that execution is morally wrong outweighs another set of reasons to think that it is morally right, then the same goes for other cases to which the same sets of reasons apply. Our rational moral beliefs are in this way principled. When we judge that certain features of the exam make it unfair, we commit ourselves to the view that any other exam with exactly the same features is also unfair. When we judge that a particular act of capital punishment is morally wrong because it has certain features, we commit ourselves to the view that any other act of capital punishment with exactly the same features is also morally wrong. Perhaps the most basic element of morality is the idea that like cases should be treated alike.

This gives us a way to approach some of the cases in which the relevant moral reasons and their varying weights are unclear. To see if a particular feature of an act is a good reason in support of its having a particular moral quality, we can apply a generality test: Is this feature, in general, a good reason to think that acts that have it also have that moral quality? Suppose I don't feel like keeping a promise to a friend. Is this a good reason in support of my moral belief that it is permissible for me to break the promise? It is, only if the fact that someone else doesn't feel like keeping her promise is a good reason in support of the belief that she is not obligated to keep it. Is it a strong enough reason to outweigh my reasons to think to think that I am obligated to keep the promise (e.g., that breaking it will harm my friend)? It is, only if the same is true in the other cases as well.

We can apply the generality test in particular cases to help determine the good reasons for and against a particular moral belief and their relative weights, but it would be helpful to have a more broad sense of what sorts of considerations are good reasons for and against moral beliefs. We would then have a general perspective from which to examine and form beliefs about various moral issues. This is where moral theorizing comes into play. Insofar as we develop our concept of a morally right punishment, we will gain a better sense of the good reasons for or against the belief that a particular punishment is right and their relative weights. The same is true for our concept of a morally right action in general and other moral concepts such as fairness and justice.

We develop our moral concepts through constructing moral theories. When philosophers construct moral theories about the nature of various moral qualities such as moral rightness and justice, they are seeking to determine, in general terms, what features make something have those qualities. What features of morally right actions make them morally right? What features of just social practices make them just? The features of an act that give it a certain moral quality are among the very features that provide us with a good reason to think that it has that quality. If morally permissible systems of punishment are permissible, in part, because they deter crimes, then the deterrent value of a particular system of capital punishment is a good reason to think that it is morally permissible. If they are permissible, in part, because they require criminals to repay a debt to their victims, then the fact that a victim has waived repayment is good reason to think the punishment is wrong. Moral theorizing about what features of actions give them various moral qualities is one good way to develop our awareness of what counts as good moral reasons and how various reasons relate to one another.

Our attempt to determine good reasons for our moral beliefs thus leads us to the activity of constructing moral theories. Yet, this may not seem to get us very far. There are, as we shall soon see, lots of different moral theories, offering lots of different accounts of what makes actions have various moral properties. There are thus lots of different accounts of good reasons for moral beliefs in the presence or absence of those qualities. Haven't we just traded the question of how to form rational moral beliefs about particular cases (e.g., the permissibility of a particular act of capital punishment) for the question of how to form rational beliefs about the correctness of competing moral theories? The answer is that we have. Fortunately, we have a method for evaluating moral theories. It has come to be called the method of **reflective equilibrium**.

The moral theories we are going to examine all present us with principles about what makes acts, either in general or of a particular sort, have some specific moral property. **Act-Utilitarianism** presents us with a principle about what makes actions in general morally right rather than wrong: an act is right just so long as it produces more net good in the world than any available alternative. **Retributivism** presents us with a principle about what makes acts of punishment morally right: an act of punishment is right only if the person punished is responsible for committing a crime and the punishment fits the crime. We can test these theories by examining what their general principles imply both for our theoretical moral commitments and for particular moral cases. This allows us to reflectively balance our commitments to moral generalizations or theory (e.g., like cases should be treated alike) with our commitments to particular moral cases (e.g., it is not morally permissible to torture children for fun).

We can start with the cases of which we are most confident. Do a theory's implications match our most confident moral judgments? Do the general principles of the theory explain those moral judgments in a plausible fashion? If a theory captures our most confident moral judgments and presents a plausible explanation of what makes those judgments correct, that fact gives us some reason to think that the theory is correct. If the theory does not do this, then that fact gives us some reason to think the theory is mistaken. If a theory of the morality of punishment captures, and gives a plausible explanation of, the truth of our moral judgment that using torture as punishment is wrong, that's a point in its favor. If it fails to do so, that's a strong reason to think it's mistaken. Whether or not a theory of fairness captures our judgment that the exam in our first case is unfair gives us good reason to accept or reject the theory.

We can also extend the testing process by examining the implications of a theory's general principles for cases that perplex us. Does the theory shed light on these difficult cases, highlighting their primary moral features in a plausible way? In this way, we can see how well each theory not only captures and explains our most confident moral convictions but also extends our moral understanding to cases of which we are unsure. That a theory does well in this regard is again a good reason to accept it.

We begin then with our most confident moral beliefs, those we hold most firmly on the basis of what we take to be our best reasons. Those beliefs are the "moral data" against which we evaluate moral theories. The theories that do best in explaining and extending that data are the most rational ones for us to accept. Note, though, that even our initial data are subject to revision in this process. None of our moral beliefs is beyond question, even those of which we are most confident. If a fundamental moral belief conflicts with a theory that has strong support from other moral beliefs of which we are confident, we have some cognitive dissonance in our beliefs. The best solution may be to retain the theory and abandon the particular moral belief that conflicts with it. When a theory thus captures our most confident, and suitably revised, moral beliefs and extends our moral understanding in a plausible way, it captures our sense of morality in reflective equilibrium. We have an equilibrium between our particular moral beliefs and our general moral theory.

The fact that this process of theory evaluation starts with our most confident moral beliefs may cause concern. Perhaps those confident beliefs are mistaken. Won't we then be evaluating moral theories on the basis of false "moral data"? Yes, we will. The lesson here is not that the method of reflective equilibrium should be rejected. The lesson is that every process of reasoning has to start somewhere. In any area of life, we have no plausible place to start except the judgments of which we are most confident. In forming factual beliefs about how the world is (e.g., that we are sitting in a chair), we assume that our sense perceptions are accurate, that the world is as it seems to us. That assumption, while not itself beyond question, is a starting point for our reasoning. So, too, our most confident moral judgments are a starting point for our evaluation of moral theories in the method of reflective equilibrium.

The achievements involved in the process of attaining reflective equilibrium relative to a moral theory can be described on different levels. We are discovering what moral theory best organizes, explains, and extends our moral judgments about particular cases. We are developing our moral concepts, gaining a better sense of what general considerations make actions and practices have various moral qualities. We are advancing our understanding of what does and doesn't count as a good reason in support of moral beliefs and so developing our ability to think and act rationally as moral agents. Our study of ethics promises benefits on various levels.

NOTE

1. Strictly speaking, there is a third condition that is also important: the argument must not assume what it is trying to prove. Philosophers call this begging the question. If an argument begs the question, it's circular. We won't focus on this condition since it's often obvious when an argument has this flaw.

CHAPTER 3

True for You, but Not for Me

University = uni (one) veritas (truth)

INTRODUCTION

Philosophy is an attempt to uncover deep and important truths about the world and ourselves. Reflective equilibrium (Chapter §2.6) can help us do that. But what if what's true about the world varies from person to person? Consider the following:

> Chocolate tastes good. True or false?
> It's always wrong to have an abortion. True or false?
> There is life after death. True or false?

Some people reject the question in each case as misleading. The claim that chocolate tastes good is not just true or false; it is true for some people and false for others. The same goes for the claims about abortion and life after death. This view can be very attractive. After all, if what's true for you need not be true for me, then we don't have to disagree about chocolate, abortion, or life after death. We can both be right. Perhaps because of this attractive feature, the "true for you, but not for me" distinction is ubiquitous in pop culture. Yet, what do we mean when we say that something could be true for you but not for me? And what reason might we have for thinking that there is such a distinction?

It is fairly clear what it is for something to be just plain true or false rather than true or false *for someone*. First and foremost, truth and falsehood are properties of declarative sentences. Declarative sentences are sentences that state facts. For example, "God exists" is a declarative sentence, whereas "Do you like the movies?" and "Shut the door!" are not. The relationship between just plain truth and falsity and declarative sentences is pretty straightforward: the sentence "God exists" is either true or false, as is the sentence "God doesn't exist."

We often take various mental attitudes toward declarative sentences. We believe them, assert them, deny them, or withhold belief about them. Such attitudes are themselves true or false insofar as the declarative sentences they concern are true or false. For example, the Pope's belief that God exists is true just in case the declarative sentence "God exists" is true. Second, a declarative sentence is true just in case it correctly describes reality. The sentence "God exists" for example, is true just in case God is one of the things in the world; the sentence "Barack Obama is president" is true just in case Barack Obama is, in fact, president.

What, then, might it be for a sentence to be, not just true or false, but true or false *for someone*? Each of the next sections presents a possible answer to this question. On each of these interpretations, the claim that something can be true for one person but not another turns out to be false, infelicitous, or indefensible.

3.1 MORAL INTERPRETATION

Sometimes when we say that something is true for you, but not for me, we are really expressing a *moral claim*. In particular, we want to convey the idea that each person has a right to her own beliefs. It may be morally wrong for one person to force her views on others. If you believe that God exists and I believe that God doesn't exist, I should not try to force you to change your belief and you shouldn't try to force me to change mine. In this sense, the claim that God exists can be true for you but not for me. We each have a right to our opinion on the matter.

On this reading, the use of the phrase "true for you, but not for me" is what philosophers call *infelicitous*. It means that it's a phrase that is used improperly. That's because when we use the phrase this way, we are really trying to say something about how we ought to behave, instead of something about how a particular declarative sentence is true or false. What we really want to convey has nothing to do with how the sentence "God exists" might be true or false. We simply want to say that each person has a right to form and retain a belief on the topic. And, importantly, that each person has such a right does not have any implications for how the sentence "God exists" is true or false.

3.2 DOXASTIC INTERPRETATION

Imagine two people are having an intense religious debate. One says to the other, "Look, as a Christian, it's true for you that Jesus was God's son. But that's just not true for me since I'm a Buddhist." This looks like another instance of something's being true for one person but not for another. It's true for you that Jesus was God's son, but not for me.

Like the first use of "true for you, but not for me," this use is infelicitous. The speaker doesn't really want to say that whether Jesus was God's son depends on who you are (that would be a strange world indeed!). Rather, he means that whether you *believe* that Jesus was God's son depends on who you are. A Christian will accept this claim. A Buddhist will reject it. So, once again, this use of "true for you, but not for me" doesn't really have anything to do with truth,

either. It has to do with our *doxastic* states (*doxa* is Greek for belief). What the speaker is trying to say is better put in the following manner: "As a Christian, you are committed to the belief that Jesus was God's son. As a Buddhist, I don't believe that." But what is time is the same for both of us.

3.3 EPISTEMIC INTERPRETATION

A similar use of "true for you, but not for me" is as follows. Suppose you're a detective on a murder case. You find the murder weapon. You discover that the accused had a motive. You find the accused's prints on the weapon. Finally, you have a DNA match between the victim's blood and the accused's clothing. I, however, am a member of the jury who has yet to hear all of these discoveries. We might say in this case that it's true for you that the accused is guilty, but this is not yet true for me.

It should be fairly easy to see that this use of "true for you, but not for me" commits the same mistake as that considered in the foregoing section. The idea that we want to express in this instance is that you as the detective have evidence that I as a member of the jury do not. Or perhaps we want to say that from your perspective, the accused is guilty whereas from my perspective he is not. In either case, what really varies from you to me is evidence, perspective, experience, etc. In other words, the facts that are relative in this case are *epistemic* facts (*episteme* is Greek for knowledge). We don't *really* want to say that whether the accused is guilty of the murder depends on who is talking. So this use of "true for you, but not for me" is also infelicitous—it's saying something we don't really mean to say.

3.4 SEMANTIC INTERPRETATION

But there is another use of the phrase "true for you, but not for me" that is less deceptive. Take the example of chocolate presented at the outset of this chapter. It may very well be true that the claim "chocolate tastes good" is true for you, but not for me. Perhaps you like chocolate. I hate it. So perhaps it makes sense after all to say that some things are true for you, but not for me.

Actually, this use also engenders confusion. In this case, it is a *semantic* confusion, which is to say, a confusion in the way we use words. Whether a declarative sentences is true or false depends on its meaning. And sometimes a sentence is ambiguous and has more than one meaning. That is what happens here. The sentence "chocolate tastes good" is ambiguous. It could mean any of the following:

1. Chocolate tastes good to *everybody*.
2. Chocolate tastes good to *some people but not others*.
3. Chocolate tastes good to *the current reader of this book*.
4. Chocolate tastes good to *the author of this book*.

When we say that "chocolate tastes good" is true for you but not for me, what we're really saying is that sentence (3) is true and sentence (4) is false. So, in reality, there is no one declarative sentence with a univocal meaning that is true for some person but false for another. We both agree that (1) is just plain false and that (2) is just plain true. Same goes for (3) and (4): you and I agree that (3) is just plain true (i.e., chocolate tastes good to you) and that (4) is just plain false (i.e., chocolate doesn't taste good to me). So it appears once again that there is no sense in which a proposition is ever true for you, but not for me.

3.5 METAPHYSICAL INTERPRETATION

There is one final interpretation of the claim that something could be "true for you, but not for me," and this final interpretation is neither infelicitous nor the result of ambiguity. It's expressing exactly what we mean to convey: one and the same unambiguous declarative sentence is true for one person and false for another (at the same time). This interpretation is really talking about truth and the world, and thus it's a *metaphysical* reading of the phrase "true for you, but not for me" (metaphysics is the study of ultimate reality). On this reading, the property of being true is genuinely relative.

It's hard to know what to make of this claim. It might help to get clearer on what it means for something to be true. Suppose I say that Atlanta is the capital of Georgia. This declarative sentence is true if and only if (a) there really is a city denoted by the term 'Atlanta,' (b) there really is a place denoted by the term 'Georgia,' and (c) the city denoted by 'Atlanta' bears the relation 'is the capital of' the place denoted by 'Georgia.' If it turns out that the capital of Georgia is not Atlanta but Athens, then the sentence, and my assertion of it, are false.

So truth is the property of corresponding to the way the world really is. But now suppose that truth is relative. This means that when we say that a sentence is "true for you, but not for me," we are *really* saying that the world is one way for you, but another way for me. But how could that be? By "world" we mean "reality"—and how could there be more than one reality? And how could reality change with our beliefs?

Let's apply this to a concrete example. Ashley believes that there is life elsewhere in the universe. Becker denies this. He believes that there is no life elsewhere in the universe. Suppose Ashley decides to settle the debate by saying that what's true for her isn't true for Becker. Suppose, too, that Becker attempts to clarify her claim, and Ashley insists on the metaphysical interpretation: what's true for her isn't true for him. They can both be right. What is Becker to think? What is reality like if Ashley is right?

Well, we can't say that there really is life elsewhere in the universe, for if so, Becker's belief is false. And we can't say that there really isn't life elsewhere in the universe, for if so, Ashley's belief is false. And there are no further options: there either is life elsewhere in the universe or there isn't. So on either reading, at least one of them holds a false belief. There is no sense in which the sentence "there is life elsewhere in the universe" is true for Ashley and false for Becker.

But suppose Ashley won't accept this response. She digs in her heels and insists that it's begging the question to simply assume that the world has to be one way or the other—that's the very thing she is denying! How might we proceed? Well, we might ask Ashley why she thinks her view is true. It's hard to see how she would defend it. Suppose she says that truth is person-relative. Given what we mean by 'truth,' this commits her to the view that *reality* is person-relative. But suppose you ask Ashley what she means by this. She can't mean the following: the world is such that what is real is person-relative. Why not? Because then you could ask Ashley about that declarative sentence itself. Is *that* person-relative? In other words, is it person-relative that the world is person-relative or are you saying that it's just plain true that reality is person-relative? See the problem? It appears that Ashley's view is self-refuting: if she's right that reality is person-relative, then it's just plain true that reality is person-relative.

I suppose Ashley might say that she doesn't mean the word 'true' to describe reality. She has some other sense of the word in mind. This may absolve her of the earlier difficulty, but now it seems like we're just talking about different things. We started this discussion—and philosophy more generally—in an attempt to find out what's true about the world. If a relativist like Ashley wants to use the word 'true' to mean something different than what the rest of us mean, she's not engaging in the same intellectual task. There is no defensible sense of the phrase "true for you, but not for me."

In conclusion, it seems best to avoid the appeal to something's being true for you, but not for me. On some readings this phrase expresses a trivial claim that is best conveyed in a more careful way (e.g., the claim that you and I believe different things). On other readings, the phrase papers over an ambiguity of language (e.g., the claim that I am six feet tall is true for you, but not for me). Finally, on the last reading the phrase expresses a view about truth that is either hard to defend, self-refuting, or irrelevant.

CHAPTER 4

Reading Philosophy

[T]he man who does not read has no advantage over the man who cannot read.

—MARK TWAIN

INTRODUCTION

Many students have difficulty reading philosophical texts. This may be due, in part, to the fact that philosophy is simply unlike much of the material that college-age students read. Philosophy is (typically) not written in the style of a news article or a novel. At its best, philosophy is a careful and detailed examination of a difficult issue, and reading material of this sort requires patience and skill. As already noted in the sections on logic, the meat of philosophy is evaluating arguments for and against important philosophical claims. But you can't evaluate an argument until you know what the argument is! So the philosophical enterprise really has two components: exegesis (i.e., figuring out what the argument is) and evaluation (i.e., figuring out whether or not the argument is any good). The chapter on logic will help you to learn to do the latter. The remainder of this chapter will help you to learn to do the former.

In particular, for every piece of philosophy that you read, you should ask yourself two questions:

1. What is the main point that the author wishes to convince me to accept? In other words, what is the author's thesis?
2. What reason(s) does the author present for me to agree with her? In other words, what is the author's argument?

Each of the sections below provides guidelines for determining the answer to each of these two questions.

4.1 DETERMINING THE THESIS

Far and away the most important thing to figure out for any given piece of philosophy that you will read is the thesis—what is the point of the essay? What is the author trying to convince you to believe? If you don't know what the author's main point is, you will have great difficulty discerning the crucial argument. There are basically two suggestions for determining the thesis of any piece of philosophy. First, you should use any "outside" help that is available. For instance, in this anthology, we have taken the time to highlight certain features of each essay in an effort to make important claims and distinctions more apparent (see Chapter §4.3 below). In particular, the thesis of the essay is usually mentioned in the opening précis, and it is usually found in *italics* in the reading itself.

Second, and of greater importance, you should look for "signal words" that flag the conclusion of an argument or the thesis of a paper. Each of the following can be used to indicate the thesis of an essay:

Therefore. . .
Wherefore. . .
So. . .

Hence. . .
As a result. . .
For this reason. . .
Consequently. . .
It follows that. . .
Accordingly. . .
We may infer that. . .
I will argue that. . .

Each of these words/phrases can be used to indicate the conclusion of an argument, and the conclusion of the central argument in any essay is the thesis of that essay. Knowing these "signal words" in advance will help you identify the main point of the essays you read.

4.2 RECONSTRUCTING AN ARGUMENT

As noted above (chapter 2.1), an argument is a series of statements in which some of the statements are offered as a reason to accept some further statement. In order to understand the precise structure of an argument, you will need be able to identify the arguments and distinguish the premises from the conclusion(s). Premises are the assumptions that are used as evidence in favor of the conclusion. Just as conclusions are often flagged by "signal words" (see above), premises are also indicated by words or phrases like the following:

since. . .
because. . .
given that. . .
inasmuch as. . .
as indicated by. . .
for. . .
seeing that. . .

Knowing these "signal words" in advance will help you identify the premises of an argument in the essays you read.

Eventually, you need to be able to identify both the premises and the conclusions of arguments in the text. This will enable you to "reconstruct" the argument in your own terms. Consider the following example:

In the *Phaedo*, Socrates talks about his impending death, and he suggests that there is an afterlife. However, seeing that all men are mortal and since Socrates is a man, it follows that Socrates is mortal.

This passage contains a short and simple argument for the conclusion that Socrates is mortal. We know that it is the conclusion since it is flagged by the signal words 'it follows that.' The argument has two premises. First is the claim that all men are mortal. This premise is flagged by the signal words 'seeing that.' Second is the claim that Socrates is a man. This premise is flagged by the signal word 'since.' We can reconstruct the argument as follows:

1. All men are mortal.
2. Socrates is a man.
3. Therefore, Socrates is mortal.

Now that the argument is reconstructed, we're in a position to turn to the other task of philosophy: evaluation. This argument is good just in case (a) the premises properly support the conclusion and (b) the arguments has true premises.

Of course, the arguments in this text will often be more subtle than this. Here is another for practice:

Cloning is morally wrong. After all, to clone a person is really to play God—it's to decide who lives and what that life shall be like. Only God has that power, and rightfully so.

This short passage includes an argument, but discerning the argument is a bit trickier since the order of the prose is a little different, "signal words" are noticeably absent, and there is a premise that is suppressed or not explicitly stated in the prose. The conclusion of this argument is clearly stated in the first line (i.e., cloning is morally wrong). The suppressed premise is indicated at the end of the paragraph, but it is not stated explicitly (i.e., it is morally wrong to play God). We can reconstruct the argument as follows:

1. It is morally wrong to play God.
2. Cloning people is a way of playing God.
3. Therefore, it is morally wrong to clone people.

Now that the argument is clearly reconstructed, we are in a position to determine its quality. Is it a good argument?

4.3 HOW TO USE THIS TEXT

The readings in this text have been edited in order to make your job as a reader a bit easier. Remember: The overarching goal in reading philosophy is to find out what the author's view is (i.e., her thesis) and why she thinks it's true (i.e., her argument). Knowing how to use the special features of the readings in this text will help you to reach both of these goals.

Précis: Each reading opens with a short summary or précis that introduces the author in historical reference to other authors that you will read in this text. The précis will also give you an idea of the main thesis that the author is interested in defending.

Reading Questions: After the précis, you will find a short list of reading questions. These are questions that you should think about *before* reading the essay selection. Each question picks out some important thesis, distinction, or concept in the reading, and thus knowing what the questions are will help you to pick up on the more important sections of the essay. After you finish reading the essay, you should be able to answer each of the questions.

Subheadings: Any given article in philosophy will likely attempt to do several things (e.g., present a thesis, compare it to related theses, argue for a thesis, defend a premise in an argument for a thesis, offer objections, respond to objections, etc.). This back-and-forth that represents the progression of an argument is called the dialectic. Some philosophers include subheadings in their work to make it clear to the reader exactly how the dialectic goes. Where philosophers have not done so, we have added subheadings to make the structure of the article clearer. Pay attention to these subheadings—doing so is a good way to ensure that you know how each portion of the article relates to the overall thesis.

Boldface words: Some of the material in each reading is of crucial importance. When key concepts, distinctions, or phrases are first introduced, these words will be in **bold** font. A bolded term will be found in the glossary at the end of the text. For example:

> According to the **Principle of Utility,** the right acts or social policies are the ones that produce the greatest net intrinsic good.

Italicized sentences: At various points in the readings, the author will try to bring together various considerations to draw a conclusion or to state a principle that will play a crucial role in her overall argument. To help you pick out important conclusions, principles, and assumptions, these words will be in italics. For example:

> The creed which accepts as the foundation of morals, Utility, or the **Greatest Happiness Principle,** holds that *actions are right in proportion as they tend to promote happiness, wrong as they tend to produce the reverse of happiness.* To give a clear view of the moral standard set up by the theory. . .

Discussion Questions: After each reading selection, you will find some discussion questions that are designed to promote reflection on crucial aspects of the reading. Some of these questions will ask you to apply the distinctions and conclusions of the reading to novel ethical cases. Others will prompt reflection on some of the more abstruse or complex assumptions made by the author. The overall point of these questions is to move you beyond the first stage of determining what the author said to the second stage of determining whether what she said is correct.

Argument Reconstruction Exercises: Finally, each reading is followed by some argument reconstruction exercises. Each exercise contains an excerpt of the reading selection that contains an implicit argument for an important conclusion. Your job is to make the argument explicit by identifying the premises and conclusion(s) of the argument. As a helpful guide, the answer key in the back of the book provides suggested reconstructions for some of the exercises after each reading.

Writing Philosophy

. . .in my life, writing has been an important exercise to clarify what I believe, what I see, what I care about, what my deepest values are. . .the process of converting a jumble of thoughts into coherent sentences makes you ask tougher questions.
— PRESIDENT BARACK OBAMA (*TIME* INTERVIEW, DECEMBER 2012)

INTRODUCTION

We're rarely clear about an argument or position until we have written about it. It often happens that we think we understand an argument or position until we're asked to verbally explain it or to write on it, and then we realize that we didn't know the argument or position as well as we previously thought. In that sense, writing is thinking. For this reason, it is very likely that you will be asked to write a philosophy paper at some point during your study of ethics. Since a paper in philosophy is different in both content and style than a paper in other academic fields, it's important that you have a good grasp of these differences before you begin. And it's important to avoid simply emulating the writing styles of some of the authors in this text—not all of these pieces are well-written works of philosophy despite their important insights. Some are included in this text *in spite* of their writing style, not because of it. This chapter is broken into the following topics: the *goal* of a philosophy paper, the *evaluation* of a philosophy paper, the *content* of a philosophy paper, and the *structure* of a philosophy paper.

5.1 GOAL

It is *not* the point of a philosophy paper to use big words, anger your reader, ask rhetorical questions, or show off your intellectual prowess. The point of

a philosophy paper is deceptively simple: to clearly articulate and defend a philosophical thesis. Let's break that down. First, a philosophy paper needs to *clearly articulate* a position. A good philosophy paper is one that explains the position or issue at hand in simple, easy-to-understand terminology, using examples, definitions, and distinctions when appropriate. When a paper is sufficiently clear, anyone in the intended audience should be able to read the paper and easily grasp the view under consideration and the author's overall point.

Consider the following two paper theses:

This paper argues that it is not at all clear that the arguments against stem-cell research are good enough to counterweight the *prima facie* case for the moral permissibility of stem-cell research.

This paper argues that stem-cell research is morally permissible.

It's obvious that the latter is preferable to the former in terms of clarity. In particular, using everyday language instead of arcane terminology and using everyday examples can make a paper much more accessible to the reader. Consider the following two explanations:

It is obvious that epistemology plays a paramount role in the determination of moral responsibility. An agent is morally responsible for a consequence only if he knew (or should have known) about the possibility of that consequence.

What we know is important for what we're responsible for. In particular, a person is responsible for the consequences of her action only if she knew (or should have known) about that consequence beforehand. For example, suppose starting your car detonates a nearby bomb. We wouldn't hold you morally responsible for the explosion if you didn't know that starting your car would set off the bomb.

Again, the latter is obviously preferable as it uses clearer language and includes a helpful example. Don't shoot for literary greatness; shoot for simplicity. Read each sentence aloud. If it sounds strained to your ear, it will be strained for your reader as well.

Second, a philosophy paper focuses on a *philosophical* thesis. Recall that philosophy is the search for reasoned answers to important, non-empirical questions. As such, a good philosophy paper is one that tackles a uniquely philosophical issue. Consider the following theses:

There are more abortions performed in the U.S.A. than in Europe.

The Catholic Church is opposed to abortions.

Many women who have abortions suffer from Post Abortion Syndrome (PAS).

Many women feel guilty after having abortions.

The Bible indicates that having an abortion is morally wrong.

Some of these theses are exegetical (e.g., the claim that the Bible says a particular thing). Some are empirical (e.g., the claim that many women feel guilty after having abortions). None is a suitable thesis for a philosophy paper, and that's because none is philosophical. Now consider the following theses:

It is never morally permissible to obtain an abortion.

Abortion doctors should be killed.

Thomson's argument for the moral permissibility of abortion is unsound.

Late-term abortions should be illegal.

The most common pro-life arguments contain a false premise.

Some of these theses are moral claims (e.g., it is never morally permissible to obtain an abortion). Some are logical claims (e.g., Thomson's argument for the moral permissibility of abortion is unsound). All are suitable theses for a philosophy paper because all are philosophical claims.

Third, a philosophy paper *defends* a philosophical thesis. The goal of a philosophy paper is not just to report—it's not your job simply to relay the facts to your reader. Your job is to make a case for or against a philosophical claim. In that sense, a philosophy paper is like a persuasive paper in English, with the exception that a philosophy paper aims to persuade only by means of rational argumentation (as opposed to rhetoric, etc.). A good philosophy paper aims to persuade its audience by making a reasoned case for its thesis. Consider the following theses:

I believe that every woman has the choice to have an abortion.

This paper will explain Thompson's view on abortion.

This paper will compare Kant's view of ethics with Mill's view of ethics.

The first is inadequate as it is merely stating one's opinion. Surely you don't need to argue for or present a defense of the fact that you believe something. This thesis merely reports your mental state. The more important question is whether or not your belief is true! Instead of just reporting your belief, you should state the philosophical issue more clearly—it is morally permissible for any woman to choose to have an abortion—and then argue for this view. The second thesis suffers a similar deficiency: it is merely reporting the view of another. A good philosophy paper is not a book report—it's an argument for a particular conclusion. The third thesis is risky. If it merely presents what Kant thought and what Mill thought, then it, too, is merely reporting facts.

That's not philosophy; that's a book report. On the other hand, if the paper makes some substantive *philosophical* points of its own—not merely reporting what these two philosophers thought—then it has merit as a *philosophical* paper.

Recall that one of the key reasons we write philosophy is to become clearer and better thinkers. When it comes time to turn in your final draft, it's important that the paper you turn in is the sort of paper that contributes to better thinking. To ensure that your paper is one that's doing some real philosophy, read over it and ensure that the answers to the following questions are all "yes":

1. Is the paper *clear* and *articulate?*
2. Is the thesis of the paper *philosophical* in nature?
3. Does the body of the paper *defend* the thesis as opposed to merely reporting facts?

5.2 EVALUATION

To write a good paper, it's important to know how your professor will evaluate your work. Isn't philosophy just a bunch of opinions? Are there really right answers to philosophical questions? How can I get a bad grade on a paper as long as I give my honest opinion?

First, you should know by now that philosophy is *not* just a bunch of opinions. To be totally honest, your professor probably doesn't even care what your opinion is. What your professor cares about is your ability to provide a well-reasoned case for your opinion. Philosophers prize rigorous argument. And while the standards of evaluation may vary a bit from professor to professor, you can bet that the following three features will play a prominent role in the overall grading scheme:

(1) Presentation. The ideas in the paper must be presented in a clear and coherent fashion. This is a necessary (but not sufficient) condition for a good philosophy paper. There are at least two issues that are important to keep in mind with regard to presentation. First, is the overall structure of the paper clear and easy to follow? For example, a nicely structured essay will include a clear thesis statement, a "road map" at the outset of the essay, transitional markers as the paper moves from point to point, etc. Second, does the paper use written language appropriately? For example, a well-written essay will avoid sentence fragments, run-on sentences, confusing syntax, misspelled words, subject–verb disagreement, etc. If you need help with any of these things, see the writing center at your school or refer to one of the many handbooks on grammar available in the library or on the web.

(2) Content. A clearly presented essay that says nothing of philosophical merit will still receive a poor grade. *What* you say is just as important as *how* you say it. When it comes to content, keep the following questions in mind: Does the paper have a *philosophical* (as opposed to, say, empirical) thesis? Is there a clear line of argument in the paper? Is the paper generally convincing? Does the paper make any good points? Does the paper make it obvious why this issue matters? Are all necessary explanations given and all necessary distinctions noted? One final note about content—it's important that the essay contain ALL of the information necessary to establish the thesis and ONLY the information necessary to establish the thesis. Don't burden your reader with information/arguments that are tangential to the central issue of the paper. This will detract from the overall quality of the philosophical content.

(3) Originality. Finally, your professor will likely care that at least some of the content in your essay is original. This doesn't mean that you are the first person in the world to ever have this idea or criticism. Instead, it means that you came up with the ideas/criticisms on your own or while thinking through the issue with others. The gist is that your professor wants you to do a little bit of philosophy of your own and not just rehearse basic points made in class on in the text. It's important not to dwell too much on this element of the grading—your professor doesn't expect you to write something philosophically brilliant. Instead, your professor only expects that you deal seriously with an issue in your own mind and clearly record the outcome of this deliberation in a way that's accessible for another reader.

5.3 CONTENT

Because content plays a significant role in the evaluation of a philosophy paper, it's important to have some idea of how to come up with a topic that is suitable. This section provides some help in that area. The most important point is to keep the goal of the paper appropriate to the length of the paper. Don't try to prove the existence of God in one short paper; the result will be a poorly explained, sloppy, and ill-defended piece of work. Short papers call for a clear defense of an important but modest thesis.

The most important step in writing a good philosophy paper is determining your topic. If the topic is not philosophical, the paper will not be a work of *philosophy*. If the topic is too broad, the paper will not be able to do justice to the issue at hand. If the topic is too narrow, the paper will be trivial or repetitive or both.

First of all, pick something that interests you. Chances are that you'll put more effort into thinking and writing about something that you care about. Perhaps your professor has provided you with a list of topics from which to choose. If so, examine these topics and pick several that interest you. If your professor has not provided a preset list of paper topics, choose three or four issues from class that you have found interesting. Spend some time thinking about these topics, discussing them with friends, and researching them on in the library. Talking through an issue with others can often help you to figure out not only what the relevant issues are but what you really think about the issues. Your professor is likely to be another good source of help at this stage. He or she will be able to make sure the thesis is appropriate, help you further refine it, and direct you to helpful sources.

Once you've settled on a topic, the next challenge is to narrow it to something that can be adequately handled in a short paper. Suppose you settle on the following topic:

Abortion

As it stands, this topic is much too broad and ill defined for a short paper. Try narrowing down the topic to something like the following:

Abortion is always morally wrong.
Abortion is always morally permissible.
Abortion ought to be illegal.
Abortion ought to be legal.

Spend some more time thinking about these more narrow topics. Is there one in particular you'd like to defend? If so, try to sketch an outline of how your argument or defense might go. You may find that these topics are *still* too broad. In that case, you should narrow the topic further:

In at least some cases, abortions are morally wrong.
Thomson's argument for the moral permissibility of abortion is unsound.
There is at least one good argument for the legality of abortion.

When you feel that you can adequately address the topic in your paper, your topic is probably narrow enough. The statement of your topic has now become the focal point of the paper—the thesis statement.

All of the content of your paper should relate—in some way or another—to the thesis statement you have chosen. Sometimes it will relate directly, for example, when you offer the argument in favor of your thesis. Sometimes it will relate indirectly, for example, when you take the time to explain a possible objection to the argument for your thesis. Ensure that the connection between each paragraph and your overall thesis is clear for your reader by using connectives like the following:

My argument assumes that X. For this reason, it's important to see why X is true. . .
Having just shown that my argument is valid, I will now show that the premises are true. . .

Here's an objection that might be offered
    against my argument. . .
I claimed above that Thomson is committed
    to *X*. Here's why. . .

The use of such constructions ensures that your
reader can follow the connection between the
issue under discussion and the thesis of the paper.

Two other devices can be used to focus the
content of a paper: examples and distinctions.
Examples are useful ways to communicate an
otherwise abstract concept or suggestion to a
reader. Consider the following:

> In at least some cases, it is morally permissible to
> inflict pain on one's child. For example, suppose
> the child suffers from an illness that can only be
> cured by an injection. In this case, it would be
> morally permissible to give the child the injection
> despite the fact that it causes her pain.

Upon first reading the claim that it is morally
permissible to hurt one's child, the reader is
incredulous. But the example presents a concrete scenario in which it's obvious that doing
the right thing involves causing some short-term
pain. Thus the example functions to prove the
author's point without further elaboration.

Second, and just as important, is the use of
distinctions. Often one wants to make a limited point or a point about a limited number of
cases. It's a good idea to avoid sweeping generalizations; instead, use distinctions to draw your
reader's attention to a subset of cases. Consider
the following excerpt from a paper on the moral
permissibility of abortion:

> In this paper, I will argue that it is morally
> wrong to abort a viable fetus. To understand
> the scope of my thesis, it is important to see the
> difference between a viable and non-viable fetus.
> A fetus is viable if and only if it is able to survive
> outside of the womb. Otherwise, the fetus is
> non-viable.

This distinction is clearly drawn and helps the
reader to see that the content of the paper is
not going to cover all cases of abortion but only
those in which the fetus has a certain property
described here as viability. The point of using
such distinctions and examples is to distinguish
your thesis from other, related claims that you
won't be focusing on in your paper.

5.4 STRUCTURE

The structure of a philosophy paper is every bit
as important as its content. If the paper is structured poorly, it will be difficult for you to make
your points in a way that is both intelligible and
convincing. This section provides some guidelines for structuring your paper effectively.

Any good philosophy paper has at least two
broad sections: an introduction and a body. Let's
look at each. First, consider the introduction to
a philosophy paper. A good introduction will
do three things: (a) clearly state the thesis of the
paper, (b) explain why this thesis is important,
and (c) provide a "road map" of what's to come in
the body of the paper. Without the first, the reader
won't know what the paper is about, and thus she
will be confused when she gets to the body of the
paper. Without the second, the reader won't know
why she should bother reading the paper. What's
at stake in this debate? Why waste my time?
Without the third, the reader will be lost as she
tries to follow your reasoning in the body of the
paper. Each of these elements is discussed below.

(a) Thesis. When stating the thesis of the
paper, be clear and obvious. Don't be afraid to
use the first person (i.e., "I") if that helps to make
the point obvious. You should just come out and
write something like the following:

In this paper, I argue that. . . .
I will show that. . .
This paper will demonstrate that. . .
It is the case that. . .

It is best to do this right away in a philosophy
paper. Beware of what's often called the "running start." This is where a paper begins by stating a series of generalities and truisms that are
superfluous to the issue at hand. For example,
consider the following:

People have long debated the morality of abortion. Some people think that abortions are always morally permissible. Others think that abortions are always morally wrong. This divide has gotten even more serious in the United States since the Supreme Court decision in *Roe v. Wade* in 1973. It is probably not possible to evaluate all of the reasons that pro-choicers and pro-lifers use to defend their views in one paper. In this paper, I will argue that. . .

This introduction is a running start. The first 5 sentences are truisms that anyone would agree with and that do nothing to advance the central point of the paper. Much better is the following:

> Though there are many views on the moral permissibility of abortion, I will argue that. . .

This is short, clear, and to the point.

(b) Motivation. There is a lot of stuff to read out there. Why should the reader bother with your paper? Who cares whether or not you're right about the issue you're discussing? What hangs on whether or not you're right? A good introduction is one that motivates the reader to continue reading your paper. Tell the reader why the issue bothers you or what is to be gained (or lost) by dealing with (or avoiding) your topic. Consider the following:

> Though there are many views on the moral permissibility of abortion, I will argue that having an abortion is never morally permissible because it is always the killing of an innocent person. The issue is an important one for both legal and moral reasons. On the legal front, U.S. law guarantees almost unrestricted access to abortions at any stage in pregnancy. If I am right that an abortion is the killing of an innocent person, then for almost 40 years U.S. law has sanctioned the death of hundreds of thousands of innocent persons. When it comes to matters of morality, the conclusion that the fetus is an innocent person has important ramifications not just for abortion (i.e., whether or not it is wrong to harm the fetus) but for the ethics of parenting as well (i.e.,

pregnant mothers might have positive duties to protect the fetus).

Whether or not the author of this introduction is right that abortion is the killing of an innocent person, the thesis of the essay is clearly motivated. It's obvious why this author wants to prove her point and what hangs in the balance until she does.

(c) "Road map." Suppose we are on a road trip together, but I don't inform you of our final destination. Without such information, it will be hard for you to get a clear sense of our journey. Any time I make a turn, you'll wonder whether that turn was necessary or not, but you won't know since you won't know where we're going. At any point in the journey you won't even know if we're halfway there, almost there, etc.

It's the same in written work. If a reader doesn't know the point of the paper or how the author is going to get there, it's difficult to evaluate the twists and turns of the narrative flow. Is this point necessary or not? Is there a point that the author needs to make but hasn't? Are we there yet?

For this reason, it's best that your introduction gives the reader a "road map" of the overall paper. Tell the reader explicitly where you hope to end up (i.e., your thesis statement) and exactly how you hope to get there (i.e., what your argument for your thesis will be). The following is an excellent example of a road map for a paper:

> Though there are many views on the moral permissibility of abortion, I will argue that having an abortion is never morally permissible because it is always the killing of an innocent person. I will first explain what makes something a person, then explain what makes something innocent, and then I will apply these two concepts to the fetus. Given the obvious point that an abortion kills a fetus, it will follow from these two points that abortion is the killing of an innocent person. I will close the paper by responding to two potential objections to my argument.

Chapter 5: Writing Philosophy **31**

The body of the paper should simply follow this ready-made outline.

Second, consider the body of a philosophy paper. The body of the paper should basically make good on the promises made in the introduction. For example, given the thesis and road map from the foregoing paragraph, the body of the paper should follow roughly this outline:

A. Explain the conditions for personhood.
B. Explain the conditions for innocence.
C. Apply these conditions to the case of the fetus.
D. Offer and respond to two objections to the positions defended in A–C.

It will be extremely helpful to your reader to include "signposts" or transitional phrases throughout the paper to make it clear exactly where you are in your defense of your thesis. For example, the following is a good transition between point A and point B:

> Now that it's clear what it takes to count as a person, what are the conditions for innocence?

And the following is a nice transition between C and D:

> Given my argument above, it's clear that abortion is the killing of an innocent person. But there are at least two objections that one might offer to my account. The first objection is that. . .

Notice that the overall structure of the paper will vary according to its goal. Philosophy papers fall into roughly three categories: positive, critical, and defensive. A positive paper seeks to establish some point (e.g., I will argue that abortion is sometimes morally permissible.). A critical paper seeks to show that some particular effort to establish a point fails (e.g., I will argue that so-and-so's argument is unsound). A defensive paper defends a point or an argument against the criticism of another (e.g., I will argue that so-and-so's criticism of utilitarianism is a bad one). All three types have theses, but they differ in what they attempt to prove. Furthermore, since

the overall structure of these papers tends to be different, it might be helpful to compare a basic outline for each.

Positive Paper

   i. Introduction (thesis: I will argue that X.)
  ii. Argument for X.
 iii. Show that argument for X is valid.
  iv. Show that all the premises in argument for X are true.
   v. Conclude and respond to objections to the *argument* for X.

Critical Paper

   i. Introduction (thesis: I will argue that so-and-so's argument for X fails.)
  ii. Explain so-and-so's argument for X.
 iii. Explain the defect in so-and-so's argument for X (i.e., invalid or false premise).
  iv. Conclude and respond to objections so-and-so might have about the interpretation of her argument in (ii) or the criticism of her argument in (iii).

Defensive Paper

   i. Introduction (thesis: I will argue that so-and-so's criticism of X fails.)
  ii. Explain X.
 iii. Explain so-and-so's criticism of X.
  iv. Explain why so-and-so's criticism is a bad one.
   v. Conclude and respond to objections so-and-so might have about the interpretation of her criticism in (iii) or the criticism of her argument in (iv).

Finally, several strategies can help you convince your reader of your thesis by rational argumentation. One helpful strategy is to be clear about the difference between *rebutting a claim* and *undermining a claim*. To *rebut* a claim is to show that it is false. To *undermine* a claim is to remove a reason for thinking that it is true. These are very different strategies as you might think that an argument for claim is a bad one even though you're not sure whether or not the claim is true or false. Think about the difference in the context of the debate over the existence of God. To *rebut* the claim that God exists would be to show that God does not exist. This sort of paper aims to convince the reader to be an atheist. To *undermine* the claim that God exists would be to remove all or one of the reasons for thinking that God exists. This sort of paper aims to convince the reader to be an agnostic. Keep this distinction clearly in mind. If your thesis is that Thomson's argument for the moral permissibility of abortion is a bad one, you are arguing for an undermining thesis. You need not take a stand on whether abortion is right or wrong—you only need to show that the reasons she presents for thinking abortion is permissible are bad ones.

Other strategies are outlined in Chapter 2 on the methods of philosophy (page 12). For example, **counterexamples** and **analysis** often play a big role in philosophy papers. Suppose you are considering the conditions for moral responsibility, and you begin with the following analysis of moral responsibility:

> A person is responsible for a state of affairs if and only if that person caused the state of affairs.

The analysis includes an "if and only if," which means that the connection between the clauses goes in both directions (for a refresher, see page 13). This provides two possibilities for counterexamples. One counterexample would be an instance where a person is responsible for a state of affairs that she didn't cause (this shows that the left is not sufficient for the right). The second style of counterexample would be an instance where a person caused an outcome but is not responsible for that state of affairs (this shows that the right is not sufficient for the left). If we can find an instance of either sort of counterexample, the analysis fails, and the claim is false.

A paper that is seeking to rebut this analysis of moral responsibility could do so by making a persuasive case for either of the two sorts of counterexamples. And in this instance, it's not hard to do with the use of **thought experiments**. *A thought experiment is a hypothetical scenario that we can examine to illustrate a certain point.* Here's an easy example of a thought experiment: Suppose that a mother knowingly watches her child drink a glass of poison and does not intervene to stop her. Would we say that the mother is morally responsible for the child's death? Surely we would. In that case, people can be morally responsible for things that they don't directly cause—this is the first style of counterexample. We can invent another thought experiment to support a counterexample in the opposite direction. Recall the example from the beginning of this chapter: Unbeknownst to you, a bomb has been wired to your car so that when you start your car, the bomb explodes. If this happened, would we hold you morally responsible for the explosion? Surely not. In that case, people may not be morally responsible for things that they directly cause— this is the second style of counterexample.

A good philosophy paper will employ strategies like these in order to make a persuasive case for the thesis of the paper. One final piece of advice is in order. Sometimes it seems to an author that a point, argument, or criticism is crystal clear when in reality it presupposes a great deal of information that the author has not made explicit. To avoid finding yourself in this predicament, try one of two strategies. First, type out a draft of a paper and put it aside for several days. Pick the paper up only after some time to clear your head. When you do so, do you still find the reasoning persuasive? Are all of the necessary definitions and distinctions in the paper? Are the points still clear? A second strategy is also helpful: let a friend (who's not in the class) read the paper. When she's finished, ask her to state the thesis and the main argument for the thesis. If she can do so, it's a good sign that the paper is well done. If not, keep working on the draft.

UNIT

2

Foundations of Ethics

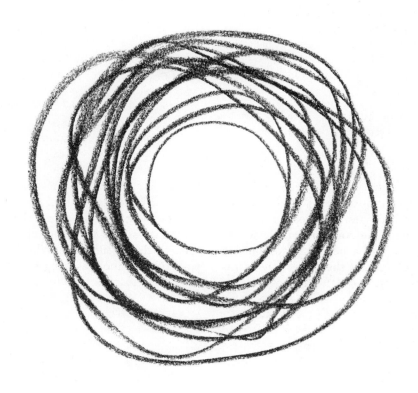

CHAPTER 6

Moral Facts

[M]orality has no philosophically objective foundation. It is just an illusion, fobbed off on us [by evolution] to promote biological "altruism."

—MICHAEL RUSE "EVOLUTIONARY ETHICS"

INTRODUCTION

As noted in the Introduction, (page 3) there are three ways to approach ethics. One approach is to develop general theories that seek to explain ethical facts. Given the fact that it is wrong to torture small animals for fun, what makes it wrong to do so? This is the field of normative ethics. A second approach is to apply general theories to particular, concrete situations. Assuming that we have a general account of what makes some acts right and other acts wrong, what does this general theory imply about the morality of, say, abortion? This is applied ethics. A third approach is to investigate the assumptions made by those working in either normative or applied ethics. Are there really any objective moral facts to explain? How are such facts related to cultural mores and taboos? How are such facts related to God? Are we really capable of *knowing*, rather than just *believing*, that certain acts are right, while others are wrong? Can we know that a particular ethical theory is correct? This is the field of **metaethics** (*meta* is Greek for "beyond"). Since metaethics is devoted to investigating the assumptions behind normative and applied ethics, it is appropriate to begin our study of ethics here.

In this first section on metaethics, we'll focus our attention on two fundamental assumptions of normative and applied ethics. First, each

assumes that there really are some moral facts, and, second, each assumes that we are capable of knowing at least some of them. But initially, these assumptions appear strained. Consider this quote from philosopher Simon Blackburn:

> The natural world is the world revealed by the senses, and described by the natural sciences: physics, chemistry, and notably biology, including evolutionary theory. However we think of it, ethics seems to fit badly into that world. Neither the senses nor the sciences seem to be good detectors of obligations, duties, or the order of value of things. (*Ruling Passions* [Oxford: Clarendon Press, 1998], p. 49.)

Blackburn's quote raises two concerns. Let's take each one in turn. The first concern is that the natural world—the world in which we live and act—seems to be described completely by the natural sciences. Yet, if these sciences *completely* describe the natural world, then there are no moral facts, for these sciences do not mention moral facts. A theory in physics can tell us how nuclear weapons work; it cannot tell us when, if ever, it is morally permissible to use them.

Is Blackburn's concern a legitimate one? The suggestion that there are no moral facts may seem too outrageous to consider. After all, even though we sometimes disagree about the morality of particular acts and practices, we all share a general framework of moral principles in terms of which we understand our behavior and that of others. We take someone who lacks such a framework to have a severe mental deficit. The suggestion that there are no moral facts whatsoever seems to imply not simply that our moral framework is mistaken in some particular ways, but that it is wholly and completely mistaken. The dimension of reality that it purports to describe just isn't there. How could we make such a mistake?

Well, consider the case of a culture in which the people understand physical illness in terms of possession by demon spirits. For example, such people might claim that headaches are caused by demons inhabiting one's skull. Even as they argue about fine points, whether possession by this or that demon is responsible for this or that physical symptom, such people would find it hard to imagine what we know to be the case: their theory of illness is mistaken. There are no demons in the first place, much less do they cause physical illness. Might we be like such people? Might we be committed to describing the world in a way that is grossly mistaken? Might there be no moral facts?

Second, note that we cannot avoid Blackburn's concern by extending his list of sciences to include the social and behavioral sciences, such as psychology, anthropology, and sociology. The basic problem remains the same: all of these sciences concern themselves with various aspects of how the natural world *is*, while morality is concerned with how it *ought to be*. Psychology tells us how the mind works and what causes people to be happy, sad, or insecure. Anthropology tells us how humankind developed and how human societies first began using moral language. But neither tell us if there are any moral facts. If the sciences *completely* describe the natural world, if the natural world consists just of *what is the case* as distinguished from *what ought to be*, nature contains no moral facts.

Finally, we cannot avoid this concern by simply "reducing" normative ethics to one of the natural sciences. Some may propose, for example, that our moral judgments about moral right and wrong are simply judgments about what is permitted or prohibited by the moral norms of our culture. The fact that an act is morally right *just is* the fact that it is prohibited by the moral norms of our culture; the fact that one is wrong *just is* the fact that it is permitted by the moral norms of our culture. Moral facts are really just facts about the moral practices of various cultures. Such facts concern what is the case—what the culture's moral norms require—and those kinds of facts really are within the scope of one or more of the social sciences that study the natural world. Among other things, the problem with this response to the first concern is that we just eliminated normative and applied ethics as distinctive intellectual disciplines. The question of whether and why certain acts are wrong, for example, has been reduced to that of whether and why those acts are prohibited by moral code of the culture at hand, and that is a question for social scientists, not philosophers. Furthermore, almost none of us think this to be the case: many people think that what the Nazis did was morally wrong *regardless* of what their culture said.

Blackburn's second concern is not so much with the *existence* of moral facts but with our *knowledge* of such facts. Suppose that the natural world does contain some moral facts. How can we discover them? As Blackburn notes, our senses are our primary, perhaps only, source of information about the natural world, and our senses do not seem to be "good detectors of obligations, duties, or the order of value of things." The difficult moral issues that confront us cannot be resolved just by sensory observation. We cannot determine the morality of abortion, capital punishment, torture, or euthanasia just by observing these activities. Watching such activities might show that they cause pain or that they relieve suffering, etc., but watching them cannot show us whether it is *wrong* to cause pain or *right* to relieve suffering. The limitation doesn't rest in lack of suitable technological devices to aid us.

No moral microscope or virtue meter will enable us to just see, hear, taste or smell the difference between right and wrong. Thus, even if the natural world contains moral facts, it is unclear how we can discover them. The defining agenda of normative and applied ethics—to explain the theoretical structure undergirding moral facts and to extend those explanations to gain additional moral knowledge in others areas—seems to be a fool's errand.

The readings in this section focus on these two concerns and, in doing so, offer very different perspectives on the moral dimension of our lives.

SUGGESTIONS FOR FURTHER READING

Brink, David. *Moral Realism and the Foundations of Ethics*. (New York: Cambridge University Press, 1989)

Huemer, Michael. *Ethical Intuitionism*. (New York: Palgrave Macmillan, 2005)

Joyce, Richard. *The Evolution of Morality*. (Cambridge, MA: MIT Press, 2006)

Mackie, J. L. *Ethics: Inventing Right and Wrong*. (Penguin Books, 1977)

McNaughton, David. *Moral Vision: An Introduction to Ethics*. (Oxford: Blackwell, 1988)

Sayre-McCord, Geoffrey (ed.). *Essays on Moral Realism*. (Ithaca: Cornell University Press, 1988)

Shafer-Landau, Russ. *Moral Realism: A Defence*. (Oxford: Clarendon Press, 2003)

Sinnott-Armstrong, Walter & Timmons, Mark. *Moral Knowledge? New Readings in Moral Epistemology*. (Oxford: Oxford University Press, 1996)

Sturgeon, Nicholas, "Moral Explanations," in *Essays on Moral Realism*, ed. Sayre-McCord, Geoffrey. (Ithaca: Cornell University Press, 1988, 229–255)

6.1 MORAL NIHILISM

GILBERT HARMAN (1977)

Gilbert Harman is the James S. McDonnell Distinguished University Professor of Philosophy at Princeton University. His work has been influential in many fields of philosophy, including normative ethics, metaethics, epistemology, and philosophy of language. In this essay, Harman argues for the thesis that moral nihilism should be taken seriously. **Moral nihilism** is the view that there are no moral facts (*nihil* is Latin for "nothing"). Harman argues for nihilism by showing that our scientific beliefs are different in kind from our moral beliefs. The observations we make about the world provide evidence for our scientific beliefs, but they do not serve as evidence for our moral beliefs. Unless we can understand moral facts as explaining some feature of our experience, there is no reason to think that such facts exist.

Reading Questions:

1. What is Harman's example involving a cat?

2. What does it mean to say that observation is theory laden?

3. According to Harman, why does observation play a unique role in science that it does not play in ethics?

4. According to Harman, why don't we need to posit the truth of moral facts in order to explain our "moral observations"?

5. What is nihilism?

6. What is the point of the example about average American citizens?

7. How might moral facts be reducible to natural facts about a thing's function or purpose?

Ethics and Observation

Can moral principles be tested and confirmed in the way scientific principles can? . . .

You can observe someone do something, but can you ever perceive the rightness or wrongness of what he does? If you round a corner and see a group of young hoodlums pour gasoline on a cat and ignite it, you do not need to *conclude* that what they are doing is wrong; you do not need to figure anything out; you can *see* that it is wrong. But is your reaction due to the actual wrongness of what you see or is it simply a reflection of your moral "sense," a "sense" that you have acquired perhaps as a result of your moral upbringing?

The issue is complicated. There are no pure observations. *Observations are always "theory laden." What you perceive depends to some extent on the theory you hold, consciously or unconsciously.* You see some children pour gasoline on a cat and ignite it. To really see that, you have to possess a great deal of knowledge, know about a considerable number of objects, know about people: that people pass through the life stages infant, baby, child, adolescent, adult. You must know what flesh and blood animals are, and in particular, cats. You must have some idea of life. You must know what gasoline is, what burning is, and much more. In one sense, what you "see" is a pattern of light on your retina, a shifting array of splotches, although even that is theory, and you could never adequately describe what you see in that sense. In another sense, you see what you do because of the theories you hold. Change those theories and you would see something else, given the same pattern of light.

Similarly, if you hold a moral view, whether it is held consciously or unconsciously, you will be able to perceive rightness or wrongness, goodness or badness, justice or injustice. There is no difference in this respect between moral propositions and other theoretical propositions. If there is a difference, it must be found elsewhere.

Observation depends on theory because perception involves forming a belief as a fairly direct result of observing something; you can form a belief only if you understand the relevant concepts and a concept is what it is by virtue of its role in some theory or system of beliefs. To recognize a child as a child is to employ, consciously or unconsciously, a concept that is defined by its place in a framework of the stages of human life. Similarly, burning is an empty concept apart from its theoretical connections to the concepts of heat, destruction, smoke, and fire.

Moral concepts—Right and Wrong, Good and Bad, Justice and Injustice—also have a place in your theory or system of beliefs and are the concepts they are because of their context. If we say that observation has occurred whenever an opinion is a direct result of perception, we must allow that there is moral observation, because such an opinion can be a moral opinion as easily as any other sort. In this sense, observation may be used to confirm or disconfirm moral theories. The observational opinions that, in this sense, you find yourself with can be in either agreement or conflict with your consciously explicit moral principles. When they are in conflict, you must choose between your explicit theory and observation. In ethics, as in science, you sometimes opt for theory, and say that you made an error in observation or were biased or whatever, or you sometimes opt for observation, and modify your theory.

In other words, *in both science and ethics, general principles are invoked to explain particular cases* and, therefore, in both science and ethics, the general principles you accept can be tested by appealing to particular judgments that certain things are right or wrong, just or unjust, and so forth; and these judgments are analogous to direct perceptual judgments about facts.

Nevertheless, *observation plays a role in science that it does not seem to play in ethics.* The difference is that you need to make assumptions about certain physical facts to explain the occurrence of the observations that support a scientific theory, but you do not seem to need to make assumptions about any moral facts to explain the occurrence of the so-called moral observations I have been talking about. In the moral case, it would seem that you need only make assumptions about the psychology or moral sensibility of the person making the moral observation. In the scientific case, theory is tested against the world.

The point is subtle but important. Consider a physicist making an observation to test a scientific theory. Seeing a vapor trail in a cloud chamber, he thinks, "There goes a proton." Let us suppose that this is an observation in the relevant sense, namely, an immediate judgment made in response to the situation without any conscious reasoning having taken place. Let us also suppose that his observation confirms his theory, a theory that helps give meaning to the very term "proton" as it occurs in his observational judgment. Such a confirmation rests on inferring an explanation. He can count his making the observation as confirming evidence for his theory only to the extent that it is reasonable to explain his making the observation by assuming that, not only is he in a certain psychological "set," given the theory he accepts and his beliefs about the experimental apparatus, but furthermore, there really was a proton going through the cloud chamber, causing the vapor trail, which he saw as a proton. (This is evidence for the theory to the extent that the theory can explain the proton's being there better than competing theories can.) But, if his having made that observation could have been equally well explained by his psychological set alone, without the need for any assumption about a proton, then the observation would not have been evidence for the existence of that proton and therefore would not have been evidence for the theory. His making the observation supports the theory only because, in order to explain his making the observation, it is reasonable to assume something about the world over and above the assumptions made about the observer's psychology. In particular, it is reasonable to assume that there was a proton going through the cloud chamber, causing the vapor trail.

Compare this case with one in which you make a moral judgment immediately and without conscious reasoning, say, that the children are wrong to set the cat on fire. In order to explain your making [this] judgment, it would be reasonable to assume,

perhaps, that the children really are pouring gasoline on a cat and you are seeing them do it. But, there is no obvious reason to assume anything about "moral facts," such as that it really is wrong to set the cat on fire. Indeed, an assumption about moral facts would seem to be totally irrelevant to the explanation of your making the judgment you make. It would seem that all we need assume is that you have certain more or less well articulated moral principles that are reflected in the judgments you make, based on your moral sensibility. It seems to be completely irrelevant to our explanation whether your intuitive immediate judgment is true or false.

The observation of an event can provide observational evidence for or against a scientific theory in the sense that the truth of that observation can be relevant to a reasonable explanation of why that observation was made. A moral observation does not seem, in the same sense, to be observational evidence for or against any moral theory, since the truth or falsity of the moral observation seems to be completely irrelevant to any reasonable explanation of why that observation was made. The fact that an observation of an event was made at the time it was made is evidence not only about the observer but also about the physical facts. *The fact that you made a particular moral observation when you did does not seem to be evidence about moral facts, only evidence about you and your moral sensibility.* Facts about protons can affect what you observe, since a proton passing through the cloud chamber can cause a vapor trail that reflects light to your eye in a way that, given your scientific training and psychological set, leads you to judge that what you see is a proton. But there does not seem to be any way in which the actual rightness or wrongness of a given situation can have any effect on your perceptual apparatus. In this respect, ethics seems to differ from science. . . .

Moral Nihilism

We have seen that observational evidence plays a role in science it does not seem to play in ethics. Moral hypotheses do not help explain why people observe what they observe. So ethics is problematic and **nihilism** must be taken seriously. *Nihilism is the doctrine that there are no moral facts, no moral* *truths, and no moral knowledge.* This doctrine can account for why reference to moral facts does not seem to help explain observations, on the grounds that what does not exist cannot explain anything.

Nihilism holds that *morality is simply an illusion:* nothing is ever right or wrong, just or unjust, good or bad. In this version, we should abandon morality, just as an atheist abandons religion after he has decided that religious facts cannot help explain observations. Some nihilists have even suggested that morality is merely a superstitious remnant of religion.

Such nihilism is hard to accept. It implies that there are no moral constraints—that everything is permitted. As Dostoevsky observes, it implies that there is nothing wrong with murdering your father. It also implies that slavery is not unjust and that Hitler's extermination camps were not immoral. These are not easy conclusions to accept.

This, of course, does not refute nihilism. Nihilism does not purport to reflect our ordinary views; and the fact that it is difficult to believe does not mean that it must be false. At one time in the history of the world people had difficulty in believing that the earth was round; nevertheless the earth was round. A truly religious person could not easily come to believe that God does not exist; that is no argument against atheism. Nihilism is a possible view and it deserves to be taken seriously. . . .

Our previous discussion suggests the following argument for moral nihilism:

> Moral hypotheses never help explain why we observe anything. So we have no evidence for our moral opinions.

The argument depends upon this assumption:

> We can have evidence for hypotheses of a certain sort only if such hypotheses sometimes help explain why we observe what we observe.

But that assumption is too strong. Hypotheses about the average American citizen never help explain why we observe anything about a particular American, but we can obtain evidence for such hypotheses by obtaining evidence for hypotheses about American citizens. The reason is that facts about the average American citizen are definable in terms of facts about American citizens. Facts of the first sort are constructed out of and therefore reducible to facts of the second sort. Even if assumptions about moral facts do not directly help explain observations, it may be that moral facts can be reduced to other sorts of facts and that assumptions about these facts do help explain observations. In that case, there could be evidence for assumptions about moral facts.

To take another example, we might be able to account for color perception without making the supposition that objects actually have colors. For we might be able to explain how objects whose surfaces have certain physical characteristics will reflect light of a particular wave length; this light then strikes the retina of an observer's eye, affecting him in a way that might be described by an adequate neurophysiological psychology. That is, we might be able to explain perception of color entirely in terms of the physical characteristics of the objects perceived and the properties of light together with an account of the perceptual apparatus of the observer. This would not prove that there are no facts about colors; it would only show that facts about colors are not additional facts, over and above physical and psychological facts. If we could explain color perception in this way, we would conclude that facts about color are somehow reducible to facts about the physical characteristics of perceived objects, facts about light, and facts about the psychology and perceptual apparatus of perceivers. We might consider whether moral facts are in a similar way constructible out of or reducible to certain other facts that can help explain our observations.

This is certainly a plausible suggestion for certain *nonmoral* evaluative facts. Consider, for example, what is involved in something's being a good thing of its kind, a good knife, a good watch, or a good heart. Associated with these kinds of things are certain functions. A knife is something that is used for cutting; a watch is used to keep time; a heart is that organ that pumps the blood. Furthermore, something is a good thing of the relevant kind to the extent that it adequately fulfills its proper function. A good knife cuts well; a good watch keeps accurate time; a good heart pumps blood at the right pressure without faltering. Let us use the letter "K" to stand for a kind of thing. Then, for these cases, a good K is a K that adequately fulfills its function. It is a factual question whether or not something is a good K because it is a factual question whether or not K's have that function and a factual question whether or not this given something adequately fulfills that function.

Moreover, a K ought to fulfill its function. If it does not do so, something has gone wrong. Therefore, it is a factual question whether a given K of this sort is as it ought to be and does what it ought to do, and it is a factual question whether anything is wrong with a K of this sort. A knife ought to be sharp, so that it will cut well. There is something wrong with a heart that fails to pump blood without faltering. . . .

More complex cases involve roles that a person can have in one way or another: a good farmer, a good soldier, a good teacher, a good citizen, a good thief. A person is evaluated in terms of functions, roles, and various interests in a way that is hard to specify. Here too the words "ought" and "wrong" are relevant as before. During battle, we say, a soldier ought to obey his superior officers without question. It is wrong for a teacher to play favorites. A thief ought to wear gloves.

Some kinds of things are not associated with functions, purposes, or sets of interests; for example, rocks per se are not. Therefore, it does not make sense to ask apart from a specific context whether something is a good rock. We can answer such a question only in relation to interests that we might have in possible uses of the rock. For example, it might be a good rock to use as a paperweight; but, if it is to be used as a doorstop, maybe it ought to be heavier.

The relevant evaluative judgments are factual. The facts are natural facts though somewhat complex facts. We judge that something is good or bad, that it is right or wrong, that it ought or ought not to have certain characteristics or do certain things, relative to a cluster of interests, roles, and functions. We can abbreviate this by saying that something X is good to the extent that it adequately answers to the relevant interests. To specify those interests is to specify what X is good as. Similarly, a person P ought to do D if and only if P's doing D would answer to the relevant interests.

This analysis is a realistic one for many cases and it suggests how evaluative facts might be constructed out of observable facts even when the evaluative facts themselves do not figure in explanations of observations. That my watch is a good one may not explain anything about my observations of it; but that it keeps fairly accurate time does help to explain its continual agreement with the announcements of

the time on the radio and perhaps the goodness of my watch consists in facts of this sort.

But a problem manifests itself when this sort of analysis is applied in ethics. Consider a case in which you are a doctor who either can save five patients by cutting up the healthy patient in Room 306 and distributing his organs to the other patients or can do nothing and let the five other patients die. The problem is that in either case you would be satisfying certain interests and not others. The interests of the five dying patients conflict with the interests of the healthy patient in Room 306. The moral question is what you ought to do, taking all interests into account. Our intuitive judgment is that you ought not to sacrifice the one patient in Room 306 to save the five other patients. Is this a factual judgment? If we suppose that it is a fact that you ought not to sacrifice the patient in Room 306, how is that fact related to facts that can help explain observations? It is not at all obvious how we can extend our analysis to cover this sort of case. . . .

Although we are in no position to assume that nihilism is correct, we are now in a position to see more clearly the way in which ethics is problematic. Our starting point was that moral judgments do not seem to help explain observations. This led us to wonder whether there are moral facts, moral truths, and moral knowledge. We saw that there could be moral facts if these facts were reducible in some way or other to other facts of a sort that might help explain observations. For we noticed that there are facts about the average American citizen, even though such facts do not themselves help explain observations, because such facts are reducible to facts about American citizens that can help explain observations. Similarly, we noticed that we would not decide that there are no facts about colors even if we were able to explain color perception without appealing to facts about colors; we would instead suppose that facts about colors are reducible to facts about the physical surfaces of objects, the properties of light, and the neurophysiological psychology of observers. So, we concluded that we did not have to accept ethical nihilism simply because moral facts do not seem to help explain observations; instead we might hope for a naturalistic reduction of moral facts.

With this in mind, we considered the possibility that moral facts might be reduced to facts about interests, roles, and functions. We concluded that, if they were to be, the reduction would have to be complex, vague, and difficult to specify. Ethics remains problematic. . . .

We are willing to suppose that there are facts about color, despite our not knowing precisely how to reduce them, because in practice we assume that there are such facts in many of our explanations of color perception, even if in theory this assumption is dispensable. We are willing to suppose that there are facts about the average American citizen, despite our never using such an assumption to explain observations, because we can precisely reduce these facts to facts of a sort that can help explain observations. Since moral facts seem to be neither precisely reducible nor useful even in practice in our explanations of observations, it remains problematic whether we have any reason to suppose that there are any moral facts.

DISCUSSION QUESTIONS:

1. Do you think that you can literally see that some actions are right and that others are wrong? What does the rightness or wrongness look like? If you don't think you can literally sense rightness and wrongness, how do you come to know what's right and wrong?

2. Suppose you can't literally observe moral facts. What about other moral observations that you make? For example, what about "thought experiments" like when you imagine what you should do in a particular situation? Should we assume that your responses to such imagined scenarios give you a reason to believe in one moral theory over another?

3. Do you think that you would make the same judgments about right and wrong had you grown up with a different family? What about a different culture? Does this prove that moral facts are not necessary to explain your moral observations or moral beliefs?

4. Do you think moral nihilism is true? If so, is there no way to legitimately criticize the behavior of mass murderers and terrorists? If not, why do you think that moral nihilism is false?

Argument Reconstruction Exercises:

I. Harman initially tries to show how scientific theorizing is akin to moral theorizing. They both share a similar feature, and this shows that the two practices are similar in an important respect. Identify the premises and conclusion in this excerpt:

> In other words, in both science and ethics, general principles are invoked to explain particular cases and, therefore, in both science and ethics, the general principles you accept can be tested by appealing to particular judgments that certain things are right or wrong, just or unjust, and so forth. (page 38)

II. Despite their initial similarity, Harman argues that observation plays a very different role in science than it does in ethics. Identify the premises and conclusion in this excerpt:

> The observation of an event can provide observational evidence for or against a scientific theory in the sense that the truth of that observation can be relevant to a reasonable explanation of why that observation was made. A moral observation does not seem, in the same sense, to be observational evidence for or against any moral theory, since the truth or falsity of the moral observation seems to be completely irrelevant to any reasonable explanation of why that observation was made. (page 39)

III. At one point, Harman states the argument for moral nihilism rather explicitly. Identify the premises and conclusion in this excerpt:

> Our previous discussion suggests the following argument for moral nihilism:
>
> > Moral hypotheses never help to explain why we observe anything. So we have no evidence for our moral opinions.

The argument depends upon this assumption:

> We can have evidence for hypotheses of a certain sort only if such hypotheses sometimes help explain why we observe what we observe. (page 40)

IV. Harman notes that if we could find a way to reduce moral facts to natural facts, this would allow us to say that moral facts could be explanatory in the same sense as other natural facts. One way to do this is to understand moral facts as evaluative facts about functions. Identify the premises and conclusion in the following paraphrased argument:

> Some knives are good, and some knives are not good. If a knife is dull, it's true that it ought not be this way. Similarly, some people are good, and some people are not good. When a person acts wrongly, it's true that he ought not behave in this way. And since facts about knives being good are natural facts, so, too are facts about people being good.

6.2 VALUES IN A SCIENTIFIC WORLD

RUSS SHAFER-LANDAU (2004)

Russ Shafer-Landau is professor of philosophy at the University of Wisconsin-Madison. Much of his professional work is in the foundations of ethics. In this essay, he is concerned not so much with the *content* of morality (e.g., which acts are right and which acts are wrong) but the *status* of morality (e.g., whether *any* acts are right or wrong in the first place and how we can know which acts are which). He considers the argument from explanation that shows that moral facts do not exist. According to this argument, it is reasonable to believe in something only if that thing explains something else. But since moral facts do not explain anything, it is not reasonable to believe in them. Shafer-Landau sketches ways that a **moral objectivist** might respond to this argument and ultimately concludes that it is reasonable to believe in at least some things that do not explain anything else.

Reading Questions:

1. What is ontology?

2. What is moral objectivism?

3. What is Occam's razor?

4. According to Shafer-Landau, why don't moral facts explain non-moral facts?

5. According to Shafer-Landau, why is it illegitimate for the moral objectivist to insist that moral facts explain other moral facts?

6. What is a *normative* fact?

7. What is the confirmation test?

Good and evil are values. But what could a value be? It seems to be something unique, unlike anything else in the world. In an inventory of the world's contents—philosophers call this an **ontology,** a list or theory of what exists—will we really find anything that answers to our notions of good and evil?

Suppose, with moral objectivis, that moral judgments are true, and true quite independently of what we happen to think of them. They are true, when they are, because they accurately report objective moral facts. But the nature of such facts can appear very mysterious. We readily grant that geologists and chemists, physicists and astronomers deal in objective truth, because we believe that their findings are targeted on a natural world whose features exist independently of whether anyone recognizes them. Botanical facts are facts about plants; geological facts are facts about rocks. In botany and geology, evidence is supplied by three-dimensional, tangible, physical stuff. We can taste it, smell it, touch it, and see it. We can't taste wrongness or hear rightness. *Moral facts, if they were to exist, would have to be quite odd sorts of things, certainly nothing at all like the kinds of phenomena studied by the recognized sciences.*

Suppose we make an effort to understand the nature of objective reality, and are searching, in particular, for what exists prior to our contributions to the world. This ontology will surely include such things as molecules, stars, catfish, clouds, and atomic particles. It will include such features as having six sides, a symmetrical structure, or a hard surface, and being colorless, a foot long, a micron in width, and soluble in water. Is there any room in there for good and evil?

The basic reason for suspicion stems from an application of **Occam's razor**. William of Occam, a medieval philosopher, instructed us not to multiply entities (or suppositions) beyond necessity. *If there are competing theories to explain some phenomenon, then the better theory is the one that makes the fewest assumptions, or posits the fewest mechanisms.* His maxim, which is basically a counsel to adopt the simplest, most economical view of things, is almost universally embraced within philosophy, mathematics, and the natural sciences.

To see how Occam's razor works, consider one of its more famous applications: the vindication of the Copernican theory of planetary orbit. The Ptolemaic conception that it replaced was positively baroque by comparison. Copernicus explained the same phenomena that Ptolemy sought to, only with far fewer assumptions, positing far fewer entities. Conversion to the Copernican system didn't occur overnight. Conceptual revolutions rarely do. But its ultimate triumph lay primarily in its ability to explain all that Ptolemy's theory was able to do, with the added benefit of employing fewer assumptions into the bargain. Occam's razor at work.

We can deploy this stratagem in the service of a powerful *Argument from Occam's Razor* against ethical objectivism. This argument asks us to survey the world and report on its contents. And it tells us to do so by employing the following test: is the thing in question required to help us to explain what we see in our world? If the answer is No, then we have

reason to abandon any belief in it. And the moral skeptic claims that when we have a careful look at what surrounds us, we'll have no need of the objectivist's assumption that the world contains moral features:

The Argument from Occam's Razor

1. We have reason to believe that something exists only if it is explanatorily indispensable.
2. Moral facts are not explanatorily indispensable.
3. Therefore we lack reason to believe in the existence of moral facts.

To get a better sense of what is at stake here, consider what has happened to once-predominant views about the existence of God, or the immortal soul, or leprechauns and trolls. Though many still believe in God and the soul, why have we seen so great an increase in skepticism about their existence? Why have we seen the *complete* abandonment of belief in leprechauns and trolls? Doubtless there are a variety of cultural factors involved. But there is also, and perhaps primarily, a philosophical source of such doubt, That source is Occam's razor, and the eponymous Argument that gives expression to it.

Supernatural forces were once invoked to explain why regions suffered drought, why people died, why rivers ran their course, why volcanoes erupted. These explanations have been threatened by modern science. Since there is a scientific explanation for all of these happenings, what is left for God (or those other supernatural beings) to do?

We can put the question even more sharply. Consider any given event in the world—how about catching a cold? There is, it seems, a complete medical explanation for this occurrence. Perhaps no one has all of the details for any given case, but science tells us that, in principle, we could cite an extremely complex biochemical story that explains how a person (say) contracts influenza.

With this story in hand, what room is there for anything else to get into the picture? Knowing what we now know, we *need* to refer to microbes, immune systems, and viruses or bacteria in order to explain why people get sick. That's why we are justified in thinking that such things exist, even though we can't see them with the naked eye. But given that the biochemical story can offer us a complete picture of the origins of a cold, we haven't any need to go beyond its details. The reason we don't believe in leprechauns or trolls is that they don't explain anything. Everything they were once invoked to explain has been better, more efficiently explained by the workings of modern science.

In effect, what the moral skeptic is giving us is a universe exclusively regulated by scientific laws, containing only the things that are ratified by science. Ethical objectivists give us a fuller, more expansive ontology. This includes all that science does, but adds an additional layer—moral principles and facts. In addition to protons, neutrons, electrons, molecules, gases and liquids, we also get good and evil, virtue and vice. Skeptics wield the razor to pare away such superfluous things. All that needs explaining can be taken care of strictly within the scientific viewpoint.

When we ask what is in our world, where should we begin? It's natural to begin with what we can see. And we quickly move to what we can hear, and touch, taste, and smell. In short, we take in the evidence of the senses and then ask how they can be best explained. What in the world (literally) is causing us to have the experiences we do? When we find out what it is, we can add that to our ontological catalogue. And not before.

We are justified in thinking that there are trees, and buildings, and rocks, because if we walk long enough, we'll bump into them. We've got some evidence—a bruised shoulder, a bumped shin—and we need to account for it. And once our curiosity gets the best of us, we'll want to know what made the trees the way they are, what made our shins as vulnerable as they are, etc. In pursuit of such knowledge, we develop and apply ever finer instruments and hypotheses to account for the phenomena we are investigating. We've gotten all the way to nucleotides and string theory. Who knows where we'll end?

The question for ethics is whether or not all the evidence of our senses requires the postulation of moral facts to explain them. Do we need the categories of good and evil, of right and wrong, to explain how clouds form, why rainbows appear, why people succumb to disease? It doesn't seem so. In fact, it doesn't seem that moral qualities help to explain *anything* that occurs in the natural world. But then we have

two choices: either they aren't needed to explain anything at all, in which case Occam's razor tells us that they don't really exist, or they *are* needed to explain something, but something that isn't part of the natural world.

Two Options for the Moral Objectivist

[1] There are problems either way we go. If moral facts explain nothing at all, then why believe that there are any such things? The best reason we have for discrediting belief in trolls and ghosts, after all, is that (i) we've never seen any such things, and (ii) these things aren't needed to explain anything we *have* seen. It seems that we can tell a perfectly parallel story in the case of morality.

Have you ever seen evil? You may think so. Perhaps only in films, if you're lucky. But what have you really seen? Two persons, perhaps, one with a rifle, hauling a child out of her home and pushing her to her knees. Soldiers nearby, laughing and encouraging their comrade. The one with the rifle casually lifts it to the chest of the little girl. You hear a noise. The girl falls in a heap. Blood leaks from her body. The soldiers move on, buoyant, looking for another victim.

If you've seen such a thing, you've seen evil—if that's not evil, what is? But you could provide a full description of all the actions of such a scene, and never once mention evil. You'd mention the position of the rifleman and his victim, the soldier's words, the way he manhandled his victim, her look of fear, the impact of the bullet, etc. *You don't need to cite the evil of the action to completely explain what happened.* All the explanatory work can be done without it. The girl didn't die because of evil—she died because of a bullet to the chest. You have to mention that to explain her death. You don't have to mention evil at all.

Because reference to the moral quality of the interaction is optional, it isn't required. And Occam's razor tells us that, therefore, we have no reason to believe that it's real. Moral skeptics capitalize on this and allege that either evil is nonexistent, or that evil is a human construct. There is no such thing as evil, really. If evil exists at all, it is only as a result of our projecting onto a value-free world our emotional repugnance at actions that, taken in themselves, are entirely morally neutral.

David Hume, the most brilliant of the philosophers of the Scottish enlightenment, captured this very idea more than two hundred years ago:

> Take any action allow'd to be vicious: Wilful murder, for instance. Examine it in all lights, and see if you can find that matter of fact, or real existence, which you call *vice*. In whichever way you take it, you find only certain passions, motives, volitions and thoughts. There is no other matter of fact in the case. The vice entirely escapes you, as long as you consider the object. You never can find it, till you turn your reflexion into your own breast, and find a sentiment of disapprobation, which arises in you, towards this action. . . . [W]hen you pronounce any action or character to be vicious, you mean nothing, but that from the constitution of your nature you have a feeling or sentiment of blame from the contemplation of it. (*Treatise of Human Nature,* Book III, Part I, Section I)

In a thorough description of all that the world contains, we will require no mention of virtue or vice. Even wilful murder, the epitome of vice, can be wholly described without the use of any moral vocabulary at all. Just the facts, ma'am. A coroner's report or a police blotter may include a full description of truly sociopathic behavior. But it needn't go on to register a moral verdict of the matter. That is gratuitous, at least from an explanatory standpoint. Adding the fact that the gunman's actions were depraved, evil, vicious, etc., tells us nothing we didn't already know about the cause of death.

So Occam's razor supports Hume's moral skepticism. *Because we don't need to cite moral facts in order to explain the goings-on in the natural world, we have no reason to believe in them.* There is the world that science tells us about. There are our emotional responses to that world (e.g., our "sentiments of disapprobation"). And that's it.

[2] The alternative for the ethical objectivist is to claim that moral facts *are* needed to explain things, but things that lay outside the purview of the natural sciences. If moral facts really are explanatorily indispensable, then Occam's razor will insist that we keep them in our catalogue of the world's contents. But are they really indispensable in this way?

A problem arises when we ask, specifically, about what moral facts might be needed to explain. *There are two possibilities: moral facts could explain nonmoral facts, or moral facts might explain other moral facts.* The first option isn't promising. We have seen, in considering the wilful murder case, that moral facts (such as an agent's evil nature, or evil action) don't really add anything to an explanation of the nonmoral occurrences in the world. All that takes place in the natural world can be explained without citing the moral qualities of things.

So that leaves us with the second possibility—moral facts are needed to explain things, but only other moral facts. Hitler's callousness, depravity, and cruel indifference explain why he was evil, for instance. This is all right, as far as it goes. But it doesn't go very far, and that's putting it kindly. For the objectivist strategy here is really nothing other than a classic case of begging the question. You beg the question when you presuppose what must be proved. The present strategy is to defend the objective existence of moral facts by claiming that they pass the Occam's razor test. They are explanatorily indispensable. If that's so, then what are they required to explain? Other moral facts. But this just *assumes* that there are moral facts in need of explanation, and that is the very point at issue. Skeptics are in the business of challenging the existence of such facts. We can't just assume that they're there, and then go looking for what will explain them (other moral facts). That puts the cart before the horse.

Well, now we're in trouble. Morality is in real danger of being cut out of the ontological inventory. We said goodbye to trolls and mermaids and centaurs. We never laid eyes on them, and we didn't need to rely on them in order to explain anything in our experience. Perhaps we must take our leave of moral facts for the very same reasons.

There is only one way out, and that is the hard way.

The Hard Way

Ethical objectivists must reject the claim that something exists only if there is an explanatory need that it fulfills. Moral facts aren't necessary to explain anything. But they may exist for all that.

There are at least three arguments that objectivists can rely on to defend such a claim.

[1] The first tries to reveal the absurd implications of the skeptical position. The skeptic insists that something exists only if it is needed to explain what we experience. But, as it turns out, only a very few things are needed for such a task. According to the skeptic's own test, therefore, everything else is nonexistent.

Let's make this a little less mysterious. Recall Hume's example of wilful murder, and my gloss on it. I had said there that if we want to understand why the victim died, we *must* make reference to the bullet that killed her, whereas we needn't make any mention of the evil or wrongness involved. According to Occam's razor, that entitles us to believe that bullets really exist. And that moral facts don't.

But must we really make mention of bullets to explain the cause of death? Couldn't we do as well, or better, by citing the biochemistry that led to the death? Surely there is a biochemical story to tell about what occurred during the fateful moments of the shooting. If we had that in hand, then why bring in bullets (and blood, and cessation of breath, etc.)? We *could* mention such things, but we wouldn't *need* to. And that consigns such things as bullets to the ontological dustbin. They don't really exist.

There's a general point here: Occam's razor forces us to abandon belief in most things we think are real. There's nothing special about bullets. Cars, pumpkins, hammers, dishwashers . . . the list is endless. Though we often do cite such things in explaining what goes on in our world, we don't need to. We could just as well talk in terms of molecules or atoms. Likewise, though we often do invoke moral features to explain things in the world, Occam's razor tells us that we haven't any need of such things. Someone's goodness explains why she cared for that lost child. The chairman's integrity explains why he votes according to the rules, rather than rigging the ballot to suit his preferences. A state's iniquity explains why so many rebel against it. All of these seem like perfectly good explanations. But if we are to do away with moral features, because they aren't really needed to explain what occurs, then we should be equally prepared to do away with most things.

We have two choices. Each is based on the claim that there is a parity between moral features and most other features of the world. We either keep such things as bullets and hammers in our ontology, or we scrap them. If we keep them, then we keep the moral features, too. We can do that either by abandoning Occam's razor, or by sticking with it and finding a way to conclude that such things pass its test. Alternatively, we might stick with Occam's razor, and claim that it cuts moral features out of the ontology. They aren't needed to explain what happens in the world. But then we need to get rid of most of what we think is real, since bullets, etc., would also be unnecessary to do any explaining. (All references to such thing could be replaced by references to molecules and atoms.) As long as you're prepared to accept the reality of dishwashers and hammers (and bullets and blood and . . .), then you should be prepared to accept the reality of good and evil.

[2] Here is a second objectivist argument to show that moral facts can exist, even if they aren't needed to explain anything. The key claim here is that moral facts are a species of *normative fact*. Normative facts are those that tell us what we *ought* to do. Normative facts don't explain anything. Yet they exist for all that.

In my own opinion, moral facts are most similar to another kind of normative fact—epistemic facts. **Epistemic facts** concern what we ought to *believe*, provided that our beliefs are aimed at the truth. If you believe something on the basis of excellent evidence, and know that your belief entails another, then you *ought* to believe that further proposition. This is a true epistemic principle.

Moral facts, like epistemic ones, are normative. Their existence, if I am right, does not depend on our finding an explanatory need that they satisfy. *Occam's razor is too strict a test for the existence of normative principles and facts.*

Here is an epistemic fact: you ought to believe that two and two are four. What does this fact (i.e., the fact that you ought to believe this equation) explain? Nothing. But surely there are things that you ought to believe, and just as surely, you (or your culture) don't get to have the final say about every such matter. You *ought* to believe a whole host of things that you don't, or don't want, to believe. Many of these are things that your culture doesn't believe, and doesn't want you to believe, either. The scope of our epistemic duties is not limited by personal or cultural opinion. There really are such duties. And they don't explain a thing.

The parallel with morality should be clear. We have good reason to think that moral duties exist, and do not ultimately depend on personal or cultural ratification. The question is whether the force of that cumulative case can be overridden by morality's failure to pass some explanatory test.

I don't believe that the test can be that powerful. I don't mean to suggest for a moment that Occam's razor is useless. Rather, I think we should recognize its limits. It doesn't work when applied to the normative realm. When we consider all of our oughts—what we ought to do in order to believe the truth, or behave morally, or maximize our self-interest, etc.—then we will expect answers that, as it turns out, have no ability to explain the workings of the natural order. Our epistemic and moral duties cannot explain why chameleons change their color, why cyclones form, or why heat rises. They may exist for all that.

Surely there are certain things that you ought to believe. If all the evidence is staring you in the face, then there's something you ought to believe, even if it's easier, or psychologically more comforting, to put your head in the sand. If your second-grader comes home and tells you that six times six is thirty-five, then there's something else she ought to believe—no matter how stubbornly she resists your counsel. It's easy to multiply examples. The point is that we all agree that there are certain things that each of us ought to believe. You don't really suppose that every such duty is just a fiction, or merely a matter of conforming to your own standards, or those of your culture. There really are epistemic oughts, epistemic duties. And there are moral ones, too. This despite the fact that such normative truths fail to pull their weight in the network of explanations that tells us how the natural world operates.

If we think about it for a moment, this shouldn't be all that surprising. The kinds of principles that science vindicates are essentially *causal* and *predictive*. We are justified in believing in them because they accurately cite the causes of events and predict what

is going to happen. Their explanatory power consists in precisely this ability. The law of gravity tells me that every time I drop my keys, they're going to fall to the ground. And they always do. We are justified in believing in a gravitational force just because it can explain so many things better than any competing hypothesis.

But moral rules are not like that. The rule enjoining us not to perjure ourselves is true even if it is honored only in the breach. Moral rules don't depend for their justification on an ability to predict what will happen. Moral principles aren't meant to describe what people do, or anticipate their actions, but rather to *prescribe* how they ought to behave. They don't cite the causes of outcomes, but rather indicate what sort of conduct would merit approval, or justify our gratitude, or legitimate some result. Science can't tell us such things.

So we are really faced with a choice. If we take up an exclusively scientific view of the world, then there is no room for normative principles and normative facts. But such things do exist. There are genuine reasons to believe things, and genuine moral reasons to do things. Science cannot verify the existence of such reasons, duties, or principles. But that only points to the limits of science, rather than to the limits of a credible ontology.

[3] One final argument. Think of the big picture here. What kind of world view is being advanced by those who would do away with moral features? My hunch is that something like **the confirmation test** is what underlies so much suspicion about morality. The confirmation test says that *a claim is true only if it is scientifically confirmable.* Since we can't confirm moral claims scientifically, they aren't confirmable at all. And if they aren't scientifically confirmable, then we have no reason to think that any of them are true.

Importantly, the confirmation test *cannot* be true. And so there can be truths whose existence escapes scientific confirmation. If I am right, objective principles that state our moral obligations are such truths.

Why can't the confirmation test be true? Simple: *if we suppose that the test is true, then it is self-refuting.* If we correctly apply the test, then it turns out that the test itself flunks. It doesn't measure up to its own standards. So it must be false.

Here's the basic idea: if the confirmation test were true, then it would be an instance of a true claim that cannot be scientifically confirmed. Science is totally ill-equipped to render a verdict on the merits of the confirmation test. The discipline best suited to assessing that test is *philosophy*. And philosophical claims are not the sort that can be verified exclusively by scientific means.

Since the confirmation test cannot be true, we needn't decide what is real and unreal just by reference to what science can tell us. Indeed, based on arguments that we have already seen, and some yet to come, we have excellent reason for thinking that there is more to the world than science can reveal. Among these extra ingredients are normative facts and principles. And foremost among these are moral duties and moral rules. The fact that science cannot tell us how to behave doesn't mean that we are free to do as we please. It just means that science can't tell us everything we need to know.

DISCUSSION QUESTIONS:

1. Do you think that Occam's razor is true? Why should we prefer simpler theories or explanations over more complex ones? Is simplicity, as such, really a guide to truth?
2. Shafer-Landau doesn't think that it is legitimate for a moral objectivist to argue that moral facts explain other moral facts. He thinks this begs the question against the moral skeptic who denies that there are any moral facts. Is this correct? Suppose someone said that light bulbs don't exist because they don't explain anything. To the contrary, you claim that the light bulb explains the fact that there is light in the room, the fact that the lamp is warm to the touch, etc. In response, the skeptic announces that she doesn't believe in light, lamps, etc. Is that a reason for you to give up your belief in light bulbs?
3. Do you think that there are any entities or properties that exist but do not explain anything? Like what?

Argument Reconstruction Exercises:
I. Shafer-Landau ultimately concludes that there are things that exist in our world that are outside of the bounds of science. Identify the premises and conclusion in this excerpt:

> If we take up an exclusively scientific view of the world, then there is no room for normative principles and normative facts. But such things do exist. There are genuine reasons to believe things, and genuine moral reasons to do things. Science cannot verify the existence of such reasons, duties, or principles. But that only points to the limits of science, rather than the limits of a credible ontology. (page 48)

II. Shafer-Landau takes up Harman's challenge to show how moral facts help to explain the moral observations that we make. In this argument, he reconstructs Harman's reasoning in order to clarify the assumptions his argument makes. Identify the premises and conclusion in this excerpt:

> Because reference to the moral quality of the interaction is optional, it isn't required. And Occam's razor tells us that, therefore, we have no reason to believe that it's real. Moral skeptics capitalize on this and allege that either evil is nonexistent, or that evil is a human construct. There is no such thing as evil, really. (page 45)

III. Shafer-Landau thinks that the nihilist position is often defended by an appeal to what he calls the confirmation test. Here he shows how the confirmation test plays a crucial role in the argument for the claim that we have no evidence for our moral beliefs. Identify the premises and conclusion in this excerpt:

> My hunch is that something like the confirmation test is what underlies so much suspicion about morality. The confirmation test says that a claim is true only if it is scientifically confirmable. Since we can't confirm moral claims scientifically, they aren't confirmable at all. And if they aren't scientifically confirmable, then we have no reason to think that any of them are true. (page 48)

IV. Shafer-Landau argues that, despite its initial attraction, the confirmation test cannot be true. This argument attempts to clarify why it is self-refuting. Identify the premises and conclusion in this excerpt:

The confirmation test says that a claim is true only if it is scientifically confirmable. . . . Why can't the confirmation test be true? Simple: if we suppose that the test is true, then it is self-refuting. If we correctly apply the test, then it turns out that the test itself flunks. It doesn't measure up to its own standards. So it must be false. (page 48)

6.3 FOUR ARGUMENTS AGAINST MORAL KNOWLEDGE

RUSS SHAFER-LANDAU (2004)

Russ Shafer-Landau is professor of philosophy at the University of Wisconsin-Madison. In this essay, he reviews four of the most common arguments for the claim that humans can't have any **moral knowledge.** These are the argument from certainty, the epistemic argument from disagreement, the perspectival argument, and the argument from inadequate evidence. He concludes that each of the arguments is unsound. If it's true that we can't have moral knowledge, it must be for different (and better!) reasons than those provided here.

Reading Questions:

1. What does it mean to say that there are moral facts?

2. According to Shafer-Landau, what is the difference between feeling certain and being genuinely certain?

3. According to Shafer-Landau, what did Descartes prove about what's certain for us?

4. What does it mean to say that disagreement is intractable?

5. Shafer-Landau refers to an "ideal perspective" on moral issues. What is an ideal perspective? Does anyone have an ideal perspective on ethical matters? How about on scientific matters?

6. What is the difference between evidence and *empirical* evidence?

7. According to Shafer-Landau, what kinds of things count as evidence for moral beliefs?

Surely one of the great obstacles to a belief in objective moral truths is our puzzlement at how we might gain knowledge of them. If you are like most people, you'll assume that you are imperfect, can make moral mistakes, and that some of the moral convictions you now hold are mistaken (though you aren't sure which). Wouldn't it be nice to discover a method to sort out the true beliefs from the false ones? The problem is that there doesn't seem to be any good way to do this.

To get knowledge in any area is to have, at the least, some beliefs about it that are both true *and* justified. True beliefs aren't good enough. They might be the result of guesswork, of dependence on unreliable sources, of misconstruing the evidence. We want true beliefs that are well supported.

The problem, says the skeptic, is that we can't have justified moral beliefs. Ever. And so moral knowledge is an impossibility. [**Skepticism** . . . refers to doubts about the possibility of moral knowledge, rather than to doubts about the existence of objective moral truth.]

There are [four] major arguments that skeptics offer to defeat our hopes of gaining moral knowledge. Here is a preview . . . starting with the argument that presents the least difficulty to the defender of moral knowledge.

That would be the *Argument from Certainty*, which relies on the impossibility of ever being certain about one's moral claims. Knowledge, it is thought, requires certainty. But certainty is unobtainable in ethics. So moral knowledge itself is impossible.

Why is moral certainty unobtainable? Simple: for any moral belief you hold, there will be someone who is informed and rational, and who will remain unconvinced to the bitter end. This is the second skeptical worry, expressed in the *Epistemic Argument from Disagreement*. The existence of rational, informed people with views that are diametrically opposed to yours undermines any justification you have for your beliefs. And yet this is precisely the situation that holds for *all* of our ethical beliefs. Therefore we can have no justification for our moral outlooks. And without justification, there can be no knowledge.

The *Perspectival Argument* begins with the assumption that there is no uniquely best perspective from which to make moral judgments. Once we grant that assumption, and make the further claim that justified belief can be had only when one has adopted the best perspective for viewing a matter, then we get the result that we cannot be justified in any of our moral beliefs. Hence moral knowledge is an impossibility.

The fourth worry, which serves as the basis for the *Argument from Inadequate Evidence*, concerns the kind of evidence we can have in support of our moral judgments. We have a clear idea of what counts as evidence in all other areas we acknowledge to be objective. Botanists study plants; geologists study rock formations; hydrologists study water. We know such things exist because we can see them. Moral facts aren't like that. It seems that all the evidence

we have for our moral beliefs is our feeling that they must be right. But that is a notoriously shaky basis for knowledge. Since ethics can do no better, any claim to moral knowledge is equally shaky.

Let's take these criticisms in order. This has the virtue of bolstering the spirit, since the first argument, as it turns out, is also the easiest to handle. Having disposed of it, we can buck up our confidence and tackle those that are substantially more difficult.

The Argument from Certainty

The 1st argument claims that we can't have moral knowledge because we can't have moral certainty. How should we plead? Guilty. *We can't have certainty in ethics.* But we are facing trumped-up charges here. *The claim that knowledge requires certainty is mistaken.* Or, if it is correct, then we can know almost nothing at all.

Before we show this, it is important to get clear on a terminological point. Of course people can *feel* certain about their views on moral issues. They may be absolutely unwavering in their commitments, totally sure that, at least in some moral matters, they can't be mistaken. But this feeling is compatible with error—indeed, it must be, if there are people who feel equally strongly about such matters, and yet disagree. They can't both be right. (That would be a contradiction.) *So a feeling of certainty isn't the same thing as genuine certainty.* Genuine certainty, like knowledge, entails that the proposition you are certain of is true.

Genuine certainty is almost nonexistent. Philosophy students learn this when they encounter Rene Descartes's *Meditations* for the first time. In his classic work, Descartes decides to cast aside all of his beliefs, in the hopes of starting with a clean slate. Only those beliefs that are literally indubitable—incapable of being doubted—will be retained, in order to serve as foundations for a reconstructed, pure edifice of knowledge. Every new belief will be either indubitable itself, or derived by pure logic from indubitable beliefs, so as to ensure the security of the entire network of beliefs. A classic philosophical dream. Everything is guaranteed, every belief underwritten by certainty and logic. Like many a beautiful dream, it was never destined to be realized.

To purge himself of possibly false beliefs, Descartes imagined an evil demon, who was manipulating him into thinking his present thoughts. He believed he was sitting before a fire, watching a candle burn. But he might have been dreaming. He was sure that two and three are five, but the certitude he felt at such a thought may have been just a manufactured confidence, implanted by an evil genius bent on deception. The basic problem is this: all the evidence that Descartes used to justify his beliefs (namely, other beliefs and experiences) could be equally explained on the assumption that an evil demon was deceiving him. Until he could eliminate that assumption, he couldn't be sure that his beliefs were true. And absent such certainty, he couldn't *know* whether they were true or false.

OK, not everything can be subject to this sort of sweeping doubt. In particular, Descartes came upon his famous maxim, *cogito ergo sum*: I think, therefore I am. So long as he was thinking—even thinking that he might be systematically deceived—there was someone doing the thinking. And so he could at least be certain of *that*. As it turns out, Descartes couldn't be sure of any other aspect of his own biography, for any such impressions might have been implanted in him by the evil demon. But he *could* be sure that so long as he was thinking, then there was something, he knew not what, that was doing the thinking.

And what else could he know? Just about nothing . . . You think you are reading this now? You might be mistaken. You think you're living in the twenty-first century? (Possibly) wrong again. You think you know what town you're in, what the names of your family and friends are, what teacher you had in the third grade? Think again. You can't be certain of any of it.

You might be dreaming right now. Didn't you ever dream that you were awake, thankful that, at least this time, you weren't dreaming your good luck? Didn't you ever wish, within a dream, that it were only a dream, "knowing" all the while that it was an awful reality you had to go and face? If this has never happened to you, try a contemporary spin on Descartes's fantasy for a moment. It might be the case that, right at this very moment,

you are just a brain in a vat, your cerebral cortex being manipulated by ingenious neuroscientists to simulate the activity of reading a book [on ethics]. Can you prove that this is *not* what is happening to you? How would you do such a thing? All the evidence you bring forward is compatible with both hypotheses—the one that says you're a real, live person, just as you think you are, and the other, which says that, as a perfectly manipulated brain in a vat, even the appearances of your protesting your full-bodied existence are being fed into your cortex by the neuroscientists who control the brain that you are.

Here's a distressing bit of news. Philosophers have never solved this problem. They have never demonstrated the existence of an external world—a world that exists outside of your thoughts, a world whose details are mirrored in your thoughts, a world of 3-D stuff that exists independently of you. We all believe that there is such a world. And none of us can prove it.

What follows? Just this. *If you insist on certainty as a precondition of knowledge, then you can know almost nothing.* You can know that you exist, so long as you are thinking, though you can't know anything much about yourself. You can also know that things appear to you in certain ways—you can be certain that there *seems* to be a page here, right in front of your nose, that there *appears* to be a sun and a moon and other people about. Of that you can be sure. But you can't be sure that there *really* is a page here, a sun, a moon, and other people. You can't be sure that there is anything outside of you, and you can't even be certain about who you are—what your history is, what you look like, when you are living, etc. You could be dreaming. Or systematically deceived. You can't prove that you're not.

So here is the choice. Insist on certainty, and foreclose the chance of getting any real knowledge. Or relax the standards required for gaining knowledge. This latter is what almost every philosopher has done. Philosophers have taken from Descartes precisely the opposite message that he intended to convey: *don't* insist on certainty as a requirement for knowledge. It sets the bar too high.

If we can have knowledge without certainty, then, for all we've said so far, we might have *moral* knowledge without certainty. It would be unfair to hold morality to standards higher than those in any other area. Certainty promises a kind of epistemic purity. But it is a false promise, holding out hopes that can never be realized. *If knowledge requires certainty, then we must abandon hopes for moral knowledge. But then we must give up on every other kind of knowledge as well.*

Epistemic Argument from Disagreement

Rather than do that, let's take up the second skeptical criticism, which tries to show that there is something especially troublesome about *moral* knowledge. Here, in the Epistemic Argument from Disagreement we confront a variation on a familiar theme, one that seeks to undermine [moral] objectivism by pointing to the greater lack of consensus within ethics, as opposed to that found within the natural sciences and mathematics. Here the claim is *not* that intractable disagreement reveals an absence of objective ethical truth. Rather, the claim is that such disagreement undercuts the possibility of ever knowing what it is.

The basic idea is that persistent disagreement, at least among those who know all the relevant facts and are thinking them through efficiently, defeats the justification you might otherwise have for your beliefs. If you can't convince such a person, then maybe you shouldn't be convinced yourself. Though that sounds pretty plausible, there are two problems with it, one in practice, one in theory.

[1] The practical problem is that you can never really be sure whether you have reached a point where an opponent's intransigence is reason for you to withdraw your endorsement of some moral belief. After all, he might not really have all the information he claims to have. He might be making some error of reasoning that isn't obvious in the heat of debate, or even after, in a cool moment of reflection. He might be failing to imaginatively place himself in some relevant position. He might be advancing a view that isn't really as coherent as he makes it out to be. These sorts of failings are often extremely hard to detect. So, in practice, just because another smart person morally disagrees with you, doesn't mean that his view is as well honed as yours. The

disagreement itself isn't enough to force you to give up your beliefs.

[2] We can reach the same result in theory as in practice. Suppose now that you are faced with an opponent whose moral views *are* as integrated, informed, and reasonable as your own. You certainly aren't required to go over to his side—remember, he's in the same position, and it would be odd were you two simply forced to switch belief systems. Rather, the thought must be that you are both required to suspend judgment about the controversial issue.

But if you are, then you're in trouble (and so are the rest of us). You will have to abandon just about every belief you presently hold. Every belief about the external world, for instance, must go. For there is a very sophisticated, internally consistent, well-informed position that tells us that if we can't discount the possibility of an evil demon, then we cannot know whether there is an external world. This was Descartes's position. You may not like it (neither do I), but that doesn't prove that it's wrong.

The bottom line is that for just about any belief at all, there will be detractors who are very smart, well informed, possessed of consistent views, and imaginatively flexible. *If you think that any party to such a debate ought to suspend judgment, then you ought to suspend judgment about nearly everything.* Brilliant skeptics have doubted the existence of an external world. Nothing you could say would convince them. Therefore (if the Epistemic Argument from Disagreement works) you must abandon belief in an external world. Do you really believe that?

If you're willing to bite that bullet, there's nothing I could do to convince you that moral disagreements aren't epistemically crippling. Instead, we have a dilemma. You choose the least painful option. Either intractable disagreement among consistent, intelligent parties forces them to suspend judgment about their contested views, or it doesn't. If it does, then we must suspend judgment about *all* of our philosophical views, as well as our belief that there is an external world, that I am an embodied being, that the earth is older than a second, etc. All of these have been challenged by brilliant, consistent, informed skeptics over the millennia.

Alternatively, if we are warranted in any of our beliefs, despite the presence of such skepticism, then justified belief is possible, even in the face of persistent disagreement. And so we could retain our moral beliefs, especially those that we have carefully thought through, despite an inability to convince all of our intelligent opponents. Take your pick.

The Perspectival Argument

The Perspectival Argument represents another familiar challenge to the possibility of acquiring moral knowledge. The argument says, in effect, that *gaining knowledge requires us to occupy a special vantage point. But, in ethics, there is no special vantage point—no best perspective from which to render moral judgments. And, absent that best perspective, there is no basis for knowing whether any given moral belief is true or not.*

Consider a simple analogy. Suppose you are an insurance investigator, looking into the causes of an accident. You get a number of different stories from the eyewitnesses. When that happens, you (rightly) trust the account of the person who was best situated to view the accident. One person had the best perspective. That is the person who knows what really happened.

The skeptic says that there's nothing like this in ethics; no best perspective from which to assess competing moral claims. But without that sort of privileged point of view, we are just seeing things through our limited, parochial, lenses. Such vision is cloudy and unreliable. It can't give us knowledge.

There are two ways to reply to this kind of argument. The *first* defends the claim that there really is a best perspective on moral matters. The *second* allows that there may be no such vantage point, but then says that such a perspective isn't needed for knowledge.

[1] There is a lot of controversy about the first strategy. Many philosophers have tried to identify the elements of this preferred standpoint. One familiar try is given by a variation on the **Golden Rule.** To know whether an act is right or wrong, you need only ask: would you like it if that were done to you? If you would, then your act is right. If you wouldn't,

then your act is wrong. But this often fails as a good standpoint. The sadomasochist wouldn't mind being hit, hard. But that doesn't make it right for him to go hitting others.

Another familiar picture of the ideal moral perspective is one in which a person is purged of his false beliefs, knows all of the relevant nonmoral information, has no personal interest in the matter at hand, and is impartial in his concern for others. The thought is that anyone who manages to occupy such an exalted position will have knowledge of what is right and wrong—her opinions, if formed under these conditions, can't be mistaken.

Philosophers call people who satisfy all of these conditions **"ideal observers."** Though this has been, historically, a popular option for specifying a moral vantage point, it remains a controversial position. In fact, there are three standard criticisms of ideal observer theories.

- First, many think that it's impossible for any of us mere mortals to become an ideal observer. No one can be perfectly impartial, be rid of all of her false beliefs, etc. So even if this is the morally best perspective, no one can ever occupy it.
- Second, many think that this isn't, in fact, the morally best perspective. Some think that the best moral decisions are made from an engaged, passionate standpoint, rather than a neutral, detached one. Others think that impartiality isn't always a good thing, that it's sometimes morally advisable to give preference to parents, children, and spouses over others who are equally needy, talented, deserving, etc.
- Third, many allege that the ideal observers will disagree with one another. And if they do, then contradiction ensues. And any theory that generates a contradiction is false. So the ideal observer theory is false.

Why would ideal observers disagree with one another (if they would)? Well, imagine a scenario where ideal observers consider the case of a woman seeking an abortion. Each observer, being ideal, is purged of all false beliefs. And each knows all there is to know about embryology, and the facts of the woman's situation. Neither observer has any special attachment to the woman. Both are relevantly impartial. Still, mightn't these two disagree about whether she should have the abortion? Most have thought such disagreement possible.

But being ideal entails knowing what's right and wrong. And knowing something entails its truth. So one ideal observer knows that the woman should have an abortion. And the other knows that she shouldn't. It follows that she both should and shouldn't have that abortion. And that's a contradiction.

Now it's important to note that the Golden Rule position, and the ideal observer strategy, are but two in a long line of attempts to discover a uniquely best perspective from which to make moral judgments. We can't investigate all such efforts. Instead, let's content ourselves with a couple of points.

First, despite the controversy that attaches to each such effort, there might, after all, be a morally best perspective. For instance, some version of the ideal observer view might be correct after all. To give us what we needed, it would have to be a version that was humanly achievable, one that gave us moral advice that we found deeply satisfying, and that ensured unanimity among ideal observers. *Perhaps* such a thing is impossible. Yet skeptics haven't given a decisive argument for thinking it so.

[2] But suppose they do. Suppose there is no morally ideal perspective. It doesn't follow that we can't have moral knowledge. For there might be a number of quite good moral viewpoints, a number of strategies for obtaining moral knowledge, even if there isn't a perfect one. Utilizing one of these strategies, we might often gain moral knowledge, even if we don't always do so. We might know many things, even if we can't know them all.

To make this plausible, consider other areas where you think that knowledge is obtainable. If you're a moral skeptic, for instance, then you think that philosophy is one such area. *By your lights, we can know at least this philosophical claim: that moral skepticism is true.* But no one, to my knowledge, has offered any remotely plausible view of a uniquely best perspective from which to do philosophy. Of course, that might just be ignorance on my part.

But if it is, then we've got just as much reason to suppose that there is a uniquely best moral perspective, since any "best" philosophical viewpoint is going to be at least as controversial as a similar one for ethics.

And matters don't end here. Physicists and biologists are in the same boat. There is no uniquely best vantage point from which to do physics, or biology (or economics, or chemistry, etc.). Scientists arrive at their results by means of different methods. They approach their subjects from different angles, some more intuitively, others more analytically, for example. Some view the world as if there must be some simple design underlying its complex manifestations; others are more comfortable accepting complexity at face value. There is no one thing properly called "the scientific method," or, if there is, it is sketched at a such a high level of generality (test hypotheses, gather evidence, use your senses) that many people, employing this same method, will arrive at contradictory results. And there is also no uniquely best manual for experimental design, which is a central element in scientific discovery. Instead, there are a variety of experimental paths to gaining knowledge in any given scientific field.

Try it for yourself:

one is best poised to gain knowledge in
_____ (fill in your favorite area of inquiry)
just in case one meets these conditions:
_____ (fill 'em in).

If those who meet these conditions are allowed to make mistakes in their given field, then the chances that we can fill in the blanks for ethics rise a good deal. If those who meet these conditions can never be wrong, then the chance that the conditions can really be specified, for any area of inquiry, go way, way down.

I am in fact quite sympathetic to the idea that there is no uniquely best perspective from which to gain moral knowledge. But I could be wrong about that. And even if I am right, such a perspective isn't needed for moral knowledge. For it isn't needed elsewhere. On the assumption that we actually can have knowledge in other fields, we must ask whether there is any decent specification of an optimal vantage point for getting it. And there doesn't seem to be. So we may have moral knowledge after all, even if there is no uniquely best perspective that guarantees us access to it.

The Argument from Inadequate Evidence

The last argument . . . concerns the kind of evidence that is available to defend one's moral views. *The Argument from Inadequate Evidence claims that moral evidence is inferior to the evidence relied upon in recognized objective disciplines, because moral evidence is intangible and not quantifiable.* Really, all the ethical evidence we can muster amounts to a recitation of our already-held opinions. And the fact that we hold a given view is no indication of its truth.

I think we must admit that ethical evidence is different in kind from the sort we find in the natural sciences. Provided we are entitled to trust our senses, scientists can rely on them to supply evidence to test a wide array of hypotheses. Ethics cannot rely on sense evidence in the same way, for any moral theory is perfectly compatible with such evidence. That is just a result of the observation that moral principles are not in the business of describing the natural world, or predicting its occurrences, but rather in evaluating it and telling us how we ought to conduct ourselves within it.

Our senses can tell us what is actually happening in the world. But they can't tell us what *ought* to happen in the world. All the empirical evidence there is leaves all the important ethical questions quite open. Two embryologists may know all there is to know about fetal development, and all there is to know about a woman's circumstances, and yet, consistently, come to absolutely opposed views about the morality of her intended abortion. True, our experience of the world may tell us what is impossible for us to achieve, and so it may, in that respect, narrow the moral options (provided that we aren't obligated to do the impossible). But that still leaves a huge variety of moral alternatives, each of which is perfectly compatible with all the empirical evidence there is.

If we can't rely exclusively (or even primarily) on empirical evidence to fix the content of our moral principles, then how can we justify our moral commitments? The answer comes when we recall the place of ethics in the larger scheme of things. *Ethics is a branch of philosophy.* We can't settle the debate about God's existence, or that of free will, or the nature of ethics, just by paying a visit to the Physics or Chemistry department and consulting their journals. *Knowledge of moral standards, like philosophical knowledge quite generally, is not attainable solely by relying on the evidence and methods of science.*

Unsurprisingly, philosophers disagree amongst themselves about how to discover and confirm philosophical truths. The reason is that this question is itself a philosophical one, and can be expected to be as controversial as most philosophical questions (i.e., very). There is intractable disagreement within philosophy about all of its major assumptions. As we have seen, this isn't enough to show that there isn't any objective philosophical truth.

But the question before us is not about whether there is such truth, but about whether we can ever retrieve it. In particular, we must ask whether the absence of determinative empirical evidence must cripple our hopes of gaining ethical knowledge. Since, it seems to me, that is just a more specific version of the general question as applied to philosophical knowledge, we won't get very far without tackling that last question.

If we wanted to find out whether there really was such a thing as (say) free will, what would we have to do? Well, a number of things. First, we'd have to get clear about precisely what we mean when we use the term. Then we would have to get all the relevant facts under our belt. We would solicit the views of those whose opinions we trust. We'd have to engage with the best of our critics to see whether we could answer their challenges, and whether they could answer ours. We must test our claims for logical consistency, and decide, in the face of contradiction, which of our competing views is least well supported. And we must investigate to see whether ours, among competitors, best exemplifies a host of theoretical virtues—economy, stability across cases, avoidance of *ad hoc* assumptions, preservation of existing beliefs, explanatory breadth, etc.

Every single stage of this process is fraught with controversy, since all but the second primarily involves philosophical exploration. The meaning of free will is itself a contested issue within philosophical circles. The appraisal of a critic's challenges is no less a philosophical task. The logical consistency of one's views isn't always transparent. The comparative assessment of whether one view best exemplifies a theoretical virtue is not to be resolved by appealing just to the evidence of the senses. We might as well face it. There is no way to pursue the philosophical method, as described in the previous paragraph, and expect that all of its intelligent practitioners will come to agreement at the end of the day.

In working through the method, we are prevented from relying primarily on empirical evidence to direct our findings. We must instead rely on our own considered views, as they emerge from this extensive battery of tests. This is what critics object to when they claim that, in ethics, the only evidence for our views is how we feel about things. We can now see that this is only a caricature of the philosophical method. The evidence we have is that of logical consistency, a check against recognized theoretical virtues, trial by fire in the face of criticism, and an obligation to defend, via argument, the claims that we believe to be true. All of this evidence is more controversial, typically, than that relied upon by natural scientists. But that, by itself, can't be a knock-down objection against the possibility of moral knowledge, since any claim to philosophical knowledge will be equally controversial.

The major lesson is this. If there can be philosophical knowledge at all, then it will not come primarily through empirical evidence, but via the a priori application of the philosophical method. The routes we traced a few paragraphs back will result in great controversy, but the existence of even intractable disagreement is not enough to undermine possibilities of philosophical truth or philosophical knowledge.

And, to get right down to it, doesn't everyone really believe that there can be philosophical knowledge? Those who doubt the existence of objective moral truths are taking a philosophical stance. If there is no philosophical knowledge, then either there is no philosophical truth, or there are no justified philosophical beliefs. But there are philosophical truths, and there are justified philosophical beliefs. So there is philosophical knowledge.

There is philosophical truth—it is true that God exists (or does not exist). It is true that we have free will (or true that we lack it). It is true that knowledge requires true belief. It is true that we have a soul (or true that we don't).

And everyone, even a moral skeptic, assumes that at least some of our philosophical beliefs are justified. Skeptics assume, for instance, that their own philosophical views, which deny the existence of moral truth or moral knowledge, are themselves justified. If such skeptical views, being philosophical, are not justified, then we needn't pay much attention to them!

. . . If the sort of evidence we rely on to establish our moral claims is thought to be, by its nature, insufficient to justify our moral beliefs, then all philosophical justification must be discredited, since the pursuit of ethical truth exactly mirrors that of philosophical truth. Are any of your own philosophical views justified? You have opinions about whether God exists, about whether we have free will, about whether scientific reality is all the reality there is. You have beliefs about the morality of abortion, capital punishment, euthanasia, pacifism, and slavery. Are *any* of these beliefs justified? Don't you think so? (If you don't, why continue to hold them?) If any are, then there must be a way to justify them. However that is done, ethics can avail itself of precisely the same method.

If you abandon hope for moral knowledge, because you can't conceive of plausible evidence that can support moral claims, then you must also abandon all hope for philosophical knowledge. The very same kind of evidence, and the very same method of verification, are found for philosophy generally, and ethics in particular. This shouldn't be surprising, since ethics is, after all, a branch of philosophy. Both ethics, and philosophy generally, rely on considered judgments that are not primarily a matter of marshaling empirical evidence. Both proceed to confirm their claims by means of the a priori method described a few pages above. *If there's no good evidence for ethical judgments, then there's no good evidence for any philosophical judgments.*

We are now in a position to see why there must be good evidence to support our moral views. Remember **modus tollens**? If one claim implies another, and this second one is false, then the original one must be false, too. Well, here's one claim:

(E) There's no adequate evidence for moral judgments.

If (E) is true, then so is:

(P) There's no adequate evidence for philosophical views.

But (P) isn't true. Since that's so, then the original claim that implies it, (E), isn't true, either. And if (E) is false, then there is, after all, adequate evidence for moral judgments. In short, if (E) is true, then (P) is true. (P) is false. Therefore (E) is false. If there's no adequate evidence for moral claims, then there's no such evidence for philosophical claims. But philosophical claims can be well supported. Therefore moral claims can be, too. *Modus tollens.*

Who says that (P) is false—that philosophical claims can be well supported? You do. You have some philosophical beliefs, don't you? That God does (or does not) exist. That some people do evil and deserve punishment (or that everyone is a product of conditioning, and so should be immune from punishment). That morality is all a human construct (or something objective). That you can (or cannot) know that you are not presently dreaming. We all operate on the assumption that our philosophical beliefs are justified, even if we admit, as we should, that we aren't certain of their truth. But if any of these beliefs are justified, then (P) is false. And if (P) is false, so is (E). And if (E) is false, then there is adequate evidence for moral judgments.

Here is another way to show that (P) isn't plausible. A dilemma: (P) is either supported by evidence or it isn't. If it isn't, then forget about it. But what if (P) *is* supported by evidence? Then (P) is self-refuting! For (P) is a philosophical claim. (What else could it be?) If there is evidence to support it, then it can't be true. So either way—whether (P) is or isn't supported by evidence—we do best to reject (P). In rejecting it, we admit that there's good evidence to support philosophical claims. And if there is this good evidence, then there is also good evidence to support moral claims, which are, after all, a kind of philosophical claim. Moral knowledge is a real possibility.

In brief: if moral knowledge requires certainty, widespread consensus, a uniquely best perspective, or determinative empirical evidence for its support, then we can have no moral knowledge. But we can do without certainty. We can do without consensus. We can do without a best perspective. And we can do without determinative empirical support. We may have moral knowledge after all.

DISCUSSION QUESTIONS:

1. Do you think that you know anything at all? If so, what kinds of claims do you know? How are those claims similar to or different from moral claims? Is your belief that there is such a place as Fiji or that $a^2 + b^2 = c^2$ relevantly different from your belief that it is wrong to torture children? If so, how?

2. Is it true that there is widespread disagreement about ethical issues? Think about the moral views held by people you know. When there is disagreement, how often is the disagreement the result of a disagreement over non-moral facts (e.g., whether a fetus counts as a person) rather than over moral principles (e.g., it is wrong to kill innocent people)? If there is genuine disagreement about moral principles, how different is this than disagreement about religious claims, political claims, etc.?

3. Do we have evidence for anything in philosophy (e.g., the existence of free will, the existence of God, the existence of souls, etc.)? If so, why can't we have evidence for ethical claims? If not, is it unreasonable to hold any philosophical view whatsoever? Is the view that it is unreasonable to hold any philosophical view *itself* a philosophical view?

Argument Reconstruction Exercises:

I. The argument from certainty is one of the major reasons to think that, even if there are moral facts, no one knows what they are. Identify the premises and conclusion in this excerpt:

Knowledge, it is thought, requires certainty. But certainty is unobtainable in ethics. So moral knowledge itself is impossible. (page 51)

II. According to the epistemic argument from disagreement, no one knows any moral claims because people disagree about all moral claims. Shafer-Landau challenges one of the assumptions behind this argument, namely the claim that intractable disagreement is incompatible with knowledge. In this passage, he forces defenders of this principle into a dilemma. Identify the premises and conclusion in this excerpt:

> Either intractable disagreement among consistent, intelligent parties forces them to suspend judgment about their contested views, or it doesn't. If it does, then we must suspend judgment about *all* of our philosophical views, as well as our belief that there is an external world, that I am an embodied being, that the earth is older than a second, etc. All of these have been challenged by brilliant, consistent, informed skeptics over the millennia. Alternatively, if we are warranted in any of our beliefs, despite the presence of such skepticism, then justified belief is possible, even in the face of persistent disagreement. And so we could retain our moral beliefs, especially those that we have carefully thought through, despite an inability to convince all of our intelligent opponents. (pages 53–54)

III. The perspectival argument claims that knowing something requires having a special perspective on the truth of that claim. Shafer-Landau reconstructs this argument in a tidy fashion. Identify the premises and conclusion in this excerpt:

> [G]aining knowledge requires us to occupy a special vantage point. But, in ethics, there is no special vantage point—no best perspective from which to render moral judgments. And, absent that best perspective, there is no basis for knowing whether any given moral belief is true or not. (page 54)

IV. Shafer-Landau agrees that the kind of evidence we have available for moral claims is of a different sort than the kind of evidence we have available for scientific claims. But he insists that this isn't a problem. In the following argument, he attempts to show the implications of accepting the view that the kind of evidence we have for moral claims is insufficient for moral knowledge. Identify the premises and conclusion in this excerpt:

> If the sort of evidence we rely on to establish our moral claims is thought to be, by its nature, insufficient to justify our moral beliefs, then all philosophical justification must be discredited, since the pursuit of ethical truth exactly mirrors that of philosophical truth. . . . If there is no good evidence for ethical judgments, then there's no good evidence for any philosophical judgments. (pages 57)

CHAPTER 7

Morality and Authority

I learned that all moral judgments are "value judgments," that all value judgments are subjective, and that none can be proved to be either "right" or "wrong."
—SERIAL KILLER TED BUNDY (TRANSCRIBED FROM A TAPE-RECORDING AND PUBLISHED IN HARRY JAFFA, *HOMOSEXUALITY AND THE NATURAL LAW* [CLAREMONT, CA, 1990])

INTRODUCTION

Metaethics is the study of the assumptions that underlie our theories of what is right and wrong, good and bad, just and unjust, etc. One such assumption is that the claims of morality have authority over us as rational beings. There are things that we ought to do and things we ought not to do. The exact nature of this authority will be explored in Chapter 9, but for now we need to address a related issue. If the demands of morality have authority over us, does this require that the demands of morality stem from some authority *figure*?

This idea seems quite plausible. Doesn't it make sense to say that if I ought to do something, that's because there is someone who commanded me to do it? We can think about it this way: if there are things that I morally ought to do, then there must be moral rules that make this so. If there are moral rules, then there are moral rule-makers. So it is reasonable to believe in moral obligations only if it is reasonable to believe in an authority figure who could establish moral rules.

This chapter will explore the connection, if any, between our actual beliefs, desires, commands, and wishes (along with those of other beings) and our moral obligations. Historically, the two most common authority figures who have played the role of "rule-makers" are God and culture. This chapter explores both possibilities.

The first possibility has a long history in the West: our moral obligations depend upon the existence of God. The idea is that what we ought to do and what we ought not to do depends on the existence of a divine creator to serve as rule-maker. Ivan Karamazov, one of the foils in Dostoevsky's famous work *The Brothers Karamazov*, puts the point this way: if there is no God, then everything is permissible. If there is no God, then we're just highly evolved apes who learned to think about things in a special way. Nothing is ultimately good or bad. Nothing is ultimately right or wrong.

Is Ivan right? Well, there is certainly a trivial sense in which he is correct. If there is such a being as God, he exists of necessity. That is to say, no one created God. If God exists, he's always existed. And so in that sense, it's true that moral facts depend on divine facts: if there weren't divine facts, there wouldn't be any facts at all! So in *some* very weak sense, if there is a God, then everything depends on that being.

But many people think that there is a tighter connection between God and morality. Some argue that what we ought to do is based on God's *character*. God is the ultimately good thing. Thus, he is the defining feature of our universe that distinguishes the good from the bad. Others hold a view known as **Divine Command Theory** that says that what we ought to do is determined by God's *commands* or God's *will*. To say that something is morally wrong is just to say that it's the kind of thing that God has commanded us not to do.

We've got to be careful here, too. All theists should agree that if God prohibits a certain behavior, then the behavior is morally wrong. The question is whether or not God's prohibition is what *makes* the action wrong. For example, one might think that what makes an action wrong is that it causes pain to others, but then insist that God would prohibit the action since, knowing everything, he knows that the action would cause pain to others. In other words, given that God is omniscient, he obviously knows all of the moral facts. The question under consideration here is not whether God *knows* all the moral facts but whether or not God *determines* what those moral facts are. The latter is a view known as **Divine Moral Voluntarism**.

Given that the question of God's existence is not presupposed for our investigation into ethical matters, the question of the connection between divine authority and morality is a crucial one. Does God's approval make things right? Is the only reason it's wrong to murder that God disapproves of it? If there is no God, how can we make sense out of what we ought to do? Is it even coherent to try to construct a purely secular ethical system? The first two readings of this chapter explore these and related questions. In his essay, John Arthur examines and rejects several ways in which morality might be thought to depend upon religion. Kai Nielsen next argues that a secular person is just as able as her religious counterpart to give adequate answers to ultimate moral questions.

If there is no God or if God's existence alone won't establish moral facts, then what will? The second plausible connection between moral facts and authority is human culture. Perhaps it's as simple as this: To say that something is wrong is just to say that someone's culture disapproves of it. This view would make moral facts relative. **Moral Relativism** says that there are moral facts,

but that the standards for these facts are relative either to individual people or to cultures. The first is known as **Individual Relativism**, and the second is **Cultural Relativism**. According to the latter, to say that something is right is just to say that someone's culture approves of it. What's right for me might be wrong for you. Thus, moral facts are determined by the authority of a local culture.

This proposal is both interesting and yet difficult. It's interesting because, if true, it might explain why it's a mistake for people in one culture to criticize the behavior and practices of people in another culture. What's right for people in the Middle East is not right for people in the contemporary United States, and vice versa. And this view would also provide an easy explanation for how there might be moral facts despite the nonexistence of God. When groups of people agree to behave in certain ways, this consensus gives rise to facts about what we ought to do. Just as there are facts about etiquette, there are facts about morality—each is determined by local culture.

However, the proposal is difficult as well. What counts as a culture? Think of yourself: Which of your potential associations counts as the culture that determines what's right for you? Your planet? Your civilization (e.g., West vs. East)? Your country? State? City? School? Ethnicity? Religious culture? Gender? What happens when these cultural groups disagree? Suppose your family culture says one thing, but your national culture says another? Which determines what you ought to do?

And even if we could decide to which culture we belong, what do we say about inter-cultural activities? Suppose a person from culture A visits culture B. Which set of cultural norms determines what's morally right to do in that situation? Do we "carry our culture" with us wherever we go? Or is it true that when in Rome we should act as the Romans do?

Finally, suppose it's true that moral facts are culture-relative. Does that mean that a culture can never make a moral mistake? Consider Third

Reich Germany. Was its stance on the moral status of Jews a correct one? What about cultures that endorse slavery, sexism, or child abuse? The readings of this section grapple with these issues in an attempt to determine whether or not we can make sense out of morality in the absence of some authority figure or other. Gilbert Harman offers a defense of moral relativism. Paul Taylor critically examines cultural relativism in particular.

SUGGESTIONS FOR FURTHER READING

Adams, Robert M. "A Modified Divine Command Conception of Ethical Wrongness." *The Virtue of Faith and Other Essays in Philosophical Theology.* (Oxford: Oxford University Press, 1987, 97–122)

Alston, William P. "Some Suggestions for Divine Command Theorists." In Beaty, Michael (ed). *Christian Theism and the Problems of Philosophy.* (Notre Dame: University of Notre Dame Press, 1990, 303–326)

Harman, Gilbert. "Moral Relativism Defended." In Harman, *Explaining Value: And Other Essays in Moral Philosophy.* (Oxford: Clarendon Press, 2000, 3–19; original publication date 1975)

Harman, Gilbert & Thomson, Judith Jarvis. *Moral Relativism and Moral Objectivity.* (Cambridge, MA: Blackwell, 1996)

Moser, P. K., and T. L. Carson (eds.). *Moral Relativism: A Reader.* (New York: Oxford University Press, 2001)

Murphy, Mark C. *An Essay on Divine Authority.* (Ithaca: Cornell University Press, 2002)

Quinn, Philip. "An Argument for Divine Command Ethics." In Beaty, Michael (ed). *Christian Theism and the Problems of Philosophy.* (Notre Dame: University of Notre Dame Press, 1990, 289–302)

Wainwright, William J. *Religion and Morality.* (Aldershot: Ashgate, 2005)

7.1 DOES MORALITY DEPEND UPON RELIGION?

JOHN ARTHUR (1984)

Until his death in 2007, John Arthur taught for many years as professor of philosophy at the State University of New York, Binghamton. He worked primarily in ethics and social/political philosophy, in particular the philosophy of law. In this essay, Arthur considers several ways in which morality might be dependent upon religion and argues that each is mistaken. We do not need to posit God to explain moral motivation, moral knowledge, or moral facts. Additionally, **divine command theory**—the most popular account that connects moral facts to divine facts—suffers from serious defects. So although it's true as a contingent fact that one's religion often affects one's moral outlook and vice versa, there is no essential connection between the two.

Reading Questions:

1. According to Arthur, what makes something a religion?

2. What does it mean to say that religion is necessary to provide people with moral motivation?

3. Why doesn't Arthur think that religion is helpful for moral knowledge?

4. What is divine command theory?

5. Arthur explains the relationship between moral laws and God of human laws and the New York legislature. How are the two similar?

6. What is the example of Plato's fictional character Euthyphro supposed to illustrate?

7. What does it mean to say that God's commands are morally arbitrary?

8. Even though there is no essential connection between religion and morality, in the final section of the paper, Arthur grants that the two often influence one another. Find one example.

The question I discuss in this paper was famously captured by a character in Dostoevsky's novel *The Brothers Karamazov*: "Without God" said Ivan, "everything is permitted." I want to argue that this is wrong: *there is in fact no important sense in which morality depends on religion.* Yet, I will also argue, there do remain important other respects in which the two are related. First, however, I want to say something about the subjects: just what are we referring to when we speak of morality and of religion?

Morality and Religion

A useful way to approach the first question—the nature of morality—is to ask what it would mean for a society to exist without a social moral code. How would such people think and behave? What would that society look like? First, it seems clear that such people would never feel guilt or resentment. For example, the notions that I ought to remember my parents' anniversary, that he has a moral responsibility to help care for his children after the divorce, that she has a right to equal pay for equal work, and that discrimination on the basis of race is unfair would be absent in such a society. Notions of duty, rights, and obligations would not be present, except perhaps in the legal sense; concepts of justice and fairness would also be foreign to these people. In short, people would have no tendency to evaluate or criticize the behavior of others, nor to feel remorse about their own behavior. Children would not be taught to be ashamed when they steal or hurt others, nor would they be allowed to complain when others treat them badly. (People might, however, feel regret at a decision that didn't turn out as they had hoped; but that would only be because their expectations were frustrated, not because they feel guilty.)

Such a society lacks a moral code. What, then, of religion? Is it possible that people lacking a morality would nonetheless have religious beliefs? It seems clear that it is possible. Suppose every day these same people file into their place of worship to pay homage to God (they may believe in many gods or in one all-powerful creator of heaven and earth). Often they can be heard praying to God for help in dealing with their problems and thanking Him for their good fortune. Frequently they give sacrifices to God, sometimes in the form of money spent to build beautiful, temples and churches, other times by performing actions they believe God would approve such as helping those in need. These practices might also be institutionalized, in the sense that certain people are assigned important leadership roles. Specific texts might also be taken as authoritative, indicating the ways God has acted in history and His role in their lives or the lives of their ancestors.

To have a moral code, then, is to tend to evaluate (perhaps without even expressing it) the behavior of others and to feel guilt at certain actions when we perform them. Religion, on the other hand, involves beliefs in supernatural power(s) that created and perhaps also control nature, the tendency to worship and pray to those supernatural forces or beings, and the presence of organizational structures and authoritative texts. The practices of morality and religion are thus importantly different. One involves our attitudes toward various forms of behavior (lying and killing, for example), typically expressed using the notions of rules, rights, and obligations. The other, religion, typically involves prayer, worship, beliefs about the supernatural, institutional forms, and authoritative texts.

We come, then, to the central question: What is the connection, if any, between a society's moral code and its religious practices and beliefs? Many people have felt that morality is in some way dependent on religion or religious truths. But what sort of "dependence" might there be? In what follows I distinguish various ways in which one might claim that religion is necessary for morality, arguing against those who claim morality depends in some way on religion. I will also suggest, however, some other important ways in which the two are related, concluding with a brief discussion of conscience and moral education.

Religious Motivation

One possible role which religion might play in morality relates to motives people have. *Religion, it is often said, is necessary so that people will do right.* Typically, the argument begins with the important point that doing what is right often has costs: refusing to shoplift or cheat can mean people go without some good or fail a test; returning a billfold means they don't get the contents. Religion is therefore said to be necessary in that it provides motivation to do the right thing. God rewards those who follow His commands by providing for them a place in heaven or by insuring that they prosper and are happy on earth. He also punishes those who violate the moral law. Others emphasize less self-interested ways in which religious motives may encourage people to act rightly. Since God is the creator of the universe and has ordained that His plan should be followed, they point out, it is important to live one's life in accord with this divinely ordained plan. Only by living a moral life, it is said, can people live in harmony with the larger, divinely created order.

The first claim, then, is that religion is necessary to provide moral motivation. The problem with that argument, however, is that religious motives are far from the only ones people have. For most of us, a decision to do the right thing (if that is our decision) is made for a variety of reasons: "What if I get caught? What if somebody sees me—what will he or she think? How will I feel afterwards? Will I regret it?" Or maybe the thought of cheating just doesn't arise. We were raised to be a decent person, and that's what we are—period. Behaving fairly and treating others well is more important than whatever we might gain from stealing or cheating, let alone seriously harming another person. *So it seems clear that many motives for doing the right thing have nothing whatsoever to do with religion.* Most of us, in fact, do worry about getting caught, being blamed, and being looked down on by others. We also may do what is right just because it's right, or because we don't want to hurt others or embarrass family and friends. To say that we need religion to act morally is mistaken; indeed it seems to me that many of us, when it really gets down to it, don't give much of a thought to religion when making moral decisions. All those other reasons are the ones which we tend to consider, or else we just don't consider cheating and stealing at all. So far, then, there seems to be no reason to suppose that people can't be moral yet irreligious at the same time.

Moral Knowledge

A second argument that is available for those who think religion is necessary to morality, however, focuses on moral guidance and knowledge rather than on people's motives. However much people may want to do the right thing, according to this view, we cannot ever know for certain what is right without the guidance of religious teaching. *Human understanding is simply inadequate to this difficult and controversial task; morality involves immensely complex problems, and so we must consult religious revelation for help.*

Again, however, this argument fails. First, consider how much we would need to know about religion and revelation in order for religion to provide moral guidance. Besides being sure that there is a God, we'd also have to think about which of the many religions is true. How can anybody be sure his or her religion is the right one? But even if we assume the Judeo-Christian God is the real one, we still need to find out just what it is He wants us to do, which means we must think about revelation.

Revelation comes in at least two forms, and not even all Christians agree on which is the best way to understand revelation. Some hold that revelation occurs when God tells us what He wants by providing us with His words: The Ten Commandments are an example. Many even believe, as evangelist Billy Graham once said, that the entire Bible was written by God using thirty-nine secretaries. Others, however, doubt that the "word of God" refers literally to the words God has spoken, but believe instead that the Bible is an historical document, written by human beings, of the events or occasions in which God revealed Himself. It is an especially important document, of course, but nothing more than that. So on this second view, revelation is not understood as statements made by God but rather as His acts such as leading His people from Egypt, testing Job, and sending His son as an example of the ideal life. The Bible is not itself revelation; it's the historical account of revelatory actions.

If we are to use revelation as a moral guide, then, we must first know what is to count as revelation—words given us by God, historical events, or both? But even supposing that we could somehow answer those questions, the problems of relying on revelation are still not over since we still must *interpret* that revelation. Some feel, for example, that the Bible justifies various forms of killing, including war and capital punishment, on the basis of such statements as "An eye for an eye." Others, emphasizing such sayings as "Judge not lest ye be judged" and "Thou shalt not kill," believe the Bible demands absolute pacifism. How are we to know which interpretation is correct? It is likely, of course, that the answer people give to such religious questions will be influenced in part at least by their own moral beliefs: if capital punishment is thought to be unjust, for example, then an interpreter will seek to read the Bible in a way that is consistent with that moral truth. That is not, however, a happy conclusion for those wishing to rest morality on revelation, for it means that their understanding of what God has revealed is itself dependent on their prior moral views. *Rather than revelation serving as a guide for morality, morality is serving as a guide for how we interpret revelation.*

So my general conclusion is that far from providing a short-cut to moral understanding, looking to revelation for guidance often creates more questions and problems. It seems wiser under the circumstances to address complex moral problems like abortion, capital punishment, and affirmative action directly, considering the pros and cons of each side, rather than to seek answers through the much more controversial and difficult route of revelation.

Moral Facts

It may seem, however, that we have still not really gotten to the heart of the matter. Even if religion is not necessary for moral motivation or knowledge, it is often claimed, religion is necessary in another more fundamental sense. According to this view, *religion is necessary for morality because without God there could be no right or wrong.* God, in other words, provides the foundation or bedrock on which morality is grounded. This idea was expressed by Bishop R. C. Mortimer:

> God made us and all the world. Because of that He has an absolute claim on our obedience .... From [this] it follows that a thing is not right simply because we think it is. It is right because God commands it.[1]

What Bishop Mortimer has in mind can be seen by comparing moral rules with legal ones. Legal statutes, we know, are created by legislatures; if the state assembly of New York had not passed a law limiting the speed people can travel, then there would be no such legal obligation. Without the statutory enactments, such a law simply would not exist. *Mortimer's view,* the **divine command theory**, *would mean that God has the same sort of relation to moral law as the legislature has to statutes it enacts: without God's commands there would be no moral rules, just as without a legislature there would be no statutes.*

Defenders of the divine command theory often add to this a further claim, that only by assuming God sits at the foundation of morality can we explain the objective difference between right and wrong. This point was forcefully argued by F. C. Copleston in a 1948 British Broadcasting Corporation radio debate with Bertrand Russell. . . .[2]

Against those who, like Bertrand Russell, seek to ground morality in feelings and attitudes, Copleston argues that there must be a more solid foundation if we are to be able to claim truly that the Nazis were evil. God, according to Copleston, is able to provide the objective basis for the distinction, which we all know to exist, between right and wrong. *Without divine commands at the root of human obligations, we would have no real reason for condemning the behavior of anybody, even Nazis.* Morality, Copleston thinks, would then be nothing more than an expression of personal feeling.

Assessing Divine Command Theory

To begin assessing the divine command theory, let's first consider this last point. Is it really true that only the commands of God can provide an objective basis for moral judgments? Certainly many philosophers have felt that morality rests on its own perfectly sound footing, be it reason, human nature, or natural sentiments. It seems wrong to conclude, automatically, that morality cannot rest on anything but religion. And it is also possible that morality doesn't have any foundation or basis at all, so that its claims should be ignored in favor of whatever serves our own self-interest....

I think that, in fact, theists should reject the divine command theory. One reason is what it implies. Suppose we were to grant (just for the sake of argument) that the divine command theory is correct, so that actions are right just because they are commanded by God. The same, of course, can be said about those deeds that we believe are wrong. If God hadn't commanded us not to do them, they would not be wrong.

But now notice this consequence of the divine command theory. Since God is all-powerful, and since right is determined solely by His commands, is it not possible that He might change the rules and make what we now think of as wrong into right? It would seem that according to the divine command theory the answer is "yes": it is theoretically possible that tomorrow God would decree that virtues such as kindness and courage have become vices while actions that show cruelty and cowardice will henceforth be the right actions. (Recall the analogy with a legislature and the power it has to change law.) So now rather than it being right for people to help each other out and prevent innocent people from suffering unnecessarily, it would be right (God having changed His mind) to create as much pain among innocent children as we possibly can! *To adopt the divine command theory therefore commits its advocate to the seemingly absurd position that even the greatest atrocities might be not only acceptable but morally required if God were to command them.*

Plato made a similar point in the dialogue *Euthyphro.* Socrates is asking Euthyphro what it is that makes the virtue of holiness a virtue, just as we have been asking what makes kindness and courage virtues. Euthyphro has suggested that holiness is just whatever all the gods love.

> SOCRATES: Well, then, Euthyphro, what do we say about holiness? Is it not loved by all the gods, according to your definition?
> EUTHYPHRO: Yes.
> SOCRATES: Because it is holy, or for some other reason?
> EUTHYPHRO: No, because it is holy.
> SOCRATES: Then it is loved by the gods because it is holy: it is not holy because it is loved by them?
> EUTHYPHRO: It seems so.
> SOCRATES: ... Then holiness is not what is pleasing to the gods, and what is pleasing to the gods is not holy as you say, Euthyphro. They are different things.
> EUTHYPHRO: And why, Socrates?
> SOCRATES: Because we are agreed that the gods love holiness because it is holy: and that it is not holy because they love it.[3]

This raises an interesting question: Why, having claimed at first that virtues are merely what is loved (or commanded) by the gods, would Euthyphro so quickly contradict this and agree that the gods love holiness *because* it's holy, rather than the reverse? One likely possibility is that Euthyphro believes that whenever the gods love something they do so with good reason, not without justification and arbitrarily. To deny this, and say that it is merely the gods' love that makes holiness a virtue, would mean that the gods have no basis for their attitudes, that they are arbitrary in what they love. Yet—and this is the crucial point—it's far from clear that a religious person would want to say that God is arbitrary in that way. If we say that it is simply God's loving something that makes it right, then what sense would it make to say God wants us to do right? All that could mean, it seems, is that God wants us to do what He wants us to do; He would have no reason for wanting it. Similarly "God is good" would mean little more than "God does what He pleases." *The divine command theory therefore leads us to the results that God is morally arbitrary, and that His wishing us to do good or even God's being just mean nothing more than that God does what He does and wants whatever He wants.* Religious people who reject that consequence would also, I am suggesting, have reason to reject the divine command theory itself, seeking a different understanding of morality.

This now raises another problem, however. If God approves kindness because it is a virtue and hates the Nazis because they were evil, then it seems that God discovers morality rather than inventing it. So haven't we then identified a limitation on God's power, since He now, being a good God, must love kindness and command us not to be cruel? Without the divine command theory, in other words, what is left of God's omnipotence?

But why, we may ask, is such a limitation on God unacceptable? It is not at all clear that God really can do anything at all. Can God, for example, destroy Himself? Or make a rock so heavy that He cannot lift it? Or create a universe which was never created by Him? Many have thought that God cannot do these things, but also that His inability to do them does not constitute a serious limitation on His power since these are things that cannot be done at all: to do them would violate the laws of logic. Christianity's most influential theologian, Thomas Aquinas, wrote in this regard that "whatever implies contradiction does not come within the scope of divine omnipotence, because it cannot have the aspect of possibility. Hence it is more appropriate to say that such things cannot be done than that God cannot do them."[4]

How, then, ought we to understand God's relationship to morality if we reject the divine command theory? Can religious people consistently maintain their faith in God the Creator and yet deny that what is right is right because He commands it? I think the answer to this is "yes." Making cruelty good is not like making a universe that wasn't made, of course. It's a moral limit on God rather than a logical one. But why suppose that God's limits are only logical?

One final point about this. Even if we agree that God loves justice or kindness because of their

nature, not arbitrarily, there still remains a sense in which God could change morality even having rejected the divine command theory. That's because if we assume, plausibly I think, that morality depends in part on how we reason, what we desire and need, and the circumstances in which we find ourselves, then morality will still be under God's control since God could have constructed us or our environment very differently. Suppose, for instance, that he created us so that we couldn't be hurt by others or didn't care about freedom. Or perhaps our natural environment were created differently, so that all we have to do is ask and anything we want is given to us. If God had created either nature or us that way, then it seems likely our morality might also be different in important ways from the one we now think correct. In that sense, then, morality depends on God whether or not one supports the divine command theory.

The Contingent Relationship between Religion & Morality

I have argued here that religion is not necessary in providing moral motivation or knowledge and against the divine command theory's claim that God is necessary for there to be morality at all. In this last section, I want first to look briefly at how religion and morality sometimes *do* influence each other. . . .

Nothing I have said so far means that morality and religion are independent of each other. But in what ways are they related, assuming I am correct in claiming morality does not *depend* on religion? First, of course, we should note the historical influence religions have had on the development of morality as well as on politics and law. Many of the important leaders of the abolitionist and civil rights movements were religious leaders, as are many current members of the pro-life movement. The relationship is not, however, one-sided: morality has also influenced religion, as the current debate within the Catholic church over the role of women, abortion, and other social issues shows. In reality, then, it seems clear that the practices of morality and religion have historically each exerted an influence on the other.

But just as the two have shaped each other historically, so, too, do they interact at the personal level. I have already suggested how people's understanding of revelation, for instance, is often shaped by morality as they seek the best interpretations of revealed texts. Whether trying to understand a work of art, a legal statute, or a religious text, interpreters regularly seek to understand them in the best light—to make them as good as they can be, which requires that they bring moral judgment to the task of religious interpretation and understanding.

The relationship can go the other direction as well, however, as people's moral views are shaped by their religious training and beliefs. These relationships between morality and religion are often complex, hidden even from ourselves, but it does seem clear that our views on important moral issues, from sexual morality and war to welfare and capital punishment, are often influenced by our religious outlook. So not only are religious and moral practices and understandings historically linked, but for many religious people the relationship extends to the personal level—to their understanding of moral obligations as well as their sense of who they are and their vision of who they wish to be.

NOTES

1. R. C. Mortimer, *Christian Ethics* (London: Hutchinson's University Library, 1950) pp. 7–8.
2. This debate was broadcast on the "Third Program" of the British Broadcasting Corporation in 1948.
3. Plato, *Euthyphro*, trans. H. N. Fowler (Cambridge, MA: Harvard University Press, 1947).
4. Thomas Aquinas, *Summa Theologica*, Part I, Q. 25, Art. 3.

DISCUSSION QUESTIONS:

1. Arthur seems to think that many people would act the same way even in the absence of a belief in the existence of a God who is able to reward and punish humans. Is that true? What role do religious beliefs play in your deliberations about how to behave?
2. Arthur argues that reliance on divine testimony is not a good strategy for gaining moral knowledge. Yet it seems that we rely on non-divine testimony all the time. We learn from our parents, teachers, peers, etc. all on the basis of what they tell us the world is like. So why is it any different to trust the revelations of a divine being? If the fact that my mother tells me that it's wrong to hurt others is a good enough reason to give me moral knowledge, then why isn't the fact that God tells me that it's wrong to hurt others also a good enough reason to give me moral knowledge?
3. In the section on moral facts, Arthur assumes that if moral facts depend on God, then they must depend on God's commands. In other words, he assumes that the only plausible view in which moral facts depend on divine facts is divine command theory. But is that correct? Might someone think that moral facts are deeply connected to facts about God in another way besides relying on God's commands? What are some other options?
4. Arthur thinks that theists can still say that God is omnipotent even though he can't control the facts of morality. Is that correct? What reason does Arthur offer for this perhaps surprising conclusion? Do you agree? Would God be somehow "better" if he had the power to make harming innocent children morally permissible?

Argument Reconstruction Exercises:

I. Some people think that God is necessary in order for us to know any moral claim. Arthur reconstructs the line of reasoning for this conclusion here. Identify the premises and conclusion in this excerpt:

> However much people may want to do the right thing, according to this view, we cannot ever know for certain what is right without the guidance of religious teaching. Human understanding is simply inadequate to this difficult and controversial task; morality involves immensely complex problems, and so we must consult religious revelation for help. (page 64)

II. Other people think that we could KNOW what's right and wrong or be motivated to DO the right thing without God's intervention, but they insist that it wouldn't make sense to even talk about right and wrong if there weren't a God. Identify the premises and conclusion in this excerpt:

Even if religion is not necessary for moral motivation or guidance, it is often claimed, religion is necessary in another more fundamental sense. According to this view, religion is necessary for morality because without God there could be no right or wrong. God, in other words, provides the foundation or bedrock on which morality is grounded. (page 65)

III. To argue by *reductio ad absurdum* (Latin: reduce to absurdity) you assume a claim is true and then see what follows from it. If the claim implies absurd results, then you know the assumption you started out with is false. In this argument, Arthur sets up a *reductio* against divine command theory. Identify the thesis that he assumes is true and the absurd conclusion in this excerpt:

> I think that, in fact, theists should reject the divine command theory. One reason is what it implies. Suppose we were to grant (just for the sake of argument) that the divine command theory is correct, so that actions are right just because they are commanded by God. The same, of course, can be said about those deeds that we believe to be wrong. If God hadn't commanded us not to do them, they would not be wrong . . . But now notice this

consequence of the divine command theory. Since God is all-powerful, and since right is determined solely by His commands, is it not possible that He might change the rules and make what we now think of as wrong into right? . . . To adopt the divine command theory therefore commits its advocate to the seemingly absurd position that even the greatest atrocities might be not only acceptable but morally required if God were to command them. (page 66)

IV. Arthur entertains the worry that if theists agree that God does not "invent" morality, then they cannot say that God is omnipotent. Instead of stating the argument explicitly, he instead employs a series of rhetorical questions. Identify the premises and conclusion in the implicit argument made in this excerpt:

> If God approves kindness because it is a virtue and hates the Nazis because they were evil, then it seems that God discovers morality rather than inventing it. So haven't we then identified a limitation on God's power, since He now, being a good God, must love kindness and command us not to be cruel? Without the divine command theory, in other words, what is left of God's omnipotence? (page 67)

7.2 HUMANISTIC ETHICS
KAI NIELSEN (1973)

Kai Nielsen is professor emeritus at the University of Calgary, though much of his teaching career was at New York University. His work ranges widely from ethics and metaethics to philosophy of religion. In the latter, Nielsen has been one of the foremost defenders of atheism in the twentieth century. In this essay, he argues that we need not posit the existence of God in order to make sense out of ethics. Human lives can have meaning even if there is no ultimate purpose for our lives, and striving for human happiness and against human suffering are two important components of a meaningful life. In particular, he thinks that the secular person has responses to ultimate questions about morality that are at least as good as—and sometimes better than—the answers offered by religious counterparts.

Reading Questions:

1. What does Nielsen mean when he says that there is no "overarching purpose" to human life?

2. Nielsen thinks that our desire to be happy can give us meaning in a Godless world. What kinds of things does he claim are necessary for human happiness?

3. What is the relationship between human suffering and the meaning of life?

4. What does it mean to derive an "ought" from an "is"?

5. What argument, if any, does Nielsen provide for the claim that human happiness is morally good?

6. Nielsen thinks that we would have good reason to act morally even in the absence of a God, and he presents that reason in the section on the "problem of others." What is that reason?

Religious Morality vs. Secular Morality

Religious morality—and Christian morality in particular—may have its difficulties, but religious apologists argue that secular morality has still greater difficulties. It leads, they claim, to ethical skepticism, nihilism, or, at best, to a pure conventionalism. Such apologists could point out that if we look at morality with the cold eye of an anthropologist, we will find morality to be nothing more than the often conflicting *mores* of the various tribes spread around the globe.

If we eschew the kind of insight that religion can give us, we will have no Archimedean point in accordance with which we can decide how it is that we ought to live and die. If we look at ethics from such a purely secular point of view, we will discover that it is constituted by tribal conventions, conventions that we are free to reject if we are sufficiently free from ethnocentrism. We can continue to act in accordance with them or we can reject them and adopt a different set of conventions; but whether we act in accordance with the old conventions or forge "new tablets," we are still acting in accordance with certain conventions. In relation to these conventions certain acts are right or wrong, reasonable or unreasonable, but we cannot justify the fundamental moral conventions themselves or the ways of life which they partially codify.

When these points are conceded, theologians are in a position to press home a powerful apologetic point: *when we become keenly aware of the true nature of such conventionalism and when we become aware that there is no overarching purpose that men were destined to fulfill, the myriad purposes, the aims and goals humans create for themselves, will be seen to be inadequate.* When we realize that life does not have a meaning that is there to be found, but that we human beings must by our deliberate decisions give it whatever meaning it has, we will (as Sartre so well understood) undergo estrangement and despair. We will drain our cup to its last bitter drop and feel our alienation to the full. Perhaps there are human purposes, purposes to be found in life, and we can and do have them even in a Godless world; but *without God there can be no one overarching purpose, no one basic scheme of human existence in virtue of which we could find a meaning for our grubby lives.* It is this overall sense of meaning that man so ardently strives for, but it is not to be found in a purely secular worldview. You secularists, a new Pascal might argue, must realize, if you really want to be clear-headed, that no purely human purposes are ultimately worth striving for. What you humanists can give us by way of a scheme of human existence will always be a poor second-best and not what the human heart most ardently longs for.

The considerations for and against an ethics not rooted in a religion are complex and involuted; a fruitful discussion of them is difficult, for in considering the matter of our passions, our anxieties, our ultimate concerns (if you will) are involved, and they tend to blur our vision, enfeeble our understanding of what exactly is at stake. But we must not forget that what is at stake here is just what kind of ultimate commitments or obligations a man could have without evading any issue, without self-deception or without delusion. I shall be concerned to display and assess, to make plain and also to weigh, some of the most crucial considerations for and against a purely secular ethic. While I shall try to make clear in an objective fashion what the central issues are, I shall also give voice to my reflective convictions on this matter. *I shall try to make evident my reasons for believing that we do not need God or any religious belief to support our moral convictions.* I shall do this, as I think one should in philosophy, by making apparent the dialectic of the problem, the considerations for and against, and by arguing for what I take to be their proper resolution.

Human Happiness

I am aware that crisis theologians would claim that I am being naive, but I do not see why purposes of purely human devising are not ultimately worth striving for. There is much that we humans prize and would continue to prize even in a Godless world. Many things would remain to give our lives meaning and point even after "the death of God."

Take a simple example. *All of us want to be happy.* But in certain bitter or skeptical moods we question what happiness is or we despairingly ask ourselves whether anyone can really be happy. Is this, however, a sober, sane view of the situation? I do not think that it is. Indeed, we cannot adequately define 'happiness' in the way that we can 'bachelor', but neither can we in that way define 'chair', 'wind', 'pain', and the vast majority of words in everyday discourse. For words like 'bachelor', 'triangle', or 'father' we can specify a consistent set of properties that all the things and only the things denoted by these words have, but we cannot do this for 'happiness', 'chair', 'pain', and the like. Yet there is no great loss here. Modern philosophical analysis has taught us that such an essentially Platonic conception of definition is unrealistic and unnecessary.[1] I may not be able to define 'chair' in the way that I can define 'bachelor', but I understand the meaning of chair perfectly well. In normal circumstances, at least, I know what to sit on when someone tells me to take a chair. I may not be able to define 'pain', but I know what it is like to be in pain and sometimes I can know when others are in pain. Similarly, though I cannot define 'happiness' in the

same way that I can define 'bachelor', I know what it is like to be happy, and sometimes I can judge with considerable reliability whether others are happy or sad. 'Happiness' is a slippery word, but it is not so slippery that we are justified in saying that nobody knows what happiness is.

A man could be said to have lived a happy life if he had found lasting sources of satisfaction in his life and if he had been able to find certain goals worthwhile and to achieve at least some of them. He could indeed have suffered some pain and anxiety, but his life, for the most part, must have been free from pain, estrangement and despair and must, on balance, have been a life that he has liked and found worthwhile. Surely we have no good grounds for saying that no one achieves such a balance or that no one is ever happy even for a time. We all have some idea of what would make us happy and of what would make us unhappy; many people, at least, can remain happy even after "the death of God." At any rate, we need not strike Pascalian attitudes, for even in a purely secular world there are permanent sources of human happiness of which anyone may avail himself.

What are these relatively permanent sources of human happiness that we all want or need? What is it that, if we have it, will give us the basis for a life that could properly be said to be happy? We all desire to be free from pain and want. [Even masochists do not seek pain for its own sake; they endure pain because this is the only psychologically acceptable way of achieving something else (usually sexual satisfaction) that is so gratifying to them that they will put up with the pain to achieve it.] We all want a life in which sometimes we can enjoy ourselves and in which we can attain our fair share of some of the simple pleasures that we all desire. They are not everything in life, but they are important, and our lives would be impoverished without them.

We also need security and emotional peace. We need and want a life in which we will not be constantly threatened with physical or emotional harassment. Again, this is not the only thing worth seeking, but it is an essential ingredient in any adequate picture of the good life.

Human love and companionship are also central to a happy life. We prize them and a life without them is most surely an impoverished life, a life that no man, if he would take the matter to heart, would desire. But I would most emphatically assert that human love and companionship are quite possible in a Godless world, and the fact that life will some day inexorably come to an end and cut off love and companionship altogether enhances rather than diminishes their present value.

Furthermore, we all need some sort of creative employments or meaningful work to give our lives point, to save them from boredom, drudgery and futility. A man who can find no way to use the talents he has, or a man who can find no work that is meaningful to him, will indeed be a miserable man. But again there is work—whether it be as a surgeon, a farmer, or a fisherman—that has a rationale even in a world without God. And poetry, music, and art retain their beauty and enrich our lives even in the complete absence of God or the gods.

We want and need art, music, and the dance. We find pleasure in travel and conversation and in a rich variety of experiences. The sources of human enjoyment are obviously too numerous to detail, but all of them are achievable in a Godless universe. If some can be ours, we can attain a reasonable measure of happiness. Only a Steppenwolfish personality, beguiled by impossible expectations and warped by irrational guilts and fears, can fail to find happiness in the realization of such ends. But to be free of impossible expectations people must clearly recognize that there is no "one big thing" (or, for that matter, "one small thing") that would make them permanently happy; almost anything permanently and exclusively pursued will lead to that nausea that Sartre has so forcefully brought to our attention. But *we can, if we are not too sick and if our situation is not too precarious, find lasting sources of human happiness in a purely secular world.*

Human Suffering

It is not only happiness for ourselves that can give us something of value, but there is the need to do what we can to diminish the awful sum of human misery in the world. I have never understood those who say that they find contemporary life meaningless because they find nothing worthy to which they can devote their energies. Throughout the world there is an immense amount of human suffering, suffering that can be partially alleviated through a variety of human efforts. Why can we not find a meaningful life in devoting ourselves, as did Doctor Rieux in Albert Camus's *La Peste*, to relieving somewhat the sum total of human suffering? Why cannot this give our lives point and an overall rationale? It is childish to think that by human effort we will some day totally rid the world of suffering and hate, of deprivation and sadness; they are a permanent feature of the human condition. But specific instances of human suffering can be alleviated. The plague is always potentially with us, but we can destroy the Nazis and we can fight for racial and social equality throughout the world. And as isolated people, as individuals in a mass society, we find people turning to us in dire need, in suffering and in emotional deprivation, and we can as individuals respond to those people and alleviate or at least acknowledge that suffering and deprivation. A man who says, "If God is dead, nothing matters," is a spoilt child who has never looked at his fellowman with compassion.

Yet, it might be objected, if we abandon a Judeo-Christian *Weltanschauung*, there can, in a secular world, be no "one big thing" to give our lives an overall rationale. We will not be able to see written in the stars the final significance of human effort. There will be no architectonic purpose to give our lives such a rationale. Like Tolstoy's Pierre in *War and Peace*, we desire somehow to gather the sorry scheme of things entire into one intelligible explanation so that we can finally crack the riddle of human destiny. We long to understand why it is that men suffer and die. If it is a factual answer that is wanted when such a question is asked, the answer is evident enough: ask any physician. But clearly that is no answer to people who seek such a general account of human existence. They want some justification for suffering; they want some way of showing that suffering is after all for a good purpose. It can, of course, be argued that suffering sometimes is a good thing, for it occasionally gives us insight and at times even brings about in the man who suffers an increased capacity to love and to be kind. But there is plainly an excessive amount of human suffering—the suffering of children in hospitals, the suffering of people devoured by cancer and the sufferings of millions of Jews under the

Nazis—for which there simply is no justification. Neither the religious man nor the secularist can explain, that is, justify, such suffering and find some overall scheme of life in which it has some place, but only the religious man needs to do so. The secularist understands that suffering is not something to be justified but simply to be struggled against with courage and dignity. And in this fight, even the man who has been deprived of that which could give him some measure of happiness can still find or make for himself a meaningful human existence.

Confusing 'Is' with 'Ought'

I have argued that purely human purposes—those goals we set for ourselves, the intentions we form— are enough to give meaning to our lives.[2] We desire happiness and we can find, even in a purely secular world, abundant sources of it. Beyond this we can find a rationale for seeking to mitigate the awful burden of human suffering. These two considerations are enough to make life meaningful. But it might be objected that I have put far too great a stress on the value of human happiness; that there, are other considerations in life, other values that are intrinsically worthwhile. We desire self-consciousness and some sense of self-identity as well as happiness. And we do not desire them for the enjoyment and happiness that will come from them but for their own sakes.

I am inclined to agree that this is so; human happiness and the desire to avoid suffering are central but are not the only facets of morality. To acknowledge this, however, only complicates the secular picture of morality: it gives us no reason to bring in theistic concepts. I admire human beings who are non-evasive and who have a sense of their own identity, and I regard an understanding of myself as something to be prized for its own sake. I do not need a deity to support this appreciation or give it value.

Philosophers, and some theologians as well, might challenge what I have said in a slightly different way. It could be said that even if we add consciousness as another intrinsic good *there is not the close connection between happiness and self-awareness on the one hand and virtue or moral good on the other that I have claimed there is.* That men do seek happiness as an end is one thing; that they ought to seek

it as an end is another. As G. E. Moore has in effect shown,[3] we cannot derive 'X is good' from 'People desire X' or from 'X makes people happy', for it is always meaningful to ask whether or not happiness is good and whether or not we ought to seek it for its own sake. It will be argued that I, like all secularists, have confused factual and moral issues. *An 'ought' cannot be derived from an 'is': we cannot deduce that something is good from a discovery that it will make people happy.* My hypothetical critic could well go on to claim that we must first justify the fundamental claim that happiness is good. Do we really have any reason to believe that happiness is good? Is the secularist in any more of a position to justify his claim than is the religionist to justify his claim that whatever God wills is good?

I would first like to point out that I have not confused factual and moral issues. One of the basic reasons I have for rejecting either a natural-law ethics or an ethics of divine commands is that both systematically confuse factual and moral issues. We cannot deduce that people ought to do something from discovering that they do it or seek it; nor can we conclude from the proposition that a being exists whom people call God that we ought to do whatever that being commands. In both cases we unjustifiably pass from a factual premise to a moral conclusion. Moral statements are not factual statements about what people seek or avoid, or about what a deity commands. But we do justify moral claims by an appeal to factual claims, and there is a close connection between what human beings desire on reflection and what they deem to be good. 'X is good' does not mean 'X makes for happiness', but in deciding that something is good, it is crucial to know what makes human beings happy. Both the Christian moralist and the secular moralist lay stress on human happiness. The Christian moralist—St. Augustine and Pascal are perfect examples—argues that only the Christian has a clear insight into what human happiness really is and that there is no genuine happiness without God. But we have no valid grounds for believing that only in God can we find happiness and that there are no stable sources of human happiness apart from God.

I cannot prove that happiness is good, but Christian and non-Christian alike take it in practice to be a very fundamental good. I can only appeal to your sense of psychological realism to persuade you to admit intellectually what in practice you acknowledge, namely, that happiness is good and that pointless suffering is bad. If you will acknowledge this, you must accept that I have shown that man can attain happiness even in a world without God.

Suppose some Dostoyevskian "underground man" does not care a fig about happiness. Suppose he does not even care about the sufferings of others. How, then, can you show him to be wrong? But suppose a man does not care about God or about doing what He commands either. How can you show that such an indifference to God is wrong? If we ask such abstract questions, we can see a crucial feature about the nature of morality. Sometimes a moral agent may reach a point at which he can give no farther justification for his claims but must simply, by his own deliberate decision, resolve to take a certain position. Here the claims of the existentialists have a genuine relevance. We come to recognize that, in the last analysis, nothing can take the place of a decision or resolution. *In the end, we must simply decide.* This recognition may arouse our anxieties and stimulate rationalization, but the necessity of making a decision is inherent in the logic of the situation. Actually, the religious moralist is in a worse position than the secularist, for he not only needs to subscribe to the principle that human happiness is good and that pain and suffering have no intrinsic value; he must also subscribe to the *outré* claims that only in God can man find happiness and that one ought to do whatever it is that God commands. 'Man can find lasting happiness only if he turns humbly to his Savior' has the look of a factual statement and is a statement that most assuredly calls for some kind of rational support. It is not something we must or can simply decide about. But the assertion that one ought to do what is commanded by God, like the assertion that happiness is good, does appear simply to call for a decision for or against. But what it is that one is deciding for when one "decides for God or for Christ" is so obscure as to be scarcely intelligible. Furthermore, the man who subscribes to that religious principle must subscribe to the secular claim as well. But why subscribe to this obscure second principle when there is no evidence

at all for the claim that man can find happiness only in God?

Morality is not science. Moral claims direct our actions; they tell us how we ought to act; they do not simply describe what we seek or explain our preferential behavior.[4] A secular morality need not view morality as a science or as an activity that is simply descriptive or explanatory. It can and should remain a normative activity. *Secular morality starts with the assumption that happiness and self-awareness are fundamental human goods and that pain and suffering are never desirable in themselves.* It may finally be impossible to prove that this is so, but if people will be honest with themselves they will see that in their behavior they clearly show that they subscribe to such a principle; and a philosopher can demonstrate that criticisms of such moral principles rest on confusions. Finally, I have tried to show that a man with secular knowledge alone can find clear and permanent sources of happiness such that whoever will avail himself of these sources of happiness can, if he is fortunate, lead a happy and purposeful life.

Secular Morality & the Problem of Others

The dialectic of our problem has not ended. The religious moralist might acknowledge that human happiness is indeed plainly a good thing while contending that secular morality, where it is consistent and reflective, will inevitably lead to some variety of egoism. *An individual who recognized the value of happiness and self-consciousness might, if he were free of religious restraints, ask himself why he should be concerned with the happiness and self-awareness of others, except where their happiness and self-awareness would contribute to his own good.* We must face the fact that sometimes, as the world goes, people's interests clash. Sometimes the common good is served only at the expense of some individual's interests. An individual must therefore, in such a circumstance, sacrifice what will make him happy for the common good. Morality requires this sacrifice of us, when it is necessary for the common good; morality, any morality, exists in part at least to adjudicate between the conflicting interests and demands of people. It is plainly evident that everyone cannot be happy all the time and that sometimes one person's happiness or the happiness of a group is at the expense of another person's happiness.

Morality requires that we attempt to distribute happiness as evenly as possible. We must be fair: each person is to count for one and none is to count for more than one. Whether we like a person or not, whether he is useful to his society or not, his interests and what will make him happy, must be considered in any final decision as to what ought to be done. The requirements of justice make it necessary that each person be given equal consideration. I cannot justify my neglect of another person in some matter of morality simply on the grounds that I do not like him, that he is not a member of my set or that he is not a productive member of society. The religious apologist will argue that behind these requirements of justice as fairness there lurks the ancient religious principle that men are creatures of God, each with an infinite worth, and that men are never to be treated only as means but as persons deserving of respect in their own right. They have an infinite worth simply as persons.

My religious critic, following out the dialectic of the problem, should query why you should respect someone, why you should treat all people equally, if doing this is not in your interest or not in the interests of your group. No purely secular justification can be given for so behaving. My critic now serves his *coup de grâce*: the secularist, as does the "knight of faith," acknowledges that the principle of respect for persons is a precious one—a principle that he is unequivocally committed to, but the religious man alone can justify adherence to this principle. The secularist is surreptitiously drawing on Christian inspiration when he insists that all men should be considered equal and that people's rights must be respected. For a secular morality to say all it wants and needs to say, it must, at this crucial point, be parasitical upon a God-centered morality. Without such a dependence on religion, secular morality collapses into egoism.

It may well be the case that, as a historical fact, our moral concern for persons came from our religious conceptions, but it is a well-known principle of logic that the truth of a belief is independent of its origin. *What the religious moralist must do is to show*

that only on religious grounds could such a principle of respect for persons be justifiably asserted. But he has not shown that this is so; and there are good reasons for thinking that it is not so. . . .

There is a purely secular rationale for treating people fairly, for regarding them as persons. Let me show how this is so. We have no evidence that men ever lived in a pre-social state of nature. Man, as we know him, is an animal with a culture, he is part of a community, and the very concept of community implies binding principles and regulations—duties, obligations and rights. Yet, imaginatively we could conceive, in broad outline at any rate, what it would be like to live in a pre-social state.

In such a state no one would have any laws or principles to direct his behavior. In that sense, man would be completely free. But such a life, as Hobbes graphically depicted, would be a clash of rival egoisms. Life in that state of nature would be, in his celebrated phrase, "nasty, brutish, and short." Now if men were in such a state and if they were perfectly rational egoists, what kind of community life would they choose, given the fact that they were, very roughly speaking, nearly equal in strength and ability? (The fact that in communities as we find them men are not so nearly equal in power is beside the point for our hypothetical situation.) Given that they all start from scratch and have roughly equal abilities, it seems to me that it would be most reasonable, even for rational egoists, to band together into a community where each man's interests were given equal consideration, where each person was treated as deserving of respect.[5]

Each rational egoist would want others to treat him with respect, for his very happiness is contingent upon that; and he would recognize that he could attain the fullest cooperation of others only if other rational egoists knew or had good grounds for believing that their interests and their persons would also be respected. Such cooperation is essential for each egoist if all are to have the type of community life that would give them the best chance of satisfying their own interests to the fullest degree. Thus, even if men were thorough egoists, we would still have rational grounds for subscribing to a principle of respect for persons. That men are not thoroughly rational, do not live in a state of nature, and are not thorough egoists does not gainsay the fact that we have rational grounds for regarding social life, organized in accordance with such a principle, as being objectively better than a social life which ignores this principle. The point here is that even rational egoists could see that this is the best possible social organization where men are nearly equal in ability.

What about the world we live in—a world in which, given certain extant social relationships, men are not equal or even nearly equal in power and opportunity? What reason is there for an egoist who is powerfully placed to respect the rights of others, when they cannot hurt him? We can say that his position, no matter how strong, might change and he might then need his rights protected; but this is surely not a strong enough reason for respecting human rights. To be moral involves respecting those rights, but our rational egoist may not propose to be moral. In considering such questions, we reach a point in reasoning at which we must simply decide what sort of person we shall strive to become. The religious moralist also reaches the same point. He, too, must make a decision of principle, but the principle he adopts is a fundamentally incoherent one. He not only must decide, but his decision must involve the acceptance of an absurdity.

It is sometimes argued by religious apologists that men will respect the rights of others only if they fear a wrathful and angry God. Without such a punitive sanction or threat, men will go wild. Yet it hardly seems to be the case that Christians, with their fear of hell, have been any better at respecting the rights of others than non-Christians. A study of the Middle Ages or the conquest of the non-Christian world makes this plain enough. And even if it were true that Christians were better in this respect than non-Christians, it would not show that they had a superior moral reason for their behavior, for in so acting and in so reasoning, they are not giving a morally relevant reason at all but are simply acting out of fear for their own hides. Yet Christian morality supposedly takes us beyond the clash of the rival egoisms of secular life.

In short, Christian ethics has not been able to give us a sounder ground for respecting persons than we have with a purely secular morality. The Kantian principle of respect for persons is actually bound up in the very idea of morality, either secular or religious; and there are good reasons, of a perfectly mundane sort, why we should have the institution of morality as we now have it, namely, that our individual welfare is dependent on having a device that equitably resolves social and individual conflicts. Morality has an objective rationale in complete independence of religion. Even if God is dead, it does not really matter.

NOTES

1. This is convincingly argued in Michael Scriven's "Definitions, Explanations and Theories" in H. Feigl, M. Scriven, and G. Maxwell, *Minnesota Studies in the Philosophy of Science*, vol. 2. (Minneapolis: University of Minnesota Press, 1958), pp. 99–195.
2. I have argued this point in considerably more detail in Kai Nielsen, "Linguistic Philosophy and 'The Meaning of Life,'" *Cross Currents* 15, no. 3 (1964): 313–34.
3. G. E. Moore, *Principia Ethica* (Cambridge: Cambridge University Press, 1903), chapters 1 and 2.
4. This crucial claim is ably argued by P. H. Nowell-Smith, *Ethics*, (London: Blackwell, 1957), chapters 1–4; by John Ladd, "Reason and Practice," in John Wild, (ed.), *The Return to Reason* (Chicago: Chicago University Press, 1953) pp. 253–358; and by A. E. Murphy, "The Common Good," in *Proceedings and Addresses of the American Philosophy Association* 24 (1950–1951): pp. 3–18.
5. Some of the very complicated considerations relevant here have been brought out subtly by John Rawls's "Justice as Fairness," in *The Philosophical Review* 57 (1958): pp. 164–94, and by Georg von Wright, *The Varieties of Goodness* (London: Routledge, 1963), chapter 10. I think it could be reasonably maintained that my argument is more vulnerable here than at any other point. I would not, of course, use it if I did not think it could be sustained; but if anyone should find unconvincing the argument as presented here, I would beg him to consider the argument that precedes it and the one that immediately follows it. They alone are sufficient to establish my general case.

DISCUSSION QUESTIONS:

1. Nielsen writes that, "A man could be said to have lived a happy life if he had found lasting sources of satisfaction in his life and if he had been able to find certain goals worthwhile and to achieve at least some of them," (page 71)

But what if a person found lasting satisfaction from raping and killing women? Would that make his life a happy one? Even if it made his life happy, would his life have been a *morally* good one? If not, then there is more to a morally good life than happiness. But where could this come from if there is not a God?

2. Nielsen claims that he cannot prove that happiness is good. "In the end," he writes, "we must simply decide", (page 74) Is that true? Is there no rational argument to support the claim that happiness is a morally good thing? If it's true that we're just supposed to decide in the absence of argument, why isn't it just as reasonable to decide that God is required for moral facts?

3. Nielsen argues that it's in our own self-interest to respect the rights of others, and he appeals to a Hobbesian-type social contract to prove this. But he openly grants that there are cases in which "people's interests clash." What secular reason can he provide for thinking that one should respect the rights of others in those rare cases where one can get away with not doing so?

4. Nielsen argues forcefully that we need not posit the existence of God to make sense out of morality. But can one agree with everything that Nielsen says about morality and still believe in God? Why or why not?

Argument Reconstruction Exercises:

I. Nielsen is initially sympathetic to the view that a meaningful life can be found only if God exists. Identify the premises and conclusion in this excerpt:

> . . .without God there can be no one overarching purpose, no one basic scheme of human existence in virtue of which we could find a meaning for our grubby lives. It is this overall sense of meaning that man so ardently strives for, but it is not to be found in a purely secular worldview. (page 70)

II. The thesis of Nielsen's essay is that we don't need to posit the existence of God in order to make sense out of a meaningful life, and he thinks that human happiness plays a crucial role in the meaning of life. Identify the premises and conclusion in this excerpt:

Human love and companionship are also central to a happy life. We prize them and a life without them is most surely an impoverished life, a life that no man, if he would take the matter to heart, would desire. But I would most emphatically assert that human love and companionship are quite possible in a Godless world. . . (pages 71–72)

III. Nielsen worries that a secular ethic will not be able to explain why we should care about the welfare of others or respect the rights of others when doing so is not in our best interests. Some religious philosophers have accused secularists of trying to have their cake and eat it too. The following excerpt makes this charge clear and forms the basis for an implicit argument against a purely secular ethic. Identify the premises and conclusion in this excerpt:

> . . .the secularist, as does the "knight of faith," acknowledges that the principle of respect for persons is a precious one—a principle that he is unequivocally committed to, but the religious man alone can justify adherence to this principle. The secularist is surreptitiously drawing on Christian inspiration when he insists that all men should be considered equal and that people's rights must be respected. (page 75)

IV. The whole point of Nielsen's essay is to show how we could have moral duties even if there were no God. But there is a powerful case against this claim. Identify the premises and conclusion in this argument:

> If there is no God, then there is nothing that humans were created to do—there would be no ultimate purpose for our lives. And if there is no purpose for our lives, then it doesn't make any sense to say that there are things that we ought and ought not do. It's like the difference between a rock in a field and a watch in a field. There are things that the watch ought to do, given the fact that it has a purpose. There is no meaningful sense in which the rock ought to do anything, for it has no purpose. Similarly, if we have no purpose, it is meaningless to say that we ought to do anything at all. So Nielsen is mistaken that we can have a purely secular ethic.

7.3 MASTER & SLAVE MORALITIES

FRIEDERICH NIETZSCHE (1886)

Friederich Nietzsche was a 19th century German thinker who made contributions to a wide range of academic fields. His work in philosophy is eclectic but bound by the central themes of postmodernism: a denial of objective truth, a denial of objective value, and a deep skepticism of human progress. The present selection is taken from his book *Beyond Good and Evil*, and it represents an attempt to show that our conceptions of good and evil are reflective of the power structures in which we find ourselves. Those in power will define the good one way while those without power will define it another way. In either case, the moral values are determined by humans.

Reading Questions:

1. How do masters typically define moral goodness?

2. Who, according to the "noble type of man," is the determiner of values?

3. Why would a master morality have a deep reverence for both age and the traditional ways of doing things?

4. How do slaves typically define moral goodness or moral virtue?

5. What is Nietzsche's explanation for why humans are prone to vanity?

In a tour of the many finer and coarser moralities which have ruled or still rule on earth I found certain traits regularly recurring together and bound up with one another: until at length two basic types were revealed and, a basic distinction emerged. There is **master morality** and **slave morality**—I add at once that in all higher and mixed cultures attempts at mediation between the two are apparent and more frequently confusion and mutual misunderstanding between them, indeed sometimes their harsh juxtaposition—even within the same man, within *one* soul. The moral value-distinctions have arisen either among a ruling order which was pleasurably conscious of its distinction from the ruled—or among the ruled, the slaves and dependants of every degree.

Master Morality

In the former case, *when it is the rulers who determine the concept 'good', it is the exalted, proud states of soul which are considered distinguishing and determine the order of rank.* The noble human being separates from himself those natures in which the opposite of such exalted proud states find expression: he despises them. It should be noted at once that in this first type of morality the antithesis 'good' and 'bad' means the same thing as 'noble' and 'despicable'—the antithesis 'good' and 'evil' originates elsewhere. The cowardly, the timid, the petty, and those who think only of narrow utility are despised; as are the mistrustful with their constricted glance, those who abase themselves, the dog-like type of man who lets himself be mistreated, the fawning flatterer, above all the liar—it is a fundamental belief of all aristocrats that the common people are liars. 'We who are truthful'—thus did the nobility of ancient Greece designate themselves.

It is immediately obvious that designations of moral value were everywhere first applied to *human beings*, and only later and derivatively to *actions*: which is why it is a grave error when moral historians start from such questions as 'why has the compassionate action been praised?' *The noble type of man feels himself to be the determiner of values*, he does not need to be approved of, he judges 'what harms me is harmful in itself', he knows himself to be that which in general first accords honour to things, he *creates values*. Everything he knows to be part of himself, he honours: such a morality is self-glorification. In the foreground stands the feeling of plenitude, of power which seeks to overflow, the happiness of high tension, the consciousness of a wealth which would like to give away and bestow—the noble human being too aids the unfortunate but not, or almost not, from pity, but more from an urge begotten by superfluity of power. The noble human being honours in himself the man of power, also the man who has power over himself, who understands how to speak and how to keep silent, who enjoys practising severity and harshness upon himself and feels reverence for all that is severe and harsh. 'A hard heart has Wotan set in my breast', it says in an old Scandinavian saga: a just expression coming from the soul of a proud Viking. A man of this type is actually proud that he is *not* made for pity: which is why the hero of the saga adds as a warning: 'he whose heart is not hard in youth will never have a hard heart'. Brave and noble men who think that are at the farthest remove from that morality which sees the mark of the moral precisely in pity or in acting for others or in *désintéressement;* belief in oneself, pride in oneself, a fundamental hostility and irony for 'selflessness' belong just as definitely to noble morality as does a mild contempt for and caution against sympathy and the 'warm heart'.—It is the powerful who *understand* how to honour, that is their art, their realm of invention. *Deep reverence for age and the traditional—all law rests on this twofold reverence—belief in and prejudice in favour of ancestors and against descendants, is typical of the morality of the powerful;* and when, conversely, men of 'modern ideas' believe almost instinctively in 'progress' and 'the future' and show an increasing lack of respect for age, this reveals clearly enough the ignoble origin of these 'ideas'.

A morality of the rulers is, however, most alien and painful to contemporary taste in the severity of its principle that one has duties only towards one's equals; that towards beings of a lower rank, towards everything alien, one may act as one wishes or 'as the heart dictates' and in any case 'beyond good and evil'—: it is here that pity and the like can have a place. The capacity for and the duty of protracted gratitude and protracted revenge—both only among one's equals—subtlety in requittal, a refined conception of friendship, a certain need to have enemies (as conduit systems, as it were, for the emotions of envy, quarrelsomeness, arrogance—fundamentally so as to be able to be a good *friend*): all these are typical marks of noble morality which, as previously indicated, is not the morality of 'modem ideas' and is therefore hard to enter into today, also hard to unearth and uncover.

Slave Morality

It is otherwise with the second type of morality, *slave morality*. Suppose the abused, oppressed, suffering, unfree, those uncertain of themselves and weary should moralize: what would their moral evaluations have in common? Probably a pessimistic mistrust of the entire situation of man will find expression, perhaps a condemnation of man together with his situation. *The slave is suspicious of the virtues of the powerful*: he is sceptical and mistrustful, *keenly* mistrustful, of everything 'good' that is honoured among them—he would like to convince himself that happiness itself is not genuine among them. On the other hand, those qualities which serve to make easier the existence of the suffering will be brought into prominence and flooded with light: here it is that pity, the kind and helping hand, the warm heart, patience, industriousness, humility, friendliness come into honour—for here these are the most useful qualities and virtually the only means of enduring the burden of existence. *Slave morality is essentially the morality of utility.* Here is the source of the famous antithesis 'good' and 'evil'—power and danger were felt to exist in evil, a certain dreadfulness, subtlety and strength which could not admit of contempt. Thus, according to slave morality, the 'evil' inspire fear; according to master morality, it is precisely the 'good' who inspire fear and want to inspire it, while the 'bad' man is judged contemptible. The antithesis reaches its height when, consistently with slave morality, a breath of disdain finally also comes to be attached to the 'good' of this morality—it may be a slight and benevolent disdain—because within the slaves' way of thinking the good man has in any event to be a *harmless* man: he is good-natured, easy to deceive, perhaps a bit stupid, *un bonhomme*. Wherever slave morality comes to predominate, language exhibits a tendency to bring the words 'good' and 'stupid' closer to each other. . . .

Vanity

Among the things which a noble human being perhaps finds hardest to understand is vanity: he will be tempted to deny its existence where a different type of human being will think it palpably evident. For him the problem is to imagine creatures who try to awaken a good opinion of themselves which they themselves do not hold—and thus do not 'deserve' either—and yet subsequently come to *believe* this good opinion themselves. This seems to him in part so tasteless and lacking in self-respect and in part so baroquely irrational that he would prefer to consider vanity exceptional and in most cases where it is spoken of he doubts its existence. He will say, for example: 'I can rate my value incorrectly and yet demand that others too should recognize my value exactly as I rate it—but that is not vanity (but self-conceit, or, more usually, what is called "humility" or "modesty").' Or he will say: 'I can, for many reasons, take pleasure in the good opinion of others, perhaps because I love and honour them and take pleasure in all their pleasures, perhaps because their good opinion sustains me in my faith in my own good opinion, perhaps because the good opinion of others, even when I do not share it, is still useful to me or promises to be useful—but none of this is vanity.'

The noble human being requires the assistance of history if he is to see that, from time immemorial, in all strata which were in any way dependent, the common man *was* only that which he *counted as*—in no way accustomed to positing values himself, he also accorded himself no other value than that which his master accorded him (*it is the intrinsic right of masters to create values*). It can be conceived as the consequence of a tremendous atavism that even now the ordinary man still always *waits* for an opinion about himself and then instinctively submits to it: but this happens not merely in the case of

a 'good' opinion, but also in that of a bad and unfair one (consider, for instance, the greater part of the self-estimates and self-underestimates which believing women acquire from their father-confessors and the believing Christian acquires from his Church). Now it is a fact that, in accordance with the slow rise of the democratic order of things (and its cause, the mixing of the blood of masters and slaves), the originally noble and rare impulse to ascribe a value to oneself on one's own account and to 'think well' of oneself will be increasingly encouraged and spread wider and wider: but it has at all times an older, more widespread and more thoroughly ingrained inclination against it—and in the phenomenon of 'vanity' this older inclination masters the younger. The vain man takes pleasure in *every* good opinion he hears about himself (quite apart from any point of view of utility and likewise regardless of truth or falsehood), just as he suffers from every bad opinion: for he submits to both, he *feels* subject to them from that oldest instinct of subjection which breaks out in him.—It is 'the slave' in the vain man's blood, a remnant of the craftiness of the slave—and how much 'slave' still remains in woman, for example!—which seeks to *seduce* him to good opinions about himself; it is likewise the slave who immediately afterwards falls down before these opinions as if he himself had not called them forth.

DISCUSSION QUESTIONS:

1. Do you think it's true that people in power often have different moral values than people who are not in power? Think of some concrete cases: millionaires vs. those on food stamps, politicians vs. school teachers, corporate CEO's vs. average employees, etc. Will these people have different views of our moral obligations and what is right and what is fair? If so, will the differences of opinion be along the lines suggested by Nietzsche?

2. Think of your own set of moral beliefs. What kinds of things do you think are right or fair or required of us? In Nietzsche's terms, is your morality more of a master morality or a slave morality? What does that say about you?

3. Suppose it's true that those in power view their moral obligations differently from those outside of power. How can we explain that fact? Perhaps it's

easier to think about the scenario in a concrete case: suppose a chicken farmer and a vegetarian have a debate over the ethics of eating meat. How can we explain the fact that they will inevitably disagree about the farmer's treatment of chickens? Need we conclude, as Nietzsche apparently does, that each of us creates our own values?

Argument Reconstruction Exercises:

I. Nietzsche points out that those in the master class argue for moral virtues only by conflating what they find noble with the good and what they find despicable with the bad. Identify the premises and conclusion in this excerpt; note that the conclusion is suppressed, so you'll have to provide it:

> It should be noted at once that in this first type of morality [master morality] the antithesis 'good' and 'bad' means the same thing as 'noble' and 'despicable'...the cowardly, the timid, the petty, and those who think only of narrow utility are despised. (page 78)

II. Nietzsche spends most of his time cataloging the differences between master and slave moralities. But his ultimate conclusions seem to be that humans are the determiners or creators of value. One way of looking at his overall argument is as an argument from the best explanation of the data. Identify the premises and conclusion in this paraphrase:

> Those in power think of morality in terms of honor, rights, honesty, tradition, etc. Those without power think of morality in terms of the value of pity,

kindness, patience, humility, friendship, etc. How can we explain the differences between these two groups? Easily—each group determines what is morally valuable for themselves. Hence, morality is subjective.

III. Nietzsche notes what we might think of as a "convenient" coincidence between the moral codes we espouse and our own personal situations. Identify the premises and conclusion in this argument:

> People tend to accept only those moral principles that are good for them. Maybe it's all subconscious, but when a moral principle would be in one's favor, chances are that it will be accepted. And what kind of moral principles would favor those in power? Principles about how we should defer to authority and tradition, principles about how important it is not to steal, etc. And when we look at those in power, we find that these are exactly the moral principles that they champion.

IV. Nietzsche worries about our tendencies to be vain, and he explains our tendencies in terms of "the slave" in our blood. Identify the premises and conclusion in this paraphrased argument:

> The vain man takes pleasure in every good opinion he hears about himself...just as he suffers from every bad opinion: for he submits to both..." But we should rise above the level of being vain. We are not subjects to the opinions of others. So we should neither take pleasure in every compliment nor suffer with every criticism of others. (page 80)

7.4 MORAL RELATIVISM

GILBERT HARMAN (1996)

Gilbert Harman is the James S. McDonnell Distinguished University Professor of Philosophy at Princeton University. His work has been influential in many fields of philosophy, including normative ethics, metaethics, epistemology, and philosophy of language. In this essay, Harman argues for **moral relativism** by rejecting both **moral absolutism** and **moral nihilism**. Harman argues that just as there are no "absolute" facts about motion or mass, so, too, there are no "absolute" facts about morality. Actions are right or wrong only in comparison with a specific moral framework and no moral framework is more correct than any other. The argument in favor of this view stems from the wide variety of moral diversity we find in actual human societies.

Reading Questions:

1. What is the difference between Moral Relativism and Moral Absolutism?

2. What is the difference between Moral Relativism and Moral Nihilism?

3. What does Harman mean by "moral diversity"?

4. According to Harman, what is the best explanation for the range of moral diversity that actually exists?

5. According to Harman, what is an alternative explanation for the range of moral diversity that might be offered by a moral absolutist?

6. What is "evaluative relativity"?

7. What is the point of the horse race analogy pressed by Harman in the section entitled *Evaluative Relativity: "Good For"*?

Motion is a relative matter. Motion is always relative to a choice of spatio-temporal framework. Something that is moving in relation to one spatio-temporal framework can be at rest in relation to another. And no spatio-temporal framework can be singled out as the one and only framework that captures the truth about whether something is in motion.

According to Einstein's Theory of Relativity even an object's mass is relative to a choice of spatio-temporal framework. An object can have one mass in relation to one such framework and a different mass in relation to another. Again, there is no privileged spatio-temporal framework that determines the real mass of an object.

I am going to argue for a similar claim about moral right and wrong. I am going to defend **moral relativism**. *I am going to argue that moral right and wrong (good and bad, justice and injustice, virtue and vice, etc.) are always relative to a choice of moral framework*. What is morally right in relation to one moral framework can be morally wrong in relation to a different moral framework. And no moral framework is objectively privileged as the one true morality. . . .

It is important to distinguish moral relativism both from moral absolutism on the one side and from moral nihilism on the other side. **Moral**

absolutism holds that there is a single true morality. Moral relativism claims instead:

> There is no single true morality. There are many different moral frameworks, none of which is more correct than the others.

Moral nihilism agrees with this and takes that conclusion to be a reason to reject morality altogether including any sort of relative morality.

Moral nihilism can be compared to religious nihilism. Religious nihilism would be a natural response to the conclusion that there is no single true religion but only many different religious outlooks, none of which is more correct than the others. Such a conclusion would seem to provide a reason to reject religion and religious judgments altogether, rather than a reason to accept "religious relativism." It might then be possible to assign objective truth conditions to religious judgments in relation to one or another religious framework, but it is hard to see how such relative religious judgments could play a serious role in religious practices. Moral nihilism argues that the same is true of morality: there is no point to engaging in morality and moral judgment.

Moral relativism rejects moral nihilism and asserts instead

> Morality should not be abandoned.

Furthermore, moral relativism insists

Relative moral judgments can continue to play a serious role in moral thinking.

In the next two sections I mainly argue against moral absolutism. In particular, I argue that moral relativism is made very plausible by actual moral diversity. In the last two sections I discuss the sort of relativity involved in moral relativism. . . .

Explaining Moral Diversity

In this and the following section I argue that moral relativism is a reasonable inference from the most plausible explanation of moral diversity.

There is no single true morality. There are many different moral frameworks, none of which is more correct than the others.

I begin by mentioning data to be explained: the nature and extent of moral diversity.

Members of different cultures often have very different beliefs about right and wrong and often act quite differently on their beliefs. To take a seemingly trivial example, different cultures have different rules of politeness and etiquette: burping after eating is polite in one culture, impolite in another. Less trivially, some people are cannibals, others find cannibalism abhorrent.

The institution of marriage takes different forms in different societies. In some, a man is permitted to have several wives, in others bigamy is forbidden. More generally, the moral status of women varies greatly from one society to another in many different ways.

Some societies allow slavery, some have caste systems, which they take to be morally satisfactory, others reject both slavery and caste systems as grossly unjust.

It is unlikely that any nontrivial moral principles are universally accepted in all societies. The anthropologist George Silberbauer (1993, p. 15) is able to say only that "there are values which can be seen as common to nearly all societies," a remark limited by the phrases "can be seen as" and "nearly all." He further limits this claim by adding, "there are sometimes strong contrasts in the ways in which [these values] are expressed in precepts, principles and evaluations of behaviour."

Some say that there is a universally recognized central core of morality consisting of prohibitions against killing and harming others, against stealing, and against lying to others. Walzer (1987, p. 24) offers a more limited list of universal prohibitions: "murder, deception, betrayal and gross cruelty." It makes sense for Walzer to leave theft off the list, since some societies do not recognize private property, so they would have no rules against stealing. (Without property, there can be no such thing as stealing. It is trivial to say that all societies that recognize private property have rules against stealing, because having such rules is a necessary condition of recognizing private property!)

It may be that *murder* is always considered wrong, if murder is defined as "wrongful killing." But few societies accept *general* moral prohibitions on killing or harming other people. There are societies in which a "master" is thought to have an absolute right to treat his slaves in any way he chooses, including arbitrarily beating and killing them. Similarly, there may be no limitations on what a husband can do to his wife, or a father to his young children. Infanticide is considered acceptable in some societies. When moral prohibitions on harming and killing and lying exist, they are sometimes supposed to apply only with respect to the local group and not with respect to outsiders. A person who is able successfully to cheat outsiders may be treated as an admirable person. Similarly for someone who is able to harm and kill outsiders.

Any universally accepted principle in this area must verge on triviality, saying, for example, that one must not kill or harm members of a certain group, namely the group of people one must not kill or harm![1]

Thomson (1990) appears to disagree. She states certain principles and says of them, "it is not at all clear how their negations could be accommodated into what would be recognizable as a moral code" (Thomson, 1990, p. 20). The principles she mentions are, "Other things being equal, one ought not act rudely," "Other things being equal, one ought to do what one promised," "Other things being equal, one ought not cause others pain," and "One ought not torture babies to death for fun."

On the contrary, it is clear that many moral codes have accommodated the negations of all these general principles by accepting instead principles restricted to insiders. And, if the phrase "other things being equal" is supposed to include a restriction to insiders, then triviality looms in the manner I have already mentioned.

Now, *mere moral diversity is not a disproof of moral absolutism.* Where there are differences in custom, there are often differences in circumstance. Indeed, differences in custom are themselves differences in circumstance that can affect what is right or wrong without entailing moral relativism. You do not need to be a moral relativist to recognize that in England it is wrong to drive on the right, whereas in France it is not wrong to drive on the right.

Even where circumstances are relevantly the same, mere differences in moral opinion no more refute moral absolutism than scientific differences in opinion about the cause of canal-like features on the surface of Mars establish that there is no truth to that matter.

But, even though the rejection of moral absolutism is not an immediate logical consequence of the existence of moral diversity, it is a reasonable inference from the most plausible explanation of the range of moral diversity that actually exists (Wong, 1984).

One of the most important things to explain about moral diversity is that it occurs not just between societies but also within societies and in a way that leads to seemingly intractable moral disagreements. In the contemporary United States, deep moral differences often seem to rest on differences in basic values rather than on differences in circumstance or information. Moral vegetarians, who believe that it is wrong to raise animals for food, exist in the same community as nonvegetarians, even in the same family. A disagreement between moral vegetarians and nonvegetarians can survive full discussion and full information and certainly appears to rest on a difference in the significance assigned to animals as compared with humans. Is there a nonrelative truth concerning the moral importance of animals? How might that "truth" be discovered?

In a similar way, disagreements about the moral acceptability of abortion or euthanasia survive extensive discussion and awareness of all relevant information about abortion. Such disagreements appear to depend on basic disagreements concerning the intrinsic value or "sanctity" of human life as compared with the value of the things that life makes possible, such as pleasurable experience and fulfilling activity (Dworkin, 1993).

There are similarly intractable disagreements about the relative value of artifacts of culture as compared with human life. Some people think that it is worse when terrorists bomb famous old museums than when they bomb crowded city streets; others feel that the loss of human life is worse than the loss of architecture and art. Again, there are disagreements about how much help one person should be prepared to give to others. Is it morally wrong to purchase a new record player instead of trying to help people who cannot afford food? Singer (1972) says yes; others say no. There are intractable disputes about whether it is morally worse to kill someone than it is to let that person die (Rachels, 1975) and about the relative importance of liberty versus equality in assessing the justice of social arrangements (Rawls, 1971; Nozick, 1972).

Furthermore, some people in the United States and elsewhere are strict egoists in the sense that they are concerned only with what is to be gained for themselves. These are not just people who give in to temptation, but rather people who think it is stupid and irrational not to restrict their activities to "looking out for number one" (Ringer, 1977). They see no point in telling the truth to others, to helping others in time of need, in keeping agreements with others, or in avoiding injury or even death to others, apart from expected gain to themselves. Many other people disagree with egoism, believing that there are often reasons to keep agreements, etc., even when doing so is not in one's interest.

It is hard to see how to account for all moral disagreements in terms of differences in situation or beliefs about nonmoral facts. *Many moral disagreements seem to rest instead on basic differences in moral outlook.*

Explaining Basic Differences

Suppose that many moral disagreements do indeed rest on basic differences in moral outlook rather than on differences in situation or beliefs about nonmoral facts. What explanation might there be for that?

An "absolutist" explanation might be that some people are simply not well placed to discover the right answers to moral questions.[2] The point to this response is not just that different people have different evidence but that what one makes of evidence depends on one's antecedent beliefs, so that starting out with some beliefs can help one reach the truth, whereas starting out with other beliefs can prevent one from reaching the truth. Rational change in belief tends to be conservative. It is rational to make the least change in one's view that is necessary in order to obtain greater coherence in what one believes (Goodman, 1965; Rawls, 1971; Harman, 1986). *Different people with different starting points will rationally respond in different ways to the same evidence. There is no guarantee that people who start sufficiently far apart in belief will tend to converge in view as the evidence comes in.* Someone whose initial view is relatively close to the truth may be led by the evidence to come closer to the truth. Someone who starts further away from the truth may be led even further away by the same evidence. Such a person is simply not well placed to discover the truth.

Here then is an one absolutist's explanation of why moral disagreements that rest on basic differences in moral outlook cannot be rationally resolved, supposing that is in fact the case.

Moral relativists instead see an analogy with other kinds of relativity.

Consider the ancient question whether the earth moves or the sun moves. Here the relativistic answer is correct. Motion is a relative matter. Something can be in motion relative to one system of spatio-temporal coordinates and not in motion relative to another system. The particular motion an object exhibits will differ from one system to another. There is no such thing as absolute motion, apart from one or another system of coordinates.

A relativistic answer is also plausible in the moral case. *Moral right and wrong are relative matters. A given act can be right with respect to one system of moral coordinates and wrong with respect to another system of moral coordinates.* And nothing is absolutely right or wrong, apart from any system of moral coordinates.

By "a moral system of coordinates" I mean a set of values (standards, principles, etc.), perhaps on the model of the laws of one or another state. Whether something is wrong in relation to a given system of coordinates is determined by the system together with the facts of the case in something like the way

in which whether something is illegal in a given jurisdiction is determined by the laws of that jurisdiction together with the facts of the case.

Why does it seem (to some people) that there are objective nonrelative facts about moral right and wrong? Well, why does it seem to some people that there are objective nonrelative facts about motion or mass? In the case of motion or mass, one particular system of coordinates is so salient that it seems to have a special status. Facts about motion or mass in relation to the salient system of coordinates are treated as nonrelational facts.

In a similar way, *the system of moral coordinates that is determined by a person's own values can be so salient that it can seem to that person to have a special status.* Facts about what is right or wrong in relation to that system of coordinates can be misidentified as objective nonrelational facts.

To be sure, the system of moral coordinates that is determined by a given person's values cannot in general be *identified* with all and only exactly those very values. Otherwise a person could never be mistaken about moral issues (in relation to the relevant system of coordinates) except by being mistaken about his or her own values!

For the same reason, a legal system cannot be simply identified with existing legislation, the record of prior court decisions, and the principles currently accepted by judges. Otherwise legislation could not be unconstitutional and judges could not be mistaken in the legal principles they accept or the decisions they reach. . . .

Furthermore, relativists deny that the persistence of such basic moral disagreement is due simply to some people being better placed to discover the moral truth, the absolutist explanation of the persistence of disagreement. To a relativist, that is like saying that people in one particular spatio-temporal framework are better placed than other people are to discover what the objectively correct spatio-temporal framework is.

Evaluative Relativity: "Good For"

We might compare the relativity of moral wrongness with the way in which something that is good for one person may not be good for another person. If

Tom has bet on a horse that runs well in the rain and Sue has bet on a horse that does not run well in the rain, then rain is good for Tom and bad for Sue. This is an uncontroversial example of evaluative relativity. The rain is good in relation to Tom's goals and bad in relation to Sue's.

Similarly, abortion can be immoral with respect to (the moral coordinates determined by) Tom's values and not immoral with respect to Sue's. Moral relativists sometimes express this by saying that abortion is immoral "for Tom" and not immoral "for Sue." Of course, what is meant here is not that abortion is bad for Tom but not bad for Sue in the sense of harmful to one but not the other, nor is it just to say that Tom may think abortion immoral and Sue may think it moral. The rain might be good for Tom even if he doesn't realize it and abortion might be immoral for Tom whether or not he realizes that it is.

Notice, by the way, that a speaker does not always have to make explicit for whom a given situation is good. In particular, if Max has bet on the same horse as Alice and he is speaking to Alice, out of the hearing of Sue, he can say simply. "This rain is bad," meaning that it is bad for him and Alice.

Similarly, a moral relativist talking to another moral relativist can suppress reference to a particular set of values if the judgment is supposed to hold in relation both to the (moral coordinates determined by the) values accepted by the speaker and to the (moral coordinates determined by the) values accepted by the hearer. If Sue and Arthur both have values with the same implications for abortion, and Tom isn't listening, Sue might say simply, "Abortion is not morally wrong", meaning that it is not wrong in relation to her and Arthur's values. It is not wrong for either of them.

In saying, "This rain is bad," Tom means (roughly) that it is bad for himself and his audience; not just that it is bad for himself. The remark, "This rain is bad" is not normally equivalent to "This rain is bad for me." When Tom tells someone else that the rain is bad, he means (roughly) that it is bad in relation to certain goals, purposes, aims, or values that he takes himself to share with his audience. If Mary knows that Tom has bet on a horse that runs well in the rain and she has bet on

a horse that does not run well in the rain, it would normally be misleading for her to tell Tom, simply, "This rain is bad." Such a remark would be overly self-centered. In the absence of some more or less clearly indicated qualification, evaluative remarks are understood as having been made from a point of view that is presumed to be shared by speaker and audience. If Mary is only talking about herself, she should make that explicit and say, "This rain is bad for me."

Notice that the rain can be bad for a group of people without being bad for each of them taken individually. It might be bad for them taken collectively. If the other school's football team plays better in the rain, "This rain is bad" might mean "this rain is bad for our side." (Similarly, the values of a group might not be the values of any individual in the group (Gilbert, 1989).)

Thomson (1992, 1994) takes the remark, "This rain is bad," to be "incomplete." That seems right. However, in the present instance we cannot simply equate the remark, "This rain is bad," with the more complete remark, "This rain is bad for us." There is a subtle difference. To see the difference, consider a situation in which Mary has bet on a horse that does not run well in the rain and she thinks, incorrectly, that Tom has also bet on that horse. Suppose Tom has bet on the horse that runs well in the rain, but Mary does not realize this. If in this context she says to Tom, "This rain is bad for us," then it is clear how to evaluate her remark. What she says is simply false, since it is not the case that the rain is bad for both of them. But if instead she were to say to Tom, "This rain is bad," then it is far from clear that what she says is false. Her remark to Tom presupposes shared interests or outlook. If that presupposition is incorrect, we do not normally try to assign truth or falsity to her remark. So in certain circumstances there is a difference between. "This rain is bad" and "This rain is bad for us."

Similarly, suppose the moral relativist, Sue, thinking she and Tom have relevantly similar standards, says to him, "abortion is morally permissible," suppressing mention of standards. Sue's remark is not to be treated as false merely because she is wrong in supposing she and Tom share principles that permit abortion.

Relativity Theory

Something that is good for some people is bad for others, indifferent to yet others. Moral relativism says that the same is true of moral values and moral norms. According to moral relativism whether something is morally good, right, or just is always relative to a set of moral coordinates, a set of values or moral standards, a certain moral point of view.

Moral relativism holds that there are various sets of moral coordinates or moral outlooks with different standards of right and wrong. People's values differ with respect to the relative weight given to liberty versus equality, and to general welfare versus the development of art and science. They also differ with respect to the extent of the moral community: some restrict it to family and friends; others include all people of a certain race or caste or country; some include all people of whatever race or class; others count animals and even plants as part of the moral community to be protected by the moral rules. . . .

Recall that moral relativism is not by itself a claim about meaning. It does not say that speakers always *intend* their moral judgments to be relational in this respect. It is clear that many speakers do not. Moral relativism is a thesis about how things are and a thesis about how things aren't! *Moral relativism claims that there is no such thing as objectively absolute good, absolute right, or absolute justice; there is only what is good, right, or just in relation to this or that moral framework.* What someone takes to be absolute rightness is only rightness in relation to (a system of moral coordinates determined by) that person's values.

Earlier, I compared moral relativism with Einstein's theory of relativity in physics, which says that physical magnitudes, like mass, length, or temporal duration, are relative to a frame of reference, so that two events that are simultaneous with respect to one frame of reference can fail to be simultaneous with respect to another. In saying this, Einstein's theory does not make a claim about speakers' intentions. It does not claim that speakers intend to be making relational judgments when they speak of mass or simultaneity. The claim is, rather, that there is no such thing as absolute simultaneity or absolute mass. There is only simultaneity or mass with respect to one or another frame of reference. What someone might take to be absolute magnitudes are really relative magnitudes: magnitudes that are relative to that person's frame of reference.

Imagine a difference of opinion about whether event E precedes event F. According to Einstein's theory of relativity, there may be no uniform answer to this question: perhaps, in relation to one framework E precedes F, while in relation to a different framework E does not precede F.

Similarly, consider a moral disagreement about whether we are right to raise animals for food. Moral relativism holds that there is no uniform answer to this question: in relation to (the system of moral coordinates determined by) one person's values it is permissible to raise animals for food and in relation to (the system of moral coordinates determined by) a different person's values it is not permissible to raise animals for food. To repeat: what someone takes to be absolute rightness is only rightness in relation to (a system of moral coordinates determined by) that person's values.

Moral relativism does not claim that moral differences by themselves entail moral relativism, any more than Einstein claimed that differences in opinion about simultaneity by themselves entailed relativistic physics. We have to consider what differences there are or could be and why this might be so. How are we to explain the sorts of moral differences that actually occur? Can we seriously suppose that there is an answer to the question about the justice of our treatment of animals that is independent of one or another moral framework? What is the best explanation of differences in this and other areas of seeming intractability?

I emphasize again that moral relativism does not identify what is right in relation to a given moral framework with whatever is taken to be right by those who accept that framework. That would be like saying Einstein's theory of relativity treats two events as simultaneous with respect to a given coordinate system if people at rest with respect to the coordinate system believe the events are simultaneous.

REFERENCES
Dworkin, R. (1993). *Life's Dominion*, New York: Knopf.
Gilbert, M. (1989). *On Social Facts*, London: Routledge.

Goodman, N. (1965). *Fact, Fiction, and Forecast*. Cambridge, Mass.: Harvard University Press.

Harman, G. (1986). *Change in View: Principles of Reasoning,* Cambridge, Massachusetts: Bradford Books/MIT Press.

Mackie, J. (1977). *Ethics: Inventing Right and Wrong*, London: Penguin Books.

Nozick, R. (1972). *Anarchy, State, and Utopia*, New York: Basic Books.

Rachels, J. (1975). "Active and passive euthanasia," *New England Journal of Medicine* 292.

Rawls, J. (1971). *A Theory of Justice*, Cambridge, Mass.: Harvard University Press.

Ringer, R. J. (1977). *Looking Out for Number One*, New York: Fawcett Crest Books.

Silberbauer, G. (1993). "Ethics in small-scale societies," *A Companion to Ethics*, ed. Peter Singer, Oxford: Blackwell.

Singer, P. (1972). "Famine, affluence, and morality," *Philosophy and Public Affairs* 1.

Thomson, J. (1990). *The Realm of Rights*, Cambridge, Mass.: Harvard University Press.

Thomson, J. (1992). "On some ways in which a thing can be good." *Social Philosophy & Policy* 9: 96–117.

Thomson, J. (1994). "Goodness and utilitarianism," *Proceedings and Addresses of The American Philosophical Association* 67.4: 7–21.

Walzer, M. (1987). *Interpretation and Social Criticism,* Cambridge, Massachusetts: Harvard University Press.

Wong, D. B. (1984). *Moral Relativity*, Berkeley, California: University of California Press.

NOTES

1. There will be universal truths about moralities just as there are universal truths about spatio-temporal frameworks. Perhaps all spatio-temporal frameworks must admit of motion and rest. And perhaps all moralities have some rules against killing, harm, and deception. The existence of universal features of spatio-temporal frameworks is compatible with and is even required by Einstein's Theory of Relativity and the existence of universal features of morality is compatible with moral relativism.

2. I am indebted to Nicholas Sturgeon for this suggestion.

DISCUSSION QUESTIONS:

1. Harman argues that moral diversity is so widespread that there are no non-trivial moral rules that all human societies would agree on. Is that true? Can you think of a moral prohibition that all human cultures would agree to live by?

2. Harman thinks that the best explanation for the diversity of moral opinion in our world is that there are no "absolute" moral facts. Can you think of other reasons why moral disagreement in the actual world might be so trenchant? How much do our ethnocentric tendencies, our vested interests, and our ignorance play into our deep moral disagreements with one another?

3. As Harman noted, we don't appeal to fact-relativity to explain disagreement in other areas of inquiry. Using his example, we don't see the diversity of opinion among scientists as to what caused the canal-like marks on the surface of Mars as indicative of the fact that there is no objective answer as to what caused those marks. How is morality different? Why should diversity of opinion cause us to doubt the existence of objective answers in the one case but not the other?

4. Suppose Harman is right that no moral framework is more correct than any other. What can we say about the moral frameworks held by others, including those of serial killers and Nazi guards? Is it really true that there's no moral reason to prefer one moral framework to another? If not, how are we to choose which to endorse?

Argument Reconstruction Exercises:

I. Harman grants that mere moral diversity does not entail moral relativism, but he thinks that this is the most reasonable conclusion to draw. His argument is one that proceeds by appealing to the best explanation for a set of data. Compare this sort of argument to what happens in the courtroom: matching fingerprints and blood type do not entail that the accused with matching prints and blood is guilty, but the guilt of the accused is the best explanation for that data. Identify the premises and conclusion in this excerpt:

> Now, mere moral diversity is not a disproof of moral absolutism. Where there are differences in custom, there are often differences in circumstance....But, even though the rejection of moral absolutism is not an immediate logical consequence of the existence of moral diversity, it is a reasonable inference from the most plausible explanation of the range of moral diversity that actually exists. (page 84)

II. Identify the premises and conclusion in this argument:

> If moral absolutism is correct, then there is only one, single true morality. But anyone who has ever read a newspaper or traveled abroad knows that people have very different beliefs about what they ought to do. Some people think that it's always wrong to have an abortion, and others think that it's sometimes permissible to have one. So it's obvious that there is no single, true morality. That's why I'm a moral relativist.

III. Harman thinks that our moral disagreement cannot be due merely to differences in non-moral beliefs. He thinks that we are aware of too many cases of disagreement in the real world to conclude that all such disagreement stems from differences of opinion about empirical matters of fact. Identify the premises and conclusion in this excerpt:

> Moral vegetarians, who believe that it is wrong to raise animals for food, exist in the same community as nonvegetarians, even in the same family. A disagreement between moral vegetarians and nonvegetarians can survive full discussion and full information and certainly appears to rest on a difference in the significance assigned to animals as compared to humans. . . . It is hard to see how to account for all moral disagreements in terms of differences in situation or beliefs about nonmoral facts. Many moral disagreements seem to rest instead on basic differences in moral outlook. (page 84)

IV. Many people identify moral relativism with tolerance. Insofar as it is a good thing to be tolerant of the beliefs and practices of those who disagree with you, moral relativism seems to explain this. Identify the premises and conclusion in this argument:

> No one should be intolerant of people who hold different moral beliefs from us. To think that you're always right and that others are always wrong is hubris at best or ethnocentric at worst. And since we ought to be tolerant of the moral beliefs of others, this shows that all moral beliefs are on par. No moral framework is any better than any other. So moral relativism is true.

7.5 ETHICAL RELATIVISM AND ETHICAL ABSOLUTISM

PAUL TAYLOR (1975)

Paul Taylor is professor emeritus at Brooklyn College, New York. His work focuses on normative ethics and in particular the norms that govern our relationship to the natural world. In addition to an introductory textbook in ethics (from which the following essay is taken), in 1986 Taylor published *Respect for Nature*—one of the seminal works in environmental ethics. In this essay, he distinguishes **descriptive relativism** from both **cultural relativism (normative ethical relativism)** and **ethical universalism**. Taylor argues that descriptive relativism is obviously true, but that it provides little support for cultural relativism. He closes the essay by distinguishing two different senses of **moral absolutism**.

Reading Questions:

1. Taylor claims that the term "ethical relativism" is ambiguous. What does it mean for a term to be ambiguous? What are the different senses of "ethical relativism" that he distinguishes?

2. What is the view that Taylor calls "descriptive relativism?"

3. What is the view that Taylor calls "ethical normative relativism?"

4. What are the three facts that Taylor explains to show that descriptive relativism is true?

5. What is an ultimate moral principle?

6. According to Taylor, the term "absolute" is also ambiguous. What are the two different senses of absolute that he distinguishes?

One of the most commonly held opinions in ethics is that all moral norms are relative to particular cultures. The rules of conduct that are applicable in one society, it is claimed, do not apply to the actions of people in another society. Each community has its own norms, and morality is entirely a matter of conforming to the standards and rules accepted in one's own culture. To put it simply: *What is right is what my society approves of; what is wrong is what my society disapproves of.*

This view raises serious doubts about the whole enterprise of normative ethics. For if right and wrong are completely determined by the given moral code of a particular time and place, and if moral codes vary from time to time and place to place, it would seem that there are no unchanging cross-cultural principles that could constitute an ideal ethical system applicable to everyone. Since the purpose of normative ethics is to construct and defend just such a universal system of principles, belief in the relativity of moral norms denies the possibility of normative ethics. It is therefore important at the outset to examine the theory of ethical relativism.

The question raised by the ethical relativist may be expressed thus: Are moral values absolute, or are they relative? We may understand this question as asking, Are there any moral standards and rules of conduct that are universal (applicable to all mankind) or are they all culture-bound (applicable only to the members of a particular society or group)? Even when the question is interpreted in this way, however, it still remains unclear. For *those who answer the question by claiming that all moral values are relative or culture-bound may be expressing either of two different ideas.* They may, first, be making an empirical or factual assertion. Or secondly, they may be making a normative claim. The term

"ethical relativism" has been used to refer to either of these positions. In order to keep clear the differences between them, the following terminology will be used. We shall call the first position '**descriptive relativism**' and the second '**normative ethical relativism**'. Let us consider each in turn.

Descriptive Relativism

Certain facts about the moral values of different societies and about the way an individual's values are dependent on those of his society have been taken as empirical evidence in support of the claim that all moral values are relative to the particular culture in which they are accepted. These facts are cited by the relativist as reasons for holding a general theory about moral norms, namely, that no such norms are universal. This theory is what we shall designate "descriptive relativism." *It is a factual or empirical theory because it holds that, as a matter of historical and sociological fact, no moral standard or rule of conduct has been universally recognized to be the basis of moral obligation.* According to the descriptive relativist there are no moral norms common to all cultures. Each society has its own view of what is morally right and wrong and these views vary from society to society because of the differences in their moral codes. Thus it is a mistake to think there are common norms that bind all mankind in one moral community.

Those who accept the position of descriptive relativism point to certain facts as supporting evidence for their theory. These facts may be conveniently summed up under the following headings:

    (1) The facts of cultural variability.
    (2) Facts about the origin of moral beliefs and moral codes.
    (3) The fact of ethnocentrism.

(1) The facts of cultural variability are now so familiar to everyone that they need hardly be enumerated in detail. We all know from reading anthropologists' studies of primitive cultures how extreme is the variation in the customs and taboos, the religions and moralities, the daily habits and the general outlook on life to be found in the cultures of different peoples. But we need not go beyond our own culture to recognize the facts of variability. Historians of Western civilization have long pointed out the great differences in the beliefs and values of people living in different periods. Great differences have also been discovered among the various socioeconomic classes existing within the social structure at any one time. Finally, our own contemporary world reveals a tremendous variety of ways of living. No one who dwells in a modern city can escape the impact of this spectrum of different views on work and play, on family life and education, on what constitutes personal happiness, and on what is right and wrong.

(2) When we add to these facts of cultural and historical variability the recent psychological findings about how the individual's values reflect those of his own social group and his own time, we may begin to question the universal validity of our own values. For it is now a well-established fact that *no moral values or beliefs are inborn.* All our moral attitudes and judgments are learned from the social environment. Even our deepest convictions about justice and the rights of man are originally nothing but the "introjected" or "internalized" views of our culture, transmitted to us through our parents and teachers. Our very conscience itself is formed by the internalizing of the sanctions used by our society to support its moral norms. When we were told in childhood what we ought and ought not to do, and when our parents expressed their approval and disapproval of us for what we did, we were being taught the standards and rules of conduct accepted in our society. The result of this learning process (sometimes called "acculturation") was to ingrain in us a set of attitudes about our own conduct, so that even when our parents were no longer around to guide us or to blame us, we would guide or blame ourselves by thinking, "This is what I ought to do"; "That would be wrong to do"; and so on. If we then

did something we believed was wrong we would feel guilty about it, whether or not anyone caught us at it or punished us for it.

It is this unconscious process of internalizing the norms of one's society through early childhood training that explains the origin of an individual's moral values. If we go beyond this and ask about the origin of society's values, we find a long and gradual development of traditions and customs which have given stability to the society's way of life and whose obscure beginnings lie in ritual magic, taboos, tribal ceremonies, and practices of religious worship. Whether we are dealing with the formation of an individual's conscience or the development of a society's moral code, then, the origin of a set of values seems to have little or nothing to do with rational, controlled thought. Neither individuals nor societies originally acquire their moral beliefs by means of logical reasoning or through the use of an objective method for gaining knowledge.

(3) Finally, the descriptive relativist points out another fact about people and their moralities that must be acknowledged. This is the fact that *most people are ethnocentric (group centered).* They think not only that there is but one true morality for all mankind, but that the one true morality is their own. They are convinced that the moral code under which they grew up and which formed their deepest feelings about right and wrong—namely, the moral code of their own society—is the only code for anyone to live by. Indeed, they often refuse even to entertain the possibility that their own values might be false or that another society's code might be more correct, more enlightened, or more advanced than their own. Thus ethnocentrism often leads to intolerance and dogmatism. It causes people to be extremely narrow-minded in their ethical outlook, afraid to admit any doubt about a moral issue, and unable to take a detached, objective stance regarding their own moral beliefs. Being absolutely certain that their beliefs are true, they can think only that those who disagree with them are in total error and ignorance on moral matters. Their attitude is: We are advanced, they are backward. We are civilized, they are savages. . . .

The argument for descriptive relativism, then, may be summarized as follows. Since every culture varies with respect to its moral rules and standards, and since each individual's moral beliefs—including his inner conviction of their absolute truth—have been learned within the framework of his own culture's moral code, it follows that there are no universal moral norms. If a person believes there are such norms, this is to be explained by his ethnocentrism, which leads him to project his own culture's norms upon everyone else and to consider those who disagree with him either as innocent but "morally blind" people or as sinners who do not want to face the truth about their own evil ways.

Assessing Descriptive Relativism

In order to assess the soundness of this argument it is necessary to make a distinction between (a) specific moral standards and rules, and (b) ultimate moral principles. Both (a) and (b) can be called "norms," and it is because the descriptive relativist often overlooks this distinction that his argument is open to doubt. A specific moral standard (such as personal courage or trustworthiness) functions as a criterion for judging whether and to what degree a person's character is morally good or bad. A specific rule of conduct (such as "Help others in time of need" or "Do not tell lies for one's own advantage") is a prescription of how people ought or ought not to act. It functions as a criterion for judging whether an action is right or wrong. In contrast with specific standards and rules, *an ultimate moral principle is a universal proposition or statement about the conditions that must hold if a standard or rule is to be used as a criterion for judging any person or action.* Such a principle will be of the form: Standard S or rule R applies to a person or action if and only if condition C is fulfilled. An example of an ultimate moral principle is that of utility. The principle of utility may be expressed thus: A standard or rule applies to a person or action if, and only if, the use of the standard or rule in the actual guidance of people's conduct will result in an increase in everyone's happiness or a decrease in everyone's unhappiness.

Now it is perfectly possible for an ultimate moral principle to be consistent with a variety of specific standards and rules as found in the moral codes of different societies. For if we take into account the traditions of a culture, the beliefs about reality and the attitudes toward life that are part of each culture's world-outlook, and if we also take into account the physical or geographical setting of each culture, we will find that a standard or rule which increases people's happiness in one culture will not increase, but rather decrease, people's happiness in another. In one society, for example, letting elderly people die when they can no longer contribute to economic production will be necessary for the survival of everyone else. But another society may have an abundant economy that can easily support people in their old age. Thus the principle of utility would require that in the first society the rule "Do not keep a person alive when he can no longer produce" be part of its moral code, and in the second society it would require a contrary rule. In this case the very same kind of action that is wrong in one society will be right in another. *Yet there is a principle that makes an action of that kind right (in one set of circumstances) and another action of that kind right (in a different set of circumstances).* In other words, the reason why one action is wrong and the other right is based on one and the same principle, namely utility.

Having in mind this distinction between specific standards and rules on the one hand and ultimate moral principles on the other, what can we say about the argument for descriptive relativism given above? It will immediately be seen that *the facts pointed out by the relativist as evidence in support of his theory do not show that ultimate moral principles are relative or culture-bound.* They show only that specific standards and rules are relative or culture-bound. The fact that different societies accept different norms of good and bad, right and wrong, is a fact about the standards and rules that make up the various moral codes of those societies. Such a fact does not provide evidence that there is no single ultimate principle which, explicitly or implicitly, every society appeals to as the final justifying ground for its moral code. For if there were such a common ultimate principle, the actual variation in moral codes could be explained in terms of the different world-outlooks, traditions, and physical circumstances of the different societies. . . .

Normative Ethical Relativism

The statement, "What is right in one society may be wrong in another," is a popular way of explaining what is meant by the "relativity of morals." It is usually constrasted with **"ethical universalism"** taken as the view that "right and wrong do not vary from society to society." These statements are ambiguous, however, and it is important for us to be mindful of their ambiguity. For they may be understood either as factual claims or as normative claims, and it makes a great deal of difference which way they are understood.

When it is said that what is right in one society may be wrong in another, this may be understood to mean that what is *believed* to be right in one society is *believed* to be wrong in another. And when it is said that moral right and wrong vary from society to society, this may be understood to mean that different moral norms are adopted by different societies, so that an act which fulfills the norms of one society may violate the norms of another. If this is what is meant, then we are here being told merely of the cultural variability of specific standards and rules, which we have already considered in connection with descriptive relativism.

But the statement, "What is right in one society may be wrong in another," may be interpreted in quite a different way. It may be taken as a normative claim rather than as a factual assertion. *Instead of asserting the unsurprising fact that what is believed to be right in one society is believed to be wrong in another, it expresses the far more radical and seemingly paradoxical claim that what actually is right in one society may actually be wrong in another.* According to this view, moral norms are to be considered valid only within the society which has adopted them as part of its way of life. Such norms are not to be considered valid outside that society. The conclusion is then drawn that is is not legitimate to judge people in other societies by applying the norms of one's own society to their conduct. This is the view we shall designate "normative ethical relativism." In order to be perfectly clear about what it claims, we shall examine two ways in which it can be stated, one focusing our attention upon moral judgments, the other on moral norms.

With regard to moral judgments, normative ethical relativism holds that two *apparently* contradictory statements can both be true. The argument runs as follows. Consider the two statements:

(1) It is wrong for unmarried women to have their faces unveiled in front of strangers.
(2) It is not wrong for . . . (as above).

Here it seems as if there is a flat contradiction between two moral judgments, so that if one is true the other must be false. But the normative ethical relativist holds that they are both true, because the statements as given in (1) and (2) are incomplete. They should read as follows:

(3) It is wrong for unmarried women *who are members of society S* to have their faces unveiled in front of strangers.
(4) It is not wrong for unmarried women *outside of society S* to have their faces unveiled in front of strangers.

Statements (3) and (4) are not contradictories. To assert one is not to deny the other. The normative ethical relativist simply translates all moral judgments of the form "Doing act X is right" into statements of the form Doing X is right when the agent is a member of society S." The latter statement can then be seen to be consistent with statements of the form "Doing X is wrong when the agent is not a member of society S."

The normative ethical relativist's view of moral norms accounts for the foregoing theory of moral judgments. A moral norm, we have seen, is either a standard used in a judgment of good and bad character or a rule used in a judgment of right and wrong conduct. Thus a person is judged to be good insofar as he fulfills the standard, and an action is judged to be right or wrong according to whether it conforms to or violates the rule. Now when a normative ethical relativist says that moral norms vary from society to society, he does not intend merely to assert the fact that different societies have adopted different norms. He is going beyong descriptive relativism and is making a normative claim. He is denying any universal validity to moral norms. He is saying that *a moral standard or rule is correctly applicable only to the members of the particular society which has adopted the standard or rule as part of its actual moral code.* He therefore thinks it is illegitimate to judge the character or conduct of those outside the society by such a standard or rule. Anyone who uses the norms of one society as the basis for judging the character or conduct of persons in another society is consequently in error.

It is not that a normative ethical relativist necessarily believes in *tolerance* of other people's norms. Nor does his position imply that he grants others the *right* to live by their own norms, for he would hold a relativist view even about tolerance itself. A society whose code included a rule of tolerance would be right in tolerating others, while one that denied tolerance would be right (relative to its own norm of intolerance) in prohibiting others from living by different norms. The normative ethical relativist would simply say that *we* should not judge the tolerant society to be any better than the intolerant one, for this would be applying our own norm of tolerance to other societies. Tolerance, like any other norm, is culture-bound. *Anyone who claims that every society has a right to live by its own norms, provided that it respects a similar right in other societies, is an ethical universalist, since he holds at least one norm valid for all societies,* namely, the right to practice a way of life without interference from others. And he deems this universal norm a valid one, whether or not every society does in fact accept it.

Assessing Normative Relativism

If the normative ethical relativist is challenged to prove his position, he may do either of two things. On the one hand, he may try to argue that his position follows from, or is based on, the very same facts that are cited by the descriptive relativist as evidence for *his* position. . . .

The most frequent argument given in defense of normative ethical relativism is that, if the facts pointed out by the descriptive relativist are indeed true, then we must accept normative ethical relativism as the only position consistent with those facts. For it seems that if each person's moral judgments are formed within the framework of the norms of his own culture

and historical epoch, and if such norms vary among cultures and epochs, it would follow necessarily that it is unwarranted for anyone to apply his own norms to conduct in other societies and times. To do so would be ethnocentrism, which is, as the descriptive relativist shows, a kind of blind, narrow-minded, dogmatism. To escape the irrationality of being ethnocentric, we need but realize that the only norms one may legitimately apply to any given group are the ones accepted by that group. Since different peoples accept different norms, there are no universal norms applicable to everyone throughout the world. Now, to say that there are no universal norms applicable worldwide is to commit oneself to normative ethical relativism. Thus, the argument concludes, normative ethical relativism follows from the facts of descriptive relativism.

Is this a valid argument? Suppose one accepts the facts pointed out by the descriptive relativist. Must he then also accept normative ethical relativism? Let us examine some of the objections that have been raised to this argument. In the first place, it is claimed that the facts of cultural variability do not, *by themselves,* entail normative ethical relativism. The reason is that it is perfectly possible for someone to accept those facts and deny normative ethical relativism without contradicting himself. No matter how great may be the differences in the moral beliefs of different cultures and in the moral norms they accept, it is still possible to hold that some of these beliefs are true and others false, or that some of the norms are more correct, justified, or enlightened than others. The fact that societies differ about what is right and wrong does not mean that one society may not have better reasons for holding its views than does another. After all, *just because two people (or two groups of people) disagree about whether a disease is caused by bacteria or by evil spirits does not lead to the confusion that there is no correct or enlightened view about the cause of the disease.* So it does not follow from the fact that two societies differ about whether genocide is right that there is no correct or enlightened view about this moral matter.

A similar argument can be used with regard to the second set of facts asserted by the descriptive relativist. No contradiction is involved, in affirming that all moral beliefs come from the social environment and denying normative ethical relativism. *The fact that a belief is learned from one's society does not mean that it is neither true nor false, or that if it is true, its truth is "relative" to the society in which it was learned.* All of our beliefs, empirical ones no less than moral ones, are learned from our society. We are not born with any innate beliefs about chemistry or physics; we learn these only in our schools. Yet this does not make us skeptical about the universal validity of these sciences. So the fact that our moral beliefs come from our society and are learned in our homes and schools has no bearing on their universal validity. The origin or cause of a person's *acquiring* a belief does not determine whether the *content* of the belief is true or false, or even whether there are good grounds for his accepting that content to be true or false. . .

The same kind of argument also holds with respect to the third fact of descriptive relativism: ethnocentrism. People who are ethnocentric *believe* that the one true moral code is that of their own society. But this leaves open the question, Is their belief true or false? Two people of different cultures, both ethnocentric but with opposite moral beliefs, may each think his particular moral norms are valid for everyone; however, this has no bearing on whether either one—or neither one—is correct. We must inquire independently into the possibility of establishing the universal validity of a set of moral norms, regardless of who might or might not believe them to be universally true.

It should be noted that these various objections to the first argument for normative ethical relativism, even if sound, are not sufficient to show that normative ethical relativism is false. They only provide reasons for rejecting one argument in support of that position. To show that the position is false, it would be necessary to give a sound argument in defense of ethical universalism. It is only if one or more of these arguments proves acceptable that normative ethical relativism is refuted.

Ethical Absolutism

When someone asks, "Are moral norms relative or absolute?" there is often an ambiguity in his question, not only with respect to the word 'relative' but also with respect to the word 'absolute.' We have seen that 'relative' can mean, among other things, 'causally dependent on variable factors in different cultures' (descriptive relativism); *or* 'validly applicable only within the culture which accepts the norm' (normative ethical relativism). Let us now examine an important ambiguity in the term 'absolute' as it is applied to moral norms. For unless this ambiguity is cleared up, we cannot give a straightforward answer to the question of whether moral norms are relative or absolute.

That moral norms (that is, specific moral rules and standards) are 'absolute' can mean either of two things. It can mean that at least some moral norms are justifiable on grounds that can be established by a cross-cultural method of reasoning and that, consequently, these norms correctly apply to the conduct of all human beings. This, we have seen, is **ethical universalism**. It entails the denial of normative ethical relativism. Hence, in this first sense of the term "absolute," ethical absolutism may simply be equated with ethical universalism.

The second meaning of the term 'absolute' is entirely different from the first. According to the second meaning, to say that moral norms are 'absolute' is to say that they *have no exceptions.* Thus, if the rule "It is wrong to break a promise" is an absolute moral norm in this second sense, then one must never break a promise no matter what the circumstances. It follows that it is our duty to keep a promise, even if doing so brings suffering to innocent people. It means, for example, that a hired gunman who promises his boss to murder someone should commit the murder. It signifies that, if we have promised a friend to go to a movie with him on Saturday night, we must do so even if our parents are injured in an automobile accident Saturday afternoon and desperately need our help. Extreme cases like these show that, at least in our ordinary unreflective moral judgments, the rule "Do not break promises" has exceptions and that, consequently, ethical absolutism in the second sense of the term is not true of that particular moral rule.

Are there *any* rules of conduct that are absolute in the second sense? The reader should try to work out his own answer to this question for himself. What is important for present purposes is to notice the *logical independence* of the two meanings of "ethical absolutism."

According to the first meaning, an ethical absolutist holds that there are moral norms that apply to everyone, no matter what norms are actually accepted in a given society. According to the second meaning, an ethical absolutist is one who claims that at least some moral norms allow for no legitimate or justifiable exceptions. It is clear that the first meaning of ethical absolutism does not necessarily entail the second. In other words, it is possible to be an ethical absolutist in the first sense but not in the second. For it may be that all moral norms valid for everyone in any society are norms that allow for legitimate exceptions in special circumstances, *whenever* those circumstances occur. Let us consider an example.

Suppose we think that in almost all situations of life it is wrong for one person to take the life of another. Suppose, further, that we hold the rule "Thou shalt not kill" to be a universal moral norm, believing that it applies to all persons in all societies (even if a certain group of people in a given society do not accept the rule). Thus, with respect to this rule we are ethical universalists. Now suppose that we also think that there are very unusual conditions which, when they occur, make it permissible for one person to kill another. For instance, we might think that if a person's only means of defending his life or the lives of his children against the attack of a madman is to kill him, then it is not wrong to kill him. Or we might think that killing is permissible when such an act is necessary to overthrow a totalitarian government carrying out a policy of systematic genocide. If we hold these cases to be legitimate exceptions to the rule "Thou shalt not kill," are we contradicting our position of ethical universalism with regard to that rule? The answer is no, since we may be willing to consider these exceptions universally legitimate whenever they occur, no matter whether a given society accepts them as legitimate exceptions or not. In this case the *full* statement of our rule against killing would be expressed thus: It is wrong for anyone, in any society, to take the life of another, except when such an act is necessary

for self-defense or the prevention of systematic genocide.

When a moral rule is stated in this manner, it encompasses its own exceptions. In other words, the complete rule stipulates all the kinds of situations in which an action of the sort *generally* forbidden by the rule is right. If we then accept the rule in its complete form, *including the list of exceptions,* as validly applicable to all human beings, we are ethical universalists (and hence ethical absolutists in the first sense of the term) with respect to this rule. However, we are not ethical absolutists in the second sense of the term, since we hold that the simple rule "Thou shalt not kill" does have legitimate exceptions.

It is true that in this case we may not be willing to allow for exceptions to the whole rule in its *complete* form, since we may think our statement of the rule includes all the possible exceptions it could have. With regard to the rule in its complete form, we would then be ethical absolutists in both senses of the term. On the other hand, if we are not sure we have included all the exceptions that could possibly be legitimate, then with regard to such an incomplete rule we would not be ethical absolutists in the second sense. The rule as we have formulated it may still have legitimate exceptions which we have overlooked, but we can nevertheless be ethical universalists about such an incomplete rule. For we might believe that, even in its *incomplete* form, it correctly applies to all mankind.

The main point of this discussion may now be indicated. When an ethical universalist says that there are moral norms applicable to everyone everywhere, he does not mean that the application of these norms to particular circumstances must determine that one kind of action is always right (or that it is always wrong). He means only that, whenever the norms do apply, they apply regardless of whether a given society may have accepted them in its actual moral code and another society may have excluded them from *its* moral code. The (normative) ethical relativist, on the other hand, claims that what makes an act right is precisely its conformity to the accepted norms of the society in which it occurs, while its violation of such accepted norms makes it wrong. Consider, then, two acts of the very same kind done in the very same sort of circumstances, but each occurring in a different society. One can be right and the other wrong, according to the relativist, since the moral norms of the two societies may disagree concerning the behavior in question. The ethical universalist (or "absolutist" in the first sense), however, would say that if one act is right the other is too and if one is wrong so is the other. For both are acts of an identical kind performed in identical circumstances. Therefore a rule which required or prohibited the one would also require or prohibit the other, and only one rule validly applies to such actions performed in circumstances of that sort. Thus the universalist holds that the rightness and wrongness of actions do not change according to variations in the norms accepted by different societies, even though (contrary to what the "absolutist" in the second sense says) the rightness and wrongness of actions do vary with differences in the sorts of circumstances in which they are performed.

If we keep this distinction between the two meanings of ethical absolutism clearly in mind, we can then see that it is possible to be an absolutist in one sense and not in the other. Whether either sense of absolutism is a correct view is a matter that cannot be settled without further study of normative and analytic ethics. Perhaps the reader will be able to decide these questions for himself as he pursues his own ethical inquiry.

DISCUSSION QUESTIONS:

1. Do you think that descriptive relativism is true? Why do you think so? Can one think that descriptive relativism is true while maintaining, for example, that it was wrong for people in Nazi Germany to torture Jews?

2. Do you think that normative ethical relativism is true? Do you have an argument for this conclusion? If so, what is it?

3. What does it mean for a culture to "approve" of an action or "disapprove" of an action? What if people in your culture dislike wiping one's mouth on one's sleeve; does that mean that it's *morally* wrong to do so? Perhaps a culture disapproves of something only if it makes it illegal. If so, then given the truth of ethical normative relativism, only that which is illegal is immoral. Is that right?

4. Suppose normative ethical relativism is true. What happens when a person from one culture visits another culture? Which moral rules properly govern his behavior? What if many people from many cultures meet in international space: which moral rules properly govern their behavior?

5. One sense of "absolute" means something like unbreakable or without exception. On this understanding, if a moral rule is absolute, then it is never permissibly broken. Do you think that there are such rules? If so, list some of them. If not, why not?

Argument Reconstruction Exercises:

I. Taylor provides an argument for a version of relativism that he calls descriptive relativism. Identify the premises and conclusion in this excerpt:

> The argument for descriptive relativism, then, may be summarized as follows. Since every culture varies with respect to its moral rules and standards, and since each individual's moral beliefs—including his inner conviction of their absolute truth—have been learned within the framework of his own culture's moral code, it follows that there are no universal moral norms. (pages 91–92)

II. One of the most common ways to argue for cultural relativism is to show that it follows from facts about moral diversity (i.e., descriptive relativism). Harman argued in such a way in the previous reading. Here Taylor reconstructs this line of reasoning. Identify the premises and conclusion in this excerpt:

> According to the descriptive relativist there are no moral norms common to all cultures. Each society has its own view of what is morally right and wrong and these views vary from society to society because of the differences in their moral codes. Thus it is a mistake to think there are common norms that bind all mankind in one moral community. (page 90)

III. Here Taylor reconstructs the argument from descriptive relativism to normative ethical relativism. Identify the premises and conclusion in this excerpt:

> Since different peoples accept different norms, there are no universal norms applicable to everyone throughout the world. Now, to say that there are no universal norms applicable worldwide is to

commit oneself to normative ethical relativism. Thus, the argument concludes, normative ethical relativism follows from the facts of descriptive relativism. (page 94)

IV. Taylor thinks that the argument from descriptive relativism to normative ethical relativism is invalid. Here he argues that since the origins of scientific beliefs are similar to the origins of moral beliefs, we should treat the two similarly. Identify the premises and conclusion in this excerpt:

All of our beliefs, empirical ones no less than moral ones, are learned from our society. We are not born with any innate beliefs about chemistry or physics; we learn these only in our schools. Yet this does not make us skeptical about the universal validity of these sciences. So the fact that our moral beliefs come from our society and are learned in our homes and schools has no bearing on universal validity. (page 95)

CHAPTER 8

Moral Responsibility

Morality is concerned with what men ought and ought not to do. But if a man has no freedom to choose what he will do, if whatever he does is done under compulsion, then it does not make sense to tell him that he ought not to have done what he did and that he ought to do something different. All moral precepts would in such case be meaningless. Also, if he acts always under compulsion, how can he be morally responsible for his actions? How can he, for example, be punished for what he could not help doing?
—W. T. STACE, *RELIGION AND THE MODERN MIND*

INTRODUCTION

In our commonsense, everyday moral judgments, we take ourselves to be morally responsible for much of what we do. We praise good deeds and blame bad ones. Many of us also think we have some objective moral obligations: it is wrong for us not to do some actions, not because we or others strongly approve of them, but just because of what those acts involve. What must we be like for these assumptions regarding the existence of moral responsibility and objective morality to be true?

At a minimum, it seems that we must have some control over what we do and the sort of people we are. A lack of control seems to give us a perfect excuse that relieves us of all moral responsibility. It is not Anne's fault that she is selfish if she can't help being that sort of person. It is not to Joan's credit that she is kind if she can't help being kind any more than Anne can help being selfish. It is not my fault that I didn't keep my promise if I have no control over my behavior. In taking one another to be morally responsible, we assume that we have an appropriate amount of control over what we do and the sort of people we are. In similar fashion, the existence of objective moral obligations also seems to require the existence of self-control. We can only have an objective moral obligation to do what we are capable of doing in the first place. If we can't do something else, we have no objective moral obligation to do something else. Yet, if we never have an objective moral obligation to do something else, we never do anything that is objectively wrong. Morality as a set of subjective judgments reflecting our or our society's attitudes may still survive, but morality as a set of objective duties that we can sometimes honor and sometimes violate seems to have disappeared.

None of this is especially worrisome, until we realize that there are some good reasons to doubt that we have the required control over our actions and character. One of those reasons is based on an assumption that is at least as compelling as the assumption that we are morally responsible and subject to objective moral duties: Whatever happens is caused to happen. If our car won't start, there's a cause for that. If it does start, there's a cause for that, too. The same is true of every other event. If I break a promise, something caused me to act that way. If Anne grows up to be selfish, something caused her to become that sort of person. Yet, since we have no control over the past events or the laws of causation by which the past determines the present, we have no control over our present choices, our actions or the kinds of persons they lead us to become. Some philosophers reason about control in this way and conclude that a view known as **Incompatibilism** is true. According to incompatibilism, no action can be both free and determined.

Incompatiblism is plausible. However, it's also plausible that every event, including each of our choices and actions, is caused by a prior event, and—combined with incompatibilism—this fact implies that we never act freely and so are never morally responsible for our behavior. This is the view known as **Hard Determinism**. From the Hard Determinist perspective, it may make sense to develop a moral code for our society, since the issuing of moral rules and sanctions may help cause people to act in ways we prefer, but our doing so is not substantially different from our developing and enforcing a code of conduct for a pet dog in order to causally influence its behavior. People are not objectively responsible for their behavior or obligated to follow the code any more than the dog is. In this chapter, Galen Strawson offers a compelling argument against moral responsibility. He takes his argument to be one that Hard Determinists can adopt, even without relying on their claim that every event has a cause. The argument simply focuses on how the way we are at any particular time is determined by how we were previously.

Despite the plausibility of Hard Determinism, most philosophers deny it, and both of the main competing views allow for moral responsibility and objective moral obligations. **Soft Determinism** is the view that while human actions are determined, such determinism doesn't rule out the sort of control necessary for moral responsibility. For this reason, Soft Determinists endorse a view known as **Compatibilism**—the view that even if every event is indeed caused by another event, we can still sometimes act freely. Even if we live in a deterministic universe in which the causal determination by past events extends all the way to our choices and actions, we can have enough control over our behavior to allow for moral responsibility and objective moral obligations. Compatibilists offer us two important insights into the nature of moral responsibility. First, our choices must be caused by prior events in order for us to be morally responsible for them; otherwise they are mere accidents for which no one is responsible. Second, the kind of freedom that is required for moral responsibility and objective moral obligations is compatible with causal determinism. We can have this freedom even though all of our choices and actions are caused by past events. A. J. Ayer's essay presents a version of Soft Determinism. Ayer offers a detailed defense of the claim that moral responsibility requires causal determinism and the claim that such causal determinism does not rule out our being free in a way required for moral responsibility.

Libertarianism is the third alternative to both Hard Determinism and Soft Determinism. According to Libertarians, at least some of our choices are exceptions to the general causal determination of the present by the past. We are able to make choices that are not caused by past events. Our control over these choices allows for the possibility of moral responsibility and objective moral obligations. Roderick Chisholm presents a classic statement of the Libertarian perspective, arguing that, because some of our choices are caused by us, rather than past events, we can be morally responsible for our conduct.

The issues raised in these essays are part of a long-running and sophisticated debate in metaphysics over the basic nature of a human being, and these essays come nowhere close to covering all the dimensions of that debate. They do, though, illustrate an important way in which our moral philosophy, in this case our position on the possibility of moral responsibility and objective moral obligations, depends on our more general conception of the human condition.

SUGGESTIONS FOR FURTHER READING

Dennett, Daniel. *Elbow Room: The Varieties of Free Will Worth Having.* (Cambridge, MA: MIT Press, 1984)

Fischer, John Martin. *The Metaphysics of Free Will.* (Oxford: Blackwell, 1994)

Frankfurt, Harry. "Alternative Possibilities and Moral Responsibility," *Journal of Philosophy,* 66 (1969) pp. 829–839.

———. "Freedom of the Will and the Concept of a Person," *Journal of Philosophy,* 68 (1971), pp. 5–20.

Kane, Robert. *The Significance of Free Will.* (New York: Oxford University Press, 1996)

———. *Oxford Handbook on Free Will.* (New York: Oxford University Press, 2002)

Nagel, Thomas. *Mortal Questions.* (Cambridge: Cambridge University Press, 1979), Chapter Three.

O'Connor, Timothy. *Agents, Causes, and Events: Essays on Indeterminism and Free Will.* (New York: Oxford University Press, 1995)

———. *Persons and Causes: The Metaphysics of Free Will.* (Oxford: Oxford University Press, 2000)

Schoeman, Ferdinand. *Responsibility, Character and the Emotions: New Essays in Moral Psychology.* (Cambridge: Cambridge University Press, 1988)

Van Inwagen, Peter. *An Essay on Free Will.* (Oxford: Oxford University Press, 1983)

Watson, Gary. *Free Will.* (New York: Oxford University Press, 2003)

8.1 THE IMPOSSIBILITY OF MORAL RESPONSIBILITY

GALEN STRAWSON (1994)

Galen Strawson is a professor of philosophy at the University of Reading. In this essay, he presents what he terms "the Basic Argument" for the conclusion that we are not morally responsible for our actions. He describes the kind of moral responsibility he has in mind as the kind that is required to make sense of our common practices of reward and punishment as being sometimes just, and he claims that we regularly believe, incorrectly, that we are responsible for many of our actions in this way. After he presents the Basic Argument, Strawson considers and rejects three objections to it.

Reading Questions:

1. How does Strawson explain our common concept of moral responsibility?

2. Strawson's Basic Argument contains the premise that we are not responsible for how we are. What is his argument in defense of this premise?

3. What reason does each of the following give for rejecting Strawson's Basic Argument: The Compatibilist Reply, the Libertarian Reply, the Independent Self Reply?

4. What reason does Strawson give for rejecting each of these replies?

There is an argument, which I will call the Basic Argument, which appears to prove that we cannot be truly or ultimately morally responsible for our actions. According to the Basic Argument, it makes no difference whether determinism is true or false. We cannot be truly or ultimately morally responsible for our actions in either case.

The Basic Argument has various expressions in the literature of free will, and its central idea can be quickly conveyed. (1) Nothing can be causa sui—nothing can be the cause of itself. (2) In order to be truly morally responsible for one's actions one would have to be causa sui, at least in certain crucial mental respects. (3) Therefore nothing can be truly morally responsible.

In this paper I want to reconsider the Basic Argument, in the hope that anyone who thinks that we can be truly or ultimately morally responsible for our actions will be prepared to say exactly what is wrong with it. I think that the point that it has to make is obvious, and that it has been underrated in recent discussion of free will—perhaps because it admits of no answer. I suspect that it is obvious in such a way that insisting on it too much is likely to make it seem less obvious than it is, given the innate contrasuggestibility of human beings in general and philosophers in particular. But I am not worried about making it seem less obvious than it is so long as it gets adequate attention. As far as its validity is concerned, it can look after itself.

A more cumbersome statement of the Basic Argument goes as follows.[1]

(1) Interested in free action, we are particularly interested in actions that are performed for a reason (as opposed to 'reflex' actions or mindlessly habitual actions).

(2) When one acts for a reason, what one does is a function of how one is, mentally speaking. (It is also a function of one's height, one's strength, one's place and time, and so on. But the mental factors are crucial when moral responsibility is in question.)

(3) So if one is to be truly responsible for how one acts, one must be truly responsible for how one is, mentally speaking—at least in certain respects.

(4) But to be truly responsible for how one is, mentally speaking, in certain respects, one must have brought it about that one is the way one is, mentally speaking, in certain respects. And it is not merely that one must have caused oneself to be the way one is, mentally speaking. One must have consciously and explicitly chosen to be the way one is, mentally speaking, and one must have succeeded in bringing it about that one is that way.

(5) But one cannot really be said to choose, in a conscious, reasoned, fashion, to be the way one is mentally speaking, in any respect at all, unless one already exists, mentally speaking, already equipped with some principles of choice, 'P1'—preferences, values, pro-attitudes, ideals—in the light of which one chooses how to be.

(6) But then to be truly responsible, on account of having chosen to be the way one is, mentally speaking, in certain respects, one must be truly responsible for one's having the principles of choice PI in the light of which one chose how to be.

(7) But for this to be so one must have chosen P1, in a reasoned, conscious, intentional fashion.

(8) But for this, i.e. (7), to be so one must already have had some principles of choice P2, in the light of which one chose P1.

(9) And so on. Here we are setting out on a regress that we cannot stop. True self-determination is impossible because it requires the actual completion of an infinite series of choices of principles of choice.[2]

(10) So true moral responsibility is impossible, because it requires true self-determination, as noted in (3).

This may seem contrived, but essentially the same argument can be given in a more natural form. (1) It is undeniable that one is the way one is, initially, as a result of heredity and early experience, and it is undeniable that these are things for which one cannot be held to be in any responsible (morally or otherwise). (2) One cannot at any later stage of life hope to accede to true moral responsibility for the way one is by trying to change the way one already is as a result of heredity and previous experience. For (3) both the particular way in which one is moved to try to change oneself, and the degree of one's success in one's attempt at change, will be determined by how one already is as a result of heredity and previous experience. And (4) any further changes that one can bring about only after one has brought about certain initial changes will in turn be determined, via the initial changes, by heredity and previous experience. (5) This may not be the whole story, for it may be that some changes in the way one is are traceable not to heredity and experience but to the influence of indeterministic or random factors. But it is absurd to suppose that indeterministic or random factors, for which one is ex hypothesi in no way responsible, can in themselves contribute in any way to one's being truly morally responsible for how one is.

The claim, then, is not that people cannot change the way they are. They can, in certain respects (which tend to be exaggerated by North Americans and underestimated, perhaps, by Europeans). The claim is only that people cannot be supposed to change themselves in such a way as to be or become truly or ultimately morally responsible for the way they are, and hence for their actions.

The Importance of the Basic Argument

If one wants to think about free will and moral responsibility, consideration of some version of the Basic Argument is an overwhelmingly natural place to start. It certainly has to be considered at some point in a full discussion of free will and moral responsibility, even if the point it has to make is obvious. Belief in the kind of absolute moral responsibility that it shows to be impossible has for a long time been central to the Western religious, moral, and cultural tradition, even if it is now slightly on the wane (a disputable view).

In saying that the notion of moral responsibility criticized by the Basic Argument is central to the Western tradition, I am not suggesting that it is some artificial and local Judaeo-Christian-Kantian construct that is found nowhere else in the history of the peoples of the world, although even if it were that would hardly diminish its interest and importance for us. It is natural to suppose that Aristotle also subscribed to it[3], and it is significant that anthropologists have suggested that most human societies can be classified either as 'guilt cultures' or as 'shame cultures'. It is true that neither of these two fundamental moral emotions necessarily presupposes a conception of oneself as truly morally responsible for what one has done. But the fact that both are widespread does at least suggest that a conception of moral responsibility similar to our own is a natural part of the human moral-conceptual repertoire.

In fact the notion of moral responsibility connects more tightly with the notion of guilt than with the notion of shame. In many cultures shame can attach to one because of what some member of one's family—or government—has done, and not because of anything one has done oneself; and in such cases the feeling of shame need not (although it may) involve some obscure, irrational feeling that one is somehow responsible for the behaviour of one's family or government. The case of guilt is less clear. There is no doubt that people can feel guilty (or can believe that they feel guilty) about things for which they are not responsible, let alone morally responsible. But it is much less obvious that they can do this without any sense or belief that they are in fact responsible.

True Moral Responsibility

Such complications are typical of moral psychology, and they show that it is important to try to be precise about what sort of responsibility is under discussion. What sort of 'true' moral responsibility is being said to be both impossible and widely believed in?

An old story is very helpful in clarifying this question. This is the story of heaven and hell. *As I understand it, true moral responsibility is responsibility of such a kind that if we have it, then it makes sense, at least, to suppose that it could be just to punish some of us with (eternal) torment in hell and reward others with (eternal) bliss in heaven.* The stress on the words 'makes sense' is important, for one certainly does not have to believe in any version of the story of heaven and hell in order to understand the notion of true moral responsibility that it is being used to illustrate. Nor does one have to believe in any version of the story of heaven and hell in order to believe in the existence of true moral responsibility. On the contrary: many atheists have believed in the existence of true moral responsibility. The story of heaven and hell is useful simply because it illustrates, in a peculiarly vivid way, the kind of absolute or ultimate accountability or responsibility that many have supposed themselves to have, and that many do still suppose themselves to have. It very clearly expresses its scope and force.

But one does not have to refer to religious faith in order to describe the sorts of everyday situation that are perhaps primarily influential in giving rise to our belief in true responsibility. Suppose you set off for a shop on the evening of a national holiday, intending to buy a cake with your last ten pound note. On the steps of the shop someone is shaking an Oxfam tin. You stop, and it seems completely clear to you that it is entirely up to you what you do next. That is, it seems to you that you are truly, radically free to choose, in such a way that you will be ultimately morally responsible for whatever you do choose. Even if you believe that determinism is true, and that you will in five minutes time be able to look back and say that what you did was determined, this does not seem to undermine your sense of the absoluteness and inescapability of your freedom, and of your moral responsibility for your choice. The same seems to be true even if you accept the validity of the Basic Argument stated in section I, which concludes that one cannot be in any way ultimately responsible for the way one is and decides. In both cases, it remains true that as one stands there, one's freedom and true moral responsibility seem obvious and absolute to one.

Large and small, morally significant or morally neutral, such situations of choice occur regularly in human life. I think they lie at the heart of the experience of freedom and moral responsibility. They are the fundamental source of our inability to give up belief in true or ultimate moral responsibility. There are further questions to be asked about why human beings experience these situations of choice as they do. It is an interesting question whether any cognitively sophisticated, rational, self-conscious agent must experience situations of choice in this way.[4] But they are the experiential rock on which the belief in true moral responsibility is founded.

Our Common Belief in Responsibility

I will restate the Basic Argument. First, though, I will give some examples of people who have accepted that some sort of true or ultimate responsibility for the way one is is a necessary condition of true or ultimate moral responsibility for the way one acts, and who, certain that they are truly morally responsible for the way they act, have believed the condition to be fulfilled.[5]

E.H. Carr held that "normal adult human beings are morally responsible for their own personality". Jean-Paul Sartre talked of "the choice that each man makes of his personality", and held that "man

is responsible for what he is". In a later interview he judged that his earlier assertions about freedom were incautious; but he still held that "in the end one is always responsible for what is made of one" in some absolute sense. Kant described the position very clearly when he claimed that "man *himself* must make or have made himself into whatever, in a moral sense, whether good or evil, he is to become. Either condition must be an effect of his free choice; for otherwise he could not be held responsible for it and could therefore be *morally* neither good nor evil." Since he was committed to belief in radical moral responsibility, Kant held that such self-creation does indeed take place, and wrote accordingly of "man's character, which he himself creates", and of "knowledge of oneself as a person who . . . is his own originator". John Patten, the current British Minister for Education, a Catholic apparently preoccupied by the idea of sin, has claimed that "it is . . . self-evident that as we grow up each individual chooses whether to be good or bad." It seems clear enough that he sees such choice as sufficient to give us true moral responsibility of the heaven-and-hell variety.[6]

The rest of us are not usually so reflective, but it seems that we do tend, in some vague and unexamined fashion, to think of ourselves as responsible for—answerable for—how we are. The point is quite a delicate one, for we do not ordinarily suppose that we have gone through some sort of active process of self-determination at some particular past time. Nevertheless it seems accurate to say that we do unreflectively experience ourselves, in many respects, rather as we might experience ourselves if we did believe that we had engaged in some such activity of self-determination.

Sometimes a part of one's character—a desire or tendency—may strike one as foreign or alien. But it can do this only against a background of character traits that are not experienced as foreign, but are rather 'identified' with (it is a necessary truth that it is only relative to such a background that a character trait can stand out as alien). Some feel tormented by impulses that they experience as alien, but in many a sense of general identification with their character predominates, and this identification seems to carry within itself an implicit sense that one is, generally, somehow in control of and answerable for how one is (even, perhaps, for aspects of one's character that one does not like). Here, then, I suggest that we find, semi-dormant in common thought, an implicit recognition of the idea that true moral responsibility for what one does somehow involves responsibility for how one is. Ordinary thought is ready to move this way under pressure.

There is, however, another powerful tendency in ordinary thought to think that one can be truly morally responsible even if one's character is ultimately wholly non-self-determined—simply because one is fully self-consciously aware of oneself as an agent facing choices. I will return to this point later on.

The Basic Argument Restated

Let me now restate the Basic Argument in very loose—as it were conversational—terms. New forms of words allow for new forms of objection, but they may be helpful none the less.

(1) You do what you do, in any situation in which you find yourself, because of the way you are.

So

(2) To be truly morally responsible for what you do you must be truly responsible for the way you are—at least in certain crucial mental respects.

Or:

(1) What you intentionally do, given the circumstances in which you (believe you) find yourself, flows necessarily from how you are.

Hence

(2) you have to get to have some responsibility for how you are in order to get to have some responsibility for what you intentionally do, given the circumstances in which you (believe you) find yourself.

Comment. Once again the qualification about 'certain mental respects' is one I will take for granted. Obviously one is not responsible for one's sex, one's basic body pattern, one's height, and so on. But if one

were not responsible for anything about oneself, how could be one responsible for what one did, given the truth of (1)? This is the fundamental question, and it seems clear that if one is going to be responsible for any aspect of oneself, it had better be some aspect of one's mental nature.

I take it that (1) is incontrovertible, and that it is (2) that must be resisted. For if (1) and (2) are conceded the case seems lost, because the full argument runs as follows.

(1) You do what you do because of the way you are.

So

(2) To be truly morally responsible for what you do you must be truly responsible for the way are—at least in certain crucial mental respects.

But

(3) You cannot be truly responsible for the way you are, so you cannot be truly responsible for what you do.

Why can't you be truly responsible for the way you are? Because

(4) To be truly responsible for the way you are, you must have intentionally brought it about that you are the way you are, and this is impossible.

Why is it impossible? Well, suppose it is not. Suppose that

(5) You have somehow intentionally brought it about that you are the way you now are, and that you have brought this about in such a way that you can now be said to be truly responsible for being the way you are now.

For this to be true

(6) You must already have had a certain nature N in the light of which you intentionally brought it about that you are as you now are.

But then

(7) For it to be true you and you alone are truly responsible for how you now are, you must

be truly responsible for having had the nature N in the light of which you intentionally brought it about that you are the way you now are.

So

(8) You must have intentionally brought it about that you had that nature N, in which case you must have existed already with a prior nature in the light of which you intentionally brought it about that you had the nature N in the light of which you intentionally brought it about that you are the way you now are . . .

Here one is setting off on the regress. Nothing can be *causa sui* in the required way. Even if such causal 'aseity' is allowed to belong unintelligibly to God, it cannot be plausibly be supposed to be possessed by ordinary finite human beings. "The *causa sui* is the best self-contradiction that has been conceived so far", as Nietzsche remarked in 1886:

> it is a sort of rape and perversion of logic. But the extravagant pride of man has managed to entangle itself profoundly and frightfully with just this nonsense. The desire for "freedom of the will" in the superlative metaphysical sense, which still holds sway, unfortunately, in the minds of the half-educated; the desire to bear the entire and ultimate responsibility for one's actions oneself, and to absolve God, the world, ancestors, chance, and society involves nothing less than to be precisely this causa sui and, with more than Baron Münchhausen's audacity, to pull oneself up into existence by the hair, out of the swamps of nothingness . . . (*Beyond Good and Evil*, § 21).

The rephrased argument is essentially exactly the same as before, although the first two steps are now more simply stated. . . .

We are what we are, and we cannot be thought to have made ourselves *in such a way* that we can be held to be free in our actions *in such a way* that we can be held to be morally responsible for our actions *in such a way* that any punishment or reward for our actions is ultimately just or fair. Punishments and rewards may seem deeply appropriate or intrinsically 'fitting' to us in spite of this argument, and

many of the various institutions of punishment and reward in human society appear to be practically indispensable in both their legal and non-legal forms. *But if one takes the notion of justice that is central to our intellectual and cultural tradition seriously, then the evident consequence of the Basic Argument is that there is a fundamental sense in which no punishment or reward is ever ultimately just.* It is exactly as just to punish or reward people for their actions as it is to punish or reward them for the (natural) colour of their hair or the (natural) shape of their faces. The point seems obvious, and yet it contradicts a fundamental part of our natural self-conception, and there are elements in human thought that move very deeply against it. When it comes to questions or responsibility, we tend to feel that we are somehow responsible for the way we are. Even more importantly, perhaps, we tend to feel that our explicit self-conscious awareness of ourselves as agents who are able to deliberate about what to do, in situations of choice, suffices to constitute us as morally responsible free agents, in the strongest sense, whatever the conclusion of the Basic Argument.

Three Replies

I have suggested that it is step (2) of the restated Basic Argument that must be rejected, and of course it can be rejected, because the phrases 'truly responsible' and 'truly morally responsible' can be defined in many ways. I will briefly consider three sorts of response to the Basic Argument, and I will concentrate on their more simple expressions, in the belief that truth in philosophy, especially in areas of philosophy like the present one, is almost never very complicated.

(I) The first is **compatibilist**. *Compatibilists believe that one can be a free and morally responsible agent even if determinism is true.* Roughly, they claim, with many variations of detail, that one may correctly be said to be truly responsible for what one does, when one acts, just so long as one is not caused to act by any of a certain set of constraints (kleptomaniac impulses, obsessional neuroses, desires that are experienced as alien, post-hypnotic commands, threats, instances of *force majeure*, and so on). Clearly, this sort of compatibilist responsibility does not require that one should be truly responsible for how one is in any way at all, and so step (2) of the Basic Argument comes out as false. One can have compatibilist responsibility even if the way one is is totally determined by factors entirely outside one's control.

It is for this reason, however, that *compatibilist responsibility famously fails to amount to any sort of true moral responsibility, given the natural, strong understanding of the notion of true moral responsibility (characterized above by reference to the story of heaven and hell)*. One does what one does entirely because of the way one is, and one is in no way ultimately responsible for the way one is. So how can one be justly punished for anything one does? Compatibilists have given increasingly refined accounts of the circumstances in which punishment may be said to be appropriate or intrinsically fitting. But they can do nothing against this basic objection.

Many compatibilists have never supposed otherwise. They are happy to admit the point. They observe that the notions of true moral responsibility and justice that are employed in the objection cannot possibly have application to anything real, and suggest that the objection is therefore not worth considering. In response, proponents of the Basic Argument agree that the notions of true moral responsibility and justice in question cannot have application to anything real; but they make no apologies for considering them. They consider them because they are central to ordinary thought about moral responsibility and justice. So far as most people are concerned, they are the subject, if the subject is moral responsibility and justice.

(II) The second response is ***libertarian***. *Incompatibilists believe that freedom and moral responsibility are incompatible with determinism, and some of them are libertarians, who believe that that we are free and morally responsible agents, and that determinism is therefore false.* In an ingenious statement of the incompatibilist-libertarian case, Robert Kane argues that agents in an undetermined world can have free will, for they can "have the power to make choices for which they have ultimate responsibility". That is, they can "have the power to make choices which can only and finally be explained in terms of their own wills (i.e. character, motives, and efforts of will)."[7] Roughly, Kane sees this power as grounded in the possible occurrence, in agents, of efforts of will that have two main features: first, they are partly indeterministic in their nature, and hence indeterminate in their outcome; second, they occur in cases in which agents are trying to make a difficult choice between the options that their characters dispose them to consider. (The paradigm cases will be cases in which they face a conflict between moral duty and non-moral desire.)

But the old objection to libertarianism recurs. How can this indeterminism help with moral responsibility? Granted that the truth of determinism rules out true moral responsibility, how can the falsity of determinism help? How can the occurrence of partly random or indeterministic events contribute in any way to one's being truly morally responsible either for one's actions or for one's character? If my efforts of will shape my character in an admirable way, and in so doing are partly indeterministic in nature, while also being shaped (as Kane grants) by my already existing character, why am I not merely lucky?

The general objection applies equally whether determinism is true or false, and can be restated as follows. We are born with a great many genetically determined predispositions for which we are not responsible. We are subject to many early influences for which we are not responsible. These decisively shape our characters, our motives, the general bent and strength of our capacity to make efforts of will. We may later engage in conscious and intentional shaping procedures—call them S-procedures—designed to affect and change our characters, motivational structure, and wills. Suppose we do. The question is then why we engage in the particular S-procedures that we do engage in, and why we engage in them in the particular way that we do. The general answer is that we engage in the particular S-procedures that we do engage in, given the circumstances in which we find ourselves, because of certain features of the way we already are. (Indeterministic factors may also play a part in what happens, but these will not help to make us responsible for what we do.) And these features of the way we already are—call them character features, or C-features—are either wholly the products of genetic or environmental influences, deterministic or random, for which we are not responsible, or are at least partly the result of earlier S-procedures, which are in turn either wholly the product of C-features for which we are not responsible, or are at least partly the product of still earlier S-procedures, which are in turn either the products of C-features for which we are not responsible, or the product of such C-features together with still earlier S-procedures—and so on. In the end, we reach the first S-procedure, and this will have been engaged in, and engaged in the particular way in which it was engaged in, as a result of genetic or environmental factors, deterministic or random, for which we were not responsible.

Moving away from the possible role of indeterministic factors in character or personality formation, we can consider their possible role in particular instances of deliberation and decision. Here too it seems clear that indeterministic factors cannot, in influencing what happens, contribute to true moral responsibility in any way. In the end, whatever we do, we do it either as a result of random influences for which we are not responsible, or as a result of non-random influences for which we are not responsible, or as a result of influences for which we are proximally responsible but not ultimately responsible. The point seems obvious. Nothing can be ultimately *causa sui* in any respect at all. Even if God can be, we can't be.

Kane says little about moral responsibility in his paper, but his position seems to be that true moral responsibility is possible if indeterminism is true. It is possible because in cases of "moral, prudential and practical struggle we . . . are truly 'making ourselves' in such a way that we are ultimately responsible for the outcome." This 'making of ourselves' means that "we can be ultimately responsible for our present motives and character by virtue of past choices which helped to form them and for which we were ultimately responsible" (op. cit., p. 252). It is for this reason that we can be ultimately responsible and morally responsible not only in cases of struggle in which we are 'making ourselves', but also for choices and actions which do not involve struggle, flowing unopposed from our character and motives.

In claiming that we can be ultimately responsible for our present motives and character, Kane appears to *accept* step (2) of the Basic Argument. He appears to accept that we have to 'make ourselves', and so be ultimately responsibly for ourselves, in order to be morally responsible for what we do.[8] The problem with this suggestion is the old one. In Kane's view, a person's 'ultimate responsibility' for the outcome of an effort of will depends essentially on the partly indeterministic nature of the outcome. This is because it is only the element of indeterminism that prevents prior character and motives from fully explaining the outcome of the effort of will (op. cit, p. 236). But how can this indeterminism help with moral responsibility? How can the fact that my effort of will is indeterministic in such a way that its outcome is indeterminate make me truly responsible for it, or even help to make me truly responsible for it? How can it help in any way at all with moral responsibility? How can it make punishment—or reward—ultimately just?

There is a further, familiar problem with the view that moral responsibility depends on indeterminism. If one accepts the view, one will have to grant that it is impossible to know whether any human being is ever morally responsible. For moral responsibility now depends on the falsity of determinism, and determinism is unfalsifiable. There is no more reason to think that determinism is false than that it is true, in spite of the impression sometimes given by scientists and popularizers of science.

(III) The *third option* begins by accepting that one cannot be held to be ultimately responsible for one's character or personality or motivational structure. It accepts that this is so whether determinism is true or false. It then directly challenges step (2) of the Basic Argument. *It appeals to a certain picture of the self in order to argue that one can be truly free and morally responsible in spite of the fact that one cannot be held to be ultimately responsible for one's character or personality or motivational structure.* This picture has some support in the 'phenomenology' of human choice—we sometimes experience our choices and decisions as if the picture were an accurate one. But it is easy to show that it cannot be accurate in such a way that we can be said to be truly or ultimately morally responsible for our choices or actions.

It can be set out as follows. One is free and truly morally responsible because one's self is, in a crucial sense, independent of one's character or personality or motivational structure—one's CPM, for short. Suppose one is in a situation which one experiences as a difficult choice between A, doing one's duty, and B, following one's non-moral desires. Given one's CPM, one responds in a certain way. One's desires and beliefs develop and interact and constitute reasons for both A and B. One's CPM makes one tend towards A or B. So far the problem is the same as ever: whatever one does, one will do what one does because of the way one's CPM is, and since one neither is nor can be ultimately responsible for the way one's CPM is, one cannot be ultimately responsible for what one does.

Enter one's self, S. S is imagined to be in some way independent of one's CPM. S (i.e. one) considers the deliverances of one's CPM and decides in the light of them, but it—S—incorporates a power of decision that is independent of one's CPM in such a way that one can after all count as truly and ultimately morally responsible in one's decisions and actions, even though one is not ultimately responsible for one's CPM. Step (2) of the Basic Argument is false because of the existence of S.[9]

The trouble with the picture is obvious. S (i.e. one) decides on the basis of the deliverances of one's CPM. But whatever S decides, it decides as it does because of the way it is (or else because partly or wholly because of the occurrence in the decision process of indeterministic factors for which it—i.e. one—cannot be responsible, and which cannot plausibly be thought to contribute to one's true moral responsibility). And this returns us to where we started. To be a source of true or ultimate responsibility, S must be responsible for being the way it is. But this is impossible, for the reasons given in the Basic Argument.

The story of S and CPM adds another layer to the description of the human decision process, but it cannot change the fact that human beings cannot be ultimately self-determining in such a way as to be ultimately morally responsible for how they are,

and thus for how they decide and act. The story is crudely presented, but it should suffice to make clear that no move of this sort can solve the problem.

'Character is destiny', as Novalis is often reported as saying.[10] The remark is inaccurate, because external circumstances are part of destiny, but the point is well taken when it comes to the question of moral responsibility. Nothing can be *causa sui*, and in order to be truly morally responsible for one's actions one would have to be *causa sui*, at least in certain crucial mental respects. One cannot institute oneself in such a way that one can take over *true or* assume moral responsibility for how one is in such a way that one can indeed be truly morally responsible for what one does. This fact is not changed by the fact that we may be unable not to think of ourselves as truly morally responsible in ordinary circumstances. Nor is it changed by the fact that it may be a very good thing that we have this inability—so that we might wish to take steps to preserve it, if it looked to be in danger of fading. As already remarked, many human beings are unable to resist the idea that it is their capacity for fully explicit self-conscious deliberation, in a situation of choice, that suffices to constitute them as truly morally responsible agents in the strongest possible sense. The Basic Argument shows that this is a mistake. However self-consciously aware we are, as we deliberate and reason, every act and operation of our mind happens as it does as a result of features for which we are ultimately in no way responsible. But the conviction that self-conscious awareness of one's situation can be a sufficient foundation of strong free will is very powerful. It runs deeper than rational argument, and it survives untouched, in the everyday conduct of life, even after the validity of the Basic Argument has been admitted.

Conclusion

There is nothing new in the somewhat incantatory argument of this paper. It restates certain points that may be in need of restatement. "Everything has been said before," said André Gide, echoing La Bruyère, "but since nobody listens we have to keep going back and beginning all over again." This is an exaggeration, but it may not be a gross exaggeration, so far as general observations about the human condition are concerned.

The present claim, in any case, is simply this: time would be saved, and a great deal of readily available clarity would be introduced into the discussion of the nature of moral responsibility, if the simple point that is established by the Basic Argument were more generally acknowledged and clearly stated. Nietzsche thought that thorough-going acknowledgement of the point was long overdue, and his belief that there might be moral advantages in such an acknowledgement may deserve further consideration.[11]

NOTES

1. Adapted from G. Strawson, 1986, pp. 28–30.
2. That is, the infinite series must have a beginning and an end, which is impossible.
3. Cf. *Nichomachean Ethics* III. 5.
4. Cf. MacKay (1960), and the discussion of the 'Genuine Incompatibilist Determinist' it G. Strawson (1986, pp. 281–6).
5. I suspect that they have started out from their subjective certainty that they have true moral responsibility. They have then been led by reflection to the realization that they cannot really have such moral responsibility if they are not in some crucial way responsible for being the way they are. They have accordingly concluded that they are indeed responsible for being the way they are.
6. Carr in *What Is History*?, p. 89; Sartre in *Being and Nothingness, Existentialism and Humanism*, p. 29, and in the *New Left Review* 1969 (quoted in Wiggins, 1975); Kant in *Religion within the Limits of Reason Alone*, p. 40, *The Critique of Practical Reason*, p. 101 (Ak. V. 98), and in *Opus Postumum*, p. 213; Patten in *The Spectator*, January 1992.

These quotations raise many questions which I will not consider. It is often hard, for example, to be sure what Sartre is saying. But the occurrence of the quoted phrases is significant on any plausible interpretation of his views. As for Kant, it may be thought to be odd that he says what he does, in so far as he grounds the possibility of our freedom in our possession of an unknowable, non-temporal noumenal nature. It is, however, plausible to suppose that he thinks that radical or ultimate self-determination must take place even in the noumenal realm, in some unintelligibly non-temporal manner, if there is, to be true moral responsibility.
7. Kane (1989) p. 254. I have omitted some italics.
8. He cites Van Inwagen (1989) in support of this view.

9. Cf. C.A. Campbell (1957).
10. e.g. by George Eliot in *The Mill on the Floss*, book 6, chapter 6. Novalis wrote "Oft fühl ich jetzt . . . [und] je tiefer einsehe, dass Schicksal und Gemüt Namen eines Begriffes sind"—"I often feel, and ever more deeply realize, that fate and character are the same concept". He was echoing Heracleitus, Fragment 119 DK.
11. Cf. R. Schacht (1983) pp. 304–9. The idea that there might be moral advantages in the clear headed admission that true or ultimate moral responsibility is impossible has recently been developed in another way by Saul Smilansky (1994).

REFERENCES

Aristotle, 1953. *Nichomachean Ethics*, trans. J. A. K. Thomson, Allen and Unwin, London.

Campell, C.A., 1957. 'Has the Self "Free Will"?', in C.A. Campbell, *On Selfhood and Godhood*, Allen and Unwin, London.

Carr, E.H., 1961. *What Is History*'?, Macmillan, London.

Kane, R., 1989. 'Two Kinds of Incompatibilism', *Philosophy and Phenomenological Research* 50, pp. 219–254.

Kant, I., 1956. *Critique of Practical Reason*, trans. L. W. Beck, Bobbs-Merrill, Indianapolis.

Kant, I., 1960. *Religion within the Limits of Reason Alone*, trans. T. M. Greene and H. H. Hudson, Harper and Row, New York.

Kant, I., 1993. *Opus postumum*, trans. E. Förster and M. Rosen, Cambridge University Press, Cambridge.

MacKay, D.M., 1960. 'On the Logical Indeterminacy of Free Choice', *Mind* 69, pp. 31–40.

Mele, A., 1995. *Autonomous Agents: From Self-Control to Autonomy*, Oxford University Press, New York.

Nietzsche, F., 1966. *Beyond Good and Evil*, trans. Walter Kaufmann, Random House, New York.

Novalis, 1802. *Heinrich von Ofterdingen*.

Sartre, J.-P., 1969. *Being and Nothingness*, trans. Hazel E. Barnes, Methuen, London.

Sartre, J.-P., 1989. *Existentialism and Humanism*, trans. Philip Mairet, Methuen, London.

Schacht, R., 1983. *Nietzsche*, Routledge and Kegan Paul, London.

Smilansky, S., 1994. 'The Ethical Advantages of Hard Determinism', *Philosophy and Phenomenological Research*.

Strawson, G., 1986. *Freedom and Belief*, Clarendon Press, Oxford.

Van Inwagen, P., 1989. 'When Is the Will Free?', *Philosophical Perspectives* 3, pp. 399–422.

Wiggins, D., 1975. 'Towards a Reasonable Libertarianism', in T. Honderich, ed., *Essays on Freedom of Action*, Routledge, London.

DISCUSSION QUESTIONS:

1. If, as Strawson argues, we are not morally responsible for our actions, why, as he acknowledges, do we persist in believing that we are?

2. What are the implications for our social practices, if we accept Strawson's position that we are never morally responsible for our actions in the way, as he puts it, required "to make sense" of our view that reward and punishment are sometimes just? Must we abandon or at least modify our practices of reward or punishment in some way? Our current system of criminal justice provides for the punishment of some people, while others are excused from punishment on the ground that they were not responsible for their conduct. If we adopt Strawson's view, must we revise our criminal justice system?

3. To what extent are our individual actions determined by what Strawson calls our CPM, our character, personality, or motivational structure? To what extent do we act as we do because of how we are? Do we ever act in such a way that there is no explanation of our action in terms of our CPM? Do you know of any examples of such cases?

4. If you have already read them, reconsider Ayer's essay, "Freedom and Necessity," and Chisholm's essay, "Human Freedom and the Self." How might Ayer best defend his version of Compatibilism against Strawson's arguments? How might Chisholm best defend his version of Libertarianism? Does either have a successful response to Strawson's arguments?

Argument Reconstruction Exercises:

I. Strawson states the compatibilist reply to his position as follows. Identify its premises and conclusion:

> [Compatibilists claim] that one may correctly be said to be truly responsible for what one does, when one acts, just so long as one is not caused to act by any of a certain set of contraints [e.g., kleptomanic impulses, obsessional neuroses]. . . .

Clearly, this sort of compatibilist responsibility does not require that one should be truly responsible for how one is in any way at all, and so step (2) of the Basic Argument comes out to be false, (pages 106–107)

II. Strawson gives the following response to the Libertarian reply. Identify the premises and conclusion in this excerpt:

> But how can this indeterminism help with moral responsibility? How can the fact that my effort of will is indeterministic in such a way that its outcome is indeterminate make me truly responsible for it, or even help to make me truly responsible for it? How can it help in any way at all with moral responsibility? How can it make punishment—or reward—ultimately just? (pages 108)

III. Strawson presents the Independent Self Reply to his view as follows. Identify the premises and conclusion in this excerpt:

> Enter one's self, S. S is imagined to be in some way independent of one's CPM. S (i.e. one) considers the deliverances of one's CPM and decides in the light of them, but it—S—incorporates a power of decision that is independent of one's CPM in such a way that one can after all count as truly and ultimately morally responsible in one's decisions and actions even though one is not ultimately responsible for one's CPM. (page 109)

IV. Strawson gives the following response to the Independent Self Reply. Identify the premises and conclusion in this excerpt:

> The trouble with the picture is obvious. S (i.e. one) decides on the basis of the deliverances of one's CPM. But whatever S decides, it does so because of the way it is (or else because partly or wholly because of the occurrence in the decision process of indeterministic factors for which it—i.e. one—cannot be responsible, and which cannot plausibly be thought to contribute to one's true moral responsibility). And this returns us to where we started. To be a source of true or ultimate responsibility, S must be responsible for being the way it is. But this is impossible for the reasoning given in the Basic Argument, (page 109)

8.2 FREEDOM AND NECESSITY

A. J. AYER (1954)

A. J. Ayer was a professor of philosophy at Oxford University and is perhaps best known for his book *Language, Truth and Logic* (1936). The essay here is taken from his work *Philosophical Essays* (1954). In this selection, Ayer presents a version of **Soft Determinism** with a defense of **Compatibilism**. He develops a definition of freedom that is designed both to capture the kind of freedom that is required for moral responsibility and to reveal that our actions can be both free and causally determined. According to Ayer, moral responsibility requires freedom, at least in the form of the ability to have acted otherwise, and he provides an elegant argument to show that moral responsibility requires causal determinism: if our act is not caused, then it is an accident. But if our act is an accident, and so merely a matter of chance, then we are not responsible for it. Moral responsibility thus requires causal determinism.

Reading Questions:

1. Some philosophers respond to the apparent conflict between causal determinism and freedom by rejecting causal determinism. Ayer considers some reasons for doing just this: that we often have a "feeling" of freedom when we act, that the assumption of causal determinism, that every event has a cause, has not been proven and is not a necessary presupposition of scientific thought. What is Ayer's basis for setting aside these reasons against causal determinism?

2. Ayer notes that some moralists will reject his claim that moral responsibility requires causal determinism. They will say that we are responsible for our actions because they are the result of our character and we are responsible for our character. What is Ayer's response to this objection to his view?

3. Ayer claims that, while all of our choices and actions are causally determined by past events, it is only in some cases that those causes prevent us from acting freely. In this regard, he confronts the question, "Why should we distinguish, with regard to a person's freedom, between the operations of one sort of cause and those of another?" What is his answer to this question?

Responsibility Requires Freedom

When I am said to have done something of my own free will it is implied that I could have acted otherwise: and it is only when it is believed that I could have acted otherwise that I am held to be morally responsible for what I have done. For a man is not thought to be morally responsible for an action that it was not in his power to avoid. But if human behaviour is entirely governed by causal laws, it is not clear how any action that is done could ever have been avoided. It may be said of the agent that he would have acted otherwise if the causes of his action had been different, but they being what they were, it seems to follow that he was bound to act as he did. Now it is commonly assumed both that men are capable of acting freely, in the sense that is required to make them morally responsible, and that human behaviour is entirely governed by causal laws: and it is the apparent conflict between these two assumptions that gives rise to the philosophical problem of the freedom of the will.

Confronted with this problem, many people will be inclined to agree with Dr. Johnson; 'Sir, we *know* our will is free, and *there's* an end on't.' But, while this does very well for those who accept Dr. Johnson's premiss, it would hardly convince anyone who denied the freedom of the will. Certainly, if we do know that our wills are free, it follows that they are so. But the logical reply to this might be that since our wills are not free, it follows that no one can know that they are: so that if anyone claims, like Dr. Johnson, to know that they are, he must be mistaken. What is evident, indeed, is that people often believe themselves to be acting freely; and it is to this 'feeling' of freedom that some philosophers appeal when they wish, in the supposed interests of morality, to prove that not all human action is causally determined. But if these philosophers are right in their assumption that a man cannot be acting freely if his action is causally determined, then the fact that someone feels free to do, or not to do, a certain action does not prove that he really is so. It may prove that the agent does not himself know what it is that makes him act in one way rather than another: but from the fact that a man is unaware of the causes of his action, it does not follow that no such causes exist.

Responsibility Requires Determinism

So much may be allowed to the determinist; but his belief that all human actions are subservient to causal laws still remains to be justified. If, indeed, it is necessary that every event should have a cause, then the rule must apply to human behaviour as much as to anything else. But why should it be supposed that every event must have a cause? The contrary is not unthinkable. Nor is the law of universal causation a necessary presupposition of scientific thought. The scientist may try to discover causal laws, and in many cases he succeeds; but sometimes he has to be content with statistical laws, and sometimes he comes upon events which, in the present state of his knowledge, he is not able to subsume under any law at all. In the case of these events he assumes that if he

From *Philosophical Essays* by Professor Sir Alfred Ayer (1954, pp. 271–84). Reprinted by permission of Macmillan, London and Basingstoke.

knew more he would be able to discover some law, whether causal or statistical, which would enable him to account for them. And this assumption cannot be disproved. For however far he may have carried his investigation, it is always open to him to carry it further; and it is always conceivable that if he carried it further he would discover the connection which had hitherto escaped him. Nevertheless, it is also conceivable that the events with which he is concerned are not systematically connected with any others: so that the reason why he does not discover the sort of laws that he requires is simply that they do not obtain.

Now in the case of human conduct the search for explanations has not in fact been altogether fruitless. Certain scientific laws have been established; and with the help of these laws we do make a number of successful predictions about the ways in which different people will behave. But these predictions do not always cover every detail. We may be able to predict that in certain circumstances a particular man will be angry, without being able to prescribe the precise form that the expression of his anger will take. We may be reasonably sure that he will shout, but not sure how loud his shout will be, or exactly what words he will use. And it is only a small proportion of human actions that we are able to forecast even so precisely as this. But that, it may be said, is because we have not carried our investigations very far. The science of psychology is still in its infancy and, as it is developed, not only will more human actions be explained, but the explanations will go into greater detail. The ideal of complete explanation may never in fact be attained: but it is theoretically attainable. Well, this may be so: and certainly it is impossible to show *a priori* that it is not so: but equally it cannot be shown that it is. This will not, however, discourage the scientist who, in the field of human behaviour, as elsewhere, will continue to formulate theories and test them by the facts. And in this he is justified. For since he has no reason *a priori* to admit that there is a limit to what he can discover, the fact that he also cannot be sure that there is no limit does not make it unreasonable for him to devise theories, nor, having devised them, to try constantly to improve them.

But now suppose it to be claimed that, so far as men's actions are concerned, there is a limit: and that this limit is set by the fact of human freedom.

An obvious objection is that in many cases in which a person feels himself to be free to do, or not to do, a certain action, we are even now able to explain, in causal terms, why it is that he acts as he does. But it might be argued that even if men are sometimes mistaken in believing that they act freely, it does not follow that they are always so mistaken. For it is not always the case that when a man believes that he has acted freely we are in fact able to account for his action in causal terms. A determinist would say that we should be able to account for it if we had more knowledge of the circumstances, and had been able to discover the appropriate natural laws. But until those discoveries have been made, this remains only a pious hope. And may it not be true that, in some cases at least, the reason why we can give no causal explanation is that no causal explanation is available; and that this is because the agent's choice was literally free, as he himself felt it to be?

The answer is that this may indeed be true, inasmuch as it is open to anyone to hold that no explanation is possible until some explanation is actually found. But even so it does not give the moralist what he wants. For he is anxious to show that men are capable of acting freely in order to infer that they can be morally responsible for what they do. *But if it is a matter of pure chance that a man should act in one way rather than another, he may be free but can hardly be responsible.* And indeed when a man's actions seem to us quite unpredictable, when, as we say, there is no knowing what he will do, we do not look upon him as a moral agent. We look upon him as a lunatic.

To this it may be objected that we are not dealing fairly with the moralist. For when he makes it a condition of my being morally responsible that I should act freely, he does not wish to imply that is purely a matter of chance that I act as I do. What he wishes to imply is that my actions are the result of my own free choice: and it is because they are the result of my own free choice that I am held to be morally responsible for them.

But now we must ask how it is that I come to make my choice. Either it is an accident that I choose to act as I do or it is not. If it is an accident, then it is merely a matter of chance that I did not choose otherwise; and if it is merely a matter of chance that I did not choose otherwise, it is surely irrational to hold me morally responsible for choosing as I did. But if it is not an accident that I choose to do one thing rather than another, then presumably there is some causal explanation of my choice: and in that case we are led back to determinism.

Again, the objection may be raised that we are not doing justice to the moralist's case. His view is not that it is a matter of chance that I choose to act as I do, but rather that my choice depends upon my character. Nevertheless he holds that I can still be free in the sense that he requires; for it is I who am responsible for my character. But in what way am I responsible for my character? Only, surely, in the sense that there is a causal connection between what I do now and what I have done in the past. It is only this that justifies the statement that I have made myself what I am: and even so this is an over-simplification, since it takes no account of the external influences to which I have been subjected. But, ignoring the external influences, let us assume that it is in fact the case that I have made myself what I am. Then it is still legitimate to ask how it is that I have come to make myself one sort of person rather than another. And if it be answered that it is a matter of my strength of will, we can put the same question in another form by asking how it is that my will has the strength that it has and not some other degree of strength. Once more, either it is an accident or it is not. If it is an accident, then by the same argument as before, I am not morally responsible, and if it is not an accident we are led back to determinism.

Furthermore, to say that my actions proceed from my character or, more colloquially, that I act in character, is to say that my behaviour is consistent and to that extent predictable: and since it is, above all, for the actions that I perform in character that I am held to be morally responsible, it looks as if the admission of moral responsibility, so far from being incompatible with determinism, tends rather to presuppose it. But how can this be so if it is a necessary condition of moral responsibility that the person who is held responsible should have acted freely? It seems that if we are to retain this idea of moral responsibility, we must either show that men can be held responsible for actions which they do not do freely, or else find some way of reconciling determinism with the freedom of the will.

It is no doubt with the object of effecting this reconciliation that some philosophers have defined freedom as the consciousness of necessity. And by so doing they are able to say not only that a man can be acting freely when his action is causally determined, but even that his action must be causally determined for it to be possible for him to be acting freely. Nevertheless this definition has the serious disadvantage that it gives to the word 'freedom' a meaning quite different from any that it ordinarily bears. It is indeed obvious that if we are allowed to give the word 'freedom' any meaning that we please, we can find a meaning that will reconcile it with determinism: but this is no more a solution of our present problem than the fact that the word 'horse' could be arbitrarily used to mean what is ordinarily meant by 'sparrow' is a proof that horses have wings. For suppose that I am compelled by another person to do something 'against my will'. In that case, as the word 'freedom' is ordinarily used, I should not be said to be acting freely: and the fact that I am fully aware of the constraint to which I am subjected makes no difference to the matter. I do not become free by becoming conscious that I am not. It may, indeed, be possible to show that my being aware that my action is causally determined is not incompatible with my acting freely: but it by no means follows that it is in this that my freedom consists. Moreover, I suspect that one of the reasons why people are inclined to define freedom as the consciousness of necessity is that they think that if one is conscious of necessity one may somehow be able to master it. But this is a fallacy. It is like someone's saying that he wishes he could see into the future, because if he did he would know what calamities lay in wait for him and so would be able to avoid them. But if he avoids the calamities then they don't lie in the future and it is not true that he foresees them. And similarly if I am able to master necessity, in the sense of escaping the operation of a necessary law, then the law in question is not necessary. And if the law is not necessary, then neither my freedom nor anything else can consist in my knowing that it is.

Let it be granted, then, when we speak of reconciling freedom with determination we are using the word 'freedom' in an ordinary sense. It still remains for us to make this usage clear: and perhaps the best way to make it clear is to show what it is that freedom, in this sense, is contrasted with. Now we began with the assumption that freedom is contrasted with causality: so that a man cannot be said to be acting freely if his action is causally determined. But this assumption has led us into difficulties and I now wish to suggest that it is mistaken. For it is not, I think, causality that freedom is to be contrasted with, but constraint. And while it is true that being constrained to do an action entails being caused to do it, I shall try to show that the converse does not hold. *I shall try to show that from the fact that my action is causally determined it does not necessarily follow that I am constrained to do it: and this is equivalent to saying that it does not necessarily follow that I am not free.*

Determinism and Freedom Are Compatible

If I am constrained, I do not act freely. But in what circumstances can I legitimately be said to be constrained? An obvious instance is the case in which I am compelled by another person to do what he wants. In a case of this sort the compulsion need not be such as to deprive one of the power of choice. It is not required that the other person should have hypnotized me, or that he should make it physically impossible for me to go against his will. It is enough that he should induce me to do what he wants by making it clear to me that, if I do not, he will bring about some situation that I regard as even more undesirable than the consequences of the action that he wishes me to do. Thus, if the man points a pistol at my head I may still choose to disobey him: but this does not prevent its being true that if I do fall in with his wishes he can legitimately be said to have compelled me. And if the circumstances are such that no reasonable person would be expected to choose the other alternative, then the action that I am made to do is not one for which I am held to be morally responsible.

A similar, but still somewhat different, case is that in which another person has obtained an habitual ascendancy over me. Where this is so, there may be no question of my being induced to act as the other person wishes by being confronted with a still more disagreeable alternative: for if I am sufficiently under his influence this special stimulus will not be necessary. Nevertheless I do not act freely, for the reason that I have been deprived of the power of choice. And this means that I have acquired so strong a habit of obedience that I no longer go through any process of deciding whether or not to do what the other person wants. About other matters I may still deliberate; but as regards the fulfillment of this other person's wishes, my own deliberations have ceased to be a causal factor in my behaviour. And it is in this sense that I may be said to be constrained. It is not, however, necessary that such constraint should take the form of subservience to another person. A kleptomaniac is not a free agent, in respect of his stealing, because he does not go through any process of deciding whether or not to steal. Or rather, if he does go through such a process, it is irrelevant to his behaviour. Whatever he resolved to do, he would steal all the same. And it is this that distinguishes him from the ordinary thief.

But now it may be asked whether there is any essential difference between these cases and those in which the agent is commonly thought to be free. No doubt the ordinary thief does go through a process of deciding whether or not to steal, and no doubt it does affect his behaviour. If he resolved to refrain from stealing, he could carry his resolution out. But if it be allowed that his making or not making this resolution is causally determined, then how can he be any more free than the kleptomaniac? It may be true that unlike the kleptomaniac he could refrain from stealing if he chose: but if there is a cause, or set of causes, which necessitate his choosing as he does, how can he be said to have the power of choice? Again, it may be true that no one now compels me to get up and walk across the room: but if my doing so can be causally explained in terms of my history or my environment, or whatever it may be, then how am I any more free than if some other person had compelled me? I do not have the feeling of constraint that I have when a pistol is manifestly pointed at my head; but the chains of causation by which I am bound are no less effective for being invisible.

The answer to this is that the cases I have mentioned as examples of constraint do differ from the others: and they differ just in the ways that I have tried to bring out. If I suffered from a compulsion neurosis, so that I got up and walked across the room, whether I wanted to or not, or if I did so because somebody else compelled me, then I should not be acting freely. But if I do it now, I shall be acting freely, just because these conditions do not obtain; and the fact that my action may nevertheless have a cause is, from this point of view, irrelevant. For it is not when my action has any cause at all, but only when it has a special sort of cause, that it is reckoned not to be free.

But here it may be objected that, even if this distinction corresponds to ordinary usage, it is still very irrational. For why should we distinguish, with regard to a person's freedom, between the operations of one sort of cause and those of another? Do not all causes equally necessitate? And is it not therefore arbitrary to say that a person is free when he is necessitated in one fashion but not when he is necessitated in another?

That all causes equally necessitate is indeed a tautology, if the word 'necessitate' is taken merely as equivalent to 'cause': but if, as the objection requires, it is taken as equivalent to 'constrain' or 'compel', then I do not think that this proposition is true. For all that is needed for one event to be the cause of another is that, in the given circumstances, the event which is said to be the effect would not have occurred if it had not been for the occurrence of the event which is said to be the cause, or vice versa, according as causes are interpreted as necessary, or sufficient, conditions; and this fact is usually deducible from some causal law which states that whenever an event of the one kind occurs then, given suitable conditions, an event of the other kind will occur in a certain temporal or spatio-temporal relationship to it. In short, there is an invariable concomitance between the two classes of events; but there is no compulsion, in any but a metaphorical sense. Suppose, for example, that a psycho-analyst is able to account for some aspect of my behaviour by referring it to some lesion that I suffered in my childhood. In that case, it may be said that my childhood experience, together with certain other events, necessitates my behaving as I do. But all that this involves is that it is found to be true in general that when people have had certain experiences as children, they subsequently behave in certain specifiable ways; and my case is just another instance of this general law. It is in this way indeed that my behaviour is explained. But from the fact that my behaviour is capable of being explained, in the sense that it can be subsumed under some natural law, it does not follow that I am acting under constraint.

If this is correct, to say that I could have acted otherwise is to say, first, that I should have acted otherwise if I had so chosen; secondly, that my action was voluntary in the sense in which the actions, say, of the kleptomaniac are not; and thirdly, that nobody compelled me to choose as I did: and these three conditions may very well be fulfilled. When they are fulfilled, I may be said to have acted freely. But this is not to say that it was a matter of chance that I acted as I did, or, in other words, that my action could not be explained. And that my actions should be capable of being explained is all that is required by the postulate of determinism.

If more than this seems to be required it is, I think, because the use of the very word 'determinism' is in some degree misleading. For it tends to suggest that one event is somehow in the power of another, whereas the truth is merely that they are factually correlated. And the same applies to the use, in this context, of the word 'necessity' and even of the word 'cause' itself. Moreover, there are various reasons for this. One is the tendency to confuse causal with logical necessitation, and so to infer mistakenly that the effect is contained in the cause. Another is the uncritical use of a concept of force which is derived from primitive experiences of pushing and striking. A third is the survival of an animistic conception of causality, in which all causal relationships are modelled on the example of one person's exercising authority over another. As a result we tend to form an imaginative picture of an unhappy effect trying vainly to escape from the clutches of an overmastering cause. But, I repeat, the fact is simply that when an event of one type occurs, an event of another type occurs also, in a certain temporal or spatio-temporal relation to the first. The rest is only metaphor. And it is because of the metaphor, and not because of the fact, that we come to think that there is an antithesis between causality and freedom.

Nevertheless, it may be said, if the postulate of determinism is valid, then the future can be explained in terms of the past; and this means that if one knew enough about the past one would be able to predict the future. But in that case what will happen in the future is already decided. And how then can I be said to be free? What is going to happen is going to happen and nothing that I do can prevent it. If the determinist is right, I am the helpless prisoner of fate.

But what is meant by saying that the future course of events is already decided? If the implication is that some person has arranged it, then the proposition is false. But if all that is meant is that it is possible, in principle, to deduce it from a set of particular facts about the past, together with the appropriate general laws, then, even if this is true, it does not in the least entail that I am the helpless prisoner of fate. It does not even entail that my actions make no difference to the future: for they are causes as well as effects; so that if they were different their consequences would be different also. What it does entail is that my behaviour can be predicted: but to say that my behaviour can be predicted is not to say that I am acting under constraint. It is indeed true that I cannot escape my destiny if this is taken to mean no more than that I shall do what I shall do. But this is a tautology, just as it is a tautology that what is going to happen is going to happen. And such tautologies as these prove nothing whatsoever about the freedom of the will.

DISCUSSION QUESTIONS:

1. Ayer reasons that if our choice to perform an action is uncaused, then it is an accident and, if it is an accident, then we are not responsible for it. Do you agree with him that our choice must be caused for us to be responsible for it?

2. Ayer claims that his account of freedom captures one of our ordinary meanings of "freedom." Does it do so? Suppose that we are created by a god who, at the moment of creation, predetermines all of our future mental states (from all our experiences to all our desires, thoughts, and choices). Will our subsequent actions be free in the sense of "freedom" that we associate with moral responsibility? Will they meet Ayer's three conditions for being free?

3. Ayer claims that we are responsible for some of our actions, even though they are just as causally determined as those acts of theft for which kleptomaniacs are not responsible. According to Ayer, the causes of our behavior do not "constrain" us in the way in which the causes of kleptomaniacs' behavior "constrain" them. How does Ayer explain this difference between causality and constraint? Is there such a difference?

4. Ayer assumes that we are morally responsible for an action only if our act is free in the sense that we could have done otherwise. In this regard, he writes that "a man in not thought to be morally responsible for an action that was not in his power to avoid." Some philosophers have questioned this claim. Suppose that Smith can tell what you are about to choose and, if he doesn't like the choice you're about to make, he can cause you to make another. Suppose too that he monitors your deliberations as you choose to tell a lie and then do so. Since your behavior is just what he wants it to be, he doesn't intervene. Yet, if he had detected that you were going to choose to tell the truth, he would have intervened in order to cause you to choose to lie instead. In this case, it seems that it was not in your power to avoid telling the lie. If you had not told it on your own, Smith would have intervened to make sure you did. Nothing you could have done would have kept you from telling the lie. Ayer's condition for moral responsibility is not met. Yet, it also seems that you, not Smith, are responsible for your lie. After all, he never does intervene to make you lie. If moral responsibility does not require freedom in the form of an ability to have done otherwise, what does it require?

5. If you have already read it, reconsider Strawson's position in his essay, "The Impossibility of Moral Responsibility." Which aspects of Ayer's position will Strawson accept? Which ones will he reject? Where they disagree, who, if either, is correct?

6. If you have already read it, reconsider Chisholm's position in his essay, "Human Freedom and the Self." Which aspects of Ayer's position will Chisholm accept? Which will he reject? Where they disagree, who, if either, is correct?

Argument Reconstruction Exercises:

I. Ayer opens his essay with the following argument intended to show that there is a conflict between the assumption that we are capable of acting freely in the way required for moral responsibility and the assumption that our behavior is governed by causal laws. Identify the premises and conclusion in this excerpt:

> When I am said to have done something of my own free will, it is implied that I could have acted otherwise; and it is only when it is believed that I could have acted otherwise that I am held to be morally responsible for what I have done. For a man is not thought to be morally responsible for an action that it was not in his power to avoid. But if human behavior is entirely governed by causal laws, it is not clear how any action that is done could ever have been avoided. It may be said of the agent that he would have acted otherwise if the causes of his action had been different, but they being what they were, it seems to follow that he was bound to act as he did. (page 112)

II. Ayer offers the following argument to show that moral responsibility requires causal determinism. Identify the premises and conclusion in this excerpt:

> Either it is an accident that I choose to act as I do or it is not. If it is an accident, then it is merely a matter of chance that I did not choose otherwise; and if it is merely a matter of chance that I did not choose otherwise, it is surely irrational to hold me morally responsible for choosing as I did. But if it is not an accident that I choose to do one thing rather than another, then presumably there is some causal explanation of my choice: and in that case we are led back to determinism. (page 114)

III. Ayer considers and rejects the following argument for the incompatibility of freedom and causal determinism. Identify the premises and conclusion in this excerpt:

> Nevertheless, it may be said, if the postulate of determinism is valid, then the future can be explained in terms of the past: and this means that if one knew enough about the past one would be able to predict

the future. But in that case what will happen in the future is already decided. And how then can I be said to be free? What is going to happen is going to happen and nothing I do can prevent it. If the determinist is right, I am the helpless prisoner of fate. (page 117)

IV. Consider the following objection to Ayer's account of freedom. Identify the premises and conclusion.

Suppose that we are created by a powerful being who at the moment of creation predetermines all of the thoughts, including all the desires and choices, we will ever have. Since they are all predetermined in this way, our choices and the resulting actions are beyond our control, and we therefore, cannot be responsible for them. Since Ayer's account of freedom implies that we can be responsible for our actions, his account must be mistaken.

8.3 HUMAN FREEDOM AND THE SELF

RODERICK M. CHISHOLM (1964)

Roderick Chisholm was a professor of philosophy at Brown University, well known for his original and significant contributions to work in epistemology, metaphysics, and ethics. In this essay, he defends a version of **Libertarianism**, the view that some of our choices are not caused by other events, so that we sometimes act freely and are responsible for our actions. Chisholm opens his defense with a statement of the problem of human freedom. He then offers a solution to the problem by distinguishing between two types of causation, **transeunt causation** and **immanent causation**. He ends his essay by considering the implications of his solution for our ability to understand and explain human behavior.

Reading Questions:

1. Chisholm opens his essay with a statement of the Metaphysical Problem of Human Freedom; state the problem in your own terms.

2. In section 5 of his essay, Chisholm writes:

   We must not say that every event involved in the act is caused by some other event; and we must not say that the act is something that is not caused at all. The possibility that remains, therefore, is this: We should say that at least one of the events that are involved in the act is caused, not by any other events but by something else instead. And this something else can only be the agent—the man. (page 122)

   Why does Chisholm set aside each of the first two alternatives he considers here? Why don't his reasons for setting aside those alternatives apply to his proposal that the cause of one of the events involved in an action is the agent?

3. What is the difference between transeunt causation and immanent causation?

4. Suppose you want to pick up a pen, you decide to do so, you extend your arm, and you pick it up. Suppose too that you do this freely. What forms of causation are involved in each step in the sequence between your initial desire and your action, according to Chisholm?

5. Chisholm says that when we act, our desires, intentions, and the like influence our action without necessitating it. What is the difference between influencing and necessitating?

'A staff moves a stone, and is moved by a hand, which is moved by a man.' Aristotle, *Physics*, 256a.

1. The metaphysical problem of human freedom might be summarized in the following way: Human beings are responsible agents; but this fact appears to conflict with a deterministic view of human action (the view that every event that is involved in an act is caused by some other event): and it *also* appears to conflict with an indeterministic view of human action (the view that the act, or some event that is essential to the act, is not caused at all). To solve the problem, I believe, we must make somewhat far-reaching assumptions about the self or the agent—about the man who performs the act.

Perhaps it is needless to remark that, in all likelihood, it is impossible to say anything significant about this ancient problem that has not been said before.[1]

Responsibility Requires Ability to Do Otherwise

2. Let us consider some deed, or misdeed, that may be attributed to a responsible agent: one man, say, shot another. If the man *was* responsible for what he did, then, I would urge, what was to happen at the time of the shooting was something that was entirely up to the man himself. There was a moment at which it was true, both that he could have fired the shot and also that he could have refrained from firing it. And if this is so, then, even though he did fire it, he could have done something else instead. (He didn't find himself firing the shot 'against his will', as we say.) *I think we can say, more generally, then, that if a man is responsible for a certain event or a certain state of affairs (in our example, the shooting of another man), then that event or state of affairs was brought about by some act of his, and the act was something that was in his power either to perform or not to perform.*

But now if the act which he *did* perform was an act that was also in his power *not* to perform, then it could not have been caused or determined by any event that was not itself within his power either to bring about or not to bring about. For example, if what we say he did was really something that was brought about by a second man, one who forced his hand upon the trigger, say, or who by means of hypnosis, compelled him to perform the act, then since the act was caused by the *second* man it was nothing that was within the power of the *first* man to prevent. And precisely the same thing is true, I think, if instead of referring to a second man who compelled the first one, we speak instead of the *desires* and *beliefs* which the first man happens to have had. For if what we say he did was really something that was brought about by his own beliefs and desires, if these beliefs and desires in the particular situation in which he happened to have found himself caused him to do just what it was that we say he did do, then, since *they* caused it *he* was unable to do anything other than just what it was that he did do. It makes no difference whether the cause of the deed was internal or external; if the cause was some state or event for which the man himself was not responsible, then he was not responsible for what we have been mistakenly calling his act. If a flood caused the poorly constructed dam, to break, then, given the flood and the constitution of the dam. the break, we may say, *had* to occur and nothing could have happened in its place. And if the flood of desire caused the weak-willed man to give in, then he, too, had to do just what it was that he did do and he was no more responsible than was the dam for the results that followed. (It is true, of course, that if the man is responsible for the beliefs and desires that he happens to have, then he may also be responsible for the things they lead him to do. But the question now becomes: *is* he responsible for the beliefs and desires he happens to have? If he is, then there was a time when they were within his power either to acquire or not to acquire, and we are left, therefore, with our general point.)

One may object: But surely if there were such a thing as a man who is really *good*, then he would be responsible for things that he would do: yet, he would be unable to do anything other than just what it is that he does do, since, being good, he will always choose to do what is best. The answer, I think, is suggested by a comment that Thomas Reid makes upon an ancient author. The author had said of Cato, 'He was good because he could not be otherwise', and Reid observes: 'This saying, if understood literally and strictly, is not the praise of Cato, but of his constitution, which was no more the work of Cato than his existence'.[2] If Cato was himself responsible for the good things that he did, then Cato, as Reid suggests, was such that, although he had the power to do what was not good, he exercised his power only for that which was good.

All of this, if it is true, may give a certain amount of comfort to those who are tender-minded. But we should remind them that it also conflicts with a familiar view about the nature of God—with the view that St. Thomas Aquinas expresses by saying that 'every movement both of the will and of nature proceeds from God as the Prime Mover'.[3] If the act of the sinner *did* proceed from God as the Prime Mover, then God was in the position of the second agent we just discussed—the man who forced the trigger finger, or the hypnotist—and the sinner, so-called, was *not* responsible for what he did. (This may be a bold assertion, in view of the history of western theology, but I must say that I have never encountered a single good reason for denying it.)

There is one standard objection to all of this and we should consider it briefly.

Responsibility Conflicts with Determinism

3. The objection takes the form of a stratagem—one designed to show that determinism (and divine providence) is consistent with human responsibility. The stratagem is one that was used by Jonathan Edwards and by many philosophers in the present century, most notably, G. E. Moore.[4]

One proceeds as follows: The expression

(a) He could have done otherwise, it is argued, means no more nor less than
(b) If he had chosen to do otherwise, then he would have done otherwise.

(In place of 'chosen', one might say 'tried', 'set out', 'decided', 'undertaken', or 'willed'.) The truth of statement (b), it is then pointed out, is consistent with determinism (and with divine providence); for even if all of the man's actions were causally determined, the man could still be such that, *if* he had chosen otherwise, then he would have done otherwise. What the murderer saw, let us suppose, along with his beliefs and desires, *caused* him to fire the shot; yet he was such that *if,* just then, he had chosen or decided *not* to fire the shot, then he would not have fired it. All of this is certainly possible. Similarly, we could say, of the dam, that the flood caused it to break and also that the dam was such that, *if* there had been no flood or any similar pressure, then the dam would have remained intact. And therefore, the argument proceeds, if (b) is consistent with determinism, and if (a) and (b) say the same thing, then (a) is also consistent with determinism; hence we can say that the agent *could* have done otherwise even though he was caused to do what he did do; and therefore determinism and moral responsibility are compatible.

Is the argument sound? The conclusion follows from the premises, but the catch, I think, lies in the first premiss—the one saying that statement (a) tells us no more nor less than what statement (b) tells us. For (b), it would seem, could be true while (a) is false. That is to say, our man might be such that, if he had chosen to do otherwise, then he would have done otherwise, and yet *also* such that he could not have done otherwise. Suppose, after all, that our murderer could not have *chosen,* or could not have *decided,* to do otherwise. Then the fact that he happens also to be a man such that, if he had chosen not to shoot he would not have shot, would make no difference. For if he could *not* have chosen *not* to shoot, then he could not have done anything other than just what it was that he did do. In a word: from our statement (b) above ('If he had chosen to do otherwise, then he would have done otherwise'), we cannot make an inference to (a) above ('He could have done otherwise') unless we can also assert:

(c) He could have chosen to do otherwise.

And therefore, if we must reject this third statement (c), then, even though we may be justified in asserting (b), we are not justified in asserting (a). If the man could not have chosen to do otherwise, then he would not have done otherwise—*even if* he was such that, if he *had* chosen to do otherwise, then he would have done otherwise.

The stratagem in question, then, seems to me not to work, and *I would say, therefore, that the ascription of responsibility conflicts with a deterministic view of action.*

Responsibility Conflicts with Indeterminism

4. Perhaps there is less need to argue that the ascription of responsibility also conflicts with an indeterministic view of action—with the view that the act, or some event that is essential to the act, is not caused at all. *If the act—the firing of the shot—was not caused at all, if it was fortuitous or capricious, happening so to speak out of the blue, then, presumably, no one—and nothing—was responsible for the act.* Our conception of action, therefore, should be neither deterministic nor indeterministic. Is there any other possibility?

Agents As Causes

5. We must not say that every event involved in the act is caused by some other event; and we must not say that the act is something that is not caused at all. The possibility that remains, therefore, is this: *We should say that at least one of the events that are involved in the act is caused, not by any other events, but by something else instead. And this something else can only be the agent—the man.* If there is an event that is caused, not by other events, but by the man, then there are some events involved in the act that are not caused by other events. But if the event in question is caused by the man then it is caused and we are not committed to saying that there is something involved in the act that is not caused at all.

But this, of course, is a large consequence, implying something of considerable importance about the nature of the agent or the man.

6. If we consider only inanimate natural objects, we may say that causation, if it occurs, is a relation between *events* or *states of affairs*. The dam's breaking was an event that was caused by a set of other events—the dam being weak, the flood being strong, and so on.

But if a man is responsible for a particular deed, then, if what I have said is true, there is some event, or set of events, that is caused, *not* by other events or states of affairs, but by the agent, whatever he may be.

I shall borrow a pair of medieval terms, using them, perhaps, in a way that is slightly different from that for which they were originally intended. I shall say that when one event or state of affairs (or set of events or states of affairs) causes some other event or state of affairs, then we have an instance of **transeunt causation**. And I shall say that when an *agent*, as distinguished from an event, causes an event or state of affairs, then we have an instance of **immanent causation**.

The nature of what is intended by the expression 'immanent causation' may be illustrated by this sentence from Aristotle's *Physics:* 'Thus, a staff moves a stone, and is moved by a hand, which is moved by a man.' (VII, 5, 256a, 6–8) If the man was responsible, then we have in this illustration a number of instances of causation—most of them transeunt but at least one of them immanent. What the staff did to the stone was an instance of transeunt causation, and thus we may describe it as a relation between events: 'the motion of the staff caused the motion of the stone.' And similarly for what the hand did to the staff: 'the motion of the hand caused the motion of the staff'. And, as we know from physiology, there are still other events which caused the motion of the hand. Hence we need not introduce the agent at this particular point, as Aristotle does—we *need* not, though we *may. We may say that the hand was moved by the man, but we may also say that the motion of the hand was caused by the motion of certain muscles; and we may say that the motion of the muscles was caused by certain events that took place within the brain. But some event, and presumably one of those that took place within the brain, was caused by the agent and not by any other events.*

There are, of course, objections to this way of putting the matter; I shall consider the two that seem to me to be most important.

First Objection and Reply

7. One may object, firstly: 'If the *man* does anything, then, as Aristotle's remark suggests, what he does is to

move the *hand*. But he certainly does not *do* anything to his brain—he may not even know that he *has* a brain. And if he doesn't do anything to the brain, and if the motion of the hand was caused by something that happened within the brain, then there is no point in appealing to "immanent causation" as being something incompatible with "transeunt causation"—for the whole thing, after all, is a matter of causal relations among events or states of affairs.

The answer to this objection, I think, is this: It is true that the agent does not *do* anything with his brain, or to his brain, in the sense in which he *does* something with his hand and does something to the staff. But from this it does not follow that the agent was not the immanent cause of something that happened within his brain.

We should note a useful distinction that has been proposed by Professor A. I. Melden—namely, the distinction between 'making something A happen' and 'doing A'.[5] If I reach for the staff and pick it up, then one of the things that I *do* is just that—reach for the staff and pick it up. And if it is something that I do, then there is a very clear sense in which it may be said to be something that I know that I do. If you ask me, 'Are you doing something, or trying to do something, with the staff?', I will have no difficulty in finding an answer. But in doing something with the staff, I also make various things happen which are not in this same sense things that I do: I will make various air-particles move; I will free a number of blades of grass from the pressure that had been upon them: and I may cause a shadow to move from one place to another. If these are merely things that I make happen, as distinguished from things that I do, then I may know nothing whatever about them; I may not have the slightest idea that, in moving the staff, I am bringing about any such thing as the motion or air-particles, shadows, and blades of grass.

We may say, in answer to the first objection, therefore, that it is true that our agent does nothing to his brain or with his brain; but from this it does not follow that the agent is not the immanent cause of some event within his brain; for the brain event may be something which, like the motion of the air-particles, he made happen in picking up the staff. The only difference between the two cases is this: in each case, he made something happen when he picked up the staff; but in the one case—the motion of the air-particles or of the shadows—it was the motion of the staff that caused the event to happen; and in the other case—the event that took place in the brain—it was this event that caused the motion of the staff.

The point is, in a word, that whenever a man does something A, then (by 'immanent causation') he makes a certain cerebral event happen, and this cerebral event (by 'transeunt causation') makes A happen.

Second Objection and Reply

8. The second objection is more difficult and concerns the very concept of 'immanent causation', or causation by an agent, as this concept is to be interpreted here. The concept is subject to a difficulty which has long been associated with that of the prime mover unmoved. We have said that there must be some event A, presumably some cerebral event, which is caused not by any other event, but by the agent. Since A was not caused by any other event, then the agent himself cannot be said to have undergone any change or produced any other event (such as 'an act of will' or the like) which brought A about. But if, when the agent made A happen, there was no event involved other than A itself, no event which could be described as *making* A happen, what did the agent's causation consist of? What, for example, is the difference between A's just happening, and the agent's *causing* A to happen? We cannot attribute the difference to any event that took place within the agent. And so far as the event A itself is concerned, there would seem to be no discernible difference. Thus Aristotle said that the activity of the prime mover is nothing in addition to the motion that it produces, and Suarez said that 'the action is in reality nothing but the effect as it flows from the agent'.[6] Must we conclude, then, that there is no more to the man's action in causing event A than there is to the event A's happening by itself? Here we would seem to have a distinction without a difference—in which case we have failed to find a *via media* between a deterministic and an indeterministic view of action.

The only answer, I think, can be this: that the difference between the man's causing A, on the one hand, and the event A just happening, on the other, lies in the fact that, in the first case but not the second, the event A *was* caused and was caused by the man. There was a brain event A: the agent did, in fact, cause the brain event; but there was nothing that he did to cause it.

This answer may not entirely satisfy and it will be likely to provoke the following question: 'But what are you really *adding* to the assertion that A happened when you utter the words "The agent *caused* A to happen"?' As soon as we have put the question this way, we see, I think, that whatever difficulty we may have encountered is one that may be traced to the concept of causation generally—whether 'immanent' or 'transeunt'. The problem, in other words, is not a problem that is peculiar to our conception of human action, it is a problem that must be faced by anyone who makes use of the concept of causation at all; and therefore, I would say, it is a problem for everyone but the complete indeterminist.

For the problem, as we put it, referring just to 'immanent causation', or causation by an agent, was this: 'What is the difference between saying, of an event A, that A just happened and saying that someone caused A to happen?' The analogous problem, which holds for 'transeunt causation', or causation by an event, is this: 'What is the difference between saying, of two events A and B, that B happened and then A happened, and saying that B's happening was the *cause* of A's happening?' And the only answer that one can give is this—that in the one case the agent was the cause of A's happening and in the other case event B was the cause of A's happening. The nature of transeunt causation is no more clear than is that of immanent causation.

9. But we may plausibly say—and there is a respectable philosophical tradition to which we may appeal—that the notion of immanent causation, or causation by an agent, is in fact more clear than that of transeunt causation, or causation by an event, and that it is only by understanding our own causal efficacy, as agents, that we can grasp the concept of *cause* at all. Hume may be said to have shown that we do not derive the concept of *cause* from what we perceive of external things. How, then, do we derive it? The most plausible suggestion, it seems to me, is that of Reid, once again: namely that 'the conception of an efficient cause may very probably be derived from

the experience we have had . . . of our own power to produce certain effects'.[7] If we did not understand the concept of immanent causation, we would not understand that of transeunt causation.

10. It may have been noted that I have avoided the term 'free will' in all of this. For even if there is such a faculty as 'the will', which somehow sets our acts agoing, the question of freedom, as John Locke said, is not the question '*whether the will be free*'; it is the question '*whether a man be free*'.[8] For if there is a 'will', as a moving faculty, the question is whether the man is free to will to do these things that he does will to do—and also whether he is free *not* to will any of those things that he does will to do, and, again, whether he is free to will any of those things that he does not will to do. Jonathan Edwards tried to restrict himself to the question—'Is the man free to do what it is that he wills?'—but the answer to this question will not tell us whether the man is responsible for what it is that he *does* will to do. Using still another pair of medieval terms, we may say that the metaphysical problem of freedom does not concern the *actus imperatus;* it does not concern the question whether we are free to accomplish whatever it is that we will or set out to do; it concerns the *actus elicitus,* the question whether we are free to will or to set out to do those things that we do will or set out to do.

11. If we are responsible, and if what I have been trying to say is true, then we have a prerogative which some would attribute only to God: each of us, when we act, is a prime mover unmoved. In doing what we do, we cause certain events to happen, and nothing—or no one—causes us to cause those events to happen.

No Strict Science of Human Action

12. If we are thus prime movers unmoved and if our actions, or those for which we are responsible, are not causally determined, then they are not causally determined by our *desires*. And this means that the relation between what we want or what we desire, on the one hand, and what it is that we do, on the other, is not as simple as most philosophers would have it.

We may distinguish between what we might call the 'Hobbist approach' and what we might call the 'Kantian approach' to this question. The Hobbist approach is the one that is generally accepted at the present time, but the Kantian approach, I believe, is the one that is true. According to Hobbism, if we *know*, of some man, what his beliefs and desires happen to be and how strong they are, if we know what he feels certain of, what he desires more than anything else, and if we know the state of his body and what stimuli he is being subjected to, then we may *deduce*, logically, just what it is that he will do—or, more accurately, just what it is that he will try, set out, or undertake to do. Thus Professor Melden has said that 'the connection between wanting and doing is logical'.[9] But according to the Kantian approach to our problem, and this is the one that I would take, there is no such logical connection between wanting and doing, nor need there even be a causal connection. No set of statements about a man's desires, beliefs, and stimulus situation at any time implies any statement telling us what the man will try, set out, or undertake to do at that time. As Reid put it, though we may 'reason from men's motives to their actions and, in many cases, with great probability', we can never do so 'with absolute certainty'.[10]

This means that, in one very strict sense of the terms, there can be no science of man, if we think of science as a matter of finding out what laws happen to hold, and if the statement of a law tells us what kinds of events are caused by what other kinds of events, then there will be human actions which we cannot explain by subsuming them under any laws. We cannot say, 'It is causally necessary that, given such and such desires and beliefs, and being subject to such and such stimuli, the agent will do so and so'. For at times the agent, if he chooses, may rise above his desires and do something else instead.

But all of this is consistent with saying that, perhaps more often than not, our desires do exist under conditions such that those conditions necessitate us to act. And we may also say, with Leibniz, that at other times our desires may 'incline without necessitating'.

The Role of Desires

13. Leibniz's phrase presents us with our final philosophical problem. What does it mean to say that a desire, or a motive, might 'incline without necessitating'? There is a temptation, certainly, to say that 'to incline' means to cause and that 'not to necessitate' means not to cause, but obviously we cannot have it both ways.

Nor will Leibniz's own solution do. In his letter to Coste, he puts the problem as follows: 'When a choice is proposed, for example to go out or not to go out, it is a question whether, with all the circumstances, internal and external, motives, perceptions, dispositions, impressions, passions, inclinations taken together, I am still in a contingent state, or whether I am necessitated to make the choice, for example, to go out; that is to say, whether this proposition true and determined in fact, *In all these circumstances taken together I shall choose to go out*, is contingent or necessary.'[11] Leibniz's answer might be put as follows: in one sense of the terms 'necessary' and 'contingent', the proposition 'In all these circumstances taken together I shall choose to go out', may be said to be contingent and not necessary, and in another sense of these terms, it may be said to be necessary and not contingent. But the sense in which the proposition may be said to be contingent, according to Leibniz, is only this: there is no logical contradiction involved in denying the proposition. And the sense in which it may be said to be necessary is this: since 'nothing ever occurs without cause or determining reason', the proposition is causally necessary. 'Whenever all the circumstances taken together are such that the balance of deliberation is heavier on one side than on the other, it is certain and infallible that that is the side that is going to win out'. But if what we have been saying is true, the proposition 'In all these circumstances taken together I shall choose to go out', may be causally as well as logically contingent. Hence we must find another interpretation for Leibniz's statement that our motives and desires may incline us, or influence us, to choose without thereby necessitating us to choose.

Let us consider a public official who has some moral scruples but who also, as one says, could be had. Because of the scruples that he does have, he would never take any positive steps to receive a bribe—he would not actively solicit one. But his morality has its limits and he is also such that, if we were to confront him with a *fait accompli* or to let him see what is about to happen ($10,000 in cash is being deposited behind the garage), then he would succumb and be unable to resist. The general situation is a familiar one and this is one reason that people pray to be delivered from temptation. It also justifies Kant's remark: 'And how many there are who may have led a long blameless life, who are only *fortunate* in having escaped so many temptations'.[12] Our relation to the misdeed that we contemplate may not be a matter simply of being able to bring it about or not to bring it about. As St. Anselm noted, there are at least four possibilities. We may illustrate them by reference to our public official and the event which is his receiving the bribe, in the following way: (i) he may be able to bring the event about himself (*facere esse*), in which case he would actively cause himself to receive the bribe; (ii) he may be able to refrain from bringing it about himself (*non facere esse*), in which case he would not himself do anything to insure that he receive the bribe; (iii) he may be able to do something to prevent the event from occurring (*facere non esse*), in which case he would make sure that the $10,000 was *not* left behind the garage; or (iv) he may be unable to do anything to prevent the event from occurring (*non facere non esse*), in which case, though he may not solicit the bribe, he would allow himself to keep it.[13] We have envisaged our official as a man who can resist the temptation to (i) but cannot resist the temptation to (iv): he can refrain from bringing the event about himself, but he cannot bring himself to do anything to prevent it.

Let us think of 'inclination without necessitation', then, in such terms as these. First we may contrast the two propositions:

(1) He can resist the temptation to do something in order to make A happen;
(2) He can resist the temptation to allow A to happen (i.e. to do nothing to prevent A from happening).

We may suppose that the man has some desire to have A happen and thus has a motive for making A happen. His motive for making A happen, I suggest,

is one that *necessitates* provided that, because of the motive, (1) is false; he cannot resist the temptation to do something in order to make A happen. His motive for making A happen is one that *inclines* provided that, because of the motive, (2) is false; like our public official, he cannot bring himself to do anything to prevent A from happening. And therefore we can say that this motive for making A happen is one that *inclines but does not necessitate* provided that, because of the motive, (1) is true and (2) is false; he can resist the temptation to make it happen but he cannot resist the temptation to allow it to happen.

NOTES

1. The general position to be presented here is suggested in the following writings, among others: Aristotle. *Eudemian Ethics*, bk. ii ch. 6: *Nicomachean Ethics*. bk. iii. ch. 1-5: Thomas Reid. *Essays on the Active Powers of Man*: C. A. Campbell. 'Is "Free Will" a Pseudo-Problem?' *Mind*. 1951. 441–65: Roderick M. Chisholm. 'Responsibility and Avoidability', and Richard Taylor. 'Determination and the Theory of Agency', in *Determinism and Freedom at the Age of Modem Science*. ed. Sidney Hook (New York. 1958).
2. Thomas Reid. *Essays on the Active Powers of Man*. essay iv. ch. 4 (*Works*, 600).
3. *Summa Theologica*. First Part of the Second Part. qu. vi ('On the Voluntary and Involuntary").
4. Jonathan Edwards, *Freedom of the will* (New Haven, 1957); G. E. Moore, *Ethics* (Home University Library. 1912). ch. 6.
5. A. I. Melden. *Free Action* (London. 1961), especially ch. 3. Mr. Melden's own views, however, are quite the contrary of those that are proposed here.
6. Aristotle. *Physics*, bk. iii. ch. 3: Suarez, *Disputations Metaphysicae*, Disputation 18, s. 10.
7. Reid, *Works*:. 524.
8. *Essay concerning Human Understanding*, bk. ii, ch. 21.
9. Melden, 166.
10. Reid. *Works*, 608, 612.
11. Lettre a Mr. Coste de la Nècessité de la Contingence' (1707) in *Opera Philosophica*. ed. Erdmann. 447-9.
12. In (the Preface to the *Metaphysical Elements of Ethics*, in Kant's *Critique of Practical Reason and Other Works on the Theory of Ethics*, ed. T. K. Abbott (London. 1959). 303.
13. Cf. D. P. Henry. 'Saint Anselm's De '*Grammotica*''; *Philosophical Quarterly*, x (1960). 1-15–26. St. Anselm noted that (i) and (iii). respectively, may be thought of as forming the upper left and the upper right corners of a square of opposition, and (ii) and (iv) the lower left and the lower right.

DISCUSSION QUESTIONS:

1. Is there such a thing as immanent causation? Consider the following reply to Chisholm's proposal. To say we cause our choice is to say that some event that happens in us causes the event of our making a particular choice. Perhaps that event is a particularly strong desire to act in a certain way. Whatever it is, it is an event and the causation behind our choice is transeunt causation after all. How will Chisholm respond to this objection?

2. As Chisholm himself admits, his view implies that there can never be a science of human beings in terms of a series of general laws that explain how our actions are caused by prior events through transeunt causation. Yet, as we learn more and more about the brain we seem to be on the verge of developing just such a science. Is Chisholm's view at odds with progress in this area?

3. If, as Chisholm claims, the question, "Why did she do that?" cannot be correctly answered by presenting various mental states of the agent (e.g., her desires and intentions) that cause her choice and subsequent behavior, then how is it to be correctly answered?

4. If you have already read it, reconsider Strawson's essay, "The Impossibility of Moral Responsibility." Which aspects of Strawson's position does Chisholm accept? Which aspects does Chisholm reject? Where they disagree, who, if either, is correct?

5. If you have already read it, reconsider Ayer's essay "Freedom and Necessity." What aspects of Ayer's position does Chisholm accept? Which aspects does Chisholm reject? Where they disagree, who, if either, is correct?

Argument Reconstruction Exercises:

I. Chisholm considers and rejects the following sort of reasoning for the view that causal determinism and free will are compatible. Identify the premises and conclusion.

Moral responsibility requires free choice in the following way: We are morally responsible for an action only if we could have acted otherwise. But to say that we could have acted otherwise is just to say that we could have done something else, if we had chosen to do something else. So moral responsibility simply requires that we could have done something else if we had chosen to do something else. This sort of hypothetical ability (the ability to do something else if we had chosen to do something else) is consistent with our actual choice being causally determined.

Therefore, we can be free in the way required for moral responsibility, even if we are causally determined.

II. The following argument attempts to show that the freedom required for moral responsibility involves more than the hypothetical ability to have acted differently if one had chosen to act differently. Identify the premises and conclusion.

Suppose that Jones murders Smith and cannot help choosing to do so. Someone has gained control of his thoughts and has caused in him an irresistible desire to kill Smith. That desire has caused him to choose to kill Smith and his choice has caused his action. Jones lacks the freedom required to make him morally responsible for his action. Yet, he could have done something else if he had chosen to do something else. Therefore, the freedom required for moral responsibility demands more than the hypothetical ability to have done something else if one had decided to do something else.

III. The following argument offers an objection to Chisholm's theory: his view actually implies that we are not morally responsible for our actions. Identify the premises and conclusion.

If Chisholm's theory is true, then whenever we make a choice, the event that is our making that choice was not caused by any prior events. Yet if that event was not caused by any prior events, then nothing happened in the world to bring it about. But if nothing happened in the world to being it about, it was an accident after all. We are not responsible for accidents. If Chisholm's theory is correct, we are not responsible for our choices after all.

IV. The following argument offers an objection to Chisholm's theory: there is no such thing as immanent causation. Identify the premises and conclusion.

> Every physical event can be causally explained in terms of prior physical events and transeunt causation. It follows then that no physical event is caused by an agent through immanent causation. Our choices are simply physical events in our brain. Therefore, none of our choices is caused by us through immanent causation.

8.4 EXISTENTIALISM IS A HUMANISM

JEAN-PAUL SARTRE (1946)

Jean-Paul Sartre was a major French philosopher and literary figure, best known as a proponent of atheistic **existentialism**. In this essay, Sartre claims that, given the nonexistence of God, existence precedes essence for human beings. No given human nature, no set of defining traits, determines the manner of our existence. And so unlike a manufactured object like a paper-cutter, we exist without being defined by any concept. We are what we make of ourselves. We choose what we will be. Moreover, our freedom carries significant responsibility. We are responsible for ourselves and for everyone else. Our condition involves elements of anguish, forlornness, and despair.

Reading Questions:

1. Sartre contrasts a human being with a paper-cutter. For the paper-cutter, essence precedes existence; for the human, existence precedes essence. What difference does he have in mind?

2. Why, according to Sartre, does the fact that our existence precedes our essence make us responsible both for ourselves and everyone else?

3. What is anguish?

4. What is forlornness?

5. What is despair?

What is meant by the term *existentialism?*

Most people who use the word would be rather embarrassed if they had to explain it, since, now that the word is all the rage, even the work of a musician or painter is being called existentialist. A gossip columnist in *Clartés* signs himself *The Existentialist,* so that by this time the word has been so stretched and has taken on so broad a meaning, that it no longer means anything at all. It seems that for want of an advance-guard doctrine analogous to **surrealism** the kind of people who are eager for scandal and flurry turn to this philosophy which in other respects does not at all serve their purposes in this sphere.

Actually, it is the least scandalous, the most austere of doctrines. It is intended strictly for specialists and philosophers. Yet it can be defined easily. What complicates matters is that there are two kinds of existentialist; first, those who are

Christian, among whom I would include Jaspers and Gabriel Marcel, both Catholic; and on the other hand the atheistic existentialists, among whom I class Heidegger, and then the French existentialists and myself. What they have in common is that they think that existence precedes essence, or, if you prefer, that subjectivity must be the starting point.

Just what does that mean? Let us consider some object that is manufactured, for example, a book or a paper-cutter: here is an object which has been made by an artisan whose inspiration came from a concept. He referred to the concept of what a paper-cutter is and likewise to a known method of production, which is part of the concept, something which is, by and large, a routine. Thus, the paper-cutter is at once an object produced in a certain way and, on the other hand, one having a specific use; and one can not postulate a man who produces a paper-cutter but does not know what it is used for. Therefore, let us say that, for the paper-cutter, essence—that is, the ensemble of both the production routines and the properties which enable it to be both produced and defined—precedes existence. Thus, the presence of the paper-cutter or book in front of me is determined. Therefore, we have here a technical view of the world whereby it can be said that production precedes existence.

When we conceive God as the Creator, He is generally thought of as a superior sort of artisan. Whatever doctrine we may be considering, whether one like that of Descartes or that of Leibnitz, we always grant that will more or less follows understanding or, at the very least, accompanies it, and that when God creates He knows exactly what He is creating. Thus, the concept of man in the mind of God is comparable to the concept of paper-cutter in the mind of the manufacturer, and, following certain techniques and a conception, God produces man, just as the artisan, following a definition and a technique, makes a paper-cutter. Thus, the individual man is the realization of a certain concept in the divine intelligence.

In the eighteenth century, the atheism of the philosophers discarded the idea of God, but not so much for the notion that essence precedes existence. To a certain extent, this idea is found everywhere; we find it in Diderot, in Voltaire, and even in Kant. Man has a human nature; this human nature, which is the concept of the human, is found in all men, which means that each man is a particular example of a universal concept, man. In Kant, the result of this universality is that the wild-man, the natural man, as well as the bourgeois, are circumscribed by the same definition and have the same basic qualities. Thus, here too the essence of man precedes the historical existence that we find in nature.

Atheistic existentialism, which I represent, is more coherent. *It states that if God does not exist, there is at least one being in whom existence precedes essence, a being who exists before he can be defined by any concept, and that this being is man*, or, as Heidegger says, human reality. What is meant here by saying that existence precedes essence? It means that, first of all, man exists, turns up, appears on the scene, and, only afterwards, defines himself. If man, as the existentialist conceives him, is indefinable, it is because at first he is nothing. Only afterward will he be something, and he himself will have made what he will be. Thus, there is no human nature, since there is no God to conceive it. Not only is man what he conceives himself to be, but he is also only what he wills himself to be after this thrust toward existence.

Man is nothing else but what he makes of himself. Such is the first principle of existentialism. It is also what is called subjectivity, the name we are labeled with when charges are brought against us. But what do we mean by this, if not that man has a greater dignity than a stone or table? For we mean that man first exists, that is, that man first of all is the being who hurls himself toward a future and who is conscious of imagining himself as being in the future. Man is at the start a plan which is aware of itself, rather than a patch of moss, a piece of garbage, or a cauliflower; nothing exists prior to this plan; there is nothing in heaven; man will be what he will have planned to be. Not what he will want to be. Because by the word "will" we generally mean a conscious decision, which is subsequent to what we have already made of ourselves. I may want to belong to a political party, write a book, get married; but all that is only a manifestation of an earlier, more spontaneous choice that is called "will." But if existence really does precede essence, man is responsible for what he is. Thus, existentialism's first move is to make every man aware of what he is and to make the full responsibility of his existence rest on him. And when we say that a man is responsible for himself, we do not only mean that he is responsible for his own individuality, but that he is responsible for all men.

The word subjectivism has two meanings, and our opponents play on the two. Subjectivism means, on the one hand, that an individual chooses and makes himself; and, on the other, that it is impossible for man to transcend human subjectivity. The second of these is the essential meaning of existentialism. When we say that man chooses his own self, we mean that every one of us does likewise; but we also mean by that that in making this choice he also chooses all men. In fact, in creating the man that we want to be, there is not a single one of our acts which does not at the same time create an image of man as we think he ought to be. To choose to be this or that is to affirm at the same time the value of what we choose, because we can never choose evil. We always choose the good, and nothing can be good for us without being good for all.

If, on the other hand, existence precedes essence, and if we grant that we exist and fashion our image at one and the same time, the image is valid for everybody and for our whole age. Thus, our responsibility is much greater than we might have supposed, because it involves all mankind. If I am a workingman and choose to join a Christian trade-union rather than be a communist, and if by being a member I want to show that the best thing for man is resignation, that the kingdom of man is not of this world, I am not only involving my own case—I want to be resigned for everyone. As a result, my action has involved all humanity. To take a more individual matter, if I want to marry, to have children; even if this marriage depends solely on my own circumstances or passion or wish, I am involving all humanity in monogamy and not merely myself. *Therefore, I am responsible for myself and for everyone else. I am creating a certain image of man of my own choosing. In choosing myself, I choose man.*

This helps us understand what the actual content is of such rather grandiloquent words as anguish, forlorness, despair. As you will see, it's all quite simple.

First, what is meant by anguish? The existentialists say at once that man is anguish. What that means is this: the man who involves himself and who realizes that he is not only the person he chooses to be, but also a lawmaker who is, at the same time, choosing all mankind as well as himself, can not help escape the feeling of his total and deep responsibility. Of course, there are many people who are not anxious; but we claim that they are hiding their anxiety, that they are fleeing from it. Certainly, many people believe that when they do something, they themselves are the only ones involved, and when someone says to them, "What if everyone acted that way?" they shrug their shoulders and answer, "Everyone doesn't act that way." But really, one should always ask himself, "What would happen if everybody looked at things that way?" There is no escaping this disturbing thought except by a kind of double-dealing. A man who lies and makes excuses for himself by saying "not everybody does that," is someone with an uneasy conscience, because the act of lying implies that a universal value is conferred upon the lie.

Anguish is evident even when it conceals itself. This is the anguish that Kierkegaard called the anguish of Abraham. You know the story: an angel has ordered Abraham to sacrifice his son; if it really were an angel who has come and said, "You are Abraham, you shall sacrifice your son," everything would be all right. But everyone might first wonder, "Is it really an angel, and am I really Abraham? What proof do I have?"

There was a madwoman who had hallucinations; someone used to speak to her on the telephone and give her orders. Her doctor asked her, "Who is it who talks to you?" She answered, "He says it's God." What proof did she really have that it was God? If an angel comes to me, what proof is there that it's an angel? And if I hear voices, what proof is there that they come from heaven and not from hell, or from the subconscious, or a pathological condition? What proves that they are addressed to me? What proof is there that I have been appointed to impose my choice and my conception of man on humanity? I'll never find any proof or sign to convince me of that. If a voice addresses me, it is always for me to decide that this is the angel's voice; if I consider that such an act is a good one, it is I who will choose to say that it is good rather than bad.

Now, I'm not being singled out as an Abraham, and yet at every moment I'm obliged to perform exemplary acts. For every man, everything happens as if all mankind had its eyes fixed on him and were guiding itself by what he does. And every man ought to say to himself, "Am I really the kind of man who has the right to act in such a way that humanity might guide itself by my actions?" And if he does not say that to himself, he is masking his anguish.

There is no question here of the kind of anguish which would lead to quietism, to inaction. It is a matter of a simple sort of anguish that anybody who has had responsibilities is familiar with. For example, when a military officer takes the responsibility for an attack and sends a certain number of men to death, he chooses to do so, and in the main he alone makes the choice. Doubtless, orders come from above, but they are too broad; he interprets them and on this interpretation depend the lives of ten or fourteen or twenty men. In making a decision he can not help having a certain anguish. All leaders know this anguish. That doesn't keep them from acting; on the contrary, it is the very condition of their action. For it implies that they envisage a number of possibilities, and when they choose one, they realize that it has value only because it is chosen. We shall see that this kind of anguish, which is the kind that existentialism describes, is explained, in addition, by a direct responsibility to the other men whom it involves. It is not a curtain separating us from action, but is part of action itself.

When we speak of forlornness, a term Heidegger was fond of, we mean only that God does not exist and that we have to face all the consequences of this. The existentialist is strongly opposed to a certain kind of secular ethics which would like to abolish God with the least possible expense. About 1880, some French teachers tried to set up a secular ethics which went something like this: God is a useless and costly hypothesis; we are discarding it; but, meanwhile, in order for there to be an ethics, a society, a civilization, it is essential that certain values be taken seriously and that they be considered as having an *a priori* existence. It must be obligatory, *a priori*, to be honest, not to lie, not to beat your

wife, to have children, etc., etc. So we're going to try a little device which will make it possible to show that values exist all the same, inscribed in a heaven of ideas, though otherwise God does not exist. In other words—and this, I believe, is the tendency of everything called reformism in France—nothing will be changed if God does not exist. We shall find ourselves with the same norms of honesty, progress, and humanism, and we shall have made of God an outdated hypothesis which will peacefully die off by itself.

The existentialist, on the contrary, thinks it very distressing that God does not exist, because all possibility of finding values in a heaven of ideas disappears along with Him; there can no longer be an *a priori* Good, since there is no infinite and perfect consciousness to think it. Nowhere is it written that the Good exists, that we must be honest, that we must not lie; because the fact is we are on a plane where there are only men. Dostoevsky said, "If God didn't exist, everything would be possible." That is the very starting point of existentialism. Indeed, everything is permissible if God does not exist, and as a result man is forlorn, because neither within him nor without does he find anything to cling to. He can't start making excuses for himself.

If existence really does precede essence, there is no explaining things away by reference to a fixed and given human nature. In other words, there is no determinism, man is free, man is freedom. On the other hand, if God does not exist, we find no values or commands to turn to which legitimize our conduct. So, in the bright realm of values, we have no excuse behind us, nor justification before us. We are alone, with no excuses.

That is the idea I shall try to convey when I say that man is condemned to be free. Condemned, because he did not create himself, yet, in other respects is free; because, once thrown into the world, he is responsible for everything he does. The existentialist does not believe in the power of passion. He will never agree that a sweeping passion is a ravaging torrent which fatally leads a man to certain acts and is therefore an excuse. He thinks that man is responsible for his passion.

The existentialist does not think that man is going to help himself by finding in the world some omen by which to orient himself. Because he thinks that man will interpret the omen to suit himself. Therefore, he thinks that man, with no support and no aid, is condemned every moment to invent man. Ponge, in a very fine article, has said, "Man is the future of man." That's exactly it. But if it is taken to mean that this future is recorded in heaven, that God sees it, then it is false, because it would really no longer be a future. If it is taken to mean that, whatever a man may be, there is a future to be forged, a virgin future before him, then this remark is sound. But then we are forlorn.

To give you an example which will enable you to understand forlornness better, I shall cite the case of one of my students who came to see me under the following circumstances: his father was on bad terms with his mother, and, moreover, was inclined to be a collaborationist; his older brother had been killed in the German offensive of 1940, and the young man, with somewhat immature but generous feelings, wanted to avenge him. His mother lived alone with him, very much upset by the half-treason of her husband and the death of her older son; the boy was her only consolation.

The boy was faced with the choice of leaving for England and joining the Free French Forces—that is, leaving his mother behind—or remaining with his mother and helping her to carry on. He was fully aware that the woman lived only for him and that his going-off—and perhaps his death—would plunge her into despair. He was also aware that every act that he did for his mother's sake was a sure thing, in the sense that it was helping her to carry on, whereas every effort he made toward going off and fighting was an uncertain move which might run aground and prove completely useless; for example, on his way to England he might, while passing through Spain, be detained indefinitely in a Spanish camp; he might reach England or Algiers and be stuck in an office at a desk job. As a result, he was faced with two very different kinds of action: one, concrete, immediate, but concerning only one individual; the other concerned an incomparably vaster group, a national collectivity, but for that very reason was dubious, and might be interrupted en route. And, at the same time, he was wavering between two kinds of ethics. On the one hand, an ethics of sympathy, of personal devotion; on the other hand, a broader ethics, but

one whose efficacy was more dubious. He had to choose between the two.

Who could help him choose? Christian doctrine? No. Christian doctrine says, "Be charitable, love your neighbor, take the more rugged path, etc., etc." But which is the more rugged path? Whom should he love as a brother? The fighting man or his mother? Which does the greater good, the vague act of fighting in a group, or the concrete one of helping a particular human being to go on living? Who can decide *a priori*? Nobody. No book of ethics can tell him. The Kantian ethics says, "Never treat any person as a means, but as an end." Very well, if I stay with my mother, I'll treat her as an end and not as a means; but by virtue of this very fact, I'm running the risk of treating the people around me who are fighting, as means; and, conversely, if I go to join those who are fighting, I'll be treating them as an end, and, by doing that, I run the risk of treating my mother as a means.

If values are vague, and if they are always too broad for the concrete and specific case that we are considering, the only thing left for us is to trust our instincts. That's what this young man tried to do; and when I saw him, he said, "In the end, feeling is what counts. I ought to choose whichever pushes me in one direction. If I feel that I love my mother enough to sacrifice everything else for her—my desire for vengeance, for action, for adventure—then I'll stay with her. If, on the contrary, I feel that my love for my mother isn't enough, I'll leave."

But how is the value of a feeling determined? What gives his feeling for his mother value? Precisely the fact that he remained with her. I may say that I like so-and-so well enough to sacrifice a certain amount of money for him, but I may say so only if I've done it. I may say "I love my mother well enough to remain with her" if I have remained with her. The only way to determine the value of this affection is, precisely, to perform an act which confirms and defines it. But, since I require this affection to justify my act, I find myself caught in a vicious circle.

On the other hand, Gide has well said that a mock feeling and a true feeling are almost indistinguishable; to decide that I love my mother and will remain with her, or to remain with her by putting on an act, amount somewhat to the same thing. In other words, the feeling is formed by the acts one performs; so, I can not refer to it in order to act upon it. Which means that I can neither seek within myself the true condition which will impel me to act, nor apply to a system of ethics for concepts which will permit me to act. You will say, "At least, he did go to a teacher for advice." But if you seek advice from a priest, for example, you have chosen this priest; you already knew, more or less, just about what advice he was going to give you. In other words, choosing your adviser is involving yourself. The proof of this is that if you are a Christian, you will say, "Consult a priest." But some priests are collaborating, some are just marking time, some are resisting. Which to choose? If the young man chooses a priest who is resisting or collaborating, he has already decided on the kind of advice he's going to get. Therefore, in coming to see me he knew the answer I was going to give him, and I had only one answer to give: "You're free, choose, that is, invent." No general ethics can show you what is to be done; there are no omens in the world. The Catholics will reply, "But there are." Granted—but, in any case, I myself choose the meaning they have.

When I was a prisoner, I knew a rather remarkable young man who was a Jesuit. He had entered the Jesuit order in the following way: he had had a number of very bad breaks; in childhood, his father died, leaving him in poverty, and he was a scholarship student at a religious institution where he was constantly made to feel that he was being kept out of charity; then, he failed to get any of the honors and distinctions that children like; later on, at about eighteen, he bungled a love affair; finally at twenty-two, he failed in military training, a childish enough matter, but it was the last straw.

This young fellow might well have felt that he had botched everything. It was a sign of something, but of what? He might have taken refuge in bitterness or despair. But he very wisely looked upon all this as a sign that he was not made for secular triumphs, and that only the triumphs of religion, holiness, and faith were open to him. He saw the hand of God in all this, and so he entered the order. Who can help seeing that he alone decided what the sign meant?

Some other interpretation might have been drawn from this series of set-backs; for example, that he might have done better to turn carpenter or

revolutionist. Therefore, he is fully responsible for the interpretation. Forlornness implies that we ourselves choose our being. Forlornness and anguish go together.

As for despair, the term has a very simple meaning. It means that we shall confine ourselves to reckoning only with what depends upon our will, or on the ensemble of probabilities which make our action possible. When we want something, we always have to reckon with probabilities. I may be counting on the arrival of a friend. The friend is coming by rail or street-car; this supposes that the train will arrive on schedule, or that the street-car will not jump the track. I am left in the realm of possibility; but possibilities are to be reckoned with only to the point where my action comports with the ensemble of these possibilities, and no further. The moment the possibilities I am considering are not rigorously involved by my action, I ought to disengage myself from them, because no God, no scheme, can adapt the world and its possibilities to my will. When Descartes said, "Conquer yourself rather than the world," he meant essentially the same thing.

The Marxists to whom I have spoken reply, "You can rely on the support of others in your action, which obviously has certain limits because you're not going to live forever. That means; rely on both what others are doing elsewhere to help you, in China, in Russia, and what they will do later on, after your death, to carry on the action and lead it to its fulfillment, which will be the revolution. You even *have* to rely upon that, otherwise you're immoral." I reply at once that I will always rely on fellow-fighters insofar as these comrades are involved with me in a common struggle, in the unity of a party or a group in which I can more or less make my weight felt; that is, one whose ranks I am in as a fighter and whose movements I am aware of at every moment. In such a situation, relying on the unity and will of the party is exactly like counting on the fact that the train will arrive on time or that the car won't jump the track. But, given that man is free and that there is no human nature for me to depend on, I can not count on men whom I do not know by relying on human goodness or man's concern for the good of society. I don't know what will become of the Russian revolution; I may make an example of it to the extent that at the present time it is apparent that the proletariat plays a part in Russia that it plays in no other nation. But I can't swear that this will inevitably lead to a triumph of the proletariat. I've got to limit myself to what I see.

Given that men are free and that tomorrow they will freely decide what man will be, I can not be sure that, after my death, fellow-fighters will carry on my work to bring it to its maximum perfection. Tomorrow, after my death, some men may decide to set up Fascism, and the others may be cowardly and muddled enough to let them do it. Fascism will then be the human reality, so much the worse for us.

Actually, things will be as man will have decided they are to be. Does that mean that I should abandon myself to quietism? No. First, I should involve myself; then, act on the old saw, "Nothing ventured, nothing gained." Nor does it mean that I shouldn't belong to a party, but rather that I shall have no illusions and shall do what I can. For example, suppose I ask myself, "Will socialization, as such, ever come about?" I know nothing about it. All I know is that I'm going to do everything in my power to bring it about. Beyond that, I can't count on anything. Quietism is the attitude of people who say, "Let others do what I can't do." The doctrine I am presenting is the very opposite of quietism, since it declares, 'There is no reality except in action." Moreover, it goes further, since it adds, "Man is nothing else than his plan; he exists only to the extent that he fulfills himself; he is therefore nothing else than the ensemble of his acts, nothing else than his life."

According to this, we can understand why our doctrine horrifies certain people. Because often the only way they can bear their wretchedness is to think, "Circumstances have been against me. What I've been and done doesn't show my true worth. To be sure, I've had no great love, no great friendship, but that's because I haven't met a man or woman who was worthy. The books I've written haven't been very good because I haven't had the proper leisure. I haven't had children to devote myself to because I didn't find a man with whom I could have spent my life. So there remains within me, unused and quite viable, a host of propensities, inclinations, possibilities, that one wouldn't guess from the mere series of things I've done."

Now, for the existentialist there is really no love other than one which manifests itself in a person's being in love. There is no genius other than one which is expressed in works of art; the genius of Proust is the sum of Proust's works; the genius of Racine is his series of tragedies. Outside of that, there is nothing. Why say that Racine could have written another tragedy, when he didn't write it? A man is involved in life, leaves his impress on it, and outside of that there is nothing. To be sure, this may seem a harsh thought to someone whose life hasn't been a success. But, on the other hand, it prompts people to understand that reality alone is what counts, that dreams, expectations, and hopes warrant no more than to define a man as a disappointed dream, as miscarried hopes, as vain expectations. In other words, to define him negatively and not positively. However, when we say, "You are nothing else than your life," that does not imply that the artist will be judged solely on the basis of his works of art; a thousand other things will contribute toward summing him up. *What we mean is that a man is nothing else than a series of undertakings, that he is the sum, the organization, the ensemble of the relationships which make up these undertakings.*

DISCUSSION QUESTIONS:

1. Sartre writes, "Thus, there is no human nature, since there is no God to conceive it," (page 129) He similarly writes that "there can no longer be an *a priori* Good, since there is no infinite and perfect consciousness to think it." (page 131) Is the existence of human nature dependent on the existence of God? What of the existence of objective values?

2. Sartre claims that each of us is responsible for our own individuality but also responsible for everyone else as well. In what way, if at all, are we responsible for our own individuality? Are we in any similar way responsible for everyone else as well?

3. Even as Sartre writes that we are responsible for what we are and that we choose our own self, he notes our limited ability to control or even predict the various factors on which the success of our plans often depend. To what extent can we be responsible for what we are, if we are limited in

our ability to control and predict the outcome of our choices?

4. Sartre writes that the human condition contains elements of anguish, forlornness, and despair. Is he right?

Argument Reconstruction Exercises:

I. Sartre offers the following argument about the nature of our choices. Identify its premises and conclusion.

> In fact, in creating the man that we want to be, there is not a single one of our acts which does not at the same time create an image of man as we think he ought to be. To choose to be this or that is to affirm at the same time the value of what we choose, because we can never choose evil. We always choose the good, and nothing can be good for us without being good for all. (page 130)

II. Sartre offers the following argument about the moral implications of God's nonexistence. Identify its premises and conclusion.

> The existentialist, on the contrary, thinks it is very distressing that God does not exist, because all possibility of finding values in a heaven of ideas disappears along with Him; there can no longer be an a priori Good, since there is no infinite and perfect consciousness to think it. Nowhere is it written that the Good exists, that we must be honest, that we must not lie; because the fact is we are on a plane where there are only men. (page 131)

III. Sartre writes the following about our attempts to define ourselves. Identify the premises and conclusion of his reasoning.

> The existentialist does not think that man is going to help himself by finding in the world some omen by which to orient himself. Because he thinks that man will interpret the omen to suit himself. Therefore, he thinks that man, with no support and no aid, is condemned every moment to invent man. (page 132)

IV. Sartre considers what his denial of God's existence and human nature means for our ability to know the outcome of our actions. Identify the premises and conclusion of his reasoning.

> [W]e shall confine ourselves to reckoning only with what depends upon our will, or on the ensemble of probabilities which make our action possible. When we want something, we always have to reckon with probabilities. . . . The moment the possibilities I am considering are not rigorously involved by my action, I ought to disengage myself from them, because no God, no scheme, can adapt the world and its possibilities to my will . . . [G]iven that man is free and that there is no human nature for me to depend on, I can not count on men whom I do not know by relying on human goodness or man's concern for the good of society. (pages 133–134)

CHAPTER 9

Why Be Moral?

On what principle, then, shall we any longer choose justice rather than the worst injustice?
— PLATO, *THE REPUBLIC*

INTRODUCTION

Suppose there was once an ancient sect, the Karmata, whose members developed a detailed code of conduct, the Code of the Karmata. The sect ceased to exist for reasons we don't understand, but recently we have been able to learn a bit about it, and I've just made one of the greatest discoveries of all: I've found the books that contain the Karmata Code. Impressed as I am by all things Karmata, I've decided to live my life by these rules, and I now urge you to do the same. I point out that a particular act you are contemplating is required by the Code and, on that basis, I encourage you to do it. I more generally encourage you to join me in mastering the details of the Code and living by it. You naturally respond with two questions. Noting that the particular act is indeed required by the Code of the Karmata, you ask why you should do it. You also ask why, more generally, you should adopt the Code as your guide for how to live.

In each question, you ask for reasons, a reason to follow the Karmata Code in the particular case at hand and a reason to adopt the Code as a general guide in your life. Each question is a perfectly appropriate response to my advice. There are other codes of conduct for you to choose. As a rational agent, it is appropriate for you to seek reasons for your choices. The relevance of the Karmata Code to your life hangs on your

questions. If there's no good answer to either, if you have no good reason to follow the Karmata Code in this case or in general, then the Code has no practical relevance for how you, as a rational being, live your life. It is just an interesting artifact of a long-gone culture.

Now consider a putatively analogous case. Suppose that our study of normative ethics is successful. We discover the correct moral code, a system of objectively true moral principles that tells us which acts are morally right, which ones morally wrong, and why. With the correct moral code in hand, I point out that it requires a particular act you are contemplating and, on that basis, I urge you to do it. I more generally encourage you to master the details of the correct moral code and to strive to live by it. You again respond with two questions. Noting that the particular act is indeed required by the correct moral code, you ask why you should do it. You also ask why, more generally, you should adopt the correct moral code as your guide for how to live.

Here, too, you are asking for reasons, a reason to follow the correct moral code in the particular case at hand and a reason to adopt that code as a general guide for your actions. Each question is again appropriate to ask. There are still other codes of conduct, including the Code of the Karmata, for you to choose instead, and as a rational agent, it is still appropriate for you to seek reasons for your choices. The relevance of the correct moral code—of the demands of morality—to your life hangs in the balance. If there's no good answer to either question, then the correct moral code may be an interesting bit of information for you to have, but it has no more practical relevance to how you, as a rational agent, live than the Code of the Karmata. Our search for the moral truth is a purely "academic" exercise from your perspective.

Many of us think that the demands of morality are relevant to our lives in a way in which other systems of rules are not. As Socrates tells us in Plato's *Republic*, in discussing the demands of morality, we are discussing no small matter but how we ought to live. We must then have some reason to be moral. There must be correct answers to the questions:

Given that a particular act is our moral duty, what reason do we have to do it?
Given that a set of moral rules is the correct moral code, what reason do we have to try to live in accord with it?

What are the answers?

One approach to the issue is to assume that all reasons are reasons of self-interest. If something is a reason for us to do something, then it must make reference to our interests. In asking the first question, we are asking why, given that a particular act is morally required of us, it is in our self-interest to do it. In asking the second question, we are asking why it is in our self-interest to guide our life by the correct moral code. If we understand the questions in this way, we can find some answers to them in the theory of **Ethical Egoism**, which Ayn Rand presents in her essay here. According to Ethical Egoism, the demands of morality simply are the demands of rational self-interest: An act is our moral obligation just in case it maximizes our own individual welfare. Our questions have straightforward answers. We should do our moral duty because it's good for us to do so. Guiding our life by the correct moral code is quite likely to be in our self-interest as well, for we will be trying in each case to honor our

moral obligations and that means trying in each case to do what is best for ourselves.

Therefore, if Ethical Egoism is true, our self-interest gives us at least one very good reason to do what morality requires in a particular case and to try to live a moral life generally. That reason may sometimes conflict with, and perhaps be outweighed by, reasons we have to put the demands of morality aside in particular cases or in general, but so long as the demands of morality are the demands of self-interest, they are not completely irrelevant to our rational behavior. The search for the moral truth is not a mere academic exercise.

A serious objection to the Ethical Egoist approach to our questions is that Ethical Egoism is itself deeply flawed as a moral theory, as James Rachels argues in his essay. According to Rachels, the standard arguments for Ethical Egoism are unsound, the demands of morality and self-interest often diverge in particular cases, and the Egoist's identification of the two is based on the fundamental misconception that our interests have some special weight over those of others in determining the morality of our conduct.

Rachels' concerns have their limits, however. If Ethical Egoism is mistaken as a general moral theory, there are particular cases in which our moral duty runs counter to our self-interest. Nonetheless, our self-interest may still be a powerful reason to live by the demands of morality in general. We may still be able to answer our second question in terms of a connection between living by the correct moral code and living so as to promote our self-interest. Gregory Kavka explores this possibility in his essay. He argues that, for most of us, the existence of external and internal sanctions for immoral behavior makes it in our self-interest to live morally. The external sanctions include various social penalties for immoral behavior; the internal sanctions include, on the one hand, the feelings of guilt and discomfort we experience at our moral failings and, on the other hand, the feelings of satisfaction we gain from doing what we believe to be morally correct. Kavka acknowledges an important limitation of his approach: Some people may lack the psychological dispositions required to support internal sanctions. Their wrongdoing may not make them feel guilty or uncomfortable; they may gain no satisfaction or pleasure from doing what is right. For such people, living by the demands of morality may not be in their self-interest, and, insofar as reasons are limited to self-interested considerations, they may not have a reason to do so. The discovery of the correct moral code may well be of little interest to them.

Perhaps, though, we can best answer our questions by expanding the set of reasons to be moral to include ones that go beyond self-interest. Not all reasons are reasons of self-interest. The likely effects of our conduct on others can also be reasons for us in deciding what to do. Nagel explores this option in his essay. Focusing on our first question, he rejects Ethical Egoism and argues that the considerations that determine our moral duty can themselves give us reason to do what morality requires. That an act will harm others is part of what gives us a moral obligation not to do it. It is also in itself a good reason for us not to do it. We need not equate moral obligation with our self-interest (or something else that we happen to value for that matter) to have reason to do what morality requires.

Expanding the set of reasons beyond those of self-interest does not completely end our quandary. Suppose an act is our moral duty because our failing to do it will harm others. If Nagel is right, the fact that the act is required to avoid harm to others is a reason for us to do it. Moral considerations are a source of reasons for action for us and so not merely academic. So far so good; the initial concern behind our two questions has been addressed. But now suppose that, contrary to Ethical Egoism, the act is not in our self-interest. We have a moral reason to do the act and a prudential reason not to do it. Are these reasons such that one might properly be said to outweigh or override the other; if so, by what standard is one reason the weightier of the two? Are the reasons incomparable, so that we have a moral reason to act one way, a prudential reason to act otherwise, neither outweighs or overrides the other, and that's all there is to it? If so, how are we to decide what to do? Even if moral considerations give us reasons for action and so are relevant to how we conduct our lives as rational agents, the question of how they relate to other reasons remains.

SUGGESTIONS FOR FURTHER READING

Baier, Kurt. *The Moral Point of View.* (Cornell University Press, 1958)

Frankena, William. *Ethics.* (Englewood Cliffs, NJ: Prentice Hall, 1973)

Gauthier, David, ed. *Morality and Rational Self-Interest.* (Englewood Cliffs, NJ: Prentice-Hall, 1970)

_____. *Morality By Agreement.* (Oxford: Oxford University Clarendon Press, 1986)

Hobbes, Thomas. *Leviathan*, Chapters Fourteen and Fifteen.

Melden, A. I. "Why Be Moral?" *Journal of Philosophy* 45 (1948), pp. 445–456.

Nagel, Thomas. *The View From Nowhere.* (New York: Oxford University Press, 1986)

Nielsen, Kai. "Is 'Why Should I Be Moral?' an Absurdity?" *Australasian Journal of Philosophy* 36 (1958), pp. 25–32.

Plato, *The Republic*, Book Two.

Shaver, Robert. "Egoism," *Stanford Encyclopedia of Philosophy*, http://plato.Stanford.edu.

Taylor, Richard. *Good and Evil.* (Amherst, NY: Prometheus Books, 2000)

9.1 THE VIRTUE OF SELFISHNESS

AYN RAND (1964)

Ayn Rand was born Alisa Rosenbaum in St. Petersburg, Russia. She emigrated to the United States in 1924, became a screenwriter in Hollywood, and ultimately wrote numerous plays, novels, and essays. She is perhaps best known for her novels, including *The Fountainhead* (1943) and *Atlas Shrugged* (1957). Rand developed a general philosophical position she termed "Objectivism." The central ethical component of Rand's Objectivism is **Ethical Egoism**, which she presents here. Ethical Egoism seems to provide an answer to the question, "Why be moral?" by conflating moral demands with prudential demands. We should act morally because it is in our own best interest to do so.

Reading Questions:

1. Rand rejects what she takes to be the meaning commonly ascribed to the word "selfishness" and offers a new meaning for it. What are these new and old meanings? How are they different?

2. Rand presents her ethical theory by contrasting it with a view she terms "Altruism." What are the main claims of Altruism? How does it differ from Ethical Egoism? How, if at all, is the question, "Why be moral?," to be answered from the perspective of Altruism?

3. What are Rand's reasons for rejecting Altruism?

4. Rand claims that there is an important difference between Ethical Egoism and the view of those she calls the "Nietzschean egoists;" what is the difference between these two views?

5. Rand distinguishes between our rational and our irrational desires; what does she take to determine the difference between the two?

The title of this [essay] may evoke the kind of question that I hear once in a while: "Why do you use the word 'selfishness' to denote virtuous qualities of character, when that word antagonizes so many people to whom it does not mean the things you mean?"

To those who ask it, my answer is: "For the reason that makes you afraid of it."

But there are others, who would not ask that question, sensing the moral cowardice it implies, yet who are unable to formulate my actual reason or to identify the profound moral issue involved. It is to them that I will give a more explicit answer.

It is not a mere semantic issue nor a matter of arbitrary choice. The meaning ascribed in popular usage to the word "selfishness" is not merely wrong: it represents a devastating intellectual "package-deal," which is responsible, more than any other single factor, for the arrested moral development of mankind.

In popular usage, the word "selfishness" is a synonym of evil; the image it conjures is of a murderous brute who tramples over piles of corpses to achieve his own ends, who cares for no living being and pursues nothing but the gratification of the mindless whims of any immediate moment.

Yet the exact meaning and dictionary definition of the word "selfishness" is: *concern with one's own interests.*

This concept does *not* include a moral evaluation; it does not tell us whether concern with one's own interests is good or evil; nor does it tell us what constitutes man's actual interests. It is the task of ethics to answer such questions.

The Ethics of Altruism

The ethics of altruism has created the image of the brute, as its answer, in order to make men accept two inhuman tenets: (a) that any concern with one's own interests is evil, regardless of what these interests might be, and (b) that the brute's activities are *in fact* to one's own interest (which altruism enjoins man to renounce for the sake of his neighbors). . . .

There are two moral questions which altruism lumps together into one "package-deal": (1) What are values? (2) Who should be the beneficiary of values? Altruism substitutes the second for the first; it evades the task of defining a code of moral values, thus leaving man, in fact, without moral guidance.

Altruism declares that any action taken for the benefit of others is good, and any action taken for one's own benefit is evil. Thus the *beneficiary* of an action is the only criterion of moral value—and so long as that beneficiary is anybody other than oneself, anything goes.

Hence the appalling immorality, the chronic injustice, the grotesque double standards, the insoluble conflicts and contradictions that have characterized human relationships and human societies throughout history, under all the variants of the altruist ethics.

Observe the indecency of what passes for moral judgements today. An industrialist who produces a fortune, and a gangster who robs a bank are regarded as equally immoral, since they both sought wealth for their own "selfish" benefit. A young man who gives up his career in order to support his parents and never rises beyond the rank of grocery clerk is regarded as morally superior to the young man who endures an excruciating struggle and achieves his personal ambition. A dictator is regarded as moral, since the unspeakable atrocities he committed were intended to benefit "the people," not himself.

Observe what this beneficiary-criterion of morality does to a man's life. The first thing he learns is that morality is his enemy: he has nothing to gain from it, he can only lose; self-inflicted loss, self-inflicted pain and the gray, debilitating pall of an incomprehensible duty is all that he can expect. He may hope that others might occasionally sacrifice themselves for his benefit, as he grudgingly sacrifices himself for theirs, but he knows that the relationship will bring mutual resentment, not pleasure—and that, morally, their pursuit of values will be like an exchange of unwanted, unchosen Christmas presents, which neither is morally permitted to buy for himself. Apart from such times as he manages to perform some act of self-sacrifice, he possesses no moral significance: morality takes no cognizance of him and has nothing to say to him for guidance in the crucial issues of his life; it is only his own personal, private, "selfish" life and, as such, it is regarded either as evil or, at best, *amoral*.

Since nature does not provide man with an automatic form of survival, since he has to support his life by his own effort, the doctrine that concern with one's own interests is evil means that man's desire to live is evil—that man's life, as such, is evil. No doctrine could be more evil than that.

Yet that is the meaning of altruism, implicit in such examples as the equation of an industrialist with a robber. There is a fundamental moral difference between a man who sees his self-interest in production and a man who sees it in robbery. The evil of a robber does *not* lie in the fact that he pursues his own interests, but in *what* he regards as to his own interest; *not* in the fact that he pursues his values, but in *what* he chose to value; *not* in the fact that he wants to live, but in the fact that he wants to live on a subhuman level. . . .

If it is true that what I mean by "selfishness" is not what is meant conventionally, then *this* is one of the worst indictments of altruism: it means that altruism *permits no concept* of a self-respecting, self-supporting man—a man who supports his life by his own effort and neither sacrifices himself nor others. It means that altruism permits no view of men except as sacrificial animals and profiteers-on-sacrifice, as victims and parasites—that it permits no concept of a benevolent co-existence among men—that it permits no concept of *justice*.

If you wonder about the reasons behind the ugly mixture of cynicism and guilt in which most men spend their lives, these are the reasons: cynicism, because they neither practice nor accept the altruist morality—guilt, because they dare not reject it.

The Objectivist Ethics

To rebel against so devastating an evil, one has to rebel against its basic premise. To redeem both man and morality, it is the concept of "*selfishness*" that one has to redeem.

The first step is to assert *man's right to a moral existence*—that is: to recognize his need of a moral code to guide the course and the fulfillment of his own life. . . .The reasons why man needs a moral code will tell you that the purpose of morality is to define man's proper values and interests, that *concern with his own interests* is the essence of a moral existence, and that *man must be the beneficiary of his own moral actions.*

Since all values have to be gained and/or kept by man's actions, any breach between actor and beneficiary necessitates an injustice: the sacrifice of some men to others, of the actors to the nonactors, of the moral to the immoral. Nothing could ever justify such a breach, and no one ever has.

The choice of the beneficiary of moral values is merely a preliminary or introductory issue in the field of morality. It is not a substitute for morality nor a criterion of moral value, as altruism has made it. Neither is it a moral *primary*: it has to be derived from and validated by the fundamental premises of a moral system.

The Objectivist ethics holds that the actor must always be the beneficiary of his action and that man must act for his own rational self-interest. But his right to do so is derived from his nature as man and from the function of moral values in human life—and, therefore, is applicable only in the context of a rational, objectively demonstrated and validated code of moral principles which define and determine his actual self-interest. It is not a license "to do as he pleases" and it is not applicable to the altruists' image of a "selfish" brute nor to any man motivated by irrational emotions, feelings, urges, wishes or whims.

This is said as a warning against the kind of "Nietzschean egoists" who, in fact, are a product of the altruist morality and represent the other side of the altruist coin: the men who believe that any action, regardless of its nature, is good if it is intended for one's own benefit. Just as the satisfaction of the irrational desires of others is *not* a criterion of moral value, neither is the satisfaction of one's own irrational desires. Morality is not a contest of whims. . . .

A similar type of error is committed by the man who declares that since man must be guided by his own independent judgment, any action he chooses to take is moral if *he* chooses it. One's own independent judgment is the *means* by which one must choose one's actions, but it is not a moral criterion nor a moral validation: only reference to a demonstrable principle can validate one's choices.

Just as man cannot survive by any random means, but must discover and practice the principles which his survival requires, so man's self-interest cannot be determined by blind desires or random whims, but must be discovered and achieved by the guidance of rational principles.

This is why the Objectivist ethics is a morality of *rational* self-interest—or of *rational selfishness*.

Since selfishness is "concern with one's own interests," the Objectivist ethics uses that concept in its exact and purest sense. It is not a concept that one can surrender to man's enemies, nor to the unthinking misconceptions, distortions, prejudices and fears of the ignorant and the irrational. The attack on "selfishness" is an attack on man's self-esteem; to surrender one, is to surrender the other.

DISCUSSION QUESTIONS:

1. Rand claims that Altruism is widely accepted in our society. Is she correct?
2. Rand distinguishes between Ethical Egoism (an obligatory act is one that best promotes our rational self-interest), Altruism (an obligatory act is one that best promotes not our interests, but those of others), and Nietzschean Egoism (an obligatory act is one that sacrifices the interests of others for our own). She takes Ethical Egoism to be the superior alternative of the three. Are there any other alternatives she has overlooked? How else might we understand the relation between whether an act is morally obligatory, whether it promotes our interests, and whether it promotes the interests of others?
3. Rand distinguishes between what we take to be in our interest (what we choose to value) and what really is in our interest (what really is valuable for us). Is there a difference? What are some examples of things that we sometimes take to be in our interest when they really are not? What determines whether something is really in our interest?
4. Rand takes our rational self-interest to be determined by our nature as human beings. What is human nature? What things does it determine to be in our rational self-interest and why?
5. Rand claims that a robber's mistake lies in what he takes to be in his self-interest; he chooses "to live on a subhuman level." In what way is a robber, who defines self-interest in terms of stealing the goods of others, choosing to live on a subhuman level?

Argument Reconstruction Exercises:

I. Rand presents the following criticisms of Altruism. Use them to construct an argument for the conclusion that Altruism is mistaken.

[A]ltruism permits no concept of a self-respecting, self-supporting man—a man who supports his life by his own effort and neither sacrifices himself nor others. It means that altruism permits no view of men except as sacrificial animals and profiteers-on-sacrifice, as victims and parasites—that it permits no concept of a benevolent co-existence among men—that it permits no concept of justice. (page 140)

II. Rand provides the following objection to Altruism. Identify the premises and conclusion in this excerpt.

Since nature does not provide man with an automatic form of survival, since he has to support his life by his own effort, the doctrine that concern with one's own interests is evil means that man's desire to live is evil—that man's life, as such, is evil. No doctrine could be more evil than that. (page 140)

III. Rand claims that Altruism has some clearly mistaken implications. Using her observations as premises, construct an argument for the conclusion that Altruism is false.

Observe the indecency of what passes for moral judgments today. An industrialist who produces a fortune, and a gangster who robs a bank are regarded as equally immoral, since they both sought wealth for their own "selfish" benefit. A young man who gives up his career in order to support his parents and never rises beyond the rank of grocery clerk is regarded as morally superior to the young man who endures an excruciating struggle and achieves his personal ambition. (page 140)

IV. A theory that is closely related to Ethical Egoism is Psychological Egoism, which claims that whenever we act our ultimate goal is to do what is best for ourselves. Identify the premises and conclusion in this argument for Ethical Egoism on the basis of Psychological Egoism.

Each of us is such that, whenever we act, our ultimate end is to do what is best for ourselves. That's just our nature. Every moral theory, other than Ethical Egoism, requires us to sometimes act in a way that is not best for ourselves and thus in a way that is contrary to our natural inclination. Any moral theory that requires us to act in a way contrary to our natural inclination is mistaken. Ethical Egoism then is the only correct moral theory.

9.2 ETHICAL EGOISM

JAMES RACHELS (1999)

James Rachels was a professor of philosophy at the University of Alabama-Birmingham. He is well known for his innovative and challenging work in both ethical theory and, especially, applied ethics. In this essay, he assesses the case for and against **Ethical Egoism**, the view that we act rightly so long as we do what is best for us. Rachels begins by considering and rejecting three arguments for Ethical Egoism. He then considers and rejects two standard arguments against the theory before accepting a third one. Rachels takes this last argument to reveal the fundamental flaw in Ethical Egoism: it would have us each assign greater importance to our own interests than to those of others, despite the fact that no factual difference between others and ourselves makes it appropriate for us to do so.

Reading Questions:

1. Which premise or premises does Rachels reject in setting aside each of the arguments for Ethical Egoism?

2. Which premise or premises does Rachels reject in setting aside each of the first two objections against Ethical Egoism?

3. Rachels bases his rejection of Ethical Egoism on this principle: We can justify treating people differently only if we can show that there is some factual difference between them that is relevant to justifying the difference in treatment. What support does Rachels offer for this principle?

Three Failed Arguments in Favor of Ethical Egoism

Ethical Egoism says we have no duty except to do what is best for ourselves . . . What reasons can be advanced to support this doctrine? Why should anyone think it is true? Unfortunately, the theory is asserted more often than it is argued for. Many of its supporters apparently think its truth is self-evident, so that arguments are not needed. When it is argued for, three lines of reasoning are most commonly used.

1. The first argument has several variations, each suggesting the same general point:

(a) Each of us is intimately familiar with our own individual wants and needs. Moreover, each of us is uniquely placed to pursue those wants and needs effectively. At the same time, we know the desires and needs of other people only imperfectly, and we are not well situated to pursue them. Therefore, it is reasonable to believe that if we set out to be "our brother's keeper," we would often bungle the job and end up doing more mischief than good.

(b) At the same time, the policy of "looking out for others" is an offensive intrusion into other people's privacy; it is essentially a policy of minding other people's business.

(c) Making other people the object of one's "charity" is degrading to them; it robs them of their individual dignity and self-respect. The offer of charity says, in effect, that they are not competent to care for themselves; and the statement is self-fulfilling. They cease to be self-reliant and become passively dependent on others. That is why the recipients of "charity" are so often resentful rather than appreciative.

What this adds up to is that the policy of "looking out for others" is self-defeating. If we want to do what is best for people, we should not adopt so-called altruistic policies of behavior. On the contrary, if each person looks after his or her own interests, it is more likely that everyone will be better off, in terms of both physical and emotional well-being. Thus Robert G. Olson says in his book *The Morality of Self-Interest* (1965), "The individual is most likely to contribute to social betterment by rationally pursuing his own best long-range interests." Or as Alexander Pope put it,

> Thus God and nature formed the general frame
> And bade self-love and social be the same.

It is possible to quarrel with this argument on a number of grounds. Of course no one favors bungling, butting in, or depriving people of their self-respect. But is that really what we are doing when we feed hungry children? Is the starving child in Ethiopia really harmed when we "intrude" into "her business" by supplying food? It hardly seems likely. Yet we can set this point aside, for considered as an argument for Ethical Egoism, this way of thinking has an even more serious defect.

The trouble is that it isn't really an argument for Ethical Egoism at all. The argument concludes that we should adopt certain policies of action; and on the surface they appear to be egoistic policies. However, the *reason* it is said we should adopt those policies is decidedly unegoistic. It is said that we should adopt those policies because doing so will promote the "betterment of society"—but according to Ethical Egoism, that is something we should not be concerned about. Spelled out fully, with everything laid on the table, the argument says:

(1) We ought to do whatever will best promote everyone's interests.
(2) The best way to promote everyone's interests is for each of us to adopt the policy of pursuing our own interests exclusively.
(3) Therefore, each of us should adopt the policy of pursuing our own interests exclusively.

If we accept this reasoning, then we are not ethical egoists at all. Even though we might end up behaving like egoists, our ultimate principle is one of beneficence—we are doing what we think will help everyone, not merely what we think will benefit ourselves. Rather than being egoists, we turn out to be altruists with a peculiar view of what in fact promotes the general welfare.

2. The second argument was put forward with some force by Ayn Rand, a writer little heeded by professional philosophers but who was enormously popular on college campuses during the 1960s and '70s. *Ethical Egoism, in her view, is the only ethical philosophy that respects the integrity of the individual human life.* She regarded the ethics of "altruism" as a totally destructive idea, both in society as a whole and in the lives of individuals taken in by it. Altruism, to her way of thinking, leads to a denial of the value of the individual. It says to a person: Your life is merely something that may be sacrificed. "If a man accepts the ethics of altruism," she writes, "his first concern is not how to live his life, but how to sacrifice it." Moreover, those who would promote this idea are beneath contempt—they are parasites who, rather than working to build and sustain their own lives, leech off those who do. She writes:

> Parasites, moochers, looters, brutes and thugs can be of no value to a human being—nor can he gain any benefit from living in a society geared to *their* needs, demands and protections, a society that treats him as a sacrificial animal and penalizes him for his virtues in order to reward *them* for their vices, which means: a society based on the ethics of altruism.

By "sacrificing one's life" Rand does not mean anything so dramatic as dying. A person's life consists (in part) of projects undertaken and goods earned and created. Thus to demand that a person abandon his projects or give up his goods is also a clear effort to "sacrifice his life."

Rand also suggests that there is a metaphysical basis for egoistic ethics. Somehow, it is the only ethics that takes seriously the *reality* of the individual person. She bemoans "the enormity of the extent to which altruism erodes men's capacity to grasp . . . the value of an individual life; it reveals a mind from which the reality of a human being has been wiped out."

What, then, of the starving people? It might be argued, in response, that Ethical Egoism "reveals a

mind from which the reality of a human being has been wiped out"—namely, the human being who is starving. Rand quotes with approval the evasive answer given by one of her followers: "Once, when Barbara Brandon was asked by a student: 'What will happen to the poor . . .?' she answered: 'If *you* want to help them, you will not be stopped.'"

All these remarks are, I think, part of one continuous argument that can be summarized like this:

(1) A person has only one life to live. If we value the individual—that is, if the individual has moral worth—then we must agree that this life is of supreme importance. After all, it is all one has, and all one is.

(2) The ethics of altruism regards the life of the individual as something one must be ready to sacrifice for the good of others.

(3) Therefore, the ethics of altruism does not take seriously the value of the human individual.

(4) Ethical Egoism, which allows each person to view his or her own life as being of ultimate value, does take the human individual seriously—it is, in fact, the only philosophy that does so.

(5) Thus, Ethical Egoism is the philosophy that ought to be accepted.

The problem with this argument, as you may already have noticed, is that it relies on picturing the alternatives in such an extreme way. As Ayn Rand describes it, "altruism" implies that one's own interests have *no* value, and that *any* demand by others calls for sacrificing them. Thus the "ethics of altruism" would appeal to no one, with the possible exception of certain monks. If this is the alternative, then any other view, including Ethical Egoism, will look good by comparison.

But that is hardly a fair picture of the choices. What we called the commonsense view stands somewhere between the two extremes. It says that one's own interests and the interests of others are both important and must be balanced against one another. Sometimes, when the balancing is done, it will turn out that one should act in the interests of others; at other times, it will turn out that one should take care for oneself. So even if we should reject the extreme "ethics of altruism," it does not follow that one must accept the other extreme of Ethical Egoism.

3. The third line of reasoning takes a somewhat different approach. Ethical Egoism is usually presented as a *revisionist* moral philosophy, that is, as a philosophy that says our commonsense moral views are mistaken and need to be changed. It is possible, however, to interpret Ethical Egoism in a much less radical way, as a theory that *accepts* commonsense morality and offers a surprising account of its basis.

The less radical interpretation goes as follows. Ordinary morality consists in obeying certain rules. We must avoid doing harm to others, speak the truth, keep our promises, and so on. At first glance, these duties appear to be very different from one another, having little in common. Yet from a theoretical point of view, we may wonder whether there is not some hidden unity underlying the hodgepodge of separate duties. Perhaps there is some small number of fundamental principles that explain all the rest, just as in physics there are basic principles that bring together and explain diverse phenomena. From a theoretical point of view, the smaller the number of basic principles, the better. Best of all would be one fundamental principle, from which all the rest could be derived. *Ethical Egoism, then, would be the theory that all our duties are ultimately derived from the one fundamental principle of self-interest.*

Understood in this way, Ethical Egoism is not such a radical doctrine. It does not challenge commonsense morality; it only tries to explain and systematize it. And it does a surprisingly successful job. It can provide plausible explanations of the duties mentioned above, and more:

The duty not to harm others: If we make a habit of doing things that are harmful to other people, people will not be reluctant to do things that harm us. We will be shunned and despised; others will not have us as friends and will not do us favors when we need them. If our offenses against others are serious enough, we may even end up in jail. Thus it is to our own advantage to avoid harming others.

The duty not to lie: If we lie to other people, we will suffer all the ill effects of a bad reputation. People will distrust us and avoid doing business with us. We will often need for people to be honest with us, but we can hardly expect them to feel much of an obligation to be honest with us if they know we have not been honest with them. Thus it is to our own advantage to be truthful.

The duty to keep our promises: It is to our own advantage to be able to enter into mutually beneficial arrangements with other people. To benefit from those arrangements, we need to be able to rely on others to keep their parts of the bargains—we need to be able to rely on them to keep their promises to us. But we can hardly expect others to keep their promises to us if we do not keep our promises to them. Therefore, from the point of view of self-interest, we should keep our promises.

Pursuing this line of reasoning, Thomas Hobbes suggested that the principle of Ethical Egoism leads to nothing less than the Golden Rule: We should "do unto others" because if we do, others will be more likely to "do unto us."

Does this argument succeed in establishing Ethical Egoism as a viable theory of morality? It is, in my opinion at least, the best try. But there are two serious objections to it. In the first place, the argument does not prove quite as much as it needs to prove. At best, it shows only that as a general rule it is to one's own advantage to avoid harming others. It does not show that this is *always* so. And it could not show that, for even though it may usually be to one's advantage to avoid harming others, sometimes it is not. Sometimes one might even *gain* from treating another person badly. In that case, the obligation not to harm the other person could not be derived from the principle of Ethical Egoism. Thus it appears that not all our moral obligations can be explained as derivable from self-interest.

But set that point aside. There is a still more fundamental problem. Suppose it is true that, say, contributing money for famine relief is somehow to one's own advantage. It does not follow that this is the only reason, or even the most basic reason, why doing so is a morally good thing. (For example, the most basic reason might be *in order to help the starving people*. The fact that doing so is also to one's own advantage might be only a secondary, less important, consideration.) A demonstration that one *could* derive this duty from self-interest does not prove that self-interest is the only reason one has this duty. Only if you accept an additional proposition—namely, that there is no reason for giving other than self-interest—will you find Ethical Egoism a plausible theory.

Three Arguments Against Ethical Egoism

Ethical Egoism has haunted 20th-century moral philosophy. It has not been a popular doctrine; the most important philosophers have rejected it outright. But it has never been very far from their minds. Although no thinker of consequence has defended it, almost everyone has felt it necessary to explain why he was rejecting it, as though the very possibility that it might be correct was hanging in the air, threatening to smother their other ideas. As the merits of the various "refutations" have been debated, philosophers have returned to it again and again.

The following three arguments are typical of the refutations proposed by contemporary philosophers.

1. In his book The Moral Point of View (1958), Kurt Baier argues that *Ethical Egoism cannot be correct because it cannot provide solutions for conflicts of interest.* We need moral rules, he says, only because our interests sometimes come into conflict. (If they never conflicted, then there would be no problems to solve and hence no need for the kind of guidance that morality provides.) But Ethical Egoism does not help to resolve conflicts of interest; it only exacerbates them. Baier argues for this by introducing a fanciful example:

> Let B and K be candidates for the presidency of a certain country and let it be granted that it is in the interest of either to be elected, but that only one can succeed. It would then be in the interest of B but against the interest of K if B were elected, and vice versa, and therefore in the interest of B but against the interest of K if K were liquidated, and vice versa. But from this it would follow that B ought to liquidate K, that it is wrong for B not to do so, that B has not "done his duty" until he has liquidated K; and vice versa. Similarly K, knowing that his own liquidation is in the interest of B and therefore, anticipating B's attempts to secure it, ought to take steps to foil B's endeavors. It would be wrong for him not to do so. He would "not have done his duty" until he had made sure of stopping B . . .

This is obviously absurd. For morality is designed to apply in just such cases, namely, those where interests conflict. But if the point of view of morality were that of self-interest, then there could never be moral solutions of conflicts of interest.

Does this argument prove that Ethical Egoism is unacceptable? It does, *if* the conception of morality to which it appeals is accepted. The argument assumes that an adequate morality must provide solutions for conflicts of interest in such a way that everyone concerned can live together harmoniously. The conflict between B and K, for example, should be resolved so that they would no longer be at odds with one another. (One would not then have a duty to do something that the other has a duty to prevent.) Ethical Egoism does not do that, and if you think an ethical theory should, then you will not find Ethical Egoism acceptable.

But a defender of Ethical Egoism might reply that he does not accept this conception of morality. For him, life is essentially a long series of conflicts in which each person is struggling to come out on top; and the principle he accepts—the principle of Ethical Egoism—simply urges each one to do his or her best to win. On this view, the moralist is not like a courtroom judge, who resolves disputes. Instead, he is like the Commissioner of Boxing, who urges each fighter to do his best. So the conflict between B and K will be "resolved" not by the application of an ethical theory but by one or the other of them winning the struggle. The egoist will not be embarrassed by this—on the contrary, he will think it no more than a realistic view of the nature of things.

2. *Some philosophers, including Baier, have leveled an even more serious charge against Ethical Egoism. They have argued that it is logically inconsistent—that is, they say it leads to logical contradictions.* If this is true, then Ethical Egoism is indeed a mistaken theory, for no theory can be true if it is self-contradictory.

Consider B and K again. As Baier explains their predicament, it is in B's interest to kill K, and obviously it is in K's interest to prevent it. But, Baier says,

> if K prevents B from liquidating him, his act must be said to be both wrong and not wrong—wrong because it is the prevention of what B ought to do,

his duty, and wrong for B not to do it; not wrong because it is what K ought to do, his duty, and wrong for K not to do it. But one and the same act (logically) cannot be both morally wrong and not morally wrong.

Now, does *this* argument prove that Ethical Egoism is unacceptable? At first glance it seems persuasive. However, it is a complicated argument, so we need to set it out with each step individually identified. Then we will be in a better position to evaluate it. Spelled out fully, it looks like this:

(1) Suppose it is each person's duty to do what is in his own best interests.
(2) It is in B's best interest to liquidate K.
(3) It is in K's best interest to prevent B from liquidating him.
(4) Therefore B's duty is to liquidate K, and K's duty is to prevent B from doing it.
(5) But it is wrong to prevent someone from doing his duty.
(6) Therefore it is wrong for K to prevent B from liquidating him.
(7) Therefore it is both wrong and not wrong for K to prevent B from liquidating him.
(8) But no act can be both wrong and not wrong; that is a self-contradiction.
(9) Therefore the assumption with which we started that it is each person's duty to do what is in his own best interests cannot be true.

When the argument is set out in this way, we can see its hidden flaw. The logical contradiction—that it is both wrong and not wrong for K to prevent B from liquidating him—does not follow simply from the principle of Ethical Egoism. It follows from that principle *and* the additional premise expressed in step (5), namely, that "it is wrong to prevent someone from doing his duty." Thus we are not compelled by the logic of the argument to reject Ethical Egoism. Instead, we could simply reject this additional premise, and the contradiction would be avoided. That is surely what the ethical egoist would do, for the ethical egoist would never say, without qualification, that it is always wrong to prevent someone from doing his duty. He would say, instead, that whether one ought to prevent someone from doing his duty

depends entirely on whether it would be to one's own advantage to do so. Regardless of whether we think this is a correct view, it is, at the very least, a consistent view, and so this attempt to convict the egoist of self-contradiction fails.

3. Finally, we come to the argument that I think comes closest to an outright refutation of Ethical Egoism. It is also the most interesting of the arguments, because it provides some insight into why the interests of other people *should* matter to us. But before presenting this argument, we need to look briefly at a general point about moral values. So let us set Ethical Egoism aside for a moment and consider this related matter.

There is a whole family of moral views that have this in common: They all involve dividing people into groups and saying that the interests of some groups count for more than the interests of other groups. Racism is the most conspicuous example; it involves dividing people into groups according to race and assigning greater importance to the interests of one race than to others. The practical result is that members of the preferred race are to be treated better than the others. Anti-Semitism works the same way, and so can nationalism. People in the grip of such views will think, in effect: "My race counts for more," or "Those who believe in my religion count for more," or "My country counts for more," and so on.

Can such views be defended? Those who accept them are usually not much interested in argument—racists, for example, rarely try to offer rational grounds for their beliefs. But suppose they did. What could they say?

There is a general principle that stands in the way of any such defense, namely: *We can justify treating people differently only if we can show that there is some factual difference between them that is relevant to justifying the difference in treatment.* For example, if one person is admitted to law school while another is rejected, this can be justified by pointing out that the first graduated from college with honors and scored well on the admissions test, while the second dropped out of college and never took the test. However, if both graduated with honors and did well on the entrance examination—in other words, if they are in all relevant respects equally well qualified—then it is merely arbitrary to admit one but not the other.

Can a racist point to any differences between, say, white people and black people that would justify treating them differently? In the past, racists have sometimes attempted to do this by picturing blacks as stupid, lacking in ambition, and the like. If this were true, then it might justify treating them differently, in at least some circumstances. (This is the deep purpose of racist stereotypes—to provide the "relevant differences" needed to justify differences in treatment.) But of course it is not true, and in fact there are no such general differences between the races. Thus racism is an arbitrary doctrine, in that it advocates treating people differently even though there are no differences between them to justify it.

Ethical Egoism is a moral theory of the same type. It advocates that each of us divide the world into two categories of people—ourselves and all the rest—and that we regard the interests of those in the first group as more important than the interests of those in the second group. But each of us can ask, what is the difference between myself and others that justifies placing myself in this special category? Am I more intelligent? Do I enjoy my life more? Are my accomplishments greater? Do I have needs or abilities that are so different from the needs or abilities of others? *What makes me so special?* Failing an answer, it turns out that Ethical Egoism is an arbitrary doctrine, in the same way that racism is arbitrary.

The argument, then, is this:

(1) Any moral doctrine that assigns greater importance to the interests of one group than to those of another is unacceptably arbitrary unless there is some difference between the members of the groups that justifies treating them differently.

(2) Ethical Egoism would have each person assign greater importance to his or her own interests than to the interests of others. But there is no general difference between oneself and others, to which each person can appeal, that justifies this difference in treatment.

(3) Therefore, Ethical Egoism is unacceptably arbitrary.

And this, in addition to arguing against Ethical Egoism, also sheds some light on the question of why we should care about others.

We should care about the interests of other people for the same reason we care about our own interests; for their needs and desires are comparable to our own. Consider, one last time, the starving people we could feed by giving up some of our luxuries. Why should we care about them? We care about ourselves, of course—if we were starving, we would go to almost any lengths to get food. But what is the difference between us and them? Does hunger affect them any less? Are they somehow less deserving than we? If we can find no relevant difference between us and them, then we must admit that if our needs should be met, so should theirs. *It is this realization, that we are on a par with one another, that is the deepest reason why our morality must include some recognition of the needs of others, and why, then, Ethical Egoism fails as a moral theory.*

DISCUSSION QUESTIONS:

1. Consider Ayn Rand's position in "The Virtue of Selfishness" (selection 9.1). Is the second argument Rachels considers for Ethical Egoism an accurate account of her position? Does her essay contain any other arguments for Ethical Egoism that Rachels does not consider? If so, do those arguments avoid Rachels' objections?

2. Rachels claims that the first two objections to Ethical Egoism involve assumptions that the Ethical Egoist need not accept. Should we, however, accept either of those assumptions?

3. Rachels does not consider one point that might be raised in favor of Ethical Egoism: that it explains why we should be moral. How might Rachels best respond to the claim that Ethical Egoism is correct because it alone can adequately answer the question, "Why be moral?"

4. Consider the principle that it is right to treat people differently only if some factual difference between them justifies the difference in treatment. Rachels presents several factual differences between people (e.g., differences in race and religious belief) that often fail to justify differences in treatment. What sorts of factual differences between people *do*

justify differences in treatment, and under what circumstances do they do so?

5. Rachels claims that there is no general difference between oneself and others to which each person can appeal to justify assigning greater importance to his or her interests than to the interests of others. Yet, we often seem to assign greater importance to our own interests (e.g., in deciding to spend money on our own momentary pleasures when it could be used to more significantly advance the welfare of those in need). Is Rachels' position at odds with how we often behave? If so, should we reject Rachels' position or change our behavior?

Argument Reconstruction Exercises:

I. Rachels does not consider the following argument for Ethical Egoism. Identify its premises and conclusion.

An adequate ethical theory will successfully answer the question, "Why be moral?" To answer that question successfully, a theory must imply that we always have a good reason to do what is right. We have a good reason to do something only if it is in our self-interest to do it. Therefore, an adequate ethical theory will imply that what is right is always in our self-interest.

II. Consider the following response to Rachels' final argument against Ethical Egoism. Identify the premises and conclusion.

Part of friendship is making a commitment to our friends to give their interests special consideration. This commitment is a factual difference between our friends and strangers that justifies us in assigning greater importance to our friends' interests than to those of others. I have made a similar commitment to myself, a commitment to assign greater interest to my own welfare than to anyone else's. Therefore, there is a factual difference between all others and myself that justifies me in assigning greater importance to my own interests than to anyone else's.

III. Consider the following response to Rachels' final argument against Ethical Egoism. Identify the premises and conclusion.

If no factual difference between ourselves and others justifies us in assigning greater importance to our own interests than to those of others, then no factual difference between our family and others justifies us in assigning greater importance to the interests of our family than to those of others. A factual difference between our family and others does justify us in assigning greater importance to the interests of our family. Therefore, a factual difference between all others and ourselves justifies us in assigning greater importance to our interests than to those of others.

IV. Identify the premises and conclusion of the following argument directed against defenders of Ethical Egoism.

If you point out to me that my act will seriously harm your interests, you give me a good reason to believe that my act is wrong. If the fact that my act will seriously harm your interests is a good reason for me to believe that it is wrong, then the fact that your act will harm my interests is a good reason for you to believe that your act is wrong. Yet, if your act's effects on my interests are relevant to whether it is right or wrong, then Ethical Egoism is mistaken.

9.3 RIGHT AND WRONG

THOMAS NAGEL (1987)

Thomas Nagel is University Professor of Philosophy and Law at New York University and is known for his work in ethics, political philosophy, and the philosophy of mind. He here considers how moral considerations can give us reasons for action. What reason do we have to refrain from any of the things usually thought to be wrong (lying, stealing, cheating), if we can get away with them? Rejecting an identification of the demands of morality with self-interest (see the readings on **Ethical Egoism**), Nagel argues that the interests of others, which help determine our moral duty, can be reasons for us to act one way rather than another. That an act will benefit or harm a particular person is not just good or bad from that person's point of view, but it is also good or bad from a more general perspective that every thinking person can understand. Nagel takes this to imply that we each have a reason to consider the interests of others in deciding what to do.

Reading Questions:

1. Nagel rejects attempts to generate reasons to be moral by connecting the demands of morality with something else the person already cares about (e.g., honoring God, maximizing one's self-interest). What are his three objections to this approach?

2. Nagel develops his position by considering the response contained in the rhetorical question, "How would you like it if someone did that to you?" How does Nagel understand the argument contained in the rhetorical question? How does his understanding of the argument lead him to the view that each of us has a reason to consider the welfare of others in deciding what to do?

3. Nagel outlines an apparent and unwelcome implication of his view as follows:

> But if something's being wrong is supposed to be a reason against doing it, and if your reasons for doing things depend on your motives and people's motives can vary greatly, then it looks as though there won't be a single right and wrong for everybody. There won't be a single right and wrong, because if people's basic motives differ, there won't be one basic standard of behavior that everyone has a reason to follow. (pages 153–154)

   He considers and rejects three ways of avoiding this implication that morality is not universal. What are the three ways? Which step in the above reasoning does each way reject? Why does Nagel think each is unsuccessful?

4. Nagel ends his discussion with the following observation: "The difficulty of justifying morality is not that there is only one human motive, but that there are so many." What is Nagel's point here?

Why Be Moral?

Suppose you work in a library, checking people's books as they leave, and a friend asks you to let him smuggle out a hard-to-find reference work that he wants to own.

You might hesitate to agree for various reasons. You might be afraid that he'll be caught, and that both you and he will then get into trouble. You might want the book to stay in the library so that you can consult it yourself.

But you may also think that what he proposes is wrong—that he shouldn't do it and you shouldn't help him. If you think that, what does it mean, and what, if anything, makes it true?

To say it's wrong is not just to say it's against the rules. There can be bad rules which prohibit what isn't wrong—like a law against criticizing the government. A rule can also be bad because it requires something that *is* wrong—like a law that requires racial segregation in hotels and restaurants. The ideas of wrong and right are different from the ideas of what is and is not against the rules. Otherwise they couldn't be used in the evaluation of rules as well as of actions.

If you think it would be wrong to help your friend steal the book, then you will feel uncomfortable about doing it: in some way you won't want to do it, even if you are also reluctant to refuse help to a friend. Where does the desire not to do it come from; what is its motive, the reason behind it?

There are various ways in which something can be wrong, but in this case, if you had to explain it, you'd probably say that it would be unfair to other users of the library who may be just as interested in the book as your friend is, but who consult it in the reference room, where anyone who needs it can find it. You may also feel that to let him take it would betray your employers, who are paying you precisely to keep this sort of thing from happening.

These thoughts have to do with effects on others—not necessarily effects on their feelings, since they may never find out about it, but some kind of damage nevertheless. In general, the thought that something is wrong depends on its impact not just on the person who does it but on other people. They wouldn't like it, and they'd object if they found out.

But suppose you try to explain all this to your friend, and he says, "I know the head librarian wouldn't like it if he found out, and probably some of the other users of the library would be unhappy to find the book gone, but who cares? I want the book; why should I care about them?"

The argument that it would be wrong is supposed to give him a reason not to do it. But if someone just doesn't care about other people, what reason does he have to refrain from doing any of the things usually thought to be wrong, if he can get away with it: what reason does he have not to kill, steal, lie, or hurt others? If he can get what he wants by doing such things, why shouldn't he? And if there's no reason why he shouldn't, in what sense is it wrong?

Morality and Self-Interest

Of course most people do care about others to some extent. But if someone doesn't care, most of us wouldn't conclude that he's exempt from morality. A person who kills someone just to steal his wallet,

without caring about the victim, is not automatically excused. The fact that he doesn't care doesn't make it all right: He *should* care. But *why* should he care?

There have been many attempts to answer this question. *One type of answer tries to identify something else that the person already cares about, and then connect morality to it.*

For example, some people believe that even if you can get away with awful crimes on this earth, and are not punished by the law or your fellow men, such acts are forbidden by God, who will punish you after death (and reward you if you didn't do wrong when you were tempted to). So even when it seems to be in your interest to do such a thing, it really isn't. Some people have even believed that if there is no God to back up moral requirements with the threat of punishment and the promise of reward, morality is an illusion: "If God does not exist, everything is permitted."

This is a rather crude version of the religious foundation for morality. A more appealing version might be that the motive for obeying God's commands is not fear but love. He loves you, and you should love Him, and should wish to obey His commands in order not to offend Him.

But however we interpret the religious motivation, there are three objections to this type of answer. First, plenty of people who don't believe in God still make judgments of right and wrong, and think no one should kill another for his wallet even if he can be sure to get away with it. Second, if God exists, and forbids what's wrong, that still isn't what *makes* it wrong. Murder is wrong in itself, and that's *why* God forbids it (if He does.) God couldn't make just any old thing wrong—like putting on your left sock before your right—simply by prohibiting it. If God would punish you for doing that it would be inadvisable to do it, but it wouldn't be wrong. Third, fear of punishment and hope of reward, and even love of God, seem not to be the right motives for morality. If you think it's wrong to kill, cheat, or steal, you should want to avoid doing such things because they are bad things to do to the victims, not just because you fear the consequences for yourself, or because you don't want to offend your Creator.

This third objection also applies to other explanations of the force of morality which appeal to the interests of the person who must act. For example, it may be said that you should treat others with consideration so that they'll do the same for you. This may be sound advice, but it is valid only so far as you think what you do will affect how others treat you. It's not a reason for doing the right thing if others won't find out about it, or against doing the wrong thing if you can get away with it (like being a hit and run driver).

The Universality of Moral Reasons

There is no substitute for a direct concern for other people as the basis of morality. But morality is supposed to apply to everyone: and can we assume that everyone has such a concern for others? Obviously not: some people are very selfish, and even those who are not selfish may care only about the people they know, and not about everyone. So where will we find a reason that everyone has not to hurt other people, even those they don't know?

Well, there's one general argument against hurting other people which can be given to anybody who understands English (or any other language), and which seems to show that he has some reason to care about others, even if in the end his selfish motives are so strong that he persists in treating other people badly anyway, It's an argument that I'm sure you've heard, and it goes like this: "How would you like it if someone did that to you?"

It's not easy to explain how this argument is supposed to work. Suppose you're about to steal someone else's umbrella as you leave a restaurant in a rainstorm, and a bystander says, "How would you like it if someone did that to you?" Why is it supposed to make you hesitate, or feel guilty?

Obviously the direct answer to the question is supposed to be, "I wouldn't like it at all!" But what's the next step? Suppose you were to say, "I wouldn't like it if someone did that to me. But luckily no one *is* doing it to me. I'm doing it to someone else, and I don't mind that at all!"

This answer misses the point of the question. When you are asked how you would like it if someone did that to you, you are supposed to think about all the feelings you would have if someone stole your umbrella. And that includes more than

just "not liking it"—as you wouldn't "like it" if you stubbed your toe on a rock. If someone stole your umbrella you'd *resent* it. You'd have feelings about the umbrella thief, not just about the loss of the umbrella. You'd think, "Where does he get off, taking my umbrella that I bought with my hard-earned money and that I had the foresight to bring after reading the weather report? Why didn't he bring his own umbrella?" and so forth.

When our own interests are threatened by the inconsiderate behavior of others, most of us find it easy to appreciate that those others have a reason to be more considerate. When you are hurt, you probably feel that other people should care about it: you don't think it's no concern of theirs, and that they have no reason to avoid hurting you. That is the feeling that the "How would you like it?" argument is supposed to arouse.

Because if you admit that you would *resent* it if someone else did to you what you are now doing to him, you are admitting that you think he would have a reason not to do it to you. And if you admit that, you have to consider what that reason is. It couldn't be just that it's *you* that he's hurting, of all the people in the world. There's no special reason for him not to steal *your* umbrella, as opposed to anyone else's. There's nothing so special about you. Whatever the reason is, it's a reason he would have against hurting anyone else in the same way. And it's a reason anyone else would have too, in a similar situation, against hurting you or anyone else.

But if it's a reason anyone would have not to hurt anyone else in this way, then it's a reason *you* have not to hurt someone else in this way (since *anyone* means *everyone*). Therefore it's a reason not to steal the other person's umbrella now.

This is a matter of simple consistency. *Once you admit that another person would have a reason not to harm you in similar circumstances, and once you admit that the reason he would have is very general and doesn't apply only to you, or to him, then to be consistent you have to admit that the same reason applies to you now.* You shouldn't steal the umbrella, and you ought to feel guilty if you do.

Someone could escape from this argument if, when he was asked, "How would you like it if someone did that to you?" he answered, "I wouldn't resent it at all. I wouldn't *like* it if someone stole my umbrella in a rainstorm, but I wouldn't think there was any reason for him to consider my feelings about it." But how many people could honestly give that answer? I think most people, unless they're crazy, would think that their own interests and harms matter, not only to themselves, but in a way that gives other people a reason to care about them too. We all think that when we suffer it is not just bad *for us,* but *bad, period.*

The basis of morality is a belief that good and harm to particular people (or animals) is good or bad not just from their point of view, but from a more general point of view, which every thinking person can understand. That means that each person has a reason to consider not only his own interests but the interests of others in deciding what to do. And it isn't enough if he is considerate only of some others—his family and friends, those he specially cares about. Of course he will care more about certain people, and also about himself. But he has some reason to consider the effect of what he does on the good or harm of everyone. If he's like most of us, that is what he thinks others should do with regard to him, even if they aren't friends of his.

Impartiality and Universality

Even if this is right, it is only a bare outline of the source of morality. It doesn't tell us in detail how we should consider the interests of others, or how we should weigh them against the special interest we all have in ourselves and the particular people close to us. It doesn't even tell us how much we should care about people in other countries in comparison with our fellow citizens. There are many disagreements among those who accept morality in general, about what in particular is right and what is wrong.

For instance: should you care about every other person as much as you care about yourself? Should you in other words love your neighbor as yourself (even if he isn't your neighbor)? Should you ask yourself, every time you go to a movie, whether the cost of the ticket could provide more happiness if you gave it to someone else, or donated the money to famine relief?

Very few people are so unselfish. And if someone were that impartial between himself and others, he would probably also feel that he should be just as impartial *among* other people. That would rule out caring more about his friends and relatives than he does about strangers. He might have special feelings about certain people who are close to him, but complete impartiality would mean that he won't *favor* them—if for example he has to choose between helping a friend or a stranger to avoid suffering, or between taking his children to a movie and donating the money to famine relief.

This degree of impartiality seems too much to ask of most people: someone who had it would be a kind of terrifying saint. But it's an important question in moral thought, how much impartiality we should try for. You are a particular person, but you are also able to recognize that you're just one person among many others, and no more important than they are, when looked at from outside. How much should that point of view influence you? You do matter somewhat from outside—otherwise you wouldn't think other people had any reason to care about what they did to you. But you don't matter as much from the outside as you matter to yourself, from the inside—since from the outside you don't matter any more than anybody else.

Not only is it unclear how impartial we should be; it's unclear what would make an answer to this question the right one. Is there a single correct way for everyone to strike the balance between what he cares about personally and what matters impartially? Or will the answer vary from person to person depending on the strength of their different motives?

This brings us to another big issue: Are right and wrong the same for everyone?

Morality is often thought to be universal. If something is wrong, it's supposed to be wrong for everybody; for instance if it's wrong to kill someone because you want to steal his wallet, then it's wrong whether you care about him or not. But if something's being wrong is supposed to be a reason against doing it, and if your reasons for doing things depend on your motives and people's motives can vary greatly, then it looks as though there won't be a single right and wrong for everybody. There won't be a single right and wrong, because if people's basic motives differ, there won't be one basic standard of behavior that everyone has a reason to follow.

There are three ways of dealing with this problem, none of them very satisfactory.

First, we could say that the same things *are* right and wrong for everybody, but that not everyone has a reason to do what's right and avoid what's wrong: only people with the right sort of "moral" motives—particularly a concern for others—have any reason to do what's right, for its own sake. This makes morality universal, but at the cost of draining it of its force. It's not clear what it amounts to to say that it would be wrong for someone to commit murder, but he has no reason not to do it.

Second, we could say that everyone has a reason to do what's right and avoid what's wrong, but that these reasons don't depend on people's actual motives. Rather they are reasons to change our motives if they aren't the right ones. This connects morality with reasons for action, but leaves it unclear what these universal reasons are which do not depend on motives that everyone actually has. What does it mean to say that a murderer had a reason not to do it, even though none of his actual motives or desires gave him such a reason?

Third, we could say that morality is not universal, and that what a person is morally required to do goes only as far as what he has a certain kind of reason to do, where the reason depends on how much he actually cares about other people in general. If he has strong moral motives, they will yield strong reasons and strong moral requirements. If his moral motives are weak or nonexistent, the moral requirements on him will likewise be weak or nonexistent. This may seem psychologically realistic, but it goes against the idea that the same moral rules apply to all of us, and not only to good people. . . .

Impartial Motivation

I should answer one possible objection to the whole idea of morality. You've probably heard it, said that the only reason anybody ever does anything is that it makes him feel good, or that not doing it will make him feel bad. If we are really motivated only by our own comfort, it is hopeless for morality to try to

appeal to a concern for others. On this view, even apparently moral conduct in which one person seems to sacrifice his own interests for the sake of others is really motivated by his concern for himself: he wants to avoid the guilt he'll feel if he doesn't do the "right" thing, or to experience the warm glow of self-congratulation he'll get if he does. But those who don't have these feelings have no motive to be "moral."

Now it's true that when people do what they think they ought to do, they often feel good about it: similarly if they do what they think is wrong, they often feel bad. But that doesn't mean that these feelings are their motives for acting. In many cases the feelings result from motives which also produce the action. You wouldn't feel good about doing the right thing unless you thought there was some other reason to do it, besides the fact that it would make you feel good. And you wouldn't feel guilty about doing the wrong thing unless you thought that there was some other reason not to do it, besides the fact that it made you feel guilty: something which made it *right* to feel guilty. At least that's how things should be. It's true that some people feel irrational guilt about things they don't have any independent reason to think are wrong—but that's not the way morality is supposed to work.

In a sense, people do what they want to do. But their reasons and motives for wanting to do things vary enormously. I may "want" to give someone my wallet only because he has a gun pointed at my head and threatens to kill me if I don't. And I may want to jump into an icy river to save a drowning stranger not because it will make me feel good, but because I recognize that his life is important, just as mine is, and I recognize that I have a reason to save his life just as he would have a reason to save mine if our positions were reversed.

Moral argument tries to appeal to a capacity for impartial motivation which is supposed to be present in all of us. Unfortunately it may be deeply buried, and in some cases it may not be present at all. In any case it has to compete with powerful selfish motives, and other personal motives that may not be so selfish, in its bid for control of our behavior. The difficulty of justifying morality is not that there is only one human motive, but that there are so many.

DISCUSSION QUESTIONS:

1. One strategy for explaining how morality is a source of reasons for action is to assume that all our reasons for action must be based in our self-interest and then to understand the demands of morality in terms of self-interest. Nagel's approach is the opposite. He understands the demands of morality as extending beyond our self-interest to include the welfare of others, and he argues that our reasons for action include considerations of the welfare of others. In pursuing this strategy, Nagel faces the question of why someone else's welfare is a reason for us to act one way or another. How does he answer it? Is his answer successful?

2. Consider Nagel's discussion of impartiality. Is each of the following true: (i) that an act will harm others with whom we have no relationship is a reason for us not to do it; (ii) that an act will harm our friends is an even stronger reason for us not to do it? If (i) and (ii) are both true and the amount of harm to be done in each case is the same, what makes the harm to strangers a weaker reason not to do the act than the harm to friends?

3. Nagel rejects the psychological claim that "the only reason anybody ever does anything is that it makes him feel good, or that not doing it will make him feel bad." What is his basis for rejecting this claim? Is he correct?

4. In asking the question, "Why be moral?" we may be wondering how the moral character of an action can give us a reason to do it or not do it. We may also be wondering whether and how any reasons that stem from the moral character of an action can outweigh any competing reasons that stem from other sources (e.g. our self-interest, our personal goals). Has Nagel provided an answer to this second question?

Argument Reconstruction Exercises:

I. In explaining our reason to act as morality requires, Nagel appeals to the rhetorical question, "How would you like it if someone did that to you?" One way to understand the argument contained in the question is the following. Identify the premises and the conclusion.

Suppose you are about to do something that is wrong because it involves treating someone badly (e.g., stealing his umbrella). Others have a reason not to treat you in that same way (steal your umbrella). Their reason not to treat you in that way is that it is bad for you. Yet, there is nothing special about you or them. So, everyone has this same reason not to treat anyone in this way, that it is bad for the person so treated. In particular, you now have a reason not to treat the person at hand in this way. Your reason is that your behavior is bad for him. That's why you should not do what's wrong in this case.

II. Nagel considers the following problem for attempts to explain the relation between moral considerations and reasons for action. Identify the premises and conclusion in the excerpt.

But if something's being wrong is supposed to be a reason against doing it, and if your reasons for doing things depend on your motives and people's motives can very greatly, then it looks as though there won't be a single right and wrong for everybody. There won't be a single right and wrong, because if people's basic motives differ, there won't be one basic standard of behavior that everyone has a reason to follow. (pages 153–154)

III. Nagel considers the following response to his position. Identify the premises and conclusion in this excerpt.

I should answer one possible objection to the whole idea of morality. You've probably heard it said that the only reason anybody ever does anything is that it makes him feel good, or that not doing it will make him feel bad. If we are really motivated only by our own comfort, it is hopeless for morality to appeal to a concern for others. (page 154)

IV. Nagel offers the following argument to show that we are motivated by more than our self-interest. Identify the premises and conclusion in this excerpt.

Now it's true that when people do what they think they ought to do, they often feel good about it: similarly if they do what they think is wrong, they often feel bad. But that doesn't mean that these feelings are their motives for acting. In many cases, the feelings result from motives which also produce the action. You wouldn't feel good about doing the right thing unless you thought there was some other reason to do it, besides the fact that it would make you feel good. And you wouldn't feel guilty about doing the wrong thing unless you thought that there was some other reason not to do it. . . (page 154)

9.4 THE RECONCILIATION PROJECT

GREGORY S. KAVKA (1984)

Gregory S. Kavka was a professor of philosophy at the University of California at Irvine and a leading political philosopher before his untimely death at the age of 47. In this essay, Kavka's main concern is the **Reconciliation Project**: showing that moral behavior is required by, or at least consistent with, the demands of rational self-interest or prudence. After distinguishing between different versions of the project, Kavka presents Thomas Hobbes's solution to the project. Improving on Hobbes's approach, Kavka appeals to the existence of internal sanctions for immoral conduct (e.g., guilt, satisfaction, etc.) to show that "the ordinary good man . . . is not harming himself by being moral." Kavka ends his essay by arguing that that our non–self-interested motives often support moral behavior even when self-interested ones do not. For this reason, "while it is normally prudent to be moral, it is sometimes rational to be moral even if it is not prudent."

Reading Questions:

1. Kavka distinguishes between different versions of the Reconciliation Project along four dimensions. What are they?

2. What version of the Reconciliation Project does Hobbes attempt?

3. What are the premises and conclusions of the two objections Kavka presents to Hobbes's position?

4. In his attempt to improve on Hobbes' view, Kavka acknowledges a restriction to his version of the Reconciliation Project along its agent dimension. What is the restriction?

5. What is Kavka's response to the objection that his version of the Reconciliation Project does not show that morality and self-interest coincide when our moral duty requires us to sacrifice our own life?

6. What is Kavka's response to the objection that his version of the Reconciliation Project does not show that morality and self-interest coincide for powerful groups in their relations to weaker ones?

7. Explain Kavka's final observation: "While it is normally prudent to be moral, it is sometimes rational to be moral even if it is not prudent", (page 169). What is the difference between being rational and being prudent?

Four Dimensions of Reconciliation

Clarifying the nature of the relationship between ethical and self-interested conduct is one of the oldest problems of moral philosophy. As far back as Plato's *Republic,* philosophers have approached it with *the aim of reconciling morality and self-interest by showing that moral behavior is required by, or at least is consistent with, rational prudence. Let us call this undertaking the Reconciliation Project.* In modern times this project is generally viewed as doomed to failure. It is believed that unless we make an outdated and implausible appeal to divine sanctions, we cannot expect to find agreement between moral and prudential requirements.

Can this negative verdict on the Reconciliation Project be avoided? Before we can deal with this question, we must distinguish among versions of the project along four dimensions. The *audience* dimension concerns to whom our arguments about coincidence of duty and interest are addressed. Sometimes it is supposed that a successful version of the Reconciliation Project must be capable of converting to virtue a hardened cynic or immoralist such as Thrasymacus. This is too much to ask. Immoralists are not likely to understand or appreciate the benefits of living morally, nor are they usually the sort of people who will listen to, or be swayed by, abstract rational arguments. A more modest aim is to speak convincingly to the puzzled ordinary person, such as Glaucon, who fears that in following the path of morality he is being irrational and is harming himself, but who is willing to listen to and ponder arguments to the contrary. We shall here be concerned with versions of the Reconciliation Project having this more modest aim.

A second dimension concerns the sort of *agent* for whom morality and self-interest are supposed to coincide. Versions of the Reconciliation Project that are ambitious along this dimension might attempt to demonstrate such coincidence in the case of all actual human beings, or even all possible human beings. More restrained versions would concentrate on more limited classes, such as persons without severe emotional disturbances or persons capable of self-assessment and love for others. The audience and agent dimensions of the Reconciliation Project

are related. If one's aim in pursuing the project is to create or strengthen moral motivation, one would normally choose an agent class that just encompasses one's audience, so as to convince one's listeners that it pays *them* (promotes their own interests) to be moral, while at the same time exposing one's argument to the fewest possible objections. But if one aims at promoting theoretical understanding, one's agent class may be broader or narrower than one's audience. One may, for example, seek to convince reflective persons of goodwill that it pays everyone to be moral. Agent and audience classes need not even overlap; one might argue to sophisticated theorists that morality pays for the unsophisticated, who could not be expected successfully to disguise their immoralities.

The third dimension of the Reconciliation Project is the *social* one. Whether morality pays is partly a function of others' responses to one's immoralities. Are morality and prudence supposed to coincide, then, in all imaginable social environments, all feasible ones, all (or most) actual ones, some feasible ones, or some imaginable ones? Different answers to this question yield importantly different versions of the Reconciliation Project.

Fourth and finally, if we say that morality and prudence coincide, does this mean that (i) each individual ethical act is prudent or (ii) that there are sufficient prudential reasons for adopting a moral way of life and acting in accordance with moral rules? This question concerns the nature of the objects or entities to be reconciled and calls attention to the *object* dimension of the Reconciliation Project. Reconciling all particular acts of duty with prudence is so unpromising a task as to have been largely shunned by the major philosophical exponents of the project. (Although, as we shall see below, much depends on whether prudential evaluations of acts are undertaken prospectively or retrospectively.) Thus Plato argues the prudential advantages of moral dispositions or ways of life, while Hobbes focuses on providing a prudential grounding for moral rules.

Taking note of the object dimension allows us to clarify the Reconciliation Project by answering a preliminary objection to it. According to this objection, the project must fail because supposedly moral actions are not really moral if they are motivated by prudential concerns. We may, however, accept this observation about motivation and moral action without damaging the Reconciliation Project properly construed. For that project is not committed to morality and prudence being identical, or to moral and prudential motives or reasons for action being the same. Rather, prudence and morality are supposed to be reconcilable in two senses. They recommend the same courses of conduct (where conduct is described in some motive-neutral way). Further, it is consistent with the requirements of prudence to adopt and live a moral way of life, even though this involves developing a pattern of motivation in which nonprudential considerations play an important role.[1] Thus the Reconciliation Project survives the preliminary objection because it concerns, along its object dimension, acts or rules of action or ways of life, rather than motives or reasons for action.

Still, the Reconciliation Project is hopeless if we adopt very stringent interpretations of it along most or all of its four dimensions. We cannot expect to convince a clever immoralist that it pays everyone to act morally on every specific occasion in any sort of society. But why should we consider only such extreme versions of the project? *Taking account of the dimensions of variation of the Reconciliation Project, I propose instead to discuss some less extreme versions (and modifications) of it to see to what extent they can be carried out and why they fail when they do.* In the course of this investigation, I hope partly to vindicate the rationality of being moral and to clarify further the relationship between morality, prudence, and rationality.

I begin by sketching a **Hobbesian** verison of the Reconciliation Project that presupposes **psychological egoism** and relies exclusively on external sanctions (social rewards and punishments) to reconcile obligation and interest. This Hobbesian approach provides considerable illumination, but it suffers from serious defects. To correct some of these, I consider the significance of internal (self-imposed psychological) sanctions.[2] Next, I take up the two most intractable objections to all forms of the project. These concern the obligation to die for others, and those duties owed by members of strong groups

to members of weak groups who are apparently not in a position to reciprocate benefits bestowed on them. Finally, I note how the recognition of nonegoistic motives transforms the Reconciliation Project. Throughout, my remarks are largely programmatic. I sketch alternatives, problems, and general strategies for solving problems and leave much detail to be filled in later. I hope nonetheless to say enough to show that the Reconciliation Project is still philosophically interesting and important.

The Hobbesian Strategy[3]

As a starting point, let us consider Hobbes's version of the Reconciliation Project. In seeking to reconcile duty and interest, Hobbes is limited by two self-imposed restrictions: He rules out appeal to religious sanctions, and he leaves no place for internal sanctions (such as guilt feelings) in his account of human psychology. Hence, Hobbes is reduced to arguing his case solely in terms of external sanctions; that is, social rewards and punishments. He does, however, marshall these relatively meager resources to good advantage.

The core of Hobbes's view is that the general rules of conduct that a farsighted prudent man concerned with his own survival, security, and well-being would follow are essentially the rules of traditional morality. The function of these rules is to promote peace, cooperation, and mutual restraint for the benefit of all parties. The rules therefore forbid killing, assault, and robbery, and they require keeping one's agreements, settling disputes by arbitration, providing aid to others when the cost to one is small and the benefit to them is large,[4] and so on. The self-interested individual, if sufficiently rational and farsighted, will follow these rules because doing so is the best (and only reliable) way to ensure peaceful and cooperative relations with others. The person, for example, who wastes on luxuries what others need to survive is not likely to be helped by others if he later falls into want; nor will his person and property ever be safe from the desperate acts of the needy. The dangers of hostile reactions by others that confront the habitual assailant, thief, or contract-breaker are even more obvious. And while people may try to conceal their violations of moral rules, the long-run dangers of exposure and retaliation by others are great. Thus, argues Hobbes, morality is superior to immorality as a general policy, from the viewpoint of rational prudence.

One may agree that normally morality is a more prudent general policy than immorality but raise doubts about its prudential rationality in two special circumstances: when one is confident that a violation would go undiscovered and unpunished, and when others are not willing to reciprocate restraint. In the first case, it appears that one would benefit by *offensively* violating moral rules; that is, by not complying with them when others are complying. In the second case, prudence seems to call for a *defensive* violation—for noncompliance motivated by the belief that others are not complying and the desire not to put oneself at a disadvantage. Hobbes recognizes and attempts to deal with both cases.

Hobbes's argument against offensive violations of moral rules is presented in his famous reply to the Fool. He acknowledges that such violations will in some cases turn out, *in retrospect*, to best serve the agent's interests. But because they risk serious external sanctions (such as the withdrawal of all future cooperation by others[5]), they are never *prospectively* rational. Since the consequences of failure are horrible and the chances of failure are not precisely calculable, it is not a rational gamble to offensively violate moral rules. Underlying this Hobbesian argument is an intuition about rational prudence that is reflected in the usual connotation of the word *prudence*. To be prudent is to play it safe and not take large, uncontrollable risks. It is not implausible to suppose that rational pursuit of one's own interests requires being prudent in this sense when one's vital interests are at stake.

To develop this point, let us follow decision theorists in drawing a distinction between choices under *risk* and under *uncertainty*. In the former cases, one has reliable knowledge of the probabilities that the various possible outcomes would follow the different available courses of action. In choices under uncertainty, one lacks such knowledge. Rawls contends that rationality requires that, when making vitally important choices under uncertainty, one follow a Maximin Strategy—choose the act with the best worst outcome. I have argued elsewhere for

using a Disaster Avoidance Strategy in such circumstances—choosing the alternative that maximizes one's chances of avoiding all unacceptable outcomes.[6] Both strategies favor playing it safe in the sense of aiming at avoidance (or minimization) of the risk of unacceptable outcomes.

Now suppose we view choices among actions in the real world as made under uncertainty. (This is plausible for the most part, given our limited understanding of the complex factors that determine the consequences of our actions.[7]) If, as Hobbes suggests, offensive violators risk the application of serious external sanctions, offensive violations would be irrational according to both the Maximin and Disaster Avoidance viewpoints. For the offensive violator accepts, under uncertainty, an unnecessary (or greater than necessary) risk of suffering disastrous consequences. So if either Rawls's analysis of rational prudential choice under uncertainty or my own is correct, Hobbes's argument against offensive violations under uncertainty is largely vindicated.

The considerations just presented attempt in effect to reconcile the requirements of morality and prudence as applied to (a certain class of) particular actions. They may serve, that is, as part of a Reconciliation Project focusing along the object dimension on *acts*. They function ever more effectively as part of an argument for the coincidence of *rules* of morality and prudence. We can imagine someone claiming that living by some rule such as the following would better serve one's interests than following moral rules: "Follow the moral rules except when you believe (or confidently believe) you can get away with violating them." But if one lives by this sort of rule, one is likely to undergo the risks inherent in offensive violations on a good number of occasions. And even if one is cautious in selecting the occasions, the risk of getting caught and suffering serious sanctions on one or more occasions will be substantial and much greater than the chance of getting caught on one particular occasion. Hence, insofar as rational prudence requires avoiding or minimizing risks of suffering serious sanctions, it would not recommend a policy of clever "compromise" between moral and immoral conduct as exemplified in this rule.

We have seen that Hobbes tries to reconcile duty and prudence in the case of offensive violations by denying that such violations are prudential. The opposite tack is adopted for defensive violations. These, Hobbes claims, are not contrary to moral duty. Agents are not obligated to follow the constraints of traditional morality unless others are reciprocating their restraint. To comply with moral rules unilaterally is to render oneself prey to others, and this, Hobbes urges, one is not required to do.

The governing principle of Hobbesian morality, then, is what I call the Copper Rule: "Do unto others as they *do* unto you." This principle enunciates a less glittering moral ideal than the familiar Golden Rule, which requires us to treat others well regardless of whether they treat us well in return. In thus opting for a reciprocal rather than unilateral interpretation of moral requirements, is Hobbes abandoning traditional morality?

To answer this question, we must distinguish between two aspects of morality—practice morality and ideal morality. Practice morality encompasses the standards of conduct actually expected of, and generally practiced by, persons living within a given moral tradition. It is roughly the part of morality concerned with *requirements,* those standards for which people are blamed, criticized, or punished for failing to live up to. Ideal morality refers to standards of moral excellence that a tradition sets up as models to aspire to and admire. Praise, honor, and respect are the rewards of those who live by its higher, more demanding standards. But, in general, people are not blamed for falling short of such ideals, or even for not aiming at them.

Now there surely are important strands of unilateralism in the ideal morality of the Western tradition. The Golden Rule, the admonition to love thine enemy, and the principle of turning the other cheek, all concern treating well even those who do not reciprocate. But if we turn to practice, and the standards of conduct that are actually treated as moral requirements, we find Copper Rule reciprocity to be a reasonable summary of much of what we observe. For practice morality allows us considerable leeway to engage in otherwise forbidden conduct toward those who violate moral constraints, especially when this is necessary for protection. Thus individuals may

kill in self-defense, society may deprive criminals of their liberty, contracts may be broken when reciprocal fulfillment cannot be expected, and so forth.

We may then, without committing Hobbes to absurdity, attribute to him the claim that, in practice, traditional moral rules contain exception clauses allowing for defensive "violations" of the main clauses of the rule, if these are aimed at other violators. In adopting this pruned-down conception of moral requirements, Hobbes has abandoned the ambitious dream of achieving a reconciliation between ideal morality and prudence. But he has avoided one telling objection to the Reconciliation Project: that morality requires us (as prudence does not) to sacrifice our interests to the immoral, who will be all too ready to take advantage of such a sacrifice. Note, however, that the companion objection that morality sometimes requires us to sacrifice our interests for others who are moral is not dealt with by the Copper Rule interpretation of morality. Forms of this objection will be considered later.[8]

As we have seen, Hobbes treats offensive and defensive violations of moral rules quite differently. In the former case, he reconciles prudence to morality by altering cynical interpretations of what prudence demands, while in the latter case he reconciles morality to prudence by offering a nonstandard interpretation of morality. Yet in each case he draws our attention to the oft-neglected social dimension of the Reconciliation Project. His discussion of defensive violations suggests that under certain conditions—anarchy or general noncompliance with traditional moral rules—moral and prudential requirements coincide, but only as a result of the effective loosening or disappearance of the former. Hence, *how* duty and interest are reconciled is a function of the social environment. In arguing for the imprudence of offensive violations of moral rules, Hobbes presupposes threats of external sanctions that are serious enough to make such violations a bad gamble. Therefore, his argument does not apply to imaginary situations in which society rewards immoral actions, or even certain real ones in which it ignores serious immoralities when they are committed by members of some privileged groups.

Suppose, then, that our aim is to reconcile prudence with traditional moral requirements (without the exception clauses); that is, do not kill or steal, aid the needy when the costs are small, and so on. Hobbes suggests that this reconciliation is possible only in a certain sort of social environment—one we may call *punitive*. In a punitive environment, serious violators of moral norms are sought out, apprehended, and given stiff punishments frequently enough to make immorality a bad prudential risk. As a result, there is general compliance with moral rules and little need for one to undertake defensive violations. In a punitive social environment, offensive violations of moral rules are irrational and defensive ones are unnecessary. If an actual social environment is punitive, the Reconciliation Project seems to have succeeded with respect to it. And if such an environment is feasible but nonactual, those who wish people to act morally but fear the distracting influence of self-interest will have some reason to create it.

Let us now briefly summarize the Hobbesian approach to the Reconciliation Project, which is based on external sanctions. It consists first of proposing specific interpretations of that project along two of the four dimensions. With respect to the object dimension, it focuses on rules or policies rather than on individual acts. (Although the reply to the Fool fits within an act version of the project as well.) And it presupposes a punitive social environment, avoiding the dubious claim that duty and interest coincide in any social context. Further, it provides a novel interpretation of moral requirements—the Copper Rule or reciprocal interpretation—and it rests on a "playing it safe" theory of rational prudential choice under uncertainty. All of these aspects of the Hobbesian strategy make contributions to the interpretation and development of the Reconciliation Project. None is without plausibility. However, there are two fatal objections that the Hobbesian Strategy cannot adequately answer.

Two Objections to Hobbes' View

The first concerns punitive social environments. These are beneficial in discouraging immoral conduct, but they have costs. To render immorality a bad risk solely via threats of punishments, such punishments must be made very heavy and/or very probable. In a society of significant size, doing the latter would normally require a massive policing establishment with large monetary costs (borne by the citizens), interferences with personal liberty and privacy (searches, eavesdropping, surveillance), and dangers of police power and influence over the political and economic institutions of society. Heavy penalties also have social costs—monetary costs of supporting prisons, lessened chances of reconciliation between offenders and society, dangers of gross injustice if the innocent might sometimes be punished, and so on. In short, we must accept trade-offs between various things that we value and the deterrence of serious immorality. And it may not always be possible for society, by use of external sanctions alone, to ensure that "crime does not pay" without sacrificing too much in the way of individual liberty, privacy, and protection from excessive state and police power.

Our second objection concedes that immorality generally does not pay, and even allows, that immorality is prudentially irrational under genuine uncertainty. However, *some* opportunities for immoral gain may present themselves under risk; that is, the probabilities of detection and punishment may be reliably known. In these situations, maximizing expected personal utility is arguably the most rational course, and this may imply engaging in an offensive violation. A slumlord, for example, may have relatively precise statistical data that allow him to estimate reliably the odds of his getting caught and punished if he hires a professional arsonist to burn one of his buildings so that he can collect the insurance. If the chances of arrest and conviction are low and the return is high, the crime may have positive expected value for him, and it will be prudentially rational for him to undertake it. The rules of a system of rational self-interest will be formulated to allow agents to take advantage of such situations.

These two objections reveal that while external sanctions alone can take us, via the Hobbesian Strategy, some considerable way toward reconciling duty and interest, they cannot take us far enough. We at least need some device other than a punitive social environment that can alter the calculations or dispositions of the slumlord and other potential criminals. The obvious candidates here are internal sanctions, psychic structures that punish immorality and reward virtue. Unlike external sanctions, these are relatively free of problems concerning evasion and detection, since one's conscience follows one everywhere[9] and they do not threaten privacy and democracy as do secret police forces. In the next section, I will explore how their inclusion may extend and strengthen the Hobbesian arguments for the coincidence for morality and prudence.

Internal Sanctions

Internal sanctions come in two varieties, negative and positive. The negative sanctions are guilt feelings and related forms of psychic distress that most of us are subject to feel when we believe we have done wrong. We develop the tendency to experience such feelings under such circumstances as part of the socialization process we undergo in growing up. It is no mystery why society nurtures and encourages the development of this tendency, it benefits others to the extent that it inhibits or deters misconduct by the individual. And once one possesses the tendency, it imposes extra—and relatively certain[10]—costs on immorality, costs which may tip the prudential balance in favor of restraint. Arson may not be the most rational option for our slumlord, for example, if in addition to prison he risks, with high probability, significant guilt feelings over endangering the lives of tenants or over cheating his insurance company. With internal sanctions operating along with external sanctions in this way, the social environment need not be so punitive as to keep serious immorality within tolerable limits.

There is no entirely satisfactory label for the positive internal sanctions, the agreeable feelings that typically accompany moral action and the realization that one has acted rightly, justly, or benevolently. So let us opt for the vague term "the satisfactions of morality."[11] Moral people have long testified as to the strength and value of such satisfactions, often claiming that they are the most agreeable satisfactions we can attain. This last claim goes beyond what is necessary for our purposes. All we need to assert is that there are special significant pleasures or satisfactions that accompany regular moral action and the practice of a moral way of life that are not available to (unreformed) immoralists and others of their ilk.[12] For if this is so, then the forgoing of these potential satisfactions must be charged as a significant opportunity cost of choosing an immoral way of life.

Can an individual have it both ways, enjoying the psychic benefits of morality while living an immoral life? He could, perhaps, if he lived immorally while sincerely believing he was not. Certain fanatics who selflessly devote themselves to false moral ideals, such as purifying the human race by eugenics or pleasing God by destroying nonbelievers, might fall in this category. Of more concern in the present context, however, is the individual who adopts morality as a provisional way of life or policy while planning to abandon it if a chance to gain much by immorality should arise later. This person, we would say, is not truly moral, and it is hard to believe that he would perceive himself to be, so long as his motives are purely prudential and his commitment to morality is only conditional. In any case, we would not expect him to experience the satisfactions of morality in the same way, or to the same degree, as the genuinely moral individual who is aware of the (relative) purity of his motives and the nature and depth of his commitment.

Note that if this is so we have arrived at a paradox of self-interest: *being* purely self-interested will not always best serve one's interests. For there may be certain substantial personal advantages that accrue only to those who are not purely self-interested, such as moral people. Thus it may be rational for you, as a purely self-interested person, to cease being one if you can, to transform yourself into a genuinely moral person.[13] And once you are such a person, you will not be disposed to act immorally, under risk, whenever so doing promises to maximize personal expected utility.

The lesson of this paradox, and the opportunity cost of being immoral, does not apply, though, to those (if any) who are no longer capable of learning to enjoy the satisfactions of living a moral life. Further, some people may still be capable of developing an appreciation of these satisfactions, but the transition costs of moving to this state from their present immoral condition may outweigh the advantages gained. For people such as these, especially those who are immune from guilt feelings, the prudential argument for being moral must essentially rest on external sanctions. And with respect to some individuals, such as hardened but cautious immoralists or clever psychopaths, the argument may fail.

Thus we must acknowledge a restriction of the Reconciliation Project along its agent dimension. It is too much to claim that it pays one to be moral, irrespective of one's psychological characteristics. Rather, the argument from internal sanctions supports the prudential rationality of living a moral life for the two classes of people constituting the vast majority of humankind: First, those who are already endowed with conscience and moral motivations, so that they experience the satisfactions of living morally and are liable to suffering guilt feelings when they do wrong. Second, those who are capable of developing into moral persons without excessive cost—immoralists who are not fully committed to that way of life, and children.

Should we be dismayed that the Reconciliation Project may not encompass, along its agent dimension, those incapable of enjoying the satisfactions of morality? This depends upon our aims in pursuing the project and the audience to whom its arguments are addressed. Insofar as our aim is to reassure the ordinary good man that he is not harming himself by being moral, or to encourage parents who want to do the best for their children to give them moral education, we need not worry. And if we seek theoretical illumination, we achieve more by recognizing the variation along the agent dimension than by denying it. Only if our aim were the hopeless one of convincing dedicated immoralists to be moral, by using rational arguments, would we be in difficulty. Am I confessing, then, that we are helpless in the face of the immoralist? No, we are not helpless in the practical sense, for we can use external sanctions to restrain immoralists. Nor should we perceive an immoralist's gloating that it does not pay him to be moral (because the satisfactions of morality are not for him) as a victory over us. It is more like the pathetic boast of a deaf person that he saves money because it does not pay him to buy opera records.

The Ultimate Sacrifice

We have seen how the recognition of internal sanctions allows us to deal with two objections that undermine the Hobbesian external-sanctions approach to the Reconciliation Project. Two difficult objections remain, however, even when internal sanctions are taken into account. The first is that morality sometimes requires the sacrifice of one's life, and this cannot be in one's interests. The second is that morality requires powerful groups to treat weak groups fairly and decently, while it better serves the interests of the powerful group's members not to do so.

The objection concerning death runs as follows. In certain circumstances, morality requires of us that we give up our lives to protect others. We are bound by obligations of fair play, gratitude, and perhaps consent to fight in just wars of national defense. Fulfilling these obligations costs many people their lives. Extreme situations can also arise in civilian life in which morality requires one to accept one's own death. If gangsters credibly threaten to kill me unless I kill an innocent person, I must refrain. If I am a loser in a fair and necessary lifeboat lottery, I am morally bound to abide by the outcome. If half of the expedition's necessary food supply is lost as a result of my recklessness, I must be the first to agree to go without food on the long return trip so that others may survive. And so on. In each of these cases, however, self-interest seems to counsel taking the opposite course. Where there is life there is hope, and even if the likely cost of saving my life is to suffer severe internal and external sanctions (such as imprisonment, depression, and guilt for the military deserter), that cost must be less than the premature loss of my life, since such loss would deprive me of all future enjoyments and frustrate all of my main plans and desires.

In response to this objection, let us first note that there are fates worse than death. And for some people, living with the knowledge that one has preserved one's life at the cost of the lives of others, the sacrifice of one's principles, or the desertion of a cause one loves may be such a fate. In addition, society is aware of the heavy value that people place on the continuation of their own lives and typically responds by using heavy external sanctions to encourage appropriate life-risking behavior in defense of society. Thus infantry officers may stand behind their own lines and shoot those who retreat, thereby rendering advance a safer course than retreat. (Even if advance is virtually suicidal, death with honor at the hands of the enemy may be a lesser evil than death with dishonor at the hands of one's own officers.) On the positive side, those who risk or lose their lives in battle are often offered significant rewards by their fellow citizens—medals, honors, praise, and material compensation for themselves or their families.

The upshot of this is that in a substantial number of cases the sacrifice of one's life for moral ends may be consistent with the requirements of prudence because it constitutes the lesser of two extreme personal evils. It would, however, be disingenuous to suggest that this is so in most, much less all, cases. Officers cannot shoot all deserters or retreaters, nor are courts likely to sentence to death those who cheat in lifeboat lotteries. And relatively few are so committed to morality that they could not eventually recover, at least partially, from the negative psychic effects of abandoning principle to preserve their lives. *So we must concede that self-interest and morality will frequently, or usually, recommend divergent courses of action when there is a stark choice between immoral action and certain death.*

Does this concession destroy the Reconciliation Project? Only if we have in mind a version of the project that focuses, along the object dimension, on acts. If instead we consider, as we have been, whether adopting the moral *way of life* is consistent with prudence, the answer may well be different. In adopting or pursuing a moral way of life, we are, it is true, running a *risk* of sacrificing our lives imprudently. For the requirements of morality may sometimes call for us to give up (or risk) our lives. And if we do develop the habits and dispositions appropriate to the moral life, we are likely (or at least more likely than otherwise) to live up to these requirements at the cost of our lives, if we find ourselves in appropriate circumstances. Notice,

however, that in assessing this risk and weighing it against the advantages of the moral life, we must consider how likely we are to find ourselves in such circumstances.

Now this depends, in turn, on our view of what the substantive rules of morality require of us. If they demand that one right all wrongs and fight all injustices anywhere at any time with all the means one possesses and regardless of the personal cost, the likelihood that one would be morally obligated to lay down (or seriously risk) one's life at some time or another is obviously large. But surely on any reasonable conception they require much less than this. Perhaps you are obligated to give up your life (i) to protect your country in a just war; (ii) to protect those to whom you owe special duties of protection (your children, your passengers if you are a ship's captain); (iii) to protect those you owe immense debts of gratitude (your parents); (iv) to avoid seriously violating the rights of innocent others (as in the gangster threat situation); (v) to save others from dangers that your misconduct, recklessness, or negligence has created; (vi) to keep important agreements you have made (such as accepting employment as a bodyguard); or (vii) to save the lives of large numbers of innocent people when you are the only one who can do so. And perhaps there are other specific duties of sacrifice that I have left off this list. But as a whole, the duties are limited to special and quite unlikely circumstances. (Military service is the only seriously life-endangering-required activity that is at all likely to confront a significant segment of the population. Presumably such service is morally obligatory only if the war is just, which frequently is not the case. Further, in most wars the percentage of those serving who are killed is rather low.)

Now if the chances are small that you will ever confront a situation in which you are morally obligated to surrender your life, it may well pay you to adopt a moral way of life, even if doing so increases the likelihood that you would sacrifice your life in such a situation. For the relatively certain external and internal benefits of the moral life should far outweigh the very unlikely loss of one's life. Further, it is worth noting that many immoral lifestyles—crime, debauchery, deception of all those around you— may have much higher premature death rates than the moral life. Insofar as adoption of a moral way of life ensures that you will not lapse into one of these alternatives, it may even on balance increase your life expectancy.[14]

The argument, then, is that adopting a moral way of life carries at most a very small net risk to one's life. Since it provides significant benefits with high probability, it is a reasonable prudential choice.[15] It is useful in understanding this argument to compare adopting a moral way of life with two other activities that are not generally thought to be imprudent: joining the military and entering into a long-term love relationship, such as by marrying or having children. These undertakings are like becoming moral in the main respect relevant to our argument. They are likely to involve or produce changes in one's motivational structure that would render one more likely to risk or sacrifice one's life in certain circumstances, such as when your loved ones or comrades in arms are in danger. (In addition, military service carries a nonnegligible risk of finding yourself in precisely these circumstances.) But this feature of these undertakings is not usually thought to render them ineligible choices from a prudential perspective. Why, then, should the same feature render becoming moral a generally imprudent course of conduct? This activity, like entering a long-term love relationship, promises very large external and internal rewards while involving a relatively tiny risk of loss of life. The gamble is hardly more foolish in the case of virtue than in the case of love.

Group Immorality

Human beings, as has often been remarked, are social creatures. We need one another for a variety of practical and emotional reasons—for help in securing satisfaction of our material needs, for physical protection, for companionship, for love, and so on. The above arguments that duty and interest coincide all rest on this fact. Individuals need the help rather than the hostility of society to prosper, and in the process of social learning they internalize norms of conscience that further fuse their interests with those of the social group. However, one does not require the aid or cooperation of *all* others,

only of a sufficient number of those with whom one is likely to come in contact. *This fact generates the most telling objection to the Reconciliation Project: That it is not in the interests of powerful groups and their members to treat decently and to help, as morality demands, the members of weak groups, who are apparently not in a position to return good for good and evil for evil.*[16]

It is clear that when we consider relations among groups, our earlier tools for reconciling interest and obligation cannot be used in the same way. External sanctions operate effectively, to the extent they do, because it is in the general interest of society and its members to restrain individuals from harming others. But if there is a split between groups in society, there may be no effective sanction against members of a dominant group harming members of a powerless group. For the others in the dominant group may condone, or even approve, such conduct, while the members of the powerless group are too weak to punish the offenders. And if the norms of the dominant group allow, or even encourage, mistreatment of the powerless group—as throughout history they often have—even well-socialized members of the dominant group may carry out such mistreatment without suffering substantial guilt feelings.

This objection shows that there cannot be a satisfactory solution to the Reconciliation Project if the project is strictly interpreted along the social and degree dimensions. That is, we cannot hope to show that in all historically actual (much less all conceivable) social circumstances it has been (or would be) in the interests of all groups and their members to act morally toward members of other groups.[17] Instead, particular cases of supposed divergence of group duty and interest must be considered on an ad hoc basis, and the most we can reasonably aspire to is the presentation of arguments that make it plausible that obligation and interest coincide in *actual* present circumstances. This will not ease the anxiety of moralists who seek a noncontingent guarantee that interest and duty will never diverge. But it could suffice to convince the attentive moral individual, or group leader, that he or she is not being foolish in acting morally, or in leading his or her group in a moral direction.

Before discussing the three most important specific instances of the objection before us, it should be pointed out that whether there is hope of reconciling group interest and duty depends on what we take the demands of duty to be. In the case of individuals, we saw that a unilateralist-idealistic interpretation of moral requirements might render the Reconciliation Project impossible. Similarly, if we interpret morality as requiring rich and powerful groups to share so much with the poor and weak as to create absolute equality, there is very little prospect that duty and interest can be reconciled. But it is far from obvious that morality demands this much. What morality does clearly require is that the rich and powerful refrain from actively harming the poor and weak, and that the former aid the latter when the costs of giving are small and the benefits of receiving are large. We shall see that with this modest interpretation of the obligations of the powerful, reconciling their obligations with their interests may be possible.

Let us turn to our examples, the first concerning justice within a society. Why should rich and powerful groups in a nation allow the poor opportunities for education, employment, and advancement and provide social-welfare programs that benefit the poor as morality requires? Why shouldn't they simply oppress and exploit the poor? There are several reasons why, in modern times, it is most probably in the long-term interest of the rich and powerful to treat the domestic poor well. First, some rich individuals, and more likely some of their children, may be poor at some time in the future and thus benefit from programs to help the poor. Second, offering opportunities to members of all groups widens the pool of talent available to fill socially useful jobs, which should provide long-run economic benefits to members of all groups.[18] Third, and most important, there is the reason that has impressed social theorists from Hobbes to Rawls: Decent treatment of all promotes social stability and cohesion and discourages revolution. This reason is especially important in contemporary times, when ideals of human dignity, equality, and justice are known and espoused virtually everywhere, and when revolution is frequently proposed as a legitimate means of attaining such ideals.

Taken together, these reasons constitute a strong case, on prudential grounds, for decent treatment of the domestic poor by a nation's dominant groups. In fact, if we apply Disaster Avoidance reasoning, it turns out that the third reason alone shows that good treatment of the poor is prudentially rational. For if the poor find the status quo unacceptable and apply such reasoning, they will revolt. Thus Hobbes writes, "Needy men and hardy, not contented with their present condition, . . . are inclined to . . . stir up trouble and sedition; for there is no . . . such hope to mend an ill game as by causing a new shuffle." The rich, being aware of this, will (if they follow a Disaster Avoidance strategy) seek to prevent the poor from falling into such unacceptable circumstances. For the rich thereby maximize their chances of obtaining an outcome acceptable to them: preservation of something resembling the status quo.

What about a wealthy and powerful nation aiding poor, weak nations? Is this in the long-run interest of the former as well as the latter? In a world of advanced technology, international markets, ideological conflicts among powerful nations, and nuclear weapons, it most probably is. In competition with other powerful nations, allies—even poor nations—are useful for political, economic, and military reasons. And economic development of poor nations should, in the long run, produce economic benefits for richer nations, such as by providing markets and reliable supplies of various raw and finished goods.[19] Most important, continued poverty in the Third World is likely to produce continued political turmoil, civil wars, and regional wars between nations. In a world armed to the teeth with nuclear weapons, and with more and more nations acquiring such weapons, the long-run danger of rich developed countries being drawn into a devastating military conflict started by a desperate poor nation, or some desperate group within such a nation, is far from negligible.

The above arguments about domestic and international justice suggest *there is, after all, a form of reciprocity between powerful and weak groups because of interdependencies between the two in economic and security matters.* The poor cannot return the aid of the rich in kind, but they can offer their talents, their purchasing power, and so on. If not treated well, they cannot directly punish the rich and powerful, but they can stir up serious trouble for them if they are willing to experience such trouble themselves. Thus they are able, and likely, to return good for good and evil for evil to the rich in the long run, and it will be rational for the rich to act accordingly.

Even this form of reciprocity is not available, however, to deal with our third and most puzzling example—the treatment of future generations. Future generations (beyond the next few) are powerless to act upon us, since they will not exist until after we are dead. Yet we have substantial power to determine the quality of their lives by influencing their numbers and the nature of the social and natural environment into which they will be born. Given this absolute asymmetry in power to affect one another, how can it be in our interest to act morally toward future generations? Morality requires us, at a minimum, to leave our descendants with enough resources to allow future people to live decent lives. But this would necessitate having a lower material standard of living than we could obtain by depleting resources and contaminating the environment whenever it is convenient to do so. If future generations cannot punish us for ruthlessly exploiting the earth in this way, doesn't rational prudence require it of us?

The supporter of the Reconciliation Project can come some considerable way toward answering even this objection. He might point out first that misuse of resources and damage to the environment will often produce substantial negative effects within our own lifetimes. So, for the most part, it is in our own interests to follow conservation policies that will turn out to benefit future generations. This reply will take us only so far, however. For there are policies whose benefits are experienced now and most of whose costs will be borne generations later (such as building nuclear power plants without having solved the long-term waste storage problem). Also, optimal *rates* of use of scarce nonrenewable resources will vary greatly depending upon how long we care about the resource lasting. Hence, there is a far from perfect overlap between the resource and environmental policies likely to most benefit present people and those likely to ensure a decent life for future generations.

A more promising argument begins from the fact that most people care very deeply about the happiness of their own children and grandchildren, and hence their own happiness would be diminished by contemplating the prospect of these descendants having to live in a resource-depleted world. Further, they realize that their children's and grandchildren's happiness will in turn be affected by the prospects for happiness of *their* children and grandchildren, and so forth. Hence, the happiness of present people is linked, generation by generation, to the prospects for happiness of some likely members of distant future generations. This "chain-connection" argument has considerable force, but it falls short of constituting a full solution to the problem before us. This is because the perceived happiness of one's children and grandchildren is only one component of the well-being or happiness of the typical parent. And the perceived happiness of *their* children and grandchildren is, in turn, only one component of the happiness of one's children and grandchildren. So there is a multiplier effect over generations that quickly diminishes the influence on a present person's happiness of the prospects for happiness of his later descendants.[20] And we must seek some other device to link living peoples' interests firmly with those of distant future generations.

The most promising such device is an appeal to our need to give meaning to our lives and endeavors. I have suggested elsewhere that *one strong reason we have for providing future people with the means to survive and prosper is that this is our best hope for the successful continuation of certain human enterprises that we value* (and may have contributed to)— science, the arts and humanities, morality, religion, democratic government. Similarly, Ernest Partridge has argued that human beings have a psychological need for "self-transcendence"; that is, a need to contribute to projects that are outside themselves and that will continue after their deaths. Those without such goals are unlikely to find meaning in their lives, especially during the middle and later stages of life, when people typically reflect on their own mortality. Thus Partridge says, "We need the future, *now*."

There is a great deal of truth in this argument, but there are some limits to what it can show. It cannot reconcile the interests and obligations to posterity of the narcissist who has no self-transcending goals and is incapable of developing them. However, this need not worry us anymore than did the corresponding remark made earlier about the person no longer capable of becoming moral. The self-transcending life may be the happier life for the vast majority who still can live it, and these people have good prudential reasons for doing so. The more important problem is that not all self-transcending concerns need be directed toward the distant future. They may involve goals that do not extend much beyond one's lifetime (such as the prosperity of one's children, or the eventual rise to power of one's favorite political movement). Such goals may give meaning to one's life without supplying reasons to provide for the welfare of distant generations. Perhaps, though, it is a psychological fact that enterprises that promise to continue into the indefinite future are better able to provide meaning in our lives, or to provide consolation for our mortality.[21] If so, there would be powerful prudential reasons for one's adopting self-transcending concerns of unlimited temporal scope, and for protecting the social and natural environments for future generations.

These are the best arguments I can think of for a coincidence of self-interest and our obligations to posterity. Many (including myself at times) will find them only partly convincing. Does this lack of complete conviction indicate that we should abandon the Reconciliation Project? No. Instead, we may broaden our interpretation of that project.

The Wider Project

The general strategy I have followed in outlining a defense of the Reconciliation Project has been to restrain the project's ambitions where necessary. Thus the scope of the project has been narrowed in several ways. It applies to ways of life rather than particular actions and to practice morality rather than ideal morality. It succeeds with respect to most people and groups in actual social circumstances, but not with respect to all people and groups in all actual or possible circumstances. It may not convince the skeptical immoralist to change his ways, but it provides good reasons for moral people not to regret (or abandon) their way of life and for loving parents to raise their children to be moral.

However, to understand better the relationship between morality, rationality, and self-interest, we must briefly consider *an important widening of the Reconciliation Project. For that project may be viewed as but a specific instance of a more general project: reconciling morality with the requirements of practical rationality.* Given two special assumptions—the truth of Psychological Egoism and the interpretation of practical rationality as the efficient pursuit of the agent's ends (whatever they may be[22])—this Wider Reconciliation Project would collapse into our original version concerning morality and self-interest. But the first of these assumptions is surely false; on any construal that does not render all motives self-interested by definition, people sometimes do have unselfish aims and possess and act upon non-self-interested motives. As a result, the question of whether moral requirements are consistent with the rational pursuit of the actual ends that people have is both distinct from and more important than the question of whether these requirements cohere with the demands of prudence.

Would shifting our focus to the Wider Reconciliation Project render irrelevant all we have said about the original project? If self-interested concerns played only an insignificant role in human motivation, it would. But clearly this is not the case. In fact, while Psychological Egoism is false, I would venture to propose that a milder doctrine, which I call Predominant Egoism, is probably true. Predominant Egoism says that human beings are, as a matter of fact, predominantly self-interested in the following sense. At least until they have achieved a satisfactory level of security and well-being, people's self-interested concerns tend to override their other-regarding, idealistic, and altruistic motives in determining their actions. Further, those non-selfish concerns that are sufficiently powerful to move people to acts that seriously conflict with self-interest tend to be limited in scope, such as to the well-being of family and friends and the advancement of specific favored projects or institutions.

Now if it is true that people are predominantly self-interested, in this sense, many or most of their strongest motives and dearest ends are self-interested ones. And the above arguments about reconciling duty and interest will be highly relevant to the task of reconciling duty and the rational pursuit of people's actual ends. But in carrying out this Wider Reconciliation Project, there would be a new resource to appeal to—the altruistic and nonselfish ends that most everyone actually has to some degree. The presence of these ends may extend the range of cases in which the requirements of reason and morality coincide beyond those in which prudence and morality coincide.

Consider again our relationship to future generations. Most of us do have significant nonselfish concerns about the well-being of our children and grandchildren and the survival and prospering of the human species. So we have reason to provide for these things *over and above* the contribution that our awareness of such provision makes to our own psychic well-being.[23] This further strengthens both the chain-connection and self-transcendence arguments for reconciling practical rationality with our duties to posterity. For it shows that in carrying out such duties we are fulfilling ends of ours not previously considered (that is, nonselfish ends) in addition to contributing to our own happiness.

The recognition of nonselfish ends also provides a fresh perspective on the sustenance of moral motivation over generations. We suggested earlier that parents seeking to promote their children's interests would have good reasons to raise their children to be moral. This suggestion would have little significance if we were operating upon an assumption of the truth of Psychological Egoism. (For then the only relevant question would be whether it is in a *parent's* interest to raise his or her children to be moral.) Since, however, concern for the well-being of one's children is among the strongest and most universal of non-self-interested human concerns, the suggestion is crucial to our understanding of how morality is rationally passed on from generation to generation. Typical parents who care strongly

for the well-being of their children and care somewhat for the well-being of others have three significant reasons for raising those children to be moral: This will likely benefit the children (in accordance with our earlier arguments that being moral usually pays), it will likely benefit others who are affected by the children, and it will likely benefit the parents themselves (because their children will treat them better). And when children grow up as moral beings possessing consciences and the potential to experience the satisfactions of morality, it is, we have argued, most always in their interest to continue to live a moral life. Further, they, as parents, will have the same reasons for raising their children to be moral as their parents had for raising them in this manner. Thus morality can be seen to be potentially self-sustaining from generation to generation, without even taking into account socializing influences on the child from outside the family.

In raising children to be moral, and in providing for future generations, some of the ends that we seek to achieve are non-self-interested ones. Given the content of moral rules and their connection with protecting the interests of others, many morally required actions will satisfy ends of this kind. As a result, the Wider Reconciliation Project should be successful in more cases than the original project. We may restate this crucial point: *While it is normally prudent to be moral, it is sometimes rational to be moral even if it is not prudent.*

NOTES

1. See the discussion of the paradox of self-interest in section II.
2. I borrow the internal/external sanction terminology from Sidgwick.
3. I further discuss some of the issues raised in this section in my "Right Reason and Natural Law in Hobbes's Ethics," (1983).
4. This aid principle is inferred from Hobbes's explanation of his fifth law of nature requiring mutual accommodation.
5. By treating the loss of the primary social reward of morality—the goodwill and cooperation of others—as the main punishment for immorality, Hobbes implicitly takes account of both the positive and the negative external sanctions of morality.
6. To employ the Disaster Avoidance Strategy, ordinal knowledge of the relevant probabilities is required.
7. See, however, the second objection discussed at the end of this section.

8. "The Ultimate Sacrifice" and "Group Immorality."

9. This claim may be qualified to take account of self-deception and related phenomena without greatly affecting my argument.

10. This is important because experts say that in achieving deterrence, the certainty of a sanction is generally more important than its severity.

11. There may be other satisfactions that are incompatible with the psychological structure of the immoralist's mind. For example, Richmond Campbell in *Self-Love and Self Respect: A Philosophical Study of Egoism* (Canadian Library of Philosophy, Ottawa, 1979) argues that immoral egoism is incompatible with self-respect and genuine love of oneself. If this is so, these satisfactions (or the chance to obtain them) may be included as "satisfactions of morality," and their loss may be regarded as an opportunity cost of living an immoral life.

12. Are there compensating special satisfactions of the immoral life that are not available to the moral individual? Without discussing cases of obvious psychopathology, we might consider the pleasures of, for example, being strong and independent or outsmarting others. It seems, however, that all of these pleasures are available within the context of various moral lives, since being moral does not rule out being strong and independent, outsmarting others, and so on.

13. Moralists should not be too comforted by this argument. For somewhat analogous arguments suggest that the abandonment of morality may be called for in certain imaginable circumstances. See my "Some Paradoxes of Deterrence," *Journal of Philosophy*, 75 (1978).

14. If it does not, then the decrease in life expectancy, together with the other costs of the moral life (such as lost opportunities to cheat), must be added together and compared to the benefits of the moral life. The decrease, if any, in life expectancy seems unlikely to be great enough to tip the prudential balance against the moral way of life.

15. This follows from the expected value principle if we treat the choice as one under risk. If we regard the choice as under uncertainty, we can obtain the same result by applying the Disaster Avoidance Principle. For rejecting, rather than adopting, the moral life is more likely to lead to an unacceptable outcome, such as imprisonment or ostracism.

Does prudence counsel selecting a particular nondangerous moral way of life, namely pacifism? No, for if one does not believe in pacifism, it may not be an eligible choice as a moral way of life. Further, its external costs may be large (such as imprisonment for conscientious objection), and it might even commit one to actions as dangerous as armed conflict (such as interposing oneself between aggressors and victims or serving as a medic at the front).

16. See Brenard Boxill ("How Injustice Pays," *Philosophy and Public Affairs*, 9, 1980).

17. In certain cases immoral conduct might conceivably be in the interest of an oppressed group; for example, if terrorism is the only way of ending the oppression. These cases raise special problems about the morality of revolutionary violence and will not be discussed here.

18. This argument is the liberal counterpart of the conservative "trickle-down" theory, which claims that direct benefits to the rich will indirectly benefit the poor.

19. This claim should be qualified by noting that worldwide development without environmental safeguards might be disastrous. See Donella Meadows et al., *The Limits of Growth* (Universe Books, for Potomac Associates, New York, 1972).

20. We can illustrate this point using arbitrarily chosen and artificially precise numbers. Suppose that my happiness is half dependent upon my perception of my children's well-being and half dependent on other independent things, and that I assume the same will be true of them and their children, and so on. Then one-quarter of my happiness will be determined by the prospects of my grandchildren, one-eighth by the prospects of my great grandchildren, and so forth.

21. The fact that most of us do care a good deal about the future survival and prosperity of humankind may constitute evidence that this is so.

22. This is a standard conception adopted by economists, social scientists, and philosophers such as Rawls and David A. J. Richards. One could follow Richard Brandt in rejecting some *ends* as irrational and still maintain the links described below between the original project and the Wider Reconciliation Project, given the plausible assumption that many of our self-interested ends (such as security and material well-being) are rational in the relevant sense. These links would be severed, however, and the Wider Reconciliation Project trivialized, if we adopted Thomas Nagel's view that practical reasons are by nature general and not agent-relative.

23. I am here relying on a distinction, noted by critics of psychological hedonism, between desiring that X occur and experiencing pleasure at the thought that X will occur. To take an example, I purchase life insurance because I desire that my family be provided for after my death, not because I seek the peace of mind of now knowing that they will be provided for, although the latter is also a predictable and expected result of my action. This action contributes to the fulfillment of *two* of my ends: the safeguarding of my family's future after my demise and the attainment of peace of mind for me now. It is thus more likely to be rational for me (that is, worth the cost in terms of foregoing fulfillment of other ends I could use the insurance premium money to forward) than if peace of mind were the only of my ends achieved thereby.

DISCUSSION QUESTIONS:

1. Both Hobbes and Kavka are concerned with a version of the Reconciliation Project that is focused on our decision to live by moral rules rather than our decisions to perform particular actions. Their goal is to show that adopting moral rules

is rationally prudent, not to show that every act required by those rules is rationally prudent. Why does each focus on our decision to live by moral rules rather than on our decisions to perform particular actions? Is it possible to accomplish the Reconciliation Project for the case of individual actions?

2. Are Kavka's two objections to Hobbes's position successful?

3. Kavka recognizes that his version of the Reconciliation Project does not extend to the case of a "dedicated immoralist," but he claims that this is not a serious limitation to his view:

> Nor should we perceive an immoralist's gloating that it does not pay him to be moral (because the satisfactions of morality are not for him) as a victory over us. It is more like the pathetic boast of a deaf person that he saves money because it does not pay him to buy opera records. (page 163)

Is Kavka correct? Should we be as sanguine about the fact that morality and prudence do not coincide for the immoralist as we are about the fact that buying opera records and prudence do not coincide for a deaf person? If not, how might we extend the Reconciliation Project to cover the immoralist?

4. Consider Kavka's answer to the question, "Why should rich and powerful groups in a nation allow the poor opportunities for education, employment, and advancement and provide social-welfare programs that benefit the poor as morality requires?" Is his answer correct? What do you think morality requires the rich and powerful in our society to do for the poor? Is it also rationally prudent for the rich to honor those moral demands?

5. Consider Kavka's answer to the question, "Is it in the long-run interest of wealthy and powerful nations to aid poor, weak ones, as morality demands?" Is his answer correct? What do you think morality requires wealthy and powerful nations to do to aid poor, weak ones? Is it rationally prudent for each wealthy and powerful nation to provide such aid?

6. Consider Kavka's answer to the question of whether it is rationally prudent for us to honor our moral duties to future generations. Is his answer correct? What are our moral duties to future generations? Do our moral obligations to posterity coincide with our self-interest?

Argument Reconstruction Exercises:

I. Consider the following argument for a lack of coincidence between the demands of morality and those of prudence. Identify the premises and conclusion.

> Even in a society in which there are strong external sanctions for immoral behavior, we will maximize our self-interest by following the qualified moral rule: Obey the rules of morality except when a particular violation is likely to maximize your self-interest and you can reliably determine that the chances of detection and punishment are low. If following this rule will maximize our self-interest, then the rationally prudent choice is to follow it. Therefore, even in a society in which there are strong external sanctions for immoral behavior, the unqualified demands of morality and prudence do not coincide.

II. Do dedicated immoralists have a reason to reform? Not according to the following argument; identify the premises and conclusion.

> Immoralists lack any internal sanctions against immoral behavior, and they can often reliably detect that some immoral behavior to advance their ends is unlikely to result in any external sanction. Since the immoral behavior will advance their ends at no cost in terms of internal or external sanctions, it is prudentially rational for them. If morality and prudence do not coincide for immoralists, then they have no reason to be reform their immoral behavior. Therefore, immoralists have no reason to reform their behavior in these cases.

III. Kavka considers "the ultimate sacrifice objection" to the Reconciliation Project. Identify the premises and conclusion is this excerpt.

> In certain circumstances, morality requires of us that we give up our lives to protect others. We are bound by obligations of fair play, gratitude, and perhaps

consent to fight in just wars of national defense. . . . Extreme situations can also arise in civilian life in which morality requires one to accept one's own death. If gangsters credibly threaten to kill me unless I kill an innocent person, I must refrain. . . . In each of these cases, however, self-interest seems to counsel taking the opposite course. Where there is life there is hope, and even if the cost of saving my life is to suffer severe internal and external sanctions (such as imprisonment, depression, and guilt for the military deserter), that cost must be less than the premature loss of my life, since such loss would deprive me of all future enjoyments and frustrate all my main plans and desires. (page 163)

IV. Do morality and prudence coincide when it comes to our use of natural resources? Identify the premises and conclusion of the following argument.

Morality requires us to leave future generations with enough resources to live decent lives. To leave future generations that amount of resources, we will have to have a lower standard of living than we might have otherwise, and, indeed, a lower standard of living than we have now. It is not in our self-interest to have such a lower standard of living. Therefore, our moral duty to our descendants does not coincide with what is rationally prudent for us to do now.

3

Normative Ethics

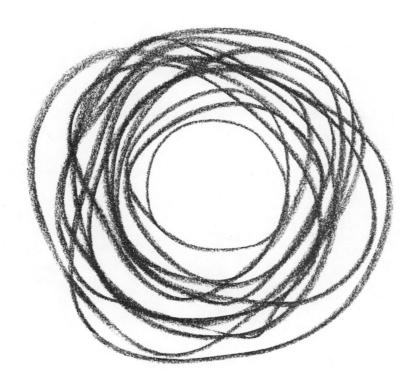

CHAPTER 10

Value and the Good Life

There is but one truly serious philosophical problem, and that is suicide. Judging whether life is or is not worth living amounts to answering the fundamental question of all philosophy.

—CAMUS, *THE MYTH OF SISYPHUS*

INTRODUCTION

Consider the opening quote (above) from Camus. If you've ever known someone who has committed suicide, you'll know how tragic such a loss can be. It is obviously terrible for the surviving friends and family. But is it terrible for the person who died as well? And if so, what makes it terrible?

Think about your own life. There are a lot of things that you want for your life. There are a lot of things that you do NOT want for your life. You probably think that it is possible for your life to go well or go badly. But why? What kind of things would make your life a success and what kind of things would make your life go well? You probably think that some things are good (like ice cream) whereas other things are bad (like suffering). But why? What makes these things good or bad?

Philosophical theories that explain what makes things good or bad are called value theories. **Value theories** are about moral concepts like good, bad, evil, etc. These are theories about what makes a state of affairs, a person's life, etc. valuable. Value theories are distinct from deontic theories. **Deontic theories** are about moral concepts like right, wrong, obligatory, etc. These theories are about what makes actions morally permissible, impermissible, required, etc. Value theories are about the nature of the good, whereas deontic theories are about the nature of the right.

So setting aside the question of what makes an action right or wrong, how should we think about goodness and badness? Here's one suggestion: There's no such thing. We saw this kind of value nihilism in Chapter 6. And just as some philosophers are skeptical about the reality of right and wrong, some philosophers are skeptical about the reality of good and bad.

And even if we grant that the world contains valuable states of affairs, it is an open question whether these values are in some sense objective. Camus, in his famous essay on suicide, provides a typically existentialist answer to the value question: the only values are ones that we create. Objectively speaking, nothing is more valuable than anything else in this world. Other philosophers have suggested that all goodness is really goodness for (or badness for) something or other. In other words, perhaps all things that are good are so because they are good *for something or someone*. In this sense, goods are person-relative, and what is good for one person might not be good for another. For example, it is good for the hunter that he finds a deer so that his family can eat, but this is plausibly not good for the deer. It is good for one business to attract a new customer but bad for the business that just lost that customer.

Those who disagree that all goodness is relative often put the point by saying that some things are good *simpliciter* (Latin: simply). To say that some things are simply good is to say that some things are just plain good and not simply good only relative to something or someone. In this sense, it might be good *simpliciter* that the hunter's family eat and bad *simpliciter* that the deer is shot. It might be simply good that one business is thriving and simply bad that another is not.

However, even philosophers who think that we can talk about things being simply good or bad recognize that not everything is good or bad in the same way. **Instrumental goods** are goods that are valuable because they help one obtain some further good. Money is a perfect example of an instrumental good. No one wants money for its own sake—we want money because it can help us get other things that are valuable. **Intrinsic goods** are goods that are valuable in their own right and not merely for what they can get you. Pleasure is a perfect example of an intrinsic good. We want pleasure simply because of what it is and not because of some further end or goal. Some goods might be mixed goods, which is to say that they are both instrumental and intrinsic. Perhaps knowledge or health are mixed goods: they are valuable because they are instrumental in procuring other things that we want, but we also want to be knowledgeable and healthy for their own sake.

What would make something intrinsically valuable? There are broadly two families of theories about intrinsic value. Monistic Value Theories say that one and only one thing is valuable. Pluralistic Value theories say that a variety or plurality of things is valuable. Philosophers hotly disagree about which sort of view is ultimately correct. The most plausible form of value monism is a view called hedonism. **Hedonism** is the view that there is only one thing in the world that is intrinsically valuable: pleasure. Furthermore, there is only one thing in the world that is intrinsically disvaluable: pain. That's it. The hedonist says that all of the value in the world is reducible to pleasure and pain.

How might a hedonist explain the value judgments we make about our own lives? Well, suicide is a tragedy in the following sense: the person who dies misses out on a wide range of pleasures that

her life would have included, the death itself is often painful, and the suicide causes serious pain in the friends and family who are left behind. And think about your own life. You want to be healthy, to be educated, to have a good job, to raise a successful family, etc. All of those things are either pleasurable in themselves or else are instrumental in getting you pleasure (e.g., a good job).

Value pluralists disagree with all of this. Sure, pleasure might be something that is intrinsically good. But, says the value pluralist, it is not the *only* thing that is intrinsically good. For example, having a friend is a good thing even if this friendship doesn't provide you with pleasure. And, sure, pain might be something that is intrinsically bad. But, says the value pluralist, it is not the *only* thing that is intrinsically bad. For example, making fun of crippled children might be bad even if the children never find out about it and hence the taunting never causes any pain. Value pluralists suggest that when we think clearly about the way we want our lives to go, we often focus on things other than pleasure and pain. Robert Nozick will explore this very issue in his selection for this section.

Thus far we've been asking a perfectly general question: what makes any sort of thing good or bad? But we might ask about the goodness and badness of a more particular range of things, for example, *human lives*. What makes a human life go well? What makes a human life a success? What makes a human life good? Theories that try to answer this question are often called **theories of well-being** or theories of self-interest. These theories attempt to explain the good life.

One might think that the answer to the well-being question is straightforward: the goal of a human life is happiness. Something like this sounds correct: your life goes well when you live a happy life or when you are truly happy. And this is the sort of thing that we say about ourselves and one another: parents want their adult children to be happy, we sympathize with those who are unhappy, etc. But saying that the good life is the happy life only pushes the question further: what does it take for one to be truly happy?

Philosophers disagree about the nature of happiness. Indeed, the very way that we use the word 'happy' suggests that the concept is ambiguous. Sometimes we use 'happy' to mean something like content or pleased with one's life. But other times we use 'happy' to mean something more robust like meeting one's goals or having a life filled with good things. Someone who is hopelessly addicted to heroin might be happy in the first sense (she is content) but unhappy in the second sense (her life is not filled with a rich variety of goods).

Despite the difficulties of the terrain, the question of what is good or what makes our life go well is a crucial component of the human experience. As Socrates rightly noted, "The unexamined life is not worth living." The readings of this section will help you to cultivate your own thinking about what you find valuable and why.

SUGGESTIONS FOR FURTHER READING

Annas, J. *The Morality of Happiness*. (New York: Oxford, 1993)

Aristotle & Irwin, Terence (translator). *Nicomachean Ethics*. (Hackett Publishing, 1999)

Camus, Albert. (translated by Justin O'Brien). *The Myth of Sisyphus*. (New York: Vintage International, 1942)

Feldman, F. *Pleasure and the Good Life*. (Oxford: Clarendon Press, 2004)

Griffin, J. *Well-Being*. (Oxford: Clarendon Press, 1986)

Mill, John Stuart. *Utilitarianism* [this volume, page 194]

Nussbaum, M., and A. Sen (ed.) *The Quality of Life*. (Oxford: Clarendon Press, 1993)

Ross, W.D. *The Right and the Good*. (Oxford University Press, 1930)

Sumner, W. *Welfare, Happiness, and Ethics*. (Oxford: Clarendon Press, 1996)

10.1 THE MEANING OF LIFE

RICHARD TAYLOR (2000)

Richard Taylor was a professor of philosophy at the University of Rochester and well known for his work in metaphysics and ethics. He here considers whether life has any meaning. He approaches the question by considering what he takes to be a clear example of meaningless activity: the pointless labors of Sisyphus, the figure from Greek mythology bound by the gods to roll a boulder up a hill only to have it roll down so he can begin the task again. Taylor takes our condition to be that of Sisyphus. He rejects the view that our lives are meaningful through the achievement of an assigned end, but he considers two ways in which Sisyphus' activity (and ours) might become meaningful.

Reading Questions:

1. Taylor claims that the labors of Sisyphus are "objectively meaningless;" what does he mean by this?

2. Taylor claims that, even though the labors of Sisyphus are objectively meaningless, they can nonetheless acquire a meaning for him. How, according to Taylor, is this possible?

3. Of the different ways in which Sisyphus' activity might gain some meaning, which does Taylor take to be the best, and why?

4. In what ways are our lives comparable to the situation of Sisyphus, according to Taylor?

5. How, according to Taylor, can our lives be meaningful?

The question whether life has any meaning is difficult to interpret, and the more you concentrate your critical faculty on it the more it seems to elude you, or to evaporate as any intelligible question.

You want to turn it aside, as a source of embarrassment, as something that, if it cannot be abolished, should at least be decently covered. And yet I think any reflective person recognizes that the question it raises is important, and that it ought to have a significant answer.

If the idea of meaningfulness is difficult to grasp in this context, so that we are unsure what sort of thing would amount to answering the question, the idea of meaninglessness is perhaps less so. If, then, we can bring before our minds a clear image of meaningless existence, then perhaps we can take a step toward coping with our original question by seeing to what extent our lives, as we actually find them, resemble that image, and draw such lessons as we are able to from the comparison.

Meaningless Existence

A perfect image of meaninglessness, of the kind we are seeking, is found in the ancient myth of Sisyphus. Sisyphus, it will be remembered, betrayed divine secrets to mortals, and for this he was condemned by the gods to roll a stone to the top of a hill, the stone then immediately to roll back down, again to be pushed to the top by Sisyphus, to roll down once more, and so on again and again, *forever*. Now in this we have the picture of meaningless, pointless toil, of a meaningless existence that is absolutely *never* redeemed. It is not even redeemed by a death that, if it were to accomplish nothing more, would at least bring this idiotic cycle to a close. If we were invited to imagine Sisyphus struggling for a while and accomplishing nothing, perhaps eventually falling from exhaustion, so that we might suppose him then eventually turning to something having some sort of promise, then the meaninglessness of that chapter of his life would not be so stark. It would be a dark and dreadful dream, from which he eventually awakens to sunlight and reality. But he does not awaken, for there is nothing for him to awaken to. His repetitive toil is his life and reality, and it goes on forever, and it is without any meaning whatever. Nothing ever

comes of what he is doing, except simply, more of the same. Not by one step, nor by a thousand, nor by ten thousand does he even expiate by the smallest token the sin against the gods that led him into this fate. Nothing comes of it, nothing at all.

This ancient myth has always enchanted people, for countless meanings can be read into it. Some of the ancients apparently thought it symbolized the perpetual rising and setting of the sun, and others the repetitious crashing of the waves upon the shore. Probably the commonest interpretation is that it symbolizes our eternal struggle and unquenchable spirit, our determination always to try once more in the face of overwhelming discouragement. This interpretation is further supported by that version of the myth according to which Sisyphus was commanded to roll the stone *over* the hill, so that it would finally roll down the other side, but was never quite able to make it.

I am not concerned with rendering or defending any interpretation of this myth, however. I have cited it only for the one element it does unmistakably contain, namely, that of a repetitious, cyclic activity that never comes to anything. We could contrive other images of this that would serve just as well, and no myth-makers are needed to supply the materials of it. Thus, we can imagine two persons transporting a stone—or even a precious gem, it does not matter—back and forth, relay style. One carries it to a near or distant point where it is received by the other; it is returned to its starting point, there to be recovered by the first, and the process is repeated over and over. Except in this relay nothing counts as winning, and nothing brings the contest to any close, each step only leads to a repetition of itself. Or we can imagine two groups of prisoners, one of them engaged in digging a prodigious hole in the ground that is no sooner finished than it is filled in again by the other group, the latter then digging a new hole that is at once filled in by the first group, and so on and on endlessly.

Now what stands out in all such pictures as oppressive and dejecting is not that the beings who enact these roles suffer any torture or pain, for it need not be assumed that they do. Nor is it that their labors are great, for they are no greater than the labors commonly undertaken by most people most of the time. According to the original myth, the stone is so large that Sisyphus never quite gets it to the top and must groan under every step, so that his enormous labor is all for nought. But this is not what appalls. It is not that his great struggle comes to nothing, but that his existence itself is without meaning. Even if we suppose, for example, that the stone is but a pebble that can be carried effortlessly, or that the holes dug by the prisoners are but small ones, not the slightest meaning is introduced into their lives. The stone that Sisyphus moves to the top of the hill, whether we think of it as large or small, still rolls back every time, and the process is repeated forever. Nothing comes of it, and the work is simply pointless. That is the element of the myth that I wish to capture.

Again, *it is not the fact that the labors of Sisyphus continue forever that deprives them of meaning. It is, rather, the implication of this: that they come to nothing.* The image would not be changed by our supposing him to push a different stone up every time, each to roll down again. But if we supposed that these stones, instead of rolling back to their places as if they had never been moved, were assembled at the top of the hill and there incorporated, say, in a beautiful and enduring temple, then the aspect of meaninglessness would disappear. His labors would then have a point, something would come of them all, and although one could perhaps still say it was not worth it, one could not say that the life of Sisyphus was devoid of meaning altogether. Meaningfulness would at least have made an appearance, and we could see what it was.

That point will need remembering. But in the meantime, let us note another way in which the image of meaninglessness can be altered by making only a very slight change. Let us suppose that the gods, while condemning Sisyphus to the fate just described, at the same time, as an afterthought, waxed perversely merciful by implanting in him a strange and irrational impulse; namely, a compulsive impulse to roll stones. We may if we like, to make this more graphic, suppose they accomplish this by implanting in him some substance that has this effect on his character and drives. I call this perverse, because from our point of view there is clearly no reason why anyone should have a persistent and insatiable desire to do something so pointless as that. Nevertheless, suppose that is Sisyphus' condition. He has but one obsession,

which is to roll stones, and it is an obsession that is only for the moment appeased by his rolling them—he no sooner gets a stone rolled to the top of the hill than he is restless to roll up another.

Now it can be seen why this little afterthought of the gods, which I called perverse, was also in fact merciful. For they have by this device managed to give Sisyphus precisely what he wants—by making him want precisely what they inflict on him. However it may appear to us, Sisyphus' fate now does not appear to him as a condemnation, but the very reverse. His one desire in life is to roll stones, and he is absolutely guaranteed its endless fulfillment. Where otherwise he might profoundly have wished surcease, and even welcomed the quiet of death to release him from endless boredom and meaninglessness, his life is now filled with mission and meaning, and he seems to himself to have been given an entry to heaven. Nor need he even fear death, for the gods have promised him an endless opportunity to indulge his single purpose, without concern or frustration. He will be able to roll stones *forever*.

What we need to mark most carefully at this point is that the picture with which we began has not really been changed in the least by adding this supposition. Exactly the same things happen as before. The only change is in Sisyphus' view of them. The picture before was the image of meaningless activity and existence. It was created precisely to be an image of that. It has not lost that meaninglessness, it has now gained not the least shred of meaningfulness. The stones still roll back as before, each phase of Sisyphus' life still exactly resembles all the others, the task is never completed, nothing comes of it, no temple ever begins to rise, and all this cycle of the same pointless thing over and over goes on forever in this picture as in the other. The *only* thing that has happened is this: Sisyphus has been reconciled to it, and indeed more, he has been led to embrace it. Not, however, by reason or persuasion, but by nothing more rational than the potency of a new substance in his veins.

The Meaninglessness of Life

I believe the foregoing provides a fairly clear content to the idea of meaninglessness and, through it, some hint of what meaningfulness, in this sense might be. *Meaninglessness is essentially endless pointlessness, and meaningfulness is therefore the opposite.* Activity, and even long, drawn out and repetitive activity, has a meaning if it has some significant culmination, some more or less lasting end that can be considered to have been the direction and purpose of the activity. *But the descriptions so far also provide something else; namely, the suggestion of how an existence that is objectively meaningless, in this sense, can nevertheless acquire a meaning for him whose existence it is.*

Now let us ask: Which of these pictures does life in fact resemble? And let us not begin with our own lives, for here both our prejudices and wishes are great, but with the life in general that we share with the rest of creation. We shall find, I think, that it all has a certain pattern, and that this pattern is by now easily recognized.

We can begin anywhere, only saving human existence for our last consideration. We can, for example, begin with any animal. It does not matter where we begin, because the result is going to be exactly the same.

Thus, for example, there are caves in New Zealand, deep and dark, whose floors are quiet pools and whose walls and ceilings are covered with soft light. As you gaze in wonder in the stillness of these caves it seems that the Creator has reproduced there in microcosm the heavens themselves, until you scarcely remember the enclosing presence of the walls. As you look more closely, however, the scene is explained. Each dot of light identifies an ugly worm, whose luminous tail is meant to attract insects from the surrounding darkness. As from time to time one of these insects draws near it becomes entangled in a sticky thread lowered by the worm, and is eaten. This goes on month after month, the blind worm lying there in the barren stillness waiting to entrap an occasional bit of nourishment that will only sustain it to another bit of nourishment until. . . . Until what? What great thing awaits all this long and repetitive effort and makes it worthwhile? Really nothing. The larva just transforms itself finally to a tiny winged adult that lacks even mouth parts to feed and lives only a day or two. These adults, as soon as they have mated and laid eggs, are themselves caught in the threads and are devoured by the cannibalist worms, often without

having ventured into the day, the only point to their existence having now been fulfilled. This has been going on for millions of years, and to no end other than that the same meaningless cycle may continue for another millions of years.

All living things present essentially the same spectacle. The larva of a certain cicada burrows in the darkness of the earth for seventeen years, through season after season, to emerge finally into the daylight for a brief flight, lay its eggs, and die—this all to repeat itself during the next seventeen years, and so on to eternity. We have already noted, in another connection, the struggles of fish, made only that others may do the same after them and that this cycle, having no other point than itself, may never cease. Some birds span an entire side of the globe each year and then return, only to insure that others may follow the same incredibly long path again and again. One is led to wonder what the point of it all is, with what great triumph this ceaseless effort, repeating itself through millions of years, might finally culminate, and why it should go on and on for so long, accomplishing nothing, getting nowhere. But then you realize that there is no point to it at all, that it really culminates in nothing, that each of these cycles, so filled with toil, is to be followed only by more of the same. The point of any living thing's life is, evidently, nothing but life itself.

This life of the world thus presents itself to our eyes as a vast machine, feeding on itself, running on and on forever to nothing. And we are part of that life. To be sure, we are not just the same, but the differences are not so great as we like to think; many are merely invented, and none really cancels the kind of meaninglessness that we found in Sisyphus and that we find all around, wherever anything lives. We are conscious of our activity. Our goals, whether in any significant sense we choose them or not, are things of which we are at least partly aware and can therefore in some sense appraise. More significantly, perhaps, we have a history, as other animals do not, such that each generation does not precisely resemble all those before. Still, if we can in imagination disengage our wills from our lives and disregard the deep interest we all have in our own existence, we shall find that they do not so little resemble the existence of Sisyphus. We toil after goals, most of them—indeed every single one of them—of transitory significance and, having gained one of them, we immediately set forth for the next, as if that one had never been, with this next one being essentially more of the same. Look at a busy street any day, and observe the throng going hither and thither. To what? Some office or shop, where the same things will be done today as were done yesterday, and are done now so they may be repeated tomorrow. And if we think that, unlike Sisyphus, these labors do have a point, that they culminate in something lasting and, independently of our own deep interests in them, very worthwhile, then we simply have not considered the thing closely enough. Most such effort is directed only to the establishment and perpetuation of home and family; that is, to the begetting of others who will follow in our steps to do more of the same. Everyone's life thus resembles one of Sisyphus's climbs to the summit of his hill, and each day of it one of his steps; the difference is that whereas Sisyphus himself returns to push the stone up again, we leave this to our children. We at one point imagined that the labors of Sisyphus finally culminated in the creation of a temple, but for this to make any difference it had to be a temple that would at least endure, adding beauty to the world for the remainder of time. Our achievements, even though they are often beautiful, are mostly bubbles; and those that do last, like the sand-swept pyramids, soon become mere curiosities while around them the rest of human-kind continues its perpetual toting of rocks, only to see them roll down. Nations are built upon the bones of their founders and pioneers, but only to decay and crumble before long, their rubble then becoming the foundation for others directed to exactly the same fate. *The picture of Sisyphus is the picture of existence of the individual man, great or unknown, of nations, of the human race, and of the very life of the world.*

On a country road one sometimes comes upon the ruined hulks of a house and once extensive buildings, all in collapse and spread over with weeds. A curious eye can in imagination reconstruct from what is left a once warm and thriving life, filled with purpose. There was the hearth, where a family once talked, sang, and made plans; there were the rooms, where people loved, and babes were born to a rejoicing mother; there are the musty remains of a sofa, infested with bugs, once

bought at a dear price to enhance an ever-growing comfort, beauty, and warmth. Every small piece of junk fills the mind with what once, not long ago, was utterly real, with children's voices, plans made, and enterprises embarked upon. That is how these stones of Sisyphus were rolled up, and that is how they became incorporated into a beautiful temple, and that temple is what now lies before you. Meanwhile other buildings, institutions, nations, and civilizations spring up all around, only to share the same fate before long. And if the question "What for?" is now asked, the answer is clear: so that just this may go on forever.

The two pictures—of Sisyphus and of our own lives, if we look at them from a distance—are in outline the same and convey to the mind the same image. It is not surprising, then, that we invent ways of denying it, our religions proclaiming a heaven that does not crumble, their hymnals and prayer books declaring a significance to life of which our eyes provide no hint whatever.[1] Even our philosophies portray some permanent and lasting good at which all may aim, from the changeless forms invented by Plato to the beatific vision of St. Thomas and the ideals of permanence contrived by the moderns. When these fail to convince, then earthly ideals such as universal justice and brotherhood are conjured up to take their places and give meaning to our seemingly endless pilgrimage, some final state that will be ushered in when the last obstacle is removed and the last stone pushed to the hilltop. No one believes, of course, that any such state will be final, or even wants it to be in case it means that human existence would then cease to be a struggle; but in the meantime such ideas serve a very real need.

The Meaning of Life

We noted that Sisyphus' existence would have meaning if there were some point to his labors, if his efforts ever culminated in something that was not just an occasion for fresh labors of the same kind. But that is precisely the meaning it lacks. And human existence resembles his in that respect. We do achieve things—we scale our towers and raise our stones to the hilltops—but every such accomplishment fades, providing only an occasion for renewed labors of the same kind.

But here we need to note something else that has been mentioned, but its significance not explored, and that is the state of mind and feeling with which such labors are undertaken. We noted that if Sisyphus had a keen and unappeasable desire to be doing just what he found himself doing, then, although his life would in no way be changed, it would nevertheless have a meaning for him. It would be an irrational one, no doubt, because the desire itself would be only the product of the substance in his veins, and not any that reason could discover, but a meaning nevertheless.

And would it not, in fact, be a meaning incomparably better than the other? For let us examine again the first kind of meaning it could have. Let us suppose that, without having any interest in rolling stones, as such, and finding this, in fact, a galling toil, Sisyphus did nevertheless have a deep interest in raising a temple, one that would be beautiful and lasting. And let us suppose he succeeded in this, that after ages of dreadful toil, all directed at this final result, he did at last complete his temple, such that now he could say his work was done, and he could rest and forever enjoy the result. Now what? What picture now presents itself to our minds? It is precisely the picture of infinite boredom! Of Sisyphus doing nothing ever again, but contemplating what he has already wrought and can no longer add anything to, and contemplating it for an eternity! Now in this picture we have a meaning for Sisyphus' existence, a point for his prodigious labor, because we have put it there; yet, at the same time, that which is really worthwhile seems to have slipped away entirely. Where before we were presented with the nightmare of eternal and pointless activity, we are now confronted with the hell of its eternal absence.

Our second picture, then, wherein we imagined Sisyphus to have had inflicted on him the irrational desire to be doing just what he found himself doing, should not have been dismissed so abruptly. The meaning that picture lacked was no meaning that he or anyone could crave, and the strange meaning it had was perhaps just what we were seeking.

At this point, then, we can reintroduce what has been until now, it is hoped, resolutely pushed aside in an effort to view our lives and human existence with objectivity; namely, our own wills, our deep interest in what we find ourselves doing. If we do this we find that our lives do indeed still resemble that of Sisyphus, but that the meaningfulness they thus lack is precisely the meaningfulness of infinite boredom. At the same time, the strange meaningfulness they possess is that of the inner compulsion to be doing just what we were put here to do, and to go on doing it forever. This is the nearest we may hope to get to heaven, but the redeeming side of that fact is that we do thereby avoid a genuine hell.

If the builders of a great and flourishing ancient civilization could somehow return now to see archaeologists unearthing the trivial remnants of what they had once accomplished with such effort—see the fragments of pots and vases, a few broken statues, and such tokens of another age and greatness—they could indeed ask themselves what the point of it all was, if this is all it finally came to. Yet, it did not seem so to them then, for it was just the building, and not what was finally built, that gave their life meaning. Similarly, if the builders of the ruined home and farm that I described a short while ago could be brought back to see what is left, they would have the same feelings. What we construct in our imaginations as we look over these decayed and rusting pieces would reconstruct itself in their very memories, and certainly with unspeakable sadness. The piece of a sled at our feet would revive in them a warm Christmas. And what rich memories would there be in the broken crib? And the weed-covered remains of a fence would reproduce the scene of a great herd of livestock, so laboriously built up over so many years. What was it all worth, if this is the final result? Yet, again, it did not seem so to them through those many years of struggle and toil, and they did not imagine they were building a Gibraltar. The things to which they bent their backs day after day, realizing one by one their ephemeral plans, were precisely the things in which their wills were deeply involved, precisely the things in which their interests lay, and there was no need then to ask questions. There is no more need of them now—the day was sufficient to itself, and so was the life.

This is surely the way to look at all of life—at one's own life, and each day and moment it contains; of the life of a nation; of the species; of the life of the world; and of everything that breathes. Even the glow worms I described, whose cycles of existence over the millions of years seem so pointless when looked at by us, will seem entirely different to us if we can somehow try to view their existence from within. Their endless activity, which gets nowhere, is just what it is their will to pursue. This is its whole justification and meaning. Nor would it be any salvation to the birds who span the globe every year, back and forth, to have a home made for them in a cage with plenty of food and protection, so that they would not have to migrate anymore. It would be their condemnation, for it is the doing that counts for them, and not what they hope to win by it. Flying these prodigious distances, never ending, is what it is in their veins to do, exactly as it was in Sisyphus's veins to roll stones, without end, after the gods had waxed merciful and implanted this in him.

You no sooner drew your first breath than you responded to the will that was in you to live. You no more ask whether it will be worthwhile, or whether anything of significance will come of it, than the worms and the birds. *The point of living is simply to be living, in the manner that it is your nature to be living.* You go through life building your castles, each of these beginning to fade into time as the next is begun; yet it would be no salvation to rest from all this. It would be a condemnation, and one that would in no way be redeemed were you able to gaze upon the things you have done, even if these were beautiful and absolutely permanent, as they never are. What counts is that you should be able to begin a new task, a new castle, a new bubble. It counts only because it is there to be done and you have the will to do it. The same will be the life of your children, and of theirs; and if the philosopher is apt to see in this a pattern similar to the unending cycles of the existence of Sisyphus, and to despair, then it is indeed because the meaning and point he is seeking is not there—but mercifully so. *The meaning of life is from within us, it is not bestowed from without, and it far exceeds in both its beauty and permanence any heaven of which men have ever dreamed or yearned for.*

NOTE
1. A popular Christian hymn, sung often at funerals and typical of many hymns, expresses this thought:

Swift to its close ebbs out life's little day;
Earth's joys grow dim, its glories pass away;
Change and decay in all around I see:
O thou who changest not, abide with me.

DISCUSSION QUESTIONS:
1. Taylor claims that, even as Sisyphus' activity remains objectively meaningless, it can acquire meaning for him by his desiring to engage in it. Is any activity capable of gaining meaning for him in this way? If any activity can be meaningful for him in this way, how valuable is this form of meaningfulness?
2. Taylor claims that the "picture of Sisyphus is the picture of existence of the individual man, great or unknown, of nations, of the human race, and of the very life of the world." Is he correct? Are our lives as pointless as the labors of Sisyphus? If not, how are they different?
3. Taylor claims that the meaning that Sisyphus can give to his labors by desiring to engage in them is "incomparably better" than any meaning those labors could have by being directed toward some external purpose, such as the building of a temple. Is he correct?

Argument Reconstruction Exercises:
I. Taylor claims that our condition is that of Sisyphus. Identify the premises and conclusion in this reasoning in support of his view.

Sisyphus toils after a goal—moving his stone up the hill—of transitory significance; as soon as he achieves it, it disappears and he starts over again. His toils lack any objective meaning. We too toil after goals of transitory significance; none is lasting and, having achieved one, we immediately set forth after the next. Therefore, our toils also lack any objective meaning.

II. Taylor claims that the meaning that Sisyphus' labors gain from his desiring to engage in them is better than any meaning they might have relative to some external goal such as building a temple. Identify the premises and conclusion in this reasoning in support of his view.

For suppose that Sisyphus' labors gain meaning by being directed toward a goal (e.g., to build a temple).

With the achievement of his goal, Sisyphus has nothing more to do. His existence is marked by the absence of activity. If Sisyphus' labors instead gain meaning by his desiring to engage in them, then Sisyphus never completes his task, and as a result, his existence is always marked by his desired activity. The meaningfulness of an existence that is marked by the achievement of an end followed by inactivity is not as good as the meaningfulness of an existence that is marked by continual, desired, activity.

III. If the meaning of our lives is wholly within us, does it follow that each life is potentially as meaningful as any other? Identify the premises and conclusion of the following argument.

Is a human life is meaningful just insofar as it consists in the pursuit of desired goals? If so, then Sisyphus' life, which consists in his desired activity of continually moving a stone up a hill, is just as meaningful as the life of a saint, which consists in her desired activity of helping those in need. Yet, surely, the saint's life is more meaningful than that of Sisyphus.

IV. Might the meaning of a life depend on the activities it contains rather than whether those activities actually serve some purpose? Identify the premises and conclusion of the following argument.

Suppose the gods condemn Sisyphus to a life of rolling his boulder up a hill and Socrates to a life of seeking knowledge that constantly eludes him. As soon as he gets close to answering a question, he discovers that its answer depends on the solution to yet another one. Neither has any desire to engage in his assigned activity. Yet, Socrates' life is more meaningful than that of Sisyphus. Since the only relevant difference between them rests in the nature of their activities, the meaning of a life is determined, at least in part, by the nature of the activities it involves.

10.2 THE EXPERIENCE MACHINE

ROBERT NOZICK (1974)

Robert Nozick was University Professor of Philosophy at Harvard University. Although he is best known for his work in social and political philosophy, Nozick also made major contributions both in epistemology and metaphysics. In this essay, he presents an argument against the view that our well-being is defined simply by our experiences. The argument employs an interesting thought experiment in which we have access to an experience machine that we can use to simulate any experience we would like, along with all the associated pleasures and pains. Nozick appeals to our intuitions about whether we would be willing to "plug into" the experience machine to argue that what is valuable includes more than our experiences.

Reading Questions:

1. What claims about the nature of human well-being does Nozick reject on the basis of his thought experiment?

2. What three conclusions about the nature of human well-being does Nozick reach on the basis of his thought experiment?

There are substantial puzzles when we ask what matters other than how people's experiences feel "from the inside." Suppose there were an experience machine that would give you any experience you desired. Superduper neuropsychologists could stimulate your brain so that you would think and feel you were writing a great novel, or making a friend, or reading an interesting book. All the time you would be floating in a tank, with electrodes attached to your brain. Should you plug into this machine for life, preprogramming your life's experiences? If you are worried about missing out on desirable experiences, we can suppose that business enterprises have researched thoroughly the lives of many others. You can pick and choose from their large library or smorgasbord of such experiences, selecting your life's experiences for, say, the next two years. After two years have passed, you will have ten minutes or ten hours out of the tank, to select the experiences of your *next* two years. Of course, while in the tank you won't know that you're there; you'll think it's all actually happening. Others can also plug in to have the experiences they want, so there's no need to stay unplugged to serve them. (Ignore problems such as who will service the machines if everyone plugs in.) Would you plug in? *What else can matter to us, other than how our lives feel from the inside?* Nor should you refrain because of the few moments of distress between the moment you've decided and the moment you're plugged. What's a few moments of distress compared to a lifetime of bliss (if that's what you choose), and why feel any distress at all if your decision *is* the best one?

What does matter to us in addition to our experiences? First, we want to *do* certain things, and not just have the experience of doing them. In the case of certain experiences, it is only because first we want to do the actions that we want the experiences of doing them or thinking we've done them. (But *why* do we want to do the activities rather than merely to experience them?)

A second reason for not plugging in is that we want to *be* a certain way, to be a certain sort of person. Someone floating in a tank is an indeterminate blob. There is no answer to the question of what a person is like who has long been in the tank. Is he courageous, kind, intelligent, witty, loving? It's not merely that it's difficult to tell; there's no way he is. Plugging into the machine is a kind of suicide. It will seem to some, trapped by a picture, that nothing about what we are like can matter except as it gets reflected in our experiences. But should it be surprising that what *we are* is important to us? Why should we be concerned only with how our time is filled, but not with what we are?

Thirdly, plugging into an experience machine limits us to a man-made reality, to a world no deeper or more important than that which people can construct. There is no *actual* contact with any deeper

reality, though the experience of it can be simulated. Many persons desire to leave themselves open to such contact and to a plumbing of deeper significance.[1] This clarifies the intensity of the conflict over psychoactive drugs, which some view as mere local experience machines, and others view as avenues to a deeper reality; what some view as equivalent to surrender to the experience machine, others view as following one of the reasons *not* to surrender!

We learn that something matters to us in addition to experience by imagining an experience machine and then realizing that we would not use it. We can continue to imagine a sequence of machines each designed to fill lacks suggested for the earlier machines. For example, since the experience machine doesn't meet our desire to *be* a certain way, imagine a transformation machine which transforms us into whatever sort of person we'd like to be (compatible with our staying us). Surely one would not use the transformation machine to become as one would wish, and thereupon plug into the experience machine![2] So something matters in addition to one's experiences *and* what one is like. Nor is the reason merely that one's experiences are unconnected with what one is like. For the experience machine might be limited to provide only experiences possible to the sort of person plugged in. Is it that we want to make a difference in the world? Consider then the result machine, which produces in the world any result you would produce and injects your vector input into any joint activity. We shall not pursue here the fascinating details of these or other machines. What is most disturbing about them is their living of our lives for us. Is it misguided to search for *particular* additional functions beyond the competence of machines to do for us? *Perhaps what we desire is to live (an active verb) ourselves, in contact with reality. (And this, machines cannot do for us.)* Without elaborating on the implications of this, which I believe connect surprisingly with issues about free will and causal accounts of knowledge, we need merely note the intricacy of the question of what matters *for people* other then their experiences. Until one finds a satisfactory answer, and determines that this answer does not *also* apply to animals, one cannot reasonably claim that only the felt experiences of animals limit what we may do to them.

NOTE

1. Traditional religious views differ on the *point* of contact with a transcendent reality. Some say that contact yields eternal bliss or Nirvana, but they have not distinguished this sufficiently from merely a *very* long run on the experience machine. Others think it is intrinsically desirable to do the will of a higher being which created us all, though presumably no one would think this if we discovered we had been created as an object of amusement by some superpowerful child from another galaxy or dimension. Still others imagine an eventual merging with a higher reality, leaving unclear its desirability, or where that merging leaves *us*.

2. Some wouldn't use the transformation machine at all; it seems like *cheating*. But the one-time use of the transformation machine would not remove all challenges; there would still be obstacles for the new us to overcome, a new plateau from which to strive even higher. And is this plateau any the less earned or deserved than that provided by genetic endowment and early childhood environment? But if the transformation machine could be used indefinitely often, so that we could accomplish anything by pushing a button to transform ourselves into someone who could do it easily, there would remain no limits we *need* to strain against or try to transcend. Would there be anything left to *do*? Do some theological views place God outside of time because an omniscient omnipotent being couldn't fill up his days?

DISCUSSION QUESTIONS:

1. Nozick writes that "we learn that something matters to us in addition to experience by imagining an experience machine and then realizing that we would not use it." Would you use the experience machine? If so, why? If not, do you agree with Nozick's analysis of what valuable aspects an experience-machine life would lack?

2. Consider the possibility of plugging into the experience machine for a limited time just to have a very pleasant experience that you would not be able to have otherwise. Suppose you could do this during a time when you would otherwise have no notable experience of pleasure or pain. Would your life as a whole be better for plugging in? Does this show that experiences of pleasure can add value to our lives even when they are not gained by interacting with reality?

3. Assuming that Hedonism is mistaken, what is intrinsically good (or evil)?

Argument Reconstruction Exercises:

I. Consider the following argument regarding the relation between our experiences and our well-being. Identify the premises and conclusion.

> Nothing adds to or detracts from our well-being unless it affects us in some way, but nothing has an effect on us except insofar as we experience it. Our well-being is, therefore, entirely defined by our experiences after all.

II. Just what does the experience-machine thought experiment show? Identify the premises and conclusion of the following argument.

> If we had the option of actually seeing a beautiful painting or instead simply having the experience of seeing it, we would prefer the former. Yet, this does not imply that the beauty of the painting is not just a function of its ability to produce a certain sort of experience in us. So too, the fact that we would prefer actually living a certain life to having the associated experiences does not imply that the value of the life is not just a function of the experiences it contains for those who live it.

III. Here is one argument inspired by Nozick's experience-machine example. Identify the premises and conclusion.

> Suppose you and I have lives of identical experiences, except that you gain all of your experiences through the experience machine and I gain mine by interacting with the world. I've had a better life than you. Yet, we've lived equally good lives, if our experiences alone define our well-being. So there's more of value for us than what we experience.

IV. If an experience-machine life is not as good as its real counterpart, what makes the latter better? Identify the premises and conclusion of the following argument.

> Suppose you and I have lives of identical experiences, except that you gain all of your experiences through the experience machine and I gain mine by interacting with the world. I've had a better life than you. The only difference between our lives is that I've gained my experiences from contact with the world. Therefore, just living in contact with the world is valuable in itself.

10.3 WHAT MAKES SOMEONE'S LIFE GO BEST

DEREK PARFIT (1984)

Derek Parfit is one of the most influential British philosophers of the twentieth century, and he currently serves as emeritus professor of philosophy at All Souls College, Oxford. His first major work, *Reasons and Persons,* was published to much acclaim in the mid-1980s, and in this book he carefully develops a theory on the metaphysics of personal identity and the use of reason in the moral life. The current selection comes from the appendix of *Reasons and Persons* where Parfit addresses the **theories of well-being.** He claims that there are three basic kinds of theory: **hedonistic theories, desire-fulfillment theories,** and **objective list theories.** Parfit explains the strengths and weaknesses of each genus before concluding with a compromise view of well-being that he calls the **composite view.**

Reading Questions:

1. What are the three basic kinds of theories of self-interest?

2. What is the difference between a narrow hedonist and a preference hedonist?

3. What are the two species of desire-fulfillment theory that Parfit considers?

4. According to preference hedonism, can something be bad for me even if I do not know about it?

5. According to success theory, can something be bad for me even if I do not know about it?

6. According to the objective list theory, what kind of things might be good for us? What kind of things might be bad for us?

7. What is the composite view of self-interest?

What would be best for someone, or would be most in this person's interests, or would make this person's life go, for him, as well as possible? Answers to this question I call *theories about self-interest.* There are three kinds of theory. On **Hedonistic Theories**, what would be best for someone is what would make his life happiest. On **Desire-Fulfillment Theories**, what would be best for someone is what, throughout his life, would best fulfil his desires. On **Objective List Theories**, certain things are good or bad for us, whether or not we want to have the good things, or to avoid the bad things.

Hedonistic Theories

Narrow Hedonists assume, falsely, that pleasure and pain are two distinctive kinds of experience. Compare the pleasures of satisfying an intense thirst or lust, listening to music, solving an intellectual problem, reading a tragedy, and knowing that one's child is happy. These various experiences do not contain any distinctive common quality.

What pains and pleasures have in common are their relations to our desires. On the use of 'pain' which has rational and moral significance, all pains are when experienced unwanted, and a pain is worse or greater the more it is unwanted. Similarly, all pleasures are when experienced wanted, and they are better or greater the more they are wanted. These are the claims of *Preference-Hedonism*. On this view, one of two experiences is more pleasant if it is preferred.

This theory need not follow the ordinary uses of the words 'pain' and 'pleasure'. Suppose that I could go to a party to enjoy the various pleasures of eating, drinking, laughing, dancing, and talking to my friends. I could instead stay at home and read *King Lear*. Knowing what both alternatives would be like, I prefer to read King Lear. It extends the ordinary use to say that this would give me more pleasure. But on Preference-Hedonism, if we add some further assumptions given below, reading King Lear would give me a better evening. Griffin cites a more extreme case. Near the end of his life Freud refused pain-killing drugs, preferring to think in torment than to be confusedly euphoric. Of these two mental states, euphoria is more pleasant. But on Preference-Hedonism thinking in torment was, for Freud, a better mental state. It is clearer here not to stretch the meaning of the word 'pleasant'. A Preference-Hedonist should merely claim that, since Freud preferred to think clearly though in torment, his life went better if it went as he preferred.

Desire-Fulfillment Theories

Consider next Desire-Fulfillment Theories. The simplest is the *Unrestricted* Theory. This claims that what is best for someone is what would best fulfil *all* of his desires, throughout his life. Suppose that I meet a stranger who has what is believed to be a fatal disease. My sympathy is aroused, and I strongly want this stranger to be cured. We never meet again. Later, unknown to me, this stranger is cured. On the **Unrestricted Desire-Fulfillment Theory**, this event is good for me, and makes my life go better. This is not plausible. We should reject this theory.

Another theory appeals only to our desires about our own lives. I call this the **Success Theory**. This theory differs from Preference-Hedonism in only one way. *The Success Theory appeals to all of our preferences about our own lives. A Preference-Hedonist appeals only to preferences about those features of our lives that are introspectively discernible.* Suppose that

I strongly want not to be deceived by other people. On Preference-Hedonism it will be better for me if I believe that I am not being deceived. It will be irrelevant if my belief is false, since this makes no difference to my state of mind. On the Success Theory, it will be worse for me if my belief is false. I have a strong desire about my own life—that I should not be deceived in this way. It is bad for me if this desire is not fulfilled, even if I falsely believe that it is. . . .

Suppose that I try to give my children a good start in life. I try to give them the right education, good habits, and psychological strength. Suppose that, unknown to me, my children's lives go badly. One finds that the education that I gave him makes him unemployable, another has a mental breakdown, another becomes a petty thief. If my children's lives fail in these ways, and these failures are in part the result of mistakes I made as their parent, these failures in my children's lives would be judged on the Success Theory to be bad for me. One of my strongest desires was to be a successful parent. What is now happening to my children, though it is unknown to me, shows that this desire is not fulfilled. My life failed in one of the ways in which I most wanted it to succeed. Though I do not know this fact, it is bad for me, and makes it true that I have had a worse life. This is like the case where I strongly want not to be deceived. Even if I never know, it is bad for me both if I am deceived and if I turn out to be an unsuccessful parent. These are not introspectively discernible differences in my conscious life; so, on Preference-Hedonism, these events are not bad for me. But on the Success Theory, they are.

Consider next the desires that some people have about what happens after they are dead. For a Preference-Hedonist, once I am dead, nothing bad can happen to me. A Success Theorist should deny this. Return to the case where all my children have wretched lives, because of the mistakes I made as their parent. Suppose that my children's lives all go badly only after I am dead. My life turns out to have been a failure, in one of the ways I cared about most. A Success Theorist should claim that, here too, this makes it true that I had a worse life.

Some Success Theorists would reject this claim, since they tell us to ignore the desires of the dead.

But suppose that I was asked, 'Do you want it to be true, even after you are dead, that you were a successful parent?' I would answer 'Yes'. It is irrelevant to my desire whether it is fulfilled before or after I am dead. These Success Theorists count it as bad for me if my attempts fail, even if, because I am an exile, I never know this. How then can it matter whether, when my attempts fail, I am dead? All that my death does is to *ensure* that I will never know this. If we think it irrelevant that I never know about the non-fulfillment of my desires, we cannot defensibly claim that my death makes a difference. . . .

Objective List Theories

Turn now to the third kind of theory that I mentioned: the Objective List Theory. According to this theory, certain things are good or bad for people, whether or not these people would want to have the good things, or to avoid the bad things. The good things might include moral goodness, rational activity, the development of one's abilities, having children and being a good parent, knowledge, and the awareness of true beauty. The bad things might include being betrayed, manipulated, slandered, deceived, being deprived of liberty or dignity, and enjoying either sadistic pleasure, or aesthetic pleasure in what is in fact ugly.

An Objective List Theorist might claim that his theory coincides with the Success Theory. On this theory, what would make my life go best depends on what I would prefer, now and in the various alternatives, if I knew all of the relevant facts about these alternatives. An Objective List Theorist might say that the most relevant facts are those just mentioned—the facts about what would be good or bad for me. And he might claim that anyone who knew these facts would want what is good for him, and want to avoid what would be bad for him.

Even if this was true, though the Objective List Theory would coincide with the Success Theory, the two theories would remain distinct. A Success Theorist would reject this description of the coincidence. On his theory, nothing is good or bad for people *whatever* their preferences are. Something is bad for someone only when, if he knew the facts, he would want to avoid it. And the relevant facts do

not include the alleged facts cited by the Objective List Theorist. *On the Success Theory it is, for instance, bad for a person to be deceived if and because this is not what this person wants. The Objective List Theorist makes the reverse claim. People want not to be deceived because this is bad for them.*

As these remarks imply, there is one important difference between on the one hand Preference-Hedonism and the Success Theory, and on the other hand the Objective List Theory. The first two kinds of theory give an account of self-interest which is purely descriptive—which does not appeal to facts about value. This account appeals only to what a person does and would prefer, given full knowledge of the purely non-evaluative facts about the alternatives. In contrast, the Objective List Theory appeals directly to what it claims to be facts about value.

In choosing between these theories, we must decide how much weight to give to imagined cases in which someone's fully informed preferences would be bizarre. If we can appeal to these cases, they cast doubt on both Preference-Hedonism and the Success Theory. Consider the man who wants to spend his life counting the numbers of blades of grass in different lawns. Suppose that this man knows that he could achieve great progress if instead he worked in some especially useful part of Applied Mathematics. Though he could achieve such significant results, he prefers to go on counting blades of grass. On the Success Theory, if we allow this theory to cover all imaginable cases, it could be better for this person if he counted his blades of grass rather than achieving great and useful mathematical results.

The counter-example might be more offensive. Suppose that what someone would most prefer, knowing the alternatives, is a life in which, without being detected, he causes as much pain as he can to other people. On the Success Theory, such a life would be what is best for this person.

We may be unable to accept these conclusions. . . . Suppose we agree that, in some imagined cases, what someone would most want both now and later, fully knowing about the alternatives, would *not* be what would be best for him. If we accept this conclusion, it may seem that we must reject both Preference-Hedonism and the Success Theory. . . .

The Composite View

Which of these different theories should we accept? I shall not attempt an answer here. But I shall end by mentioning another theory, which might be claimed to combine what is most plausible in these conflicting theories. It is a striking fact that those who have addressed this question have disagreed so fundamentally. Many philosophers have been convinced Hedonists; many others have been as much convinced that Hedonism is a gross mistake.

Some Hedonists have reached their view as follows. They consider an opposing view, such as that which claims that what is good for someone is to have knowledge, to engage in rational activity, and to be aware of true beauty. These Hedonists ask, 'Would these states of mind be good, if they brought no enjoyment, and if the person in these states of mind had not the slightest desire that they continue?' Since they answer No, they conclude that the value of these states of mind must lie in their being liked, and in their arousing a desire that they continue.

This reasoning assumes that the value of a whole is just the sum of the value of its parts. If we remove the part to which the Hedonist appeals, what is left seems to have no value, hence Hedonism is the truth.

Suppose instead, more plausibly, that the value of a whole may not be the mere sum of the value of its parts. We might then claim that what is best for people is a composite. It is not just their being in the conscious states that they want to be in. Nor is it just their having knowledge, engaging in rational activity, being aware of true beauty, and the like. What is good for someone is neither just what Hedonists claim, nor just what is claimed by Objective List Theorists. *We might believe that if we had either of these, without the other, what we had would have little or no value.* We might claim, for example, that what is good or bad for someone is to have knowledge, to be engaged in rational activity, to experience mutual love, and to be aware of beauty, while strongly wanting just these things. On this view, each side in this disagreement saw only half of the truth. Each put forward as sufficient something that was only necessary. Pleasure with many other kinds of object has no value. And, if they are entirely devoid of pleasure, there is no value in knowledge, rational activity, love,

or the awareness of beauty. *What is of value, or is good for someone, is to have both; to be engaged in these activities, and to be strongly wanting to be so engaged.*

DISCUSSION QUESTIONS:

1. Parfit claims that pleasure and pain are not distinctive kinds of experience. Instead, he suggests that what unifies all instances of pain is that they are unwanted, whereas what unifies all instances of pleasure is that they are wanted. Do you find this convincing? Does it make sense to say that someone wants an experience that is painful? Does it make sense to say that someone does not want an experience that is pleasurable?

2. According to the success theory, your life goes well just in case you get what you want. This means that if a mass murderer wants to commit heinous crimes and does so, then his life might have been as good as the life of Mother Theresa (assuming that she wanted to serve the poor and did so). Do you find this plausible?

3. The Objective List Theory says that your life goes well just in case your life contains certain features that are objectively valuable. Parfit provides a partial list of the kind of things that might have such value. Do you think that anything is valuable in-and-of itself, independent of our wants and desires? If so, what kind of things? And what makes them valuable if not our wanting them?

Argument Reconstruction Exercises:

I. Arguments from false implication are reasons to deny a particular theory or principle. If the principle entails something that is false or implausible, then the principle itself is also false or implausible. Identify the premises and conclusion in the following argument from false implication.

> The simplest [desire-fulfillment theory] is the unrestricted theory. This claims that what is best for someone is what would best fulfill all of his desires, throughout his life. Suppose that I meet a stranger who has what is believed to be a fatal disease. My sympathy is aroused, and I strongly want this stranger to be cured. We never meet again. Later, unknown to me, this stranger is cured. On the

Unrestricted Desire-Fulfillment Theory, this event is good for me, and makes my life go better. This is not plausible. We should reject this theory. (page 188)

II. Parfit argues that Success Theorists should accept the idea that what happens to someone after he dies can be bad for him. He argues for this conclusion by showing that success theorists are already committed to saying that unknown fulfillment or frustration of desires is relevant to our welfare and that death is no different. Identify the premises and conclusion in this excerpt.

> Some Success Theorists [deny that something bad can happen to someone after he is dead], since they tell us to ignore the desires of the dead. But suppose that I was asked, 'Do you want it to be true, even after you are dead, that you were a successful parent?' I would answer 'Yes'. It is irrelevant to my desire whether it is fulfilled before or after I am dead. These Success Theorists count it as bad for me if my attempts fail, even if, because I am in exile, I never know this. How then can it matter whether, when my attempts fail, I am dead? All that my death does is to *ensure* that I will never know this. If we think it irrelevant that I never know about the non-fulfillment of my desires, we cannot defensibly claim that my death makes a difference... (pages 188–189)

III. Parfit argues that both Preference-Hedonism and Success Theory should be rejected because they have false implications in what he describes as "bizarre" cases. Identify the premises and conclusion in this excerpt.

> In choosing between these theories, we must decide how much weight to give to imagined cases in which someone's fully informed preferences would be bizarre. If we appeal to these cases, they cast doubt on both Preference-Hedonism and the Success Theory.... Suppose that what someone would most prefer, knowing the alternatives, is a life in which, without being detected, he causes as much pain as he can to other people. On the Success Theory, such a life would be what is best for this person. Suppose we agree that, in some imagined cases, what someone would most want both now and later, fully knowing about the alternatives, would not be best for him. If we accept this conclusion, it may seem that we must reject both Preference-Hedonism and the Success Theory. (page 189)

IV. We often reject theories because they have what we think are false implications. Identify the premises and conclusion in this paraphrased argument:

> The success theory says that a good life is one in which a person gets what he wants. But suppose what someone wants most is to rape and torture others? Despite the fact that this might bring pleasure to this person, it wouldn't make for a good life. So the success theory is a mistake.

CHAPTER 11

Consequentialism

I do the very best I know how, the very best I can, and I mean to keep on doing so until the end.

—ABRAHAM LINCOLN

INTRODUCTION

Here's a foolproof way to do the right thing: Always do the best one can. If we always do our moral best, we can't be properly criticized for not having done better; we did the best we could. The reassuring injunction that parents give their children before every test, athletic competition, recital, and the like—just do your best—is the bedrock of ethical wisdom.

What, though, is it to do our best from a moral point of view? One very plausible answer is this: the difference between those acts that are morally best and those that are less than the best is determined solely by their consequences. This is the insight behind **Consequentialism**, which claims that the moral status of actions is determined solely by their results. One implication of Consequentialism seems to be that no acts are right or wrong just in themselves. Nothing is just plain right or just plain wrong. The moral status of an act depends on its consequences, and these can vary with the circumstances. Even an act of torture may be morally permissible if its consequences in the situation are good enough. The alternative to Consequentialism is **Nonconsequentialism**, which claims that consequences are not the *only* factors that determine what is morally best for us to do. The intrinsic nature of an action—the mere fact, for example, that it is an act of breaking a promise

or an act of torture—can play a role in determining whether it is morally best. The readings in this chapter all deal with the strengths and weaknesses of Consequentialism. We consider Nonconsequentialism in Chapter Twelve.

We have already considered one form of Consequentialism in Chapter Nine, **Ethical Egoism**. According to Ethical Egoism, an act is our moral duty just so long as it will produce more net good for us than any other available alternative. From the Egoist's perspective, to do one's moral best is simply to do what will produce the best results for oneself. No one else counts in the calculation of best consequences.

Another, more important form of Consequentalism is **Utilitarianism**. Utilitarians claim that our moral duties are the acts that produce the most net good, not only for us, but for everyone. **Act Utilitarians** develop this idea by focusing on the consequences of individual actions: A particular act is morally obligatory just so long as it will produce more net good than any other alternative available. If your act of breaking a specific promise to a friend will produce more net good than any other alternative available to you, then you are morally obligated to do so. **Rule Utilitarians** take a different approach. They focus on the consequences, not of particular actions (breaking a specific promise), but of general types of actions (promise breaking in general), and they take general types of actions to be specified by moral rules. Your act of breaking a particular promise to a friend is morally obligatory just so long as it is required by a correct moral rule for your situation, and a correct moral rule for your situation is such that more net good would result from everyone's following it than from their following any alternative rule. Put simply, you are morally obligated to break your promise to your friend, if the general practice of breaking such promises in situations like yours will produce more net good than any alternative practice.

All consequentialists (including Utilitarians) say that what is right is a function of what is good. Hence, a major task confronting all consequentialists is to develop a theory of the good (see Chapter 10). Assuming that the rightness or wrongness of our actions depends on the amount of net good they produce, just what things are good and what things are evil? We can distinguish generally between two types of goods and two types of evils. Some things are **intrinsically good** (good for their own sake); other things are **instrumentally good** or **extrinsically good** (good by virtue of producing other goods). Similarly, some things are **intrinsically evil** (evil for their own sake); other things are **instrumentally evil** or **extrinsically evil** (evil by virtue of producing other evils). Since extrinsic goods and evils gain their value or disvalue from the intrinsic goods and evils they produce, Utilitarians concentrate on the question of what is intrinsically good and what is intrinsically evil. They develop different versions of Utilitarianism by presenting different theories of intrinsic value.

Our readings open with John Stuart Mill's classic statement of Utilitarianism. According to Mill, whether acts are right or wrong is determined by the net intrinsic good they produce, not just for the person performing the act, but for everyone. In the selection "Against Moral Conservatism," Kai Nielsen defends Act-Utilitarianism against the objection of

Moral Conservatism or **Absolutism** that some actions are always wrong no matter what the circumstances and so no matter what their consequences. Denying this sometimes leads to problem cases that are tough for Act Utilitarians to explain.

Some Utilitarians adopt Rule-Utilitarianism in response to the problem cases considered by Nielsen. They acknowledge that the moral status of a particular action is sometimes disconnected from the net good contained in its consequences. Some particular acts are wrong, despite the fact that they will produce more net intrinsic good than any alternative. Some particular acts are obligatory, despite the fact that they will not produce as much net intrinsic good as some other alternative. Rule Utilitarians believe, however, that the lesson of these examples is that the moral status of a particular action is determined by the net good associated with the *type* of activity the act represents, rather than the net good produced by the act itself. A particular act of torture that is clearly morally wrong may maximize the net good in the situation at hand, but, Rule Utilitarians may insist, torture as a general practice does not maximize the net good. That's why both torture in general and particular acts of torture are wrong. The morality of an act is determined by the net good produced by the general type of behavior it represents. How though are types of behavior to be defined? Rule Utilitarians use moral rules to define types of behavior; in doing so, they face the challenge of distinguishing between relevant considerations, which should be part of a defining moral rule, and irrelevant ones, which should not. Richard Brandt develops a form of Rule-Utilitarianism in the selection "Some Merits of One Form of Rule-Utilitarianism." Finally, in the selection "Turning the Trolley," Judith Thomson presents a puzzle that involves the moral relevance of consequences. Thinking about our moral obligations in far-fetched scenarios can help us to sort out how and to what extent consequences determine the difference between right and wrong.

SUGGESTIONS FOR FURTHER READING

Bentham, J. *An Introduction to the Principles of Morals and Legislation*. (Garden City: Doubleday, 1961). Originally published in 1789.

Brandt, R. *A Theory of the Good and the Right*. (New York: Oxford University Press, 1979)

_____. "In Search of a Credible Form of Rule-Utilitarianism," *Morality and the Language of Conduct*, ed. H. N. Castaneda and George Nakhnikian. (Wayne State University, 1953)

_____. *Morality, Utilitarianism, and Rights*. (Cambridge: Cambridge University Press, 1992)

Brink, D. *Moral Realism and the Foundations of Ethics*. (New York: Cambridge University Press, 1989)

_____. "Some Forms and Limits of Consequentialism," *The Oxford Handbook of Ethical Theory*, ed. D. Copp. (Oxford: Clarendon Press, 2006)

Feldman, F. *Doing the Best We Can*. (Boston: D. Reidel, 1986)

_____. *Utilitarianism, Hedonism, and Desert*. (New York: Cambridge University Press, 1997)

Lyons, D. *Forms and Limits of Utilitarianism*. (Oxford: Clarendon Press, 1965)

Moore, G. E. *Principia Ethica*. (Cambridge: Cambridge University Press, 1903)

_____. *Ethics* (New York: Oxford University Press, 1912)

Ross, W. D. *The Right and the Good*. (Oxford: Clarendon Press, 1930)

Sen, A., and Williams, B., eds. *Utilitarianism and Beyond*. (Cambridge: Cambridge University Press, 1982)

Smart, J. J. C. "Extreme and Restricted Utilitarianism", *The Philosophical Quarterly*, 6: 344–54, 1956.

Smart, J. J. C. and Williams, B., eds. *Utilitarianism: For and Against*. (Cambridge: Cambridge University Press, 1973)

11.1 UTILITARIANISM

JOHN STUART MILL (1863)

John Stuart Mill was a British philosopher, economist, and social theorist. He made major contributions to logic, social philosophy, and ethics. In these selections from his book *Utilitarianism*, he defends the ethical theory of the same name. Given the question of what makes an action or social policy morally right rather than wrong, Utilitarians answer that the difference lies in the consequences. Mill offers a defense of both the **Principle of Utility** and **Hedonism**. He also argues that pleasures differ not only quantitatively but also qualitatively, and he supports his utilitarianism by arguing that since "there is in reality nothing desired except happiness," happiness is the sole criterion of morality.

Reading Questions:

1. How does Mill define happiness?

2. What does Mill take to be intrinsically good (good for its own sake)? What does he take to be intrinsically evil (evil for its own sake)?

3. Mill introduces the claim that some pleasures are of a higher quality than others in order to meet a particular objection to his theory. What is that objection?

4. What is Mill's argument for his claim that intellectual pleasures are of a higher quality than non-intellectual ones? How does he respond to the fact that many who have learned to enjoy intellectual pleasures when they are young subsequently prefer non-intellectual ones?

5. What weight does Mill think we should give to our own interests against those of others, when we decide how to act?

6. Mill considers five objections to the Principle of Utility. What is each objection and what is Mill's response to it?

7. What line of reasoning leads Mill to the conclusion that happiness is one of the criteria of morality, one of the factors determining the difference between right and wrong? What line of reasoning leads him to the conclusion that it is the sole criterion of morality?

The Principles of Utility and Hedonism

The creed which accepts as the foundation of morals, Utility, or the Greatest Happiness Principle, holds that actions are right in proportion as they tend to promote happiness, wrong as they tend to produce the reverse of happiness. By happiness is intended pleasure, and the absence of pain; by unhappiness, pain, and the privation of pleasure. To give a clear view of the moral standard set up by the theory, much more requires to be said; in particular, what things it includes in the ideas of pain and pleasure; and to what extent this is left an open question. But these supplementary explanations do not affect the theory of life on which this theory of morality is grounded—namely, that *pleasure, and freedom from pain, are the only things desirable as ends; and that all desirable things (which are as numerous in the utilitarian as in any other scheme) are desirable either for the pleasure inherent in themselves, or as means to the promotion of pleasure and the prevention of pain.*

The Qualitative Difference Between Pleasures

Now, such a theory of life excites in many minds, and among them in some of the most estimable in feeling and purpose, inveterate dislike. To suppose that life has (as they express it) no higher end than pleasure—no better and nobler object of desire and pursuit—they designate as utterly mean and groveling; as a doctrine worthy only of swine, to whom the followers of Epicurus were, at a very early period, contemptuously likened; and modern holders of the doctrine are occasionally made the subject of equally polite comparisons by its German, French, and English assailants.

When thus attacked, the Epicureans have always answered, that it is not they, but their accusers, who represent human nature in a degrading light; since the accusation supposes human beings to be capable of no pleasures except those of which swine are capable. . . . But there is no known **Epicurean** theory of life which does not assign to the pleasures of the intellect, of the feelings and imagination, and of the moral sentiments, a much higher value as pleasures than to those of mere sensation. It must be admitted, however, that utilitarian writers in general have placed the superiority of mental over bodily pleasures chiefly in the greater permanency, safety, uncostliness, etc., of the former—that is, in their circumstantial advantages rather than in their intrinsic nature. And on all these points utilitarians have fully proved their case; but they might have taken the other, and, as it may be called, higher ground, with entire consistency. It is quite compatible with the principle of utility to recognize the fact, that some kinds of pleasure are more desirable and more valuable than others. It would be absurd that while, in estimating all other things, quality is considered as well as quantity, the estimation of pleasures should be supposed to depend on quantity alone.

If I am asked, what I mean by difference of quality in pleasures, or what makes one pleasure more valuable than another, merely as a pleasure, except its being greater in amount, there is but one possible answer. *Of two pleasures, if there be one to which all or almost all who have experience of both give a decided preference, irrespective of any feeling of moral obligation to prefer it, that is the more desirable pleasure.* If one of the two is, by those who are competently acquainted with both, placed so far above the other that they prefer it, even though knowing it to be attended with a greater amount of discontent, and would not resign it for any quantity of the other pleasure which their nature is capable of, we are justified in ascribing to the preferred enjoyment a superiority in quality, so far outweighing quantity as to render it, in comparison, of small account.

Now it is an unquestionable fact that those who are equally acquainted with, and equally capable of appreciating and enjoying, both, do give a most marked preference to the manner of existence which employs their higher faculties. Few human creatures would consent to be changed into any of the lower animals, for a promise of the fullest allowance of a beast's pleasures; no intelligent human being would consent to be a fool, no instructed person would be an ignoramus, no person of feeling and conscience would be selfish and base, even though they should be persuaded that the fool, the dunce, or the rascal is better satisfied with his lot than they are with theirs. They would not resign what they possess more than he for the most complete satisfaction of all the desires which they have in common with him. If they ever fancy they would, it is only in cases of unhappiness so extreme, that to escape from it they would exchange their lot for almost any other, however undesirable in their own eyes. A being of higher faculties requires more to make him happy, is capable probably of more acute suffering, and certainly accessible to it at more points, than one of an inferior type; but in spite of these liabilities, he can never really wish to sink into what he feels to be a lower grade of existence. We may give what explanation we please of this unwillingness; we may attribute it to pride, a name which is given indiscriminately to some of the most and to some of the least estimable feelings of which mankind are capable: we may refer it to the love of liberty and personal independence, an appeal to which was with the Stoics one of the most effective means for the inculcation of it; to the love of power, or to the love of excitement, both of which do really enter into and contribute to it: but its most appropriate appellation is a sense of dignity, which all human beings possess in one form or other, and in some, though by no means in exact, proportion to their higher faculties, and which is so essential a part of the happiness of those in whom it is strong, that nothing which conflicts with it could be, otherwise than momentarily, an object of desire to them.

Whoever supposes that this preference takes place at a sacrifice of happiness—that the superior being, in anything like equal circumstances, is not happier than the inferior—confounds the two very different ideas, of happiness, and content. It is indisputable that the being whose capacities of enjoyment are low, has the greatest chance of having them fully satisfied; and a highly endowed being will always feel that any happiness which he can look for, as the world is constituted, is imperfect. But he can learn to bear its imperfections, if they are at all bearable; and they will not make him envy the being who is indeed unconscious of the imperfections, but only because he feels not at all the good which those imperfections qualify. It is better to be a human being dissatisfied than a pig satisfied; better to be Socrates dissatisfied than a fool satisfied. And if the fool, or the pig, are a different opinion, it is because they only know their own side of the question. The other party to the comparison knows both sides.

Two Objections to the Argument for Qualitative Difference Between Pleasures

It may be objected, that many who are capable of the higher pleasures, occasionally, under the influence of temptation, postpone them to the lower. But this is quite compatible with a full appreciation of the intrinsic superiority of the higher. Men often, from infirmity of character, make their election for the nearer good, though they know it to be the less valuable; and this no less when the choice is between two bodily pleasures, than when it is between bodily and mental. They pursue sensual indulgences to the injury of health, though perfectly aware that health is the greater good.

It may be further objected, that many who begin with youthful enthusiasm for everything noble, as they advance in years sink into indolence and selfishness. But I do not believe that those who undergo this very common change, voluntarily choose the lower description of pleasures in preference to the higher. I believe that before they devote themselves exclusively to the one, they have already become incapable of the other. Capacity for the nobler feelings is in most natures a very tender plant, easily killed, not only by hostile influences, but by mere want of sustenance; and in the majority of young persons it speedily dies away if the occupations to which their position in life has devoted them, and the society into which it has thrown them, are not favourable to keeping that higher capacity in exercise. Men lose their high aspirations as they lose their intellectual tastes, because they have not time or opportunity for indulging them; and they addict themselves to inferior pleasures, not because they deliberately prefer them, but because they are either the only ones to which they have access, or the only ones which they are any longer capable of enjoying. It may be questioned whether any one who has remained equally susceptible to both classes of pleasures, ever knowingly and calmly preferred the lower; though many, in all ages, have broken down in an ineffectual attempt to combine both.

From this verdict of the only competent judges, I apprehend there can be no appeal. On a question which is the best worth having of two pleasures, or which of two modes of existence is the most grateful to the feelings, apart from its moral attributes and from its consequences, the judgment of those who are qualified by knowledge of both, or, if they differ, that of the majority among them, must be admitted as final. And there needs be the less hesitation to accept this judgment respecting the quality of pleasures, since there is no other tribunal to be referred to even on the question of quantity. What means are there of determining which is the acutest of two pains, or the intensest of two pleasurable sensations, except the general suffrage of those who are familiar with both? Neither pains nor pleasures are homogeneous, and pain is always heterogeneous with pleasure. What is there to decide whether a particular pleasure is worth purchasing at the cost of a particular pain, except the feelings and judgment of the experienced? When, therefore, those feelings and judgment declare the pleasures derived from the higher faculties to be preferable in kind, apart from the question of intensity, to those of which the animal nature, disjoined from the higher faculties, is susceptible, they are entitled on this subject to the same regard.

I have dwelt on this point, as being a necessary part of a perfectly just conception of Utility or Happiness, considered as the directive rule of human conduct. But it is by no means an indispensable condition to the acceptance of the utilitarian standard; for that standard is not the agent's own greatest happiness, but the greatest amount of happiness altogether; and if it may possibly be doubted whether a noble character is always the happier for its nobleness, there can be no doubt that it makes other people happier, and that the world in general is immensely a gainer by it. Utilitarianism, therefore, could only attain its end by the general cultivation of nobleness of character, even if each individual were only benefited by the nobleness of others, and his own, so far as happiness is concerned, were a sheer deduction from the benefit. But the bare enunciation of such an absurdity as this last, renders refutation superfluous.

According to the Greatest Happiness Principle, as above explained, the ultimate end, with reference to and for the sake of which all other things are desirable (whether we are considering our own good or that of other people), is an existence exempt as far as possible from pain, and as rich as possible in enjoyments, both in point of quantity and quality; the test of quality, and the rule for measuring it against quantity, being the preference felt by those who in their opportunities of experience, to which must be added their habits of self-consciousness and self-observation, are best furnished with the means of comparison. This, being, according to the utilitarian opinion, the end of human action, is necessarily also the standard of morality; which may accordingly be defined, the rules and precepts for human conduct, by the observance of which an existence such as has been described might be, to the greatest extent possible, secured to all mankind; and not to them only, but, so far as the nature of things admits, to the whole sentient creation. . . .

The Equal Importance of Each Person's Happiness

I must again repeat, what the assailants of utilitarianism seldom have the justice to acknowledge, that the happiness which forms the utilitarian standard of what is right in conduct, is not the agent's own happiness, but that of all concerned. *As between his own happiness and that of others, utilitarianism requires him to be as strictly impartial as a disinterested and benevolent spectator.* In the golden rule of Jesus of Nazareth, we read the complete spirit of the ethics of utility. To do as you would be done by, and to love your neighbor as yourself, constitute the ideal perfection of utilitarian morality. As the means of making the nearest approach to this ideal, utility would enjoin, first, that laws and social arrangements should place the happiness, or (as speaking practically it may be called) the interest, of every individual, as nearly as possible in harmony with the interest of the whole; and secondly, that education and opinion, which have so vast a power over human character, should so use that power as to establish in the mind of every individual an indissoluble association between his own happiness and the good of the whole; especially between his own happiness and the practice of such modes of conduct, negative and positive, as regard for the universal happiness prescribes; so that not only he may be unable to conceive the possibility of happiness to himself, consistently with conduct opposed to the general good, but also that a direct impulse to promote the general good may be in every individual one of the habitual motives of action, and the sentiments connected therewith may fill a large and prominent place in every human being's sentient existence. If the impugners of the utilitarian morality represented it to their own minds in this its true character, I know not what recommendation possessed by any other morality they could possibly affirm to be wanting to it; what more beautiful or more exalted developments of human nature any other ethical system can be supposed to foster, or what springs of action, not accessible to the utilitarian, such systems rely on for giving effect to their mandates. . . .

Objections to the Principle of Utility and Replies

The objectors to utilitarianism cannot always be charged with representing it in a discreditable light. *On the contrary, those among them who entertain anything like a just idea of its disinterested character, sometimes find fault with its standard as being too high for humanity.* They say it is exacting too much to require that people shall always act from the inducement of promoting the general interests of society. But this is to mistake the very meaning of a standard of morals, and confound the rule of action with the motive of it. It is the business of ethics to tell us what are our duties, or by what test we may know them; but no system of ethics requires that the sole motive of all we do shall be a feeling of duty; on the contrary, ninety-nine hundredths of all our actions are done from other motives, and rightly so done, if the rule of duty does not condemn them. It is the more unjust to utilitarianism that this particular misapprehension should be made a ground of objection to it, inasmuch as utilitarian moralists have gone beyond almost all others in affirming that the motive has nothing to do with the morality of the action, though much with the worth of the agent. He who saves a fellow creature from drowning does what is morally right, whether his motive be duty, or the hope of being paid for his trouble; he who betrays the friend that trusts him, is guilty of a crime, even if his object be to serve another friend to whom he is under greater obligations. . . .

The same considerations dispose of another reproach against the doctrine of utility, founded on a still grosser misconception of the purpose of a standard of morality, and of the very meaning of the words right and wrong. *It is often affirmed that utilitarianism renders men cold and unsympathising; that it chills their moral feelings towards individuals; that it makes them regard only the dry and hard consideration of the consequences of actions, not taking into their moral estimate the qualities from which those actions emanate.* If the assertion means that they do not allow their judgment respecting the rightness or wrongness of an action to be influenced by their opinion of the qualities of the person who does it, this is a complaint not against utilitarianism, but against having any standard of morality at all; for certainly no known ethical standard decides an action to be good or bad because it is done by a good or a bad man, still less because done by an amiable, a brave, or a benevolent man, or the contrary. These considerations are relevant, not to the estimation of actions, but of persons; and there is nothing in the utilitarian theory inconsistent with the fact that there are other things which interest us in persons besides the rightness and wrongness of their actions. . . . Utilitarians are quite aware that there are other desirable possessions and qualities besides virtue, and are perfectly willing to allow to all of them their full worth. They are also aware that a right action does not necessarily indicate a virtuous character, and that actions which are blamable, often proceed from qualities entitled to praise. When this is apparent in any particular case, it modifies their estimation, not certainly of the act, but of the agent. I grant that they are, notwithstanding, of opinion, that in the long run the best proof of a good character is good actions; and resolutely refuse to consider any mental disposition as good, of which the predominant tendency is to produce bad conduct. This makes them unpopular with many people; but it is an unpopularity which they must share with every one who regards the distinction between right and wrong in a serious light; and the reproach is not one which a conscientious utilitarian need be anxious to repel. . . .

We not uncommonly hear the doctrine of utility inveighed against as a godless doctrine. If it be necessary to say anything at all against so mere an assumption, we may say that the question depends upon what idea we have formed of the moral character of the Deity. If it be a true belief that God desires, above all things, the happiness of his creatures, and that this was his purpose in their creation, utility is not only not a godless doctrine, but more profoundly religious than any other. If it be meant that utilitarianism does not recognise the revealed will of God as the supreme law of morals, I answer, that a utilitarian who believes in the perfect goodness and wisdom of God, necessarily believes that whatever God has thought fit to reveal on the subject of morals, must fulfill the requirements of utility in a supreme degree. But others besides utilitarians have been of opinion that the Christian revelation was intended, and is fitted, to inform the hearts and minds of mankind with a spirit which should enable them to find for themselves what is right, and incline them to do it when found, rather than to tell them, except in a very general way, what it is; and that we need a doctrine of ethics, carefully followed out, to interpret to us the will of God. Whether this opinion is correct or not, it is superfluous here to discuss; since whatever aid religion, either natural or revealed, can afford to ethical investigation, is as open to the utilitarian moralist as to any other. He

can use it as the testimony of God to the usefulness or hurtfulness of any given course of action, by as good a right as others can use it for the indication of a transcendental law, having no connection with usefulness or with happiness.

Again, Utility is often summarily stigmatized as an immoral doctrine by giving it the name of Expediency, and taking advantage of the popular use of that term to contrast it with Principle. But the Expedient, in the sense in which it is opposed to the Right, generally means that which is expedient for the particular interest of the agent himself; as when a minister sacrifices the interests of his country to keep himself in place. When it means anything better than this, it means that which is expedient for some immediate object, some temporary purpose, but which violates a rule whose observance is expedient in a much higher degree. The Expedient, in this sense, instead of being the same thing with the useful, is a branch of the hurtful. Thus, it would often be expedient, for the purpose of getting over some momentary embarrassment, or attaining some object immediately useful to ourselves or others, to tell a lie. But inasmuch as the cultivation in ourselves of a sensitive feeling on the subject of veracity, is one of the most useful, and the enfeeblement of that feeling one of the most hurtful, things to which our conduct can be instrumental; and inasmuch as any, even unintentional, deviation from truth, does that much towards weakening the trustworthiness of human assertion, which is not only the principal support of all present social well-being, but the insufficiency of which does more than any one thing that can be named to keep back civilization, virtue, everything on which human happiness on the largest scale depends; we feel that the violation, for a present advantage, of a rule of such transcendent expediency, is not expedient, and that he who, for the sake of a convenience to himself or to some other individual, does what depends on him to deprive mankind of the good, and inflict upon them the evil, involved in the greater or less reliance which they can place in each other's word, acts the part of one of their worst enemies. Yet that even this rule, sacred as it is, admits of possible exceptions, is acknowledged by all moralists; the chief of which is when the withholding of some fact (as of information from a malefactor, or of bad news from a person dangerously ill) would save an individual (especially an individual other than oneself) from great and unmerited evil, and when the withholding can only be effected by denial. But in order that the exception may not extend itself beyond the need, and may have the least possible effect in weakening reliance on veracity, it ought to be recognized, and, if possible, its limits defined; and if the principle of utility is good for anything, it must be good for weighing these conflicting utilities against one another, and marking out the region within which one or the other preponderates.

Again, defenders of utility often find themselves called upon to reply to such objections as this—that there is not time, previous to action, for calculating and weighing the effects of any line of conduct on the general happiness. This is exactly as if any one were to say that it is impossible to guide our conduct by Christianity, because there is not time, on every occasion on which anything has to be done, to read through the Old and New Testaments. The answer to the objection is, that there has been ample time, namely, the whole past duration of the human species. During all that time, mankind have been learning by experience the tendencies of actions; on which experience all the prudence, as well as all the morality of life, are dependent. People talk as if the commencement of this course of experience had hitherto been put off, and as if, at the moment when some man feels tempted to meddle with the property or life of another, he had to begin considering for the first time whether murder and theft are injurious to human happiness. Even then I do not think that he would find the question very puzzling; but, at all events, the matter is now done to his hand.

It is truly a whimsical supposition that, if mankind were agreed in considering utility to be the test of morality, they would remain without any agreement as to what is useful, and would take no measures for having their notions on the subject taught to the young, and enforced by law and opinion. There is no difficulty in proving any ethical standard whatever to work ill, if we suppose universal idiocy to be conjoined with it; but on any hypothesis short of that, mankind must by this time have acquired positive beliefs as to the effects of some actions on their

happiness; and the beliefs which have thus come down are the rules of morality for the multitude, and for the philosopher until he has succeeded in finding better. That philosophers might easily do this, even now, on many subjects; that the received code of ethics is by no means of divine right; and that mankind have still much to learn as to the effects of actions on the general happiness, I admit, or rather, earnestly maintain. The corollaries from the principle of utility, like the precepts of every practical art, admit of indefinite improvement, and, in a progressive state of the human mind, their improvement is perpetually going on. . . .

Of What Sort of Proof the Principle of Utility Is Susceptible

It has already been remarked, that questions of ultimate ends do not admit of proof, in the ordinary acceptation of the term. To be incapable of proof by reasoning is common to all first principles; to the first premises of our knowledge, as well as to those of our conduct. But the former, being matters of fact, may be the subject of a direct appeal to the faculties which judge of fact—namely, our senses, and our internal consciousness. Can an appeal be made to the same faculties on questions of practical ends? Or by what other faculty is cognizance taken of them?

Questions about ends are, in other words, questions what things are desirable. The utilitarian doctrine is, that happiness is desirable, and the only thing desirable, as an end; all other things being only desirable as means to that end. What ought to be required of this doctrine—what conditions is it requisite that the doctrine should fulfill—to make good its claim to be believed?

An Argument that Happiness Is Good in Itself

The only proof capable of being given that an object is visible, is that people actually see it. The only proof that a sound is audible, is that people hear it: and so of the other sources of our experience. In like manner, I apprehend, the sole evidence it is possible to produce that anything is desirable, is that people do actually desire it. If the end which the utilitarian doctrine proposes to itself were not, in theory and in practice, acknowledged to be an end, nothing could ever convince any person that it was so. *No reason can be given why the general happiness is desirable, except that each person, so far as he believes it to be attainable, desires his own happiness.* This, however, being a fact, we have not only all the proof which the case admits of, but all which it is possible to require, that happiness is a good: that each person's happiness is a good to that person, and the general happiness, therefore, a good to the aggregate of all persons. Happiness has made out its title as one of the ends of conduct, and consequently one of the criteria of morality.

An Argument That Nothing but Happiness Is Good in Itself

But it has not, by this alone, proved itself to be the sole criterion. To do that, it would seem, by the same rule, necessary to show, not only that people desire happiness, but that they never desire anything else. Now it is palpable that they do desire things which, in common language, are decidedly distinguished from happiness. They desire, for example, virtue, and the absence of vice, no less really than pleasure and the absence of pain. The desire of virtue is not as universal, but it is as authentic a fact, as the desire of happiness. And hence the opponents of the utilitarian standard deem that they have a right to infer that there are other ends of human action besides happiness, and that happiness is not the standard of approbation and disapprobation.

But does the utilitarian doctrine deny that people desire virtue, or maintain that virtue is not a thing to be desired? The very reverse. It maintains not only that virtue is to be desired, but that it is to be desired disinterestedly, for itself. Whatever may be the opinion of utilitarian moralists as to the original conditions by which virtue is made virtue; however they may believe (as they do) that actions and dispositions are only virtuous because they promote another end than virtue; yet this being granted, and it having been decided, from considerations of this description, what is virtuous, they not only place virtue at the very head of the things which are good as means to the ultimate end, but they also recognize as a psychological fact the possibility of its being, to the individual, a good in

itself, without looking to any end beyond it; and hold, that the mind is not in a right state, not in a state conformable to Utility, not in the state most conducive to the general happiness, unless it does love virtue in this manner—as a thing desirable in itself, even although, in the individual instance, it should not produce those other desirable consequences which it tends to produce, and on account of which it is held to be virtue. This opinion is not, in the smallest degree, a departure from the Happiness principle. The ingredients of happiness are very various, and each of them is desirable in itself, and not merely when considered as swelling an aggregate. The principle of utility does not mean that any given pleasure, as music, for instance, or any given exemption from pain, as for example health, is to be looked upon as means to a collective something termed happiness, and to be desired on that account. They are desired and desirable in and for themselves; besides being means, they are a part of the end. Virtue, according to the utilitarian doctrine, is not naturally and originally part of the end, but it is capable of becoming so; and in those who love it disinterestedly it has become so, and is desired and cherished, not as a means to happiness, but as a part of their happiness.

To illustrate this farther, we may remember that virtue is not the only thing, originally a means, and which if it were not a means to anything else, would be and remain indifferent, but which by association with what it is a means to, comes to be desired for itself, and that too with the utmost intensity. What, for example, shall we say of the love of money? There is nothing originally more desirable about money than about any heap of glittering pebbles. Its worth is solely that of the things which it will buy; the desires for other things than itself, which it is a means of gratifying. Yet the love of money is not only one of the strongest moving forces of human life, but money is, in many cases, desired in and for itself; the desire to possess it is often stronger than the desire to use it, and goes on increasing when all the desires which point to ends beyond it, to be compassed by it, are falling off. It may, then, be said truly, that money is desired not for the sake of an end, but as part of the end. From being a means to happiness, it has come to be itself a principal ingredient of the individual's conception of happiness. The same may be said of the majority of the great objects of human life—power, for example, or fame; except that to each of these there is a certain amount of immediate pleasure annexed, which has at least the semblance of being naturally inherent in them; a thing which cannot be said of money. Still, however, the strongest natural attraction, both of power and of fame, is the immense aid they give to the attainment of our other wishes; and it is the strong association thus generated between them and all our objects of desire, which gives to the direct desire of them the intensity it often assumes, so as in some characters to surpass in strength all other desires. In these cases the means have become a part of the end, and a more important part of it than any of the things which they are means to. What was once desired as an instrument for the attainment of happiness, has come to be desired for its own sake. In being desired for its own sake it is, however, desired as part of happiness. The person is made, or thinks he would be made, happy by its mere possession; and is made unhappy by failure to obtain it. The desire of it is not a different thing from the desire of happiness, any more than the love of music, or the desire of health. They are included in happiness. They are some of the elements of which the desire of happiness is made up. Happiness is not an abstract idea, but a concrete whole; and these are some of its parts. And the utilitarian standard sanctions and approves their being so. Life would be a poor thing, very ill provided with sources of happiness, if there were not this provision of nature, by which things originally indifferent, but conducive to, or otherwise associated with, the satisfaction of our primitive desires, become in themselves sources of pleasure more valuable than the primitive pleasures, both in permanency, in the space of human existence that they are capable of covering, and even in intensity.

Virtue, according to the utilitarian conception, is a good of this description. There was no original desire of it, or motive to it, save its conduciveness to pleasure, and especially to protection from pain. But through the association thus formed, it may be felt a good in itself, and desired as such with as great intensity as any other good; and with this difference between it and the love of money, of power, or of fame, that all of these may, and often do, render the individual noxious to the other members of the society to which he belongs, whereas there is nothing which makes him so much a blessing to them as the cultivation of the disinterested love of virtue. And consequently, the utilitarian standard, while it tolerates and approves those other acquired desires, up to the point beyond which they would be more injurious to the general happiness than promotive of it, enjoins and requires the cultivation of the love of virtue up to the greatest strength possible, as being above all things important to the general happiness.

It results from the preceding considerations, that there is in reality nothing desired except happiness. Whatever is desired otherwise than as a means to some end beyond itself, and ultimately to happiness, is desired as itself a part of happiness, and is not desired for itself until it has become so. Those who desire virtue for its own sake, desire it either because the consciousness of it is a pleasure, or because the consciousness of being without it is a pain, or for both reasons united; as in truth the pleasure and pain seldom exist separately, but almost always together, the same person feeling pleasure in the degree of virtue attained, and pain in not having attained more. If one of these gave him no pleasure, and the other no pain, he would not love or desire virtue, or would desire it only for the other benefits which it might produce to himself or to persons whom he cared for. *We have now, then, an answer to the question, of what sort of proof the principle of utility is susceptible. If the opinion which I have now stated is psychologically true—if human nature is so constituted as to desire nothing which is not either a part of happiness or a means of happiness, we can have no other proof, and we require no other, that these are the only things desirable. If so, happiness is the sole end of human action, and the promotion of it the test by which to judge of all human conduct; from whence it necessarily follows that it must be the criterion of morality, since a part is included in the whole.*

And now to decide whether this is really so; whether mankind does desire nothing for itself but that which is a pleasure to them, or of which the absence is a pain; we have evidently arrived at a question of fact and experience, dependent, like all similar questions, upon evidence. It can only be determined by practiced self-consciousness and self-observation, assisted by observation of others. I believe that these sources of evidence, impartially consulted, will declare that desiring a thing and finding it pleasant, aversion to it and thinking of it as painful, are phenomena entirely inseparable, or rather two parts of the same phenomenon; in strictness of language, two different modes of naming the same psychological fact: that to think of an object as desirable (unless for the sake of its consequences), and to think of it as pleasant, are one and the same thing; and that to desire anything, except in proportion as the idea of it is pleasant, is a physical and metaphysical impossibility.

DISCUSSION QUESTIONS:

1. Mill defines happiness in terms of pleasure and the absence of pain. Is this all there is to happiness?
2. Mill claims that happiness, understood as pleasure and the absence of pain, is the only intrinsic good. Might some other things (e.g., virtue, knowledge, self-respect) be good for their own sakes independently of any pleasure they may provide us?
3. According to Utilitarianism, whether an act is right or wrong is determined solely by its consequences. Might some other factors be relevant, such as whether the act is required to keep a promise or pay a debt of gratitude?
4. Mill insists that it "is not the agent's own happiness, but that of all concerned" that matters for morality, and, given his Hedonism, the set of "all concerned" is presumably the set of all beings capable of experiencing pleasure or pain. Is this a correct determination of the set of things whose welfare is relevant to our obligations? What of plants? Ecosystems? Natural wonders? Works of art?
5. Mill claims that in determining how to behave, we must take the perspective of a disinterested and benevolent spectator, giving equal weight to each person's welfare. Might we owe it to some people (e.g., friends or family members) to give more weight to their interests than to that of strangers? If so, what makes it appropriate to give greater consideration to the interests some persons than to others?
6. Is Mill correct that those with experience of both prefer intellectual pleasures to non-intellectual ones? Should we prefer the one to the other?
7. Consider Mill's argument for the claim that happiness is the only intrinsic good. How, if at all, can his premises about what we do in fact desire for its own sake support his conclusions about what is intrinsically good (what we ought to desire for its own sake)?

Argument Reconstruction Exercises:

I. Are some kinds of pleasure really better than others, not in terms of quantity, but quality? Identify the premises and conclusion in Mill's argument.

Of two pleasures, if there be one to which all or almost all who have experience of both give a decided preference, irrespective of any feeling of moral obligation to prefer it, that is the more desirable pleasure. If one of the two is, by those who are competently acquainted with both, placed so far above the other that they prefer it, even though knowing it to be attended with a greater amount of discontent, and would not resign it for any quantity of the other pleasure which their nature is capable of, we are justified in ascribing to the preferred enjoyment a superiority in quality, so far outweighing quantity as to render it, in comparison, of small account. Now it is an unquestionable fact that those who are equally acquainted with, and equally capable of appreciating and enjoying, both, do give a most marked preference to the manner of existence which employs their higher faculties. (pages 195–196)

II. Mill thinks not only that each person's happiness is a good for that person, but that happiness in general, not just our own happiness, is an intrinsic good and therefore something we each have a reason to promote. Identify the premises and conclusion in his argument.

[T]he sole evidence it is possible to produce that anything is desirable, is that people do actually desire it. If the end which the utilitarian doctrine proposes to itself were not, in theory and in practice, acknowledged to be an end, nothing could ever convince any person that it was so. No reason can be given why the general happiness is desirable, except that each person, so far as he believes it to be attainable, desires his own happiness. This, however, being a fact, we have not only all the proof which the case admits of, but all which it is possible to require, that happiness is a good: that each person's happiness is a good to that person, and the general happiness, therefore, a good to the aggregate of all persons. (pages 200–201)

III. At one point, Mill sums up his argument for the Principle of Utility as follows. Identify his premises and conclusion.

If the opinion which I have now stated is psychologically true—if human nature is so constituted as to desire nothing which is not either a part of happiness or a means of happiness, we can have no other proof, and we require no other, that these are the only things desirable. If so, happiness is the sole end of human action, and the promotion of it the test by which to judge of all human conduct; from whence it necessarily follows that it must be the criterion

of morality, since a part is included in the whole. (page 202)

IV. Why is each person's happiness equally relevant to what we should do? Identify the premises and conclusion of the following argument.

Whether we should do an action is determined by how much net intrinsic good the act will produce. Since happiness (unhappiness) is the only intrinsic good (evil), whether we should do an action is determined by how much net happiness the act will produce. The fact that a particular state of happiness belongs to one person rather than another is irrelevant to how much happiness it involves. The identity of those to be affected by an action is therefore irrelevant to how much happiness the act will produce and therefore irrelevant to our act's moral status.

11.2 AGAINST MORAL CONSERVATISM

KAI NIELSEN (1972)

Kai Nielsen is Professor Emeritus of Philosophy at the University of Calgary and adjunct Professor of Philosophy at Concordia University (Montreal). He is well known for his work in ethics, social and political philosophy, and the philosophy of religion. He here defends **Consequentialism** against those who would reject it in favor of what he terms **Conservatism** or **Moral Absolutism**. The Consequentialist claims that the moral status of an action depends solely on its consequences, whereas the conservative (moral absolutist) claims that "there is a privileged moral principle or cluster of moral principles, prescribing determinate actions, with which it would always be wrong not to act in accordance no matter what the consequences." According to Nielsen, Consequentialism does not have the morally unacceptable implications often raised by its critics, while Conservatism does have morally unacceptable implications.

Reading Questions:

1. What are the defining claims of Moral Conservatism (Moral Absolutism)? How does this view differ from Consequentialism?

2. Why does Nielsen reject Anscombe's view that anyone who thinks it is sometimes right to deliberately harm the innocent has "a corrupt mind"?

3. What, according to Nielsen, are the implications of Consequentialism for the case of the Magistrate? What is his reply to those who think that those implications conflict with our commonsense morality?

4. What, according to Nielsen, are the implications of Consequentialism for the case of the Innocent Fat Man? What is his reply to those who think that those implications conflict with our commonsense morality?

5. What is Nielsen's reply to the charge that if we adopt Consequentialism, we must deny the *a priori* nature of moral truths?

6. Nielsen claims that Moral Conservatism (Moral Absolutism) has morally unacceptable consequences. What does he take them to be?

Consequentialism and Conservatism

It is sometimes claimed that any consequentialist view of ethics has monstrous implications which make such a conception of morality untenable. What we must do—so the claim goes—is reject all forms of consequentialism and accept what has been labeled 'conservativism' or 'moral absolutism.' *By 'conservativism' is meant, here, a normative ethical theory which maintains that there is a privileged moral principle or cluster of moral principles, prescribing determinate actions, with which it would always be wrong not to act in accordance no matter what the consequences.* A key example of such a principle is the claim that it is always wrong to kill an innocent human, whatever the consequences of not doing so.

I will argue that such moral conservativism is itself unjustified and, indeed, has morally unacceptable consequences, while consequentialism does not have implications which are morally monstrous and does not contain evident moral mistakes.

A consequentialist maintains that actions, rules, policies, practices, and moral principles are ultimately to be judged by certain consequences: to wit (for a very influential kind of consequentialism), by whether doing them more than, or at least as much as doing anything else, or acting in accordance with them more than or at least as much as acting in accordance with alternative policies, practices, rules or principles, tends, on the whole, and for *everyone* involved, to maximize satisfaction and minimize dissatisfaction. The states of affairs to be sought are those which maximize these things to the greatest extent possible for all mankind. But while this all

sounds very humane and humanitarian, when its implications are thought through, it has been forcefully argued, it will be seen actually to have inhumane and morally intolerable implications. Circumstances could arise in which one holding such a view would have to assert that one was justified in punishing, killing, torturing, or deliberately harming the innocent, and such a consequence is, morally speaking, unacceptable.[1] As Anscombe has put it, anyone who "really thinks, *in advance*, that it is open to question whether such an action as procuring the judicial execution of the innocent should be quite excluded from consideration—I do not want to argue with him; he shows a corrupt mind."[2]

At the risk of being thought to exhibit a corrupt mind and a shallow consequentialist morality, I should like to argue that things are not as simple and straightforward as Anscombe seems to believe.

Surely, every moral man must be appalled at the judicial execution of the innocent or at the punishment, torture, and killing of the innocent. Indeed, being appalled by such behavior partially defines what it is to be a moral agent. And a consequentialist has very good utilitarian grounds for being so appalled, namely, that it is always wrong to inflict pain for its own sake. But this does not get to the core considerations which divide a conservative position such as Anscombe's from a consequentialist view. There are a series of tough cases that need to be taken to heart and their implications thought through by any reflective person, be he a conservative or a consequentialist. By doing this, we can get to the heart of the issue between conservativism and consequentialism. Consider this clash between conservativism and consequentialism arising over the problem of a 'just war.'

> If we deliberately bomb civilian targets, we do not pretend that civilians are combatants in any simple fashion, but argue that this bombing will terminate hostilities more quickly, and will minimize all around suffering. It is hard to see how any brand of utilitarian will escape Miss Anscombe's objections. We are certainly killing the innocent. . . we are not killing them for the sake of killing them, but to save the lives of other innocent persons. Utilitarians, I think, grit their teeth and put up with this as part of the logic of total war; Miss Anscombe and anyone who thinks like her surely has to either redescribe the situation to ascribe guilt to the civilians or else she has to refuse to accept this sort of military tactics as simply wrong.[3]

It is indeed true that we cannot but feel the force of Anscombe's objections here. But is it the case that anyone shows a corrupt mind if he defends such bombing when, horrible as it is, it will quite definitely lessen appreciably the total amount of suffering and death in the long run, and if he is sufficiently nonevasive not to rationalize such a bombing of civilians into a situation in which all the putatively innocent people—children and all—are somehow in some measure judged guilty? Must such a man exhibit a corrupt moral sense if he refuses to hold that such military tactics are never morally justified? Must this be the monstrous view of a fanatical man devoid of any proper moral awareness? It is difficult for me to believe that this must be so.

Consider the quite parallel actions of guerrilla fighters and terrorists in wars of national liberation. In certain almost unavoidable circumstances, they must deliberately kill the innocent. We need to see some cases in detail here to get the necessary contextual background, and for this reason the motion picture *The Battle of Algiers* can be taken as a convenient point of reference. There we saw Algerian women—gentle, kindly women with children of their own and plainly people of moral sensitivity— with evident heaviness of heart, plant bombs which they had every good reason to believe would kill innocent people, including children; and we also saw a French general, also a human being of moral fiber

and integrity, order the torture of Arab terrorists and threaten the bombing of houses in which terrorists were concealed but which also contained innocent people, including children. There are indeed many people involved in such activities who are cruel, sadistic beasts, or simply morally indifferent or, in important ways, morally uncomprehending. But the characters I have referred to from *The Battle of Algiers* were not of that stamp. They were plainly moral agents of a high degree of sensitivity, and yet they deliberately killed or were prepared to kill the innocent. And, with inessential variations, this is a recurrent phenomenon of human living in extreme situations. Such cases are by no means desert-island or esoteric cases.

It is indeed arguable whether such actions are always morally wrong—whether anyone should ever act as the Arab women or French general acted. But what could not be reasonably maintained, *pace* Anscombe, by any stretch of the imagination, is that the characters I described from *The Battle of Algiers* exhibited corrupt minds. Possibly morally mistaken, yes; guilty of moral corruption, no.

Dropping the charge of moral corruption but sticking with the moral issue about what actions are right, is it not the case that my consequentialist position logically forces me to conclude that under some circumstances—where the good to be achieved is great enough—I must not only countenance but actually advocate such violence toward the innocent? But is it not always, no matter what the circumstances or consequences, wrong to countenance, advocate, or engage in such violence? To answer such a question affirmatively is to commit oneself to the kind of moral absolutism or conservativism which Anscombe advocates. But, given the alternatives, should not one be such a conservative or at least hold that certain **deontological** principles must never be overridden?

I will take, so to speak, the papal bull by the horns and answer that there are circumstances when such violence must be reluctantly assented to or even taken to be something that one, morally speaking, must do. But, *pace* Anscombe, this very much needs arguing, and I shall argue it; but first I would like to set out some further but simpler cases which have a similar bearing. They are, by contrast, artificial cases. I use them because, in their greater simplicity, by contrast with my above examples, there are fewer variables to control and I can more coveniently make the essential conceptual and moral points. But, if my argument is correct for these simpler cases, the line of reasoning employed is intended to be applicable to those more complex cases as well.

Two Cases

Consider the following cases embedded in their exemplary tales:

1. The Case of the Innocent Fat Man

Consider the story (well known to philosophers) of the fat man stuck in the mouth of a cave on a coast. He was leading a group of people out of the cave when he got stuck in the mouth of the cave and in a very short time high tide will be upon them, and unless he is promptly unstuck, they all will be drowned except the fat man, whose head is out of the cave. But, fortunately or unfortunately, someone has with him a stick of dynamite. The short of the matter is, either they use the dynamite and blast the poor innocent fat man out of the mouth of the cave or everyone else drowns. Either one life or many lives. Our conservative presumably would take the attitude that it is all in God's hands and say that he ought never to blast the fat man out, for it is always wrong to kill the innocent. Must or should a moral man come to that conclusion? I shall argue that he should not. . . .

2. The Magistrate and the Threatening Mob

A magistrate or judge is faced with a very real threat from a large and uncontrollable mob of rioters demanding a culprit for a crime. Unless the criminal is produced, promptly tried, and executed, they will take their own bloody revenge on a much smaller and quite vulnerable section of the community (a kind of frenzied pogrom). The judge knows that the real culprit is unknown and that the authorities do not even have a good clue as to who he may be. But he also knows that there is within easy reach a disreputable, thoroughly disliked, and useless man, who, though innocent, could easily be framed so that the mob would be quite convinced that he was guilty and would be pacified if he were promptly executed.

Recognizing that he can prevent the occurrence of extensive carnage only by framing some innocent person, the magistrate has him framed, goes through the mockery of a trial, and has him executed. Most of us regard such a framing and execution of such a man in such circumstances as totally unacceptable.[4] There are some who would say that it is categorically wrong—morally inexcusable—*whatever the circumstances*. Indeed, such a case remains a problem for the consequentialist, but here again, I shall argue, one can consistently remain a consequentialist and continue to accept commonsense moral convictions about such matters.

My storytelling is at an end. The job is to see what the stories imply. We must try to determine whether thinking through their implications should lead a clearheaded and morally sensitive man to abandon consequentialism and to adopt some form of deontological absolutism. I shall argue that it does not.

Consequentialism and the Magistrate Case

I shall consider the last case first because there are good reasons why the consequentialist should stick with commonsense moral convictions for such cases. I shall start by giving my rationale for that claim. If the magistrate were a tough-minded but morally conscientious consequentialist, he could still, on straightforward consequentialist grounds, refuse to frame and execute the innocent man, even knowing that this would unleash the mob and cause much suffering and many deaths. The rationale for his particular moral stand would be that, by so framing and then executing such an innocent man, he would, in the long run, cause still more suffering through the resultant corrupting effect on the institution of justice. That is, in a case involving such extensive general interest in the issue—without that, there would be no problem about preventing the carnage or call for such extreme measures—knowledge that the man was framed, that the law had prostituted itself, would, surely, eventually leak out. This would encourage mob action in other circumstances, would lead to an increased skepticism about the incorruptibility or even the reliability of the judicial process, and would set a dangerous precedent for less clearheaded or less scrupulously humane magistrates. Given such a potential for the corruption of justice, a utilitarian or consequentialist judge or magistrate could, on good utilitarian or consequentialist grounds, argue that it was morally wrong to frame an innocent man. If the mob must rampage if such a sacrificial lamb is not provided, then the mob must rampage.

Must a utilitarian or consequentialist come to such a conclusion? The answer is no. It is the conclusion which is, as things stand, the most reasonable conclusion, but that he *must* come to it is far too strong a claim. A consequentialist could *consistently*—I did not say successfully—argue that, in taking the above tough-minded utilitarian position, we have overestimated the corrupting effects of such judicial railroading. His circumstance was an extreme one: a situation not often to be repeated even if, instead of acting as he did, he had set a precedent by such an act of judicial murder. A utilitarian rather more skeptical than most utilitarians about the claims of commonsense morality might reason that the lesser evil here is the judicial murder of an innocent man, vile as it is. He would persist in his moral iconoclasm by standing on the consequentialist rock that the lesser evil is always to be preferred to the greater evil.

The short of it is that utilitarians could disagree, as other consequentialists could disagree, about what is morally required of us in that case. The disagreement here between utilitarians or consequentialists of the same type is not one concerning fundamental moral principles but a disagreement about the empirical facts, about what course of action would in the long run produce the least suffering and the most, happiness for *everyone* involved.[5]

However, considering the effect advocating the deliberate judicial killing of an innocent man would have on the reliance people put on commonsense moral beliefs of such a ubiquitous sort as the belief that the innocent must not be harmed, a utilitarian who defended the centrality of commonsense moral beliefs would indeed have a strong utilitarian case here. But the most crucial thing to recognize is that, to regard such judicial bowing to such a threatening mob as unqualifiedly wrong, as morally intolerable, one need not reject utilitarianism and accept some form of deontological absolutism.

It has been argued, however, that, in taking such a stance, I still have not squarely faced the moral conservative's central objection to the judicial railroading of the innocent. I allow, as a consequentialist, that there could be circumstances, at least as far as logical possibilities are concerned, in which such a railroading would be justified but that, as things actually go, it is not and probably never in fact will be justified. But the conservative's point is that in *no circumstances, either actual or conceivable, would it be justified*. No matter what the consequences, it is unqualifiedly unjustified. To say, as I do, that the situations in which it might be justified are desert-island, esoteric cases which do not occur in life, is not to the point, for, as Alan Donagan argues, "Moral theory is **a priori**, as clear-headed utilitarians like Henry Sidgwick recognized. It is, as Leibniz would say, 'true of all possible worlds.'"[6] Thus, to argue as I have and as others have that the counterexamples directed against the consequentialist's appeal to conditions which are never in fact fulfilled or are unlikely to be fulfilled is beside the point.[7] Whether "a moral theory is true or false depends on whether its implications for all possible worlds are true. Hence, whether utilitarianism (or consequentialism) is true or false cannot depend on how the actual world is."[8] It is possible to specify logically conceivable situations in which consequentialism would have implications which are monstrous—for example, certain beneficial judicial murders of the innocent (whether they are even remotely likely to obtain is irrelevant)—hence consequentialism must be false.

We should not take such a short way with consequentialists, for what is true in Donagan's claim about moral theory's being a priori will not refute or even render implausible consequentialism, and what would undermine it in such a claim about the a priori nature of moral theory and presumably moral claims is not true.

To say that moral theory is a priori is probably correct if that means that categorical moral claims—fundamental moral statements—cannot be deduced from empirical statements or nonmoral theological statements, such that it is a contradiction to assert the empirical and/or nonmoral theological statements and deny the categorical moral claims or vice versa.[9] In that fundamental sense, it is reasonable and, I believe, justifiable to maintain that moral theory is autonomous and a priori. It is also a priori in the sense that moral statements are not themselves a kind of empirical statement. That is, if I assert 'One ought never to torture any sentient creature' or 'One ought never to kill an innocent man,' I am not trying to predict or describe what people do or are likely to do but am asserting what they are *to do*. It is also true that, if a moral statement is true, it holds for all possible worlds *in which situations of exactly the sort characterized in the statement obtain*. If it is true for one, it is true for all. You cannot consistently say that A ought to do B in situation Y and deny that someone exactly like A in a situation exactly like Y ought to do B.

In these ways, moral claims and indeed moral theory are a priori. But it is also evident that none of these ways will touch the consequential or utilitarian arguments. After all, the consequentialist need not be, and typically has not been, an ethical naturalist—he need not think moral claims are derivable from factual claims or that moral claims are a subspecies of empirical statement and he could accept—indeed, he must accept—what is an important truism anyway, that you cannot consistently say that A ought to do B in situation Y and deny that someone exactly like A in a situation exactly like Y ought to do B. But he could and should deny that moral claims are a priori in the sense that rational men must or even will make them without regard for the context, the situation, in which they are made. We say people ought not to drive way over the speed limit, or speed on icy roads, or throw knives at each other. But, if human beings had a kind of metallic exoskeleton and would not be hurt, disfigured, or seriously inconvenienced by knives sticking in them or by automobile crashes, we would not—so evidently at least—have good grounds for saying such speeding or knife throwing is wrong. It would not be so obvious that it was unreasonable and immoral to do these things if these conditions obtained.

In the very way we choose to describe the situation when we make ethical remarks, it is important in making this choice that we know what the world is like and what human beings are like. Our understanding of the situation, our understanding of human nature and motivation cannot but effect our structuring of the moral case. *The consequentialist is saying that as the world goes, there are good grounds for holding that judicial killings are morally intolerable, though he would have to admit that if the world (including human beings) were very different, such killings could be something that ought to be done.* But, in holding this, he is not committed to denying the universalizability of moral judgments, for, where he would reverse or qualify the moral judgment, the situation must be different. He is only committed to claiming that, where the situation is the same or relevantly similar and the persons are relevantly similar, they must, if they are to act morally, do the same thing. However, he is claiming both (1) that, as things stand, judicial killing of the innocent is always wrong and (2) that it is an irrational moral judgment to assert of reasonably determinate actions (e.g., killing an innocent man) that they are unjustifiable and morally unacceptable in all *possible* worlds, whatever the situation and whatever the consequences.

Donagan's claims about the a priori nature of moral theories do not show such a consequentialist claim to be mistaken or even give us the slightest reason for thinking that it is mistaken. What is brutal and vile, for example, throwing a knife at a human being just for the fun of it, would not be so, if human beings were invulnerable to harm from such a direction because they had a metallic exoskeleton. Similarly, what is, as things are, morally intolerable, for example, the judicial killing of the innocent, need not be morally intolerable in all conceivable circumstances.

Such considerations support the utilitarian or consequentialist skeptical of simply taking the claims of our commonsense morality as a rock-bottom ground of appeal for moral theorizing. Yet it may also well be the case—given our extensive cruelty anyway—that, if we ever start sanctioning such behavior, an even greater callousness toward life than the very extensive callousness extant now will, as a matter of fact, develop. Given a normative ethical theory which sanctions, *under certain circumstances*, such judicial murders, there may occur an undermining of our moral disapproval of killing and our absolutely essential moral principle that all human beings, great and small, are deserving of respect. This is surely enough, together with the not unimportant weight of even our unrehearsed moral feelings, to give strong utilitarian weight *here* to the dictates of our commonsense morality. Yet, I think I have also said enough to show that someone who questions their 'unquestionableness' in such a context does not thereby exhibit a 'corrupt mind' and that it is an open question whether he must be conceptually confused or morally mistaken over this matter.

Consequentialism and the Cave Case

So far, I have tried to show with reference to the case of the magistrate and the threatening mob how consequentialists can reasonably square their normative ethical theories with an important range of commonsense moral convictions. Now, I wish by reference to the case of the innocent fat man to establish that there is at least a serious question concerning whether such fundamental commonsense moral convictions should always function as 'moral facts' or a kind of moral ground to test the adequacy of normative ethical theories or positions. I want to establish that careful attention to such cases shows that we are not justified in taking the principles embodied in our commonsense moral reasoning about such cases as normative for all moral decisions. *That a normative ethical theory is incompatible with some of our 'moral intuitions' (moral feelings or convictions) does not refute the normative ethical theory*. What I will try to do here is to establish that this case, no more than the [Magistrate case], gives us adequate grounds for abandoning consequentialism and for adopting moral conservativism.

Forget the levity of the example and consider the case of the innocent fat man. If there really is no other way of unsticking our fat man and if plainly, without blasting him out, everyone in the cave will drown, then, innocent or not, he should be blasted out. This indeed overrides the principle that the innocent should never be deliberately killed, but it does not reveal a callousness toward life, for the people involved are caught in a desperate situation

in which, if such extreme action is not taken, many lives will be lost and far greater misery will obtain. Moreover, the people who do such a horrible thing or acquiesce in the doing of it are not likely to be rendered more callous about human life and human suffering as a result. Its occurrence will haunt them for the rest of their lives and is as likely as not to make them more rather than less morally sensitive. It is not even correct to say that such a desperate act shows a lack of respect for persons. We are not treating the fat man merely as a means. The fat man's person—his interests and rights—are not ignored. Killing him is something which is undertaken with the greatest reluctance. It is only when it is quite certain that there is no other way to save the lives of the others that such a violent course of action is justifiably undertaken.

Alan Donagan, arguing rather as Anscombe argues, maintains that "to use any innocent man ill for the sake of some public good is directly to degrade him to being a mere means" and to do this is of course to violate a principle essential to morality, that is, that human beings should never merely be treated as means but should be treated as ends in themselves (as persons worthy of respect).[10] But, as my above remarks show, it need not be the case, and in the above situation it is not the case, that in killing such an innocent man we are treating him *merely* as a means. The action is universalizable, all alternative actions which would save his life are duly considered, the blasting out is done only as a last and desperate resort with the minimum of harshness and indifference to his suffering and the like. It indeed sounds ironical to talk this way, given what is done to him. But if such a terrible situation were to arise, there would always be more or less humane ways of going about one's grim task. And in acting in the more humane ways toward the fat man, as we do what we must do and would have done to ourselves were the roles reversed, we show a respect for his person.[11]

In so treating the fat man—not just to further the public good but to prevent the certain death of a whole group of people (that is to prevent an even greater evil than his being killed in this way)—the claims of justice are not overidden either, for each individual involved, if he is reasoning correctly, should realize that if he were so stuck rather than the fat man, he should in such situations be blasted out. Thus, there is no question of being unfair. Surely we must choose between evils here, but is there anything more reasonable, more morally appropriate, than choosing the lesser evil when doing or allowing some evil cannot be avoided? That is, where there is no avoiding both and where our actions can determine whether a greater or lesser evil obtains, should we not plainly always opt for the lesser evil? And is it not obviously a greater evil that all those other innocent people should suffer and die than that the fat man should suffer and die? Blowing up the fat man is indeed monstrous. But letting him remain stuck while the whole group drowns is still more monstrous.

The consequentialist is on strong moral ground here, and, if his reflective moral convictions do not square either with certain unrehearsed or with certain reflective particular moral convictions of human beings, so much the worse for such commonsense moral convictions. One could even usefully and relevantly adapt here—though for a quite different purpose—an argument of Donagan's. Consequentialism of the kind I have been arguing for provides so persuasive "a theoretical basis for common morality that when it contradicts some moral intuition, it is natural to suspect that intuition, not theory, is corrupt." *Given the comprehensiveness, plausibility, and overall rationality of consequentialism, it is not unreasonable to override even a deeply felt moral conviction if it does not square with such a theory, though if it made no sense or overrode the bulk of or even a great many of our considered moral convictions, that would be another matter indeed.*

Anticonsequentialists often point to the inhumanity of people who will sanction such killing of the innocent, but cannot the compliment be returned by speaking of the even greater inhumanity, conjoined with evasiveness, of those who will allow even more death and far greater misery and then excuse themselves on the ground that they did not intend the death and misery but merely forbore to prevent it? In such a context, such reasoning and such forbearing to prevent seems to me to constitute a moral evasion. I say it is evasive because rather than steeling himself to do what in normal circumstances would be a horrible and vile act but in this circumstance is

a harsh moral necessity, he allows, when he has the power to prevent it, a situation which is still many times worse. He tries to keep his 'moral purity' and avoid 'dirty hands' at the price of utter moral failure and what Kierkegaard called 'doublemindedness.' It is understandable that people should act in this morally evasive way but this does not make it right.

My consequentialist reasoning about such cases as the case of the innocent fat man is very often resisted on the grounds that it starts a very dangerous precedent. People rationalize wildly and irrationally in their own favor in such situations. To avoid such rationalization, we must stubbornly stick to our deontological principles and recognize as well that very frequently, if people will put their wits to work or just endure, such admittedly monstrous actions done to prevent still greater evils will turn out to be unnecessary.

The general moral principles surrounding bans on killing the innocent are strong and play such a crucial role in the ever-floundering effort to humanize the savage mind—savage as a primitive and savage again as a contemporary in industrial society—that it is of the utmost social utility, it can be argued that such bans against killing the innocent not be called into question in any practical manner by consequentialist reasoning.

However, in arguing in this way, the moral conservative has plainly shifted his ground, and he is himself arguing on consequentialist grounds that we must treat certain nonconsequentialist moral principles as absolute (as principles which can never *in fact*, from a reasonable moral point of view, be overridden, for it would be just too disastrous to do so).[13] But now he is on my home court, and my reply is that there is no good evidence at all that in the circumstances I characterized, overriding these deontological principles would have this disastrous effect. I am aware that a bad precedent could be set. Such judgments must not be made for more doubtful cases. But my telling my two stories in some detail, and my contrasting them, was done in order to make evident the type of situation, with its attendant rationale, in which the overriding of those deontological principles can be seen clearly to be justified and the situations in which this does not obtain and why. My point was to specify the situations in which we ought to override our commonsense moral convictions about those matters, and the contexts in which we are not so justified or at least in which it is not clear which course of action is justified.[14]

If people are able to be sufficiently clearheaded about these matters, they can see that there are relevant differences between the two sorts of cases. But I was also carefully guarding against extending such 'moral radicalism'—if such it should be called—to other and more doubtful cases. Unless solid empirical evidence can be given that such a 'moral radicalism' would—if it were to gain a toehold in the community—overflow destructively and inhumanely into the other doubtful and positively unjustifiable situations, nothing has been said to undermine the correctness of my consequentialist defense of 'moral radicalism' in the contexts in which I defended it.[15]

NOTES

1. Alan Donagan, "Is There a Credible Form of Utilitarianism?" and H. J. Mc Closkey, "A Non-Utilitarian Approach to Punishment," both in *Contemporary Utilitarianism,* ed. Michael D. Bayles (Garden *City,* N.Y.: Doubleday & Co., 1968).

2. Elizabeth Anscombe, "Modern Moral Philosophy," *Philosophy* 23 (January 1957): 16–17.

3. Alan Ryan, "Review of Jan Narveson's *Morality and Utility,"* *Philosophical Books* 9, no. 3 (October 1958): 14.

4. Later, I shall show that there are desert-island circumstances—i.e., highly improbable situations—in which such judicial railroading might be a moral necessity. But I also shall show what little force desert-island cases have in the articulation and defense of a normative ethical theory.

5. 'Everyone' here is used distributively; i.e., I am talking about the interests of each and every one. In that sense, everyone's interests need to be considered.

6. Alan Donagan (n. 1 above), p. 189.

7. T. L. S. Sprigge argues in such a manner in his "A Utilitarian Reply to Dr. McCloskey," in *Contemporary Utilitarianism,* ed. Michael D. Bayles (Garden City, N.Y.: Doubleday & Co., 1968).

8. Alan Donagan, p. 194.

9. There is considerable recent literature about whether it is possible to derive moral claims from nonmoral claims. See W. D. Hudson, ed., *The Is-Ought Question: A Collection of Papers on the Central Problem in Moral Philosophy* (New York: St. Martin's Press, 1969).

10. Alan Donagan (n. 1 above), pp. 199–200.

11. Again, I am not asserting that we would have enough fortitude to assent to it were the roles actually reversed. I am making a conceptual remark about what as moral beings we must try to do and not a psychological observation about what we can do.

12. Alan Donagan (n. 1 above), p. 198.

13. Jonathan Bennett, "Whatever the Consequences," *Analysis,* vol. 26 (1966), has shown that this is a very common equivocation for the conservative and makes, when unnoticed, his position seem more plausible than it actually is.

14. I have spoken, conceding this to the Christian absolutist for the sake of the discussion, as if (1) it is fairly evident what our commonsense moral convictions are here and (2) that they are deontological principles taken to hold no matter what the consequences. But that either (1) or (2) is clearly so seems to me very much open to question.

15. I do not mean to suggest that I am giving a blanket defense to our common sense morality; that is one of the last things I would want to do. Much of what we or any other tribe take to be commonsense morality is little better than a set of magical charms to deal with our social environment. But I was defending the importance of such cross-culturally ubiquitous moral principles as that one ought not to harm the innocent or that promises ought to be kept. However, against Christian absolutists of the type I have been discussing. I take them to be prima facie obligations. This means that they always hold *ceteris paribus,* but the *ceteris paribus* qualification implies that they can be overridden on occasion. On my account, appeal to consequences and considerations about justice and respect for persons determines when they should on a given occasion be overridden.

DISCUSSION QUESTIONS:

1. Are there any acts that are wrong no matter what the consequences would be of not doing them? If there is such an act, what makes it wrong, given that its moral status does not depend on its consequences?

2. Nielsen defends Consequentialism against the objection that it sometimes implies that acts are morally right, when they are actually morally wrong. Might Consequentialism be open to a different objection: it sometimes implies that acts are morally obligatory when they are not? Is it always morally wrong to fail to do what has the best consequences? What if producing the best consequences will demand some great sacrifice on our part?

3. Nielsen is concerned to show that Consequentialism does not conflict with our moral judgments about what is right or wrong in the Magistrate and Fat Man cases. What Consequentialism implies to be

morally right or wrong in these cases is just what we take to be right or wrong, he argues. How well does Consequentialism do at explaining *why* particular acts are right or wrong in these cases? Does Consequentialism give us a correct account, not just of whether it is right or wrong for the judge to frame the innocent man, but also of *why* it is right or wrong for the judge to do so? Does it give a correct account of *why* it is right or wrong for those in the cave to kill the man who is stuck in the opening?

Argument Reconstruction Exercises:

I. If we adopt Moral Conservatism, what are we to say of the case where we must do an act we think is always wrong in order to prevent another act that we think is always wrong? Identify the premises and conclusion of the following argument.

> For any act we pick (e.g., killing an innocent child), we can imagine a situation in which we have to do it in order to prevent someone from doing an even worse act of the same kind (killing two innocent children). It is always wrong for us to allow a greater evil when we can prevent it by engaging in a lesser one. No act then is such that it is always wrong for us to do it no matter what the circumstances.

II. Nielsen thinks that the cave case presents a choice between a lesser evil and a greater one. Does it? Identify the premises and conclusion of the following argument.

> If those in the cave case kill the fat man to save themselves, they will be acting immorally. They will be taking the value of their lives to be greater than that of the fat man. No human being has a right to determine that the value of one person's life or the lives of any group of people is greater that than of any other person or group of people. They will be doing what they have no right to do.

III. Some might defend a form of Moral Conservatism by appealing to a particular conception of morality. Identify the premises and conclusion of the following argument.

> Our moral obligations are determined by the correct laws of morality, just as our legal obligations are determined by the laws of our state. Once they are fully spelled out, the laws of morality do not have any exceptions; insofar as consequences are ever relevant to our moral obligations, the moral laws take them into account. There are then some moral principles, namely, the correct laws of morality, which it is always wrong not to act in accord with no matter what the consequences.

IV. Consequentialists and their critics are concerned with whether Consequentialism captures our commonsense moral convictions. Identify the premises and conclusion of the following argument.

> The fact that a theory captures (or fails to capture) our commonsense moral convictions is only evidence that it captures (or fails to capture) our general conception of what is morally right rather than wrong. Yet, the fact that a theory captures (or fails to capture) our general conception of the difference between right and wrong is no indication of whether the theory captures the real difference between right and wrong. Our commonsense moral convictions are not, therefore, relevant to the truth or falsehood of a moral theory.

11.3 SOME MERITS OF ONE FORM OF RULE-UTILITARIANISM

RICHARD B. BRANDT (1965)

Richard B. Brandt was professor of philosophy at the University of Michigan; in ethics, he is best known for his defense of **Utilitarianism**. He here develops a version of **Rule-Utilitarianism**, which he calls "the Ideal Moral Code theory." Brandt opens his discussion by considering some attractive features of Utilitarianism, in general, and offering Rule-Utilitarianism as a way to avoid some of the counter-intuitive implications of **Act-Utilitarianism**. (See, though, Nielsen's defense of Act-Utilitarianism in this chapter.) Brandt's development of the Ideal Moral Code theory involves a careful discussion of two central concepts: that of a code being current in a society and that of a person subscribing to a moral principle. Brandt argues that, unlike some versions of Rule-Utilitarianism, his theory is not equivalent to Act-Utilitarianism.

Reading Questions:

1. Brandt writes that a moral code is ideal for a society, if its currency in the society would produce as much good per person as the currency of any other moral code. What is it for a code to be current in a society, according to Brandt?

2. If a code is current in a society, a high proportion of the adults subscribe to its principles. What, according to Brandt, is it for people to subscribe to a moral principle?

3. Why, according to Brandt, is a society's moral code not one of its institutions?

4. Brandt gives special consideration to whether an ideal moral code will take the behavior of others into account in determining our obligations. What specific sorts of behavior by others concern him? How does he think an ideal moral code will take those considerations into account?

5. Consider Brandt's discussion of the moral code of the Hopi Indians. To what extent does he think the acts required by the Hopi code and those required by an ideal moral code for their society are the same, and why?

6. Brandt argues that, unlike Act-Utilitarianism, his Rule Utilitarian theory does not imply "that various immoral actions (murdering one's elderly father, breaking solemn promises) are right or even obligatory if only they can be kept secret." How, according to Brandt, does his theory avoid such implications?

Advantages of Utilitarianism

Utilitarianism is the thesis that the moral predicates of an act—at least its objective rightness or wrongness, and sometimes also its moral praiseworthiness or blameworthiness—are functions in some way, direct or indirect, of consequences for the welfare of sentient creatures, and of nothing else. Utilitarians differ about what precise function they are; and they differ about what constitutes welfare and how it is to be measured. But they agree that all one needs to know, in order to make moral appraisals correctly, is the consequences of certain things for welfare. . . .

Before turning to the details of various types of utilitarian theory, it may be helpful to offer some

supporting remarks that will explain some reasons why some philosophers are favorably disposed toward a utilitarian type of normative theory.

(a) The utilitarian principle provides a clear and definite procedure for determining which acts are right or wrong (praiseworthy or blameworthy), by observation and the methods of science alone and without the use of any supplementary intuitions (assuming that empirical procedures can determine when something maximizes utility), for all cases, including the complex ones about which intuitions are apt to be mute, such as whether kleptomanic behavior is blameworthy or whether it is right to break a confidence in certain circumstances. The utilitarian presumably frames his thesis so as to conform with enlightened intuitions which are clear, but his thesis, being general, has implications for all cases, including those about which his intuitions are not clear. The utilitarian principle is like a general scientific theory, which checks with observations at many points, but can also be used as a guide to beliefs on matters inaccessible to observation (like the behavior of matter at absolute zero temperature).

Utilitarianism is not the only normative theory with this desirable property; egoism is another, and, with some qualifications, so is Kant's theory.

(b) Any reasonably plausible normative theory will give a large place to consequences for welfare in the moral assessment of actions, for this consideration enters continuously and substantially into ordinary moral thinking. Theories which ostensibly make no appeal of this sort either admit utilitarian considerations by the back door, or have counterintuitive consequences. Therefore the ideal of simplicity leads us to hope for the possibility of a pure utilitarian theory. Moreover, utilitarianism avoids the necessity of weighing disparate things such as justice and utility.

(c) If a proposed course of action does not raise moral questions, it is generally regarded as rational, and its agent well advised to perform it, if and only if it will maximize expectable utility for the agent. In a similar vein, it can be argued that society's "choice" of an institution of morality is rational and well advised, if and only if having it will maximize expectable social utility—raise the expectable level of the average "utility curve" of the population. If morality is a system of traditional and arbitrary constraints on behavior, it cannot be viewed as a rational institution. But it can be, if the system of morality is utilitarian. In that case the institution of morality can be recommended to a person of broad human sympathies, as an institution that maximizes the expectation of general welfare; and to a selfish person, as an institution that, in the absence of particular evidence about his own case, may be expected to maximize his own expectation of welfare (his own welfare being viewed as a random sample from the population). To put it in other words, a utilitarian morality can be "vindicated" by appeal either to the humanity or to the selfishness of human beings.

To say this is not to deny that nonutilitarian moral principles may be capable of vindication in a rather similar way. For instance, to depict morality as an institution that fosters human equality is to recommend it by appeal to something perhaps as deep in man as his sympathy or humanity.[1]

The type of utilitarianism on which I wish to focus is a form of rule-utilitarianism, as contrasted with act-utilitarianism. According to the latter type of theory (espoused by Sidgwick and Moore), an act is objectively right if no other act the agent could perform would produce better consequences. (On this view, an act is blameworthy if and only if it is right to perform the act of blaming or condemning it; the principles of blameworthiness are a special case of the principle of objectively right actions.) Act-utilitarianism is hence a rather atomistic theory: The rightness of a single act is fixed by its effects on the world. *Rule-utilitarianism, in contrast, is the view that the rightness of an act is fixed, not by its relative utility, but by the utility of having a relevant moral rule, or of most or all members of a certain class of acts being performed.*

The implications of act-utilitarianism are seriously counterintuitive, and I shall ignore it except to consider whether some ostensibly different theories really are different. . . .

The Ideal Moral Code Theory

The theory I wish to describe is rather similar to one proposed by J. D. Mabbott in is 1953 British Academy lecture, "Moral Rules." It is also very similar to the view defended by J. S. Mill in *Utilitarianism*, although Mill's formulation is ambiguous at some points, and he apparently did not draw some distinctions he should have drawn (I shall revert to this historical point).

For convenience I shall refer to the theory as the "ideal moral code" theory. The essence of it is as follows. *Let us first say that a moral code is "ideal" if its currency in a particular society would produce at least as much good per person (the total divided by the number of persons) as the currency of any other moral code.* (Two different codes might meet this condition, but, in order to avoid complicated formulations, the following discussion will ignore this possibility.) *Given this stipulation for the meaning of "ideal," the Ideal Moral Code theory consists in the assertion of the following thesis: An act is right if and only if it would not be prohibited by the moral code ideal for the society; and an agent is morally blameworthy (praiseworthy) for an act if, and to the degree that, the moral code ideal in that society would condemn (praise) him for it.* It is a virtue of this theory that it is a theory both about objective rightness and about moral blameworthiness (praiseworthiness) of actions, but the assertion about blameworthiness will be virtually ignored in what follows.

In order to have a clear proposal before us, however, the foregoing summary statement must be filled out in three ways: (1) by explaining what it is for a moral code to have currency; (2) by making clear what is the difference between the rules of a society's moral code and the rules of its institutions; and (3) by describing how the relative utility of a moral code is to be estimated.

First, then, the notion of a moral code having currency in a society.

For a moral code to have currency in a society, two things must be true. First, a high proportion of the adults in the society must subscribe to the moral principles, or have the moral opinions, constitutive of the code. Exactly how high the proportion should be, we can hardly decide on the basis of the ordinary meaning of "the moral code"; but probably it would not be wrong to require at least 90 percent agreement. Thus, if at least 90 percent of the adults subscribe to principle *A,* and 90 percent to principle *B,* etc., we may say that a code consisting of *A* and *B* (etc.) has currency in the society, provided the second condition is met. Second, we want to say that certain principles *A, B,* etc. belong to the moral code of a society only if they are recognized as such. That is, it must be that a large proportion of the adults of the society would respond correctly if asked, with respect to *A* and *B,* whether most members of the society subscribed to them. (It need not be required that adults base their judgments on such good evidence as recollection of moral discussions; it is enough if for some reason the correct opinion about what is accepted is widespread.) It is of course possible for certain principles to constitute a moral code with currency in a society even if some persons in the society have no moral opinions at all, or if there is disagreement, for example, if everyone in the society disagrees with every other person with respect to at least one principle.

The more difficult question is what it is for an individual to subscribe to a moral principle or to have a moral opinion. What is it, then, for someone to think sincerely that any action of the kind *F* is wrong? (1) He is to some extent motivated to avoid actions he thinks are *F,* and often, if asked why he does not perform such an action when it appears to be to his advantage, offers, as one of his reasons, that it is *F*. In addition, the person's motivation to avoid *F*-actions does not derive entirely from his belief that *F*-actions on his part are likely to be harmful to him or to persons to whom he is somehow attached. (2) If he thinks he has just performed an *F*-action, he feels guilty or remorseful or uncomfortable about it, unless he thinks he has some excuse—unless, for instance, he knows that at the time of action he did not think his action would be an *F*-action. "Guilt" (etc.) is not to be understood as implying some special origin such as interiorization of parental prohibitions, or as being a vestige of anxiety about punishment. It is left open that it might be an unlearned emotional response to the thought of being the cause of the suffering of another person. Any feeling that must be viewed simply as anxiety about anticipated consequences, for one's self or a person to whom one is attached, is not, however, to count as a "guilt" feeling. (3) If he believes that someone has performed an *F*-action, he will tend to admire him less as a person, unless he thinks that the individual has a good excuse. He thinks that action of this sort, without excuse, reflects on character—this being spelled out, in part, by reference to traits like honesty, respect for the rights of others, and so on. (4) He thinks that these attitudes of his are correct or well justified, in some sense, but with one restriction: it is not enough if he thinks that what justifies them is simply the fact that they are shared by all or most members of his society. This restriction corresponds with our distinction between a moral conviction and something else. For instance, we are inclined to think no moral attitude is involved if an Englishman disapproves of something but says that his disapproval is justified by the fact that it is shared by "well-bred Englishmen." In such cases we are inclined to say that the individual subscribes only to a custom, or to a rule of etiquette or manners. On the other hand, if the individual thinks that what justifies his attitude unfavorable to F-actions is that F-actions are contrary to the will of God (and the individual's attitude is not merely a prudential one), or inconsistent with the welfare of mankind, or contrary to human nature, we are disposed to say the attitude is a moral attitude and the opinions expressed are moral ones. And the same if he thinks his attitude justified, but can give no reason. There are perhaps other restrictions we should make on acceptable justifications (perhaps to distinguish a moral code from a code of honor), and other types of justifications we should wish to list as clearly acceptable (perhaps an appeal to human equality).

The Ideal Moral Code and Institutions

It is important to distinguish between the moral code of a society and its institutions, or the rules of its institutions. It is especially important for the Ideal Moral Code theory, for this theory involves the conception of a moral code ideal for a society in the context of its institutions, so that it is necessary to distinguish the moral code a society does or might have from its institutions and their rules. The distinction is also one we actually do make in our thinking, although it is blurred in some cases. (For instance, is "Honor thy father and thy mother" a moral rule, or a rule of the family institution, in our society?)[2]

An institution is a set of positions or statuses, with which certain privileges and jobs are associated. (We can speak of these as "rights" and "duties" if we are careful to explain that we do not mean moral rights and duties.) That is, there are certain, usually nameable, positions that consist in the fact that anyone who is assigned to the position is expected to do certain things, and at the same time is expected to have certain things done for him. The individuals occupying these positions are a group of cooperating agents in a system that as a whole is thought to have the aim of serving certain ends. (For example, a university is thought to serve the ends of education, research, etc.) The rules of the system concern jobs that must be done in order that the goals of the institution be achieved; they allocate the necessary jobs to different positions. Take, for instance, a university. There are various positions in it: the presidency, the professorial ranks, the registrars, librarians, etc. It is understood that one who occupies a certain post has certain duties, say teaching a specified number of classes or spending time working on research in the case of the instructing staff. Obviously the university cannot achieve its ends unless certain persons do the teaching, some tend to the administration, some do certain jobs in the library, and so on. Another such system is the family. We need not speculate on the "purpose" of the family, whether it is primarily a device for producing a new generation, etc. But it is clear that when a man enters marriage, he takes a position to which certain jobs are attached, such as providing support for the family to the best of his ability, and to which also certain rights are attached, such as exclusive sexual rights with his wife, and the right to be cared for should he become incapacitated.

If an "institution" is defined in this way, it is clear that the moral code of a society cannot itself be construed as an institution, nor its rules as rules of an institution. The moral code is society-wide, so if we were to identify its rules as institutional rules, we should presumably have to say that everyone belongs to this institution. But what is the "purpose" of society as a whole? Are there any distinctions of status, with rights and duties attached, that we could identify as the "positions" in the moral system? Can we say that moral rules consist in the assignment of jobs in such a way that the aims of the institution may be achieved? It is true that there is a certain analogy: society as a whole might be said to be aiming at the good life for all, and the moral rules of the society might be viewed as the rules with which all must conform in order to achieve this end. But the analogy is feeble. Society as a whole is obviously not an organization like a university, an educational system, the church, General Motors, etc.; there is no specific goal in the achievement of which each position has a designated role to play. Our answer to the above questions must be in the negative: Morality is not an institution in the explained sense, nor are moral rules institutional expectations or rules.

The moral code of a society may, of course, have implications that bear on institutional rules. For one thing, the moral code may imply that an institutional system is morally wrong and ought to be changed. Moreover, the moral code may imply that a person has also a moral duty to do something that is his institutional job. For instance, it may be a moral rule that a person ought to do whatever he has undertaken to do, or that he ought not to accept the benefits of a position without performing its duties. Take for instance the rules, "A professor should meet his classes" or "Wives ought to make the beds." Since the professor has undertaken to do what pertains to his office, and the same for a wife, and since these tasks are known to pertain to the respective offices, the moral rule that a person is morally bound (with certain qualifications) to do what he has undertaken to do implies, in context, that the professor is morally bound to meet his classes and the wife to make the beds, other things being equal (that is, there being no contrary moral obligations in the situation). But these implications are not themselves part of the moral code. No one would say that a parent had neglected to teach his child the moral code of the society if he had neglected to teach him that professors must meet classes, and that wives must make the beds. A person becomes obligated to do these things only by participating in an institution, by taking on the status of professor or wife. Parents do not teach children to have guilt feelings about missing classes, or making beds. The moral code consists only of more general rules, defining what is to be done in certain types of situations in which practically everyone will find himself. ("Do what you have promised!")

Admittedly some rules can be both moral and institutional: "Take care of your father in his old age" might be both an institutional rule of the family organization and also a part of the moral code of a society. (In this situation, one can still raise the question whether this moral rule is optimific in a society with that institutional rule; the answer could be negative.)

It is an interesting question whether "Keep your promises" is a moral rule, an institutional rule (a rule of an "institution" of promises), or both. Obviously it is a part of the moral code of western societies. But is it also a rule of an institution?

There are difficulties in the way of affirming that it is. There is no structure of cooperating individuals with special functions, serving to promote certain aims. Nor, when one steps into the "role" of a promiser, does one commit one's self to any specific duties; one fixes one's own duties by what one promises. Nor, in order to understand what one is committing one's self to by promising, need one have any knowledge of any system of expectations prevalent in the society. A three-year-old, who has never heard of any duties incumbent on promisers, can tell her friends, who wish to play baseball that afternoon, that she will bring the ball and bat, and that they need give no thought to the availability of these items. Her invitation to rely on her for something needed for their common enjoyment, and her assurance that she will do something and encouraging them thereby to set their minds at rest, is to make a promise. No one need suppose that the promiser is stepping into a socially recognized position, with all the rights and duties attendant on the same, although it is true she has placed herself in a position where she will properly be held responsible for the disappointment if she fails, and where inferences about her reliability as a person will properly be drawn if she forgets, or worse, if it turns out she was never in a position to perform. The bindingness of a promise is no more dependent on a set of expectations connected with an institution than is the wrongness of striking another person without justifying reason.

Nevertheless, if one thinks it helpful to speak of a promise as an institution or a practice, in view of certain analogies (promiser and promisee may be said to have rights and duties like the occupants of roles in an institution, and there is the ritual word "promise" the utterance of which commits the speaker to certain performances), there is no harm in this. The similarities and dissimilarities are what they are, and as long as these are understood it seems to make little difference what we say. Nevertheless, even if making a promise is participating in a practice or institution, there is still the *moral* question whether one is morally bound to perform, and in what conditions, and for what reasons. This question is left open; given the institution is whatever it is—as is the case with all rules of institutions.

Determining The Ideal Moral Code

It has been proposed above that an action is right if and only if it would not be prohibited by the moral code ideal for the society in which it occurs, where a moral code is taken to be "ideal" if and only if its currency would produce at least as much good per person as the currency of any other moral code.[3] We must now give more attention to the conception of an ideal moral code, and how it may be decided when a given moral code will produce as much good per person as any other. We may, however, reasonably bypass the familiar problems of judgments of comparative utilities, especially when different persons are involved, since these problems are faced by all moral theories that have any plausibility. We shall simply assume that rough judgments of this sort are made and can be justified.

(a) We should first notice that, as "currency" has been explained above, a moral code could not be current in a society if it were too complex to be learned or applied. We may therefore confine our consideration to codes simple enough to be absorbed by human beings, roughly in the way in which people learn actual moral codes.

(b) We have already distinguished the concept of an institution and its rules from the concept of a moral rule, or a rule of the moral code. (We have, however, pointed out that in some cases a moral rule may prescribe the same thing that is also an institutional expectation. But this is not a necessary situation, and a moral code could condemn an institutional expectation.) Therefore, in deciding how much good the currency of a specific moral system would do, we consider the institutional setting as it is, as part of the situation. We are asking which moral code would produce the most good in the long run in this setting. One good to be reckoned, of course, might be that the currency of a given moral code would tend to change the institutional system.

(c) In deciding which moral code will produce the most per person good, we must take into account the probability that certain types of situations will arise in the society. For instance, we must take for granted that people will make promises and subsequently want to break them, that people

will sometimes assault other persons in order to achieve their own ends, that people will be in distress and need the assistance of others, and so on. We may not suppose that, because an ideal moral code might have certain features, it need not have other features because they will not be required; for instance, we may not suppose, on the ground that an ideal moral system would forbid everyone to purchase a gun, that such a moral system needs no provisions about the possession and use of guns—just as our present moral and legal codes have provisions about self-defense, which would be unnecessary if everyone obeyed the provision never to assault anyone.

It is true that the currency of a moral code with certain provisions might bring about a reduction in certain types of situations, for example, the number of assaults or cases of dishonesty. And the reduction might be substantial, if the moral code were current which prohibited these offenses very strongly. (We must remember that an ideal moral code might differ from the actual one not only in what it prohibits or enjoins, but also in how strongly it prohibits or enjoins.) But it is consistent to suppose that a moral code prohibits a certain form of behavior very severely, and yet that the behavior will occur, since the "currency" of a moral code requires only 90 percent subscription to it, and a "strong" subscription, on the average, permits a great range from person to person. In any case there must be doubt whether the best moral code will prohibit many things very severely, since there are serious human costs in severe prohibitions: the burden of guilt feelings, the traumas caused by the severe criticism by others which is a part of having a strong injunction in a code, the risks of any training process that would succeed in interiorizing a severe prohibition, and so on.

(d) It would be a great oversimplification if, in assessing the comparative utility of various codes, we confined ourselves merely to counting the benefits of people doing (refraining from doing) certain things, as a result of subscribing to a certain code. To consider only this would be as absurd as estimating the utility of some feature of a legal system by attending only to the utility of people behaving in the way the law aims to make them behave—and overlooking the fact that the law only reduces and does not eliminate misbehavior, as well as the disutility of punishment to the convicted, and the cost of the administration of criminal law. In the case of morals, we must weigh the benefit of the improvement in behavior as a result of the restriction built into conscience, against the cost of the restriction—the burden of guilt feelings, the effects of the training process, etc. There is a further necessary refinement. In both law and morals we must adjust our estimates of utility by taking into account the envisaged system of excuses. That *mens rea* is required as a condition of guilt in the case of most legal offenses is most important; and it is highly important for the utility of a moral system whether accident, intent, and motives are taken into account in deciding a person's liability to moral criticism. A description of a moral code is incomplete until we have specified the severity of condemnation (by conscience or the criticism of others) to be attached to various actions, along with the excuses to be allowed as exculpating or mitigating.

The Ideal Moral Code and Others' Behavior

Philosophers have taken considerable interest in the question what implications forms of rule-utilitarianism have for the moral relevance of the behavior of persons other than the agent. Such implications, it is thought, bring into focus the effective difference between any form of rule-utilitarianism, and act-utilitarianism. In particular, it has been thought that the implications of rule-utilitarianisms for two types of situation are especially significant: (a) for situations in which persons are generally violating the recognized moral code, or some feature of it; and (b) for situations in which, because the moral code is generally respected, maximum utility would be produced by violation of the code by the agent. An example of the former situation (sometimes called a "state of nature" situation) would be widespread perjury in making out income-tax declarations. An example of the latter situation would be widespread conformity to the rule forbidding walking on the grass in a park.

What are the implications of the suggested form of rule-utilitarianism for these types of situations?

Will it prescribe conduct which is not utility-maximizing in these situations? If it does, it will clearly have implications discrepant with those of act-utilitarianism—but perhaps unpalatable to some people.

It is easy to see how to go about determining what is right or wrong in such situations, on the above-described form of rule-utilitarianism—it is a question of what an "ideal" moral code would prescribe. But it is by no means easy to see where a reasonable person would come out, after going through such an investigation. Our form of rule-utilitarianism does not rule out, as morally irrelevant, reference to the behavior of other persons; it implies that the behavior of others is morally relevant precisely to the extent to which an optimific moral code (the one the currency of which is optimific) would take it into account. How far, then, we might ask, would an optimific moral code take into account the behavior of other persons, and what would its specific prescriptions be for the two types of situations outlined?

It might be thought, and it has been suggested, that an ideal moral code could take no cognizance of the behavior of other persons, and in particular of the possibility that many persons are ignoring some prohibitions of the code, sometimes for the reason, apparently, that it is supposed that a code of behavior would be self-defeating if it prescribed for situations of its own breach, on a wide scale. It is a sufficient answer to this suggestion, to point out that our actual moral code appears to contain some such prescriptions. For instance, our present code seems to permit, for the case in which almost everyone is understating his income, that others do the same, on the ground that otherwise they will be paying more than their fair share. It is, of course, true that a code simple enough to be learned and applied cannot include prescriptions for all possible types of situations involving the behavior of other persons; but it can contain some prescriptions pertinent to some general features of the behavior of others.

Granted, then, that an ideal moral code may contain some special prescriptions which pay attention to the behavior of other persons, how in particular will it legislate for special situations such as the examples cited above? The proper answer to this question is that there would apparently be no blanket provision for all cases of these general types, and that a moral agent faced with such a concrete situation would have to think out what an ideal moral code would imply for his type of concrete situation. Some things do seem clear. An ideal moral code would not provide that a person is permitted to be cruel in a society where most other persons are cruel; there could only be loss of utility in any special provision permitting that. On the other hand, if there is some form of cooperative activity that enhances utility only if most persons cooperate, and nonparticipation in which does not reduce utility when most persons are not cooperating, utility would seem to be maximized if the moral code somehow permitted all to abstain—perhaps by an abstract formula stating this very condition. (This is on the assumption that the participation by some would not, by example, eventually bring about the participation of most or all.) Will there be any types of situations for which an ideal moral code would prescribe infringement of a generally respected moral code, by a few, when a few infringements (provided there are not many) would maximize utility? The possibility of this is not ruled out. Obviously there will be some regulations for emergencies; one may cut across park grass in order to rush a heart-attack victim to a hospital. And there will be rules making special exceptions when considerable utility is involved; the boy with no other place to play may use the grass in the park. But, when an agent has no special claim others could not make, it is certainly not clear that ideal moral rules will make him an exception on the ground that some benefit will come to him, and that restraint by him is unnecessary in view of the cooperation of others.

The implications of the above form of rule-utilitarianism, for these situations, are evidently different from those of act-utilitarianism.[4]

Mill's Utilitarianism

The Ideal Moral Code theory is very similar to the view put forward by J.S. Mill in Utilitarianism.

Mill wrote that his creed held that "actions are right in proportion as they tend to promote happiness; wrong as they tend to produce the reverse of happiness." Mill apparently did not intend by this any form of act-utilitarianism. He was—doubtless

with much less than full awareness—writing of act-*types,* and what he meant was that an act of a certain type is morally obligatory (wrong) if and only if acts of that type tend to promote happiness (the reverse). Mill supposed that it is known that certain kinds of acts, for instance, murder and theft, promote unhappiness, and that therefore we can say, with exceptions only for very special circumstances, that murder and theft are wrong. Mill recognized that there can be a discrepancy between the tendency of an act-type, and the probable effects, in context, of an individual act. He wrote: "In the case of abstinences, indeed—of things which people forbear to do from moral considerations, though the consequences in the particular case might be beneficial, it would be unworthy of an intelligent agent not to be consciously aware that the action is of a class which, if practiced generally, would be generally injurious, and that this is the ground of the obligation to abstain from it."[5] Moreover, he specifically denied that one is morally obligated to perform (avoid) an act just on the ground that it can be expected to produce good consequences; he says that "there is no case of moral obligation in which some secondary principle is not involved" (op. cit., p. 33).

It appears, however, that Mill did not quite think that it is morally obligatory to perform (avoid) an act according as its general performance would promote (reduce) happiness in the world. For he said (p. 60) that "We do not call anything wrong unless we mean to imply that a person ought to be punished in some way or other for doing it—if not by law, by the opinion of his fellow creatures; if not by opinion, by the reproaches of his own conscience. This seems the real turning point of the distinction between morality and simple expediency." The suggestion here is that it is morally obligatory to perform (avoid) an act according as it is beneficial to have a system of sanctions (with what this promises in way of performance), whether formal, informal (criticism by others), or internal (one's own conscience), for enforcing the performance (avoidance) of the type of act in question. This is very substantially the Ideal Moral Code theory.

Not that there are no differences. Mill is not explicit about details, and the theory outlined above fills out what he actually said. Moreover, Mill noticed that an act can fall under more than one secondary principle and that the relevant principles may give conflicting rulings about what is morally obligatory. In such a case, Mill thought, what one ought to do (but it is doubtful whether he believed there is a strict moral obligation in this situation) is what will maximize utility in the concrete situation. This proposal for conflicts of "ideal moral rules" is not a necessary part of the Ideal Moral Code theory as outlined above.

Act-Utilitarianism

It is sometimes thought that a rule-utilitarianism rather like Mill's cannot differ in its implication about what is right or wrong from the act-utilitarian theory. This is a mistake.

The contention would be correct if two dubious assumptions happened to be true. The first is that one of the rules of an optimific moral code will be that a person ought always to do whatever will maximize utility. The second is that, when there is a conflict between the rules of an optimific code, what a person ought to do is to maximize utility. For then, either the utilitarian rule is the only one that applies (and it always will be relevant), in which case the person ought to do what the act-utilitarian directs; or if there is a conflict among the relevant rules, the conflict-resolving principle takes over, and this, of course, prescribes exactly what act-utilitarianism prescribes. Either way, we come out where the act-utilitarian comes out.

But there is no reason at all to suppose that there will be a utilitarian rule in an optimific moral code. In fact, obviously there will not be. It is true that there should be a directive to relieve the distress of others, when this can be done, say, at relatively low personal cost; and there should be a directive not to injure other persons, except in special situations. And so on. But none of this amounts to a straight directive to do the most good possible. Life would be chaotic if people tried to observe any such moral requirement.

The second assumption was apparently acceptable to Mill. But a utilitarian principle is by no means the only possible conflict-resolving principle. For if we say, with the Ideal Moral Code theory, that what is right is fixed by the content of

the moral system with maximum utility, the possibility is open that the utility-maximizing moral system will contain some rather different device for resolving conflicts between lowest-level moral rules. The ideal system might contain several higher-level conflict-resolving principles, all different from Mill's. Or, if there is a single one, it could be a directive to maximize utility; it could be a directive to do what an intelligent person who had fully interiorized the rest of the ideal moral system would feel best satisfied with doing; and so on. But the final court of appeal need not be an appeal to direct utilities. Hence the argument that Mill-like rule-utilitarianism must collapse into direct utilitarianism is doubly at fault.[6]

In fact, far from "collapsing" into act-utilitarianism, the Ideal Moral Code theory appears to avoid the serious objections which have been leveled at direct utilitarianism. One objection to the latter view is that it implies that various immoral actions (murdering one's elderly father, breaking solemn promises) are right or even obligatory if only they can be kept secret. The Ideal Moral Code theory has no such implication. For it obviously would not maximize utility to have a moral code which condoned secret murders or breaches of promise. W. D. Ross criticized act-utilitarianism on the ground that it ignored the personal relations important in ordinary morality, and he listed a half-dozen types of moral rule which he thought captured the main themes of thoughtful morality: obligations of fidelity, obligations of gratitude, obligations to make restitution for injuries, obligations to help other persons, to avoid injuring them, to improve one's self, and to bring about a just distribution of good things in life. An ideal moral code, however, would presumably contain substantially such rules in any society, doubtless not precisely as Ross stated them. So the rule-utilitarian need not fail to recognize the personal character of morality. . . .

Institutional Duties

According to the Ideal Moral Code theory, an institutional system forms the setting within which the best (utility-maximizing) moral code is to be applied, and one's obligation is to follow the best moral rules in that institutional setting—not to do what the best moral rules would require for some other, more ideal, setting.

Let us examine the implications of the Ideal Moral Code theory by considering a typical example. Among the Hopi Indians, a child is not expected to care for his father (he is always in a different clan), whereas he is expected to care for his mother, maternal aunt, and maternal uncle, and so on up the female line (all in the same clan). It would be agreed by observers that this system does not work very well. The trouble with it is that the lines of institutional obligation and the lines of natural affection do not coincide, and, as a result, an elderly male is apt not to be cared for by anyone.

Can we show that an "ideal moral code" would call on a young person to take care of his maternal uncle, in a system of this sort? (It might also imply he should try to change the system, but that is another point.) One important feature of the situation of the young man considering whether he should care for his maternal uncle is that, the situation including the expectations of others being what it is, if he does nothing to relieve the distress of his maternal uncle, it is probable that it will not be relieved. His situation is very like that of the sole observer of an automobile accident; he is a mere innocent bystander, but the fact is that if he does nothing, the injured persons will die. So the question for us is whether an ideal moral code will contain a rule that, if someone is in a position where he can relieve serious distress, and where it is known that in all probability it will not be relieved if he does not do so, he should relieve the distress. The answer seems to be that it will contain such a rule: we might call it an "obligation of humanity." But there is a second, and more important point. Failure of the young person to provide for his maternal uncle would be a case of unfairness or free-riding. For the family system operates like a system of insurance; it provides one with various sorts of privileges or protections, in return for which one is expected to make certain payments, or accept the risk of making certain payments. Our young man has already benefited by the system, and stands to benefit further; he has received care and education as a child, and later on his own problems

of illness and old age will be provided for. On the other hand, the old man, who has (we assume) paid such premiums as the system calls on him to pay in life, is now properly expecting, in accordance with the system, certain services from a particular person whom the system designates as the one to take care of him. Will the ideal moral code require such a person to pay the premium in such a system? I suggest that it will, and we can call the rule in question an "obligation of fairness".[7] So, we may infer that our young man will have a moral obligation to care for his maternal uncle, on grounds both of humanity and fairness.

We need not go so far as to say that such considerations mean that an ideal moral code will underwrite morally every institutional obligation. An institution may be grossly inequitable; or some part of it may serve no purpose at all but rather be injurious (as some legal prohibitions may be). But I believe we can be fairly sure that Professor Diggs went too far in saying that a system of this sort "deprives social and moral rules of their authority and naturally is in sharp conflict with practice" and that it "collapses into act-utilitarianism."

Other Forms of Rule-Utilitarianism

It may be helpful to contrast the Ideal Moral Code theory with a rather similar type of rule-utilitarianism, which in some ways is simpler than the Ideal Moral Code theory, and which seems to be the only form of rule-utilitarianism recognized by some philosophers. This other type of theory is suggested in the writings of R. F. Harrod, Jonathan Harrison, and perhaps John Hospers and Marcus Singer, although, as I shall describe it, it differs from the exact theory proposed by any of these individuals, in more or less important ways.

The theory is a combination of act-utilitarianism with **Kantian universalizability requirement** for moral action. It denies that an act is necessarily right if it will produce consequences no worse than would any other action the agent might perform; rather, it affirms that an act is right if and only if universal action on the "maxim" of the act would not produce worse consequences than universal action on some other maxim on which the agent could act. Or, instead of talking of universal action on the "maxim" of the act in question, we can speak of all members of the class of relevantly similar actions being performed; then the proposal is that an action is right if and only if universal performance of the class of relevantly similar acts would not have worse consequences than universal performance of the class of acts relevantly similar to some alternative action the agent might perform. Evidently it is important how we identify the "maxim" of an act or the class of "relevantly similar" acts.

One proceeds as follows. One may begin with the class specified by the properties one thinks are the morally significant ones of the act in question. (One could as well start with the class defined by all properties of the act, if one practically could do this!) One then enlarges the class by omitting from its definition those properties that would not affect the average utility that would result from all the acts in the class being performed. (The total utility might be affected simply by enlarging the size of the class; merely enlarging the class does not affect the average utility.) Conversely, one must also narrow any proposed class of "relevantly similar" acts if it is found that properties have been omitted from the specification of it, the presence of which would affect the average utility that would result if all the acts in the class were performed. The relevant class must not be too large, because of omission of features that define subclasses with different utilities; or too small, because of the presence of features that make no difference to the utilities.

An obvious example of an irrelevant property is that of the agent having a certain name (in most situations), or being a certain person. On the other hand, the fact that the agent wants (does not want) to perform a certain act normally is relevant to the utility of the performance of that act.

So much by way of exposition of the theory.

For many cases this theory and the Ideal Moral Code theory have identical implications. For, when it is better for actions of type *A* to be performed in a certain situation than for actions of any other type to be performed, it will often be a good thing to have type *A* actions prescribed by the moral code, directly or indirectly.

The theory also appears more simple than the Ideal Moral Code theory. In order to decide whether a given act is right or wrong we are not asked to do anything as grand as decide what some part of an ideal moral code would be like, but merely whether it would be better, or worse, for all in a relevant class of acts to be performed, as compared with some other relevant class. Thus it offers simple answers to questions such as whether one should vote ("What if nobody did?"), pick wildflowers along the road ("What if everyone did?"), join the army in wartime, or walk on the grass in a park.[8] Furthermore, the theory has a simple way of dealing with conflicts of rules: one determines whether it would be better, or worse, for all members of the more complex class (about which the rules conflict) of actions to be performed (for example, promises broken in the situation where the breach would save a life).

In one crucial respect, however, the two theories are totally different. For, in contrast with the Ideal Moral Code theory, this theory implies that exactly those acts are objectively right which are objectively right on the act-utilitarian theory. Hence the implications of this theory for action include the very counterintuitive ones which led its proponents to seek an improvement over act-utilitarianism.

It must be conceded that this assessment of the implications of the theory is not yet a matter of general agreement,[9] and depends on a rather complex argument. In an earlier paper I argued that the theory does have these consequences, although my statement of the theory was rather misleading. More recently Professor David Lyons has come to the same conclusion, after an extensive discussion in which he urges that the illusion of a difference between the consequences of this theory and those of act-utilitarianism arises because of failure to notice certain important features of the context of actions, primarily the relative frequency of similar actions at about the same time, and "threshold effects" an action may have because of these features.[10]

It may be worthwhile to draw attention to the features of the Ideal Moral Code theory that avoid this particular result. In the first place, the Ideal Moral Code theory sets a limit to the number and complexity of the properties that define a class of morally similar actions. For, on this theory, properties of an act make a difference to its rightness, only if a moral principle referring to them (directly or indirectly) can be learned as part of the optimific moral code. Actual persons, with their emotional and intellectual limitations, are unable to learn a moral code that incorporates all the distinctions the other theory can recognize as morally relevant; and even if they could learn it, it would not be utility-maximizing for them to try to apply it. In the second place, we noted that to be part of a moral code a proscription must be public, believed to be part of what is morally disapproved of by most adults. *Thus whereas some actions (for instance, some performed in secret) would be utility-maximizing, the Ideal Moral Code theory may imply that they are wrong, because it would be a bad thing for it to be generally recognized that a person is free to do that sort of thing.*

I do not know of any reason to think that the Ideal Moral Code theory is a less plausible normative moral theory than any other form of utilitarianism. Other types of rule-utilitarianism are sufficiently like it, however, that it might be that relatively minor changes in formulation would make their implications for conduct indistinguishable from those of the Ideal Moral Code theory.

Two questions have not been here discussed. One is whether the Ideal Moral Code theory is open to the charge that it implies that some actions are right which are unjust in such an important way that they cannot be right. The second question is one a person would naturally wish to explore if he concluded that the right answer to the first question is affirmative: It is whether a rule-utilitarian view could be combined with some other principles like a principle of justice in a plausible way, without loss of all the features that make utilitarianism attractive. The foregoing discussion has not been intended to provide an answer to these questions.

NOTES

1. It would not be impossible to combine a restricted principle of utility with a morality of justice or equality. For instance, it might be said that an act is right only if it meets a certain condition of justice, and also if it is one which, among all the just actions open to the agent, meets a requirement of utility as well as any other.
2. The confusion is compounded by the fact that terms like "obligation" and "duty" are used sometimes to speak about moral obligations and duties, and sometimes not. The fact

that persons have a certain legal duty in certain situations is a rule of the legal institutions of the society; a person may not have a moral duty to do what is his legal duty. The fact that a person has an obligation to invite a certain individual to dinner is a matter of manners or etiquette, and at least may not be a matter of moral obligation. See R. B. Brandt, "The Concepts of Duty and Obligation," *Mind* 73 (1964), especially pp. 380–4.
3. Some utilitarians have suggested that the right act is determined by the total net intrinsic good produced. This view can have embarrassing consequences for problems of population control. The view here advocated is that the right act is determined by the per person, average, net intrinsic good produced.
4. The above proposal is different in various respects from that set forth in the writer's "Toward a Credible Form of Utilitarianism," in Castaneda and Nakhnikian, *Morality and the Language of Conduct,* 1963. The former paper did not make a distinction between institutional rules and moral rules. (The present paper, of course, allows that both may contain a common prescription.) A result of these differences is that the present theory is very much simpler, and avoids some counterintuitive consequences which some writers have pointed out in criticism of the earlier proposal.
5. *Utilitarianism,* Library of Liberal Arts, New York, 1957, p. 25.
6. Could some moral problems be so unique that they would not be provided for by the set of rules it is best for the society to have? If so, how should they be appraised morally? Must there be some appeal to rules covering cases most closely analogous, as seems to be the procedure in law? If so, should we say that an act is right if it is not prohibited, either explicitly or by close analogy, by an ideal moral code? I shall not attempt to answer these questions.
7. See John Rawls, in "Justice as Fairness," *Philosophical Review* 67 (1958), 164–94, especially pp. 179–84.
It seems to be held by some philosophers that an ideal moral code would contain no rule of fairness. The line of argument seems to be as follows: Assume we have an institution involving cooperative behavior for an end which will necessarily be of benefit to all in the institution. Assume further that the cooperative behavior required is burdensome. Assume finally that the good results will be produced even if fewer than all cooperate—perhaps 90 percent is sufficient. It will then be to an individual's advantage to shirk making his contribution, since he will continue to enjoy the benefits. Shirking on the part of some actually maximizes utility, since the work is burdensome, and the burdensome effort of those who shirk (provided there are not too many) is useless.

I imagine that it would be agreed that, in this sort of system, there should be an agreed and known rule for exempting individuals from useless work. (For example, someone who is ill would be excused.) In the absence of this, a person should feel free to excuse himself for good and special reason. Otherwise, I think we suppose everyone should do his share, and that it is not a sufficient reason for shirking, to know that enough are cooperating to produce the desired benefits. Let us call this requirement, of working except for special reason (etc.), a "rule of fairness."

Would an ideal moral code contain a rule of fairness? At least, there could hardly be a public rule permitting people to shirk while a sufficient number of others work. For what would the rule be? It would be all too easy for most people to believe that a sufficient number of others were working (like the well-known difficulty in farm planning, that if one plants what sold at a good price the preceding year, one is apt to find that prices for that product will drop, since most other farmers have the same idea). Would it even be a good idea to have a rule to the effect that if one absolutely knows that enough others are working, one may shirk? This seems highly doubtful.

Critics of rule-utilitarianism seem to have passed from the fact that the best system would combine the largest product with the least effort, to the conclusion that the best moral code would contain a rule advising not to work when there are enough workers already. This is a non sequitur.
8. One should not, however, overemphasize the simplicity. Whether one should vote in these circumstances is not decided by determining that it would have bad consequences if no one voted at all. It is a question whether it would be the best thing for all those people to vote (or not vote) in the class of situations relevantly similar to this one. It should be added, however, that if I am correct in my (below) assessment of the identity of this theory with act-utilitarianism, in the end it is simple, on the theory, to answer these questions.

It hardly seems that an ideal moral code would contain prescriptions as specific as rules about these matters. But the implications for such matters would be fairly direct if, as suggested above, an ideal moral code would contain a principle enjoining fairness, that is, commanding persons to do their share in common enterprises (or restraints), when everyone benefits if most persons do their share, when persons find doing their share a burden, and when it is not essential that everyone do his share although it is essential that most do so, for the common benefit to be realized.
9. See, for instance, the interesting paper by Michael A. G. Stocker, *Consistency in Ethics, Analysis* supplement, vol. 25, January 1965, pp. 116–122
10. David Lyons, *Forms and Limits of Utilitarianism*, Clarendon Press, Oxford, 1965.

DISCUSSION QUESTIONS:

1. Brandt claims that "a utilitarian morality can be 'vindicated' by appeal either to the humanity or to the selfishness of human beings." How, if at all, does Utilitarianism, in general, and Brant's Ideal Moral Code theory, in particular, provide an answer to the question of Chapter 9, "Why Be Moral?"

2. Consider an Act Utilitarian moral code that consists just of one principle: Always do the act that, of all the available alternatives, will produce the greatest net good for all. Given Brandt's account of what it is for a code to be current in a society, including what it is for someone to subscribe to a moral principle, will this Act Utilitarian moral code have high or low currency utility for our society?

3. Brandt is concerned that his theory be sensitive to the fact that the actual institutional arrangements of our society can play a role in determining our moral obligations. See in this regard his discussion of how the behavior of others can be relevant to our obligations and his discussion of the institutional arrangements in the Hopi Indian case. Sometimes, especially when social institutions are unjust, our moral obligations are contrary to the institutional rules. Consider such a case; does Brandt's theory capture the fact that, in this case, our moral obligations are at odds with the institutional arrangements?

4. A correct moral theory should explain what it is that makes the right acts right and the wrong acts wrong. Brandt claims that, unlike Act-Utilitarianism, his Rule Utilitarian theory does not imply "that various immoral actions (murdering one's elderly father, breaking solemn promises) are right or even obligatory if only they can be kept secret." (page 222) Does Brandt's theory also give a correct explanation of why such acts are wrong?

Argument Reconstruction Exercises:

I. Brandt argues that Utilitarianism can be "vindicated" by appeal to either our humanity or our selfishness. Identify the premises and conclusion of the argument.

> [If the system of morality is utilitarian, it] can be recommended to a person of broad human sympathies, as an institution that maximizes the expectation of the general welfare; and to a selfish person, as an institution that, in the absence of particular evidence about his own case, may be expected to maximize his own expectation of welfare . . . To put it in other words, a utilitarian morality can be "vindicated" by appeal to either the humanity or to the selfishness of human beings. (page 215)

II. Does Rule-Utilitarianism give us the very same moral assessments as Act-Utilitarianism? Identify the premises and conclusion of the following argument.

> Rule-Utilitarianism gives us the same moral guidance as Act-Utilitarianism. Take any type of situation, say one in which we have to decide whether to keep a promise. There are lots of moral rules we might adopt to guide us in such a situation (e.g., if you have made a promise, keep it; if you've made a promise and it's to a friend, keep it; etc.). One such rule is: If you've made a promise, then keep it or break it, depending on which alternative will produce the most net good in the circumstances. Our adopting this rule will produce the greatest good, for in following it, we will always, in each case, do what produces the greatest good. This rule is then the one that determines how we should behave, according to Rule-Utilitarianism. Yet, this rule and Act-Utilitarianism tell us to do the same thing: in each case, do the act with the best consequences.

III. A correct moral theory has to do more than capture which acts are right and which ones are wrong. It has to give us a correct explanation of what makes the right acts right and the wrong acts wrong.

Identify the premises and conclusion of the following argument.

> According to Rule-Utilitarianism, if an act is wrong, it is wrong because it is prohibited by a rule or code our adoption of which will produce the most net good. Killing an innocent person, for example, is wrong because as a general policy killing innocent people fails to produce the most net good. That's not why killing innocent people is wrong. It's wrong because it violates the human right to life. Rule-Utilitarianism does not, therefore, correctly explain what makes wrong acts wrong.

IV. What is the good of discovering the correct moral theory, if we can't put it to use? Identify the premises and conclusion of the following argument.

> If Rule-Utilitarianism is true, then to determine whether an act is right or wrong, we have to determine whether it is permitted or prohibited by a correct moral rule or code, one our adoption of which will produce the most net good. There is no way for us to determine this, at least not when it comes to the most difficult and pressing moral issues we face (e.g., capital punishment, abortion, euthanasia). Rule-Utilitarianism cannot, therefore, give us the guidance we need on our most pressing moral issues.

11.4 TURNING THE TROLLEY

JUDITH JARVIS THOMSON (2008)

Judith Jarvis Thomson is Emerita Professor of Philosophy at the Massachusetts Institute of Technology. She is known for her work in both moral philosophy and metaphysics. She here considers what has come to be known as "the Trolley Problem." This is an experimental case in which a bystander has the opportunity to save the lives of some in exchange for the life of another. Most people seem to think that in some cases it is morally acceptable to sacrifice some for others but not in other cases. But this is hard to explain if the rightness of an action is solely a function of its consequences. Thomson's subtle analysis reveals some of the ways in which the difference between right and wrong seems to depend on more than considerations of utility.

Reading Questions:

1. Thomson begins her discussion by considering Philippa Foot's analysis of two cases: Judge's Two Options and Driver's Two Options. What problem do the

cases present? What is Foot's proposed solution to it? What does Thomson present as a past objection on her part to Foot's view?

2. Consider the case, Bystander's Three Options; why does Thomson think it is not permissible for the bystander to take the second option—save the five at the cost of killing the one—in this case?

3. Thomson uses our intuition about Bystander's Three Options, that the bystander may not save the five at the cost of killing the one, to support her view about Bystander's Two Options, that here too the bystander may not save the five at the cost of killing the one. What line of argument takes Thomson from our intuition about Bystander's Three Options to her conclusion about Bystander's Two Options?

4. Consider the cases, Driver's Two Options and Driver's Three Options. What is Thomson's position about what is permissible in each? How does her position about these cases differ from her position about Bystander's Two Options and Bystander's Three Options? How does she explain that difference?

5. According to Thomson, many people have been mistaken about what it is permissible for the bystander to do in Bystander's Two Options. What is her explanation for their mistake?

The Trolley Problem

The trolley problem is by now thoroughly familiar, but it pays to begin with a description of its origins.

In "The Problem of Abortion and the Doctrine of the Double Effect," Philippa Foot described a variety of hypothetical cases, in some of which we regard it as permissible for the agent to act, in others of which we regard it as impermissible for the agent to act, and she asked the good question what explains the differences among our verdicts about them.[1] Her aim was to assess whether the **Doctrine of Double Effect** provides a plausible answer. She concluded that it doesn't, and went on to offer an answer of her own. It is her own answer that will interest us.

Here are two of her hypothetical cases. In the first, which I will call Judge's Two Options, a crime has been committed, and some rioters have taken five innocent people hostage; they will kill the five unless the judge arranges for the trial, followed by the execution, of the culprit. The real culprit is unknown, however. So the judge has only two options:

Judge's Two Options: he can
(i) let the rioters kill the five hostages, or

(ii) frame an innocent person for the crime, and have him executed.

Most people would say that the judge must not choose option (ii).

In the second case, which I will call Driver's Two Options, the driver of a runaway tram has only the following two options:

Driver's Two Options: he can
(i) continue onto the track ahead, on which five men are working, thereby killing the five, or
(ii) steer onto a spur of track off to the right on which only one man is working, thereby killing the one.

Most people would say that the driver may choose option (ii).

What explains the difference between our verdicts about what the agents may do in these two cases? After all, in both cases, the agents must choose between five deaths and one death.

Foot suggested that the difference is explainable by appeal to two principles. "There is worked into our moral system a distinction between what we owe to people in the form of aid and what we owe to them in the way of non-interference." She suggested that we call what we owe to people in the form of aid our positive duties, and what we owe to people in the way of non-interference our negative duties. She then invited us to accept that negative duties are weightier than positive duties. Markedly weightier. So much so that, as I will express her first principle:

> *Letting Five Die Vs. Killing One Principle*: A must let five die if saving them requires killing B.

That explains why the judge must not choose option (ii).

Things are otherwise in Driver's Two Options. The driver doesn't face a choice between letting five die and killing one, so the first principle is irrelevant to his case. So Foot appealed to a second principle, namely

> *Killing Five Vs. Killing One Principle*: A must not kill five if he can instead kill one.

Given this principle, the driver must choose option (ii), and, a fortiori, he may choose it. So that explains why the driver may choose option (ii). So we now have an explanation of the difference between our verdicts in the two cases.

Her proposal is very attractive. The ideas about negative and positive duties expressed in the two principles are not new, but they are intuitively very plausible, and Foot shows that given those two principles, we have a satisfying explanation of the differences among our verdicts in all of the cases she drew attention to. I should perhaps add that the principles she appeals to are intended merely as *ceteris paribus* principles, since further information about the six potential victims might make a difference in our views about what the agent may do. For example, finding out that one or more of the six potential victims is at fault for the coming about of the situation they now face might well make such a difference. What she had in mind is just that *other things being equal* the agent must or must not choose such and such an option. It will perhaps be useful, however, if I make explicit the assumption I make throughout that no one of the six in any of the cases we consider is at fault.

But are those two principles true? . . . I will assume that the second principle is satisfactory, and

focus instead on a doubt that was in fact raised about the first.

In an article provoked by Foot's, I suggested that we should take our eyes off the driver; we should eliminate him.[2] (Make him have dropped dead of a heart attack.) Then let us imagine the situation to be as in the case I will call Bystander's Two Options. A bystander happens to be standing by the track, next to a switch that can be used to turn the tram off the straight track, on which five men are working, onto a spur of track to the right on which only one man is working. The bystander therefore has only two options:

> Bystander's Two Options: he can
> (i) do nothing, letting five die, or
> (ii) throw the switch to the right, killing one.

Most people say that he may choose option (ii).

If the bystander may choose option (ii) in Bystander's Two Options, however, then Foot's first principle won't do. For if the *Letting Five Die Vs. Killing One Principle* is true, then the bystander must not choose option (ii)—for if he chooses option (ii), he kills one, whereas if he chooses option (i), he merely lets five die.

But if the *Letting Five Die Vs. Killing One Principle* is not true, then it cannot be appealed to to explain why the judge must not choose option (ii) in Judge's Two Options.

Perhaps there is some other answer to the question why the judge must not choose option (ii) in Judge's Two Options? An answer resting on the role of a judge in a legal system? No doubt there is. So let us bypass that case. Consider a case I called Fat Man. In this case a fat man and I happen to be on a footbridge over the track. I have two options:

> Fat Man: I can
> (i) do nothing, letting five die, or
> (ii) shove the fat man off the footbridge down onto the track, thereby killing him, but also, since he's very big, stopping the tram and saving the five.

Most people would say that I must not choose option (ii)—just as they would say that the judge must not choose option (ii) in Judge's Two Options. Yet I am not a judge, and no facts about the role of a judge in a legal system could be appealed to to explain why I must not choose option (ii).

Indeed, Foot might have presented us at the outset, not with Judge's Two Options and Driver's Two Options, but with Fat Man and Driver's Two Options, and asked why I must not choose option (ii) in Fat Man, whereas the driver may choose option (ii) in Driver's Two Options. Let us call that Philippa Foot's problem. We might well have been tempted to answer, as Foot would have answered, that the *Letting Five Die Vs. Killing One Principle* explains why I must not choose option (ii) in Fat Man, whereas the *Killing Five Vs. Killing One Principle* explains why the driver may choose option (ii) in Driver's Two Options.

But of course that answer won't do if the *Letting Five Die Vs. Killing One Principle* is false. So Philippa Foot's problem remains with us.

What is of interest is that we also have a second, different, problem before us. As I said, most people say that the bystander may choose option (ii) in Bystander's Two Options. In both Fat Man and Bystander's Two Options, the agent can choose option (i), letting the five die; in both, the agent who chooses option (ii) kills one. *Why is it impermissible for the agent in Fat Man to choose option (ii), but permissible for the agent in Bystander's Two Options to choose option (ii)?* Nothing we have in hand even begins to explain this second difference.

Moreover, it is not in the least easy to see what might explain it. Since trams are trolleys on this side of the Atlantic, I called this "the trolley problem." (Besides, that is more euphonious than "the tram problem.")

It spawned a substantial literature. Unfortunately, nobody produced a solution that anyone else thought satisfactory, and the trolley problem therefore also remains with us.

A Possible Solution

A few years ago, an MIT graduate student, Alexander Friedman, devoted a chapter of his thesis to a discussion of the most interesting solutions to the trolley problem on offer in the literature.[3] He did a very good job: he showed clearly that none of them worked. What was especially interesting, though, was what he concluded. He said: the reason why no adequate solution has been found is that something went wrong at the outset. He said: *it just isn't true that the bystander may choose option (ii) in Bystander's Two Options!*

Friedman didn't offer an independent argument to that effect. He drew his conclusion from two premises. First, there is the fact, which, as I say, he showed clearly, that none of the most interesting solutions on offer worked. We shouldn't take that fact lightly. It is, of course, consistent with there actually being a solution to the trolley problem that nobody has been clever enough to find it. But we should be troubled by the fact that so many people have tried, for so many years—well over a quarter of a century by now—and come up wanting. Friedman's second premise was that it just is intuitively plausible that negative duties really are weightier than positive duties. Thus, in particular, that the *Letting Five Die Vs. Killing One Principle* is true. And if it is true, then of course the bystander must not, after all, choose option (ii) in Bystander's Two Options.

Friedman therefore said that we should see the (so-called) trolley problem "for what it really is—a very intriguing, provocative, and eye-opening non-problem."

Well, there's an unsettling idea! But if you mull over Friedman's unsettling idea for a while, then perhaps it can come to seem worth taking very seriously. So let us mull over it.

Altruism

Here is a case that I will call Bystander's Three Options. The switch available to this bystander can be thrown in two ways. If he throws it to the right, then the trolley will turn onto the spur of track to the right, thereby killing one workman. If he throws it to the left, then the trolley will turn onto the spur of track to the left. The bystander himself stands on that left-hand spur of track, and will himself be killed if the trolley turns onto it. Or, of course, he can do nothing, letting five workmen die. In sum,

Bystander's Three Options: he can
  (i)   do nothing, letting five die, or
  (ii) throw the switch to the right, killing one, or
  (iii) throw the switch to the left, killing himself.

What is your reaction to the bystander's having the following thought? "Hmm. I want to save those five workmen. I can do that by choosing option (iii), that is by throwing the switch to the left, saving the five but killing myself. I'd prefer not dying today, however, even for the sake of saving five. So I'll choose option (ii), saving the five but killing the one on the right-hand track instead."

I hope you will agree that choosing (ii) would be unacceptable on the bystander's part. If he *can* throw the switch to the left and turn the trolley onto himself, how dare he throw the switch to the right and turn the trolley onto the one workman? The bystander doesn't feel like dying today, even for the sake of saving five, but we can assume, and so let us assume, that the one workman also doesn't feel like dying today, even if the bystander would thereby save five.

Let us get a little clearer about why this bystander must not choose option (ii). He wants to save the five on the straight track ahead. That would be good for them, and his saving them would be a good deed on his part. But his doing that good deed would have a cost: his life or the life of the one workman on the right-hand track. What the bystander does if he turns the trolley onto the one workman is to make the one workman pay the cost of his good deed because he doesn't feel like paying it himself.

Compare the following possibility. I am asked for a donation to Oxfam. I want to send them some money. I am able to send money of my own, but I don't feel like it. So I steal some from someone else and send *that* money to Oxfam. That is pretty bad. But if the bystander proceeds to turn the trolley onto the one on the right-hand track in Bystander's Three Options, then what he does is markedly worse, because the cost in Bystander's Three Options isn't money, it is life.

In sum, if A wants to do a certain good deed, and can pay what doing it would cost, then—other things being equal—A may do that good deed only if A pays the cost himself. In particular, here is a third *ceteris paribus* principle:

> *Third Principle*: A must not kill B to save five if he can instead kill himself to save the five.

So the bystander in Bystander's Three Options must not kill the one workman on the right-hand track in

furtherance of his good deed of saving the five since he can instead save the five by killing himself. Thus he must not choose option (ii).

On the other hand, morality doesn't require him to choose option (iii). If A wants to do a certain good deed, and discovers that the only permissible means he has of doing the good deed is killing himself, then he may refrain from doing the good deed. In particular, here is a fourth *ceteris paribus* principle:

> *Fourth Principle*: A may let five die if the only permissible means he has of saving them is killing himself.

So the bystander in Bystander's Three Options may choose option (i).

Let us now return to Bystander's Two Options. We may imagine that the bystander in this case can see the trolley headed for the five workmen, and wants to save them. He thinks: "Does this switch allow for me to choose option (iii), in which I turn the trolley onto myself? If it does, then I must not choose option (ii), in which I turn the trolley onto the one workman on the right-hand track, for as the *Third Principle* says, I must prefer killing myself to killing him. But I don't want to kill myself, and if truth be told, I wouldn't if I could. So if the switch does allow for me to choose option (iii), then I have to forgo my good deed of saving the five: I have to choose option (i)—thus I have to let the five die. As, of course, the *Fourth Principle* says I may."

As you can imagine, he therefore examines the switch *very* carefully. Lo, he discovers that the switch doesn't allow him to choose option (iii). "What luck," he thinks, "I can't turn the trolley onto myself. So it's perfectly all right for me to choose option (ii)!" His thought is that since he can't himself pay the cost of his good deed, it is perfectly all right for him to make the workman on the right-hand track pay it—despite the fact that he wouldn't himself pay it if he could.

I put it to you that that thought won't do. Since he wouldn't himself pay the cost of his good deed if he could pay it, there is no way in which he can decently regard himself as entitled to make someone else pay it.

Of how many of us is it true that if we could permissibly save five only by killing ourselves, then we would? *Doing so would be altruism, for as the Fourth Principle says, nobody is required to do so, and doing so would therefore be altruism: moreover, doing so would be doing something for others at a major cost to oneself, and doing so would therefore be major altruism. Very few of us would. Then very few of us could decently regard ourselves as entitled to choose option (ii) if we were in the bystander's situation in Bystander's Two Options.*

The Impermissibility of Killing One to Save Five

Very well, suppose that the bystander in Bystander's Two Options is among the very few major altruists who would choose option (iii) if it were available to them. Should we agree that *he* anyway can decently regard himself as entitled to choose option (ii)?

I stop to mention my impression that altruism that rises to this level is not morally attractive. Quite to the contrary. A willingness to give up one's life *simply* on learning that five others will live if and only if one dies is a sign of a serious moral defect in a person. "They're my children," "They're my friends," "They stand for things that matter to me," "They're young, whereas I haven't much longer to live," "I've committed myself to doing what I can for them": these and their ilk would make sacrificing one's life to save five morally intelligible. Consider, by contrast, the man who learns that five strangers will live if and only if they get the organs they need, and that his are the only ones that are available in time, and who therefore straightway volunteers. No reputable surgeon would perform the operation, and no hospital would allow it to be performed under its auspices. I would certainly not feel proud of my children if I learned that they value their own lives as little as that man values his.

Perhaps you disagree. I therefore do not rely on that idea. It remains the case that the altruistic bystander is not entitled to assume that the one workman is equally altruistic, and would therefore consent to the bystander's choosing option (ii). Altruism is by hypothesis not morally required of us.

Suppose, then, that the bystander knows that the one workman would not consent, and indeed is not

morally required to consent, *to his choosing option (ii). The bystander has a permissible alternative, namely choosing option (i)—that is letting the five die. I think it very plausible therefore that there is no way in which he can justify to himself or to anyone else his choosing option (ii), and thus that he cannot decently regard himself as entitled to choose it.*

A Remaining Question

If those arguments succeed, then Friedman was right:

Letting Five Die Vs. Killing One Principle: A must let five die if saving them requires killing B

is safe against the objection I made to it in drawing attention to Bystander's Two Options, since the bystander may not in fact proceed in that case. And if so, two consequences follow. First, Bystander's Two Options is no threat to solving Philippa Foot's problem as she would have done. She *can* explain the difference between our verdicts about the agents in Fat Man and Driver's Two Options as she would have done—that is, she *can* say that the *Letting Five Die Vs. Killing One Principle* explains why I may not proceed in Fat Man, whereas the

Killing Five Vs. Killing One Principle: A must not kill five if he can instead kill one

explains why the driver may proceed in Driver's Two Options. Second, as Friedman said, the (so-called) trolley problem is a nonproblem. The bystander in Bystander's Two Options is no more free to turn the trolley than I am to shove the fat man off the footbridge into the path of the trolley; a fortiori, there is no difference between our verdict about the agent in Fat Man and our (now corrected) verdict about the agent in Bystander's Two Options to *be* explained.

But even if the (so-called) trolley problem is therefore in one way a nonproblem, it is therefore in another way a real problem, for *if the bystander must not turn the trolley in Bystander's Two Options, then we need to ask why so many people who are presented with that case think it obvious that he may.* I will make a suggestion about why they do.

There is a question that we need to answer first, however.

Positive and Negative Duties

What I have in mind is this. I have suggested that consideration of Bystander's Three Options brings out that there is trouble for the idea that the bystander may turn the trolley in Bystander's Two Options. What has to be asked is whether consideration of an analogous case, namely Driver's Three Options, brings out that there is analogous trouble for the idea that the driver may turn the trolley in Driver's Two Options. If it does, then something must be wrong with my arguments in the preceding sections. Let us see why.

By way of reminder, here is Driver's Two Options again.

Driver's Two Options: he can
  (i)   continue onto the track ahead, on which five men are working, thereby killing the five, or
  (ii) steer onto a spur of track off to the right on which only one man is working, thereby killing the one.

Most people would say that the driver may choose option (ii). What would make that true? According to the *Killing Five Vs. Killing One Principle*, the driver must choose option (ii). I said in Section I that a doubt might be raised about that principle, but I also said that I would ignore it—thus that I would assume the principle is true. Very well then, the driver must choose option (ii). It follows that he may.

Here, now, is Driver's Three Options:
Driver's Three Options: he can
  (i)   continue onto the track ahead, on which five men are working, thereby killing the five, or
  (ii)   steer onto a spur of track off to the right on which only one man is working, thereby killing the one, or
  (iii) steer onto a spur of track off to the left, which ends in a stone wall, thereby killing himself.

If consideration of this case makes trouble for the idea that the driver in Driver's Two Options may choose option (ii), then, as I said, something must be wrong with my argument in the preceding sections.

Before attending to the question whether it does, we should take note of an objection that some

people make when presented with these cases. If the bystanders in Bystander's Two Options and Bystander's Three Options choose option (i), then they on any view don't kill the five; they merely let the five die. But the people I refer to object that that is also true of the drivers in these cases. After all, choosing option (i) in these cases isn't *steering* onto the track ahead. The drivers merely continue onto the track ahead. We may assume that they don't turn the steering wheel. Indeed, we may assume that they take their hands entirely off the steering wheels—letting the trolleys continue onto the tracks ahead, where *they* (the trolleys) will kill the five.

It really won't do, however, if we can also assume that the drivers themselves started their trolleys, and were steering them up to the time at which the brakes failed—so let us assume it. Suppose Alfred takes out his car and drives toward a restaurant where he expects to meet his friends. He suddenly sees five people on the street ahead of him, but his brakes fail: he cannot stop his car, he can only continue onto the street ahead or steer to the right (killing one) or steer to the left (killing himself). If he doesn't steer to one or the other side, if he simply takes his hands off the wheel, he runs the five down and kills them. He cannot at all plausibly insist that he merely lets them die. So similarly for the trolley drivers. Let us therefore return to them.

In Section III, I argued that if the bystander in Bystander's Two Options is not a major altruist, and, in particular, would not choose option (iii) if he could, then he cannot decently regard himself as entitled to choose option (ii). Here is a reminder of that argument. The bystander in Bystander's Three Options can choose option (iii)—that is, he can kill himself—and

Third Principle: A must not kill B to save five if he can instead kill himself to save the five

therefore yields that he must not choose option (ii). He isn't required to choose option (iii), for choosing option (iii) would be major altruism, and he therefore may instead choose option (i). But he must not choose option (ii). I then went on to say that if the bystander in Bystander's Two Options is not a major altruist, and in particular, would not choose option (iii) if it were available to him, then he cannot decently regard himself as entitled to choose option (ii).

Does that argument have an analogue for the driver in Driver's Two Options? Well, should we accept yet another *ceteris paribus* principle? Namely

> *Variant Third Principle*: A must not kill B to avoid killing five if he can instead kill himself to avoid killing the five.

If so, then since the driver in Driver's Three Options can choose option (iii)—he can kill himself—he must not choose option (ii). Are we to go on to say that if the driver in Driver's Two Options would not choose option (iii) if it were available to him, then he cannot decently regard himself as entitled to choose option (ii)? Can that be right—given that the *Killing Five Vs. Killing One Principle* yields that the driver in Driver's Two Options must choose option (ii)?

Should we accept the *Variant Third Principle?* One thing that might incline us to accept it should be set aside. We might be moved to accept it because we are moved by the fact that it is trolley drivers, and track workmen, whom we are concerned with here. Perhaps we think of a trolley driver as charged, as part of his duties, with seeing to the safety of the men who are working on the tracks. If we do, then perhaps we will think it true that since the driver in Driver's Three Options can choose option (iii)—he can kill himself—he must not choose option (ii). And the quite general *Variant Third Principle* may strike us as true for that reason.

But we should prescind from the possibility that the agents in the cases we are considering have special duties towards the other parties—special in that they are duties beyond those that any (private) human beings have towards any other (private) human beings. So let us return to Alfred. I invited you to imagine that he took out his car to drive toward a restaurant where he expects to meet his friends. He suddenly sees five people on the street ahead of him, but his brakes fail: he cannot stop his car, he can only continue onto the street ahead, or steer to the right (killing one), or steer to the left (killing himself). I said that if he doesn't steer to one

or the other side, if he simply takes his hands off the wheel, then he kills the five. If the *Variant Third Principle* is true, then he must steer to the left, killing himself. Should we agree?

There is reason to believe that we should. Alfred is driving the car; *he* is the threat to people. He will kill five if he does nothing, and it is not morally optional for him to do nothing: he must not kill the five. But since he will kill the five if he does nothing, *he* must be the one to pay the cost of his avoiding killing them. And if the cost is a life, then so be it: he is the one who must pay it.

(This rationale for saying that Alfred must pay the cost in this case is clearly very different from the rationale for saying that the bystander in Bystander's Three Options must pay the cost of saving the five if he is to save them. The difference lies in the fact that it is morally optional for the bystander, but not Alfred, to do nothing: the bystander may decline to do the good deed he would like to do, whereas Alfred must not kill five.)

On the other hand, there is the fact that Alfred is not at fault for the situation in which he now finds himself. Admittedly, it is not morally optional for him to do nothing, but why does he have to kill himself? Somebody has to pay the cost of his avoiding killing the five, but why him? Wouldn't it be fair in him to flip a coin? Is it mere high-mindedness that lies behind the thought that he had better kill himself?

(By contrast, the bystander in Bystander's Three Options must not flip a coin. It is not fair in him to impose a 0.5 risk of death on a person in order to do what it is morally optional for him to not do.)

On balance, I am more moved by the former consideration than by the latter, and thus prefer the idea that though Alfred is without fault, he must kill himself. (After all, the one on the right is also without fault.) And in sum, that we should accept the *Variant Third Principle*.

But I leave it open.[4] What matters, anyway, is what conclusion should be drawn about the driver in Driver's Two Options, whether or not the *Variant Third Principle* is true. Or, to avoid possible interference due to the thought that trolley drivers have special duties to track workmen, what conclusion should be drawn about Alfred, if it turns out that he cannot after all steer his car to the left, killing himself. Thus if it turns out that he has only the following two options: continue straight (killing five), or steer to the right (killing one). Suppose now that it is true of him that if he had the third alternative of steering to the left (killing himself), he wouldn't choose it. Suppose he wouldn't even flip a coin. Can he decently regard himself as entitled to steer to the right?

It is unjust in him that he would not only not steer to the left, but not flip a coin, if the option of steering to the left were available to him. That remains the case whatever he does. But his not steering to the right would itself be unjust, for his only alternative to steering to the right is killing five. If he knows that those are his only two options, then he cannot decently regard himself as entitled to *not* steer to the right.

Both of those facts mark Alfred off from the non-altruistic bystander in Bystander's Two Options. It is not the case that it is unjust in the bystander that he would not only not throw the switch to the left, killing himself, but not flip a coin as to whether or not to do so, if the option of throwing the switch to the left were available to him. And it is not the case that his not throwing the switch to the right would itself be unjust. For it is morally open to him to do nothing.

This difference between Alfred and the bystander is obviously due to the fact that whereas Alfred kills five if he does nothing, the bystander instead lets five die. Thus it is due to the very difference in weight between positive and negative duties that Foot said we should bring to bear on the cases she drew attention to, and that Friedman said was so plausible. I find myself strongly inclined to think they were right.

I add a proviso, though. I am sure it could go without saying, but it won't: it is one thing to say there is a difference in weight between positive and negative duties, and quite another to say what the source of that difference is. I know of no thoroughly convincing account of its source, and regard the need for one as among the most pressing in all of moral theory.

The Explanation of Our Mistaken Intuition

We should return now to the question I set aside earlier, namely why so many people who are presented with Bystander's Two Options think it obvious that the bystander may turn the trolley.

Friedman suggested that they think this for two reasons, first because of "the subconscious pull of utilitarianism," and second because the bystander's turning the trolley would not be as strikingly abhorrent as the agent's acting in some of the other hypothetical cases described in the literature, such as Fat Man and another case that I will get to shortly.

Friedman's first reason is over-strong. As we know, a number of psychologists have recently been collecting data on people's reactions to cases of the kind we are looking at. Ninety-three percent of the seniors at South Regional High School in Dayton, Ohio, say that the bystander may turn the trolley in Bystander's Two Options! (Actually, I just invented that statistic, but it's in the right ballpark.) I doubt that those students were pulled, consciously or subconsciously, by anything as sophisticated as utilitarianism.

It is surely right, however, to think that the psychologists' informants are moved by the fact that more people will live if the bystander turns the trolley than if he doesn't. A utilitarian would of course be moved by that fact; but so also would many others.[5]

Friedman's second reason is not so much a reason as a restatement of what has to be explained. Consider Fat Man again. It would be strikingly abhorrent for me to shove the fat man off the footbridge down onto the track, thereby killing him, even though more people will live if I do than if I don't. Consider a case often called Transplant: I am a surgeon, and can save my five patients who are in need of organs only by cutting up one healthy bystander—a bystander who has not volunteered—and distributing his organs among the five. Here too it would be strikingly abhorrent for me to proceed. Even more so, in fact. By contrast, it does not strike people generally as abhorrent for the bystander to turn the trolley. However, that difference cannot be thought to explain why people think that the bystander may proceed whereas the agents in Fat Man and Transplant may not. Rather it is what has to *be* explained.

Perhaps the explanation is not deep but right up at the surface?

In those three hypothetical cases, more will live if the agent proceeds than if he or she does not. Yet it isn't open to any of the agents to arrange, by magic, as it were, that there be just that difference, namely that more live. The agents have to *do* something to bring that outcome about. By what means are they to bring it about? Here are the only means by which I can bring it about in Fat Man: move the one into the path of the trolley currently headed toward the five. Here are the only means by which I can bring it about in Transplant: carve the one up and distribute his organs to the five who need them.

There is a wild efflorescence of hypothetical cases in this literature, and much strenuous theorizing about the differences among them. My impression is that when one backs off from all those cases—and one has to back off, lest one get bemused by the details, some of them thoroughly weird—*what seems to vary is at heart this: how drastic an assault on the one the agent has to make in order to bring about, thereby, that the five live.* The more drastic the means, the more strikingly abhorrent the agent's proceeding. That, I suspect, may be due to the fact that the more drastic the means, the more striking it is that the agent who proceeds infringes a negative duty to the one.

By contrast, if the bystander proceeds, then here are the means by which he brings about that more live: merely turn the trolley.

Some early attempts to explain why the bystander may proceed appealed to that fact about his means. Alas, they didn't succeed, since by turning the trolley, the bystander will kill the one, and thus will infringe a negative duty to the one; and there is no good reason to think that that fact about his means makes his infringing the negative duty count any the less heavily against his proceeding. No matter. We are not asking here why the bystander *may* turn the trolley. What we are asking is only why it seems to so many people that he may. The answer, then, may simply lie in our

being overly impressed by the fact that if he proceeds, he will bring about that more live by merely turning a trolley.

NOTE

1. Foot's article was first published in the *Oxford Review* in 1967; it is reprinted in her collection *Virtues and Vices* (Oxford: Basil Blackwell, 1978).

2. "Killing, Letting Die, and the Trolley Problem," *The Monist* 59 (1976): 204–17. In that article, the driver was eliminated in favor of a passenger. The case I will call Bystander's Two Options—in which the driver is eliminated in favor of a bystander—comes from my second article provoked by Foot's, namely "The Trolley Problem, " *The Yale Law Journal* 94 (1985): 1395–415. Those two articles, along with Foot's and several others on the topic, were helpfully reprinted and discussed. *Ethics: Problems and Principles,* ed. John Martin Fischer and Mark Ravizza (Orlando, Fla.: Harcourt Brace Jovanovich, 1992).

3. A. W. Friedman, *Minimizing Harm: Three Problems in Moral Theory.* Unpublished doctoral dissertation, Department of Linguistics and Philosophy, Massachusetts Institute of Technology (2002).

4. The view one holds on this matter has a bearing on the views one can consistently hold on other issues in moral theory, on the moral limits to self-defense in particular.

5. My own account of how facts of that kind figure in support of a conclusion about what a person ought to do appears in *Normativity* (Chicago: Open Court Publishing, 2008).

DISCUSSION QUESTIONS:

1. Foot and, ultimately, Thomson propose that our negative duties (e.g., our duty not to kill) are weightier than our positive duties (e.g., our duty to save). Are they correct? If so, what makes the former sort of duty weightier than the latter, given that the consequence of violating either is the same: someone dies?

2. Thomson argues that, in Bystander's Three Options, it would be wrong for the bystander to save the five by killing the one. Is she correct?

3. Thomson claims that in Bystander's Two Options, "Since [bystander] wouldn't himself pay the cost of his good deed if he could pay it, there is no way in which he can decently regard himself as entitled to make someone else pay it." Is she correct? Does our hypothetical unwillingness to pay a cost we are not in fact in a position to pay

imply that it is wrong for us to act in a way that would result in that cost being paid by others who are in fact able to pay it? Might an act by which we impose a burden on others still be right, even though we would not impose the same burden on ourselves if we could?

4. Thomson offers an explanation for why many people have the intuition that it is permissible for the bystander to redirect the trolley in Bystander's Two Options. Insofar as you have that intuition, is Thomson's explanation an accurate account of what leads you to it?

5. If you have read Kai Nielsen's essay, "Against Moral Conservatism," compare his treatment of the cave case, in which those trapped in a cave can save themselves only by blowing up the person stuck in the exit, to Thomson's treatment of the Fat Man case. How are the cases relevantly similar? How are they relevantly different? How do you think Thomson would deal with Nielsen's cave case? How do you think Nielsen would deal with Thomson's Fat Man case?

6. Can Act-Utilitarianism capture our intuitions about the cases Thomson presents? Can Rule-Utilitarianism do so? Is there any way in which either Utilitarian approach can accommodate the insight that our negative duties are weightier than our positive ones?

Argument Reconstruction Exercises:

I. Thomson considers the case of a bystander who can save five people from the oncoming trolley by using a switch to turn the trolley onto a track where it will only kill one person; the bystander is also someone who would not turn the trolley onto himself in order to save the five. Identify the premises and conclusion of her argument.

> "What luck," he thinks, "I can't turn the trol-ley onto myself. So it's perfectly all right for me to choose option (ii) [and turn the trolley onto the one]!" His thought is that since he can't him-self pay the cost of his good deed, it is perfectly all right for him to make the workman on the right-hand track pay it—despite the fact that he wouldn't himself pay it if he could. I put it to you that that thought won't do. Since he wouldn't

himself pay the cost of his good deed if he could pay it, there is no way in which he can decently regard himself as entitled to make someone else pay it. (page 231)

II. Can the fact of our selfishness relieve us of an obligation to help others? Identify the premises and conclusion of the following argument.

> May we perform a good deed that imposes a cost on others only if we would be willing to pay that cost ourselves if we were in a position to do so? Suppose a bystander can save five people by turning a trolley at the cost of a minor injury to someone else. Suppose too that the bystander is so selfish that he would not be willing to save the five if he were the one to suffer the minor injury. It is still permis-sible for the bystander to save the five by turning the trolley at the cost of a minor injury to someone else. We need not, therefore, always be willing to pay the costs of our good deeds in order for them to be permissible.

III. How might a Utilitarian think about the Trolley Problem? Identify the premises and conclusion of the following argument.

> A social practice is morally incorrect if it produces less net good than any alternative. The practice of killing some people to save others produces less net good than other alternatives, so long as the difference between the number of lives lost and the number of lives saved is minimal. Therefore, the practice of killing some people to save others is morally incorrect, so long as the difference between the number of lives lost and the number of lives saved is minimal. In Fat Man and Bystander Two Options, the difference in the number of lives to be lost (one) and the number of lives to be saved (five) is minimal. Therefore, in each case, it is mor-ally incorrect for the bystander to save the five by killing the one.

IV. Might the lesson of the Trolley Problem be that it is wrong to use people solely as a means? Identify the premises and conclusion of the following argument.

> The bystander's efforts to save the five are restricted by the moral principle that we must never treat

anyone solely as a means to our ends, no matter how good those ends may be. In Fat Man, the bystander uses the fat man solely as a means to her end of saving the five. She saves the five by using the fat man to stop the trolley. In Bystander's Two Choices, the bystander does not use the person on the alternate track as a means to save the five. She saves the five by shifting the trolley to the other track, the one person who happens to be there need not be present for her act to save the five. Therefore, the bystander's act of saving the five is wrong in Fat Man, but permissible in Bystander's Two Options.

CHAPTER 12

Nonconsequentialism

As I have said, I believe torture produces unreliable information, hinders our fight against global terrorism, and harms our national interest and reputation. But ultimately, this debate is about far more than . . . whether torture works or does not work. It is about far more than utilitarian matters. Ultimately, this is about morality. . . . Individuals might forfeit their life and liberty as punishment for breaking laws, but even then, as recognized in our Constitution's prohibition of cruel and unusual punishment, they are still entitled to respect for their basic human dignity, even if they have denied that respect to others.

—SENATOR JOHN McCAIN, REMARKS ON THE FLOOR OF
THE UNITED STATES SENATE, MAY 12, 2011

INTRODUCTION

When we puzzle over moral issues, be they as ordinary as whether to keep a slightly burdensome promise to a friend or as notable as whether to commit an act of torture, we often find that our deliberations take us past considering the good and evil consequences of our actions to considering how well our actions measure up to various moral standards about such things as human dignity, justice and rights. As we've seen, some philosophers reject **Consequentialism**, because it does not seem to give such standards their due. The alternative to Consequentialism is **Nonconsequentialism**. Where the Consequentialists say that acts and social practices are made right or wrong just by their good and evil consequences, Nonconsequentialists say that other factors are relevant as well.

It is, of course, one thing to say that the morality of our actions involves considerations beyond their consequences, and another to determine what those considerations are, what the basis for them is, and how they relate to one another to determine the difference between right and

wrong. There are thus many different forms of Nonconsequentialism. The readings in this chapter cover some of the main ones.

The selections by St. Thomas Aquinas and Alfonzo Gomez-Lobo represent the long tradition of **Natural Law Theory**. According to this tradition, we, as human beings, have a good that is the fulfillment or perfection of our nature; this good determines the moral standards, principles of the natural law, that together define how we ought to behave. Traditionally, natural law theory had a theological basis, as is most evident in Aquinas' presentation. Our good is the fulfillment or perfection of our God-given nature; the natural law, and so our moral obligations, are thus determined by God. However, Natural Law ethics need not explicitly invoke God to define either our natures or our obligations, and the selection by Gomez-Lobo sketches a natural law theory that emphasizes the relation between our moral obligations and our rationality. Our reason enables us to know the moral standards of the natural law, and the acts dictated by those standards are rational for us to perform as they support the fulfillment of our nature. (In considering Natural Law Theory, it may be helpful to reflect on the points presented in Chapter 8.4 by Sartre in his version of **atheistic existentialism**.)

Obviously not all nonconsequentialists seek to ground our moral obligations in the divine or in principles of nature. For example, Immanuel Kant attempts to ground moral obligations in reason alone, and he thereby offers another stark alternative to Consequentialism. In defending his fundamental moral principle, the **Categorical Imperative**, Kant assumes that whenever we act, we act on a maxim, a principle that states the policy that we take ourselves to be implementing. Kant formulates the Categorical Imperative in terms of maxims: "Act as though the maxim of your action were to become by your will a universal law of nature." In this principle, Kant captures the insight that morally correct action is universalizable: if it is morally permissible for us to act in a certain way, say break a promise to serve our self-interest, then the same is true of all others in the same situation.

Notice that both Kant and Utilitarianism agree about one important thing: there is a single rule, principle or consideration that determines our moral duty in any given situation. Many nonconsequentialists disagree with this sort of reduction of morality. For example, where Kant and Consequentialism offer one consideration as determining our moral duty, W. D. Ross in his selection offers us several. Ross sees us as having a variety of different moral relations to our self and to others. We are in a position to help or harm others. We make commitments to them. We receive benefits from them that need to be recognized, and we harm them in ways that need to be rectified. Our various moral relations are a source of different, sometimes mutually reinforcing and sometimes conflicting, moral duties. To do what is right in any situation, we should do whatever act, on balance, is our most stringent moral duty. If one alternative will produce the greatest net good and another will honor a promise we have made, we have a duty

to do each of them, and the right act is whichever one of these duties is the most stringent in the situation.

The selection by John Rawls illustrates a different way of understanding the moral principles. Rawls focuses his attention on the principles that define the requirements of distributive justice. Distributive justice refers to the just distribution of the rights and responsibilities in any given society. Rawls' approach is a contemporary version of the **Social Contract Theory** of morality. According to a social contract theory, rightness and wrongness are a function of the correct moral rules, and the correct moral rules are those that equal and rational self-interested individuals freely agree upon to govern their relations (or, in Rawls' case, *would* freely agree upon, under appropriate conditions). The correct moral rules are in this way an expression of our rational nature. We can discover them by specifying the appropriate conditions for the choice of rules and then determining what rules equal and rational self-interested, persons would choose under those conditions.

Social contract theorists face some difficult questions and challenges: Just what are the appropriate conditions by which to define the contractual situation? How will this approach give due consideration to the moral status of those who are not part of the contractual situation (e.g., non-human animals and children)? Are our moral relations to one another best understood by thinking of ourselves as rational individuals relating to one another in terms of agreements based in self-interest? In her essay, Virginia Held pursues this last concern. She argues that in thinking of morality as founded on agreements between rational, self-interested individuals, we overlook important moral aspects of our social relationships, especially ones that are based in attitudes of care and affection for others. Held suggests that, to best understand many aspects of morality, we should think of moral relations using the model of the caring relation between a mothering person and a child. Her suggestion is developed in still another approach to morality considered in Chapter Thirteen, the ethics of care.

SUGGESTIONS FOR FURTHER READING

Daniels, Norman, ed. *Reading Rawls.* (Palo Alto, CA: Stanford University Press, 1989)

Darwall, Stephen. *Deontology.* (Hoboken, N.J.: Wiley-Blackwell, 2002)

Finnis, John. *Natural Law and Natural Rights.* (Oxford: Oxford University Press, 1980)

Foot, Philippa. "The Problem of Abortion and the Doctrine of Double Effect", *Oxford Review,* 5, 1967, pp. 5–15.

_____. *Natural Goodness.* (Oxford: Oxford University Press, 2001)

Gauthier, D. *Morals By Agreement.* (Oxford: Clarendon Press, 1986)

McNaughten, David. "An Unconnected Heap of Duties?" *Philosophical Quarterly* 46, 1996, pp. 433–47.

Nozick, R. *Anarchy, State and Utopia.* (New York: Basic Books, 1974)

O'Neill, Onora. "Kantian Ethics." *A Companion to Ethics,* ed. Peter Singer (Oxford: Basil Blackwell, 1991), pp. 175–185.

Scheffler, S., ed. *Consequentialism and Its Critics.* (Oxford: Oxford University Press, 1988)

Woodward, P.A. *The Doctrine of Double Effect.* (Notre Dame: University of Notre Dame Press, 2001)

12.1 NATURAL LAW

ST. THOMAS AQUINAS (1265)

St. Thomas Aquinas was a Dominican monk and is the most famous medieval theologian and philosopher. He is best known for his interpretation of Aristotle's philosophy and his development of Aristotelianism within the context of Christian doctrines. In this selection from his *Summa Theologica,* Aquinas develops his view that our moral obligations are determined by a natural law, which derives from our God-given nature and is knowable by us. All creatures, as part of God's design, have a good that is the fulfillment of their nature. Humans, as rational and free, are able to discover their natural good and to direct their actions toward it. The precepts of the natural law define how we must behave to achieve our natural good. They determine our moral obligations.

Reading Questions:

1. What is Aquinas' definition of law in general, and how does that definition apply to each type of law (eternal, divine, natural, human)?

2. What is the relation between the eternal law and the natural law, according to Aquinas?

3. Aquinas distinguishes between the common or first principles of the natural law and the secondary principles. What are the main points of difference between the two?

4. Aquinas distinguishes between practical reason and speculative reason and draws analogies between the principles known by each. What is practical reason? What is speculative reason? What are some analogies between the principles known by each?

Whether There Is an Eternal Law?

Law is nothing else but a dictate of practical reason emanating from the ruler who governs a perfect community. *Now it is evident, granted that the world is ruled by divine providence, as was stated in the First Part that the whole community of the universe is governed by the divine reason.* Therefore the very notion of the government of things in God, the ruler of universe, has the nature of a law. And since the divine reason's conception of things is not subject to time, but is eternal, according to *Prov.* viii. 23, therefore it is that this kind of law must be called eternal.

Whether There Is in Us a Natural Law?

Romans 2:14— When the Gentiles, who have not the law, do by those nature *things that are of the law) Although they have no written law, yet they have the natural law, whereby each one knows, and is conscious of, what is good and what is evil.*

Law, being a rule and measure, can be in a person in two ways: in one way, as in him that rules and measures; in another way, as in that which is ruled and measured, since a thing is ruled and measured in so far as it partakes of the rule or measure. Therefore, since all things subject to divine providence are ruled and measured by the eternal law . . . it is evident that all things partake in some way in the eternal law, in so far as, namely from its being imprinted on them, they derive their respective inclinations to their proper acts and ends. Now among all others, the rational creature is subject to divine providence in a more excellent way, in so far as itself partakes of a share of providence, by being provident both for itself and for others. Therefore it has a share of the eternal reason, whereby it has a natural inclination to its proper act and end; and *this participation of the eternal law in the rational creature is called the natural law.* Hence the Psalmist, after saying (*Ps.* iv. 6): *Offer up the sacrifice of justice,* as though someone asked what the works of justice are, adds: *Many say, Who showeth us good things?* in answer to which question he says: *The light of Thy countenance, O Lord, is signed upon us.* He thus implies that the light of natural reason, whereby we discern what is good and what is evil, which is the function of the natural law, is nothing else than an imprint on us of the divine light. It is therefore evident that the natural law is nothing else than the rational creature's participation of the eternal law.

Whether There Is a Human Law?

Augustine distinguishes two kinds of law, the one eternal, the other temporal, which he calls human. . . .

As we have stated above, a law is a dictate of the practical reason. Now it is to be observed that the same procedure takes place in the practical and in the speculative reason, for each proceeds from principles to conclusions. . . . Accordingly, we conclude that, just as in the speculative reason, from naturally known indemonstrable principles we draw the conclusions of the various sciences, the knowledge of which is not imparted to us by nature, but acquired by the efforts of reason, so too it is that *from the precepts of the natural law, as from common and indemonstrable principles, the human reason needs to proceed to the more particular determination of certain matters. These particular determinations, devised by human reason, are called human laws,* provided that the other essential conditions of law be observed. . . .

Just as on the part of the speculative reason, by a natural participation of divine wisdom, there is in us the knowledge of certain common principles, but not a proper knowledge of each single truth, such as that contained in the divine wisdom, so, too, on the part of the practical reason, man has a natural participation of the eternal law, according to certain common principles, but not as regards the particular determinations of individual cases, which are, however, contained in the eternal law. Hence the need for human reason to proceed further to sanction them by law.

Whether There Was Any Need for a Divine Law?

Besides the natural and the human law it was necessary for the directing of human conduct to have a divine law. And this for four reasons. First, because it is by law that man is directed how to perform his proper acts in view of his last end. Now if man were ordained to no other end than that which is proportionate to his natural ability, there would be no need for man to have any further direction, on the part of his reason, in addition to the natural law and humanly devised law which is derived from it. *But since man is ordained to an end of eternal happiness which exceeds man's natural ability . . . therefore it was necessary that, in addition to the natural and the human law, man should be directed to his end by a law given by God.*

Secondly, because, by reason of the uncertainty of human judgment, especially on contingent and particular matters, different people form different judgments on human acts; whence also different and contrary laws result. In order, therefore, that man may know without any doubt what he ought to do and what he ought to avoid, it was necessary for man to be directed in his proper acts by a law given by God, for it is certain that such a law cannot err.

Thirdly, because man can make laws in those matters of which he is competent to judge. But man is not competent to judge of interior movements, that are hidden, but only of exterior acts which are observable; and yet for the perfection of virtue it is necessary for man to conduct himself rightly in both kinds of acts. Consequently, human law could not sufficiently curb and direct interior acts, and it was necessary for this purpose that a divine law should supervene.

Fourthly, because, as Augustine says, human law cannot punish or forbid all evil deeds, since, while aiming at doing away with all evils, it would do away with many good things, and would hinder the advance of the common good, which is necessary for human living. In order, therefore, that no evil might remain unforbidden and unpunished, it was necessary for the divine law to supervene, whereby all sins are forbidden. . . .

Whether the Natural Law Contains Several Precepts, or Only One?

. . . The precepts of the natural law are to the practical reason what the first principles of demonstrations are to the speculative reason, because both are self-evident principles. Now a thing is said to be self-evident in two ways: first, in itself; secondly, in relation to us. Any proposition is said to be self-evident in itself, if its predicate is contained in the notion of the subject; even though it may happen

that to one who does not know the definition of the subject, such a proposition is not self-evident. For instance, this proposition, *Man is a rational being* is in its very nature, self-evident, since he who says *man*, says a *rational being* and yet to one who does not know what a man is, this proposition is not self-evident. Hence it is that, as Boethius says, certain axioms or propositions are universally self-evident to all; and such are the propositions whose terms are known to all, as, *Every whole is greater than its part,* and, *Things equal to one and the same are equal to one another.* But some propositions are self-evident only to the wise, who understand the meaning of the terms of such propositions. Thus to one who understands that an angel is not a body, it is self-evident that an angel is not circumscriptively in a place. But this is not evident to the unlearned, for they cannot grasp it.

Now a certain order is to be found in those things that are apprehended by men. For that which first falls under apprehension is *being*, the understanding of which is included in all things whatsoever a man apprehends. Therefore the first indemonstrable principle is that *the same thing cannot be affirmed and denied at the same time*, which is based on the notion of *being* and *not-being*: and on this principle all others are based . . . Now as *being* is the first thing that falls under the apprehension absolutely, so *good* is the first thing that falls under the apprehension of the practical reason, which is directed to action (since every agent acts for an end, which has the nature of good). Consequently, the first principle in the practical reason is one founded on the nature of good, viz., that *good is that which all things seek after.* Hence this is the first precept of law, that *good is to be done and promoted, and evil is to be avoided.* All other precepts of the natural law are based upon this; so that all the things which the practical reason naturally apprehends as man's good belong to the precepts of the natural law under the form of things to be done or avoided.

Since, however, good has the nature of an end, and evil, the nature of the contrary, hence it is that all those things to which man has a natural inclination are naturally apprehended by reason as being good, and consequently as objects of pursuit, and their contraries as evil, and objects of avoidance. Therefore, the order of the precepts of the natural law is according to the order of natural inclinations. For there is in man, first of all, an inclination to good in accordance with the nature which he has in common with all substances, inasmuch, namely, as every substance seeks the preservation of its own being, according to its nature; and by reason of this inclination, whatever is a means of preserving human life, and of warding off its obstacles, belongs to the natural law. Secondly, there is in man an inclination to things that pertain to him more specially, according to that nature which he has in common with other animals; and in virtue of this inclination, those things are said to belong to the natural law *which nature has taught to all animals,* such as sexual intercourse, the education of offspring and so forth. Thirdly, there is in man an inclination to good according to the nature of his reason, which nature is proper to him. Thus man has a natural inclination to know the truth about God, and to live in society; and in this respect, whatever pertains to this inclination belongs to the natural law: e.g., to shun ignorance, to avoid offending those among whom one has to live, and other such things regarding the above inclination. . . .

Whether All the Acts of the Virtues Are Prescribed by the Natural Law?

. . .We may speak of virtuous acts in two ways: first, in so far as they are virtuous; secondly, as such and such acts considered in their proper species. If, then, we are speaking of the acts of the virtues in so far as they are virtuous, thus all virtuous acts belong to the natural law. For it has been stated that to the natural law belongs everything to which a man is inclined according to his nature. Now each thing is inclined naturally to an operation that is suitable to it according to its form: *e.g.,* fire is inclined to give heat. Therefore, since the rational soul is the proper form of man, there is in every man a natural inclination to act according to reason; and this is to act according to virtue. Consequently, considered thus, all the acts of the virtues are prescribed by the natural law, since each one's reason naturally dictates to him to act virtuously. But if we speak of virtuous acts, considered in themselves, *i.e.,* in their proper species, thus not all virtuous acts are prescribed by the natural law. For many things are done virtuously, to which nature does not primarily incline, but which, through the inquiry of reason, have been found by men to be conducive to well living.

. . .Temperance is about the natural concupiscences of food, drink and sexual matters, which are indeed ordained to the common good of nature, just as other matters of law are ordained to the moral common good. . . .

By human nature we may mean either that which is proper to man, and in this sense all sins, as being against reason, are also against nature, as Damascene states; or we may mean that nature which is common to man and other animals, and in this sense, certain special sins are said to be against nature: *e.g.* contrary to sexual intercourse, which is natural to all animals, is unisexual lust, which has received the special name of the unnatural crime. . . .

Whether the Natural Law Is the Same in All Men?

. . .As we have stated above, to the natural law belong those things to which a man is inclined naturally; and among these it is proper to man to be inclined to act according to reason. Now it belongs to the reason to proceed from what is common to what is proper. . . . The speculative reason, however, is differently situated, in this matter, from the practical reason. For, since the speculative reason is concerned chiefly with necessary things, which cannot be otherwise than they are, its proper conclusions, like the universal principles, contain the truth without fail. The practical reason, on the other hand, is concerned with contingent matters, which is the domain of human actions; and, consequently, although there is necessity in the common principles, the more we descend towards the particular, the more frequently we encounter defects. Accordingly, then, in speculative matters truth is the same in all men, both as to principles and as to conclusions; although the truth is not known to all as regards the conclusions but only as regards the principles which are called *common notions.* But in matters of action, truth or practical rectitude is not the same for all as to what is particular, but only as to the common principles; and where there is the same rectitude in relation to particulars, it is not equally known to all.

It is therefore evident that, as regards the common principles whether of speculative or of practical reason, truth or rectitude is the same for all, and is equally known by all. But as to the proper conclusions of the speculative reason, the truth is the same for all, but it is not equally known to all. Thus, it is true for all that the three angles of a triangle are together equal to two right angles, although it is not known to all. But as to the proper conclusions of the practical reason, neither is the truth or rectitude the same for all, nor, where it is the same, is it equally known by all. Thus it is right and true for all to act according to reason, and from this principle follows, as a proper conclusion, that goods entrusted to another should be restored to their owner. Now this is true for the majority of cases. But it may happen in a particular case that it would be injurious, and therefore unreasonable, to restore goods held in trust; for instance, if they are claimed for the purpose of fighting against one's country. And this principle will be found to fail the more, according as we descend further towards the particular, *e.g.,* if one were to say that goods held in trust should be restored with such and such a guarantee, or in such and such a way; because the greater the number of conditions added, the greater the number of ways in which the principle may fail, so that it be not right to restore or not to restore.

Consequently, we must say that the natural law, as to the first common principles, is the same for all both as to rectitude and as to knowledge. But as to certain more particular aspects, which are conclusions, as it were, of those common principles, it is the same for all in the majority of cases, both as to rectitude and as to knowledge; and yet in some few cases it may fail both as to rectitude, by reason of certain obstacles (just as natures subject to generation and corruption fail in some few cases because of some obstacle), and as to knowledge, since in some the reason is perverted by passion, or evil habit, or an evil disposition of nature. Thus at one time theft, although it is expressly contrary to the natural law, was not considered wrong among the Germans, as Julius Caesar relates.

Whether the Natural Law Can Be Changed?

A change in the natural law may be understood in two ways. First, by way of addition. In this sense,

nothing hinders the natural law from being changed, since many things for the benefit of human life have been added over and above the natural law, both by the divine law and by human laws.

Secondly, a change in the natural law may be understood by way of subtraction, so that what previously was according to the natural law, ceases to be so. In this sense, the natural law is altogether unchangeable in its first principles. But in its secondary principles, which, as we have said, are certain detailed proximate conclusions drawn from the first principles, the natural law is not changed so that what it prescribes be not right in most cases. But it may be changed in some particular cases of rare occurrence, through some special causes hindering the observance of such precepts, as stated above.

Whether the Natural Law Can Be Abolished from the Heart of Man?

As we have stated above, there belong to the natural law, first, certain most common precepts that are known to all; and secondly, certain secondary and more particular precepts, which are, as it were, conclusions following closely from first principles. As to the common principles, the natural law, in its universal meaning, cannot in any way be blotted out from men's hearts. But it is blotted out in the case of a particular action, in so far as reason is hindered from applying the common principle to the particular because of concupiscence or some other passion. . . .

But as to the other, i.e., the secondary precepts, the natural law can be blotted out from the human heart, either by evil persuasions, just as in speculative matters errors occur in respect of necessary conclusions; or by vicious customs and corrupt habits, as, among some men, theft, and even unnatural vices, as the Apostle states (Rom. i. 24), were not esteemed sinful.

DISCUSSION QUESTIONS:

1. Aquinas appeals to certain beliefs about the nature and existence of God in presenting his version of Natural Law theory. How, if at all, might we develop a Natural Law theory that does not include any such theological claims?

2. An essential claim of Natural Law theory is that human beings have a natural end or good;

the precepts of the natural law detail how we are to behave to achieve that end. Do we have such a natural end? If so, what is it and how is it determined?

3. According to Natural Law theory, immoral actions are contrary to our nature. Consider some clearly immoral acts. In what way, if at all, are these acts "unnatural" for human beings?

4. Critics of Natural Law theory sometimes object that the theory involves a mistaken inference from what "is" to what "ought to be." Even if we have a particular nature, that fact about how we are is insufficient to support conclusions about how we morally ought to behave. How might Aquinas best respond to this objection?

Argument Reconstruction Exercises:

I. Aquinas argues that all acts of virtue are prescribed by the natural law. Identify the premises and conclusion of his reasoning.

> [T]here is in every man a natural inclination to act according to reason; and this to act according to virtue. Consequently, considered, thus, all the acts of the virtues are prescribed by the natural law, since each one's reason naturally dictates him to act virtuously. (page 244)

II. Does morality require that we have a natural end or purpose? Identify the premises and conclusion of the following argument.

> The difference between right and wrong is the difference between what does and does not promote the welfare of human beings. Human beings have a welfare to promote only if they have some natural end or purpose relative to which their welfare is defined. There is, therefore, a difference between right and wrong only if human beings have some natural end or purpose.

III. Some acts seem to be just plain wrong, independently of any considerations about our natural goals or ends. Identify the premises and conclusion of the following argument.

> The act of the rapist, thief, or murderer may in some way be "unnatural," but that is not what makes it wrong. The act would be immoral even if were "natural." Such acts are wrong in and of themselves.

IV. What is it for an action to be unnatural and how, if at all, is that fact relevant to our moral obligations? Identify the premises and conclusion of the following argument.

> Any argument of the form, "That act is unnatural, therefore it's wrong," is defective. On one reading, the first premise is just the claim that the act is unusual, in which case it doesn't support the conclusion that the act is wrong. On another reading, the first premise is the claim that the act is in some way improper, in which case it assumes the truth of the conclusion and the argument begs the question.

12.2 NATURAL LAW ETHICS

ALFONSO GOMEZ-LOBO (2001)

Alfonso Gomez-Lobo was a professor of philosophy at Georgetown University and a specialist in Greek philosophy, the history of ethics, and natural law ethics. In this selection, he offers a contemporary defense of **Natural Law theory** that starts with a principle he takes to be true by definition: one should pursue what is good and one should avoid what is evil. He then develops a theory of basic human goods as those things that are fundamental ingredients of human flourishing (e.g., friendship), and he uses that theory of goods to support a system of moral norms, some of which are **absolute** or exceptionless. Gomez-Lobo notes that **consequentialist** philosophers reject such moral conservatism (see Kai Nielsen's essay in Section 11.2, "Against Moral

Conservatism") and introduces the **Principle of Double Effect** to reconcile the conflicting intuitions that an appeal to absolute norms sometimes generates.

Reading Questions:

1. Gomez-Lobo notes that his attempt to persuade his readers must begin with certain shared assumptions. What claims does he offer as shared assumptions to be the basis for his argument?

2. What is Gomez-Lobo's argument for the claim that biological human life is intrinsically good?

3. Gomez-Lobo takes each basic human good he presents to be a "basic ingredient of human flourishing." What does he mean by this? Is his view that it is impossible to have a good life unless one's life contains each of these goods? Is his claim that each of these goods is something that contributes to the excellence of a human life? Does he have in mind some other relation between each good, on the one hand, and having an excellent human life, on the other?

4. For each good he presents, what is Gomez-Lobo's basis for his claim that it is a basic ingredient of a good life?

5. What moral norms does Gomez-Lobo associate with each basic human good?'

6. What is Gomez-Lobo's reason for thinking that, when negative and positive norms conflict, the negative norms take precedence?

7. What are implications of the Principle of Double Effect for one of the cases of potential moral conflict cited by Gomez-Lobo in his discussion of exceptionless norms?

The First Principle of Practical Rationality

Any attempt to reason with other human beings has to start somewhere. If I can show you that statement Q logically follows from statement P, and I get you to agree that P is true, then I am in a position to persuade you that Q is also true. In this case, our agreement on P is an adequate starting point. . . .

The purpose of this chapter is to invite you, the reader, to agree on something that will allow us to make further progress. If we do not agree on anything, you would be well-advised to close this book and throw it in the trash (or sell it second-hand to diminish your losses).

Perhaps you will agree that, in general, it makes sense to refrain from eating food that smells bad. If it smells bad, it is probably spoiled, and you want to avoid the ensuing sickness. You also may agree that exercising

regularly is something worth doing (although, in real life, you may well be a couch potato). I may ask, however, "Why is it worthwhile?" And you will probably answer, "Because it keeps you in good health."

We seem to be starting to agree on two things here: that it is bad to be sick and good to be healthy and that it is reasonable to avoid being sick and to try to stay healthy.

Illness is not the only bad thing for us, nor is health the only good one. We are surrounded by many good and bad things, so the normal attitude toward sickness and health reasonably can be adopted toward other things.

Hence, I suggest that we agree on the following, which I call "The Formal Principle" (FP):

One should pursue what is good, and one should avoid what is bad.

Several things must be said about this principle before we continue. The verbs ("to pursue," "to avoid") should be taken to stand for a wide variety of actions. The former can be replaced by, for example, "try to obtain," "secure," "do," "foster," "perform," and so forth, the latter by "to refrain from," "eschew," "shun," "run away from," and so forth. These verbs describe actions that we humans deliberately perform as a result of taking a positive or a negative stand toward something. The reasons to take a positive or a negative stand, to do or to refrain from doing something, are encapsulated in the words "good" and "bad," respectively.

How are the terms "good" and "bad" being used here? They are surely evaluative terms. If one values something, one says it is good; contrariwise, we say it is bad. The evaluation we are considering here is the usual nonmoral evaluation: Illness and health are not morally bad and morally good things, respectively. We are implicitly appealing to this principle whenever we exhort someone to go to a good college, avoid bad grades, buy a good pair of sneakers, get rid of a bad car, and so forth.

The FP, therefore, is not a moral principle but a general principle of practical rationality. In the absence of further specifications, it cannot tell us whether some action is morally right or wrong. Because of its generality, it also leaves open whose good ought to be pursued and when. Sometimes it will be rational for me to pursue my good, sometimes the good of someone else. The principle does not enjoin me to actively pursue on each occasion every single good that is within my grasp. What the principle rejects in broad terms is the pursuit of something bad (for anyone) and the deliberate neglect of something good (for someone). By itself, the principle does not resolve practical conflicts.

The term "practical" is not meant here in its standard sense (where "practical" means the same as "useful," "capable of being put to immediate use"). I am relying heavily on the Greek roots of the term. The adjective "practical" is derived from *praxis*, the Greek word for "action." This is why in philosophy it has been used to mean "pertaining to human action." "Practical reason," then, stands for our capacity to use our rational powers to guide us in what we *do* as opposed to what we *make* or what we *figure out* without any intention of putting it into practice. Aristotle called these two further uses of reason "productive reason" and "theoretical reason," respectively.[1] . . .

What reasons do we have to think that it is true that we should pursue what is good and avoid what is bad? Surely no observation of empirical facts will provide us with such reasons because the claim itself is not an empirical claim. It is not a claim about the world and our experience of it. By "empirical claim" we mean a statement that can be known to be true (or false) by observation and experimentation. Typically, chemistry makes empirical claims, and that is why chemistry students need to conduct experiments and observe their results. There are no labs for ethics courses.

The first principle of practical reason does not make a claim about the world of nature, nor about cities and their institutional roles. It does not make a claim about the world at all. As we have seen, it makes a claim about how we should act. It tells us that if something is good, it is rational to pursue it, and if it is bad, it is rational to avoid it. . . .

The first principle of practical rationality . . . is true by virtue of the meaning of its terms. Any person who understands what we are talking about when we say (in any language) that something is good should be able to realize that the principle is true and hence have no objection to our positing it as the first step in our moral philosophy.

If the truth of the principle is analogous to that of the statement that a bachelor is an unmarried male, we can immediately see that, by itself, it is not very helpful. To know that all bachelors are unmarried males does not tell a woman at a party which of the three men talking to her is, in fact, a bachelor. Likewise, to have the basic practical understanding that good things are the things worth pursuing does not tell us which things are indeed good for myself or for other people.

To flag this insufficiency, I qualify the principle under consideration by saying that it is a *formal* principle. I mean by this that it does not provide us with actual criteria to determine which things are good. Thus, it is analogous to the claim that if this creature swimming under my boat is a whale, it is a mammal. This is true, of course, but it does not tell me whether the creature is a whale or not.

Basic Human Goods

The next questions you naturally will ask are: Which things are good? How can you tell a good from a bad thing? Moreover, good for whom? . . .

I would like to cast some doubt on the prospect of finding a single criterion for goodness. If we look around, we will see that the many good things that surround us differ considerably from each other. There are good cars, good classes, good vacations, good museums, good friends, and so forth. We praise all these things by characterizing them as good, but if we are asked to say why the Metropolitan Museum in New York is a good museum and a Mercedes-Benz is a good car, we will give quite different answers. It would be intolerably vague and unsatisfactory to say that both provide pleasure. In one case we will mention certain works of art to be seen there, in the second perhaps the durability of its engine. The pleasant feeling experienced by people who visit the former and drive the latter does not tell us much about the goodness of either one.

The criteria (note the plural form) differ widely from one class of things to the next. There is no single criterion of goodness across all classes. Likewise, there is no reason to expect that fundamental human goods can be discerned by applying a single criterion. Hence, my strategy will be to assume that there is a plurality of criteria, and then question the view that they are all reducible to one.

Criteria often are articulated by means of general propositions that can be used as premises for inferences. Let me provide an example: "Any number that is divisible by 2 is an even number." This proposition functions as a starting point for the following inference: "The number 6 is a particular instance of a number divisible by 2; therefore, 6 is an even number."

I plan to adopt a similar pattern for the criteria that should allow us to distinguish real goods from apparent goods. This pattern will be as follows:

X is a basic human good, and if Y is an instance of X, then Y is a real good.

The challenge is to find the correct substitutions for X. They have to be general terms that stand for things that are basic ingredients of human flourishing. A basic human good is to the good life roughly as pasta is to an Italian meal. Pasta is one of its key ingredients, and it can appear under many particular guises (spaghetti, fettucine, tortellini, etc.). Just as a meal without any pasta is unlikely to qualify as a product of Italian cooking, a life that is totally lacking in one or more of the basic human goods can hardly be said to be an excellent one.

I will present my candidates for basic goods; you must decide whether you agree with my list. I will have to give you reasons to agree (recall the nature of moral philosophy as a rational discussion among people regarded as equals); reasons will be difficult to provide, however, because, for the most part, one cannot appeal to something *more* universal than each basic good. Occasionally, I will appeal to the ordinary notion of "being well off." I plan to do this in cases that I expect to be fairly uncontroversial and thus capable of commanding wide-ranging assent. . . .

Let us start with something truly basic:

(P.1) Life is a basic human good.

By "life" I mean here human life at the basic biological level, manifesting itself in the typical functions of a human organism (taking nourishment, growing, etc.). Whether a certain organism is human depends on whether it has the complete set of standard human chromosomes or a deviation therefrom that counts as a human genetic abnormality. An egg or a sperm by itself does not qualify. Neither of them, as we now know, has the complete set. It also matters whether it is a complete organism with its own self-developing life and not just a part of one. A toe or a tumor or some drops of blood do have cells each of which as the required chromosomes, but none of them is a complete organism. . . .

These are all descriptive statements and therefore not strictly part of moral philosophy. Let us make the transition into the latter by placing our consideration of these matters under the concepts of good and bad.

Would you consent, as you read this page, that your life be taken? I suspect you would not. You probably think, as I do, that death is awful—whether it is your own death or that of your boyfriend, your girlfriend, your spouse, your child, your mother, or. . . . The list can go on indefinitely. You can agree that even the execution of a murderer is a terrible thing; if you are in favor of the death penalty, you would add that something so terrible is precisely what that individual deserves. Death, with its implication of one's final dissolution and annihilation, is the ultimate evil, the ultimate thing we wish to avoid.

By contrast, life appears to be a good worth enjoying and celebrating, as we implicitly acknowledge when we celebrate our own and other peoples' birthdays.

Life is not the sole good (we can possess many other goods beyond being merely alive), but it is surely the very first one. Without it we cannot partake in any other goods. In this sense, it is the grounding good. It also is worth having on its own: It is good to be alive. The closest analogy to this claim is that health also is good in the same way: When we are not ill we can pursue other goods, but being healthy is just plain good in itself.

I am sure that you can easily come up with an objection that is gaining social acceptance today because it underpins arguments for voluntary euthanasia and physician-assisted suicide: There are people for whom life is simply bad. . . .

Why do some people regard their lives as bad? Why do some people long to die? What makes life bad surely is one or more of the following: chronic illness, acute physical pain, extreme poverty and destitution, being lonely and forsaken by friends and relatives, realizing that one has committed a terrible crime (like Oedipus, who killed his father and married his mother), or experiencing unrequited love or clinical depression. You may add to the list as you see fit.

The list is necessary, however, because without reference to items such as these one would be at a loss to understand how a person could regard her life as bad. If by fiat one could do away with illness, pain, poverty, and so forth, would it be sensible to say that life itself is bad for that person? Surely not, because, strictly speaking, it is not life that is bad (unless perhaps "life" is understood in a different, not strictly biological sense). The illness, pain, poverty, and so forth are the bad things. Life as such is different from those evils, and one cannot conclude that in its own right it is an evil.

Perhaps, however, life is a purely neutral thing that derives all of its value or disvalue from other goods.

To prove that B has derivative or instrumental value, one must show that B is instrumental in attaining A and that A has intrinsic value. Assume, however, that B sometimes can be instrumental to the attainment of C. If one shows that C is bad, one will have shown in turn that B also is instrumentally bad. B, then, will be instrumentally both good and bad, but in itself neither (this is exactly what "neutral" means).

How can we persuade each other that something has intrinsic value? If we have reason to agree that G is intrinsically good and that D, E, and F are neither extrinsically nor instrumentally conducive to G but are internal constituents of G, we also have reason to think that they are intrinsically valuable. We all doubtless agree that happiness or the good life is the ultimate worthwhile thing—something that we value not because it will lead to something else but because it is good itself. Surely life is not external or instrumental to the good life. The good life is not a product or a consequence of life. It is life fully realized. Life, then—as the key ingredient of the good life (though not the only one)—is worth having for its own sake. Life is not neutral, nor is death. Death is totally incompatible with the ultimate goal of human beings. . . .

As I have just mentioned, there is a good that is closely connected with life and analogous to it: the good of health. This good, in turn, manifests itself in other worthwhile bodily operations such as perceiving, sensing, and moving on one's own.

Health does not play a strictly grounding role, however, because it is possible to be in poor health and yet enjoy other, nonbodily goods (such as the friendship of those caring for you with love and devotion), although a life lived for the most part in good health will be better than one with long periods of illness. For most people (including you, I trust), it is indeed axiomatic that health is something good. By "axiomatic" I mean "akin to the axioms of geometry" (i.e., to propositions that are readily accepted as true without proof). . . .

Beyond the preservation of life and the promotion of health, most people also would grant that the healthy transmission of life is valuable. This realization leads us to a second item in our list of basic goods:

(P.2) The family is a basic human good.

Here we enter a controversial and complex subject. The family is a matter of vigorous controversy mainly because marriages fail today at an astonishing rate. There also is the charge that it is inevitably a patriarchal, male-dominated institution that is detrimental to the well-being of women, which can be replaced by new arrangements, such as single-parent households. We often hear too about parents whose children have made them suffer a lot and children whose abusive parents have made *them* suffer quite a bit. You may remember the old bumper-sticker: "Live long enough to be a burden for your children." How can the family be all that good?

One also could challenge the idea of listing the family as a *basic* good from a different perspective. There are many people who, as a matter of fact, do not have a family and seem to be doing fine, and there are religious persons—notably Roman Catholic men and women—who decline to have a family in spite of their being committed to an ethical outlook that is very much like the one presented in this book.

Let us not lose sight of our strategy and ask not factual questions but evaluative ones. Is a child better off being raised in an orphanage or in a family? Is an adult better off having a loving spouse with whom to have sex, children, companionship, fun, and common projects or being alone? Is a senior citizen better off having an affectionate daughter to drive her to a chemotherapy session or having to drive herself in spite of the pain and the nausea?

What makes the family a basic good is that in the hypothetical absence of any family ties, in the total deprivation of a loving spouse and close relatives, in the case of a life starting in an orphanage and ending in solitude, one can hardly speak of a fully flourishing existence: What makes the family a basic good is its contribution to the good life. Just as the fact that we are sometimes sick does not contradict the claim that health is a basic good, likewise failure in family life or simply not having a family (either by design or by the circumstances of life) do not entail that it would not be good to have one.

The reflection on family failure discloses an important aspect of the complex human good we are analyzing. Family life fails when other goods are missing—notably the excellence of communities that Aristotle calls *philia*, "friendship."[2] If spouses are not good friends and lovers of each other, if parents are not good friends of their children or the children of their parents, or the siblings among themselves, families fall apart. Familial friendship is to the family what health is to the body. You can cope with illness or lack of love, but you would be better off if you were in the opposite condition. . . .

Hence, the next supplementary principle will be as follows:

(P.3) Friendship is a basic human good.

As we have seen, there is an inevitable overlap with the previous good, but now we are going explicitly beyond the narrow confines of the family. . . .

By 'friendship' I mean the kind of relationship that develops between you and a small number of people you are willing to see every day, hang out with, help when they need you, seek help from when you need them. To such people we open our hearts; we tell them what burdens us; we phone them when we have good news. These are the persons we are willing to call "friends."

Three things seem to be core ingredients of this form of relationship. First, there is affection involved (though not intense, erotic affection). We like these people; we feel comfortable with them. Second, there has to be reciprocity. I may like someone, but if that other person is unaware of me or is not willing to spend time with me or does not open his or her heart to me, I would not say we are friends. Third, friends are individuals who wish the best for each other; moreover, each does it for the other's sake. Asking for favors and never returning them or outright ill will toward a person are clear signs that friendship has vanished or has never existed.

Because friendship requires more than one person and entails mutual good will, it follows that friendship also is a good of communities. The forms and rituals of friendship may vary from culture to culture (some cultures, for example, require a formal declaration of the newly established friendship), but its beneficial effect is common to all of those forms. . . .

Communities also are connected to two other basic goods that may be considered jointly.

(P.4) Work and play are basic human goods.

By "work" I mean the myriad activities by means of which human beings produce goods and services for each other and thus earn their living. I emphasize that work can take many different forms in our culture, as well as across cultures. A man begging on a street corner is not working, but a man playing the guitar may be. If his performance is appreciated, people will give him a few coins. A service has been rendered, and a reward has been reaped. . . .

The key ingredient that makes work (including schoolwork) a human good seems to be the experience of achievement and self-realization that is at its very core. At work we activate at least some of our talents, and this is a source of personal satisfaction. Because volunteer work can contribute to these grounds of self-esteem, one can hold that remuneration is not essential to the goodness of work. For most of us, however, a paycheck at the end of the month also is vital.

Another important aspect of work is that it links us to our communities. We do not work alone. Most of us work within institutions— such as corporations, federal agencies, small companies, professional basketball teams, or philosophy departments—but even the most isolated producer has to sell her products to someone. Her wares or services have to be appreciated by other human beings. Work, then, puts us in contact with various communities. We make a contribution to them, and we get something in return, in the form of a salary or gratitude and recognition. Volunteers get only the latter, but they are not deprived of the core goods of work.

We may agree that work is good and unemployment bad. Does this entail that it would be sensible to make work the supreme value in our lives? Should we think highly of the fanatic, relentless workaholic? I myself do not.

There is value in relaxation—in doing something just for the fun of it. If you never take time off from work, go out to shoot baskets with your friends, swim at a local beach, go with a kid to fly a kite, or . . . the list can be very long! I try to capture it by means of the label "play." . . .

The infinite variety of forms of play should not distract us from the claim that it represents an important aspect of human fulfillment. Although play seems to be the direct opposite of work, it ends up as work's natural complement. A life of work without play is hardly attractive, but neither is a life of play without work. Without work, the relaxation aspect of play probably would be lost—and with it a key reason to engage in play.

Some people in their work and in their play aim at a goal that leads us to our next item: the production of beauty.

(P.5) The experience of beauty is a basic human good.

Again, we are facing a vast domain. There is, of course, the active production of beauty (a task that is carried out primarily by artists) and the passive enjoyment of the aesthetic experience (an activity that is open to anyone).

Beauty comes in so many forms—in nature and in the works crafted by human hands—that it is simply impossible to canvass all of its different manifestations. Indeed, any object, gesture, shade of color, or musical performance can display beauty, and a second look often is needed for us to realize that it is there. In a sense, the history of art is the progressive discovery of beauty where at first no one thought it could be found. Most of what was produced by the modern industrial revolution initially was perceived as ugly until, among others, the first photographers started to show the astonishing aesthetic qualities of cranes and machines, pipes and towers. Something similar can be said about the progression in music from classical to romantic to contemporary to jazz to rock, etc. (I add "etc." because of my own limitations in this area, but you can supply your favorite new releases).

The possibilities are endless. What I invite agreement on is the claim that lives are enriched by the experience of beauty (any form thereof) and that lives without it are sorely less desirable.

[For the next good,] I start, as usual, with a bold generalization and then try to justify it

(P.6) Knowledge is a basic human good.

The target of inquiry and knowledge is truth. If you are going through this book with a critical eye—if you are trying to find errors or mistakes, if you wish to know whether its claims are true or not—you are already granting that truth is valuable, that it is a good. . . .

We can know many things, but we are not equally interested in being acquainted with all possible items of knowledge, particularly in an era of technological explosion of information. We are more eager to know some things than other things. If we try to identify the things that all of us are most interested in, a reasonable beginning can be to say that we would like to know what is good for us and what is bad for us. Again, this knowledge clearly is cross-cultural.

The reason for the widely shared appreciation of insight into what will benefit us and what will harm us is that all human beings are agents. We cannot sit idly. We have to do things, and we have to choose to do X or Y. Moreover, as we have seen, our choices will be rational if we choose what we correctly determine to be good for us.

Because we could be mistaken, which could have dire consequences for us, we want to *know* whether X is good for us. Knowledge of goods for action expressed by means of standard evaluative propositions can be labeled "practical knowledge," and we are thus justified in claiming that

(P.6a) Practical knowledge is a basic human good.

This good is about other goods. The purpose of engaging in the practice of practical knowledge is to identify the remaining human goods, generically and specifically, and to develop strategies to attain them. An example of practical knowledge would be to realize generically how important friendship is for life and to develop a good eye to choose one's friends among a crowd of acquaintances. Nourishing an already initiated friendship also requires some kind of policy—such as, for instance, postponing instant gratification to be available to attend to one's friend's needs. To realize this (and to act on it) is also to be practically smart.

Sometimes one also wants to know things that do not have an immediate impact on one's decisions. It would be good to know more about the history of India or the latest discoveries in molecular biology—perhaps not for me, but in general. I am aware of the fact that many sciences and theories are beyond my reach, but if I turn to the other extreme I can make a

reliable evaluation: Am I better off if I am ignorant—if I am muddled in my thoughts about the world, its basic structures, its wide variety of manifestations? Isn't theoretical knowledge (whether it will have an impact on technology later on or not) something that fulfills us as human beings? If so, then

(P.6b) Theoretical knowledge is a basic human good.

This claim, like each of the previous claims, is quite general. Theoretical knowledge is understood here broadly and in opposition to practical knowledge. It embraces all forms of descriptive knowledge ranging from knowledge of particular facts to the most abstract scientific and philosophical theories. The key to the distinction is that theoretical knowledge is pursued for its own sake, whereas practical knowledge is pursued for the sake of action. Typically, a theoretical proposition states something about the world as it is, whereas practical proposition will include an evaluative or normative component (expressed by terms such as "good," "right," and similar words that endows it with action-guiding force.

What if someone denies that knowledge, at least of the theoretical sort, is a basic good? The person who issues this denial seems to be trapped in an inevitable paradox, for to deny that knowledge is a good is to claim that it is true that knowledge is not a good. This claim surely betrays an interest in the truth and a willingness to avoid error. To thus value truth over error, however, is to conceive of knowledge as a better state than ignorance. Indeed, any truth claim—any claim that one is right about something (and someone else is wrong)—is a claim that assumes the goodness of knowledge.

A more serious challenge to this view comes from those who agree that knowledge is generally a good but that in certain particular cases it is better not to know than to know because it would be painful to know. One such scenario is the case of a patient whose physician has diagnosed her as being terminally ill. I submit that knowledge of the fact that one is ill, as well as theoretical awareness of the features and stages of the illness, is better than ignorance; it is something worth having by virtue of the fact that it satisfies one's curiosity and on account of some of its practical implications. There is less of the fear caused by uncertainty, and there is so much one would like to be able to settle before dying: There are friends to talk to, grudges to smooth, and opportunities for reconciliation to be sought. All of these, I should think, are good things for a human being that are made possible by knowledge of the descriptive (i.e., theoretical) sort. . . .

[This] brings us to a new item on our list:

(P.7) Integrity is a basic human good.

What this principle seeks to identify is a complex phenomenon that I am not evaluating now from a moral point of view. By "integrity" I mean the inner harmony of a human being who does not let her thoughts, attitudes, desires, emotions, utterances, and actions go asunder but brings them into fundamental consistency. To say one thing and do something radically different is to be hypocritical; it is to fail to keep the utterance of one's thoughts and the performance of one's actions in mutual harmony. Self-deception also is indicative of lack of integrity because it fails to bring into harmony what one pretends not to know and what one, in a veiled manner, does know.

Integrity, in fact, is the result of bringing the good of practical knowledge to bear on our choices. The mere intellectual realization that it would be good, say, to give up a higher salary in exchange for more time with the family is insufficient if one does not act on it. Practical knowledge, by its very nature, makes immediate claims on our actions, so we would hardly attribute practical wisdom or reasonableness to a person who makes a correct list of things that would be good for her to do but fails to do them.

Some treatments of traditional moral philosophy add a further item to the list of human goods:

Religion is a basic human good.

Moral philosophers who include religion among the items that make a human life a flourishing one usually are following Cicero and many medieval thinkers and hence are invoking a period in the history of philosophy that antedates modern criticism of the assumption that one can prove rationally that God exists.

If God does not exist, then religion—in spite of the benefits of hope in salvation and afterlife or the uplifting joys of communal worship—would be an illusory good. At its very heart there would be a promise of something it cannot deliver. From this belief it is only a short step to the claim that religion in fact is quite detrimental for human beings because it also tends to generate bigotry, intolerance, and certain forms of fanaticism.

On the other hand, if God does exist but there are no satisfactory arguments to prove that, it would still be far from self-evident that religion is a good. Even if it were possible to find such proofs, however, they would take the form of highly complex metaphysical arguments that require advanced philosophical training; thus, their conclusion would hardly be understood by nonspecialists. The goodness of religion, then, would be even more obscure to the layperson than the metaphysical proofs, which would set religion apart from the rest of the goods on our list. Indeed, the expectation for each basic human good was that it would be readily admissible by anyone considering it attentively, without the need or possibility of metaphysical proof.

Someone could claim, of course, that religious faith warrants belief both in the existence of God and in the goodness of religion, but to make this move would be to place the discussion outside the boundaries defined at the outset for moral philosophy. It would be an incursion into theology—a domain of knowledge to whose tenets we cannot request assent from everybody.

We are well advised, then, to take the integrity of human persons as the last item on the list of basic goods that you and I, and anybody else, can accept after a modicum of reflection on their notions and on how they impact on our lives.

Moral Norms

Morality is not an optional social arrangement; we cannot do without it because it is crucial for the enhancement and protection of the things that are most cherished by all of us. If this is correct, then *moral norms must be justified by showing that they are grounded on basic goods*. . . .

Let us now turn to the norms themselves. I have hitherto used the term 'norms' with the implication that there is a unique set of them. . . .

The reason to think that there is a definite set of norms is their rationale. If norms promote and protect basic goods, and there is a unique, set of basic goods that are objective and universal, it is natural to expect that norms form a unique set. If members of a community do not appear to acknowledge a norm protecting a basic good (such as the norm protecting the physical integrity of young women in places where female genital mutilation is practiced), we have reason to criticize that culture for its insensitivity to a dreadful form of harm, and we could add that although the corresponding norm is not presently acknowledged, it exists and it certainly *ought* to be acknowledged.

Introduction of new norms, on the other hand, is fine as long as they are properly justified. Then, however, there is a good chance that they will not be really "new" but merely better or more specific formulations of generally acknowledged norms. There is the further possibility of arguing that the proposed list of basic goods is incomplete (i.e., that one or more items should be added); in this case, we might get norms that have not been generally acknowledged heretofore. I suspect that the development of environmental ethics will lead us in this direction.

In spite of having been recognized in the past, there surely is room for variation in the formulation of each of the moral norms and in the way of setting up the list.

For the sake of consistency with the proposed rationale, my preference has been to present clusters of norms classified under the good primarily affected by the immediate point of the action. We should not forget that, given the complexity of human life, what we do often affects more than one good and that therefore the corresponding norm could be classified under different headings. Lying to a friend is an attack on knowledge and on friendship. Thus, the classification presented here is not unalterable. It represents one way of reaching some degree of clarity about things that are important to know when choosing and acting.

Because the aim of this book is to provide only a broad outline of the foundations of "our common morality," I introduce the moral norms in their most general form. I make few attempts to resolve questions of **casuistry** or particular application to hard cases. Such inquiries should come *after* the general norms have been formulated and justified. Moreover, the following exposition does not claim to be exhaustive. A comprehensive treatment would have to include at least norms for sexual ethics and private property.

(R.1) Norms Concerning Human Life

Life is so basic that the moral command "Do not kill" (i.e., the norm forbidding the intentional killing of a fellow human being or oneself), can be regarded rightly as fundamental in moral thought.

From this norm it appears to follow at first sight that abortion, infanticide, murder, suicide, and active euthanasia, as well as the death penalty, killing in warfare, and self-defense, are all morally wrong actions.

Much of the debate centers on the question of whether a given case falls under the norm. If a fetus is not a human being, abortion does not fall under the norm; neither does self-defense, if the killing is not intentional. One also might claim that there are justifiable exceptions to the norm. If the good of the community requires the execution of a criminal, the death penalty would be a justifiable exception; likewise, if one's country is attacked, killing in its defense also would be permissible. The key point, however, is that all parties to the debate acknowledge, implicitly or explicitly, that *there is a norm to the effect that one should not intentionally kill people.* Any deviation from the norm calls for painstaking justification. . .

On the positive side are all kinds of actions that entail saving and preserving human lives, directly or indirectly. If you come upon a child drowning in a pool, and you are a good swimmer, you are bound by a norm that requires you to jump in and save the child. Moreover, if you are the lifeguard on duty, you are bound by an even stricter norm to do so: The good to be preserved appears explicitly in the name of your job! On the other hand, if you are at a lake, if the temperature is near freezing, if you are a poor swimmer, if you have had heart problems, it may be heroic for you to jump in, but you are not strictly under the norm that makes it obligatory for you to do so. The reason is that the very same norm bids you to preserve your own life.

The preceding example shows something that will hold for an moral norms: Consideration of the circumstances is crucial for deciding if and when the norm applies. The circumstances must be examined in light of the generic goods at stake, however. Refusal to jump in to avoid ruining your new outfit obviously will not do. . .

(R.2) Norms Concerning the Basic Human Community

The best-known traditional moral norm relating primarily to this good is "Do not commit adultery." To appreciate it fully, the defining traits of the family should be called to mind.

The family is a community that arises out of the marriage contract which in turn determines the institution itself. Here I am employing moral terms, not legal ones; sometimes a contract may be assumed even if no civil (or religious) wedding ceremony has taken place.

If marriage is a contract, it is a particular case of a much broader human practice—that of making mutual agreements, mutual promises, mutual commitments. A brief reflection on our everyday life shows that we live immersed in a thick network of agreements. A college agrees to educate a young person in exchange, for a fee, a teacher undertakes to teach for a salary, a student promises to abide by the rules of dorm life, a person makes a commitment to have lunch with a friend, and so forth. It seems clear that agreements generate obligations to abide by them if certain conditions are met, the two most important of which are that the agreement has been freely entered into and that there has been no deception. Coercion and fraud normally make a contract or agreement null and void.

Why do we make contracts in the first place? The rationale for this practice—which at first sight seems to involve the irrational step of giving up one's freedom—is to be sought, as usual, in the human pursuit of goods. Because many goods (certainly the most important ones) cannot be attained in isolation from other people, we see that it is reasonable to make commitments and to accept commitments from others. An individual who shies away from commitments simply will not be able to enjoy certain goods. If you never sign a contract committing you to the purchase of a house, you will never own a house. A person who is "free" from all commitments inevitably will end up empty-handed.

The reference to goods explains why some agreements are more strictly binding than others. Breaking a casual agreement to meet at the cafeteria is not a serious matter, unless there is reason to think your friend will be offended and your friendship might be imperiled.

(R.3) Norms Concerning Friendship within Broader Communities

Perhaps the most general negative norm with regard to this all-pervasive good can be conveyed by the injunction "Don't be selfish." Friendships are threatened by lack of generosity—by giving oneself undue preference in the assignment of advantages or the avoidance of discomforts and burdens.

Intimate friendships are harmed by insincerity, hypocrisy, infidelity, and so forth. Less intimate ones, such as business associations, are harmed by breaking of contracts and formal agreements. Attempts to dominate and exercise power over others also are destructive of friendship; so is the use of force. Date rape surely is a serious violation of the good of friendship, especially if the persons involved were more than passing acquaintances.

Norms on the positive side—those bidding us to act with reasonable selflessness—are quite general and hence subject to imaginative deliberation for particular situations. The right answer to the question "How can I advance the good of my friend in the present circumstances?" will vary from person to person and even from day to day. Incidentally, this observation does not open the door to moral relativism (some answers will be definitely wrong); it does show, however, that moral reasoning leaves plenty of room for new and creative developments in the effort to abide by norms whose aim is the flourishing of all kinds of friendship.

Friendship, insofar as it makes of a community a good community, satisfies *a fortiori* another set of important moral claims: the claims of justice. Friendship is "stronger" (this is what the expression *a fortiori* implies) in that real friends do not need to worry about treating each other fairly: They do, and do much more than that. When friendship declines or disappears, however, justice acquires special prominence. In a happy marriage, visitation rights make no sense (parents and kids live in the same house); after a divorce, however, a fair and clear settlement of such rights is imperative because the welfare of the children still requires coordination between the estranged parents—and thus generates a community of sorts. Justice is necessary for it to work.

We also are members of larger communities (e.g., a big corporation or a huge country), within which the bonds of affection are very weak or practically impossible. Our moral obligations toward these communities and toward fellow members, therefore, also will entail requirements of justice.

Although justice has made its appearance in our conversation in connection with the good of communities, it seems to be omnipresent in the moral universe. Thus, the norms that govern duties of justice are best treated as pervasive norms after more specific norms have been enumerated—among them norms pertaining to protection of the next set of basic goods.

(R.4) Norms Concerning Work and Play

The most general negative norm with regard to these goods is "Do not cheat." Cheating at work or in play is surely wrong. The game breaks down, and the trust most jobs require thereby is destroyed.

Although the foregoing assertion is true, you will agree, it is highly insufficient. Today, virtually everywhere, the good of work directly intersects with a social mechanism called the free market. This mechanism, in turn, generates new and complex situations that can hardly be judged by means of traditional moral norms.

If having a job is good for an individual, it seems to follow that firing an employee is wrong. Yet we know today that artificially subsidizing jobs that are no longer needed has a cost that also will be borne by other segments of the economy, sometimes in the form of inflation. Hence, it may not be immoral to lay off workers even of a whole sector. Losing one's job is not as serious as losing one's life. A new job can be found, and unemployment benefits can temporarily compensate for the lost good. Conversely, it may be immoral to fire employees if the whole point is to move the jobs to a place abroad where labor laws are seriously defective or simply are not enforced. Sometimes the agents claim that decisions such as these are justified by efficiency within market conditions, but we should not assume that all assignments of goods made through the free market are morally right. . . .

To decide which are right and which are not, philosophers and economists must collaborate in formulating or revising the norms that spell out appropriate and inappropriate behavior in the domain that directly affects the good of work. Some companies and large corporations already have adopted ethics codes with the assistance of specialists in business ethics, and further developments can be expected in this direction. The same can be said of the domain where work and play intersect: professional sports. The need for a code of sports ethics already is being felt.

(R.5) Norms Concerning Aesthetic Experience

Moral norms within this domain have not been the subject of sustained reflection because of the natural tendency to distinguish between aesthetic and moral values. Artists and poets often claim that their works disclose a dimension that is "beyond good and evil," and they probably are right. Morality, after all, is not the whole story of human existence. A play, a movie, a photograph that defies morality may well be the occasion of a moving and disturbing experience that has a place in a rich and fulfilled human life.

Moral norms in reference to beauty, then, have nothing to do with dictating standards for the production or admissibility of works of art. Among the negative norms are those that ban actions that deprive people of the experience of beauty, such as the wanton destruction of works of art (Hitler's kicking the paintings of the German expressionists would be a good example).

What counts as a genuine instance of artistic beauty is not for moral philosophers to decide; hence, no criteria can be proposed here. That there is beauty in nature, however, and that it makes an important contribution to human well-being should be uncontroversial. Therefore, some of the concerns of the emerging field of ecological ethics should be addressed under this heading. Nature ought (in the moral sense of "ought") to be preserved not just because its destruction can have serious negative effects on human health and physical well-being but also because destroying or impoverishing the environment deprives us of the fundamental experience of natural beauty.

(R.6) Norms Concerning Knowledge

The most general norm protecting this good is reflected in the traditional injunction not to lie. The Greek historian Herodotus (fifth century B.C.) reports that the ancient Persians taught their young three basic things: to ride, to use the bow, and to speak the truth *(Histories* 1.136). This suggests that they regarded the habit of honesty in utterance as no less valuable than their two most basic military skills. The reason is that just as being able to shoot from the saddle was vital to the defense and expansion of the nation, telling the truth was regarded as crucial for the internal unity and preservation of the community.

Lying—expressing in words the contrary of what one thinks with the intention of deceiving someone who is entitled to know—is destructive of trust and an obstacle in the pursuit of common goals. Friendships break down and partnerships dissolve if there is habitual lying on the part of one or more individuals. Sometimes the discovery of even one instance of lying and deceiving someone else may have sad consequences. . . .

At this point it is common to raise the objection that veracity (i.e., always telling the truth) may have bad consequences—such as the horrible ones that ensue when you tell a Nazi officer that there is a Jewish neighbor hiding in your basement. For a consequentialist, there is an easy solution: Lying is justified, perhaps even obligatory, in a case such as this.

For the human goods tradition and its unwillingness to give up too easily when important values are at stake, there is a genuine perplexity that has generated a complex casuistry involving subtle distinctions such as that between lying and deceiving and between having a right to know and not having it. Strategies of silence, evasion, equivocation, or mental reservation also have been recommended. Deception of the officer by saying, "I saw him walking past the house" (withholding any utterance about the fact that the neighbor then turned around

to enter her basement through the back door) would be perfectly permissible as part of an heroic effort to remain faithful to the truth. . . .

The norms of positive care for truth are manifold and perhaps best illustrated by the duties involved in scholarly and scientific research. Among them are duties to be open-minded, to strive for clear thinking, to engage in painstaking research and verification, to admit unfavorable results or unpalatable opinions, and so forth. In a broader setting, it is reasonable to affirm that upholding freedom of speech is a moral obligation under a norm that is grounded on the good of truth.

(R.7) Norms Concerning Integrity

The good of integrity or inner harmony is protected by negative norms that forbid us from engaging in actions that tear us asunder by letting certain passions have the upper hand. Greed—the passion to possess more and more material goods—if catered to, is destructive of inner harmony; so is vanity, the passion to strive for more and more honors and public recognition. Pornography, sexual promiscuity, rape, and so forth also are attacks on the integrity of the perpetrators (as well as the dignity of the victims). The traditional norm forbidding fornication (i.e., sexual activity) outside the setting of marriage and love has its place here.

Integrity has its limitations, however. A person of integrity is someone who acts invariably in accordance with her convictions. Thus, in the examples I have just given I assume an individual who is convinced that action motivated by greed, vanity, or mere sexual desire is wrong. What if an individual lacks these convictions, however, and thinks on the contrary that, for example, indiscriminate sexual activity with competent and willing adults is OK, and acts accordingly? For him there is no lack of harmony between thought and action. The same holds, incidentally, for the Nazi who thinks all Jews should be exterminated. Neither can be accused of hypocrisy or lack of integrity.

These examples show once more that human goods are not absolute goods—that is, beneficial in isolation from all others. Just as the family (or sex) is not really good without love and friendship, likewise integrity without the good of practical knowledge can be seriously detrimental for a given person (and those around her). However, a person who is mistaken about some of the goods, and hence some of the norms, need not be morally blameworthy—as we shall see when we discuss the role of conscience in human action.

Positive norms that protect integrity can be summarized under the norm "Act always in accordance with your convictions," in the understanding that a reasonable person is willing critically to examine those convictions. Restraint and self-control should be natural fruits of the exercise of care for the good of integrity.

(NJ) Norms of Justice

The requirements of justice are present everywhere on the map of morality. The reason, as I have argued, is that, for the most part, basic human goods can be pursued effectively only in community, and justice is required for the adequate functioning of any community—even the community of sorts that is formed by divorced parents. The demands of justice will be vastly exceeded, as we have seen, by the deeds of friendship.

Justice can be approached fruitfully from the perspective of community or from the perspective of the individual. Here we follow the second approach because it best suits our plan of providing a sketch of the good life for persons such as you and me. . . .

An honest person follows the elementary norm of justice encapsulated in the traditional command: "Do not steal." Appropriating an instrumental good that belongs to someone else with no intention of giving it back is a paradigmatic instance of dishonesty that prevents the rightful owner from making use of the item in his own pursuits. Fraud, misappropriation, embezzlement, and so forth are sophisticated forms of stealing, and all are wrong for the same reason: They prevent individuals from enjoying certain goods and thus should be considered attacks on the negatively affected communities. The norms of justice add a further conceptual determination to the norms that ban attacks on communal friendship: They include a reference *not only to other persons but also to what is rightfully due to them.* A person who rightfully owns a car can demand that it be returned to her (after being driven away from the company parking lot) as a duty in justice. This is owed to her by whoever drove it away.

The next step in this direction would be to explain property rights and, more generally, human and legal rights. This explanation, however, is beyond the limits set for this book.

As we move from external goods to the internal good of freedom, we can identify kinds of action that are clearly unjust because they fail to give due respect to this good. Enslavement, kidnapping, coerced prostitution, and so forth are seriously wrong not because they violate property rights but for a deeper reason: They fail to give due respect to human dignity. Respect for their dignity doubtless is the most basic thing we owe to persons, to all persons.

Is every restriction of freedom, therefore, a failure to respect persons? Is there a negative moral norm that prevents individuals or communities from imposing limitations of liberty? Surely not. The reason not to restrict freedom is that individuals need to exercise self-direction in the successful pursuit of the good life. To try to force people to attain a fulfilled existence is simply irrational. In the midst of their pursuits, however, individuals can deprive each other of goods; they can harm each other. Hence, the grounding norm of classical liberalism advocated by Mill and others ("Do not restrict freedom except to prevent someone from harming others") is perfectly sensible from the human goods perspective.

Individuals sometimes can harm themselves, however. Here the classical liberal (and libertarian) reply is, "It's up to them!" Restricting the freedom of an individual for his own good is called "paternalism" and is unwarranted under the liberal norm. Thus, upholders of classical liberalism have to reject certain social policies (e.g., seat belt laws or Social Security contributions) or otherwise find convoluted arguments to show that their deeper-lying rationale is to avoid harm to others. From the human goods perspective, this is unnecessary. If the inconvenience is not significant and the goods at stake are of great weight (life, limb, and income in old age), there is nothing immoral in requiring people to wear seat belts or save for retirement. . . .

Justice requires us not only to respect free choices (unless they are seriously detrimental to others or to the person herself); it requires us to treat people equally. Arbitrary discrimination on the basis of race, gender, national origin, religious belief, or sexual orientation is unjust. An act of preferential treatment, however, ceases to be arbitrary if there are strong grounds for it. An adequate example would be the preferential hiring of female guards for women's jails to prevent well-documented abuses by male guards. The discrimination in this case is justified because it is grounded on the need to protect the dignity of the inmates. If no instance of a human good is being directly attacked, norms based on the guideline of care can take precedence.

If respect for the dignity of other human beings, then, is to be explained in terms of due respect for their goods, the norms protecting those goods also will be susceptible of formulation in terms of dignity and justice. Justice, in sum, entails essential reference to others and requires treating equals equally. It also requires treating unequals (in relevant respects) unequally, but in all cases it is the good of others that provides the ultimate reference point for just behavior.

Remarks on Norms

The foregoing norms constitute a catalog of general injunctions that should be accepted by anyone who accepts the list of basic goods and prudential guidelines, especially those of impartial respect and care and, ultimately, the first principle of practical rationality.

Sometimes people speak disparagingly of moral norms, calling them "abstract"—as if they were somehow unconnected to real life and its requirements. Moral norms are, indeed, abstract because they need to be general to provide guidance for large classes of similar cases. "Do not lie" abstracts from differences among particular contemplated lies—and that is precisely how such a command discharges the function of protecting particular instances of truth and trust. . . .

Moral norms provide useful guidance for action, but they do not resolve all moral dilemmas. Many perplexities arise from the fact that, as we have seen, they are general. We often do not know for sure whether a particular kind of action falls under a given norm. Norms require specification—that is, a process of practical thinking that involves consideration of the particular circumstances to see if the norm covers the case at hand. . . .

There may be conflicts for an agent who is torn between two conflicting moral demands. . . .

Violation of a negative norm requires that Jill choose to perform an action that directly violates a good. The agent is the cause of the harm.

Violation of a positive norm, on the other hand, requires that Jill fail to act to prevent a harm. The cause of the harm has to be another person (such as Jack) or simply a case of nonhuman agency (such as the drowning of a child who has accidentally slipped and fallen into a pool). If we do not assume that the harm is caused by someone or something else, we are back to the previous alternative—violation of a negative norm.

As we have seen, a person has a direct responsibility for what she intentionally does, not for what others do or what happens accidentally. Any responsibility she might have in the latter cases would be derivative. It would be derived from choices or facts outside her direct control.

Therefore, if the action directly under a person's control falls under a negative norm, she should judge her action by this norm. If it does not fall under a negative norm—that is, if no important good is intentionally under attack in her own action—the action should be judged by any positive norm that may apply. . . .

If certain specific negative norms always take precedence over any positive ones, it becomes apparent that there are at least some exceptionless moral norms (or "absolutes," as they are sometimes, misleadingly, called). Indeed, there is a long tradition—going back at least to the ancient Greek philosophers—that is committed to the view that certain kinds of action are always wrong.

In Plato's *Crito*, Socrates defends the thesis that one should *never* do something unjust to another person. Having been treated unjustly oneself does not justify an exception. Retaliation is wrong because it too is a form of injustice (the corresponding Greek term, *antadikein,* means literally "to treat unjustly in return") and hence falls under the general norm.

Against the Socratic thesis it could be argued that the injunction "never do wrong" is valid universally simply because it is analytically true (i.e., true by virtue of the meaning of the terms). To state that something is wrong or unjust is to state that it is one of the things that should not be done. One still needs a criterion to figure out whether some particular action is just or unjust. If what we do in return for an injustice done to us, for example, is not unjust (under this criterion), it would not be retaliation and hence would not violate the injunction. It would be legitimate punishment. The universality of the norm stands; the key problem for the application of the Socratic thesis becomes judgment about a specific kind of action.

Is it possible to have exceptionless moral norms that are not analytic—that is, that do not include moral terms in the descriptions of the kinds of action that are declared to be right or wrong? Aristotle claimed that adultery, theft, and murder are always wrong and that their names already imply badness.[3] He does not make this claim explicitly in terms of norms, but the claim itself is logically equivalent to a set of three exceptionless norms. Are they analytic? It is not totally clear because Aristotle may mean simply that in his moral community, everyone would agree on the moral wrongness of those actions—a fact reflected in linguistic usage that does not preclude the possibility of describing the same actions without using moral terms. If adultery was defined in Greece as a sexual act involving a married woman with a man who is not her spouse, the claim that adultery is always wrong turns out not to be analytic, even though it does not acknowledge exceptions.

Talk of exceptionless moral norms usually generates uneasiness these days, however. Shouldn't we be more flexible? Isn't it irrational to deny that in special circumstances exceptions should be allowed? Consequentialist philosophers invariably are in favor of exceptions because, as we have seen, they shift their attention from the act itself (and the goods thereby affected) to outcomes, intended or not. . . .

I would insist once again that imaginary examples in which important goods are "maximized" at the price of attracting a single good tend to obscure important aspects of morality. In this case, we may lose sight of the unconditional claim a single basic good may place on us. Indeed, many people in the past and even today report that they experience certain moral claims as unconditional, as an obligation to follow the moral law regardless of consequences—such as the duty of a judge or a jury always to hand down a just verdict, regardless of the riots or political turmoil it may generate.

The Principle of Double Effect (PDE)

Introduction of exceptionless, moral rules, however, seems to create a moral quandary of its own by prescribing inaction when something could be done to preserve certain goods. When a child is being attacked or tortured, shouldn't one intervene even at the cost of inflicting harm and, ultimately, death? If one's country is being invaded (with all the ensuing rapes, destruction, and killings on the part of the occupying forces), shouldn't one fight and kill in its defense?

Traditional moral philosophy has struggled with these problems and has come to deal with them by distinguishing sharply between cases in which the intentionally caused harm is instrumental to the good effect (and therefore remain impermissible under the guideline of respect) and cases in which the harm is an unintended side effect of the pursuit of a good.

We now introduce a normative principle that narrows the application of FP, the formal principle of practical rationality, to actions that are indeed causes of double effect.

The PDE may be formulated as follows:

An action that has two effects, one of which is bad, is morally permissible if and only if the following conditions are satisfied:

(1) The action itself is morally permissible—that is, its main immediate goal is neither to attack an instance of a basic human good nor to fail to prevent a harm. The action itself must follow the moral norms.

(2) The intended good effect will not be obtained by means of the bad effect.

(3) The agent does not intend the bad effect. The bad effect should not be a desired and sought goal. It can be foreseen, predicted, or tolerated, but not directly willed.

(4) There will be a favorable proportion or balance (prudentially judged) between the good and bad effects. If the good effect is minimal (e.g., avoiding an inconvenience or protecting an instrumental good) and the bad effect is significant (loss of a basic good), the action is not morally justified.[4]

The PDE is not a blanket excuse to carve exceptions to the strict protection of the basic human goods. It represents a good-faith effort to affirm the value of the good protected by exceptionless norms *and* the need to take action in certain extreme cases. Not that consequentialists need not worry about a principle to mediate in such cases because they are committed to the view that, for example, a human life, in suitable expectations of abundant good consequences, may be considered an instrument to be disposed of intentionally. Acceptance of the normative system introduced thus far should lead to firm rejection of such a view. . . .

NOTES

1. Aristotle *Metaphysics* 6.1.102sb25.
2. Aristotle *Nicomachean Ethics* 7–9.
3. Aristotle *Nicomachean Ethics* 2.6.1107a9–12.
4. See Fagothey (1976), 32–33; Beauchamp and Childress (1989), 128.

DISCUSSION QUESTIONS:

1. Gomez-Lobo argues that biological human life is intrinsically good because it is a key ingredient of the good life. Are all the premises of his argument true? Do they support his conclusion?

2. Gomez-Lobo argues that various items are basic goods by appealing to the premise that they are basic ingredients of human flourishing, that without them we could not have a "fully flourishing existence." Do some ways of living constitute a less flourishing human existence than others? What are some examples of pairs of lives, one of which constitutes a less flourishing human existence than another?

3. Is each candidate for a basic human good presented by Gomez-Lobo an ingredient of a fully flourishing human existence?

4. Some of the goods presented by Gomez-Lobo are such that the extent to which we can possess them depends on the extent to which we have certain abilities. For example, our ability to possess the good of knowledge depends on our intellectual abilities. Our ability to possess the good of friendship may depend on our personality traits. This seems to imply that some people are capable of living better lives than others; everything else being equal, someone of superior intellectual ability is capable of living a better life than someone of lesser intellectual ability. Is this correct?

5. Gomez-Lobo claims that when a negative moral norm conflicts with a positive one, the negative norm takes precedence. Presumably, then, if we have to choose between letting someone die, on the one hand, and saving her by killing someone else, on the other, we should let her die. The negative norm not to kill outweighs the positive norm to save. Does this remain the case, if the good to be accomplished changes; if, say, our choice is between saving five people at the cost of killing one?

6. Consider the implications of the Principle of Double Effect for some of the cases discussed in the readings on Consequentialism, e.g., those contained in Kai Nielsen's essay, "Against Moral Conservatism," and Judith Thomson's essay, "Turning the Trolley." Are the principle's implications for these cases correct? Why or why not?

Argument Reconstruction Exercises:

I. Gomez-Lobo presents the following argument with regard to the goodness of human life. Identify the premises and conclusion of his argument.

If we have reason to agree that G is intrinsically good and that D, E and F are neither extrinsically nor instrumentally conducive to G but are internal constituents of G, we also have reason to think that they are intrinsically valuable. We all doubtless agree that happiness or the good life is the ultimate worthwhile thing—something that we value not because it will lead to something else but because it is good in itself. Surely life is not external or instrumental to the good life. . . . Life, then—as the key ingredient of the good life (though not the only one)—is worth having for its own sake, (page 250)

II. To what extent do variations in natural abilities result in variations in how good a life different people can have? Identify the premises and conclusion of the following argument.

All other things being equal, someone with severe mental disabilities is not as capable of experiencing all the basic human goods as someone without those disabilities. A necessary condition for human flourishing is experiencing basic human goods. Therefore, all other things being equal, someone with severe mental disabilities is not able to have as flourishing a human existence as someone without those disabilities. And since a life is good only to the extent that it is flourishing, all other things being equal, someone with severe mental disabilities will not have as good a life as someone without those disabilities.

III. If our nature determines certain goods, which then support particular norms about how we may treat one another, then the same may be true with regard to other living things. Identify the premises and conclusion of the following argument.

Human beings have a natural good, human flourishing, which supports moral norms that restrict how we may treat them. Other living things also have a natural good. Animals and plants have their own natural ways of flourishing. Therefore, there are moral norms that restrict how we may treat other living things.

IV. That human lives can vary with regard to the amount of good they involve suggests that some human lives can be more valuable than others. Identify the premises and conclusion of the following reasoning.

The lives of some people are more valuable than the lives of others. The lives of some people involve more basic human goods than the lives of others, and those lives that involve the most basic human goods are the best.

12.3 THE GROUNDWORK FOR THE METAPHYSICS OF MORALS

IMMANUEL KANT (1785)

Immanuel Kant is a dominant figure in the history of philosophy whose revolutionary ideas changed the nature of philosophical work in metaphysics, epistemology and ethics. In this selection, he considers two issues: What qualities of a person are good without qualification? What fundamental principle determines our moral obligations? In answer to the first, Kant claims that only one quality is good without qualification, a good will. In answer to the second, Kant takes the fundamental law of morality to be a **categorical imperative**, rather than a **hypothetical imperative**. According to this categorical imperative we should "Act only on that maxim by which we can at the same time will that it should become a universal law." He then restates this fundamental moral principle in two ways, one emphasizing the universality of morality and one emphasizing the intrinsic dignity of every person.

Reading Questions:

1. While Kant claims that a good will is the only thing good without qualification, he acknowledges that other things are also good. What are these things and why, according to Kant, are they not good without qualification?

2. What, according to Kant, is the relation between happiness and a good will?

3. What would it be for you to do an act with a good will? Describe such a case.

4. Consider the case you described in answering Question 3. How does the case illustrate each of Kant's three principles about a good will?

5. Kant distinguishes between categorical and hypothetical imperatives. What is the difference?

6. Why, according to Kant, must the fundamental imperative of morality be a categorical, rather than a hypothetical, imperative?

7. What are Kant's different versions of the categorical imperative? How do they differ from one another?

8. How does each version of the categorical imperative differ from the moral principles presented in other essays you have read (e.g., the principles of Act and Rule-Utilitarianism)?

9. What is Kant's reasoning in each of his four examples of the application of the categorical imperative?

The Unqualified Value of a Good Will

It is impossible to imagine anything at all in the world, or even beyond it, that can be called good without qualification—except a good will. Intelligence, wit, judgement, and the other mental talents, whatever we may call them, or courage, decisiveness, and perseverance, are, as qualities of *temperament,* certainly good and desirable in many respects; but they can also be extremely bad and harmful when the will which makes use of these *gifts of nature* and whose specific quality we refer to as *character,* is not good. It is exactly the same with *gifts of fortune.* Power, wealth, honour, even health and that total well-being and contentment with one's condition which we call *'happiness',* can make a person bold but consequently often reckless as well, unless a good will is present to correct their influence on the mind, thus adjusting the whole principle of one's action to render it conformable to universal ends. It goes without saying that the sight of a creature enjoying uninterrupted prosperity, but never feeling the slightest pull of a pure and good will, cannot excite approval in a rational and impartial spectator. Consequently, a good will seems to constitute the indispensable condition even of our worthiness to be happy.

Some qualities, even though they are helpful to this good will and can make its task very much easier, nevertheless have no intrinsic unconditional worth. Rather, they presuppose a good will which puts limits on the esteem in which they are rightly held and forbids us to regard them as absolutely good. Moderation in emotions and passions, self-control, and sober reflection are not only good in many respects: they may even seem to constitute part of the inner worth of a person. Yet they are far from being properly described as good without qualification (however unconditionally they were prized by the ancients). For without the principles of a good will those qualities may become exceedingly bad; the passionless composure of a villain makes him not merely more dangerous but also directly more detestable in our eyes than we would have taken him to be without it.

A good will is not good because of its effects or accomplishments, and not because of its adequacy to achieve any proposed end: it is good only by virtue of its willing—that is, it is good in itself. Considered in itself it is to be treasured as incomparably higher than anything it could ever bring about merely in order to satisfy some inclination or, if you like, the sum total of all inclinations. Even if it were to happen that, because of some particularly unfortunate fate or the miserly bequest of a step-motherly nature, this will were completely powerless to carry out its aims; if with even its utmost effort it still accomplished nothing, so that only good will itself remained (not, of course, as a mere wish, but as the summoning of every means in our power), even then it would still, like a jewel, glisten in its own right, as something that has its full worth in itself. Its utility or ineffectuality can neither add to nor subtract from this worth. Utility would be merely, as it were, its setting, enabling us to handle it better in our ordinary dealings or to attract to it the attention of those who are not yet experts, but not why we recommend it to experts and determine its worth.

The Nature of a Good Will

I will here omit all actions already recognized as opposed to duty, even if they may be useful from this or that perspective; for about these it makes no sense even to ask the question whether they might have been done *out of duty* since they are directly opposed to it. I will also set aside actions that in fact accord with duty, yet for one has no *direct inclination,* but which one performs because impelled to do so by some other inclination. For in such a case it is easy to decide whether the action [which accords with duty] was done *out of duty* or for some self-interested goal. This distinction is far more difficult to perceive when the action accords with duty but the agent has in addition a *direct* inclination to do it. For example, it is certainly in accord with duty that a shopkeeper should not overcharge an inexperienced customer; and, where there is much business, a prudent merchant refrains from doing this and maintains a fixed general price for everybody, so that a child can buy from him just as well as anyone else. People thus get *honest* treatment. But this is not nearly enough to justify our believing that the shopkeeper acted in this way out of duty or from principles of honesty; his interests required him to act as he did. We cannot assume him to have in addition a direct inclination towards his customers, leading him, as it were out of love, to give no one preferential

treatment over another person in the matter of price. Thus the action was done neither out of duty nor from immediate inclination, but solely out of self-interest.

On the other hand, it is a duty to preserve one's life, and every one also has a direct inclination to do it. But for that reason the often-fearful care that most people take for their lives has no intrinsic worth, and the maxim of their action has no moral merit. They do protect their lives *in conformity with duty,* but not *out of duty.* If, by contrast, disappointments and hopeless misery have entirely taken away someone's taste for life; if that wretched person, strong in soul and more angered at fate than faint-hearted or cast down, longs for death and still preserves life without loving it—not out of inclination or fear but out of duty—then indeed that person's maxim has moral worth.

It is a duty to help others where one can, and besides this many souls are so compassionately disposed that, without any further motive of vanity or self-interest, they find an inner pleasure in spreading joy around them, taking delight in the contentment of others, so far as they have brought it about. Yet I maintain that, however dutiful and kind an action of this sort may be, it still has no genuinely moral worth. It is on a level with other inclinations—for example, the inclination to pursue honour, which if fortunate enough to aim at something generally useful and consistent with duty, something consequently honourable, deserves praise and encouragement but not esteem. For its maxim lacks the moral merit of such actions done not out of inclination but out of *duty.* Suppose then that the mind of this humanitarian were overclouded by sorrows of his own which extinguished all compassion for the fate of others, but that he still had the power to assist others in distress; suppose though that their adversity no longer stirred him, because he is preoccupied with his own; and now imagine that, though no longer moved by any inclination, he nevertheless tears himself out of this deadly apathy and does the action without any inclination, solely out of duty. Then for the first time his action has its genuine moral worth. Furthermore, if nature had put little sympathy into this or that person's heart; if he, though an honest man, were cold in temperament and indifferent to the sufferings of others—perhaps because he has the special gifts of patience and fortitude in his own sufferings and he assumes or even demands the same of others; if such a man (who would in truth not be the worst product of nature) were not exactly fashioned by nature to be a humanitarian, would he not still find in himself a source from which he might give himself a worth far higher than that of a good-natured temperament? Assuredly he would. *It is precisely in this that the worth of character begins to show—a moral worth, and incomparably the highest—namely, that he does good, not out of inclination, but out of duty.* . . .

The second proposition is this: *The moral worth of an action done out of duty has its moral worth, not in the objective to be reached by that action, but in the maxim in accordance with which the action is decided upon*; it depends, therefore, not on actualizing the object of the action, but solely on the *principle of volition* in accordance with which the action was done, without any regard for objects of the faculty of desire. It is clear from our previous discussion that the objectives we may have in acting, and also our actions' effects considered as ends and as what motivates our volition, can give to actions no unconditional or moral worth. Where then can this worth be found if not in the willing of the action's hoped for effect? It can be found nowhere but *in the principle of the will*, irrespective of the ends that can be brought about by such action. For the will stands, so to speak, at the crossroads between its a priori principle, which is formal, and its a posteriori motivation, which is material; and since it must be determined by something, it will have to be determined by the formal principle of volition, since every material principle is ruled out when an action is done out of duty.

The third proposition, which follows from the two preceding, I would express in this way: Duty is the necessity of an act done out of respect for the law. While I can certainly have an *inclination* for an object that results from my proposed action, I can never *respect it*, precisely because it is nothing but an effect of a will and not its activity. Similarly I cannot respect any inclination whatsoever, whether it be my own inclination or that of another. At most I can

approve of that towards which I feel an inclination, and occasionally I can like the object of somebody else's inclination myself—that is, see it as conducive to my own advantage. But the only thing that could be an object of respect (and thus a commandment) for me is something that is conjoined with my will purely as a ground and never as a consequence, something that does not serve my inclination but overpowers it or at least excludes it entirely from my decision-making—consequently, nothing but the law itself. Now if an action done out of duty is supposed to exclude totally the influence of inclination, and, along with inclination, every object of volition, then nothing remains that could determine the will except objectively *the law* and subjectively *pure respect* for this practical law. What is left therefore is the maxim,[1] to obey this sort of law even when doing so is prejudicial to all my inclinations. . . .

The Moral Imperative

All imperatives are expressed by a 'must'. Thereby they mark a constraint, that is to say, the relation of an objective law of reason to a will that in its subjective constitution is not necessarily determined by this law. Imperatives say that something would be good to do or to leave undone; but they say this to a will that does not always do something simply because it has been informed that it is a good thing to do. . . .

All imperatives command either hypothetically or categorically. **Hypothetical imperatives** declare a possible action to be practically necessary as a means to the attainment of something else that one wants (or that one may want). A **categorical imperative** would be one that represented an action as itself objectively necessary, without regard to any further end.

Since every practical law presents a possible action as good and therefore as necessary for a subject whose actions are determined by reason, all imperatives are therefore formulae for determining an action which is necessary according to the principle of a will in some way good. If the action would be good only as a means to something else, the imperative is hypothetical; if the action is thought of as good in itself and therefore as necessary for a will which of itself conforms to reason as its principle, then the imperative is categorical.

An imperative therefore states which of my possible actions would be good. The imperative formulates a practical rule for a will that does not perform an action immediately just because that action is good, partly because, the subject does not always know that a good action is good, partly because, even if he did know this, his maxims might still be contrary to the objective principles of practical reason.

A hypothetical imperative thus says only that an action is good for some purpose or other, either possible or actual. . . .

There is one imperative which commands a certain line of conduct directly, without assuming or being conditional on any further goal to be reached by that conduct. This imperative is categorical. It is concerned not with the material of the action and its anticipated result, but with its form and with the principle from which the action itself results. And what is essentially good in the action consists in the [agent's] disposition, whatever the result may be. This imperative may be called the imperative of morality.

If I think of a *hypothetical* imperative as such, I do not know before-hand what it will contain—not until I am given its condition. But if I think of a *categorical imperative,* I know right away what it contains. For since this imperative contains, besides the law, only the necessity that the maxim[2] conform to this law, while the law, as we have seen, contains no condition limiting it, there is nothing left over to which the maxim of action should conform except the universality of a law as such; and it only this conformity that the imperative asserts to be necessary.

There is therefore only one categorical imperative and it is this: 'Act only on that maxim by which you can at the same time will that it should become a universal law.'

Now if all imperatives of duty can be derived from this one imperative as their principle, then even though we leave it unsettled whether what we call duty is or is not an empty concept, we shall still be able to indicate at least what we understand by it and what the concept means.

Because the universality of law according to which effects occur constitutes what is properly called nature in its most general sense (nature as regards its form)—that is, the existence of things so far as this is determined by universal laws—*the universal imperative of duty could also be formulated as follows: 'Act as though the maxim of your action were to become by your will a universal law of nature.'*

Four Examples

We shall now enumerate some duties, dividing them in the usual way into duties towards ourselves and duties towards others and into perfect and imperfect duties.[3]

1. A man feels sick of life as the result of a mounting series of misfortunes that has reduced him to hopelessness, but he still possesses enough of his reason to ask himself whether it would not be contrary to his duty to himself to take his own life. Now he tests whether the maxim of his action could really become a universal law of nature. His maxim, however, is: 'I make it my principle out of self-love to shorten my life if its continuance threatens more evil than it promises advantage.' The only further question is whether this principle of self-love can become a universal law of nature. But one sees at once that a nature whose law was that the very same feeling meant to promote life should actually destroy life would contradict itself, and hence would not endure as nature. The maxim therefore could not possibly be a general law of nature and thus it wholly contradicts the supreme principle of all duty.

2. Another finds himself driven by need to borrow money. He knows very well that he will not be able to pay it back, but he sees too that nobody will lend him anything unless he firmly promises to pay it back within a fixed time. He wants to make such a promise, but he still has enough conscience to ask himself, 'Isn't it impermissible and contrary to duty to get out of one's difficulties this way?' Suppose, however, that he did decide to do it. The maxim of his action would run thus: 'When I believe myself short of money, I will borrow money and promise to pay it back, even though I know that this will never be done.' Now this principle of self-love or personal advantage is perhaps quite compatible with my own

entire future welfare; only there remains the question 'Is it right?' I therefore transform the unfair demand of self-love into a universal law and frame my question thus: 'How would things stand if my maxim became a universal law?' I then see immediately that this maxim can never qualify as a self-consistent universal law of nature, but must necessarily contradict itself. For the universality of a law that permits anyone who believes himself to be in need to make any promise he pleases with the intention of not keeping it would make promising, and the very purpose one has in promising, itself impossible. For no one would believe he was being promised anything, but would laugh at any such utterance as hollow pretence.

3. A third finds in himself a talent that, with a certain amount of cultivation, could make him a useful man for all sorts of purposes. But he sees himself in comfortable circumstances, and he prefers to give himself up to pleasure rather than to bother about increasing and improving his fortunate natural aptitudes. Yet he asks himself further 'Does my maxim of neglecting my natural gifts, besides agreeing with my taste for amusement, agree also with what is called duty?' He then sees that a nature could indeed endure under such a universal law, even if (like the South Sea Islanders) every man should let his talents rust and should be bent on devoting his life solely to idleness, amusement, procreation—in a word, to enjoyment. Only he cannot possibly *will* that this should become a universal law of nature or should be implanted in us as such a law by a natural instinct. For as a rational being he necessarily wills that all his powers should be developed, since they are after all useful to him and given to him for all sorts of possible purposes.

4. A fourth man, who is himself flourishing but sees others who have to struggle with great hardships (and whom he could easily help) thinks to himself: 'What do I care? Let every one be as happy as Heaven intends or as he can make himself; I won't deprive him of anything; I won't even envy him; but I don't feel like contributing anything to his well-being or to helping him in his distress!' Now admittedly if such an attitude were a universal law of nature, the human race could survive perfectly well and doubtless even better than when everybody chatters about

sympathy and good will, and even makes an effort, now and then, to practise them, but, when one can get away with it, swindles, traffics in human rights, or violates them in other ways. But although it is possible that a universal law of nature in accord with this maxim could exist, it is impossible to *will* that such a principle should hold everywhere as a law of nature. For a will that intended this would be in conflict with itself, since many situations might arise in which the man needs love and sympathy from others, and in which, by such a law of nature generated by his own will, he would rob himself of all hope of the help he wants. . . .

Humanity as an End

Now, I say, a human being, and in general every rational being, does exist as an end in himself not merely as a means to be used by this or that will as it pleases. In all his actions, whether they are directed to himself or to other rational beings, a human being must always be viewed at the same time as an end. All the objects of inclination have only a conditional worth; for if these inclinations and the needs based on them did not exist, their object would be worthless. But inclinations themselves, as sources of needs, are so far from having absolute value to make them desirable for their own sake that it must rather be the universal wish of every rational being to be wholly free of them. Thus the value of any object *that is to be acquired* by our action is always conditional. Beings whose existence depends not on our will but on nature still have only a relative value as means and are therefore called *things*, if they lack reason. Rational beings, on the other hand, are called *persons* because, their nature already marks them out as ends in themselves—that is, as something which ought not to be used *merely* as a means—and consequently imposes restrictions on all choice making (and is an object of respect). Persons, therefore, are not merely subjective ends whose existence as an effect of our actions has a value *for us*. They are *objective ends*—that is, things whose existence is in itself an end, and indeed an end such that no other end can be substituted for it, no end to which they should serve *merely* as a means. For if this were not so, there would be nothing at all having *absolute value* anywhere. But if all value were conditional, and thus contingent, then no supreme principle could be found for reason at all.

If then there is to be a supreme practical principle and a categorical imperative for the human will, it must be such that it forms an objective principle of the will from the idea of something which is necessarily an end for everyone because *it is an end in itself,* a principle that can therefore serve as a universal practical law. The ground of this principle is: *Rational nature exists as an end in itself.* This is the way in which a human being necessarily conceives his own existence, and it is therefore a *subjective* principle of human actions. But it is also the way in which every other rational being conceives his existence, on the same rational ground which holds also for me;* hence it is at the same time an *objective* principle from which, since it is a supreme practical ground, it must be possible to derive all laws of the will. *The practical imperative will therefore be the following: Act in such a way that you treat humanity, whether in your own person or in any other person, always at the same time as an end, never merely as a means.* We will now see whether this can be carried out in practice.

Let us keep to our previous examples.

First, as regards the concept of necessary duty to oneself, the man who contemplates suicide will ask himself whether his action could be compatible with the Idea of humanity as *an end in itself.* If he damages himself in order to escape from a painful situation, he is making use of a person *merely as a means* to maintain a tolerable state of affairs till the end of his life. But a human being is not a thing—not something to be used *merely* as a means: he must always in all his actions be regarded as an end in himself. Hence I cannot dispose of a human being in my own person, by maiming, corrupting, or killing him. (I must here forego a more precise definition of this principle that would forestall any misunderstanding—for example, as to having limbs amputated to save myself or exposing my life to danger in order to preserve it, and so on—this discussion belongs to ethics proper.)

Secondly, as regards necessary or strict duty owed to others, the man who has in mind making a false promise to others will see at once that he is intending to make use of another person *merely as a means* to an end which that person does not share. For the person whom I seek to use for my own purposes by such a promise cannot possibly agree with my way of treating him, and so cannot himself share the end of the action. This incompatibility with the principle of duty to others can be seen more distinctly when we bring in examples of attacks on the freedom and property of others. For then it is manifest that a violator of the rights of human beings intends to use the person of others merely as a means without taking into consideration that, as rational beings, they must always at the same time be valued as ends—that is, treated only as beings who must themselves be able to share in the end of the very same action.

Thirdly, as regards contingent (meritorious) duty to oneself, it is not enough that an action not conflict with humanity in our own person as an end in itself: it must also *harmonize with this end.* Now there are in humanity capacities for greater perfection that form part of nature's purpose for humanity in our own person. To neglect these can perhaps be compatible with the *survival* of humanity as an end in itself, but not with the *promotion* of that end.

Fourthly, as regards meritorious duties to others, the natural end that all human beings seek is their own perfect happiness. Now the human race might indeed exist if everybody contributed nothing to the happiness of others but at the same time refrained from deliberately impairing it. This harmonizing with humanity *as an end in itself* would, however, be merely negative and not positive, unless everyone also endeavours, as far as he can, to further the ends of others. For the ends of any person who is an end in himself must, if this idea is to have its full effect in me, be also, as far as possible, *my* ends.

NOTES

1. A *maxim* is the subjective principle of volition: an objective principle (that is, one which would also serve subjectively as a practical principle for all rational beings if reason had full control over the faculty of desire) is a practical *law.*

---

*This proposition I put forward here as a postulate.

2. A *maxim* is a subjective principle of action and must be distinguished from an *objective principle*—namely, a practical law. The former contains a practical rule determined by reason in accordance with the conditions of the subject (often his ignorance or his inclinations); it is thus a principle on which the subject *acts*. A law, on the other hand, is an objective principle, valid for every rational being; and it is a principle on which he *ought to act*—that is, an imperative.

3. It should be noted that I reserve the division of duties entirely for a future *Metaphysic of Morals* and that my present division is put forward as an arbitrary one (merely for the purpose of arranging my examples). Further, I understand here by a perfect duty one that allows no exception in the interests of inclination, and so I recognize among *perfect duties*, both outer and inner duties. This runs contrary to the standard usage in the schools, but I do not intend to justify it here, since for my purpose it makes no difference whether this point is conceded or not.

DISCUSSION QUESTIONS:

1. Suppose that one person gives to famine relief and does so acting with a good will. Another does the same act but, instead of doing it with a good will, simply acts out of a feeling of compassion. A third does the same act without either a good will or a feeling of compassion but out of a desire to impress others. Do the acts differ in their moral worth, according to Kant? Is Kant correct?

2. Consider Kant's explanations of how the acts described in his four examples violate each version of the Categorical Imperative. Is the act described in each case morally wrong? What is Kant's account of how the act violates the Categorical Imperative? Is he correct?

3. In applying the Natural Law version of the Categorical Imperative ("Act as though the maxim of your action were to become by your will a universal law of nature") to some of his examples, Kant appeals to what we can will insofar as we are rational. He claims, for example, that every rational being "necessarily wills that all his powers should be developed." Are there some things we all will in so far as we are rational? What are they?

4. Kant's Natural Law version of the Categorical Imperative directs us to only act on maxims we can rationally will to be a universal law of nature. One and the same act can be done on the basis of different maxims, however. In failing to help someone in need, Jones may act on the maxim, "Whenever others are in need and I can help, I

won't do so." Smith may do the same act on the maxim, "Whenever others are in need and I can help, I'll only do so if they will use my help to better their situation." Might Kant's theory imply that an act is wrong when done on one maxim but right when done on another? If so, is this a problem for Kant's theory?

5. Kant says very little to explain what it is to treat someone solely as a means. Develop your own explanation. What are some examples of such treatment? What, if any, defining traits do they have in common?

Argument Reconstruction Exercises:

I. To what extent are our motives relevant to the moral worth of our actions? Identify the premises and conclusion of the following reasoning.

> If we happen to hit the center of a target when actually trying to do something else (e.g., we are instead trying to show how high our arrow can fly), our hitting the target's center is an accident. We don't deserve any credit as an archer for targets we hit accidentally. Analogously, if we happen to honor our moral obligations when actually trying to do something else, we honor our moral obligation by accident, and we don't deserve any credit as moral agents for obligations we honor by accident. Only acts done with a good will then count to our credit as moral agents.

II. Kant claims that there is only one categorical imperative. Identify the premises and conclusion of his reasoning.

> But if I think of a categorical imperative, I know right away what it contains. For since this imperative contains, besides the law, only the necessity that the maxim conform to this law, while the law, as we have seen, contains no conditions limiting it, there is nothing left over to which the maxim of action should conform except the universality of a law as such; and it is only this conformity that the imperative asserts to be necessary. There is therefore only one categorical imperative and it is this: "Act only on that maxim by which you can at the same time will that it should become a universal law." (page 267)

III. Kant argues that suicide is immoral, relying on the assumption that those engaged in suicide act on the maxim, "I make it my principle out of self-love to shorten my life if its continuance threatens more evil than it promises advantage" (page 267). Identify the premises and conclusion of his argument.

> The only . . . question is whether this principle of self-love can become a universal law of nature. But one sees at once that a nature whose law was that the very same feeling meant to promote life should actually destroy life would contradict itself, and hence would not endure as nature. The maxim therefore could not possibly be a general law of nature and thus it wholly contradicts the supreme principle of all duty. (page 267)

IV. True fanatics stick to their cause, no matter what. Identify the premises and conclusion of the following argument.

> People from Sneech-land are without worth. My maxim for interacting with them is to enslave them whenever possible. I'd be quite happy to have my maxim be a universal law of nature so that all those from Sneech-land are enslaved. If it should turn out that, unbeknownst to me, I and those I love are actually Sneech-landers, then others should enslave us as well, for we too are without worth. Since I can will that my maxim be a universal law of nature, it is morally correct for me to treat Sneech-landers as I do.

12.4 WHAT MAKES RIGHT ACTS RIGHT

W. D. ROSS (1930)

William David Ross taught at Oxford University and specialized in ethics and the history of philosophy, especially the work of Kant and Aristotle. This selection is from his book *The Right and the Good*, one of the classics of contemporary ethical theory. Ross opens his discussion by arguing that **Act-Utilitarianism** mistakenly assumes that we have only one significant moral relation to others (they are the possible beneficiaries of our actions) and only one moral duty (to produce the most good we can). On the contrary, Ross argues, we have many significant moral relations to others and many, sometimes overlapping and sometimes conflicting, moral duties. He calls these duties that arise from our relations with others *'prima facie duties,'* to indicate that there are various considerations that go into determining what we are morally obligated to do, all things considered.

Reading Questions:

1. Why does Ross think that utilitarianism fails to give adequate attention to the personal character of moral duty?

2. According to Ross, what is it for an act to be a *prima facie* moral duty for us?

3. How are our *prima facie* moral duties related to what Ross calls our "duty proper" or "actual duty"?

4. What are the different types of *prima facie* moral duty listed by Ross?

5. How, according to Ross, can we come to know that certain types of action (e.g., keeping our promises) are *prima facie* moral duties for us?

6. How, according to Ross, can we determine which action is our actual duty in a particular situation?

7. In what way, according to Ross, is the right act often a fortunate act?

8. How does Ross respond to the objection that his theory gives us no principle by which to discern what our actual duty is in particular circumstances?

Utilitarianism and *Prima Facie* Duties

The real point at issue between hedonism and utilitarianism on the one hand and their opponents on the other is not whether "right" means "productive of so and so"; for it cannot with any plausibility be maintained that it does. *The point at issue is that to which we now pass, viz. whether there is any general character which makes right acts right, and if so, what it is.* Among the main historical attempts to state a single characteristic of all right actions which is the foundation of their rightness are those made by egoism and utilitarianism. But I do not propose to discuss these, not because the subject is unimportant, but because it has been dealt with so often and so well already, and because there has come to be so much agreement among moral philosophers that neither of these theories is satisfactory. A much more attractive theory has been put forward by Professor Moore: that what makes actions right is that they are productive of more *good* than could have been produced by any other action open to the agent. . . .

In fact the theory of "ideal utilitarianism," if I may for brevity refer so to the theory of Professor Moore, seems to simplify unduly our relations to our fellows. It says, in effect, that the only morally significant relation in which my neighbours stand to me is that of being possible beneficiaries by my action. They do stand in this relation to me, and this relation is morally significant. But they may also stand to me in the relation of promisee to promiser, of creditor to debtor, of wife to husband, of child to parent, of friend to friend, of fellow countryman to fellow countryman, and the like; and each of these relations is the foundation of a *prima facie* duty, which is more or less incumbent on me according to the circumstances of the case. When I am in a situation, as perhaps I always am, in which more than one of these *prima facie* duties is incumbent on me, what I have to do is to study the situation as fully as I can until I form the considered opinion (it is never more) that in the circumstances one of them

is more incumbent than any other; then I am bound to think that to do this *prima facie* duty is my duty *sans phrase* in the situation.

*I suggest "**prima facie duty**" or "conditional duty" as a brief way of referring to the characteristic (quite distinct from that of being a duty proper) which an act has, in virtue of being of a certain kind (e.g. the keeping of a promise), of being an act which would be a duty proper if it were not at the same time of another kind which is morally significant. Whether an act is a duty proper or actual duty depends on all the morally significant kinds it is an instance of.* The phrase "*prima facie* duty" must be apologized for, since (1) it suggests that what we are speaking of is a certain kind of duty, whereas it is in fact not a duty, but something related in a special way to duty. Strictly speaking, we want not a phrase in which duty is qualified by an adjective, but a separate noun. (2) "*Prima*" *facie* suggests that one is speaking only of an appearance which a moral situation presents at first sight, and which may turn out to be illusory; whereas what I am speaking of is an objective fact involved in the nature of the situation, or more strictly in an element of its nature, though not, as duty proper does, arising from its *whole* nature. I can, however, think of no term which fully meets the case. . . .

There is nothing arbitrary about these *prima facie* duties. Each rests on a definite circumstance which cannot seriously be held to be without moral significance. Of *prima facie* duties I suggest, without claiming completeness or finality for it, the following division.

(1) Some duties rest on previous acts of my own. These duties seem to include two kinds, *(a)* those resting on a promise or what may fairly be called an implicit promise, such as the implicit undertaking not to tell lies which seems to be implied in the act of entering into conversation (at any rate by civilized men), or of writing books that purport to be history and not fiction. These may be called the duties of fidelity. (*b*) Those resting on a previous wrongful

act. These may be called the duties of reparation. (2) Some rest on previous acts of other men, i.e. services done by them to me. These may be loosely described as the duties of gratitude. (3) Some rest on the fact or possibility of a distribution of pleasure or happiness (or of the means thereto) which is not in accordance with the merit of the persons concerned; in such cases there arises a duty to upset or prevent such a distribution. These are the duties of justice. (4) Some rest on the mere fact that there are other beings in the world whose condition we can make better in respect of virtue, or of intelligence, or of pleasure. These are the duties of beneficence. (5) Some rest on the fact that we can improve our own condition in respect of virtue or of intelligence. These are the duties of self-improvement. (6) I think that we should distinguish from (4) the duties that may be summed up under the title of "not injuring others." No doubt to injure others is incidentally to fail to do them good; but it seems to me clear that non-maleficence is apprehended as a duty distinct from that of beneficence, and as a duty of a more stringent character. It will be noticed that this alone among the types of duty has been stated in a negative way. An attempt might no doubt be made to state this duty, like the others, in a positive way. It might be said that it is really the duty to prevent ourselves from acting either from an inclination to harm others or from an inclination to seek our own pleasure, in doing which we should incidentally harm them. But on reflection it seems clear that the primary duty here is the duty not to harm others, this being a duty whether or not we have an inclination that if followed would lead to our harming them; and that when we have such an inclination the primary duty not to harm others gives rise to a consequential duty to resist the inclination. The recognition of this duty of non-maleficence is the first step on the way to the recognition of the duty of beneficence; and that accounts for the prominence of the commands "thou shalt not kill," "thou shalt not commit adultery," "thou shalt not steal," "thou shalt not bear false witness," in so early a code as the Decalogue. But even when we have come to recognize the duty of beneficence, it appears to me that the duty of non-maleficence is recognized as a distinct one, and as *prima facie* more binding. We should not in general consider it justifiable to kill one person in order to keep another alive, or to steal from one in order to give alms to another.

The essential defect of the "ideal utilitarian" theory is that it ignores, or at least does not do full justice to, the highly personal character of duty. If the only duty is to produce the maximum of good, the question who is to have the good—whether it is myself, or my benefactor, or a person to whom I have made a promise to confer that good on him, or a mere fellow man to whom I stand in no such special relation—should make no difference to my having a duty to produce that good. But we are all in fact sure that it makes a vast difference.

One or two other comments must be made on this provisional list of the divisions of duty. (1) The nomenclature is not strictly correct. For by "fidelity" or "gratitude" we mean, strictly, certain states of motivation; and, as I have urged, it is not our duty to have certain motives, but to do certain acts. By "fidelity," for instance, is meant, strictly, the disposition to fulfil promises and implicit promises *because we have made them*. We have no general word to cover the actual fulfilment of promises and implicit promises *irrespective of motive*; and I use "fidelity," loosely but perhaps conveniently, to fill this gap. So too I use "gratitude" for the returning of services, irrespective of motive. The term "justice" is not so much confined, in ordinary usage, to a certain state of motivation, for we should often talk of a man as acting justly even when we did not think his motive was the wish to do what was just simply for the sake of doing so. Less apology is therefore needed for our use of "justice" in this sense. And I have used the word "beneficence" rather than "benevolence," in order to emphasize the fact that it is our duty to do certain things, and not to do them from certain motives.

(2) If the objection be made, that this catalogue of the main types of duty is an unsystematic one resting on no logical principle, it may be replied, first, that it makes no claim to being ultimate. It is a *prima facie* classification of the duties which reflection on our moral convictions seems actually to reveal. And if these convictions are, as I would claim that they are, of the nature of knowledge, and if I have not misstated them, the list will be a list of authentic conditional duties, correct as far as it goes though

not necessarily complete. The list of *goods* put forward by the rival theory is reached by exactly the same method—the only sound one in the circumstances—viz. that of direct reflection on what we really think. Loyalty to the facts is worth more than a symmetrical architectonic or a hastily reached simplicity. If further reflection discovers a perfect logical basis for this or for a better classification, so much the better.

(3) It may, again, be objected that our theory that there are these various and often conflicting types of *prima facie* duty leaves us with no principle upon which to discern what is our actual duty in particular circumstances. But this objection is not one which the rival theory is in a position to bring forward. For when we have to choose between the production of two heterogeneous goods, say knowledge and pleasure, the "ideal utilitarian" theory can only fall back on an opinion, for which no logical basis can be offered, that one of the goods is the greater; and this is no better than a similar opinion that one of two duties is the more urgent. And again, when we consider the infinite variety of the effects of our actions in the way of pleasure, it must surely be admitted that the claim which *hedonism* sometimes makes, that it offers a readily applicable criterion of right conduct, is quite illusory.

I am unwilling, however, to content myself with an *argumentum ad hominem,* and I would contend that in principle there is no reason to anticipate that every act that is our duty is so for one and the same reason. Why should two sets of circumstances, or one set of circumstances, *not* possess different characteristics, any one of which makes a certain act our *prima facie* duty? When I ask what it is that makes me in certain cases sure that I have a *prima facie* duty to do so and so, I find that it lies in the fact that I have made a promise; when I ask the same question in another case, I find the answer lies in the fact that I have done a wrong. And if on reflection I find (as I think I do) that neither of these reasons is reducible to the other, I must not on any *a priori* ground assume that such a reduction is possible.

An attempt may be made to arrange in a more systematic way the main types of duty which we have indicated. In the first place it seems self-evident that if there are things that are intrinsically good, it

is *prima facie* a duty to bring them into existence rather than not to do so, and to bring as much of them into existence as possible. It will be argued in our fifth chapter that there are three main things that are intrinsically good—virtue, knowledge, and, with certain limitations, pleasure. And since a given virtuous disposition, for instance, is equally good whether it is realized in myself or in another, it seems to be my duty to bring it into existence whether in myself or in another. So too with a given piece of knowledge.

The case of pleasure is difficult; for while we clearly recognize a duty to produce pleasure for others, it is by no means so clear that we recognize a duty to produce pleasure for ourselves. This appears to arise from the following facts. The thought of an act as our duty is one that presupposes a certain amount of reflection about the act; and for that reason does not normally arise in connexion with acts towards which we are already impelled by another strong impulse. So far, the cause of our thinking of the promotion of our own pleasure as a duty is analogous to the cause which usually prevents a highly sympathetic person from thinking of the promotion of the pleasure of others as a duty. He is impelled so strongly by direct interest in the well-being of others towards promoting their pleasure that he does not stop to ask whether it is his duty to promote it; and we are all impelled so strongly towards the promotion of our own pleasure that we do not stop to ask whether it is a duty or not. But there is a further reason why even when we stop to think about the matter it does not usually present itself as a duty: viz. that, since the performance of most of our duties involves the giving up of some pleasure that we desire, the doing of duty and the getting of pleasure for ourselves come by a natural association of ideas to be thought of as incompatible things. This association of ideas is in the main salutary in its operation, since it puts a check on what but for it would be much too strong, the tendency to pursue one's own pleasure without thought of other considerations. Yet if pleasure is good, it seems in the long run clear that it is right to get it for ourselves as well as to produce it for others, when this does not involve the failure to discharge some more stringent *prima facie* duty. The question is a very difficult one, but it seems that this conclusion can be denied only on one or other of three grounds: (1) that pleasure is not *prima facie* good (i.e. good when it is neither the actualization of a bad disposition nor undeserved), (2) that there is no *prima facie* duty to produce as much that is good as we can, or (3) that though there is a *prima facie* duty to produce other things that are good, there is no *prima facie* duty to produce pleasure which will be enjoyed by ourselves. I give reasons later for not accepting the first contention. The second hardly admits of argument but seems to me plainly false. The third seems plausible only if we hold that an act that is pleasant or brings pleasure to ourselves must for that reason not be a duty; and this would lead to paradoxical consequences, such as that if a man enjoys giving pleasure to others or working for their moral improvement, it cannot be his duty to do so. Yet it seems to be a very stubborn fact, that in our ordinary consciousness we are not aware of a duty to get pleasure for ourselves; and by way of partial explanation of this I may add that though, as I think, one's own pleasure is a good and there is a duty to produce it, it is only if we *think* of our own pleasure not as simply our own pleasure, but as an objective good, something that an impartial spectator would approve, that we can think of the getting it as a duty; and we do not habitually think of it in this way.

If these contentions are right, what we have called the duty of beneficence and the duty of self-improvement rest on the same ground. No different principles of duty are involved in the two cases. If we feel a special responsibility for improving our own character rather than that of others, it is not because a special principle is involved, but because we are aware that the one is more under our control than the other. It was on this ground that Kant expressed the practical law of duty in the form "seek to make yourself good and other people happy." He was so persuaded of the internality of virtue that he regarded any attempt by one person to produce virtue in another as bound to produce, at most, only a counterfeit of virtue, the doing of externally right acts not from the true principle of virtuous action but out of regard to another person. It must be admitted that one man cannot compel another to be virtuous; compulsory virtue would just not be

virtue. But experience clearly shows that Kant overshoots the mark when he contends that one man cannot do anything to *promote* virtue in another, to bring such influences to bear upon him that his own response to them is more likely to be virtuous than his response to other influences would have been. And our duty to do this is not different in kind from our duty to improve our own characters.

It is equally clear, and clear at an earlier stage of moral development, that if there are things that are bad in themselves we ought, *prima facie*, not to bring them upon others; and on this fact rests the duty of non-maleficence.

The duty of justice is particularly complicated, and the word is used to cover things which are really very different—things such as the payment of debts, the reparation of injuries done by oneself to another, and the bringing about of a distribution of happiness between other people in proportion to merit. I use the word to denote only the last of these three. In the fifth chapter I shall try to show that besides the three (comparatively) simple goods, virtue, knowledge, and pleasure, there is a more complex good, not reducible to these, consisting in the proportionment of happiness to virtue. The bringing of this about is a duty which we owe to all men alike, though it may be reinforced by special responsibilities that we have undertaken to particular men. This, therefore, with beneficence and self-improvement, comes under the general principle that we should produce as much good as possible, though the good here involved is different in kind from any other.

But besides this general obligation, there are special obligations. These may arise, in the first place, incidentally, from acts which were not essentially meant to create such an obligation, but which nevertheless create it. From the nature of the case such acts may be of two kinds—the infliction of injuries on others, and the acceptance of benefits from them. It seems clear that these put us under a special obligation to other men, and that only these acts can do so incidentally. From these arise the twin duties of reparation and gratitude.

And finally there are special obligations arising from acts the very intention of which, when they were done, was to put us under such an obligation. The name for such acts is "promises"; the name is wide enough if we are willing to include under it implicit promises, i.e. modes of behaviour in which without explicit verbal promise we intentionally create an expectation that we can be counted on to behave in a certain way in the interest of another person.

These seem to be, in principle, all the ways in which *prima facie* duties arise. In actual experience they are compounded together in highly complex ways. Thus, for example, the duty of obeying the laws of one's country arises partly (as Socrates contends in the *Crito*) from the duty of gratitude for the benefits one has received from it; partly from the implicit promise to obey which seems to be involved in permanent residence in a country whose laws we know we are *expected* to obey, and still more clearly involved when we ourselves invoke the protection of its laws (this is the truth underlying the doctrine of the social contract); and partly (if we are fortunate in our country) from the fact that its laws are potent instruments for the general good.

Or again, the sense of a general obligation to bring about (so far as we can) a just apportionment of happiness to merit is often greatly reinforced by the fact that many of the existing injustices are due to a social and economic system which we have, not indeed created, but taken part in and assented to; the duty of justice is then reinforced by the duty of reparation.

Prima Facie Duty and Actual Duty

It is necessary to say something by way of clearing up the relation between *prima facie* duties and the actual or absolute duty to do one particular act in particular circumstances. If, as almost all moralists except Kant are agreed, and as most plain men think, it is sometimes right to tell a lie or to break a promise, it must be maintained that there is a difference between *prima facie* duty and actual or absolute duty. When we think ourselves justified in breaking, and indeed morally obliged to break, a promise in order to relieve some one's distress, we do not for a moment cease to recognize a *prima facie* duty to keep our promise, and this leads us to feel, not indeed shame or repentance, but certainly compunction, for behaving as we do; we recognize, further, that it is

our duty to make up somehow to the promisee for the breaking of the promise. We have to distinguish from the characteristic of being our duty that of tending to be our duty. Any act that we do contains various elements in virtue of which it falls under various categories. In virtue of being the breaking of a promise, for instance, it tends to be wrong; in virtue of being an instance of relieving distress it tends to be right. *Tendency to be one's duty may be called a parti-resultant attribute, i.e. one which belongs to an act in virtue of some one component in its nature*: *Being one's duty is a toti-resultant attribute, one which belongs to an act in virtue of its whole nature and of nothing less than this*. This distinction between parti-resultant and toti-resultant attributes is one which we shall meet in another context also.

Another instance of the same distinction may be found in the operation of natural laws. *Qua* subject to the force of gravitation towards some other body, each body tends to move in a particular direction with a particular velocity, but its actual movement depends on *all* the forces to which it is subject. It is only by recognizing this distinction that we can preserve the absoluteness of laws of nature, and only by recognizing a corresponding distinction that we can preserve the absoluteness of the general principles of morality. But an important difference between the two cases must be pointed out. When we say that in virtue of gravitation a body tends to move in a certain way, we are referring to a causal influence actually exercised on it by another body or other bodies. When we say that in virtue of being deliberately untrue a certain remark tends to be wrong, we are referring to no causal relation, to no relation that involves succession in time, but to such a relation as connects the various attributes of a mathematical figure. And if the word "tendency" is thought to suggest too much a causal relation, it is better to talk of certain types of act as being *prima facie* right or wrong (or of different persons as having different and possibly conflicting claims upon us), than of their tending to be right or wrong.

Knowledge of Our Duty

Something should be said of the relation between our apprehension of the *prima facie* rightness of certain types of act and our mental attitude towards particular acts. It is proper to use the word "apprehension" in the former case and not in the latter. *That an act, qua fulfilling a promise, or qua effecting a just distribution of good, or qua returning services rendered, or qua promoting the good of others, or qua promoting the virtue or insight of the agent, is prima facie right, is self-evident*: not in the sense that it is evident from the beginning of our lives, or as soon as we attend to the proposition for the first time, but in the sense that when we have reached sufficient mental maturity and have given sufficient attention to the proposition it is evident without any need of proof, or of evidence beyond itself. It is self-evident just as a mathematical axiom, or the validity of a form of inference, is evident. The moral order expressed in these propositions is just as much part of the fundamental nature of the universe (and, we may add, of any possible universe in which there were moral agents at all) as is the spatial or numerical structure expressed in the axioms of geometry or arithmetic. In our confidence that these propositions are true there is involved the same trust in our reason that is involved in our confidence in mathematics; and we should have no justification for trusting it in the latter sphere and distrusting it in the former. In both cases we are dealing with propositions that cannot be proved, but that just as certainly need no proof.

Some of these general principles of *prima facie* duty may appear to be open to criticism. It may be thought, for example, that the principle of returning good for good is a falling off from the Christian principle, generally and rightly recognized as expressing the highest morality, of returning good for evil. To this it may be replied that I do not suggest that there is a principle commanding us to return good for good and forbidding us to return good for evil, and that I do suggest that there is a positive duty to seek the good of all men. What I maintain is that an act in which good is returned for good is recognized as *specially* binding on us just because it is of that character, and that *ceteris paribus* any one would think it his duty to help his benefactors rather than his enemies, if he could not do both; just as it is generally recognized that *ceteris paribus* we should pay our debts rather than give our money in charity, when we cannot do both. A benefactor is not only

a man, calling for our effort on his behalf on that ground, but also our benefactor, calling for our *special* effort on *that* ground.

Our judgements about our actual duty in concrete situations have none of the certainty that attaches to our recognition of the general principles of duty. A statement is certain, i.e. is an expression of knowledge, only in one or other of two cases: when it is either self-evident, or a valid conclusion from self-evident premises. And our judgements about our particular duties have neither of these characters. (1) They are not self-evident. Where a possible act is seen to have two characteristics, in virtue of one of which it is *prima facie* right, and in virtue of the other *prima facie* wrong, we are (I think) well aware that we are not certain whether we ought or ought not to do it; that whether we do it or not, we are taking a moral risk. We come in the long run, after consideration, to think one duty more pressing than the other, but we do not feel certain that it is so. And though we do not always recognize that a possible act has two such characteristics, and though there *may* be cases in which it has not, we are never certain that any particular possible act has not, and therefore never certain that it is right, nor certain that it is wrong. For, to go no further in the analysis, it is enough to point out that any particular act will in all probability in the course of time contribute to the bringing about of good or of evil for many human beings, and thus have a *prima facie* rightness or wrongness of which we know nothing. (2) Again, our judgements about our particular duties are not logical conclusions from self-evident premises. The only possible premises would be the general principles stating their *prima facie* rightness or wrongness *qua* having the different characteristics they do have; and even if we could (as we cannot) apprehend the extent to which an act will tend on the one hand, for example, to bring about advantages for our benefactors, and on the other hand to bring about disadvantages for fellow men who are not our benefactors, there is no principle by which we can draw the conclusion that it is on the whole right or on the whole wrong. In this respect the judgement as to the rightness of a particular act is just like the judgement as to the beauty of a particular natural object or work of art. A poem is, for instance, in respect of certain qualities beautiful and in respect of certain others not beautiful; and our judgement as to the degree of beauty it possesses on the whole is never reached by logical reasoning from the apprehension of its particular beauties or particular defects. Both in this and in the moral case we have more or less probable opinions which are not logically justified conclusions from the general principles that are recognized as self-evident.

There is therefore much truth in the description of the right act as a fortunate act. If we cannot be certain that it is right, it is our good fortune if the act we do is the right act. This consideration does not, however, make the doing of our duty a mere matter of chance. There is a parallel here between the doing of duty and the doing of what will be to our personal advantage. We never *know* what act will in the long run be to our advantage. Yet it is certain that we are more likely in general to secure our advantage if we estimate to the best of our ability the probable tendencies of our actions in this respect, than if we act on caprice. And similarly we are more likely to do our duty if we reflect to the best of our ability on the *prima facie* rightness or wrongness of various possible acts in virtue of the characteristics we perceive them to have, than if we act without reflection. With this greater likelihood we must be content.

Many people would be inclined to say that the right act for me is not that whose general nature I have been describing, viz. that which if I were omniscient I should see to be my duty, but that which on all the evidence available to me I should think to be my duty. But suppose that from the state of partial knowledge in which I think act A to be my duty, I could pass to a state of perfect knowledge in which I saw act B to be my duty should I not say "act B was the right act for me to do"? I should no doubt add "though I am not to be blamed for doing act A." But in adding this am I not passing from the question "what is right" to the question "what is morally good"? At the same time I am not making the *full* passage from the one notion to the other; for in order that the act should be morally good, or an act I am not to be blamed for doing, it must not merely be the act which it is reasonable for me to think my duty; it must also be done for that reason, or from some other morally good motive. Thus the

conception of the right act as the act which it is reasonable for me to think my duty is an unsatisfactory compromise between the true notion of the right act and the notion of the morally good action.

The general principles of duty are obviously not self-evident from the beginning of our lives. How do they come to be so? The answer is, that they come to be self-evident to us just as mathematical axioms do. We find by experience that this couple of matches and that couple make four matches, that this couple of balls on a wire and that couple make four balls; and by reflection on these and similar discoveries we come to see that it is of the nature of two and two to make four. In a precisely similar way, we see the *prima facie* rightness of an act which would be the fulfilment of a particular promise, and of another which would be the fulfilment of another promise, and when we have reached sufficient maturity to think in general terms, we apprehend *prima facie* rightness to belong to the nature of any fulfilment of promise. What comes first in time is the apprehension of the self-evident *prima facie* rightness of an individual act of a particular type. From this we come by reflection to apprehend the self-evident general principle of *prima facie* duty. From this, too, perhaps along with the apprehension of the self-evident *prima facie* rightness of the same act in virtue of its having another characteristic as well, and perhaps in spite of the apprehension of its *prima facie* wrongness in virtue of its having some third characteristic, we come to believe something not self-evident at all, but an object of probable opinion, viz. that this particular act is (not *prima facie* but) actually right.

In this respect there is an important difference between rightness and mathematical properties. A triangle which is isosceles necessarily has two of its angles equal, whatever other characteristics the triangle may have—whatever, for instance, be its area, or the size of its third angle. The equality of the two angles is a parti-resultant attribute. And the same is true of all mathematical attributes. It is true, I may add, of *prima facie* rightness. But no act is ever, in virtue of falling under some general description, necessarily actually right; its rightness depends on its whole nature and not on any element in it. The reason is that no mathematical object (no figure, for instance, or angle) ever has two characteristics that tend to give it opposite resultant characteristics, while moral acts often (as every one knows) and indeed always (as on reflection we must admit) have different characteristics that tend to make them at the same time *prima facie* right and *prima facie* wrong; there is probably no act, for instance, which does good to any one without doing harm to some one else, and *vice versa*.

DISCUSSION QUESTIONS:

1. How might a utilitarian best respond to Ross' concern that the utilitarian approach oversimplifies our moral relations to others? Is the utilitarian response successful?

2. Ross claims that the principles of *prima facie* duty are self-evident for us in the way that mathematical axioms are self-evident. In what way are mathematical axioms self-evident for us? Do the principles of *prima facie* duty have the same status for us?

3. What sometimes seems self-evident to us is really nothing more than a moral prejudice that we have been brought up to believe. If Ross' theory is correct, how and to what extent can we distinguish between the principles of *prima facie* duty that are self-evident moral truths and mere moral prejudices that seem equally self-evident to us?

4. Is Ross correct in his claim that the fundamental nature of the universe has a moral dimension just as it has a mathematical one? Do we have any reasons to doubt the objectivity of moral claims that we don't have to doubt the objectivity of mathematical claims?

5. Ross seeks to answer the question, "What makes right acts right?" What is his answer and just how informative is it? Is it as informative as the answers offered by other moral theories you have examined?

Argument Reconstruction Exercises:

I. The theory of "ideal utilitarianism" claims that what makes actions right is that they are productive of more good than could be produced by any other action open to the agent. Ross gives the following objection to the theory. Identify the premises and conclusion of his argument.

The essential defect of the "ideal utilitarian" theory is that it ignores, or at least does not do full justice to, the highly personal character of duty. If the only duty is to produce the maximum amount of good, the question who is to have the good—whether it is myself, or my benefactor, or a person to whom I have made a promise to confer good on him, or a mere fellow man to whom I stand in no special relationship—should make no difference to my having a duty to produce that good. But we are all in fact sure that it makes a vast difference. (page 273)

II. Ross considers some objections to his theory that are captured in the following argument. Identify its premises and conclusion.

According to the theory of *prima facie* duties what makes a right act right is the fact that it is the most stringent of our various, perhaps competing, *prima facie* duties. But the theory does not go on to explain what makes one *prima facie* duty more stringent than another. Without such an explanation the theory does not fully explain what makes right acts right.

III. Ross claims that the principles of *prima facie* duty are self-evident in the same way that mathematical truths are self-evident. He also claims that they describe features of the fundamental nature of the universe. Identify the premises and conclusion of this objection to his view.

Any mathematical truths that are self-evident are self-evident because they simply tell us how our concepts are related to one another (e.g., the claim that all squares have four sides is self-evident because all it says is that our concept of a square contains the concept of being four-sided). If principles of *prima facie* duty are similarly self-evident, then they too are just claims about how our concepts are related to one another (e.g., the claim that we have a *prima facie* duty to keep our promises is self-evident because all it says is that our concept of a promise contains the concept of being a moral reason to do something). Yet, if principles of *prima facie* duty are just about the relations between our concepts, then they do not describe fundamental features of the universe.

IV. If principles of *prima facie* duty are self-evident in the same way that mathematical truths are, then what are we to make of moral disagreements between cultures? Identify the premises and conclusion of the following argument.

If principles of *prima facie* duty are self-evident as mathematical truths are, then there won't be significant disagreement among cultures over principles of *prima facie* duty, just as there isn't significant disagreement among cultures over truths of mathematics. Yet, there is significant moral disagreement among cultures and that disagreement extends even to principles of *prima facie* obligation.

12.5 HYPOTHETICAL CONTRACTARIANISM

JOHN RAWLS (1971)

John Rawls was a professor of philosophy at Harvard University. The selection here is taken from his influential book *A Theory of Justice*. Rawls is concerned with specifying the conditions for a just distribution of primary social goods (rights and liberties, powers and opportunities, income and wealth) by the major institutions of a society, what he calls the society's "basic structure." He offers a version of a hypothetical **Social Contract Theory**, and he argues that at least two principles are defensible by this methodology, one about basic rights and one about social/economic inequalities. Rawls takes these two principles to match our considered judgments about what justice requires in various cases and to be ones that would be chosen by rational persons under reasonable conditions as the principles to govern their social relations.

Reading Questions:

1. Rawls describes his view as "justice as fairness;" what does he mean by this description?

2. What does Rawls mean by "reflective equilibrium?" What role does this concept play in his argument for his principles?

3. Rawls presents his principles as applying to the distribution of primary social goods by the basic structure of society; what is the basic structure of society and what are the primary social goods?

4. What does each of Rawls' principles require? What is the most extensive scheme of equal basic liberties compatible with a similar scheme of liberties for others? How can social and economic inequalities be to everyone's advantage, including to the advantage of those worst off?

   What is it for positions and offices to be open to all?

5. What do the parties in the original position know? What don't they know?

6. What goal guides parties in the original position in their choice of principles of justice? What is the maximin strategy, and why does Rawls think that it is the appropriate strategy for them to use in choosing principles of justice?

The Main Idea of the Theory of Justice

My aim is to present a conception of justice which generalizes and carries to a higher level of abstraction the familiar theory of the social contract as found, say, in Locke, Rousseau, and Kant.[1] In order to do this we are not to think of the original contract as one to enter a particular society or to set up a particular form of government. *Rather, the guiding idea is that the principles of justice for the basic structure of society are the object of the original agreement. They are the principles that free and rational persons concerned to further their own interests would accept in an initial position of equality as defining the fundamental terms of their association.* These principles are to regulate all further agreements; they specify the kinds of social cooperation that can be entered into and the forms of government that can be established. This way of regarding the principles of justice I shall call justice as fairness.

Thus we are to imagine that those who engage in social cooperation choose together, in one joint act, the principles which are to assign basic rights and duties and to determine the division of social benefits. Men are to decide in advance how they are to regulate their claims against one another and what is to be the foundation charter of their society. Just as each person must decide by rational reflection what constitutes his good, that is, the system of ends which it is rational for him to pursue, so a group of persons must decide once and for all what is to count among them as just and unjust. The choice which rational men would make in this hypothetical situation of equal liberty, assuming for the present that this choice problem has a solution, determines the principles of justice.

In justice as fairness the original position of equality corresponds to the state of nature in the traditional theory of the social contract. This original position is not, of course, thought of as an actual historical state of affairs, much less as a primitive condition of culture. It is understood as a purely hypothetical situation characterized so as to lead to a certain conception of justice.[2] Among the essential features of this situation is that no one knows his place in society, his class position or social status, nor does any one know his fortune in the distribution of natural assets and abilities, his intelligence, strength, and the like. I shall even assume that the parties do not know their conceptions of the good or their special psychological propensities. The principles of justice are chosen behind a veil of ignorance. This ensures that no one is advantaged or disadvantaged in the choice of principles by the outcome of natural chance or the contingency of social circumstances. Since all are similarly situated and no one is able to design principles to favor his particular condition, the principles of justice are the result of a fair agreement or bargain. For given the circumstances of the original position, the symmetry of everyone's relations to each other, this initial situation is fair between individuals as moral persons, that is, as rational beings with their own ends and capable, I shall assume, of a sense of justice. The original position is, one might say, the appropriate initial status quo, and thus the fundamental agreements reached in it are fair. This explains the propriety of the name "justice as fairness": it conveys the idea that the principles of justice are agreed to in an initial situation that is fair. The name does not mean that the concepts of justice and fairness are the same, any more than the phrase "poetry as metaphor" means that the concepts of poetry and metaphor are the same.

Justice as fairness begins, as I have said, with one of the most general of all choices which persons might make together, namely, with the choice of the first principles of a conception of justice which is to regulate all subsequent criticism and reform of institutions. Then, having chosen a conception of justice, we can suppose that they are to choose a constitution and a legislature to enact laws, and so on, all in accordance with the principles of justice initially agreed upon. Our social situation is just if it is such that by this sequence of hypothetical agreements we would have contracted into the general system of rules which defines it. Moreover, assuming that the original position does determine a set of principles (that is, that a particular conception of justice would be chosen), it will then be true that whenever social institutions satisfy these principles those engaged in them can say to one another that they are cooperating on terms to which they would agree if they were free and equal persons whose relations with respect to one another were fair. They could all view their arrangements as meeting the stipulations which they would acknowledge in an initial situation that embodies widely accepted and reasonable constraints on the choice of principles. The general recognition of this fact would provide the basis for a public acceptance of the corresponding principles of justice. No society can, of course, be a scheme of cooperation which men enter voluntarily in a literal sense; each person finds himself placed at birth in some particular position in some particular society, and the nature of this position materially affects his life prospects. Yet a society satisfying the principles of justice as fairness comes as close as a society can to being a voluntary scheme, for it meets the principles which free and equal persons would assent to under circumstances that are fair. In this sense its members are autonomous and the obligations they recognize self-imposed.

One feature of justice as fairness is to think of the parties in the initial situation as rational and mutually disinterested. This does not mean that the parties are egoists, that is, individuals with only certain kinds of interests, say in wealth, prestige, and domination. But they are conceived as not taking an interest in one another's interests. They are to presume that even their spiritual aims may be opposed, in the way that the aims of those of different religions may be opposed. Moreover, the concept of rationality must be interpreted as far as possible in the narrow sense, standard in economic theory, of taking the most effective means to given ends. I shall modify this concept to some extent, as explained later, but one must try to avoid introducing into it any controversial ethical elements. The initial situation must be characterized by stipulations that are widely accepted. . . .

I shall maintain . . . that the persons in the initial situation would choose two . . . different principles: the first requires equality in the assignment of basic rights and duties, while the second holds that social and economic inequalities, for example inequalities of wealth and authority, are just only if they result in compensating benefits for everyone, and in particular for the least advantaged members of society. These principles rule out justifying institutions on the grounds that the hardships of some are offset by a greater good in the aggregate. It may be expedient but it is not just that some should have less in order that others may prosper. But there is no injustice in the greater benefits earned by a few provided that the situation of persons not so fortunate is thereby improved. The intuitive idea is that since everyone's well-being depends upon a scheme of cooperation without which no one could have a satisfactory life, the division of advantages should be such as to draw forth the willing cooperation of everyone taking part in it, including those less well situated. The two principles mentioned seem to be a fair basis on which those better endowed, or more fortunate in their social position, neither of which we can be said to deserve, could expect the willing cooperation of others when some workable scheme is a necessary condition of the welfare of all.[3] Once we decide to look for a conception of justice that prevents the use of the accidents of natural endowment and the contingencies of social circumstance as counters in a quest for political and economic advantage, we are led to these principles. They express the result of leaving aside those aspects of the social world that seem arbitrary from a moral point of view.

The problem of the choice of principles, however, is extremely difficult. I do not expect the answer I shall suggest to be convincing to everyone. It is, therefore, worth noting from the outset that justice as fairness, like other contract views, consists of two parts: (1) an interpretation of the initial situation and of the problem of choice posed there, and (2) a set of principles which, it is argued, would be agreed to. One may accept the first part of the theory (or some variant thereof), but not the other, and conversely. The concept of the initial contractual situation may seem reasonable although the particular principles proposed are rejected. To be sure, I want to maintain that the most appropriate conception of this situation does lead to principles of justice contrary to utilitarianism and perfectionism, and therefore that the contract doctrine provides an alternative to these views. Still, one may dispute this contention even though one grants that the contractarian method is a useful way of studying ethical theories and of setting forth their underlying assumptions.

Justice as fairness is an example of what I have called a contract theory. . . .

The merit of the contract terminology is that it conveys the idea that principles of justice may be conceived as principles that would be chosen by rational persons, and that in this way conceptions of justice may be explained and justified. The theory of justice is a part, perhaps the most significant part, of the theory of rational choice. Furthermore, principles of justice deal with conflicting claims upon the advantages won by social cooperation; they apply to the relations among several persons or groups. The word "contract" suggests this plurality as well as the condition that the appropriate division of advantages must be in accordance with principles acceptable to all parties. The condition of publicity for principles of justice is also connoted by the contract phraseology. Thus, if these principles are the outcome of an agreement, citizens have a knowledge of the principles that others follow. It is characteristic of contract theories to stress the public nature of political principles. Finally there is the long tradition of the contract doctrine. Expressing the tie with this line of thought helps to define ideas and accords with natural piety. There are then several advantages in the use of the term "contract." With due precautions taken, it should not be misleading. . . .

The Original Position and Justification

I have said that the original position is the appropriate initial status quo which insures that the fundamental agreements reached in it are fair. This fact yields the name "justice as fairness." It is clear, then, that *I want to say that one conception of justice is more reasonable than another, or justifiable with respect to it, if rational persons in the initial situation would choose its principles over those of the other for the role of justice.* Conceptions of justice are to be ranked by their acceptability to persons so circumstanced. Understood in this way the question of justification is settled by working out a problem of deliberation: we have to ascertain which principles it would be rational to adopt given the contractual situation. This connects the theory of justice with the theory of rational choice.

If this view of the problem of justification is to succeed, we must, of course, describe in some detail the nature of this choice problem. A problem of rational decision has a definite answer only if we know the beliefs and interests of the parties, their relations with respect to one another, the alternatives between which they are to choose, the procedure whereby they make up their minds, and so on. As the circumstances are presented in different ways, correspondingly different principles are accepted. The concept of the original position, as I shall refer to it, is that of the most philosophically favored interpretation of this initial choice situation for the purposes of a theory of justice.

But how are we to decide what is the most favored interpretation? I assume, for one thing, that there is a broad measure of agreement that principles of justice should be chosen under certain conditions. To justify a particular description of the initial situation one shows that it incorporates these commonly shared presumptions. One argues from widely accepted but weak premises to more specific conclusions. Each of the presumptions should be itself be natural and plausible; some of them may seem innocuous or even trivial. The aim of the contract approach is to establish that taken together they impose significant bounds on acceptable principles of justice. The ideal outcome would be that these conditions determine a unique set of principles; but I shall be satisfied if they suffice to rank the main traditional conceptions of social justice.

One should not be misled, then, by the somewhat unusual conditions which characterize the original position. The idea here is simply to make vivid to ourselves the restrictions that it seems reasonable to impose on arguments for principles of justice, and therefore on these principles themselves. Thus it seems reasonable and generally acceptable that no one should be advantaged or disadvantaged by natural fortune or social circumstances in the choice of principles. It also seems widely agreed that it should be impossible to tailor principles to the circumstances of one's own case. We should insure further that particular inclinations and aspirations, and persons' conceptions of their good do not affect the principles adopted. The aim is to rule out those principles that it would be rational to propose for acceptance, however little the chance of success, only if one knew certain things that are irrelevant from the standpoint of justice. For example, if a man knew that he was wealthy, he might find it rational to advance the principle that various taxes for welfare measures be counted unjust; if he knew that he was poor, he would most likely propose the contrary principle. To represent the desired restrictions one imagines a situation in which everyone is deprived of this sort of information. One excludes the knowledge of those contingencies which sets men at odds and allows them to be guided by their prejudices. In this manner the veil of ignorance is arrived at in a natural way. This concept should cause no difficulty if we keep in mind the constraints on arguments that it is meant to express. At any time we can enter the original position, so to speak, simply by following a certain procedure, namely, by arguing for principles of justice in accordance with these restrictions.

It seems reasonable to suppose that the parties in the original position are equal. That is, all have the same rights in the procedure for choosing principles; each can make proposals, submit reasons for their acceptance, and so on. Obviously the purpose of these conditions is to represent equality between human beings as moral persons, as creatures having a conception of their good and capable of a sense of justice. The basis of equality is taken to be similarity in these two respects. Systems of ends are not ranked in value; and each man is presumed to have the requisite ability to understand and to act upon whatever principles are adopted. Together with the veil of ignorance, these conditions define the principles of justice as those which rational persons concerned to advance their interests would consent to as equals when none are known to be advantaged or disadvantaged by social and natural contingencies.

There is, however, another side to justifying a particular description of the original position. This is to see if the principles which would be chosen match our considered convictions of justice or extend them in an acceptable way. We can note whether applying these principles would lead us to make the same judgments about the basic structure of society which we now make intuitively and in which we have the greatest confidence; or whether, in cases where our present judgments are in doubt and given with hesitation, these principles offer a resolution which we can affirm on reflection. There are questions which we feel sure must be answered in a certain way. For example, we are confident that religious intolerance and racial discrimination are unjust. We think that

we have examined these things with care and have reached what we believe is an impartial judgment not likely to be distorted by an excessive attention to our own interests. These convictions are provisional fixed points which we presume any conception of justice must fit. But we have much less assurance as to what is the correct distribution of wealth and authority. Here we may be looking for a way to remove our doubts. We can check an interpretation of the initial situation, then, by the capacity of its principles to accommodate our firmest convictions and to provide guidance where guidance is needed.

In searching for the most favored description of this situation we work from both ends. We begin by describing it so that it represents generally shared and preferably weak conditions. We then see if these conditions are strong enough to yield a significant set of principles. If not, we look for further premises equally reasonable. But if so, and these principles match our considered convictions of justice, then so far well and good. But presumably there will be discrepancies. In this case we have a choice. We can either modify the account of the initial situation or we can revise our existing judgments, for even the judgments we take provisionally as fixed points are liable to revision. *By going back and forth, sometimes altering the conditions of the contractual circumstances, at others withdrawing our judgments and conforming them to principle, I assume that eventually we shall find a description of the initial situation that both expresses reasonable conditions and yields principles which match our considered judgments duly pruned and adjusted. This state of affairs I refer to as reflective equilibrium.*[4] It is an equilibrium because at last our principles and judgments coincide; and it is reflective since we know to what principles our judgments conform and the premises of their derivation. At the moment everything is in order. But this equilibrium is not necessarily stable. It is liable to be upset by further examination of the conditions which should be imposed on the contractual situation and by particular cases which may lead us to revise our judgments. Yet for the time being we have done what we can to render coherent and to justify our convictions of social justice. We have reached a conception of the original position.

I shall not, of course, actually work through this process. Still, we may think of the interpretation of the original position that I shall present as the result of such a hypothetical course of reflection. It represents the attempt to accommodate within one scheme both reasonable philosophical conditions on principles as well as our considered judgments of justice. In arriving at the favored interpretation of the initial situation there is no point at which an appeal is made to self-evidence in the traditional sense either of general conceptions or particular convictions. I do not claim for the principles of justice proposed that they are necessary truths or derivable from such truths. A conception of justice cannot be deduced from self-evident premises or conditions on principles; instead, its justification is a matter of the mutual support of many considerations, of everything fitting together into one coherent view.

A final comment. We shall want to say that certain principles of justice are justified because they would be agreed to in an initial situation of equality. I have emphasized that this original position is purely hypothetical. It is natural to ask why, if this agreement is never actually entered into, we should take any interest in these principles, moral or otherwise. The answer is that the conditions embodied in the description of the original position are ones that we do in fact accept. Or if we do not, then perhaps we can be persuaded to do so by philosophical reflection. Each aspect of the contractual situation can be given supporting grounds. Thus what we shall do is to collect together into one conception a number of conditions on principles that we are ready upon due consideration to recognize as reasonable. These constraints express what we are prepared to regard as limits on fair terms of social cooperation. One way to look at the idea of the original position, therefore, is to see it as an expository device which sums up the meaning of these conditions and helps us to extract their consequences. On the other hand, this conception is also an intuitive notion that suggests its own elaboration, so that led on by it we are drawn to define more clearly the standpoint from which we can best interpret moral relationships. We need a conception that enables us to envision our objective from afar: the intuitive notion of the original position is to do this for us.[5] . . .

Two Principles of Justice

I shall now state in a provisional form the two principles of justice that I believe would be agreed to in the original position. The first formulation of these principles is tentative. As we go on I shall consider several formulations and approximate step by step the final statement to be given much later. I believe that doing this allows the exposition to proceed in a natural way.

The first statement of the two principles reads as follows

First: each person is to have an equal right to the most extensive scheme of equal basic liberties compatible with a similar scheme of liberties for others.

Second: social and economic inequalities are to be arranged so that they are both (a) reasonably expected to be to everyone's advantage, and (b) attached to positions and offices open to all. . . .

These principles primarily apply, as I have said, to the basic structure of society and govern the assignment of rights and duties and regulate the distribution of social and economic advantages. Their formulation presupposes that, for the purposes of a theory of justice, the social structure may be viewed as having two more or less distinct parts, the first principle applying to the one, the second principle to the other. Thus we distinguish between the aspects of the social system that define and secure the equal basic liberties and the aspects that specify and establish social and economic inequalities. Now it is essential to observe that the basic liberties are given by a list of such liberties. Important among these are political liberty (the right to vote and to hold public office) and freedom of speech and assembly; liberty of conscience and freedom of thought; freedom of the person, which includes freedom from psychological oppression and physical assault and dismemberment (integrity of the person); the right to hold personal property and freedom from arbitrary arrest and seizure as defined by the concept of the rule of law. These liberties are to be equal by the first principle.

The second principle applies, in the first approximation, to the distribution of income and wealth and to the design of organizations that make use of differences in authority and responsibility. While the distribution of wealth and income need not be equal, it must be to everyone's advantage, and at the same time, positions of authority and responsibility must be accessible to all. One applies the second principle by holding positions open, and then, subject to this constraint, arranges social and economic inequalities so that everyone benefits.

These principles are to be arranged in a serial order with the first principle prior to the second. This ordering means that infringements of the basic equal liberties protected by the first principle cannot be justified, or compensated for, by greater social and economic advantages. These liberties have a central range of application within which they can be limited and compromised only when they conflict with other basic liberties. Since they may be limited when they clash with one another, none of these liberties is absolute; but however they are adjusted to form one system, this system is to be the same for all. It is difficult, and perhaps impossible, to give a complete specification of these liberties independently from the particular circumstances—social, economic, and technological—of a given society. The hypothesis is that the general form of such a list could be devised with sufficient exactness to sustain this conception of justice. Of course, liberties not on the list, for example, the right to own certain kinds of property (e.g., means of production) and freedom of contract as understood by the doctrine of laissez-faire are not basic; and so they are not protected by the priority of the first principle. Finally, in regard to the second principle, the distribution of wealth and income, and positions of authority and responsibility, are to be consistent with both the basic liberties and equality of opportunity.

The two principles are rather specific in their content, and their acceptance rests on certain assumptions that I must eventually try to explain and justify. For the present, it should be observed that these principles are a special case of a more general conception of justice that can be expressed as follows.

> All social values—liberty and opportunity, income and wealth, and the social bases of self-respect— are to be distributed equally unless an unequal distribution of any, or all, of these values is to everyone's advantage.

Injustice, then, is simply inequalities that are not to the benefit of all. Of course, this conception is extremely vague and requires interpretation.

As a first step, suppose that the basic structure of society distributes certain primary goods, that is, things that every rational man is presumed to want. These goods normally have a use whatever a person's rational plan of life. For simplicity, assume that the chief primary goods at the disposition of society are rights, liberties, and opportunities, and income and wealth. (Later on in Part Three the primary good of self-respect has a central place.) These are the social primary goods. Other primary goods such as health and vigor, intelligence and imagination, are natural goods; although their possession is influenced by the basic structure, they are not so directly under its control. Imagine, then, a hypothetical initial arrangement in which all the social primary goods are equally distributed: everyone has similar rights and duties, and income and wealth are evenly shared. This state of affairs provides a benchmark for judging improvements. If certain inequalities of wealth and differences in authority would make everyone better off than in this hypothetical starting situation, then they accord with the general conception.

Now it is possible, at least theoretically, that by giving up some of their fundamental liberties men are sufficiently compensated by the resulting social and economic gains. The general conception of justice imposes no restrictions on what sort of inequalities are permissible; it only requires that everyone's position be improved. We need not suppose anything so drastic as consenting to a condition of slavery. Imagine instead that people seem willing to forego certain political rights when the economic returns are significant. It is this kind of exchange which the two principles rule out; being arranged in serial order they do not permit exchanges between basic liberties and economic and social gains except under extenuating circumstances . . . .

The fact that the two principles apply to institutions has certain consequences. First of all, the rights and basic liberties referred to by these principles are those which are defined by the public rules of the basic structure. Whether men are free is determined by the rights and duties established by the major institutions of society. Liberty is a certain pattern of social forms. The first principle simply requires that certain sorts of rules, those defining basic liberties, apply to everyone equally and that they allow the most extensive liberty compatible with a like liberty for all. The only reason for circumscribing basic liberties and making them less extensive is that otherwise they would interfere with one another.

Further, when principles mention persons, or require that everyone gain from an inequality, the reference is to representative persons holding the various social positions, or offices established by the basic structure. Thus in applying the second principle I assume that it is possible to assign an expectation of well-being to representative individuals holding these positions. This expectation indicates their life prospects as viewed from their social station. In general, the expectations of representative persons depend upon the distribution of rights and duties throughout the basic structure. Expectations are connected: by raising the prospects of the representative man in one position we presumably increase or decrease the prospects of representative men in other positions. Since it applies to institutional forms, the second principle (or rather the first part of it) refers to the expectations of representative individuals. As I shall discuss below, neither principle applies to distributions of particular goods to particular individuals who may be identified by their proper names. The situation where someone is considering how to allocate certain commodities to needy persons who are known to him is not within the scope of the principles. They are meant to regulate basic institutional arrangements. We must not assume that there is much similarity from the standpoint of justice between an administrative allotment of goods to specific persons and the appropriate design of society. Our common sense intuitions for the former may be a poor guide to the latter.

Now the second principle insists that each person benefit from permissible inequalities in the basic structure. This means that it must be reasonable for each relevant representative man defined by this structure, when he views it as a going concern, to prefer his prospects with the inequality to his prospects without it. One is not allowed to justify differences in income or in positions of authority and responsibility on the ground that the disadvantages of those in one position are outweighed by the greater advantages of those in another. Much less can infringements of liberty be counterbalanced in this way. It is obvious, however, that there are indefinitely many ways in which all may be advantaged when the initial arrangement of equality is taken as a benchmark. How then are we to choose among these possibilities? The principles must be specified so that they yield a determinate conclusion. . .

Democratic Equality and the Difference Principle

The democratic interpretation . . . is arrived at by combining the principle of fair equality of opportunity with the difference principle. . . . Assuming the framework of institutions required by equal liberty and fair equality of opportunity, the higher expectations of those better situated are just if and only if they work as part of a scheme which improves the expectations of the least advantaged members of society. The intuitive idea is that the social order is not to establish and secure the more attractive prospects of those better off unless doing so is to the advantage of those less fortunate. . . .

To illustrate the difference principle, consider the distribution of income among social classes. Let us suppose that the various income groups correlate with representative individuals by reference to whose expectations we can judge the distribution. Now those starting out as members of the entrepreneurial class in property-owning democracy, say, have a better prospect than those who begin in the class of unskilled laborers. It seems likely that this will be true even when the social injustices which now exist are removed. What, then, can possibly justify this kind of initial inequality in life prospects? According to the difference principle, it is justifiable only if the difference in expectation is to the advantage of the representative man who is worse off, in this case the representative unskilled worker. The inequality in expectation is permissible only if lowering it would make the working class even more worse off. Supposedly, given the rider in the second principle concerning open positions, and the principle of liberty generally, the greater expectations allowed to entrepreneurs encourages them to do things which raise the prospects of laboring class. Their better prospects act as incentives so that the economic process is more efficient, innovation proceeds at a faster pace, and so on. I shall not consider how far these things are true. The point is that something of this kind must be argued if these inequalities are to satisfy by the difference principle. . .

The Tendency to Equality

I wish to conclude this discussion of the two principles by explaining the sense in which they express an egalitarian conception of justice. . . .

The difference principle represents, in effect, an agreement to regard the distribution of natural talents as in some respects a common asset and to share in the greater social and economic benefits made possible by the complementarities of this distribution. Those who have been favored by nature, whoever they are, may gain from their good fortune only on terms that improve the situation of those who have lost out. The naturally advantaged are not to gain merely because they are more gifted, but only to cover the costs of training and education and for using their endowments in ways that help the less fortunate as well. No one deserves his greater natural capacity nor merits a more favorable starting place in society. But, of course, this is no reason to ignore, much less to eliminate these distinctions. Instead, the basic structure can be arranged so that these contingencies work for the good of the least fortunate. Thus we are led to the difference principle if we wish to set up the social system so that no one gains or loses from his arbitrary place in the distribution of natural assets or his initial position in society without giving or receiving compensating advantages in return.

In view of these remarks we may reject the contention that the ordering of institutions is always defective because the distribution of natural talents and the contingencies of social circumstance are unjust, and this injustice must inevitably carry over to human arrangements. Occasionally this reflection is offered as an excuse for ignoring injustice, as if the refusal to acquiesce in injustice is on a par with being unable to accept death. The natural distribution is neither just nor unjust; nor is it unjust

that persons are born into society at some particular position. These are simply natural facts. What is just and unjust is the way that institutions deal with these facts. Aristocratic and caste societies are unjust because they make these contingencies the ascriptive basis for belonging to more or less enclosed and privileged social classes. The basic structure of these societies incorporates the arbitrariness found in nature. But there is no necessity for men to resign themselves to these contingencies. The social system is not an unchangeable order beyond human control but a pattern of human action. Injustice as fairness men agree to avail themselves of the accidents of nature and social circumstance only when doing so is for the common benefit. The two principles are a fair way of meeting the arbitrariness of fortune; and while no doubt imperfect in other ways, the institutions which satisfy these principles are just.

A further point is that the difference principle expresses a conception of reciprocity. It is a principle of mutual benefit. At first sight, however, it may appear unfairly biased towards the least favored. To consider this question in an intuitive way, suppose for simplicity that there are only two groups in society, one noticeably more fortunate than the other. Subject to the usual constraints (defined by the priority of the first principle and fair equality of opportunity), society could maximize the expectations of either group but not both, since we can maximize with respect to only one aim at a time. It seems clear that society should not do the best it can for those initially more advantaged; so if we reject the difference principle, we must prefer maximizing some weighted mean of the two expectations. But if we give any weight to the more fortunate, we are valuing for their own sake the gains to those already more favored by natural and social contingencies. No one had an antecedent claim to be benefited in this way, and so to maximize a weighted mean is, so to speak, to favor the more fortunate twice over. Thus the more advantaged, when they view the matter from a general perspective, recognize that the well-being of each depends on a scheme of social cooperation without which no one could have a satisfactory life; they recognize also that they can expect the willing cooperation of all only if the terms of the scheme are reasonable. So they regard themselves as already compensated, as it were, by the advantages to which no one (including themselves) had a prior claim. They forego the idea of maximizing a weighted mean and regard the difference principle as a fair basis for regulating the basic structure.

One may object that those better situated deserve the greater advantages they could acquire for themselves under other schemes of cooperation whether or not these advantages are gained in ways that benefit others. Now it is true that given a just system of cooperation as a framework of public rules, and the expectations set up by it, those who, with the prospect of improving their condition, have done what the system announces it will reward are entitled to have their expectations met. In this sense the more fortunate have title to their better situation; their claims are legitimate expectations established by social institutions and the community is obligated to fulfill them. But this sense of desert is that of entitlement. It presupposes the existence of an ongoing cooperative scheme and is irrelevant to the question whether this scheme itself is to be designed in accordance with the difference principle or some other criterion.

Thus it is incorrect that individuals with greater natural endowments and the superior character that has made their development possible have a right to a cooperative scheme that enables them to obtain even further benefits in ways that do not contribute to the advantages of others. We do not deserve our place in the distribution of native endowments, any more than we deserve our initial starting place in society. That we deserve the superior character that enables us to make the effort to cultivate our abilities is also problematic; for such character depends in good part upon fortunate family and social circumstances in early life for which we can claim no credit. The notion of desert does not apply here. To be sure, the more advantaged have a right to their natural assets, as does everyone else; this right is covered by the first principle under the basic liberty protecting the integrity of the person. And so the more advantaged are entitled to whatever they can acquire in accordance with the rules of a fair system of social cooperation. Our problem is how this scheme, the basic structure of society, is to be designed. From a suitably general standpoint, the difference principle

appears acceptable to both the more advantaged and the less advantaged individual. Of course, none of this is strictly speaking an argument for the principle, since in a contract theory arguments are made from the point of view of the original position. But these intuitive considerations help to clarify the principle and the sense in which it is egalitarian. . . .

The Veil of Ignorance

The idea of the original position is to set up a fair procedure so that any principles agreed to will be just. The aim is to use the notion of pure procedural justice as a basis of theory. Somehow we must nullify the effects of specific contingencies which put men at odds and tempt them to exploit social and natural circumstances to their own advantage. Now in order to do this *I assume that the parties are situated behind a veil of ignorance. They do not know how the various alternatives will affect their own particular case and they are obliged to evaluate principles solely on the basis of general considerations.*[6]

It is assumed, then, that the parties do not know certain kinds of particular facts. First of all, no one knows his place in society, his class position or social status; nor does he know his fortune in the distribution of natural assets and abilities, his intelligence and strength, and the like. Nor, again, does anyone know his conception of the good, the particulars of his rational plan of life, or even the special features of his psychology such as his aversion to risk or liability to optimism or pessimism. More than this, I assume that the parties do not know the particular circumstances of their own society. That is, they do not know its economic or political situation, or the level of civilization and culture it has been able to achieve. The persons in the original position have no information as to which generation they belong. These broader restrictions on knowledge are appropriate in part because questions of social justice arise between generations as well as within them, for example, the question of the appropriate rate of capital saving and of the conservation of natural resources and the environment of nature. There is also, theoretically anyway, the question of a reasonable genetic policy. In these cases too, in order to carry through the idea of the original position, the parties must not know the contingencies that set them in opposition. They must choose principles the consequences of which they are prepared to live with whatever generation they turn out to belong to.

As far as possible, then, the only particular facts which the parties know is that their society is subject to the circumstances of justice and whatever this implies. It is taken for granted, however, that they know the general facts about human society. They understand political affairs and the principles of economic theory; they know the basis of social organization and the laws of human psychology. Indeed, the parties are presumed to know whatever general facts affect the choice of the principles of justice. There are no limitations on general information, that is, on general laws and theories, since conceptions of justice must be adjusted to the characteristics of the systems of social cooperation which they are to regulate, and there is no reason to rule out these facts. It is, for example, a consideration against a conception of justice that, in view of the laws of moral psychology, men would not acquire a desire to act upon it even when the institutions of their society satisfied it. For in this case there would be difficulty in securing the stability of social cooperation. An important feature of a conception of justice is that it should generate its own support. Its principles should be such that when they are embodied in the basic structure of society men tend to acquire the corresponding sense of justice and develop a desire to act in accordance with its principles. In this case a conception of justice is stable. This kind of general information is admissible in the original position.

The notion of the veil of ignorance raises several difficulties. Some may object that the exclusion of nearly all particular information makes it difficult to grasp what is meant by the original position. Thus it may be helpful to observe that one or more persons can at any time enter this position, or perhaps better, simulate the deliberations of this hypothetical situation, simply by reasoning in accordance with the appropriate restrictions. In arguing for a conception of justice we must be sure that it is among the permitted alternatives and satisfies the stipulated formal constraints. No considerations can be advanced in its favor unless they would be rational ones for us to urge were we to lack the kind of knowledge that is excluded. The evaluation of principles must proceed in terms of the general consequences of their public recognition and universal application, it being assumed that they will be complied with by everyone. To say that a certain conception of justice would be chosen in the original position is equivalent to saying that rational deliberation satisfying certain conditions and restrictions would reach a certain conclusion. If necessary, the argument to this result could be set out more formally. I shall, however, speak throughout in terms of the notion of the original position. It is more economical and suggestive, and brings out certain essential features that otherwise one might easily overlook.

These remarks show that the original position is not to be thought of as a general assembly which includes at one moment everyone who will live at some time or, much less, as an assembly of everyone who could live at some time. It is not a gathering of all actual or possible persons. If we conceived of the original position in either of these ways, the conception would cease to be a natural guide to intuition and would lack a clear sense. In any case, the original position must be interpreted so that one can at any time adopt its perspective. It must make no difference when one takes up this viewpoint, or who does so: the restrictions must be such that the same principles are always chosen. The veil of ignorance is a key condition in meeting this requirement. It insures not only that the information available is relevant, but that it is at all times the same.

It may be protested that the condition of the veil of ignorance is irrational. Surely, some may object, principles should be chosen in the light of all the knowledge available. There are various replies to this contention. Here I shall sketch those which emphasize the simplifications that need to be made if one is to have any theory at all. . . . To begin with, it is clear that since the differences among the parties are unknown to them, and everyone is equally rational and similarly situated, each is convinced by the same arguments. Therefore, we can view the agreement in the original position from the standpoint of one person selected at random. If anyone after due reflection prefers a conception of justice to another, then they all do, and a unanimous agreement can be reached. We can, to make the circumstances more vivid, imagine that the parties are required to communicate with each other through a referee as intermediary, and that he is to announce which alternatives have been suggested and the reasons offered in their support. He forbids the attempt to form coalitions, and he informs the parties when they have come to an understanding. But such a referee is actually superfluous, assuming that the deliberations of the parties must be similar.

Thus there follows the very important consequence that the parties have no basis for bargaining in the usual sense. No one knows his situation in society or his natural assets, and therefore no one is in a position to tailor principles to his advantage. We might imagine that one of the contractees threatens to hold out unless the others agree to principles favorable to him. But how does he know which principles are especially in his interests? The same holds for the formation of coalitions: if a group were to decide to band together to the disadvantage of the others, they would not know how to favor themselves in the choice of principles. Even if they could get everyone to agree to their proposal, they would have no assurance that it was to their advantage, since they cannot identify themselves either by name or description. The one case where this conclusion fails is that of saving. Since the persons in the original position know that they are contemporaries (taking the present time of entry interpretation), they can favor their generation by refusing to make any sacrifices at all for their successors; they simply acknowledge the principle that no one has a duty to save for posterity. Previous generations have saved or they have not; there is nothing the parties can now do to affect that. So in this instance the veil of ignorance fails to secure the desired result. Therefore, to handle the question of justice between generations, I modify the motivation assumption and add a further constraint. . . . With these adjustments, no generation is able to formulate principles especially designed to advance its own cause and some significant limits on savings principles can be derived. . . . Whatever a person's temporal position, each is forced to choose for all.[7]

The restrictions on particular information in the original position are, then, of fundamental importance. Without them we would not be able to work out any definite theory of justice at all. We would have to be content with a vague formula stating that justice is what would be agreed to without being able to say much, if anything, about the substance of the agreement itself. The formal constraints of the concept of right, those applying to principles directly, are not sufficient for our purpose. The veil of ignorance makes possible a unanimous choice of a particular conception of justice. Without these limitations on knowledge the bargaining problem of the original position would be hopelessly complicated. Even if theoretically a solution were to exist, we would not, at present anyway, be able to determine it. . . .

The Reasoning Leading to the Two Principles of Justice

. . . It seems from these remarks that the two principles are at least a plausible conception of justice. The question, though, is how one is to argue for them more systematically. Now there are several things to do. One can work out their consequences for institutions and note their implications for fundamental social policy. In this way they are tested by a comparison with our considered judgments of justice. . . . But one can also try to find arguments in their favor that are decisive from the standpoint of the original position. In order to see how this might be done, *it is useful as a heuristic device to think of the two principles as the maximin solution to the problem of social justice.* There is a relation between the two principles, and the maximin rule for choice under uncertainty.[8] This is evident from the fact that the two principles are those a person would choose for the design of a society in which his enemy is to assign him his place. The maximin rule tells us to rank alternatives by their worst possible outcomes: we are to adopt the alternative the worst outcome of which is superior to the worst outcomes of the others.[9] The persons in the original position do not, of course, assume that their initial place in society is decided by a malevolent opponent. As I note below, they should not reason from false premises. The veil of ignorance does not violate this idea, since an absence of information is not misinformation. But that the two principles of justice would be chosen if the parties were forced to protect themselves against such a contingency explains the sense in which this conception is the maximin solution. And this analogy suggests that if the original position has been described so that it is rational for the parties to adopt the conservative attitude expressed by this rule, a conclusive argument can indeed be constructed for these principles. Clearly the maximin rule is not, in general, a suitable guide for choices under uncertainty. But it holds only in situations marked by certain special features. My aim, then, is to show that a good case can be made for the two principles based on the fact that the original position has these features to a very high degree.

Now there appear to be three chief features of situations that give plausibility to this unusual rule.[10] First, since the rule takes no account of the likelihoods of the possible circumstances, there must be some reason for sharply discounting estimates of these probabilities. Offhand, the most natural rule of choice would seem to be to compute the expectation of monetary gain for each decision and then to adopt the course of action with the highest prospect. . . . Thus it must be, for example, that the situation is one in which a knowledge of likelihoods is impossible, or at best extremely insecure. In this case it is unreasonable not to be skeptical of probabilistic calculations unless there is no other way out, particularly if the decision is a fundamental one that needs to be justified to others.

The second feature that suggests the maximin rule is the following: the person choosing has a conception of the good such that he cares very little, if anything, for what he might gain above the minimum stipend that he can, in fact, be sure of by following the maximin rule. It is not worthwhile for him to take a chance for the sake of a further advantage, especially when it may turn out that he loses much that is important to him. This last provision brings in the third feature, namely, that the rejected alternatives have outcomes that one can hardly accept. The situation involves grave risks. Of course these features work most effectively in combination. The paradigm situation for following the maximin rule is when all three features are realized to the highest degree.

Let us review briefly the nature of the original position with these three special features in mind.

To begin with, the veil of ignorance excludes all knowledge of likelihoods. The parties have no basis for determining the probable nature of their society, or their place in it. Thus they have no basis for probability calculations. They must also take into account the fact that their choice of principles should seem reasonable to others, in particular their descendants, whose rights will be deeply affected by it. These considerations are strengthened by the fact that the parties know very little about the possible states of society. Not only are they unable to conjecture the likelihoods of the various possible circumstances, they cannot say much about what the possible circumstances are, much less enumerate them and foresee the outcome of each alternative available. Those deciding are much more in the dark than illustrations by numerical tables suggest. It is for this reason that I have spoken only of a relation to the maximin rule.

Several kinds of arguments for the two principles of justice illustrate the second feature. Thus, if we can maintain that these principles provide a workable theory of social justice, and that they are compatible with reasonable demands of efficiency, then this conception guarantees a satisfactory minimum. There may be, on reflection, little reason for trying to do better. Thus much of the argument . . . is to show, by their application to some main questions of social justice, that the two principles are a satisfactory conception. These details have a philosophical purpose. Moreover, this line of thought is practically decisive if we can establish the priority of liberty. For this priority implies that the persons in the original position have no desire to try for greater gains at the expense of the basic equal liberties. The minimum assured by the two principles in lexical order is not one that the parties wish to jeopardize for the sake of greater economic and social advantages.

Finally, the third feature holds if we can assume that other conceptions of justice may lead to institutions that the parties would find intolerable. For example, it has sometimes been held that under some conditions the utility principle (in either form) justifies, if not slavery or serfdom, at any rate serious infractions of liberty for the sake of greater social benefits. We need not consider here the truth of this claim. For the moment, this contention is only to illustrate the way in which conceptions of justice may allow for outcomes which the parties may not be able to accept. And having the ready alternative of the two principles of justice which secure a satisfactory minimum, it seems unwise, if not irrational, for them to take a chance that these conditions are not realized. . . .

NOTES

1. As the text suggests, I shall regard Locke's *Second Treatise of Government*, Rousseau's *The Social Contract*, and Kant's ethical works beginning with *The Foundations of the Metaphysics of Morals* as definitive of the contract tradition. For all of its greatness, Hobbes's *Leviathan* raises special problems. A general historical survey is provided by J. W. Gough, *The Social Contract*, 2nd ed. (Oxford, The Clarendon Press, 1957), and Otto Gierke, *Natural Law and the Theory of Society*, trans. with an introduction by Ernest Barker (Cambridge, The University Press, 1934). A presentation of the contract view as primarily an ethical theory is to be found in G. R. Grice, *The Grounds of Moral Judgment* (Cambridge, The University Press, 1967). . . .

2. Kant is clear that the original agreement is hypothetical. See *The Metaphysics of Morals*, pt. I *(Rechtslehre),* especially §§47,52; and pt. II of the essay "Concerning the Common Saying: This May Be True in Theory but It Does Not Apply in Practice," in *Kant's Political Writings*, ed. Hans Reiss and trans. by H. B. Nisbet (Cambridge, The University Press, 1970), pp. 73–87. See Georges Vlachos, *La Pensee politique de Kant* (Paris, Presses Universitaires de France, 1962), pp. 326–335; and I. G. Murphy, *Kant: The Philosophy of Right* (London, Macmillan. 1970), pp. 109–112,133–136, for a further discussion.

3. For the formulation of this intuitive idea I am indebted to Allan Gibbard.

4. The process of mutual adjustment of principles and considered judgments is not peculiar to moral philosophy. See Nelson Goodman, *Fact, Fiction, and Forecast* (Cambridge, Mass., Harvard University Press, 1955), pp. 65–68, for parallel remarks concerning the justification of the principles of deductive and inductive inference.

5. Henri Poincaré remarks: "Il nous faut une faculté qui nous fasse voir le but de loin, et, cette faculté, c'est l'intuition." *La Valeur de la science* (Paris, Flammarion, 1909), p. 27.

6. The veil of ignorance is so natural a condition that something like it must have occurred to many. The formulation in the text is implicit, I believe, in Kant's doctrine of the categorical imperative, both in the way this procedural criterion is defined and the use Kant makes of it. Thus when Kant tells us to test our maxim by considering what would be the case were it a universal law of nature, he must suppose that we do not know our place within this imagined system of nature. See, for example, his discussion of the topic of practical judgment in *The Critique of Practical Reason,* Academy Edition, vol. 5, pp. 68–72. A similar restriction on information is found in J. C. Harsanyi, "Cardinal Utility in Welfare Economics and in the Theory of Risk-taking," *Journal of Political Economy*, vol. 61 (1953). However, other aspects of Harsanyi's view are quite different, and he uses the restriction to develop a utilitarian theory. . . .

7. II Rousseau, *The Social Contract*, bk. I, ch. IV, par. 5.

8. An accessible discussion of this and other rules of choice under uncertainty can be found in W. J. Baumol, *Economic Theory and Operations Analysis*. 2nd ed. (Englewood Cliffs, N. J., Prentice-Hall Inc., 1965), ch. 24. Baumol gives a geometric interpretation of these rules. . . to illustrate the difference principle. See pp. 558–562. See also R. D. Luce and Howard Raiffa, *Games and Decisions* (New York, John Wiley and Sons, Inc., 1957), ch. XIII, for a fuller account.

9. Consider the gain-and-loss table below. It represents the gains and losses for a situation which is not a game of strategy. There is no one playing against the person making the decision; instead he is faced with several possible circumstances which may or may not obtain. Which circumstances happen to exist does not depend upon what the person choosing decides or whether he announces his moves in advance. The numbers in the table are monetary values (in hundreds of dollars) in comparison with some initial situation. The gain (g) depends upon the individual's decision (d) and the circumstances (c). Thus $g = f(d, c)$. Assuming that there are three possible decisions and three possible circumstances, we might have this gain-and-loss table.

Decisions	Circumstances		
	c_1	c_2	c_3
d_1	−7	8	12
d_2	−8	7	14
d_3	5	6	8

The maximin rule requires that we make the third decision. For in this case the worst that can happen is that one gains five hundred dollars, which is better than the worst for the other actions. If we adopt one of these we may lose either eight or seven hundred dollars. Thus, the choice of d_3 maximizes $f(d,c)$ for that value of c, which for a given d, minimizes f. The term "maximin" means the *maximum minimorum;* and the rule directs our attention to the worst that can happen under any proposed course of action, and to decide in the light of that.

10. Here I borrow from William Fellner, *Probability and Profit* (Homewood, Ill., R. D. Irwin, Inc., 1965), pp. 140–142, where these features are noted.

DISCUSSION QUESTIONS:

1. Might different people be such that different principles of justice capture their judgments of justice in reflective equilibrium? If so, in what way does the (assumed) fact that Rawls' principles capture our judgments in reflective equilibrium give us a good reason to believe them?

2. Rawls describes the conditions that define the original position as ones that "we are prepared to regard as limits on the fair terms of cooperation." Is he correct?

3. Suppose we were to modify the original position, say by removing the veil of ignorance and changing the motivation of the parties to a desire for social relations that maximize the common good. What principles of justice, if any, would the parties select?

4. Is Rawls correct that the maximin strategy is the correct one for parties in the original position to use and that it will lead them to choose his principles of justice?

5. Rawls notes that, under his principles of justice, the higher expectations of those better situated are justified only if they help improve the expectations of the least advantaged. Is this implication of his principles correct?

6. Rawls formulates his principles of justice as principles for the distribution of primary social goods by a combination of social institutions, the basic structure of society. Are the primary social goods, as he explains them, distributed by a combination of social institutions?

Argument Reconstruction Exercises:

I. Rawls argues that his two principles of justice characterize our considered judgments of justice in reflective equilibrium. Identify the premises and conclusion of this objection to his view.

> That Rawls' principles of justice characterize our considered judgments of justice in reflective equilibrium indicates that they capture our sense of justice. Analogously, that the members of some culture adopt a particular moral code upon consideration indicates that the moral code captures their general sense of morality. Yet, that that code captures their general sense of morality does not justify them in

concluding that it is correct, especially given that other cultures adopt different codes upon consideration. So too, that Rawls' principles capture our sense of justice does not justify us in concluding that they are correct.

II. One objection to Rawls' theory is that the original position is irrelevant to the justification of principles of justice because it is completely hypothetical. Identify the premises and conclusion of his response.

> The answer is that the conditions embodied in the description of the original position are ones we do in fact accept. Or if we do not, then perhaps we can be persuaded to do so by philosophical reflection. . . . These conditions express what we are prepared to regard as limits on fair terms of social cooperation. (page 285)

III. Rawls' principles of justice will require that any inequalities in primary social goods, including income and wealth, work to the benefit of the least advantaged. It seems that, to meet this standard, the basic structure will either have to restrict individuals' economic activities or redistribute the benefits they gain from those activities. Identify the premises and conclusion of this objection to Rawls' theory:

> To meet Rawls' demands of justice on a continual basis, a society must either restrict individuals' economic activities or redistribute the benefits they gain from those activities. Such restrictions on their activities will violate their right to liberty, and such redistribution of the benefits of their activities will violate their right to property. The demands of Rawls' theory can only be met through the violation of individual rights. His theory is, therefore, incorrect.

IV. Rawls admits that those who are better off in a society may well have a legitimate claim to their goods, whether or not their good fortune benefits the least advantaged, but he distinguishes between this kind of entitlement and the form of justice that interests him. Identify the premises and conclusion in his reasoning.

> [T]he more fortunate have title to their better situation; their claims are legitimate expectations established by social institutions and the community is

obligated to fulfill them. But this sense of desert is that of entitlement. It presupposes the existence of an ongoing cooperative scheme and is irrelevant

to the question whether this scheme itself is to be designed in accordance with the difference principle or some other criterion. (page 289)

12.6 NON-CONTRACTUAL SOCIETY: A FEMINIST VIEW

VIRGINIA HELD (1987)

Virginia Held is Distinguished Professor of Philosophy at the City University of New York, Graduate School, and Professor Emerita of Philosophy and Women's Studies at Hunter College; she is especially known for her work in social and political philosophy and feminist ethics. She here offers a feminist critique of a contractual model of human relations. In a contractual model, human relations are understood in terms of agreements between rational, self-interested individuals. Labeling this perspective the model of "economic man," Held offers an alternative view that emphasizes the very different relationship between a mothering person and child. According to Held, this alternative model is more appropriate than the contractual model for understanding the moral aspects of many social relations and it highlights important dimensions of morality that the contractual model obscures.

Reading Questions:

1. What are the main elements of a contractual model for social relations?

2. What are the main elements of a mothering-person model for social relations?

3. What, according to Held, are the limitations of a contractual model?

4. According to Held, what aspects of our moral relations are obscured by a contractual model but highlighted by a mothering-person model?

Rational Contractors and Mothering Persons

Contemporary society is in the grip of contractual thinking. Realities are interpreted in contractual terms, and goals are formulated in terms of rational contracts. The leading current conceptions of

rationality begin with assumptions that human beings are independent, self-interested or mutually disinterested, individuals; they then typically argue that it is often rational for human beings to enter into contractual relationships with each other.

On the side of description, assumptions characteristic of a contractual view of human relations underlie the dominant attempts to view social realities through the lenses of the social sciences.[1] They also underlie the principles upon which most persons in contemporary Western society claim their most powerful institutions to be founded. We are told that modern democratic states rest on a social contract,[2] that their economies should be thought of as a free market where producers and consumers, employers and employees make contractual

This paper was first presented at a conference at Loyola University on April 18, 1983. It has also been discussed at philosophy department or women's studies colloquia at Hamilton and Dartmouth, at a conference on feminist theory at the University of Cincinnati, and at a conference on contractarianism at the University of Western Ontario. I am grateful to the many persons who have commented on the paper on these occasions, and also to Elise Boulding, Marsha Hanen, Kai Nielsen, Carole Pateman, Elizabeth Potter, and Sara Ruddick for additional comments.

agreements.³ And we should even, it is suggested, interpret our culture as a free market of ideas.⁴

On the side of prescription, leading theories of justice and equality such as those of Rawls, Nozick, and Dworkin, suggest what social arrangements should be like to more fully reflect the requirements of contractual rationality.⁵ And various philosophers claim that even morality itself is best understood in contractual terms.⁶ . . .

When subjected to examination, the assumptions and conceptions of contractual thinking seem highly questionable. As descriptions of reality they can be seriously misleading. Actual societies are the results of war, exploitation, racism, and patriarchy far more than of social contracts. Economic and political realities are the outcomes of economic strength triumphing over economic weakness more than of a free market. And rather than a free market of ideas, we have a culture in which the loudspeakers that are the mass media drown out the soft voices of free expression. As expressions of normative concern, moreover, contractual theories hold out an impoverished view of human aspiration.

To see contractual relations between self-interested or mutually disinterested individuals as constituting a paradigm of human relations is to take a certain historically specific conception of 'economic man' as representative of humanity. And it is, many feminists are beginning to agree, to overlook or to discount in very fundamental ways the experience of women.

I shall try in this paper to look at society from a thoroughly different point of view than that of economic man. I shall take the point of view of women, and especially of mothers, as the basis for trying to rethink society and its possible goals. Certainly there is no single point of view of women; the perspectives of women are potentially as diverse as those of men. But since the perspectives of women have all been to a large extent discounted, across the spectrum, I shall not try to deal here with diversity among such views, but rather to give voice to one possible feminist outlook. . . .

On the face of it, it seems plausible to take the relation between mother and child as *the* primary social relation, since before there could have been any self-sufficient, independent men in a hypothetical state of nature, there would have had to have

been mothers, and the children these men would have had to have been. And the argument could be developed in terms of a conceptual as well as a causal primacy. However, let me anticipate a likely reaction and say before I begin this exploration that I doubt that the view I am going to present is the one we should end up with. I doubt that we should take any one relation as paradigmatic for all the others. And I doubt that morality should be based on any one type of human relation. . . .

I am inclined at this point to think that we will continue to need conceptions of different types of relations for different domains, such as the domains of law, of economic activity, and of the family.

To think of relations between mothers and children as paradigmatic, however, may be an important stage to go through in reconstructing a view of human relationships that will be adequate from a feminist point of view. Since the image of rational economic man in contractual relations is pervasive in this society, and expanding constantly, it may be a useful endeavor to try to see everything in this different way, as if the primary social relation is that between mother and child, and as if all the others could and should be made over in the image of this one, or be embedded in a framework of such relations. *In any case, if we pay attention to this neglected relation between mother and child, perhaps we can put a stop to the imperialism of the model of economic man, and assert with conviction that at least there are some or perhaps many domains where this model is definitely not appropriate. And perhaps we can show that morality must be as relevant to, and moral theory as appropriately based on, the context of mothering as the context of contracting.*

Since it is the practice of mothering with which I shall be concerned in what follows, rather than with women in the biological sense, I shall use the term 'mothering person' rather than 'mother.' A 'mothering person' can be male or female. So I shall speak of 'mothering persons' in the same gender-neutral way that various writers now try to speak of 'rational contractors.' If men feel uncomfortable being referred to as, or even more so in being, 'mothering persons,' this may possibly mirror the discomfort many mothers feel adapting to the norms and practices, and language, of 'economic man.'

It is important to emphasize that I shall look at the practice of mothering not as it has in fact existed in any patriarchal society, but in terms of what the characteristic features of this practice would be without patriarchal domination. In method this may be comparable to what has been done in developing a concept of rational contracting. This concept of course developed while large segments of society were in fact still feudal, and of course actual human beings are not in fact fully rational. These realities have not prevented the contractual relation from being taken as paradigmatic. . . .

Human Mothering

. . .Human mothering is an extremely different activity from the mothering engaged in by other animals. It is as different from the mothering of other animals as is the work and speech of men different from the 'work' and 'speech' of other animals. Since humans are also animals, one should not exaggerate the differences between humans and other animals. But to whatever extent it is appropriate to recognize a difference between 'man' and other animals, so would it be appropriate to recognize a comparable difference between human mothering and the mothering of other animals.

Human mothering shapes language and culture, and forms human social personhood. Human mothering develops morality, it does not merely transmit techniques of survival; impressive as the latter can be, they do not have built into them the aims of morality. Human mothering teaches consideration for others based on moral concern; it does not merely follow and bring the child to follow instinctive tendency. *Human mothering creates autonomous persons; it does not merely propagate a species. It can be fully as creative an activity as most other human activities; to create new persons, and new types of persons, is surely as creative as to make new objects, products, or institutions.* Human mothering is no more 'natural' than any other human activity. It may include many dull and repetitive tasks, as does farming, industrial production, banking, and work in a laboratory. But degree of dullness has nothing to do with degree of 'naturalness.' In sum, human mothering is as different from animal mothering as humans are from animals. . . .

Clearly, the view that contractual relations are a model for human relations generally is especially unsuitable for considering the relations between mothering persons and children. It stretches credulity even further than most philosophers can tolerate to imagine babies as little rational calculators contracting with their mothers for care. Of course the fundamental contracts have always been thought of as hypothetical rather than real. But one cannot imagine hypothetical babies contracting either. And mothering persons, in their care of children, demonstrate hardly any of the 'trucking' or trading instinct claimed by Adam Smith to be the *most* characteristic aspect of human nature.[7] If the epitome of what it is to be human is thought to be a disposition to be a rational contractor, human persons creating other human persons through the processes of human mothering are overlooked. And human children developing human personhood are not recognized as engaged in a most obviously human activity.

David Hume, whom some admire for having moral views more compatible with 'women's moral sense' than most philosophers have had,[8] had the following to say about the passion of avarice: 'Avarice, or the desire of gain, is a universal passion which operates at all times, in all places, and upon all persons.'[9] Surely we can note that in the relation between mothering person and child, not only as it should be but often enough as it is, avarice is hard to find. One can uncover very many emotions in the relation, but the avarice that fuels the model of 'economic man' with his rational interest is not prominent among them.

There is an exchange in Charlotte Perkins Gilman's *Herland* that illustrates the contrast between the motives ascribed to rational economic man building contractual society, and those central to the practice of mothering. Herland is an imaginary society composed entirely of women. They reproduce by parthenogenesis, and there are only mothers and daughters in the society. Everything is arranged to benefit the next generation and the society has existed peacefully for hundreds of years, with a high level of technological advancement but without any conception of a 'survival of the fittest' ethic. Three young men from twentieth century America manage to get to Herland. They acknowledge that in Herland there are no wars, no kings, no priests, no aristocracies, that the women are all like sisters to each other and work together not by competition but by united action. But they argue that things are much better at home. In one exchange they try to explain how important it is to have competition. One of them expounds on the advantages of competition, on how it develops fine qualities, saying that 'without it there would be "no stimulus to industry."[10] He says competition is necessary to provide an incentive to work; 'competition,' he explains, 'is the motor power' of society.

The women of Herland are genuinely curious and good-naturedly skeptical, as they so often are in Gilman's novel. 'Do you mean,' they ask, 'that no mother would work for her children without the stimulus of competition?' In Herland, the entire, industrious society works on the strong motivation of making the society better for the children. As one women explains, 'The children in this country are the one center and focus of all our thoughts. Every step of our advance is always considered in its effects on them . . . You see, we are *Mothers*.'[11]

Of course, this is an idealized picture of mothering. But I am contrasting it with an idealized picture of rationally contracting. Quite probably we would not want a society devoted entirely to mothering. But then we might not want a society devoted entirely to better bargains either. In developing these suggestions, it is instructive to see what is most seriously overlooked by a contractual view of society, and to see how important what is overlooked is.

Family and Society

In recent years, many feminists have demanded that the principles of justice and freedom and equality on which it is claimed that democracy rests be extended to women and the family. They have demanded that women be treated as equals in the polity, in the workplace, and, finally, at home. They have demanded, in short, to be accorded full rights to enter freely the contractual relations of modern society. They have asked that these be extended to take in the family.

But some feminists are now considering whether the arguments should perhaps, instead, run the other way. Instead of importing into the household principles derived from the marketplace, perhaps we should export to the wider society the relations suitable for mothering persons and children. This approach suggests that just as relations between persons within the family should be based on concern and caring, rather than on egoistic or non-tuistic contracts, so various relations in the wider society should be characterized by more care and concern and openness and trust and human feeling than are the contractual bargains that have developed so far in political and economic life, or even than are aspired to in contractarian prescriptions. Then, the household instead of the marketplace might provide a model for society. . . .

The major question remains: what are the possibilities of remaking society by remaking what have been thought of as 'personal' relations? Societies are composed of persons in relation to one another. The 'personal' relations among persons are the most affective and influential in many ways. But the extent to which they are central to wider social relations, or could possibly provide a model for social and political relations of a kind that has been thought of as 'public,' remains an open question.

Western liberal democratic thought has been built on the concept of the 'individual' seen as a theoretically isolatable entity. This entity can assert interests, have rights, and enter into contractual relations with other entities. But this individual is not seen as related to other individuals in inextricable or intrinsic ways. This individual is assumed to be motivated primarily by a desire to pursue his own interests, though he can recognize the need to agree to contractual restraints on the ways everyone may pursue their interests. To the extent that groups have been dealt with at all, they have been treated *as* individuals.

The difficulties of developing trust and cooperation and society itself on the sands of self-interested individuals pursuing their own gain are extreme.[12] Contractual society is society perpetually in danger of breaking down. Perhaps what are needed for even adequate levels of social cohesion are persons tied together by relations of concern and caring and empathy and trust rather than merely by contracts it may be in their interests to disregard. Any enforcement mechanisms put in place to keep persons to their contracts will be as subject to disintegration as the contracts themselves; at some point contracts must be embedded in social relations that are non-contractual.

The relation between mothering person and child, hardly understandable in contractual terms, may be a more fundamental human relation, and a more promising one on which to build our recommendations for the future, than is any relation between rational contractors. Perhaps we should look to the relation between mothering person and child for suggestions of how better to describe such society as we now have. And perhaps we should look to it especially for a view of a future more fit for our children than a global battleground for rational, egoistic entities trying, somehow, to restrain their antagonisms by fragile contracts. . . .

The Mother/Child Relation

Let us examine in more detail the relation between mothering person and child. *A first aspect of the relation that we can note is the intent to which it is not voluntary and, for this reason among others, not contractual.* The ties that bind mothering person and child are affectional and solicitous on the one hand, and emotional and dependent on the other. The degree to which bearing and caring for children has been voluntary for most mothers throughout most of history has been extremely limited; it is still quite limited for most mothering persons. The relation *should* be voluntary for the mothering person but it cannot possibly be voluntary for the young child, and it can only become, gradually, slightly more voluntary.

A woman can have decided voluntarily to have a child, but once that decision has been made, she will never again be unaffected by the fact that she has brought this particular child into existence. And even if the decision to have a child is voluntary, the decision to have this particular child, for either parent, cannot be. Technological developments can continue to reduce the uncertainties of childbirth, but unpredictable aspects are likely to remain great for most parents. Unlike that contract where buyer and seller can know what is being exchanged, and which is void if the participants cannot know what they are agreeing to, a parent cannot know what a particular child will be like. And children are totally

unable to choose their parents and, for many years, any of their caretakers.

The recognition of how limited are the aspects of voluntariness in the relation between mothering person and child may help us to gain a closer approximation to reality in our understanding of most human relations, especially at a global level, than we can gain from imagining the purely voluntary trades entered into by rational economic contractors to be characteristic of human relations in other domains.

Society may impose certain reciprocal obligations: on parents to care for children when the children are young, and on children to care for parents when the parents are old. But if there is any element of a bargain in the relation between mothering person and child, it is very different from the bargain supposedly characteristic of the marketplace. If a parent thinks 'I'll take care of you now so you'll take care of me when I'm old,' it must be based, unlike the contracts of political and economic bargains, on enormous trust and on a virtual absence of enforcement.[13] And few mothering persons have any such exchange in mind when they engage in the activities of mothering. At least the bargain would only be resorted to when the callousness or poverty of the society made the plight of the old person desperate. This is demonstrated in survey after survey; old persons certainly hope not to have to be a burden on their children.[14] And they prefer social arrangements that will allow them to refuse to cash in on any such bargain. So the intention and goal of mothering is to give of one's care without obtaining a return of a self-interested kind. The emotional satisfaction of a mothering person is a satisfaction in the well-being and happiness of another human being, and a satisfaction in the health of the relation between the two persons, not the gain that results from an egoistic bargain. The motive behind the activity of mothering is thus entirely different from that behind a market transaction. And so is, perhaps even more clearly, the motive behind the child's project of growth and development.

A second aspect of the contrast between market relations and relations between mothering person and child is found in the qualities of permanence and non-replaceability. The market makes of everything, even human labor and artistic expression and sexual desire, a commodity to be bought and sold, with one unit of economic value replaceable by any other of equivalent value. To the extent that political life reflects these aspects of the market, politicians are replaceable and political influence is bought and sold. Though rights may be thought of as outside the economic market, in contractual thinking they are seen as inside the wider market of the social contract, and can be traded against each other. But the ties between parents and children are permanent ties, however strained or slack they become at times. And no person within a family should be a commodity to any other. Although various persons may participate in mothering a given child, and a given person may mother many children, still no child and no mothering person is to the other a merely replaceable commodity. The extent to which more of our attitudes, for instance toward our society's cultural productions, should be thought of in these terms rather than in the terms of the marketplace, should be considered.

A third aspect of the relation between mothering person and child that may be of interest is the insight it provides for our notions of equality. It shows us unmistakably that equality is not equivalent to having equal legal rights. All feminists are committed to equality and to equal rights in contexts where rights are what are appropriately at issue. But in many contexts, concerns other than rights are more salient and appropriate. And the equality that is at issue in the relation between mothering person and child is the equal consideration of persons, not a legal or contractual notion of equal rights.

Parents and children should not have equal rights in the sense that what they are entitled to decide or to do or to have should be the same. A family of several small children, an adult or two, and an aged parent should not for instance, make its decisions by majority vote in most cases.[15] But every member of a family is worthy of equal respect and consideration. Each person in a family is as important as a person as every other.

Sometimes the interests of children have been thought in some sense to count for more, justifying 'sacrificing for the children.' Certainly, the interests of mothers have often counted for less than those of either fathers or children. Increasingly, we may come to think that the interests of all should count equally, but we should recognize that this claim is appropriately invoked only if the issue should be thought of as one of interest. Often, it should not. Much of the time we can see that calculations of interest, and of equal interests, are as out of place as are determinations of equal rights. Both the rights and the interests of individuals seen as separate entities, and equality between them all, should not exhaust our moral concerns. The flourishing of shared joy, of mutual affection, of bonds of trust and hope between mothering persons and children can illustrate this as clearly as anything can. Harmony, love, and cooperation cannot be broken down into individual benefits or burdens. They are goals we ought to share and relations *between* persons. And although the degree of their intensity may be different, many and various relations *between* persons are important also at the level of communities or societies. We can consider, of a society, whether the relations between its members are trusting and mutually supportive, or suspicious and hostile. To focus only on contractual relations and the gains and losses of individuals obscures these often more important relational aspects of societies.

A fourth important feature of the relation between mothering person and child is that we obviously do not fulfil our obligations by merely leaving people alone. If one leaves an infant alone he will starve. If one leaves a two-year old alone she will rapidly harm herself. The whole tradition that sees respecting others as constituted by non-interference with them is most effectively shown up as inadequate. It assumes that people can fend for themselves and provide through their own initiatives and efforts what they need. This Robinson Crusoe image of 'economic man' is false for almost everyone, but it is totally and obviously false in the case of infants and children, and recognizing this can be salutary. It can lead us to see very vividly how unsatisfactory are those prevalent political views according to which we fulfil our obligations merely by refraining from interference. We ought to acknowledge that our fellow citizens, and fellow inhabitants of the globe, have moral rights to what they need to live—to the food, shelter, and medical care that are the necessary conditions of living and growing—and that when the resources exist for honoring such rights there are few excuses for not doing so. Such rights are not rights to be left to starve unimpeded. Seeing how unsatisfactory rights merely to be left alone are as an interpretation of the rights of children may help us to recognize a similar truth about other persons. And the arguments—though appropriately in a different form—can be repeated for interests as distinct from rights.[16]

A fifth interesting feature of the relation between mothering person and child is the very different view it provides of privacy. We come to see that to be in a position where others are *not* making demands on us is a rare luxury, not a normal state. To be a mothering person is to be subjected to the continual demands and needs of others. And to be a child is to be subjected to the continual demands and expectations of others. Both mothering persons and children need to extricate themselves from the thick and heavy social fabric in which they are entwined in order to enjoy any pockets of privacy at all.

Here the picture we form of our individuality and the concept we form of a 'self' is entirely different from the one we get if we start with the self-sufficient individual of the 'state of nature.' If we begin with the picture of rational contractor entering into agreements with others, the 'natural' condition is seen as one of individuality and privacy, and the problem is the building of society and government. From the point of view of the relation between mothering person and child, on the other hand, the problem is the reverse. The starting condition is an enveloping tie, and the problem is individuating oneself. The task is to carve out a gradually increasing measure of privacy in ways appropriate to a constantly shifting interdependency. For the child, the problem is to become gradually more independent. For the mothering person, the problem is to free oneself from an all-consuming involvement. For both, the progression is from society to greater individuality rather than from self-sufficient individuality to contractual ties. . . .

[W]e should expect that a new concept of 'self' or 'person' should have as much significance for our views of politics and society, and for our conceptualizations of the supposedly 'impersonal' and 'public' domain distinct from the supposedly 'personal' and 'private' sphere of the family, as has the concept of the self as rational calculator and the conceptualization of society as contractual. The same real 'persons' can act in and inhabit both marketplace and household contexts. It is open to them to decide what sorts of institutions to encourage for the sake of what sorts of persons.

A sixth aspect of the relation between mothering person and child which is noteworthy is the very different view of power it provides. We are accustomed to thinking of power as something that can be wielded by one person over another, as a means by which one person can bend another to his will. An ideal has been to equalize power so that agreements can be forged and conflicts defused. But consider now the very different view of power in the relation between mothering person and child. The superior power of the mothering person over the child is relatively useless for most of what the mothering person aims to achieve in bringing up the child. The mothering person seeks to *empower* the child to act responsibly, she neither wants to 'wield' power nor to defend herself against the power 'wielded' by the child. The relative powerlessness of the child is largely irrelevant to most of the project of growing up. When the child is physically weakest, as in infancy and illness, the child can 'command' the greatest amount of attention and care from the mothering person because of the seriousness of the child's needs.

The mothering person's stance is characteristically one of caring, of being vulnerable to the needs and pains of the child, and of fearing the loss of the child before the child is ready for independence. It is not characteristically a stance of domination. The child's project is one of developing, of gaining ever greater control over his or her own life, of relying on the mothering person rather than of submitting to superior strength. Of course the relation may in a degenerate form be one of domination and submission, but this only indicates that the relation is not what it should be. In a form in which the relation between mothering person and child is even adequately exemplified, the conceptions of power with which we are familiar, from Hobbes and Locke to Hegel and Marx, are of little use for understanding the aspects of power involved in the relation.[17] The power of a mothering person to empower others, to foster transformative growth, is a different sort of power than that of a stronger sword or dominant will. And the power of a child to call forth tenderness and care is perhaps more different still.

Mothering and Moral Theory

A final aspect of the relation between mothering person and child about which I would like to speculate is what a focus on this relation might imply for our views of morality itself, and of ethical theory itself. . . .

Mothering persons are vulnerable to the demands and needs of children. We do not know if this is instinctive or innate, or not. Some claim that women lack a mothering instinct. Others claim that the experiences of carrying a child, of laboring and suffering to give birth, of suckling, inevitably cause mothers to be especially sensitive to the cries and needs of a child. Others claim that fathers, placed in the position of being the only persons capable of responding to the needs of a child, develop similar responsiveness. Whatever the truth, one can admit that *no one can become a mothering person without becoming sensitive to the needs of relatively helpless or less powerful others*. And to become thus sensitive is to become vulnerable. If the vulnerability is chosen, so much the better. Mothering persons become in this way vulnerable to the claims of morality.

It is not, however, the morality of following abstract, universal rules so much as the morality of being responsive to the needs of actual, particular others in relations with us. The traditional view, reasserted in the psychological studies of Lawrence Kohlberg, that women are less likely than men to be guided by the highest forms of morality, would only be plausible if morality were no more than the abstract and rational rules of pure and perfect principle.[18] For traditional morality, increasingly recognizable as developed from a male point of view, there seems to be either the pure principle of the rational law-giver, or the self-interest of the individual contractor. There is the unreal universality of *all*, or the real *self* of individual interest.

Both views, however, lose sight of acting *for* particular others in actual contexts. Mothering persons cannot lose sight of the particularity of the child being mothered nor of the actuality of the circumstances in which the activity is taking place.

Mothering persons may tend to resist harming or sacrificing those particular others for the sake of abstract principles or total faith; on the other hand, it is for the sake of *others,* or for the sake of relationships between persons, rather than to further their own interests, that such resistance is presented by mothering persons. *Morality, for mothering persons, must guide us in our relations with actual, particular children, enabling them to develop their own lives and commitments. For mothering persons, morality can never seem adequate if it offers no more than ideal rules for hypothetical situations: morality must connect with the actual context of real particular others in need. At the same time, morality, for mothering persons, cannot possibly be a mere bargain between rational contractors. That morality in this context could not be based on self-interest or mutual disinterest directly is obvious; that a contractual escape is unavailable or inappropriate is clear enough.*

The morality that could offer guidance for those engaged in mothering might be a superior morality to those available at present. It would be a morality based on caring and concern for actual human others, and it would have to recognize the limitations of both egoism and perfect justice.[19] When we would turn to the social and political theories that would be compatible with such a view of morality, we would see that they would have to be very different not only from the patriarchial models of pre-contractual conceptions, but also from the contractual models that so dominate current thinking. Contractual relations would not be ruled out, but they would cease to seem paradigmatic of human relations, and the regions within which they could be thought to be justified would be greatly reduced.

The Child's Perspective

What about the point of view of the child? *A most salient characteristic of the relation between mothering person and child is the child's relative powerlessness. . . .*

The child in relation to the mothering person is permanently in the best possible position from which to recognize that right is *not* equivalent to might, that power, including the power to teach and enforce a given morality, is not equivalent to morality itself.

Becoming a person is not so much learning a morality that is being taught as it is developing the ability to decide for oneself what morality requires of one. Children characteristically go beyond the mothering persons in their lives, becoming autonomous beings. They do not characteristically then respond to the mothering persons they leave behind with proposals for better bargains for themselves now that they have the power to enforce their terms. The relation between mothering person and child is such that disparities of power are given. Though the positions may reverse themselves, unequal power is almost ever-present. But it is often also irrelevant to the relation.

When young men are invited to enter the public realm of contractual relations they are encouraged to forget their past lack of power and to assume a position of equality or superiority. But we should probably none of us ever forget what it is like to lack power. Taking the relation between child and mothering person as the primary social relation might encourage us to remember the point of view of those who cannot rely on the power of arms to uphold their moral claims. It might remind us of the distinction between the morality that, as developed autonomous persons, we come to construct for ourselves, and the moral injunctions which those with superior force can hold us to. Though I cannot develop these suggestions further in this particular paper, *much* more needs to be felt from the point of view of children.

Models for Society

. . .There are good reasons to believe that a society resting on no more than bargains between self-interested or mutually disinterested individuals will not be able to withstand the forces of egoism and dissolution pulling such societies apart. Although there may be some limited domains in which rational contracts are the appropriate form of social relations, as a foundation for the fundamental ties which ought to bind human beings together, they are clearly inadequate. Perhaps we can learn from a non-patriarchal household better than from further searching in the marketplace what the sources might be for justifiable trust, cooperation, and caring.

On the first occasion when I spoke about considering the relation between mothering person and child as the primary social relation, a young man in the audience asked: but in society, by which he meant society outside the family, who are the mothers and who are the children? It was meant as a hostile question, but it is actually a very good question. The very difficulty so many persons have in imagining an answer may indicate how distorted are the traditional contractual conceptions. Such persons can imagine human society on the model of 'economic man,' society built on a contract between rationally self-interested persons, because these are the theories they have been brought up with. But they cannot imagine society resembling a group of persons tied together by on-going relations of caring and trust between persons in positions such as those of mothers and children where, as adults, we would sometimes be one and sometimes the other. Suppose now we ask: in the relation between mothering person and child, who are the contractors? Where is the rational self-interest? The model of 'economic man' makes no sense in this context. Anyone in the social contract tradition who has noticed the relation of mothering person and child at all has supposed it to belong to some domain outside the realm of the 'free market' and outside the 'public' realm of politics and the law. Such theorists have supposed the context of mothering to be of much less significance for human history and of much less relevance for moral theory than the realms of trade and government, or they have imagined mothers and children as somehow outside human society altogether in a region labelled 'nature,' and engaged wholly in 'reproduction.' But mothering is at the heart of human society.

If the dynamic relation between mothering person and child is taken as the primary social relation, then it is the model of 'economic man' that can be seen to be deficient as a model for society and morality, and unsuitable for all but a special context. A domain such as law, if built on no more than contractual foundations, can then be recognized as one limited domain among others; law protects some moral rights when people are too immoral or weak to respect them without the force of law. But it is hardly a majestic edifice that can serve as a model for morality. Neither can the domain of politics, if built on no more than self-interest or mutual disinterest, provide us with a model with which to understand

and improve society and morality. And neither, even more clearly, can the market itself.

When we explore the implications of these speculations we may come to realize that instead of seeing the family as an anomalous island in a sea of rational contracts composing economic and political and social life, perhaps it is instead 'economic man' who belongs on a relatively small island surrounded by social ties of a less hostile, cold, and precarious kind.

NOTES

1. As Carole Pateman writes, 'One of the most striking features of the past two decades is the extent to which the assumptions of liberal individualism have permeated the whole of social life.' Carole Pateman, *The Problem of Political Obligation: A Critique of Liberal Theory* (Berkeley: University of California Press 1985), 182-3. All those fields influenced by rational choice theory—and that includes most of the social sciences—thus 'hark back to classical liberal contract doctrines,' Pateman writes, 'and claims that social order is founded on the interactions of self-interested, utility-maximizing individuals, protecting and enlarging their property in the capitalist market' (183).
2. E.g. Thomas Hobbes, *Leviathan*, C.B. Macpherson, ed. (Baltimore: Penguin 1971); John Locke, *Two Treatises of Government*, Peter Laslett, ed. (New York: Mentor 1965); Jean-Jacques Rousseau, *The Social Contract*, Charles Frankel, ed. (New York: Hafner 1947); The U. S. Declaration of Independence; and of course a literature too vast to mention. As Carole Pateman writes of this tradition, 'a corollary of the liberal view . . . is that social contract theory is central to liberalism. Paradigmatically, contract is the act through which two free and equal individuals create social bonds, or a collection of such individuals creates the state' (180).
3. E.g. Adam Smith, *The Wealth of Nations*, M. Lerner, ed. (New York: Random House 1937) and virtually the whole of classical and neo-classical economics.
4. The phrase has been entrenched in judicial and social discussion since Oliver Wendell Holmes used it in *Abrams v. United States* (250 U.S. 616, 630 [1919]).
5. E.g. John Rawls, *A Theory of Justice* (Cambridge, MA: Harvard University Press 1971); Robert Nozick, *Anarchy, State, and Utopia* (New York: Basic Books 1974); and Ronald Dworkin, *Taking Rights Seriously* (Cambridge, MA: Harvard University Press 1977).
6. E.g. David A. J. Richards, *A Theory of Reasons for Action* (New York: Oxford University Press 1971); and David Gauthier, *Morals by Agreement* (New York: Oxford University Press 1986).
7. Adam Smith, Book I, Chap. II

8. See, e.g., Annette Baier, 'Hume: The Women's Moral Theorist?' in *Women and Moral Theory*, Eva Kittay and Diana Meyers, eds. (Totowa, NJ: Rowman and Littlefield 1986).
9. David Hume, *Essays Moral, Political, and Literary*, vol. 1, Green and T.H. Grose, eds. (London: Longmans 1898), 176
10. Charlotte Perkins Gilman, *Herland* (New York: Pantheon 1979), 60; orginally publ. 1915
11. Ibid., 66
12. See especially Virginia Held, *Rights and Goods Justifying Social Action* (New York: Free Press/Macmillan 1984) chapter 5.
13. In some societies, social pressures to conform with the norms of reciprocal care—of children by parents and later of parents by children—can be very great. But these societies are usually of a kind which are thought to be at a stage of development antecedent to that of contractual society.
14. The gerontologist Elaine Brody says about old people that 'what we hear over and over again—and I'm talking gross numbers of 80 to 90 percent in survey after survey—is "I don't want to be a burden on my children."' Interview by Lindsy Van Gelder, *Ms.* Magazine (January 1986), 48.
15. For a different view see Howard Cohen, *Equal Rights for Children* (Totowa, NJ: Littlefield, Adams 1980)
16. See Virginia Held, *Rights and Goods Justifying Social Action.* (New York: Free Press/Macmillan, 1984)
17. For related discussions, see Nancy Hartsock, *Money, Sex, and Power: Toward a Feminist Historical Materialism* (New York: Longmans 1983); and Sara Ruddick, 'Maternal Thinking,' in Trebilcot, *Mothering.*
18. For examples of the view that women are more deficient than men in understanding morality and acting morally, see e.g. Mary Mahowald, ed., *Philosophy of Woman: Classical to Current Concepts* (Indianapolis: Hackett 1978). See also Lawrence Kohlberg, *The Philosophy of Moral Development* (San Francisco: Harper and Row 1981), and L. Kohlberg and R. Kramer, 'Continuities and Discontinuities in Child and Adult Moral Development,' *Human Development* 12 (1969) 93–120.
19. For further discussion, see Virginia Held, 'Feminism and Moral Theory,' in *Women and Moral Theory*, Eva Kittay and Diana Meyers, eds. (Totowa, NJ: Rowman & Littlefield 1987)

DISCUSSION QUESTIONS:

1. Does the contractual model obscure or at least neglect any important moral aspects of our relations with others (e.g., our relations with children or others in our care, our relation to future generations, our relation to the environment)?
2. Does the mothering-person model, as described by Held, obscure or misrepresent any important moral aspects of our relations with others (e.g., our relations with others to whom we have made no commitments)?

3. Held expresses the "doubt that morality should be based on any one type of human relation" and suggests that "we will continue to need conceptions of different types of relations for different domains, such as the domains of law, of economic activity, and of the family" (page 296). Are there particular domains (types of activity) for which the contractual model is appropriate? Are there particular ones for which the mothering-person model is appropriate? Are there domains for which neither of these models is especially well suited?

Argument Reconstruction Exercises:

I. Held takes the contractual model to be clearly unsuitable for understanding the relation between mothering persons and children. Identify the premises and conclusion of her argument.

> It stretches credulity even further than most philosophers can tolerate to imagine babies as little rational contractors contracting with their mothers for care. . . . [O]ne cannot imagine hypothetical babies contracting either. And mothering persons, in their care of children, demonstrate hardly any of the "trucking" or trading instinct claimed by Adam Smith to be the *most* characteristic aspect of human nature. (page 297)

II. Held argues that the contractual model ignores important moral relations between persons. Identify the premises and conclusion of the following argument.

> Harmony, love, and cooperation cannot be broken down into individual benefits or burdens. They are goals we ought to share and relations *between* persons. And although the degree of their intensity may be different, many and various relations *between* persons are important also at the level of communities and societies. We can consider, of a society, whether the relations between its members are trusting and

mutually supportive, or suspicious and hostile. To focus only on contractual relations and the gains and losses of individuals obscures these often more important relational aspects of societies. (page 300)

III. Held argues that the contractual model of morality does not provide an adequate basis for lasting social relationships. Identify the premises and conclusion in her reasoning.

> The difficulties of developing trust and cooperation and society itself on the sands of self-interested individuals pursuing their own gain are extreme. Contractual society is society perpetually in danger of breaking down. Perhaps what are needed for even adequate levels of social cohesion are persons tied together by relations of caring and empathy and trust rather than merely by contracts it may be in their interests to disregard. Any enforcement mechanisms put in place to keep persons to their contracts will be subject to disintegration as the contracts themselves; at some point contracts must be embedded in social relations that are non-contractual. (pages 298–299)

IV. Held claims that the model of mothering persons helps us appreciate the dimensions of our duty to respect others. Identify the premises of conclusion in her reasoning.

> [An] important feature of the relation between mothering person and child is that we obviously do not fulfill our obligations by merely leaving people alone. If one leaves an infant alone he will starve. If one leaves a two-year-old alone, she will rapidly harm herself. The whole tradition that sees respecting others as constituted by non-interference with them is most effectively shown up as inadequate. It assumes that people can fend for themselves and provide through their own initiatives and efforts what they need. This Robinson Crusoe image of "economic man" is false for almost everyone. (page 300)

CHAPTER 13

Virtue and Care Ethics

It isn't enough to stand up and fight darkness. You've got to stand apart from it, too. You've got to be different from it.

—JIM BUTCHER, *FOOL MOON*

INTRODUCTION

In the last two chapters, we attempted to discover the essential difference between right and wrong action. According to **Consequentialists,** the only difference between right and wrong action is the consequence of an action. **Nonconsequentialists** deny this. Consequences may be important, but they're not the whole of the story. However in both cases, these views are focused on the moral quality of an *action*.

Doesn't this emphasis leave something out of morality? Perhaps it's not enough just to *do* something; perhaps morality demands that we *be* something. Suppose you meet someone who never acted wrongly but who was a miserable person nonetheless. This person desperately wants to act wickedly, but she changes her mind only at the last moment. She also hates the people around her and secretly enjoys the tragedies of others. Or suppose you meet someone who never acts wrongly only because she "blindly" follows her moral duty. If you ask her why she feeds her children, she would respond by telling you that she has a moral duty to do so. It's not because they are her children or because she loves them. She just feeds them because she is supposed to. That's all.

Many of us would feel that these people are the appropriate targets of moral criticism despite the fact that they don't technically act wrongly.

And this indicates that there is more to our normative moral scheme than merely evaluating states of affairs as good or bad and actions as right or wrong. Our moral concepts also appropriately target *people*. There is a moral difference between some character traits and others, some motivations and others, etc.

Virtue Ethics is a family of normative ethical theories that attempts to rectify this oversight. According to virtue theory, a person's character plays a crucial role in understanding the good life. Precisely how evaluations of persons are related to evaluations of actions and states of affairs is an open question. But what seems obvious enough is that this focus on character is important to the way many of us think about the world.

For example, think about when you've had to deliberate over a tough moral decision (e.g., whether or not to donate some of your resources to a worthy cause). It's unlikely that you thought about the issue by appealing to abstract principles like the one proposed by Kant (see Chapter 12.3). And it's unlikely that you tried to perform a utility calculus to figure out which action would bring about the most units of happiness for the most people (see Chapter 11.1). Instead, if you are like many of us, you probably asked yourself something like this: what would a really good person do in this situation? Some of us have our own particular paradigms of good people in mind: what would Jesus do? Or my grandmother? Or Gandhi?

Thinking about a moral problem this way focuses on people's character. But this isn't the only place character shows up in our thinking about morality. Think of some of the goals you've set for your own life. Surely some of those goals are character-related: you want to be known as a person of integrity, honesty, charity, etc. And just as we often define our own success in terms of character, we often define the failure of others in the same way: "he is so selfish" or "she is so unfaithful."

All of this shows that we are committed to evaluating persons and not just actions. Virtue theorists accommodate this fact by drawing a distinction between virtues and vices. A **virtue** is a trained disposition that produces morally good results, for example, honesty, courage, conscientiousness, etc. A **vice** is a trained disposition that produces morally bad results, for example, stinginess, cowardice, selfishness, etc.

Virtue theorists do not agree on a complete list of virtues and vices. And they do not agree on the exact nature of the relationship between virtues and human life. One promising proposal is that offered by Aristotle. Aristotle thinks of all things as having a purpose or a function. For example, the function of a knife is to cut well. Virtues are then defined in relation to this function. If something is a virtue, then it helps an object to achieve its function or goal. For example, a virtue of a knife is to be sharp. If this picture of virtue is correct, what is the function of human beings? And what character traits contribute to the execution of this function? These are questions that will be explored in the first selection of this chapter.

Another important question regards not merely defining virtues and vices but illustrating their relation to right action. Some philosophers posit a tight correlation among virtues, right action and good consequences. For example, the virtue of honesty corresponds with the duty to tell the truth which often results in the happiness of others. The virtue of faithfulness corresponds with the duty to be loyal which often results in the happiness of others. And so on.

However, despite the correspondence among these various elements, virtue theorists do not agree on the precise nature of the connection. Some seem to think of virtue theory as replacing normative views about right and wrong. One way to do so is to make virtue theoretically basic, which means that all other moral values can be defined in terms of virtue. For example, one might say that the right thing to do in a particular scenario *just is* whatever the perfectly virtuous person would do in that scenario. Indeed, Aristotle himself writes that, "actions, then, are called just and temperate when they are such as the just or temperate man would do."

Others reject this approach on the grounds that it invites charges of circularity. If we say that right action just is whatever the virtuous person would do, then how do we define the virtuous person? Here's one thing we can't say: it's the person whose character traits often result in right action. That would be circular. For this reason, some philosophers have argued that virtue theory should supplement, not replace, our other normative theories about right and wrong or good and bad. We should develop views about the moral goodness of particular character traits, motivations, etc. in tandem with our views about what makes an action right or wrong without making either sort of concept theoretically basic.

This chapter closes with a feminist suggestion that parallels that of the virtue theorist. The latter argue that mainstream views about right and wrong have sidelined the crucial role that character plays in our moral lives. Feminist philosophers have lodged a related complaint: mainstream views about right and wrong have sidelined the crucial role that emotions, relationships, and care play in our moral lives. The fact of the matter is that almost all of the historical figures who developed the mainstream views about right and wrong were men who lived in societies that systematically exploited and denigrated women. It would be nothing short of a miracle if the theoretical views that came out of such a time didn't, in some measure, reflect the biases of the time. Feminists argue that a cursory inspection of these views bears out this worry: each focuses on elements that are typically associated with men—an emphasis on reason rather than emotion, impartiality rather than special relationships, rights rather than duties, justice rather than care, etc.

Contemporary feminist philosophers attempt to rectify this oversight. In particular, they have offered two suggestions that are explored in the final essays of this chapter. The first suggestion is that context can alter our moral obligations. Where we are and who we have relationships with can change what it is we ought to do. The second suggestion is that emotions are morally important. Emotions may play an epistemic role by getting us to notice things about others (e.g., that someone is embarrassed) and ourselves (e.g., our guilty feelings help us to see that we've acted badly). Furthermore, emotions may help to motivate right action (e.g., your love for your children might motivate you to make a sacrifice on their behalf). Insofar as mainstream normative views about right and wrong do not acknowledge these features, they have missed crucial features of the moral life.

SUGGESTIONS FOR FURTHER READING

Blum, Lawrence. "Gilligan and Kohlberg: Implications for Moral Theory." *Ethics* 1988; 98(3):472–491.

Foot, Philippa. *Virtues and Vices.* (Oxford: Blackwell, 1978)

Gilligan, Carol. *In a Different Voice: Psychological Theory and Women's Development.* (Harvard University Press, 1993)

Grimshaw, Jean. "The Idea of a Female Ethic." *Philosophy East & West* 1992; 42(2): 221–238.

Held, Virginia. "Reason, Gender and Moral Theory." *Philosophy and Phenomenological Research*, 1990 Fall Supplement, pp. 321–344.

MacIntyre, Alasdair. *After Virtue: A Study in Moral Theory*, 3e. (South Bend: University of Notre Dame Press, 2007)

Noddings, Nel. *Caring: A Feminine Approach to Ethics and Moral Education.* (Berkeley: University of California Press, 2003)

Slote, Michael. "Agent-Based Virtue Ethics." *Midwest Studies in Philosophy* 1995; 20(1):83–101.

Urmson, J.O. *Aristotle's Ethics.* (Wiley-Blackwell, 1991)

13.1 VIRTUE

ARISTOTLE CIRCA 350 BCE, TRANSLATED BY W. D. ROSS (1925)

Aristotle is one of the three major thinkers of Classical Greece, along with Plato (his teacher) and Socrates. A prolific writer and teacher, including serving as tutor to Alexander the Great, Aristotle left behind an enormous corpus of work that shaped thought in both the Arab and the European worlds for much of the Middle Ages and Renaissance. This essay is an excerpt from the first two chapters of his primary work in normative ethics, entitled *Nicomachean Ethics*, a book named for his son, Nicomachus. In this excerpt, Aristotle argues that the supreme goal of human life is to be happy, and he describes the necessary conditions for living a happy life. Chief among these conditions is that we develop virtues that will help us to reach our goal, and he develops a theory of virtues in which they are states of character that cultivate moderation instead of extremes.

Reading Questions:

1. How does Aristotle define "the good"?

2. What does Aristotle say that all men agree on as the highest of all goods achievable by action?

3. How do the "vulgar" and "people of superior refinement" identify happiness?

4. Why does Aristotle think that happiness is humankind's chief good?

5. What is the function of a human?

6. What kind of "external goods" does Aristotle say that we need in order to be happy?

7. What are the two kinds of virtue?

8. What is the relation between an excess or deficiency in something and a virtue?

9. How does Aristotle define a moral virtue?

10. Why does Aristotle conclude that it is no easy task to be a good person?

BOOK I · THE GOOD FOR MAN

All Human Activities Aim at Some Good: Some Goods Subordinate to Others

Every art and every inquiry, and similarly every action and pursuit, is thought to aim at some good; and for this reason *the good has rightly been declared to be that at which all things aim.* But a certain difference is found among ends; some are activities, others are products apart from the activities that produce them. Where there are ends apart from the actions, it is the nature of the products to be better than the activities. Now, as there are many actions, arts, and sciences, their ends also are many; the end of the medical art is health, that of shipbuilding a vessel, that of strategy victory, that of economics wealth. But where such arts fall under a single capacity—as bridle-making and the other arts concerned with the equipment of horses fall under the art of riding, and this and every military action under strategy, in the same way other arts fall under yet others—in all of these the ends of the master arts

are to be preferred to all the subordinate ends; for it is for the sake of the former that the latter are pursued. It makes no difference whether the activities themselves are the ends of the actions, or something else apart from the activities, as in the case of the sciences just mentioned.

The Science of the Good for Man Is Politics

If, then, there is some end of the things we do, which we desire for its own sake (everything else being desired for the sake of this), and if we do not choose everything for the sake of something else (for at that rate the process would go on to infinity, so that our desire would be empty and vain), clearly this must be the good and the chief good. Will not the knowledge of it, then, have a great influence on life? Shall we not, like archers who have a mark to aim at, be more likely to hit upon what is right? If so, we must try, in outline at least, to determine what it is, and of which of the sciences or capacities it is the object. It would seem to belong to the most authoritative art and that which is most truly the master art. And politics appears to be of this nature. . . .

Translator's footnotes have been excised.

It Is Generally Agreed to be Happiness, But There Are Various Views as to what Happiness Is. What Is Required at the Start Is an Unreasoned Conviction about the Facts, Such as Is Produced by a Good Upbringing

Let us resume our inquiry and state, in view of the fact that all knowledge and every pursuit aims at some good, what it is that we say political science aims at and what is the highest of all goods achievable by action.

Verbally there is very general agreement; *for both the general run of men and people of superior refinement say that it is happiness, and identify living well and faring well with being happy*; but with regard to what happiness is they differ, and the many do not give the same account as the wise. For the former think it is some plain and obvious thing, like pleasure, wealth, or honour; they differ, however, from one another—and often even the same man identifies it with different things, with health when he is ill, with wealth when he is poor; but, conscious of their ignorance, they admire those who proclaim some great thing that is above their comprehension. Now some thought that apart from these many goods there is another which is good in itself and causes the goodness of all these as well. To examine all the opinions that have been held were perhaps somewhat fruitless; enough to examine those that are most prevalent or that seem to be arguable. . . .

Discussion of the Popular Views that the Good Is Pleasure, Honour, Wealth; A Fourth Kind of Life, That of Contemplation, Deferred for Future Discussion

. . .To judge from the lives that men lead, *most men, and men of the most vulgar type, seem (not without some ground) to identify the good, or happiness, with pleasure*; which is the reason why they love the life of enjoyment. *For there are, we may say, three prominent types of life–that just mentioned, the political, and thirdly the contemplative life.* Now the mass of mankind are evidently quite slavish in their tastes, preferring a life suitable to beasts, but they get some ground for their view from the fact that many of those in high places share the tastes of Sardanapallus. A consideration of the prominent types of life shows

that *people of superior refinement and of active disposition identify happiness with honour*; for this is, roughly speaking, the end of the political life. But it seems too superficial to be what we are looking for, since it is thought to depend on those who bestow honour rather than on him who receives it, but the good we divine to be something of one's own and not easily taken from one. Further, men seem to pursue honour in order that they may be assured of their merit; at least it is by men of practical wisdom that they seek to be honoured, and among those who know them, and on the ground of their virtue; clearly, then, according to them, at any rate, virtue is better. And perhaps one might even suppose this to be, rather than honour, the end of the political life. But even this appears somewhat incomplete; for possession of virtue seems actually compatible with being asleep, or with lifelong inactivity, and, further, with the greatest sufferings and misfortunes; but a man who was living so no one would call happy, unless he were maintaining a thesis at all costs. But enough of this; for the subject has been sufficiently treated even in the popular discussions. Third comes the contemplative life, which we shall consider later.

The life of money-making is one undertaken under compulsion, and wealth is evidently not the good we are seeking; for it is merely useful and for the sake of something else. And so one might rather take the aforenamed objects to be ends; for they are loved for themselves. But it is evident that not even these are ends; yet many arguments have been wasted on the support of them. Let us leave this subject, then. . . .

The Good Must Be Something Final and Self-Sufficient. Definition of Happiness Reached by Considering the Characteristic Function of Man

Let us again return to the good we are seeking, and ask what it can be. It seems different in different actions and arts; it is different in medicine, in strategy, and in the other arts likewise. *What then is the good of each? Surely that for whose sake everything else is done.* In medicine this is health, in strategy victory, in architecture a house, in any other sphere something else, and in every action and pursuit the end; for it is for the sake of this that all men do whatever else they do. *Therefore, if there is an end for all that we do, this will be the good achievable by action, and if there are more than one, these will be the goods achievable by action.*

So the argument has by a different course reached the same point; but we must try to state this even more clearly. Since there are evidently more than one end, and we choose some of these (e.g. wealth, flutes, and in general instruments) for the sake of something else, clearly not all ends are final ends; but *the chief good is evidently something final.* Therefore, if there is only one final end, this will be what we are seeking, and if there are more than one, the most final of these will be what we are seeking. Now we call that which is in itself worthy of pursuit more final than that which is worthy of pursuit for the sake of something else, and that which is never desirable for the sake of something else more final than the things that are desirable both in themselves and for the sake of that other thing, and therefore *we call final without qualification that which is always desirable in itself and never for the sake of something else.*

Now such a thing happiness, above all else, is held to be; for this we choose always for itself and never for the sake of something else, but honour, pleasure, reason, and every virtue we choose indeed for themselves (for if nothing resulted from them we should still choose each of them), but we choose them also for the sake of happiness, judging that through them we shall be happy. Happiness, on the other hand, no one chooses for the sake of these, nor, in general, for anything other than itself. . . .

Presumably, however, to say that happiness is the chief good seems a platitude, and a clearer account of what it is is still desired. This might perhaps be given, if we could first ascertain *the function of man.* For just as for a flute-player, a sculptor, or any artist, and, in general, for all things that have a function or activity, the good and the 'well' is thought to reside in the function, so would it seem to be for man, if he has a function. Have the carpenter, then, and the tanner certain functions or activities, and has man none? Is he born without a function? Or as eye, hand, foot, and in general each of the parts evidently has a function, may one lay it down that man similarly has a function apart from all these? What

then can this be? Life seems to belong even to plants, but *we are seeking what is peculiar to man.* Let us exclude, therefore, the life of nutrition and growth. Next there would be a life of perception, but it also seems to be shared even by the horse, the ox, and every animal. There remains, then, *an active life of the element that has a rational principle*; of this, one part has such a principle in the sense of being obedient to one, the other in the sense of possessing one and exercising thought. And, as 'life of the rational element' also has two meanings, we must state that life in the sense of activity is what we mean; for this seems to be the more proper sense of the term. Now if the function of man is an activity of soul which follows or implies a rational principle, and if we say 'a so-and-so' and 'a good so-and-so' have a function which is the same in kind, e.g. a lyre-player and a good lyre-player, and so without qualification in all cases, eminence in respect of goodness being added to the name of the function (for the function of a lyre-player is to play the lyre, and that of a good lyre-player is to do so well): if this is the case [and we state the function of man to be a certain kind of life, and this to be an activity or actions of the soul implying a rational principle, and the function of a good man to be the good and noble performance of these, and if any action is well performed when it is performed in accordance with the appropriate excellence: if this is the case], *human good turns out to be activity of soul exhibiting excellence, and if there are more than one excellence, in accordance with the best and most complete.*

But we must add 'in a complete life'. For one swallow does not make a summer, nor does one day; and so too one day, or a short time, does not make a man blessed and happy. . . .

Happiness then is the best, noblest, and most pleasant thing in the world, and these attributes are not severed as in the inscription at Delos—

> Most noble is that which is justest, and best is health;
> But most pleasant it is to win what we love.

For all these properties belong to the best activities; and these, or one—the best—of these, we identify with happiness.

Yet evidently, as we said, it needs the external goods as well; for it is impossible, or not easy, to do noble acts without the proper equipment. In many actions we use friends and riches and political power as instruments; and there are some things the lack of which takes the lustre from happiness—good birth, goodly children, beauty; for the man who is very ugly in appearance or ill-born or solitary and childless is not very likely to be happy, and perhaps a man would be still less likely if he had thoroughly bad children or friends or had lost good children or friends by death. As we said, then, happiness seems to need this sort of prosperity in addition; for which reason some identify happiness with good fortune, though others identify it with virtue. . . .

Division of the Faculties, and Resultant Division of Virtue into Intellectual and Moral

Since *happiness is an activity of soul in accordance with perfect virtue*, we must consider the nature of virtue; for perhaps we shall thus see better the nature of happiness. The true student of politics, too, is thought to have studied virtue above all things; for he wishes to make his fellow citizens good and obedient to the laws. As an example of this we have the lawgivers of the Cretans and the Spartans, and any others of the kind that there may have been. And if this inquiry belongs to political science, clearly the pursuit of it will be in accordance with our original plan. But clearly the virtue we must study is human virtue; for the good we were seeking was human good and the happiness human happiness. By human virtue we mean not that of the body but that of the soul; and happiness also we call an activity of soul. But if this is so, clearly the student of politics must know somehow the facts about the soul, as the man who is to heal the eyes must know about the whole body also; and all the more since political science is more prized and better than medical; but even among doctors the best educated spend much labour on acquiring knowledge of the body. The student of politics, then, must study the soul, and must study it with these objects in view, and do so just to the extent which is sufficient for the questions we are discussing; for further precision would perhaps involve more labour than our purposes require. . . .

Virtue is distinguished into kinds in accordance with this difference; for we say that some of the virtues are intellectual and others moral, philosophic wisdom and understanding and practical wisdom being intellectual, liberality and temperance moral. For in speaking about a man's character we do not say that he is wise or has understanding, but that he is good-tempered or temperate; yet we praise the wise man also with respect to his state of mind; and of states of mind we call those which merit praise virtues.

BOOK II · MORAL VIRTUE

Moral Virtue, Like the Arts, Is Acquired by Repetition of the Corresponding Acts

Virtue, then, being of two kinds, intellectual and moral, *intellectual virtue in the main owes, both its birth and its birth and its growth to teaching* (for which reason it requires experience and time), *while moral virtue comes about as a result of habit,* whence also its name (ἠθική) is one that is formed by a slight variation from the word ἔθος (habit). From this it is also plain that none of the moral virtues arises in us by nature; for nothing that exists by nature can form a habit contrary to its nature. For instance the stone which by nature moves downwards cannot be habituated to move upwards, not even if one tries to train it by throwing it up ten thousand times; nor can fire be habituated to move downwards, nor can anything else that by nature behaves in one way be trained to behave in another. *Neither by nature, then, nor contrary to nature do the virtues arise in us: rather we are adapted by nature to receive them, and are made perfect by habit.*

Again, of all the things that come to us by nature we first acquire the potentiality and later exhibit the activity (this is plain in the case of the senses; for it was not by often seeing or often hearing that we got these senses, but on the contrary we had them before we used them, and did not come to have them by using them); but the virtues we get by first exercising them, as also happens in the case of the arts as well. *For the things we have to learn before we can do them, we learn by doing them,* e.g. men become builders by building and lyre-players by playing the lyre; so too we become just by doing just acts, temperate by doing temperate acts, brave by doing brave acts.

This is confirmed by what happens in states; for legislators make the citizens good by forming habits in them, and this is the wish of every legislator, and those who do not effect it miss their mark, and it is in this that a good constitution differs from a bad one.

Again, it is from the same causes and by the same means that every virtue is both produced and destroyed, and similarly every art; for it is from playing the lyre that both good and bad lyre-players are produced. And the corresponding statement is true of builders and of all the rest; men will be good or bad builders as a result of building well or badly. For if this were not so, there would have been no need of a teacher, but all men would have been born good or bad at their craft. This, then, is the case with the virtues also; *by doing the acts that we do in our transactions with other men we become just or unjust*, and by doing the acts that we do in the presence of danger, and by being habituated to feel fear or confidence, we become brave or cowardly. The same is true of appetites and feelings of anger; some men become temperate and good-tempered, others self-indulgent and irascible, by behaving in one way or the other in the appropriate circumstances. Thus, in one word, *states of character arise out of like activities*. This is why the activities we exhibit must be of a certain kind; it is because the states of character correspond to the differences between these. It makes no small difference, then, whether we form habits of one kind or of another from our very youth; it makes a very great difference, or rather *all* the difference.

These Acts Cannot Be Prescribed Exactly, but Must Avoid Excess and Defect

Since, then, the present inquiry does not aim at theoretical knowledge like the others (for we are inquiring not in order to know what virtue is, but in order to become good, since otherwise our inquiry would have been of no use), we must examine the nature of actions, namely how we ought to do them; for these determine also the nature of the states of character that are produced, as we have said. . . .

But though our present account is of this nature we must give what help we can. First, then, let us consider this, that it is the nature of such things to be destroyed by defect and excess, as we see in the case of strength and of health (for to gain light on things imperceptible we must use the evidence of sensible things); exercise either excessive or defective destroys the strength, and similarly drink or food which is above or below a certain amount destroys the health, while that which is proportionate both produces and increases and preserves it. So too is it, then, in the case of temperance and courage and the other virtues. For the man who flies from and fears everything and does not stand his ground against anything becomes a coward, and the man who fears nothing at all but goes to meet every danger becomes rash; and similarly the man who indulges in every pleasure and abstains from none becomes self-indulgent, while the man who shuns every pleasure, as boors do, becomes in a way insensible; *temperance and courage, then, are destroyed by excess and defect, and preserved by the mean.*

But not only are the sources and causes of their origination and growth the same as those of their destruction, but also the sphere of their actualization will be the same; for this is also true of the things which are more evident to sense, e.g. of strength; it is produced by taking much food and undergoing much exertion, and it is the strong man that will be most able to do these things. So too is it with the virtues; by abstaining from pleasures we become temperate, and it is when we have become so that we are most able to abstain from them; and similarly too in the case of courage; for by being habituated to despise things that are fearful and to stand our ground against them we become brave, and it is when we have become so that we shall be most able to stand our ground against them. . . .

The Actions That Produce Moral Virtue Are not Good in the Same Sense as Those that Flow from It: The Latter Must Fulfill Certain Conditions not Necessary in the Case of the Arts

The question might be asked, what we mean by saying that we must become just by doing just acts, and temperate by doing temperate acts; for if men do just and temperate acts, they are already just and temperate, exactly as, if they do what is in accordance with the laws of grammar and of music, they are grammarians and musicians.

Or is this not true even of the arts? It is possible to do something that is in accordance with the laws of grammar, either by chance or under the guidance of another. A man will be a grammarian, then, only when he has both said something grammatical and said it grammatically; and this means doing it in accordance with the grammatical knowledge in himself.

Again, the case of the arts and that of the virtues are not similar; for the products of the arts have their goodness in themselves, so that it is enough that they should have a certain character, but if the acts that are in accordance with the virtues have themselves a certain character it does not follow that they are done justly or temperately. The agent also must be in a certain condition when he does them; in the first place he must have knowledge, secondly he must choose the acts, and choose them for their own sakes, and thirdly his action must proceed from a firm and unchangeable character. These are not reckoned in as conditions of the possession of the arts except the bare knowledge; but as a condition of the possession of the virtues knowledge has little or no weight, while the other conditions count not for a little but for everything, i.e. the very conditions which result from often doing just and temperate acts.

Actions, then, are called just and temperate when they are such as the just or the temperate man would do; but it is not the man who does these that is just and temperate, but the man who also does them *as* just and temperate men do them. It is well said, then, that it is by doing just acts that the just man is produced, and by doing temperate acts the temperate man; without doing these no one would have even a prospect of becoming good.

But most people do not do these, but take refuge in theory and think they are being philosophers and will become good in this way, behaving somewhat like patients who listen attentively to their doctors, but do none of the things they are ordered to do. As the latter will not be made well in body by such a course of treatment, the former will not be made well in soul by such a course of philosophy.

The Genus of Moral Virtue: It Is a State of Character, not a Passion, nor a Faculty

Next we must consider what virtue is. *Since things that are found in the soul are of three kinds—passions, faculties, states of character—virtue must be one of these.* By passions I mean, appetite, anger, fear, confidence, envy, joy, friendly feeling, hatred, longing, emulation, pity, and in general the feelings that are accompanied by pleasure or pain; by faculties the things in virtue of which we are said to be capable of feeling these, e.g. of becoming angry or being pained or feeling pity; by states of character the things in virtue of which we stand well or badly with reference to the passions, e.g. with reference to anger we stand badly if we feel it violently or too weakly, and well if we feel it moderately; and similarly with reference to the other passions.

Now neither the virtues nor the vices are *passions,* because we are not called good or bad on the ground of our passions, but are so called on the ground of our virtues and our vices, and because we are neither praised nor blamed for our passions (for the man who feels fear or anger is not praised, nor is the man who simply feels anger blamed, but the man who feels it in a certain way), but for our virtues and our vices we *are* praised or blamed.

Again, we feel anger and fear without choice, but the virtues are modes of choice or involve choice. Further, in respect of the passions we are said to be moved, but in respect of the virtues and the vices we are said not to be moved but to be disposed in a particular way.

For these reasons also they are not *faculties;* for we are neither called good or bad, nor praised or blamed, for the simple capacity of feeling the passions; again, we have the faculties by nature, but we are not made good or bad by nature; we have spoken of this before.

If, then, the virtues are neither passions nor faculties, all that remains is that they should be *states of character*.

Thus we have stated what virtue is in respect of its genus.

The Differentia of Moral Virtue: It Is a Disposition to Choose the Mean

We must, however, not only describe virtue as a state of character, but also say what sort of state it is.

We may remark, then, that every virtue or excellence both brings into good condition the thing of which it is the excellence and makes the work of that thing be done well; e.g. the excellence of the eye makes both the eye and its work good; for it is by the excellence of the eye that we see well. Similarly the excellence of the horse makes a horse both good in itself and good at running and at carrying its rider and at awaiting the attack of the enemy. Therefore, if this is true in every case, *the virtue of man also will be the state of character which makes a man good and which makes him do his own work well.*

How this is to happen we have stated already, but it will be made plain also by the following consideration of the specific nature of virtue. In everything that is continuous and divisible it is possible to take more, less, or an equal amount, and that either in terms of the thing itself or relatively to us; and the equal is an intermediate between excess and defect. By the intermediate in the object I mean that which is equidistant from each of the extremes, which is one and the same for all men; by the intermediate relatively to us that which is neither too much nor too little—and this is not one, nor the same for all. For instance, if ten is many and two is few, six is the intermediate, taken in terms of the object; for it exceeds and is exceeded by an equal amount; this is intermediate according to arithmetical proportion. But the intermediate relatively to us is not to be taken so; if ten pounds are too much for a particular person to eat and two too little, it does not follow that the trainer will order six pounds; for this also is perhaps too much for the person who is to take it, or too little—too little for Milo, too much for the beginner in athletic exercises. The same is true of running and wrestling. Thus a master of any art avoids excess and defect, but seeks the intermediate and chooses this—the intermediate not in the object but relatively to us.

If it is thus, then, that every art does its work well—by looking to the intermediate and judging its works by this standard (so that we often say of good works of art that it is not possible either to take away or to add anything, implying that excess and defect destroy the goodness of works of art, while the mean preserves it; and good artists, as we say, look to this in their work), and if, further, virtue is

more exact and better than any art, as nature also is, then *virtue must have the quality of aiming at the intermediate.* I mean moral virtue; for it is this that is concerned with passions and actions, and in these there is excess, defect, and the intermediate. For instance, both fear and confidence and appetite and anger and pity and in general pleasure and pain may be felt both too much and too little, and in both cases not well; but to feel them at the right times, with reference to the right objects, towards the right people, with the right motive, and in the right way, is what is both intermediate and best, and this is characteristic of virtue. Similarly with regard to actions also there is excess, defect, and the intermediate. Now virtue is concerned with passions and actions, in which excess is a form of failure, and so is defect, while the intermediate is praised and is a form of success; and being praised and being successful are both characteristics of virtue. *Therefore virtue is a kind of mean, since, as we have seen it aims at what is intermediate.*

Again, it is possible to fail in many ways (for evil belongs to the class of the unlimited, as the Pythagoreans conjectured, and good to that of the limited), while to succeed is possible only in one way (for which reason also one is easy and the other difficult—to miss the mark easy, to hit it difficult); for these reasons also, then, *excess and defect are characteristic of vice, and the mean of virtue;*

For men are good in but one way, but bad
  in many.

Virtue, then, is a state of character concerned with choice, lying in a mean, i.e. the mean relative to us, this being determined by a rational principle, and by that principle by which the man of practical wisdom would determine it. Now it is a mean between two vices, that which depends on excess and that which depends on defect; and again it is a mean because the vices respectively fall short of or exceed what is right in both passions and actions, while virtue both finds and chooses that which is intermediate. Hence in respect of what it is, i.e. the definition which states its essence, virtue is a mean, with regard to what is best and right an extreme.

But not every action nor every passion admits of a mean; for some have names that already imply badness, e.g. spite, shamelessness, envy, and in the case of actions adultery, theft, murder; for all of these and suchlike things imply by their names that they are themselves bad, and not the excesses or deficiencies of them. It is not possible, then, ever to be right with regard to them; one must always be wrong. Nor does goodness or badness with regard to such things depend on committing adultery with the right woman, at the right time, and in the right way, but simply to do any of them is to go wrong. It would be equally absurd, then, to expect that in unjust, cowardly, and voluptuous action there should be a mean, an excess, and a deficiency; for at that rate there would be a mean of excess and of deficiency, an excess of excess, and a deficiency of deficiency. But as there is no excess and deficiency of temperance and courage because what is intermediate is in a sense an extreme, so too of the actions we have mentioned there is no mean nor any excess and deficiency, but however they are done they are wrong; for in general there is neither a mean of excess and deficiency, nor excess and deficiency of a mean.

The Above Proposition Illustrated by Reference to Particular Virtues

We must, however, not only make this general statement, but also apply it to the individual facts. For among statements about conduct those which are general apply more widely, but those which are particular are more true, since conduct has to do with individual cases, and our statements must harmonize with the facts in these cases. We may take these cases from our table. With regard to feelings of fear and confidence **courage** is the mean; of the people who exceed, he who exceeds in fearlessness has no name (many of the states have no name), while the man who exceeds in confidence is rash, and he who exceeds in fear and falls short in confidence is a coward. With regard to pleasures and pains—not all of them, and not so much with regard to the pains—the mean is temperance, the excess self-indulgence. Persons deficient with regard to the pleasures are not often found; hence such persons also have received no name. But let us call them 'insensible'. With regard to giving and taking of money the mean is **liberality** the excess and the defect prodigality and meanness. In these actions people exceed and fall short in contrary ways; the prodigal exceeds in spending and falls short in taking, while the mean man exceeds in taking and falls short in spending. (At present we are giving a mere outline or summary, and are satisfied with this; later these states will be more exactly determined.) With regard to money there are also other dispositions—a mean, magnificence (for the magnificent man differs from the liberal man; the former deals with large sums, the latter with small ones), an excess, tastelessness and vulgarity, and a deficiency, niggardliness; these differ from the states opposed to liberality, and the mode of their difference will be stated later.

With regard to honour and dishonour the mean is **proper pride**, the excess is known as a sort of 'empty vanity', and the deficiency is undue humility; and as we said liberality was related to magnificence, differing from it by dealing with small sums, so there is a state similarly related to proper pride, being concerned with small honours while that is concerned with great. For it is possible to desire honour as one ought, and more than one ought, and less, and the man who exceeds in his desires is called ambitious, the man who falls short unambitious, while the intermediate person has no name. The dispositions also are nameless, except that that of the ambitious man is called ambition. Hence the people who are at the extremes lay claim to the middle place; and we ourselves sometimes call the intermediate person ambitious and sometimes unambitious, and sometimes praise the ambitious man and sometimes the unambitious. The reason of our doing this will be stated in what follows; but now let us speak of the remaining states according to the method which has been indicated.

With regard to anger also there is an excess, a deficiency, and a mean. Although they can scarcely be said to have names yet since we call the intermediate person **good-tempered** let us call the mean good temper; of the persons at the extremes let the one who exceeds be called irascible, and his vice irascibility, and the man who falls short an unirascible sort of person, and the deficiency unirascibility.

There are also three other means, which have a certain likeness to one another, but differ from one another: for they are all concerned with intercourse in words and actions, but differ in that one is concerned with truth in this sphere, the other two with pleasantness; and of this one kind is exhibited in giving amusement, the other in all the circumstances of life. We must therefore speak of these too, that we may the better see that in all things the mean is praiseworthy, and the extremes neither praiseworthy nor right, but worthy of blame. Now most of these states also have no names, but we must try, as in the other cases, to invent names ourselves so that we may be clear and easy to follow. With regard to truth, then, the intermediate is a truthful sort of person and the mean may be called **truthfulness**, while the pretence which exaggerates is boastfulness and the person characterized by it a boaster, and that which understates is mock modesty and the person characterized by it mock-modest. With regard to pleasantness in the giving of amusement the intermediate person is ready-witted and the disposition ready wit, the excess is buffoonery and the person characterized by it a buffoon, while the man who falls short is a sort of boor and his state is boorishness. With regard to the remaining kind of pleasantness, that which is exhibited in life in general, the man who is pleasant in the right way is friendly and the mean is friendliness, while the man who exceeds is an obsequious person if he has no end in view, a flatterer if he is aiming at his own advantage, and the man who falls short and is unpleasant in all circumstances is a quarrelsome and surly sort of person.

There are also means in the passions and concerned with the passions; since shame is not a virtue, and yet praise is extended to the modest man. For even in these matters one man is said to be intermediate, and another to exceed, as for instance the bashful man who is ashamed of everything; while he who falls short or is not ashamed of anything at all is shameless, and the intermediate person is modest. **Righteous indignation** is a mean between envy and spite, and these states are concerned with the pain and pleasure that are felt at the fortunes of our neighbours; the man who is characterized by righteous indignation is pained at undeserved good fortune, the envious man, going beyond him, is pained at all good fortune, and the spiteful man falls so far short of being pained that he even rejoices. But these states there will be an opportunity of describing elsewhere; with regard to justice, since it has not one simple meaning, we shall, after describing the other states, distinguish its two kinds and say how each of them is a mean; and similarly we shall treat also of the rational virtues.

The Extremes Are Opposed to Each Other and to the Mean

There are three kinds of disposition, then, two of them vices, involving excess and deficiency respectively, and one a virtue, viz. the mean, and all are in a sense opposed to all; for the extreme states are contrary both to the intermediate state and to each other, and the intermediate to the extremes; as the equal is greater relatively to the less, less relatively to the greater, so the middle states are excessive relatively to the deficiencies, deficient relatively to the excesses, both in passions and in actions. For the brave man appears rash relatively to the coward, and cowardly relatively to the rash man; and similarly the temperate man appears self-indulgent relatively to the insensible man, insensible relatively to the self-indulgent, and the liberal man prodigal relatively to the mean man, mean relatively to the prodigal. Hence also the people at the extremes push the intermediate man each over to the other, and the brave man is called rash by the coward, cowardly by the rash man, and correspondingly in the other cases.

These states being thus opposed to one another, the greatest contrariety is that of the extremes to each other, rather than to the intermediate; for these are further from each other than from the intermediate, as the great is further from the small and the small from the great than both are from the equal. Again, to the intermediate some extremes show a certain likeness, as that of rashness to courage and that of prodigality to liberality; but the extremes show the greatest unlikeness to each other; now contraries are defined as the things that are furthest from each other, so that things that are further apart are more contrary.

To the mean in some cases the deficiency, in some the excess, is more opposed; e.g. it is not rashness, which is an excess, but cowardice, which is a deficiency, that is more opposed to courage, and not insensibility, which is a deficiency, but self-indulgence, which is an excess, that is more opposed to temperance. This happens from two reasons, one being drawn from the thing itself; for because one extreme is nearer and liker to the intermediate, we oppose not this but rather its contrary to the intermediate. E.g., since rashness is thought liker and nearer to courage, and cowardice more unlike, we, oppose rather the latter to courage; for things that are, further from the intermediate are thought more contrary to it. This, then, is one cause, drawn from the thing itself; another is drawn from ourselves; for the things to which we ourselves more naturally tend seem more contrary to the intermediate. For instance, we ourselves tend more naturally to pleasures, and hence are more easily carried away towards self-indulgence than towards propriety. We describe as contrary to the mean, then, rather the directions in which we more often go to great lengths; and therefore self-indulgence, which is an excess, is the more contrary to temperance.

The Mean Is Hard to Attain, and Is Grasped by Perception, not by Reasoning

That moral virtue is a mean, then, and in what sense it is so, and that it is a mean between two vices, the one involving excess, the other deficiency, and that it is such because its character is to aim at what is intermediate in passions and in actions, has been sufficiently stated. Hence also *it is no easy task to be good.* For in everything it is no easy task to find the middle, e.g. to find the middle of a circle is not for everyone but for him who knows; so, too, anyone can get angry—that is easy—or give or spend money; but to do this to the right person, to the right extent, at the right time, with. the right motive, and in the right way, *that* is not for everyone, nor is it easy; wherefore goodness is both rare and laudable and noble.

Hence he who aims at the intermediate must first depart from what is the more contrary to it, as Calypso advises—

Hold the ship out beyond that surf and spray.

For of the extremes one is more erroneous, one less so: therefore, since to hit the mean is hard in the extreme, we must as a second best, as people say, take the least of the evils; and this will be done best in the way we describe.

But we must consider the things towards which we ourselves also are easily carried away; for some of us tend to one thing, some to another; and this will be recognizable from the pleasure and the pain we feel. We must drag ourselves away to the contrary extreme; for we shall get into the intermediate state by drawing well away from error, as people do in straightening sticks that are bent.

Now in everything the pleasant or pleasure is most to be guarded against; for we do not judge it impartially. We ought, then, to feel towards pleasure as the elders of the people felt towards Helen, and in all circumstances repeat their saying; for if we dismiss pleasure thus we are less likely to go astray. It is by doing this, then, (to sum the matter up) that we shall best be able to hit the mean.

But this is no doubt difficult, and especially in individual cases; for it is not easy to determine both how and with whom and on what provocation and how long one should be angry; for we too sometimes praise those who fall short and call them good-tempered, but sometimes we praise those who get angry and call them manly.

The man, however, who deviates little from goodness is not blamed, whether he do so in the direction of the more or of the less, but only the man who deviates more widely; for *he* does not fail to be noticed. But up to what point and to what extent a man must deviate before he becomes blameworthy it is not easy to determine by reasoning, any more than anything else that is perceived by the senses; such things depend on particular facts, and the decision rests with perception. So much, then, is plain, that the intermediate state is in all things to be praised, but that we must incline sometimes towards the excess, sometimes towards the deficiency; for so shall we most easily hit the mean and what is right.

DISCUSSION QUESTIONS:

1. Aristotle says that we need "external goods" in order to be happy. For example, he says that we need friends, riches, political power, good birth, prosperity, etc. If this is true, then it's not ultimately up to us whether or not we achieve happiness. That's because it's not ultimately up to us whether or not we have friends, are rich, etc. Is Aristotle right about this? If you think he's wrong, would you be willing to say that anyone can be happy regardless of circumstance?

2. Aristotle defines virtues as the mean between extremes. For example, the virtue of courage has an excess on "both sides": one could have too little and thus be cowardly or one could have too much and thus be rash. Is this true for all virtues? Can you think of a virtuous character trait that one cannot have too much or too little of?

3. Aristotle closes this excerpt with advice for those of us who fail to meet the intermediate virtue but instead tend toward the extremes: "We must drag ourselves away to the contrary extreme; for we shall get into the intermediate state by drawing well away from error, as people do in straightening sticks that are bent" (page 318). What does this advice mean? Is Aristotle right about this? Can you think of a concrete example?

Argument Reconstruction Exercises:

I. Aristotle argues that there is only one chief good for mankind, and that is happiness. In this passage he argues that happiness is the only good that is "final without qualification." Identify the premises and conclusion in this excerpt:

> . . .the chief good is evidently something final. . . . we call final without qualification that which is always desirable in itself and never for the sake of something else. Now such a thing happiness, above all else, is held to be; for this we choose always for itself and never for the sake of something else, but honour, pleasure, reason, and every virtue we choose indeed for themselves (for if nothing resulted from them we should still choose each of them), but we choose them also for the sake of happiness, judging that through them we shall be happy. (page 311)

II. Aristotle argues that just as a flute-player or sculptor have functions, so, too, humankind has a function. He argues for a particular function by trying to isolate something that is unique to humankind. Identify the premises and conclusion in this excerpt:

> Presumably, however, to say that happiness is the chief good seems a platitude, and a clearer account of what it is is still desired. This might perhaps be given, if we could first ascertain the function of man. . . . What then can this be? Life seems to belong even to plants, but we are seeking what is peculiar to man. Let us exclude, therefore, the life of nutrition and growth. Next there would be a life of perception, but it also seems to be shared even by the horse, the ox, and every animal. There remains, then, an active life of the element that has rational principle. (page 311)

III. Aristotle argues that a virtue is a state of character. He does this by eliminating other possible candidates for virtue. Identify the premises and conclusion in the following excerpt:

> Next we must consider what a virtue is. Since things that are found in the soul are of three kinds— passions, faculties, states of character—virtue must be one of these. . . . Now neither the virtues nor the vices are passions, because we are not called good or bad on the ground of our passions. . . . For these reasons also they are not faculties; for we are neither called good or bad, nor praised or blamed, for the simple capacity of feeling the passions; again, we have the faculties by nature, but we are not made good or bad by nature; we have spoken of this before. If, then, the virtues are neither passions nor faculties, all that remains is that they should be states of character. (page 314)

IV. Not just any state of character is a virtue; some states of character are vices. Aristotle distinguishes between the two by their contribution to a human's function. Identify the premises and conclusion in the following excerpt.

> We must, however, not only describe virtue as a state of character, but also say what sort of state it is. We may remark, then, that every virtue or excellence both brings into good condition the thing of which it is the excellence and makes the work of that thing be done well; e.g. the excellence of the eye makes both the eye and its work good; for it is by the excellence of the eye that we see well. Similarly, the excellence of the horse makes a horse both good in itself and good at running and at carrying its rider and at awaiting the attack of the enemy. Therefore, if this is true in every case, the virtue of man also will be the state of character which makes a man good and which makes him do his own work well (pages 314–315)

13.2 ARISTOTLE ON VIRTUE

ROSALIND HURSTHOUSE (1986)

Rosalind Hursthouse is a professor at the University of Auckland in New Zealand. Most of her professional work is in the field of normative and applied ethics, and she is one of the world's foremost Aristotle scholars. In this essay, Hursthouse develops the basic outlines of a virtue theory as sketched by Aristotle in *Nicomachean Ethics*. She contrasts the modem moral philosophy approach to ethics with the virtue theory approach to ethics and shows how the answer to the central question of virtue ethics (How am I to live well?) is essentially connected with the moral virtues. Going further, she responds to two objections to virtue theory—namely, the objection that virtues are not sufficient for a good life and the objection that virtues are not necessary for the good life. She closes the essay with some thoughts on moral education and development.

Reading Questions:

1. What is the difference between how modem moral philosophers and ancient Greeks approached the issue of ethics?

2. According to Hursthouse, how should we understand the Greek concept of *eudaimonia*?

3. What is the difference between the materialistic and non-materialistic sense of success?

4. According to Hursthouse, what is the connection between the answer to the question "How am I to live?" and the moral virtues?

5. Why might generosity, honesty, and courage be important for a successful life?

6. What are the two objections to virtue theory that Hursthouse considers and how are they different from one another?

7. What is the connection between virtues and consequences?

8. According to Hursthouse, what kinds of things should we think about or remind ourselves of as we try to develop virtues in ourselves?

Our understanding of the moral philosophy of Aristotle is hampered by a number of modern assumptions we make about the subject.[1] For a start, we are accustomed to thinking about ethics or moral philosophy as being concerned with theoretical questions about actions—what makes an action right or wrong? Modern moral philosophy [claims that] what makes an action right or wrong is whether it promotes the greatest happiness, or whether it is in accordance with or violates a moral rule, or whether it promotes or violates a moral right. *But the ancient Greeks start with a totally different question. Ethics is supposed to answer, for each one of us, the question 'How am I to live well?'* What this question means calls for some discussion.

What Is the Question?

The question can be expressed in a variety of ways; none is perfect, but one comes to understand it by grasping the variety.

'How $\begin{Bmatrix} \text{Should} \\ \text{ought} \\ \text{Must} \end{Bmatrix}$ I live in order to $\begin{Bmatrix} \text{live the best life} \\ \text{flourish} \\ \text{be successful} \end{Bmatrix}$?'

The first comment which needs to be made is that one should not be misled by the presence of so-called 'value' words ('well', 'should', 'best', etc.) into thinking that these are specifically moral words. For then one will understand the question as 'How am I to live morally well?' 'What's the morally best life?' 'How should I live from the moral point of view?' And although, as we shall see, one would not be entirely wrong to do so, it is nevertheless not the proper understanding of the question. We should/must/ought not read in a 'morally' qualification, any more than we would at the beginning of this sentence. This point shows up particularly clearly in any versions of the question involving 'flourish' or 'be successful'. Compare 'How should this plant be treated in order that it will flourish?' and 'How ought I to study if I am to be a successful student?' where once again we wouldn't think that these were moral 'shoulds' or 'oughts'.

The next comment that needs to be made is also about these versions—about what is meant by 'flourish' and 'successful'. 'Flourishing' is one of the standard translations of the Greek word **eudaimonia**, a concept that beginning readers of Aristotle find hard to grasp. It is used in ways which lead us to translate it (when it is an abstract noun) as good fortune, happiness, prosperity, flourishing, success, the good/best life; where it is an adjective of a person as fortunate, happy, prospering, flourishing, successful, living well.[2] The extent to which any one of these is and is not an adequate translation can be seen by comparing what we say about them and what Aristotle says about **eudaimonia** in Book I. For a start, he tells us that it is what we all want to get in life (or get out of it); what we are all aiming at, ultimately (1094a1–26); the way we all want to be. And we all agree in one sense about what it consists in, namely, living well or faring well. But another truth about it is that we can disagree about what it consists in too, to the point where some of us can say it consists in wealth, others that it consists in pleasure or enjoyment and others that it consists of honour or virtue (1095a14–25).

What do we say about success and prospering? Well, 'successful' and 'prosperous' have a materialistic sense in which they connote wealth and power; when

we use them in this way it is obvious to us (a) that one can be happy and count oneself as fortunate without them and (b) that they do not necessarily bring with them happiness and the good fortune of loyal friends, loving relationships, the joys of art and learning and so on. So many of us will say that (material) success and prosperity is not what we want; that having it doesn't amount to faring well. But 'success' has a non-materialistic sense as well. Someone who possesses wealth and power may yet count her life to be not a success but a failure, perhaps because she finds herself to be lonely and lacking the conviction that anything she does is worthwhile. Similarly, someone who lacks wealth and power may still count their lives a success, thinking of themselves as rich in the things that matter. And it is the possibility of this non-materialistic sense of 'success' which makes it a suitable translation of 'eudaimonia'. Perhaps nowadays 'prosperous' can have only the materialistic sense—but the non-materialistic one still lurks in 'May you prosper', the wishes for a prosperous New Year, and indeed the non-materialistic use of 'rich' I just exploited. . . .

I said above that one of the truths that determines the concept of *eudaimonia* is that it is something everyone wants, the way everyone wants to be. Someone who said that she didn't want to be *eudaimon* would be incomprehensible. Some philosophers, for instance Mill, have maintained that this is true of happiness, and 'happiness' is certainly the most common translation that has been given. 'True (or real) happiness' would be better, since we tend to say that someone may be happy (though not truly happy) if they are living in a fool's paradise, or engaged in what we know is a fruitless activity, or brain damaged and leading the life of a happy child; whereas such people are not flourishing or leading successful lives and none of us would want to be that way.

But even 'true (or real) happiness' is not obviously something everyone wants—unless, as I am sure was true of Mill, one is already thinking of 'true happiness' *as eudaimonia*. For, thinking of (true) happiness as something like (well-founded) contentment or satisfaction or enjoyment one might intelligibly deny that one wanted to be happy. For surely one can think that happiness is not the most important thing in life—'We're not put on this earth to enjoy ourselves' people say. I might want not just to be happy, but to do great deeds, discover great truths, change the world for the better, no matter what it cost me in terms of happiness.

Of course, rather than saying 'no matter what it costs me in terms of happiness' I might say instead 'Then I would count myself as happy or content, no matter what it cost me'. This, I think, shows that *'happiness' does not have to connote bovine contentment or a life full of pleasure and free from striving and suffering*, and, as with 'success' above, it is the possibility of this second sense—happiness despite a lot of striving, effort and suffering—which makes it a suitable translation of '*eudaimonia*'.

Bearing all these points in mind, let us return to our question 'How am I to live well?' and its various versions—'How should/ought/must I live in order to flourish/be happy/successful?' We have seen that when 'success', 'happiness', etc., are construed in the intended way, this is a question any one of us is bound to be interested in because we all want to flourish/be happy/successful; the very idea that someone interested in life should not want to 'make a go of it' in this way is deeply puzzling.[3] This, one might say, contrasts with wanting to be *morally* successful or wanting to lead a morally good life—there is nothing puzzling about someone who doesn't want to do that. As we noted above, the 'should/ought/must' in the various versions of the question should not be given a particularly moral reading, any more than they would be in 'How should/ought I to live in order to be healthy?'

How Is This an Ethical Question?

So much for the discussion of what the question means. But now we are clear about that a new difficulty arises. *How can the question, understood in the right way, have anything to do with ethics?* If we understand it as asking 'How am I to live morally well?' we can see why it counts as a question for ethics to (try to) answer. But this interpretation is the one that has just been ruled out. It now seems to be an entirely self-seeking or egoistic question which has nothing to do with ethics.

Another obstacle we have in understanding the ancient Greek view of ethics is that it does not clearly embody the contrast—between the moral and the self-seeking or egoistic—which this new difficulty

relies on. But the obstacle may be surmounted by looking carefully at the answer Aristotle gives to this question that apparently has nothing to do with ethics. For his answer is: '*If you want to flourish/be happy/successful you should acquire and exercise the virtues—courage, temperance, liberality, patience, truthfulness, friendship, justice. . . .*'. Or, as we might say, be a morally virtuous person.[4] With this answer we are clearly back in the business of doing ethics—but how could this have come about when we started with the self-seeking or egoistic question?

The claim that is basic to Aristotle's view is that it comes about because *qua* human beings we naturally have certain emotions and tendencies and that it is simply a brute fact (made up of a vastly complex set of other facts) that *given that we are as we naturally are we can only flourish/be happy/successful by developing and exercising those character traits that are called the virtues—courage, justice, benevolence and so on*. For reasons that I shall go into later, Aristotle does not in fact give the argument for each such character trait, but it is worth briefly considering some examples as an illustration of (roughly) how the argument goes and what sorts of facts are relevant.

Take one of the simplest cases for us—**generosity**. Here are some of the relevant facts; we are naturally sociable creatures who like to have friends and want to be loved by friends and family. We also like and love people who do things for us rather than always putting themselves first. We also are not merely sympathetic but empathetic—the pleasure of others is pleasurable to us. Given that this is how we are, *someone who is mean and selfish is unlikely to be liked and loved and hence likely to be lonely and unhappy*; someone who is generous is likely to enjoy the benefits of being liked and loved and, moreover, in the exercise of their generosity will find much added enjoyment, for the pleasures of those they benefit will be pleasures to them.

Take another—**honesty**. Amongst the relevant facts there are some similar to the preceding ones—that we want friends, want them to be trustworthy, want them to trust us—and some that are rather different, for instance that there are likely to be occasions in our lives when we need to be believed—as the many fables on the theme of crying 'wolf' too often illustrate. Folk wisdom also contains the adage that 'honesty is the best policy' and the conviction that 'the truth will out' to the discomfort of those who have lied about it. The exercise of this virtue is not as immediately enjoyable as the exercise of generosity, but the honest person has the advantage of not having to keep a constant guard on her tongue and has peace of mind thereby. One should also note that the honest person can tell the truth effortlessly in circumstances in which doing so would be embarrassing, frightening, unpleasant or unfortunately impossible for the person who lacks the virtue. Literature abounds with scenes in which a character desperately needs to tell the truth for if she does not a profound relationship in her life is going to be destroyed—she will lose her lover, or her closest friend will feel betrayed, or her son will turn in bitterness from her, or she will put herself in the hands of the blackmailer or . . . to her subsequent irremediable regret and misery. But the truth in question is one of those truths it is hard to own up to—and she can't bring herself to do so. But had she armed herself with the virtue of honesty she would have been able to. Much more could be said here too about the harm one does oneself through self-deception and how difficult it is to be simultaneously ruthlessly honest with oneself but dishonest to other people.

Even more than honesty, **courage** is a character trait one needs to arm oneself with given that we are the sorts of creatures we are—subject to death and pain and frightened of them. It is not so much that we need courage to endure pain and face death as ends in themselves, but that we are likely to have to face the threat of pain or danger for the sake of some good that we shall otherwise lose. I read of someone who had the opportunity to save someone's life by donating bone marrow; one might see this as a wonderful opportunity but lack the courage to do it, to one's subsequent bitter regret. And how much worse the regret would be if one's cowardice led to the death of someone one loved. If I have managed to make myself courageous I am ready to save my child from the burning house at whatever risk to myself, to stand up to the terrorists who threaten my friends' lives and to my racist neighbours who are trying to hound me and my family from our home. In a society in which cancer has become one of the most common ways to die we also need courage to enable us to die well, not only so that we may not waste the last years or months of our lives but also for the sake of the people we love who love us.

All the above is schematic. I do not pretend to have shown conclusively that generosity, honesty and courage are necessarily part of flourishing or living well, and of course much of what I have said is open to detailed disagreement. I cannot go through many of the details here, but I will discuss one pair of objections that spring very naturally to mind, since the responses to them form part of the further exposition.

The two objections one wants to make are that, contrary to what has been claimed, *the virtues are surely neither sufficient nor necessary for living well.* Not sufficient because my generosity, honesty and courage (for example) might, any one of them, lead to my being harmed or indeed to my whole life being ruined or ended. Not necessary because, as we all know, the wicked may flourish like the green bay tree.

Objection 1: Virtue Is not Sufficient for Living Well

How do we envisage that my virtue might lead to my downfall? It is not quite right to say that it is obviously the case that, having the virtue of generosity I might fall foul of a lot of people who exploit me or find myself poverty-stricken. For built into each concept of a virtue is the idea of getting things *right*. (This is what distinguishes full virtue from natural virtue—see 1144b 1–17.) *In the case of generosity this involves giving the right things or amount for the right reasons on the right occasions to the right people. The right amount,* in many cases, would be *an amount I can afford* or *an amount I can give without depriving someone else.* So, for instance, I do not count as mean, or even ungenerous when, being relatively poor, or fairly well off but with a large and demanding family, I do not give lavish presents to richer friends at Christmas. *The right people* do not include the exploiters for I do not count as mean or ungenerous if I refuse to let people exploit me; moreover generosity does not require me to help support someone who is simply bone lazy, nor to finance the self-indulgence of a spendthrift. Any virtue may contrast with several vices or failings and generosity is to be contrasted not only with meanness or selfishness but also with being prodigal, too open-handed, a sucker.[5]

Once this point is borne in mind, examples in which I may suffer because of my virtue are harder to find. Nevertheless, there are some; sudden financial disaster might befall many of us, leaving the generous in dire straits where the mean do much better. Just as, in the past, people have been burnt at the stake for refusing to lie about what they believed, so now, under some regimes, people are shut in asylums and subjected to enforced drugging for the same reason while the hypocrites remain free. My courage may lead me to go to the defence of someone being attacked in the street to no avail and with the result that I am killed or maimed for life while the coward goes through her life unscathed. Given these possibilities, how can anyone claim that the question 'How am I to flourish?' is to be honestly answered by saying 'Be virtuous'?

There are two possible responses to this. [1] The first is to grit one's teeth and deny that the virtuous person can be harmed by her possession of virtue. To be virtuous *is* to flourish, to be (truly) happy or successful. *Nothing counts as being harmed except doing evil, and nothing counts as a genuine benefit, or advantage, or being better off than doing what is right.* There is more than a grain of truth in this view, to which I shall return later on, but, on the face of it, it is, as a response to the sorts of examples we have envisaged, simply absurd. As Aristotle says, 'Those who maintain that, provided he is good, a man is happy (*eudaimon*) on the rack, or when fallen amongst great misfortunes are talking nonsense . . .' (NE1153b17) (The point of these examples is that I become unable to exercise virtue, either because I am dead, or because I have become physically, mentally or materially incapable of doing so.)

[2] The second response is to *deny that the answer to the question was ever supposed to offer a guarantee.* If I ask my doctor 'How am I to flourish physically/be healthy?' she gives me the right answer when she says 'Give up smoking, don't work with asbestos, lose weight, take some exercise . . .' Even if, despite following her advice I subsequently develop lung cancer or heart disease, this does not impugn its correctness; I can't go back to her and say 'You were wrong to tell me I should give up smoking, etc.' She and I both know that doing as she says does not guarantee perfect health; nevertheless, if perfect health is what I want, the only thing I can do to achieve it is follow her advice. Continuing to smoke, work with asbestos, etc, is asking for trouble—even though, it is agreed, I may be lucky and live to be a hearty ninety.

Similarly, the claim is not that being virtuous guarantees that one will flourish. It is, rather, probabilistic—'true for the most part' (1094b21–22). *Virtue is the only reliable bet*; it will probably bring flourishing—though, it is agreed, I might be unlucky and, because of my virtue, wind up on the rack.[6] So virtue is not being made out to be guaranteed sufficient for flourishing.

Objection 2: Virtue Is not Necessary for Living Well

But now we move to the second objection. Is it not being made out to be necessary? It was just said to be the *only* reliable bet, as if, as in the medical case, making no effort to acquire the virtues was asking for trouble. *But don't the wicked, as we said above, flourish? In which case virtue can't be necessary.* The two possible responses to this objection are elaborations on the two that were given to the other. [1] The first denies that the wicked ever do flourish, for nothing counts as having an advantage or being well off or . . . except doing what is right. [2] The second, continuing to pursue the medical analogy, still insists that virtue is the only reliable bet and, agreeing that occasionally the non-virtuous flourish, maintains that this is, like fat smokers living to be ninety, rare and a matter of luck. So, for instance, it is usually true that people who are entirely selfish and inconsiderate miss out on being loved—but such a person might be lucky enough to be blessed with particular beauty or charm, or by lucky chance come across someone else very loving who just fell for them in the mysterious way that sometimes happens. But, the claim is, we can all recognize that this is a matter of luck—one could never rely on it.

However, many people may feel that this response is implausible. Surely it is not simply by pure chance and luck that the non-virtuous flourish. Isn't power just as good a bet as virtue, if not a better one, for flourishing? If one has power, people do, as a matter of fact, love one for that; one is respected and honoured, people treat one with special concern and consideration—and all despite the fact that in order to get and maintain power one will undoubtedly have to be selfish, dishonest, callous, unjust . . . to a certain extent. So the answer to 'How am I to flourish?' should not be 'Acquire virtue' but 'Acquire power'[7]. This objection can be seen as a form of one of the oldest, and still current, debates in moral philosophy. In Plato's *Republic* it takes on a form specifically related to the virtue of justice—if injustice is more profitable than justice to the man of strength, then practising injustice is surely the best way of life for the strong. Its most modern version is entirely general—'What reason have I to be moral?' One very important question it brings up is whether morality, or moral judgments, give reasons for acting to everyone. If some action ought not to be done (because, say, it is dishonest or unjust) does this mean that everyone has a reason not to do it, or is it open to the powerful to say truly that there is no reason for them to refrain?

What then, should be said about this old, but still hotly debated issue? When we were considering how 'success' could work as a translation of *eudaimonia*, we noted that one could be successful in a materialistic sense—wealthy and powerful—while still counting one's life not a success but a failure, because, say, one felt lonely and unfulfilled. Now let us consider someone who is (a) successful in the materialistic sense, (b) non-virtuous—they have acquired their power by cheating and lying, ruthlessly sacrificing people when it suited them, but (c) perfectly happy—they don't feel guilty, or lonely, or unfulfilled or worried about what would happen to them if they lost their power, or that their life is a failure in any sense. The question we then ask ourselves is—do we find this person's life enviable or desirable? And part of the truth I said was contained in the view that nothing counts as a genuine advantage or being better off than doing what is right is that many of us are going to say 'No'. We may

be hard put to explain *why* we say 'No'; perhaps we cannot say anything more than that we couldn't live like that, or that we wouldn't want to have cheated our friends or to have let our parents or children down. But our inability to say more than this does not matter; all that matters is that *we can view a life containing every apparent benefit and advantage as one that we don't want because it contains having acted wrongly in various ways. . . .*

Indeed, thinking back, we might wonder whether the alternative position is even intelligible. If there cannot be common agreement on the application of words such as 'benefit', 'advantage', 'pleasure', 'enjoyment', 'good' and 'harm', 'loss', etc., how can such words be taught? So why might anyone hold such a position—for it is held and expressed as the first responses to the two objections considered above. It seems that in part people are led into it by finding it necessary to make the first response rather than the second to the first objection. So, for instance, Phillips, responding to the point that my virtue may require me to lay down my life, insists that when this is so the virtuous 'see death as a good'.[8] He would presumably want to say the same about other 'evils', 'disadvantages' or 'losses' such as being tortured, or reduced to physical or mental incapacity, or being made destitute too, and indeed, generalizing his point in this way, McDowell maintains that the virtuous understand the notions of 'benefit, advantage, harm, loss and so forth' in such a way that no 'sacrifice' necessitated by virtue counts as a loss, and that the virtuous life cannot, even under such circumstances, contain any ground for regret.[9]

But here an important distinction seems to have been missed. Let us agree that there are cases in which the virtuous person may see her death or pain 'as a good', namely those cases in which some other good will be (or may be) achieved by them— say that others live or do not suffer. But these are not the only sorts of cases in which virtue may require me to die or suffer—what of the cases in which a tyrant tries to force me to do something wicked by threatening me with death or torture? As Aristotle says, there are some things we must sooner die (and, by implication submit to torture, destitution, etc.) than do, but this does not entail that the virtuous must see their death or pain in such circumstances as a good. Rather, they see it as the lesser of two evils—lesser, but a great evil all the same. Freedom from pain, health, modest possessions, the way of life, life itself, these are all goods and precious to the virtuous person; their loss is a real loss and she may regret them as such, regretting that circumstances made it necessary.[10]

Phillips seems to have overlooked this distinction, and been led to the position of the first response through a confusion over what Aristotle's answer is an answer to and hence over what it amounts to. *It is an answer to the question 'How am I to live the best life, to flourish?' and the answer is 'Be virtuous, i.e. acquire and practise the virtues'. The question is not 'How should I act on this particular occasion?' nor is the answer 'Be virtuous', in its other sense, i.e. 'Act now in the way required by virtue because if you do you'll flourish'.* Inevitably, if one takes the question and answer this wrong way the Aristotelian position becomes very peculiar. For a start, the probabilistic second response is ruled out as unintelligible. I ask 'How should I act on this particular occasion?' in circumstances in which virtue requires me to bring some great evil upon myself and the answer of the second response is made out to be 'Act in accordance with virtue because if you do you'll probably flourish, though of course you won't on this occasion', or 'Act in accordance with virtue because when other people less unluckily circumstanced than you are now act that way *they* flourish'. If this were what the second response amounted to, no wonder philosophers reject it and are drawn to the first. For if one takes the question and answer this wrong way something else seems attractive about the first response too. If I ask 'How should I act on this particular occasion?' in quite ordinary circumstances and am told that I should tell the truth, or share my cloak, i.e. be virtuous, because I will flourish if I do (and won't if I don't) I surely have not been given the right answer.

Acting virtuously, we want to say (as does Aristotle. cf.1105a26–1105b1. 1144a14–20), is an end in itself, something you do for its own sake, not because you have calculated that on this occasion it *will pay off.* If you think that each virtuous act is supposed to benefit you and is to be done for that reason you have missed the whole point of morality—unless, that is, you have become fully virtuous and respecified the concept of 'benefit' in such a way that for you to act virtuously, even when it brings evil upon you, *counts* as a benefit, as the first response holds. . . .

Moral Education

I do not think that moral education does or should consist simply in insisting that wrong acts are not worth doing because they do not secure 'real' advantages and, correspondingly, I do not think that the (theoretical) disagreement between the virtuous and the vicious over whether the virtuous characteristically flourish while the vicious do not is simply a disagreement about what flourishing consists in. It is also a disagreement about the explanation of why the virtuous and vicious don't flourish when they don't. For each side attributes its own failures to bad luck or odd circumstances and the failures of the other side to being the way things were bound to fall out—it's a disagreement about how life works.

I should like to suggest that the belief that we are so constituted that the virtuous characteristically flourish (so the failures are due to bad luck) while the wicked do not (so their failures are just what was to be expected) is part of virtue itself. It used to be called the belief in providence, and to doubt it while still believing that one must do as virtue requires is to fall into the vice of despair. To doubt it while not yet believing that one must do as virtue requires (because one is unsettled and not yet virtuous) is to be (still) in the grip of a number of beliefs that are corrupting and to which the above belief is the proper corrective.

One is the belief that one can get away with certain things, that the occasional bare-faced lie or piece of cruelty won't come home to roost. Another is that one can have things both ways, reaping the advantages of virtue and vice simultaneously. Another very tempting thought is that one is particularly clever, and hence that even if most people can't manage this, one will be able to oneself, that although, as Foot says, people cannot be manipulated like household objects in general, nevertheless you will be able to manage being the manipulator but never the manipulated. Another is that one is blessed with some special characteristic like beauty or social position which will command love and respect from some and mysteriously guarantee that you won't find yourself wanting love and respect from anyone who is unimpressed.

Maybe these are all just versions of the same belief—a denial of the one I have claimed is part of virtue. It is not that many people consciously hold such beliefs; rather they are expressed in reactions people have to events in their lives; the surprise and feeling of having been unfairly punished when just that one lie does come home to roost or when one reaps the whirlwind; the thought 'How can this have happened to *me*?'; the shock when one finds oneself the sucker; the difficulty in understanding how one's beautiful self can *not* be loved. They are expressed too in one's reactions to other people's lives be they real or fictional. Perhaps one of the most corrupting things about the lives that are portrayed in films and on television is the way in which they do show the wicked flourishing and the (token) good being tricked and victimized. One is encouraged to believe that this is realistic, and to the extent that one believes what one is shown, rather than reacting with sceptical scorn, one is settling towards vice rather than virtue. . . .

Aristotle's account of full virtue—that perfectly harmonious state in which we always do what is right gladly and never knowingly fall into wrongdoing—sets the standard very high. Probably none of us has got there yet, and to the extent that we are still unsettled we still need to correct our tendency to think that we can get away with acting wrongly. It is true that, in line with the idea that to be virtuous is to have a view of flourishing according to which acting wrongly *cannot* count as securing one any benefit, we may sometimes correct this tendency by reminding ourselves that we won't be 'getting away' with anything, but rather throwing away something it is worth hanging on to. But let us frankly acknowledge that this doesn't always

secure inner conviction. When it doesn't, reminding oneself of the corrective belief nevertheless may. *I can't convince myself that I haven't got away with acting wrongly, but I can convince myself that I got away with running a great risk and might not be so lucky again.* I can't convince myself that in acting rightly I haven't suffered a real disadvantage but I can convince myself that this was bad luck and shouldn't give me a reason to act otherwise next time. And in this way I may gradually settle into the belief that acting wrongly is never worth doing, serene confidence in which would be virtue indeed.

This debate that I have been going through is often discussed under the heading 'Must morality have a point?' I have maintained that, according to Aristotle, the fact of the matter is that it *does* have a point. If that is so, but it is nevertheless not true that it must have, this could only mean that virtue's constituting a flourishing life (in the sense of 'flourishing' that the unsettled can grasp) was a happy accident, something that is not necessarily so, but could be otherwise. But this seems to me to be a dangerous thought. If we allow our society to degenerate into a state in which it is extremely difficult for many of the people within it to exercise the virtues of honesty, generosity, courage and justice, because their best chances of minimal comfort and even survival lie in the opposing vices, and think that, since morality doesn't have to have a point, it will still be teachable, we may be in for a nasty surprise. And even if, under such circumstances, we were able to convince the next generation that there really is a concept of flourishing, grasped only by the virtuous, in terms of which one can flourish when too poor to be able to do anything for one's family and friends, even save them from starvation or hypothermia, and circumstanced in such a way that even the minimal physical pleasures are denied one, we would, I think, be offering them false coin. Aristotle recognises as a constraint on his account of *eudaimonia* that the flourishing life should contain the real advantages of (some) material wealth and pleasure to which the vicious attach such importance, and we should be honest enough to do the same.

NOTES

1. I am grateful to Gavin Lawrence for his detailed and helpful criticism of an earlier draft of this paper and for much discussion on the topics discussed herein over the years. All references to the *Nicomachean Ethics* have been given in terms of the so-called 'Bekker numbers' which are standardly used for giving exact references to Aristotle's writings. They also enable one to identify a passage on the page of any good translation, for instance the current Penguin edition of the *Ethics* introduced by Jonathan Barnes.

2. Etymologically it means 'well (*eu*) demoned/genuised', i.e. blessed with a good genius or attendant spirit (*daimon*).

3. Though perhaps not incomprehensible, if we can understand a certain sort of neuroticism in which the person seems bent on misery and self-destruction. Aristotle appears not to recognize the existence of such people.

4. The translation of some of Aristotle's terms for virtues makes them sound a little odd, and they are best understood by noting what vices they are opposed to. So, for instance, 'temperance' is not a matter of eschewing alcohol, but having the right disposition in respect of alcohol and food and sex—being neither an alcoholic, nor a glutton, nor sexually licentious. Of the virtue called, in translation, 'patience', Aristotle himself remarks that it doesn't really have a name, but we can readily grasp it by seeing that it is opposed to the vices of being bad tempered in various ways on the one hand, and poor spirited on the other. It is also important to realize that the term we translate as 'virtue' (*arete*) has not specifically moral overtones and is better translated as 'excellence'. So it should come as no surprise to us that Aristotle's list contains non-moral virtues or excellences such as wittiness. But we need not even take many of these very seriously as excellences, for in his other ethical work, the *Eudemian Ethics,* Aristotle makes a point of denying that they are excellences (of character) on the grounds that they do not involve choice (EE1234a25). Finally, we should note that Aristotle's list is open-ended—he nowhere claims that it is exhaustive—so it is open to us to add to it virtues with which we are more familiar, e.g. benevolence, compassion, honesty, kindness. . . .

5. Cf. for example, 1106b1–22 and 1109a, 20–29. Note in the latter passage the comparison with finding the centre of a circle, which is a better image than finding a midpoint ('mean') between just two opposing vices.

6. It is important to note that the only similarity I am claiming between the two cases is on this point. Giving up smoking, etc., is not constitutive of flourishing physically the way exercising the virtues is constitutive of flourishing as a human being, and there are other disanalogies too.

7. We might of course think of further alternatives—what for instance of the life of the entirely selfish but dedicated great artist? Aristotle does recognize an analogous alternative in Book 10. There he argues that the best life consists in intellectual activity (contemplation) not in the practical activity necessitated by the exercise of the (moral) virtues. And this apparently allows that, if I am to live well, I should *not* acquire and practise the virtues but acquire some other set of character traits which best armed me for becoming a successful contemplator. How this can be reconciled, if at all, with what has been said in the earlier books of the *Ethics* is a major problem in Aristotelian scholarship and raises questions that are interesting in their own right. Are there ways of flourishing which actually necessitate vice or must any flourishing human life resemble the fully virtuous one to some extent?

8. D. Z. Phillips, 'Does it Pay to be Good?', *Proc. Arist. Soc.* n.s. 65 (1964–65).

9. John McDowell, 'The Role of *Eudaimonia* in Aristotle's Ethics', reprinted in *Essays on Aristotle's Ethics*, Amelie Rorty (ed.) (California: University of California Press, 1980), 369–370.

10. Aristotle explicitly acknowledges the existence of such cases in his section on 'mixed' actions (Book 3, ch. i). The characteristic of these is that what is chosen—say death or torture or the enduring of disgrace—is something that considered 'in itself' is *not* a good, not the sort of thing that anyone would go for. In so far as he takes something that he recognizes not to be a good but an evil the agent acts involuntarily and can be pitied.

DISCUSSION QUESTIONS:

1. According to the ancient Greeks, ethics is supposed to tell us how to live well. But aren't the standards for living well relative to each person? It seems incredible that what would make life good for a 16th-century painter in Italy is the same as what would make life good for a 21st-century Asian farmer. What constitutes a good life for you might not necessarily constitute the good life for me. So is virtue theory a kind of moral relativism? Why or why not?

2. One might think that a life is good if and only if one *thinks* it is good. In other words, some people seem to think that ignorance is bliss, and that being in a state of bliss is sufficient for being truly happy. Is there a way to properly criticize the life of someone who thinks her life is good despite the fact that it is devoid of the kind of things mentioned by Aristotle (e.g., friends, courage, knowledge, generosity, etc.)?

3. One potential benefit of virtue theory is that it is able to offer a straightforward answer to why we should care about living a morally good life. The answer is that a morally good life is one in which we cultivate the virtues, and cultivating the virtues is the most reliable way to live well. But Hursthouse considers two objections to this view. Some think that we can live well without virtues (i.e., virtues are not *necessary* for a good life) and others think that having the virtues is not enough to live well (i.e., virtues are not *sufficient* for a good life). Do you think that you could live a good life without being virtuous? Why or why not? Do you think that it is possible that your life not be good even if you had successfully cultivated the virtues? Why or why not?

4. Is there a virtue that you would like to have but currently lack (e.g., generosity)? If so, how do you go about developing such a virtue in yourself?

Argument Reconstruction Exercises:

I. Hursthouse thinks that a proper understanding of *eudaimonia* will not limit success to merely the possession of material goods. Here is the passage in which she argues for this conclusion. Identify the premises and conclusion in the following excerpt.

> For a start, [Aristotle] tells us that [*eudaimonia*] is what we all want to get in life (or get out of it); what we are all aiming at, ultimately (1094a1–26); the way we all want to be. And we all agree in one sense about what it consists in, namely, living well or faring well . . . What do we say about success and prospering? Well, "successful" and "prosperous" have a materialistic sense in which they connote wealth and power; when we use them in this way it is obvious to us (a) that one can be happy and count oneself as fortunate without them and (b) that they do not necessarily bring with them happiness and the good fortune of loyal friends, loving relationships, the joys of art and learning and so on. So many of us will say that (material) success and prosperity is not what we want; that having it doesn't amount to faring well. (page 321)

II. The question "How can I live the best life?" appears to be egoistic. That is, it appears to be a selfish sort of question that is unrelated to the issue of ethics or morality. Hursthouse disagrees and cites Aristotle in support of her view. The following argument attempts to conclude that there is an essential connection between the egoistic question of how we can have the best life possible and the role of ethics in our lives. Identify the premises and conclusion in this excerpt.

> But the obstacle may be surmounted by looking carefully at the answer Aristotle gives to this question that apparently has nothing to do with ethics. For his answer is: "If you want to flourish/be happy/successful you should acquire and exercise the virtues—courage, temperance, liberality, patience, truthfulness, friendship, justice. . ." Or, as we might say, be a morally virtuous person. (page 322)

III. Hursthouse offers generosity as an example of a virtue that we have a reason to cultivate. Identify the premises and conclusion in the following excerpt.

> Take one of the simplest cases for us—generosity. Here are some of the relevant facts; we are naturally sociable creatures who like to have friends and want to be loved by friends and family. We also like and love people who do things for us rather than always putting themselves first. We also are not merely sympathetic but empathetic—the pleasure of others is pleasurable to us. Given that this is how we are, someone who is mean and selfish is unlikely to be liked and loved and hence likely to be lonely and unhappy. . . (page 322)

IV. Hursthouse entertains the objection that virtue is not necessary for a good life. Identify the premises and conclusion in the following excerpt.

> But now we move to the second objection. Is [virtue] not being made out to be necessary? It was just said to be the only reliable bet, as if, as in the medical case, making no effort to acquire the virtues was asking for trouble. But don't the wicked, as we said above, flourish? In which case, virtue can't be necessary. (page 324)

13.3 MORAL SAINTS

SUSAN WOLF (1982)

Susan Wolf is Edna J. Koury Distinguished Professor at the University of North Carolina, Chapel Hill. Her work falls mainly in the areas of ethics, value theory, and action theory. In this essay, she questions the value of being a moral saint (i.e., someone who is as morally good as possible). She argues that the role model of the moral saint is at odds both with other commonsense role models and with leading normative theories of ethics. The result, she argues, is that we ought to have a broader understanding of human excellence—one that certainly includes moral excellence but one that refuses to rank non-moral excellences as less valuable.

Reading Questions:

1. What is a moral saint?

2. What is the difference between a Loving Saint and a Rational Saint?

3. According to commonsense, what is an example of a non-moral trait or virtue that the moral saint will lack?

4. What is one of the objections that Wolf considers against her case from common sense?

5. According to Wolf, will a utilitarian aspire to be a moral saint? Why or why not?

6. According to Wolf, will a Kantian aspire to be a moral saint? Why or why not?

7. According to Wolf, why won't understanding morality in the kinds of virtue-theoretic terms described by Aristotle solve the tension between our commonsense life goals and moral sainthood?

I don't know whether there are any moral saints. But if there are, I am glad that neither I nor those about whom I care most are among them. *By **moral saint** I mean a person whose every action is as morally good as possible, a person, that is, who is as morally worthy as can be.* Though I shall in a moment acknowledge the variety of types of person that might be thought to satisfy this description, it seems to me that none of these types serve as unequivocally compelling personal ideals. In other words, *I believe that moral perfection, in the sense of moral saintliness, does not constitute a model of personal well-being toward which it would be particularly rational or good or desirable for a human being to strive.*

Outside the context of moral discussion, this will strike many as an obvious point. But, within that context, the point, if it be granted, will be granted with some discomfort. For within that context *it is generally assumed that one ought to be as morally good as possible* and that what limits there are to morality's hold on us are set by features of human nature of which we ought not to be proud. If, as I believe, the ideals that are derivable from common sense and philosophically popular moral theories do not support these assumptions, then something has to change. Either we must change our moral theories in ways that will make them yield more palatable ideals, or, as I shall argue, we must change

I have benefited from the comments of many people who have heard or read an earlier draft of this paper. I wish particularly to thank Douglas MacLean, Robert Nozick, Martha Nussbaum, and the Society for Ethics and Legal Philosophy.

our conception of what is involved in affirming a moral theory.

In this paper, I wish to examine the notion of a moral saint, first, to understand what a moral saint would be like and why such a being would be unattractive, and, second, to raise some questions about the significance of this paradoxical figure for moral philosophy. I shall look first at the model(s) of moral sainthood that might be extrapolated from the morality or moralities of common sense. Then I shall consider what relations these have to conclusions that can be drawn from utilitarian and Kantian moral theories. Finally, I shall speculate on the implications of these considerations for moral philosophy.

Moral Saints and Common Sense

Consider first what, pretheoretically, would count for us—contemporary members of Western culture—as a moral saint. *A necessary condition of moral sainthood would be that one's life be dominated by a commitment to improving the welfare of others or of society as a whole.* As to what role this commitment must play in the individual's motivational system, two contrasting accounts suggest themselves to me which might equally be thought to qualify a person for moral sainthood.

[1] First, a moral saint might be someone whose concern for others plays the role that is played in most of our lives by more selfish, or, at any rate, less morally worthy concerns. For the moral saint, the promotion of the welfare of others might play the role that is played for most of us by the enjoyment of material comforts, the opportunity to engage in the intellectual and physical activities of our choice, and the love, respect, and companionship of people whom we love, respect, and enjoy. The happiness of the moral saint, then, would truly lie in the happiness of others, and so he would devote himself to others gladly, and with a whole and open heart.

[2] On the other hand, a moral saint might be someone for whom the basic ingredients of happiness are not unlike those of most of the rest of us. What makes him a moral saint is rather that he pays little or no attention to his own happiness in light of the overriding importance he gives to the wider concerns of morality. In other words, this person sacrifices his own interests to the interests of others, and feels the sacrifice as such.

Roughly, *these two models may be distinguished according to whether one thinks of the moral saint as being a saint out of love or one thinks of the moral saint as being a saint out of duty* (or some other intellectual appreciation and recognition of moral principles). We may refer to the first model as the model of the **Loving Saint**; to the second, as the model of the **Rational Saint**.

The two models differ considerably with respect to the qualities of the motives of the individuals who conform to them. But this difference would have limited effect on the saints' respective public personalities. The shared content of what these individuals are motivated to be—namely, as morally good as possible—would play the dominant role in the determination of their characters. Of course, just as a variety of large-scale projects, from tending the sick to political campaigning, may be equally and maximally morally worthy, so a variety of characters are compatible with the ideal of moral sainthood. One moral saint may be more or less jovial, more or less garrulous, more or less athletic than another. But, above all, a moral saint must have and cultivate those qualities which are apt to allow him to treat others as justly and kindly as possible. He will have the standard moral virtues to a nonstandard degree. He will be patient, considerate, even-tempered, hospitable, charitable in thought as well as in deed. He will be very reluctant to make negative judgments of other people. He will be careful not to favor some people over others on the basis of properties they could not help but have.

Perhaps what I have already said is enough to make some people begin to regard the absence of moral saints in their lives as a blessing. For there comes a point in the listing of virtues that a moral saint is likely to have where one might naturally begin to wonder whether the moral saint isn't, after all, too good—if not too good for his own good, at least too good for his own well-being. *For the moral virtues, given that they are, by hypothesis, all present in the same individual, and to an extreme degree, are apt to crowd out the nonmoral virtues, as well as many of the interests and personal characteristics that we generally think contribute to a healthy, well-rounded, richly developed character.*

332 UNIT THREE: NORMATIVE ETHICS

In other words, if the moral saint is devoting all his time to feeding the hungry or healing the sick or raising money for Oxfam, then necessarily he is not reading Victorian novels, playing the oboe, or improving his backhand. Although no one of the interests or tastes in the category containing these latter activities could be claimed to be a necessary element in a life well lived, a life in which *none* of these possible aspects of character are developed may seem to be a life strangely barren.

The reasons why a moral saint cannot, in general, encourage the discovery and development of significant nonmoral interests and skills are not logical but practical reasons. There are, in addition, a class of nonmoral characteristics that a moral saint cannot encourage in himself for reasons that are not just practical. There is a more substantial tension between having any of these qualities unashamedly and being a moral saint. These qualities might be described as going against the moral grain. For example, a cynical or sarcastic wit, or a sense of humor that appreciates this kind of wit in others, requires that one take an attitude of resignation and pessimism toward the flaws and vices to be found in the world. A moral saint, on the other hand, has reason to take an attitude in opposition to this—he should try to look for the best in people, give them the benefit of the doubt as long as possible, try to improve regrettable situations as long as there is any hope of success. This suggests that, although a moral saint might well enjoy a good episode of *Father Knows Best*, he may not in good conscience be able to laugh at a Marx Brothers movie or enjoy a play by George Bernard Shaw.

An interest in something like gourmet cooking will be, for different reasons, difficult for a moral saint to rest easy with. For it seems to me that no plausible argument can justify the use of human resources involved in producing a *paté de canard en croute* against possible alternative beneficent ends to which these resources might be put. If there is a justification for the institution of haute cuisine, it is one which rests on the decision *not* to justify every activity against morally beneficial alternatives, and this is a decision a moral saint will never make. Presumably, an interest in high fashion or interior design will fare much the same; as will, very possibly, a cultivation of the finer arts as well.

A moral saint will have to be very, very nice. It is important that he not be offensive. The worry is that, as a result, he will have to be dull-witted or humorless or bland.

This worry is confirmed when we consider what sorts of characters, taken and refined both from life and from fiction, typically form our ideals. One would hope they would be figures who are morally good—and by this I mean more than just not morally bad—but one would hope, too, that they are not *just* morally good, but talented or accomplished or attractive in nonmoral ways as well. We may make ideals out of athletes, scholars, artists—more frivolously, out of cowboys, private eyes, and rock stars. We may strive for Katharine Hepburn's grace, Paul Newman's "cool"; we are attracted to the high-spirited passionate nature of Natasha Rostov; we admire the keen perceptiveness of Lambert Strether. Though there is certainly nothing immoral about the ideal characters or traits I have in mind, they cannot be superimposed upon the ideal of a moral saint. For although it is a part of many of these ideals that the characters set high, and not merely acceptable, moral standards for themselves, it is also essential to their power and attractiveness that the moral strengths go, so to speak, alongside of specific, independently admirable, nonmoral ground projects and dominant personal traits.

When one does finally turn one's eyes toward lives that are dominated by explicitly moral commitments, moreover, one finds oneself relieved at the discovery of idiosyncrasies or eccentricities not quite in line with the picture of moral perfection. One prefers the blunt, tactless, and opinionated Betsy Trotwood to the unfailingly kind and patient Agnes Copperfield; one prefers the mischievousness and the sense of irony in Chesterton's Father Brown to the innocence and undiscriminating love of St. Francis.

It seems that, as we look in our ideals for people who achieve nonmoral varieties of personal excellence in conjunction with or colored by some version of high moral tone, we look in our paragons of moral excellence for people whose moral achievements occur in conjunction with or colored by some interests or traits that have low moral tone. In other words, *there seems to be a limit to how much morality we can stand.*

Three Objections to the Case from Common Sense

[1] One might suspect that the essence of the problem is simply that there is a limit to how much of *any* single value, or any single type of value, we can stand. Our objection then would not be specific to a life in which one's dominant concern is morality, but would apply to any life that can be so completely characterized by an extraordinarily dominant concern. The objection in that case would reduce to the recognition that such a life is incompatible with well-roundedness. If that were the objection, one could fairly reply that well-roundedness is no more supreme a virtue than the totality of moral virtues embodied by the ideal it is being used to criticize. But I think this misidentifies the objection. For the way in which a concern for morality may dominate a life, or, more to the point, the way in which it may dominate an ideal of life, is not easily imagined by analogy to the dominance an aspiration to become an Olympic swimmer or a concert pianist might have. . . .

In other words, the ideal of a life of moral sainthood disturbs not simply because it is an ideal of a life in which morality unduly dominates. The normal person's direct and specific desires for objects, activities, and events that conflict with the attainment of moral perfection are not simply sacrificed but removed, suppressed, or subsumed. The way in which morality, unlike other possible goals, is apt to dominate is particularly disturbing, for it seems to require either the lack or the denial of the existence of an identifiable, personal self.

This distinctively troubling feature is not, I think, absolutely unique to the ideal of the moral saint, as I have been using that phrase. It is shared by the conception of the pure aesthete, by a certain kind of religious ideal, and, somewhat paradoxically, by the model of the thorough-going, self-conscious egoists. It is not a coincidence that the ways of comprehending the world of which these ideals are the extreme embodiments are sometimes described as "moralities" themselves. At any rate, they compete with what we ordinarily mean by 'morality'. Nor is it a coincidence that these ideals are naturally described as fanatical. But it is easy to see that these other types of perfection cannot serve as satisfactory personal ideals; for the

realization of these ideals would be straightforwardly immoral. It may come as a surprise to some that there may in addition be such a thing as a *moral* fanatic.

[2] Some will object that I am being unfair to "common-sense morality"—that it does not really require a moral saint to be either a disgusting goody-goody or an obsessive ascetic. Admittedly, there is no logical inconsistency between having any of the personal characteristics I have mentioned and being a moral saint. It is not morally wrong to notice the faults and shortcomings of others or to recognize and appreciate nonmoral talents and skills. Nor is it immoral to be an avid Celtics fan or to have a passion for caviar or to be an excellent cellist. With enough imagination, we can always contrive a suitable history and set of circumstances that will embrace such characteristics in one or another specific fictional story of a perfect moral saint.

If one turned onto the path of moral sainthood relatively late in life, one may have already developed interests that can be turned to moral purposes. It may be that a good golf game is just what is needed to secure that big donation to Oxfam. Perhaps the cultivation of one's exceptional artistic talent will turn out to be the way one can make one's greatest contribution to society. Furthermore, one might stumble upon joys and skills in the very service of morality. If, because the children are short a ninth player for the team, one's generous offer to serve reveals a natural fielding arm or if one's part in the campaign against nuclear power requires accepting a lobbyist's invitation to lunch at Le Lion d'Or, there is no moral gain in denying the satisfaction one gets from these activities. The moral saint, then, may, by happy accident, find himself with nonmoral virtues on which he can capitalize morally or which make psychological demands to which he has no choice but to attend. *The point is that, for a moral saint, the existence of these interests and skills can be given at best the status of happy accidents—they cannot be encouraged for their own sakes as distinct, independent aspects of the realization of human good.*

It must be remembered that from the fact that there is a tension between having any of these qualities and being a moral saint it does not follow that having any of these qualities is immoral. For it is not part of common-sense morality that one ought to be a moral saint. Still, if someone just happened to want to be a moral saint, he or she would not have or encourage these qualities, and, on the basis of our common-sense values, this counts as a reason *not* to want to be a moral saint.

[3] One might still wonder what kind of reason this is, and what kind of conclusion this properly allows us to draw. For the fact that the models of moral saints are unattractive does not necessarily mean that they are unsuitable ideals. Perhaps they are unattractive because they make us feel uncomfortable—they highlight our own weaknesses, vices, and flaws. If so, the fault lies not in the characters of the saints, but in those of our unsaintly selves.

To be sure, some of the reasons behind the disaffection we feel for the model of moral sainthood have to do with a reluctance to criticize ourselves and a reluctance to committing ourselves to trying to give up activities and interests that we heartily enjoy. These considerations might provide an *excuse* for the fact that we are not moral saints, but they do not provide a basis for criticizing sainthood as a possible ideal. Since these considerations rely on an appeal to the egoistic, hedonistic side of our natures, to use them as a basis for criticizing the ideal of the moral saint would be at best to beg the question and at worst to glorify features of ourselves that ought to be condemned.

The fact that the moral saint would be without qualities which we have and which, indeed, we like to have, does not in itself provide reason to condemn the ideal of the moral saint. The fact that some of these qualities are good qualities, however, and that they are qualities we *ought* to like, does provide reason to discourage this ideal and to offer other ideals in its place. In other words, some of the qualities the moral saint necessarily lacks are virtues, albeit nonmoral virtues, in the unsaintly characters who have them. The feats of Groucho Marx, Reggie Jackson, and the head chef at Lutèce are impressive accomplishments that it is not only permissible but positively appropriate to recognize as such. In general, the admiration of and striving toward achieving any of a great variety of forms of personal excellence are character traits it is valuable and desirable for people to have. In advocating the development of these varieties of excellence, we advocate nonmoral reasons for acting, and in

thinking that it is good for a person to strive for an ideal that gives a substantial role to the interests and values that correspond to these virtues, we implicitly acknowledge the goodness of ideals incompatible with that of the moral saint. Finally, if we think that it is *as* good, or even better for a person to strive for one of these ideals than it is for him or her to strive for and realize the ideal of the moral saint, we express a conviction that it is good not to be a moral saint.

Moral Saints and Moral Theories

I have tried so far to paint a picture—or, rather, two pictures—of what a moral saint might be like, drawing on what I take to be the attitudes and beliefs about morality prevalent in contemporary, common-sense thought. To my suggestion that common-sense morality generates conceptions of moral saints that are unattractive or otherwise unacceptable, it is open to someone to reply, "so much the worse for common-sense morality." After all, it is often claimed that the goal of moral philosophy is to correct and improve upon common-sense morality, and I have as yet given no attention to the question of what conceptions of moral sainthood, if any, are generated from the leading moral theories of our time.

A quick, breezy reading of utilitarian and Kantian writings will suggest the images, respectively, of the Loving Saint and the Rational Saint. A utilitarian, with his emphasis on happiness, will certainly prefer the Loving Saint to the Rational one, since the Loving Saint will himself be a happier person than the Rational Saint. A Kantian, with his emphasis on reason, on the other hand, will find at least as much to praise in the latter as in the former. Still, both models, drawn as they are from common sense, appeal to an impure mixture of utilitarian and Kantian intuitions. *A more careful examination of these moral theories raises questions about whether either model of moral sainthood would really be advocated by a believer in the explicit doctrines associated with either of these views.*

Utilitarianism and Moral Saints

Certainly, the utilitarian in no way denies the value of self-realization. He in no way disparages the development of interests, talents, and other personally attractive traits that I have claimed the moral saint would be without. Indeed, since just these features enhance the happiness both of the individuals who possess them and of those with whom they associate, the ability to promote these features both in oneself and in others will have considerable positive weight in utilitarian calculations.

This implies that *the utilitarian would not support moral sainthood as a universal ideal.* A world in which everyone, or even a large number of people, achieved moral sainthood—even a world in which they *strove* to achieve it—would probably contain less happiness than a world in which people realized a diversity of ideals involving a variety of personal and perfectionist values. More pragmatic considerations also suggest that, if the utilitarian wants to influence more people to achieve more good, then he would do better to encourage them to pursue happiness-producing goals that are more attractive and more within a normal person's reach. . . .

[It] may be that a limited and carefully monitored allotment of time and energy to be devoted to the pursuit of some nonmoral interests or to the development of some nonmoral talents would make a person a better contributor to the general welfare than he would be if he allowed himself no indulgences of this sort. The enjoyment of such activities in no way compromises a commitment to utilitarian principles as long as the involvement with these activities is conditioned by a willingness to give them up whenever it is recognized that they cease to be in the general interest.

This will go some way in mitigating the picture of the loving saint that an understanding of utilitarianism will on first impression suggest. But I think it will not go very far. For the limitations on time and energy will have to be rather severe, and the need to monitor will restrict not only the extent but also the quality of one's attachment to these interests and traits. They are only weak and somewhat peculiar sorts of passions to which one can consciously remain so conditionally committed. Moreover, the way in which the utilitarian can enjoy these "extra-curricular" aspects of his life is simply not the way in which these aspects are to be enjoyed insofar as they figure into our less saintly ideals.

The problem is not exactly that the utilitarian values these aspects of his life only as a means to an end, for the enjoyment he and others get from these aspects are not a means to, but a part of, the general happiness. Nonetheless, he values these things only because of and insofar as they *are* a part of the general happiness. He values them, as it were, under the description 'a contribution to the general happiness'. This is to be contrasted with the various ways in which these aspects of life may be valued by nonutilitarians. A person might love literature because of the insights into human nature literature affords. Another might love the cultivation of roses because roses are things of great beauty and delicacy. It may be true that these features of the respective activities also explain why these activities are happiness-producing. But, to the nonutilitarian, this may not be to the point. For if one values these activities in these more direct ways, one may not be willing to exchange them for others that produce an equal, or even a greater amount of happiness. From that point of view, it is not because they produce happiness that these activities are valuable; it is because these activities are valuable in more direct and specific ways that they produce happiness.

To adopt a phrase of Bernard Williams', the utilitarian's manner of valuing the not explicitly moral aspects of his life "provides (him) with one thought too many".[1] The requirement that the utilitarian have this thought—periodically, at least—is indicative of not only a weakness but a shallowness in his appreciation of the aspects in question. Thus, the ideals toward which a utilitarian could acceptably strive would remain too close to the model of the common-sense moral saint to escape the criticisms of that model which I earlier suggested. Whether a Kantian would be similarly committed to so restrictive and unattractive a range of possible ideals is a somewhat more difficult question.

Kantianism and Moral Saints

The Kantian believes that being morally worthy consists in always acting from maxims that one could will to be universal law, and doing this not out of any pathological desire but out of reverence for the moral law as such. Or, to take a different formulation of the categorical imperative, the Kantian believes that moral action consists in treating other persons always as ends and never as means only. Presumably, and according to Kant himself, the Kantian thereby commits himself to some degree of benevolence as well as to the rules of fair play. But we surely would not will that *every* person become a moral saint, and treating others as ends hardly requires bending over backwards to protect and promote their interests. On one interpretation of Kantian doctrine, then, moral perfection would be achieved simply by unerring obedience to a limited set of side-constraints. *On this interpretation, Kantian theory simply does not yield an ideal conception of a person of any fullness comparable to that of the moral saints I have so far been portraying.*

On the other hand, Kant does say explicitly that we have a duty of benevolence, a duty not only to allow others to pursue their ends, but to take up their ends as our own. In addition, we have positive duties to ourselves, duties to increase our natural as well as our moral perfection. These duties are unlimited in the degree to which they *may* dominate a life. If action in accordance with and motivated by the thought of these duties is considered virtuous, it is natural to assume that the more one performs such actions, the more virtuous one is. Moreover, of virtue in general Kant says, "it is an ideal which is unattainable while yet our duty is constantly to approximate to it".[2] *On this interpretation, then, the Kantian moral saint, like the other moral saints I have been considering, is dominated by the motivation to be moral.*

Which of these interpretations of Kant one prefers will depend on the interpretation and the importance one gives to the role of the imperfect duties in Kant's over-all system. Rather than choose between them here, I shall consider each briefly in turn.

On the second interpretation of Kant, the Kantian moral saint is, not surprisingly, subject to many of the same objections I have been raising against other versions of moral sainthood. Though the Kantian saint may differ from the utilitarian saint as to *which* actions he is bound to perform and which he is bound to refrain from performing, I suspect that the range of activities acceptable to the Kantian saint will remain objectionably restrictive. Moreover, the manner in which the Kantian saint must think about and justify the activities he pursues and the

character traits he develops will strike us, as it did with the utilitarian saint, as containing "one thought too many." As the utilitarian could value his activities and character traits only insofar as they fell under the description of 'contributions to the general happiness', the Kantian would have to value his activities and character traits insofar as they were manifestations of respect for the moral law. If the development of our powers to achieve physical, intellectual, or artistic excellence, or the activities directed toward making others happy are to have any moral worth, they must arise from a reverence for the dignity that members of our species have as a result of being endowed with pure practical reason. This is a good and noble motivation, to be sure. But it is hardly what one expects to be dominantly behind a person's aspirations to dance as well as Fred Astaire, to paint as well as Picasso, or to solve some outstanding problem in abstract algebra, and it is hardly what one hopes to find lying dominantly behind a father's action on behalf of his son or a lover's on behalf of her beloved.

Since *the basic problem with any of the models of moral sainthood we have been considering is that they are dominated by a single, all-important value under which all other possible values must be subsumed*, it may seem that the alternative interpretation of Kant, as providing a stringent but finite set of obligations and constraints, might provide a more acceptable morality. According to this interpretation of Kant, one is as morally good as can be so long as one devotes some limited portion of one's energies toward altruism and the maintenance of one's physical and spiritual health, and otherwise pursues one's independently motivated interests and values in such a way as to avoid overstepping certain bounds. Certainly, if it be a requirement of an acceptable moral theory that perfect obedience to its laws and maximal devotion to its interests and concerns be something we can wholeheartedly strive for in ourselves and wish for in those around us, it will count in favor of this brand of Kantianism that its commands can be fulfilled without swallowing up the perfect moral agent's entire personality.

Even this more limited understanding of morality, if its connection to Kant's views is to be taken at all seriously, is not likely to give an unqualified seal of approval to the nonmorally directed ideals I have been advocating. For Kant is explicit about what he calls "duties of apathy and self-mastery" (69/70)– duties to ensure that our passions are never so strong as to interfere with calm, practical deliberation, or so deep as to wrest control from the more disinterested, rational part of ourselves. The tight and self-conscious rein we are thus obliged to keep on our commitments to specific individuals and causes will doubtless restrict our value in these things, assigning them a necessarily attenuated place.

A more interesting objection to this brand of Kantianism, however, comes when we consider the implications of placing the kind of upper bound on moral worthiness which seemed to count in favor of this conception of morality. For to put such a limit on one's capacity to be moral is effectively to deny, not just the moral necessity, but the moral goodness of a devotion to benevolence and the maintenance of justice that passes beyond a certain, required point. It is to deny the possibility of going morally above and beyond the call of a restricted set of duties. Despite my claim that all-consuming moral saintliness is not a particularly healthy and desirable ideal, it seems perverse to insist that, were moral saints to exist, they would not, in their way, be remarkably noble and admirable figures. Despite my conviction that it is as rational and as good for a person to take Katharine Hepburn or Jane Austen as her role model instead of Mother Theresa, it would be absurd to deny that Mother Theresa is a morally better person.

I can think of two ways of viewing morality as having an upper bound. First, we can think that altruism and impartiality are indeed positive moral interests, but that they are moral only if the degree to which these interests are actively pursued remains within certain fixed limits. Second, we can think that these positive interests are only incidentally related to morality and that the essence of morality lies elsewhere, in, say, an implicit social contract or in the recognition of our own dignified rationality. According to the first conception of morality, there is a cut-off line to the amount of altruism or to the extent of devotion to justice and fairness that is worthy of moral praise. But to draw this line earlier than the line that brings the altruist in question into a worse-off position than all those to whom he devotes

himself seems unacceptably artificial and gratuitous. According to the second conception, these positive interests are not essentially related to morality at all. But then we are unable to regard a more affectionate and generous expression of good will toward others as a natural and reasonable extension of morality, and we encourage a cold and unduly self-centered approach to the development and evaluation of our motivations and concerns.

A moral theory that does not contain the seeds of an all-consuming ideal of moral sainthood thus seems to place false and unnatural limits on our opportunity to do moral good and our potential to deserve moral praise. Yet the main thrust of the arguments of this paper has been leading to the conclusion that, when such ideals are present, they are not ideals to which it is particularly reasonable or healthy or desirable for human beings to aspire. These claims, taken together, have the appearance of a dilemma from which there is no obvious escape. In a moment, I shall argue that, despite appearances, these claims should not be understood as constituting a dilemma. But, before I do, let me briefly describe another path which those who are convinced by my above remarks may feel inclined to take.

Virtue Theory and Moral Saints

If the above remarks are understood to be implicitly critical of the views on the content of morality which seem most popular today, an alternative that naturally suggests itself is that we revise our views about the content of morality. More specifically, my remarks may be taken to support a more Aristotelian, or even a more Nietzschean, approach to moral philosophy. Such a change in approach involves substantially broadening or replacing our contemporary intuitions about which character traits constitute moral virtues and vices and which interests constitute moral interests. If, for example, we include personal bearing, or creativity, or sense of style, as features that contribute to one's *moral* personality, then we can create moral ideals which are incompatible with and probably more attractive than the Kantian and utilitarian ideals I have discussed. Given such an alteration of our conception of morality, the figures with which I have been concerned above might, far from being considered to be moral saints, be seen as morally inferior to other more appealing or more interesting models of individuals.

This approach seems unlikely to succeed, if for no other reason, because it is doubtful that any single, or even any reasonably small number of substantial personal ideals could capture the full range of possible ways of realizing human potential or achieving human good which deserve encouragement and praise. Even if we could provide a sufficiently broad characterization of the range of positive ways for human beings to live, however, I think there are strong reasons not to want to incorporate such a characterization more centrally into the framework of morality itself. For, in claiming that a character trait or activity is morally good, one claims that there is a certain kind of reason for developing that trait or engaging in that activity. Yet, lying behind our criticism of more conventional conceptions of moral sainthood, there seems to be a recognition that among the immensely valuable traits and activities that a human life might positively embrace are some of which we hope that, if a person does embrace them, he does so *not* for moral reasons. In other words, no matter how flexible we make the guide to conduct which we choose to label "morality," no matter how rich we make the life in which perfect obedience to this guide would result, *we will have reason to hope that a person does not wholly rule and direct his life by the abstract and impersonal consideration that such a life would be morally good.*

Once it is recognized that morality itself should not serve as a comprehensive guide to conduct, moreover, we can see reasons to retain the admittedly vague contemporary intuitions about what the classification of moral and nonmoral virtues, interests, and the like should be. That is, *there seem to be important differences between the aspects of a person's life which are currently considered appropriate objects of moral evaluation and the aspects that might be included under the altered conception of morality we are now considering, which the latter approach would tend wrongly to blur or to neglect.* Moral evaluation now is focused primarily on features of a person's life over which that person has

control; it is largely restricted to aspects of his life which are likely to have considerable effect on other people. These restrictions seem as they should be. Even if responsible people could reach agreement as to what constituted good taste or a healthy degree of well-roundedness, for example, it seems wrong to insist that everyone try to achieve these things or to blame someone who fails or refuses to conform.

If we are not to respond to the unattractiveness of the moral ideals that contemporary theories yield either by offering alternative theories with more palatable ideals or by understanding these theories in such a way as to prevent them from yielding ideals at all, how, then, are we to respond? Simply, I think, by admitting that *moral ideals do not, and need not, make the best personal ideals.* Earlier, I mentioned one of the consequences of regarding as a test of an adequate moral theory that perfect obedience to its laws and maximal devotion to its interests be something we can wholeheartedly strive for in ourselves and wish for in those around us. Drawing out the consequences somewhat further should, I think, make us more doubtful of the proposed test than of the theories which, on this test, would fail. Given the empirical circumstances of our world, it seems to be an ethical fact that we have unlimited potential to be morally good, and endless opportunity to promote moral interests. But this is not incompatible with the not-so-ethical fact that we have sound, compelling, and not particularly selfish reasons to choose not to devote ourselves univocally to realizing this potential or to taking up this opportunity.

Thus, in one sense at least, I am not really criticizing either Kantianism or utilitarianism. Insofar as the point of view I am offering bears directly on recent work in moral philosophy, in fact, it bears on critics of these theories who, in a spirit not unlike the spirit of most of this paper, point out that the perfect utilitarian would be flawed in this way or the perfect Kantian flawed in that.[3] The assumption lying behind these claims, implicitly or explicitly, has been that the recognition of these flaws shows us something wrong with utilitarianism as opposed to Kantianism, or something wrong with Kantianism as opposed to utilitarianism, or something wrong with both of these theories as opposed to some nameless third alternative. The claims of this paper suggest, however, that this assumption is unwarranted. The flaws of a perfect master of a moral theory need not reflect flaws in the intramoral content of the theory itself.

Moral Saints and Moral Philosophy

In pointing out the regrettable features and the necessary absence of some desirable features in a moral saint, I have not meant to condemn the moral saint or the person who aspires to become one. Rather, I have meant to insist that the ideal of moral sainthood should not be held as a standard against which any other ideal must be judged or justified, and that the posture we take in response to the recognition that our lives are not as morally good as they might be need not be defensive.[4] It is misleading to insist that one is *permitted* to live a life in which the goals, relationships, activities, and interests that one pursues are not maximally morally good. For our lives are not so comprehensively subject to the requirement that we apply for permission, and our nonmoral reasons for the goals we set ourselves are not excuses, but may rather be positive, good reasons which do not exist *despite* any reasons that might threaten to outweigh them. In other words, a person may be *perfectly wonderful* without being *perfectly moral.* . . .

The moral point of view, we might say, is the point of view one takes up insofar as one takes the recognition of the fact that one is just one person among others equally real and deserving of the good things in life as a fact with practical consequences, a fact the recognition of which demands expression in one's actions and in the form of one's practical deliberations. Competing moral theories offer alternative answers to the question of what the most correct or the best way to express this fact is. In doing so, they offer alternative ways to evaluate and to compare the variety of actions, states of affairs, and so on that appear good and bad to agents from other, nonmoral points of view. But it seems that alternative interpretations of the moral point of view do not exhaust the ways in which our actions, characters, and their consequences can be comprehensively and objectively evaluated. Let us call the point of view from which we consider what kinds of lives are good

lives, and what kinds of persons it would be good for ourselves and others to be, the *point of view of individual perfection.*

Since either point of view provides a way of comprehensively evaluating a person's life, each point of view takes account of, and, in a sense, subsumes the other. From the moral point of view, the perfection of an individual life will have some, but limited, value—for each individual remains, after all, just one person among others. From the perfectionist point of view, the moral worth of an individual's relation to his world will likewise have some, but limited, value—for, as I have argued, the (perfectionist) goodness of an individual's life does not vary proportionally with the degree to which it exemplifies moral goodness. . . .

If moral philosophers are to address themselves at the most basic level to the question of how people should live, however, they must do more than adjust the content of their moral theories in ways that leave room for the affirmation of nonmoral values. They must examine explicitly the range and nature of these nonmoral values, and, in light of this examination, they must ask how the acceptance of a moral theory is to be understood and acted upon. For the claims of this paper do not so much conflict with the content of any particular currently popular moral theory as they call into question a metamoral assumption that implicitly surrounds discussions of moral theory more generally. Specifically, they call into question the assumption that it is always better to be morally better.

The role morality plays in the development of our characters and the shape of our practical deliberations need be neither that of a universal medium into which all other values must be translated nor that of an ever-present filter through which all other values must pass. This is not to say that moral value should not be an important, even the most important, kind of value we attend to in evaluating and improving ourselves and our world. It is to say that our values cannot be fully comprehended on the model of a hierarchical system with morality at the top.

The philosophical temperament will naturally incline, at this point, toward asking, "What, then, is at the top—or, if there is no top, how *are* we to decide when and how much to be moral?" In other words, there is a temptation to seek a metamoral—though not, in the standard sense, metaethical—theory that will give us principles, or, at least, informal directives on the basis of which we can develop and evaluate more comprehensive personal ideals. Perhaps a theory that distinguishes among the various roles a person is expected to play within a life—as professional, as citizen, as friend, and so on—might give us some rules that would offer us, if nothing else, a better framework in which to think about and discuss these questions. I am pessimistic, however, about the chances of such a theory to yield substantial and satisfying results. For I do not see how a metamoral theory could be constructed which would not be subject to considerations parallel to those which seem inherently to limit the appropriateness of regarding moral theories as ultimate comprehensive guides for action.

This suggests that, at some point, both in our philosophizing and in our lives, we must be willing to raise normative questions from a perspective that is unattached to a commitment to any particular well-ordered system of values. It must be admitted that, in doing so, we run the risk of finding normative answers that diverge from the answers given by whatever moral theory one accepts. This, I take it, is the grain of truth in G. E. Moore's "open question" argument. In the background of this paper, then, there lurks a commitment to what seems to me to be a healthy form of intuitionism. It is a form of intuitionism which is not intended to take the place of more rigorous, systematically developed, moral theories—rather, it is intended to put these more rigorous and systematic moral theories in their place.

NOTES

1. "Persons, Character and Morality" in Amelie Rorty, ed., *The Identities of Persons* (Berkeley: Univ. of California Press, 1976), p. 214.

2. Immanuel Kant, *The Doctrine of Virtue*, Mary J. Gregor, trans. (New York: Harper & Row, 1964), p. 71.

3. See, e.g., Williams, *op. cit.* and J.J. C. Smart and Bernard Williams, *Utilitarianism: For and Against* (New York: Cambridge, 1973). Also, Michael Stocker, "The Schizophrenia of Modern Ethical Theories," this JOURNAL, LXIII, 14 (Aug. 12, 1976):453–466.

4. George Orwell makes a similar point in "Reflections on Gandhi," in *A Collection of Essays by George Orwell* (New York: Harcourt Brace Jovanovich, 1945), p. 176: "sainthood is . . .a thing that human beings must avoid . . . It is too readily assumed that . . . the ordinary man only rejects it because it is too difficult; in other words, that the average human being is a failed saint. It is doubtful whether this is true. Many people genuinely do not wish to be saints, and it is probable that some who achieve or aspire to sainthood have never felt much temptation to be human beings."

DISCUSSION QUESTIONS:

1. Do you know anyone who counts as a moral saint in Wolf's terminology? Do you aspire to be a moral saint yourself? Would it really be a bad thing to be a moral saint?

2. Many people understand God as the most perfect being possible. Among his perfections is that of moral perfection. Thus, on Wolf's terminology, it looks like God (if he exists) is a moral saint. Does Wolf's article show that God would somehow be better off if he were *not* morally perfect?

3. Suppose Wolf is right that we can evaluate our lives and character from two different points of reference: the moral point of view and the point of view of individual perfection. When these two points of view recommend different courses of action, for example, spending money on a wine tasting and spending money for famine relief, how are we supposed to make a rational choice between the two?

Argument Reconstruction Exercises:

I. Wolf ultimately wants to conclude that it is not true that we ought to be as good as possible. This passage outlines the basic structure of that argument. Identify the premises and conclusion in this excerpt:

> . . . it is generally assumed that one ought to be as morally good as possible and that what limits there are to morality's hold on us are set by features of human nature of which we ought not to be proud. If, as I believe, the ideals that are derivable from common sense and philosophically popular moral theories do not support these assumptions, then something has to change. Either we must change our moral theories in ways that will make them yield more palatable ideals, or, as I shall argue, we must change our conception of what is involved in affirming a moral theory. (pages 330–331)

II. According to the argument from common sense, we share the common assumption that there is more to life than merely doing the right thing. In other words, common sense seems to commit us to some kind of non-moral goodness in life. Wolf sees a tension between this admission and the goal to be a moral saint. Identify the premises and conclusion in this excerpt.

> The fact that the moral saint would be without qualities which we have and which, indeed, we like to have, does not in itself provide reason to condemn the ideal of the moral saint. The fact that some of these qualities are good qualities, however, and that they are qualities we ought to like, does provide reason to discourage this ideal and to offer others in its place. In other words, some of the qualities the moral saint necessarily lacks are virtues, albeit nonmoral virtues, in the unsaintly characters who have them. . . . Finally, if we think that it is as good, or even better for a person to strive for one of those [non-moral] ideals than it is for him or her to strive for and realize the ideal of the moral saint, we express a conviction that it is good not to be a moral saint. (page 334)

III. Wolf thinks that common sense is in tension with the ideal of moral sainthood. Identify the premises and conclusion in this excerpt:

> . . .it is not part of common-sense morality that one ought to be a moral saint. Still, if someone just happened to want to be a moral saint, he or she would not have or encourage these [non-moral] qualities, and, on the basis of our common-sense values, this counts as a reason *not* to want to be a moral saint. (pages 333–334)

IV. In addition to arguing that the ideal of moral sainthood is at odds with common sense, Wolf wants to show that it is at odds with contemporary moral theories. Identify the premises and conclusion in this excerpt:

> This implies that the utilitarian would not support moral sainthood as a universal ideal. A world in which everyone, or even a large number of people, achieved moral sainthood—even a world in which they strove to achieve it—would probably contain less happiness than a world in which people realized a diversity of ideals involving a variety of personal and perfectionist values. (page 335)

13.4 CARE AND CONTEXT IN MORAL REASONING

MARILYN FRIEDMAN (1993)

Marilyn Friedman is W. Alton Jones Professor of Philosophy at Vanderbilt University and Professorial Fellow, Centre for Applied Philosophy and Public Ethics, Charles Stuart University, Australia. Much of her professional work is in political philosophy, ethics, and feminist theory. In this essay, she explores the empirical findings of two developmental psychologists, Lawrence Kohlberg and Carol Gilligan, and uses these findings to elucidate the contours of our moral obligations. In particular, she argues that the realm of morality is not exhausted by concepts like justice or rights but instead that contextual features like relationships can alter our moral obligations to one another.

Reading Questions:

1. What is the difference between Gilligan's "male" moral voice and "female" moral voice?

2. What is contextual relativism?

3. Contra Gilligan, Kohlberg insists that justice is the *primary* moral issue. What does that mean?

4. What is the Heinz dilemma?

5. In the "You dilemma," what's the difference between the justice orientation and the care orientation?

6. Why does Friedman think that details of context are relevant for moral reasoning from both the care perspective *and* the justice perspective?

Modern Anglo-American moral theory, as a whole, has represented "the moral life" in a severely diminished and distorted form. Until very recently, modern ethical theory neglected the moral importance of friendship and familial ties the so-called special relationships. Although a few modern moral philosophers, Kant, Sidgwick, and, most notably, Mill, for example, gave some philosophical attention to personal relationships, these investigations have not figured among the canonical texts or textual passages that have dominated Anglo-American moral theorizing over the past several centuries. The prevailing theoretical developments and research priorities of modern Anglo-American ethics have substantially ignored all intimate and special human affiliations.

In addition to neglecting close personal relationships, Anglo-American moral philosophy, like most of the Western academic tradition, has, until recent decades, almost entirely omitted the voices of women. The marked absence of women's voices, concerns, and perspectives has contributed to a near-total philosophical silence about the gender hierarchies of social life and the gender-specific nature of many norm-governed social roles and practices (again, with the notable exception of writings by Mill).

Since the 1970s, feminist philosophers have sought to rectify these deficiencies and enrich the scope of philosophical theorizing. From the outset, feminist philosophical thought focused on the nature and quality of personal relationships, including their tendencies toward gender hierarchy and the subordination of women. In the early 1980s, Carol Gilligan's research into the moral orientations of women added new directions to feminist philosophical thought. Gilligan's work helped to uncover an ethic of care, a perspective on moral matters and on the self as moral agent that both diverges from traditional moral theory and appears to be closely associated with women's traditional role as nurturer. Out of the philosophical revisions inspired by this and tandem feminist developments, a new subspeciality crystallized: feminist ethics.

At the same time that feminists began to direct ethical attention toward the moral significance of personal relationships, virtue theorists were raising related concerns. Virtue theorists, however, have ignored a number of matters that are of great interest to feminists. These include the quality of close personal relationships, the heavily female responsibilities for the intimate labors of sustaining those relationships, and the need to transform our relationship practices in order more fully to promote women's flourishing. Feminist reflections on personal relationships, thus, represent a distinctly illuminating and invigorating contribution to modern moral theory....

Care and Context in Moral Reasoning

Carol Gilligan heard a "distinct moral language" in the voices of women who were subjects in her studies of moral reasoning. Though herself a developmental psychologist, Gilligan has put her mark on contemporary feminist moral philosophy by daring to claim the competence of this voice and the worth of its message. In her book *In a Different Voice*,[1] which one theorist has aptly described as a best-seller,[2] and in a number of subsequent writings,[3] Gilligan has explored the concern with care and contextual detail that she discerned in the moral reasoning of women and has contrasted it with the orientation toward justice and abstract principles that she found to typify the moral reasoning of men.

The story is, by now, very familiar. According to Gilligan, *the standard, more typically "male," moral voice articulated in moral psychology derives moral judgments about particular cases from abstract, universalized moral rules and principles that are substantively concerned with justice and rights.* For justice reasoners, the major moral imperative enjoins respect for the rights of others; the concept of duty is limited to reciprocal noninterference; the motivating vision is one of the equal worth of self and other; and one important underlying presupposition is a highly individuated conception of persons.[4]

By contrast, the different, more characteristically "female," moral voice that Gilligan heard in her studies eschews abstract rules and principles. This moral voice derives moral judgments from the contextual detail of situations grasped as specific and unique. *The substantive concern for this moral voice is care and responsibility, particularly as these arise in the context of interpersonal relationships.* Moral judgments, for care reasoners, are tied to feelings of empathy and compassion; the major moral imperatives center around caring, not hurting others, and avoiding selfishness; and the motivating vision of this ethics is "that everyone will be responded to and included, that no one will be left alone or hurt."[5]

When gender differences first appeared in the studies of moral reasoning that were based on Lawrence Kohlberg's research[6] into cognitive moral development, it seemed that women, on average, did not attain as high a level of moral reasoning as men, on average. In other words, it seemed that women's moral reasoning was typically more immature than that of men. According to Gilligan, however, women's moral reasoning is not an immature form of the cognitive moral development that men attain, despite those early research findings. Rather, women's moral reasoning characteristically incorporates a different moral perspective altogether—a morality of care and responsibility that is particularly attentive to personal relationships. This alternative framework, this "different voice" for dealing with moral dilemmas, contrasts with Kohlberg's framework, which centers around the notions of justice and rights. If Gilligan is right, Kohlberg's framework expresses the moral concerns that typify the male moral voice.

In addition to the predominance of relationships as the central substantive moral concern of Gilligan's different voice, that voice also exhibits what Gilligan calls "contextual relativism."[7] *In Gilligan's usage.* **"Contextual relativism"** *actually encompasses two distinct features: first, a great sensitivity to the details of situations, and second, a reluctance to make moral judgments.* My discussion will concentrate on the first of these two features.

Gilligan suggests that women, more often than men, respond to hypothetical dilemmas (such as the famous Heinz dilemma used in Kohlbergian tests of moral reasoning, a dilemma I will explore shortly) by evading a forced choice between two proffered alternatives and seeking more details before reaching a conclusion. Women, more than men, are likely to seek the detail that makes the suffering clear and that engages compassion and caring. In Gilligan's view, such responses have often been misunderstood by the interviewers who administered the tests in their studies of moral reasoning. Interviewers tended to regard such responses as revealing a research subject's failure to comprehend the dilemmas or the problems to be solved. On the contrary, Gilligan argues, these responses challenge the way the problem is posed; in particular, they question its capacity to allow any real or meaningful choice.

Gilligan's insights, while often unsophisticated about the technicalities of philosophical theories of justice or rights, have nevertheless inspired needed rethinking of major ethical themes and presuppositions.[8] I use Gilligan's work as a springboard for extending certain of those themes in new directions. In the section entitled 'Care', I deploy a sequence of hypothetical narratives to ferret out a few of the ways considerations of care and relationships may sometimes override considerations of justice and rights in overall moral reasoning. In the section entitled 'Context' I explore the role of contextual detail in moral reasoning, the philosophically important core of the "contextual relativism" that has caught Gilligan's attention.

Care

Gilligan's views about the differences between men's and women's moral judgments have become highly controversial. Most of the controversy has centered around two claims: first, the claim that women tend to score lower then men when measured according to Kohlberg's moral reasoning framework; and second, her contention that Kohlberg's framework is male-biased and fails to take account of the "different" moral perspective oriented toward care that is more distinctively the perspective of women.

If women did not score significantly differently from men on Kohlberg's scale when matched against men of similar educational and occupational background, then there would be little evidence of a gender difference in moral reasoning. There would also be a good deal less evidence for the second controversial claim, namely, that Kohlberg's framework is male-biased for ignoring the distinctly different moral orientation of women. Even if Kohlberg's framework were not biased toward a moral perspective typical of males, however, that would not entail the absence of all bias. If nothing else, Gilligan's research has uncovered a substantial bias toward certain particular moral considerations that comprise only a part of the whole range of our moral concerns.

Kohlberg himself acknowledges[9] that Gilligan's research prompted him to take account of the importance to overall moral development of notions of care, relationships, and responsibility and to consider how these moral concerns augment his own prior emphasis on reasoning having to do with justice and rights. . . .[10]

Kohlberg admits that the primacy of justice was not "proven" by his previous research and that, instead, it had been a guiding assumption of the research, based on certain methodological and metaethical considerations.[11] The primacy of justice is, first of all, based on a "prescriptivist conception of moral judgment"; that is, moral judgment is treated not as the interpretation of situational fact but rather as the expression of universalizable "ought" claims. Second, it derives from a search for moral universality, that is, for "minimal value conceptions on which all persons could agree." Third, the primacy of justice stems from Kohlberg's cognitive, or rational, approach to morality. In Kohlberg's words, "justice asks for 'objective' or rational reasons and justifications for choice rather than being satisfied with subjective, 'decisionistic', personal commitments to aims and to other persons."[12] Finally, the most important

reason for the primacy of justice, in Kohlberg's view, is that it is "the most structural feature of moral judgment." As Kohlberg puts it, "With the moral domain defined in terms of justice, we have been successful in . . . elaborating stages which are structural systems in the Piagetian tradition."[13] Care reasoning, according to Kohlberg, may not be capable of being represented in terms of the criteria that he takes to define Piagetian cognitive stages.

Kohlberg's arguments for according primacy to justice reasoning are unsatisfactory, for several reasons. First, the methodological considerations to which he appeals entitle us to infer only that justice is primary in that domain of morality which can be represented in terms of Piagetian hard stages but not to infer that justice is primary to morality as such. Second, his appeal to certain metaethical considerations is controversial at best, question begging at worst. Whether moral judgments express universalizable prescriptions rather than interpretations of situational facts, whether there are "minimal value conceptions on which all persons could agree," whether "personal commitments to aims and to other persons" are excluded as rational justifications of choice, as Kohlberg seems to suggest, are all issues that cannot be resolved simply by presuming the primacy of a type of reasoning that has these features. Each of these assumptions is controversial and calls for defense in its own right.

Kohlberg's definition of the moral domain in terms of the primacy of justice is troubling for a third reason. Kohlberg claims that higher scores on his scale of moral development are correlated with participation in the secondary institutions of society, such as government and the workplace outside the home. By contrast, care reasoning is supposed to be relevant only to special relationships among "family, friends, and group members."[14] These two sorts of moral reasoning exemplify, respectively, the "public," or "political," realm and the "private," or "personal," realm. Kohlberg's primacy of justice reasoning coincides with a long-standing presumption of Western thought that the world of personal relationships, of the family and of family ties and loyalties, that is, the traditional world of women, is a world of lesser moral interest and importance than the public world of government and the marketplace, that is, the male-dominated world outside the home.

For Kohlberg, considerations of justice and rights have to do with abstract persons bound together by a social contract to act in ways that show mutual respect for rights which they possess equally. Considerations of justice do not require that persons know each other personally. Relatives, friends, or perfect strangers all deserve the same fair treatment and respect. In Kohlberg's view, considerations of special relationship and of caring seem merely to enrich with compassion the judgments that are based on prior considerations of justice. In no way would considerations of special relationship, for Kohlberg, override those of justice and rights. Unless caring and community presupposed prior judgments of justice, they would seem, in Kohlberg's terms, not to be "morally valid."[15]

For those interpersonal relationships which lack mutual concern, or even personal acquaintance, considerations of justice may have to suffice morally. But this does not entail that those considerations are of overriding moral importance for those relationships which involve mutual interest and personal concern. To explore what it might mean for caring and the closeness of relationships to override the moral significance of justice and rights. . . I shall take the liberty of performing a sex-change operation on the Heinz dilemma, the most famous of the dilemmas used by Kohlberg to measure the level of moral reasoning of his research subjects. The original dilemma is as follows:

> In Europe, a woman was near death from cancer. One drug might save her, a form of radium that a druggist in the same town had recently discovered. The druggist was charging $2000, ten times what the drug cost him to make. The sick woman's husband, Heinz, went to everyone he knew to borrow the money, but he could only get together, about half of what it cost. He told the druggist that his wife was dying and asked him to sell it cheaper or let him pay later. But the druggist said, "No." The husband got desperate and broke into the man's store to steal the drug for his wife. Should the husband have done that? Why?[16]

Of course, there is already a woman in the Heinz dilemma, namely, Heinz's wife. She is easy to forget since, unlike Heinz, she has no name, and unlike both Heinz and the also unnamed druggist, she is the only person in the story who does not act. Instead she is simply the passive patient who is there to be saved, the one whose presence provides both Heinz and the druggist with their, moral opportunities for heroism and villainy. Let us remove her from this oblivion. First, she needs a name: I will call her Heidi. Next, let us change her role from that of patient to that of agent. Finally, let us suppose that the druggist, another unnamed character in the original dilemma, is also a woman; I will call her Hilda. Now we are ready for our new story: the "Heidi dilemma":

> In Europe, a man was near death from cancer. One drug might save him, a form of radium that a druggist in the same town, a woman named Hilda, had recently discovered. The druggist was charging $2000, ten times what the drug cost her to make. A *perfect stranger,* a woman named Heidi, chanced to read about the sick man's plight in the local newspaper. She was moved to act. She went to everyone she knew to borrow the money for the drug, but she could get together only about half of what it cost. She asked the druggist to sell the drug more cheaply or to let her, Heidi, pay for it later. But Hilda, the druggist, said no. Heidi broke into the woman's store to steal the drug *for a man she did not know.* Should Heidi have done that? Why?

If Kohlberg's dilemma can indeed be resolved through impartial considerations of justice and rights, then the solution to the dilemma should not depend upon the existence of any special relationship between the person who is dying of cancer and the person who might steal the drug. I suggest, however, that the conviction many of us have, that Heinz should steal the drug for his nameless wife in the original dilemma, rests at least in part on our notion of responsibilities arising out of the sort of special relationship that marriage is supposed to be. Without this relationship, our conviction that theft ought to be committed might well, on grounds provided simply by the story, be much weaker than it is. If the patient and the prospective thief were absolute strangers, I suspect that we would be far less likely to say that a serious personal risk should be undertaken to steal the drug, break the law, and harm the druggist—even to save a life.

In *Moral Stages,* Kohlberg considers the question of whether the solution to the original dilemma depends only upon considerations of justice or rather upon considerations of special relationship as well. To illustrate what he regards as cognitive improvement in answering this question, Kohlberg cites an interview with an eleven-year-old boy with whom he discussed the Heinz dilemma. The boy was asked whether a "man" should steal a drug to save the life of a stranger, "if there was no other way to save his life." The boy's first response was that it does not seem that one should steal for someone about whom one does not care.

Subsequently, the boy revised his judgment: "But somehow it doesn't seem fair to say that. The stranger has his life and wants to live just as much as your wife; it isn't fair to say you should steal it for your wife but not for the stranger."[17] For Kohlberg, as illustrated by his young respondent, a concern for universalizing a moral judgment leads to a preference for justice reasoning and away from reasoning in terms of care and special relationship.

What are we to make of such an example? First, the boy's reasoning is quite perceptive: it is *not* fair to steal the drug for one's spouse but not for a stranger. Considerations of fairness would not lead to this distinction among needy persons. If there is a moral distinction of this sort between what is owed to one's kin and what is owed to strangers, the distinction would derive from some other moral consideration, most probably the special nature of the relationship to one's kin. If my duty to steal in order to save a life is owed to my kin in virtue of my kinship relationship to them, then the fact that it is not fair that I do not have this duty toward strangers does not entail that, all things considered, I therefore have the same duty toward strangers that I have toward my kin. We cannot presuppose in advance that considerations of justice have moral primacy, never to be outweighed by considerations of special relationship. *Considerations of justice and rights do not necessarily lead to the conclusion that, all things considered, we owe to all persons the special treatment that is due to our families and friends. It may indeed not be fair, but fairness is not our only moral concern.*

This is, of course, not to deny altogether the moral importance of justice. I argue for the need to integrate considerations of justice with those of care.

. . . My approach is, thus, integrationist through and through. Neither justice nor care is necessarily overriding under any and all circumstances. The specific features of each particular case are critical in determining which moral concerns take priority in that case. In the original Heinz dilemma in particular, the marital relationship between Heinz and the sick woman, and not considerations of justice alone, seems to be what finally tips the balance of *competing* moral concerns toward the conclusion that Heinz should steal the drug to save the woman's life.

The second problem with Kohlberg's eleven-year-old respondent who thought that Heinz should steal the drug to save the life of any impoverished, dying stranger is that it is (forgivably) naive about moral practice. Kohlberg's justice framework, we should recall, is designed to measure only abstract moral reasoning, reasoning detached from any necessary connection to moral practices. Kohlberg's framework neither measures nor evaluates the sorts of moral commitments that motivate behavior. Few persons, even at the higher stage of justice reasoning, would judge, in a manner that would impel the corresponding behavior, that anyone ought to steal to save, the life of a stranger. If you are not persuaded that this is so, then please consider one final modified form of the Heinz dilemma: the *you* dilemma:

> *You* are the perfect stranger who has just read in your morning paper about a person dying of cancer and about the only drug that can save her, but which she cannot afford. *You* are the stranger who fails to convince the druggist to sell the drug more cheaply. Will you (really) take the risk of stealing the drug to save the life of someone you do not know? What moral judgment (and practical resolution) will you (really) reach in this dilemma?

How many of those who endorse the judgment that you should steal to save the life of a stranger actually act on it? Yet this failure to act does not stem from a lack of impoverished, critically ill persons in our society or from a lack of knowledge by most people about the tragic existence of such cases. (The AIDS epidemic has ensured widespread knowledge about the crisis in health care delivery.) The *you* dilemma confronts us with the gap between moral reasoning and moral behavior. It discloses the limited bearing on true moral maturity of those moral judgments upon which we do not act.

In addition, the *you* dilemma alerts us to another factor that may differentiate a justice orientation from a care orientation. With our verbalized moral judgments, we lay claim to our moral identities, to the sorts of persons we, morally, aspire to be—and wish others to think we are. We express the purported sweep of our moral visions and our moral aspirations. A justice orientation, with its strict impartiality and grandiose universality, lends itself to a more "heroic"[18] form of moral expression than does a care orientation. Judgments based upon considerations of justice and rights seem permeated with an impersonal nobility of moral concern, unlike considerations of "my husband," "my sister," or "my body."

Nobility of moral concern is especially easy to affect when one is merely responding to a test interviewer or when real commitment, for some other reason, is not measured and deeds need not follow upon words. Of course, some individuals in our world really do steal or undertake other grave risks to save the lives of strangers.[19] Moral thinking would be sorely impoverished without such heroic exemplars.[20]

Many people, however, who judge that "one" should steal to save a dying stranger are not manifesting a genuine readiness to act. Most such judgments are cut off from any link with practice. Such judgments might be naively sincere and betoken understandable moral inexperience (as with Kohlberg's eleven-year-old boy) or forgivable moral weakness; or they might, instead, be insincere and exhibit moral hypocrisy. Of greatest relevance to the present discussion, perhaps, such judgments are seldom acted upon because the complexities of our lives interweave the universalizing demands of justice with other competing and equally imperative moral concerns.

Context

In addition to a substantive orientation to care and relationships, the "different voice" of Gilligan's studies shows certain distinctive formal features

as well. *Gilligan suggests that women, more than men, respond inadequately to such dilemmas as the Heinz dilemma because of their hypothetical nature.* In Gilligan's view, the dilemmas are too abstract and, as she puts it, they separate "the moral problem from the social contingencies of its possible occurrence."[21]

Gilligan's insight can be strengthened by a change in focus. Of greater importance than whether the dilemmas are real or hypothetical, I believe, is the extent of the contextual detail in which they are described. A work of literature or a film can portray a moral crisis with enough detail to make the responses and behavior of the protagonist plausible, even compelling, to readers or viewers. The hypothetical nature of the moral dilemmas facing numerous protagonists of fiction does not at all preclude thoughtful moral consideration or profound moral insight about those fictional cases.

Perhaps Gilligan has been distracted by the fact that when we learn of real-world moral dilemmas, we typically know the people and a good bit about their lives and their current situations. We rely upon this tacit but crucial background information to help generate alternative possible solutions for those problems. Hypothetical dilemmas have no social or historical context outside their own specifications; lacking any background information, we require longer stories in order to feel that we know most of the pertinent information that can be expected in cases of this sort. What matters, I contend, is having sufficient detail for understanding the story at hand, whether the story is of a real moral dilemma or a hypothetical one.

Gilligan shows convincingly how the hypothetical Heinz dilemma would be significantly altered were it to be enriched by some very plausible details. Commenting on the response to the Heinz dilemma given by one subject, Gilligan says:

Heinz's decision to steal is considered not in terms of the logical priority of life over property, which justifies its rightness, but rather in terms of the actual consequences that stealing would have for a man of limited means and little social power.

Considered in the light of its probable outcomes—his wife dead, or Heinz in jail, brutalized by the violence of that experience and his life compromised by a record of felony—the dilemma itself changes. Its resolution has less to do with the relative weights of life and property in an abstract moral conception than with the collision between two lives, formerly conjoined but now in opposition, where the continuation of one life can occur only at the expense of the other.[22]

In order to emphasize the importance of contextual detail, let us elaborate the Heinz-Heidi dilemma even further.

The woman who is dying of cancer is weary and depressed from the losing battle she has been fighting for several years. It all began with cancer of the colon, and her doctors convinced her to resort to a colostomy. Now, several years later, it is clear that the malignancy was not stopped by this drastic measure. Experiencing her own present embodiment as unacceptably disfigured, weakened, and in pain from the cancer that continues to poison her system, bedridden and dependent on others for her daily functioning, she has lost hope and grown despondent about a fate that, to her, is worse than death. How does this woman really measure the value of her own life?

And perhaps there is more to the druggist's story as well. Her husband deserted her and her three children years ago and has paid not a penny of his court-ordered child-support money, So the druggist struggles mightily day after day to keep her family together and tends a small pharmacy that barely meets the material needs of her children, let alone her own. Moreover, she lives in a society that jealousy guards the private ownership of its property. Were she and her children to fall into poverty, that society would throw her a few crumbs of welfare support, but only after she had exhausted all other resources and at the cost of her dignity and the invasion of her privacy.

In this society, the tiny share of goods on which she can labor and whose fruits she can sell are the slender means of livelihood for her and her family. The notion of property does not mean the same thing to a single mother with dependent children, living at the margins under the constraints of a "free

enterprise" economy, as it does to the affluent shareholders of General Dynamics. The druggist, too, is a person of flesh and blood with a story of her own to tell.

There are other contingencies that could be imaginatively explored. I have already referred to one of Gilligan's interviews in which the subject ponders the risks and uncertainties of theft for a person who lacks the skill or experience to bring the job off successfully—burglary is no mean accomplishment. Then there are the possible deleterious side effects of drugs that are proclaimed as cancer cures in all the glittering hyperbole of the mass media before they have been adequately tested. When the story is filled out with such additional considerations, it is no longer possible to resolve the dilemma with a simple principle asserting the primacy of life over property. Economic constraints can turn property into a family's only means to life and can force a competition of life *against* life in a desperate struggle not all can win.

Indeed, the most pervasive and universalizable problems of justice in the Heinz dilemma lie entirely outside the scope of its narrowly chosen details. The significance of the larger justice problem in the Heinz dilemma is neglected in Kohlberg's discussions. His construction of the dilemma as one individual's own moral problem forces a choice between two alternatives that actually are identical in at least one important respect: neither threatens the institutional context that partly structures Heinz's (and his wife's) problem.

The significance of this more fundamental justice problem has also not been commented on by Gilligan, although she perceptively sees the importance of grasping the situation in terms of rich contextual detail. Gilligan seems to think that contextual detail is a concern only of people whose moral reasoning centers on care and relationships. She does not appear to realize that in reasoning about justice and rights, it is equally inappropriate to draw conclusions from highly abbreviated descriptions of situations. Gilligan's position would be strengthened, I believe, by incorporating this insight.

In Heinz's hypothetical situation, in addition to the justice dilemma of life vs. property, there are also broad issues of social justice at stake regarding the delivery of health care. These issues cannot be resolved or even properly understood from the scanty detail that is provided in any of Kohlberg's formulations of the dilemma. We must have background knowledge about the inadequacy of health care provided for people without financial resources in a society that allows most health care resources to be privately owned, privately sold for profit in the marketplace, and privately withheld from people who cannot afford the market price or the insurance rates. And before we can resolve the problem, we must know what the alternatives are and must assess them for the degree to which they approximate an ideal of fair and just health care available to all and the degree to which they achieve, or fall short of, other relevant moral ideals.

Should we, for example, allow health care resources to remain privately owned while we simply implement a Medicaid-like program of government transfer payments to subsidize the cost of health care to the needy? Or should the government provide mandatory health insurance for everyone, with premiums taken from those who can pay, as a kind of health care tax, and premiums waived for those who cannot pay, as an in-kind welfare benefit? Or should we instead abolish private ownership of health care resources altogether, and, if so, should our alternative be grassroots-organized health care cooperatives or state-run socialized medicine? Selecting an answer to these questions and resolving the larger justice dilemma that the Heidi-Heinz situation merely intimates requires an inordinate amount of detail as well as a complex theoretical perspective on matters of economics, politics, and social and domestic life. Thus, contextual detail is of overriding importance to matters of justice as well as to matters of care and relationships.

Despite my general agreement with Gilligan's emphasis on contextual detail in moral reasoning, there is a second feature of her approach that I question. Gilligan believes that a concern for contextual detail moves a moral reasoner away from principled moral reasoning in the direction of "contextual relativism." She suggests that persons who exemplify this form of moral reasoning have "difficulty in arriving at definitive answers to moral questions" and show a "reluctance to judge" others.[23] Obviously, many people experience this reluctance at some time or other, and some people experience it all the time. But we misunderstand moral reasoning if we regard this as a necessary or inevitable outcome of being concerned with contextual detail.

Kohlberg's response to Gilligan on this point, however, is over-simple. In Kohlberg's view, the notion of a principle is the notion of that which guides moral judgment in a way that allows for exceptions. On this construal, a responsiveness to contextual details and a willingness to alter moral judgments depending upon the context do not, therefore, imply an abandonment of moral principles or a genuine moral relativism.[24] For Kohlberg, an increasing awareness of context need only indicate an increasing awareness of the difficulties of applying one's principles to specific cases. There is something to this: *sensitivity to contextual detail need not carry with it the relativistic view that there simply are no moral rights or wrongs, or the slightly weaker view that there is merely no way to decide such matters.* Contextual sensitivity need only reflect uncertainties about just which principles to apply to a particular case, or a concern that one does not yet have sufficient knowledge to apply one's principles, or a worry that one's principles are themselves too general and abstract to deal with the endless moral variety of human life.

This last alternative merits special emphasis. Kohlberg seems unconcerned about the excess generality and abstractness of most moral rules and principles. Yet, when we heed attentively the variety and complexity of contextual detail in real everyday situations we see how limited is the help afforded by abstract moral principles in reaching conclusive moral judgments. A principle that asserts the primacy of life over property is obviously not wrong; in the abstract, few of us would challenge the point. Its relevance to a particular situation, however, depends on countless details about the quality of the particular lives at stake, the meaning of that particular property, the identities of those involved, the range of available options, the potential benefits and harms of each, the institutional setting that structures the situation and the lives of its participants, and the crucial possibility (or its absence) of changing that institutional context.

These details are ordinarily very complex; some sway us in one direction, some in another. In no time at all, we need principles for the *ordering* of our principles. Kohlberg's suggestion that contextual detail helps one to figure out which principle to apply simply does not get us very far in understanding how we finally decide what ought to be done in the complex, institutionally structured situations of our everyday lives. And this is true whether the reasoning is about care and relationships or about matters of social justice.

Kohlberg acknowledges that his scale of moral development does not measure the whole of moral reasoning; it is limited to what he calls structural stages in the development of reasoning about justice and rights. Drawing upon Gilligan's gender-based critique of Kohlberg, I have discussed two other limitations: first, the absence of any genuine integration of moral considerations having to do with care and relationships; and second, the absence of an adequate account of how people reason about complex and richly specified situations in terms of general and abstract moral rules and principles.

NOTES

1. *In a Different Voice* (Cambridge: Harvard University Press, 1982).
2. Frigga Haug, "Morals Also Have Two Genders," trans. Rodney Livingstone, *New Left Review* 143 (1984): 55.
3. "Do the Social Sciences Have an Adequate Theory of Moral Development?" in Norma Haan, Robert N. Bellah, Paul Rabinow, and William M. Sullivan, eds., *Social Science as Moral Inquiry* (New York: Columbia University Press 1983), pp. 33–51; "Reply," *Signs* 11 (1986): 324–33; "Moral Orientation and Moral Development," in Eva Feder Kittay and Diana T. Meyers, eds., *Women and Moral Theory* (Totowa, N.J.: Rowman & Littlefield, 1987), pp. 19–33; and "Remapping the Moral Domain: New Images of the Self in Relationship," in Thomas C. Heller, Morton Sosna, and David E. Wellbery, eds., *Reconstructing Individualism* (Stanford: Stanford University Press, 1986), pp. 237–52; reprinted in Carol Gilligan, Janie Victoria Ward, Jill McLean Taylor, with Betty Bardige, eds., *Mapping the Moral Domain* (Cambridge: Harvard Center for the Study of Gender, Education, and Human Development, 1988), pp. 3–20.

4. *In a Different Voice*, pp. 63, 100, 147.
5. Ibid., pp. 19, 63, 69, 90, 100.
6. Lawrence Kohlberg, *The Philosophy of Moral Development* (San Francisco: Harper & Row, 1981).
7. *In a Different Voice*, p. 22.
8. The literature on these themes has mushroomed rapidly in recent years. The following are important collections of papers that, in whole or in part, deal with care ethics: *Social Research* 50 (Fall 1983); Kittay and Meyers, eds., *Women and Moral Theory*; Marsha Hanen and Kai Nielsen, eds., *Science, Morality, and Feminist Theory, Canadian Journal of Philosophy* suppl. Vol. 13 (1987); Claudia Card, ed., *Feminist Ethics* (Lawrenceville: University Press of Kansas, 1991); and Eve Browning Cole and Susan Coultrap-McQuin, eds., *Explorations in Feminist Ethics* (Bloomington: Indiana University Press, 1992).
9. In Lawrence Kohlberg, Charles Levine, and Alexandra Hewer, *Moral Stages: A Current Reformulation and Response to Critics* (Basel: S. Karger, 1983).
10. Ibid., pp. 20, 122–23.
11. Ibid., pp. 93–95.
12. Ibid., p. 93.
13. Ibid., p. 92.
14. Ibid., pp. 129–31. Kohlberg relied heavily for this assessment on Lawrence J. Walker's meta-analysis of research into cognitive moral development: "Sex Difference in the Development of Moral Reasoning," *Child Development* 55, no.3 (1984): 677–91. This meta-analysis has more recently been challenged: see Diana Baumrind, "Sex Differences in Moral Reasoning: Response to Walker's (1984) Conclusion That There Are None," *Child Development* 57 (1986):511–21.
15. Kohlberg et al., *Moral Stages,* p. 92.
16. Lawrence Kohlberg, "Stage and Sequence: The Cognitive-Developmental Approach to Socialization," in D. A. Goslin, ed., *Handbook of Socialization Theory and Research* (Chicago: Rand McNally, 1969), p. 379.
17. Kohlberg et al., *Moral Stages,* p. 92.
18. Eva Kittay suggested the relevance of heroism to this part of my discussion.
19. See Philip Hallie, *Lest Innocent Blood Be Shed* (New York: Harper & Row, 1979); and Lawrence Blum, "Moral Exemplars: Reflections on Schindler, the Trocmes, and Others," *Midwest Studies in Philosophy* 13(1988): 196–221.
20. For example, the way the orientation of a moral theory is revealed in part by its particular choice of heroic exemplars.
21. *In a Different Voice*, p. 100.
22. Ibid., p. 101.
23. Ibid., pp. 101–2.
24. Kohlberg et al., *Moral Stages*, pp. 145–48.

DISCUSSION QUESTIONS:

1. Do you think that matters of justice have priority from a moral standpoint? What defense can you offer for this meta-ethical conclusion?

2. What would you do in the "You dilemma"? Why?

3. Do you think that you have moral obligations to friends or family that you don't have to strangers? If so, what accounts for this fact? Can a Kantian or Utilitarian explain why these special moral obligations hold?

Argument Reconstruction Exercises:

I. Friedman is interested in showing that the Heinz dilemma can be solved in a number of different ways, and that if this is so, then impartial considerations do not exhaust the moral considerations of any given scenario. Identify the premises and conclusion in this excerpt.

> If Kohlberg's dilemma can indeed be resolved through impartial considerations of justice and rights, then the solution to the dilemma should not depend upon the existence of any special relationship between the person who is dying of cancer and the person who might steal the drug. I suggest, however, that the conviction that many of us have, that Heinz should steal the drug for his nameless wife in the original dilemma, rests at least in part on our notion of responsibilities arising out of the sort of special relationship that marriage is supposed to be. (page 345)

II. Kohlberg argues that justice is "primary" in moral reasoning. The following text paraphrases the argument presented on page 344.

> Morality is based on a prescriptivist conception of judgment (i.e., a system that will generate universalizable "ought" claims that apply to all moral agents regardless of situational facts). And since justice is the attempt to treat all individuals fairly regardless of situational fact, justice is the primary moral concept.

III. Friedman argues that context is crucial for solving moral dilemmas, and she illustrates this with her modified version of the Heinz dilemma. Solving the dilemma, she thinks, requires addressing questions concerning social structure, availability of healthcare, taxation schemes, extent of private property, etc. Identify the premises and conclusion in this excerpt.

> Selecting an answer to these questions and resolving the larger justice dilemma that the Heidi-Heinz situation merely intimates requires an inordinate amount of detail as well as a complex theoretical perspective on matters of economics, politics, and social and domestic life. Thus contextual detail is of overriding importance to matters of justice as well as to matters of care and relationships. (page 349)

IV. Friedman accuses Kohlberg of drawing a mistaken inference about the implications of contextual moral thinking (page 349). Re-create Kohlberg's criticized argument from the following proses:

> Women seem to adjust their moral conclusions on the basis of contextual details of a case. But if there are objective moral principles, these principles are not context dependent and so what we ought to do in a given situation would not fluctuate in this way. Only if principles were context-relative could this be so. It follows then that the way most women reason assumes a kind of moral relativism.

13.5 THE ETHICS OF CARE AS MORAL THEORY

VIRGINIA HELD (2006)

Virginia Held is Distinguished Professor of Philosophy at the City University of New York, Graduate School, and Professor Emerita of Philosophy and Women's Studies at Hunter College; she is especially known for her work in social and political philosophy and feminist ethics. In this essay, Held develops the ethics of care as an alternative moral theory to such traditional approaches as **Kantian ethics, utilitarianism,** and

virtue ethics. As she puts it, the ethics of care "takes the experience of women in caring activities such as mothering as central, interprets and emphasizes the values inherent in caring practices, shows the inadequacies of other theories for dealing with the moral aspects of caring activity, and then considers generalizing the insights of caring to other questions of morality." (page 356)

Reading Questions:

1. What features of the ethics of care distinguish it from the ethical theories offered by utilitarians, Kantians, and virtue theorists?

2. How, according to Held, is the concept of a person presented by the ethics of care different from that presented by such moral theories as Kantianism and utilitarianism?

3. Held describes the ethics of care as a response to feminist critiques of Kantian and utilitarian moral theories. What is the nature of those critiques? How is the ethics of care a response to them?

4. Held describes care as both a practice and a value. In what way is it a practice and in what way is it a value?

5. Held considers several views on the relationship between the values of justice and care. What are the views she considers? Which ones does she reject and why? Which one does she accept?

6. Held rejects the view that "universal, impartial, liberal moral principles of justice and right should always be accorded priority over the concerns of caring relationships, which include considerations of trust, friendship and loyalty" (page 360). What is her argument against this view?

By now, the ethics of care has moved far beyond its original formulations, and any attempt to evaluate it should consider much more than the one or two early works so frequently cited. It has been developed as a moral theory relevant not only to the so-called private realms of family and friendship but to medical practice, law, political life, the organization of society, war, and international relations.

The ethics of care is sometimes seen as a potential moral theory to be substituted for such dominant moral theories as Kantian ethics, utilitarianism, or Aristotelian virtue ethics. It is sometimes seen as a form of virtue ethics. It is almost always developed as emphasizing neglected moral considerations of at least as much importance as the considerations central to moralities of justice and rights or of utility and preference satisfaction. And many who contribute to the understanding of

the ethics of care seek to integrate the moral considerations, such as justice, which other moral theories have clarified, satisfactorily with those of care, though they often see the need to reconceptualize these considerations.

Features of the Ethics of Care

I think one can discern among various versions of the ethics of care a number of major features.

First, the central focus of the ethics of care is on the compelling moral salience of attending to and meeting the needs of the particular others for whom we take responsibility. Caring for one's child, for instance, may well and defensibly be at the forefront of a person's moral concerns. The ethics of care recognizes that human beings are dependent for many years of their lives, that the moral claim of those dependent on us for the care they need is pressing and that there are highly important moral aspects in developing the relations of caring that enable human beings to live and progress. . . . Moralities built on the image of the independent, autonomous, rational individual largely overlook the reality of human dependence and the morality for which it calls. The ethics of care attends to this central concern of human life and delineates the moral values involved. It refuses to relegate care to a realm "outside morality." How caring for particular others should be reconciled with the claims of, for instance, universal justice is an issue that needs to be addressed. But the ethics of care starts with the moral claims of particular others, for instance, of one's child, whose claims can be compelling regardless of universal principles.

Second, in the epistemological process of trying to understand what morality would recommend and what it would be morally best for us to do and to be, the ethics of care values emotion rather than rejects it. Not all emotion is valued, of course, but in contrast with the dominant rationalist approaches, such emotions as sympathy, empathy, sensitivity, and responsiveness are seen as the kind of moral emotions that need to be cultivated not only to help in the implementation of the dictates of reason but to better ascertain what morality recommends. . . Since even the helpful emotions can often become misguided or worse—as when excessive empathy with others leads to a wrongful degree of self-denial or when benevolent concern crosses over into controlling domination—we need an *ethics* of care, not just care itself. The various aspects and expressions of care and caring relations need to be subjected to moral scrutiny and *evaluated,* not just observed and described.

Third, the ethics of care rejects the view of the dominant moral theories that the more abstract the reasoning about a moral problem the better because the more likely to avoid bias and arbitrariness, the more nearly to achieve impartiality. The ethics of care respects rather than removes itself from the claims of particular others with whom we share actual relationships[2]. . .

To most advocates of the ethics of care, the compelling moral claim of the particular other may be valid even when it conflicts with the requirement usually made by moral theories that moral judgments be universalizeable, and this is of fundamental moral importance.[3] Hence the potential conflict between care and justice, friendship and impartiality, loyalty and universality. To others, however, there need be no conflict if universal judgments come to incorporate appropriately the norms of care previously disregarded. . . .

The ethics of care may seek to limit the applicability of universal rules to certain domains where they are more appropriate, like the domain of law, and resist their extension to other domains. Such rules may simply be inappropriate in, for instance, the contexts of family and friendship, yet relations in these domains should certainly be *evaluated,* not merely described, hence morality should not be limited to abstract rules. We should be able to give moral guidance concerning actual relations that are trusting, considerate, and caring and concerning those that are not. . . .

A fourth characteristic of the ethics of care is that like much feminist thought in many areas, it reconceptualizes traditional notions about the public and the private. . . . Dominant moral theories have seen "public" life as relevant to morality while missing the moral significance of the "private" domains of family and friendship. Thus the dominant theories have assumed that morality should be sought for unrelated, independent, and mutually indifferent individuals assumed to be equal. They have posited an abstract, fully rational "agent as such" from which to construct morality[4], while missing the moral issues that arise between interconnected persons in the contexts of family, friendship, and social groups. In the context of the family, it is typical for relations to be between persons with highly unequal power who did not choose the ties and obligations in which they find themselves enmeshed. For instance, no child can choose her parents yet she may well have obligations to care for them. Relations of this kind are standardly noncontractual, and conceptualizing them as contractual would often undermine or at least obscure the trust on which their worth depends. The ethics of care addresses rather than neglects moral issues arising in relations among the unequal and dependent, relations that are often laden with emotion and involuntary, and then notices how often these attributes apply not only in the household but in the wider society as well. For instance, persons do not choose which gender, racial, class, ethnic, religious, national, or cultural groups to be brought up in, yet these sorts of ties may be important aspects of who they are and how their experience can contribute to moral understanding.

A fifth characteristic of the ethics of care is the conception of persons with which it begins. . . .

The ethics of care usually works with a conception of persons as relational, rather than as the self-sufficient independent individuals of the dominant moral theories. The dominant theories can be interpreted as importing into moral theory a concept of the person developed primarily for liberal political and economic theory, seeing the person as a rational, autonomous agent, or a self-interested individual. On this view, society is made up of "independent, autonomous units who cooperate only when the terms of cooperation are such as to make it further the ends of each of the parties," in Brian Barry's words.[5] Or, if they are Kantians, they refrain from actions that they could not will to be universal laws to which all fully rational and autonomous individual agents could agree. What such views hold, in Michael Sandel's critique of them, is that "what separates us is in some important sense prior to what connects us—epistemologically prior as well as morally prior. We are distinct individuals first and *then* we form relationships.[6] In Martha Nussbaum's liberal feminist morality, "the flourishing of human beings taken one by one is both analytically and normatively prior to the flourishing" of any group.[7]

The ethics of care, in contrast, characteristically sees persons as relational and interdependent, morally and epistemologically. Every person starts out as a child dependent on those providing us care, and we remain interdependent with others in thoroughly fundamental ways throughout our lives. That we can think and act as if we were independent depends on a network of social relations making it possible for us to do so. And our relations are part of what constitute our identity. This is not to say that we cannot become autonomous; feminists have done much interesting work developing an alternative conception of autonomy in place of the liberal individualist one.[8] Feminists have much experience rejecting or reconstituting relational ties that are oppressive. But it means that from the perspective of an ethics

of care, to construct morality *as if* we were Robinson Crusoes, or, to use Hobbes's image, mushrooms sprung from nowhere, is misleading.[9]

Even if the liberal ideal is meant only to instruct us on what would be rational in the terms of its ideal model, thinking of persons as the model presents them has effects that should not be welcomed. As Annette Baier writes, "Liberal morality, if unsupplemented, may *unfit* people to be anything other than what its justifying theories suppose them to be, ones who have no interest in each others' interests.[10] There is strong empirical evidence of how adopting a theoretical model can lead to behavior that mirrors it. Various studies show that studying economics, with its "repeated and intensive exposure to a model whose unequivocal prediction" is that people will decide what to do on the basis of self-interest, leads economics students to be less cooperative and more inclined to free ride than other students.[11]

The conception of the person adopted by the dominant moral theories provides moralities at best suitable for legal, political, and economic interactions between relative strangers, once adequate trust exists for them to form a political entity.[12] The ethics of care is, instead, hospitable to the relatedness of persons. It sees many of our responsibilities as not freely entered into but presented to us by the accidents of our embeddedness in familial and social and historical contexts. It often calls on us to *take* responsibility, while liberal individualist morality focuses on how we should leave each other alone. The view of persons as embedded and encumbered seems fundamental to much feminist thinking about morality and especially to the ethics of care. . . .

The Ethics of Care and Virtue Ethics

Insofar as the ethics of care wishes to cultivate in persons the characteristics of a caring person and the skills of activities of caring, might an ethic of care be assimilated to virtue theory?. . .

In my view, although there are similarities between them and although to be caring is no doubt a virtue, *the ethics of care is not simply a kind of virtue ethics. Virtue ethics focuses especially on the states of character of individuals, whereas the ethics of care concerns itself especially with caring relations. Caring relations have primary value. . . .*

If virtue ethics is interpreted as less restricted to motives, and if it takes adequate account of the results of the virtuous person's activities for the persons cared for, it may better include the concerns of the ethics of care. It would still, however, focus on the dispositions of individuals, whereas the ethics of care focuses on social relations and the social practices and values that sustain them. The traditional Man of Virtue may be almost as haunted by his patriarchal past as the Man of Reason. The work of care has certainly not been among the virtuous activities to which he has adequately attended. . . .

The ethics of care is sometimes thought inadequate because of its inability to provide definite answers in cases of conflicting moral demands. Virtue theory has similarly been criticized for offering no more than what detractors call a "bag of virtues," with no clear indication of how to prioritize the virtues or apply their requirements, especially when they seem to conflict. Defenders of the ethics of care respond that the adequacy of the definite answers provided by, for instance, utilitarian and Kantian moral theories is illusory. Cost-benefit analysis is a good example of a form of utilitarian calculation that purports to provide clear answers to questions about what we ought to do, but from the point of view of moral understanding, its answers are notoriously dubious. So, too, often are casuistic reasonings about deontological rules. To advocates of the ethics of care, its alternative moral epistemology seems better. It stresses sensitivity to the multiple relevant considerations in particular contexts, cultivating the traits of character and of relationship that sustain caring, and promoting the, dialogue that corrects and enriches the perspective of any one individual.[13] The ethics of care is hospitable to the methods of discourse ethics, though with an emphasis on actual dialogue that empowers its participants to express themselves rather than on discourse so ideal that actual differences of viewpoint fall away. . . .[14]

The Feminist Background

. . . The dominant moral theories when the feminism of the late twentieth century appeared on the scene were Kantian moral theory and utilitarianism. These were the theories that, along with their relevant metaethical questions, dominated the literature in moral philosophy and the courses taught to students.[15] They were also the moral outlooks that continued to have a significant influence outside philosophy in the field of law, one of the few areas that had not banished moral questions in favor of purportedly value-free psychology and social science.

These dominant moral theories can be seen to be modeled on the experience of men in public life and in the marketplace. When women's experience is thought to be as relevant to morality as men's, a position whose denial would seem to be biased, these moralities can be seen to fit very inadequately the morally relevant experience of women in the household. Women's experience has typically included cultivating special relationships with family and friends, rather than primarily dealing impartially with strangers, and providing large amounts of caring labor for children and often for ill or elderly family members. Affectionate sensitivity and responsiveness to need may seem to provide better moral guidance for what should be done in these contexts than do abstract rules or rational calculations of individual utilities. . . .

Both Kantian moralities of universal, abstract moral laws, and utilitarian versions of the ethics of Bentham and Mill advocating impartial calculations to determine what will produce the most happiness for the most people have been developed for interactions between relative strangers. Contractualism treats interactions between mutually disinterested individuals. All require impartiality and make no room at the foundational level for the partiality that connects us to those we care for and to those who care for us. Relations of family, friendship, and group identity have largely been missing from these theories, though recent attempts, which I find unsuccessful, have been made to handle such relations within them.

Although their conceptions of reason differ significantly, with Kantian theory rejecting the morality of instrumental reasoning and utilitarian theory embracing it, both types of theory are rationalistic. Both rely on one very simple supreme and universal moral principle: the Kantian categorical imperative, or the utilitarian principle of utility, in accordance with which everyone ought always to act. Both ask us to be entirely impartial and to reject emotion in determining what we ought to do. Though Kantian ethics enlists emotion in carrying out the dictates of reason, and utilitarianism allows each of us to count ourselves as one among all whose pain or pleasure will be affected by an action, for both kinds of theory we are to disregard our emotions in the epistemological process of figuring out what we ought to do. These characterizations also hold for contractualism.

These theories generalize from the ideal contexts of the state and the market, addressing the moral decisions of judges, legislators, policy makers, and citizens. But because they are *moral* theories rather than merely political or legal or economic theories, they extend their recommendations to what they take to be *all* moral decisions about how we ought to act in any context in which moral problems arise.

In Margaret Walker's assessment, these are idealized "theoretical-juridical" accounts of actual moral practices. They invoke the image of "a fraternity of independent peers invoking laws to deliver verdicts with authority."[16] Fiona Robinson asserts that in dominant moral theories, values such as autonomy, independence, noninterference, self-determination, fairness, and rights are given priority, and there is a "systematic devaluing of notions of interdependence, relatedness, and positive involvement" in the lives of others.[17] The theoretical-juridical accounts, Walker shows, are presented as appropriate for "the" moral agent, as recommendations for how "we" ought to act, but their canonical forms of moral judgment are the judgments of those who resemble "a judge, manager, bureaucrat, or gamesman.[18] They are abstract and idealized forms of the judgments made by persons who are dominant in an established social order. They do not represent the moral experiences of women caring for children or aged parents, or of minority service workers providing care for minimal wages. And they do not deal with the judgments of groups who must rely on communal solidarity for survival. . . .

In place of the dominant moral theories found inadequate, feminists have offered a variety of alternatives. There is not any single "feminist moral theory," but a number of approaches sharing a basic commitment to

eliminate gender bias in moral theorizing as well as elsewhere.[19]

Some feminists defend versions of Kantian moral theory[20] or utilitarianism[21] or of such related theories as contractualism[22] and liberal individualist moral theory.[23] But they respond to different concerns and interpret and apply these theories in ways that none or few of their leading nonfeminist defenders do. . . .

Other feminist theorists, at the same time, have gone much further in a distinctive direction. Rather than limiting themselves to extending traditional theories in nontraditional ways, they have developed a more distinctively different ethics: the ethics of care. Although most working within this approach share the goals of justice and equality for women that can be dealt with using traditional theories, they see the potential of a very different set of values for a more adequate treatment of moral issues not only within the family but in the wider society as well. *The ethics of care is a deep challenge to other moral theories. It takes the experience of women in caring activities such as mothering as central, interprets and emphasizes the values inherent in caring practices, shows the inadequacies of other theories for dealing with the moral aspects of caring activity, and then considers generalizing the insights of caring to other questions of morality. . . .*

Care as Practice and Value

What *is* care? What do we mean by the term 'care'? Can we define it in anything like a precise way? There is not yet anything close to agreement among those writing on care on what exactly we should take the meaning of this term to be, but there have been many suggestions, tacit and occasionally explicit. . . .

. . .In my view, as we clarify care, we need to see it in terms of *caring relations*.

Care is a practice involving the work of care-giving and the standards by which the practices of care can be evaluated. Care must concern itself with the effectiveness of its efforts to meet needs, but also with the motives with which care is provided. It seeks good caring relations. In normal cases, recipients of care sustain caring relations through their responsiveness—the look of satisfaction in the child, the smile of the patient. Where such responsiveness is not possible—with a severely mentally ill person, for instance—sustaining the relation may depend entirely on the caregiver, but it is still appropriate to think in terms of caring relations: The caregiver may be trying to form a relation or must imagine a relation.²⁴ Relations between persons can be criticized when they become dominating, exploitative, mistrustful, or hostile. Relations of care can be encouraged and maintained. . . .

Practices of justice such as primitive revenge and an eye for an eye have from the earliest times been engaged in and gradually reformed and refined. By now we have legal, judicial, and penal practices that only dimly resemble their ancient forerunners, and we have very developed theories of justice and of different kinds of justice with which to evaluate such practices. Practices of care—from mothering to caring for the ill to teaching children to cultivating social relations—have also changed a great deal from their earliest forms, but to a significant extent without the appropriate moral theorizing. That, I suggest, is part of what the ethics of care should be trying to fill in. The practices themselves already incorporate various values, often unrecognized, especially until recently by the philosophers engaged in moral theorizing who ought to be attending to them. And the practices themselves as they exist are often riddled with the gender injustices that pervade societies in most ways but that especially characterize most practices of care. So, moral theorizing is needed to understand the practices and to reform them.

Consider, for instance, mothering, in the sense of caring for children. It had long been imagined in the modern era after the establishment of the public/private distinction to be "outside morality" because it was based on instinct. Feminist critique has been needed to show how profoundly mistaken such a view is. Moral issues are confronted constantly in the practice of mothering and other caring work. There is constant need for the cultivation of the virtues appropriate to these practices, and of moral evaluation of how the practices are being carried out. To get a hint of how profoundly injustice has been embedded in the practice of mothering, one can compare the meaning of "mothering" with that

of "fathering," which standardly has meant no more than impregnating a woman and being the genetic father of a child. "Mothering" suggests that this activity must or should be done by women, whereas, except for lactation, there is no part of it that cannot be done by men as well. Many feminists argue that for actual practices of child care to be morally acceptable, they will have to be radically transformed to accord with principles of equality, though existing conceptions of equality should probably not be the primary moral focus of practices of care. This is only the beginning of the moral scrutiny to which they should be subject.

This holds also for other practices that can be thought of as practices of care. We need, then, not only to examine the practices and discern with new sensitivities the values already embedded or missing within them but also to construct the appropriate normative theory with which to evaluate them, reform them, and shape them anew. This, I think, involves understanding care as a value worthy of the kind of theoretical elaboration justice has received. Understanding the value of care involves understanding how it should not be limited to the household or family; care should be recognized as a political and social value also.

We all agree that justice is a value. There are also practices of justice: law enforcement, court proceedings, and so on. Practices incorporate values but also need to be evaluated by the normative standards values provide. A given actual practice of justice may only very inadequately incorporate within it the value of justice, and we need justice as a value to evaluate such a practice. The value of justice picks out certain aspects of the overall moral spectrum, those having to do with fairness, equality, and so on, and it would not be satisfactory to have only the most general value terms, such as 'good' and 'right,' 'bad' and 'wrong,' with which to do the evaluating of a practice of justice. Analogously, *for actual practices of care we need care as a value to pick out the appropriate cluster of moral considerations, such as sensitivity, trust, and mutual concern, with which to evaluate such practices.* It is not enough to think of care as simply work, describable empirically, with 'good' and 'right' providing all the normative evaluation of actual practices of care. Such practices are often morally deficient in ways specific to care as well as to justice. . . .

Care as relevant to an ethics of care incorporates the values we decide as feminists to find acceptable in it. And the ethics of care does not accept and describe the practices of care as they have evolved under actual historical conditions of patriarchal and other domination; it evaluates such practices and recommends what they morally ought to be like.

I think, then, of care as practice and value. The practices of care are of course multiple, and some seem very different from others. Taking care of a toddler so that he does not hurt himself yet is not unduly fearful is not much like patching up mistrust between colleagues and enabling them to work together. Dressing a wound so that it will not become infected is not much like putting up curtains to make a room attractive and private. Neither are much like arranging for food aid to be delivered to families who need it half a world away. Yet all care involves attentiveness, sensitivity, and responding to needs. Needs are of innumerable subtle emotional and psychological and cultural kinds, as well as of completely basic and simple kinds, such as for sufficient calories to stay alive. It is helpful to clarify what different forms of care have in common, as it is to clarify how justice in all its forms requires impartiality, treating persons as equals, and recognizing their rights. This is not at all to say that a given practice should involve a single value only. On the contrary, as we clarify the values of care we can better advocate their relevance for many practices from which they have been largely excluded.

Consider police work. Organizationally a part of the "justice system," it must have the enforcement of the requirements of justice high among its priorities. But as it better understands the relevance of care to its practices, as it becomes more caring, it can often accomplish more through educating and responding to needs, building trust between police and policed, and thus preventing violations of law than it can through traditional "law enforcement" after prevention has failed. Sometimes the exclusion of the values of care is more in theory than in practice. An ideal market that treats all exchanges as impersonal and all participants as replaceable has no room for caring. But actual markets often include significant

kinds of care and concern, of employers for employees, of employees for customers, and so on. As care is better understood, the appropriate places for caring relations in economic activity may be better appreciated.

At the same time, *practices of care are not devorted solely to the values of care.* They often need justice as well. Consider mothering or fathering in the sense of caring for a child, or "parenting," if one prefers this term. This is probably the most caring of the caring practices since the emotional tie between carer and cared-for is characteristically so strong. This practice has caring well for the child as its primary value. But as understanding of what this involves becomes more adequate, it should include normative guidance on how to avoid such tendencies as parents may have to unduly interfere and control, and it can include the aspect well delineated by Ruddick: "respect for 'embodied willfulness.'"[25] Moreover, practices of parenting must include justice in requiring the fair treatment of multiple children in a family and in fairly distributing the burdens of parenting. . . .

The Meshing of Care and Justice

Feminist understandings of justice and care have enabled us to see that these are different values, reflecting different ways of interpreting moral problems and expressing moral concern. Feminist discussion has also shown, I think, that neither justice nor care can be dispensed with: Both are extremely important for morality. Not all feminists agree, by any means, but this is how I see the debates of the last few decades on these issues.

How does the framework that structures justice, equality, rights, and liberty mesh with the network that delineates care, relatedness, and trust? Or are they incompatible views we must (at least at a given time and in a given context) choose between?

One clearly unsatisfactory possibility is to think that justice is a value appropriate to the public sphere of the political, whereas care belongs to the private domains of family and friends and charitable organizations. Feminist analyses have shown how faulty are traditional divisions between public and private, the political and the personal, but even if we use cleaned-up versions of these concepts, we can see how unsatisfactory it is to assign justice to public life and care to private, although in earlier work I may have failed to say enough along these lines.[26] I have argued that we need different moral approaches for different domains, and I have mapped out which are suitable for which domains. There is an initial plausibility, certainly, in thinking of justice as a primary value in the domain of law and care as a primary value in the domain of the family. But more needs to be said.

Justice is badly needed in the family as well as in the state: in a more equitable division of labor between women and men in the household, in the protection of vulnerable family members from domestic violence and abuse, in recognizing the rights of family members to respect for their individuality. In the practice of caring for children or the elderly, justice requires us to avoid paternalistic and maternalistic domination.

At the same time, we can see that care is badly needed in the public domain. Welfare programs are an intrinsic part of what contemporary states with the resources to do so provide, and no feminist should fail to acknowledge the social responsibilities they reflect, however poorly. The nightwatchman state is not a feminist goal. Almost all feminists recognize that there should be much more social and public concern for providing care than there now is in the United States, although it should be provided in appropriate and empowering ways very different from those in place. There should be greatly increased public concern for child care, education, and health care, infused with the values of care. . . .

One possibility I have considered in the past is that justice deals with moral minimums, a floor of moral requirements beneath which we should not sink as we avoid the injustices of assault and disrespect. In contrast, care deals with what is above and beyond the floor of duty. Caring well for children, for instance, involves much more than honoring their rights to not be abused or deprived of adequate food; good care brings joy and laughter. But as a solution to our problem, I have come to think that this is not clear. Perhaps one can have ever more justice in the sense of more understanding of rights, equality, and respect. Certainly there are minimums

of care, even of the kind that cannot be handled by a right to them, such as by rights to adequate nourishment or medical care, that must be provided for persons to develop normally, though excellent care will far exceed them.

Another possible metaphor is that justice and rights set more or less absolute bounds or moral constraints within which we pursue our various visions of the good life, which would for almost everyone include the development of caring relationships. But this metaphor collapses for many of the same reasons as does that of justice as a floor of moral minimums. For instance, if there is anything that sets near absolute constraints on our pursuit of anything, including justice, it is responding to the needs of our children for basic, including emotional, care.

I now think that *caring relations should form the wider moral framework into which justice should be fitted. Care seems the most basic moral value.* As a practice, we know that without care we cannot have anything else, since life requires it. All human beings require a great deal of care in their early years, and most of us need and want caring relationships throughout our lives. As a value, care indicates what many practices ought to involve. When, for instance, necessities are provided without the relational human caring children need, children do not develop well, if at all. When in society individuals treat each other with only the respect that justice requires but no further consideration, the social fabric of trust and concern can be missing or disappearing.

Though justice is surely among the most important moral values, much life has gone on without it, and much of that life has had moderately good aspects. There has, for instance, been little justice within the family in almost all societies but much care; so we know we can have care without justice. Without care, however, there would be no persons to respect and no families to improve. Without care, there would be no public system of rights—even if it could be just. But care is not simply causally primary, it is more inclusive as a value. Within a network of caring, we can and should demand justice, but justice should not then push care to the margins, imagining justice's political embodiment as the model of morality, which is what has been done.

From a perspective of care, persons are relational and interdependent, not the individualistic autonomous rational agents of the perspective of justice and rights. This relational view is the better view of human beings, of persons engaged in developing human morality. We can decide to treat such persons *as* individuals, to be the bearers of individual rights, for the sake of constructing just political and legal and other institutions. But we should not forget the reality and the morality this view obscures. Persons *are* relational and interdependent. We can and should value autonomy, but it must be developed and sustained within a framework of relations of trust.

At the levels of global society and our own communities, we should develop frameworks of caring about and for one another as human beings who are members of families and groups. We should care for one another as persons in need of a habitable environment with a sufficient absence of violence and with sufficient provision of care for human life to flourish. We need to acknowledge the moral values of the practices and family ties underlying the caring labor on which human life has always depended, and we need to consider how the best of these values can be better realized. Within a recognized framework of care we should see persons as having rights and as deserving of justice, most assuredly. And we might even give priority to justice in certain limited domains. But we should embed this picture, I think, in the wider tapestry of human care. . .

A Look at Some Cases

Let me now try to examine in greater detail what can be thought to be at issue between the ethics of care and morality built on impartiality and why a satisfactory feminist morality should not accept the view that universal, impartial, liberal moral principles of justice and right should always be accorded priority over the concerns of caring relationships, which include considerations of trust, friendship, and loyalty. The argument needs to be examined both at the level of "personal" relationships and at the level of societies. . . .

Consider, first, the story of Abraham. It has been discussed by a number of defenders of the ethics of care who do not agree with the religious and moral teaching that Abraham made the right decision when be chose to obey the command of God and kill his infant son.[27] (That God intervened later to prevent the killing is not relevant to an evaluation of Abraham's decision for anyone but a religious consequentialist, if such a position can be thought coherent.) From the perspective of the ethics of care, the relationship between child and parent should not always be subordinated to the command of God or of universal moral rules. But let's consider a secular case in which there is a genuine conflict between impartialist rules and the parent/child relation. . . .

Suppose the father of a young child is by profession a teacher with a special skill in helping troubled young children succeed academically. Suppose now that on a utilitarian calculation of how much overall good will be achieved, he determines that from the point of view of universal utilitarian rules he ought to devote more time to his work, staying at his school after hours and so on, and letting his wife and others care for his own young child. But he also thinks that from the perspective of care, he should build the relationship he has with his child, developing the trust and mutual consideration of which it is capable. Even if the universal rules allow him some time for family life, and even if he places appropriate utilitarian value on developing his relationship with his child—the good it will do the child, the pleasure it will give him, the good it will enable the child to do in the future, and so on—the calculation still comes out, let's say, as before: He should devote more time to his students. But the moral demands of care suggest to him that he should spend more time with his child. . . .

If it would be objected that this is not the way such calculations would in fact come out, my response is that in evaluating alternative moral theories, we can be interested in imagined situations where it would be the case that the calculations came out a certain way. The force of the deontologists' objections to utilitarianism can appropriately rest on such arguments as that if, on a utilitarian calculation, a torture show would produce more pleasure for those who enjoyed it than pain for its victims and critics, then it would be morally recommended. That is enough of an argument against utilitarianism; we don't also need to show that the example is empirically likely.

Suppose the argument the father considers is presented in Kantian rather than utilitarian forms. Then we could say he considers increasing his work at the school an **imperfect duty**, he considers his duty to spend more time with his child an imperfect duty also, and he thinks the former outweighs die latter. Even if he interprets such duties only negatively . . .in terms of what we must avoid, the father concludes in this example that with respect to the time he spends fulfilling both duties, his duty to avoid neglecting his students outweighs his duty to avoid neglecting his child.

Kantians can of course, like utilitarians, try to reinterpret the problem so that the conflict dissolves, but defenders of the ethics of care can try to formulate hypothetical problems less easy to reinterpret in ways that refuse to acknowledge the conflict. Whether we can come up with cases that will convince committed universalists is unclear. But many persons are convinced there *is* a conflict between their commitments to the particular persons for whom they care and what morality might ask from an impartial point of view.

Returning to our example, the argument for impartiality might go something like this: Reasoning as an abstract agent as such,[28] I should act on moral rules that all could accept from a perspective of impartiality. Those rules recommend that we treat all persons equally, including our children, with respect to exercising our professional skills, and that when we have special skills we should use them for the benefit of all persons equally. For example, a teacher should not favor his own child if his child happens to be one of his students. If one has the abilities and has had the social advantages to become a teacher, one should exercise those skills when they are needed, especially when they are seriously needed.

But the father in my example also considers the perspective of care. From this perspective, his relationship with his child is of enormous and irreplaceable value. He thinks that out of concern for this particular relationship he should spend more time with his child. He experiences the relationship as one of love, trust, and loyalty and thinks that in the case being considered he should subordinate such other considerations as exercising his professional skills to this relationship. He thinks he should free

himself from extra work to help his child feel the trust and encouragement from which his development will benefit, even if this conflicts with impartial morality.

He reflects on what the motives would be in choosing between the alternatives. For one alternative, the motive would be: because universal moral rules recommend it. For the other the motive would be: because this is my child and I am the father of this child and the relationship between us is no less important than universal rules. He reflects on whether the latter can be a moral motive and concludes that it can in the sense that he can believe it is the motive he ought to act on. And he can do this without holding that every father ought to act similarly toward his child. He can further conclude that if Kantian and utilitarian moralities deny that such a motive can be moral then they have mistakenly defined the moral to suit their purposes and, by arbitrary fiat, excluded whatever might challenge their universalizing requirements. . .

The father in my example may think fathers should join mothers in paying more attention to relationships of care and in resisting the demands of impartial rules when they are excessive. From the perspective of all, or everyone, perhaps particular relationships should be subordinated to universal rules. But from the perspective of particular persons in relationships, it is certainly meaningful to ask: Why must we adopt the perspective of all and everyone when it is a particular relationship that we care about at least as much as "being moral" in the sense required by universal rules? This relationship, we may think, is central to the identities of the persons in it. It is relationships between persons, such as in families, that allow persons to develop and to become aware of themselves as individuals with rights. And relationships between persons sustain communities within which moral and political rights can be articulated and protected. Perhaps the perspective of universal rules should be limited to the domain of law, rather than expected to serve for the whole of morality. Then, in my example, the law should require gender fairness in parental leaves. Beyond this, it might allow persons with professional skills to work more or fewer hours as they choose; but the case as I developed it was to consider the moral decision that would still face the father in question after the law had spoken. *Even if the law permitted him to work less, would it be what he morally ought to do? From the perspective of universal impartial utilitarian rules: no. But from the perspective of care: yes.* This is the moral issue I am trying to explore. What I argue is that the ethics of care considers the moral claims of caring as no less valid than the moral claims of impartial rules. This is not to say that considerations of impartiality are unimportant; it does deny that they morally ought always to have priority. *This makes care ethics a challenge to liberalism as a moral theory, not a mere supplement.* . . .

Models of Morality

At the level of morality, we need to decide which "models" are appropriate for which contexts. Many of the arguments of recent decades about the priority of justice were developed against a background of utilitarian ascendancy. . . .

The ethics of care suggests that the priority of impartial justice is at best persuasive for the legal-judicial context. It might also suggest that calculations of general utility are at best appropriate for some choices about public policy. Moral theories are still needed to show us how, within the relatedness that should exist among all persons as fellow human beings—and that does exist in many personal contexts and numerous group ones—we should apply the various possible models. We will then be able to see how the model of caring relations can apply and have priority in some contexts, and how it should not be limited to the personal choices made by individuals after they have met all the requirements of impartial rules. A comprehensive moral theory might show, indeed, how care and its related values are the most comprehensive and satisfactory model within which to locate more familiar components.

NOTES

1. See, for example, Annette C. Baier, *Moral Prejudices: Essays on Ethics* (Cambridge, Mass.: Harvard University Press, 1994) Virginia Held, *Feminist Morality: Transforming Culture, Society, and Politics* (Chicago: University of Chicago Press, 1993); Diana Tietjens Meyers, *Subjection and Subjectivity* (New York: Routledge, 1994); and Margaret Urban Walker, *Moral Understandings: A Feminist Study in Ethics* (New York: Routledge, 1998).

2. See, for example, Seyla Benhabib, *Situating the Self: Gender, Community, and Postmodernism in Contemporary Ethics* (New York: Routledge, 1992); Marilyn Friedman, *What Are Friends For? Feminist Perspectives on Personal Relationships* (Ithaca, N.Y.: Cornell University Press, 1993); Held, *Feminist Morality*, and Eva Feder Kittay, *Love's Labor: Essays on Women, Equality, and Dependency* (New York: Routledge, 1999).

3. It is often asserted that to count as moral, a judgment must be universalizeable: If we hold that it would be right (or wrong) for one person to do something, then we are committed to holding that it would be right (or wrong) for anyone similar in similar circumstances to do it. The subject terms in moral judgments must thus be universally quantified variables and the predicates universal. "I ought to take care of Jane because she is my child" is not universal; "all parents ought to take care of their children" is. The former judgment could be universalizeable if it were derived from the latter, but if, as many advocates of the ethics of care think, it is taken as a *starting* moral commitment (rather than as dependent on universal moral judgments), it might not be universalizeable.

4. Good examples are Stephen L. Darwall, *Impartial Reason* (Ithaca, N.Y.: Cornell University Press, 1983), and David Gauthier, *Morals by Agreement* (Oxford: Oxford University Press, 1986).

5. Brian Barry, *The Liberal Theory of Justice* (London: Oxford University Press, 1973), p. 166.

6. Michael Sandel, *Liberalism and the Limits of Justice* (Cambridge: Cambridge University Press, 1982), p. 133. Other examples of the communitarian critique that ran parallel to the feminist one are Alasdair MacIntyre, *After Virtue: A Study in Moral Theory* (Notre Dame, Ind.: University of Notre Dame Press, 1981), and *Whose Justice? Which Rationality?* (Notre Dame, Ind.: University of Notre Dame Press, 1988); Charles Taylor, *Hegel and Modem Society* (Cambridge: Cambridge University Press, 1979); and Roberto Mangabeire Unger, *Knowledge and Politics* (New York: Free Press, 1975).

7. Martha Nussbaum, *Sex and Social Justice* (New York: Oxford University Press, 1999), p. 62.

8. See, for example, Diana T. Meyers, *Self, Society, and Personal Choice* (New York: Columbia University Press, 1989); Grace Clement, *Care, Autonomy, and Justice* (Boulder, Colo.: Westview Press, 1996); Diana T. Meyers, ed., *Feminists Rethink the Self* (Boulder, Colo.: Westview Press, 1997); and Catriona MacKenzie and Natalie Stoljar, eds.. *Relational Autonomy: Feminist Perspectives on Autonomy, Agency, and the Social Self* (New York: Oxford University Press, 2000). See also Marina Oshana, "Personal Autonomy and Society," *Journal of Social Philosophy* 29(1) (spring 1998): 81–102.

9. This image is in Thomas Hobbes's *The Citizen: Philosophical Rudiments Concerning Government and Society*, ed. B. Gert

(Garden City, N.Y.: Doubleday, 1972), p. 205. For a contrasting view, see Sibyl Schwarzenbach, "On Civic Friendship," *Ethics* 107(1) (1996): 97–128.

10. Baier, *Moral Prejudices*, p. 29.

11. See Robert A. Frank, Thomas Gilovich, and Dennis T. Regan, "Does Studying Economics Inhibit Cooperation?" *Journal of Economic Perspectives* 7(2) (spring 1993): 159–71; and Gerald Marwell and Ruth Ames, "Economists Free Ride, Does Anyone Else?: Experiments on the Provision of Public Goods, IV," *Journal of Public Economics* 15(3) (June 1981): 295–310.

12. See Virginia Held, *Rights and Goods: Justifying Social Action* (Chicago: University of Chicago Press, 1989), chap. 5, "The Grounds for Social Trust".

13. For another view, see Richmond Campbell, *Illusions of Paradox: A Feminist Epistemology Naturalized* (Lanham, Md.: Rowman and Littlefield, 1998).

14. See Jürgen Habermas, "Discourse Ethics," in his *Moral Consciousness and Communicative Action* (Cambridge, Mass.: MIT Press, 1995); and Benhabib, *Situating the Self.*

15. I share Stephen Darwall's view that normative ethics and metaethics are highly interrelated and cannot be clearly separated. See his *Philosophical Ethics* (Boulder, Co. Westview Press, 1998), esp. chap. 1.

16. Walker, *Moral Understandings*, p. 1.

17. Fiona Robinson, *Globalizing Care: Ethics, Feminist Theory and International Affairs* (Boulder, Co. Westview Press, 1999).

18. Walker, *Moral Understandings*, p. 21.

19. See especially Alison M. Jaggar, "Feminist Ethics: Some Issues for the Nineties," *Journal of Social Philosophy* 20 (spring-fall 1989): 91–107.

20. For example, Marcia Baron, *Kantian Ethics Almost without Apology* (Ithaca, N.Y.: Cornell University Press, 1995); and Barbara Herman, *The Practice of Moral Judgment* (Cambridge, Mass.: Harvard University Press, 1993).

21. For example, Laura M. Purdy, *Reproducing Persons: Issues in Feminist Bioethics* (Ithaca, N.Y.: Cornell University Press, 1996).

22. For example, Jean Hampton, "Feminist Contractarianism," in *A Mind of One's Own: Feminist Essays on Reason and Objectivity,* 2nd ed., eds. Louise M. Antony and Charlotte Witt (Boulder, Colo.: Westview Press, 2002); and Okin, *Justice, Gender, and the Family.*

23. For example, Nussbaum, *Sex and Social Justice.*

24. I thank Tucker Lennox for his comment on this issue in connection with a different paper.

25. Sara Ruddick, "Injustice in Families: Assault and Domination," in *Justice and Care: Essential Readings in Feminist Ethics,* ed. Virginia Held (Boulder, Colo.: Westview, 1995).

26. Held, *Rights and Goods.*

27. For example, Nel Noddings, *Caring: A Feminine Approach to Ethics and Moral Education* (Berkeley: University of California Press, 1986).

28. Stephen Darwall, *Impartial Reason* (Ithaca, N.Y.: Cornell University Press, 1983).

DISCUSSION QUESTIONS:

1. Consider the five major features of the ethics of care presented by Held. Can a utilitarian, Kantian, or virtue theory of ethics be adapted to include any of these features?

2. Consider Held's reply to the objection that the ethics of care is inadequate as a moral theory because it is unable to provide definite answers in cases of conflicting moral demands. Is her reply successful?

3. Held outlines a feminist critique of Kantian and utilitarian moral theories. Does the critique, as she presents it, give us good reason to reject those theories? Can some traditional theories be modified to avoid the concerns presented in the critique?

4. What is the correct way to understand the relation between the sometimes conflicting values of justice and care? Does one always take precedence over the other? Do they apply to different areas of human conduct? Is one, in some way, more fundamental than the other?

5. According to Held, a major difference between the ethics of care and many traditional moral theories is that the ethics of care correctly implies that considerations of impartiality do not always outweigh claims of caring. Does the ethics of care have this implication? Do utilitarianism and Kantianism imply otherwise? Do claims of caring sometimes outweigh considerations of impartiality?

Argument Reconstruction Exercises:

I. Held claims that dominant moral theories, such as Kantianism and utilitarianism, employ a concept of a person that limits their application. Identify the premises and conclusion of the following argument on this topic.

> Dominant moral theories, such as Kantianism and utilitarianism, conceive of persons as rational, autonomous, or self-interested individuals. This conception of a person may be suitable for understanding the moral dimensions of legal,

political, or economic interactions between strangers, but it is not suitable for understanding the moral dimensions of interactions between interconnected persons in the context of the family and friendships. The dominant moral theories are, therefore, unable to give an adequate account of the moral dimensions of interactions between persons in such contexts and are limited in their application.

II. As Held notes, the ethics of care is sometimes criticized for not being definitive enough. Identify the premises and conclusion of the following argument.

While the ethics of care directs our attention to moral considerations that may well be overlooked by such theories as Kantianism and utilitarianism, it does not provide us with any principles that determine the right thing to do when these and other moral considerations conflict. As a result, it does not provide an adequate answer to the primary question of normative ethics: What makes right acts right?

III. Held criticizes the dominant moral theories (e.g., Kantianism and utilitarianism) on the ground that they do not represent the moral experiences of women and others. Identify the premises and conclusion of the following argument.

These dominant moral theories can be seen to be modeled on the experience of men in public life and the marketplace. When women's experience is thought to be as relevant to morality as men's,

a position whose denial would seem to be biased, these moralities can be seen to fit very inadequately the morally relevant experience of women in the household. Women's experience has typically included cultivating special relationships with family and friends. . . . Affectionate sensitivity and responsiveness to need may seem to provide better moral guidance for what should be done in these contexts than do abstract rules or rational calculations of individual utilities. (page 355)

IV. Held (pages 360–361) presents the case of a father who is also a teacher with a special talent for helping troubled students. He faces the choice of whether to devote more time to his students or to invest that same time in improving his relationship with his son. According to Held, the case illustrates the shortcomings of utilitarianism and Kantianism and the strength of an ethics of care. Identify the premises and conclusion in the following statement of her view.

It is right that the father devote the time to his son rather than to his students. Moral theories such as utilitarianism and Kantianism, which require the father to make moral decisions from an impartial point of view, falsely imply that he is morally required to devote his time to his students rather than to his son. The ethics of care, however, directs him to take a different perspective on his conduct: that of a particular person in a particular caring relationship. From this perspective, the proper decision is to devote the time to his son.

4

Applied Ethics

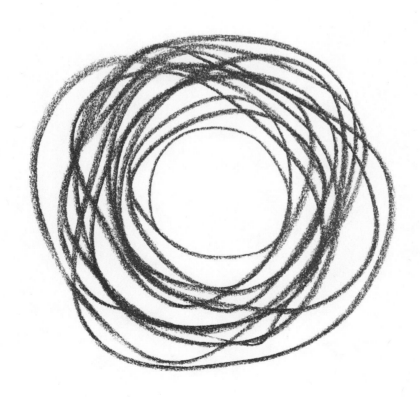

CHAPTER 14

The Moral Community

The day may come, when [animals] may acquire those rights which never could have been withholden from them but by the hand of tyranny. The French have already discovered that the blackness of skin is no reason why a human being should be abandoned without redress to the caprice of a tormentor. It may come one day to be recognized, that the number of legs, the villosity of the skin, or the termination of the os sacrum, are reasons equally insufficient for abandoning a sensitive being to the same fate. What else is it that should trace the insuperable line? Is it the faculty of reason, or perhaps, the faculty for discourse?... [T]he question is not, Can they reason? nor, Can they talk? but, Can they suffer?

—JEREMY BENTHAM, *INTRODUCTION TO THE PRINCIPLES OF MORALS*

INTRODUCTION

The last few chapters have explored our moral concepts. We've canvassed different theoretical answers for what makes an action right or wrong, what makes a state of affairs good or bad, and what makes a person virtuous or vicious. We now have a much better grasp of what these concepts are and how they relate to one another. But there remains another significant theoretical question to ask: *to whom* do these moral concepts apply?

We can put the question another way by invoking some new terminology. Let's say that a **moral patient** is any being whose welfare counts when it comes to morality. When you're deliberating about what you should do, you need to take all moral patients into account. In other words, the moral community consists of all and only moral patients. Furthermore, let's say that a **moral agent** is a special type of moral patient; a moral agent is a being that can have moral obligations and can grant valid consent. There are things that they morally ought to do and morally

ought not to do. These are the kinds of beings that can rightly be praised or blamed for what they do or fail to do.

On this definition, almost everyone would agree that adult humans are moral patients. What you do to other adult humans falls under the umbrella of morality. Their welfare counts. And almost everyone would agree that most (but not all) adult humans are also moral agents. Unless an adult human is severely mentally disabled, etc., she is capable of having moral obligations and giving consent. There are ways that she morally ought to act, and if she fails to act in these ways, we may appropriately blame her.

With these distinctions in hand, we can now rephrase the theoretical question with which we began: which beings in our world are moral patients? Which beings are moral agents? What is the essential difference between something that is a moral patient and something that is not?

As you might imagine, these questions have been answered in a variety of ways. For quite a long time, for example, many people seemed to hold the view that the only moral patients were adult males. Women and children were seen as property, not as moral patients. And even as such views evolved to include women and children as appropriate targets of moral concern, racial barriers persisted. For example, a white American slaveholder at the turn of the 18th century might have held a view like the following: "All white humans are moral patients. Their welfare matters for morality. But only adult white males are moral agents. They are the only beings capable of having moral obligations (children being too immature and women being too emotionally fragile to face moral dilemmas). Furthermore, black humans are not moral patients. Their welfare is important for economic reasons, but not moral ones." Even people who viewed women and people of color as moral patients were very likely to view the welfare of such people as counting for less than the welfare of other humans.

But questions of the moral community are not anachronistic or merely academic. They undergird some of the most emotionally charged ethical dilemmas of our day. The issue of abortion involves, in part, the question of whether the fetus counts as a moral patient. Do we need to keep the welfare of the fetus in mind when deliberating about what we morally ought to do in a case of abortion? Does the fetus "count" as one of us? Some say yes, while others say no. The issue of euthanasia often raises similar issues about moral agency. Are those who are elderly, sick, and dying still genuine moral agents, capable of consenting to an early death?

Notice furthermore that the class of moral patients might well extend beyond human beings. What about other species of animals? Many of us want to say that there are things that we could do to our pets that are morally wrong. If so, that means that pets are moral patients—their welfare is accurately captured in moral concepts. Suppose we agree that our pets are, indeed, moral patients. Does that mean that their welfare is just as important as ours? According to Peter Singer in his selection

in this chapter, the answer is yes. On the other hand, David Schmidtz denies that we have reason to endorse such **species egalitarianism**, and he argues that there a good reason to draw a distinction between human welfare and non-human welfare when it comes to how we morally ought to behave. But if there is a good reason, what is it?

We might not just stop at pets. We could include wild animals as well. But how far can we go? Are there ways of treating plants that are morally wrong? How about viruses, rivers, or ecosystems? How about the planet as a whole? In his selection, Paul Taylor will address some of these concerns. But even if we agree that some of these beings count as legitimate moral patients, do any of them meet the requirements to be a moral agent? Can squirrels do things that are morally wrong? Are dogs capable of giving consent? The readings in this chapter will explore these and other questions as we move from the theoretical to applied issues in morality.

SUGGESTIONS FOR FURTHER READING

DeGrazia, David. *Taking Animals Seriously: Mental Life and Moral Status.* (Cambridge: Cambridge University Press, 1996)

Fox, Michael A. *The Case for Animal Experimentation: An Evolutionary and Ethical Perspective.* (Berkeley: The University of California Press, 1986)

Goodpaster, Kenneth. "On Being Morally Considerable". *The Journal of Philosophy* 1978; 75, pp. 308–25.

Harrison, Peter. "Do Animals Feel Pain?" *Philosophy* 1991; 66, pp. 25–40.

Narveson, Jan. "Animal Rights." *Canadian Journal of Philosophy* 1977; 7, pp. 161–78.

Singer, Peter. *Animal Liberation.* (New York: Harper Collins, 1975)

Steinbock, Bonnie. "Speciesism and the Idea of Equality." *Philosophy* 1978; 53, pp. 247–56.

Warren, Mary Anne. *Moral Status: Obligations to Persons and Other Living Things.* (London: Oxford University Press, 2000)

Wilson, Holly. "The Green Kant: Kant's Treatment of Animals." *In Environmental Ethics: Readings in Theory and Application,* 5e, ed. Louis P. Pojman and Paul Pojman. (Thomson-Wadsworth, 2008, pp. 65–72.)

14.1 ALL ANIMALS ARE EQUAL

PETER SINGER (1974)

Peter Singer is Ira W. DeCamp Professor of Bioethics at Princeton University. He is widely regarded as one of the most influential philosophers of the late 20th century. The vast majority of Singer's work focuses on issues in applied ethics, in particular the moral status of non-human animals. For example, his groundbreaking book *Animal Liberation* (1975) is seen as one of the ancestors to today's growing animal welfare movement. In this article, he argues that the best reasons that we have for granting all humans equality of consideration regardless of their personal differences apply equally well to many non-human animals. There is no essential moral difference between human animals and non-human animals that would justify our treating members of these two categories so differently. Just as a racist treats members of different races differently despite a lack of a justified difference, so, too, a **speciesist** treats members of different species differently despite a lack of justified difference. He closes the article with several gruesome examples of speciesism in action.

Reading Questions

1. What is equality of consideration?

2. Why does Singer think that the claim that all humans are morally equal cannot be defended by appeal to actual, empirical facts?

3. What does it mean to say that "equality is a moral ideal, not a simple assertion of fact"?

4. What is speciesism?

5. According to Singer, what is a precondition for having legitimate interests?

6. What is sentience?

7. How does our diet suggest a speciesist attitude?

8. How does our scientific research suggest a speciesist attitude?

A liberation movement demands an expansion of our moral horizons and an extension or reinterpretation of the basic moral principle of equality.[1] Practices that were previously regarded as natural and inevitable come to be seen as the result of an unjustifiable prejudice. Who can say with confidence that all his or her attitudes and practices are beyond criticism? If we wish to avoid being numbered amongst the oppressors, we must be prepared to rethink even our most fundamental attitudes. We need to consider them from the point of view of those most disadvantaged by our attitudes, and the practices that follow from these attitudes. If we can make this unaccustomed mental switch we may discover a pattern in our attitudes and practices that consistently operates so as to benefit one group—usually the one to which we ourselves belong—at the expense of another. In this way we may come to see that there is a case for a new liberation movement. My aim is to advocate that we make this mental switch in respect of our attitudes and practices towards a very large group of beings: members of species other than our own—or, as we popularly though misleadingly call them, animals. In other words, *I am urging that we extend to other species the basic principle of equality that most of us recognize should be extended to all members of our own species.*

All this may sound a little far-fetched, more like a parody of other liberation movements than a serious objective. . . .

[After all,] There *are* important differences between humans and other animals, and these differences must give rise to *some* differences in the rights that each have. Recognizing this obvious fact, however, is no barrier to the case for extending the basic principle of equality to nonhuman animals. The differences that exist between men and women are equally undeniable, and the supporters of Women's Liberation are aware that these differences may give rise to different rights. Many feminists hold that women have the right to an abortion on request. It does not follow that since these same people are campaigning for equality between men and women they must support the right of men to have abortions too. Since a man cannot have an abortion, it is meaningless to talk of his right to have one. Since a pig can't vote, it is meaningless to talk of its right to vote. There is no reason why either Women's Liberation or Animal Liberation should get involved in such nonsense. *The extension of the basic principle of equality from one group to another does not imply that we must treat both groups in exactly the same way, or grant exactly the same rights to both groups.* Whether we should do so will depend on the nature of the members of the two groups. *The basic principle of equality, I shall argue, is equality of consideration:* and equal consideration for different beings may lead to different treatment and different rights. . . .

Theoretical Defense of Equality

When we say that all human beings, whatever their race, creed or sex, are equal, what is it that we are asserting? Those who wish to defend a hierarchical, inegalitarian society have often pointed out that, by whatever test we choose, it simply is not true that all humans are equal. Like it or not, we must face the fact that humans come in different shapes and sizes; they come with differing moral capacities, differing intellectual abilities, differing amounts of benevolent feeling and sensitivity to the needs of others, differing abilities to communicate effectively, and differing capacities to experience pleasure and pain. In short, if the demand for equality were based on the actual equality of all human beings, we would have to stop demanding equality. It would be an unjustifiable demand.

Still, one might cling to the view that the demand for equality among human beings is based on the actual equality of the different races and sexes. Although humans differ as individuals in various ways, there are no differences between the races and sexes *as such*. From the mere fact that a person is black, or a woman, we cannot infer anything else about that person. This, it may be said, is what is wrong with racism and sexism. The white racist claims that whites are superior to blacks, but this is false—although there are differences between individuals, some blacks are superior to some whites in all of the capacities and abilities that could conceivably be relevant. The opponent of sexism would say the same: a person's sex is no guide to his or her abilities, and this is why it is unjustifiable to discriminate on the basis of sex.

This is a possible line of objection to racial and sexual discrimination. It is not, however, the way that someone really concerned about equality would choose, because taking this line could, in some circumstances, force one to accept a most inegalitarian society. The fact that humans differ as individuals, rather than as races or sexes, is a valid reply to someone who defends a hierarchical society like, say, South Africa, in which all whites are superior in status to all blacks. The existence of individual variations that cut across the lines of race or sex, however, provides us with no defence at all against a more sophisticated opponent of equality, one who proposes that, say, the interests of those with ratings above 100. Would a hierarchical society of this sort really be so much better than one based on race or sex? I think not. But if we tie the moral principle of equality to the factual equality of the different races or sexes, taken as a whole, our opposition to racism and sexism does not provide us with any basis for objecting to this kind of inegalitarianism.

There is a second important reason why we ought not to base our opposition to racism and sexism on any kind of factual equality, even the limited kind that asserts that variations in capacities and abilities are spread evenly between the different races and sexes: we can have no absolute guarantee that these abilities and capacities really are distributed evenly, without regard to race or sex, among human beings. So far as actual abilities are concerned, there do seem to be certain measurable differences between both races and sexes. These differences do not, of course, appear in each case, but only when averages are taken. More important still, we do not yet know how much of these differences is really due to the different genetic endowments of the various races and sexes, and how much is due to environmental differences that arc the result of past and continuing discrimination. Perhaps all of the important differences will eventually prove to be environmental rather than genetic. Anyone opposed to racism and sexism will certainly hope that this will be so, for it will make the task of ending discrimination a lot easier; nevertheless it would be dangerous to rest the case against racism and sexism on the belief that all significant differences are environmental in origin. The opponent of, say, racism who takes this line will be unable to avoid conceding that if differences in ability did after all prove to have some genetic connection with race, racism would in some way be defensible.

It would be folly for the opponent of racism to stake his whole case on a dogmatic commitment to one particular outcome of a difficult scientific issue which is still a long way from being settled. While attempts to prove that differences in certain selected abilities between races and sexes are primarily genetic in origin have certainly not been conclusive, the same must be said of attempts to prove that these differences are largely the result of environment. At this stage of the investigation we cannot be certain which view is correct, however much we may hope it is the latter.

Fortunately, there is no need to pin the case for equality to one particular outcome of this scientific investigation. The appropriate response to those who claim to have found evidence of genetically-based differences in ability between the races or sexes is not to stick to the belief that the genetic explanation must be wrong, whatever evidence to the contrary may turn up: instead we should make it quite clear that the claim to equality does not depend on intelligence, moral capacity, physical strength, or similar matters of fact. *Equality is a moral ideal, not a simple assertion of fact.* There is no logically compelling reason for assuming that a factual difference in ability between two people justifies any difference in the amount of consideration we give to satisfying their needs and interests. *The principle of the equality of human beings is not a description of an alleged actual equality among humans: it is a prescription of how we should treat humans.*

Equality and Interests

Jeremy Bentham incorporated the essential basis of moral equality into his **utilitarian system** of ethics in the formula: "Each to count for one and none for more than one." In other words, the interests of every being affected by an action are to be taken into account and given the same weight as the like interests of any other being. A later utilitarian, Henry Sidgwick, put the point in this way: "The good of any one individual is of no more importance, from the point of view (if I may say so) of the Universe, than the good of any other."[2] More recently, the leading figures in contemporary moral philosophy have shown a great deal of agreement in specifying as a fundamental presupposition of their moral theories some similar requirement which operates so as to give everyone's interests equal consideration—although they cannot agree on how this requirement is best formulated.[3]

It is an implication of this principle of equality that our concern for others ought not to depend on what they are like, or what abilities they possess—although precisely what this concern requires us to do may vary according to the characteristics of those affected by what we do. It is on this basis that the case against racism and the case against sexism must both ultimately rest; and it is in accordance with this principle that **speciesism** is also to be condemned. *If possessing a higher degree of intelligence does not entitle one human to use another for his own ends, how can it entitle humans to exploit non-humans?*

Many philosophers have proposed the principle of equal consideration of interests, in some form or other, as a basic moral principle; but not many of them have recognized that this principle applies to members of other species as well as to our own. Bentham was one of the few who did realize this. In a forward-looking passage, written at a time when black slaves in the British dominions were still being treated much as we now treat nonhuman animals, Bentham wrote:

> The day *may* come when the rest of the animal creation may acquire those rights which never could have been withholden from them but by the hand of tyranny. The French have already discovered that the blackness of the skin is no reason why a human being should be abandoned without redress to the caprice of a tormentor. It may one day come to be recognized that the number of the legs, the villosity of the skin, or the termination of the *os sacrum*, are reasons equally insufficient for abandoning a sensitive being to the same fate. What else is it that should trace the insuperable line? Is it the faculty of reason, or perhaps the faculty of discourse? But a full-grown horse or dog is beyond comparison a more rational, as well as a more conversable animal, than an infant of a day, or a week, or even a month, old. But suppose they were otherwise, what would it avail? The question is not, Can they *reason*? nor, Can they *talk*? but, Can they *suffer*?[4]

In this passage Bentham points to the capacity for suffering as the vital characteristic that gives a being the right to equal consideration. The capacity for suffering—or more strictly, for suffering and/or enjoyment or happiness—is not just another characteristic like the capacity for language, or for higher mathematics. Bentham is not saying that those who try to mark "the insuperable line" that determines whether the interests of a being should be considered happen to have selected the wrong characteristic. *The capacity for suffering and enjoying things is a prerequisite for having interests at all, a condition that must be satisfied before we can speak of interests in any meaningful way.* It would be nonsense to say that it was not in the interests of a stone to be kicked along the road by a schoolboy. A stone does not have interests because it cannot suffer. Nothing that we can do to it could possibly make any difference to its welfare. A mouse, on the other hand, does have an interest in not being tormented, because it will suffer if it is.

If a being suffers, there can be no moral justification for refusing to take that suffering into consideration. No matter what the nature of the being, the principle of equality requires that its suffering be counted equally with the like suffering—in so far as rough comparisons can be made—of any other being. If a being is not capable of suffering, or of experiencing enjoyment or happiness, there is nothing to be taken into account. This is why the limit of **sentience** (using the term as a convenient, if not strictly accurate, shorthand for the capacity to suffer or experience enjoyment or happiness) is the only defensible boundary of concern for the interests of others. To mark this boundary by some characteristic like intelligence or rationality would be to mark it in an arbitrary way. Why not choose some other characteristic, like skin color?

The racist violates the principle of equality by giving greater weight to the interests of members of his own race, when there is a clash between their interests and the interests of those of another race. Similarly the speciesist allows the interests of his own species to override the greater interests of members of other species.[5] The pattern is the same in each case. Most human beings are speciesists. I shall now very briefly describe some of the practices that show this.

Speciesism at Work

For the great majority of human beings, especially in urban, industrialized societies, the most direct form of contact with members of other species is at meal-times: we eat them. In doing so we treat them purely as means to our ends. We regard their life and well-being as subordinate to our taste for a particular kind of dish. I say "taste" deliberately—this is purely a matter of pleasing our palate. There can be no defence of eating flesh in terms of satisfying nutritional needs, since it has been established beyond doubt that we could satisfy our need for protein and other essential nutrients far more efficiently with a diet that replaced animal flesh by soy beans, or products derived from soy beans, and other high-protein vegetable products.[6]

It is not merely the act of killing that indicates what we are ready to do to other species in order to gratify our tastes. The suffering we inflict on the animals while they are alive is perhaps an even clearer indication of our speciesism than the fact that we are prepared to kill them.[7] In order to have meat on the table at a price that people can afford, our society tolerates methods of meat production that confine sentient animals in cramped, unsuitable conditions for the entire durations of their lives. Animals are treated like machines that convert fodder into flesh, and any innovation that results in a higher "conversion ratio" is liable to be adopted. As one authority on the subject has said, "cruelty is acknowledged only when profitability ceases."[8] So hens are crowded four or five to a cage with a floor area of twenty inches by eighteen inches, or around the size of a single page of the *New York Times*. The cages have wire floors, since this reduces cleaning costs, though wire is unsuitable for the hens' feet; the floors slope, since this makes the eggs roll down for easy collection, although this makes it difficult for the hens to rest comfortably. In these conditions all the birds' natural instincts are thwarted: they cannot stretch their wings fully, walk freely, dust-bathe, scratch the ground, or build a nest. Although they have never known other conditions, observers have noticed that the birds vainly try to perform these actions. Frustrated at their inability to do so, they often develop what farmers call "vices", and peck each other to death. To prevent this, the beaks of young birds are often cut off.

This kind of treatment is not limited to poultry. Pigs are now also being reared in cages inside sheds. These animals are comparable to dogs in intelligence, and need a varied, stimulating environment if they are not to suffer from stress and boredom. Anyone who kept a dog in the way in which pigs are frequently kept would be liable to prosecution, in England at least, but, because our interest in exploiting pigs is greater than our interest in exploiting dogs, we object to cruelty to dogs while consuming the produce of cruelty to pigs. Of the other animals, the condition of veal calves is perhaps worst of all, since these animals are so closely confined that they cannot even turn around or get up and lie down

freely. In this way they do not develop unpalatable muscle. They are also made anaemic and kept short of roughage, to keep their flesh pale, since white veal fetches a higher price; as a result they develop a craving for iron and roughage, and have been observed to gnaw wood off the sides of their stalls, and lick greedily at any rusty hinge that is within reach.

Since, as I have said, none of these practices cater for anything more than our pleasures of taste, *our practice of rearing and killing other animals in order to eat them is a clear instance of the sacrifice of the most important interests of other beings in order to satisfy trivial interests of our own.* To avoid speciesism we must stop this practice, and each of us has a moral obligation to cease supporting the practice. Our custom is all the support that the meat industry needs. The decision to cease giving it that support may be difficult, but it is no more difficult than it would have been for a white Southerner to go against the traditions of his society and free his slaves; if we do not change our dietary habits, how can we censure those slave holders who would not change their own way of living?

The same form of discrimination may be observed in the widespread practice of experimenting on other species in order to see if certain substances are safe for human beings, or to test some psychological theory about the effect of severe punishment on learning, or to try out various new compounds just in case something turns up. People sometimes think that all this experimentation is for vital medical purposes, and so will reduce suffering overall. This comfortable belief is very wide of the mark. Drug companies test new shampoos and cosmetics that they are intending to put on the market by dropping them into the eyes of rabbits, held open by metal clips, in order to observe what damage results. Food additives, like artificial colorings and preservatives, are tested by what is known as the "LD50" —a test designed to find the level of consumption at which 50 per cent of a group of animals will die. In the process, nearly all of the animals are made very sick before some finally die, and others pull through. If the substance is relatively harmless, as it often is, huge doses have to be force-fed to the animals, until in some cases sheer volume or concentration of the substance causes death.

Much of this pointless cruelty goes on in the universities. In many areas of science, nonhuman animals are regarded as an item of laboratory equipment, to be used and expended as desired. In psychology laboratories experimenters devise endless variations and repetitions of experiments that were of little value in the first place. To quote just one example, from the experimenter's own account in a psychology journal: at the University of Pennsylvania, Perrin S. Cohen hung six dogs in hammocks with electrodes taped to their hind feet. Electric shock of varying intensity was then administered through the electrodes. If the dog learnt to press its head against a panel on the left, the shock was turned off, but otherwise it remained on indefinitely. Three of the dogs, however, were required to wait periods varying from 2 to 7 seconds while being shocked' before making the response that turned off the current. If they failed to wait, they received further shocks. Each dog was given from 26 to 46 "sessions" in the hammock, each session consisting of 80 "trials" or shocks, administered at intervals of one minute. The experimenter reported that the dogs, who were unable to move in the hammock, barked or bobbed their heads when the current was applied. The reported findings of the experiment were that there was a delay in the dogs' responses that increased proportionately to the time the dogs were required to endure the shock, but a gradual increase in the intensity of the shock had no systematic effect in the timing of the response. The experiment was funded by the National Institutes of Health and the United States Public Health Service.[9]

In this example, and countless cases like it, the possible benefits to mankind are either nonexistent or fantastically remote; while the certain losses to members of other species are very real. This is, again, a clear indication of speciesism.

In the past, argument about vivisection has often missed this point, because it has been put in absolutist terms: would the abolitionist be prepared to let thousands die if they could be saved by experimenting on a single animal? The way to reply to this purely hypothetical question is to pose another: would the experimenter be prepared to perform his experiment on an orphaned human infant, if that were the only way to save many lives? (I say "orphan" to avoid the complication of parental feelings, although in doing so I am being overfair to the experimenter, since the non-human subjects of experiments are not orphans.) *If the experimenter is not prepared to use an orphaned human infant, then his readiness to use nonhumans is simple discrimination, since adult apes, cats, mice, and other mammals are more aware of what is happening to them, more self-directing and, so far as we can tell at least as sensitive to pain, as any human infant.* There seems to be no relevant characteristic that human infants possess that adult mammals do not have to the same or a higher degree. (Someone might try to argue that what makes it wrong to experiment on a human infant is that the infant will, in time and if left alone, develop into more than the nonhuman, but one would then, to be consistent, have to oppose abortion, since the fetus has the same potential as the infant—indeed, even contraception and abstinence might be wrong on this ground, since the egg and sperm, considered jointly, also have the same potential. In any case, this argument still gives us no reason for selecting a nonhuman, rather than a human with severe and irreversible brain damage, as the subject for our experiments.)

The experimenter, then, shows a bias in favor of his own species whenever he carries out an experiment on a nonhuman for a purpose that he would not think justified him in using a human being at an equal or lower level of sentience, awareness, ability to be self-directing, etc. No one familiar with the kind of results yielded by most experiments on animals can have the slightest doubt that if this bias were eliminated the number of experiments performed would be a minute fraction of the number performed today. . . .

In case there are those who still think it may be possible to find some relevant characteristic that distinguishes all humans from all members of other species, I shall refer again, before I conclude, to the existence of some humans who quite clearly are below the level of awareness, self-consciousness, intelligence, and sentience of many nonhumans. I am thinking of humans with severe and irreparable brain damage, and also of infant humans. To avoid the complication of the relevance of a being's potential, however, I shall henceforth concentrate on permanently retarded humans.

Philosophers who set out to find a characteristic that will distinguish humans from other animals rarely take the course of abandoning these groups of humans by lumping them in with the other animals. It is easy to see why they do not. To take this line without rethinking our attitudes to other animals would entail that we have the right to perform painful experiments on retarded humans for trivial reasons; similarly it would follow that we had the right to rear and kill these humans for food. To most philosophers these consequences are as unacceptable as the view that we should stop treating non-humans in this way.

Of course, when discussing the problem of equality it is possible to ignore the problem of mental defectives, or brush it aside as if somehow insignificant.[14] This is the easiest way out. What else remains? My final example of speciesism has been selected to show what happens when a writer is prepared to face the question of human equality and animal inequality without ignoring the existence of mental defectives, and without resorting to obscurantist mumbo-jumbo. Stanley Benn's clear and honest article "Egalitarianism and Equal Consideration of Interests"[15] fits this description.

Benn, after noting the usual "evident human inequalities" argues, correctly I think, for equality of consideration as the only possible basis for egalitarianism. Yet Benn, like other writers, is thinking only of "equal consideration of human interests". Benn is quite open in his defence of this restriction of equal consideration:

> not to possess human shape *is* a disqualifying condition. However faithful or intelligent a dog may be, it would be a monstrous sentimentality to attribute to him interests that could be weighed in an equal balance with those of human beings . . . if, for instance, one had to decide between feeding a hungry baby or a hungry dog, anyone who chose the dog would generally be reckoned morally defective, unable to recognize a fundamental inequality of claims.
>
> This is what distinguishes our attitude to animals from our attitude to imbeciles. It would be odd to say that we ought to respect equally the dignity or personality of the imbecile and of the rational man . . . but there is nothing odd about saying that we should respect their interests equally, that is, that we should give to the interests of each the same serious consideration as claims to considerations

necessary for some standard of well-being that we can recognize and endorse.

Benn's statement of the basis of the consideration we should have for imbeciles seems to me correct, but why should there be any fundamental inequality of claims between a dog and a human imbecile? Benn sees that, if equal consideration depended on rationality, no reason could be given against using imbeciles for research purposes, as we now use dogs and guinea pigs. This will not do: "But of course we do distinguish imbeciles from animals in this regard," he says. That the common distinction is justifiable is something Benn does not question; his problem is how it is to be justified. The answer he gives is this:

> we respect the interests of men and give them priority over dogs not *insofar* as they are rational, but because rationality is the human norm. We say it is *unfair* to exploit the deficiencies of the imbecile who falls short of the norm, just as it would be unfair, and not just ordinarily dishonest, to steal from a blind man. If we do not think in this way about dogs, it is because we do not see the irrationality of the dog as a deficiency or a handicap, but as normal for the species. The characteristics, therefore, that distinguish the normal man from the normal dog make it intelligible for us to talk of other men having interests and capacities, and therefore claims, of precisely the same kind as we make on our own behalf. But although these characteristics may provide the point of the distinction between men and other species, they are not in fact the qualifying conditions for membership, or the distinguishing criteria of the class of morally considerable persons; and this is precisely because a man does not become a member of a different species, with its own standards of normality, by reason of not possessing these characteristics.

The final sentence of this passage gives the argument away. An imbecile, Benn concedes, may have no characteristics superior to those of a dog; nevertheless this does not make the imbecile a member of "a different species" as the dog is. *Therefore* it would be "unfair" to use the imbecile for medical research as we use the dog. But why? That the imbecile is not rational is just the way things have worked out, and the same is true of the dog—neither is any more responsible for their mental level. If it is unfair to take advantage of an isolated defect, why is it fair to take advantage of a more general limitation? I find it hard to see anything in this argument except a defence of preferring the interests of members of our own species because they are members of our own species. To those who think there might be more to it, I suggest the following mental exercise. Assume that it has been proven that there is a difference in the average, or normal, intelligence quotient for two different races, say whites and blacks. Then substitute the term "white" for every occurrence of "men" and "black" for every occurrence of "dog" in the passage quoted; and substitute "high IQ" for "rationality" and when Benn talks of "imbeciles" replace this term by "dumb whites"—that is, whites who fall well below the normal white IQ score. Finally, change "species" to "race." Now reread the passage. It has become a defence of a rigid, no exceptions division between whites and blacks, based on IQ scores, *not withstanding an admitted overlap* between whites and blacks in this respect. The revised passage is, of course, outrageous, and this is not only because we have made fictitious assumptions in our substitutions. The point is that in the original passage Benn was defending a rigid division in the amount of consideration due to members of different species, despite admitted cases of overlap. If the original did not, at first reading, strike us as being as outrageous as the revised version does, this is largely because, although we are not racists ourselves, most of us are speciesists. Like the other articles, Benn's stands as a warning of the ease with which the best minds can fall victim to a prevailing ideology.

NOTES

1. Passages of this article appeared in a review of *Animals, Men and Morals*, edited by S. and R. Godlovitch and J. Harris (London: Gollancz and Taplinger, 1972) in the *New York Review of Books*, April 5, 1973. The whole direction of my thinking on this subject I owe to talks with a number of friends in Oxford in 1970–1, especially Richard Keshen, Stanley Godlovitch, and, above all, Roslind Godlovitch.
2. *The Methods of Ethics*, 7th edn, p. 382.
3. For example, R. M. Hare, *Freedom and Reason* (Oxford, 1963) and J. Rawls, *A Theory of Justice* (Harvard, 1972); for a brief account of the essential agreement on this issue between these and other positions, see R. M. Hare, "Rules of War and Moral Reasoning," *Philosophy and Public Affairs*, 1, no. 2 (1972).

4. *Introduction to the Principles of Morals and Legislation*, ch. XVII.
5. I owe the term "speciesism" to Dr Richard Ryder.
6. In order to produce 1 lb of protein in the form of beef or veal, we must feed 21 lb of protein to the animal. Other forms of livestock are slightly less inefficient, but the average ratio in the US is still 1:8. It has been estimated that the amount of protein lost to humans in this way is equivalent to 90% of the annual world protein deficit. For a brief account, see Frances Moore Lappe, *Diet for a Small Planet* (New, York: Friends of the Earth/Ballantine, 1971), pp. 4–11.
7. Although one might think that killing a being is obviously the ultimate wrong one can do to it, I think that the infliction of suffering is a clearer indication of speciesism because it might be argued that at least part of what is wrong with killing a human is that most humans are conscious of their existence over time, and have desires and purposes that extend into the future — see, for instance, M. Tooley, "Abortion and Infanticide", *Philosophy and Public Affairs*, 2, no. 1 (1972). Of course, if one took this view one would have to hold — as Tooley does — that killing a human infant or mental defective is not in itself wrong, and is less serious than killing certain higher mammals that probably do have a sense of their own existence over time.
8. Ruth Harrison, *Animal Machines* (London: Stuart, 1964). This book provides an eye-opening account of intensive farming methods for those unfamiliar with the subject.
9. *Journal of the Experimental Analysis of Behavior*, 13, no. 1 (1970). Any recent volume of this journal, or of other journals in the field, like the *Journal of Comparative and Physiological Psychology*, will contain reports of equally cruel and trivial experiments. For a fuller account, see Richard Ryder, "Experiments on Animals" in *Animals, Men and Morals*.
10. For example, Bernard Williams, "The Idea of Equality", in *Philosophy, Politics and Society* (second series), ed. P. Laslett and W. Runciman (Oxford: Blackwell, 1962), p. 118; J. Rawls, *A Theory of Justice*, pp. 509–10.
11. *Nomos IX: Equality*, the passages quoted are on pp. 62ff.

DISCUSSION QUESTIONS:

1. Do you think that you are a speciesist? If so, which of your daily practices confirms this moral vice? If you don't think that you're a speciesist, why not?
2. Singer grants that "the extension of the basic principle of equality from one group to another does not imply that we must treat both groups in exactly the same way" (page 370). If that's true, is it possible for us to extend the basic principle of equality to non-human animals but continue to treat them in the same way? Why or why not?
3. Singer thinks that all beings with legitimate interests should be given equality of consideration,

and furthermore that only beings who can suffer have interests. Is that true? It seems obvious enough that plants don't suffer (they lack nervous systems, etc.), but doesn't it seem as if plants have interests in being watered, receiving sufficient sunlight, etc.? If so, should we conclude that plants are owed equality of consideration, too?

Argument Reconstruction Exercises:

I. Singer sketches one possible way to defend human equality by appealing to averages. While it may be true that some individual humans are faster, smarter, etc. than other individual humans, no sexual or racial subgroup exhibits such a difference across the board. Identify the premises and conclusion in this excerpt:

> Although humans differ as individuals in various ways, there are no differences between the races and sexes as such. From the mere fact that a person is black, or a woman, we cannot infer anything else about that person. This, it may be said, is what is wrong with racism and sexism. (page 370)

II. Singer wants to show that the boundaries of the moral community extend to all sentient beings. Identify the premises and conclusion in this paraphrase:

> No matter what the nature of the being, the principle of equality requires that its interests be given equal consideration. And any being who can suffer will have an interest in not suffering. Therefore, the principle of equality requires that any being who can suffer be given equal consideration.

III. Sometimes philosophers are not careful in stating their arguments and instead rely on rhetorical questions or claims to do the work. Once we add a suppressed premise (i.e., an unstated assumption), the following conditional statement can be formed into an argument for speciesism in experimental research. Use the following excerpt along with the suppressed premise to form an argument:

> If the experimenter is not prepared to use an orphaned human infant, then his readiness to use nonhumans is simple discrimination, since adult apes, cats, mice, and other mammals are more aware of what is happening to them, more self-directing, and, so far as we can tell, at least as sensitive to pain, as any human infant. (page 374)

IV. Here is another instance of a passage using a rhetorical question instead of a clearly stated argument. In this case, it is the conclusion of the argument that is suppressed. Identify the premises and conclusion in the following excerpt:

> . . .our concern for others ought not to depend on what they are like, or what abilities they possess. . .It is on this basis that the case against racism and the case against sexism must both ultimately rest; and it is in accordance with this principle that speciesism is also to be condemned. If possessing a higher degree of intelligence does not entitle one human to use another for his own ends, how can it entitle humans to exploit non-humans? (page 371)

14.2 THE ETHICS OF RESPECT FOR NATURE

PAUL TAYLOR (1981)

Paul Taylor is professor emeritus at Brooklyn College in New York. His most important contributions have been to normative ethics and environmental ethics. In this essay, he sketches a view in environmental ethics that he calls respect for nature. This is an attitude of respect that generates moral duties to all living things. It is notable for being a **biocentric view**, as opposed to an **anthropocentric view**, and for defending our duties to living things on a nonconsequentialist framework. Taylor suggests that once we take seriously what he calls the biocentric outlook on nature, we'll come to see that all other living things have inherent worth, and that, as such, we have moral obligations to respect their pursuit of what is good for them.

Reading Questions:

1. What is an anthropocentric view of ethics?

2. What is a life-centered or biocentric view of ethics?

3. What does it mean to say that something has a good of its own?

4. What does it mean to say that something possesses inherent worth?

5. What is the principle of intrinsic value?

6. What are the four components of the biocentric outlook on nature?

7. What are the three main traditions that Taylor cites in defense of the view that humans have more inherent worth than other living things?

I. Human-Centered and Life-Centered Systems of Environmental Ethics

In this paper I show how the taking of a certain ultimate moral attitude toward nature, which I call "respect for nature," has a central place in the foundations of a life-centered system of environmental ethics. I hold that a set of moral norms (both standards of character and rules of conduct) governing human treatment of the natural world is a rationally grounded set if and only if, first, commitment to those norms is a practical entailment of adopting the attitude of respect for nature as an ultimate moral attitude, and second, the adopting of that attitude on the part of all rational agents can itself be justified. When the basic characteristics of the attitude of respect for nature are made clear, it will be seen that a life-centered system of environmental ethics need not be holistic or organicist in its conception of the kinds of entities that are deemed the appropriate objects of moral concern and consideration. Nor does such a system require that the concepts of ecological homeostasis, equilibrium, and integrity provide us with normative principles from which could be derived (with the addition of factual knowledge) our obligations with regard to natural ecosystems. The "balance of nature" is not itself a moral norm, however important may be the role it plays in our general outlook on the natural world that underlies the attitude of respect for nature. I argue that finally *it is the good (well-being, welfare) of individual organisms, considered as entities having* **inherent worth**, *that determines our moral relations with the Earth's wild communities of life.*

In designating the theory to be set forth as **life-centered** I intend to contrast it with all **anthropocentric** views. According to the latter, human actions affecting the natural environment and its nonhuman inhabitants are right (or wrong) by either of two criteria: they have consequences which are favorable (or unfavorable) to human well-being, or they are consistent (or inconsistent) with the system of norms that protect and implement human rights. *From this human-centered standpoint it is to humans and only to humans that all duties are ultimately owed.* We may have responsibilities *with regard to* the natural ecosystems and biotic communities of our planet, but these responsibilities are in every case based on the contingent fact that our treatment of those ecosystems and communities of life can further the realization of human values and/or human rights. We have no obligation to promote or protect the good of nonhuman living things, independently of this contingent fact.

A life-centered system of environmental ethics is opposed to human-centered ones precisely on this point. *From the perspective of a life-centered theory, we have prima facie moral obligations that are owed to wild plants and animals themselves as members of the Earth's biotic community.* We are morally bound (other things being equal) to protect or promote their good for *their* sake. Our duties to respect the integrity of natural ecosystems, to preserve endangered species, and to avoid environmental pollution stem from the fact that these are ways in which we can help make it possible for wild species populations to achieve and maintain a healthy existence in a natural state. *Such obligations are due those living things out of recognition of their inherent worth. They are entirely additional to* and independent of the obligations we owe to our fellow humans. Although many of the actions that fulfill one set of obligations will also fulfill the other, two different grounds of obligation are involved. Their well-being, as well as human well-being, is something to be realized *as an end in itself*.

If we were to accept a life-centered theory of environmental ethics, a profound reordering of our moral universe would take place. We would begin to look at the whole of the Earth's biosphere in a new light. Our duties with respect to the "world" of nature would be seen as making *prima facie* claims upon us to be balanced against our duties with respect to the "world" of human civilization. We could no longer simply take the human point of view and consider the effects of our actions exclusively from the perspective of our own good.

II. The Good of a Being and the Concept of Inherent Worth

What would justify acceptance of a life-centered system of ethical principles? In order to answer this it is first necessary to make clear the fundamental moral attitude that underlies and makes intelligible the commitment to live by such a system. It is then necessary to examine the considerations that would justify any rational agent's adopting that moral attitude.

Two concepts are essential to the taking of a moral attitude of the sort in question. These concepts are, first, that of the good (well-being, welfare) of a living thing, and second, the idea of an entity possessing inherent worth. I examine each concept in turn.

[1] Every organism, species population, and community of life has a good of its own which moral agents can intentionally further or damage by their actions. *To say that an entity has a good of its own is simply to say that, without reference to any other entity, it can be benefited or harmed.* One can act in its overall interest or contrary to its overall interest, and environmental conditions can be good for it (advantageous to it) or bad for it (disadvantageous to it). What is good for an entity is what "does it good" in the sense of enhancing or preserving its life and well-being. What is bad for an entity is something that is detrimental to its life and well-being.[1]

We can think of the good of an individual nonhuman organism as consisting in the full development of its biological powers. Its good is realized to the extent that it is strong and healthy. It possesses whatever capacities it needs for successfully coping with its environment and so preserving its existence throughout the various stages of the normal life cycle of its species. The good of a population or community of such individuals consists in the population or community maintaining itself from generation to generation as a coherent system of genetically and ecologically related organisms whose average good is at an optimum level for the given environment. (Here *average good* means that the degree of realization of the good of *individual organisms* in the population or community is, on average, greater than would be the case under any other ecologically functioning order of interrelations among those species populations in the given ecosystem.)

The idea of a being having a good of its own, as I understand it, does not entail that the being must have interests or take an interest in what affects its life for better or for worse. We can act in a being's interest or contrary to its interest without its being interested in what we are doing to it in the sense of wanting or not wanting us to do it. It may, indeed, be wholly unaware that favorable and unfavorable events are taking place in its life. I take it that trees, for example, have no knowledge or desires or feelings. Yet it is undoubtedly the case that trees can be harmed or benefited by our actions. We can crush their roots by running a bulldozer too close to them. We can see to it that they get adequate nourishment and moisture by fertilizing and watering the soil around them. Thus we can help or hinder them in the realization of their good. It is the good of trees themselves that is thereby affected. We can similarly act so as to further the good of an entire tree population of a certain species (say, all the redwood trees in a California valley) or the good of a whole community of plant life in a given wilderness area, just as we can do harm to such a population or community.

When construed in this way, the concept of a being's good is not coextensive with sentience or the capacity for feeling pain. . . .

[2] The second concept essential to the moral attitude of respect for nature is the idea of inherent worth. We take that attitude toward wild living things (individuals, species populations, or whole biotic communities) when and only when we regard

them as entities possessing **inherent worth**. Indeed, it is only because they are conceived in this way that moral agents can think of themselves as having validly binding duties, obligations, and responsibilities that are *owed* to them as their *due*.

What does it mean to regard an entity that has a good of its own as possessing inherent worth? Two general principles are involved: the principle of moral consideration and the principle of intrinsic value.

According to the **principle of moral consideration**, wild living things are deserving of the concern and consideration of all moral agents simply in virtue of their being members of the Earth's community of life. From the moral point of view their good must be taken into account whenever it is affected for better or worse by the conduct of rational agents. This holds no matter what species the creature belongs to. The good of each is to be accorded some value and so acknowledged as having some weight in the deliberations of all rational agents. Of course, it may be necessary for such agents to act in ways contrary to the good of this or that particular organism or group of organisms in order to further the good of others, including the good of humans. But the principle of moral consideration prescribes that, with respect to each being an entity having its own good, *every individual is deserving of consideration*.

The **principle of intrinsic value** states that, regardless of what kind of entity it is in other respects, if it is a member of the Earth's community of life, the realization of its good is something *intrinsically* valuable. This means that *its good is prima facie worthy of being preserved or promoted as an end in itself* and for the sake of the entity whose good it is. Insofar as we regard any organism, species population, or life community as an entity having inherent worth, we believe that it must never be treated as if it were a mere object or thing whose entire value lies in being instrumental to the good of some other entity. The well-being of each is judged to have value in and of itself.

Combining these two principles, we can now define what it means for a living thing or group of living things to possess inherent worth. *To say that it possesses inherent worth is to say that its good is deserving of the concern and consideration of all moral agents, and that the realization of its good has intrinsic value, to be pursued as an end in itself and for the sake of the entity whose good it is.*

The duties owed to wild organisms, species populations, and communities of life in the Earth's natural ecosystems are grounded on their inherent worth. When rational, autonomous agents regard such entities as possessing inherent worth, they place intrinsic value on the realization of their good and so hold themselves responsible for performing actions that will have this effect and for refraining from actions having the contrary effect.

III. The Attitude of Respect for Nature

Why should moral agents regard wild living things in the natural world as possessing inherent worth? To answer this question we must first take into account the fact that, when rational, autonomous agents subscribe to the principles of moral consideration and intrinsic value and so conceive of wild living things as having that kind of worth, such agents are *adopting a certain ultimate moral attitude toward the natural world*. This is the attitude I call "respect for nature." It parallels the attitude of respect for persons in human ethics. When we adopt the attitude of respect for persons as the proper (fitting, appropriate) attitude to take toward all persons as persons, we consider the fulfillment of the basic interests of each individual to have intrinsic value. We thereby make a moral commitment to live a certain kind of life in relation to other persons. We place ourselves under the direction of a system of standards and rules that we consider validly binding on all moral agents as such.[4]

Similarly, when we adopt the attitude of respect for nature as an ultimate moral attitude we make a commitment to live by certain normative principles. These principles constitute the rules of conduct and standards of character that are to govern our treatment of the natural world. This is, first, an *ultimate* commitment because it is not derived from any higher norm. The attitude of respect for nature is not grounded on some other, more general, or more fundamental attitude. It sets the total framework for our responsibilities toward the natural world. It can be justified, as I show below, but its justification cannot consist in referring to a more general attitude or a more basic normative principle.

Second, the commitment is a *moral* one because it is understood to be a disinterested matter of principle. It is this feature that distinguishes the attitude of respect for nature from the set of feelings and dispositions that comprise the love of nature. The latter stems from one's personal interest in and response to the natural world. Like the affectionate feelings we have toward certain individual human beings, one's love of nature is nothing more than the particular way one feels about the natural environment and its wild inhabitants. And just as our love for an individual person differs from our respect for all persons as such (whether we happen to love them or not), so love of nature differs from respect for nature. *Respect for nature is an attitude we believe all moral agents ought to have simply as moral agents, regardless of whether or not they also love nature.* Indeed, we have not truly taken the attitude of respect for nature ourselves unless we believe this. To put it in a Kantian way, to adopt the attitude of respect for nature is to take a stance that one wills it to be a universal law for all rational beings. It is to hold that stance categorically, as being validly applicable to every moral agent without exception, irrespective of whatever personal feelings toward nature such an agent might have or might lack. . . .

. . .The attitude we take toward living things in the natural world depends on the way we look at them, on what kind of beings we conceive them to be, and on how we understand the relations we bear to them. Underlying and supporting our attitude is a certain *belief system* that constitutes a particular world view or outlook on nature and the place of human life in it. To give good reasons for adopting the attitude of respect for nature, then, we must first articulate the belief system which underlies and supports that attitude. If it appears that the belief system is internally coherent and well-ordered, and if, as far as we can now tell, it is consistent with all known scientific truths relevant to our knowledge of the object of the attitude (which in this case includes the whole set of the Earth's natural ecosystems and their communities of life), then there remains the task of indicating why scientifically informed and rational thinkers with a developed capacity of reality awareness can find it acceptable as a way of conceiving of the natural world and our place in it. To the extent we can do this we provide at least

a reasonable argument for accepting the belief system and the ultimate moral attitude it supports.

I do not hold that such a belief system can be *proven* to be true, either inductively or deductively. As we shall see, not all of its components can be stated in the form of empirically verifiable propositions. Nor is its internal order governed by purely logical relationships. But the system as a whole, I contend, constitutes a coherent, unified, and rationally acceptable "picture" or "map" of a total world. By examining each of its main components and seeing how they fit together, we obtain a scientifically informed and well-ordered conception of nature and the place of humans in it.

This belief system underlying the attitude of respect for nature I call (for want of a better name) "the **biocentric outlook** on nature." Since it is not wholly analyzable into empirically confirmable assertions, it should not be thought of as simply a compendium of the biological sciences concerning our planet's ecosystems. It might best be described as a philosophical world view, to distinguish it from a scientific theory or explanatory system. However, one of its major tenets is the great lesson we have learned from the science of ecology: the interdependence of all living things in an organically unified order whose balance and stability are necessary conditions for the realization of the good of its constituent biotic communities.

Before turning to an account of the main components of the biocentric outlook, it is convenient here to set forth the overall structure of my theory of environmental ethics as it has now emerged. The ethics of respect for nature is made up of three basic elements: a belief system, an ultimate moral attitude, and a set of rules of duty and standards of character. These elements are connected with each other in the following manner. The belief system provides a certain outlook on nature which supports and makes intelligible an autonomous agent's adopting, as an ultimate moral attitude, the attitude of respect for nature. It supports and makes intelligible the attitude in the sense that, when an autonomous agent understands its moral relations to the natural world in terms of this outlook, it recognizes the attitude of respect to be the only *suitable* or *fitting* attitude to take toward all wild forms of life in the Earth's biosphere. Living things are now viewed as *the appropriate objects of the attitude of respect* and are accordingly regarded as entities possessing inherent worth. One then places intrinsic value on the promotion and protection of their good. As a consequence of this, one makes a moral commitment to abide by a set of rules of duty and to fulfill (as far as one can by one's own efforts) certain standards of good character. Given one's adoption of the attitude of respect, one makes that moral commitment because one considers those rules and standards to be validly binding on all moral agents. They are seen as embodying forms of conduct and character structures in which the attitude of respect for nature is manifested. . . .

IV. The Biocentric Outlook on Nature

The biocentric outlook on nature has four main components. (1) Humans are thought of as members of the Earth's community of life, holding that membership on the same terms as apply to all the nonhuman members. (2) The Earth's natural ecosystems as a totality are seen as a complex web of interconnected elements, with the sound biological functioning of each being dependent on the sound biological functioning of the others. (This is the component referred to above as the great lesson that the science of ecology has taught us). (3) Each individual organism is conceived of as a teleological center of life, pursuing its own good in its own way. (4) Whether we are concerned with standards of merit or with the concept of inherent worth, the claim that humans by their very nature are superior to other species is a groundless claim and, in the light of elements (1), (2), and (3) above, must be rejected as nothing more than an irrational bias in our own favor.

The conjunction of these four ideas constitutes the biocentric outlook on nature. In the remainder of this [section] I give a brief account of the first three components, followed by a more detailed analysis of the fourth. I then conclude by indicating how this outlook provides a way of justifying the attitude of respect for nature.

[1] We share with other species a common relationship to the Earth. In accepting the biocentric outlook we take the fact of our being an animal species to be a fundamental feature of our existence. We

consider it an essential aspect of "the human condition." We do not deny the differences between ourselves and other species, but we keep in the forefront of our consciousness the fact that in relation to our planet's natural ecosystems we are but one species population among many. Thus we acknowledge our origin in the very same evolutionary process that gave rise to all other species and we recognize ourselves to be confronted with similar environmental challenges to those that confront them. The laws of genetics, of natural selection, and of adaptation apply equally to all of us as biological creatures. In this light we consider ourselves as one with them, not set apart from them. We, as well as they, must face certain basic conditions of existence that impose requirements on us for our survival and well-being. Each animal and plant is like us in having a good of its own. Although our human good (what is of true value in human life, including the exercise of individual autonomy in choosing our own particular value systems) is not like the good of a nonhuman animal or plant, it can no more be realized than their good can without the biological necessities for survival and physical health.

When we look at ourselves from the evolutionary point of view, we see that not only are we very recent arrivals on Earth, but that our emergence as a new species on the planet was originally an event of no particular importance to the entire scheme of things. The Earth was teeming with life long before we appeared. Putting the point metaphorically, we are relative newcomers, entering a home that has been the residence of others for hundreds of millions of years, a home that must now be shared by all of us together.

The comparative brevity of human life on Earth may be vividly depicted by imagining the geological time scale in spatial terms. Suppose we start with algae, which have been around for at least 600 million years. (The earliest protozoa actually predated this by several *billion* years.) If the time that algae have been here were represented by the length of a football field (300 feet), then the period during which sharks have been swimming in the world's oceans and spiders have been spinning their webs would occupy three quarters of the length of the field; reptiles would show up at about the center of the field; mammals would cover the last third of the field; hominids (mammals of the family *Hominidae*) the last two feet; and the species *Homo sapiens* the last six inches. . . .

The possibility of the extinction of the human species, a possibility which starkly confronts us in the contemporary world, makes us aware of another respect in which we should not consider ourselves privileged beings in relation to other species. This is the fact that the well-being of humans is dependent upon the ecological soundness and health of many plant and animal communities, while their soundness and health does not in the least depend upon human well-being. Indeed, from their standpoint the very existence of humans is quite unnecessary. Every last man, woman, and child could disappear from the face of the Earth without any significant detrimental consequence for the good of wild animals and plants. On the contrary, many of them would be greatly benefited. The destruction of their habitats by human "developments" would cease. The poisoning and polluting of their environment would come to an end. The Earth's land, air, and water would no longer be subject to the degradation they are now undergoing as the result of large-scale technology and uncontrolled population growth. . . .

Our presence, in short, is not needed. If we were to take the standpoint of the community and give voice to its true interest, the ending of our six-inch epoch would most likely be greeted with a hearty "Good riddance!"

[2] To accept the biocentric outlook and regard ourselves and our place in the world from its perspective is to see the whole natural order of the Earth's biosphere as a complex but unified web of interconnected organisms, objects, and events. The ecological relationships between any community of living things and their environment form an organic whole of functionally interdependent parts. Each ecosystem is a small universe itself in which the interactions of its various species populations comprise an intricately woven network of cause-effect relations. Such dynamic but at the same time relatively stable structures as food chains, predator-prey relations, and plant succession in a forest are self-regulating, energy-recycling mechanisms that preserve the equilibrium of the whole.

As far as the well-being of wild animals and plants is concerned, this ecological equilibrium must not be destroyed. The same holds true of the well-being of humans. When one views the realm of nature from the perspective of the biocentric outlook, one never forgets that in the long run the integrity of the entire biosphere of our planet is essential to the realization of the good of its constituent communities of life, both human and nonhuman. . . .

[3] As our knowledge of living things increases, as we come to a deeper understanding of their life cycles, their interactions with other organisms, and the manifold ways in which they adjust to the environment, we become more fully aware of how each of them is carrying out its biological functions according to the laws of its species-specific nature. But besides this, our increasing knowledge and understanding also develop in us a sharpened awareness of the uniqueness of each individual organism. Scientists who have made careful studies of particular plants and animals, whether in the field or in laboratories, have often acquired a knowledge of their subjects as identifiable individuals. Close observation over extended periods of time has led them to an appreciation of the unique "personalities" of their subjects. Sometimes a scientist may come to take a special interest in a particular animal or plant, all the while remaining strictly objective in the gathering and recording of data. Nonscientists may likewise experience this development of interest when, as amateur naturalists, they make accurate observations over sustained periods of close acquaintance with an individual organism. As one becomes more and more familiar with the organism and its behavior, one becomes fully sensitive to the particular way it is living out its life cycle. One may become fascinated by it and even experience some involvement with its good and bad fortunes (that is, with the occurrence of environmental conditions favorable or unfavorable to the realization of its good). The organism comes to mean something to one as a unique, irreplaceable individual. The final culmination of this process is the achievement of a genuine understanding of its point of view and, with that understanding, an ability to "take" that point of view. *Conceiving of it as a center of life, one is able to look at the world from its perspective.*

This development from objective knowledge to the recognition of individuality, and from the recognition of individuality to full awareness of an organism's standpoint, is a process of heightening our consciousness of what it means to be an individual living thing. We grasp the particularity of the organism as a teleological center of life, striving to preserve itself and to realize its own good in its own unique way. . . .

[4] This fourth component of the biocentric outlook on nature is the single most important idea in establishing the justifiability of the attitude of respect for nature. Its central role is due to the special relationship it bears to the first three components of the outlook. This relationship will be brought out after the concept of human superiority is examined and analyzed.⁷

The Case From Capacities

In what sense are humans alleged to be superior to other animals? We are different from them in having certain capacities that they lack. But why should these capacities be a mark of superiority? From what point of view are they judged to be signs of superiority and what sense of superiority is meant? After all, various nonhuman species have capacities that humans lack. There is the speed of a cheetah, the vision of an eagle, the agility of a monkey. Why should not these be taken as signs of *their* superiority over humans?

One answer that comes immediately to mind is that these capacities are not as *valuable* as the human capacities that are claimed to make us superior. Such uniquely human characteristics as rational thought, aesthetic creativity, autonomy and self-determination, and moral freedom, it might be held, have a higher value than the capacities found in other species. Yet we must ask: valuable to whom, and on what grounds?

The human characteristics mentioned are all valuable to humans. They are essential to the preservation and enrichment of our civilization and culture. Clearly it is from the human standpoint that they are being judged to be desirable and good. It is not difficult here to recognize a begging of the question. Humans are claiming human superiority from a strictly human point of view, that is, from a point of view in which the good of humans is taken as the standard of judgment. All we need to do is to look at the capacities of nonhuman animals (or plants, for that matter) from the standpoint of *their* good to find a contrary judgment of superiority. The speed of the cheetah, for example, is a sign of its superiority to humans when considered from the standpoint of the good of its species. If it were as slow a runner as a human, it would not be able to survive. And so for all the other abilities of nonhumans which further their good but which are lacking in humans. In each case the claim to human superiority would be rejected from a nonhuman standpoint.

When superiority assertions are interpreted in this way, they are based on judgments of *merit*. To judge the merits of a person or an organism one must apply grading or ranking standards to it. . . .

The question that naturally arises at this juncture is: why should standards that are based on human values be assumed to be the only valid criteria of merit and hence the only true signs of superiority? This question is especially pressing when humans are being judged superior in merit to nonhumans. It is true that a human being may be a better mathematician than a monkey, but the monkey may be a better tree climber than a human being. If we humans value mathematics more than tree climbing, that is because our conception of civilized life makes the development of mathematical ability more desirable than the ability to climb trees. But is it not unreasonable to judge nonhumans by the values of human civilization, rather than by values connected with what it is for a member of *that* species to live a good life? *If all living things have a good of their own, it at least makes sense to judge the merits of nonhumans by standards derived from their good.* To use only standards based on human values is already to commit oneself to holding that humans are superior to nonhumans, which is the point in question.

The Case From Moral Agency

A further logical flaw arises in connection with the widely held conviction that humans are *morally* superior beings because they possess, while others lack, the capacities of a moral agent (free will, accountability, deliberation, judgment, practical reason). This view rests on a conceptual confusion. As far as moral standards are concerned, only beings that have the capacities of a moral agent can properly be judged to be *either* moral (morally good) *or* immoral (morally deficient). Moral standards are simply not applicable to beings that lack such capacities. Animals and plants cannot therefore be said to be morally inferior in merit to humans. Since the only beings that can have moral merits *or be deficient in such merits* are moral agents, it is conceptually incoherent to judge humans as superior to nonhumans on the ground that humans have moral capacities while nonhumans don't.

The Case From Inherent Worth

Up to this point I have been interpreting the claim that humans are superior to other living things as a grading or ranking judgment regarding their comparative merits. There is, however, another way of understanding the idea of human superiority. According to this interpretation, humans are superior to nonhumans not as regards their merits but as regards their inherent worth. Thus the claim of human superiority is to be understood as asserting that all humans, simply in virtue of their humanity, have *a greater inherent worth* than other living things.

The inherent worth of an entity does not depend on its merits.[8] To consider something as possessing inherent worth, we have seen, is to place intrinsic value on the realization of its good. This is done regardless of whatever particular merits it might have or might lack, as judged by a set of grading or ranking standards. In human affairs, we are all familiar with the principle that one's worth as a person does not vary with one's merits or lack of merits. The same can hold true of animals and plants. To regard such entities as possessing inherent worth entails disregarding their merits and deficiencies, whether they are being judged from a human standpoint or from the standpoint of their own species.

The idea of one entity having more merit than another, and so being superior to it in merit, makes perfectly good sense. Merit is a grading or ranking concept, and judgments of comparative merit are based on the different degrees to which things satisfy a given standard. But what can it mean to talk about one thing being superior to another in inherent worth? In order to get at what is being asserted in such a claim it is helpful first to look at the social origin of the concept of degrees of inherent worth.

The idea that humans can possess different degrees of inherent worth originated in societies having rigid class structures. Before the rise of modern democracies with their egalitarian outlook, one's membership in a hereditary class determined one's social status. People in the upper classes were looked up to, while those in the lower classes were looked down upon. In such a society one's social superiors and social inferiors were clearly defined and easily recognized.

Two aspects of these class-structured societies are especially relevant to the idea of degrees of inherent worth. First, those born into the upper classes were deemed more worthy of respect than those born into the lower orders. Second, the superior worth of upper class people had nothing to do with their merits nor did the inferior worth of those in the lower classes rest on their lack of merits. One's superiority or inferiority entirely derived from a social position one was born into. The modern concept of a meritocracy simply did not apply. One could not advance into a higher class by any sort of moral or nonmoral achievement. Similarly, an aristocrat held his title and all the privileges that went with it just because he was the eldest son of a titled nobleman. Unlike the bestowing of knighthood in contemporary Great Britain, one did not earn membership in the nobility by meritorious conduct.

We who live in modern democracies no longer believe in such hereditary social distinctions. Indeed, we would wholeheartedly condemn them on moral grounds as being fundamentally unjust. We have come to think of class systems as a paradigm of social injustice, it being a central principle of the democratic way of life that among humans there are no superiors and no inferiors. Thus *we have rejected the whole conceptual framework in which people are judged to have different degrees of inherent worth.* That idea is incompatible with our notion of human equality based on the doctrine that all humans, simply in virtue of their humanity, have the same inherent worth. (The belief in universal human rights is one form that this egalitarianism takes.)

The vast majority of people in modem democracies, however, do not maintain an egalitarian outlook when it comes to comparing human beings with other living things. *Most people consider our own species to be superior to all other species and this superiority is understood to be a matter of inherent worth, not merit.* There may exist thoroughly vicious and depraved humans who lack all merit. Yet because they are human they are thought to belong to a higher class of entities than any plant or animal. That one is born into the species *Homo sapiens* entitles one to have lordship over those who are one's inferiors, namely, those born into other species. The parallel with hereditary social classes is very close. Implicit in this view is a hierarchical conception of nature according to which an organism has a position of superiority or inferiority in the Earth's community of life simply on the basis of its genetic background. The "lower" orders of life are looked down upon and it is considered perfectly proper that they serve the interests of those belonging to the highest order, namely humans. The intrinsic value we place on the well-being of our fellow humans reflects our recognition of their rightful position as our equals. No such intrinsic value is to be placed on the good of other animals, unless we choose to do so out of fondness or affection for them. But their well-being imposes no moral requirement on us. In this respect there is an absolute difference in moral status between ourselves and them.

This is the structure of concepts and beliefs that people are committed to insofar as they regard humans to be superior in inherent worth to all other species. I now wish to argue that this structure of concepts and beliefs is completely groundless. *If we accept the first three components of the biocentric outlook and from that perspective look at the major philosophical traditions which have supported that structure, we find it to be at bottom nothing more than the expression of an irrational bias in our own favor.* The philosophical traditions themselves rest on very questionable assumptions or else simply beg the question. I briefly consider three of the main traditions to substantiate the point. These are classical Greek humanism, Cartesian dualism,

and the Judeo-Christian concept of the Great Chain of Being.

The inherent superiority of humans over other species was implicit in the Greek definition of man as a rational animal. Our animal nature was identified with "brute" desires that need the order and restraint of reason to rule them (just as reason is the special virtue of those who rule in the ideal state). Rationality was then seen to be the key to our superiority over animals. It enables us to live on a higher plane and endows us with a nobility and worth that other creatures lack. This familiar way of comparing humans with other species is deeply ingrained in our Western philosophical outlook. The point to consider here is that this view does not actually provide an argument *for* human superiority but rather makes explicit the framework of thought that is implicitly used by those who think of humans as inherently superior to nonhumans. The Greeks who held that humans, in virtue of their rational capacities, have a kind of worth greater than that of any nonrational being, never looked at rationality as but one capacity of living things among many others. But when we consider rationality from the standpoint of the first three elements of the ecological outlook, we see that its value lies in its importance for *human* life. Other creatures achieve their species-specific good without the need of rationality, although they often make use of capacities that humans lack. So the humanistic outlook of classical Greek thought does not give us a neutral (nonquestion-begging) ground on which to construct a scale of degrees of inherent worth possessed by different species of living things.

The second tradition, centering on the Cartesian dualism of soul and body, also fails to justify the claim to human superiority. That superiority is supposed to derive from the fact that we have souls while animals do not. Animals are mere automata and lack the divine element that makes us spiritual beings. I won't go into the now familiar criticisms of this two-substance view. I only add the point that, even if humans are composed of an immaterial, unextended soul and a material, extended body, this in itself is not a reason to deem them of greater worth than entities that are only bodies. Why is a soul substance a thing that adds value to its possessor? Unless some theological reasoning is offered here (which many, including myself, would find unacceptable on epistemological grounds), no logical connection is evident. An immaterial something which thinks is better than a material something which does not think only if thinking itself has value, either intrinsically or instrumentally. Now it is intrinsically valuable to humans alone, who value it as an end in itself, and it is instrumentally valuable to those who benefit from it, namely humans.

For animals that neither enjoy thinking for its own sake nor need it for living the kind of life for which they are best adapted, it has no value. Even if "thinking" is broadened to include all forms of consciousness, there are still many living things that can do without it and yet live what is for their species a good life. The anthropocentricity underlying the claim to human superiority runs throughout Cartesian dualism.

A third major source of the idea of human superiority is the Judeo-Christian concept of the Great Chain of Being. Humans are superior to animals and plants because their Creator has given them a higher place on the chain. It begins with God at the top, and then moves to the angels, who are lower than God but higher than humans, then to humans, positioned between the angels and the beasts (partaking of the nature of both), and then on down to the lower levels occupied by nonhuman animals, plants, and finally inanimate objects. Humans, being "made in God's image," are inherently superior to animals and plants by virtue of their being closer (in their essential nature) to God.

The metaphysical and epistemological difficulties with this conception of a hierarchy of entities are, in my mind, insuperable. Without entering into this matter here, I only point out that if we are unwilling to accept the metaphysics of traditional Judaism and Christianity, we are again left without good reasons for holding to the claim of inherent human superiority.

The foregoing considerations (and others like them) leave us with but one ground for the assertion that a human being, regardless of merit, is a higher kind of entity than any other living thing. This is the mere fact of the genetic makeup of the species *Homo sapiens*. But this is surely irrational and arbitrary. Why should the arrangement of genes of a certain type be a mark of superior value, especially when this fact about an organism is taken by itself, unrelated to any other aspect of its life? We might just as well refer to any other genetic makeup as a ground of superior value. Clearly we are confronted here with a wholly arbitrary claim that can only be explained as an irrational bias in our own favor. . . .

Rejecting the notion of human superiority entails its positive counterpart: **the doctrine of species impartiality**. One who accepts that doctrine regards *all living things as possessing inherent worth—the same inherent worth, since no one species has been shown to be either "higher" or "lower" than any other.* Now we saw earlier that, insofar as one thinks of a living thing as possessing inherent worth, one considers it to be the appropriate object of the attitude of respect and believes that attitude to be the only fitting or suitable one for all moral agents to take toward it.

Here, then, is the key to understanding how the attitude of respect is rooted in the biocentric outlook on nature. The basic connection is made through the denial of human superiority. Once we reject the claim that humans are superior either in merit or in worth to other living things, we are ready to adopt the attitude of respect. The denial of human superiority is itself the result of taking the perspective on nature built into the first three elements of the biocentric outlook.

Now the first three elements of the biocentric outlook, it seems clear, would be found acceptable to any rational and scientifically informed thinker who is fully "open" to the reality of the lives of nonhuman organisms. Without denying our distinctively human characteristics, such a thinker can acknowledge the fundamental respects in which we are members of the Earth's community of life and in which the biological conditions necessary for the realization of our human values are inextricably linked with the whole system of nature. In addition, the conception of individual living things as teleological centers of life simply articulates how a scientifically informed thinker comes to understand them as the result, of increasingly careful and detailed observations. Thus, the biocentric outlook recommends itself as an acceptable system of concepts and beliefs to anyone who is clear-minded, unbiased, and factually enlightened, and who has a developed capacity of reality awareness with regard to the lives of individual organisms. This, I submit, is as good a reason for making the moral commitment involved in adopting the attitude of respect for nature as any theory of environmental ethics could possibly have.

NOTES

1. The conceptual links between an entity *having* a good, something being good *for* it, and events doing good *to* it are examined by G. H. Von Wright in *The Varieties of Goodness* (New York: Humanities Press, 1963), chaps. 3 and 5.

4. I have analyzed the nature of this commitment of human ethics in "On Taking the Moral Point of View," *Midwest Studies in Philosophy*, vol. 3, *Studies in Ethical Theory* (1978), pp. 35–61.

7. My criticisms of the dogma of human superiority gain independent support from a carefully reasoned essay by R. and V. Routley showing the many logical weaknesses in arguments for human-centered theories of environmental ethics. R. and V. Routley, "Against the Inevitability of Human Chauvinism," in K. E. Goodpaster and K. M. Sayre, eds., *Ethics and Problems of the 21st Century* (Notre Dame: University of Notre Dame Press, 1979), pp. 36–59.

8. For this way of distinguishing between merit and inherent worth, I am indebted to Gregory Vlastos, "Justice and Equality," in R. Brandt, ed., *Social Justice* (Englewood Cliffs, N. J.: Prentice-Hall, 1962), pp. 31–72.

DISCUSSION QUESTIONS:

1. Taylor makes much of the distinction between anthropocentric and biocentric outlooks on the moral community. But consider some of the world's most pressing environmental problems: global warming, pollution, overfishing of the seas, extinction of species, etc. Isn't it plausible that all of these things are very bad for humans? If so, do we really need a biocentric account to explain why these things are bad and why we ought not contribute to them?

2. Taylor writes that "every organism, species population, and community of life has a good of its own. . ." Is that true? How does the North American goldfinch population have a good of its own? And if we allow that it does have a good of its own, what about other groups of individuals? Does the Republican Party have a good of its own? How about cars or computers? If these things DO have goods of their own, does that mean that we have moral duties to each of them?

3. In the previous reading, Peter Singer makes the point that no empirical claims about beings on the earth will help to justify our moral claims about how we ought to treat them. David Hume, a famous 18th-century philosopher, put this point as saying that you cannot infer a statement about what *ought* to be the case from what *is* the case. But in this reading, Taylor claims that the biocentric outlook on nature ". . .supports and makes intelligible an autonomous agent's adopting, as an ultimate moral attitude, the attitude of respect for nature" (page 381). This appears to violate Hume's dictum by starting with a claim about how things *are* and drawing a conclusion about how we *ought* to behave. But how could reflecting on the fact that life on earth is interdependent, that other living things have biological goals, etc. provide us with a reason to think that we have certain moral obligations to those things?

4. Taylor notes that "[m]ost people consider our species to be superior to all other species and this superiority is understood to be a matter of inherent worth. . ." (page 386). Yet, he thinks that the three main philosophical traditions that he surveys (Greek, Cartesian, and Christian) provide little reason to think that this is true. Do you agree? Is one of these traditions really better than Taylor has suggested? Or is there another, independent reason for thinking that humans have more inherent worth than other species?

Argument Reconstruction Exercises:

I. Taylor claims that living things have inherent value, and he bases this claim on the principle of moral consideration and the principle of intrinsic value. Identify the premises and conclusion in the following paraphrase.

> To say that something has inherent worth is to say that (a) it deserves the consideration of all moral agents and (b) the realization of its good is intrinsically valuable. And according to the principle of moral consideration, every individual living thing is deserving of moral consideration from all moral agents. And according to the principle of intrinsic value, the realization of the good for every individual living thing is intrinsically valuable. Therefore, all living things have inherent worth.

II. Taylor spends a portion of his essay trying to debunk the idea that humans are morally superior to non-humans. One of the central lines of defense for this view appeals to capacities. Identify the premises and the suppressed conclusion in this excerpt:

> In what sense are humans alleged to be superior to other animals? We are different from them in having certain capacities that they lack. . . .Such uniquely human characteristics as rational thought, aesthetic creativity, autonomy and self determination, and moral freedom, it might be held, have a higher value than the capacities found in other species. (page 384)

III. One of the ways that the inherent worth of humans has been defended is by appeal to the idea that humans have souls. This view is most often cashed out in terms of substance dualism as defended by Descartes and others. Identify the premises and conclusion in the following paraphrase:

> Nothing without a soul can think. And it is better to be a thinking thing than a non-thinking thing. According to many philosophers, only humans have souls. Therefore, it is better to be a human than a non-human.

IV. Identify the premises and conclusion in the following argument:

> Taylor claims that "to say that an entity has a good of its own is simply to say that, without reference to any other entity, it can be benefited or harmed." It seems like the Republican party, the country of Greece, and a computer virus can be benefited or harmed. So these entities must have goods of their own.

14.3 ARE ALL SPECIES EQUAL?[1]

DAVID SCHMIDTZ (1998)

David Schmidtz is Kendrick Professor of Philosophy and Director of the Freedom Center at the University of Arizona. His work ranges widely from decision theory and social/political philosophy to environmental ethics and theories of justice. In this article, Schmidtz does three things. First, he contends that Paul Taylor's defense of species egalitarianism fails. Second, he argues that Peter Singer's rejection of speciesism fails. Third, Schmidtz offers his own view of the moral community in which all living things command our respect, though some command more respect than others.

Reading Questions:

1. What is species egalitarianism?

2. Schmidtz suggests two ways of responding to Taylor's argument for the claim that humans are not inherently superior to other living beings (i.e., claim (d) in Taylor's biocentric theory). What are they?

3. Why does Schmidtz think that species egalitarianism implies that it is no worse to kill a cow than a carrot?

4. Why does Schmidtz think that Singer is really a speciesist?

5. What is a failure of self-respect?

6. Why does Schmidtz think that living things command respect?

7. What are we supposed to learn from the example of Johnson and native Australian species?

Species egalitarianism *is the view that all living things have equal moral standing.* To have moral standing is, at a minimum, to command respect, to be more than a mere thing. Is there reason to believe that all living things have moral standing in even this most minimal sense? If so—that is, if all living things command respect—is there reason to believe that they all command *equal* respect?

I will try to explain why members of other species command our respect but also why they do not command equal respect. The intuition that we should have respect for nature is one motive for embracing species egalitarianism, but we need not be species egalitarians to have respect for nature. Indeed, I will question whether species egalitarianism is even compatible with respect for nature.

1. Respect for Nature

According to Paul Taylor, anthropocentrism "gives either exclusive or primary consideration to human interests above the good of other species."[2] The alternative to anthropocentrism is biocentrism, and it is biocentrism that, in Taylor's view, grounds species egalitarianism:

The beliefs that form the core of the biocentric outlook are four in number:

(a) The belief that humans are members of the Earth's Community of life in the same sense and on the same terms in which other living things are members of that community.

(b) The belief that the human species, along with all other species, are integral elements in a system of interdependence. . . .

(c) The belief that all organisms are teleological centers of life in the sense that each is a unique individual pursuing its own good in its own way.

(d) The belief that humans are not inherently superior to other living beings.[3]

Taylor concludes: "Rejecting the notion of human superiority entails its positive counterpart: the doctrine of species impartiality. One who accepts that doctrine regards all living things as possessing inherent worth—the *same* inherent worth, since no one species has been shown to be either higher or lower than any other."[4]

Taylor does not call this a valid argument, but he thinks that if we concede (a), (b), and (c), it would be unreasonable not to move to (d), and then to his egalitarian conclusion. Is he right? For those who accept Taylor's three premises (and who thus interpret those premises in terms innocuous enough to render them acceptable), there are two responses. First, we may go on to accept (d), following Taylor, but then still deny that there is any warrant for moving from there to Taylor's egalitarian conclusion. Having accepted that our form of life is not superior, we might choose instead to regard it as inferior. More plausibly, we might view our form of life as noncomparable. We simply do not have the same kind of value as nonhumans. The question of how we compare to nonhumans has a simple answer: we do not compare to them. We are not equal. We are not unequal. We are simply different.

Alternatively, we may reject (d) and say that humans are indeed inherently superior but that humans' superiority is a moot point. Whether humans are inherently superior (that is, superior as a form of life) does not matter much. Even if humans are superior, the fact remains that within the web of ecological interdependence mentioned in premises (a) and (b), it would be a mistake to ignore the needs and the telos of the other species referred to in premise (c). *Thus, there are two ways of rejecting Taylor's argument for species egalitarianism. Each, on its face, is compatible with the respect for nature that motivates Taylor's egalitarianism in the first place.*

These are preliminary worries, then, about Taylor's argument. Taylor's critics have been harsh—perhaps too harsh. After building on some criticisms while rejecting others, I explore some of our reasons to have respect for nature and ask whether they translate into reasons to be species egalitarians.

2. Is Species Egalitarianism Hypocritical?

Paul Taylor is among the most intransigent of species egalitarians, yet he allows that human needs override the needs of nonhumans. In response, French argues that species egalitarians cannot have it both ways. French perceives a contradiction between the egalitarian principles Taylor officially endorses and the unofficial principles Taylor offers as the real principles by which we should live. Having proclaimed that we are all equal, French asks, what licenses Taylor to say that, in cases of conflict, non-human interests can legitimately be sacrificed to vital human interests?[5]

Good question. Yet, somehow Taylor's alleged inconsistency is too obvious. Perhaps his position is not as blatantly inconsistent as it appears. Let me suggest how Taylor could respond. Suppose I find myself in a situation of mortal combat with an enemy soldier. If I kill my enemy to save my life, that does not entail that I regard my enemy as inherently inferior (i.e., as an inferior form of life). Likewise, if I kill a bear to save my life, that does not entail that I regard the bear as inherently inferior. Therefore, Taylor can, without hypocrisy, deny that species egalitarianism requires a radically self-effacing pacifism.

What, then, does species egalitarianism require? It requires us to avoid mortal combat whenever we can, not just with other humans but with living things in general. On this view, we ought to regret finding ourselves in kill-or-be-killed situations that we could have avoided. There is no point in regretting the fact that we must kill in order to eat, though, for there is no avoiding that. Species egalitarianism is compatible with our having a limited license to kill.

What seems far more problematic for species egalitarianism is that it seems to suggest that it makes no difference what we kill. Vegetarians typically think it is worse to kill a cow than to kill a carrot. Are they wrong? Yes, according to species egalitarianism. In this respect, species egalitarianism cannot be right. I believe we have reason to respect nature. However, *we fail to give nature due respect if we say we should have no more respect for a cow than for a carrot.*

3. Is Species Egalitarianism Arbitrary?

Suppose interspecies comparisons are possible. Suppose the capacities of different species, and whatever else gives living things moral standing, are commensurable. In that case, it could turn out that all living things are equal, but that would be quite a fluke.

Taylor says a being has intrinsic worth just in case it has a good of its own. And Taylor thinks even plants have a good of their own in the relevant sense. They

seek their own good in their own way. As mentioned earlier, Taylor defines anthropocentrism as giving exclusive or primary consideration to human interests above the good of other species. So, when we acknowledge the ability to think as a valuable capacity, and acknowledge that some but not all living things possess this valuable capacity, are we giving exclusive or primary consideration to human interests? Probably not. Is there something wrong with noticing that there are valuable capacities that not all living things possess? Put it this way: if biocentrism involves resolving to ignore the fact that cognitive capacity is something we value—if biocentrism amounts to a resolution to value only those capacities that all living things share—then biocentrism is as arbitrary and as question-begging as anthropocentrism.

It will not do to defend species egalitarianism by singling out a property that all living things possess, arguing that this property is morally important, then concluding that all living things are therefore of equal moral importance. The problem with this sort of argument is that, where there is one property that provides a basis for moral standing, there might be others. Other properties might be possessed by some but not all living things, and might provide bases for different kinds or degrees of moral standing.

Obviously, Taylor knows that not all living things can think, and he would not deny that the capacity for thought is valuable. What he would say, though, is that it begs the question to rank the ability to think as *more* valuable than the characteristic traits of plants and other animals. Taylor himself assumes that human rationality is on a par with, for example, a cheetah's foot-speed: no less valuable, but no more valuable either.[6] In this case, though, perhaps it is Taylor who begs the question. The difference between the foot-speed of chimpanzees and cheetahs is at least arguably a difference of degree, while the difference between the intelligence of a chimpanzee and the intelligence of a carrot is something else: a difference in kind. Chimpanzees are very smart. Carrots, in contrast, are not merely a lot less smart. Carrots are not smart at all. They do not even make it into the same category.

Here, though, is the more telling point. Anthropocentrists might argue, against Taylor, that the good associated with the ability to think is superior to the good associated with a tree's ability to grow and reproduce. Could they be wrong? Let us suppose they are wrong. For argument's sake, suppose the ability to grow and reproduce is *superior* to the ability to think. Wouldn't that mean trees are superior to chimpanzees? No. The point is not that chimpanzees have one singular virtue, the ability to think, while trees have another singular virtue, the ability to grow and reproduce. Rather, both trees and chimpanzees share one virtue: they can grow and reproduce. They are both teleological centers of life, to use Taylor's phrase. But chimpanzees have a second virtue as well: they can think.

Of course, it is more complicated than this, for in fact both trees and chimpanzees have innumerable capacities. The crucial point, though, is this. *Although both trees and chimpanzees are teleological centers of life, and we can agree that this is valuable, and that trees and chimpanzees share equally in this particular value, we cannot infer that trees and chimpanzees have equal value.* We are entitled to conclude only that they are of equal value so far as being a teleological center of life is concerned.[7] From that, we may of course infer that *one* ground of our moral standing (i.e., that we grow and reproduce) is shared by all living things. Beyond that, nothing about equality even suggests itself. In particular, *it begs no questions to notice that there are grounds for moral standing that humans do not share with all living things.*

None of this presumes that the unshared capacity for thought is more valuable than the shared capacity for reproduction. In this argument, it does not matter which has more value. It matters only that the capacity for thought has *some* value.

4. Speciesism and Social Policy

Peter Singer and others talk as if **speciesism**—the idea that some species are superior to others—is necessarily a kind of bias favor of humans and against nonhuman animals. (Singer has no problem with being "biased" against plants.) This is a mistake. If we have more respect for chimpanzees than for mice, then we are speciesists, no matter what status we accord to human beings. But we *should* have more respect for chimpanzees than for mice,

shouldn't we? Or if not, then shouldn't we at least have more respect for chimpanzees than for carrots?

Suppose we take an interest in how chimpanzees rank compared to mice. Perhaps we wonder what we would do in an emergency where we could save a drowning chimpanzee or a drowning mouse but not both. More realistically, suppose we conclude we must do experiments involving animals (because, let's say, there is no other way to develop an effective treatment for an otherwise catastrophic disease) and now we have to choose which animals. Whichever we use, the animals we use will die. We decide to use mice. Then a species egalitarian says, "Why not use chimpanzees? They're all the same anyway, morally speaking, and you'll get more reliable data." Wouldn't that sort of egalitarianism be monstrous? I say yes, and I expect that Singer would agree. *But if we believe (with Taylor) all living things are equal, or even if we think only (with Singer) that all animals are equal, then why not use the chimpanzee instead of the mouse?*

In reality, chimpanzees are, morally speaking, the wrong *kind* of animal to experiment on when researchers could get by with mice. To that extent, speciesism is closer to the moral truth than is species egalitarianism. Moreover, although in philosophy we tend to use science fiction examples, the situation just described is an ordinary problem, every day, in the scientific community. Suppose researchers had to choose between harvesting the organs of a chimpanzee or a brain-damaged human baby. Peter Singer says we cannot have it both ways. He argues that if the ability to think makes the difference, then the brain-damaged infant commands no more respect than a chimpanzee, and may indeed command less. Singer concludes that if we need to use one or the other in a painful and/or lethal medical experiment, and if it does not matter which one we use so far as the experiment is concerned, then we ought to use the brain-damaged child, not the chimpanzee.[8]

Does this seem obvious? It should not. Actually, Singer appears to be the one trying to have it both ways here. The mistake here is subtle, but it is, nevertheless, a mistake. Singer does not reject speciesism so much as what he considers to be a bad kind of speciesism. If we claimed that the rightness of eating beef has to be settled individual cow by individual cow, it would be Singer who would insist that cows are the wrong *kind* of thing for us to be eating, and that we need a policy governing our exploitation of cows as a species. Yet, when Singer criticizes those who exalt the value of rationality, he says rationality is relevant to justification only at the individual level.

Some speciesists are impressed with humanity's characteristic rationality. They say this characteristic justifies respect for humanity, not merely for particular humans who exemplify human rationality. Other speciesists such as Singer are more impressed with the ability to feel pain. They say this ability justifies respecting cows in general, not just those individual cows that have proven they can feel pain.

Singer is indeed a speciesist of the latter kind. Singer has to agree that if most chimpanzees have morally important characteristics that most mice lack, we do not need to compare individual chimpanzees and mice on a case-by-case basis in order to have a moral justification for passing laws that stop researchers from using chimpanzees in their experiments when mice would do just as well. It is Singer who would insist that researchers cannot be allowed to decide on a case-by-case basis whether to use mice or chimpanzees or defective people in their experiments, when turnips would do just as well. Likewise, it is Singer who wants to insist that individual consumers should not decide on a case-by-case basis whether to eat cows or turnips—rather, they ought to quit eating cows, period. In the medical research policy area, what we actually do, and rightly so, is ignore Singer's point that some animals are smarter than some people, and instead formulate policy on the basis of characteristic features of the species. And if Singer objects to the policy we choose, it will not be because our policy is based on features of the species. His objection will be that we used the wrong feature. He will say the feature we ought to have used is the ability to feel pain.

Of course, some chimpanzees lack characteristic features in virtue of which chimpanzees command respect as a species, just as some humans lack characteristic features in virtue of which humans command respect as a species. Just as obviously, some chimpanzees have cognitive capacities superior to those of some humans. But when it comes to questions of practical policy, such as we face when trying to formulate policy regarding animal experimentation, whether every human being is superior in every respect to every chimpanzee is beside the point. The point is that *we can, we do, and we must make policy decisions on the basis of our recognition that turnips, mice, chimpanzees, and humans are relevantly different types.*

5. Equality and Transcendence

Even if speciesists are right to see a nonarbitrary distinction between humans and other living things, though, the fact remains that *claims of superiority do not easily translate into justifications of domination.*[9] We can have reasons to treat nonhuman species with respect, regardless of whether we consider them to be on a moral par with *Homo sapiens.*

What kind of reasons do we have for treating members of other species with respect? We might have respect for chimpanzees or even mice on the grounds that they are sentient. Even mice have a rudimentary point of view and rudimentary hopes and dreams, and we might well respect them for that. But what about plants? Plants, unlike mice and chimpanzees, do not care what happens to them. It is literally true that they could not care less. So, why should we care? Is it even possible for us to have any good reason, other than a purely instrumental reason, to care what happens to plants?

When we are alone in a forest, wondering whether it would be fine to chop down a tree for fun, our perspective on what happens to the tree is, so far as we know, the only perspective there is. The tree does not have its own. Thus, explaining why we have reason to care about trees requires us to explain caring from our point of view, since that (we are supposing) is all there is. In that case, we do not have to satisfy *trees* that we are treating them properly; rather, we have to satisfy ourselves. So, again, can we have noninstrumental reasons for caring about trees—for treating them with respect?

One reason to care (not the only one) is that gratuitous destruction is a failure of self-respect. It is a repudiation of the kind of self-awareness and self-respect we can achieve by repudiating wantonness. So far as I know, no one finds anything puzzling in the idea that we have reason to treat our lawns or living rooms with respect. Lawns and living rooms have instrumental value, but there is more to it than that. Most of us have the sense that taking reasonable care of our lawns and living rooms is somehow a matter of self-respect, not merely a matter of preserving their instrumental value. Do we have similar reasons to treat forests with respect? I think we do. There is an aesthetic involved, the repudiation of which would be a failure of self-respect. (Obviously, not everyone feels the same way about forests. Not everyone feels the same way about lawns and living rooms, either. But the point here is to make sense of respect for nature, not to argue that respect for nature is in fact universal or that failing to respect nature is irrational.) If and when we identify with a redwood, in the sense of being inspired by it, having respect for its size and age and so on, then as a psychological fact, we really do face questions about how we ought to treat it. If and when we come to see a redwood in that light, subsequently turning our backs on it becomes a kind of self-effacement. The values we thereby fail to take seriously are *our* values, not the tree's.

So, I am saying the attitude we take toward gazelles (for example) raises issues of self-respect, insofar as we see ourselves as relevantly like gazelles. Here is a different and complementary way of looking at the issue. Consider that lions owe nothing to gazelles. Therefore, if we owe it to gazelles not to hunt them, it must be because we are *unlike* lions, not (or not only) because we are *like* gazelles.

Unlike lions, we have a choice about whether to hunt gazelles, and we are capable of deliberating about that choice in a reflective way. We are capable of caring about the gazelle's pain, the gazelle's beauty, the gazelle's hopes and dreams (such as they are), and so forth. If we do care, then in a more or less literal way, something is wrong with us—we are less than fully, magnificently, human—if we cannot adjust our behavior in light of what we care about. And if we do not care, then we are missing something. *For a human being, to lack a broad respect for living things and beautiful things and well-functioning things is to be stunted in a way.*

Our coming to see members of other species as commanding respect is itself a way of transcending our animal natures. It is part of our natures

unthinkingly to see ourselves as superior, and to try to dominate accordingly; our capacity to see ourselves as equal is one of the things that makes us different. (It may be one of the things that makes us superior.)[10] Coming to see all living things as equal may not be the best way of transcending our animal natures—it doesn't work for me—but it is one way.

Another way of transcending our animal natures and expressing due respect for nature is simply to not bother to keep score. This way is, I think, better. It is more respectful of our own reflective natures. It does not dwell on rankings. It does not insist on seeing equality where a more reflective being simply would see what is there to be seen and would not shy away from respecting what is unique as well as what is common. Someone might say we need to rank animals as our equals so as to be fair, but that appears to be false. I can be fair to my friends without ranking them. Imagine a friend saying, "I disagree! In fact, failing to rank us is insulting! You have to rank us as equals!" What would be the point? Perhaps my friends are each other's equals (in some respect?). Even so, we are left with no need at all to *rank* them as equal. For most purposes, it is better for them simply to be the unique and priceless friends that they are. Sometimes, respect is simply respect. It need not be based on a pecking order.

Children rank their friends. It is one of the things children do not yet understand about friendship. Sometimes, the idea of ranking things, even as equals, is a child's game. It is beneath us.

6. Respect for Everything

Thus, *a broad respect for living or beautiful or well-functioning things need not translate into equal respect.* It need not translate into universal respect, either. Part of our responsibility as moral agents is to be somewhat choosy about what we respect and how we respect it. I can see why people shy away from openly accepting that responsibility, but they still have it.

We might suppose speciesism is as arbitrary as racism unless we can show that the differences are morally relevant. This is, to be sure, a popular sentiment among animal liberationists such as Peter Singer and Tom Regan. But are we really like racists when we think it is worse to kill a dolphin than to kill a tuna? The person who asserts that there is a relevant similarity between speciesism and racism has the burden of proof: go ahead and identify the similarity. Is seeing moral significance in biological differences between chimpanzees and mice anything like seeing moral significance in biological differences between races? I think not.

To be sure, burden of proof, crucial though it is to many philosophical arguments, is a slippery notion. Do we need good reason to exclude plants and animals from the realm of things we regard as commanding respect? Or do we need reason to include them? Should we be trying to identify properties in virtue of which a thing forfeits presumptive (equal) moral standing? Or does it make more sense to be trying to identify properties in virtue of which a thing *commands* respect? The latter seems more natural to me, so I am left supposing the burden of proof lies with those who claim we should have respect for all living things. I could be wrong.

But even if I am right, I would not say this burden is unbearable. One reason to have regard for other living things has to do with self-respect. (As I said earlier, when we mistreat a tree that we admire, the values we fail to respect are our values, not the tree's.) A second reason has to do with self-realization. (As I said, exercising our capacity for moral regard is a form of self-realization.) Finally, at least some species seem to share with human beings precisely those characteristics that lead us to see human life as especially worthy of esteem. For example, Lawrence Johnson describes experiments in which rhesus monkeys show extreme reluctance to obtain food by means that would subject monkeys in neighboring cages to electric shock. He describes the case of Washoe, a chimpanzee who learned sign language.[11] Anyone who has tried to learn a foreign language ought to be able to appreciate how astonishing an intellectual feat it is that an essentially nonlinguistic creature could learn a language—a language that is not merely foreign but the language of another species.[12]

However, although he believes Washoe has moral standing, Johnson does not believe that the moral standing of chimpanzees, and indeed of all living creatures, implies we must resolve never to kill. Thus, Johnson (an Australian) supports killing introduced

animal species (feral dogs, rabbits, and so forth) to protect Australia's native species, including native plant species.[13]

Is Johnson advocating a speciesist version of the Holocaust? Has he shown himself to be no better than a racist? I think not. Johnson is right to want to take drastic measures to protect Australia's natural flora, and the idea of respecting trees is intelligible. Certainly one thing I feel in the presence of redwoods (or Australia's incredible eucalyptus forests) is something like a feeling of respect. But I doubt that what underlies Johnson's willingness to kill feral dogs is mere respect for Australia's native plants. I suspect his approval of such killings turns to some extent on needs and aesthetic sensibilities of human beings, not just interests of plants. For example, if the endangered native species happened to be a malaria-carrying mosquito, I doubt Johnson would advocate wiping out an exotic species of amphibian simply to protect the mosquitoes.

Aldo Leopold urged us to see ourselves as plain citizens of, rather than conquerors of, the biotic community.[14] But there are some species with whom we can never be fellow citizens. The rabbits that once ate flowers in my backyard in Ohio (or the cardinals currently eating my cherry tomatoes in Arizona) are neighbors, and I cherish their company, minor frictions notwithstanding. I feel no sense of community with mosquitoes, though, and not merely because they are not warm and fuzzy. Some mosquito species are so adapted to making human beings miserable that mortal combat is not accidental; rather, combat is a natural state. It is how such creatures live. I think it is fair to say human beings are not able to respond to malaria-carrying mosquitoes in a caring manner. At very least, most of us would think less of a person who did respond to them in a caring manner. We would regard the person's caring as a parody of respect for nature.[15]

The conclusion that *all* living things have moral standing is unmotivated. For human beings, viewing apes as having moral standing is a form of self-respect. Viewing viruses as having moral standing is not. It is good to have a sense of how amazing living things are, but being able to marvel at living things is not the same as thinking all living things have moral standing. Life as such commands respect only in the limited but important sense that for self-aware and reflective creatures who want to act in ways that make sense, deliberately killing something is an act that does not make sense unless we have good reason to do it. Destroying something for no good reason is (at best) the moral equivalent of vandalism.

NOTES

1. This essay revises David Schmidtz, "Are All Species Equal?" *Journal of Applied Philosophy* 15 (1998): 57–67. Reprinted by permission of Blackwell Publishers.
2. Taylor (1983) 240.
3. Taylor(1986) 99. See also Taylor (1981).
4. Taylor (1981) 217.
5. French (1995) 44. See also James Anderson (1993) 350.
6. Taylor (1981) 211.
7. For a similar critique of Taylor from an Aristotelian perspective, see Anderson (1993) 348. See also Lombardi (1993).
8. Singer (1990) 1–23. See also Johnson (1991) 52.
9. This is effectively argued by Anderson (1993) 362.
10. When the Cincinnati Zoo erected a monument to the passenger pigeon, Aldo Leopold expressed a related thought. "We have erected a monument to commemorate the funeral of a species. . . .For one species to mourn the death of another is a new thing under the sun. . . .In this fact. . .lies objective evidence of our superiority over the beasts" (1966, 116–17).
11. Johnson (1991) 64n.
12. This is what I wrote in the original version of this essay. I since have heard that families of low-land gorillas have their own fairly complicated language of hand signals, which leads me to suspect I may have been mistaken in describing chimpanzees as essentially nonlinguistic.
13. Johnson (1991) 174.
14. Leopold (1966) 240.
15. Martha Ramsey has asked me, what about Buddhists who consider it a sign of great spiritual advancement when a monk refrains from killing mosquitoes? What if the mosquitoes were known to be transmitters of malaria parasites? In that case, would letting them live be a way of respecting life, or disrespecting it?

DISCUSSION QUESTIONS:

1. Schmidtz thinks that species egalitarians must hold the view that it is no worse to kill a carrot than a chimpanzee. Is he right about that implication? If so, how would this affect our own lives, for example our diets? Given that it takes enormous quantities of plants to produce meat, isn't there still a moral reason for a species egalitarian to be a vegetarian?

2. Schmidtz anchors our respect for nature in respect for ourselves. Anyone who has certain values and cares about certain kinds of things will be rationally required to respect other living things. But what if a person has no self-respect? Is it morally permissible for such a person to abuse non-human animals, cut down forests at a whim, etc.? If not, why not?

3. At one point, Schmidtz notes that it may not be possible, or even preferable, to rank the moral value of various living things. It might not be possible because the different values exhibited by different things may be incommensurable, and it might not be preferable because it might be the equivalent of a child's game—something that detracts from the value of the relationship between humans and non-human living things. Do you rank the moral value of other beings that you have a relationship with? Why or why not?

Argument Reconstruction Exercises:

I. In Section 2, Schmidtz dismisses an objection to biocentrism levied by French. Instead of parsing the objection into a clear argument, he states it in terms of a contradiction and ends with a rhetorical question. The conclusion of the argument is suppressed. Identify the premises and conclusion in this excerpt:

> French perceives a contradiction between the egalitarian principles Taylor officially endorses and the unofficial principles Taylor offers as the real principles by which we should live. Having proclaimed that we are all equal, French asks, what licenses Taylor to say that, in cases of conflict, nonhuman interests can legitimately be sacrificed to vital human interests? (page 391)

II. Like French, Schmidtz thinks that we should reject species egalitarianism because it has false implications about how we should treat non-humans in cases of conflict. Identify the premises and conclusion in this excerpt:

> Species egalitarianism is compatible with our having a limited license to kill. What seems far more problematic for species egalitarianism is that it seems to suggest that it makes no difference what we kill. Vegetarians typically think that it is worse to kill a cow than to kill a carrot. Are they wrong? Yes,

according to species egalitarianism. In this respect, species egalitarianism cannot be right. (page 391)

III. Schmidtz argues that Singer's speciesist criticism of anthropomorphic views in ethics misses the mark. Rightly understood, he thinks that we should all be speciesist and that this is what morality requires of us. Identify the premises and conclusion in the following excerpt:

> Peter Singer and others talk as if speciesism—the idea that some species are superior to others—is necessarily a kind of bias in favor of humans and against nonhuman animals. (Singer has no problem with being "biased" against plants.) This is a mistake. If we have more respect for chimpanzees than for mice, then we are speciesists, no matter what the status we accord to human beings. But we *should* have more respect for chimpanzees than for mice, shouldn't we? Or if not, then shouldn't we at least have more respect for chimpanzees than for carrots? (page 392)

IV. Schmidtz's central argument for his own view of the moral community relies on an analogy, but the central passage leaves the inference unclear. Identify the premises and conclusion in this excerpt:

> One reason to care [about nonhuman living things like forests] is that gratuitous destruction is a failure of self-respect. It is a repudiation of the kind of self-awareness and self-respect we can achieve by repudiating wantonness. So far as I know, no one finds anything puzzling in the idea that we have reason to treat our lawns or living rooms with respect. Lawns and living rooms have instrumental value, but there is more to it than that. Most of us have the sense that taking reasonable care of our lawns and living rooms is somehow a matter of self-respect, not merely a matter of preserving their instrumental value. Do we have similar reasons to treat forests with respect? I think we do. (page 393–394)

CHAPTER 15

Abortion

No woman can call herself free who does not control her own body.
—MARGARET SANGER, "A PARENT'S PROBLEM OR A WOMAN'S?"

It is a poverty to decide that a child must die so that you may live as you wish.
—MOTHER TERESA (ALLEGED)

INTRODUCTION

Morgan is a junior in college and has been dating Jeremy for almost 6 months. The two of them are wonderful together, but they are careful to keep the relationship from getting too serious. After all, Jeremy has plans to attend graduate school after college, and Morgan has always wanted to follow in her family's footsteps by spending at least two years in the Peace Corps after graduation. Like many college students, they have big plans for their lives.

Unfortunately, like many college students, they also have unprotected sex, and Morgan becomes pregnant. Her world is turned upside down, and she doesn't know what she should do. On the one hand, it seems miraculous that there is a tiny human living inside of her that depends solely on her for protection and nourishment. On the other hand, it seems impossible for her to fulfill her life dreams while being a mother. What should she do? Morgan has three live options: deliver the baby and keep it, deliver the baby and surrender it for adoption, or terminate the pregnancy via abortion.

What moral reasons are there for her to carry the fetus to term? What moral reasons are there for terminating the pregnancy? Is there a moral reason to prefer keeping the child over surrendering the child for adoption? What role

should Jeremy play in the decision process? Is it morally permissible to abort the fetus even if Jeremy protests?

Furthermore, even if we can answer the questions about *what* Morgan should do in such a situation, this begs the deeper question: *why?* If it's true that she ought to carry the fetus to term, is that because the fetus has moral rights? Or is it because the fetus would feel pain if killed via an abortion? If it's true that it is permissible for her to have an abortion, is that because she has rights over her body that trump the rights of the fetus? Or is it because the fetus has no rights at all and is due no moral consideration?

No doubt you already have a view about what Morgan should do in this situation. And no doubt you feel strongly about the issue. The topic of abortion is one of the most emotionally fraught of the topics covered in this book. However, if you're like most people who have not had a course in ethics or philosophy before, your view on abortion is probably not very sophisticated. It's not what you might call a *considered* view. This chapter is your chance to refine your moral views about abortion. And to do so, we need to make some distinctions and clear up some misunderstandings.

First, it's a mistake to talk about the abortion issue in terms of pro-life and pro-choice. One reason for this is that all of the intelligent participants in the debate think that both life and choice are good things, so the labels are misleading. Also, not everyone who holds a "pro-life" view agrees about when, if ever, an abortion is morally permissible. And not everyone who holds a "pro-choice" view agrees about how far a woman's right to choose goes. So the labels are not very enlightening. Instead, we should face the fact that there is a continuum of views about the permissibility of abortion ranging from the very strict to the very permissive. Here is one way of drawing such a continuum regarding the permissibility of having an abortion:

> Never.
> Only to protect the mother's life.
> Only to protect the mother's life or health.
> Only to protect the mother's life or health or cases of rape.
> Only to protect the mother's life or health or cases of rape or . . .
> Always.

Notice that the only relevant factor, according to this continuum of views, is how the pregnancy affects the mother. Some people view this as the morally crucial factor.

However, other people think that the pregnancy's impact on the mother is irrelevant. What matters is the moral status of the fetus, and this can change with time. So here is another way of drawing the continuum regarding the permissibility of having an abortion:

> Never.
> Only in the first two weeks.
> Only in the first trimester.
> Only in the first or second trimesters.
> Anytime.

The point is that it's a mistake to talk about abortion simply in terms of pro-life and pro-choice. There are a variety of subtle differences and more complex views that are more carefully described and defensible than the simplistic pro-life/pro-choice dichotomy.

Second, it's important to know something about the empirical facts surrounding abortions.

The fertilized human egg becomes an embryo shortly after conception (which doesn't happen in a moment but takes about 24 hours) and morphs into a zygote and then a fetus. Most philosophers refer to the conceptus at any stage of the pregnancy as a fetus both for simplicity's sake and to keep from begging the question by assuming that the fetus is a person (as insisted by some) or just a lump of tissue (as insisted by others). Furthermore, all sides of the debate agree that the fetus is fully human from the time it first begins to exist. Note that being human is a *biological* characteristic and not a *moral* one. Whether the fetus's human nature is morally relevant is an issue addressed in some of the readings of this chapter.

Fetuses can feel pain and raw emotions at later stages of the pregnancy. Precisely when this occurs is some matter of debate, but scientists largely agree that at least by 22 weeks the fetus is **sentient** in the sense that it can suffer. When doctors perform intrauterine surgery on fetuses after this point, they administer general anesthesia of the sort you would receive were you to have an operation at a hospital. So late-term abortions cause significant pain to the fetus.

Abortions are successful and intentional actions to terminate the pregnancy by killing the fetus. On this definition, a natural miscarriage is not an abortion—there was no agent who intended to kill the fetus. Furthermore, intentionally inducing labor to deliver a late-term fetus ends the pregnancy but does not count as an abortion.

How an abortion is performed depends upon many factors, including the age/size of the fetus. Very early abortions can be performed using noninvasive drugs that force the woman's body to miscarry. Later abortions involve using mechanical devices or chemical solutions or both to kill and dismember the fetus before removing it from the woman's womb. Very late abortions require partially delivering the fetus before killing it (so-called "partial birth abortions").

Finally, it is useful to recall the legal/moral distinction. In the United States, it is legal to procure an abortion at any stage of pregnancy. This fact alone has no bearing on the moral question.

If it is morally permissible to have an abortion at any stage of pregnancy, then this was true *before* the landmark *Roe v. Wade* case was issued and would continue to be true even if abortion were criminalized. The present issue is not whether or not an abortion is ever legal (it is, at least in the United States), but whether procuring an abortion is ever morally permissible.

Like many of the contentious moral issues you will think about while reading this text, the abortion issue is a difficult one. There are good things to be said about a wide variety of different ways of understanding the issue. As you read the following selections, it will help if you keep the following two questions clearly in your mind:

1. Is the fetus a **moral patient** (see Chapter 14)? If so, why?
2. How ought we to balance the interests of one moral patient against the interests of another?

In her selection, Mary Anne Warren will argue that the answer to the first question is no, and hence abortions are always morally permissible. Judith Jarvis Thomson concedes that a fetus is often a moral patient, but she answers question two by insisting that the rights of the mother almost always trump the moral consideration due to the fetus. On the other hand, Don Marquis thinks that we can settle the abortion debate without having to decide whether the fetus is a full-fledged person. As you work through these questions for yourself, your view of the moral permissibility of abortion is sure to become more reasonable and sophisticated than the view that you first showed up with.

SUGGESTIONS FOR FURTHER READING

Beckwith, Francis. *Politically Correct Death: Answering Arguments for Abortion Rights.* (Grand Rapids, Michigan: Baker Books, 1993)

English, Jane. "Abortion and the Concept of a Person." *The Canadian Journal of Philosophy* 1975; 5:2, pp. 233–243.

Hursthouse, Rosalind. "Virtue Theory and Abortion." *Philosophy and Public Affairs* 1991; 20, pp. 223–246.

Kamm, Francis Myrna. *Creation and Abortion: A Study in Moral and Legal Philosophy.* (Oxford: Oxford University Press, 1992)

McMahan, Jeff. *The Ethics of Killing: Problems at the Margins of Life.* (Oxford: Oxford University Press, 2002)

Noonan, Jr., John T. "An Almost Absolute Value in History." in *The Morality of Abortion: Legal and Historical Perspectives.* ed. by John T. Noonan, Jr. (Cambridge, Mass: Harvard University Press, 1970)

Schwarz, Stephen. *The Moral Question of Abortion.* (Chicago: Loyola University Press, 1990)

Tooley, Michael. *Abortion and Infanticide.* (Oxford: Clarendon Press, 1983)

15.1 AN ARGUMENT THAT ABORTION IS WRONG

DON MARQUIS (1997)

Don Marquis is a professor of philosophy at the University of Kansas. His most important work has appeared in the field of applied ethics, and he is known as one of the foremost defenders of the view that abortion is a serious moral wrong. In this article, Marquis develops his argument for the conclusion that abortion is a serious moral wrong by explaining what makes killing humans a morally bad thing in general and then applying this criterion to the case of abortion. According to Marquis, the crucial issue is whether a being has a **Future Like Ours (FLO)**. If so, abortion is just as morally wrong as killing an adult human.

Reading Questions:

1. How does Marquis define 'abortion'?
2. How does Marquis define 'fetus'?

3. Why does Marquis think that it is wrong to kill one of us?

4. Why does Marquis think that the mere loss of a future biological life does not explain the misfortune of an early death?

5. What does Marquis mean by the FLO theory?

6. What is the "worst of crimes" argument for the FLO theory?

7. What is the difference between *having* an interest in something and *taking* an interest in something?

8. What is the contraception objection to the FLO theory?

The purpose of this essay is to set out an argument for the claim that abortion, except perhaps in rare instances, is seriously wrong.[1] One reason for these exceptions is to eliminate from consideration cases whose ethical analysis should be controversial and detailed for clear-headed opponents of abortion. Such cases include abortion after rape and abortion during the first fourteen days after conception when there is an argument that the fetus is not definitely an individual. Another reason for making these exceptions is to allow for those cases in which the permissibility of abortion is compatible with the argument of this essay. Such cases include abortion when continuation of a pregnancy endangers a woman's life and abortion when the fetus is anencephalic. When I speak of the wrongness of abortion in this essay, a reader should presume the above qualifications. *I mean by an abortion an action intended to bring about the death of a fetus for the sake of the woman who carries it.* (Thus, as is standard on the literature on this subject, I eliminate spontaneous abortions from consideration.) *I mean by a fetus a developing human being from the time of conception to the time of birth.* (Thus, as is standard, I call embryos and zygotes, fetuses.)

The argument of this essay will establish that *abortion is wrong for the same reason as killing a reader of this essay is wrong.* I shall just assume, rather than establish, that killing you is seriously wrong. I shall make no attempt to offer a complete ethics of killing. Finally, I shall make no attempt to resolve some very fundamental and difficult general philosophical issues into which this analysis of the ethics of abortion might lead. . . .

The "Future Like Ours" Account of the Wrongness of Killing

Opponents of abortion claim that abortion is wrong because abortion involves killing someone like us, a human being who just happens to be very young. Supporters of choice claim that ending the life of a fetus is not in the same moral category as ending the life of an adult human being. Surely *this controversy cannot be resolved in the absence of an account of what it is about killing us that makes killing us wrong.* On the one hand, if we know what property we possess that makes killing us wrong, then we can ask whether fetuses have the same property. On the other hand, suppose that we do not know what it is about us that makes killing us wrong. If this is so, we do not understand even easy cases in which killing is wrong. Surely, we will not understand the ethics of killing fetuses, for if we do not understand easy cases, then we will not understand hard cases. Both pro-choicer and anti-abortionist agree that it is obvious that it is wrong to kill us. Thus, a discussion of what it is about us that makes killing us not only wrong, but seriously wrong, seems to be the right place to begin a discussion of the abortion issue.

Who is primarily wronged by a killing? The wrong of killing is not primarily explained in terms of the loss to the family and friends of the victim. Perhaps the victim is a hermit. Perhaps one's friends find it easy to make new friends. The wrong of killing is not primarily explained in terms of the brutalization of the killer. The great wrong to the victim explains the brutalization, not the other way around. *The wrongness of killing us is understood in terms of what killing does to us. Killing us imposes on us the misfortune of premature death. That misfortune underlies the wrongness.*

Premature death is a misfortune because when one is dead, one has been deprived of life. This misfortune can be more precisely specified. Premature death cannot deprive me of my past life. That part of my life is already gone. If I die tomorrow or if I live thirty more years my past life will be no different. It has occurred on either alternative. Rather than my past, my death deprives me of my future, of the life that I would have lived if I had lived out my natural life span.

The loss of a future biological life does not explain the misfortune of death. Compare two scenarios: In the former I now fall into a coma from which I do not recover until my death in thirty years. In the latter I die now. The latter scenario does not seem to describe a greater misfortune than the former.

The loss of our future conscious life is what underlies the misfortune of premature death. Not any future conscious life qualifies, however. Suppose that I am terminally ill with cancer. Suppose also that pain and suffering would dominate my future conscious life. If so, then death would not be a misfortune for me.

Thus, *the misfortune of premature death consists of the loss to us of the future goods of consciousness.* What are these goods? Much can be said about this issue, but a simple answer will do for the purposes of this essay. The goods of life are whatever we get out of life. The goods of life are those items toward which we take a "pro" attitude. They are completed projects of which we are proud, the pursuit of our goals, aesthetic enjoyments, friendships, intellectual pursuits, and physical pleasures of various sorts. The goods of life are what makes life worth living. In general, what makes life worth living for one person will not be the same as what makes life worth living for another. Nevertheless, the list of goods in each of our lives will overlap. The lists are usually different in different stages of our lives.

What makes the goods of my future good for me? One possible, but wrong, answer is my desire for those goods now. This answer does not account for those aspects of my future life that I now believe I will later value, but about which I am wrong. Neither does it account for those aspects of my future that I will come to value, but which I don't value now. What is valuable to the young may not be valuable to the middle-aged. What is valuable to the middle-aged may not be valuable to the old. Some of life's values for the elderly are best appreciated by the elderly. Thus it is wrong to say that the value of my future to me is just what I value now. *What makes my future valuable to me are those aspects of my future that I will (or would) value when I will (or would) experience them, whether I value them now or not.*

It follows that a person can believe that she will have a valuable future and be wrong. Furthermore, a person can believe that he will not have a valuable future and also be wrong. This is confirmed by our attitude toward many of the suicidal. We attempt to save the lives of the suicidal and to convince them that they have made an error in judgment. This does not mean that the future of an individual obtains value from the value that others confer on it. It means that, in some cases, others can make a clearer judgment of the value of a person's future *to that person* than the person herself. This often happens when one's judgment concerning the value of one's own future is clouded by personal tragedy. (Compare the views of McInerney, 1990, and Shirley, 1995.)

Thus, what is sufficient to make killing us wrong, in general, is that it causes premature death. Premature death is a misfortune. Premature death is a misfortune, in general, because it deprives an individual of a future of value. An individual's future will be valuable to that individual if that individual will come, or would come, to value it. We know that killing us is wrong. What makes killing us wrong, in general, is that it deprives us of a future of value. Thus, *killing someone is wrong, in general, when it deprives her of a **future like ours**.* I shall call this "an **FLO**."

Arguments in Favor of the FLO Theory

At least four arguments support this FLO account of the wrongness of killing.

(1) The considered judgment argument
The FLO account of the wrongness of killing is correct because it fits with our considered judgment

concerning the nature of the misfortune of death. The analysis of the previous section is an exposition of the nature of this considered judgment. This judgment can be confirmed. If one were to ask individuals with AIDS or with incurable cancer about the nature of their misfortune, I believe that they would say or imply that their impending loss of an FLO makes their premature death a misfortune. If they would not, then the FLO account would plainly be wrong.

(2) The worst of crimes argument

The FLO account of the wrongness of killing is correct because it explains why we believe that killing is one of the worst of crimes. My being killed deprives me of more than does my being robbed or beaten or harmed in some other way because my being killed deprives me of all of the value of my future, not merely part of it. This explains why we make the penalty for murder greater than the penalty for other crimes.

As a corollary the FLO account of the wrongness of killing also explains why killing an adult human being is justified only in the most extreme circumstances, only in circumstances in which the loss of life to an individual is outweighed by a worse outcome if that life is not taken. Thus, we are willing to justify killing in self-defense, killing in order to save one's own life, because one's loss if one does not kill in that situation is so very great. We justify killing in a just war for similar reasons. We believe that capital punishment would be justified if, by having such an institution, fewer premature deaths would occur. The FLO account of the wrongness of killing does not entail that killing is always wrong. Nevertheless, the FLO account explains both why killing is one of the worst of crimes and, as a corollary, why the exceptions to the wrongness of killing are so very rare. A correct theory of the wrongness of killing should have these features.

(3) The appeal to cases argument

The FLO account of the wrongness of killing is correct because it yields the correct answers in many life-and-death cases that arise in medicine and have interested philosophers.

Consider medicine first. Most people believe that it is not wrong deliberately to end the life of a person who is permanently unconscious. Thus we believe that it is not wrong to remove a feeding tube or a ventilator from a permanently comatose patient, knowing that such a removal will cause death. The FLO account of the wrongness of killing explains why this is so. A patient who is permanently unconscious cannot have a future that she would come to value, whatever her values. Therefore, according to the FLO theory of the wrongness of killing, death could not, *ceteris paribus,* be a misfortune to her. Therefore, removing the feeding tube or ventilator does not wrong her.

By contrast, almost all people believe that it is wrong, *ceteris paribus,* to withdraw medical treatment from patients who are temporarily unconscious. The FLO account of the wrongness of killing also explains why this is so. Furthermore, these two unconsciousness cases explain why the FLO account of the wrongness of killing does not include present consciousness as a necessary condition for the wrongness of killing. . . .

The FLO theory of the wrongness of killing also deals correctly with issues that have concerned philosophers. It implies that it would be wrong to kill (peaceful) persons from outer space who come to visit our planet even though they are biologically utterly unlike us. Presumably, if they are persons, then they will have futures that are sufficiently like ours so that it would be wrong to kill them. The FLO account of the wrongness of killing shares this feature with the personhood views of the supporters of choice. Classical opponents of abortion who locate the wrongness of abortion somehow in the biological humanity of a fetus cannot explain this. . . .

A major respect in which the FLO account is superior to accounts that appeal to the concept of person is the explanation the FLO account provides of the wrongness of killing infants. There was a class of infants who had futures that included a class of events that were identical to the futures of the readers of this essay. Thus, reader, the FLO account explains why it was as wrong to kill you when you were an infant as it is to kill you now. This account can be generalized to almost all infants. Notice that the wrongness of killing infants can be explained in the absence of an account of what makes the future of an individual sufficiently valuable so that it is wrong to kill that individual. The absence of such an account explains why the FLO account is indeterminate with respect to the wrongness of killing non-human animals.

If the FLO account is the correct theory of the wrongness of killing, then because abortion involves killing fetuses and fetuses have FLOs for exactly the same reasons that infants have FLOs, abortion is presumptively seriously immoral. This inference lays the necessary groundwork for a fourth argument in favor of the FLO account that shows that abortion is wrong.

(4) The analogy with animals argument

Why do we believe it is wrong to cause animals suffering? We believe that, in our own case and in the case of other adults and children, suffering is a misfortune. It would be as morally arbitrary to refuse to acknowledge that animal suffering is wrong as it would be to refuse to acknowledge that the suffering of persons of another race is wrong. It is, on reflection, suffering that is a misfortune, not the suffering of white males or the suffering of humans. Therefore, *infliction of suffering is presumptively wrong: no matter on whom it is inflicted and whether it is inflicted on persons or nonpersons.* Arbitrary restrictions on the wrongness of suffering count as racism or speciesism. Not only is this argument convincing on its own, but it is the only way of justifying the wrongness of animal cruelty. Cruelty toward animals is clearly wrong. (This famous argument is due to Singer, 1979.)

The FLO account of the wrongness of abortion is analogous. We believe that, in our own case and the cases of other adults and children, the loss of a future of value is a misfortune. It would be as morally arbitrary to refuse to acknowledge that the loss of a future of value to a fetus is wrong as to refuse to acknowledge that the loss of a future of value to Jews (to take a relevant twentieth-century example) is wrong. It is, on reflection, the loss of a future of value that is a misfortune; not the loss of a future of value to adults or loss of a future of value to non-Jews. *To deprive someone of a future of value is wrong*

no matter on whom the deprivation is inflicted and no matter whether the deprivation is inflicted on persons or nonpersons. Arbitrary restrictions on the wrongness of this deprivation count as racism, genocide or ageism. Therefore, abortion is wrong. This argument that abortion is wrong should be convincing because it has the same form as the argument for the claim that causing pain and suffering to non-human animals is wrong. Since the latter argument is convincing, the former argument should be also. Thus, an analogy with animals supports the thesis that abortion is wrong.

Replies to Objections

The four arguments in the previous section establish that abortion is, except in rare cases, seriously immoral. Not surprisingly, there are objections to this view. There are replies to the four most important objections to the FLO argument for the immorality of abortion.

(1) The potentiality objection

The FLO account of the wrongness of abortion is a potentiality argument. To claim that a fetus *has* an FLO is to claim that a fetus now has the potential to be in a state of a certain kind in the future. It is not to claim that all ordinary fetuses *will* have FLOs. Fetuses who are aborted, of course, will not. To say that a standard fetus has an FLO is to say that a standard fetus either will have or would have a life it will or would value. To say that a standard fetus would have a life it would value is to say that it will have a life it will value if it does not die prematurely. The truth of this conditional is based upon the nature of fetuses (including the fact that they naturally age) and this nature concerns their potential.

Some appeals to potentiality in the abortion debate rest on unsound inferences. For example, one may try to generate an argument against abortion by arguing that because persons have the right to life, potential persons also have the right to life. Such an argument is plainly invalid as it stands. The premise one needs to add to make it valid would have to be something like: "If Xs have the right to Y, then potential Xs have the right to Y." This premise is plainly false. Potential presidents don't have the rights of the presidency; potential voters don't have the right to vote.

In the FLO argument potentiality is not used in order to bridge the gap between adults and fetuses as is done in the argument in the above paragraph. The FLO theory of the wrongness of killing adults is based upon the adult's potentiality to have a future of value. Potentiality is in the argument from the very beginning. Thus, the plainly false premise is not required. Accordingly, the use of potentiality in the FLO theory is not a sign of an illegitimate inference.

(2) The argument from interests

A second objection to the FLO account of the immorality of abortion involves arguing that even though fetuses have FLOs, nonsentient fetuses do not meet the minimum conditions for having any moral standing at all because they lack interests. Steinbock (1992, p. 5) has presented this argument clearly:

> Beings that have moral status must be capable of caring about what is done to them. They must be capable of being made, if only in a rudimentary sense, happy or miserable, comfortable or distressed. Whatever reasons we may have for preserving or protecting nonsentient beings, these reasons do not refer to their own interests. For without conscious awareness, beings cannot have interests. Without interests, they cannot have a welfare of their own. Without a welfare of their own, nothing can be done for their sake. Hence, they lack moral standing or status.

Medical researchers have argued that fetuses do not become sentient until after 22 weeks of gestation (Steinbock, 1992, p. 50). If they are correct, and if Steinbock's argument is sound, then we have both an objection to the FLO account of the wrongness of abortion and a basis for a view on abortion minimally acceptable to most supporters of choice.

Steinbock's conclusion conflicts with our settled moral beliefs. Temporarily unconscious human beings are nonsentient, yet no one believes that they lack either interests or moral standing. Accordingly,

neither conscious awareness nor the capacity for conscious awareness is a necessary condition for having interests.

The counter-example of the temporarily unconscious human being shows that there is something internally wrong with Steinbock's argument. The difficulty stems from an ambiguity. One cannot *take* an interest in something without being capable of caring about what is done to it. However, something can be *in* someone's interest without that individual being capable of caring about it, or about anything. Thus, life support can be *in* the interests of a temporarily unconscious patient even though the temporarily unconscious patient is incapable of *taking* an interest in that life support. If this can be so for the temporarily unconscious patient, then it is hard to see why it cannot be so for the temporarily unconscious (that is, nonsentient) fetus who requires placental life support. Thus the objection based on interests fails.

(3) The problem of equality

The FLO account of the wrongness of killing seems to imply that the degree of wrongness associated with each killing varies inversely with the victim's age. Thus, the FLO account of the wrongness of killing seems to suggest that it is far worse to kill a five-year-old than an 89-year-old because the former is deprived of far more than the latter. However, we believe that all persons have an equal right to life. Thus, it appears that the FLO account of the wrongness of killing entails an obviously false view (Paske, 1994).

However, the FLO account of the wrongness of killing does not, strictly speaking, imply that it is worse to kill younger people than older people. The FLO account provides an explanation of the wrongness of killing that is sufficient to account for the serious presumptive wrongness of killing. It does not follow that killings cannot be wrong in other ways. For example, one might hold, as does Feldman (1992, p. 184), that in addition to the wrongness of killing that has its basis in the future life of which the victim is deprived, killing an individual is also made wrong by the admirability of an individual's past behavior. Now the amount of admirability will presumably vary directly with age, whereas the amount of deprivation will vary inversely with age. This tends to equalize the wrongness of murder.

However, even if, *ceteris paribus,* it is worse to kill younger persons than older persons, there are good reasons for adopting a doctrine of the legal equality of murder. Suppose that we tried to estimate the seriousness of a crime of murder by appraising the value of the FLO of which the victim had been deprived. How would one go about doing this? In the first place, one would be confronted by the old problem of interpersonal comparisons of utility. In the second place, estimation of the value of a future would involve putting oneself, not into the shoes of the victim at the time she was killed, but rather into the shoes the victim would have worn had the victim survived, and then estimating from that perspective the worth of that person's future. This task seems difficult, if not impossible. Accordingly, there are reasons to adopt a convention that murders are equally wrong.

Furthermore, the FLO theory, in a way, explains why we do adopt the doctrine of the legal equality of murder. The FLO theory explains why we regard murder as one of the worst of crimes, since depriving someone of a future like ours deprives her of more than depriving her of anything else. This gives us a reason for making the punishment for murder very harsh, as harsh as is compatible with civilized society. One should not make the punishment for younger victims harsher than that. Thus, the doctrine of the equal legal right to life does not seem to be incompatible with the FLO theory.

(4) The contraception objection

The strongest objection to the FLO argument for the immorality of abortion is based on the claim that, because contraception results in one less FLO, the FLO argument entails that contraception, indeed, abstention from sex when conception is possible, is immoral. Because neither contraception nor abstention from sex when conception is possible is immoral, the FLO account is flawed.

There is a cogent reply to this objection. If the argument of the early part of this essay is correct, then *the central issue concerning the morality of abortion is the problem of whether fetuses are individuals who are members of the class of individuals whom it is seriously presumptively wrong to kill.* The properties of being human and alive, of being a person, and of having an FLO are criteria that participants in the abortion debate have offered to mark off the relevant class of individuals. The central claim of this essay is that having an FLO marks off the relevant class of individuals. A defender of the FLO view could, therefore, reply that since, at the time of contraception, there is no individual to have an FLO, the FLO account does not entail that contraception is wrong. The wrong of killing is primarily a wrong to the individual who is killed; at the time of contraception there is no individual to be wronged.

However, someone who presses the contraception objection might have an answer to this reply. She might say that the sperm and egg are the individuals deprived of an FLO at the time of contraception. Thus, there are individuals whom contraception deprives of an FLO and if depriving an individual of an FLO is what makes killing wrong, then the FLO theory entails that contraception is wrong.

There is also a reply to this move. In the case of abortion, an objectively determinate individual is the subject of harm caused by the loss of an FLO. This individual is a fetus. In the case of contraception, there are far more candidates (see Norcross, 1990). Let us consider some possible candidates in order of the increasing number of individuals harmed: (1) The single harmed individual might be the combination of the particular sperm and the particular egg that would have united to form a zygote if contraception had not been used. (2) The two harmed individuals might be the particular sperm itself, and, in addition, the ovum itself that would have physically combined to form the zygote. (This is modeled on the double homicide of two persons who would otherwise in a short time fuse. (1) is modeled on harm to a single entity some of whose parts are not physically contiguous, such as a university.) (3) The many harmed individuals might be the millions of *combinations* of sperm and the released ovum whose (small) chances of having an FLO were reduced by the successful contraception. (4) The even larger class of harmed individuals (larger by one) might be the class consisting of all of the individual sperm in an ejaculate and, in addition, the individual ovum released at the time of the successful contraception. (1) through (4) are all candidates for being the subject(s) of harm in the case of successful contraception or abstinence from sex. Which should be chosen? Should we hold a lottery? There seems to be no non-arbitrarily determinate subject of harm in the case of successful contraception. But if there is no such subject of harm, then no determinate thing was harmed. If no determinate thing was harmed, then (in the case of contraception) no wrong has been done. Thus, the FLO account of the wrongness of abortion does not entail that contraception is wrong.

Conclusion

This essay contains an argument for the view that, except in unusual circumstances, abortion is seriously wrong. Deprivation of an FLO explains why killing adults and children is wrong. Abortion deprives fetuses of FLOs. Therefore, abortion is wrong. This argument is based on an account of the wrongness of killing that is a result of our considered judgment of the nature of the misfortune of premature death. It accounts for why we regard killing as one of the worst of crimes. It is superior to alternative accounts of the wrongness of killing that are intended to provide insight into the ethics of abortion. This account of the wrongness of killing is supported by the way it handles cases in which our moral judgments are settled. This account has an analogue in the most plausible account of the wrongness of causing animals to suffer. This account makes no appeal to religion. Therefore, the FLO account shows that abortion, except in rare instances, is seriously wrong.

NOTE

1. This essay is an updated version of a view that first appeared in the *Journal of Philosophy* (1989). This essay incorporates attempts to deal with the objections of McInerney (1990), Norcross (1990), Shirley (1995), Steinbock (1992), and Paske (1994) to the original version of the view.

REFERENCES

Beckwith, F. J., *Politically Correct Death: Answering Arguments for Abortion Rights* (Grand Rapids, Michigan: Baker Books, 1993)

Benn, S. I., "Abortion, infanticide, and respect for persons," *The Problem of Abortion*, ed. J. Feinberg (Belmont, California: Wadsworth, 1973), pp. 92–104.

Engelhardt, Jr, H. T., *The Foundations of Bioethics* (New York: Oxford University Press, 1986)

Feinberg, J., "Abortion," *Matters of Life and Death: New Introductory Essays in Moral Philosophy*, ed. T. Regan (New York: Random House, 1986)

Feldman, F., *Confrontations with the Reaper: A Philosophical Study of the Nature and Value of Death* (New York: Oxford University Press, 1992)

Kant, I., *Lectures on Ethics*, tr. L. Infeld (New York: Harper, 1963)

Marquis, D. B., "A future like ours and the concept of person: a reply to McInerney and Paske," *The Abortion Controversy: A Reader*, ed. L. P. Pojman and F. J. Beckwith (Boston: Jones and Bartlett, 1994), pp. 354–68.

_____, "Fetuses, futures and values: a reply to Shirley," *Southwest Philosophy Review*, 11 (1995): 263–5.

_____, "Why abortion is immoral," *Journal of Philosophy*, 86 (1989): 183–202.

McInerney, P., "Does a fetus already have a future like ours?," *Journal of Philosophy*, 87 (1990): 264–8.

Noonan, J., "An almost absolute value in history," in *The Morality of Abortion*, ed. J. Noonan (Cambridge, Massachusetts: Harvard University Press)

Norcross, A., "Killing, abortion, and contraception: a reply to Marquis," *Journal of Philosophy*, 87 (1990): 268–77.

Paske, G., "Abortion and the neo-natal right to life: a critique of Marquis's futurist argument," *The Abortion Controversy: A Reader*, ed. L. P. Pojman and F. J. Beckwith (Boston: Jones and Bartlett, 1994), pp. 343–53.

Sacred Congregation for the Propagation of the Faith, *Declaration on Euthanasia* (Vatican City, 1980)

Shirley, E. S., "Marquis' argument against abortion: a critique," *Southwest Philosophy Review*, 11 (1995): 79–89.

Singer, P., "Not for humans only: the place of nonhumans in environmental issues," *Ethics and Problems of the 21st Century*, ed. K. E. Goodpaster and K. M. Sayre (South Bend: Notre Dame University Press, 1979)

Steinbock, B., *Life Before Birth: The Moral and Legal Status of Embryos and Fetuses.* (New York: Oxford University Press, 1992)

Thomson, J. J., "A defense of abortion," *Philosophy and Public Affairs*, 1 (1971): 47–66.

Tooley, M., "Abortion and infanticide," *Philosophy and Public Affairs*, 2 (1972): 37–65.

Warren, M. A., "On the moral and legal status of abortion," *Monist*, 57 (1973): 43–61.

DISCUSSION QUESTIONS:

1. Suppose you are driving down the road, and as you come around the corner you see two people crossing the street. There is no time to apply the brakes or swerve off the road—you must hit one of them, and at this speed the impact will kill them. The left-hand lane has a 6-year-old boy. The right-hand lane has an 89-year-old man. Do you have a moral reason to hit one of the people over the other? If so, does the FLO theory explain this? Would another theory explain it equally as well?

2. The contraception objection to the FLO theory attempts to show that the theory has a really counter-intuitive implication—namely, that it's wrong to use contraception because you're depriving something of a future like ours. Marquis' reply is that there is no determinate being that is deprived of such a future. Is that correct? Doesn't it seem true that sperm have the potential to have a future like ours? If not, how are they relevantly different from a fertilized ovum?

3. It is common to hear people defend the moral permissibility of abortion by appealing to the kind of life the child would have had if she had been carried to term. The idea is that if the mother is considering abortion, then the child must be unwanted, and unwanted children often suffer from abuse, neglect, etc. Do you think that these are relevant considerations? How does the FLO theory address such a case?

Argument Reconstruction Exercises:

I. Many arguments both in science and in philosophy are arguments from the best explanation (see page 10 in Unit 1). When one theory does a better job than another theory in explaining some given data, we take the data to be evidence for the former theory over the latter. Marquis relies on a series of arguments to the best explanation to defend his FLO theory. Identify the premises and conclusion in this excerpt:

> The FLO account of the wrongness of killing is correct because it explains why we believe that killing is one of the worst crimes. My being killed deprives me of more than does my being robbed or beaten or harmed in some other way because my being killed deprives me of all of the value of my future, not merely part of it. (page 403)

II. Identify the premises and conclusion in this excerpt:

> If the FLO account is the correct theory of the wrongness of killing, then because abortion involves killing fetuses and fetuses have FLOs for exactly the same reasons that infants have FLOs, abortion is presumptively seriously immoral. (page 404)

III. Marquis argues that drawing a distinction between an adult human's future of value and a fetus's future of value is to make an arbitrary distinction tantamount to ageism. Identify the thesis that he assumes is true and the absurd conclusion in this excerpt:

> To deprive someone of a future of value is wrong no matter on whom the deprivation is inflicted and no matter whether the deprivation is inflicted on persons or nonpersons. Arbitrary restrictions on the wrongness of this deprivation count as racism, genocide or ageism. Therefore, abortion is wrong. (page 404)

IV. Marquis attempts to handle several objections to his theory that take the form of arguments from false implications (see page x on *modus tollens*). Here is one example of such an argument. Identify the premises and conclusion in the implicit argument made in this excerpt:

> The FLO account of the wrongness of killing seems to imply that the degree of wrongness associated with each killing varies inversely with the victim's age. Thus, the FLO account of the wrongness of killing seems to suggest that it is far worse to kill a five-year-old than an 89-year-old because the former is deprived of far more than the latter. However, we believe that all persons have an equal right to life. Thus, it appears that the FLO account of the wrongness of killing entails an obviously false view. (page 405)

15.2 ON THE MORAL AND LEGAL STATUS OF ABORTION

MARY ANN WARREN (1973, UPDATED IN 1982 & 1996)

Mary Ann Warren was a professor of philosophy at San Francisco State University. She is best known for her work in feminism and applied ethics, especially her contributions regarding the moral permissibility of abortion. In this essay, Warren argues for the conclusion that a woman's right to procure an abortion is absolute because a fetus is not a person (though it is human) and hence has no rights. She closes by considering the moral relevance of the resemblance between a fetus and adult human, the fetus's potential personhood, and the implication of morally permissible infanticide.

Reading Questions:

1. What is the moral sense of the word 'human'?

2. What is the genetic sense of the word 'human'?

3. According to Warren, what are the only kinds of things that count as members of the moral community?

4. Which traits does Warren note as being central to personhood?

5. Are any of these traits *necessary* for personhood? Is any subset of these traits *sufficient* for personhood?

6. According to Warren's account, does a fetus count as a person?

7. What is the resemblance problem in applying the personhood criteria to the fetus?

8. What is the potentiality problem in applying the personhood criteria to the fetus?

9. Does Warren think that infanticide is ever morally wrong? If so, why?

The question which we must answer in order to produce a satisfactory solution to the problem of the moral status of abortion is this: *How are we to define the moral community, the set of beings with full and equal moral rights, such that we can decide whether a human fetus is a member of this community or not?* What sort of entity, exactly, has the inalienable rights to life, liberty, and the pursuit of happiness? Jefferson attributed these rights to all *men,* and it may or may not be fair to suggest that he intended to attribute them *only* to men. Perhaps he ought to have attributed them to all human beings. What reason is there for identifying the moral community with the set of all human beings, in whatever way we have chosen to define that term?

1. On the Definition of "Human"

One reason why this vital question is so frequently overlooked in the debate over the moral status of abortion is that *the term 'human' has two distinct, but not often distinguished, senses.* This fact results in a slide of meaning, which serves to conceal the fallaciousness of the traditional argument that since (1) it is wrong to kill innocent human beings, and (2) fetuses are innocent human beings, then (3) it is wrong to kill fetuses. For if 'human' is used in the same sense in both (1) and (2) then, whichever of the two senses is meant, one of these premises is question-begging. And if it is used in two different senses then of course the conclusion doesn't follow.

Thus, (1) is a self-evident moral truth,[1] and avoids begging the question about abortion, only if 'human being' is used to mean something like 'a full-fledged member of the moral community.' (It may or may not also be meant to refer exclusively to members of the species *Homo sapiens*.) We may call this the ***moral sense*** of 'human.' It is not to be confused with what we call the ***genetic sense***, i.e., the sense in which *any* member of the species is a human being, and no member of any other species could be. If (1) is acceptable only if the moral sense is intended, (2) is non-question-begging only if what is intended is the genetic sense.

Some argue for the classification of fetuses with human beings by pointing to the presence of the full genetic code, and the potential capacity for rational thought.[2] But, in the absence of any argument showing that whatever is genetically human is also morally human, *nothing more than genetic humanity can be demonstrated by the presence of the human genetic code*. And, as we will see, the *potential* capacity for rational thought can at most show that an entity has the potential for *becoming* human in the moral sense.

2. Defining the Moral Community

Can it be established that genetic humanity is sufficient for moral humanity? I think that there are very good reasons for not defining the moral community in this way. I would like to suggest an alternative way of defining the moral community, which I will argue for only to the extent of explaining why it is, or should be, self-evident. The suggestion is simply that *the moral community consists of all and only* **people**, *rather than all and only human beings*,[3] and probably the best way of demonstrating its self-evidence is by considering the concept of personhood, to see what sorts of entity are and are not persons, and what the decision that a being is or is not a person implies about its moral rights.

What characteristics entitle an entity to be considered a person? This is obviously not the place to attempt a complete analysis of the concept of personhood, but we do not need such a fully adequate analysis just to determine whether and why a fetus is or isn't a person. All we need is a rough and approximate list of the most basic criteria of personhood, and some idea of which, or how many, of these an entity must satisfy in order to properly be considered a person.

In searching for such criteria, it is useful to look beyond the set of people with whom we are acquainted, and ask how we would decide whether a totally alien being was a person or not. (For we have no right to assume that genetic humanity is necessary for personhood.) Image a space traveler who lands on an unknown planet and encounters a race of beings utterly unlike any he has ever seen or heard of. If he wants to be sure of behaving morally toward these beings, he has to somehow decide whether they are people, and hence have full moral rights, or whether they are the sort of thing which he need not feel guilty about treating as, for example, a source of food.

How should he go about making this decision? If he has some anthropological background, he might look for such things as religion, art, and the manufacturing of tools, weapons, or shelters, since these factors have been used to distinguish our human from our prehuman ancestors, in what seems to be closer to the moral than the genetic sense of 'human.' And no doubt he would be right to consider the presence of such factors as good evidence that the alien beings were people, and morally human. It would, however, be overly anthropocentric of him to take the absence of these things as adequate evidence that they were not, since we can imagine people who have progressed beyond, or evolved without ever developing, these cultural characteristics.

I suggest that the traits which are most central to the concept of personhood, or humanity in the moral sense, are, very roughly, the following:

1. Consciousness (of objects and events external and/or internal to the being), and in particular the capacity to feel pain;
2. Reasoning (the *developed* capacity to solve new and relatively complex problems);
3. Self-motivated activity (activity which is relatively independent of either genetic or direct external control);

4. The capacity to communicate, by whatever means, messages of an indefinite variety of types, that is, not just with an indefinite number of possible contents, but on indefinitely many possible topics;

5. The presence of self-concepts, and self-awareness, either individual or racial, or both.

Admittedly, there are apt to be a great many problems involved in formulating precise definitions of these criteria, let alone in developing universally valid behavioral criteria for deciding when they apply. But I will assume that both we and our explorer know approximately what (1)–(5) mean, and that he is also able to determine whether or not they apply. How, then, should he use his findings to decide whether or not the alien beings are people? *We needn't suppose that an entity must have all of these attributes to be properly considered a person;* (1) and (2) alone may well be sufficient for personhood, and quite probably (1)–(3) are sufficient. *Neither do we need to insist that any one of these criteria is necessary for personhood.* although once again (1) and (2) look like fairly good candidates for necessary conditions, as does (3), if 'activity' is construed so as to include the activity of reasoning.

All we need to claim, to demonstrate that a fetus is not a person, is that any being which satisfies none of (1)–(5) *is certainly not a person.* I consider this claim to be so obvious that I think anyone who denied it, and claimed that a being which satisfied none of (1)–(5) was a person all the same, would thereby demonstrate that he had no notion at all of what a person is—perhaps because he had confused the concept of a person with that of genetic humanity. If the opponents of abortion were to deny the appropriateness of these five criteria, I do not know what further arguments would convince them. We would probably have to admit that our conceptual schemes were indeed irreconcilably different, and that our dispute could not be settled objectively.

I do not expect this to happen, however, since I think that the concept of a person is one which is very nearly universal (to people), and that it is common to both proabortionists and antiabortionists, even though neither group has fully realized the relevance of this concept to the resolution of their dispute. Furthermore, I think that on reflection even the antiabortionists ought to agree not only that (1)–(5) are central to the concept of personhood, but also that it is a part of this concept that all and only people have full moral rights. *The concept of a person is in part a moral concept; once we have admitted that x is a person we have recognized, even if we have not agreed to respects, x's right to be treated as a member of the moral community.* It is true that the claim that x is a *human being* is more commonly voiced as part of an appeal to treat x decently than is the claim that x is a person, but this is either because 'human being' is here used in the sense which implies personhood, or because the genetic and moral sense of 'human' have been confused.

Now if (1)–(5) are indeed the primary criteria of personhood, then it is clear that genetic humanity is neither necessary nor sufficient for establishing that an entity is a person. Some human beings are not people, and there may well be people who are not human beings. A man or woman whose consciousness has been permanently obliterated but who remains alive is a human being which is no longer a person; defective human beings, with no appreciable mental capacity, are not and presumably never will be people; and a fetus is a human being which is not yet a person, and which therefore cannot coherently be said to have full moral rights. Citizens of the next century should be prepared to recognize highly advanced, self-aware robots or computers, should such be developed, and intelligent inhabitants of other worlds, should such be found, as people in the fullest sense, and to respect their moral rights. But to ascribe full moral rights to an entity which is not a person is as absurd as to ascribe moral obligations and responsibilities to such an entity.

3. Fetal Development and the Right to Life

Two problems arise in the application of these suggestions for the definition of the moral community to the determination of the precise moral status of a human fetus. Given that the paradigm example of a person is a normal adult human being, then (1) How like this paradigm, in particular how far advanced since conception, does a human being need to be before it begins to have a right to life by virtue, not of being fully a person as of yet, but of being *like* a person? and (2) To what extent, if any, does the fact that a fetus has the *potential* for becoming a person endow it with some of the same rights? Each of these questions requires some comment.

In answering the first question, we need not attempt a detailed consideration of the moral rights of organisms which are not developed enough, aware enough, intelligent enough, etc., to be considered people, but which resemble people in some respects. It does seem reasonable to suggest that the more like a person, in the relevant respects, a being is, the stronger is the case for regarding it as having a right to life, and indeed the stronger its right to life is. Thus we ought to take seriously the suggestion that, insofar as "the human individual develops biologically in a continuous fashion . . . the rights of a human person might develop in the same way."[4] But we must keep in mind that the attributes which are relevant in determining whether or not an entity is enough like a person to be regarded as having some of the same moral rights are no different from those which are relevant to determining whether or not it is fully a person—i.e., are no different from (1)–(5)—and that being genetically human, or having recognizable human facial and other physical features, or detectable brain activity, or the capacity to survive outside the uterus, are simply not among these relevant attributes.

Thus it is clear that even though a seven or eight-month fetus has features which make it apt to arouse in us almost the same powerful protective instinct as is commonly aroused by a small infant, nevertheless it is not significantly more personlike than is a very small embryo. It is *somewhat* more personlike; it can apparently feel and respond to pain, and it may even have a rudimentary form of consciousness, insofar as its brain is quite active. Nevertheless, it seems safe to say that it is not fully conscious, in the way that an infant of a few months is, and that it cannot reason, or communicate messages of indefinitely many sorts, does not engage in self-motivated activity, and has no self-awareness. *Thus, in the relevant respects, a fetus, even a fully developed one, is considerably less personlike than is the average mature mammal, indeed the average fish.* And I think that a rational person must conclude that if the right to life of a

fetus is to be based upon its resemblance to a person, then it cannot be said to have any more right to life than, let us say, a newborn guppy (which also seems to be capable of feeling pain), and that a right of that magnitude could never override a woman's right to obtain an abortion, at any stage of her pregnancy.

There may, of course, be other arguments in favor of placing legal limits upon the stage of pregnancy in which an abortion may be performed. Given the relative safety of the new techniques of artificially inducing labor during the third trimester, the danger to the woman's life or health is no longer such an argument. Neither is the fact that people tend to respond to the thought of abortion in the later stages of pregnancy with emotional repulsion, since mere emotional responses cannot take the place of moral reasoning in determining what ought to be permitted. Nor, finally, is the frequently heard argument that legalizing abortion, especially late in the pregnancy, may erode the level of respect for human life, leading, perhaps, to an increase in unjustified euthanasia and other crimes. For this threat, if it is a threat, can be better met by educating people to the kinds of moral distinctions which we are making here than by limiting access to abortion (which limitation may, in its disregard for the rights of women, be just as damaging to the level of respect for human rights).

Thus, since the fact that even a fully developed fetus is not personlike enough to have any significant right to life on the basis of its personlikeness shows that no legal restrictions upon the stage of pregnancy in which an abortion may be performed can be justified on the grounds that we should protect the rights of the older fetus; and since there is no other apparent justification for such restrictions, we may conclude that they are entirely unjustified. Whether or not it would be *indecent* (whatever that means) for a woman in her seventh month to obtain an abortion just to avoid having to postpone a trip to Europe, it would not, in itself, be *immoral*, and therefore it ought to be permitted.

4. Potential Personhood and the Right to Life

We have seen that a fetus does not resemble a person in any way which can support the claim that it has even some of the same rights. But what about its *potential,* the fact that if nurtured and allowed to develop naturally it will very probably become a person? Doesn't that alone give it at least some right to life? *It is hard to deny that the fact that an entity is a potential person is a strong prima facie reason for not destroying it;* but we need not conclude from this that a potential person has a right to life, by virtue of that potential. It may be that our feeling that it is better, other things being equal, not to destroy a potential person is better explained by the fact that potential people are still (felt to be) an invaluable resource, not to be lightly squandered. Surely, if every speck of dust were a potential person, we would be much less apt to conclude that every potential person has a right to become actual.

Still, we do not need to insist that a potential person has no right to life whatever. There may well be something immoral, and not just imprudent, about wantonly destroying potential people, when doing so isn't necessary to protect anyone's rights. *But even if a potential person does have some prima facie right to life, such a right could not possibly outweigh the right of a woman to obtain an abortion, since the rights of any actual person invariably outweigh those of any potential person, whenever the two conflict.* Since this may not be immediately obvious in the case of a human fetus, let us look at another case.

Suppose that our space explorer falls into the hands of an alien culture, whose scientists decide to create a few hundred thousand or more human beings, by breaking his body into its component cells, and using these to create fully developed human beings, with, of course, his genetic code. We may imagine that each of these newly created men will have all of the original man's abilities, skills, knowledge, and so on, and also have an individual self-concept, in short that each of them will be a bona fide (though hardly unique) person. Imagine that the whole project will take only seconds, and that its chances of success are extremely high, and that our explorer knows all of this, and also knows that these people will be treated fairly. I maintain that in such a situation he would have every right to escape if he could, and thus to deprive all of these potential people of their potential lives; for his right to life outweighs all of theirs together, in spite of the fact that they are all genetically human, all innocent, and all have a very high probability of becoming people very soon, if only he refrains from acting.

Indeed, I think he would have a right to escape even if it were not his life which the alien scientists planned to take, but only a year of his freedom, or, indeed, only a day. Nor would he be obligated to stay if he had gotten captured (thus bringing all these people-potentials into existence) because of his own carelessness, or even if he had done so deliberately, knowing the consequences. Regardless of how he got captured, he is not morally obligated to remain in captivity for *any* period of time for the sake of permitting any number of potential people to come into actuality, so great is the margin by which one actual person's right to liberty outweighs whatever right to life even a hundred thousand potential people have. And it seems reasonable to conclude that the rights of a woman will outweigh by a similar margin whatever right to life a fetus may have by virtue of its potential personhood.

Thus, neither a fetus's resemblance to a person, nor its potential for becoming a person provides any basis whatever for the claim that it has any significant right to life. Consequently, a woman's right to protect her health, happiness, freedom, and even her life,[5] by terminating an unwanted pregnancy, will always override whatever right to life it may be appropriate to ascribe to a fetus, even a fully developed one. And thus, in the absence of any overwhelming social need for every possible child, the laws which restrict the right to obtain an abortion, or limit the period of pregnancy during which an abortion may be performed, are a wholly unjustified violation of a woman's most basic moral and constitutional rights.[6]

Postscript on Infanticide, February 26, 1982

One of the most troubling objections to the argument presented in this article is that it may appear to justify not only abortion but infanticide as well. A newborn infant is not a great deal more person-like than a nine-month fetus, and thus it might seem that if late-term abortion is sometimes justified, then infanticide must also be sometimes justified. Yet most people consider that infanticide is a form of murder, and thus never justified.

While it is important to appreciate the emotional force of this objection, its logical force is far less than it may seem at first glance. *There are many reasons why infanticide is much more difficult to justify than abortion, even though if my argument is correct neither constitutes the killing of a person.* In this country, and in this period of history, the deliberate killing of viable newborns is virtually never justified. This is in part because neonates are so very *close* to being persons that to kill them requires a very strong moral justification—as does the killing of dolphins, whales, chimpanzees, and other highly personlike creatures. It is certainly wrong to kill such beings just for the sake of convenience, or financial profit, or "sport."

Another reason why infanticide is usually wrong, in our society, is that if the newborn's parents do not want it, or are unable to care for it, there are (in most cases) people who are able and eager to adopt it and to provide a good home for it. Many people wait years for the opportunity to adopt a child, and some are unable to do so even though there is every reason to believe that they would be good parents. *The needless destruction of a viable infant inevitably deprives some person or persons of a source of great pleasure and satisfaction, perhaps severely impoverishing their lives.* Furthermore, even if an infant is considered to be adoptable (e.g., because of some extremely severe mental or physical handicap) it is still wrong in most cases to kill it. For most of us value the lives of infants, and would prefer to pay taxes to support orphanages and state institutions for the handicapped rather than to allow unwanted infants to be killed. So long as most people feel this way, and so long as our society can afford to provide care for infants which are unwanted or which have special needs that preclude home care, it is wrong to destroy any infant which has a chance of living a reasonably satisfactory life.

If these arguments show that infanticide is wrong, at least in this society, then why don't they also show that late-term abortion is wrong? After all, third trimester fetuses are also highly personlike, and many people value them and would much prefer that they be preserved; even at some cost to themselves. As a potential source of pleasure to some family, a viable fetus is just as valuable as a viable infant. But there is an obvious and crucial difference between the two

cases: once the infant is born, its continued life cannot (except, perhaps, in very exceptional cases) pose any serious threat to the woman's life or health, since she is free to put it up for adoption, or, where this is impossible, to place it in a state-supported institution. While she might prefer that it die, rather than being raised by others, it is not clear that such a preference would constitute a right on her part. True, she may suffer greatly from the knowledge that her child will be thrown into the lottery of the adoption system, and that she will be unable to ensure its well-being, or even to know whether it is healthy, happy, doing well in school, etc.: for the law generally does not permit natural parents to remain in contact with their children, once they are adopted by another family. But there are surely better ways of dealing with these problems than by permitting infanticide in such cases. (It might help, for instance, if the natural parents of adopted children could at least receive some information about their progress, without necessarily being informed of the identity of the adopting family.)

In contrast, *a pregnant woman's right to protect her own life and health clearly outweighs other people's desire that the fetus be preserved*—just as, when a person's life or limb is threatened by some wild animal, and when the threat cannot be removed without killing the animal, the person's right to self-protection outweighs the desires of those who would prefer that the animal not be harmed. Thus, while the moment of birth may not mark any sharp discontinuity in the degree to which an infant possesses a right to life, it does mark the end of the mother's absolute right to determine its fate. Indeed, if and when a late-term abortion could be safely performed without killing the fetus, she would have no absolute right to insist on its death (e.g., if others wish to adopt it or pay for its care), for the same reason that she does not have a right to insist that a viable infant be killed.

It remains true that according to my argument neither abortion nor the killing of neonates is properly considered a form of murder. Perhaps it is understandable that the law should classify infanticide as murder or homicide, since there is no other existing legal category which adequately or conveniently expresses the force of our society's disapproval of this action. But the moral distinction remains, and it has several important consequences.

In the first place, it implies that when an infant is born into a society which—unlike ours—is so impoverished that it simply cannot care for it adequately without endangering the survival of existing persons, killing it or allowing it to die is not necessarily wrong—provided that there is no *other* society which is willing and able to provide such care. Most human societies, from those at the hunting and gathering stage of economic development to the highly civilized Greeks and Romans, have permitted the practice of infanticide under such unfortunate circumstances, and I would argue that it shows a serious lack of understanding to condemn them as morally backward for this reason alone.

In the second place, the argument implies that when an infant is born with such severe physical anomalies that its life would predictably be a very short and/or very miserable one, even with the most heroic of medical treatment, and where its parents do not choose to bear the often crushing emotional, financial and other burdens attendant upon the artificial prolongation of such a tragic life, it is not morally wrong to cease or withhold treatment, thus allowing the infant a painless death. It is wrong (and sometimes a form of murder) to practice involuntary euthanasia on persons, since they have the right to decide for themselves whether or not they wish to continue to live. But terminally ill neonates cannot make this decision for themselves, and thus it is incumbent upon responsible persons to make the decision for them, as best they can. *The mistaken belief that infanticide is always tantamount to murder is responsible for a great deal of unnecessary suffering,* not just on the part of infants which are made to endure needlessly prolonged and painful deaths, but also on the part of parents, nurses, and other involved persons, who must watch infants suffering needlessly, helpless to end that suffering in the most humane way.

I am well aware that these conclusions, however modest and reasonable they may seem to some people, strike other people as morally monstrous, and that some people might even prefer to abandon their previous support for women's right to abortion rather than accept a theory which leads to such conclusions about infanticide. But all that these facts show is that abortion is not an isolated moral issue; to fully understand the moral status of abortion we may have to reconsider other moral issues as well, issues not just about infanticide and euthanasia, but also about the moral rights of women and of non-human animals. It is a philosopher's task to criticize mistaken beliefs which stand in the way of moral understanding, even when—perhaps especially when—those beliefs are popular and widespread. The belief that moral strictures against killing should apply equally to *all* genetically human entities, and *only* to genetically human entities, is such an error. The overcoming of this error will undoubtedly require long and often painful struggle; but it must be done.

NOTES

1. Of course, the principle that it is (always) wrong to kill innocent human beings is in need of many other modifications, e.g., that it may be permissible to do so to save a greater number of other innocent human beings, but we may safely ignore these complications here.
2. John Noonan, "Deciding Who is Human," *Natural Law Forum,* 13 (1968), 135.
3. From here on, we will use "human' to mean genetically human, since the moral sense seems closely connected to, and perhaps derived from, the assumption that genetic humanity is sufficient for membership in the moral community.
4. Thomas L. Hayes, "A Biological View," *Commonweal,* 85 (March 17, 1967), 677–78; quoted by Daniel Callahan, in *Abortion: Law, Choice and Morality* (London: Macmillan & Co., 1970).
5. That is, insofar as the death rate, for the woman, is higher for childbirth than for early abortion.
6. My thanks to the following people, who were kind enough to read and criticize an earlier version of this paper: Herbert Gold, Gene Glass, Anne Lauterbach, Judith Thomson, Mary Mothersill, and Timothy Binkley.

DISCUSSION QUESTIONS:

1. Warren claims that the moral community consists of all and only people. This means that there is no moral reason to care for the welfare of any non-person. This appears to include non-human animals, plants, ecosystems, etc. Do you think this is correct? Do we ever have moral reasons to care for non-human animals or plants?

2. Warren offers a list of traits that she considers central to personhood. Do you think that something would have to have all five traits in order to properly count as a person? Do non-human animals exhibit any of these characteristics? Is it plausible to say that at least some non-human animals (e.g., chimpanzees) are people? Does the fetus have any of the five traits? What about traits (1) and (3)?

3. Warren's argument concludes that since a fetus is not a person, a woman's rights over her body make it morally permissible for her to kill the fetus. But if the fetus is not a person, and thus has no rights, then a newborn that is relevantly similar will not be a person and thus have no rights. Warren agrees but says that it might be wrong to kill the infant for other reasons (e.g., there might be couples who would like to adopt the infant). Do you find this plausible? Is the reason it's wrong to kill newborns because of how that action will affect *other* people?

Argument Reconstruction Exercises:

I. Warren thinks that the traditional argument to defend the wrongness of abortion appeals to the humanity of the fetus. She also thinks that this argument equivocates on the term 'human' such that there is no sense of the word in which both crucial premises are correct. Identify the premises and conclusion in this excerpt and then plug in the different senses of the term 'human' to see how the argument might be equivocating:

> . . . the traditional argument that since (1) it is wrong to kill innocent human beings, and (2) fetuses are innocent human beings, then (3) it is wrong to kill fetuses. (pages 409-410)

II. Warren's argument for the moral permissibility of abortion relies on the claim that the fetus is not a person. She argues for this claim by comparing a fetus with what she considers the five central traits of personhood: consciousness, reasoning, self-motivated activity, the capacity to communicate an indefinite variety of messages, and self-awareness. Identify the premises and conclusion in this excerpt:

> All we need to claim, to demonstrate that a fetus is not a person, is that any being which satisfies none of (1)–(5) is certainly not a person. . . . it seems safe to say that [the fetus] is not fully conscious, in the way that an infant of a few months is, and that it cannot reason, or communicate messages of indefinitely many sorts, does not engage in self-motivated activity, and has no self-awareness. Thus, in the relevant respects, a fetus, even a fully developed one, is considerably less personlike than is the average mature mammal, indeed the average fish. (pages 411-412)

III. In Section 4, Warren responds to the criticism that the fetus should be protected because it is a potential person. Instead of expressing the argument directly, she couches the concern in a series of rhetorical questions. Here is a passage that paraphrases her worry in prose form. Identify the premises and conclusion in this text.

> The fetus clearly has the potential to be a person; if it is nurtured and allowed to develop naturally it will very probably become a person. And potential persons have all of the same rights as actual persons. Actual persons have the right to life; therefore, potential persons have the right to life. And since an abortion kills a potential person, an abortion violates a right to life.

IV. One serious objection to Warren's view on abortion is that it has the false implication that infanticide is morally permissible. Identify the premises and conclusion in this excerpt:

> One of the most troubling objections to the argument presented in this article is that it may appear to justify not only abortion but infanticide as well. A newborn infant is not a great deal more personlike than a nine-month fetus, and thus it might seem that if a late-term abortion is sometimes justified, then infanticide must also be sometimes justified. Yet most people consider that infanticide is a form of murder, and thus never justified. (page 413)

15.3 A DEFENSE OF ABORTION

JUDITH JARVIS THOMSON (1971)

Judith Jarvis Thomson is Emerita Professor of Philosophy at the Massachusetts Institute of Technology. She is known for her work in both moral philosophy and metaphysics. In this essay, Thomson offers a moderate defense of abortion. Even if we grant that the fetus is a **person**, she argues, it does not thereby follow that it would always be wrong to take steps to end its life. Thus, Thomson proposes to give the critics of abortion what they want (the assumption that the fetus is a person) and yet show that there is no obvious argument from this starting point to the conclusion that abortions are always morally wrong. Besides objecting to the argument that abortion is always wrong because it involves killing a person, Thomson provides her own arguments for the conclusion that abortion is sometimes morally permissible and sometimes morally impermissible.

Reading Questions:

1. Does Thomson think that the fetus is a person?

2. Thomson compares the condition of a pregnant woman to someone kidnapped and connected to what?

3. How does rape affect Thomson's arguments for the impermissibility of abortion?

4. What is the difference between killing someone and letting someone die?

5. Does Thomson think that it is ever morally permissible to kill an innocent person whose existence threatens the existence of someone else?

6. Thomson compares the condition of a pregnant woman with a homeowner who has what blow through the window?

7. What defines the "minimum moral decency" that Thomson suggests that we are obligated to show one another?

8. According to Thomson, under what conditions do parents have special moral obligations toward their children?

The Standard Anti-Abortion Argument

Most opposition to abortion relies on the premise that the fetus is a human being, a person, from the moment of conception . . .[1] On the other hand, *I think that the premise is false, that the fetus is not a person from the moment of conception.* A newly fertilized ovum, a newly implanted clump of cells, is no more a person than an acorn is an oak tree. But I shall not discuss any of this. For it seems to me to be of great interest to ask what happens if, for the sake of argument, we allow the premise. How, precisely, are we supposed to get from there to the conclusion that abortion is morally impermissible? Opponents of abortion commonly spend most of their time establishing that the fetus is a person, and hardly any time explaining the step from there to the impermissibility of abortion. Perhaps they think the step too simple and obvious to require much comment. Or perhaps instead they are simply being economical in argument. Many of those who defend abortion rely on the premise that the fetus is not a person, but only a bit of tissue that will become a person at birth; and why pay out more arguments than you have to? Whatever the explanation, I suggest that the step they take is neither easy nor obvious, that it calls for closer examination than it is commonly given, and that when we do give it this closer examination we shall feel inclined to reject it.

I propose, then, that we grant that the fetus is a person, from the moment of conception. How does the argument go from here? Something like this, I take it.

The Pro-Life Argument

Every person has a right to life. So the fetus has a right to life. No doubt the mother has a right to decide what shall happen in and to her body; everyone would grant that. But surely a person's right to life is stronger and more stringent than the mother's right to decide what happens in and to her body, and so outweighs it. So the fetus may not be killed; an abortion may not be performed. It sounds plausible. But now let me ask you to imagine this.

The Violinist Analogy

You wake up in the morning and find yourself back to back in bed with an unconscious violinist. A famous unconscious violinist. He has been found to have a fatal kidney ailment, and the Society of Music Lovers has canvassed all the available medical records and found that you alone have the right blood type to help. They have therefore kidnapped you, and last night the violinist's circulatory system was plugged into yours, so that your kidneys can be used to extract poisons from his blood as well as your own. The director of the hospital now tells you, "Look, we're sorry the Society of Music Lovers did this to you—we would never have permitted it if we had known. But still, they did it, and the violinist now is plugged into you. To unplug you would be to kill him. But never mind, it's only for nine months. By then he will have recovered from his ailment, and can safely be unplugged from you."

Is it morally incumbent on you to accede to this situation? No doubt it would be very nice of you if you did, a great kindness. But do you *have* to accede to it? What if it were not nine months, but nine years? Or longer still? What if the director of the hospital says, "Tough luck, I agree, but you've now got to stay in bed, with the violinist plugged into you, for the rest of your life. Because remember this. All persons have a right to life, and violinists are persons. Granted you have a right to decide what happens in and to your body, but a person's right to life outweighs your right to decide what happens in and to your body. So you cannot ever be unplugged from him." *I imagine you would regard this as outrageous, which suggests that something really is wrong with that plausible-sounding argument I mentioned a moment ago.*

How Does Rape Affect the Pro-Life Argument?

In this case, of course, you were kidnapped; you didn't volunteer for the operation that plugged the violinist into your kidneys. Can those who oppose abortion on the ground I mentioned make an exception for a pregnancy due to rape? Certainly. They can say that persons have a right to life only if they didn't come into existence because of rape; or they can say that all persons have a right to life, but that some have less of a right to life than others, in particular, that those who came into existence because of rape have less. But these statements have a rather unpleasant sound. Surely the question of whether you have a right to life at all, or how much of it you have, shouldn't turn on the question of whether or not you are the product of a rape. And in fact the people who oppose abortion on the ground I mentioned do not make this distinction, and hence do not make an exception in case of rape.

Nor do they make an exception for a case in which the mother has to spend the nine months of her pregnancy in bed. They would agree that would be a great pity, and hard on the mother; but all the same, all persons have a right to life, the fetus is a person, and so on. I suspect, in fact, that they would not make an exception for a case in which, miraculously enough, the pregnancy went on for nine years, or even the rest of the mother's life.

Some won't even make an exception for a case in which continuation of the pregnancy is likely to shorten the mother's life; they regard abortion as impermissible even to save the mother's life. Such cases are nowadays very rare, and many opponents of abortion do not accept this extreme view. All the same, it is a good place to begin: a number of points of interest come out in respect to it.

Abortion in Cases Where the Mother's Life Is in Danger

Let us call the view that abortion is impermissible even to save the mother's life "**the extreme view**." I want to suggest first that it does not issue from the argument I mentioned earlier without the addition of some fairly powerful premises. Suppose a woman has become pregnant, and now learns that she has a cardiac condition such that she will die if she carries the baby to term. What may be done for her? The fetus, being a person, has a right to life, but as the mother is a person too, so has she a right to life. Presumably they have an equal right to life. How is it supposed to come out that an abortion may not be performed? If mother and child have an equal right to life, shouldn't we perhaps flip a coin? Or should we add to the mother's right to life her right to decide what happens in and to her body, which everybody seems to be ready to grant—the sum of her rights now outweighing the fetus' right to life?

Killing versus Letting Die

The most familiar argument here is the following. We are told that performing the abortion would be directly killing[2] the child, whereas doing nothing would not be killing the mother, but only letting her die. Moreover, in killing the child, one would be killing an innocent person, for the child has committed no crime, and is not aiming at his mother's death. And then there are a variety of ways in which this might be continued. (1) But as directly killing an innocent person is always and absolutely impermissible, an abortion may not be performed. Or, (2) as directly killing an innocent person is murder, and murder is always and absolutely impermissible, an abortion may not be performed.[3] Or, (3) as one's duty to refrain from directly killing an innocent person

is more stringent than one's duty to keep a person from dying, an abortion may not be performed. Or, (4) if one's only options are directly killing an innocent person or letting a person die, one must prefer letting the person die, and thus an abortion may not be performed.[4]

Some people seem to have thought that these are not further premises which must be added if the conclusion is to be reached, but that they follow from the very fact that an innocent person has a right to life.[5] But this seems to me to be a mistake, and perhaps the simplest way to show this is to bring out that while we must certainly grant that innocent persons have a right to life, the theses in (1) through (4) are all false. Take (2), for example. *If directly killing an innocent person is murder, and thus is impermissible, then the mother's directly killing the innocent person inside her is murder, and thus is impermissible. But it cannot seriously be thought to be murder if the mother performs an abortion on herself to save her life.* It cannot seriously be said that she must refrain, that she must sit passively by and wait for her death. Let us look again at the case of you and the violinist. There you are, in bed with the violinist, and the director of the hospital says to you, "It's all most distressing, and I deeply sympathize, but you see this is putting an additional strain on your kidneys, and you'll be dead within the month. But you have to stay where you are all the same. Because unplugging you would be directly killing an innocent violinist, and that's murder, and that's impermissible." If anything in the world is true, it is that you do not commit murder, you do not do what is impermissible, if you reach around to your back and unplug yourself from that violinist to save your life.

Third-Party Intervention

The main focus of attention in writings on abortion has been on what a third party may or may not do in answer to a request from a woman for an abortion. This is in a way understandable. Things being as they are, there isn't much a woman can safely do to abort herself. So the question asked is what a third party may do, and what the mother may do, if it is mentioned at all, is deduced, almost as an afterthought, from what it is concluded that third parties may do.

But it seems to me that to treat the matter in this way is to refuse to grant to the mother that very status of person which is so firmly insisted on for the fetus. For we cannot simply read off what a person may do from what a third party may do.

Tiny House Analogy

Suppose you find yourself trapped in a tiny house with a growing child. I mean a very tiny house, and a rapidly growing child—you are already up against the wall of the house and in a few minutes you'll be crushed to death. The child on the other hand won't be crushed to death; if nothing is done to stop him from growing he'll be hurt, but in the end he'll simply burst open the house and walk out a free man. Now I could well understand it if a bystander were to say, "There's nothing we can do for you. We cannot choose between your life and his, we cannot be the ones to decide who is to live, we cannot intervene." But it cannot be concluded that you too can do nothing, that you cannot attack it to save your life. However innocent the child may be, you do not have to wait passively while it crushes you to death. Perhaps a pregnant woman is vaguely felt to have the status of house, to which we don't allow the right of self-defense. But if the woman houses the child, it should be remembered that she is a person who houses it.

I should perhaps stop to say explicitly that I am not claiming that people have a right to do anything whatever to save their lives. I think, rather, that there are drastic limits to the right of self-defense. If someone threatens you with death unless you torture someone else to death, I think you have not the right, even to save your life, to do so. But the case under consideration here is very different. In our case there are only two people involved, one whose life is threatened, and one who threatens it. Both are innocent: the one who is threatened is not threatened because of any fault, the one who threatens does not threaten because of any fault. For this reason we may feel that we bystanders cannot intervene. But the person threatened can.

In sum, a woman surely can defend her life against the threat to it posed by the unborn child, even if doing so involves its death. And this shows not merely that the theses in (1) through (4) are false; it shows also that the extreme view of abortion is false, and so we need not canvass any other possible ways of arriving at it from the argument I mentioned at the outset.

Abortion in Cases Where the Mother's Life Is *Not* in Danger

Where the mother's life is not at stake, the argument I mentioned at the outset seems to have a much stronger pull. "Everyone has a right to life, so the unborn person has a right to life." And isn't the child's right to life weightier than anything other than the mother's own right to life, which she might put forward as ground for an abortion? This argument treats the right to life as if it were unproblematic. It is not, and this seems to me to be precisely the source of the mistake. *For we should now, at long last, ask what it comes to, to have a right to life.*

Right to Life = Right to the Bare Minimum Necessary for Life

In some views *having a right to life includes having a right to be given at least the bare minimum one needs for continued life.* But suppose that what in fact is the bare minimum a man needs for continued life is something he has no right at all to be given? If I am sick unto death, and the only thing that will save my life is the touch of Henry Fonda's cool hand on my fevered brow, then all the same, I have no right to be given the touch of Henry Fonda's cool hand on my fevered brow. It would be frightfully nice of him to fly in from the West Coast to provide it. It would be less nice, though no doubt well meant, if my friends flew out to the West Coast and carried Henry Fonda back with them. But I have no right at all against anybody that he should do this for me. *Or again, to return to the story I told earlier, the fact that for continued life that violinist needs the continued use of your kidneys does not establish that he has a right to be given the continued use of your kidneys.* He certainly has no right against you that you should give him continued use of your kidneys. *For nobody has any right to use your kidneys unless you give him such a right; and nobody has the right against you that you shall give him, this right—if you do allow him to go on using your kidneys, this is a kindness on your part, and not something he can claim from you as his due.* Nor has he any right against anybody else that *they* should give him continued use of your kidneys. Certainly he had no right against the Society of Music Lovers that they should plug him into you in the first place. And if you now start to unplug yourself, having learned that you will otherwise have to spend nine years in bed with him, there is nobody in the world who must try to prevent you, in order to see to it that he is given something he has a right to be given.

Right to Life = Right Not to Be Killed

Some people are rather stricter about the right to life. In their view, *it does not include the right to be given anything, but amounts to, and only to, the right not to be killed by anybody.* But here a related difficulty arises. If everybody is to refrain from killing that violinist, then everybody must refrain from doing a great many different sorts of things. Everybody must refrain from slitting his throat, everybody must refrain from shooting him—and everybody must refrain from unplugging you from him. But does he have a right against everybody that they shall refrain from unplugging you from him? To refrain from doing this is to allow him to continue to use your kidneys. It could be argued that he has a right against us that *we* should allow him to continue to use your kidneys. That is, while he had no right against us that we should give him the use of your kidneys, it might be argued that he anyway has a right against us that we shall not now intervene and deprive him of the use of your kidneys. I shall come back to third-party interventions later. But certainly the violinist has no right against you that *you* shall allow him to continue to use your kidneys. As I said, if you do allow him to use them, it is a kindness on your part, and not something you owe him.

The difficulty I point to here is not peculiar to the right to life. It reappears in connection with all the other natural rights; and it is something which an adequate account of rights must deal with. For present purposes it is enough just to draw attention to it. But I would stress that I am not arguing that people do not have a right to life—quite to the contrary. *I am arguing only that having a right to life does not*

guarantee having either a right to be given the use of or a right to be allowed continued use of another person's body—even if one needs it for life itself So the right to life will not serve the opponents of abortion in the very simple and clear way in which they seem to have thought it would.

Right to Life = Right Not to Be Killed *Unjustly*

The emendation which may be made at this point is this: *the right to life consists not in the right not to be killed, but rather in the right not to be killed unjustly.* This runs a risk of circularity, but never mind: it would enable us to square the fact that the violinist has a right to life with the fact that you do not act unjustly toward him in unplugging yourself, thereby killing him. For if you do not kill him unjustly, you do not violate his right to life, and so it is no wonder you do him no injustice.

But if this emendation is accepted, *the gap in the argument against abortion stares us plainly in the face: it is by no means enough to show that the fetus is a person, and to remind us that all persons have a right to life—we need to be shown also that killing the fetus violates its right to life, i.e., that abortion is unjust killing.* And is it?

[One way abortion might be unjust is if the woman gave the unborn child permission to use her body.] I suppose we may take it as a datum that in a case of pregnancy due to rape the mother has not given the unborn person a right to the use of her body for food and shelter. Indeed, in what pregnancy could it be supposed that the mother has given the unborn person such a right? It is not as if there were unborn persons drifting about the world, to whom a woman who wants a child says "I invite you in."

But it might be argued that there are other ways one can have acquired a right to the use of another person's body than by having been invited to use it by that person. Suppose a woman voluntarily indulges in intercourse, knowing of the chance it will issue in pregnancy, and then she does become pregnant; is she not in part responsible for the presence, in fact the very existence, of the unborn person inside her? No doubt she did not invite it in. But doesn't her partial responsibility for its being there itself give it a right to the use of her body?[6] If so, then her aborting it would . . . be doing it an injustice.

. . .[T]his argument would give the unborn person a right to its mother's body only if her pregnancy resulted from a voluntary act, undertaken in full knowledge of the chance a pregnancy might result from it. It would leave out entirely the unborn person whose existence is due to rape. Pending the availability of some further argument, then, we would be left with the conclusion that unborn persons whose existence is due to rape have no right to the use of their mothers' bodies, and thus that aborting them is not depriving them of anything they have a right to and hence is not unjust killing.

The Burglar Analogy

And we should also notice that it is not at all plain that this argument really does go even as far as it purports to. For there are cases and cases, and the details make a difference. If the room is stuffy, and I therefore open a window to air it, and a burglar climbs in, it would be absurd to say, "Ah, now he can stay, she's given him a right to the use of her house—for she is partially responsible for his presence there, having voluntarily done what enabled him to get in, in full knowledge that there are such things as burglars, and that burglars burgle." It would be still more absurd to say this if I had had bars installed outside my windows, precisely to prevent burglars from getting in, and a burglar got in only because of a defect in the bars. It remains equally absurd if we imagine it is not a burglar who climbs in, but an innocent person who blunders or falls in.

The People-Seeds Analogy

Again, suppose it were like this: people-seeds drift about in the air like pollen, and if you open your windows, one may drift in and take root in your carpets or upholstery. You don't want children, so you fix up your windows with fine mesh screens, the very best you can buy. As can happen, however, and on very, very rare occasions does happen, one of the screens is defective; and a seed drifts in and takes root. Does the person-plant who now develops have a right to the use of your house? Surely not—despite the fact that you voluntarily opened your windows, you

knowingly kept carpets and upholstered furniture, and you knew that screens were sometimes defective. Someone may argue that you are responsible for its rooting, that it does have a right to your house, because after all you *could* have lived out your life with bare floors and furniture, or with sealed windows and doors. But this won't do—for by the same token anyone can avoid a pregnancy due to rape by having a hysterectomy, or anyway by never leaving home without a (reliable!) army.

It seems to me that the argument we are looking at can establish at most that there are some cases in which the unborn person has a right to the use of its mother's body, and therefore some cases in which abortion is unjust killing. There is room for much discussion and argument as to precisely which, if any. But I think we should sidestep this issue and leave it open, for at any rate the argument certainly does not establish that all abortion is unjust killing.

Moral Rights versus Moral Decency

There is room for yet another argument here, however. *We surely must all grant that there may be cases in which it would be morally indecent to detach a person from your body at the cost of his life.* Suppose you learn that what the violinist needs is not nine years of your life, but only one hour: all you need do to save his life is to spend one hour in that bed with him. Suppose also that letting him use your kidneys for that one hour would not affect your health in the slightest. Admittedly you were kidnapped. Admittedly you did not give anyone permission to plug him into you. Nevertheless it seems to me plain you *ought* to allow him to use your kidneys for that hour—it would be indecent to refuse.

Again, suppose pregnancy lasted only an hour, and constituted no threat to life or health. And suppose that a woman becomes pregnant as a result of rape. Admittedly she did not voluntarily do anything to bring about the existence of a child. Admittedly she did nothing at all which would give the unborn person a right to the use of her body. All the same it might well be said, as in the newly emended violinist story, that she *ought* to allow it to remain for that hour—that it would be indecent in her to refuse.

Now some people are inclined to use the term "**right**" in such a way that it follows from the fact that you ought to allow a person to use your body for the hour he needs, that he has a right to use your body for the hour he needs, even though he has not been given that right by any person or act. They may say that it follows also that if you refuse, you act unjustly toward him. This use of the term is perhaps so common that it cannot be called wrong; nevertheless it seems to me to be an unfortunate loosening of what we would do better to keep a tight rein on. . . .

A further objection to so using the term "right" that from the fact that A ought to do a thing for B, it follows that B has a right against A that A do it for him, is that it is going to make the question of whether or not a man has a right to a thing turn on how easy it is to provide him with it; and this seems not merely unfortunate, but morally unacceptable. Take the case of Henry Fonda again. I said earlier that I had no right to the touch of his cool hand on my fevered brow, even though I needed it to save my life. I said it would be frightfully nice of him to fly in from the West Coast to provide me with it, but that I had no right against him that he should do so. But suppose he isn't on the West Coast. Suppose he has only to walk across the room, place a hand briefly on my brow—and lo, my life is saved. Then surely he ought to do it, it would be indecent to refuse. Is it to be said "Ah, well, it follows that in this case she has a right to the touch of his hand on her brow, and so it would be an injustice in him to refuse"? So that I have a right to it when it is easy for him to provide it, though no right when it's hard? It's rather a shocking idea that anyone's rights should fade away and disappear as it gets harder and harder to accord them to him.

So my own view is that even though you ought to let the violinist use your kidneys for the one hour he needs, we should not conclude that he has a right to do so—we should say that if you refuse, you are . . . self-centered and callous, indecent in fact, but not unjust. And similarly, that even supposing a case in which a woman pregnant due to rape ought to allow the unborn person to use her body for the hour he needs, we should not conclude that he has a right to do so; we should conclude that she is self-centered, callous, indecent, but not unjust, if she refuses. The complaints are no less grave; they are just different.

However, there is no need to insist on this point. If anyone does wish to deduce "he has a right" from "you ought," then all the same he must surely grant that there are cases in which it is not morally required of you that you allow that violinist to use your kidneys, and in which he does not have a right to use them, and in which you do not do him an injustice if you refuse. And so also for mother and unborn child. *Except in such cases as the unborn person has a right to demand it—and we were leaving open the possibility that there may be such cases—nobody is morally required to make large sacrifices, of health, of all other interests and concerns, of all other duties and commitments, for nine years, or even for nine months, in order to keep another person alive. . .*

Mothers Have Special Responsibility for the Unborn

Following the lead of the opponents of abortion, I have throughout been speaking of the fetus merely as a person, and what I have been asking is whether or not the argument we began with, which proceeds only from the fetus' being a person, really does establish its conclusion. I have argued that it does not.

But of course there are arguments and arguments, and it may be said that I have simply fastened on the wrong one. *It may be said that what is important is not merely the fact that the fetus is a person, but that it is a person for whom the woman has a special kind of responsibility issuing from the fact that she is its mother.* And it might be argued that all my analogies are therefore irrelevant—for you do not have that special kind of responsibility for that violinist, Henry Fonda does not have that special kind of responsibility for me. And our attention might be drawn to the fact that men and women both *are* compelled by law to provide support for their children.

I have in effect dealt (briefly) with this argument . . . above; but a (still briefer) recapitulation now may be in order. *Surely we do not have any such "special responsibility" for a person unless we have assumed it, explicitly or implicitly.* If a set of parents do not try to prevent pregnancy, do not obtain an abortion, and then at the time of birth of the child do not put it out for adoption, but rather take it home with them, then they have assumed responsibility for it, they have given it rights, and they cannot *now* withdraw support from it at the cost of its life because they now find it difficult to go on providing for it. But if they have taken all reasonable precautions against having a child, they do not simply by virtue of their biological relationship to the child who comes into existence have a special responsibility for it. They may wish to assume responsibility for it, or they may not wish to. And I am suggesting that if assuming responsibility for it would require large sacrifices, then they may refuse. . .

Two Objections

My argument will be found unsatisfactory on two counts by many of those who want to regard abortion as morally permissible. *First, while I do argue that abortion is not impermissible, I do not argue that it is always permissible.* There may well be cases in which carrying the child to term requires only [minimal decency] of the mother, and this is a standard we must not fall below. I am inclined to think it a merit of my account precisely that it does *not* give a general yes or a general no. It allows for and supports our sense that, for example, a sick and desperately frightened fourteen-year-old schoolgirl, pregnant due to rape, may *of course* choose abortion, and that any law which rules this out is an insane law. And it also allows for and supports our sense that in other cases resort to abortion is even positively indecent. It would be indecent in the woman to request an abortion, and indecent in a doctor to perform it, if she is in her seventh month, and wants the abortion just to avoid the nuisance of postponing a trip abroad. The very fact that the arguments I have been drawing attention to treat all cases of abortion, or even all cases of abortion in which the mother's life is not at stake, as morally on a par ought to have made them suspect at the outset.

Secondly, while I am arguing for the permissibility of abortion in some cases, I am not arguing for the right to secure the death of the unborn child. It is easy to confuse these two things in that up to a certain point in the life of the fetus it is not able to survive outside the mother's body; hence removing it from her body guarantees its death. But they are importantly different. I have argued that you are not morally required to spend nine months in bed, sustaining the life of that violinist; but to say this is by no means to say that if, when you unplug yourself, there is a miracle and he survives, you then have a right to turn round and slit his throat. You may detach yourself even if this costs him his life; you have no right to be guaranteed his death, by some other means, if unplugging yourself does not kill him. There are some people who will feel dissatisfied by this feature of my argument. A woman may be utterly devastated by the thought of a child, a bit of herself, put out for adoption and never seen or heard of again. She may therefore want not merely that the child be detached from her, but more, that it die. Some opponents of abortion are inclined to regard this as beneath contempt—thereby showing insensitivity to what is surely a powerful source of despair. All the same, I agree that the desire for the child's death is not one which anybody may gratify, should it turn out to be possible to detach the child alive.

At this place, however, it should be remembered that we have only been pretending throughout that the fetus is a human being from the moment of conception. A very early abortion is surely not the killing of a person, and so is not dealt with by anything I have said here.

NOTES

1. I am very much indebted to James Thomson for discussion, criticism, and many helpful suggestions.
2. The term "direct" in the arguments I refer to is a technical one. Roughly, what is meant by "direct killing" is either killing as an end in itself, or killing as a means to some end, for example, the end of saving someone else's life. See note 6, below, for an example of its use.
3. *Cf. Encyclical Letter of Pope Plus XI on Christian Marriage*, St. Paul Editions (Boston, n.d.), P-32: "however much we may pity the mother whose health and even life is gravely imperiled in the performance of the duty allotted to her by nature, nevertheless what could ever be a sufficient reason for excusing in any way the direct murder of the innocent? This is precisely what we are dealing with here." Noonan (*The Morality of Abortion*, p. 43) reads this as follows:

"What cause can ever avail to excuse in any way the direct killing of the innocent? For it is a question of that."
4. The thesis in (4) is in an interesting way weaker than those in (1), (2), and (3): they rule out abortion even in cases in which both mother *and* child will die if the abortion is not performed. By contrast, one who held the view expressed in (4) could consistently say that one needn't prefer letting two persons die to killing one.

5. Cf. the following passage from Pius XII, *Address to the Italian Catholic Society of Midwives:* "The baby in the maternal breast has the right to life immediately from God.—Hence there is no man, no human authority, no science, no medical, eugenic, social, economic or moral 'indication' which can establish or grant a valid juridical ground for a direct deliberate disposition of an innocent human life, that is a disposition which looks to its destruction either as an end or as a means to another end perhaps in itself not illicit.—The baby, still not born, is a man in the same degree and for the same reason as the mother" (quoted in Noonan, *The Morality of Abortion*, p. 45).

6. The need for a discussion of this argument was brought home to me by members of the Society for Ethical and Legal Philosophy, to whom this paper was originally presented.

DISCUSSION QUESTIONS:

1. Thomson's argument attempts to show that abortion is sometimes morally permissible even if the fetus is a person. What do you think? Is it true that the fetus is a person? At what stage of development? Does the fact that it's a person show that abortion is always morally wrong?

2. Thomson compares the condition of a pregnant woman to someone kidnapped and connected to a dying violinist. Is the violinist analogy a good analogy for a woman's pregnancy? If not, what are the crucial differences?

3. In many parts of the world, women practice sex-selective abortions. In a sex-selective abortion, the woman chooses to abort in large part because of the gender of the developing fetus. Given the actually-existing cultural norms, stereotypes, etc., this practice amounts to the selective abortion of female fetuses. In other words, in many parts of the world—and to some degree in the US as well—women are much more likely to abort if they find out that the fetus is female. Is this practice morally justifiable? Why would the fetus's gender be a morally relevant feature of the fetus, if the fetus isn't even a person?

4. Women can have many different reasons for obtaining an abortion. Very few choose to abort because the pregnancy endangers their life. Many choose to abort because they think that a pregnancy will hurt their chances of living a fulfilled life by getting an education, a good job, a life partner, etc. Still others choose to abort because pregnancy is a bother, because they want to hurt the father of the fetus, or simply because it's their preferred method of birth control. What role do you think a woman's intentions have to do with the moral permissibility of an abortion? Do you think that a woman's intentions affect whether or not the fetus is a person or whether or not the fetus deserves moral consideration? Do they affect whether the mother's rights with regard to her body are outweighed by those of the fetus, assuming the fetus is a person?

5. Thomson claims that a parent has special obligations to her child *only if* the parent assumes such responsibility, explicitly or implicitly. Does having unprotected sex amount to implicit assumption of responsibility for the resulting child? If so, doesn't this affect Thomson's argument? If not, why do we make fathers of children conceived in one-night stands pay child support?

Argument Reconstruction:

I. Thomson claims that the standard argument for the moral wrongness of abortion functions by showing that fetuses have a right to life that is stronger than the mother's right to control her body. Identify the premises and conclusion in this excerpt:

> Every person has a right to life. So the fetus has a right to life. No doubt the mother has a right to decide what shall happen in and to her body; everyone would grant that. But surely a person's right to life is stronger and more stringent than the mother's right to decide what happens in and to her body, and so outweighs it. So the fetus may not be killed; an abortion may not be performed. (page 418)

II. Many who see abortion as morally wrong equate it with murder. Identify the premises and conclusion in this argument:

> If directly killing an innocent person is murder, and thus is impermissible, then the mother's directly killing the innocent person inside her is murder, and thus is impermissible. (page 419)

III. Sometimes people use rhetorical questions to present a line of argument or a conclusion. Thomson does so here by asserting the conclusion of a line of reasoning as a question. Identify the premises and conclusion in this excerpt:

> But it might be argued that there are other ways one can have acquired a right to the use of another

person's body than by having been invited to use it by that person. Suppose a woman voluntarily indulges in intercourse, knowing of the chance it will issue in pregnancy, and then she does become pregnant; is she not in part responsible for the presence, in fact the very existence, of the unborn person inside her? (page 421)

IV. Thomson uses the violinist analogy to show what's wrong with the standard argument against the permissibility of abortion. Identify the premises and conclusion in this argument:

> All persons have a right to life, and violinists are persons. Granted you have a right to decide what happens in and to your body, but a person's right to life outweighs your right to decide what happens in and to your body. So you cannot ever be unplugged from him. (page 418)

15.4 CARING FOR WOMEN AND GIRLS WHO ARE CONSIDERING ABORTION

DIANA FRITZ CATES (2002)

Diana Fritz Cates is a professor of Religious Studies at the University of Iowa. Her research focuses on the intersection of religion and ethics, in particular the work of Saint Thomas Aquinas and various issues in normative and applied ethics including virtue ethics and bioethics. In this essay, Cates focuses not so much on the moral permissibility of abortion but on our moral obligations towards women and girls who are considering abortions. She employs narrative about actual cases to help describe the nuances of the kinds of concrete situations that women find themselves in, and she claims that properly understanding the complex dimensions of a decision to abort requires treating the women in such situations with both respect and compassion. In particular, she explores how respect and compassion can elucidate the relation between autonomy and moral understanding and the relation between autonomy and relations to other people.

Reading Questions:

1. What are Judy's reasons for choosing to have an abortion?

2. What is the connection between respect/compassion and understanding the moral dimensions of a decision to have an abortion?

3. According to Cates, what is respect?

4. According to Cates, what is compassion?

5. According to Cates, what is care?

6. Of the normative ethical views covered in Unit 3, which does Cates' approach to abortion follow most closely?

7. What is "bodily knowing"?

8. What are some of the ways that a person can "go wrong" in feeling guilt?

9. What does it mean to say that someone's sense of self is "fundamentally relational"?

It was an evening that I would carry with me for many years. When I arrived at Laura's, Judy was already there. The two of them had been sitting in the dimly lit living room, talking. The room seemed thick with apprehension, as if momentous words had already been spoken or were lying in wait, about to be spilled.

I had not seen Judy for a long time, so we played catch-up while Laura got some snacks and checked on the baby. As Judy and I exchanged the usual Midwestern niceties, I began instinctively to brace myself for a coming storm. When Laura returned, the niceties soon gave way to a probing emotional intensity.

Laura's eyes pulled me in. "Judy was just telling me about a difficult decision she has to make."

"I've already made the decision. There's no way that I can have a baby now." Judy hesitated and drew a difficult breath. "When I told Don that I was pregnant, he got really quiet. I was hoping that he'd be happy—that he'd be excited about starting a family—but he wasn't. He kept mumbling something about a baby not being such a good idea for us. It took a couple of days, but I managed to get him to tell me what was wrong. We've been married for a year, but this is the first time he's ever opened up to me about his family. He told me about his father—about the years of physical and emotional abuse. It was like he was trying to communicate the horror of his childhood, but without having to unleash the dreadful pain of it. I can see that he still has wounds from that abuse. And the idea of being a father himself fills him with terror. He doesn't want to be a father. He doesn't trust his instincts on this. He's not ready."

"Can't Don get some counseling to deal with his fear?" Laura pressed. "I don't see why you and he can't talk with someone about this. I mean, few people ever really feel ready to become parents. There's almost always a sense of risk and worry that you won't be strong enough or smart enough or good enough. Besides, it seems important to Don and to your marriage that Don come to terms with his past."

"I've already talked to him about that. He's willing to at least think about getting some help, but let's face it—given where he's at right now, and how deep the roots of his problem lie, and the fact that he's never had counseling before, there's little chance that he could adjust to the idea of fatherhood by the time a baby would arrive. In any case, he doesn't want to take that chance. I'm afraid that, if I were to go through with this pregnancy, I would lose Don, I mean really lose him. Our marriage would come undone, and I'd be left to raise a kid on my own. I don't want that. I can't handle it."

Laura was quick to respond. "But Judy, you told me a couple of months ago, after your dad died, that you wanted a baby more than anything else in the world. You laughed and cried about how you wanted a new life to hold, to shower with love, to fill that void in your life. You wanted a little one, and you got what you wanted. And now you want to destroy it?" It wasn't really a question.

Judy shifted in her chair. "It's not like I'm going to destroy a developed human life. The fetus is only a potential life at this point. It won't feel any pain; it'll never know the difference between being born or not being born."

The tension between Judy and Laura continued to build. "You talk about potential life as if it's just a blob of tissue. It's a potential baby, Judy. If you give it the rest of its nine months, it will be a baby, just the kind of baby that you were hoping and praying for." Tears began to stream down Laura's face. She went on and on about how much Judy had wanted a baby, how it made no sense that she could now be so sure that she didn't want this baby, how she needed to acknowledge that she got pregnant on purpose, how it didn't seem right that Don had so much influence over her choice.

Judy was becoming tearful herself and increasingly defensive. I wanted to rein Laura in somehow. I didn't know the whole story, but it was clear that Judy had wanted to see us, her friends, in order to get some support. What Laura was giving her didn't feel like support. When I suggested this to Laura, she said, "I'm sorry, but . . ." She went on, clarifying that she loved Judy and wanted to be supportive, but she had this horrible feeling that Judy hadn't really worked through her decision, and because of this, Judy was about to do something that she might regret for the rest of her life.

"Look, I'm sharing this with you because I need your support. I don't need the third degree. I've thought it through as much as I care to, and I've made my decision."

Knowing these women as well as I did, and caring for them, I could feel the power of both of their perspectives. Judy is an idealistic and sentimental person who weeps openly over beautiful and fragile things. I could imagine her gushing tearfully about having a baby. I could also hear Laura saying how wonderful it would be if Judy had a baby soon; then their children would be relatively close together in age, and Judy and Laura could share in the adventures of parenting. I could see that Laura was already grieving—and also resisting—the loss of this possibility.

At the same time, I could imagine how crushed Judy was when Don did not respond to her news as she had hoped. I felt the pull of her desperate desire to do what she could to minimize the psychological risk to Don, who was much more frail than I had realized. I knew that Judy was herself rather vulnerable, as she was still mourning her father's untimely death. I could see that she needed for us to be with her on this—to trust that she was capable of making a good choice. I imagine that she also wanted us to agree with her choice.

Yet Laura was not willing to grant that Judy had made a good choice. At least, not yet. I slowly began to figure out why. It was not simply that Laura wanted to hang on to certain possibilities for herself and her relationship with Judy; it was also that Laura was concerned about Judy's decision-making process—and the way that process reflected on Judy morally. That is to say, she was concerned about Judy's moral well-being. Laura is strikingly honest and brave when it comes to facing the most painful aspects of life. She notices when people are hiding or running from something, and she commonly wants to talk about these fears until they become workable. It seemed strange to Laura that, although Judy was upset over how the conversation was going, she did not appear to be very upset at the prospect of the abortion itself. Judy seemed to be deflecting a discussion of how it felt to conceive new life within her body, to experience the power of pregnancy, to imagine her fetus as a baby and to see herself nurturing that baby, only to have her hopes dashed. Laura suspected that Judy was deceiving herself about how

much loss she was already suffering and how much more she would suffer in getting an abortion. Laura hoped that Judy would face the truth of her situation partly by acknowledging this loss.

Judy was not entirely disengaged emotionally. She was very concerned about Don's well-being. Actually, it is a mistake to speak of Judy's well-being and Don's as though the two were straightforwardly separate, as though Judy could promote or diminish Don's well-being without at the same time indirectly promoting or diminishing parts of her own well-being. When Don suffered, Judy tended spontaneously to suffer with him. When Don experienced terror at the prospect of being a father, Judy felt his terror extend into her own body, causing her own muscles to tense up and her own palms to sweat. For Laura, this was not in itself troubling. She knew this sort of intimacy in her own marriage. What *was* troubling to Laura was that Judy's co-suffering of Don's terror—her impulse to save Don and by extension herself from disaster—seemed to be dominating Judy's deliberations. There were other important goods and evils at stake. Judy needed to experience and reflect upon the relative attractiveness and repulsiveness of these other possibilities, especially the ones that affected Judy apart from Don, before she could reach a sound decision. Or so Laura thought.

To Judy, it seemed that Laura was trying to make her feel grief-stricken or guilty for destroying her fetus and her dreams for herself and that fetus, whereas Judy had decided early on, after receiving Don's reaction, to disengage emotionally from her fetus. In my view, there was something disrespectful and even violent about the way that Laura was trying to make Judy feel the way that Laura thought she should feel. It seemed cruel to insist that Judy open up a can of worms that she would probably not be able to sort through in the limited time that was available. Yet Laura's insight (quite apart from its mode of presentation) would not let go of me. I wondered whether it was a good idea for Judy to make a decision of this magnitude in what appeared to be a state of selective emotional numbness. I was gripped by the possibility that she was making a decision in the absence of relevant information that could be gleaned only by feeling (and at the same time reflecting upon) certain painful emotions.

Regarding Don's influence on her decision-making process, Judy thought that Laura underestimated the moral weight of Don's fragile psychological state. Judy agreed that she had needs of her own that deserved to be weighed in the balance, but it was clear to her that Don's need to be protected from emotional injury—and her own need to be a wife who respected her husband's limits and honored him in his acknowledged weakness—tipped the scale toward terminating the pregnancy. This made sense, but again, Laura's perspective tugged at me. Judy had always wanted to have children, and it was an immense sacrifice for her to abort this potential child; yet it appeared that she did not feel the full weight of this sacrifice. I shared Laura's worry that a part of who Judy was apart from Don (a part of her that Laura and I had known for years) had been lost in the shuffle—not deliberately sacrificed, but simply neglected.

Judy got the abortion. I never talked to her about it. I went back to school, and we gradually lost contact. Laura never talked to her about it, either. Judy never invited her to. Laura's reaction to Judy's announcement had caused a rift in their friendship. They tried for some time to mend the relationship, but they eventually drifted apart.

To this day, I am troubled by this encounter, by the question of what friendship required of Laura and me in responding to Judy. More specifically for the purposes of this essay, I remain captivated by Laura's insights into possible problems with Judy's decision-making process. Was Judy in a good position to provide an **informed consent** to abortion? Was she well-informed? Was she doing well in exercising her **autonomy**?

. . . In what follows, I investigate first what it is to have a substantial understanding of the act of aborting one's own fetus and, accordingly, what it is to make an abortion decision partly on the basis of this understanding. The emphasis here is on *the relationship between autonomy and moral understanding.* I consider second what it is to deliberate and decide about abortion in the substantial absence of control by others. The emphasis in that section is on *the relationship between autonomy and relationality.* In each of the main sections, I follow the same pattern of inquiry. I introduce the issue and begin an analysis

of it with regard to Judy in particular. I then analyze the issue further with regard to a few other women who have shared their abortion experiences.[1] . . .

Respect and Compassion

This analysis is governed by a conviction that *attempting to be respectful and compassionate is a necessary condition for understanding the moral dimensions of abortion and making appropriate evaluations of particular abortion decisions.* No one possesses the virtues of respect and compassion in their perfect form; and most of us are probably mistaken about the degree to which we possess them; but all who wish to render moral judgments about girls' and women's choices in the matter of abortion—and this includes girls and women themselves—are morally required to cultivate these virtues and bring them to bear, as much as possible, in their reflections. Because the following analysis seeks to draw both author and reader into the work of respect and compassion, and also because I argue that respect and compassion require certain things on the part of persons who stand in relationship to those who are considering abortion, it is necessary to indicate what I mean by respect and compassion before proceeding.

Traditionally, philosophers have thought of respect as a rational attitude of reverence regarding the power that persons have to act according to universalizable maxims and in obedience to the rational moral law (Kant 1990). Recent research has done much to correct for hyper-intellectual/hypo-emotional interpretations of this attitude (Engstrom and Whiting 1996). Still, I find it more helpful to construe the reverence that is properly felt toward persons as the expression of a virtue—a moral virtue in the Aristotelian-Thomistic sense (Cates 1997). *Respect is a habit of perceiving persons as having profound moral and spiritual value, and experiencing this value on an emotional level.* It is a habit of approaching people with caution, standing at moral attention before them and perhaps also at a certain moral distance from them, giving them some privacy and leeway in the exercise of their moral agencies, and thereby honoring the separate and inviolable moral space that they occupy as personal subjects. It is a habit of being stopped short in our impulses to ignore persons, dispose of them, control them, or in other ways use them as mere means to our own ends. Respect is, at the same time, a habit of receiving and responding to persons as beings who are fundamentally like us and therefore stand with us on the same moral ground. It is a habit of approaching others with a passionate interest in protecting the basic rights and responsibilities that belong to all of us simply because we are persons.

Conceived as such, the virtue of respect is closely related to the virtue of compassion. Whereas respect disposes us to perceive every person we encounter as a being who is of immeasurable and irreplaceable value, *compassion disposes us to perceive every person we encounter as a being who is vulnerable, who suffers, and whose suffering ought ordinarily to be alleviated.* Compassion is a habit of noticing people who are suffering and approaching them with such openness and attentiveness that we are able to experience elements of their suffering as partly our own. It is a habit of responding, partly out of the experience of co-suffering, in a way that is likely to ease the suffering. Compassion is, at the same time, a habit of discerning how not to become so engrossed in the suffering of others that we are overwhelmed and thus incapacitated in our efforts to provide help. It is a disposition to help others partly from a position of leverage outside the immediacy of the other's experience.

In what follows, *I take a virtue ethics approach that considers the requirements of respect and compassion taken together.* "**Care**," as I use the term in this chapter, refers to a synthetic unity of respect and compassion. I assume that persons do best as moral agents, and that they relate best to other persons, when they exercise both virtues. One virtue may appear to be more important than the other in a given circumstance, but both are always or almost always relevant. Persons always possess basic dignity, and they are always or almost always undergoing some form of suffering. A virtuous person consistently registers these truths (in appropriate ways) in her or his relations with other persons.[2]

Autonomy and Moral Understanding

It was early in high school that Judy and I first became friends. Many things about her character drew me into her company and held me there. Most remarkable, perhaps, were her perceptual acuteness, her attentiveness to the details of experience, her intellectual curiosity and clarity, and the way that all of these gifts were infused with a palpable emotional intensity and honesty. Judy was someone who came across as being fully alive. She had a penchant for following fascinating but ultimately unanswerable questions. She sought to understand human beings and their relationships in all of their complexity, brokenness, and dignity. She was relentless, though not desperate, in her effort to discern what is most valuable in life, and what would make *her* life, in particular, most satisfying and worthwhile.

For Judy, to understand something of moral significance was, in part, to be moved. It was to receive an impression of how things are—and ought to be—with humans, partly in feeling and reflecting upon dull and inchoate or more vibrant and focused emotions. For Judy, and for those of us who learned so much from being with her, to understand the dignity of a person, for example, was partly to stand in awe before an unspeakable abyss that was not—and would never be—within our grasp or at our disposal. To understand the evil of murder was partly to be shaken and sickened by an unfathomable loss and by a human spirit so crushed that it could not feel this loss. To understand the good of friendship was partly to delight in pursuing with each other open-ended, character-forming inquiries into the meanings of life and love. Although Judy's emotional responses were not always on target (no one's are), I encountered in them a touchstone to moral value (see C. Taylor 1985, chaps. 1 and 2).[3]

J. Giles Milhaven identifies a way of knowing good and evil that he provocatively calls "bodily knowing" (Milhaven 1991; see also Milhaven 1993). This mode of moral knowing includes making truthful evaluative judgments, but for Milhaven, making such judgments properly involves being moved by the goods or evils at issue and thus experiencing pleasant or painful bodily reverberations. In Milhaven's view, a moral judgment tends to be incomplete, overly abstract, and untrue to human reality when it lacks an embodied emotional dimension. For example, Milhaven, who is white, explains that he long regarded racism as a serious moral evil. He sought to undermine it through personal acts and the exercise of institutional responsibilities. It was only in feeling compassion for a particular black person, however, who addressed him through the words of Martin Luther King, Jr. and whose suffering caused his stomach to sink, that Milhaven began to realize how weakly he had previously known the evil of racism. It was only in co-feeling the "horror, repulsion, longing, anger, despair, hope" of someone who, as Audre Lorde puts it, "[metabolized] hatred like a daily bread," that Milhaven began to grasp as a whole person what is evil about racism and how evil it is (Milhaven 1991, 241; see also Lorde 1984, 152).

Milhaven pursues with another example of what it is to know the good or evil of abortion. He explains that for many years he was unconditionally and vocally pro-choice:

> I thought long on the issue, discussed it with fellow ethicists, and arrived at what I believed was a sound, sensitive, moral position on abortion. However, on this issue I never listened attentively to the experience of women who had chosen to have abortions. Neither did I listen to the experience of women who, despite motives against having another child, chose not to have an abortion but to give birth. I knew nothing of the experience of women who were at peace with their choice, whichever it was. Of women who regretted their choice. Of women faced with the choice and struggling to make it. (Milhaven 1991, 239)

It was only when he listened and, as I interpret him, listened *with compassion* that he was able to let go of the security of his considered intellectual position and feel the heart-rending difficulty and ambiguity of many women's reproductive and moral lives. Only in the exercise of compassion did it dawn on him that, for many women who sought abortions, abortion was in their own judgment "a serious evil." Only in being moved by particular women who were caught up in unique and complex predicaments of pregnancy did he understand, intellectually and viscerally, that abortion can nevertheless be the best choice for many women. It was partly in sharing pain that he grasped that "there are other bad things, worse evils, that the continuation of the pregnancy can bring" (Milhaven 1991, 239).

Ordinarily, Judy's understanding of moral value was deeply and reflectively emotional. It included a bodily component that typically manifested itself in Judy's own verbal descriptions of her feeling states, as well as in altered physical movements and facial expressions, altered speech, sweating, crying, and the like. But as Laura saw things, Judy was not experiencing in a full-bodied way that the fetal life within her body was of value. She was not feeling in her flesh and bone the loss of the prospect of preserving and nurturing that life. Had Judy experienced an emotional acknowledgment of these features of the situation, she would have suffered more pain in her decision making. That in itself would have been sad, but in Laura's view, it would have been sad in a good way. Judy's decision would have been more truthful, it would have honored more of the different and competing goods at stake, had it been made partly in sadness.

Digging deeper into what was only implicit at the time, I believe that from Laura's perspective, making the abortion decision with emotional eyes wide open would have helped Judy to avoid self-deception and thereby exhibit courage; it would have allowed her to experience more respect and compassion for herself and for other women who are troubled by their abortions; it would have allowed her to cultivate many other moral virtues that grow only when one slogs through the pain of life, rather than skirting around it. One could judge Laura's perspective to be judgmental, moralistic, paternalistic, and even subtly sadistic. Indeed, on the face of it, Laura seemed to want Judy to suffer, to pay an emotional price for what she was about to do, so that the abortion would not be too simple or easy. I grant that Laura's motivations were probably mixed. The rather aggressive way in which she presented her concerns to Judy suggests that she wanted, for whatever reason, to exercise some control over Judy's emotional state. Still, I trust that compassionate motives predominated. Laura believed, on good evidence, that Judy had previously ascribed considerable value to the fetus and to the prospect of mothering the fetus, yet she was not presently admitting this value into her conscious awareness. Judy was suppressing relevant emotional information and sensation in order to make her decision more bearable. Laura could appreciate this, but she thought that it would be better for Judy to struggle with the pain up front than to make a decision that did not serve her well as a moral agent.

To anticipate subsequent formulations of this concern in terms of the discourse of medical ethics (even though Judy and Laura did not think in these terms), Laura wanted to help Judy make an informed choice, and she intuited that for Judy this would have to be an emotionally informed choice. She also wanted to help Judy make an autonomous choice, and she intuited that if Judy's choice was to be truly her own—if it was to express her capacity for reflective self-governance—then it would have to be based on a full or deep understanding of what she was about to do. An overly intellectual and emotionally flat understanding would not suffice. Laura believed that if Judy were to go through an abortion experience in the mode of a disembodied mind, Judy's ability to identify with her decision and thus take responsibility for it would be diminished.

Listening to Other Women

When one listens to other women's abortion stories, one hears many of the women raising similar concerns, after the fact, about their own decision-making processes. In particular, one encounters many women who seem to have engaged in forms of denial and self-deception. One woman, Fritzi, when questioned about her abortion experience, can hardly recall it. Eve Kushner narrates her story: "'I don't remember,' she answers, and then laughs, 'It must have been awful.' Fritzi continues, 'I just blanked out a lot of it. It's scary,' she says of this unfamiliar behavior. She likens it to another experience: 'Sometimes if I told a little white lie, it's the same. I try to ignore it. It's something I put behind me and I don't look back at it. I separate it from myself'" (Kushner 1997, 102). Another woman, Irene, kept so busy before and after her abortion that she did not have time to think or feel about it. "'I didn't feel it the whole time beforehand. I just laughed it off.' As the abortion occurred, however, she 'didn't feel that disconnected.' During the procedure and directly afterward, she had 'a moment of hysteria.' . . . Now, she says, thinking about 'the actual procedure' is 'the

only thing that really upsets me. I don't know if it's because that's the only part I couldn't really deny,' she muses. Otherwise, Irene notes, 'I just don't feel it. I don't let myself get like that'" (Kushner 1997, 103). Similarly, Janet, who obtained an illegal abortion in a motel off of the highway recalls, "I think also that the three of us [she and her two sisters] were in a way—well, we were scared and my boyfriend was sad—I think that we were kind of afraid to really acknowledge what was going on, because I think it would have been too hard to deal with" (Hoshiko 1993, 34). Many other women feel, as they move through their abortion experiences, like they are on "automatic pilot" or "hot and numb, lost in space" (Kushner 1997, 29–30; Winn 1988, 60).

Different women experience emotions differently. Some are characteristically less inclined than others to register events on an emotional level. Moreover, different women experience the value of human fetuses differently, and for apparently good reasons (Hoshiko 1993, 82, 138; see also Kushner 1997, 82). Nevertheless, it appears to be the case that some women who go through abortions feeling very little or no emotion do so because they are unable or unwilling to acknowledge, as whole persons, the implications of what they themselves take to be true, which is that even if a human fetus is merely a *potential* person, still it is a potential *person*, who if nurtured will likely eventuate in a thinking, feeling being just like them, with a moral standing equivalent to their own.

One woman who had an abortion proclaims, "'I think you're a cold person if it doesn't hit you. You've got a screw loose if you can do it and have no problem with it at all'" (Kushner 1997, 17). Respect and compassion require, however, recognizing that self-deception and denial are terribly common human phenomena. Few of us even notice the painful moral ambiguity that characterizes most of our actions and interactions, and few are strong enough to feel the full force of what we see. *Respect and compassion also require trying to understand women's motives for shutting down emotionally.* Some women are afraid to admit how much they care about the competing goods at stake because they want to make a decision that is as straightforward as possible. They want to make a "tight" choice that will not leave any loose ends dangling, undermining their peace of mind (they fear) for the rest of their lives. Especially in environments where people do not talk about their abortions, or in religious contexts where the voice of judgment and punishment predominates over that of forgiveness and mercy, or more specifically where women do not have a relationship with a divine power that helps them to shoulder the weight of their burden, it is hard for women to trust that they will find adequate emotional and spiritual support from others if they turn off the "auto-pilot" and attempt to navigate.

I take it that most women who choose abortion experience their fetuses to have *some* moral value and their abortions to have *some* moral significance. Some women who have abortions believe that their fetuses have the same status as a baby or a full grown person. But most women who have abortions believe that their fetuses have more limited moral value—a value that increases with fetal growth and development, but remains, at least for the first trimester, less or even much less than that of a baby or an adult person.

One would expect women who ascribe a significant amount of value to their fetuses, and who acknowledge this value on an emotional level, to experience *some* pain as they choose to destroy or withdraw support from this value (McDonnell 1984, chap. 2). Within the moral domain one would expect different women to experience this pain differently, depending partly on how they conceive of morality—whether in terms of human flourishing or a personal ideal, a standard of common human decency, a conception of virtue, a set of values, a sense of responsibility, a system of principles and rules, or convictions about religious or spiritual obligations or goals. In general terms, one would expect—and one finds—that women commonly experience pain in the form of grief and guilt (among other feelings) (Gardner 1986, 87–88; McDonnell 1984, chaps. 2 and 3). They experience grief and guilt as modes of registering their own (and other people's) judgments that their abortions and, in some cases, their broader life circumstances, are morally problematic.

Grief

One woman, Wanda, has had two abortions. For years after her first one, she continued to feel

occasional grief about it. She said to her partner, "'Honey, I'm really upset about this.' He did not understand, so Wanda insisted, 'I miss it. I miss that child. I lost something.' Wanda remembers panicking and yelling, 'You don't understand. There's something gone!' She adds, 'It's like I went into the room, they gave me the anesthetic, and all of a sudden something's gone that I will never, ever get back'" (Kushner 1997, 61). Wanda coped with her grief by leading a support group for men with HIV. Kushner narrates more of Wanda's story:

> She told the members her reason for joining: "I had an abortion and I feel like there's a little part of me missing or that I took a little something away from the world." By running the group, she gave something back. In the group, Wanda came face to face with people's grief and loss, as well as her own. Although her abortion losses caused her great pain, she did not shy away from experiencing those feelings again. . . . She believes that her grief may indeed ebb someday. But, she notes, "That's not what I'm looking for." Wanda is more interested in accepting her abortions and feeling the grief they have brought than in dulling her pain. (Kushner 1997, 63)

Another woman, Dana, began to work through her grief even before she got her abortion, by establishing a relationship with her fetus. "I thought it was a girl, I had named her, and . . . I talked to her all the time. The night before [the abortion] I kind of started this process of talking to her and telling her what was going on. And telling her, asking her how she felt about it. This may sound a little strange. And she understood, and she's at peace with it, she wasn't angry. She said to me that we would meet again, and that she will come back in my life someday." During her abortion, Dana said goodbye to her fetus and then started sobbing. "And when I cried, I've never cried as deep before. It was like, the core of my being. And it felt really good to be screaming, to cry, and just be there with all the pain" (Hoshiko 1993, 109). *For Wanda and Dana, grief appears as an embodied realization that they have lost something, not only of private, personal significance, but of broader human significance.* Grief provides them with access to a moral truth that they desire to know, and in light of which they desire to live—the truth about how precious or vulnerable or difficult or tragic human life is. *Grief contributes to their understanding of the moral dimension of their abortions.*

Guilt

In addition to grief, many women feel guilt about their abortions.[4] Some feel guilt because they believe that they are killing or have killed a "child." One Catholic woman, Annika, felt guilt because, "'There was this little life that depended on me to grow. And I was just going to toss it. The fragility and helplessness and dependency really were making it problematic for me.'" After her abortion Annika was convinced that she had violated God's will and deserved to be punished. She could not bring herself to return to church. Then one evening, "she heard 'a gentle voice.' She explains, 'It was clear to me that it was Jesus. All it said was, "Come to me." I started crying.' She fell asleep and woke up Sunday morning to find the same thing again." So she went back to church. The entire service spoke to her with the voice of forgiveness, and she was released from a lot of her guilt (Kushner 1997, 153).

Other women feel guilt because, even though they disagree with their church's stance on the morality of abortion, they cannot eradicate church teachings from their minds. Some feel brainwashed by the churches in which they were raised, and they believe that part of their spiritual task is to arrive at more autonomous judgments about their abortions. Kushner narrates the story of Abigail. After a second abortion, Abigail was overcome by the thought that God was going to punish her.

> Shocked to find herself having such thoughts, Abigail says she "had to reconsider my beliefs." She adds that she "evaluated how much I wanted to buy into a fear-driven religious system that seemed to have invaded my mind without my being conscious of it." She eventually succeeded in removing these ideas from her mind and says, "I now do not consider abortion a sin and feel sorry for those who torment themselves by that thought. I think the whole punishment ideology professed by a religious right is so manipulative and unneeded, considering everything else stressful that is caused by abortion." (Kushner 1997, 145)

Stories like these help us to realize that thoughtful, decent people disagree about the morality of abortion. People will disagree accordingly about whether guilt feelings can contribute to a sound moral understanding of one's abortion or whether, instead, they embody inauthentic, imposed-from-the-outside moral misunderstandings.

The Role of Feelings in Moral Deliberations

An ad for a feminist health care clinic reads, "NO WOMAN SHOULD EVER HAVE TO FEEL GUILTY FOR HAVING AN ABORTION." Some women who have their abortions at feminist clinics do so because they believe that abortion is an act of little or no moral significance, and they want to go to a health care facility where they can count on people to agree with them. Bernice was perturbed by what she took to be pressure to feel guilty about her abortion. Workers at the clinic that she went to "'wanted me to talk to a counselor. I was like, "No, I just need the operation. I don't have any doubts or questions. I don't need whatever you're trying to give me."'" Bernice adds, 'People at times made me feel strange because I wasn't questioning myself, because I wasn't saying, "Is it a life? Should I do this?" I was just, "I'm pregnant. I need an abortion." Bernice says slowly, 'I think I'm supposed to feel guilty and horrified, like I'm bad. But I don't feel that way, because what was right for me was having an abortion'" (Kushner 1997, 143).

Other women, including feminists, resent it when staff appear to white-wash the moral seriousness of abortion. Kushner presents Brittany: "'I didn't like the way they were talking to me.' They told her, 'It's a fetus' and 'a tissue,' not 'a baby,' the term Brittany prefers.... Smacking her hands together, she imitates how the clinic workers implied, 'There's nothing wrong with what you're doing.' She did not find their method reassuring and says, 'There wasn't really an opening for me to have an opinion. It was like, "This is the way it is."'... "'I think they were used to having to reassure people about it'" (Kushner 1997, 58). Some women report feeling chastised by feminist abortion providers for thinking that their fetuses are more than "just a collection of cells and da-da-da-da-da" (Kushner 1997, 148; see also McDonnell 1984, 34, 47). In a sense that we could finesse if we were so inclined, it may be true that no woman should ever *have* to feel guilty for having an abortion. But what if a woman already feels this way? *It is more respectful and compassionate to help women who feel ambiguous or partly at fault over their abortions to explore their moral emotions with an appropriate person than to imply that they should feel stupid, immature, or even guilty (unfeminist) for feeling guilty.*

Still, the matter is never simple, for there are many ways that one can go wrong in feeling guilt.[5] It is difficult to sort these out, and beyond the scope of this chapter to try. I would argue, in general terms, that it is not morally good to feel guilt over an act that is not, in one's soul-searching moral judgment, wrong. One ought not simply to dismiss communal moral standards as bogus, but neither ought one to be dominated by authorities with whom one has good reason to disagree. One ought not to feel guilt for acting in a way that one community judges to be wrong, when one has determined, through a discernment process involving members of other communities, that acting in that way is right. It should be noted, however, that most often when we do things that are right, we do things that are only *on balance* right or best. We do things that uphold one good while at the same time neglecting other goods. Feeling guilt may be a way of acknowledging the goods neglected or the morally mixed nature of a given choice; however, nearly all of our moral choices are impure in this way, and there are limits to the human ability to deal with impurity and ambiguity.

One can go wrong in feeling guilt by feeling it too often, too destructively, or for too long. We could perhaps identify a virtue that orders feelings of guilt—to use Aristotle's language, a disposition to feel it at the right times, with respect to the right acts, for the right end, in the right way, and so on (Aristotle 1985, 1106b, 17–24). Determining what constitutes the right kind and amount of guilt in a given situation is the work of practical wisdom. For religious believers it is also the work of prayer, the reception of grace, and the practice of religious virtue. All I can do here is to suggest that we ought not to dismiss feelings of guilt as always inauthentic, slavish, obsessively self-lacerating, or unproductive. Guilt feelings *can* be an indication that we have violated our own moral

standards or those of a community that matters to us. We may upon reflection wish to repudiate these standards, or we may judge that it was necessary to violate one standard in order to uphold another. But the fact that we appear to have violated a standard is important information for those who seek to avoid self-deception (see G. Taylor 1985).

Many women who obtain abortions experience grief and guilt (in addition to other emotions). These are painful emotions, and most people are inclined to avoid pain. Yet many women like Wanda, Dana, Annika, and Brittany choose to face this pain. They choose to undergo the grief and guilt that arise within them, rather than trying to distract themselves from these feelings. They do so, I believe, because they intuit that something good might come of this encounter. *It appears that well-formed feelings of grief and guilt can register features of an abortion event and its consequences that might otherwise be missed.* Grief and guilt help some women to acknowledge what they themselves, on some level of awareness, regard as the moral import of the deliberate destruction of fetal life. Feeling these and other feelings throughout the deliberative process, and reflecting as lucidly as possible upon them, helps some women to become more transparent to themselves, more fully present to themselves in their decision making. It helps them to understand what they are doing—or have already done— on every relevant level, and thus to make decisions that are powerfully their own. . . .

Once we admit that emotions can sometimes enhance understanding and autonomy, we are led to ask whether girls and women *ought* therefore to experience certain emotions in choosing for or against abortion. An ethic of virtue seems to require delineating the feelings that girls and women who are considering abortion ought to experience, and in what manner, in order to do well at being human and at being the particular people they are.[6] Given that most implanted human fetuses have the potential to become persons, and persons have considerable moral standing, it is prima facie morally fitting to regard developing fetuses with a degree of *something like* the respect and compassion that we extend toward persons. It is thus prima facie an indication of good human functioning to experience *some* emotional pain in choosing to end the life of a fetus. However, it is not appropriate to say categorically that a woman who feels emotionally unmoved at the thought of aborting her fetus must be in poor working order as a moral agent. Nor is it possible to specify categorically in any detail what she or any other woman ought to feel in deciding whether or not to abort. Making such judgments requires knowing a great deal about who a particular woman is, how she regards herself and the goods that are at stake for her, how she values her fetus and how she arrived at this evaluation, how she understands the responsibilities of her other relationships, and so on.

Those of us who seek answers to the problem of abortion are well-advised to start by listening to some of the people who have faced this decision. As soon as I began to ponder women's abortion stories, I found myself caring for these women to a surprising extent. I felt affection for them, and I drew close to them in my imagination, as one does with certain characters in a good novel. I extended myself into a fragment of their lives and began to glimpse their worlds partly from their perspectives, informed by their emotion-laden memories, dreams, longings, and fears. I felt their vulnerability, their need to be loved, the horror of their abusive relationships, the seductive power of their addictions and their temptations to self-hatred and suicide, the devastation of their poverty, and the constraints posed by so many other features of their lives—features that are almost never noticed, let along discussed when scholars scrutinize the morality of abortion. As I experienced all of these things, abstract ethical questions about the requirements of moral goodness slipped quietly from my mind. These questions did not cease to be of import, but their import began to re-appear in particular, personal ways, against the horizon of particular women's relational lives. It was only then, when these questions arose in relation to a whole range of other questions about the well-being of these strong and wise and fragile and injured women and the other people in their worlds, that I was in a position to reach meaningful moral insight (see Lauritzen 1994, 1998). . . .

To conclude this section, we ought in our reflections on the morality of abortion to be governed by, among other things, respect and compassion for girls and women. To focus on the matter of informed consent, respect and compassion require that we ponder what it is for a given woman to understand an act of abortion and its possible consequences for her life. Understanding the act may include understanding its moral dimensions, and reaching moral understanding may include feeling and reflecting upon certain moral emotions like grief and guilt. If we care about girls and women as moral agents—if we want them to have the experience of functioning well—we will care that they have the opportunity to engage such emotions in productive ways, in the company of wise and gentle people. Where women believe that fetal life has some moral value, we might help them to acknowledge this value, along with the other values that are at stake in their particular decisions, in a bodily-resonant way, in order that they might sort through these values with honesty, integrity, and growing clarity. Such sorting can both reflect and contribute to autonomy.[7] . . .

Autonomy and Relationality

The Judy that I knew at 25 was like a lot of people whose senses of self are fundamentally relational. She lived most of the unfolding moments of her life in more or less vague awareness of the imagined or real perspectives, thoughts, desires, and feelings of others, and she experienced the world partly as these contributions led her to experience it. Her mental-emotional life comprised a kind of community, the many members of which existed both as individuals outside of her and as resonant voices within her memory and imagination. Generally they remained at the periphery of her consciousness until their contribution became relevant. Then they would enter into her perceiving, thinking, or feeling, sometimes gently, sometimes naggingly, sometimes as strangers or well-known enemies, and sometimes as welcome familiars. Contributors to this conversation offered opinions, gave advice, moved Judy, delighted and saddened her, reminded, reprimanded, and sought to shame her, engaged in serious dialogue, and provoked heated debate. Judy's own voice, the one that seemed to her to be the dominant and organizing voice at the center of the conversation, sometimes made itself known as a voice of suspicion or resistance. Sometimes it came into prominence as a desire to quiet the chatter. Sometimes Judy's voice emerged as a lavish assemblage of relevant insights from her own and others' experiences, so that this assemblage just was, for Judy, her way of encountering the world (Cates 1991, 1997; Keller 1986; C. Taylor 1989, 35–40). . . .

Judy's inner life appeared to me to be well-organized. She was a series of shifting relational connections, but she was a reasonably coherent and stable series. Her life was full of affect, spontaneity, and creativity, yet it was focused and effective in the world. It had a great deal of narrative unity, even though Judy, like the rest of us, had to compose this unity day by day, especially in accounting for major challenges and disappointments. The apparent unity to Judy's character and story enticed those who loved her into an encounter with the secret behind or beneath the unity. To stand in relation to Judy was to encounter within her a mysterious, unfathomable depth, and a capacity hidden in that depth that enabled her to determine, to some extent, how the various contributions to her perceiving, thinking, and feeling assembled into her unique engagements with the world. As a Christian, Judy might have related this capacity to the workings of God's grace. It remains a mystery, in any case, how the exercise of this capacity of self-determination, this personal power, related to the causal forces that were exercised on every aspect of her moral agency by the persons and events of her past. Judy's power to be uniquely Judy presented itself as a result of, and in terms of, these contributions, yet also as something that caused these contributions to coalesce in certain ways rather than others.

There were a few people who were so important to Judy that she allowed them to play a substantial role in the constitution of her experience and, thus, in the exercise of her moral agency. (There were no doubt many others who entered more surreptitiously into her ways of perceiving, thinking, and feeling.) Her way of construing events, for example, was affected by a usually vague but sometimes acute awareness of how her parents would construe them. Judy slipped in and out of (what she imagined to be) her mother's perspective, her father's perspective, her perspective on their perspectives, and her own,

separate perspective on the events themselves. Her thinking about what was going on in her encounters with other people gave weight to what her friend, Sara, had said about various relationships in the past. As Judy continued to update her opinions and evaluations, she listened to internal assertions, questions, and criticisms that seemed sometimes to be attached to Sara's voice or face but seemed, at other times, to arise and persist independently of any awareness of Sara. Judy's ways of being moved emotionally were shaped by the ways that she had observed Don being moved. She found herself wanting not only what she wanted before she fell in love with Don, but also what Don wanted, precisely because he wanted it—although it also occurred to her that Don sometimes wanted things that she did not experience to be good for her or for him, which is to say that her own, separate desires created resistance. It is artificial to divide things up like this, as if each person influenced only one aspect of Judy's agency, but this provides an initial glimpse into what it is to function as an extended self (see Cates 1991, 1997).

Judy was remarkably receptive and attuned to others, yet there was something more to her, an irreducible remainder, a power capable of noticing and altering at least some of the influences that others had on her. I wonder, looking back, if it was this unspeakable power that Laura was looking for in our conversation with Judy. Laura had the impression that Judy's way of construing the prospect of bringing her fetus to term had been virtually consumed by Don's view of the matter, as if Judy's agency had been overpowered by Don's. It was doubtful that Don had manipulated Judy into feeling that his perspective was the only one worth considering, that his needs would automatically take priority, and that Judy was confused and could not trust her own feelings about the situation; Don is too humble for that. I imagine that, from Laura's point of view, it was more likely that Judy had wanted so much to please Don and protect him from injury that, after receiving his reaction to her news, all she could see were red flags. All she could feel was Don's desire to stop this racing train (the pregnancy) or jump off as soon as possible.

It is appropriate in exercising the virtue of compassion to allow oneself to be drawn into an encounter with some of the powers that constitute another's moral agency. It is fitting to experience those powers as partly one's own. When one allows oneself to see with a common set of eyes, one perceives what the other perceives with such force that one cannot easily look away. When one reasons with a common mind, one is inclined to give the other's reasoning as much of a hearing as one ordinarily gives one's own. Some of the other's reasoning may turn out to be confused, but because it comes to mind initially through a participation in the thinking of another, it is nevertheless taken seriously and not simply dismissed. When one experiences emotions within the frame of a common body, the other's terror can cause one's own heart to pound, and one can begin to understand partly in this pounding the meaning that the terror holds for the other. Yet this is only one moment in the work of virtuous compassion. Even as one participates in the perceiving, thinking, and feeling of another, one must have access to perceptions, thoughts, and feelings that one experiences as distinctively one's own, for these are what keep the self from collapsing into the other and thus becoming ineffectual in providing perspective, comfort, and aid.

In my view, Judy retained a sense of her own separateness. She was not simply a sponge for Don's terror. She had not become, like Don, incapacitated by that terror. Rather, what she experienced in co-suffering caused her to reform the desires that were previously distinctively her own. What she originally regarded as desirable, she could no longer regard as such, knowing what would likely happen to Don, and thus by extension to her, if she were to carry her fetus to term. Here we begin to see, however, how difficult it is to understand what autonomy amounts to for selves that are constituted through reciprocal movements in and out of other selves. Judy seemed to be "free from controlling interferences by others and from personal limitations that prevent choice" (Faden and Beauchamp 1986, 8). She seemed to be free to enter into a state of co-suffering with Don in the hope of showing him compassion. Yet in her co-suffering, she shared Don's desire to flee the prospect of parenthood, and this shared desire was so compelling that one wonders if any other desire could have pulled strongly enough in any other direction to make a difference in her deliberations. At what point does the beloved's desire become a controlling influence for the lover? Many women habitually put others' needs before their own, so that they make it their business to intuit the needs of others and seek above all else to meet them. *At what point does sensitivity to other people's desires compromise a person's autonomy?*

What, exactly, is the capacity or the power that we are looking for when we ask someone to make an autonomous choice? One author who seeks to articulate a new paradigm for informed consent puts forward an old and familiar conception of autonomy as involving "independence," "self-direction," "rationality," and "a developed sense of self" (Switankowsky 1998, 11). When one attends to the reflections of girls and women who are pondering abortion, one finds in many of them—or perhaps one finds oneself looking for—a power that cannot quite be captured by these terms. This is a power that sets them apart from others, but reveals itself especially in the ways that they negotiate the responsibilities of their relationships. This is a power that provides direction, but mainly by functioning like a rudder through the waves of ongoing relational exchanges. This is a power to reason through what goodness requires, but in a way that is always duly impassioned, informed by emotion. This may be a power that makes it possible for someone to "decide for him/herself precisely what s/he will endure based on his/her inner self" or "core" (Switankowsky 1998, 13), but it is also a power that comes into its own through increasingly reflective interactions with others.

The power that I am pointing to is decidedly not a power to escape the influence that others have on who we are. It appears, however, that most of us have a capacity to become increasingly aware of at least some of these influences. We have a capacity to become more deliberate about how these influences shape our character and our actions. Yet even our caring about the sorts of persons that we are— even our efforts to become more aware of the factors that are forming us, and our efforts to transform ourselves in light of this awareness—occur or fail to occur to us on account of the influences of others that have accumulated since our earliest days of consciousness (Taylor 1989, 35). It is only in being with others who regard us as persons that we become persons. It is only in choosing to spend our time with persons who share our commitment to being good that we find much success in becoming more deliberately ourselves (Cates 1997). The roots of our social formation lie much deeper than is ordinarily assumed.

In what follows, I move beyond the way that Judy's self presented itself to me—as autonomous and yet at the same time relationally constituted. I present some other women's ways of being selves-in-relation. Paying attention to the experiences of ordinary women and trying to imagine how they could become more self-governing without ceasing to share their selves intimately with others promises to help medical ethics move beyond overly simple, individualistic conceptions of autonomy.

Listening to Other Women

When one listens to a woman's abortion story, it is common to encounter a self that is composed of actual or imagined contributions from the hidden and more visible past of the woman herself, from the histories of her relationships with parents, friends, partners, and other intimates, from the anticipated looks of neighbors and strangers, from the teachings of religious figures or the convictions of religious communities, from popular media images and arguments, cultural ideologies, and more. It is common to encounter a self that gets a lot of the inspiration and direction it needs in listening and responding to this crowd, whether in feeling a surge of resistance to what is said or in recognizing an opinion as expressive of its own deepest insights. Yet one also encounters a self that struggles to establish or defend boundaries, to keep the crowd from overrunning its inmost desires and thoughts. Or one encounters a self that already has a power to engage the inner and outer crowd, at least to some extent, with a critical ear and a commanding voice.

Consider the reflections of 25-year-old Sarah, who feels "like a walking slaughter-house" as she decides in favor of a second abortion.

> Well, the pros for having the baby are all the admiration that you would get from being a single woman, alone, martyr, struggling, having the adoring love of this beautiful Gerber baby. Just more

of a home life than I have had in a long time, and that basically was it, which is pretty fantasyland. It is not very realistic. Cons against having the baby: it was going to hasten what is looking to be the inevitable end of the relationship with the man I am presently with. I was going to have to go on welfare. My parents were going to hate me for the rest of my life. I was going to lose a really good job that I have. I would lose a lot of independence. Solitude. And I would have to be put in a position of asking help from a lot of people a lot of the time. Con against having the abortion is having to face up to the guilt. And pros for having the abortion are I would be able to handle my deteriorating relation with [the father] with a lot more capability and a lot more responsibility for him and for myself. I would not have to go through the realization that for the next twenty-five years of my life I would be punishing myself for being foolish enough to get pregnant again and forcing myself to bring up a kid just because I did this. Having to face the guilt of a second abortion seemed like not exactly—well, exactly the lesser of the two evils, but also the one that would pay off for me personally in the long run because, by looking at why I am pregnant again and subsequently have decided to have a second abortion, I have to face up to some things about myself. (Gilligan 1982, 91–92)

There are many fascinating features of Sarah's description. What I wish to highlight here are the multiple, competing perspectives that eventually converge into a particular way of looking at herself and her situation that Sarah experiences to be *her* way. Sarah's perspective is relationally composed, yet there is a part of her that is beginning to make more reflective contributions to this composition. The center of her moral agency comes partially into view as a power that assesses capabilities, confronts limits—including moral limits—experiences guilt and the inclination to probe its meaning, feels a growing sense of responsibility, and makes connections between these things.

Sumi Hoshiko records a story of another woman whose mature moral agency begins to emerge only after years of painful struggle. Donna "was around a lot of drinking and fighting and arguing" from the day she was born (Hoshiko 1993, 113). Living with her mother and her mother's many boyfriends had a profound impact on Donna's power to imagine, desire, and seek a good life. "She [Donna's mother] had two other kids. I call them illegitimate, because one man, he was married, and she had a child. And the other man, he would just come by drunk and take her money and leave. But I always said I was not going to do this. And everything I said I wasn't going to do, I did it" (114). She tells of her first serious relationship:

> Somehow we started living together. We had a real heavy sexual relationship. Eventually it started getting to the point where I was losing myself. I thought he was so real. . . . So then he started throwing abusive words at me and everything. But I was past the line, I was in love or whatever, because he seemed to show some consideration or compassion that I never felt before. . . . Every other weekend I was moving out. He was putting me out, we was fighting. Because he made me leave because he wanted to see another woman. And he would mess with my girlfriends and everything. And nothing never clicked, you know, why don't you leave him alone?. . . It was a destructive relationship. . . . Because the home I came from, all I know was fighting, fucking, making up. You can scratch that out. But that's what it was like. You fight this minute, you do the thing, and then you make up. I would go stay with him, so then when he would get tired of me, would send me back home to my mother. So it was just back and forth, living out of bags. (115)

Donna married this man, and the relationship continued to deteriorate. She details her spiral into drug and alcohol addiction, murderous thoughts, prostitution, and crack houses. In the midst of this horror, she discovered an unwanted pregnancy. In a way, the decision was simple for her because the pregnancy presented itself as nothing more than an inconvenience. "Insanity told me I couldn't get pregnant. But when I did get caught, it's like: Well, that's what the abortion clinic is for" (121). Yet the decision to end the pregnancy was not fully hers because at that time she was compelled in all that she did by multiple, interlocking addictions to various people, processes, and substances, and she could not quiet these controlling

voices enough to consider how she, Donna, really felt about being pregnant or getting an abortion.

Donna began to turn the corner, after her abortion, when she went to live with her aunt, who introduced a different voice into Donna's self-awareness. "She was a positive woman. She said, 'Donna, go on. You can go on. You don't have to stay on at this. Set your mind.' She wouldn't down me, like my mother did. She wouldn't put her feet on me and keep washing me in it. She said, 'Today, start anew. You don't have to look back, just start now.' I really appreciate that woman today" (125). With the help of this aunt and other people who were committed to recovery, Donna began to experience within herself a power to submit to certain influences more than others, and to grow stronger in self-affirmation under these influences. She began to feel like "a real woman" who was capable of making her own decisions, most notably the decision to seek the right sort of support (126).

Drug and alcohol addiction complicate questions about autonomy, but it is important to see that this does not set Donna's story utterly apart from the stories of other women. As Donna's story reveals, addictions to abusive relationships can be part of the same tangled web. Moreover, many women who are not addicted to the men in their lives—and have relatively violence-free relationships—are nonetheless in the habit of turning to these men to tell them what to think, want, and do. Many women feel unable to say "no" to their lovers' demands for spontaneous and constraint-free sexual contact, fearing that if they refuse, these men will seek this pleasure elsewhere. The power we are looking and hoping for in those who are pondering abortion includes the power to experience the relational self as more than its relationship with one man. As Donna's story shows, however, the power to imagine one's life taking alternative relational forms may arise only under the preferred influence of yet other relationships.

A third woman, Dana, was "clear as a bell" about wanting a baby, but when she became pregnant, this clarity gave way to a kind of inner cacophony. To read her detailed account of how she arrived at her decision is to read the way that her thoughts, perceptions, and desires were formed and repeatedly reformed by reading and rereading the reactions of several people, focusing especially on her partner

Jim. "That first week it was like, 'My god, first, we're not ready to have it, and Jim probably doesn't want to have it, so I'm going to have to go through an abortion. But I don't want to!' And that thought would make me ill, physically ill" (Hoshiko 1993, 104). Then Dana met with some other friends and encountered another set of perspectives. "My best friend was pregnant at the time. And she had her two-year-old. And I remember it was that day that I got support from a few people . . . to not only think about not having it, but to open my mind to think about having it. I remember that day very distinctly, my thoughts shifting, opening to more possibilities" (104). After extended joint counseling, Jim and Dana decided to have the baby. "We agreed after weeks of thinking and planning, and questioning and crying, and going through our stuff. It's like I felt like we both agreed to do it, so I felt it was clean. We both believed in it, and that's the only way I would have felt good about it. Because it felt like we were doing what we wanted to be doing" (107).

But then Jim changed his mind, which was devastating for Dana. She made a decision, in anger, to have an abortion. It is as if the anger was necessary to push Jim far enough away from her to give her the moral space to make her own decision—even though her decision rested largely on the realization that Jim did not want to have a baby and she did not want to "do anything with anyone that they [didn't] want to do" (108). Dana's anger softened as she arrived at the clinic and her feelings of loss asserted themselves; it subsided further during the procedure when Jim began to cry.

> I've seen him cry before, but he was choking and
> gasping and sobbing. And it made me feel so good,
> that he was feeling some pain over it. So we were
> there crying together for a little while. Because we
> did, once, [feel] we were going to have it. So I was
> hoping some depth of feeling about it was there. So
> it was nice to see him letting himself feel it. He was
> also probably crying about the pain that he saw me
> in. I was just really glad he was crying like that; then
> I felt like I wasn't alone with it. (109)

It seems that Jim had considerable influence over Dana's feelings. Dana shifted from anger to grief to a sense of comfort and even satisfaction at least partly in response to what she perceived Jim to be doing and feeling. I would argue, however, that Dana's unique moral agency reveals itself, to some extent, in the form of insistent, mostly painful feelings that register within her what is really important to her, and in her desire to pay attention to these feelings. Dana appears to be most comfortable with her painful feelings when she perceives that Jim feels the same way, but she does not wait for Jim to share her feelings before feeling and attending to them herself.

Dana's relationship with Jim eventually came to an end. It is instructive to hear her final words concerning what she is discovering in her new relationship:

> You know something I'm noticing in this
> relationship, and comparing it? It's like I started to
> realize in the last couple months as we're together,
> how really special I am. I don't need to be with
> a man where I need to either convince him of
> anything or be tugging at . . . there's things I want,
> and either I'm going to be able to get them or not.
> Everything's a process, but being in this relationship
> now, I'm getting everything I want, without having
> to . . . it's not like I'm pulling teeth. I'm just in the
> relationship, enjoying it. (112)

As I interpret her, Dana is coming into the exercise of an increasingly autonomous moral agency, not only by attending to her own feelings and the moral lessons of those feelings, but also by attending more fundamentally to what she wants—apart from what the main man in her life wants. This separate, intentional desiring enables her to imagine and choose to be in a relationship in which her most important needs are affirmed and met with relative ease. She will probably still make many of the choices in her life in a way that depends on first reading the reactions of her partner and her other friends; yet she will be able to bring something more—something that is uniquely her/s—to that reading.

Every woman, indeed every person, is different in the way that she composes and understands what she calls her self. But Judy and the other women to whom we have listened have a few things in common. Their selves appear at the interstices of relationships, yet the way in which their selves appear is determined to some degree by a power (however inchoate) that is, in the final analysis, distinctly and irreducibly their own. In my view, these women and many others who have shared their stories are in the process of discovering and beginning to affirm within themselves a depth dimension that is both more and less than a power of independence. It is a power to become uniquely themselves by becoming more attentive to and careful about their ways of being in relation. These women and others are developing a power of self-direction, but this power does not present itself, as Switankowsky and others suggest, as a power to formulate and stick to "a solid, clearly known set of life plans and goals" (Switankowsky 1998, 3), if the implication is that such plans are set and adhered to independently, without also undergoing re-consideration and reformulation within the dynamics of ongoing relational exchanges. The power of self-direction presents itself more as a power to move with growing trust and confidence down a life path that unfolds day by day, in sometimes surprising ways. These women and others are discovering a power to hold relatively loosely to their selves and their plans, especially in times of crisis. Finally, these women and others are beginning to realize a practical rationality that makes them discerning decision makers and effective actors, but their reasoning is consistently informed by the insights of desire and emotion. . . .

Relationality and Informed Consent

Recall that an authorization amounts to an informed consent, in Faden and Beauchamp's view, "if a patient or subject with (1) substantial understanding and (2) in substantial absence of control by others (3) intentionally (4) authorizes a professional (to do [an intervention])" (Faden and Beauchamp 1986, 278). We are presently considering what it is for a woman or a girl who experiences herself to be a relational self, with a more or less open and extensible moral agency, to make an autonomous abortion decision. In their discussion of condition (2), Faden and Beachamp focus on the absence of control by others. Autonomous acts are substantially "noncontrolled" in the sense that they are "free of—that is, independent of, not governed by—controls on the person, especially controls presented by others that rob the

person of self-directedness" (Faden and Beauchamp 1985, 256). The authors have in mind acts on the part of others that go beyond rational persuasion (which is never, in their view, substantially controlling), and take the form of coercion (which is always substantially controlling) or manipulation (which can be, but is not always substantially controlling). In an act of coercion, "one party intentionally and successfully influences another by presenting a credible threat of unwanted and avoidable harm so severe that the person is unable to resist acting to avoid it" (339). In an act of manipulation, one party intentionally and successfully influences another "by noncoercively altering the actual choices available to the person or by nonpersuasively altering the other's perception of those choices" (354).

We cannot explore these definitions or their implications in depth, but it is important to note that the authors' conception of "controlled" decision making reflects a picture of the other as one who is clearly separate from the self and who exercises an intentional influence on the self from a position outside of the self (256). Substantially controlled decision making proceeds on the basis of what an external "influence agent" wills for the self, rather than on the basis of what the self wills for itself, from within itself. Typical means of control are irresistible threat, intimidation, and deceit (258). Although this sort of controlling behavior is common and can injure women who are considering abortion, what we are concerned with in this chapter are situations in which the other may have no intention to coerce or manipulate, yet his or her voice sounds so loudly within a woman's own thinking—his or her desires have so much pull within the frame of her extended self—that they threaten nonetheless to become substantially controlling influences. A lot more work needs to be done to clarify what it is to be partly constituted as a self by the reception of another without being controlled by the other's presence.[8]. . .

When it comes to making an abortion decision, many girls and women deliberate within the tension of multiple relational bonds. Because they value the experience of mutual belonging, they commonly allow their loved ones to exercise a formative influence on their ways of construing options, imagining scenarios, considering interests, and sorting through feelings that pull in different directions. To help some women make autonomous choices, one may need primarily to help them become more aware of the shape of their relational self-constitution—and more aware of what they want these selves to look like (even though they are not ultimately "in control" of the product). It can be helpful to ask them if they have discussed their decisions with the people who are most important to them and thereby to invite them to reflect on whether and why they may be privileging one perspective over another and giving more weight to certain desires than others. Where it is not possible or advisable for women to have actual discussions with relevant parties, imagined discussions can be beneficial. Being encouraged, for example, to converse with their fetuses before and after aborting them has helped many women toward greater self-awareness and autonomy (Gardner 1986).[9]

Conclusion

In sum, caring for girls and women who are considering abortion may involve encouraging some of them to become more conscious and discerning about the (welcome and unwelcome) ways that the people in their lives are at work inside their hearts and minds, shaping the exercise of their moral agencies. It may be impossible for certain women not to be swayed above all else by the desires of friends, lovers, or husbands. What is important, in my view, is that women be encouraged to make decisions that reflect a growing understanding of this influence and its power.

What this means for abortion providers is that there is no substitute for respect, compassion, and practical wisdom when it comes to treating girls and women in ways that are likely to enhance their autonomy and their overall well-being. Each woman is in a unique situation, the complexities of which we can only begin to appreciate, and each woman emerges out of the thick of these complexities as a unique agent. As Aristotle says, the decision regarding what, finally, to say and do rests with the perception of a fine moral agent (Aristotle 1985, 1109b22, 1126b2, 1143b5). Thinking of the cultivation of virtue as part of the point of one's work is more of a gift

than a burden, in my view, but that does not mean that the work is easy. . . .

I am not sure, at this point, whether Judy was able to offer a substantially informed consent to her abortion, although I trust, when all is said and done, that she was. Perhaps I extend this trust as a gesture of care toward someone whose explanation of her decision was not obviously confused or deceitful, and whose complex inner life could not possibly be made transparent to me within a single evening's conversation, even though the conversation was situated within a history of friendship. Judy probably had a substantial understanding of the abortion and its likely consequences, even though her understanding was hindered by a reluctance to confront certain of the moral and emotional meanings of her abortion. And she probably made her decision in a way that was substantially uncontrolled, even though the power that Don's emotions had on her deliberations was considerable. I take it that Judy chose to allow Don's feelings to become partly her own so that she could make a decision partly out of compassion for him. It may be that in their case, within the hiddenness of their marital relationship, Don's vulnerability to psychological debilitation and even collapse really was the most significant moral consideration. In any case, I continue to find Judy's story provocative and the act of attending to it instructive. Her experience raises profound questions for all who wish to promote women's well-being.[10]

ENDNOTES

1. It was in reflecting on Judy's story, and then turning my attention to the stories of other women, which turned out to be in important respects like Judy's, that I first began to realize that something was lacking in traditional concepts of informed consent. To some extent, I had to employ familiar formulations of this concept from the start in order to interpret the relationship between actual women's experiences and medical ethics; yet I sought to hold on to these formulations loosely, regarding them as provisional, so that I would be able to alter aspects of them that distorted, rather than illuminated, women's experiences. My method of presentation reflects my method of inquiry.
2. I use "care" as a synthetic concept that refers to both respect and compassion much as John P. Reeder, Jr. uses "agape" as a synthetic concept that refers to both justice and care. I am grateful to Prof. Reeder for helping me, in conversation, to

shift from a deontological framework for thinking about respect to a eudemonistic one.

3. I cannot develop here an account of what it is for an emotion to be "on target," but Cates (1997) addresses the issue, primarily with respect to the emotional dimension of the virtue of compassion. Cates (1996) addresses the issue with respect to the emotion of anger. Cates (forthcoming) also offers a descriptive analysis of Thomas Aquinas's view of this issue with respect to desires for food, drink, and sexual contact (many parts of which I do not endorse). For the purpose of this chapter, I simply assume an Aristotelian-Thomistic theory of virtue and emotion, according to which determining whether or not an emotion is appropriate in a given situation is a matter of perception or discernment, and is to be arrived at through the exercise of (among other things) practical wisdom or prudence, within the context of truth-seeking and character-forming friendships and communities.

4. For a philosophical analysis of the relation between guilt and shame, see G. Taylor (1985).

5. There are also many ways that one can go wrong in trying to address another person's feelings of guilt, but I cannot discuss these.

6. I assume that it is possible, at least some of the time, to summon the emotional dimensions of respect and compassion, and feelings of grief and guilt, when they do not arise spontaneously. This assumption rests on a theory of the emotions that I develop elsewhere (Cates 1997). I argue that emotions are best understood as intentional (object-directed) desires that are accompanied by feelings of pleasure or pain, and that emotions can often be evoked or changed by forming or reforming the intentions that partly constitute them.

7. In my view, acknowledging significant fetal value and feeling some measure of guilt over the destruction of this value does not settle the question of whether abortion is, all things considered, morally the best course of action in a particular situation.

8. The issue of guilt, treated earlier, reappears at this point because emotions can be modes of registering other people' attitudes toward us. The goal of relational autonomy must include the achievement of emotion-laden understandings of moral matters, but *as* persons who are always more than what we take others' moral attitudes toward us to be.

9. William LaFleur, who presented a week-long seminar in 1999 at the University of Iowa on "Religion and Biomedical Ethics in Japan," has written extensively on Japanese rituals that concern the relation between women with their aborted fetuses. His work and that of several others, including Helen Hardacre, have stimulated intense debate. See LaFleur (1992), Hardacre (1997), and the several essays on this topic in the *Journal of the American Academy of Religion* 67/4 (December 1999).

10. I want to thank Thomas A. Lewis, John P. Reeder, Jr., Paul Lauritzen, Gene Outka, Ruth L. Smith, and Joan

Henriksen Hellyer for helpful comments on earlier drafts of this chapter. I want also to thank Gene Outka for a 1999 seminar that he presented at the University of Iowa on "The Ethics of Love and the Problem of Abortion," as well as for the discussion surrounding that seminar.

REFERENCES

Appelbaum, Paul S., Charles W. Lidz, and Alan Meisel. 1987. *Informed Consent: Legal Theory and Clinical Practice.* New York: Oxford University Press.

Aristotle. 1985. *Nicomachean Ethics,* trans. Terence Irwin. Indianapolis, Ind.: Hackett Publishing Company.

Blustein, Jeffrey. 1993. The Family in Medical Decisionmaking. *Hastings Center Report* 23/3: 6–13.

Brien, Joanna, and Ida Fairbairn. 1996. *Pregnancy and Abortion Counselling.* London: Routledge.

Cates, Diana Fritz. 1991. Toward an Ethic of Shared Selfhood. *The Annual of the Society of Christian Ethics,* ed. Diane Yeager, 249–57. Washington, D.C.: Georgetown University Press.

———. 1996. Taking Women's Experience Seriously: Thomas Aquinas and Audre Lorde on Anger. In *Aquinas and Empowerment: Classical Ethics for Ordinary Lives,* ed. G. Simon Harak, S.J., 47–88. Washington, D.C.: Georgetown University Press.

———. 1997. *Choosing to Feel: Virtue, Friendship, and Compassion for Friends.* Notre Dame, Ind.: University of Notre Dame Press.

———. forthcoming. The Virtue of Temperance. In *Essays on the Ethics of St. Thomas Aquinas*, ed. Stephen J. Pope. Washington, D.C.: Georgetown University Press.

Damasio, Antonio R. 1994. *Descartes' Error: Emotion, Reason, and the Human Brain.* New York: G. P. Putnam.

Engstrom, Stephen, and Jennifer Whiting, eds. 1996. *Aristotle, Kant, and the Stoics: Rethinking Happiness and Duty.* Cambridge, U.K.: Cambridge University Press.

Faden, Ruth R., and Tom L. Beauchamp, with Nancy M. P. King. 1986. *A History and Theory of Informed Consent.* New York: Oxford University Press.

Gardner, Joy. 1986. *A Difficult Decision: A Compassionate Book About Abortion.* Trumansburg, N.Y.: The Crossing Press.

Gilligan, Carol. 1982. *In a Different Voice: Psychological Theory and Women's Development.* Cambridge, Mass.: Harvard University Press.

Hardacre, Helen. 1997. *Marketing the Menacing Fetus in Japan.* Berkeley: University of California Press.

Hardwig, John. 1990. What About the Family? *Hastings Center Report* 20/2: 5–10.

Hoshiko, Sumi. 1993. *Our Choices: Women's Personal Decisions About Abortion.* New York: The Haworth Press.

Hursthouse, Rosalind. 1997. Virtue Theory and Abortion. In *Virtue Ethics,* ed. Daniel Statman, 227–44. Washington, D.C.: Georgetown University Press.

Joffee, Carole. 1986. *The Regulation of Sexuality: Experiences of Family Planning Workers.* Philadelphia, Penn.: Temple University Press.

John, Helen J., S.N.D. 1984. Reflections on Autonomy and Abortion. In *Respect and Care in Medical Ethics,* ed. David H. Smith, 277–300. Lanham, Md.: University Press of America.

Kant, Immanuel. 1990. *Foundations of the Metaphysics of Morals,* 2d ed., revised, trans. Lewis White Beck. Englewood Cliffs, N.J.: Prentice Hall.

Keller, Catherine. 1986. *From a Broken Web: Separation, Sexism, and Self. Boston:* Beacon Press.

Kuczewski, Mark G. 1996. Reconceiving the Family: The Process of Consent in Medical Decisionmaking. *Hasting Center Report* 26/2: 30–37.

Kushner, Eve. 1997. *Experiencing Abortion: A Weaving of Women's Words.* New York: Harrington Park Press.

LaFleur, William R. 1992. *Liquid Life: Abortion and Buddhism in Japan.* Princeton, N.J.: Princeton University Press.

Lauritzen, Paul. 1994. Listening to the Different Voices: Toward a More Poetic Bioethics, in *Theological Analyses of the Clinical Encounter,* ed. Gerald P. McKenny and Jonathan R. Sande, 151–70. Dordrecht, The Netherlands: Kluwer Academic Publishers.

_____. 1998. The Knowing Heart: Moral Argument and the Appeal to Experience. *Soundings* 81/1–2: 213–34.

Lorde, Audre. 1984. Eye to Eye: Black Women, Hatred, and Anger. In *Sister Outsider,* 145–75. Trumansburg, N.Y: The Crossing Press.

McDonnell, Kathleen. 1984. *Not an Easy Choice: A Feminist Re-examines Abortion.* Boston: South End Press.

Midgley, Mary. 1986. *Wickedness: A Philosophical Essay.* London: Ark Paperbacks.

Milhaven, J. Giles. 1991. Ethics and Another Knowing of Good and Evil. *The Annual of the Society of Christian Ethics,* ed. Diane Yeager, 237–48. Washington, D.C.: Georgetown University Press.

_____. 1993. *Hadewijch and Her Sisters: Other Ways of Loving and Knowing.* Albany: State University of New York Press.

Nelson, James Lindemann. 1992. Taking Families Seriously. *Hastings Center Report* 22/4: 6–12.

Outka, Gene. 1999. The Ethics of Love and the Problem of Abortion. The Second Annual James C. Spaulding Memorial Lecture, Iowa City, IA, School of Religion.

Reeder, John P., Jr. 2001. Are Care and Justice Distinct Virtues? *Medicine and the Ethics of Care,* ed. Diana Fritz Cates and Paul Lauritzen, 3–38. Washington, D.C.: Georgetown University Press.

Simonds, Wendy. 1991. At an Impasse: Inside an Abortion Clinic. In *Current Research on Occupations and Professions,* vol. 6, ed. Helena Z. Lopata and Judith Levy, 99–115. Greenwich, Conn.: JAI Press.

_____. 1996. *Abortion at Work: Ideology and Practice in a Feminist Clinic.* New Brunswick, N.J.: Rutgers University Press.

Switankowsky, Irene S. 1998. *A New Paradigm for Informed Consent.* Lanham, Md.: University Press of America.

Taylor, Charles. 1985. *Human Agency and Language: Philosophical Papers* 1. Cambridge, U.K.: Cambridge University Press.

_____. 1989. *Sources of the Self: The Making of the Modern Identity. Cambridge,* Mass.: Harvard University Press.

Taylor, Gabriele. 1985. *Pride, Shame, and Guilt: Emotions of Self-Assessment.* Oxford: Clarendon Press.

Thomson, Judith Jarvis. 1997. A Defense of Abortion. In *The Problem of Abortion,* 3rd ed., ed. Susan Dwyer and Joel Feinberg, 75–87. Belmont, Calif.: Wadsworth.

White, Becky Cox. 1994. *Competence to Consent.* Washington, D.C.: Georgetown University Press.

Winn, Denise. 1988. *Experiences of Abortion.* London: Macdonald Optima.

DISCUSSION QUESTIONS:

1. Cates spends a great deal of time setting up the problem she wants to consider, and she does so by describing an evening with two friends, Judy and Laura. Having read the narrative, which character do you find yourself most in sympathy with: Judy, Laura, or Cates herself? Why? What does this sympathy tell you about yourself?

2. After describing Judy's situation, Cates asks a difficult question: what does friendship require of Laura and Cates in this situation? How would a good friend respond to Judy's decision? Would a good friend just listen? Is there room for "tough love" in a friendship? What would you have done for Judy or said to Judy? Why?

3. Cates concludes that "well-formed feelings of grief and guilt can register features of an abortion event and its consequences that might otherwise be missed," (page 435). Do you think this is true? In general, do you think that feelings of grief or guilt help you to see moral situations more clearly, less clearly, or no difference? Why?

4. If I take your car at gunpoint, I cannot rightly keep it. This is because you haven't consented to my having your car. But if you choose to give me your car as a gift, I may rightly keep it. Here you have consented to my having your car. But what about when your choice to give me your car is manipulated or heavily influenced by others? Does that count as valid consent? What about the external influences from family, lovers, husbands, church, etc. that a woman faces when she considers an abortion? Can she offer valid consent in such a case?

Argument Reconstruction Exercises:

I. The goal of Cates' paper is to help her readers get into a position where they can make more accurate moral evaluations of the decision to get an abortion. Assuming, as a premise, that some person doesn't attempt to be respectful or compassionate, what can we conclude given the following necessary condition?

> This analysis is governed by a conviction that attempting to be respectful and compassionate is a necessary condition for understanding the moral dimensions of abortion and making appropriate evaluations of particular abortion decisions. (page 429)

II. One issue in the background of Cates' worries is the issue of informed consent. In particular, giving truly informed consent to the abortion procedure may require dealing carefully with a woman's emotions. Identify the premises and conclusion in this excerpt:

> To focus on the matter of informed consent, respect and compassion require that we ponder what it is for a given woman to understand an act of abortion and its possible consequences for her life. Understanding the act may include understanding its moral dimensions, and reaching moral understanding may include feeling and reflecting upon certain emotions like grief and guilt. (page 436)

III. Cates argues that caring for women considering abortions requires addressing the question of how much of their agency has been affected or "co-opted" by others. Starting with the assumed premise that we should care for girls and women who are considering abortions, identify the premises and conclusion in this excerpt:

> In sum, caring for girls and women who are considering abortion may involve encouraging some of them to become more conscious and discerning about the (welcome and unwelcome) ways that the people in their lives are at work inside their hearts and minds, shaping the exercise of their moral agencies. (page 443)

CHAPTER 16

The Environment and Sustainability

We do not inherit the earth from our ancestors; we borrow it from our children.
—NATIVE AMERICAN PROVERB

INTRODUCTION

Brazil recently announced that satellite images have confirmed that the Amazonian rainforest is disappearing almost 50% faster than previously thought. Though much of the logging that takes place is technically illegal, little is done to control the damage either by Brazil or the countries that import timber from Brazil. The trees are sold for furniture and other First World products (e.g., mahogany desks), and the resulting land is often burned over and converted to grass to raise cattle for the meat-intensive diets of First World citizens.

Such an example is not restricted to Brazil. The lifestyle of the average First World citizen requires an astonishing amount of resources. Consider some of the following facts (taken from a PBS documentary entitled "Affluenza"):

- The average American home in 1950 could fit inside of a contemporary three-car garage.
- In 2008, the world's 358 billionaires owned more resources than 50% of the world's population.
- Since 1950, Americans have used more resources than all of the humans who ever lived before them combined.
- Americans throw away 2 million plastic bottles an hour.
- In 1996, Americans made up 5% of the world's population but consumed 33% of

the natural resources and produced 50% of the hazardous waste.
- The average North American citizen consumes 5 times as much as the average Mexican, 10 times as much as the average Chinese, and 30 times as much as the average Indian.
- In a 1995 survey, 86% of Americans who purposefully cut back on consumption reported being happier as a result.

Do you find these statistics troubling? If so, why?

You might worry about the destruction of natural environments and heavy consumption from a prudential or practical point of view. Given that we need some natural resources to live a good life, we are endangering the quality of life for ourselves and future generations by consuming at the present rate. In other words, you might find these statistics troubling because they indicate that our consumption choices are at odds with our long-term goals. It's that not what we're doing is morally wrong; it's that what we're doing is stupid.

However, you might also think that whatever practical import these statistics may have, they also indicate a *moral* problem. Something is wrong with living this way. Many philosophers (and other people) have argued that we have a moral obligation to live sustainably. But why is it wrong to destroy natural environments? What, precisely, is the problem with our current levels of consumption? If we have a moral obligation not to consume so much, to whom do we owe this obligation? What makes it wrong?

Perhaps it's morally wrong to consume as much as we do because of the position it puts other humans in. In other words, perhaps what's wrong with our rate of consumption is that we are inadvertently *harming* other people by leaving them without the resources necessary to make their lives better. This kind of explanation is a **consequential** one—it appeals to harm to existing humans to explain why consuming at our present rate is wrong.

But you might also worry about over consumption from a **deontological** point of view. Perhaps the problem with our current rate of consumption is that it is *unfair*. The earth's natural resources are limited, and we are taking more than our fair share of the earth's resources. Just as it is wrong for a kid to take more than his fair share of the birthday cake, it is unfair for one group of people to take more than their fair share of the resources. But how are we to determine what constitutes a fair share? And how can we divide up so vast an amount as the earth provides?

In fact, perhaps both of these explanations are short-sighted. Notice that both explanations appealed to other existing humans to explain the wrongness of our current consumption. Here are at least three other possibilities to explain the wrongness of current levels of consumption. First, you might think that our current rate of consumption is morally indefensible because of our obligations to future generations of people. Brian Barry's essay in this chapter explores this suggestion. The idea would be that it is wrong to use so much of the earth's resources in full knowledge of the fact that it is overwhelmingly probable that many more generations of humans will exist in the near future and that these humans will need these resources. This explanation appeals not to currently existing humans to ground the wrong but to humans that will exist in the future.

Second, you might think that our current rate of consumption is morally indefensible not because of what it does to other humans (either present or future) but because of what it does to the other living inhabitants of the world. The more we, as humans, consume, the less is available for wild plants and animals. Perhaps what's wrong with our overconsumption is the burden that we are placing on the non-human creatures that share the earth's resources with us. But how do we decide how much of the earth's resources are legitimately usable by humans and how much should be left alone?

Third, you might think that our current rate of consumption is morally indefensible because of what it does to us. It is not implausible to think that overconsumption can get in the way of living the good life (recall the statistic above about decreased consumption and reported happiness). The essays by Thomas Hill and Lester Milbrath in this chapter suggest as much. This more Aristotelian/virtue type of response appeals to the kinds of character needed in order to flourish. Perhaps the chase after material goods and the focus on consumption inhibits the kind of moral growth that is crucial for human flourishing.

No doubt you can think of other reasons why our present levels of consumption are morally indefensible. And then again, perhaps it only seems as if our present levels of consumption are morally problematic. As the essay in this chapter by Mark Sagoff will suggest, perhaps we are not in imminent danger of running out of resources, etc. In either case, the readings in this chapter will give you the opportunity to reflect on your current rate of consumption and the question of whether or not we have a moral obligation to live sustainably.

SUGGESTIONS FOR FURTHER READING

Daly, Herman E., and Cobb, Jr., John. *For the Common Good: Redirecting the Economy Toward Community, the Environment, and a Sustainable Future.* (Boston: Beacon Press, 1989)

De Graaf, John, Wann, David; and Naylor, Thomas. *Affluenza: The All-Consuming Epidemic.* (San Francisco: Berrett-Koehler Publishers, Inc., 2002)

Easterbrook, Gregg. "Why the Good News Shouldn't Scare You." In *A Moment on Earth.* (New York: Viking Penguin, 1995, pp. xiii-xxi)

Gardner, Gary, Assadourian, Erik, and Sarin, Radhika. "The State of Consumption Today." *In State of the World 2004: A Worldwatch Institute Report on Progress.* (New York: W. W. Norton and Company, 2004, pp. 3–21)

Hardin, Garrett. "The Tragedy of the Commons." *Science* 1968; 162, pp. 1243–48.

Pojman, Louis. *Global Environmental Ethics.* (Boston: McGraw-Hill, 1999)

Woolliams, Jessica. "Designing Cities and Buildings as if They Were Ethical Choices." *In Environmental Ethics: What Really Matters, What Really Works,* ed. David Schmidtz and Elizabeth Willott. (Oxford: Oxford University Press, 2000)

Young, John E., "Discarding the Throwaway Society." *Worldwatch Paper,* 1991, number 101, Washington, D.C.

16.1 SUSTAINABILITY AND INTERGENERATIONAL JUSTICE

BRIAN BARRY (1997)

Until his death in 2009, Brian Barry was perhaps the most important British social and political philosopher. His work brought the rigor of careful philosophy to the pressing social issues of his times, including matters of social justice and environmental policy. In this article, Barry clarifies the basic principles of justice that establish moral duties between living people, and he extends these principles to explain the duties that the current generation has for future generations. In essence, Barry argues that if we start with the principle that all humans are fundamentally equal, this principle implies (by way of three different theorems) that the current generation has a moral obligation to live sustainably.

Reading Questions:

1. What does it mean to say that all human beings are fundamentally equal?

2. How does Barry argue for the premise that all humans are fundamentally equal?

3. What are the three theorems of the premise of fundamental equality?

4. According to Barry, what are some of a human's vital interests?

5. What is the core concept of sustainability?

6. Assuming that sustainability is about maintaining some thing, X, for the indefinite future, Barry considers three possible candidates for X. What are they?

7. Does justice require that we live so that ANY amount of future humans will have the same opportunities for the good life as we do at present?

1. The Question

As temporary custodians of the planet, those who are alive at any given time can do a better or worse job of handing it on to their successors. I take that simple thought to animate concerns about what we ought to be doing to preserve conditions that will make life worth living (or indeed liveable at all) in the future, and especially in the time after those currently alive will have died ('future generations'). There are widespread suspicions that we are not doing enough for future generations, but how do we determine what is enough? Putting the question in that way leads us, I suggest, towards a formulation of it in terms of **intergenerational justice**.

We shall make most headway in asking ethical questions about the future if we start by asking them about the present and then see how the results can be extended to apply to the future. The rationale for this procedure is that we are accustomed to thinking about relations among contemporaries and have developed a quite sophisticated apparatus to help us in doing so. We have no similar apparatus to aid our thoughts about relations between people living at different times. Rather than starting from scratch, then, my proposal is that we should move from the familiar to the unfamiliar, making whatever adaptations seem necessary along the way. . . .

With that by way of preamble, I can now set out very quickly what I see as the question to be asked about the ethical status of sustainability. This is as follows: *Is sustainability (however we understand the term) either a necessary or a sufficient condition of intergenerational distributive justice?*

2. Distributive Justice

In accordance with the methodological maxim that I laid down at the beginning, I shall approach the question of the demands of intergenerational justice via the question of the demands of distributive justice among contemporaries. *The premise from which I start is one of the fundamental equality of human beings. . . .* Different treatments of different people must be justified by adducing some morally relevant ground for different treatment. This is, of course, not saying a great deal until we know what are to count

as morally relevant reasons. But even if we simply say that they are grounds which we ought reasonably to expect the person affected to accept freely, we shall rule out many historically prominent forms of domination and systematic inequality of rights, which have rested on nothing but the power of the beneficiaries to impose them.

I do not know of any way of providing a justification for the premise of fundamental equality: its status is that of an axiom. I will point out, however, that it is very widely accepted, at least in theory, and that attempts to provide a rationale for unequal treatment at least pay lip service to the obligation to square it with the premise of fundamental equality. Moreover, it seems to me that there is a good reason for this in that it is very hard to imagine any remotely plausible basis for rejecting the premise. In any case, it is presupposed in what follows.

In brief compass, then, I shall propose three principles which are, I claim, theorems of the premise of fundamental equality. These are as follows:

1. *Equal rights. Prima facie,* civil and political rights must be equal. Exceptions can be justified only if they would receive the well-informed assent of those who would be allocated diminished rights compared with others.

2. *Responsibility.* A legitimate origin of different outcomes for different people is that they have made different voluntary choices. (However, this principle comes into operation fully only against a background of a just system of rights, resources and opportunities.) The obverse of the principle is that bad outcomes for which somebody is not responsible provide a case for compensation.

3. *Vital interests.* There are certain objective requirements for human beings to be able to live healthy lives, raise families, work at full capacity, and take a part in social and political life. Justice requires that a higher priority should be given to ensuring that all human beings have the means to satisfy these vital interests than to satisfying other desires.

What implications do these principles of justice have for justice between generations? Let me take them in turn.

1. *Equal rights.* I cannot see that this principle has any *direct* intergenerational application. For it would seem to me absurd to say, for example, that it is unfair for a woman to have more rights in Britain now than a century ago, or unfair that a woman had fewer rights then. Surely, the principle of equal rights applies to contemporaries and only to contemporaries. However, the present generation may be able to affect the likelihood that there will be equal rights in the future. Thus, it seems to be a robust generalisation that rights suffer at times when large challenges to a system demand rapid and coordinated responses. (To offer a relatively modest example, I would guess that all individual university teachers and departments have lost autonomy in the last twenty years.) The more environmental stress we leave our successors to cope with, therefore, the poorer prospects for equal rights.

2. *Responsibility.* This principle will clearly apply among people who are contemporaries in the future, as it does among people who are contemporaries today, to justify inequalities of outcome that arise from choice. But what place, if any, does it have in relations between different generations? People in the future can scarcely be held responsible for the physical conditions they inherit, so it would seem that it is unjust if people in future are worse off in this respect than we are. (This, of course, leaves open the question of what is the relevant criterion of being well off, and I shall take that up in the next section.)

3. *Vital interests.* The fundamental idea that location in space and time do not in themselves affect legitimate claims has the immediate implications that the vital interests of people in the future have the same priority as the vital interests of people in the present. I shall take up the implications of this in section 4. . . .

3. Sustainability

The core concept of sustainability is, I suggest, that there is some X whose value should be maintained, in as far as it lies within our power to do so, into the indefinite future. This leaves it open for dispute what the content of X should be. Here is one candidate: utility, understood (as is orthodox in economics) as the satisfaction of wants or, as they are usually called, preferences. The obvious objection to this criterion is that wants are (quite reasonably) dependent on what is, or is expected to be, available. Perhaps people in the future might learn to find satisfaction in totally artificial landscapes, walking on the astroturf amid the plastic trees while the electronic birds sing overhead. But we cannot but believe that something horrible would have happened to human beings if they did not miss real grass, trees and birds.

The want-satisfaction criterion does not enable us to explain what would be wrong with such a world. . . .

Let us dismiss the hypothesis that X is want-satisfaction. What, then, is it? On the strength of the objection urged against want-satisfaction, it might appear that what should be maintained for future generations is their chance to live a good life as we conceive it. But even if 'we' agreed on what that is (which is manifestly not the case), this would surely be an objectionable criterion for 'what matters'. For one of the defining characteristics of human beings is their ability to form their own conceptions of the good life. It would be presumptuous—and unfair—of us to pre-empt their choices in the future. (This is what is wrong with all utopias.) We must respect the creativity of people in the future. What this suggests is that the requirement is to provide future generations with the opportunity to live good lives according to *their* conception of what constitutes a good life. This should surely include their being able to live good lives according to our conception but should leave other options open to them.

This thought leads me to the suggestion (for which I claim no originality) that X needs to be read as some notion of equal opportunity across generations. . . .

The notion of a range of opportunity cannot be reduced either to the sheer number of opportunities or to the utility of the most preferred option. We must define it in a way that tracks our reasons for wishing to make it our criterion of X in the first place. That means taking seriously the idea that conditions must be such as to sustain a range of possible conceptions of the good life. In the nature of the case, we cannot imagine in any detail what may be thought of a good life in the future. But we can be quite confident that it will not include the violation of what I have called vital interests: adequate nutrition, clean drinking water, clothing and housing, health care and education, for example. We can, in addition, at the very least leave open to people in the future the possibility of living in a world in which nature is not utterly subordinated to the pursuit of consumer satisfaction. . .

4. Sustainability and Intergenerational Justice

Having said something about intergenerational justice and something about sustainability, it is time to bring them together. We can be encouraged about the prospect of a connection if I am correct in my contention that sustainability is as much a normative concept as is justice. And I believe that there is indeed a close connection. It may be recalled that the question that I formulated at the end of section 1. asked if sustainability was either a necessary or a sufficient condition of intergenerational justice. *It appears that sustainability is at least a necessary condition of justice.* For the principle of responsibility says that, unless people in the future can be held responsible for the situation that they find themselves in, they should not be worse off than we are. And no generation can be held responsible for the state of the planet it inherits.

This suggests that we should at any rate leave people in the future with the possibility of not falling below our level. We cannot, of course, guarantee that our doing this will actually provide people in the further future with what we make possible. The next generation may, for all we know, go on a gigantic spree and leave their successors relatively impoverished. The potential for sustaining the same level of X as we enjoy depends on each successive generation playing its part. All we can do is leave

open the possibility, and that is what we are obliged by justice to do.

5. Two Objections

(1) An objection sometimes raised to the notion that it would be unjust to let future generations fall below our standard (of whatever is to count as X) is that there is something arbitrary about taking the current position as the baseline. We are, it is argued, better off materially than our ancestors. Suppose we were to pursue policies that ran down resources to such an extent that people in future would be no better off than our ancestors were a hundred years (or two hundred years) ago. Why would that be unjust? What is so special about the present as the point of comparison? In reply, it must be conceded that the expression 'intergenerational justice' is potentially misleading––though perhaps it actually misleads only those who are determined to be misled. It is a sort of shorthand for 'justice between the present generation and future generations'. Because of time's arrow, we cannot do anything to make people in the past better off than they actually were, so it is absurd to say that our relations to them could be either just or unjust. 'Ought' implies 'can', and the only people whose fate we can affect are those living now and in the future. Taking the present as our reference point is arbitrary only in some cosmic sense in which it might be said to be arbitrary that now is now and not some other time. . . .

(2) We now have to face a question of interpretation so far left aside. This is: How are we to deal with population size? On one quite natural interpretation of the concept of sustainability, the X whose value is to be maintained is to be defined over individuals. *The demands of justice will then be more stringent the larger we predict the future population to be.* Suppose we were simply to extrapolate into the indefinite future growth rates of the order of those seen in past decades. On the hypothesis that numbers double every forty years or so, we shall have a world population after two centuries of around a hundred and fifty billion and in a further two centuries a population of five thousand billion. If the increase were spread evenly round the world, this would imply a population for the UK more

than ten times the size of the whole current world population.

It is surely obvious that no degree of self-immiseration that those currently alive could engage in would be capable of providing the possibility of an equal level of X per head even that far inside the future. This would be so on any remotely plausible definition of X. (Indeed, we can be certain that some cataclysm would have occurred long before these numbers were reached.) But even far more modest increases in population would make it impossible to maintain X, if X is taken to include the preservation of so-called 'natural capital'. . .

I suggest, therefore, that the size of future population should be brought within the scope of the principle of responsibility. We must define intergenerational justice on the assumption that 'the increase of mankind shall be under the guidance of judicious foresight', as Mill put it. If future people choose to let population increase, or by default permit it to increase, that is to be at their own cost. There is no reason in justice for our having any obligation to accommodate their profligacy. Concretely, then, the conception of sustainability that makes it appropriate as a necessary condition of intergenerational justice may be formulated as follows: *Sustainability requires at any point in time that the value of some X per head of population should be capable of being maintained into the indefinite future, on the assumption that the size of the future population is no greater than the size of the present population. . . .*

My conclusion, after this vertiginous speculation, is that we would be doing very well to meet the criterion of sustainability that I originally proposed. The more we fail, and the more that world population is not checked in coming decades, the worse things will be in the future and the smaller the population at which it will be possible to maintain tolerable living conditions. Perhaps the right way to look at the matter is to think of population and resources (in the largest sense) as the two variables that enter into sustainability: we might then say that sustainability is a function of both. Realistically, any given generation can make only a limited impact on either. But what can at least then be said is that if some generation is failing to meet the condition of sustainability (defined in the standard way over a fixed

population), over a fixed population, it can at least be more just than otherwise towards its successors by ensuring that the dwindling resources will have to spread around over fewer people.

Interpreted on some such lines as these, sustainability is, I suggest, adequate as a necessary condition of intergenerational justice. *Is it also a sufficient condition? I feel strongly inclined to say that it is: if we were to satisfy it, we would be doing very well, and it is hard to see that we could reasonably be expected to do more.* My only hesitation arises from the application of the vital interests. (I noted in section 2. that this needed later discussion.) Obviously, if we give the principle of vital interests priority over the principle of responsibility, we are liable to be back at a version of the absurd idea that we are obliged to immiserate ourselves to a level capable of sustaining a hugely larger population if we predict there will be one. For if we predict an enormously greater number of people in the future, meeting their vital interests trumps any objective we might have. I have not specified priority relations among the principles, and I do not think this can be done across the board. The principles are guides to thinking, not a piece of machinery that can be cranked to grind out conclusions. However, in this case it seems to me that giving the principle of vital interests priority produces such absurd results that this cannot possibly be the right thing to do. . . .

6. Conclusion

Let me conclude with what may at first sight seem an eccentric suggestion. This is that it is not terribly difficult to know what needs to be done, though it is of course immensely difficult to get the relevant actors (governmental and other) to do it. I do not deny that there are large areas of scientific uncertainty, and probably always will be (e.g. about global warming), since the interacting processes involved are so complex. But what I am claiming is that virtually everybody who has made a serious study of the situation and whose objectivity is not compromised by either religious beliefs or being in the pay of some multinational corporation has reached the conclusion that the most elementary concern for people in the future demands big changes in the way we do things. These could start with the implementation by all signatories of what was agreed on at the Rio conference.

Moreover, whatever is actually going to get done in, say, the next decade, to move towards a sustainable balance of population and resources is going to be so pathetically inadequate that it really does not matter *how* far it falls short. We know the direction in which change is required, and we know that there is absolutely no risk that we shall find ourselves doing more than required. It really does not make any practical difference whether we think a certain given effort represents ten per cent of what needs to be done, or whether we think it is as much as twenty per cent. Either way, we have good reason to push for more. . . .

DISCUSSION QUESTIONS:

1. Barry opens with the assumption that all humans are fundamentally equal, and he uses this starting point to argue for our obligations to future generations. But this is puzzling: future generations, if they exist, are composed of future people. But future people, by definition, do not exist. But if there are no future people, then in what sense are current people fundamentally equal with non-existing people? This paradox is even stranger when we look at the principles that follow from the premise of fundamental equality. For example, Barry concludes that all humans have equal rights. But one can have a right only if one exists. And since future people do not exist, future people have no rights. So then why is it wrong for me to live in an unsustainable way if doing so does not violate the rights of others?

2. Suppose you have the opportunity to push a button that would destroy the earth. Surely Barry is right that this would be unjust given the fundamental equality of all living humans. But would it also be unjust because of its "effect" on future generations? How could that be since, *ex hypothesi*, there wouldn't be any future generations if you press the button? Are we forced to say that the only reason you shouldn't press the button is because of what it would do to currently existing beings (human or otherwise)?

3. Barry's ultimate conclusion is that members of the current generation have a moral obligation to preserve the environment so that it can "sustain a range of possible conceptions of the good life in the future" (page 452). But is it reasonable to think that we know enough at present to make such a decision about what and how much to preserve? For example, generations 100 years ago surely would have thought that they needed to preserve coal for the current generation and surely would not have thought that they needed to preserve the rare mineral tantalite (useless to their generation but crucial for electronics such as cell phones and computers). But they would have been wrong on both counts: the use of coal is terrible for our generation but tantalite is very helpful. How we decide what kind of goods will be crucial for generations hundreds or thousands of years from now?

Argument Reconstruction Exercises:

I. Barry identifies three different principles that form theorems of the premise of fundamental human equality. The first of these, *Equal Rights*, suggests that our being careless with the environment might limit the rights of future generations. Identify the premises and conclusion in this excerpt.

> I cannot see that the principle [of equal rights] has any direct intergenerational application. . . .However, the present generation may be able to affect the likelihood that there will be equal rights in the future. Thus, it seems to be a robust generalization that rights suffer at times when large challenges to a system demand rapid and coordinated responses. . . .The more environmental stress we leave our successors to cope with, therefore, the poorer prospects for equal rights. (page 451)

II. The second principle of justice identified by Barry is entitled *Responsibility*. In essence, this principle says that when someone suffers a bad outcome from someone else's choice, this is an unjust result. Identify the premises and conclusion in this excerpt.

> People in the future can scarcely be held responsible for the physical conditions they inherit, so it

would seem that it is unjust if people in the future are worse off in this respect than we are. (page 451)

III. The third principle of justice identified by Barry is entitled *Vital Interests*. In essence, this principle says that justice requires that the vital interests of all humans (e.g., food and shelter) take precedence over non-vital interests (e.g., having an iPod). In other words, justice requires that the current generation not sacrifice the vital interests of future generations in order to meet current non-vital interests. Identify the premises and conclusion in this excerpt.

> There are certain objective requirements for human beings to be able to live healthy lives, raise families, work at full capacity, and take a part in social and political life. Justice requires that a higher priority should be given to ensuring that all human beings have the means to satisfy these vital interests than to satisfying other desires. . . .The fundamental idea that location in space and time do not in themselves affect legitimate claims has the immediate implication that the vital interests of people in the future have the same priority as the vital interests of people in the present. (pages 450-451)

IV. Barry carefully investigates the question of what, exactly, should be maintained for future generations. One possibility that he considers is that we should provide future generations with the opportunity to live the good life as we currently understand it. He rejects this suggestion in the implicit argument made in this excerpt.

> . . .it might appear that what should be maintained for future generations is their chance to live a good life as we conceive it. But even if 'we' agreed on what that is (which is manifestly not the case), this would surely be an objectionable criterion for 'what matters'. For one of the defining characteristics of human beings is their ability to form their own conceptions of the good life. It would be presumptuous—and unfair—of us to pre-empt their choices in the future. (page 451)

16.2 IDEALS OF HUMAN EXCELLENCE AND PRESERVING NATURAL ENVIRONMENTS

THOMAS E. HILL, JR. (1983)

Thomas E. Hill, Jr. is Kenan Professor of Philosophy at the University of North Carolina-Chapel Hill. He is one of the country's foremost Kant scholars, and his published work includes work in the history of philosophy, social/political philosophy, and applied ethics. In this essay, Hill explores the moral significance of preserving natural environments outside of the standard concerns about harming other humans, non-human animals, future generations, etc. His suggestion is that a blatant willingness to destroy natural environments is indicative of being a certain type of person, namely a person who lacks certain moral virtues such as humility, self-acceptance, and appreciation of the good that we think of as important for the good life.

Reading Questions:

1. Why doesn't Hill consider plants to have genuine interests?

2. What does it mean to say that something is intrinsically valuable?

3. What is the example with the Nazi supposed to illustrate?

4. According to Hill, what is the connection between an indifference to non-sentient nature and the human virtues?

5. What does it mean to "appreciate one's place in the universe"?

6. What does Hill mean by "self-acceptance"?

7. What is an "aesthetic sensibility" and how is it connected to the moral virtues?

I

A wealthy eccentric bought a house in a neighborhood I know. The house was surrounded by a beautiful display of grass, plants, and flowers, and it was shaded by a huge old avocado tree. But the grass required cutting, the flowers needed tending, and the man wanted more sun. So he cut the whole lot down and covered the yard with asphalt. After all it was his property and he was not fond of plants.

It was a small operation, but it reminded me of the strip mining of large sections of the Appalachians. In both cases, of course, there were reasons for the destruction, and property rights could be cited as justification. But I could not help but wonder, "What sort of person would do a thing like that?"

Many Californians had a similar reaction when a recent governor defended the leveling of ancient redwood groves, reportedly saying, "If you have seen one redwood, you have seen them all."

Incidents like these arouse the indignation of ardent environmentalists and leave even apolitical observers with some degree of moral discomfort The reasons for these reactions are mostly obvious. Uprooting the natural environment robs both present and future generations of much potential use and enjoyment. Animals too depend on the environment; and even if one does not value animals for their own sakes, their potential utility for us is incalculable. Plants are needed, of course, to replenish the atmosphere quite aside from their aesthetic value. These reasons for hesitating to destroy forests and gardens are not only the most obvious ones, but also the most persuasive for practical purposes. But, one wonders, is there nothing more behind our discomfort? Are we concerned solely about the potential use and enjoyment of the forests, etc., for ourselves, later generations, and perhaps animals? Is there not something else

which disturbs us when we witness the destruction or even listen to those who would defend it in terms of cost/benefit analysis?

Imagine that in each of our examples those who would destroy the environment argue elaborately that, even considering future generations of human beings and animals, there are benefits in "replacing" the natural environment which outweigh the negative utilities which environmentalists cite.[1] No doubt we could press the argument on the facts, trying to show that the destruction is shortsighted and that its defenders have underestimated its potential harm or ignored some pertinent rights or interests. But is this all we could say? Suppose we grant, for a moment, that the utility of destroying the redwoods, forests, and gardens is equal to their potential for use and enjoyment by nature lovers and animals. Suppose, further, that we even grant that the pertinent human rights and animal rights, if any, are evenly divided for and against destruction. Imagine that we also concede, for argument's sake, that the forests contain no potentially useful endangered species of animals and plants. Must we then conclude that there is no further cause for moral concern? Should we then feel morally indifferent when we see the natural environment uprooted?

II

Suppose we feel that the answer to these questions should be negative. Suppose, in other words, we feel that our moral discomfort when we confront the destroyers of nature is not fully explained by our belief that they have miscalculated the best use of natural resources or violated rights in exploiting them. Suppose, in particular, we sense that *part of the problem is that the natural environment is being viewed exclusively as a natural* resource. What could be the ground of such a feeling? That is, what is there in our system of normative principles and values that could account for our remaining moral dissatisfaction?[2]

Option One: Plants

Some may be tempted to seek an explanation by appeal to the interests, or even the rights, of plants. After all, they may argue, we only gradually came to acknowledge the moral importance of all human beings, and it is even more recently that consciences have been aroused to give full weight to the welfare (and rights?) of animals. The next logical step, it may be argued, is to acknowledge a moral requirement to take into account the interests (and rights?) of plants. The problem with the strip miners, redwood cutters, and the like, on this view, is not just that they ignore the welfare and rights of people and animals; they also fail to give due weight to the survival and health of the plants themselves.

The temptation to make such a reply is understandable if one assumes that all moral questions are exclusively concerned with whether acts are right or wrong, and that this, in turn, is determined entirely by how the acts impinge on the rights and interests of those directly affected. On this assumption, if there is cause for moral concern, some right or interest has been neglected; and if the rights and interests of human beings and animals have already been taken into account, then there must be some other pertinent interests, for example, those of plants. A little reflection will show that the assumption is mistaken; but, in any case, the conclusion that plants have rights or morally relevant interests is surely untenable. We do speak of what is "good for" plants, and they can "thrive" and also be "killed." But this does not imply that they have "interests" in any morally relevant sense. Some people apparently believe that plants grow better if we talk to them, but the idea that the plants suffer and enjoy, desire and dislike, etc., is clearly outside the range of both common sense and scientific belief. The notion that the forests should be preserved to avoid hurting the trees or because they have a right to life is not part of a widely shared moral consciousness, and for good reason.[3]

Option Two: God

Another way of trying to explain our moral discomfort is to appeal to certain religious beliefs. If one believes that all living things were created by a God who cares for them and entrusted us with the use of plants and animals only for limited purposes, then one has a reason to avoid careless destruction of the forests, etc., quite aside from their future utility. Again, if one believes that a divine force is immanent in all nature, then too one might have reason to care for more than sentient things. But such arguments require strong and controversial premises, and, I suspect, they will always have a restricted audience.

Option Three: Intrinsic Value

Early in this century, due largely to the influence of G. E. Moore, another point of view developed which some may find promising.[4] Moore introduced, or at least made popular, the idea that certain states of affairs are intrinsically valuable—not just valued, but valuable, and not necessarily because of their effects on sentient beings. Admittedly Moore came to believe that in fact the only intrinsically valuable things were conscious experiences of various sorts,[5] but this restriction was not inherent in the idea of intrinsic value. The intrinsic goodness of something, he thought, was an objective, nonrelational property of the thing, like its texture or color, but not a property perceivable by sense perception or detectable by scientific instruments. In theory at least, a single tree thriving alone in a universe without sentient beings, and even without God, could be intrinsically valuable. Since, according to Moore, our duty is to maximize intrinsic value, his theory could obviously be used to argue that we have reason not to destroy natural environments independently of how they affect human beings and animals. *The survival of a forest might have worth beyond its worth to sentient beings.*

This approach, like the religious one, may appeal to some but is infested with problems. There are, first, the familiar objections to intuitionism, on which the theory depends. Metaphysical and epistemological doubts about nonnatural, intuited properties are hard to suppress, and many have argued that the theory rests on a misunder-standing of the words *good, valuable,* and the like.[6] Second, even if we try to set aside these objections and think in Moore's terms, it is far from obvious that everyone would agree that the existence of forests, etc., is intrinsically valuable. The test, says Moore, is what we would say when we imagine a universe with just the thing in question, without any effects or accompaniments, and then we ask, "Would its existence be better than its nonexis-tence?" Be careful, Moore would remind us, not to construe this question as, "Would you *prefer* the existence of that universe to its nonexistence?" The question is, "Would its existence have the objec-tive, nonrelational property, intrinsic goodness?"

Now even among those who have no worries about whether this really makes sense, we might well get a diversity of answers. Those prone to destroy natural environments will doubtless give one answer, and nature lovers will likely give another. When an issue is as controversial as the one at hand, intuition is a poor arbiter.

Option Four: Examine Character, not Action

The problem, then, is this. We want to under-stand what underlies our moral uneasiness at the destruction of the redwoods, forests, etc., even apart from the loss of these as resources for human beings and animals. But I find no adequate answer by pursuing the questions, "Are rights or inter-ests of plants neglected?" "What is God's will on the matter?" and "What is the intrinsic value of the existence of a tree or forest?" My suggestion, which is in fact the main point of this paper, is that we look at the problem from a different perspec-tive. That is, *let us turn for a while from the effort to find reasons why certain acts destructive of natu-ral environments are morally wrong to the ancient task of articulating our ideals of human excellence.* Rather than argue directly with destroyers of the environment who say, "Show me why what I am doing is *immoral,*" I want to ask, "What sort of person would want to do what they propose?" The point is not to skirt the issue with an **ad hominem,** to raise a different moral question, for even if there is no convincing way to show that the destruc-tive acts are wrong (independently of human and

animal use and enjoyment), we may find that the willingness to indulge in them reflects the absence of human traits that we admire and regard morally important.

This strategy of shifting questions may seem more promising if one reflects on certain analo-gous situations. Consider, for example, the Nazi who asks, in all seriousness, "Why is it wrong for me to make lampshades out of human skin—pro-vided, of course, I did not myself kill the victims to get the skins?" We would react more with shock and disgust than with indignation, I suspect, because it is even more evident that the question reveals a defect in the questioner than that the proposed act is itself immoral. *Sometimes we may not regard an act wrong at all though we see it as reflecting something objectionable about the person who does it.* Imagine, for example, one who laughs spontaneously to himself when he reads a newspa-per account of a plane crash that kills hundreds. Or, again, consider an obsequious grandson who, having waited for his grandmother's inheritance with mock devotion, then secretly spits on her grave when at last she dies. Spitting on the grave may have no adverse consequences and perhaps it violates no rights. The moral uneasiness which it arouses is explained more by our view of the agent than by any conviction that what he did was immoral. Had he hesitated and asked, "Why shouldn't I spit on her grave?" it seems more fitting to ask him to reflect on the sort of person he is than to try to offer reasons why he should refrain from spitting.

III

What sort of person, then, would cover his garden with asphalt, strip mine a wooded mountain, or level an irreplaceable redwood grove? Two sorts of answers, though initially appealing, must be ruled out. The first is that persons who would destroy the environment in these ways are either short-sighted, underestimating the harm they do, or else are too little concerned for the well-being of other people. Perhaps too they have insufficient regard for animal life. But these considerations have been set aside in order to refine the controversy.

Another tempting response might be that we count it a moral virtue, or at least a human ideal, to love nature. Those who value the environment only for its utility must not really love nature and so in this way fall short of an ideal. But such an answer is hardly satisfying in the present context, for what is at issue is *why* we feel moral discomfort at the activities of those who admittedly value nature only for its utility. That it is ideal to care for nonsentient nature beyond its possible use is really just another way of expressing the general point which is under controversy.

What is needed is some way of showing that this ideal is connected with other virtues, or human excellences, not in question. To do so is difficult and my suggestions, accordingly, will be tentative and subject to qualification. The main idea is that, *though indifference to nonsentient nature does not necessarily reflect the absence of virtues, it often signals the absence of certain traits which we want to encourage because they are, in most cases, a natural basis for the development of certain virtues*. It is often thought, for example, that those who would destroy the natural environment must lack a proper appreciation of their place in the natural order, and so must either be ignorant or have too little humility. Though I would argue that this is not necessarily so, I suggest that, given certain plausible empirical assumptions, their attitude may well be rooted in ignorance, a narrow perspective, inability to see things as important apart from themselves and the limited groups they associate with, or reluctance to accept themselves as natural beings. Overcoming these deficiencies will not guarantee a proper moral humility, but for most of us it is probably an important psychological preliminary. Later I suggest, more briefly, that indifference to nonsentient nature typically reveals absence of either aesthetic sensibility or a disposition to cherish what has enriched one's life and that these, though not themselves moral virtues, are a natural basis for appreciation of the good in others and gratitude.[7]

Consider first the suggestion that *destroyers of the environment lack an appreciation of their place in the universe*.[8] Their attention, it seems, must be focused on parochial matters, on what is, relatively speaking, close in space and time. They seem not to understand that we are a speck on the cosmic scene, a brief stage in the evolutionary process, only one among millions of species on Earth, and an episode in the course of human history. Of course, they know that there are stars, fossils, insects, and ancient ruins; but do they have any idea of the complexity of the processes that led to the natural world as we find it? Are they aware how much the forces at work within their own bodies are like those which govern all living things and even how much they have in common with inanimate bodies? Admittedly scientific knowledge is limited and no one can master it all; but could one who had a broad and deep understanding of his place in nature really be indifferent to the destruction of the natural environment?

This first suggestion, however, may well provoke a protest from a sophisticated anti-environmentalist.[9] "Perhaps some may be indifferent to nature from ignorance," the critic may object, "but I have studied astronomy, geology, biology, and biochemistry, and I still unashamedly regard the nonsentient environment as simply a resource for our use. It should not be wasted, of course, but what should be preserved is decidable by weighing long-term costs and benefits." "Besides," our critic may continue, "as philosophers you should know the old Humean formula, 'You cannot derive an ought from an is.' All the facts of biology, biochemistry, etc., do not entail that I ought to love nature or want to preserve it. What one understands is one thing; what one values is something else. Just as nature lovers are not necessarily scientists, those indifferent to nature are not necessarily ignorant."

Although the environmentalist may concede the critic's logical point, he may well argue that, *as a matter of fact increased understanding of nature tends to heighten people's concern for its preservation*. If so, despite the objection, the suspicion that the destroyers of the environment lack deep understanding of nature is not, in most cases, unwarranted. . . .

If someone challenges the empirical assumption here, the environmentalist might develop the argument along a quite different line. The initial idea, he may remind us, was that those *who would destroy the natural environment fail to appreciate their place in the natural order.* "Appreciating one's place" is not simply an intellectual appreciation. It is also an attitude, reflecting what one values as well as what one knows. When we say, for example, that both the servile and the arrogant person fail to *appreciate* their place in a society of equals, we do not mean simply that they are ignorant of certain empirical facts, but rather that they have certain objectionable attitudes about their importance relative to other people. Similarly, to fail to appreciate one's place in nature is not merely to lack knowledge or breadth of perspective, but to take a certain attitude about what matters. A person who *understands* his place in nature but still views nonsentient nature merely as a resource takes the attitude that nothing is *important* but human beings and animals. Despite first appearances, he is not so much like the pre-Copernican astronomers who made the intellectual error of treating the Earth as the "center of the universe" when they made their calculations. He is more like the racist who, though well aware of other races, treats all races but his own as insignificant."

So construed, the argument appeals to the common idea that *awareness of nature typically has, and should have, a humbling effect.* The Alps, a storm at sea, the Grand Canyon, towering redwoods, and "the starry heavens above" move many a person to remark on the comparative insignificance of our daily concerns and even of our species, and this is generally taken to be a quite fitting response.[11] *What seems to be missing, then, in those who understand nature but remain unmoved is a proper humility.*[12] Absence of proper humility is not the same as selfishness or egoism, for one can be devoted to self-interest while still viewing one's own pleasures and projects as trivial and unimportant.[13] And one can have an exaggerated view of one's own importance while grandly sacrificing for those one views as inferior. Nor is the lack of humility identical with belief that one has power and influence, for a person can be quite puffed up about himself while believing that the foolish world will never acknowledge him. The humility we miss seems not so much a belief about one's relative effectiveness and recognition as an attitude which measures the importance of things independently of their relation to oneself or to some narrow group with which one identifies. A paradigm of a person who lacks humility is the self-important emperor who grants status to his family because it is his, to his subordinates because *he* appointed them, and to his country because *he* chooses to glorify it. Less extreme but still lacking proper humility is the elitist who counts events significant solely in proportion to how they affect his class. The suspicion about those who would destroy the environment, then, is that what they count important is too narrowly confined insofar as it encompasses only what affects beings who, like us, are capable of feeling.

This idea that proper humility requires recognition of the importance of nonsentient nature is similar to the thought of those who charge meat eaters with "species-ism." In both cases it is felt that people too narrowly confine their concerns to the sorts of beings that are most like them. But, however intuitively appealing, the idea will surely arouse objections from our nonenvironmentalist critic. "Why," he will ask, "do you suppose that the sort of humility I *should* have requires me to acknowledge the importance of nonsentient nature aside from its utility? You cannot, by your own admission, argue that nonsentient nature is important, appealing to religious or intuitionist grounds. And simply to assert, without further argument, that an ideal humility requires us to view nonsentient nature as important for its own sake begs the question at issue. If proper humility is acknowledging the relative importance of things as one should, then to show that I must lack this you must first establish that one *should* acknowledge the importance of nonsentient nature."

Though some may wish to accept this challenge, there are other ways to pursue the connection between humility and response to nonsentient nature. For example, suppose we grant that proper humility requires only acknowledging a due status to sentient beings. We must admit, then, that it is logically possible for a person to be properly humble even though he viewed all nonsentient nature simply as a resource. But this logical possibility may be a psychological rarity. It may be that, given the sort of beings we are, we would never learn humility before persons without developing the general capacity to cherish, and regard important, many things for their own sakes. The major obstacle to humility before persons is self-importance, a tendency to measure the significance of everything by its relation to oneself and those with whom one identifies. The processes by which we overcome self-importance are doubtless many and complex, but it seems unlikely that they are exclusively concerned with how we relate to other people and animals. Learning humility requires learning to feel that something matters besides what will affect oneself and one's circle of associates. What leads a child to care about what happens to a lost hamster or a stray dog he will not see again is likely also to generate concern for a lost toy or a favorite tree where he used to live.[14] *Learning to value things for their own sake, and to count what affects them important aside from their utility, is not the same as judging them to have some intuited objective property, but it is necessary to the development of humility and it seems likely to take place in experiences with nonsentient nature as well as with people and animals.* If a person views all nonsentient nature merely as a resource, then it seems unlikely that he has developed the capacity needed to overcome self-importance.

IV

This last argument, unfortunately, has its limits. It presupposes an empirical connection between experiencing nature and overcoming self-importance, and this may be challenged. Even if experiencing nature promotes humility before others, there may be other ways people can develop such humility in a world of concrete, glass, and plastic. If not, perhaps all that is needed is limited experience of nature in one's early, developing years; mature adults, having overcome youthful self-importance, may live well enough in artificial surroundings. More importantly, the argument does not fully capture the spirit of the intuition that an ideal person stands humbly before nature. That idea is not simply that experiencing nature tends to foster proper humility before other people; it is, in part, that natural surroundings encourage and are appropriate to an ideal sense of oneself as part of the natural world. Standing alone in the forest, after months in the city, is not merely good as a means of curbing

one's arrogance before others; it reinforces and fittingly expresses one's acceptance of oneself as a natural being.

Previously we considered only one aspect of proper humility, namely, a sense of one's relative importance with respect to other human beings. Another aspect, I think, is a kind of *self-acceptance*. This involves acknowledging, in more than a merely intellectual way, that we are the sort of creatures that we are. Whether one is self-accepting is not so much a matter of how one attributes *importance* comparatively to oneself, other people, animals, plants, and other things as it is a matter of understanding, facing squarely, and responding appropriately to who and what one is, e.g., one's powers and limits, one's affinities with other beings and differences from them, one's unalterable nature and one's freedom to change. Self-acceptance is not merely intellectual awareness, for one can be intellectually aware that one is growing old and will eventually die while nevertheless behaving in a thousand foolish ways that reflect a refusal to acknowledge these facts. On the other hand, self-acceptance is not passive resignation, for refusal to pursue what one truly wants within one's limits is a failure to accept the freedom and power one has. Particular behaviors, like dying one's gray hair and dressing like those twenty years younger, do not *necessarily* imply lack of self-acceptance, for there could be reasons for acting in these ways other than the wish to hide from oneself what one really is. One fails to accept oneself when the patterns of behavior and emotion are rooted in a desire to disown and deny features of oneself, to pretend to oneself that they are not there. This is not to say that a self-accepting person makes no value judgments about himself, that he likes all facts about himself, wants equally to develop and display them; he can, and should feel remorse for his past misdeeds and strive to change his current vices. The point is that he does not disown them, pretend that they do not exist or are facts about something other than himself. Such pretense is incompatible with proper humility because it is seeing oneself as better than one is.

Self-acceptance of this sort has long been considered a human excellence, under various names, but what has it to do with preserving nature? There is, I think, the following connection. As human beings we are part of nature, living, growing, declining, and dying by natural laws similar to those governing other living beings; despite our awesomely distinctive human powers, we share many of the needs, limits, and liabilities of animals and plants. These facts are neither good nor bad in themselves, aside from personal preference and varying conventional values. To say this is to utter a truism which few will deny, but to accept these facts, as facts about oneself, is not so easy—or so common. Much of what naturalists deplore about our increasingly artificial world reflects, and encourages, a denial of these facts, an unwillingness to avow them with equanimity.

Like the Victorian lady who refuses to look at her own nude body, some would like to create a world of less transitory stuff, reminding us only of our intellectual and social nature, never calling to mind our affinities with "lower" living creatures. The "denial of death," to which psychiatrists call attention,[15] reveals an attitude incompatible with the sort of self-acceptance which philosophers, from the ancients to Spinoza and on, have admired as a human excellence. My suggestion is not merely that experiencing nature causally promotes such self-acceptance, but also that *those who fully accept themselves as part of the natural world lack the common drive to disassociate themselves from nature by replacing natural environments with artificial ones*. A storm in the wilds helps us to appreciate our animal vulnerability, but, equally important, the reluctance to experience it may *reflect* an unwillingness to accept this aspect of ourselves. The person who is too ready to destroy the ancient redwoods may lack humility, not so much in the sense that he exaggerates his importance relative to others, but rather in the sense that *he tries to avoid seeing himself as one among many natural creatures*.

V

My suggestion so far has been that, though indifference to nonsentient nature is not itself a moral vice,

it is likely to reflect either ignorance, a self-importance, or a lack of self-acceptance which we must overcome to have proper humility. A similar idea might be developed connecting attitudes toward nonsentient nature with other human excellences. For example, *one might argue that indifference to nature reveals a lack of either an aesthetic sense or some of the natural roots of gratitude*.

When we see a hillside that has been gutted by strip miners or the garden replaced by asphalt, our first reaction is probably, "How ugly!" The scenes assault our aesthetic sensibilities. We suspect that no one with a keen sense of beauty could have left such a sight. Admittedly not everything in nature strikes us as beautiful, or even aesthetically interesting, and sometimes a natural scene is replaced with a more impressive architectural masterpiece. But this is not usually the situation in the problem cases which environmentalists are most concerned about. More often beauty is replaced with ugliness.

At this point our critic may well object that, even if he does lack a sense of beauty, this is no moral vice. His cost/benefit calculations take into account the pleasure others may derive from seeing the forests, etc., and so why should he be faulted?

Some might reply that, despite contrary philosophical traditions, aesthetics and morality are not so distinct as commonly supposed. Appreciation of beauty, they may argue, is a human excellence which morally ideal persons should try to develop. But, setting aside this controversial position, there still may be cause for moral concern about those who have no aesthetic response to nature. Even if aesthetic sensibility is not itself a moral virtue, many of the capacities of mind and heart which it presupposes may be ones which are also needed for an appreciation of other people. Consider, for example, curiosity, a mind open to novelty, the ability to look at things from unfamiliar perspectives, empathetic imagination, interest in details, variety, and order, and emotional freedom from the immediate and the practical. All these, and more, seem necessary to aesthetic sensibility, but they are also traits which a person needs to be fully sensitive to people of all sorts. The point is not that a moral person must be able to distinguish beautiful from ugly people; the point is rather that unresponsiveness to what is beautiful, awesome, dainty, dumpy, and otherwise aesthetically interesting in nature probably reflects a lack of the openness of mind and spirit necessary to appreciate the best in human beings.

The anti-environmentalist, however, may refuse to accept the charge that he lacks aesthetic sensibility. If he claims to appreciate seventeenth-century miniature portraits, but to abhor natural wildernesses, he will hardly be convincing. Tastes vary, but aesthetic sense is not *that* selective. He may, instead, insist that he *does* appreciate natural beauty. He spends his vacations, let us suppose, hiking in the Sierras, photographing wildflowers, and so on. He might press his argument as follows: "I enjoy natural beauty as much as anyone, but I fail to see what this has to do with preserving the environment independently of human enjoyment and use. Nonsentient nature is a resource, but one of its best uses is to give us pleasure. I take this into account when I calculate the costs and benefits of preserving a park, planting a garden, and so on. But the problem you raised explicitly set aside the desire to preserve nature as a means to enjoyment. I say, let us enjoy nature fully while we can, but if all sentient beings were to die tomorrow, we might as well blow up all plant life as well. A redwood grove that no one can use or enjoy is utterly worthless."

The attitude expressed here, I suspect, is not a common one, but it represents a philosophical challenge. The beginnings of a reply may be found in the following. When a person takes joy in something, it is a common (and perhaps natural) response to come to cherish it. To cherish something is not simply to be happy with it at the moment, but to care for it for its own sake. This is not to say that one necessarily sees it as having feelings and so wants it to feel good; nor does it imply that one judges the thing to have Moore's intrinsic value. One simply wants the thing to survive and (when appropriate) to thrive, and not simply for its utility. We see this attitude repeatedly regarding mementos. They are not simply valued as a means to remind us of happy occasions;

they come to be valued for their own sake. Thus, if someone really took joy in the natural environment, but was prepared to blow it up as soon as sentient life ended, he would lack this common human tendency to cherish what enriches our lives. While this response is not itself a moral virtue, it may be a natural basis of the virtue we call "gratitude." *People who have no tendency to cherish things that give them pleasure may be poorly disposed to respond gratefully to persons who are good to them.* Again the connection is not one of logical necessity, but it may nevertheless be important. A nonreligious person unable to "thank" anyone for the beauties of nature may nevertheless feel "grateful" in a sense; and I suspect that the person who feels no such "gratitude" toward nature is unlikely to show proper gratitude toward people.

Suppose these conjectures prove to be true. One may wonder what is the point of considering them. Is it to disparage all those who view nature merely as a resource? To do so, it seems, would be unfair, for, even if this attitude typically stems from deficiencies which affect one's attitudes toward sentient beings, there may be exceptions and we have not shown that their view of nonsentient nature is itself blameworthy. But when we set aside questions of blame and inquire what sorts of human traits we want to encourage, our reflections become relevant in a more positive way. The point is not to insinuate that all anti-environmentalists are defective, but to see that those who value such traits as humility, gratitude, and sensitivity to others have reason to promote the love of nature.

NOTES

1. When I use the expression "the natural environment," I have in mind the sort of examples with which I began. For some purposes it is important to distinguish cultivated gardens from forests, virgin forests from replenished ones, irreplaceable natural phenomena from the replaceable, and so on, but these distinctions, I think, do not affect my main points here. There is also a broad sense, as Hume and Mill noted, in which all that occurs, miracles aside, is "natural." In this sense, of course, strip mining is as natural as a beaver cutting trees for his dam, and, as parts of nature, we cannot destroy the "natural" environment but only alter it. As will be evident, I shall use *natural* in a narrower, more familiar sense.

2. This paper is intended as a preliminary discussion in *normative* ethical theory (as opposed to *metaethics*). The task, accordingly, is the limited, though still difficult, one of articulating the possible basis in our beliefs and values for certain particular moral judgments. Questions of ultimate justification are set aside. What makes the task difficult and challenging is not that conclusive proofs from the foundation of morality are attempted; it is rather that the particular judgments to be explained seem at first not to fall under the most familiar moral principles (e.g., utilitarianism, respect for rights).

3. I assume here that having a right presupposes having interests in a sense which in turn presupposes a capacity to desire, suffer, etc. Since my main concern lies in another direction, I do not argue the point, but merely note that some regard it as debatable. See, for example, W. Murray Hunt, "Are *Mere Things* Morally Considerable?" *Environmental Ethics* 2 (1980): 59–65; Kenneth E. Goodpaster, "On Stopping at Everything," *Environmental Ethics* 2 (1980): 288–94; Joel Feinberg, "The Rights of Animals and Unborn Generations," in William Blackstone, ed., *Philosophy and Environmental Crisis* (Athens: University of Georgia Press, 1974), pp. 43–68; Tom Regan, "Feinberg on What Sorts of Beings Can Have Rights," *Southern Journal of Philosophy* (1976): 485–98, Robert Elliot, "Regan on the Sort of Beings that Can Have Rights," *Southern Journal of Philosophy* (1978): 701–05; Scott Lehmann, "Do Wildernesses Have Rights?" *Environmental Ethics* 2 (1981): 129–46.

4. G. E. Moore, *Principia Ethica* (Cambridge; Cambridge University Press, 1903); *Ethics* (London: H. Holt 1912).

5. G. E. Moore, "Is Goodness a Quality?" *Philosophical Papers* (London: George Allen and Unwin, 1959), pp. 95–97.

6. See, for example, P. H. NoweH-Smith, *Ethics* (New York: Penguin Books, 1954).

7. The issues I raise here, though perhaps not the details of my remarks, are in line with Aristotle's view of moral philosophy, a view revitalized recently by Philippa Foot's *Virtue and Vice* (Berkeley University of California Press, 1979), Alaistair McIntyre's *After Virtue* (Notre Dame: Notre Dame Press, 1981), and James Wallace's *Virtues and Vices* (Ithaca and London: Cornell University Press, 1978), and other works. For other reflections on relationships between character and natural environments, see John Rodman, "The Liberation of Nature," Inquiry (1976):83–131 and L. Reinhardt, "Some Gaps in Moral Space: Reflections on Forests and Feelings," in Mannison. McRobbie, and Routley, eds. . *Environmental Philosophy* (Canberra: Australian National University Research School of Social Sciences, 1980).

8. Though for simplicity I focus upon those who do strip mining, etc, the argument is also applicable to those whose utilitarian calculations lead them to preserve the redwoods, mountains, etc., but who care for only sentient nature for its own sake. Similarly the phrase "indifferent to nature" is meant to encompass those who are indifferent *except* when considering its benefits to people and animals.

9. For convenience I use the labels *environmentalist* and *anti-environmentalist* (or *critic*) for the opposing sides in the rather special controversy I have raised. Thus, for example, my "environmentalist" not only favors conserving the forests, etc., but finds something objectionable in wanting to destroy them even aside from the costs to human beings and animals. My "anti-environmentalist" is not simply one who wants to destroy the environment; he is a person who has no qualms about doing so independent of the adverse effects on human beings and animals.

11. An exception, apparently, was Kant, who thought "the starry heavens" sublime and compared them with "the moral law within," but did not for all that see our species as comparatively insignificant.

12. By "*proper* humility" I mean that sort and degree of humility that is a morally admirable character trait. How precisely to define this is, of course, a controversial matter; but the point for present purposes is just to set aside obsequiousness, false modesty, underestimation of one's abilities, and the like.

13. I take this point from some of Philippa Foot's remarks.

14. The causal history of this concern may well depend upon the object (tree, toy) having given the child pleasure, but this does not mean that the object is then valued only for further pleasure it may bring.

15. See, for example, Ernest Becker, *The Denial of Death* (New York: Free Press, 1973).

DISCUSSION QUESTIONS:

1. Hill claims that we cannot appeal to the interests of plants to criticize the person who destroys a natural environment because it is good for sentient beings. Hill thinks that only beings who can suffer can have interests, and plants cannot suffer. Other philosophers, notably Taylor (14.2) agree that plants cannot suffer but deny that suffering is a necessary condition for having interests. Marquis (15.1) makes a similar point about the early fetus: it has an interest in what happens to it even if it is not able to take an interest in what happens to it. Do you think that sentience is a necessary condition for having the kind of interests that count, morally speaking? If not, do you think that plants have interests? How does this

affect the moral judgments about the destruction of a natural environment?

2. Hill provides a disturbing example of a case where we might pass moral judgment on someone's character even though the action that prompts this judgment is—strictly speaking—morally permissible. The example is of a Nazi who is making lampshades from the human skin of victims that he himself did not kill. Do you think that there is something morally amiss with such a person? Do you think the action of making the lampshades is itself morally wrong? If not, what is morally amiss with such a person?

3. Hill claims repeatedly that there is a contingent (i.e., non-essential) connection between having a willingness to destroy the natural environment and lacking specific virtues. For example, he writes that "destroyers of the environment lack an appreciation of their place in the universe" (page 459). However, Hill provides no serious defense of these empirical claims. Can we tell, from our armchairs, how various cognitive attitudes will be connected with the virtues? Isn't this a question for science? Do YOU think you can tell when a cognitive attitude is a good indicator of the presence of a virtue or a vice?

Argument Reconstruction Exercises:

I. Some philosophers have suggested that what is wrong with destroying a natural environment that is devoid of sentient life is that it is harmful to the plants. Hill reconstructs the argument for that conclusion in the following passage. Identify the premises and conclusion in this excerpt:

Some may be tempted to seek an explanation [of our moral discomfort] by appeal to the interests, or even the rights, of plants. . .The temptation to make such a reply is understandable if one assumes that all moral questions are exclusively concerned with whether acts are right or wrong, and this, in turn, is determined entirely by how the acts impinge on the rights and interests of those directly affected. On this assumption, if there is cause for moral concern, some right or interest has been neglected and if the rights and interests of human beings and animals

have already been taken into account, then there must be some other pertinent interests, for example, those of plants. (page 457)

II. Hill rejects the idea that we can explain the badness of destroying nonsentient nature by appealing to the interests of plants because he thinks that plants lack morally relevant interests. Although he doesn't sketch the argument fully, here is the passage in which he rejects this conclusion. Identify the premises and conclusion in this excerpt—note that his key assumption is left unstated:

. . .the conclusion that plants have rights or morally relevant interests is surely untenable. We do speak of what is "good for" plants, and they can "thrive" and also be "killed." But this does not imply that they have "interests" in any morally relevant sense. Some people apparently believe that plants grow better if we talk to them, but the idea that the plants suffer and enjoy, desire and dislike, etc. is clearly outside of the range of both common sense and scientific belief. (page 457)

III. One of Hill's central arguments for his conclusion takes the form of an argument from analogy (see page 456). See if you can employ the following material to construct an argument from analogy that concludes that the person who willingly destroys the natural environment has a defect in character:

This strategy of shifting questions may seem more promising if one reflects on certain analogous situations. Consider, for example, the Nazi who asks, in all seriousness, "Why is it wrong for me to make lampshades out of human skin. . .?" It is even more evident that the question reveals a defect in the questioner than that the proposed act is itself immoral. . .Imagine, for example, one who laughs spontaneously to himself when he reads a newspaper account of a plane crash that kills hundreds. Or, again, consider an obsequious grandson who, having waited for his grandmother's inheritance with mock devotion, then secretly spits on her grave when at last she dies. . .The moral uneasiness which it arouses is explained more by our view of the agent than by any conviction that what he did was immoral. (page 458)

IV. Hill argues for a contingent connection between one's willingness to destroy a natural environment and a lack of appreciation of one's place in the universe. Identify the premises and conclusion in the implicit argument made in this excerpt:

. . .as a matter of fact, increased understanding of nature tends to heighten people's concern for its preservation. If so, despite the objection, the suspicion that the destroyers of the environment lack deep understanding of nature is not, in most cases, unwarranted. . . (page 459)

16.3 DO WE CONSUME TOO MUCH?

MARK SAGOFF (1997, UPDATED IN 2012)

Mark Sagoff is professor of philosophy at George Mason University and Director of the Institute for Philosophy and Public Policy. His work centers on issues in social/political philosophy, especially issues in the philosophy of law and environmental policy. In this essay, Sagoff takes a hard look at the empirical facts concerning human consumption and the natural environment, and he concludes that many environmentalists have missed the big picture. He outlines five misconceptions of the present environmental situation and argues that our moral obligations lie not in consuming less but in investing more. While it is possible to consume too much, he argues, this has little to do with an impending environmental disaster and more to do with the priorities of living a good life as an individual.

Reading Questions:

1. What is the Malthusian theory?

2. According to Sagoff, what are the five misconceptions that drive the current environmental scare?

3. What is an example of economic substitution?

4. How many people could be fed a vegetarian diet on the amount of food currently grown?

5. Sagoff argues that the real problem with fossil fuels is not a chronic shortage. What two problems does he identify with the use of fossil fuels for energy?

6. According to Sagoff, the North excludes the South. What does that mean? Find an example.

7. Sagoff cites studies that show that money does not make people happier. What does he suggest personal well-being depends on?

8. According to Sagoff, when do we consume too much?

A Roz Chast cartoon in the *New Yorker* depicts two robed monks each carrying a sign. One sign reads: "The End of the World Is at Hand for Religious Reasons." The sign carried by the other declares "The End of the World is at Hand for Ecological Reasons." Conservation biologists like

David Orr have observed the convergence of the prophecies of environmentalists and some religious fundamentalists. According to Orr, there is "an interesting convergence of views between conservation biologists and religious fundamentalists" because "both agree that things are going to hell in the proverbial handbasket." Not all religious fundamentalists, however, believe the end times are at hand. Many scoff at the idea of imminent doom.[1] Conservation biologists, however, generally agree that "whether by climate change, biotic impoverishment, catastrophic pollution, resource wars, emergent diseases, or a combination of several, the end is in sight, although we can quibble about the details and the schedule."[2]

Many environmentalists believe that the world is enjoying its "final days" because they subscribe to the **Malthusian theory** that as population and consumption increase, resources inevitably diminish and become exhausted. For many decades, these environmentalists have warned that "human demand is outstripping what nature can supply - even though the great majority of human beings have not even approached the extraordinary American level of resource consumption." They deplore the "human overshoot of the Earth's carrying capacity."[3]

The Case That We Consume Too Much

Do we consume too much? To some, the answer is self-evident. *If there is only so much food, timber, petroleum, and other material to go around, the more we consume, the less must be available for others.* The global economy cannot grow indefinitely on a finite planet. As populations increase and economies expand, natural resources must be depleted; prices will rise, and humanity—especially the poor and future generations at all income levels—as a result will suffer.[4]

Other reasons to suppose we consume too much are less often stated though also widely believed. Of these reasons the simplest—a lesson we learn from our parents and from literature since the Old Testament—may be the best: although we must satisfy basic needs, *a good life is not one devoted to amassing material possessions;*

what we own comes to own us, keeping us from fulfilling commitments that give meaning to life, such as those to family, friends, and faith. The appreciation of nature also deepens our lives. As we consume more, however, we are more likely to transform the natural world, so that less of it will remain for us to learn from, communicate with, and appreciate.

During the nineteenth century preservationists forthrightly gave ethical and spiritual reasons for protecting the natural world. John Muir condemned the "temple destroyers, devotees of ravaging commercialism" who "instead of lifting their eyes to the God of the mountains, lift them to the Almighty dollar."[5] This was not a call for better cost–benefit analysis: Muir described nature not as a commodity but as a companion. Nature is sacred, Muir held, whether or not resources are scarce.

Philosophers such as Emerson and Thoreau thought of nature as full of divinity. Walt Whitman celebrated a leaf of grass as no less than the journeywork of the stars: "After you have exhausted what there is in business, politics, conviviality, love, and so on," he wrote in Specimen Days, and "found that none of these finally satisfy, or permanently wear— what remains? Nature remains."[6] These writers thought of nature as a refuge from economic activity, not as a resource for it.

An Alternative Approach

Predictions of resource depletion, food scarcity, and falling standards of living, however, may work against our moral intuitions. Consider the responsibility many of us feel to improve the lot of those less fortunate than we. By declaring consumption a **zero-sum game**, by insisting that what feeds one mouth is taken from another, environmentalists offer a counsel of despair. Must we abandon the hope that the poor can enjoy better standards of living? The Malthusian proposition that the earth's population already overwhelms the carrying capacity of the Earth—an idea associated for fifty years with mainstream environmentalist thought—may make us feel guilty but strangely relieves us of responsibility. If there are too many people some must go. Why not them?[7]

A different approach, which is consistent with our spiritual commitment to preserve nature and with our moral responsibility to help each other, rejects the apocalyptic narrative of environmentalism. *The alternative approach suggests not so much that we consume less but that we invest more.* Environmentalists could push for investment in technologies which increase productivity per unit energy, get more economic output from less material input, provide new sources of power, increase crop yields by engineering better seeds, and move from an industrial to a service economy. Technological advances of these kinds account for the remarkable improvements in living conditions most people in the world have experienced in the last decades—and this was the period over which environmentalists had predicted the steepest declines. They also account for the preservation of nature—for example, the remarkable reforestation of the eastern United States.

What should environmentalists do? Should we insist with many conservation biologists and other scientists that the earth has reached its limits and "the end is in sight although we can quibble about the details and the schedule." Or should we instead leave the End Days to the saints and work with the kinds of knowledge-based high-tech industries that seek to engineer solutions for—or if necessary ways to adapt to—the local and global challenge of preserving nature while promoting prosperity?

The Facts

Far from vindicating the environmental narrative of inevitable decline and collapse, *the last fifty or sixty years have seen a remarkable improvement in standards of living except in those specific countries in which oppression, corruption, and civil war deprive people of the blessings of technological advance and global prosperity.*[8] According to an authoritative report, "Global economic activity increased nearly sevenfold between 1950 and 2000. Despite the population growth . . ., average income per person almost doubled during this period."[9] According to a World Bank report, "Global economic output grew 4 percent a year from 2000 to 2007, led by record growth in low- and middle-income economies. Developing economies averaged 6.5 percent annual growth of GDP from 2000 to 2007, and growth in every region was the highest in three decades."[10]

War, oppression, ethnic violence will cause famines, but it is wrong to conclude, as some environmentalists have done, that there is not enough food to go around. As a major report states, "our ability to provide sufficient food and to do so in increasingly cost-effective ways has been a major human and humanitarian achievement. . . ." And according to most projections, it appears likely that growing food needs can be met in the foreseeable future.[11]

The reasons for poor standards of living can be traced to the absence of economic development—not to a lack of resources. As the world has grown wealthier, it has become healthier. At the world level, life expectancy at birth has risen from about 30 years a century ago to 47 in 1950, 58 in 1975, and stands at 67 (for men) and 71 (for women) today.[12] In high-income nations, a child born today can expect (on average) to live at least 80 years.[13] This could greatly increase with advances in medical knowledge and technology. Access to clean potable water has also improved globally over the past 50 years although—as with food and longevity—many people lack adequate access to water in nations locked in civil war and trapped in poverty, corruption, and oppression.[14]

The idea that increased consumption will inevitably lead to depletion and scarcity, as often as it is repeated, is mistaken both in principle and in fact. It is based on five misconceptions, each of which will be addressed below. The first is that we are running out of non-renewable resources, such as minerals. The second is that the world will run out of renewable resources, such as food. The third contends that energy resources will soon run out. The fourth misconception argues from the "doubling time" of world population to the conclusion that human bodies will bury the Earth. The fifth misconception supposes the wealthy North exploits the impoverished South. These misconceptions could turn into self-fulfilling prophecies if we believed them - and if we therefore failed to make the kinds of investments and reforms that have improved standards of living in most of the world.

1. Are We Running Out of Non-renewable Resources?

While commodity markets are volatile—with petroleum especially sensitive to political conditions—the prices of minerals generally declined between 1980 and the terrorist attack on September 11, 2001. From 1980 to 1990, for example, the prices of resource-based commodities declined (the price of rubber by 40 percent, cement by 40 percent, and coal by almost 50 percent), while reserves of most raw materials increased.[15] They increased because technologies greatly improved exploration and extraction, for example, the use of bacteria to leach metals from low-grade ores. Reserves of resources "are actually functions of technology," one analyst has written. "The more advanced the technology, the more reserves become known and recoverable."[16]

If price is the measure of scarcity, then metals and minerals have become more plentiful over the past decades. According to a 2004 World Bank report, the price of its index of minerals and metals (in 1990 dollars) fell from a high close to $ 160 in 1965 to a low of about $80—a decline of 50 percent—in 2001.[17] One reason for this persistent decline is that plentiful resources are quickly substituted for those that become scarce and the price of which therefore rises. Analysts speak of an Age of Substitutability and point, for example, to nanotubes, tiny cylinders of carbon whose molecular structure forms fibers a hundred times as strong as steel, at one sixth the weight.[18] As technologies that use more-abundant resources do the work of those dependent on less-abundant ones—for example, ceramics in place of tungsten, fiber optics in place of copper wire, aluminum cans in place of tin ones—the demand for and the price of scarce resources decline.

One can easily find earlier instances of substitution. During the early nineteenth century whale oil was the preferred fuel for household illumination.[19]

A dwindling supply prompted innovations in the lighting industry, including the invention of gas and kerosene lamps and Edison's carbon-filament electric bulb.[20] Whale oil has substitutes, such as electricity and petroleum-based lubricants. From an economic point of view, technology can easily find substitutes for whale products. From an aesthetic, ethical, and spiritual point of view, in contrast, whales are irreplaceable.

The more we learn about materials, the more efficiently we use them. The progress from whale oil to candles to carbon-filament to tungsten incandescent lamps, for example, decreased the energy required for and the cost of a unit of household lighting by many times. On perfecting the electric bulb which made lighting inexpensive, Thomas Edison is widely quoted as saying that "only the rich will burn candles." Compact fluorescent lights are four times as efficient as today's incandescent bulbs and last ten to twenty times as long.[21] Comparable energy savings are available in other appliances: refrigerators sold in 1993 were 23 percent more efficient than those sold in 1990 and 65 percent more efficient than those sold in 1980, saving consumers billions in electric bills.[22] Robert Solow, a Nobel laureate, says that if the future is like the past, "there will be prolonged and substantial reductions in natural-resource requirements per unit of real output."

Communications illustrates the trend toward lighter, smaller, less materials-intensive technology. Just as telegraph cables replaced frigates in transmitting messages across the Atlantic and carried more information faster, glass fibers and microwaves have replaced cables—each new technology using less materials but providing greater capacity for sending and receiving information. Areas not yet wired for telephones are expected to leapfrog directly into cellular communications.[23]

Peter Drucker and other management experts argue that any modern economy depends more on the progress of technology than on the exploitation of nature. Although raw materials will always be necessary, knowledge has become the essential factor in the production of goods and services. Technological advance—which seems to be exponential given that each discovery prompts others—promises to improve standards of living while lightening the human "footprint" on the natural world. Of course, no one believes that economic development—or technological and scientific progress—will automatically lead to environmental improvement. It only provides the means; we must gather the moral, cultural, and political will to pursue the end.[24] "Where there is effective management," Drucker has written, "that is, application of knowledge to knowledge, we can always obtain the other resources."[25] In other words, the limits to knowledge are the limits to growth.

2. Are We Running Out of Food?

A prominent agricultural economist, Gale Johnson, wrote in 2000, "People today have more adequate nutrition than ever before and acquire that nutrition at the lowest cost in all human history, while the world has more people than ever before—not by a little but by a lot."[26] This happened, he argued, because "we have found low-cost and abundant substitutes for natural resources important in the production process."[27] By around 2000, the price of food and feed grains, in real dollars (adjusted for inflation) has declined by half from what it was fifty years ago in international markets.[28] Contrary to the apocalyptic narrative,[29] at the global level "soil loss and degradation are not likely to represent a serious constraint on agricultural production."

From 1961 to 1994 global production of food doubled.[30] "The generation of farmers on the land in 1950 was the first in history to double the production of food," the Worldwatch Institute reported. Furthermore, the world produces enough cereals and oilseeds to feed a healthful vegetarian diet adequate in protein and calories to 10 billion people—a billion more than the number at which demographers predict world population will peak later this century.[31] If, however, the idea is to feed 10 billion people not healthful vegetarian diets but the kind of meat-laden, artery-clogging, obesity-causing gluttonous meals that many Americans eat, the production of grains and oilseeds may have to triple—primarily to feed livestock.[32] Conceivably, if everyone had the money to

pay for food at current prices, with technological advances particularly in bioengineering, the world could produce enough beef and donuts to fatten everyone for the slaughter of diabetes, cirrhosis, and heart disease.

Farmers worldwide could double the acreage in production, but this should not be necessary. Increasing productivity will flow from the "agricultural revolution driven by biotechnology—a field that we define as including advanced genetics and genomics, bioinformatics, genetically modified plants, and tissue culture."[33] The Worldwatch Institute points out that "there are vast opportunities for increasing water efficiency" in arid regions, ranging from installing better water-delivery systems to planting drought-resistant crops.[34] "Scientists can help push back the physical frontiers of cropping by developing varieties that are more drought resistant, salt tolerant, and early maturing. The payoff on the first two could be particularly high."[35] Biotechnology introduces "an entirely new stage in humankind's attempts to produce more crops and plants."[36] The Gene Revolution takes over where the Green Revolution left off.[37]

According to the *Millennium Ecosystem Assessment*, "Despite rising food production and falling food prices, more than 850 million people still suffer today from chronic undernourishment."[38] Many of the poorest countries, such as Chad and Congo, possess more than enough excellent agricultural land but lack social organization and investment. Institutional reform—responsible government, peace, the functioning of markets, the provision of educational and health services—in other words, development, is the appropriate response to poverty and therefore malnutrition.[39]

Second, the *Assessment* observes, "Among industrial countries, and increasingly among developing ones, diet-related risks, mainly associated with overnutrition, in combination with physical inactivity now account for one third of the burden of disease."[40] (By comparison, "worldwide, undernutrition accounted for nearly 10% of the global burden of disease."[41]) Third, to make 9 billion people obese, biotech-based agriculture would have to convert the earth to a feedlot for human beings. Farmers can now provide a healthful diet for that many people on less acreage than they use today—thus sparing land for nature.[42] In other words, we can spare nature by sparing ourselves.[43]

By locking themselves into the Malthusian rhetoric—by predicting impending world-wide starvation and using the plight of the very poor as evidence of it—environmentalists ignore and even alienate groups who emphasize the quality and safety rather than the abundance of food and who understand that undernutrition represents a local not a global problem. The discussion has moved from the question whether the earth sets "limits" to the question of how to get wealthy people to eat less and poor people to eat more.[44] Animal rights advocates deplore horrific confined animal feed-lot operations and related factory-farm methods required to overfeed people. Environmentalists have obvious allies in advocates of human development, public health, and animal rights. To have any credibility, however, environmentalists must lose the apocalyptic narrative.

3. Are We Running Out of Energy?

Predictions that the world would by now have run out of petroleum—or will do so shortly—are an industry: recent books carry titles like *Beyond Oil: The View from Hubbert's Peak; The End of Oil: On the Edge of a Perilous New World; Out of Gas: The End of the Age of Oil?* and *The Party's Over: Oil, War and the Fate of Industrial Societies.*[45] The most persistent worries about resource scarcity concern energy. "The supply of fuels and other natural resources is becoming the limiting factor constraining the rate of economic growth," a group of experts proclaimed in 1986. They predicted the exhaustion of domestic oil and gas supplies by 2020 and, within a few decades, "major energy shortages as well as food shortages in the world."[46]

In stark contrast with the dire projections of the 1980s, the U.S. Department of Energy projected in 2009 that U.S. domestic production of petroleum would continue to increase slowly to a plateau over the following decades. "U.S. crude oil production increases from 5 million barrels per day in 2008 to over 6 million barrels per day in 2027 and remains at just over 6 million barrels per day through 2035."[47]

The same report projects domestic natural gas production to "grow from 20.6 trillion cubic feet in 2008 to 23.3 trillion cubic feet in 2035," owing largely to new methods of mining.[48]

The most abundant fossil or carbon-based fuel is coal, and some of the largest reserves of it are found in the United States. These will last for more than a century. In this respect, no global shortages of hydrocarbon fuels are imminent. "One sees no immediate danger of 'running out' of energy in a global sense," writes John P. Holdren, a professor at Harvard University who became the principal science advisor in the Obama administration. He concludes that "running out of energy resources in any global sense is not what the energy problem is all about."[49]

The real energy problem is two-fold: global climatic instability and global political instability. Reasonable minds can disagree about which problem is worse—but both require that the world move away from its dependence on fossil fuels and toward reliance on cleaner and smarter kinds of energy, as well as greater efficiencies in its use.

First, the burning of hydrocarbon fuels contributes to global warming and climate change. In 1958, the concentration of carbon dioxide (CO_2) stood at 315 parts per million (ppm). Today, it has reached 380ppm, which is about one-third higher than the historical norm over 400,000 years. Levels of CO_2 are increasing so fast that in four or five decades concentrations may be twice as great as historic levels.[50] Since the planetary climate may already be changing in response to current CO_2 loadings, scientists consider the situation urgent. The global energy problem has less to do with depleting resources than with controlling pollutants.

The second problem has to do with geopolitical stability, in other words, world peace. Thomas Friedman observes that oil-rich states tend to be the least democratic—and the wealthier the ruling class gets, the more tyrannical, truculent, obstructive, and dangerous it becomes.[51] The petrocracies destabilize global balances of power while holding oil-dependent states hostage. While the food problem is best understood as local—giving the very poor access to nutrition—the energy problem is global. The principal concern is not the supply of energy but the effects of its use on geopolitics and climate.

To provide leadership and direction—rather than simply reiterate their apocalyptic projections—environmentalists should advocate investment in some mix of power-producing climate-sparing technologies. There is a smorgasbord of suggestions. These include hybrid, plug-in hybrid, and electric vehicles; greater energy efficiency in housing, appliances; and the production of liquid fuels from renewable sources, some produced by genetically engineered or synthesized microorganisms capable of creating biomass cheaply or even directly splitting the carbon dioxide molecule. Other approaches include the expansion of nuclear power generation, including smaller "distributed" and sealed units, the development of geothermal and wind energy, and basic and applied research in battery technology, fuel cell technology, tidal, and other forms of power. Efforts are underway to construct a "smarter" and more efficient electric energy transmission grid.

4. Are There Too Many People?

In the 1970s, the population crisis was easy to define and dramatize. The Malthusian logic of exponential growth or "doubling times," so forcefully presented in books such as *The Population Bomb* (1968) and *The Population Explosion* (1990), proved that the "battle to feed all of humanity is over," and analogized the spread of population with cancer. "A cancer is an uncontrolled multiplication of cells; the population explosion is an uncontrolled multiplication of people. . . . The [surgical] operation will demand many apparently brutal and heartless decisions. The pain may be intense. But the disease is so far advanced that only with radical surgery does the patient have a chance of survival."[52]

By emphasizing the exponential mathematics of population growth—as if people were cancerous cells whose reproductive freedom had to be controlled by radical surgery—environmentalists made four mistakes. First, they missed the opportunity to endorse the belief that people should have all—but only—the children they want. The goal of assisting parents world-wide to plan for their children might appeal to "family values" and thus to social conservatives in a way that concerns about "too many people" did not. Efforts to improve the status of women—a key factor in fertility—may enjoy more political support and may be more effective than conventional fertility-control policies.

Second, by inveighing against economic growth—by demanding a small economy for a small earth—environmentalists alienated potential allies in the development community. Leading environmentalists explicitly rejected "the hope that development can greatly increase the size of the economic pie and pull many more people out of poverty." This hope expresses a "basically a humane idea," Paul Ehrlich wrote, "made insane by the constraints nature places on human activity."[53]

Third, by invoking "doubling times" as if that concept could be as meaningfully applied to people as to tumors, environmentalists ignored science and reason, that is, everything demographers knew about the transition then underway to a stable global population. As people move to cities—where children are not needed to do agricultural labor—and as they are assured their children will survive (so they can have fewer), and as the status of women improves, families become smaller. World population growth, which resulted from lower mortality not higher fertility, had been decelerating since the 1950s and dramatically after the 1970s. The United Nations now projects the global population "to reach 7 billion in late 2011, up from the current 6.8 billion, and surpass 9 billion people by 2050," at which it will stabilize and probably decline.[54] Most demographers believe that population will stop increasing during this century and then decline slowly to perhaps 8.4 billion in 2100.[55]

Fourth, the environmental community has yet to respond to the principal moral problem that confronts population policy—one that involves longevity not fertility.[56] The oldest segments of the population increase the fastest as science and technology extend the length of life. A U.N. report observes that in developed regions of the world, "the population aged 60 or over is increasing at the fastest pace ever (growing at 2.0 per cent annually) and is expected to increase by more than 50 per cent over the next four decades, rising from 264 million in 2009 to 416 million in 2050." The developing world is aging even more rapidly. "Over the next two decades, the population aged 60 or over in the developing world is projected to increase at rates far surpassing 3 per cent per year and its numbers are expected to rise from 473 million in 2009 to 1.6 billion in 2050."[57]

Environmentalists confront population growth with an entrance strategy, that is, birth control. Bill McKibben's *Maybe One: A Case for Smaller Families* (1999) now sets the pace. Even with one-child-per-couple, however, world population will continue to increase if families reach four, five, or more generations. Environmentalists need to develop an exit strategy. A book with the title *Maybe Eighty: A Case for Shorter Life-Spans* could provide one approach to the question environmentalists must confront.

The problem is no longer Malthus—it's Methuselah. What do environmentalists say about this? Oddly the writers of the 1960s and 70s in the updated versions of their original studies—published 30 to 40 years later—have little to say about this. As long as environmental leaders argue there are "too many people" without suggesting how long a life should last, they seem self-serving. They appear to comprise a vast and growing gerontocracy outraged that younger people whom they may need to take care of them presume to care for their own children.

5. Does the North Exploit the South?

William Reilly, when he served as administrator of the Environmental Protection Agency in the Bush the Elder Administration, encountered a persistent criticism at international meetings on the environment. "The problem for the world's environment is your consumption, not our population," delegates from the developing world told him. Some of these delegates later took Reilly aside. "The North buys too little from the South," they confided. "The real problem is too little demand for our exports."[58]

The delegates who told Reilly that the North consumes too little of what the South produces have a point. "With a few exceptions (notably petroleum)," a report from the World Resources Institute observes, "most of the natural resources consumed in the United States are from domestic sources."[59] Throughout the later decades of the 20th century, the United States and Canada were the world's leading exporters of raw materials.[60] The United States consistently leads the world in farm exports, running huge agricultural trade surpluses. The share of raw materials used in the North that it buys from the South recently stood at a thirty-year low; industrialized nations trade largely among themselves.[61] The World Resources Institute reported that "the United States is largely self-sufficient in natural resources." Again, excepting petroleum, bauxite, "and a few other industrial minerals, its material flows are almost entirely internal."[62]

Sugar provides an instructive example of how the North excludes—rather than exploits—the resources of the South. Since 1796 the United States has protected domestic sugar against imports.[63] American sugar growers, in part as a reward for large contributions to political campaigns, have long enjoyed a system of quotas and prohibitive tariffs against foreign competition.[64] American consumers paid about three times world prices for sugar in the 1980s, enriching a small cartel of U.S. growers. Forbes magazine has estimated that a single family, the Fanjuls, of Palm Beach, reaps more than $65 million a year as a result of quotas for sugar.[65]

As the United States tightened sugar quotas (imports fell from 6.2 to 1.5 million tons annually from 1977 to 1987), the Dominican Republic and other nations with ideal environments for growing cane experienced political turmoil and economic collapse. Many farmers in Latin America, however, did well by switching from sugar to coca, which is processed into cocaine—perhaps the only high-value imported crop for which the United States is not developing a domestic substitute.[66]

An article in *Foreign Policy* observed that the biotechnological innovations that create "substitutes for everything from vanilla to cocoa and coffee threaten to eliminate the livelihood of millions of Third World agricultural workers."[67] Vanilla cultured in laboratories costs a fifth as much as vanilla extracted from beans, and thus jeopardizes the livelihood of tens of thousands of vanilla farmers in Madagascar.[68] In the past, farms produced agricultural commodities and factories processed them. In the future, factories may "grow" as well as process many of the most valuable commodities—or the two functions will become one. As one plant scientist has said, "We have to stop thinking of these things as plant cells, and start thinking of them as new microorganisms, with all the potential that implies"—for example, that cells could be made to grow in commercially feasible quantities in laboratories in the North, not fields in the South.[69]

The North not only balks at buying sugar and other crops from developing countries; it also dumps its excess agricultural commodities, especially grain, on them. After the Second World War, American farmers, using price supports left over from the New Deal, produced vast wheat surpluses, which the United States exported at concessionary prices to Europe and then the Third World. These enormous transfers of cereals to the South, institutionalized during the 1950s and 1960s by U.S. food aid, continued during the 1970s and 1980s, as the United States and the European Community vied for markets, each outdoing the other in subsidizing agricultural exports.[70]

It might be better for the environment if the North exchanged the crops for which it is ecologically suited—wheat, for example—for crops easily grown in the South, such as coffee, cocoa, palm oil, and tea. Contrary to common belief, these tropical export crops—which grow on trees and bushes, providing canopy and continuous root structures to protect the soil—are less damaging to the soil than are traditional staples such as cereals and root crops.[71] Better markets for tropical crops could help developing nations to employ their rural populations and to protect their natural resources. Allen Hammond, of the World Resources Institute, points out that "if poor nations cannot export anything else, they will export their misery—in the form of drugs, diseases, terrorism, migration, and environmental degradation."[72]

Many environmentalists have argued that economic activity, affluence, and growth automatically lead to resource depletion, environmental deterioration, and ecological collapse. Yet greater productivity and prosperity—which is what economists mean by growth—have become prerequisite for feeding urban populations and protecting sensitive ecological systems such as rain forests by helping the world, as it urbanizes, to farm more efficiently and trade more effectively. Without economic development, destitute people who are unable to buy food and fuel will perforce create pollution by burning whatever they can find and thus destroying forests. Without economic growth, which also correlates with lower fertility, the environmental and population problems of the South will only get worse. For impoverished countries facing environmental disaster, economic growth or development may be the one thing that is sustainable.

What Is Wrong with Consumption?

No one has written a better critique of the assault that commerce makes on the quality of our lives than Thoreau provides in *Walden*. We are always in a rush—a "Saint Vitus' dance," as he called it.[73] Idleness is suspect. Americans today spend less time with their families, neighbors, and friends than they did in the 1950s. Juliet B. Schor, an economist at Harvard University, argues that "Americans are literally working themselves to death."[74] A fancy car, video equipment, or a complex computer program can exact a painful cost in the form of maintenance, upgrading, and repair. We are possessed by our possessions; they are often harder to get rid of than to acquire.

That money does not make us happier, once our basic needs are met, is a commonplace overwhelmingly confirmed by sociological evidence. Paul Wachtel, who teaches social psychology at the City University of New York, has concluded that bigger incomes "do not yield an increase in feelings of satisfaction or well-being, at least for populations who are above a poverty or subsistence level."[75] This cannot be explained simply by the fact that people have to work harder to earn more money: even those who hit jackpots in lotteries often report that their lives are not substantially happier as a result.[76] *Well-being depends upon health, membership in a community in which one feels secure, friends, faith, family, love, and virtues that money cannot buy. Whether or not economic growth is sustainable, there is little reason to think that once people attain a decent standard of living, continued growth is desirable.*

Economist Robert H. Nelson wrote that it is no longer possible for most people to believe that economic progress will "solve all the problems of mankind, spiritual as well as material."[77] Environmentalists will not make convincing arguments as long as they frame the debate over sustainability in terms of the physical limits to growth rather than the moral purpose of it. Even if technology overcomes the physical limits nature sets on the amount we can produce and consume, however, there are moral, spiritual, and cultural limits to growth. Environmentalists defeat themselves by denying the power of technological progress. If the debate were couched not in economic but in moral or social terms—if it centered on the values we seek to serve rather than the resources we may exhaust—environmentalists might more easily win the argument.

According to Thoreau, "a man's relation to Nature must come very near to a personal one."[78] For environmentalists in the tradition of Thoreau and John Muir, stewardship is a form of fellowship; although we must use nature, we do not value it primarily for the economic purposes it serves. We take our bearings from the natural world—our sense of time from its days and seasons, our sense of place from the character of a landscape and the particular plants and animals native to it. An intimacy with nature ends our isolation in the world. We know where we belong, and we can find the way home.

Rather than having the courage of our moral and cultural convictions, however, *we too often rely on economic arguments for protecting nature, in the process attributing to natural objects more instrumental value than they have.* By imputing to an endangered species an economic value or a price much greater than it fetches in a market, we "save the phenomena" for economic theory but do little for the environment. When environmentalists make the prices come out "right" by imputing market demand to aspects of nature which in fact have moral, spiritual, or aesthetic value, we confuse ourselves and fail to convince others.

The world has the wealth and the resources to provide everyone the opportunity for a decent life. We consume too much when market relationships displace the bonds of community, compassion, culture, and place. We consume too much when consumption becomes an end in itself and makes us lose affection and reverence for the natural world.

NOTES

1. In 2005, Richard Cizik, then leader of the 30-million-member National Association of Evangelicals, espoused a doctrine of sustainability and told the *New York Times*, "There's a certain gloom and doom about environmentalists. They tend to prophecies of doom that don't happen." *New York Times Magazine*, April 3, 2005; "Questions for Richard Cizik: Earthly Evangelist," Interview by Deborah Solomon, available on line at http://www.clas.ulf.edu/users/kschwart/earthy%20evangelist.pdf
2. David W. Orr, "Armageddon versus Extinction," *Conservation Biology* 19(April 2005), p. 290.
3. Paul R. Ehrlich and Anne H. Ehrlich, *One With Nineveh: Politics, Consumption, and the Human Future* (Washington, DC: Island Press, 2004), p. 69.
4. See, for example, Herman E. Daly, "From Empty-world Economics to Full-world Economics: Recognizing an Historical Turning Point in Economic Development," in Robert Goodland, Herman E. Daly, and Salah El Serafy, eds., *Population, Ecology, and Lifestyle* (Washington, DC: Island Press, 1992), pp. 23–37.
5. John Muir, *The Yosemite* (New York: Century Co., 1912), p. 256.
6. Walt Whitman, *Specimen Days* (Boston: David R. Godine, Publisher, 1971), p. 61
7. See Paul R. Ehrlich, *The Population Bomb* (New York: Ballantine Books, 1971), pp. 146–8, endorsing an end to food aid to impoverished areas.
8. The World Bank, *World Development Indicators* 2005 (Washington, DC, 2005) reports: "Since 1990 extreme poverty in developing countries has fallen from 28 percent to 21 percent. Over the same time population grew 15 percent to 5 billion people, leaving 1.1 billion people in extreme poverty. If economic growth rates in developing countries are sustained, global poverty will fall to 10 percent—a striking success.

But hundreds of million of people will still be trapped in poverty, especially in Sub-Saharan Africa and south Asia and wherever poor health and lack of education deprive people of productive employment; environmental resources have been depleted or spoiled; and corruption, conflict, and misgovernance waste public resources and discourage private investment."

9. Millennial Ecosystem Assessment, *Ecosystems and Human Well-being: Current State and Trends*, p. 74.

10. World Bank, *2009 World Development Indicators* (Washington, DC. 2009). "World View," p. 2.

11. Millennial Assessment Chapter 8, "Food", p. 212.

12. Millennial Ecosystem Assessment, *Ecosystems & Human Well-Being: Volume 1: Current State and Trends*: Chapter 28, "Synthesis," p. 829. United Nations Population Division, World Population Prospects: The 2002 Revision (February 2003). On line at: http://www.un.org/esa/population/publications/wpp2002/WPP2002-HIGHLIGHTSrevl.PDF (Also noting that because of HIV/AIDS and other scourges, "But whereas more developed regions, whose life expectancy today is estimated at 76 years, will see it rise to 82 years, that of less developed regions will remain considerably below, reaching 73 years by mid-century (up from 63 years today)."

13. For these statistics, see World Bank, *World Development Report 2010: Development and Climate Change* (Washington, DC, 2009), pp. 378–379.

14. Millennial Ecosystem Assessment, *Ecosystems and Human Well-being: Current State and Trends*.

15. See Stephen Moore, "The Coming Age of Abundance," in Ronald Bailey, ed., *The True State of the Planet*, pp. 126–27.

16. Thomas H. Lee, "Advanced Fossil Fuel Systems and Beyond," in Jesse H. Ausubel and Hedy E. Sladovich, eds., *Technology and Environment* (Washington, DC: National Academy Press, 1989), pp. 114–136; quotation at p. 116.

17. World Bank, *Global Economic Prospects 2004* (Washington, DC): Appendix 2. http://siteresources.worldbank.org/TNTRGEP2004/Resources/appendix2.pdf

18. H. E. Goeller and Alvin M. Weinberg, "The Age of Substitutability," *Science* 191 (February 20, 1976): 683–689. Curt Suplee, "Infinitesimal Carbon Structures May Hold Gigantic Potential," *Washington Post*, Dec. 2, 1996, p. A3.

19. See Daniel Yergin, *The Prize: The Epic Quest for Oil, Money, and Power* (New York: Simon and Schuster, 1992), p. 122.

20. See Jesse Ausubel, "The Liberation of the Environment," in Jesse Ausubel, ed. The Liberation of the Environments, *Daedalus* 125(3), Summer 1996, pp. 1–19.

21. See Jesse Ausubel, "Can Technology Spare the Earth?" *American Scientist* 84(March-April 1996): 166–78; esp. pp. 164–170. For further information see, Solstice: Internet Information Service of the Center for Renewable Energy and Sustainable Technology, http://www.crest.org/.

22. See "Appliance Standards are Getting Results," *Energy Conservation News*, Vol. 18, No. 2, Sept. 1, 1995.

23. See Peter Blomquist, "Fighting Poverty in the Information Age," *Seattle Times*, October 18, 1995, p. B5.

24. Recently, a group of ecological economists has conceded, "Knowledge is now recognized as a primary factor of production." They state the obvious as follows: "The acquired knowledge must be put to good use. Appropriate institutions, such as new financial institutions to securitize the biosphere, have a vital role in meeting this challenge." Similarly no one can doubt that "Even if knowledge is becoming a more important factor of production in more-developed economies, and even if this allows more-developed economies to achieve a higher rate of economic growth, this is not automatically good news for the environment. After all, economic growth is not always accompanied by an increase in environmental quality—especially under conventional definitions of economic growth. Thus it is necessary to examine closely the connection between knowledge as a production input and environmental quality." For these and similar insights see, Paul R. Ehrlich, Gary Wolff, Gretchen C. Daily, Jennifer B. Hughes, Scott Daily, Michael Dalton, and Lawrence Goulder, "Knowledge and the Environment," *Ecological Economics* 30 (1999): 267–284.1

25. Peter Drucker, *Post Capitalist Society* (New York: Harper Business, 1993), p. 45.

26. D. Gale Johnson, "Population, Food, and Knowledge," *American Economic Review* 90:1 (March 2000): 1–14; quotation at p. 1.

27. Ibid p. 2.

28. Robert E. Evenson, "Besting Malthus: The Green Revolution," *Proceedings of the American Philosophical Society* 149(4) (December 2005): 469–486; see p. 471.

29. See, for example, D. Pimental et al., "Environmental and Economic Costs of soil Erosion and Conservation Benefits," *Science*, 267(24 February 1995).

30. See Lester R. Brown, Christopher Flavin, and Hal Kane, *Vital Signs 1996* (New York: W.W. Norton, 1996), p. 25; see also Ronald Bailey, ed., *The True State of the Planet*, p. 409.

31. For discussion, see Robert Fogel, *The Escape from Hunger and Premature Death, 1700–2100*.

32. See Paul Waggoner, *How Much Land Can 10 Billion People Spare for Nature?* Task Force Report 121 (Ames, IA: Council for Agricultural Science and Technology, February, 1994), esp. Ch. 5. See also *World Resources 1994–95*, Ch. 6, esp. pp. 107–08. For a useful updates, see Pamela Matson and Peter Vitousek, "Agricultural Intensification: Will Land Spared from Farming be Land Spared for Nature?" *Conservation Biology* 20 (3)(2006), 709–710;

and A. Balmford, R. E. Green, and J. P. W. Scharlemann, "Sparing Land for Nature: Exploring the Potential Impact of Changes in Agricultural Yield on the Area Needed for Crop Production," *Global Change Biology* 11(2005): 1594–1605.

33. Rosamond Naylor and Richard Manning, "Unleashing the Genius of the Genome to Feed the Developing World" *Proceedings of the American Philosophical Society* 149(4) (December 2005): 515–528; quotation at p. p. 516. See the excellent discussion of marker-assisted breeding starting at p. 19. See also Ruttan, "Scientific and Technical Constraints," p. 462 ("At a more fundamental level, increases in crop yields would come from genetic advances that would change plant architecture to make possible higher plant populations per hectare and would increase the ratio of grain to straw in individual plants. Increases in production of animals and animal products would come about by genetic and management changes that would decrease the proportion of feed devoted to animal maintenance and increase the proportion used to produce usable animal products).

34. Lester R. Brown, Christopher Flavin, and Sandra Postel, *Saving the Planet* (New York: Norton, 1991), p. 87.

35. Lester R. Brown, "The Grain Drain," *The Futurist* 23(4) (July-August 1989), pp. 17–18.

36. Paul Kennedy, *Preparing for the Twenty-First Century* (New York: Vintage Books, 1993), p. 70.

37. Royce Rensberger, "New 'Super Rice' Nearing Fruition," *Washington Post,* Oct. 24, 1994, p. A1. For a thorough study of the prospects of improvement in rice yields in Asia and Latin America, see James Lang, *Feeding a Hungry Planet: Rice, Research and Development in Asia and Latin America* (Chapel Hill: University of North Carolina Press, 1996).

38. *Millenium Ecosystem Assessment, Ecosystems and Human Well-being: Current State and Trends,* p. 212.

39. See for example Jeffrey Sachs, *The End of Poverty: Economic Possibilities for Our Time* (Penguin Press: New York, 2005).

40. *Millennial Ecosystem Assessment Report, Ecosystems & Human Well-Being:* Volume 1: Chapter 8, "Food and Ecosystem Services," pp. 233–34. (reporting an epidemic of obesity. "At present, over 1 billion adults are overweight, with at least 300 million considered clinically obese, up from 200 million in 1995").

41. *Ecosystems and Human Well-Being Synthesis,* p. 51.

42. Waggoner, *How Much Land Can 10 Billion People Spare for Nature?* Task Force Report 121 (Ames, IA: Council for Agricultural Science and Technology, February, 1994).

43. Waggoner, *How Much Land Can 10 Billion People Spare for Nature?* Task Force Report 121 (Ames, IA: Council for Agricultural Science and Technology), pp. 26–27, citing National Corngrowers Association 1993 Tabulation of the

1992 Maize Yield Contest. Annual yields of biomass up to 550 tons per hectare are theoretically possible for algal cultures; yields half as great have been achieved. See Richard Radmer and Bessel Kok, "Photosynthesis: Limited Yields, Unlimited Dreams," *Bioscience* 27(9)(Sept. 1977): 599–604. See also, Paul Waggoner, "How Much Land Can Ten Billion People Spare for Nature?" in Jesse Ausubel, ed., *The Liberation of the Environment, Daedalus,* Summer 1996, pp. 73–94; see esp. p. 81.

44. See Nikos Alexandras, Countries with rapid population growth and resource constraints: issues of food, agriculture, and development.T. Lang, "Food Policy and Markets: Structural Challenges and Options," paper presented at the OECD Conference on Changing Dimensions of the Food Economy: Exploring the Policy Issues, The Hague, Netherlands, 6–7 February.

45. Kenneth S. Deffeyes, *Beyond Oil: The View from Hubbert's Peak* (New York: Farrar, Straus and Giroux, 2005); Paul Roberts, *The End of Oil: On the Edge of a Perilous New World* (Boston and New York: Houghton Mifflin, 2005); David Goodstein, *Out of Gas: The End of the Age of Oil* (New York and London: Norton, 2004; and Richard Heinberg, *The Party's Over: Oil, War and the Fate of Industrial Societies* (Gabriola Island, Canada: New Society Publishers, 2003).

46. John Gever, Robert Kaufmann, David Skole, Charles Vorosmarty, *Beyond Oil: The Threat to Food and Fuel in the Coming Decades* (a Project of Carrying Capacity, Inc.) (Cambridge, MA: Ballinger, 1986) pp. 9, xxix, and xxx. These authors announced that "the supply of fuels and other natural resources is becoming the limiting factor constraining the rate of economic growth" (p. 9, italics removed).

47. U.S. Energy Information Administration (EIA), "EIA Energy Outlook Projects Moderate Growth in U.S. Energy Consumption, Greater Use of Renewables, and Reduced Oil and Natural Gas Imports." Press Release December 14, 2009; available on line at http://www.eia.doe.gov/neic/press/press334.html. The press release explains, "Growth in crude oil production results from increases in offshore production and in onshore production using enhanced oil recovery techniques."

48. Ibid.

49. John Holdren, "The Energy Predicament in Perspective" in Irving M. Mintzer, ed., *Confronting Climate Change: Risks, Implications and Responses* (New York: Cambridge University Press 1992), pp. 163–169; quotation at p. 165.

50. These data are widely available. See, for example, Jonathan Shaw, Fueling Our Future, *Harvard Magazine* 108(3)(May-June 2006), p. 43.

51. Thomas L. Friedman, "As Energy Prices Rise, It's All Downhill for Democracy," *New York Times,* p. 23, Section A, col. 1.

52. Paul Ehrlich, *The Population Bomb* (New York: Ballantine Books, 1971), p. 152.

53. Paul R. Ehrlich and Anne H. Ehrlich, *The Population Explosion* (New York: Simon and Schuster, 1990), p. 269, n. 29.

54. United Nations, Department of Economic and Social Affairs, Population Division (2009). World Population Prospects: The 2008 Revision, Highlights, Working Paper No. ESA7P/WP.210 . Page vii. On line at: http://www.un.org/esa/population/publications/wpp2008/wpp2008_highlights pdf

55. See W. Lutz, W. Sanderson, and S. Scherbov, "The End of World Population Growth," *Nature* 412(2001): 543–546.

56http://www.silvereconomy-europe.org/daten/demographie en.htm

57. United Nations, Department of Economic and Social Affairs, Population Division (2009). World Population Prospects: The 2008 Revision, Highlights, Working Paper No. ESA/P/WP.210 . Page viii. On line at: http://www.un.org/esa/population/publications/wpp2008/wpp2008_highlights .pdf

58. In a phone interview, December 21, 1994, Mr. Reilly vouched for these remarks, noting that this incident happened more than once.

59. World Resources Institute, *World Resources 1994–95*, p. 16.

60. World Resources Institute, *World Resources 1994–95*, p. 291.

61. World Resources Institute, *World Resources 1994–95*, pp. 13–16.

62. Albert Adriannse et al., *Resource Flows*, p. 13.

63. See "America's Farm Subsidies," *The Economist*, June 27,1992.

64. Sean Holton, "Sugar Growers Reap Bonanza in Glades," *Orlando Sentinel Tribune*, September 18, 1990, p. A1.

65. Phyllis Berman and Alexandra Alger, "The Set-aside Charade," *Forbes*, March 13, 1995, p. 78.

66. For an excellent account of the political costs of the sugar program internationally, see Anne O. Krueger, "The Political Economy of *Controls: American Sugar," in Maurice Scott and Deepak Lal, eds., Public Policy and Economic Development: Essays in Honor of Ian Little* (New York: Oxford University Press, 1990).

67. Robin Broad and John Cavanaugh, "Don't Neglect the Impoverished South's Developing Countries," *Foreign Policy*, December 22, 1995, pp. 18–27.

68. Sally Lehrman, "Splicing Genes, Slicing Exports? U.S. Firms' Bioengineered Tropical Plants May Threaten Third World Farmers," *Washington Post*, September 22, 1992, p. H1.

69. Quoted in Mary Ellen Curtin, "Harvesting Profitable Products from Plant Tissue Culture," *Bio/Technology* 1(1983): 657. See also, R. S. Chaleff, "Isolation of Agronomically Useful Mutants from Plant Cell Cultures," *Science* 219(1983): 676–82. ("With recognition of the similarities between cultured plant cells and microorganisms came the expectation that all the extraordinary feats of genetic experimentation accomplished with microbes would soon be realized with plants." Id. at

679. Chaleff enumerates the difficulties that must be resolved before this expectation may be fulfilled.)

70. For documentation and further analysis, see Bruce L. Gardner, "The Political Economy of U.S. Export Subsidies for Wheat," in Anne Krueger, ed., *The Political Economy of American Trade Policy* (Chicago: University of Chicago Press, 1996), pp. 291–331. See also, Derek Biyearly, "The Political Economy of Third World Food Imports: The Case of Wheat," *Economic Development and Cultural Change* 35(1987): 307–328.

71. Partha Dasgupta, Carl Folke, and Karl-Goren Maler, "The Environmental Resource Base of Human Welfare," *Population, Economic Development, and the Environment* (New York: Oxford University Press, 1994), p. 31.

72. Personal communication, April 2, 1997.

73. *Walden*, previous note, p. 174.

74. Juliet B. Schor, *The Overworked American* (New York: Basic Books, 1991), p. 11.

75. Paul Wachtel, "Consumption, Satisfaction and Self-Deception," paper presented at a conference on Consumption, Steward and Good Life, University of Maryland, College Park, September 29–October 2, 1994, quotation at p. 5.

76. People "who win large sums of money in football pools or lotteries are not found to be on the whole more happy afterwards. . ." Michael Argyle, *The Psychology of Happiness* (New York: Methuen & Co., Ltd., 1986) See also Mary Jordan, "Millions Don't Turn Everything Into Gold" *The Washington Post*, July 21, 1991, p. A1, A21; and P. D. Brickman, D. Coates, and R. Janoff-Bulman, "Lottery Winners and Accident Victims: Is Happiness Relative?" *Journal of Personality and Social Psychology* 36(8)(19787): 917–27.

77. Robert H. Nelson, "In Memoriam: On the Death of the 'Market Mechanism,'" *Ecological Economics* 20(1997): 187–97; quotation at p. 188.

78. H. D. Thoreau, *The Journal of Henry David Thoreau*, vol. 10, ed. by Bradford Torrey and Francis H. Allen (Boston: Houghton Mifflin Company, 1949); quotation at p. 252.

DISCUSSION QUESTIONS:

1. Sagoff repeats the point made earlier in the chapter that although we must satisfy our basic needs, ownership and consumption of material goods can get in the way of living a good life. Do you think that this is true? Can you think of an example in your own life where living with less or giving something up made you more content or fulfilled or left you with more time and energy for things that really matter?

2. Suppose Sagoff is right that overconsumption displaces the bonds of family, community, and

place and that the current level of consumption often makes us lose affection and reverence for the natural world. Why is this a *moral* issue? Do we have moral obligations to maintain the bonds of family, community, etc.? Or is it a matter of moral virtue to have affection and reverence for the natural world?

3. In his alternative approach to the environmental crisis, Sagoff suggests "not so much that we consume less but that we invest more" (page 468). What does it mean to "invest more?" On commonsense understandings of what it means to invest more, isn't the dilemma that Sagoff presents a mistaken one? Why not consume less AND invest more? Need it be one or the other?

4. Although Sagoff seems to disagree, almost everyone else in the environmental literature agrees that a booming human population is bad for the planet. Do you think that this is true? If so, what morally permissible actions and morally just policies ought we to focus on to ameliorate this problem?

Argument Reconstruction Exercises:

I. Sagoff identifies what he sees as the central, "apocalyptic" argument against consumption as one that relies on the premise that the planet's resources are limited. Identify the premises and conclusion in this excerpt.

Do we consume too much? To some, the answer is self-evident. If there is only so much food, timber, petroleum, and other material to go around, the more we consume, the less must be available for others. The global economy cannot grow indefinitely on a finite planet. As populations increase and economies expand, natural resources must be depleted; prices will rise, and humanity—especially the poor and future generations at all income levels—will suffer. (page 467)

II. Sagoff's preferred argument against overconsumption appeals to the effects of such consumption on the quality of our lives. Identify the premises and conclusion in this argument.

Do we consume too much? . . .although we must satisfy basic needs, *a good life is not one devoted to amassing material possessions*; what we own comes to own us, keeping us from fulfilling commitments that give meaning to life, such as those to family, friends, and faith. The appreciation of nature also deepens our lives. As we consume more, however, we are more likely to transform the natural world, so that less of it will remain for us to learn from, communicate with, and appreciate. (page 467)

III. Yet a different argument for preserving natural environments and guarding our level of consumption appeals to the quasi-spiritual value of nature. Identify the premises and conclusion in this excerpt.

Do we consume too much? . . . nineteenth century preservationists forthrightly gave ethical and spiritual reasons for protecting the natural world. John Muir condemned the "temple destroyers, devotees of ravaging commercialism" who "instead of lifting their eyes to the God of the mountains, lift them to the Almighty dollar." This was not a call for better cost-benefit analysis: Muir described nature not as a commodity but as a companion. Nature is sacred, Muir held, whether or not resources are scarce. . .These writers thought of nature as a refuge from economic activity, not as a resource for it. (page 467)

IV. As noted in discussion question #3 above, Sagoff's article "suggests not so much that we consume less but that we invest more" (page 468). One might worry about whether or not this argumentative strategy embraces a false dilemma. Identify the premises and conclusion in this paraphrased text.

Environmentalists who are concerned about what we morally ought to do in this situation face a dilemma: either invest more or consume less. But there are no good empirical reasons why we should consume less—the world has the wealth and the resources to provide everyone with the opportunity for a decent life. So we should invest more instead.

16.4 REDEFINING THE GOOD LIFE IN A SUSTAINABLE SOCIETY

LESTER W. MILBRATH (1993)

Until his death in 2007, Lester Milbrath was a professor of political science at the State University at Buffalo, where he worked on environmental policy and related issues. One of the central thrusts of his work in political science was to make room for understanding a flourishing society not in terms of growth but in terms of sustainability and harmony with the natural world. In this essay, he makes some initial steps toward defining what he see as quality in living, and he emphasizes the minor role that material consumption plays in that schema. Instead, he advocates for what he calls living with simplicity—a strategy of living that pursues non-**zero sum** goods such as interpersonal relations, enjoyment of nature, learning, creative arts, etc.

Reading Questions:

1. According to Milbrath, what is wrong with defining progress and the good life in terms of material consumption?

2. What four experiences are common to people with a high quality of life?

3. What four experiences are common to people with a low quality of life?

4. According to Milbrath, does a good or decent life require ANY material goods?

5. What is Milbrath's advice as to how to order priorities when the interests of a person come into conflict with the preservation of the biocommunity? Why?

6. What does it mean to say that a good is a zero-sum good?

7. What are some examples of non-zero-sum goods that Milbrath recommends?

8. What is voluntary simplicity?

9. What is the difference between "embedded consciousness" and "self-reflective consciousness"?

Everyone wants a good life. The criminal who steals, the gambler who hopes for a "killing," the monk who meditates, the scientist who searches, the shopper who buys and buys, the outdoorsman who hunts and fishes, the tycoon who grabs for power and wealth, the religious person who prays for salvation—all are seeking what they believe to be the good life. Obviously a good life can be defined in many ways. Economists, politicians, and advertisers assume that consuming goods leads to quality of life and constantly remind us that we should want prosperity. Does prosperity equate with a good life? Should we let them define for us what a good life is? Why not give some thought to redefining the good life and take charge of our own destiny?

The physical conditions in which we live our lives set some boundaries that must be observed as we proceed with our redefinition. To be sure, we

Lester W. Milbrath, "Redefining the Good Life in a Sustainable Society." *Environmental Values* 2 (1993): 261–69. Reprinted with permission of White Horse Press, Cambridge, U.K.

can do a lot to redefine our physical conditions. We might move to another place, assuming that someone does not already occupy the place we want to take. Proffering lots of money may encourage the present occupant to allow us to take possession. Having lots of power can allow us to take over by force in the way that we routinely seize habitat from wildlife. Our cleverness and technology have stretched many boundaries and opened up many possibilities. Some people believe we can proceed indefinitely to manipulate nature and extend its boundaries.

Ironically, our very success as a species has created unforeseen consequences that set new boundaries and force us to redefine what the good life is.

1. We have successfully extended human longevity by improving public health and by appropriating more and more of the biosphere to our purposes. We have unintentionally achieved a human population explosion which is ruining quality of life in many parts of the world. The planet's ecosphere and resource base may not tolerate even two more doublings of world population (to 20 billion). Either we thoughtfully limit our reproduction or nature will limit it for us by starvation and disease.

2. At the very time of our population explosion, we are achieving a drastic increase in throughput of materials in our economy. Not only does accelerating economic activity swiftly draw down our resource stocks (many of them nonrenewable) but it also creates so much waste that it is seriously injuring ecosystems and changing global geosphere/biosphere patterns. We are recklessly perturbing biospheric systems that are so complex that we cannot know the consequences of our actions. Swift and powerful changes in global climate patterns would devastate our economies, destroy many of our resource stocks, and bring death to billions of humans.

Even if some drastic technological breakthrough enabled humans to keep growing in population and economic activity, would we want to live in the world that continuing growth would create? Within a century there would be 20 billion or more people. To prosperously support that many people, most of the biosphere's productivity would have to be turned to human needs. Most of the wilderness would be gone and those species that escaped extinction would be confined to reserves. To prevent feverish economic activity from constantly changing geosphere/biosphere patterns, and to make life somewhat comfortable, our daily existence would be confined to artificial city environments where air, water, and material processing were all carefully controlled. With that many people, life would be made tolerable only by severely restricting personal freedom. Is that the kind of world you want? Would that be a good life? *By continuing to define progress and the good life as growth in material consumption, that is where we are headed.*

A key aspect of my argument, then, is that continuing growth in human population and material consumption is not desirable (we do not want to go there) and very likely not possible.

If growth is a false god, no longer deserving of our worship, our society must rethink what living a good life means. One fundamental mistake we must correct is our penchant for trying to define the good life in material quantities and express it in monetary terms. Quality in living is not a thing, it is a feeling; it is necessarily a matter of subjective experience. Recognizing its subjective character does not mean we cannot have a rational discourse about it. To advance that discourse, I offer a definition of quality of life that I worked out with a graduate seminar several years ago. It addresses quality of life as experienced by individuals.

Quality in living is experienced only by individuals and is *necessarily* subjective. Objective conditions may contribute to or detract from the experience of quality but human reactions to physical conditions are not automatic: the experience occurs only subjectively. Personal reports of experiences of quality are much better indicators of these subjective experiences than physical measures of physical conditions. (We should carefully distinguish environmental conditions that can be measured with objective indicators from the experience of quality that can only be measured with subjective indicators.)

Quality is not a constant state but a variable ranging from high quality to low quality. Persons usually experience some combination of high and low quality; they seldom experience only one extreme or the other.

Persons have high quality of life when they experience the following:

1. A sense of happiness but not simply a momentary happiness; rather a long-run sense of joy in living.
2. A sense of physical well-being; usually this means good health but the sense of physical well-being can be realized by persons having lost certain capacities.
3. A sense of completeness or fullness of life; a sense that one is on the way to achieving, or has achieved, what one aspires to become as a person.
4. A sense of zestful anticipation of life's unfolding drama, greeting each day with hope and confidence that living it will be good.

Persons have a low quality of life when they experience the following:

1. A sense of hopelessness and despair; mornings are greeted with fear and dread. A sense that one is buffeted by fate and has lost control of one's life.
2. A sense of having failed to live up to one's image of oneself; that one's life has been a failure.
3. A sense of poor physical well-being; illness, injury, hunger, discomfort.
4. A pervading sense of unhappiness.

We should carefully distinguish quality of life judgements that are individual (personal) and subjective, from prescriptions for a good society. Individual experiences with the quality of this or that aspect of life do not translate directly into policy even though they are important informational inputs for policy makers. Ecosystem and social system values must be served in policy making as well as quality of life values.

We want a society and an environment that will allow people, as individuals, to work out their own quality of life. But there is a heavy responsibility on individuals to make the best of their situation and to take personal actions to achieve quality in living. We should be cautious about making the inference that a person living in what most people would assess as favourable conditions will experience high quality; or, conversely, that a person living in what most would assess as poor conditions will experience low quality. Yet, policy makers frequently make such inferences (when they report that per capita income has risen, or fallen, for example).

It is easy to recognize that *a decent life requires minimal provision of food, shelter, and clothing, and that society bears an obligation to provide at least that minimum.* In most developed countries those minima have been achieved for nearly everyone. But how do we decide what society should do to enhance quality of life beyond providing the minima? For example, we often hear the outcry of someone, or group, whose economic situation may be diminished in order to preserve some aspect of the ecosystem: they complain that they will starve if they cannot keep their job (and continue to injure the ecosystem). We need some clear thinking about values and what it means to live a good life in order to arrive at appropriate policies.

Is it true, for example, that loggers in the Pacific Northwest of the USA will starve if they cannot continue to log old-growth forests on national forest lands (owned by all the people)? The central question is not whether people or spotted owls are more important; they are both important. No one is suggesting that people must die for spotted owls to live. The question, rather, is what values should have the greatest priority as such policies are made? I use this syllogism to clarify value priorities:

> I can imagine a biocommunity thriving well without any human members but I cannot imagine human society thriving without a well-functioning biocommunity. Similarly, I can imagine human society functioning well without a given individual but I cannot imagine an individual thriving without a well-functioning biocommunity and a well-functioning human community. Therefore, individuals desiring quality of life must give top priority to protection and preservation of their biocommunity (their ecosystem). Second priority must go to preservation and protection of the good functioning of their social community. Only when people are careful to protect the viability of their two communities is it acceptable for

individuals to pursue quality of life according to their own personal desires.

Being allowed to cut logs on national forests is a privilege granted by society and not a basic right that society is obliged to fulfil. As society decides whether or not to grant that privilege, it should give highest priority to protecting the integrity of the ecosphere. Societies that fail to keep that top priority firmly in mind will undercut their long-run sustainability. Leaders of contemporary societies constantly make this same basic error when they persistently press for economic growth.

It is clear we must find the good life in some other way than continuing to grow in material consumption. Finding a good life is more a search of our own minds than it is a search of a shopping mall.

New but Old Ways to Enjoy Life with Fewer Material Goods

The toy industry is now very big business. The inventiveness of designers using advanced technology has produced some fantastic creations. Children with a closet full of such toys can have stimulating and happy days (though a poor kid could envy a rich kid). But what did children do to enjoy life before they had the largess of affluent parents and the cleverness of the modern toy industry? While travelling recently in a developing country I watched some boys rolling an old auto tyre, guiding it with a stick; they seemed every bit as happy with their "toy" as the modern American child with a closet full of expensive toys.

The same question applies to adults. Thousands of generations of people enjoyed life with only a small fraction of our material goods. Were they less happy than we? We all have inner resources for meditation, conversation, loving, communion with nature, reading, writing, playing music, dancing, and engaging in sports. These talents may need to be developed further because our present society lures us to buy and consume, buy and be entertained, buy and be pampered. People who have given in to those inducements have become more bystanders than participants in life's unfolding drama.

Goods That Are Not Zero Sum

Economists characterize most goods exchanged in the market as "zero sum." Because I have it, you cannot have it—that is **zero sum**. *Our conditioning toward material consumption inclines us to think of all enjoyment as zero sum.* Actually, many of the most satisfying and fulfilling things in life are enhanced when shared.

You would think that everyone would know that love is good for people, that it is easy to give and to share, that fulfilment from loving is enhanced, not diminished by sharing. Leo Buscaglia is a well known professor, author and lecturer who colourfully and effectively conveys the message that love is good for people and society. Buscaglia's message is so popular because many people sense that our modern affluent society has somehow lost its understanding of the meaning of love. Ironically, Buscaglia reports numerous instances where persons reject his claims for the virtue of love. If some day our society turns away from trying to find fulfilment in material goods, we may, indeed, find much greater fulfilment in love. We should be actively learning from each other how best to love.

Some years ago I conducted a study of quality of life in the Niagara Frontier and discovered that the ways people sought fulfilment in life clustered into lifestyle patterns. As might be expected, some persons emphasized a consumer lifestyle; their greatest enjoyment came from buying and consuming. They were a minority, however.

Another lifestyle, favoured by many, emphasized fulfilment in interpersonal relations. These people loved to socialize with friends and relatives. Rewarding companionships with friends are not difficult to find and most of these people felt quite fulfilled. Most importantly, this lifestyle is not zero-sum, is not highly consuming of goods, does not waste scarce resources, and does not injure the environment. If we slowed down our frantic production pace, demanded less and consumed less, we would have more time for enjoying companionship; chances are, we also would enhance our quality of life.

Enjoyment of nature emerged as another lifestyle in our study; it is not consumed in the same way as restaurant meals, autos, or tickets to seats in a football stadium, and thus is not zero-sum. Normally, my enjoyment of nature does not detract from your enjoyment, but, nature can be overrun and destroyed by too many people. Having to contend with a crowded beach, or bumper-to-bumper traffic heading for a national park, or elbow-to-elbow fishing in a trout pool is not a fulfilling experience. Many U.S. National Parks have had to ration nature experiences by advance reservations, quotas, and admission tickets. They are so crowded in China that they have had to assign people to take holidays in nature on different days. The obvious demand for nature experiences makes it all the more important that nature be protected and, where necessary, restored to beauty. Nature protection and beautification is a fulfilling activity that many people can join in, derive satisfaction from, and strengthen rather than diminish by their sharing. Urgent joint action also is needed to obtain and maintain such vital natural elements as clean air, water, and soils. Cutting back on consumption would help a lot, but collective political action to assure environmental protection also is imperative.

Learning is another pleasurable and fulfilling activity that is developed rather than diminished by sharing. Philosophical understanding, especially, is deepened by interpersonal discourse. Cultivation of the mind has been emphasized in many cultural traditions and surely would be an important activity to emphasize in a sustainable society. Deepening one's understanding requires time and periods of quiet contemplation; ironically, these are scarce goods that many frantically busy people today fervently wish they could have. If we slowed down, produced less, and consumed less, perhaps we could find more quiet times for learning and for deepening our understanding.

Enjoyment in creating, and appreciating literature, music, and art, similarly are not diminished if shared and should be emphasized in a sustainable society. Instead of life being bleak and cold when we are forced to slow down, it could be a flourishing period of creativity and learning.

If we can understand how our possessions have failed us, we can more readily decrease our thralldom. Turning instead to a focus on the quality of our relations with others; on the clarity and intensity of our experiences; on intimacy, sensuality, aesthetic sensibility, and emotional freedom, we can see how a more ecologically sound society can be a more exciting and enjoyable one as well. (Wachtel 1983: 143)

Play is another pleasurable and fulfilling activity that typically consumes few resources and need not damage nature. I do not speak of energy consuming and nature destroying thrill contests such as off-road vehicle racing; they are incompatible with a good society. Nor do I speak of sporting events with large crowds of spectators; they should be seen as a branch of the entertainment industry. Rather, the sustainable society should emphasize widespread participation by nearly everyone in games that bring pleasure and are not wasteful or destructive; there certainly is sufficient variety to serve almost any taste. Games requiring vigorous activity not only pass the time pleasurably but also nurture good health.

Self governance also is non-zero-sum in the sense that everyone benefits when better laws are passed or when better community programs are undertaken. (Many elections are zero-sum when the winner takes all.) Self governance does require interest, concern, and time from people. Persons caught up in the rat race for money often claim that they are too busy to participate. However, if life were restructured to give less emphasis to getting rich and consuming, people could more likely see the relevance of their participation for a better life; furthermore, schedules would be more flexible, allowing people to take the time for political affairs—it could become a natural and expected aspect of everyday life.

Leisure?

So far I have not given specific attention to leisure, although I have strongly urged people to take time for personally fulfilling activities. Entrepreneurs in modern affluent society try to sell expensive goods and services to help people use their leisure "to the fullest"; that approach to leisure appropriately could be called an industry: it fits with our delusion that happiness must be bought. Most of the activities discussed above that people do to fulfill themselves might also be thought of as leisure but they do not make up an industry. People engage in such activities to enjoy their leisure but they consume few leisure goods. The sustainable society would have little need for a "leisure industry."

Voluntary Simplicity

Duane Elgin's (1981) book *Voluntary Simplicity: Toward a Way of Life That Is Outwardly Simple, Inwardly Rich* is a much deeper examination of philosophy, lifestyles, social forces, and revolutionary changes than one might expect from the title. His central thesis is that *people voluntarily choose a life of simplicity because it is richer than modern consuming lifestyles*. To live *voluntarily* means to live more deliberately, intentionally, purposefully, and to do so consciously. "We cannot be deliberate when we are distracted from our critical life circumstances. We cannot be purposeful when we are not being present. Therefore, crucial to acting in a voluntary manner is being aware of ourselves as we move through life." (Elgin 1981, p. 32)

He distinguishes "embedded consciousness" from "self-reflective consciousness." Embedded consciousness is our normal or waking consciousness so embedded within a stream of inner-fantasy dialogue that little attention can be paid to the moment-to-moment experiencing of ourselves. Self-reflective consciousness is a more advanced level of awareness in which we are continuously and consciously "tasting" our experience of ourselves. It is "marked by the progressive and balanced development of the ability to be simultaneously concentrated (with a precise and delicate attention to the details of life) and mindful (with a panoramic appreciation of the totality of life)" (Elgin 1981, p. 151).

Living more consciously has several enabling qualities:

1. Being more consciously attentive to our moment-to-moment experiences enhances our capacity to see things as they really are; thus, life will go more smoothly.
2. Living more consciously enables us to respond more quickly to subtle feedback that something is amiss, so that we can move with greater speed towards corrective action.
3. When we are conscious of our habitual patterns of thought and behaviour, we are less

bound by them and can have greater choice in how we will respond.

4. Living more consciously promotes an ecological orientation toward all of life; we sense the subtle though profound connectedness of all life more directly.

These four enabling qualities are not trivial enhancements of human capacity; they are essential to our further evolution and to our survival. . . .

Self-reflective consciousness can open the door to a much larger journey in which our "self" is gradually but profoundly transformed. The inner and outer person gradually merge into one continuous flow of experience. Simone de Beauvoir said, "Life is occupied in both perpetuating itself and surpassing itself; if all it does is maintain itself, then living is only not dying."

To live with *simplicity* is not an ascetic but rather an aesthetic simplicity because it is consciously chosen; in doing so we unburden our lives to live more lightly, cleanly, and aerodynamically. Each person chooses a pattern or level of consumption to fit with grace and integrity into the practical art of daily living on this planet. We must learn the difference between those material circumstances that support our lives and those that constrict our lives. Conscious simplicity is not self-denying but life-affirming.

> Simplicity, then, should not be equated with poverty. Poverty is involuntary whereas simplicity is consciously chosen. Poverty is repressive, simplicity is liberating. Poverty generates a sense of helplessness, passivity, and despair; simplicity fosters personal empowerment, creativity, and a sense of ever present opportunity. Poverty is mean and degrading to the human spirit; simplicity has both beauty and functional integrity that elevate our lives. Poverty is debilitating; simplicity is enabling. (Elgin 1981, p. 34)

Simplicity is not turning away from progress; it is crucial to progress. It should not be equated with isolation and withdrawal from the world; most who choose this way of life build a personal network of people who share a similar intention. It also should not be equated with living in a rural setting; it is a "make the most of wherever we are" movement. *Voluntary simplicity would evolve both the material and the conscious aspects of life balance with each other—allowing each aspect to infuse and inform the other.*

We can get from where we are now to this new, yet old, way of defining the good life by assisting each other in our social learning. When it becomes obvious that material consumption does not lead to the good life, or that growth in material consumption is not possible, it will be somewhat easier for us to make this transformation to a new way of thinking. Life without material growth very likely will be better than the frantic chase after money and goods that now blights our lives and the ecosphere; it surely will be more sustainable.

Conclusion

Living a good life in a sustainable society could be a realization of the Greek concept of *Paideia*—the lifelong, transformation of our own person as an art form. It is ridiculous to characterize life with fewer material goods as "freezing in the dark," as some environmental critics have painted it. It would be a very *different* way of life: more contemplative, less frantic; more serene, less thrilling; valuing cooperation and love more, valuing competition and winning less; with more personal involvement, less being a spectator; more tuned to nature, less tuned to machines. Changes this sweeping may take several generations to come about. Many people have already begun the journey and their learning can help others find the way. Necessity may well hasten our relearning.

REFERENCES

Duane Elgin, *Voluntary Simplicity: Toward a Way of Life that is Outwardly Simple, Inwardly Rich* (New York: William Morrow, 1981).

Paul L. Wachtel, *The Poverty of Affluence* (New York: The Free Press, 1983).

DISCUSSION QUESTIONS:

1. Milbrath makes a number of empirical claims about how many humans the earth could support, what the world would be like if there were 20 billion humans, etc. But, of course, Milbrath is a political theorist, not an empirical scientist. Does he provide any evidence that these claims about the earth are true? How are we to judge? Where should you turn to figure out these answers for yourself?

2. At one point, Milbrath writes that "Quality in living is not a thing, it is a feeling; it is necessarily a matter of subjective experience" (page 481). Do you agree? Why or why not? Think back to Aristotle's conception of the good life in Chapter 12—would he agree with Milbrath that the good life is simply feeling a certain way? Why or why not? Suppose destroying the environment at a reckless pace made you feel good. Would Milbrath conclude that you have a high quality of life?

3. On the one hand, Milbrath claims that personal reports are good indicators of quality of life, but on the other hand, he insists that the consumptive lifestyle that many of us lead is not conducive to a high quality of life. How could this be? If I am good at determining the quality of my life, then wouldn't I naturally choose a lifestyle that increased this felt quality? Can Milbrath hang on to both of these claims or do you think he should give up either the idea that we are good judges of the overall quality of our life or the idea that the consumptive life is not a high-quality one?

Argument Reconstruction Exercises:

I. Milbrath thinks that we should rethink the good life in light of empirical facts about the earth's resources. See if you can use the following claim as a premise in his overall argument for the conclusion that continued growth both in population and consumption are inimical to a high-quality of living:

> A key aspect of my argument, then, is that continuing growth in human population and material consumption is not desirable (we do not want to go there) and very likely not possible. (page 481)

II. Milbrath offers a ranking of priorities for adjudicating disputes between competing interests. Identify the premises and conclusion in this excerpt:

> I can imagine a biocommunity thriving well without any human members, but I cannot imagine human

members thriving without a well-functioning bio-community. . . Therefore, individuals desiring quality of life must give top priority to protection and preservation of their biocommunity (their ecosystem). (page 482)

III. Milbrath appears to be worried about two separate features of consumption. First, it doesn't appear sustainable given certain empirical facts about the earth's resources. But second, he doesn't see it as advancing our interests in leading a high quality of life. Identify the premises and conclusion in this paraphrase of this second worry:

No matter what level of material property we possess, we continue to want more. Owning stuff does not satisfy our desires for more stuff. A high quality

of life, on the other hand, requires that we pursue ends that satisfy our desires. So insofar as we want to live a high quality life, we will not pursue our desires to own more stuff.

IV. Some people have objected to Milbrath by pointing out the important role that economic growth has played in giving a good life to so many people. Identify the premises and conclusion in this version of the response:

People need basic material things in order to survive, much less have a good life. This means that economic progress and material possessions are necessary conditions for the good life. Since we all want a good life, we all need to continue to pursue material possessions.

CHAPTER 17

Famine Relief

For I was hungry and you gave me something to eat, I was thirsty and you gave me something to drink, I was a stranger and you invited me in, I needed clothes and you clothed me, I was sick and you looked after me, I was in prison and you came to visit me.

—JESUS (MATTHEW 25:35–6)

INTRODUCTION

Americans spend over $7.5 billion per year on greeting cards,[1] $18 billion per year on coffee,[2] and $41 billion per year on their pets.[3] The average American consumer spends $2,693 per year on entertainment.[4] Not everyone in the world lives this way. Consider the following:

- 40% of the people on the planet live in poverty (less than $2 a day).[5]
- 1 in 7 people in the world suffer chronic hunger—more than 925 million people.[5]
- More people die from hunger each year than from AIDS, malaria, and tuberculosis combined.[5]
- World agriculture produces 17% more calories per person today than it did 30 years ago, despite a 70 percent population increase.[6]
- Poor nutrition plays a role in the deaths of over 5 million children per year. The estimated proportions of deaths in which undernutrition is an underlying cause are roughly similar for diarrhea (61%), malaria (57%), pneumonia (52%), and measles (45%).[7]

Of course, it's hard to know how much money it would take to alleviate these difficult problems.

At least, that's what many people say. But it's not that difficult once one has seen the numbers side by side. Compare the following:

$6 billion	**Estimated annual cost to achieve basic education for all people**
$6 billion	Actual annual spending on cosmetics in the United States alone
$9 billion	**Estimated annual cost to provide clean water and sanitation for all people**
$11 billion	Actual annual spending on ice cream in Europe
$12 billion	**Estimated annual cost to provide reproductive services to all women**
$12 billion	Actual annual spending on perfumes in the United States and Europe
$13 billion	**Estimated annual cost to ensure basic health and nutrition for all people**
$ 17 billion	Actual annual spending on pet foods in the United States and Europe

The comparisons are even more drastic when we consider bigger-ticket items like cigarettes ($50 billion annually in Europe alone), alcoholic drinks ($105 billion annually in Europe alone), or military spending ($780 billion worldwide).[8]

What should we think about this situation? One thing seems obvious: we could give up relatively little by way of luxury and make an enormous difference in the lives of those who are suffering from hunger and disease. If we all gave up ice cream and perfume for a year, we would save enough money to ensure that the entire world population was fed and educated. Almost no one doubts that most of us in the First World are *able* to do this. And no one doubts that, in some sense, it would be a morally *good* thing for us to do this. But do we have a moral *obligation* to do so? Must we help those who are less fortunate then ourselves? In his essay in this chapter, Peter Singer argues that we are obligated to do exactly that.

Other authors in this chapter argue for a less radical conclusion. If we rightly own the goods that we have, then others are not entitled to them. In either case, the readings of this chapter challenge us to think carefully about our moral obligations in scenarios like these. Like many applied ethical issues, the issue of famine relief may be one that is uncomfortable for us to read and think about. Perhaps that discomfort should tell us something about ourselves or about our moral responsibilities to those who are less fortunate.

REFERENCES

1. http://www.greetingcard.org/AbouttheIndustry/tabid/58/Default.aspx
2. http://www.businessweek.com/magazine/content/07 32/b4045001.htm
3. National Coffee Association online statistics.
4. US Department of Labor, US Bureau of Labor Statistics, Consumer Expenditure Survey 2010.
5. http://www.oxfamamerica.org/files/food-for-all-fact-sheet.pdf
6. Food and Agriculture Organization, International Fund for Agricultural Development, World Food Program. 2002 "Reducing Poverty and Hunger, the Critical Role of Financing for Food. Agriculture, and Rural Development." p. 9.
7. Black RE, Morris SS, Bryce J. "Where and why are 10 million children dying every year?"*Lancet.* 2003 Jun 28;361(9376):2226–34.
8. Euromonitor 1997; UN 1997g; UNDp, UNFPA and UNICEF 1994; Worldwide Research. Advisory and Business Intelligence Services 1997.

SUGGESTIONS FOR FURTHER READING

Braybrooke, David. "A Progressive Approach to Personal Responsibility for Global Beneficence." *The Monist,* 2003; 86: 301–22.
Cullity, Garrett. "International Aid and the Scope of Kindness." *Ethics* 1994; 105, pp. 99–127.
Engel, Jr., Mylan. "Hunger, Duty, and Ecology: On What We Owe Starving Humans." In *Environmental Ethics: Readings in Theory and Application,* ed. Louis Pojman (Belmont, CA: Wadsworth/Thomson, 2003, pp. 426–441)
Filice, Carlo. "On the Obligation to Keep Informed about Distant Atrocities." *Human Rights Quarterly* 1990; 12:3, pp. 397–414.
Hardin, Garrett. "Living on a Lifeboat." *Bioscience* 1974; 24:10, pp. 561–568.
Miller, Richard W. "Beneficence, Duty, and Distance." *Philosophy & Public Affairs.* 2004; 32: 357–83.
Narveson, Jan. "We Don't Owe Them a Thing! A Tough-Minded but Soft-Hearted View of Aid to the Faraway Needy." *The Monist* 2003; 86: 419–33.
Pogge, Thomas W. (ed.). *Freedom from Poverty as a Human Right: Who Owes What to the Very Poor?* (Oxford: Oxford University Press, 2007)
Slote, Michael A. "The Morality of Wealth." In *World Hunger and Moral Obligation,* W. Aiken and H. LaFollette (eds.). (Englewood Cliffs, NJ: Prentice-Hall, 1977, pp. 124–47)
Singer, Peter. *The Life You Can Save: How to Do Your Part to End World Poverty.* (Random House, 2010)
Unger, Peter. *Living High and Letting Die: Our Illusion of Innocence.* (Oxford: Oxford University Press, 1996)

17.1 FAMINE, AFFLUENCE, AND MORALITY

PETER SINGER (1972)

Peter Singer is Ira W. DeCamp Professor of Bioethics at Princeton University. He is widely regarded as one of the most influential philosophers of the late 20th century. The vast majority of Singer's work focuses on issues in applied ethics, in particular the moral status of non-human animals. His most recent book, *The Life You Can Save* (2009), is one of the most careful defenses of our moral obligations to donate to famine relief. In this essay, Singer sketches his argument for famine relief. The argument relies on two premises: one about the badness of suffering and death and the second a moral rule called the **Greater Moral Evil Principle.** Combined with trivial economic facts about the level of wealth and standard of living in First World countries, these two premises imply that many of us have moral obligations to give money to famine relief.

Reading Questions:

1. What is happening in East Bengal?

2. What moral assumption does Singer begin with and not argue for?

3. What is the difference between what Singer calls the moderate and strong view of the crucial principle in his argument?

4. What is the point of Singer's thought experiment with the child drowning in the shallow pond?

5. What is marginal utility?

6. What is the difference between duty and charity?

7. What does it mean for an action to be supererogatory?

8. What is the practical objection to Singer's conclusion on the basis of population control?

The Empirical Facts

As I write this, in November 1971, people are dying in East Bengal from lack of food, shelter, and medical care. The suffering and death that are occurring there now are not inevitable, not unavoidable in any fatalistic sense of the term. Constant poverty, a cyclone, and a civil war have turned at least nine million people into destitute refugees; nevertheless, it is not beyond the capacity of the richer nations to give enough assistance to reduce any further suffering to very small proportions. The decisions and actions of human beings can prevent this kind of suffering. Unfortunately, human beings have not made the necessary decisions. At the individual level, people have, with very few exceptions, not responded to the situation in any significant way. Generally speaking, people have not given large sums to relief funds; they have not written to their parliamentary representatives demanding increased government assistance; they have not demonstrated in the streets, held symbolic fasts, or done anything else directed toward providing the refugees with the means to satisfy their essential needs. At the government level, no government has given the sort of massive aid that would enable the refugees to survive for more than a few days. Britain, for instance, has given rather more than most countries. It has, to date, given £14,750,000. For comparative purposes, Britain's share of the nonrecoverable development costs of the Anglo-French Concorde project is already in excess of £275,000,000, and on present estimates will reach £440,000,000. The implication is that the British government values a supersonic transport more than thirty times as highly as it values the lives of the nine million refugees. Australia is another country which, on a per capita basis, is well up in the "aid to Bengal" table. Australia's aid, however, amounts to less than one-twelfth of the cost of Sydney's new opera house. The total amount given, from all sources, now stands at about £65,000,000. The estimated cost of keeping the refugees alive for one year is £464,000,000. Most of the refugees have now been in the camps for more than six months. The World Bank has said that India needs a minimum of £300,000,000 in assistance from other countries before the end of the year. It seems obvious that assistance on this scale will not be forthcoming. India will be forced to choose between letting the refugees starve or diverting funds from her own development program, which will mean that more of her own people will starve in the future.[1]

These are the essential facts about the present situation in Bengal. So far as it concerns us here, there is nothing unique about this situation except its magnitude. The Bengal emergency is just the latest and most acute of a series of major emergencies in various parts of the world, arising both from natural and from man-made causes. There are also many parts of the world in which people die from malnutrition and lack of food independent of any special emergency. I take Bengal as my example only because it is the present concern, and because the size of the problem has ensured that it has been given adequate publicity. Neither individuals nor governments can claim to be unaware of what is happening there.

The Moral Facts

What are the moral implications of a situation like this? In what follows, *I shall argue that the way people in relatively affluent countries react to a situation like that in Bengal cannot be justified*; indeed, the whole way we look at moral issues—our moral conceptual scheme—needs to be altered, and with it, the way of life that has come to be taken for granted in our society.

In arguing for this conclusion I will not, of course, claim to be morally neutral. I shall, however, try to argue for the moral position that I take, so that anyone who accepts certain assumptions, to be made explicit, will, I hope, accept my conclusion.

I begin with the assumption that suffering and death from lack of food, shelter, and medical care are bad. I think most people will agree about this, although one may reach the same view by different routes. I shall not argue for this view. People can hold all sorts of eccentric positions, and perhaps from some of them it would not follow that death by starvation is in itself bad. It is difficult, perhaps impossible, to refute such positions, and so for brevity I will henceforth take this assumption as accepted. Those who disagree need read no further.

My next point is this: *if it is in our power to prevent something bad from happening, without thereby sacrificing anything of comparable moral importance, we ought, morally, to do it* (the strong version of the principle). By "without sacrificing anything of comparable moral importance" I mean without causing anything else comparably bad to happen, or doing something that is wrong in itself, or failing to promote some moral good, comparable in significance to the bad thing that we can prevent. This principle seems almost as uncontroversial as the last one. It requires us only to prevent what is bad, and not to promote what is good, and it requires this of us only when we can do it without sacrificing anything that is, from the moral point of view, comparably important. I could even, as far as the application of my argument to the Bengal emergency is concerned, qualify the point so as to make it: if it is in our power to prevent something *very* bad from happening, without thereby sacrificing *anything* morally significant, we ought, morally, to do it (the moderate version of the principle). An application of this principle would be as follows: if I am walking past a shallow pond and see a child drowning in it, I ought to wade in and pull the child out. This will mean getting my clothes muddy, but this is insignificant, while the death of the child would presumably be a very bad thing.

A Clarification: Distance and Numbers

The uncontroversial appearance of the principle just stated is deceptive. If it were acted upon, even in its qualified form, our lives, our society, and our world would be fundamentally changed. For the principle takes, firstly, no account of proximity or distance. It makes no moral difference whether the person I can help is a neighbor's child ten yards from me or a Bengali whose name I shall never know, ten thousand miles away. Secondly, the principle makes no distinction between cases in which I am the only person who could possibly do anything and cases in which I am just one among millions in the same position.

I do not think I need to say much in defense of the refusal to take proximity and distance into account. *The fact that a person is physically near to us, so that we have personal contact with him, may make it more likely that we shall assist him, but this does not show that we ought to help him rather than another who happens to be further away.* If we accept any principle of impartiality, universalizability, equality, or whatever, we cannot discriminate against someone merely because he is far away from us (or we are far away from him). Admittedly, it is possible that we are in a better position to judge what needs to be done to help a person near to us than one far away, and perhaps also to provide the assistance we judge to be necessary. If this were the case, it would be a reason for helping those near to us first. This may once have been a justification for being more concerned with the poor in one's own town than with famine victims in India. Unfortunately for those who like to keep their moral responsibilities limited, instant communication and swift transportation have changed the situation. From the moral point of view, the development of the world into a "global village" has made an important, though still unrecognized, difference to our moral situation. Expert observers and supervisors, sent out by famine relief organizations or permanently stationed in famine-prone areas, can direct our aid to a refugee in Bengal almost as effectively as we could get it to someone in our own block. There would seem, therefore, to be no possible justification for discriminating on geographical grounds.

There may be a greater need to defend the second implication of my principle—that *the fact that there are millions of other people in the same position, in respect to the Bengali refugees, as I am, does not make the situation significantly different from a situation in which I am the only person who can prevent something very bad from occurring.* Again, of course, I admit that there is a psychological difference between the cases; one feels less guilty about doing nothing if one can point to others, similarly placed, who have also done nothing. Yet this can make no real difference to our moral obligations.[2] Should I consider that I am less obliged to pull the drowning child out of the pond if on looking around I see other people, no further away than I am, who have also noticed the child but are doing nothing? One has only to ask this question to see the absurdity of the view that numbers lessen obligation. It is a view that is an ideal excuse for inactivity; unfortunately most of the major evils—poverty, overpopulation, pollution—are problems in which everyone is almost equally involved.

The view that numbers do make a difference can be made plausible if stated in this way: if everyone in circumstances like mine gave £5 to the Bengal Relief Fund, there would be enough to provide food, shelter, and medical care for the refugees; there is no reason why I should give more than anyone else in the same circumstances as I am; therefore I have no obligation to give more than £5. Each premise in this argument is true, and the argument looks sound. It may convince us, unless we notice that it is based on a hypothetical premise, although the conclusion is not stated hypothetically. The argument would be sound if the conclusion were: if everyone in circumstances like mine were to give £5, I would have no obligation to give more than £5. If the conclusion were so stated, however, it would be obvious that the argument has no bearing on a situation in which it is not the case that everyone else gives £5. This, of course, is the actual situation. It is more or less certain that not everyone in circumstances like mine will give £5. So there will not be enough to provide the needed food, shelter, and medical care. Therefore by giving more than £5 I will prevent more suffering than I would if I gave just £5.

Absurd Consequences

It might be thought that this argument has an absurd consequence. Since the situation appears to be that very few people are likely to give substantial amounts, it follows that I and everyone else in similar circumstances ought to give as much as possible, that is, at least up to the point at which by giving more one would begin to cause serious suffering for oneself and one's dependents—perhaps even beyond this point to the point of **marginal utility** at which by giving more one would cause oneself and one's dependents as much suffering as one would prevent in Bengal. If everyone does this, however, there will be more than can be used for the benefit of the refugees, and some of the sacrifice will have been unnecessary. Thus, if everyone does what he ought to do, the result will not be as good as it would be if everyone did a little less than he ought to do, or if only some do all that they ought to do.

The paradox here arises only if we assume that the actions in question—sending money to the relief funds—are performed more or less simultaneously, and are also unexpected. For if it is to be expected that everyone is going to contribute something, then clearly each is not obliged to give as much as he would have been obliged to had others not been giving too. And if everyone is not acting more or less simultaneously, then those giving later will know how much more is needed, and will have no obligation to give more than is necessary to reach this amount. To say this is not to deny the principle that people in the same circumstances have the same obligations, but to point out that *the fact that others have given, or may be expected to give, is a relevant circumstance: those giving after it has become known that many others are giving and those giving before are not in the same circumstances.* So the seemingly absurd consequence of the principle I have put forward can occur only if people are in error about the actual circumstances—that is, if they think they are giving when others are not, but in fact they are giving when others are. The result of everyone doing what he really ought to do cannot be worse than the result of everyone doing less than he ought to do, although the result of everyone doing what he reasonably believes he ought to do could be.

Duty vs. Charity

If my argument so far has been sound, neither our distance from a preventable evil nor the number of other people who, in respect to that evil, are in the same situation as we are, lessens our obligation to mitigate or prevent that evil. I shall therefore take as established the principle I asserted earlier. As I have already said, I need to assert it only in its qualified form: if it is in our power to prevent something *very* bad from happening, without thereby sacrificing anything else morally significant, we ought, morally, to do it.

The outcome of this argument is that our traditional moral categories are upset. *The traditional distinction between* **duty** *and* **charity** *cannot be drawn, or at least, not in the place we normally draw it.* Giving money to the Bengal Relief Fund is regarded as an act of charity in our society. The bodies which collect money are known as "charities." These organizations see themselves in this way—if you send them a check, you will be thanked for your "generosity." Because giving money is regarded as an act of charity, it is not thought that there is anything wrong with not giving. The charitable man may be praised, but the man who is not charitable is not condemned. People do not feel in any way ashamed or guilty about spending money on new clothes or a new car instead of giving it to famine relief. (Indeed, the alternative does not occur to them.) This way of looking at the matter cannot be justified. When we buy new clothes not to keep ourselves warm but to look "well-dressed" we are not providing for any important need. We would not be sacrificing anything significant if we were to continue to wear our old clothes, and give the money to famine relief. By doing so, we would be preventing another person from starving. It follows from what I have said earlier that we ought to give money away, rather than spend it on clothes which we do not need to keep us warm. To do so is not charitable, or generous. Nor is it the kind of act which philosophers and theologians have called **"supererogatory"**—an act which it would be good to do, but not wrong not to do. On the contrary, *we ought to give the money away, and it is wrong not to do so.*

I am not maintaining that there are no acts which are charitable, or that there are no acts which it would be good to do but not wrong not to do. It may be possible to redraw the distinction between duty and charity in some other place. All I am arguing here is that the present way of drawing the distinction, which makes it an act of charity for a man living at the level of affluence which most people in the "developed nations" enjoy to give money to save someone else from starvation, cannot be supported. It is beyond the scope of my argument to consider whether the distinction should be redrawn or abolished altogether. There would be many other possible ways of drawing the distinction—for instance, one might decide that it is good to make other people as happy as possible, but not wrong not to do so. . . .

Practical Objections

I now want to consider a number of points, more practical than philosophical, which are relevant to the application of the moral conclusion we have reached. These points challenge not the idea that we ought to be doing all we can to prevent starvation, but the idea that giving away a great deal of money is the best means to this end.

[1] It is sometimes said that overseas aid should be a government responsibility, and that therefore one ought not to give to privately run charities. Giving privately, it is said, allows the government and the noncontributing members of society to escape their responsibilities.

This argument seems to assume that the more people there are who give to privately organized famine relief funds, the less likely it is that the government will take over full responsibility for such aid. This assumption is unsupported, and does not strike me as at all plausible. The opposite view—that if no one gives voluntarily, a government will assume that its citizens are uninterested in famine relief and would not wish to be forced into giving aid—seems more plausible. In any case, unless there were a definite probability that by refusing to give one would be helping to bring about massive government assistance, people who do refuse to make voluntary contributions are refusing to prevent a certain amount of suffering without being able to point to any tangible

beneficial consequence of their refusal. So the onus of showing how their refusal will bring about government action is on those who refuse to give.

I do not, of course, want to dispute the contention that governments of affluent nations should be giving many times the amount of genuine, no-strings-attached aid that they are giving now. I agree, too, that giving privately is not enough, and that we ought to be campaigning actively for entirely new standards for both public and private contributions to famine relief. Indeed, I would sympathize with someone who thought that campaigning was more important than giving oneself, although I doubt whether preaching what one does not practice would be very effective. Unfortunately, for many people the idea that "it's the government's responsibility" is a reason for not giving which does not appear to entail any political action either.

[2] Another, more serious reason for not giving to famine relief funds is that until there is effective population control, relieving famine merely postpones starvation. If we save the Bengal refugees now, others, perhaps the children of these refugees, will face starvation in a few years' time. In support of this, one may cite the now well-known facts about the population explosion and the relatively limited scope for expanded production.

This point, like the previous one, is an argument against relieving suffering that is happening now, because of a belief about what might happen in the future; it is unlike the previous point in that very good evidence can be adduced in support of this belief about the future. I will not go into the evidence here. I accept that the earth cannot support indefinitely a population rising at the present rate. This certainly poses a problem for anyone who thinks it important to prevent famine. Again, however, one could accept the argument without drawing the conclusion that it absolves one from any obligation to do anything to prevent famine. The conclusion that should be drawn is that the best means of preventing famine, in the long run, is population control. It would then follow from the position reached earlier that one ought to be doing all one can to promote population control (unless one held that all forms of population control were wrong in themselves, or would have significantly bad consequences). Since there are organizations working specifically for population control, one would then support them rather than more orthodox methods of preventing famine.

[3] A third point raised by the conclusion reached earlier relates to the question of just how much we all ought to be giving away. One possibility, which has already been mentioned, is that we ought to give until we reach the level of marginal utility—that is, the level at which, by giving more, I would cause as much suffering to myself or my dependents as I would relieve by my gift. This would mean, of course, that one would reduce oneself to very near the material circumstances of a Bengali refugee. It will be recalled that earlier I put forward both a strong and a moderate version of the principle of preventing bad occurrences. The strong version, which required us to prevent bad things from happening unless in doing so we would be sacrificing something of *comparable* moral significance, does seem to require reducing ourselves to the level of marginal utility. I should also say that the strong version seems to me to be the correct one. I proposed the more moderate version—that we should prevent bad occurrences unless, to do so, we had to sacrifice something morally significant—only in order to show that even on this surely undeniable principle a great change in our way of life is required. On the more moderate principle, it may not follow that we ought to reduce ourselves to the level of marginal utility, for one might hold that to reduce oneself and one's family to this level is to cause something significantly bad to happen. Whether this is so I shall not discuss, since, as I have said, I can see no good reason for holding the moderate version of the principle rather than the strong version. Even if we accepted the principle only in its moderate form, however, it should be clear that we would have to give away enough to ensure that the consumer society, dependent as it is on people spending on trivia rather than giving to famine relief, would slow down and perhaps disappear entirely. There are several reasons why this would be desirable in itself. The value and necessity of economic growth are now being questioned not only by conservationists, but by economists as well.[3] There is no doubt, too, that the consumer society has had a distorting effect on the goals and purposes of its members. Yet looking at the matter purely from the point of view of overseas aid, there must be a limit to the extent to which we should deliberately slow down our economy; for it might be the case that if we gave away, say, forty percent of our Gross National Product, we would slow down the economy so much that in absolute terms we would be giving less than if we gave twenty-five percent of the much larger GNP that we would have if we limited our contribution to this smaller percentage.

I mention this only as an indication of the sort of factor that one would have to take into account in working out an ideal. Since Western societies generally consider one percent of the GNP an acceptable level for overseas aid, the matter is entirely academic. Nor does it affect the question of how much an individual should give in a society in which very few are giving substantial amounts.

It is sometimes said, though less often now than it used to be, that philosophers have no special role to play in public affairs, since most public issues depend primarily on an assessment of facts. On questions of fact, it is said, philosophers as such have no special expertise, and so it has been possible to engage in philosophy without committing oneself to any position on major public issues. No doubt there are some issues of social policy and foreign policy about which it can truly be said that a really expert assessment of the facts is required before taking sides or acting, but the issue of famine is surely not one of these. *The facts about the existence of suffering are beyond dispute. Nor, I think, is it disputed that we can do something about it, either through orthodox methods of famine relief or through population control or both.* This is therefore an issue on which philosophers are competent to take a position. The issue is one which faces everyone who has more money than he needs to support himself and his dependents, or who is in a position to take some sort of political action. These categories must include practically every teacher and student of philosophy in the universities of the Western world. If philosophy is to deal with matters that are relevant to both teachers and students, this is an issue that philosophers should discuss.

Discussion, though, is not enough. What is the point of relating philosophy to public (and personal) affairs if we do not take our conclusions seriously? In this instance, taking our conclusion seriously means acting upon it. The philosopher will not find it any easier than anyone else to alter his attitudes and way of life to the extent that, if I am right, is involved in doing everything that we ought to be doing.

At the very least, though, one can make a start. The philosopher who does so will have to sacrifice some of the benefits of the consumer society, but he can find compensation in the satisfaction of a way of life in which theory and practice, if not yet in harmony, are at least coming together.

NOTES

1. There was also a third possibility: that India would go to war to enable the refugees to return to their lands. Since I wrote this paper, India has taken this way out. The situation is no longer that described above, but this does not affect my argument, as the next paragraph indicates.

2. In view of the special sense philosophers often give to the term, I should say that I use "obligation" simply as the abstract noun derived from "ought," so that "I have an obligation to" means no more, and no less, than "I ought to." This usage is in accordance with the definition of "ought" given by the *Shorter Oxford English Dictionary*: "the general verb to express duty or obligation." I do not think any issue of substance hangs on the way the term is used; sentences in which I use "obligation" could all be rewritten, although somewhat clumsily, as sentences in which a clause containing "ought" replaces the term "obligation."

3. See, for instance, John Kenneth Galbraith, *The New Industrial State* (Boston, 1967); and E. J. Mishan, *The Costs of Economic Growth* (London, 1967).

DISCUSSION QUESTIONS:

1. Suppose you and a friend were going out to dinner. As you walk up to the restaurant, you notice a small child sitting on the curb outside of the door. His eyes are sunken, and his belly is swollen. His knees form the widest part of his legs. He is obviously starving. For the price of a dessert you could save his life. Do you think you have a moral obligation to save him in this case? Would you think anyone who simply walked past him to be a moral monster? Given that you know that there are millions of such children in the world, how is this case any different from reality?

2. Suppose you don't find the Greater Moral Evil Principle plausible. If the principle is false, Singer's argument for the moral obligation to give to famine relief is unsound. However, what would you say about the case in which the small child is drowning in the muddy pond? Do you think that you have a moral obligation to save him, or, in other words, do you think that you would be acting wrongly by leaving him to drown? If so, what moral principle explains why you have a moral obligation to save the drowning child but no moral obligation to save the starving?

3. According to the moderate version of what we've called the Greater Moral Evil Principle, if it is in our power to prevent something very bad from happening, without thereby sacrificing anything morally significant, we ought, morally, to do it. Aside from death by starvation, can you think of other things that are significantly bad that we could prevent at little cost to ourselves? How about population control, environmental degradation, illiteracy, etc.? Must Singer think that we have moral obligations to alleviate all of these?

Argument Reconstruction Exercises:

I. Singer rejects the conclusion that our moral obligations extend only as far as what it would take to alleviate the harm if everyone contributed. Identify the premises and conclusion in this excerpt and then try to figure out what Singer thinks is wrong with the argument (hint: see his criticism on the same page):

> . . .if everyone in circumstances like mine gave £ 5 to the Bengal Relief Fund, there would be enough to provide food, shelter, and medical care for the refugees; there is no reason why I should give more than anyone else in the same circumstances as I am; therefore, I have no obligation to give more than £5. (page 492)

II. Singer doesn't present a premise/conclusion form argument for the crucial premise in his overall argument, the Greater Moral Evil Principle. However, he does offer a thought experiment that an application of his principle seems to explain. Can you take this data and construct an inference to the best explanation that concludes that the Greater Moral Evil Principle is correct?

> I could even as far as the application of my argument to the Bengal emergency is concerned, qualify the point so as to make it: if it is in our power to prevent something very bad from happening, without

thereby sacrificing anything morally significant, we ought, morally, to do it. An application of this principle is as follows: if I am walking past a shallow pond and see a child drowning in it, I ought to wade in and pull the child out. This will mean getting my clothes muddy, but this is insignificant, while the death of the child would presumably be a very bad thing. (pages 4491-492)

III. At no place in the article does Singer present his overall argument in premise/conclusion form. See if you can take the following excerpts, add a missing premise, and draw the conclusion that many of us have a moral obligation to donate to famine relief:

> I begin with the assumption that suffering and death from lack of food, shelter, and medical care are bad. . . . My next point is this: if it is in our power to prevent something bad from happening, without

thereby sacrificing anything of comparable moral importance, we ought, morally, to do it. (page 491)

IV. Singer considers a variety of practical objections to his view. One of these objections appeals to facts about population control. On the assumption that we have an obligation to donate to famine relief funds *only* if doing so prevents something bad from happening, use the following excerpt to construct an argument for the conclusion that we do not have a moral obligation to donate to famine relief funds:

> Another, more serious reason for not giving to famine relief funds is that until there is effective population control, relieving famine merely postponed starvation. If we save the Bengal refugees now, others, perhaps the children of these refugees, will face starvation in a few years' time. (page 494)

17.2 FAMINE RELIEF AND THE IDEAL MORAL CODE

JOHN ARTHUR (1996)

Until his recent death in 2007, John Arthur taught for many years as professor of philosophy at the State University of New York, Binghamton. He worked primarily in ethics and social/political philosophy, in particular the philosophy of law. In this essay, Arthur responds to Peter Singer's argument on famine relief. His criticism of Singer is that he fails to capture the moral dimensions of entitlements, desert, and rights in his case for a moral obligation to save those dying of hunger. Since the ideal moral code will recognize our rights to our belongings and the fact that we deserve what we work for, Arthur concludes that in some (but not all) cases, the ideal moral code will not require us to give our wealth away to save the lives of others.

Reading Questions:

1. How does "moral equality" enter Singer's defense of the Greater Moral Evil Principle?

2. What is an entitlement?

3. What is the difference between a negative right and a positive right?

4. What is a just desert?

5. What is a moral code?

6. According to Arthur, any action is right if and only if what?

7. According to Arthur, which moral code is the ideal moral code?

8. Arthur gives two reasons why the ideal moral code will not ignore rights. What are they?

9. Does Arthur ultimately conclude that we ever have moral obligations to help others even when they don't deserve or have a right to our help?

What do those of us who are relatively affluent owe, from a moral standpoint, to those who are hungry and sick and who may die without assistance?[1] In a provocative and important article "Famine, Affluence, and Morality" Peter Singer defends what he terms an "uncontroversial" moral principle, that we ought to prevent evil whenever we can do so without sacrificing something of comparable moral significance. In doing so, he argues there is a duty to provide aid whenever others are in greater need and will suffer without our help.[2] Other philosophers, relying on the principle that all human life is of equal value, have reached similar conclusions.[3] My first concern, then, is to assess such arguments on their own terms, asking whether these arguments do, in fact, establish a duty to give aid. I will argue, in response, that our moral "intuitions" include not only the commitments they emphasize but also entitlements, which suggests that people who deserve or have rights to their earnings may be allowed to keep them.

But the fact that our social moral code includes entitlements is not a complete answer, for it is possible that contemporary moral attitudes are mistaken and our accepted code is defective. So, in the final sections I ask whether a moral reformer might reasonably claim that an "ideal" moral code would reject entitlements, arguing that in fact it would not.

Singer's Argument

In his essay, Singer argues that two general moral principles are widely accepted and then that those principles imply an obligation to eliminate starvation.

The first of the two principles he thinks we accept is simply that "suffering and death from lack of food, shelter, and medical care are bad." Some may be inclined to think that the mere existence of such an evil in itself places an obligation on others, but

that is, of course, the problem that Singer addresses. I take it that he is not begging the question in this obvious way and will *argue* from the existence of evil to the obligation of others to eliminate it. But how, exactly, does he establish this? The second principle, he thinks, shows the connection, but it is here that I wish to raise some questions. This second principle, which I call the "greater moral evil principle," states that:

> If it is in our power to prevent something bad from happening, without thereby sacrificing anything of comparable moral importance, we ought, morally, to do it.[4]

In other words, *people are entitled to keep their earnings only if there is no way for them to prevent a greater evil by giving them away.* Providing others with food, clothing, and housing is generally of more importance than buying luxuries, so the greater moral evil principle now requires substantial redistribution of wealth.

Certainly few of us live by that principle, although, as Singer emphasizes, that hardly means that we are justified in behaving as we do. We often fail to live up to our own standards. Why does Singer think our shared morality requires that we follow the greater moral evil principle? What argument does he give for it?

He begins with an analogy. Suppose, you came across a child drowning in a shallow pond. Certainly we feel it would be wrong for you not to help. Even if saving a child meant you would dirty your clothes, we would emphasize that those clothes are not of comparable significance to the child's life. The greater moral evil principle thus seems a natural way of capturing why we think it would be wrong not to help.

But the argument for the greater moral evil principle is not limited to Singer's claim that it explains our feelings about the drowning child or that it appears "uncontroversial." Moral equality also enters the picture, in the following way.[5] In addition to the idea that we share certain rights equally, most of us are also attracted to another conception of equality, namely, that *like amounts of suffering (or happiness) are of equal significance, no matter who is experiencing them.* I cannot reasonably say that, while my pain is no more severe than yours, I am somehow special and that it's therefore more important, objectively speaking, that mine be alleviated. Impartiality requires us to admit the opposite—that no one has a unique status that warrants such special consideration.

But if we fail to give money to famine relief and instead purchase a new car when the old one will do, or buy fancy clothes for a friend when his or her old ones are perfectly good, are we not assuming that the relatively minor enjoyment we or our friends may get is as important as another person's life? And that, it seems, is a form of prejudice; we are acting as if people were not equal in the sense that their interests deserve equal consideration. We are giving special consideration to ourselves or to our group, rather as a racist does. Equal consideration of interests thus leads naturally to the greater moral evil principle.

Entitlements

Equal consideration seems to require that we prevent harm to others if in doing so we do not sacrifice anything of comparable moral importance. But there is also another side to the coin, which Singer ignores. This idea can be expressed rather awkwardly by the notion of **entitlements,** by which I have in mind the thought that *having either a right or justly deserving something can also be important as we think about our obligations to others.* A few examples will show what I mean.

One way we can help others is by giving away body parts. While your life may be shortened by the loss of a kidney or less enjoyable if lived with only one eye, those cases are probably not comparable to the loss experienced by a person who will die without a kidney transplant or who is totally blind. Or perhaps, using Judith Thomson's analogy, somebody needs to remain hooked up to you for an extended period of time while awaiting a transplant.[6] It seems clear, however, that our code does not *require* such heroism; you are entitled to your second eye and kidney and to control who uses your body, and that entitlement blocks the inference from the fact that you could prevent harm to the conclusion that you ought to let others have or use your body.

We express these ideas in terms of rights; it's your body, you have a right to it, and that weighs against whatever duty you have to help. To give up your right to your kidney for a stranger is more than is required; it's heroic—unless, of course, you have freely agreed to let the person use your body, which brings us to the next point.

There are two types of rights, negative and positive. **Negative rights** *are rights against interference by others.* The right to life, for example, is a right not to be killed by others; the right against assault is a right not to suffer physical harm from others. The right to one's body, the right to property, the right to privacy, and the right to exercise religious freedom are also negative, requiring only that people leave others alone and not interfere. **Positive rights,** *however, are rights to receive some benefit.* By contracting to pay wages, employers acquire the duty to pay the employees who work for them; if the employer backs out of the deal, the employees' positive right to receive a paycheck is violated.

Negative rights also differ from positive rights in that the former are natural or human, in the sense that they depend on what you are, not what you've done. All persons, we assume, have the right to life. If lower animals lack negative moral rights to life or liberty, it is because there is a relevant difference between them and us. *But the positive rights you may have are not natural in that sense; they arise because others have promised, agreed or contracted to do something,* just as you may have an obligation to let them use your property or even your body if you have so agreed. The right not to be killed does not depend on anything you or anybody else has done, but the right to be paid a wage makes sense only on the basis of prior agreements.

None of that is to say that rights, whether negative or positive, are beyond controversy. Rights come in a variety of shapes and sizes, and people often disagree about both their shape and their size. And while some rights are part of our generally shared moral code and widely accepted, others are controversial and hotly disputed.

Normally, then, a duty to help a stranger in need is based not on a *right* the person has but, instead, on the general duty all people have to aid those in need (as Singer's drowning child illustrates). A genuine right to be aided requires something more, such as a contract or promise to accept responsibility for the child. Consider, for example a babysitter who agrees to watch out for someone else's children but instead allows a child to drown. We would think that under the circumstances the parent whose child has drowned would in fact be doubly wronged. First, like everybody else, the person who agreed to watch the child should not have cruelly or thoughtlessly let it drown. But it's also the case that here, unlike Singer's example, we can also say there are rights at stake; promises were made that imposed special obligations on the babysitter. Other bystanders also act wrongly by cruelly ignoring the child, but the babysitter violates rights as well.

I am not suggesting that rights are all we need to take into account. Moral rights are one—but only one—factor to be weighed; we also have other obligations that should be considered. This view, like the greater moral evil principle, is an oversimplification. *In reality, our moral code expects us to help people in need as well as to respect negative and positive rights.* But it also seems clear that, besides being asked by our moral code to respect the rights of others, we are entitled, at least sometimes, to invoke our own rights as justification for what we do. It is not as if we promised to help, or are in any way responsible for the person's situation. Our social moral code teaches that *although passing by a drowning child whom we can easily save is wrong, we need not ignore our own rights and give away our savings to help distant strangers solely on the basis of the greater moral evil principle.*

A second form of entitlement involves **just deserts,** the idea that *sometimes people deserve to keep what they have acquired.* To see its role in our moral code, imagine an industrious farmer who manages through hard work to produce a surplus of food for the winter while a lazy neighbor spends the summer relaxing. Must our industrious farmer give the surplus away because without it that neighbor, who refused to work, will suffer? Under certain circumstances, we might say because of the greater moral evil principle the farmer should help, but not necessarily. What this shows is that once again we have more than one factor to weigh. Besides, the evil that could be prevented, we (and the hard-working farmer, too) should also consider the fact that one person earned the food, through hard work. And while it might be the case that just desert is outweighed by the greater need of a neighbor, being outweighed is in any case not the same as weighing nothing!

Sometimes just desert can be negative in the sense of unwanted, as well as something regarded as a good. The fact that the Nazi war criminals did what they did means they deserve punishment: We have a good reason to send them to jail, on the basis of just desert. Other considerations, for example, the fact that nobody will be deterred or that the criminal is old and harmless, may weigh against punishment, and we may even decide not to pursue the case for that reason. But, again, that does not mean that deserving to be punished is irrelevant, just that we've decided for other reasons to ignore desert in this case. But again I repeat: *A principle's being outweighed is not the same as its having no importance.*

Our social moral code thus honors both the greater moral evil principle and entitlements. The former emphasizes equality, claiming that from an objective point of view all comparable suffering, whomever its victim, is equally significant. It encourages us to take an impartial look at all the various effects of our actions and is therefore forward-looking. When we consider entitlements, however, our attention is directed to the past. Whether we have rights to money, property, or even our body depends on how we came to possess them. If money was stolen, for example, then the thief has no right to it. Or perhaps a person has promised to trade something; this would again (under normal circumstances) mean loss of entitlement. Like rights, just desert is also backward-looking, emphasizing past effort or past transgressions that now warrant responses such as reward, gratitude, or punishment.

I am suggesting, then, that, expressing both equality and entitlements, our social moral code pulls in different directions. How, then, are we to determine when one principle is more important? Unless we are moral relativists, the mere fact that equality and entitlements are both part of our moral code does not in itself justify a person's reliance on them, any more than the fact that our moral code once condemned racial mixing while condoning sexual discrimination and slavery should convince us that those principles are justified. We all assume (I trust) that the more enlightened moral code—the one we now subscribe to—is better in part just because it condemns discrimination and slavery. Because we know that the rules that define acceptable behavior are continually changing, and sometimes changing for the better, we must allow for the replacement of inferior principles with more reasonable guidelines.

Viewed in that light, *the issue posed by Singer's argument is really whether we should reform our current social moral code and reject entitlements, at least insofar as they conflict with the greater moral evil principle.* What could justify our practice of evaluating actions by looking backward to rights and just desert instead of only to their consequences? To pursue these questions, we need to look more closely at how we might justify the moral rules and principles that constitute a society's moral code; we will then be able to ask whether, although entitlements are part of our current code, we would improve that code—bring it closer to an ideal code—if they were not included.

The Concept of a Social Moral Code

So I suggest that we first say something more about the nature and purpose of social moral codes in general; then we will turn to entitlements. We can begin with the obvious: *A moral code is a system of principles, rules, and other standards that guide people's conduct.*[7] As such, it has characteristics in common with other systems of rules and standards, such as the rules of organizations. Social clubs, sports leagues, corporations, bureaucracies, professional associations, all have standards that govern the behavior of members.

Such rules function in various ways, imposing different sanctions depending on the nature of the organization. Violation of a university's code of conduct leads to one sort of punishment, while different

types of sanctions are typically imposed by a social club or by the American Bar Association.

Some standards of conduct are not limited to members of a specific organization but instead apply more broadly, and it is to those that we now turn. Law, for example, is a social practice rather than an organization. So are etiquette and customs. All these codes apply broadly, not just to members of an organization who have chosen to join. It will be most helpful in our thinking about the nature of a moral code to compare it with these other social practices, along a variety of dimensions.

As we noted with organizations, here too the form sanctions take varies among the different types of codes.[8] While in our legal system transgressions are punished by fines, jail, or even execution, informal sanctions of praise, criticism, and ostracism encourage conformity to the standards of morality and etiquette. Besides the type of sanctions, a second difference among these codes is that while violation of a moral principle is always a serious affair, this need not be so for legal rules or the norms of etiquette and custom. Many of us think it unimportant whether a fork is on the left side of a plate or the right, or whether an outmoded and widely ignored Sunday closing law is violated. But violation of a moral principle is not ignored or thought trivial; indeed, the fact that a moral principle has lost its importance is often indicated by its "demotion" to mere custom.

A third contrast, in addition to differences in sanctions and in importance, is that, unlike morality, custom, and etiquette, legal systems include, besides criminal and civil rules, other "constitutional" rules governing how those laws are to be created, modified, and eliminated.[9] Under the U.S. Constitution, for instance, if Congress acts to change the tax laws, then as of the date stated in the statute the rules are changed.[10] Moral rules, etiquette, and customs also change, of course, but they do so without benefit of any agreed procedure identifying who or how the changes occur or when they take effect.

So far, then, we've noted that different codes and standards of behavior can vary widely, along a number of dimensions. Some apply narrowly, only to members of a specific organization, while others extend broadly. And while all codes include rules or other standards to guide conduct, the sanctions that are imposed by different codes differ widely, as do the ways rules for change and the importance assigned to violations of the different codes.

The final point I want to make about rules generally, before looking specifically at morality, is that *all standards serve a purpose*, although what that purpose is will again vary with the organization or practice in question. Rules that govern games, for example, are often changed, either informally among players or by a governing organization like the National Football League. This is done in order to more effectively achieve the goals of the game, although the goals often vary and are sometimes open to dispute. Sometimes, for example, rules may be changed to improve safety (e.g., car design in auto racing) or even to make the sport more exciting but less safe. Other times rules might be changed to accommodate younger players, such as abolishing the walk in kids' baseball. Similar points can be made about organizations, as, for example, when a corporation changes its standards for how many hours people work or a university changes the deadline for dropping a class.

Like the rules that govern games and organizations, legal and moral rules and principles also change in ways that serve their purposes either better or worse. But here enters one final, important point—*because there can be deep disagreement about the purpose of such practices, there can also be disagreement about the rules themselves*, including when there should be exceptions, what exactly they require, and the circumstances under which they can be ignored. Such a dispute about rules can rest on deeper, sometimes hidden disagreements about the purposes of the organization, just as differences between fundamentalists and liberals over religious rules and principles can also uncover disagreements about the purposes of religious practices.

Turning to morality, first consider a traditional rule such as the one prohibiting homosexual behavior. Assuming people could agree that the rule serves no useful purpose but instead only increases the burden of guilt, shame, and social rejection borne by a significant portion of society, then it seems that people would have good reason to alter their rules about sexual conduct and no longer condemn homosexuality. But people who see morality as serving another purpose, for instance, encouraging behavior that is compatible with God's will or with "natural" law, might oppose such a change. Or suppose, less controversially, that rules against killing and lying help us to accomplish what we want from a moral code. In that case, we have good reason to include those rules in our "ideal" moral code.

My suggestion, then, is that there is a connection between what we ought to do and how well a code serves its purposes. If a rule serves well the goals of a moral code, then we have reason to obey it. But if, on the other hand, a rule is useless, or if it frustrates the purposes of morality, we have reason neither to support it, teach it, nor to follow it (assuming, as I said, we agree what the purpose of a social moral code is).

This suggests, then, the following conception of a right action: *Any action is right if and only if it conforms with an ideal moral code for the society in which we are living.* We will say more about this shortly, but most basically we must consider what, exactly, an *ideal* moral code is. In order to answer that, we must first ask ourselves the purpose that we hope to accomplish by creating, teaching, and enforcing a moral code for society.

The Ideal Social Moral Code

One possibility, already suggested, is that morality's purpose depends on God—that morality serves to encourage people to act in accord with God's will. But I want to suggest, and very briefly defend, another view, namely, that *the ideal moral code is the one that, when recognized and taught by members of society, would have the best consequences.* By best consequences, I mean that it would most effectively promote the collective well-being of those living under it.[11] (It's worth noting right off, however, that a religious person need not reject this out of hand but instead might reason that the general well-being is also what God would wish for creation.)

In pursuing this idea, it is helpful to return to the comparison between legal and moral standards. Clearly, both morality and law serve to *discourage* some of the same types of behavior—killing, robbing, and beating—while they both also *encourage* other acts, such as repaying debts, keeping important agreements, and providing for one's children.

The reason for rules that discourage acts like killing and beating seems clear enough, for imagine the disastrous consequences for human life absent such moral and legal rules. This idea is further substantiated when we think about how children are taught that it is wrong to hit a baby brother or sister. Parents typically explain such rules in terms of their purpose, emphasizing that it hurts and can harm others when we hit them. *At root, then, it seems at least plausible to suppose that these rules of morality and law function to keep people from causing unjustified harm to each other.* A world in which people were allowed to kill and assault each other without fear of legal or moral sanctions would be far more miserable than a world in which such behavior is discouraged. Concern for general welfare explains how we learn moral standards as children and why we support them as adults.

In addition to justifying rules that prevent harmful behavior, the other rules I mentioned that encourage different types of behavior can also be justified by their social consequences. Our own well-being, as well as that of our friends, family, and indeed, society as a whole, depends on people's generally keeping promises and fulfilling agreements. Without laws and moral rules to encourage such behavior, the institutions of promising and contracting would likely be unsustainable, and with their passing would be lost all the useful consequences that flow from our ability to bind ourselves and others by promising and contracting.

Moral rules thus promote our own welfare by discouraging acts of violence and by creating and maintaining social conventions like promising and paying debts. They also perform the same service for our family, friends, and, indeed, all of us. A life wholly without legal and moral codes would be in danger of deteriorating into what Thomas Hobbes long ago feared: a state of nature in which life is solitary, poor, nasty, brutish, and short. . . .

This line of thought, emphasizing the practical side of the ideal moral code, brings us finally to the issue with which we began: Would an ideal moral code include principles that respect rights and just deserts, or would it, as Singer suggested, reject them completely in favor of the greater moral evil principle? The answer, I will argue, rests on the fact that *an ideal moral code must not only be one that can hope to win public support but must be practical and workable in other important ways as well.* The ideal code is one that works for people as they are, or at least can be encouraged to become.

Are Rights Part of the Ideal Code?

What we want to know is whether rights (and also just desert) would be included in the ideal code, understood as the one that, in the real world, would have the best consequences. Initially, it may seem they would not, since it appears that the best consequences could be realized by substituting the greater moral evil principle for entitlements, requiring people to prevent something bad whenever the cost to them is less significant than the benefit to another. This is true because, unlike entitlements, the greater moral evil principle more clearly and directly expresses the consequentialism I have been defending.

But would such a single moral principle, recognized by society as its ideal, really have the best consequences? I suggest that *the ideal code would not in fact ignore rights, for two reasons*, each based on the fact that the ideal moral code must rest on realistic, accurate assumptions about human beings and our life in this world.

[1] [First], *It is important that a social moral code not assume people are more altruistic than they are.* Rules that would work only for angels are not the ideal ones for a society of human beings. While we do care about others' well-being, especially those we love, we also care very deeply about ourselves. It would therefore be quite difficult to get people to accept a code that requires that they give away their savings or duplicate organs to a stranger simply because doing so would avoid even more evil, as would be required by the greater moral evil rule if not balanced by entitlements. Many people simply wouldn't do as that rule required; they care too deeply about their own lives and welfare, as well as the welfare of loved ones.

Indeed, were the moral code to attempt to require such saintliness despite these problems, three results would likely follow. First, because many would not live up to the rules, despite having been taught they should, feelings of guilt would increase. Second, such a code would encourage conflict between those who met what they thought of as their moral obligations and those who did not. Such a situation is in contrast, of course, to one in which people who give generously and selflessly are thought of as heroes who have gone beyond what is morally required; in that event, unlike instances in which people don't live up to society's demands of them, the normal response is to praise them for exceeding the moral minimum. And, third, a realistic code that doesn't demand more than people can be expected to do might actually result in more giving than a code that ignores rights in favor of the greater moral evil rule. Think about how parents try to influence how their children spend their money. Perhaps the children will buy less candy if they are allowed to do so occasionally but are also praised for spending on other things than they would if the purchase of candy were prohibited. We cannot assume that making what is now a charitable act into a requirement will always encourage such behavior. In summary, *impractical rules would not only create guilt and social conflict, neither of which is compatible with the ideal code, but would also tend to encourage the opposite of the desired result.* By giving people the right to keep their property yet praising those who do not exercise the right but help others instead, we have struck a good balance.

[2] My second point is that *an ideal moral code must not assume that people are more objective, informed, and unbiased than they are.* People often tend, we know, to rationalize when their interests are at stake—a fact that has many implications for the sorts of principles we would include in an ideal, welfare maximizing code. For example, we might at first be tempted to discourage slavish conformity to counter-productive rules, teaching people to break promises whenever doing so would have the best consequences. But again practicality enters: An ideal code would not be blind to people's tendency to give special weight to their own welfare or to their inability always to be objective in tracing the effects of different actions even when they want to be. So, while an ideal code would not teach that promises must never be broken no matter what the consequences, we also would not want to encourage breaking promises whenever people convince themselves that doing so would produce less evil.

Similar considerations apply to property. Imagine a situation in which a person contemplates preventing an evil to herself or himself by taking something from a large store where it won't be missed. Such theft could easily be rationalized by the greater moral evil principle on grounds that stealing prevents something bad from happening (to the person who decides to steal) without sacrificing anything of comparable moral significance (the store won't miss the goods). So, although a particular act of theft may sometimes be welfare maximizing, it does not follow that a principle like Singer's is part of an ideal code. To recognize and teach that theft is right whenever the robber is preventing greater evil, even to himself, would work only if people were far more objective, less liable to self-deception, and more knowledgeable about the long-term consequences than they are. So here again, including rights that block such conclusions in our moral code serves a useful role, discouraging the tendency to rationalize our behavior by underestimating the harm we may cause to others or exaggerating the benefits that may accrue to ourselves.

Is Just Desert Part of the Ideal Moral Code?

Similar practical considerations argue for including desert as well as rights in the ideal moral code. The case of the farmers, recall, was meant to illustrate that our current social moral code encourages the attitude that people who work hard deserve to be rewarded, just as people who behave badly deserve to be punished. Most of us feel that while it would be nice of the hard worker to help out a lazy neighbor, the worker also has reason—based on his past effort—to refuse. But, as I have stressed, it's still an open question whether an ideal code would allow such "selfishness."

But as with rights, here again we must be careful that our conception of an ideal code is realistic and practical and does not assume people are more altruistic, informed, or objective than they are. To see why this is relevant to the principle of just desert, we should first notice that for many people, at least, working and earning a living is not their favorite activity. People would often prefer to spend time doing something else, but they know they must work if they and their family hope to have a decent life. Indeed, if humans generally are to live well, then goods and services must be produced and made available for wide use, which means that (I argue) incentives to work are an important factor in motivating people.

One such incentive, of course, is income. A moral code can encourage hard work by allowing people to keep a large part of what they earn, by respecting both rights and the principle of just desert. "I worked hard for it, so I can keep it" is a familiar thought that expresses this attitude.

But suppose we eliminated the notion of deserving what we work for from our code and asked people to follow the greater moral evil rule instead. What might happen? There are three possibilities. First, they might continue to produce as before, only this time motivated by the desire, derived from their social moral code, to prevent whatever evil they could, as long as the cost to them of doing so was not greater evil. But this seems to me quite unrealistic: While people are not egoists, neither are they that saintly and altruistic.

Given that, one of two other outcomes could be expected. Perhaps people would stop working as hard, feeling that it is no longer worth the effort to help strangers rather than themselves or their family since they are morally required to give away all but what they can use without imposing a greater evil on anybody else. Suppose, to make it vivid, that the tax system enforces the greater moral evil rule, taking away all income that could be used to prevent a greater evil's befalling somebody else. The result would be less work done, less total production of useful commodities, and therefore a general reduction in people's well-being. The other possibility is that people would simply fail to live up to the standards of society's moral code (having replaced desert with the greater moral evil rule), leading to widespread feelings of guilt and resentment by those (few?) who did behave as the code commands. In either case, I am suggesting, replacing the principle of just desert with the greater moral evil principle would actually worsen the situation. Like rights, the principle of just desert is also part of an ideal code.

Conclusion

The first sections of this paper attempted to show that our moral code is a bit self-contradictory. It seems to pull us in opposite directions, sometimes toward helping people who are in need and other times toward the view that rights and desert justify keeping things we have even if greater evil could be avoided were we to give away our extra eye or our savings account. This apparent inconsistency led us to a further question: Is the emphasis on rights and desert really defensible, or should we try to resolve the tension in our own code by rejecting entitlements in favor of the greater moral evil rule? In the last sections I have considered this question, focusing on the idea that we should understand the ideal moral code as the one that, if acknowledged and taught, would have the overall best consequences. Having suggested why it might seem sensible to conceive the ideal code this way, as the one that would produce the best consequences, I concluded by showing that an ideal code would not reject entitlements in favor of the greater moral evil rule. Concern that our moral code encourage effort and not fail because it unrealistically assumes people are more altruistic, informed, or objective than they are means that our rules giving people rights to their possessions and encouraging distribution according to desert are part of an ideal moral code. The ideal moral code would therefore not teach people to try to seek the best consequences in each individual case, insisting they give entitlements no weight whatsoever. But neither have I argued, nor do I believe, that an ideal moral code would allow people to overlook those in desperate need by making entitlements absolute, any more than it would ignore entitlements in favor of the greater moral evil rule discussed earlier.

But where would it draw the line? It's hard to know, of course, but the following seems to me to a sensible stab at an answer. Concerns of the sort I have outlined argue strongly against expecting too much of people's selflessness or ability to make objective and informed decisions. *A more modest proposal would require people to help strangers when there is no substantial cost to themselves,* that is, when what they are sacrificing would not mean *significant* reduction in their own or their family's level of happiness. Since most people's savings accounts and nearly everybody's second kidney are not insignificant, entitlements would in those cases outweigh another's need. But if what is at stake is truly trivial, as dirtying one's clothes would normally be, then an ideal moral code would not allow rights to override the greater evil that can be prevented.

Another point is that, again mindful of the need to be realistic in what it expects of people, an ideal code might also distinguish between cases in which the evil is directly present to a person (as in the drowning child) and cases involving distant people. The reason, of course, is again practical: People are more likely to help people with whom they have direct contact and when they can see immediately the evil they will prevent than they are to help strangers. So while such a distinction may seem morally arbitrary, viewed from the perspective of an ideal moral code it seems to make good sense.

Despite our code's unclear and sometimes self-contradictory posture, it seems to me that these conclusions are not that different from our current moral attitudes; an ideal moral code thus might not be a great deal different from our own. We tend to fault selfish people who give little or nothing to charity and expect those with more to give more. Yet we do not ask people to make large sacrifices of their own or their family's well-being in order to aid distant strangers. Singer's arguments do remind us, however, that entitlements are not absolute and that we all have some duty to help. But the greater moral evil rule expresses only part of the story and is not needed to make that point.[12]

NOTES

1. © 1996 by John Arthur. This paper refines and extends some of the arguments in an earlier paper of mine, "Equality, Entitlements, and the Distribution of Income." Reprinted by permission of the author.

2. Peter Singer, "Famine, Affluence, and Morality," *Philosophy & Public Affairs* 1, No. 3 (1972): 229–243.

3. For example, Richard Watson, "Reason and Morality in a World of Limited Food," in William Aiken and Hugh LaFollette, eds., *World Hunger and Moral Obligation* (Englewood Cliffs, N.J.: Prentice-Hall, 1977).

4. Singer also offers a "weak" version of this principle that, it seems to me, is *too* weak. It requires giving aid only if the gift is of *no* moral significance to the giver. But since even minor embarrassment or small amounts of unhappiness are not completely without moral importance, this weak principle would imply no obligation to aid, even to the drowning child.

5. See, for example, Singer's "Postscript" to "Famine, Affluence, and Morality" in Aiken and LaFollette, ibid., p. 36.

6. Judith Jarvis Thomson, "A Defense of Abortion," *Philosophy & Public Affairs* 1, No. 1 (1971).

7. Ronald Dworkin argues that there are important differences between principles and rules: while rules apply in an "all or nothing" fashion and have specific exceptions, principles are not either-or but instead have "weight" that must be considered in light of competing principles. Both of these can also be distinguished from moral ideals, which guide people toward the best, most valuable life. For purposes of this essay, however, these distinctions are not important; I do assume, however, that standards can compete, as Dworkin's analogy with the "weight" of principles suggests.

8. This discussion follows H. L. A. Hart, *The Concept of Law,* 2d ed. (Oxford: Oxford University Press, 1995).

9. But Ronald Dworkin has argued that legal interpretation is partly moral and normative, making this claim more difficult to make in that context. See, for example, *Law's Empire* (Cambridge: Harvard University Press, 1986), chap. 2 and 7.

10. Assuming, of course, the courts do not hold the law unconstitutional.

11. I leave aside here just how we can best understand "well-being" except to note that it should include whatever states of affairs have intrinsic value, however that is understood.

12. One final qualification is worth emphasizing. The subject of this essay has been the ideal moral code that we should adopt for our *private*, nonpolitical relations, not the character of a just constitution and tax structure. It is therefore possible to argue that while the ideal moral code correctly captures the personal duties we owe to everybody, including foreigners and strangers, a just political order requires more extensive help to fellow citizens with whom we share the basic institutions of society. Many reasons could be given for making such a distinction, including the fact that it may be more practical to expect people to provide welfare when undertaken collectively, by government, than to do so on their own in the form of private charity enforced only by morality's informal sanctions. People may also be more inclined to look to the needs of people near home, who share a common national identity and history. Nor, finally, should we conclude that political justice must be understood in the same, utilitarian way that I have been defending here. While understanding private morality in terms of an ideal moral code that has the best overall consequences, we might nevertheless conceive of political relationships and social justice in terms of the social contract, asking which constitutional arrangements could win universal consent. (The major proponent of this view of course is John Rawls, *A Theory of Justice* [Cambridge: Harvard University Press, 1971].)

It is therefore possible that justice is both philosophically distinct and also more demanding than is the ideal social moral code. Tax provisions securing a minimum income and fair equality of opportunity, for example, may be owed to other citizens on grounds of social justice (though many of the points I made earlier would apply in both contexts, including especially the need to provide incentives.) That Rawlsean approach to political justice seems to me quite consistent with the idea that we need not, as private citizens, give away our savings merely because we can prevent evil to another human being who would benefit more from them.

DISCUSSION QUESTIONS:

1. Arthur thinks that Singer's conclusion in the argument of the previous reading is false. Given that Singer's argument is valid, this means that Singer's argument for famine relief must have a false premise. Which premise does Arthur think is false and why?

2. Arthur provides the example of giving up a kidney or an eye to someone who needed one. His suggestion is that the Greater Moral Evil Principle would require this of us. Is he right? If so, do you still think the Greater Moral Evil Principle is true?

3. A negative right is a right against others not to interfere with you, whereas a positive right is a right against others that they provide you with some benefit. Arthur claims that negative rights are "natural or human," whereas positive rights arise "because others have promised, agreed, or contracted to do something." (page 499). Do you think that this is right? Do newborn children only have rights that others not interfere with them, or do you think that their rights require that others provide for them in some way? Could it be that people who find themselves starving to death through no fault of their own have a positive right to assistance? If so, how does that change the famine relief issue?

4. Despite his talk of rights, entitlements, and desert, even Arthur ultimately concludes that we have moral obligations "to help strangers when there is no substantial cost" to ourselves (page 505). If he's right, don't all of us still have some pretty serious moral obligations to relieve the suffering of others? After all, giving up $20 or even $40 a month would not result in a *significant* reduction in our happiness, and this is what the ideal moral code might suggest as the threshold for not giving.

Argument Reconstruction Exercises:

I. One way of arguing against a principle is to show that it has a false implication (see *modus tollens* on page 8). Arthur provides this sort of argument against the Greater Moral Evil Principle. See if you can reconstruct the argument using the excerpts provided below:

> If it is in our power to prevent something bad from happening, without thereby sacrificing anything of comparable moral importance, we ought, morally, to do it. (page 498)

> One way we can help others is by giving away body parts. While your life may be shortened by the loss of a kidney or less enjoyable if lived with only one eye, those cases are probably not comparable to the loss experienced by a person who will die without a kidney transplant or who is totally blind. . . It seems clear, however, that our code does not require such heroism; you are entitled to your second eye and kidney. (page 499)

II. Arthur concludes that the people who are dying of starvation do not have a right to assistance. The argument for this claim relies on the fact that a right to assistance would be an instance of a positive right. Examine this passage and construct an argument for the conclusion that those who are dying of starvation do not have a right to assistance. (Hint: There is a suppressed premise.)

> Positive rights, however, are rights to receive some benefit. By contracting to pay wages, employers acquire the duty to pay the employees who work for them; if the employer backs out of the deal, the employees' positive right to receive a paycheck is violated. . . . . The positive rights you may have are not natural in that sense; they arise because others have promised, agreed, or contracted to do something. (page 499)

III. To refute Singer, Arthur needs to show that the ideal moral code will not include the Greater Moral Evil Principle. Identify the premises and (suppressed) conclusion in the following excerpt.

. . . an ideal moral code must not only be one that can hope to win public support but must be practical and workable in other important ways as well. The ideal code is one that works for people as they are, or at least can be encouraged to become. . . . It would therefore be quite difficult to get people to accept a code that requires that they give away their savings or duplicate organs to a stranger simply because doing so would avoid even more evil, as would be required by the greater moral evil rule if not balanced by entitlements. (page 503)

IV. Despite his disagreement with Singer, Arthur ultimately concludes that the ideal moral code will sometimes obligate us to give some of our wealth or income away to help those who are dying of starvation. Use this passage to construct an argument for the conclusion that you have a moral obligation to donate some amount of money or other to help those who are dying of starvation. (Hint: The amount you will be morally obligated to give will vary from person to person according to its connection with a significant reduction in overall happiness.)

A more modest proposal would require people to help strangers when there is no substantial cost to themselves, that is, when what they are sacrificing would not mean significant reduction in their own or their family's level of happiness. (page 505)

17.3 FEEDING THE HUNGRY

JAN NARVESON (1999)

Jan Narveson is Distinguished Professor Emeritus at the University of Waterloo. One of the foremost social/political philosophers of the 20th century, he made important contributions both to normative ethical theory and to the study of the relationship between the state and the individual. In this essay, Narveson addresses our moral obligations regarding starvation. The crucial question is whether the starvation of others is a case of **killing** or **letting die**. If the former, we have an obligation to help, but if the latter, while we have reasons of charity to aid those who are dying, such duties are not a matter of justice. Furthermore, given the empirical facts, it is unlikely that our charitable contributions make much of a difference to the lives of those who are suffering.

Reading Questions:

1. What is the difference between the passive and active sense of 'starve'?

2. Why does Narveson think that active instances of starvation are morally wrong?

3. What does Narveson mean by justice?

4. What does Narveson mean by charity?

5. What is the "ethics of the hair shirt"?

6. Why does Narveson deny that killing and letting die are morally equivalent?

7. Does Narveson think that we sometimes have duties of charity to help others?

8. According to Narveson, what is it that causes or explains why most people in the actual world are starving?

Throughout history it has been the lot of most people to know that there are others worse off than they, and often enough of others who face starvation. In the contemporary world, television and other mass media enable all of us in the better-off areas to hear about starvation in even the most remote places. What, if any, are our obligations toward the victims of such a terrible situation?

This can be a rather complex subject, for different cases differ significantly. We must begin, then, by distinguishing the main ones. First, we should note that the word 'starve' functions both as a passive verb, indicating something that happens to one, and as an active verb, designating something inflicted by one person on another. In the latter case, starvation is a form of killing and comes under the same strictures that any other method of killing is liable to. But when the problem is plague, crop failure due to drought, or sheer lack of know-how, there is no obviously guilty party. Then *the question is whether we, the amply fed, are guilty parties if we fail to come to the rescue of those unfortunate people.*

Starvation and Murder

If I lock you in a room with no food and don't let you out, I have murdered you. If group A burns the crops of group B, it has slaughtered the Bs. There is no genuine issue about such cases. It is wrong to kill innocent people, and one way of killing them is as eligible for condemnation as any other. Such cases are happily unusual, and we need say no more about them here other than to note, as I will, that the most substantial recent cases could readily be regarded as cases of something amounting to murder, rather than the other kind.

Our interest, then, is in the cases where murder is not the relevant category, or at least not obviously so. But some writers, hold that **letting someone die** is *morally equivalent* to **killing** them or, at least, "basically" equivalent.[1] Is this so? Most people do not think so; it takes a subtle philosophical argument to persuade them of this. The difference between a bad thing that I intentionally or at least forseeably brought about and one that just happened, through no fault of my own, matters to most of us in practice. Is our view sustainable in principle, too? Suppose

the case is one I could do something about, as when you are starving and my granary is burgeoning. Does that make a difference?

Duties of Justice and Duties of Charity

Another important question, which has cropped up in some of our discussions but is nowhere more clearly relevant than here, is the distinction between **justice** and **charity**. *By justice I here intend those things that we may, if need be, be forced to do—* where our actions can be constrained by others to ensure our performance. Charity, on the other hand, "comes from the heart": *'charity' means, roughly, caring, an emotionally tinged desire to benefit other people just because they need it.*

We should note a special point about this. It is often said that charity "cannot be compelled." Is this true? In one clear sense, it is, for in this sense charity consists *only* of benefits motivated by love or concern. If instead you regard an act as one that we may forcibly compel people to do, then you are taking that act to be a case of *justice.* Can it at the same time be charity? It can if we detach the motive from the act and define charity simply as doing good for others. But the claim that charity in this second sense cannot be compelled is definitely not true by definition—and is in fact false. People are frequently compelled to do good for others, especially by our governments, which tax us in order to benefit the poor, educate the uneducated, and so on. Whether they *should* be thus compelled is a genuine moral question, however, and must not be evaded by recourse to semantics. (Whether those programs produce benefits that outweigh their costs is a very complex question; but that they do often produce some benefits, at whatever cost, is scarcely deniable.)

On which side of the moral divide, then, shall we place feeding the hungry? Is it to be regarded as unenforceable charity, to be left to individual consciences, or enforceable justice, perhaps to be handled by governments? Here, we are asking whether feeding the hungry is not only something we ought to do but also something we must do, as a matter of justice. It is especially this latter that concerns us [here]. A great deal turns on it. . . .

Our general question is what sort of moral concerns we have with the starving. The question breaks down into two. First, *is there a basic duty of justice to feed the starving?* And second, if there isn't, then *is there a basic requirement of charity that we be disposed to do so, and if so, how strong is that requirement?*

Justice and Starvation

Let's begin with the first. Is it *unjust* to let others starve to death? We must distinguish two very different ways in which someone might try to argue for this. First, there are those who argue that there is no fundamental distinction between killing and letting die. If that is right, then the duty not to kill is all we need to support the conclusion that there is a duty of justice not to let people starve, and the duty not to kill (innocent) people is uncontroversial. Second, however, some insist that feeding the hungry is a duty of justice even if we don't accept the equivalence of killing and letting-die. They therefore need a different argument, in support of a positive right to be fed. The two different views call for very different discussions.

Starving and Allowing to Starve

Starving and allowing to starve are special cases of killing and letting die. Are they the same, as some insist? [There is] the need for a crucial distinction here: between the view that they are literally indistinguishable and the view that even though they are logically distinguishable, they are nevertheless *morally* equivalent.

As to the first, the argument for non-identity of the two is straightforward. When you kill someone, you do an act, x, which brings it about that the person is dead *when he would otherwise still be alive.* You induce a *change* (for the worse) in his condition. But when you let someone die, this is not so, for she would have died even if you had, say, been in Australia at the time. How can *you* be said to be the "cause" of something that would have happened if you didn't exist?

To be sure, we do often attribute causality to human inaction. But the clear cases of such attribution are those where the agent in question had an antecedent *responsibility* to do the thing in question. The geraniums may die because you fail to water them, but to say that you thus *caused* them to die is to imply that you were *supposed* to water them. Of course, we may agree that if we have a duty to feed the poor and we don't feed them, then we are at fault. But the question before us is *whether* we have this duty, and the argument we are examining purports to prove this by showing that even when we do nothing, we still "cause" their deaths. If the argument presupposes that very responsibility, it plainly begs the question rather than giving us a good answer to it.

What about the claim that killing and letting die are morally equivalent? Here again, there is a danger of begging the question. *If* we have a duty to feed the hungry and we don't, then not doing so might be morally equivalent to killing them, perhaps—though I doubt that any proponents would seriously propose life imprisonment for failing to contribute to the cause of feeding the hungry! But again, the consequence clearly doesn't follow if we don't have that duty, which is in question. Those who think we do not have fundamental duties to take care of each other, but only duties to refrain from killing and the like, will deny that they are morally equivalent.

The liberty proponent will thus insist that when Beethoven wrote symphonies instead of using his talents to grow food for the starving, like the peasants he depicted in his Pastorale symphony, he was doing what he had a perfect right to do. A connoisseur of music might go further and hold that he was also doing *the right thing*: that someone with the talents of a Beethoven does more for people by composing great music than by trying to save lives, even if he would have been *successful* in saving those lives—which is not very likely anyway.

How do we settle this issue? If we were all connoisseurs, it would be easy: if you know and love great music, you will find it easy to believe that a symphony by Beethoven or Mahler is worth more than prolonging the lives of a few hundred starvelings for another few miserable years. If you are one of those starving persons, your view might well be different. (But it might not. Consider the starving artist in his garret, famed in romantic novels and operas: they lived voluntarily in squalor, believing that what they were doing was worth the sacrifice.)

We are not all connoisseurs, nor are most of us starving. Advocates of welfare duties talk glibly as though there were a single point of view ("welfare") that dominates everything else. But it's not true. There are all kinds of points of view, diverse and to a large extent incommensurable. Uniting them is not as simple as the welfarist or utilitarian may think. It is *not* certain, not obvious, that we "add more to the sum of human happiness" by supporting, the opera than by supporting OXFAM.[2] How are we to unite diverse people on these evaluative matters? The most plausible answer, I think, is the point of view that allows different people to live their various lives by forbidding interference with the lives of others. Rather than insisting, with threats to back it up, that I *help* someone for whose projects and purposes I have no sympathy whatever, let us all agree to *respect* each other's pursuits. We'll agree to let each person live as that person sees fit, with only our bumpings into each other being subject to public control. To do this, we need to draw a sort of line around each person and insist that others not cross that line without the permission of the occupant. The rule will be not to intervene forcibly in the lives of others, thus requiring that our relations be mutually agreeable. Enforced feeding of the starving, however, does cross the line, invading the farmer or the merchant, forcing him to part with some of his hard-earned produce and give it without compensation to others. That, says the advocate of liberty, is theft, not charity.

So if someone is starving, we may pity him or we may be indifferent, but the question so far as our obligations are concerned is this: how did he get that way? If it was not the result of my previous activities, then I have no obligation to him and may help him out or not, as I choose. If it was a result of my own doing, then of course I must do something. If you live and have long lived downstream from me, and I decide to dam up the river and divert the water elsewhere, then I have deprived you of your water and must compensate you, by supplying you with the equivalent, or else desist. But if you live in the middle of a parched desert and it does not rain, so that you are faced with death from thirst, that is not my doing and I have no compensating to do. . . .

The Ethics of the Hair Shirt

In stark contrast to the liberty-respecting view stands the idea that we are to count the satisfactions of others as equal in value to our own. If I can create a little more pleasure for some stranger by spending my dollar on him than I would create for myself by spending it on an ice cream cone, I then have a putative *obligation* to spend it on him. Thus I am to defer continually to others in the organization of my activities and shall be assailed by guilt whenever I am not bending my energies to the relief of those allegedly less fortunate than I. "Benefit others, at the expense of yourself—and keep doing it until you are as poor and miserable as those whose poverty and misery you are supposed to be relieving!"[3] That is the ethics of the hair shirt.

How should we react to this idea? Negatively, I suggest. Doesn't that view really make us the slaves of the (supposedly) less well off? Surely a rule of conduct that permits people to be themselves and to try to live the best and most interesting lives they can is better than one that makes us all, in effect, functionaries in a welfare state? The rule that *neither* the rich *nor* the poor ought to be enslaved by the others is surely the better rule. . .

Mutual Aid

The anti-welfarist idea, however, can be taken too far. Should people be disposed to assist each other in time of need? Certainly they should. But the appropriate rule for this is not that each person is dutybound to minister to the poor until he himself is a pauper or near-pauper as well. Rather, the appropriate rule is what the characterization "in time of need" more nearly suggests. There are indeed emergencies in life when a modest effort by someone will do a great deal for someone else. *People who aren't ready to help others when it is comparatively easy to do so are people who deserve to be avoided when they themselves turn to others in time of need.*

But this all assumes that these occasions are, in the first place, relatively unusual, and in the second, that the help offered is genuinely of modest cost to the provider. If a stranger on the street asks for directions, a trifling expenditure of time and effort saves him great frustration and perhaps also makes for a pleasant encounter with another human (which that other human should try to make so, for example, by being polite and saying "thanks!"). But if as I walk down the street I am accosted on all sides by similar requests, then I shall never get my day's work done if I can't just say, "Sorry, I've got to be going!" or merely ignore them and walk right on. If instead I must minister to each, then soon there will be nothing to give, since its existence depends entirely on the activities of people who produce it. If the stranger asks me to drive him around town all day looking for a long-lost friend, then that's going too far, though of course, I should be free to help him out even to that extent if I am so inclined.

What about parting with the means for making your sweet little daughter's birthday party a memorable one in order to keep a dozen strangers alive on the other side of the world? Is this something you are morally required to do? It is not. She may well *matter* to you more than they—and well she should. This illustrates again the point that *people do not "count equally" for most of us*. Normal people care more about some people than others, and build their very lives around those carings. It is both absurd and arrogant for theorists, talking airily about the equality of all people, to insist on cramming it down our throats—which is how ordinary people do see it.

It is reasonable, then, to arrive at a general understanding that we shall be ready to help when help is urgent and when giving it is not very onerous to us. But a general understanding that we shall help everyone as if they were our spouses or dearest friends is quite another matter. Only a thinker whose heart has been replaced by a calculating machine could suppose that to be reasonable. . . .

Charity

One of the good things we can do in life is to make an effort to care about people whom we don't ordinarily care or think about. This can benefit not only the intended beneficiaries in distant places, but it can also benefit you, by broadening your perspective. There is a place for the enlargement of human sympathies. But then, these are *sympathies*, matters of the heart; and for such matters, family, friends, colleagues, and co-workers are rightly first on your agenda. Why so? First, just because you are you and not somebody else—not, for example, a godlike "impartial observer." But there is another reason of interest, even if you think there is something right about the utilitarian view. This is what amounts to a consideration of *efficiency*. We know ourselves and our loved ones; we do not, by definition, know strangers. We can choose a gift for people we know and love, but are we wise to try to benefit someone of alien culture and diet? If we do a good thing for someone we know well, we make an investment that will be returned as the years go by; but we have little idea of the pay-off from charity for the unknown. Of course, that can be overcome, once in awhile—you might end up pen pals with a peasant in Guatemala. But it would not be wise to count on it.

The tendency and desire to do good for others is a virtue. Moreover, it is a *moral* virtue, for we all have an interest in the general acquisition of this quality. Just as anyone can kill anyone else, so anyone can benefit anyone else; and so long as the cost to oneself of participating in the general scheme of helpfulness is low—namely, decidedly less than the return—then it is likely to be worth it. But it is not reasonable to take the matter beyond that. In particular, it is not reasonable to become a busybody, or a fanatic like Dickens's character Mrs. Jellyby, who is so busy with her charitable work for the natives in darkest Africa that her own children run around in rags and become the terror of the neighbourhood. Nor is it reasonable to be so concerned for the welfare of distant persons that you resort to armed robbery in your efforts to help them out ("Stick 'em up! I'm collecting for OXFAM!").

Notes on the Real World

If we are persuaded by the above, then as decent human beings we will be concerned about starvation and inclined to do something to help out if we can. But taking this seriously, as a realistic program for action in the world we actually live in, raises two questions. First, what is the situation? Are there lots of people in danger of imminent demise from lack of food? And second, just what should we do about it if there are?

Regarding the first question, one notes that contemporary philosophers and many others talk as though the answer is obviously and overwhelmingly in the affirmative. They write as though people by the millions are starving daily. It is of interest to realize that they are, generally speaking, wrong, and in the special cases where there really is hunger at that level, its causes are such as to make a very great difference to our answer to the second question.

In fact, starvation in the contemporary world is *not at all* due to the world's population having "outrun its resources . . . " On the contrary, we now know that the world can support an indefinite number of people, certainly vastly more than there are now. If people have more children, they can be fed, or at least there is no reason why they couldn't be, so far as the actual availability of resources is concerned; nor does anyone in the affluent part of the world need to give up eating meat or driving Porsches to enable them to do so. In 1970, harbingers of gloom and doom on these matters were reporting that by the 1990s there would be massive starvation in the world unless we got to work right away, clamping birth-control measures on the recalcitrant natives and enforcing vegetarianism on us affluent North Americans. But events have shown them to be totally wrong about all this. Now at the end of the twentieth century there are perhaps a half-billion more people than there were then, and rather than starving, they are not only eating, but eating better than ever before. All, that is, *except* for those being starved at gunpoint by their governments or by warring political factions. Meanwhile, Western nations piled up food surpluses and wondered what to do to keep their farmers from going broke for lack of demand for their burgeoning products.

In fact, *all of the substantial starvation (as opposed to the occasional flood) in the middle to later parts of the twentieth century has been due to politics, not agriculture.* In several African countries, in Nicaragua for awhile, in China until not long ago, in the Soviet Union for most of its unhappy career, the regimes, in power, propelled by ideology or a desire for cheap votes, imposed artificially low food prices or artificially inefficient agricultural systems on their people, thus providing remarkably effective disincentives to their farmers to grow food. Not surprisingly, they responded by not growing it. The cure is to let the farmers farm in peace, and charge

whatever they like for their produce; it is astonishing how rapidly they will then proceed to grow food to meet the demand. But the cure isn't to have Western countries send over boatloads of wheat. Even if the local government will let people have this bounty (they often don't—corrupt officials have been known to go out and privately resell the grain elsewhere instead of distributing it to their starving subjects), providing it indiscriminately hooks them on Western charity instead of enabling them to regain the self-sufficiency they enjoyed in earlier times, before modern Western benefits such as "democracy" enabled incompetent local governments to disrupt the food supply.[4]

We must also mention countries with governments that drive people forcibly off their land, burn their crops, or outrightly steal it from the peasantry, as in Ethiopia and Somalia in the early 1990s. Those countries combined such barbarities with the familiar tendency to prevent Western aid from getting to its intended recipients. Nature has nothing to do with starvation in such cases, and improvements in agriculture are not the cure. Improvements in politics are.

This means that the would-be charitable person faces a pretty difficult problem when he turns to the second question: What to do? In cases of natural disaster, as when a huge flood inundates the coast of Bangladesh, there will be short-term problems, and charitable agencies are excellent at responding quickly with needed food and medical supplies. Supporting some of those for dealing with such emergencies is likely a good idea. But in many other cases, there is very little that an outside agency can do. Tinpot dictators equipped with modern assault weapons and armoured cars are not exactly examples of sweet reason at work, and only governments normally have the kind of clout that can open doors, even a crack, to the sort of aid we might like to give their beleaguered peoples.

There are many organizations whose enthusiastic volunteers go to Third World communities to try to help them in various ways. Their efforts meet with variable success, especially because the fundamental question of what constitutes "help" is so hard to answer. Do we help a native tribe in Africa that has maintained its way of life for thousands of years when we get their children learning arithmetic and wearing jeans? Or do we only destroy what they have and replace it with something very difficult for them to cope with? As a case in point, a travel writer[5] describes how one community in Madagascar was given an efficient modern pump for its communal water supply, which provided plenty of clean water and relieved people of long trips to polluted wells. It stopped some years later, by which time the people who installed it had long since gone, and nobody knew how to repair it. Interestingly, they didn't seem terribly concerned about this turn of events and made no effort whatever to get someone to fix the pump, but simply went back to the old ways, uncomplainingly and inefficiently. Apparently *they* didn't realize how terribly "essential" this pump was. Do we really know better than they? Why are we so sure that we do?

Helping people who are *very* different from us is not an easy matter. Did all those missionaries who descended on the hapless Africans in the past centuries do them a lot of good by teaching them Christianity, or by bringing the infant mortality rate way down so that families accustomed to having a manageable number of children surviving to maturity suddenly found themselves with six or seven mouths to feed instead of two? Or by building a road to enable tourists to drive up to the village and give the natives all sorts of Western diseases their immune systems were totally unprepared for? There is surely a real question here for thoughtful people, however well-intentioned. *Our efforts could well create disasters for the people we are trying to help, as well as impose pointless costs on ourselves.*

The sober conclusion from all this is that, with the best will in the world, it might still be better to spend our money on the opera after all. We are unlikely to act well when we act in ignorance, and when we deal with people vastly differently from ourselves, ignorance is almost certain to afflict our efforts.

Summing Up

The basic question of this chapter is whether the hungry have a **positive right** to be fed. Of course, we have a right to feed them if we wish, and they have a **negative right** to be fed. But may we forcibly impose

a duty on others to feed them? We may not. If the fact that others are starving is not our fault, then we do not need to provide for them as a duty of justice. To think otherwise is to suppose that we are, in effect, slaves to the badly off. And so we can in good conscience spend our money on the opera instead of on the poor. Even so, feeding the hungry and taking care of the miserable is a nice thing to do and is morally recommended. Charity is a virtue. Moreover, starvation turns out to be almost entirely a function of bad governments rather than of nature's inability to accommodate the burgeoning masses. Our charitable instincts can handle easily the problems that are due to natural disaster. We can feed the starving *and* go to the opera!

NOTES

1. See James Rachels, "Killing and Starving to Death," in Narveson, ed., *Moral Issues*.
2. In my late utilitarian days, I addressed this problem in "Aesthetics, Charity, Utility, and Distributive Justice," *The Monist* 36, 4 (Autumn, 1972): 527–51. Compare with Peter Singer's famous article, "Famine, Affluence, and Morality," *Philosophy and Public Affairs* 1, 3 (Spring 1972): 229–43. Of closely related interest is his "Rich and Poor," in Soifer, *Ethical Issues*, 60–76.
3. Lest this be thought a caricature, it is just about the conclusion that Singer comes to: "it does follow from my argument that we ought to be working full-time to relieve great suffering of the sort that occurs as a result of famine and other disasters." Singer, "Famine, Affluence, and Morality," 238.
4. For example see Jack Powelson, *Facing Social Revolution* (Boulder, Co: Horizon Society, 1987); Julian Simon, Population Matters (Rutgers, NJ: Transaction Press, 1991).
5. Dervla Murphy, *Muddling Through in* Madagascar (London, 1985).

DISCUSSION QUESTIONS:

1. Of the three authors we've read on the subject, Narveson is by far the most skeptical of our having a serious moral obligation to feed those dying of starvation. Still, even he ultimately concludes that, "there are indeed emergencies in life when a modest effort by someone will do a great deal for someone else" (page 511). If he's right about this, then is it plausible that everyone reading this text

has some obligation to help the starving? After all, if you're affluent enough to be reading this text, chances are that you could spare $10 or $20 a month to save the life of another. That seems like what Narveson should consider a "modest effort" to "do a great deal for someone else." Do you agree? Why or why not?'

2. Philosophers who are sympathetic to utilitarianism, like Singer in Chapter 17.1, rely on the idea that people count equally. Narveson describes this as the view that "we are to count the satisfactions of others as equal in value to our own," (page 511). Narveson argues against this thesis by insisting that "people do not 'count equally' for most of us. Normal people care more about some people than others" (page 512). Is this objection a good one? Is it plausible to understand both Singer and Narveson as being correct because they are talking about different things when they say that people count equally?

3. Narveson flatly contradicts some of the empirical claims seen earlier in this book about how many people the earth can support (e.g., compare his article with that by Mark Sagoff in Chapter 16.3). For example, Narveson writes that "we now know that the world can support an indefinite number of people, certainly vastly more than there are now. If people have more children, they can be fed, or at least there is no reason why they couldn't be, so far as the actual availability of resources is concerned; nor does anyone in the affluent part of the world need to give up eating meat or driving Porsches to enable them to do so," (page 513). How can we find out who is correct in this empirical debate? What sources should we use? After having a good sense of where to go for such information, do some research for yourself. Who is right?

4. Narveson makes much of the point that often the people who need help the most are the victims of corrupt and dictatorial governments. Providing the governments directly with aid seems like a particularly ineffective way of helping those people. So should we conclude that there is nothing that we can do to help? What about programs that provide microloans directly to budding entrepreneurs in the Third World (e.g.,

www.kiva.org) or those that provide food or animals directly to the starving people (e.g., www.heifer.org)? What about getting involved politically to urge the government not to support such corrupt governments with money/weapons/food in the form of foreign aid?

Argument Reconstruction Exercises:

I. Narveson argues that "active starvation" is morally wrong. Use the following excerpt to construct an argument for the conclusion that it is wrong to actively starve people to death:

> If I lock you in a room with no food and don't let you out, I have murdered you. If group A burns the crops of group B, it has slaughtered the Bs. There is no genuine issue about such cases. It is wrong to kill innocent people, and one way of killing them is as eligible for condemnation as any other.(page 509)

II. Narveson argues for the conclusion that feeding those who are starving through no fault of our own (i.e., passive starvation) is not a matter of justice. This is because he equates justice with things that may be rightfully enforced. Identify the premises and conclusion in this argument.

> Rather than insisting, with threats to back it up, that I help someone for whose projects and purposes I have no sympathy whatever, let us all agree to respect each other's pursuits. We'll agree to let each person live as that person sees fit, with only our bumpings into each other being subject to public control. To do this, we need to draw a sort of line around each person and insist that others not cross that line without the permission of the occupant . . . Enforced feeding of the starving, however, does cross the line, invading the farmer or the merchant, forcing him to part with some of his hard-earned produce and give it without compensation to others. That, says the advocate of liberty, is theft, not charity. (page 511)

III. Narveson's ultimate conclusion is that whether or not we have an obligation—meaning a duty of justice—to aid the starving depends on whether we are the cause of the starvation. And in the final section of his essay, he offers some empirical reason to think that we are rarely the cause of the actual starvation in the world. Using that latter claim as a premise, use the following excerpt to construct an argument with a conclusion about the scope of our moral obligations to help the starving.

> So if someone is starving, we may pity him or we may be indifferent, but the question so far as our obligations are concerned is this: how did he get that way? If it was not the result of my previous activities, then I have no obligation to him and may help him out or not, as I choose. If it was a result of my own doing, then of course I must do something. (page 511)

IV. Some philosophers have agreed with Narveson's basic starting point—that we have moral obligations to aid the starving if and only if we were part of the cause of the starvation—but have gone on to draw the conclusion that many of us who are citizens of First World countries DO have a moral obligation to aid the starving. Construct such an argument using Narveson's principle as a premise. Do you find this version of the argument convincing? Why or why not?

CHAPTER 18

Terrorism

America is at war with a transnational terrorist movement fueled by a radical ideology of hatred, oppression, and murder.
—NATIONAL STRATEGY FOR COMBATING TERRORISM, 2006

INTRODUCTION

It is good to know your enemy. If we are engaged in a war on terror, we should understand just what it is, and, from the perspective of our study of ethics, we face three questions in particular: What is terrorism? What is its moral status? How should we respond to it?

Philosophers and others have offered a variety of answers to the first question. Consider four examples.

(A) [Terrorism is] premeditated, politically motivated violence perpetrated against noncombatant targets by subnational groups or clandestine agents. [Section 140(d)(2) of the Foreign Relations Authorization Act, Fiscal Years 1988 and 1989]

(B) Terrorism is the deliberate use of violence, or the threat of such, directed upon civilians in order to achieve political objectives. [Thomas Kapitan, "The Terrorism of 'Terrorism'"]

(C) Terrorism is a type of political violence that intentionally targets civilians (noncombatants) in a ruthlessly destructive, often unpredictable, manner. [It employs] horrific violence against unsuspecting civilians, as well as combatants, in order to inspire fear and create panic, which in turn will advance the terrorists' political or religious agenda. [Louis Pojman, "The Moral Response to Terrorism and Cosmopolitianism"]

(D) [Terrorism is] a political tactic, involving the deliberate frightening of people for political advantage. [Robert Goodin, *What's Wrong With Terrorism?*]

Each of these definitions captures a good bit of what we generally have in mind when we talk of terrorism, though there are important differences among them.

All of the definitions take terrorism to be an activity that involves the deliberate use of violence or, in the case of definition (D), the deliberate creation of fear in a population. All of them also take terrorism to be a goal-directed activity. Terrorists are not engaged in violence and the production of fear for their own sake; they employ them in the service of some end. Definition (C) notes that terrorism often creates fear through the unpredictability of its violence.

There is a striking difference between definition (A) and the rest, however. Definition (A) restricts terrorism to "subnational or clandestine groups." Although this definition allows for such a thing as "state-sponsored terrorism," it does not allow for the possibility of state terrorism. Insofar as states deliberately and directly use violence against a population to advance a political end, they are not, on this approach, engaged in terrorism. There is also a striking difference between definition (D) and the rest. Definition (D) does not include the restriction that terrorism is always targeted on civilian or noncombatant populations. A third difference worth noting is that between definition (C) and the rest. Where the other definitions specify terrorism as having a political goal, definition (C) provides for the possibility of a religious one as well.

The various components in the definition of terrorism are of substantive significance. First, if states are incapable of directly engaging in terrorism, then the issue of whether state acts of conventional warfare, such as the fire bombing of a city or the use (or threat of use) of nuclear weapons, are ever acts of terrorism is automatically foreclosed. The essay by McPherson in this chapter examines the moral status of terrorist acts in comparison to acts of conventional warfare, and concludes that we should adopt either a more critical attitude toward conventional war or a less critical one toward terrorism.

Second, there is a very strong moral presumption against the use of violence, or even the threat of violence, against innocents. If terrorism, by its very definition, involves such violence, then it is, by its very nature, *prima facie* morally wrong in such a way that only powerful moral considerations could ever make it morally permissible. Given this presumption against it, the essay by Walzer in this chapter questions whether terrorists ever have a good excuse for what he takes to be their immoral conduct.

Third, activities that are directed toward achieving some end generally have at least part of their moral justification in the value of that end and the likelihood of their achieving it. The defining ends of any act of terrorism will be relevant to its moral status.

Let's assume that terrorism, by its very nature, involves violence in a way that supports a strong presumption that it is immoral. The moral status of individual acts of terrorism then hinges on whether they, the situation in which they occur,

or the end they promote has some distinctive feature that overrides the presumption against their permissibility. Each act of terrorism, as an act of terrorism, involves violence in a way that makes it presumptively immoral. Does any act of terrorism ever have any properties that override that presumption and make it justified? For many **consequentialists**, the primary focus of the question will be whether the consequences of the act or the type of act it represents are sufficiently better than those of the available alternatives. (Consider, in this regard, Kai Nielsen's discussion in his essay, "Against Moral Conservatism," in Chapter 11.2.) For many **nonconsequentialists**, the focus of the question will extend beyond consequences to such considerations as basic rights and justice. Are those engaged in terrorism themselves victims of a rights violation or other injustice that makes their actions justified?

And how does our moral evaluation of terrorism shape what we ought to do about it? David Luban's essay considers how we should respond to terrorism. In particular, he argues that the current response of the United States government, in its declared "war on terror," involves a hybrid war-law model: terrorists are treated in some ways as if they are enemy soldiers and in other ways as if they are criminals. Luban takes the main argument for this approach to be that it is the most effective way to meet the terrorist threat, but he finds that it also involves fundamental violations of human rights.

SUGGESTIONS FOR FURTHER READING

Coady, T., and O'Keefe, M., eds. *Terrorism and Justice: Moral Argument in a Threatened World.* (Melbourne: Melbourne University Press, 2002)

Frey, R. G., and Morris, C., eds. *Violence, Terrorism and Justice.* (Cambridge: Cambridge University Press, 1991)

Goodin, Robert. *What's Wrong with Terrorism?* (Oxford: Polity, 2006)

Held, Virginia. "Terrorism, Rights, and Political Goals," *In Terrorism: The Philosophical Issues*, ed. Igor Primoratz (Basinstoke and New York: Palgrave Macmillan, 2004)

_____. "Legitimate Authority in Non-state Groups Using Violence." *Journal of Social Philosophy*, 36, 2005, pp. 175–93.

Miller, Richard W. "Terrorism and Legitimacy: A Response to Virginia Held." *Journal of Social Philosophy*, 36, 2005, pp. 194–201.

Nielsen, Kai. "Violence and Terrorism: Its Uses and Abuses." *Values in Conflict*, ed. Burton Leiser. (New York: Macmillan, 1981)

Primoratz, Igor, ed. *Terrorism: The Philosophical Issues.* (Basingstoke and New York: Palgrave Macmillan, 2004)

Sterba, James, ed. *Terrorism and International Justice.* (New York: Oxford University Press, 2003)

Walzer, Michael. *Just and Unjust Wars: A Moral Argument with Historical Illustrations*, 3rd ed. (New York: Basic Books, 2000)

_____. *Arguing about War.* (Ithaca, N.Y.: Yale University Press, 2004)

Wellman, Carl. "On Terrorism Itself." *Journal of Value Inquiry*, 13, 1979, pp. 250–258.

18.1 TERRORISM: A CRITIQUE OF EXCUSES

MICHAEL WALZER (1988)

Michael Walzer is Professor Emeritus at the Institute for Advanced Study at Princeton University. He is the author of numerous books and essays in political philosophy and ethics. In this essay, he takes it as a given that terrorist acts, as an intentional and indiscriminate attack on the innocent, are wrong, and he focuses his attention on attempts to provide excuses for terrorism. Walzer considers and rejects four general excuses, and he closes with a discussion about how best to respond to terrorism. In particular, he argues both that acts of repression and retaliation must not repeat the wrongs of terrorism but also that while we ordinarily think of oppression as a cause of terrorism, terrorism is itself a primary means of oppression.

Reading Questions:

1. What are Walzer's reasons in the first three paragraphs of his essay for ruling out a moral justification for terrorism?

2. Walzer sets aside the possibility that terrorism is morally permissible and focuses on whether it is ever morally excusable. What is the difference between an action's being morally permissible and its being morally excusable?

3. What are the four general excuses Walzer considers for acts of terrorism? What is his basis for rejecting each one?

4. Walzer acknowledges that there may sometimes be good reasons to excuse the action of a particular terrorist, but he claims that we ought never to excuse the leaders of terrorist campaigns. What does he take to be the difference between the two cases?

5. What does Walzer offer as the best way to respond to terrorism?

6. Walzer describes a circle of terrorism. What is it and what does he offer as the best way to break out of it?

No one these days advocates terrorism, not even those who regularly practice it. The practice is indefensible now that it has been recognized, like rape and murder, as an attack upon the innocent. In a sense, indeed, terrorism is worse than rape and murder commonly are, for in the latter cases the victim has been chosen for a purpose; he or she is the direct object of attack, and the attack has some reason, however twisted or ugly it may be. The victims of a terrorist attack are third parties, innocent bystanders; there is no special reason for attacking them; anyone else within a large class of (unrelated) people will do as well. The attack is directed indiscriminately against the entire class. Terrorists are like killers on a rampage, except that their rampage is not just expressive of rage or madness; the rage is purposeful and programmatic. It aims at a general vulnerability: Kill these people in order to terrify those. A relatively small number of dead victims makes for a very large number of living and frightened hostages.

This, then, is the peculiar evil of terrorism—not only the killing of innocent people but also the intrusion of fear into everyday life, the violation of private purposes, the insecurity of public spaces, the endless coerciveness of precaution. A crime wave might, I suppose, produce similar effects, but no one plans a crime wave; it is the work of a thousand individual decision makers, each one independent of the others, brought together only by the invisible hand. Terrorism is the work of visible hands; it is an organizational project, a strategic choice, a conspiracy to murder and intimidate . . . you and me. No wonder the conspirators have difficulty defending, in public, the strategy they have chosen.

The moral difficulty is the same, obviously, when the conspiracy is directed not against you and me but against *them*— Protestants, say, not Catholics; Israelis, not Italians or Germans; blacks, not whites. These "limits" rarely hold for long; the logic of terrorism steadily expands the range of vulnerability. The more hostages they hold, the stronger the terrorists are. No one is safe once whole populations have been put at risk. Even if the risk were contained, however, the evil would be no different. So far as individual Protestants or Israelis or blacks are concerned, terrorism is random, degrading, and frightening. That is its hallmark, and that, again, is why it cannot be defended.

But when moral justification is ruled out, the way is opened for ideological excuse and apology. We live today in a political culture of excuses. This is far better than a political culture in which terrorism is openly defended and justified, for the excuse at least acknowledges the evil. But the improvement is precarious, hard won, and difficult to sustain. *It is not the case, even in this better world, that terrorist organizations are without supporters. The, support is indirect but by no means ineffective. It takes the form of apologetic descriptions and explanations, a litany of excuses that steadily undercuts our knowledge of the evil.* Today that knowledge is insufficient unless it is supplemented and reinforced by a systematic critique of excuses. That is my purpose here. I take the principle for granted: that every act of terrorism is a wrongful act. The wrongfulness of the excuses, however, cannot be taken for granted; it has to be argued. The excuses themselves are familiar enough, the stuff of contemporary political debate. I shall state them in stereotypical form. There is no need to attribute them to this or that writer, publicist, or commentator; my readers can make their own attributions.[1]

Four Failed Excuses For Terrorism

The most common excuse for terrorism is that it is a last resort, chosen only when all else fails. The image is of people who have literally run out of options. One by one, they have tried every legitimate form of political and military action, exhausted every possibility, failed everywhere, until no alternative remains but the evil of terrorism. They must be terrorists or do nothing at all. The easy response is to insist that, given this description of their case, they should do nothing at all; they have indeed exhausted their possibilities. But this response simply reaffirms the principle, ignores the excuse; this response does not attend to the terrorists' desperation. Whatever the cause to which they are committed, we have to recognize that, given the commitment, the one thing they cannot do is "nothing at all."

But the case is badly described. It is not so easy to reach the "last resort." To get there, one must indeed try everything (which is a lot of things) and not just once, as if a political party might organize a single demonstration, fail to win immediate victory, and claim that it was now justified in moving on to murder. Politics is an art of repetition. Activists and citizens learn from experience, that is, by doing the same thing over and over again. It is by no means clear when they run out of options, but even under conditions of oppression and war, citizens have a good run short of that. The same argument applies to state officials who claim that they have tried "everything" and are now compelled to kill hostages or bomb peasant villages. Imagine such people called before a judicial tribunal and required to answer the question, What exactly did you try? Does anyone believe that they could come up with a plausible list? "Last resort" has only a notional finality; the resort to terror is ideologically last, not last in an actual series of actions, just last for the sake of the excuse. In fact, most state officials and movement militants who recommend a policy of terrorism recommend it as a first resort; they are for it from the beginning, although they may not get their way at the beginning. If they are honest, then, they must make other excuses and give up the pretense of the last resort. . . .

The second excuse is designed for national liberation movements struggling against established and powerful states. Now the claim is that nothing else is possible, that no other strategy is available except terrorism. This is different from the first excuse because it does not require would-be terrorists to run through all the available options. Or, the second excuse requires terrorists to run through all the options in their heads, not in the world, notional finality is enough. Movement strategists consider their options and conclude that they have no alternative to terrorism. They think that they have no alternative to terrorism. They think that they do not have the political strength to try anything else, and thus they do not try anything else. Weakness is their excuse.

But two very different kinds of weakness are commonly confused here: the weakness of the movement vis-à-vis the opposing state and the movement's weakness vis-à-vis its own people. This second kind of weakness, the inability of the movement to mobilize the nation, makes terrorism the "only" option because it effectively rules out all the others: nonviolent resistance, general strikes, mass demonstrations, unconventional warfare, and so on.

These options are only rarely ruled out by the sheer power of the state, by the pervasiveness and intensity of oppression; Totalitarian states may be immune to nonviolent or guerrilla resistance, but all the evidence suggests that they are also immune to terrorism. Or, more exactly, in totalitarian states state terror dominates every other sort. Where terrorism is a possible strategy for the oppositional movement (in liberal and democratic states, most obviously), other strategies are also possible if the movement has some significant degree of popular support. In the absence of popular support, terrorism may indeed be the one available strategy, but it is hard to see how its evils can then be excused. For it is not weakness alone that makes the excuse, but the claim of the terrorists to represent the weak; and the particular form of weakness that makes terrorism the only option calls that claim into question.

One might avoid this difficulty with a stronger insistence on the actual effectiveness of terrorism. *The third excuse* is simply that terrorism works (and nothing else does); it achieves the ends of the oppressed even without their participation. "When the act accuses, the result excuses."[2] This is a consequentialist argument, and given a strict understanding of consequentialism, this argument amounts to a justification rather than an excuse. In practice, however, the argument is rarely pushed so far. More often, the argument begins with an acknowledgment of the terrorists' wrongdoing. Their hands are dirty, but we must make a kind of peace with them because they have acted effectively for the sake of people who could not act for themselves. But, in fact, have the terrorists' actions been effective? I doubt that terrorism has ever achieved national liberation—no nation that I know of owes its freedom to a campaign of random murder—although terrorism undoubtedly increases the power of the terrorists within the national liberation movement. Perhaps terrorism is also conducive to the survival and notoriety (the two go together) of the movement, which is now dominated by terrorists. But even if we were to grant some means-end relationship between terror and national liberation, the third excuse does not work unless it can meet the further requirements of a consequentialist argument. It must be possible to say that the desired end could not have been achieved through any other, less wrongful, means. The third excuse depends, then, on the success of the first or second, and neither of these look likely to be successful.

The fourth excuse avoids this crippling dependency. This excuse does not require the apologist to defend either of the improbable claims that terrorism is the last resort or that it is the only possible resort. *The fourth excuse is* simply that terrorism is the universal resort. All politics is (really) terrorism. The appearance of innocence and decency is always a piece of deception, more or less convincing in accordance with the relative power of the deceivers. The terrorist who does not bother with appearances is only doing openly what everyone else does secretly.

This argument has the same form as the maxim "All's fair in love and war." Love is always fraudulent, war is always brutal, and political action is always terrorist in character. Political action works (as Thomas Hobbes long ago argued) only by generating fear in innocent men and women. Terrorism is the politics of state officials and movement militants alike. This argument does not justify either the officials or the militants, but it does excuse them all. We hardly can be harsh with people who act the way everyone else acts. Only saints are likely to act differently, and sainthood in politics is supererogatory, a matter of grace, not obligation.

But this fourth excuse relies too heavily on our cynicism about political life, and cynicism only sometimes answers well to experience. In fact, legitimate states do not need to terrorize their citizens, and strongly based movements do not need to terrorize their opponents. Officials and militants who live, as it were, on the margins of legitimacy and strength sometimes choose terrorism and sometimes do not. Living in terror is not a universal experience. The world the terrorists create has its entrances and exits.

If we want to understand the choice of terror, the choice that forces the rest of us through the door, we have to imagine what in fact always occurs, although we often have no satisfactory record of the occurrence: A group of men and women, officials or militants, sits around a table and argues about whether or not to adopt a terrorist strategy. Later on, the litany of excuses obscures the argument. But at the time, around the table, it would have been no use for defenders of terrorism to say, "Everybody does it," because there they would be face to face with people proposing to do something else. Nor is it historically the case that the members of this last group, the opponents of terrorism, always lose the argument. They can win, however, and still not be able to prevent a terrorist campaign; the would-be terrorists (it does not take very many) can always split the movement and go their own way. Or, they can split the bureaucracy or the police or officer corps and act in the shadow of state power. Indeed, terrorism often has its origin in such splits. The first victims are the terrorist's former comrades or colleagues. What reason can we possibly have, then, for equating the two? If we value the politics of the men and women who oppose terrorism, we must reject the excuses of their murderers. Cynicism at such a time is unfair to the victims.

The fourth excuse can also take, often does take, a more-restricted form. Oppression, rather than political rule more generally, is always terroristic in character, and thus, we must always excuse the opponents of oppression. When they choose terrorism, they are only reacting to someone else's previous choice, repaying in kind the treatment they have long received. Of course, their terrorism repeats the evil—innocent people are killed, who were never themselves oppressors—but repetition is not the same as initiation. The oppressors set the terms of the struggle. But if the struggle is fought on the oppressors' terms, then the oppressors are likely to win. Or, at least, oppression is likely to win, even if it takes on a new face. The whole point of a liberation movement or a popular mobilization is to change the terms. We have no reason to excuse the terrorism reactively adopted by opponents of oppression unless we are confident of the sincerity of their opposition, the seriousness of their commitment to a nonoppressive politics. But the choice of terrorism undermines that confidence.

We are often asked to distinguish the terrorism of the oppressed from the terrorism of the oppressors. What is it, however, that makes the difference? The message of the terrorist is the same in both cases: a denial of the peoplehood and humanity of the groups among whom he or she finds victims.

Terrorism anticipates, when it does not actually enforce, political domination. Does it matter if one dominated group is replaced by another? Imagine a slave revolt whose protagonists dream only of enslaving in their turn the children of their masters. The dream is understandable, but the fervent desire of the children that the revolt be repressed is equally understandable. In neither case does understanding make for excuse—not, at least, after a politics of universal freedom has become possible. Nor does an understanding of oppression excuse the terrorism of the oppressed, once we have grasped the meaning of "liberation."

These are the four general excuses for terror, and each of them fails. They depend upon statements about the world that are false, historical arguments for which there is no evidence, moral claims that turn out to be hollow or dishonest. This is not to say that there might not be more particular excuses that have greater plausibility, extenuating circumstances in particular cases that we would feel compelled to recognize. As with murder, we can tell a story (like the story that Richard Wright tells in *Native Son*, for example) that might lead us, not to justify terrorism, but to excuse this or that individual terrorist. We can provide a personal history, a psychological study, of compassion destroyed by fear, moral reason by hatred and rage, social inhibition by unending violence—the product, an individual driven to kill or readily set on a killing course by his or her political leaders.[3] But the force of this story will not depend on any of the four general excuses, all of which grant what the storyteller will have to deny: that terrorism is the deliberate choice of rational men and women. Whether they conceive it to be one option among others or the only one available, they nevertheless argue and choose. Whether they are acting or reacting, they have made a decision. The human instruments they subsequently find to plant the bomb or, shoot the gun may act under some psychological compulsion, but the men and women who choose terror as a policy act "freely." They could not act in any other way, or accept any other description of their action, and still pretend to be the leaders of the movement or the state. We ought never to excuse such leaders.

Responses to Terrorism

What follows from the critique of excuses? There is still a great deal of room for argument about the best way of responding to terrorism. Certainly, terrorists should be resisted, and it is not likely that a purely defensive resistance will ever be sufficient. In this sort of struggle, the offense is always ahead. The technology of terror is simple; the weapons are readily produced and easy to deliver. It is virtually impossible to protect people against random and indiscriminate attack. Thus, resistance will have to be supplemented by some combination of repression and retaliation. This is a dangerous business because repression and retaliation so often take terroristic forms and there are a host of apologists ready with excuses that sound remarkably like those of the terrorists themselves. It should be clear by now, however, that counterterrorism cannot be excused merely because it is reactive. Every new actor, terrorist or counterterrorist, claims to be reacting to someone else, standing in a circle and just passing the evil along. But the circle is ideological in character; in fact, every actor is a moral agent and makes an independent decision.

Therefore, repression and retaliation must not repeat the wrongs of terrorism, which is to say that repression and retaliation must be aimed systematically at the terrorists themselves, never at *the people for whom the terrorists claim to be acting*. That claim is in any case doubtful, even when it is honestly made. The people do not authorize the terrorists to act in their name. Only a tiny number actually participate in terrorist activities; they are far more likely to suffer than to benefit from the terrorist program. Even if they supported the program and hoped to benefit from it, however, they would still be immune from attack—exactly as civilians in time of war who support the war effort but are not themselves part of it are subject to the same immunity. Civilians may be put at risk by attacks on military targets, as by attacks on terrorist targets, but the risk must be kept to a minimum, even at some cost to the attackers. The refusal to make ordinary people into targets, whatever their nationality or even their politics, is the only way to say no to terrorism. Every act of repression and retaliation has to be measured by this standard.

But what if the "only way" to defeat the terrorists is to intimidate their actual or potential supporters? It is important to deny the premise of this question: that terrorism is a politics dependent on mass support. In fact, it is always the politics of an elite, whose members are dedicated and fanatical and more than ready to endure, or to watch others endure, the devastations of a counterterrorist campaign. Indeed, terrorists will welcome counterterrorism; it makes the terrorists' excuses more plausible and is sure to bring them, however many people are killed or wounded, however many are terrorized, the small number of recruits needed to sustain the terrorist activities.

Repression and retaliation are legitimate responses to terrorism only when they are constrained by the same moral principles that rule out terrorism itself. But there is an alternative response that seeks to avoid the violence that these two entail. The alternative is to address directly, ourselves, the oppression the terrorists claim to oppose. Oppression, they say, is the cause of terrorism. But that is merely one more excuse. The real cause of terrorism is the decision to launch a terrorist campaign, a decision made by that group of people sitting around a table whose deliberations I have already described. However, terrorists do exploit oppression, injustice, and human misery generally and look to these at least for their excuses. There can hardly be any doubt that oppression strengthens their hand. Is that a reason for us to come to the defense of the oppressed? It seems to me that we have our own reasons to do that, and do not need this one, or should not, to prod us into action. We might imitate those movement militants who argue against the adoption of a terrorist strategy—although not, as the terrorists say, because these militants are prepared to tolerate oppression. They already are opposed to oppression and now add to that opposition, perhaps for the same reasons, a refusal of terror. So should we have been opposed before, and we should now make the same addition.

But there is an argument, put with some insistence these days, that we should refuse to acknowledge any link at all between terrorism and oppression—as if any defense of oppressed men and women, once a terrorist campaign has been launched, would concede the effectiveness of the campaign. Or, at least, the defense would give terrorism the appearance of effectiveness and so increase the likelihood of terrorist campaigns in the future. Here we have the reverse side of the litany of excuses; we have turned over the record. First oppression is made into an excuse for terrorism, and then terrorism is made into an excuse for oppression. The first is the excuse of the far left; the second is the excuse of the neoconservative right.[4] I doubt that genuine conservatives would think it a good reason for defending the status quo that it is under terrorist attack; they would have independent reasons and would be prepared to defend the status quo against any attack. Similarly, those of us who think that the status quo urgently requires change have our own reasons for thinking so and need not be intimidated by terrorists or, for that matter, antiterrorists.

If one criticizes the first excuse, one should not neglect the second. But I need to state the second more precisely. It is not so much an excuse for oppression as an excuse for doing nothing (now) about oppression. The claim is that the campaign against terrorism has priority over every other political activity. If the people who take the lead in this campaign are the old oppressors, then we must make a kind of peace with them—temporarily, of course, until the terrorists have been beaten. This is a strategy that denies the possibility of a two-front war. So long as the men and women who pretend to lead the fight against oppression are terrorists, we can concede nothing to their demands. Nor can we oppose their opponents.

But why not? It is not likely in any case that terrorists would claim victory in the face of a serious effort to deal with the oppression of the people they claim to be defending. The effort would merely expose the hollowness of their claim, and the nearer it came to success, the more they would escalate their terrorism. They would still have to be defeated, for what they are after is not a solution to the problem but rather the power to impose their own solution. No decent end to the conflict in Ireland, say, or in Lebanon, or in the Middle East generally, is going to look like a victory for terrorism—if only because the different groups of terrorists are each committed, by the strategy they have adopted, to an indecent end.[5] By working for our own ends, we expose the indecency.

Terror and Oppression

It is worth considering at greater length the link between oppression and terror. To pretend that there is no link at all is to ignore the historical record, but the record is more complex than any of the excuses acknowledge. The first thing to be read out of it, however, is simple enough: *Oppression is not so much the cause of terrorism as terrorism is one of the primary means of oppression.* This was true in ancient times, as Aristotle recognized, and it is still true today. Tyrants rule by terrorizing their subjects; unjust and illegitimate regimes are upheld through a combination of carefully aimed and random violence.[6] If this method works in the state, there is no reason to think that it will not work, or that it does not work, in the liberation movement. Wherever we see terrorism, we should look for tyranny and oppression. Authoritarian states, especially in the moment of their founding, need a terrorist apparatus—secret police with unlimited power, secret prisons into which citizens disappear, death squads in unmarked cars. Even democracies may use terror, not against their own citizens, but at the margins, in their colonies, for example, where colonizers also are likely to rule tyrannically. Oppression is sometimes maintained by a steady and discriminate pressure, sometimes by intermittent and random violence—what we might think of as terrorist melodrama—designed to render the subject population fearful and passive.

This latter policy, especially if it seems successful, invites imitation by opponents of the state. But terrorism does not spread only when it is imitated. If it can be invented by state officials, it can also be invented by movement militants. Neither one need take lessons from the other; the circle has no single or necessary starting point. Wherever it starts, terrorism in the movement is tyrannical and oppressive in exactly the same way as is terrorism in the state. The terrorists aim to rule, and murder is their method. They have their own internal police, death squads, disappearances. They begin by killing or intimidating those comrades who stand in their way, and they proceed to do the same, if they can, among the people they claim to represent. If terrorists are successful, they rule tyrannically, and their people bear, without consent, the costs of the terrorists' rule. (If the terrorists are only partly successful, the costs to the people may be even greater: What they have to bear now is a war between rival terrorist gangs.) But terrorists cannot win the ultimate victory they seek without challenging the established regime or colonial power and the people it claims to represent, and when terrorists do that, they themselves invite imitation. The regime may then respond with its own campaign of aimed and random violence. Terrorist tracks terrorist, each claiming the other as an excuse.

The same violence can also spread to countries where it has not yet been experienced; now terror is reproduced not through temporal succession but through ideological adaptation. State terrorists wage bloody wars against largely imaginary enemies: army colonels, say, hunting down the representatives of "international communism." Or movement terrorists wage bloody wars against enemies with whom, but for the ideology, they could readily negotiate and compromise: nationalist fanatics committed to a permanent irredentism. These wars, even if they are without precedents, are likely enough to become precedents, to start the circle of terror and counterterror, which is endlessly oppressive for the ordinary men and women whom the state calls its citizens and the movement its "people."

The only way to break out of the circle is to refuse to play the terrorist game. Terrorists in the state and the movement warn us, with equal vehemence, that any such refusal is a sign of softness and naiveté. The self-portrait of the terrorists is always the same. They are tough-minded and realistic; they know their enemies (or privately invent them for ideological purposes); and they are ready to do what must be done for victory. Why then do terrorists turn around and around in the same circle? It is true: Movement terrorists win support because they pretend to deal energetically and effectively with the brutality of the state. It also is true: State terrorists win support because they pretend to deal energetically and effectively with the brutality of the movement. Both feed on the fears of brutalized and oppressed people. But there is no way of overcoming brutality with terror. At most, the burden is shifted from these people to those; more likely, new burdens are added for everyone. *Genuine libera-tion can come only through a politics that mobilizes the victims of brutality and takes careful aim at its agents, or by a politics that surrenders the hope of victory and domination and deliberately seeks a compromise settle-ment.* In either case, once tyranny is repudiated, terrorism is no longer an option. For what lies behind all the excuses, of officials and militants alike, is the predilection for a tyrannical politics.

NOTES

1. I cannot resist a few examples: Edward Said, "The Terrorism Scam," *The Nation*, June 14, 1986; and (more intelligent and circumspect) Richard Falk; "Thinking About Terrorism," *The Nation*, June 28, 1986.
2. Machiavelli, *The Discourses* I:ix. As yet, however, there have been no results that would constitute a Machiavellian excuse.
3. See, for example, Daniel Goleman, "The Roots of Terrorism Are Found in Brutality of Shattered Childhood," *New York Times*, September 2, 1986, pp. C1, 8. Goleman discusses the psychological and social history of particular terrorists, not the roots of terrorism.
4. The neoconservative position is represented, although not as explicitly as I have stated it here, in Benjamin Netanyahu, ed., *Terrorism: How the West Can Win* (New York: Farrar, Straus & Giroux, 1986).
5. The reason the terrorist strategy, however indecent in itself, cannot be instrumental to some decent political purpose is because any decent purpose must somehow accommodate the people against whom the terrorism is aimed, and what terrorism expresses is precisely the refusal of such an accommodation, the radical devaluing of the Other. See my argument in *Just and Unjust Wars* (New York: Basic Books, 1977), 197–206, especially 203.
6. Aristotle, *The Politics* 1313–1314a.

DISCUSSION QUESTIONS:

1. Does Walzer give us good reasons for ruling out a moral justification for terrorism?
2. In his essay in this text, "Against Moral Conservatism," Nielsen considers a variety of acts, including ones of terrorism, and claims that "there are circumstances when such violence must be reluctantly assented to or even taken to be something that one, morally speaking, must do" (p. 204). What are the fundamental points of disagreement between Walzer and Nielsen? Which of them is correct? Why?
3. Walzer considers four attempts to excuse terrorism. Sometimes when we describe an act as morally

excusable, we mean that, while it is generally impermissible, it is permissible in the present circumstances. Other times, we mean that the act is morally impermissible but the agent is not morally blameworthy for his or her behavior. Do any of the excuses Walzer considers show that terrorists are not morally blameworthy for their (presumed) immoral acts; do any of them give us a good reason to think that, in some situations, acts of terrorism are morally permissible?
4. What is the appropriate way to respond to terrorism, especially when it is done in opposition to extreme political oppression? Walzer proposes a "two-front" response that seeks to end both the acts of terrorism and any political oppression that gives rise to it. Does such a response make the mistake of conceding to the demands of terrorists and unwittingly encouraging further acts of terrorism? Should governments always refuse to recognize or negotiate with terrorist organizations?
5. Walzer writes that the cycle of terror and counter-terror can only be ended in the following way:

> Genuine liberation can come only through a politics that mobilizes the victims of brutality and takes careful aim at its agents, or by a politics that surrenders the hope of victory and domination and deliberately seeks a compromise. (page 526)

Some terrorists might agree with Walzer but argue that, under some conditions, acts of terrorism are required to create an environment in which such a politics can exist. How might Walzer best respond to this claim? Would he be correct?

Argument Reconstruction Exercises:

I. Walzer describes the evil of terrorism in the following terms. Reconstruct an argument for the conclusion that terrorism is always morally wrong from his description.

> The victims of a terrorist attack are third parties, innocent bystanders; there is no special reason for attacking them; anyone else within a large class of (unrelated) people will do as well. The attack is directed indiscriminately against the entire class . . . [Terrorism is] not only the killing of innocent people but also the intrusion of fear into

everyday life, the violation of private purposes, the insecurity of public spaces, the endless coerciveness of precaution. . . . Terrorism is the work of visible hands; it is an organizational project, a strategic choice, a conspiracy to murder and intimidate. . . [T]errorism is random, degrading and frightening. (page 520)

II. As Walzer notes (pages 520–521), the first three excuses he considers can be combined to form a **consequentialist** argument for the conclusion that terrorism is sometimes morally permissible. Identify the premises and conclusion of the following argument.

> Terrorism is sometimes justified, for it sometimes achieves the ends of the oppressed where those ends could not have been achieved through any other, less wrongful, means.

III. The fourth excuse Walzer considers for terrorism provides the basis for an argument for the conclusion that terrorism, when done in response to equally brutal oppression, is morally excusable. Identify the premises and conclusion of the argument.

When [terrorists] choose terrorism, they are only reacting to someone else's previous choice, repaying in kind the treatment they have long received. Of course, their terrorism repeats the evil—innocent people are killed, who were never themselves oppressors—but repetition is not the same as initiation. The oppressors set the terms of the struggle. (page 522)

IV. Walzer rejects the following argument regarding the proper response to terrorism. Identify its premises and conclusion.

> But there is an argument, put with some insistence these days, that we should refuse to acknowledge any link at all between terrorism and oppression—as if any defense of oppressed men and women, once a terrorist campaign has been launched, would concede the effectiveness of the campaign. Or, at least, the defense would give terrorism the appearance of effectiveness and so increase the likelihood of terrorist campaigns in the future. (page 524)

18.2 IS TERRORISM DISTINCTIVELY WRONG?

LIONEL K. MCPHERSON (2007)

Lionel K. McPherson is Associate Professor of Philosophy at Tufts University. His philosophical writings focus on issues in ethics, including ones related to war, terrorism, and race. In this essay, he considers what he terms "the dominant view" that terrorism is necessarily and egregiously wrong, and he argues in response that terrorism is not distinctively wrong in comparison to conventional warfare. McPherson concludes that insofar as we believe that terrorism is evil because of the harm that it inflicts on innocent persons, we should be ready to accept a similar conclusion about conventional warfare, and, insofar as we think that war can justified by the absence of less harmful means to achieve a just cause, we should take seriously the possibility that the same can be true of terrorism.

Reading Questions:

1 What does McPherson take to be "the dominant view" on the morality of terrorism, and how is his view different from the dominant view?

2. What is McPherson's definition of terrorism?

3. How does McPherson respond to the claim that terrorism is wrong because it involves killing the innocent and spreading fear among ordinary noncombatants?

4. What is the proportionality principle, and why does McPherson believe that it does not provide the basis for a moral distinction between conventional warfare and terrorism?

5. What is the **Doctrine of Double Effect** and why does McPherson believe that it does not provide the basis for a moral distinction between conventional warfare and terrorism?

6. What is it for a group to have representative authority? Why does McPherson think that such authority is a necessary condition for the justified use of political violence? Does McPherson believe that terrorist groups can have such authority for their actions? What does he take to be "the argument from representative authority"?

7. What does McPherson claim to be the relevant similarities between terrorism and conventional warfare?

Many people, including philosophers, believe that terrorism is necessarily and egregiously wrong. I will call this "the dominant view." The dominant view maintains that terrorism is akin to murder. This forecloses the possibility that terrorism, under any circumstances, could be morally permissible—murder, by definition, is wrongful killing. The unqualified wrongness of terrorism is thus part of this understanding of terrorism. . .

I will argue that the dominant view's condemnatory attitude toward terrorism as compared to conventional war cannot be fully sustained. . . .

Too often, criticism of the prevailing discourse has been dismissed as an attempt to excuse terrorism.[2] I seek to offer no excuse for terrorism, any more than I would for war as such. The principal challenge for those who believe that terrorism is distinctively wrong lies in morally accounting for noncombatant casualties of conventional war. This challenge holds even when wars are fought according to international law, for example, as codified in the 1977 Geneva Protocol I on International Armed Conflicts.[3] Terrorism might be morally objectionable for reasons that hardly apply less to conventional war, for the laws of war are not beyond moral scrutiny. A credible argument that would demonstrate

the distinctive wrongness of terrorism is not as obvious as proponents of the dominant view believe.

Definitional Issues

The dominant view finds characteristic expression in the following definition: "Terrorism is a type of political violence that intentionally targets civilians (noncombatants) in a ruthlessly destructive, often unpredictable manner. . . . Essentially, terrorism employs horrific violence against unsuspecting civilians, as well as combatants, in order to inspire fear and create panic, which in turn will advance the terrorists' political or religious agenda."[4] Much of this language is not helpful in morally distinguishing terrorism, since conventional war tends to be at least as "ruthlessly destructive," "unpredictable," and "horrific" for noncombatants and combatants.

I will define 'terrorism' as the deliberate use of force against ordinary noncombatants, which can be expected to cause wider fear among them, for political ends. My definition focuses on the aspect of terrorism—namely, targeting of ordinary noncombatants—that commonly is thought to characterize its distinctive wrongness as compared to conventional war. Left out of the definition, for instance, is the claim that noncombatants are "innocent." The relevant understanding of innocence in war is a contested matter, and my argument will not depend on how this is settled.[5] I will assume provisionally that ordinary noncombatants in general are innocent. . . .

Challenging the Dominant View

Moral evaluation of terrorism might begin with the question of what makes terrorism wrong. A better opening question, I believe, is whether use of force that leads to casualties among ordinary noncombatants is morally objectionable. The latter question prompts comparison of terrorism and conventional war. Judging by practice and common versions of just war theory, the answer js plainly no. The journalist Chris Hedges reports these facts: "Between 1900 and 1990, 43 million soldiers died in wars. During the same period, 62 million civilians were killed. . . . In the wars of the 1990s, civilian deaths constituted between 75 and 90 percent of all war deaths."[6] Such numbers may seem counterintuitive. More noncombatants than combatants have died in war, by a sizable margin, and the margin has only grown in an era of the most advanced weapons technology. We must conclude that war generally is highly dangerous for noncombatants. I will characterize this as the brute reality of war for noncombatants. This reality cannot be attributed simply to the conduct of war departing from the laws of war.

There is an ambiguity in the data I have cited: they do not clearly support the claim that most noncombatants who died in these wars were killed by military actions, for example, through the use of bombs, artillery, and land mines. Many noncombatant deaths in war have been the result of displacement and the lack of shelter, inability to get food, and the spread of disease. At the same time, modern warfare is marked by a nontrivial number of noncombatant deaths that are the direct result of military actions. The ratio of war to "war-related" noncombatant casualties and the distribution of moral responsibility for these casualties will not be at issue here. I proceed on the assumption that evaluating the ethics of war involves recognizing that war, directly or indirectly, leads to a great many noncombatant casualties. Modern, warfare and widespread harm to noncombatants are virtually inextricable. In fact, this motivates a strain of pacifist skepticism about the just war tradition.[7] Although I would defend a revisionist version of just war theory, I do not believe we can deny that modem warfare raises the moral stakes to a degree that calls for reevaluating the view that terrorism is intrinsically worse than war.

Immediately doubtful is the popular notion that terrorism is distinctively wrong because of the fear it usually spreads among ordinary noncombatants. Recall that my nonmoral definition of terrorism includes a fear-effects clause which descriptively distinguishes terrorism from other forms of political violence. However, this does not morally distinguish terrorism and conventional war. The brute reality of war for noncombatants indicates that in general they have more to fear from conventional war than (nonstate) terrorism, particularly since (nonstate) terrorists rarely have had the capacity to employ violence on a mass scale.)[8] Noncombatants in states that are military powers might have more to fear from terrorism than conventional war, since these states are relatively unlikely to be conventionally attacked. But surely this situational advantage that does not extend more broadly to noncombatants cannot ground the claim that terrorism is distinctively wrong.

The laws of war recognize a principle that prohibits disproportionate or excessive use of force, with an emphasis on noncombatants. For example, Article 51 (5) (b) of the 1977 Geneva Protocol I rules out use of force "which may be expected to cause incidental loss of civilian life, injury to civilians, damage to civilian objects, or a combination thereof, which would be excessive in relation to the concrete and direct military advantage anticipated."[9] Standard just war theory considers this the proportionality principle. *Proponents of the dominant view might take the proportionality principle to illuminate an essential moral difference between conventional war and terrorism. They might claim that, unlike proper combatants, terrorists do not care about disproportionate harm to noncombatants. But the full impact of this charge is not easily sustained for two reasons.*

The first reason is that terrorists could have some concern about disproportionate harm to noncombatants. This point is most salient when proportionality is understood in instrumental terms of whether violence is gratuitous, namely, in exceeding what is minimally necessary to achieve particular military or political goals, despite the availability of an alternative course of action that would be less harmful and no less efficacious. Terrorists may possess a normative if flawed sensibility that disapproves of instrumentally gratuitous violence, for the harm done would serve no strategic purpose. So the plausible charge is that terrorists reject the proportionality principle as conventionally construed (since it implicitly rules out deliberate use of force against noncombatants), not that they lack all concern for disproportionate harm to noncombatants.

The second reason is that the proportionality principle requires rather modest due care for noncombatants. Force may be used against them, provided that the incidental, or collateral, harm to them is not excessive when measured against the expected military gains. According to one legal scholar, "the interpretation by the United States and its allies of their legal obligations concerning the prevention of collateral casualties and the concept of proportionality comprehends prohibiting only two types of attacks: first, those that intentionally target civilians; and second, those that involve negligent behavior in ascertaining the nature of a target or the conduct of the attack itself."[10] Such an interpretation seems accurately to reflect the principle's leniency. Indeed, the U.S. general and military theorist James M. Dubik argues that commanders have a special moral duty "not to waste lives of their soldiers" in balancing the responsibility to ensure that due care is afforded to noncombatants.[11] A commander may give priority to limiting risk of harm to his own combatants, for their sake, at the expense of noncombatants on the other side.

We find, then, that the proportionality principle does not express a commitment to minimizing noncombatant casualties. The principle more modestly would reduce noncombatant casualties in requiring that they be worth military interests. Perhaps my reading appears too narrow. A prominent reason for thinking that terrorism is distinctively wrong is that terrorists, unlike combatants who comply with the laws of war, do not acknowledge the moral significance of bearing burdens in order to reduce noncombatant casualties for the sake of noncombatants themselves. To reply that terrorists might well be motivated to reduce noncombatant casualties on strategic grounds, for example, to avoid eroding sympathy for their political goals, would miss the point. Basic respect for the lives of noncombatants seems evidenced instead by a willingness to bear burdens in order to reduce harm to them. Terrorists, the objection goes, do not have this respect for noncombatant lives, which is a major source of the sense that terrorism is distinctively wrong as compared to conventional war.

There are difficulties with this objection. It suggests that the laws of war are imbued with a certain moral character, namely, fundamental moral concern for noncombatants. These laws, though, are part of the war convention, adopted by states and codified in international law for reasons that seem largely to reflect their shared interests, at least in the long run.[12] We do not have to be political realists to see this. Given that noncombatants are vulnerable enough on all sides and no state generally has much to gain by harming them, states usually are prudent to accept mutually a principle that seeks to reduce noncombatant casualties. States usually are also prudent to comply with the laws of war, since this compliance is a benchmark of moral and political respectability on the world stage. Simply put, states, like terrorists, would seem contingently motivated to accept the proportionality principle on broadly strategic grounds.

Now the objection might go that, even if a realist analysis of the proportionality principle's place in the war convention is correct, this is no barrier to states' recognizing that the principle has independent, nonprudential moral standing. But the same can be true for terrorists. Familiar characterizations of them as "evil" or unconstrained by moral boundaries are an unreliable indication of moral indifference to harming noncombatants. As Virginia Held observes, "Terrorists often believe, whether mistakenly or not, that violence is the only course of action open to them that can advance their political objectives."[13] When terrorism is seen by its agents as a means of last resort, this provides some evidence that they acknowledge the moral significance of bearing burdens out of respect for the lives of noncombatants. Such agents will not have employed terrorism earlier, despite their grievances.

A model case is the African National Congress (ANC) in its struggle against apartheid in South Africa. Nelson Mandela, during the 1964 trial that produced his sentence of life imprisonment, summed up the ANC's position as follows:

> *a.* It was a mass political organization with a political function to fulfill. Its members had joined on the express policy of nonviolence.
> *b.* Because of all this, it could not and would not undertake violence. This must be stressed.
> *c.* On the other hand, in view of this situation I have described, the ANC was prepared to depart from its fifty-year-old policy of nonviolence. . . . There is sabotage, there is guerrilla warfare, there is terrorism, and there is open revolution. We chose to adopt the first method and to exhaust it before taking any other decision.[14]

Mandela was implying that violence, including terrorism, became an option "only when all else had failed, when all channels of peaceful protest had been barred to us," which led the ANC to conclude that "to continue preaching peace and nonviolence at a time when the government met our peaceful demands with force would be "unrealistic and wrong.[15] By the 1980s, at the height of government repression, the ANC did resort to acts of terrorism before reaffirming its earlier position on controlled violence that does not target civilians.[16] The case of the ANC demonstrates that those who employ terrorism can have and sometimes have had fundamental moral concern for noncombatants. Such moral concern, however, is overriding neither for terrorists nor for proper combatants.

Thus considerations other than proportionality and basic respect for the lives of noncombatants would *have to show that terrorism is intrinsically worse than conventional war. . . .*

Justice Beyond the Doctrine of Double Effect

Roughly, the **Doctrine of Double Effect** holds that one may never intend to cause an evil, even to achieve a greater good. One may pursue a good end through neutral means, even if foreseeing that this will have evil effects, provided that the evil is proportionate to the good and there is no better way of achieving the good.[17] *On standard just war theory, the DDE rules out terrorism, since intending to harm ordinary noncombatants would be to aim at causing an evil. Acts of conventional war that unintentionally harm noncombatants are not necessarily ruled out, since such acts have only military targets. . . .*

Some philosophers directly challenge the DDE as a test of the permissibility of acts by challenging the relevance of intention, Judith Thomson presents the following case: A bomber pilot seeks advice from his superior officers about the permissibility of an attack that would destroy a munitions factory and an adjacent hospital in which noncombatants would be killed.[18] The superiors assure the pilot that the military gains would be necessary and proportionate in relation to the noncombatant casualties. Still, the superiors want to know whether the pilot intends to destroy the factory or intends to destroy the hospital. Thomson finds absurd the notion that their advice would turn on which intention the pilot has. The properties of the bombing are known in advance and seem on their own to render the act impermissible or not under the circumstances.[19] The pilot's moral character or his disposition to act on objectionable motives in other situations is not at issue.

Perhaps Thomson's charge of absurdity against the DDE is overstated. If the pilot intends to destroy the hospital and not the factory, it would be better for his superiors to send a different pilot on the mission to destroy the factory. But if no other pilot is available, the DDE might not prohibit sending the pilot who intends to destroy the hospital: his superiors might exploit his bad moral character and wrongful intention in order to fulfill their acceptable intention to destroy the factory.[20] The intention of the pilot would make a moral difference but need not make a decisive moral difference to what his superiors could permissibly have him do, which could save the DDE from absurdity. Yet the cost of this save is high. If the pilot's superiors know that he would be acting wrongly due to his wrongful intention, it seems plausible to think that they would be acting wrongly in allowing him to act wrongly. Presumably, advocates of the DDE do not want to maintain that we can act permissibly regarding our own ultimate, acceptable intentions when the good ends would have to be brought about by exploiting the bad moral character and wrongful intentions of others. No less a friend of the importance of intention than Elizabeth Anscombe would scorn this as "double-think about double effect.[21] The proposed save looks like a moral responsibility shell game, marked by bad faith if not absurdity. . .

The DDE is susceptible to yielding dubious results. Frances Kamm describes a threshold deontological point of view. Suppose that it would be permissible to kill a million noncombatants as an unintended effect of tactical bombing in a war of just cause; a permissible alternative might be to kill a few hundred different noncombatants as an intended effect of terror bombing.[22] The DDE would not be an overriding deontological constraint, since the cost of acting within the constraint exceeds any reasonable threshold. How could it be impermissible to kill through terrorism so many fewer persons of the same type, who otherwise would be killed through conventional war? We are not presupposing that the agent's intention makes an essential moral difference. A ready response comes from an objection to consequentialism: noncombatants have a right not to be harmed that cannot simply be traded off against the collectivized interests of a greater plumber of noncombatants or against some other greater good.[23]

Whether or not this is seen as a viable objection to consequentialism, it is much less compelling in support of the DDE. The threshold deontological argument can be reformulated. Suppose that the few hundred noncombatants who would be killed intentionally are among the million noncombatants who otherwise would be killed collaterally. The presumptive right not to be harmed that the prospective terror bombing victims have would be violated anyway,

since they are a subset of the prospective tactical bombing victims who also have this right. There is no consequentialist sacrifice of the lives of noncombatants who would not be harmed, only minimization of the loss of life among noncombatants who would be killed through the alternative. Still, the DDE would prohibit the course of action through which fewer noncombatants would be killed, since the doctrine rules out intentionally killing them. Even proponents of agent-centered moral theories might balk at this conclusion. Christine Korsgaard, for example, defends a Kantian view on which "To treat someone as an end . . . is to respect his right to use his own reason to determine whether and how he will contribute to what happens [to him]."[24] The prospective terror bombing victims may well elect to be killed intentionally if confronted with the narrow choice, in order to minimize loss of life among the larger set of noncombatants that includes them. To deny them this measure of influence over their fate suggests a doctrinaire refusal to share their sensible perspective. The DDE's overwhelming emphasis on the intentions of the harm-doing agents would amount to indifference to the victims' choice and their concern for the good of their people.

Standard just war theory's application of the Doctrine of Double Effect is all too compatible with the brute reality of war for noncombatants. The conventional interpretation of the DDE permits use of force against noncombatants once its prohibition on intending to harm them and its requirements of necessity and proportionality have been satisfied. If we believe that fewer noncombatant casualties is a goal morally worth striving for, we are led to the discomfiting conclusion that terrorism in some situations might better achieve this goal than use of force that satisfies the limited noncombatant immunity principle. While this conclusion does not require accepting that terrorism can be justifiable, it does call into question the moral integrity of standard just war theory. . .

The Argument from Representative Authority

Terrorism often is not backed by *representative authority*, by which I mean adequate license for acting on behalf of a people through their approval.

The argument from representative authority that I will elaborate is related to a familiar argument from legitimate authority. While the latter is too restrictive, the former provides a qualified basis for the view that terrorism is a distinctively objectionable form of political violence.

The large and difficult topic of legitimate authority will have to be confined to a brief discussion for present purposes. One prominent approach draws from Hobbesian social contract theory, a state's authority depends on its ability to impose law and order on the persons within its domain.[25] They must fare better than they could expect to if left to their own devices. That is, the state would have legitimate authority by virtue of being able to mediate the aggressive pursuit of self-interest by individual members, who rationally would agree to be governed through coercive power for the sake of their mutual interest. Another prominent approach, which also utilizes a social contract model, regards members of a state as political constituents and moral agents, not mainly as subjects. This is exemplified when the members of a state are organized around a substantially just and democratic government. Rawls gives the following characterization: "The government is effectively under their political and electoral control, and . . . it answers to and protects their fundamental interests as specified in a written or unwritten constitution and in its interpretation. The regime is not an autonomous agency pursuing its own bureaucratic ambitions. Moreover, it is not directed by the interests of large concentrations of private economic and corporate power veiled from public knowledge and almost entirely free from accountability."[26] The state's legitimate authority would derive from the people, whose government operates through and for them. At the same time, advancing their interests must be compatible with justice.

It might be thought, as the political status definition implies, that terrorism is distinctively wrong because terrorist groups by their nature lack legitimate authority. But this would presuppose that legitimate authority could be a decisive condition for permissible resort to political violence. A plausible argument for such a position is not obvious, especially on a view that grounds the state's authority merely on its ability to provide civil order. Indeed,

authoritarian states are capable of achieving civil order. They do not thereby have moral standing, despite the claim they may have to political sovereignty under international law and custom. A decent state must do more than protect its members against internal anarchy and external threats: it also must protect their other fundamental interests and do so through acceptable means. That nonstate terrorism would offend against a morally weak, Hobbesian account of legitimate authority hardly seems a compelling reason for judging that nonstate terrorism is wrong. . . .

A limited appeal to adequate license does help to draw a moral boundary between terrorism and conventional war. In the ideal scenario, a democratic state functions with a considerable degree of control by its people and transparency regarding political processes. This provides no guarantee that political decisions will be substantively just. Nor am I suggesting that the ideal scenario of decision making in democratic states is closely approximated in real-world scenarios. There are no official referenda about decisions to go to war, let alone about how a war is fought, and political leaders can shape public opinion through selective dissemination of information and appeals to national interest that have a chilling effect on public debate. Yet political representatives in a democracy are under pressure from their constituents to justify going to war and to maintain support for a war that is already under way. Reasonable institutional procedures can provide checks and balances on the exercise of political power, presumably with a tendency to yield political decisions that are not egregiously unjust. What about states that are not democratic? Consider Rawls's proposal that their regimes might have a "decent consultation hierarchy": although the citizens are not granted equal political representation as individuals, they could belong to groups represented in a consultation hierarchy, having by proxy "the right at some point in the procedure of consultation (often at the stage of selecting a group's representatives) to express political dissent."[26] Substantial political representation of a people and accountability to them are possible in the absence of democracy. Representative authority is not exclusive to democratic states.

The deeply distinctive problem for nonstate terrorists now emerges. That they lack legitimate authority is only a rough indication of the problem. *Political violence by nonstate actors is objectionable when they employ it on their own initiative, so that their political goals, their violent methods, and, ultimately, their claim to rightful use of force do not go through any process of relevant public review and endorsement.* Nonstate terrorism's distinctive wrongness does not lie in the terrorism but rather in the resort to political violence without adequate license from a people on whose behalf the violence is purportedly undertaken.

We must recognize a distinction here between legitimate authority and representative authority. For nonstate actors, representative authority is the crucial kind of authority. While states are usually treated as the entities that have legitimacy in international relations, lack of statehood does not strictly indicate the deeper problem with political violence by nonstate actors. A nonstate group may have representative authority: the group not only would take itself to act on behalf of a people but also would be acting on the people's behalf given credible measures of approval by that people. Such measures, for example, mass demonstrations, general strikes, and polling, might lie outside formal political procedures. This raises concerns about the reliability of the measures and their interpretation by actors unfettered by the responsibilities of formal political leadership. These concerns are less of an issue when the right to resort to political violence belongs only to the state, that is, when the state has morally robust legitimate authority. Viable states function with established lines of authority for political decision making, which undergirds domestic stability and practicable international relations. In addition, states are more susceptible than nonstate actors to inducements and deterrents (e.g., economic cooperation, political sanctions, the threat of military action) aimed at promoting justice at home and abroad. Considerations of this sort motivate the prevailing view that statehood is prerequisite to permissible resort to political violence.

But the argument from the importance of statehood seems mainly pragmatic. The tendency that a state monopoly of political violence has to yield morally salient advantages does not indicate that political violence by nonstate actors is always morally objectionable. That a nonstate group does not have control of a state, does not exercise the full functions of a government, and has not conducted elections or put into place a just consultation hierarchy is not a sufficient basis for denying that the group has representative authority as a condition for permissible resort to political violence. The representative authority that nonstate groups may have, if in fact they often lack it, can be morally analogous to the legitimate authority of states. For instance, the FLN (National Liberation Front) came to have representative authority in relation to the Algerian people during Algeria's fight for independence from France, whereas Al-Qaeda does not have representative authority in pursuing militant Islamist goals in the name of the Muslim people. Appropriate wariness about nonstate groups claiming to have representative authority does not warrant rejecting all such claims tout court.

There is an apparent difficulty with how to construe a people. Individuals may be thought of as a people when they collectively identify on the basis of their self-ascribed nationality, ethnicity, culture, or religion, or on the basis of being victims of common oppressors (e.g., members of non-Arab ethnic groups in the Darfur region of Sudan vis-à-vis the Janjaweed militia). This differs from an understanding on which "the concept of 'people' belongs to the same social category as 'family' or 'tribe', that is, a people is one of those social units whose existence is independent of their members' consciousness."[27] The former, more expansive understanding is at work in my argument from representative authority, which leads to a worry. If individuals can collectively identify to comprise a people, there could be a proliferation of peoples, with the result that all kinds of groups could have gerrymandered representative authority.[28] Al-Qaeda could have representative authority that derives from the support of militant, fundamentalist Muslims in particular rather than of Muslims generally.

While my account of representative authority seems open to such a possibility, the worry is not as pressing as it may seem. Nonstate actors usually purport to represent as broad a constituency as possible in undertaking political violence. The reason is clear: the broader and less gerrymandered the constituency, for example, "the Muslim people" or "the nation," the greater the appearance of representative authority that is morally compelling. "In a verse applicable to all Muslims," contends Zayn Kassam Quran 5:32 states, 'whosoever kills a human being for other than manslaughter or corruption in the earth, it shall be as if he had killed all humankind. . . .' Can the assertion of what constitutes 'manslaughter' or 'corruption' be left to the judgment of individual not accountable to civic institutions? Surely not.[29] While I would substitute accountability to a people in place of accountability to civic institutions, Kassam's point is well taken. Any morally serious claim to having adequate license to employ political violence, namely, through having representative authority, will not come from a parochial source that answers only to the edicts of leaders who lack relevant public approval. . ."

The requirement of representative authority as a condition for employing political violence on behalf of a people expresses the value of autonomy. Typically, nonstate actors engaged in terrorism do not meet this requirement, though there have been notable exceptions that include the ANC, the FLN, and the PLO (Palestinian Liberation Organization) at some periods in their histories. Tyrannical regimes, despite having control of a state, never meet this requirement, though dictatorial regimes that have the majority support of their people might. A state that lacks legitimate authority is also likely to lack representative authority to act on behalf of the major substate groups or peoples within its territory, such as Kurds, Shiites, and Sunnis in Iraq. More precisely, then, my claim that there is a distinctive sense in which terrorism can be wrong holds with regard to a defeasible perspective from which nonstate actors lack representative authority and states have it.

The ultimate source of the value of autonomy as expressed by the requirement of representative authority is internal to a people on whose behalf political violence would be undertaken. It is true that, in order to meet this requirement, the goals and methods of political violence must go through a process of relevant public review and endorsement—a process that seems more likely than some nonrepresentative route to yield courses of action that are, at least, less unjust. To this extent, outsiders to a people have moral reason to care about representative authority. But the requirement of representative authority is not driven by the interests of outsiders, even as prospective victims. The internal moral importance of representative authority might make no difference to them. If the cause for political violence is just, victims on the other side would not be wronged with respect to the fact that the violence does not meet the representative authority requirement. When the cause is unjust, the representative authority requirement is morally moot from any perspective.

Conclusion

Let there be no misunderstanding: nonstate groups that have representative authority do not thereby have carte blanche to employ political violence. The same is true for states that legitimate authority. Representative authority for nonstate groups, like legitimate authority for states, is not sufficient to permit resorting to political violence without just cause. Also worth emphasizing is that the argument from representative authority belongs to my moral evaluation of terrorism. Political violence that has adequate license through relevant public approval may descriptively constitute terrorism, and I have not argued whether terrorism could ever be justifiable. However, when nonstate actors lack morally compelling representative authority, as is often the case, this preempts the possibility of their resort to political violence of any kind being justifiable, except in cases of indisputable humanitarian disaster. States that have morally robust legitimate authority do not face this hurdle—but adequate license is only one condition for permissible resort to political violence. While nonstate groups often fail at the level of representative authority and often would subsequently fail at the level of just cause, states often directly fail at the level of just cause. The distinctive wrongness of much nonstate terrorism does not support the dominant view that terrorism is necessarily wrong and intrinsically worse than conventional war.

I have argued that terrorism is not distinctively wrong as compared to conventional war in the following respects. Both types of political violence may be waged for just or unjust causes. Both types employ use of force against noncombatants, with conventional war usually causing them many more casualties. War and terrorism hence can be expected to produce fear widely among noncombatants where force is used. Further, states do not necessarily have and nonstate groups do not necessarily lack an adequate kind of authority that is a condition for permissible resort to political violence.

If we believe that terrorism is an evil because of the harm it does to ordinary noncombatants, we should be prepared to accept that the brute reality of war for noncombatants is an evil that is at least on par. The notion that an essential moral difference lies in whether the agents using force intend to harm noncombatants is, in the context of political violence, misplaced. If we believe that war can be justifiable on grounds of just cause and the unavailability of less harmful means, despite the harm it does to noncombatants, we must take seriously whether these same grounds could ever justify terrorism. The failures of the dominant view of terrorism should lead us to adopt either a more critical attitude toward conventional war or a less condemnatory attitude toward terrorism.

NOTES

2. See, e.g., Michael Walzer, "Terrorism: A Critique of Excuses," in *Arguing about War* (New Haven, CT: Yale University Press, 2004), 51–66.

3. See Adam Roberts and Richard Guelff, eds., *Documents on the Laws of War*, 3rd ed. (Oxford: Oxford University Press, 1982).

4. Louis P. Pojman, "The Moral Response to Terrorism and Cosmopolitanism," in *Terrorism and International Justice,* ed. James P. Sterba (New York: Oxford University Press, 2003), 135–57, 140.

5. For the revisionist view of the relevance of moral innocence and noninnocence, see Lionel K. McPherson, "Innocence and Responsibility in War," *Canadian Journal of Philosophy* 34 (2004): 485–506; and Jeff McMahan, "The Ethics of Killing in War," *Ethics* 114 (2004): 693–733.

6. Chris Hedges, *What Every Person Should Know about War* (New York: Free Press, 2003), 7.

7. See, e.g., A. J. Coates, *The Ethics of War* (Manchester: Manchester University Press, 1997), 80.

8. I add the qualification "nonstate" since states have employed tactics (e.g., fire-bombing of cities) and weapons (e.g., chemical, biological, and nuclear) that could count as terrorist.

9. Roberts and Guelff, *Documents on the Laws of War*, 449.

10. Judith Gail Gardam, "Proportionality and Force in International Law," *American Journal of International Law* 87 (1993): 391–413,410. To be clear, Gardam is not endorsing this interpretation. For a critical assessment of standard treatments of proportionality and an alternative approach, see Lionel K. McPherson, "Excessive Force in War: A 'Golden Rule' Test," *Theoretical Inquiries in Law* 7 (2005): 81–95.

11. James M. Dubik, *Philosophy & Public Affairs* 11 (1982): 354–71, 368. Dubik is responding to Waizer's more demanding requirement that combatants must accept greater costs to themselves for the sake of minimizing harm to noncombatants. See Walzer, *Just and Unjust Wars*, 155.

12. For criticism of the war convention as a source of moral obligation, see Lionel K. McPherson, "The Limits of the War Convention," *Philosophy and Social Criticism* 31 (2005): 147–63.

13. Virginia Held, "Terrorism and War," *Journal of Ethics* 8 (2004): 59–75, 69.

14. Nelson Mandela, "I Am Prepared to Die," in *Mandela, Tambo, and the African National Congress: The Struggle against Apartheid, 1948–1990: A Documentary Survey*, ed. Sheridan Johns and R. Hunt Davis Jr. (New York: Oxford University Press, 1991), 115–83, 121.

15. Ibid., 120.

16. Sheridan Johns and R. Hunt Davis Jr., "Conclusion: Mandela, Tambo, and the ANC in the 1990s," in their *Mandela, Tambo, and the African National Congress*, 309–17, 312.

17. See, e.g., F. M. Kamm, "Failures of Just War Theory: Terror, Harm, and Justice," *Ethics* 114 (2004): 650–92, 652–53.

18. Judith Jarvis Thomson, "Self-Defense," *Philosophy & Public Affairs* 20 (1991): 283–310, 293.

19. See also Kamm, "Failures of Just War Theory," 667–68; and T. M. Scanlon, "Intention and Permissibility," *Proceedings of the Aristotelian Society* 74 (2000): S301–S317, S310–S312.

20. This response to Thomson was suggested to me by Jeff McMahan.

21. G. E. M. Anscombe, "War and Murder," in her *Ethics, Religion and Politics* (Minneapolis: University of Minnesota Press, 1981), 51–61, 58. It is tempting to believe that Thomson-type cases are peculiarly unrepresentative and thus misleading about the DDE's application to conventional war. In typical cases, combatants do not have prior knowledge of the evil effects of their acts. Instead, they foresee the risk of harm to noncombatants, and even foreseeable high risk is not knowledge. Yet the DDE does not invoke a distinction between prior knowledge of evil effects and risk of evil effects. The agent's intention is supposed to make a moral difference in its own right.

22. Kamm, "Failures of Just War Theory," 664.

23. A similar point, albeit against the DDE and its requirements of necessity and proportionality, is made by Rodin, "Terrorism without Intention," 765.

24. Christine M. Korsgaard, "The Reasons We Can Share: An Attack on the Distinction between Agent-Relative and Agent-Neutral Values," *Social Philosophy and Policy* 10 (1993): 24–51, 46.

25. See Thomas Hobbes, *Leviathan* (1651), ed. C. B. Macpherson (Harmondsworth: Penguin, 1968), chaps. 13–14. Also see Charles R. Beitz, *Political Theory and International Relations* (Princeton, NJ: Princeton University Press, 1979), chaps. 2-4; and David Rodin, *War and Self-Defense* (New York: Oxford University Press, 2002), 144–48.

26. John Rawls, *The Law of Peoples* (Cambridge, MA: Harvard University Press, 1999), 24.

26. Rawls, *The Law of Peoples*, 71–72.

27. Yael Tamir, *Liberal Nationalism* (Princeton, NJ: Princeton University Press, 1993), 65.

28. Sharon Street pressed me on this point.

29. Zayn Kassarn, "Can a Muslim Be a Terrorist?" in Sterba, *Terrorism and International Justice*, 113–34, 130.

DISCUSSION QUESTIONS:

1. Is McPherson's definition of terrorism better than that associated with the dominant view? How is terrorism best defined?

2. Suppose that terrorism, by its very nature, violates certain generally accepted rules that governments have adopted for conventional warfare. Does that fact in itself imply that terrorism is morally wrong in a way that conventional warfare, when conducted in accord with those rules, is not?

3. Like many moral standards, the proportionality principle can be given more than one interpretation, some of which are more demanding than others. What is the morally best interpretation of the principle? Does the principle so interpreted provide the basis for a fundamental moral difference between just warfare, which is in accord with the principle, and terrorism?

4. Are McPherson's objections to the Doctrine of Double Effect successful? Even if the Doctrine of Double Effect is defective, might the different intentions of the parties with regard to harming noncombatants still make for an important moral difference between terrorism and conventional warfare?

5. Is McPherson correct in his claim that acts of political violence are justified only if those engaged in them act with representative authority?

What conditions must a group meet to have representative authority for its actions?

6. McPherson ends his essay with the conclusion that we should "adopt either a more critical attitude toward conventional war or a less condemnatory attitude toward terrorism." Assuming that his conclusion is correct, which of these two options should we adopt?

Argument Reconstruction Exercises:

I. Some claim that terrorism is distinctively wrong because it involves an essential failure to respect the lives and welfare of noncombatants. Identify the premises and conclusion of this argument, as McPherson presents it.

> A prominent reason for thinking that terrorism is distinctively wrong is that terrorists, unlike combatants who comply with the laws of war, do not acknowledge the moral significance of bearing burdens in order to reduce noncombatant casualties for the sake of the noncombatants themselves. . . Basic respect for the lives of noncombatants seems evidenced . . . by a willingness to bear burdens in order to reduce harm to them. Terrorists . . . do not have this respect for noncombatant lives. (page 530)

II. McPherson appeals to the example of the African National Congress (ANC) to support his view that considerations of proportionality and basic respect for innocent lives are insufficient to show that terrorism is morally worse than conventional war. Identify the premises and conclusion of his reasoning.

> The case of the ANC demonstrates that those who employ terrorism can have and sometimes have had fundamental moral concerns for noncombatants. Such moral concern . . . is overriding neither for terrorists nor for proper combatants. Thus considerations other than proportionality and basic respect for the lives of noncombatants would have to show that terrorism is intrinsically worse than conventional war. (page 531)

III. McPherson objects that the Doctrine of Double Effect has counter-intuitive implications. Identify the premises and conclusion of the following reasoning.

Suppose we have two alternatives. In Option A, a million noncombatants are killed as an unintended effect of tactical bombing in a war of just cause. In Option B, a few hundred of the same people are killed as the intended effect of terror bombing. The Doctrine of Double Effect implies, counterintuitively, that, while Option A is permissible, Option B is impermissible, despite the obvious fact that it involves killing many fewer people.

IV. McPherson takes at least some acts of terrorism to be wrong in a way that some acts of conventional war are not: the terrorists do not act with representative authority. Identify the premises and conclusion of the following argument:

> Political violence by non-state actors is objectionable when they employ it on their own initiative, so that their political goals, their violent methods, and, ultimately, their claim to rightful use of force do not go through any process of relevant public review and endorsement. Typically, non-state actors engaged in terrorism do not meet this requirement of representative authority. Tyrannical regimes, despite having control of a state, never meet it.

18.3 THE WAR ON TERRORISM AND THE END OF HUMAN RIGHTS

DAVID LUBAN (2002)

David Luban is University Professor and Professor of Law and Philosophy at Georgetown University. He is a specialist in legal ethics, just war theory, and human rights. In this essay, he argues that in its "war on terrorism," the U.S. government has combined elements of two conceptual models: the war model and the law model. As a result, terrorist suspects are in a "legal limbo" of rightlessness, and hence the hybrid war-law model involves the suspension of human rights. Luban considers one argument in favor of the model's adoption and then offers his own case against it.

Reading Questions:

1. Luban contrasts the model of war with the model of law; what are the main characteristics of each?

2. Luban claims that the U.S. government has adopted a hybrid war-law model in its response to terrorism. What are the main characteristics of that model?

3. How, according to Luban, does a government's adoption of the hybrid war-law model place suspected terrorists in a "limbo of rightlessness"?

4. What does Luban offer as the main argument in support of a government's adoption of the hybrid war-law model?

5. What does Luban offer as the main argument against a government's adoption of the hybrid war-law model?

In the immediate aftermath of September 11, President Bush stated that the perpetrators of the deed would be brought to justice. Soon afterwards, the President announced that the United States would engage in a war on terrorism. The first of these statements adopts the familiar language of criminal law and criminal justice. It treats the September 11 attacks as horrific crimes—mass murders—and the government's mission as apprehending and punishing the surviving planners and conspirators for their roles in the crimes. The War on Terrorism is a different proposition, however, and a different model of governmental action—not law but war. Most obviously, it dramatically broadens the scope of action, because now terrorists who knew nothing about September 11 have been earmarked as enemies. But that is only the beginning.

The Hybrid War-Law Approach

The model of war offers much freer rein than that of law, and therein lies its appeal in the wake of 9/11. First, in war but not in law it is permissible to use lethal force on enemy troops regardless of their degree of personal involvement with the adversary. The conscripted cook is as legitimate a target as the enemy general. Second, in war but not in law "collateral damage," that is, foreseen but unintended killing of non-combatants, is permissible. (Police cannot blow up an apartment building full of people because a murderer is inside, but an air force can bomb the building if it contains a military target.) Third, the requirements of evidence and proof are drastically weaker in war than in criminal justice. Soldiers do not need proof beyond a reasonable doubt, or even proof by a preponderance of evidence, that someone is an enemy soldier before firing on him or capturing and imprisoning him. They don't need proof at all, merely plausible intelligence. Thus, the US military remains regretful but unapologetic about its January 2002 attack on the Afghani town of Uruzgan, in which twenty-one innocent civilians were killed, based on faulty intelligence that they were al Qaeda fighters. Fourth, in war one can attack an enemy without concern over whether he has done anything. Legitimate targets are those who in the course of combat *might* harm us, not those who *have* harmed us. No doubt there are other significant differences as well. But the basic point should be clear: given Washington's mandate to eliminate the danger of future 9/11s, so far as humanly possible, the model of war offers important advantages over the model of law.

There are disadvantages as well. Most obviously, in war but not in law, fighting back is a *legitimate* response of the enemy. Second, when nations fight a war, other nations may opt for neutrality. Third, because fighting

back is legitimate, in war the enemy soldier deserves special regard once he is rendered harmless through injury or surrender. It is impermissible to punish him for his role in fighting the war. Nor can he be harshly interrogated after he is captured. The Third Geneva Convention provides: "Prisoners of war who refuse to answer [questions] may not be threatened, insulted, or exposed to unpleasant or disadvantageous treatment of any kind." And, when the war concludes, the enemy soldier must be repatriated.

Here, however, Washington has different ideas, designed to eliminate these tactical disadvantages in the traditional war model. Washington regards international terrorism not only as a military adversary, but also as a criminal activity and criminal conspiracy. In the law model, criminals don't get to shoot back, and their acts of violence subject them to legitimate punishment. That is what we see in Washington's prosecution of the War on Terrorism. Captured terrorists may be tried before military or civilian tribunals, and shooting back at Americans, including American troops, is a federal crime (for a statute under which John Walker Lindh was indicted criminalizes anyone regardless of nationality, who "outside the United States attempts to kill, or engages in a conspiracy to kill, a national of the United States" or "engages in physical violence with intent to cause serious bodily injury to a national of the United States; or with the result that serious bodily injury is caused to a national of the United States"). Furthermore, the US may rightly demand that other countries not be neutral about murder and terrorism. Unlike the war model, a nation may insist that those who are not with us in fighting murder and terror are against us, because by not joining our operations they are providing a safe haven for terrorists or their bank accounts. *By selectively combining elements of the war model and elements of the law model, Washington is able to maximize its own ability to mobilize lethal force against terrorists while eliminating most traditional rights of a military adversary, as well as the rights of innocent bystanders caught in the crossfire.*

A Limbo of Rightlessness

The legal status of al Qaeda suspects imprisoned at the Guantanamo Bay Naval Base in Cuba is emblematic of this hybrid war-law approach to the threat of terrorism. In line with the war model, they lack the usual rights of criminal suspects—the presumption of innocence, the right to a hearing to determine guilt, the opportunity to prove that the authorities have grabbed the wrong man. But, in line with the law model, they are considered *unlawful* combatants. Because they are not uniformed forces, they lack the rights of prisoners of war and are liable to criminal punishment. Initially, the American government declared that the Guantanamo Bay prisoners have no rights under the Geneva Conventions. In the face of international protests, Washington quickly backpedaled and announced that the Guantanamo Bay prisoners would indeed be treated as decently as POWs—but it also made clear that the prisoners have no right to such treatment. Neither criminal suspects nor POWs, neither fish nor fowl, they inhabit a limbo of rightlessness. Secretary of Defense Rumsfeld's assertion that the US may continue to detain them even if they are acquitted by a military tribunal dramatizes the point.

To understand how extraordinary their status is, consider an analogy. Suppose that Washington declares a War on Organized Crime. Troops are dispatched to Sicily, and a number of Mafiosi are seized, brought to Guantanamo Bay, and imprisoned without a hearing for the indefinite future, maybe the rest of their lives. They are accused of no crimes, because their capture is based not on what they have done but on what they might do. After all, to become "made" they took oaths of obedience to the bad guys. Seizing them accords with the war model: they are enemy foot soldiers. But they are foot soldiers out of uniform; they lack a "fixed distinctive emblem," in the words of the Hague Convention. That makes them unlawful combatants, so they lack the rights of POWs. They may object that it is only a unilateral declaration by the American President that has turned them into combatants in the first place—he called it a war, they didn't—and that, since they do not regard themselves as literal foot soldiers it never occurred to them to wear a fixed distinctive emblem. They have a point. It seems too easy for the President to divest anyone in the world of rights and liberty simply by announcing that the US is at war with them and then declaring them unlawful combatants

if they resist. But, in the hybrid war-law model, they protest in vain.

Consider another example. In January 2002, US forces in Bosnia seized five Algerians and a Yemeni suspected of al Qaeda connections and took them to Guantanamo Bay. The six had been jailed in Bosnia, but a Bosnian court released them for lack of evidence, and the Bosnian Human Rights Chamber issued an injunction that four of them be allowed to remain in the country pending further legal proceedings The Human Rights Chamber, ironically, was created under US auspices in the Dayton peace accords, and it was designed specifically to protect against treatment like this. Ruth Wedgwood, a well-known international law scholar at Yale and a member of the Council on Foreign Relations, defended the Bosnian seizure in war-model terms. "I think we would simply argue this was a matter of self-defense. One of the fundamental rules of military law is that you have a right ultimately to act in self-defense. And if these folks were actively plotting to blow up the US embassy, they should be considered combatants and captured as combatants in a war." Notice that Professor Wedgwood argues in terms of what the men seized in Bosnia were *planning to do,* not what they *did*; notice as well that the decision of the Bosnian court that there was insufficient evidence does not matter. These are characteristics of the war model.

More recently, two American citizens alleged to be al Qaeda operatives (Jose Padilla, a.k.a. Abdullah al Muhajir, and Yasser Esam Hamdi) have been held in American military prisons, with no crimes charged, no opportunity to consult counsel, and no hearing. The President described Padilla as "a bad man" who aimed to build a nuclear "dirty" bomb and use it against America; and the Justice Department has classified both men as "enemy combatants" who may be held indefinitely. Yet, as military law expert Gary Solis points out, "Until now, as used by the attorney general, the term 'enemy combatant' appeared nowhere in US criminal law, international law or in the law of war." The phrase comes from the 1942 Supreme Court case *Ex parte Quirin,* but all the Court says there is that "an enemy combatant who without uniform comes secretly through the lines for the purpose of waging war by destruction of life or property" would "not... be entitled to the status of prisoner of war, but... [they would] be offenders against the law of war subject to trial and punishment by military tribunals." For the Court, in other words, the status of a person as a nonuniformed enemy combatant makes him a criminal rather than a warrior, and determines *where* he is tried (in a military, rather than a civilian, tribunal) but not *whether* he is tried. Far from authorizing open-ended confinement, *Ex parte Quirin* presupposes that criminals are entitled to hearings: without a hearing how can suspects prove that the government made a mistake? *Quirin* embeds the concept of "enemy combatant" firmly in the law model. In the war model, by contrast, POWs may be detained without a hearing until hostilities are over. But POWs were captured in uniform, and only their undoubted identity as enemy soldiers justifies such open-ended custody. Apparently, Hamdi and Padilla will get the worst of both models— open-ended custody with no trial, like POWs, but no certainty beyond the US government's say-so that they really are "bad men." *This is the hybrid war-law model. It combines the Quirin category of "enemy combatant without uniform." used in the law model to justify a military trial, with the war model's indefinite confinement with no trial at all.*

The Case for the Hybrid Approach

Is there any justification for the hybrid war-law model, which so drastically diminishes the rights of the enemy? An argument can be offered along the following lines. In ordinary cases of war among states, enemy soldiers may well be morally and politically innocent. Many of them are conscripts, and those who aren't do not necessarily endorse the state policies they are fighting to defend. But enemy soldiers in the War on Terrorism are, by definition, those who have embarked on a path of terrorism. They are neither morally nor politically innocent. Their sworn aim—"Death to America!"—is to create more 9/11s. In this respect, they are much more akin to criminal conspirators than to conscript soldiers. Terrorists will fight as soldiers when they must, and metamorphose into mass murderers when they can.

Furthermore, suicide terrorists pose a special, unique danger. Ordinary criminals do not target innocent bystanders. They may be willing to kill them if necessary, but bystanders enjoy at least some measure of security because they are not primary targets. Not so with terrorists, who aim to kill as many innocent people as possible. Likewise, innocent bystanders are protected from ordinary criminals by whatever deterrent force the threat of punishment and the risk of getting killed in the act of committing a crime offer. For a suicide bomber, neither of these threats is a deterrent at all—after all, for the suicide bomber one of the hallmarks of a *successful* operation is that he winds up dead at day's end. Given the unique and heightened danger that suicide terrorists pose, a stronger response that grants potential terrorists fewer rights may be justified. Add to this the danger that terrorists may come to possess weapons of mass destruction, including nuclear devices in suitcases. *Under circumstances of such dire menace, it is appropriate to treat terrorists as though they embody the most dangerous aspects of both warriors and criminals. That is the basis of the hybrid war-law model.*

The Case Against Expediency

The argument against the hybrid war-law model is equally clear. The US has simply chosen the bits of the law model and the bits of the war model that are most convenient for American interests, and ignored the rest. The model abolishes the rights of potential enemies (and their innocent shields) by fiat—not for reasons of moral or legal principle, but solely because the US does not want them to have rights. The more rights they have, the more risk they pose. But Americans' urgent desire to minimize our risks doesn't make other people's rights disappear. Calling our policy a War on Terrorism obscures this point.

The theoretical basis of the objection is that the law model and the war model each comes as a package, with a kind of intellectual integrity. The law model grows out of relationships within states, while the war model arises from relationships between states. The law model imputes a ground-level community of values to those subject to the law—paradigmatically, citizens of a state, but also visitors and foreigners who choose to engage in conduct that affects a state. Only because law imputes shared basic values to the community can a state condemn the conduct of criminals and inflict punishment on them. Criminals deserve condemnation and punishment because their conduct violates norms that we are entitled to count on their sharing. But, for the same reason—the imputed community of values—those subject to the law ordinarily enjoy a presumption of innocence and an expectation of safety. The government cannot simply grab them and confine them without making sure they have broken the law, nor can it condemn them without due process for ensuring that it has the right person, nor can it knowingly place bystanders in mortal peril in the course of fighting crime. They are our fellows, and the community should protect them just as it protects us. The same imputed community of values that justifies condemnation and punishment creates rights to due care and due process.

War is different. War is the ultimate acknowledgment that human beings do not live in a single community with shared norms. If their norms conflict enough, communities pose a physical danger to each other, and nothing can safeguard a community against its enemies except force of arms. That makes enemy soldiers legitimate targets; but it makes our soldiers legitimate targets as well, and, once the enemy no longer poses a danger, he should be immune from punishment, because if he has fought cleanly he has violated no norms that we are entitled to presume he honors. Our norms are, after all, *our* norms, not his.

Because the law model and war model come as conceptual packages, it is unprincipled to wrench them apart and recombine them simply because it is in America's interest to do so. To declare that Americans can fight enemies with the latitude of warriors, but if the enemies fight back they are not warriors but criminals, amounts to a kind of heads-I-win-tails-you-lose international morality in which whatever it takes to reduce American risk, no matter what the cost to others, turns out to be justified. This, in brief, is the criticism of the hybrid war-law model.

To be sure, the law model could be made to incorporate the war model merely by rewriting a handful of statutes. Congress could enact laws permitting imprisonment or execution of persons who pose a significant threat of terrorism whether or not they have already done anything wrong. The standard of evidence could be set low and the requirement of a hearing eliminated. Finally, Congress could authorize the use of lethal force against terrorists regardless of the danger to innocent bystanders, and it could immunize officials from lawsuits or prosecution by victims of collateral damage. Such statutes would violate the Constitution, but the Constitution could be amended to incorporate antiterrorist exceptions to the Fourth, Fifth, and Sixth Amendments. In the end, we would have a system of law that includes all the essential features of the war model.

It would, however, be a system that imprisons people for their intentions rather than their actions, and that offers the innocent few protections against mistaken detention or inadvertent death through collateral damage. Gone are the principles that people should never be punished for their thoughts, only for their deeds, and that innocent people must be protected rather than injured by their own government. In that sense, at any rate, repackaging war as law seems merely cosmetic, because it replaces the ideal of law as a protector of rights with the more problematic goal of protecting some innocent people by sacrificing others. The hypothetical legislation incorporates war into law only by making law as partisan and ruthless as war. It no longer resembles law as Americans generally understand it.

The Threat to International Human Rights

In the War on Terrorism, what becomes of international human rights? It seems beyond dispute that the war model poses a threat to international human rights, because honoring human rights is neither practically possible nor theoretically required during war. Combatants are legitimate targets; noncombatants maimed by accident or mistake are regarded as collateral damage rather than victims of atrocities; cases of mistaken identity get killed or confined without a hearing because combat conditions preclude due process. To be sure, the laws of war specify minimum human rights, but these are far less robust than rights in peacetime—and the hybrid war-law model reduces this schedule of rights even further by classifying the enemy as unlawful combatants.

One striking example of the erosion of human rights is tolerance of torture. It should be recalled that a 1995 al Qaeda plot to bomb eleven US airliners was thwarted by information tortured out of a Pakistani suspect by the Philippine police—an eerie real-life version of the familiar philosophical thought-experiment. The *Washington Post* reports that since September 11 the US has engaged in the summary transfer of dozens of terrorism suspects to countries where they will be interrogated under torture. But it isn't just the United States that has proven willing to tolerate torture for security reasons. Last December, the Swedish government snatched a suspected Islamic extremist to whom it had previously granted political asylum, and the same day had him transferred to Egypt where Amnesty International reports that he has been tortured to the point where he walks only with difficulty. Sweden is not, to say the least, a traditionally hard-line nation on human rights issues. None of this international transportation is lawful—indeed, it violates international treaty obligations under the Convention against Torture that in the US have constitutional status as "supreme Law of the Land"—but that may not matter under the war model, in which even constitutional rights may be abrogated.

It is natural to suggest that this suspension of human rights is an exceptional emergency measure to deal with an unprecedented threat. This raises the question of how long human rights will remain suspended. When will the war be over?

Here, the chief problem is that the War on Terrorism is not like any other kind of war. The enemy, Terrorism, is not a territorial state or nation or government. There is no opposite number to negotiate with. There is no one on the other side to call a truce or declare a ceasefire, no one among the enemy authorized to surrender. In traditional wars among states, the war aim is, as Clausewitz argued, to impose one state's political will on another's. The *aim* of the war is not to kill the enemy—killing the enemy is the *means* used to achieve the real end, which is to force capitulation. In the War on Terrorism, no capitulation is possible. That means that the real aim of the war is, quite simply, to kill or capture all of the terrorists—to keep on killing and killing, capturing and capturing, until they are all gone.

Of course, no one expects that terrorism will ever disappear completely. Everyone understands that new anti-American extremists, new terrorists, will always arise and always be available for recruitment and deployment. Everyone understands that even if al Qaeda is destroyed or decapitated, other groups, with other leaders, will arise in its place. It follows, then, that the War on Terrorism will be a war that can only be abandoned, never concluded. The War has no natural resting point, no moment of victory or finality. It requires a mission of killing and capturing, in territories all over the globe, that will go on in perpetuity. It follows as well that *the suspension of human rights implicit in the hybrid war-law model is not temporary but permanent.*

Perhaps with this fear in mind, Congressional authorization of President Bush's military campaign limits its scope to those responsible for September 11 and their sponsors. But the War on Terrorism has taken on a life of its own that makes the Congressional authorization little more than a technicality. Because of the threat of nuclear terror, the American leadership actively debates a war on Iraq regardless of whether Iraq was implicated in September 11; and the President's yoking of Iraq, Iran, and North Korea into a single axis of evil because they back terror suggests that the War on Terrorism might eventually encompass all these nations. If the US ever unearths tangible evidence that any of these countries is harboring or abetting terrorists with weapons of mass destruction, there can be little doubt that Congress will support military action. So too, Russia invokes the American War on Terrorism to justify its attacks on Chechen rebels, China uses it to deflect criticisms of its campaign against Uighur separatists, and Israeli Prime Minister Sharon explicitly links military actions against Palestinian insurgents to the American War on Terrorism. No doubt there is political opportunism at work in some or all of these efforts to piggyback onto America's campaign, but the opportunity would not exist if "War on Terrorism" were merely the code name of a discrete, neatly-boxed American operation. Instead, the War on Terrorism has become a model of politics, a worldview with its own distinctive premises and consequences. As I have argued, it includes a new model of state action, the hybrid war-law model, which depresses human rights from their peacetime standard to the war-time standard, and indeed even further. So long as it continues, the War on Terrorism means the end of human rights, at least for those near enough to be touched by the fire of battle.

SOURCES

On the January 2002 attack on the Afghani town of Uruzgan, see: John Ward Anderson, "Afghans Falsely Meld by U.S. Tried to Explain; Fighters Recount Unanswered Pleas, Beatings—and an Apology on Their Release," *Washington Post* (March 26, 2002); see also Susan B. Glasser, "Afghans Live and Die With U.S. Mistakes; Villagers Tell of Over 100 Casualties," *Washington Post* (Feb. 20, 2002).

On the Third Geneva Convention, see: Geneva Convention (III) Relative to the Treatment of Prisoners of War, 6 U.S.T. 3317, signed on August 12, 1949, at Geneva, Article 17. Although the US has not ratified the Geneva Convention, it has become part of customary international law, and certainly belongs to the war model. Count One of the Lindh indictment charges him with violating 18 U.S.C. 2332(b), "Whoever outside the United States attempts to kill, or engages in a conspiracy to kill, a national of the United States" may be sentenced to 20 years (for attempts) or life imprisonment (for conspiracies). Subsection (c) likewise criminalizes "engag[ing] in physical violence with intent to cause serious bodily injury to a national of the United States; or with the result that serious bodily injury is caused to a national of the United States." Lawful combatants are defined in the Hague Convention (IV) Respecting the Laws and Customs of War on Land, Annex to the Convention, 1 Bevans 631, signed on October 18, 1907, at The Hague, Article 1. The definition requires that combatants "have a fixed distinctive emblem recognizable at a distance." Protocol I Additional to the Geneva Conventions of 1949, 1125 U.N.T.S. 3, adopted on June 8, 1977, at Geneva, Article 44 (3) makes an important change in the Hague Convention, expanding the definition of combatants to include nonuniformed irregulars. However, the United States has not agreed to Protocol I. The source of Ruth Wedgwood's remarks: Interview with Melissa Block, National Public Radio program, "All Things Considered" (January 18, 2002); Gary Solis, "Even a 'Bad Man' Has Rights," *Washington Post* (June 25,2002); *Ex parte Quirin*, 317 U.S. 1 (1942).

On the torture of the Pakistani militant by Philippine police: Doug Struck et al., "Borderless Network Of Terror; Bin Laden Followers Reach Across Globe," *Washington Post* (September 23, 2001): "'For weeks, agents hit him with

a chair and a long piece of wood, forced water into his mouth, and crushed lighted cigarettes into his private parts,' wrote journalists Marites Vitug and Glenda Gloria in *Under the Crescent Moon,* an acclaimed book on Abu Sayyaf. 'His ribs were almost totally broken and his captors were surprised he survived.'"

On US and Swedish transfers of Isamic militants to countries employing torture: Rajiv Chandrasakaran & Peter Finn, "U.S. Behind Secret Transfer of Terror Suspects," *Washington Post* (March 11, 2002); Peter Finn, "Europeans Tossing Terror Suspects Out the Door," *Washington Post* (January 29, 2002); Anthony Shadid, "Fighting Terror/ Atmosphere in Europe, Military Campaign/Asylum Bids; in Shift, Sweden Extradites Militants to Egypt," *Boston Globe* (December 31, 2001). Article 3(1) of the Convention against Torture provides that "No State Party shall expel, return ('*refouler*') or extradite a person to another State where there are substantial grounds for believing that he would be in danger of being subjected to torture." Article 2(2) cautions that "No exceptional circumstances whatsoever, whether a state of war or a threat of war, internal political instability or any other public emergency, may be invoked as a justification of torture." But no parallel caution is incorporated into Article 3(l)'s non-*refoulement* rule, and a lawyer might well argue that its absence implies that the rule may be abrogated during war or similar public emergency. *Convention against Torture and Other Cruel, Inhuman or Degrading Treatment or Punishment*, 1465 U.N.T.S. 85. Ratified by the United States, Oct. 2, 1994. Entered into force for the United States, Nov. 20, 1994. (Article VI of the US Constitution provides that treaties are the "supreme Law of the Land.")

DISCUSSION QUESTIONS:

1. How would our response to terrorism change if we were to exchange the hybrid war-law model for a pure war model? How would it change if we were to exchange the hybrid war-law model for a pure law model?

2. Is the argument that Luban presents for the adoption of the hybrid war-law model successful?

3. As an objection to the adoption of the hybrid war-law model, Luban claims that the law and war models are distinct conceptual packages and it is "unprincipled to wrench them apart and combine them simply because it is in America's interest to do so" (page 542). In what way is the adoption of the hybrid war-law model "unprincipled"? Is that enough to make our adoption of the hybrid model wrong?

4. Is Luban correct that the adoption of the hybrid war-law model, especially since it involves the classification of terrorists as unlawful combatants, poses a serious threat to international human rights?

Argument Reconstruction Exercises:

I. Luban presents an argument in support of the adoption of the hybrid war-law model. Identify the premises and conclusion of this restatement of the argument:

> Terrorists, unlike soldiers in a just war, are neither morally nor politically innocent. . . . They will fight as soldiers when they must, and metamorphose into mass murderers when they can. They also aim to kill as many innocent people as possible and cannot be deterred by threats of punishment or the risk of dying in their attack. They pose a dire threat, and given that threat, it is appropriate to treat them as the hybrid war-law model provides. (page 541)

II. Luban offers the following objection to the hybrid war-law model. Identify the argument's premises and conclusion:

> The model abolishes the rights of potential enemies (and their innocent shields) by fiat—not for reasons of moral or legal principle, but solely because the US does not want them to have rights. The more rights they have, the more risk they pose. But Americans' urgent desire to minimize our risks doesn't make other people's rights disappear. . . . [T]he law model and the war model each comes as a package, with a kind of intellectual integrity. The law model grows out of relationships within states, while the war model arises from relationships between states.

Because the law model and war model come as conceptual packages, it is unprincipled to wrench them apart and recombine them simply because it is America's interest to do so. (pages 541-542)

III. Luban (page 542) describes how the law model might be made to incorporate the war model through some changes in the law, including the U.S. Constitution. He also notes the cost of those changes. Identify the premises and conclusion of the following argument:

> We are justified in adopting the provisions of the hybrid war-law model only if we do so though legislation that incorporates the relevant provisions from the war model into the legal model. Such legislation is unjustified, however, as it eliminates the legal principle that people should never be punished for their thoughts, but only their deeds, and the principle that people must be protected rather than injured by their government. (page 542)

IV. One response to Luban's concerns about the adoption of the hybrid war-law model is that the model is only a limited response to a temporary national emergency. Identify the premises and conclusion of the following argument:

> Every nation is justified in adopting policies necessary to its own defense, even if those policies involve the suspension of the human rights of certain groups or individuals, so long as the policies are appropriately limited in their scope and duration. The policies contained in the hybrid war-law model are necessary to the defense of the U.S. and appropriately limited in their scope and duration.

CHAPTER 19

Torture

The secret authorization of brutal interrogations is an outrageous betrayal of our core values, and a grave danger to our security. We must do whatever it takes to track down and capture or kill terrorists, but torture is not a part of the answer.
—PRESIDENT BARACK OBAMA ("TORTURE AND SECRECY BETRAY CORE AMERICAN VALUES," 2007)

INTRODUCTION

You work for the CIA, and you've just detained a man arrested in the heart of Manhattan. The man was carrying a large number of documents from a nearby terrorist cell. The documents suggest an imminent terrorist attack on the city, perhaps even the detonation of a dirty nuclear weapon. If such a weapon were deployed within the city limits, millions and millions of innocent lives would be lost.

Your job is to interrogate this suspect. However, after working with him for several hours, it's obvious that the man won't budge. He insists on a lawyer and will divulge nothing about his alleged involvement in terrorist activities. Time is of the essence. Given past experience, you know that sometimes waterboarding a suspect can coerce him into talking. (Waterboarding is a technique that simulates a drowning experience for the subject by smothering his face in a towel and pouring water over his covered face.) What you don't know is how accurate the information received from waterboarding really is. Maybe people who are in such pain and panic will say anything to make it stop. Furthermore, most countries in the world have categorized waterboarding as a form of torture. Still, you're short on time and short on options. Your director gives you the green light to waterboard the suspect. Ought you to do so?

As you can imagine, philosophers disagree. And this case is another instance where we can see the differences from some of the moral theories explored in Unit 3. **Consequentialists** will want to know whether or not waterboarding the suspect will have good consequences. For example, to determine whether you ought to waterboard him, a **utilitarian** will want to know whether doing so will produce more net happiness in the world than not. If so, you ought to torture him. But this is a hard thing to decide. Is it really true that tortured subjects are reliable sources of information? In his essay in this chapter, Miller will argue that torture is at least sometimes morally permissible given good enough consequences of the action.

Nonconsequentialists like **deontologists** will ask different questions to determine whether you ought to torture the subject. For example, are there any **absolute** moral principles? If so, then we need to know whether there is an absolute prohibition on torture. Perhaps torture is wrong no matter how good the consequences might be. But if it's wrong, why? Is it because it violates the subject's rights? And what if his rights were forfeited by engaging in terrorism? In his essay in this chapter, Hill will argue that basic moral principles preclude the torturing of an individual no matter what the consequences might be.

However, deciding whether some "one-off" act of torture is morally permissible is not the end of the controversy. It's one thing to say that occasionally acts of type X are morally permissible; it's quite another thing to say that acts of type X should be legal or encouraged or sanctioned. Perhaps it's true that some occasional acts of torture have good enough consequences to make them morally permissible, but it's also true that if we authorized our police or military to torture subjects, terrible, terrible results might follow. So it's at least plausible that torture might be the kind of action that is very occasionally permissible but ought always to be outlawed and resisted.

In either case, the issue of the moral status of torture is central both to international diplomacy and police/military operations. We need to think carefully through what might justify an act of torture, what a policy of torture might do to our community, and what kind of people we will be if we sanction it.

SUGGESTIONS FOR FURTHER READING

Bagaric, Mirko, and Clarke, Julie. *Torture: When the Unthinkable is Permissible.* (Albany: State University of New York Press, 2007)

Brecher, Bob. *Torture and the Ticking Bomb.* (Oxford: Blackwell, 2008)

Davis, Michael. "The Moral Justification of Torture and Other Cruel, Inhuman, or Degrading Treatment." *International Journal of Applied Philosophy*, 2005; 19:2, pp. 161–178.

Kershnar, Stephan. "For Interrogational Torture." *International Journal of Applied Philosophy*, 2005; 19:2, pp. 223–241.

Levinson, Sanford (ed.). *Torture: A Collection.* (Oxford: Oxford University Press, 2004)

Machan, Tibor. "Exploring Extreme Violence (Torture)." *Journal of Social Philosophy*, 1990; 21:1, pp. 92–97.

Shue, Henry. "Torture." *Philosophy & Public Affairs*, 7, pp. 124–143.

Sussman, David. "What's Wrong with Torture?" *Philosophy & Public Affairs*, 2005; 33:1, pp. 1–33.

Walzer, Michael. "Political Action: The Problem of Dirty Hands." *Philosophy and Public Affairs*, 1973: 2, 160–180.

19.1 IS TORTURE EVER MORALLY JUSTIFIABLE?

SEUMAS MILLER (2005)

Seumas Miller is Professor of Philosophy at Charles Sturt University, Australia. Professor Miller has also served as the director for an Australian-sponsored think-tank called the Centre for Applied Ethics and Public Ethics. His work focuses on issues in social and political philosophy, with an emphasis on government/policing ethics and business ethics. In the current selection, Professor Miller argues for a two-fold thesis. First, he claims that torture is sometimes morally justifiable, but, second, he insists that it would be morally and socially problematic to institutionalize or legalize torture.

Reading Questions:

1. How does Miller define torture?

2. What does it mean to break a person's will?

3. What is the difference between minimalist and maximalist torture?

4. Who is tortured in case 1? Who is tortured in case 2?

5. What does it mean to say that torture is an *absolute* moral wrong?

6. What does it mean to say that the law is a "blunt instrument" whereas morality is a "sharp instrument"?

7. According to Miller, what should happen to public officials who commit an act of torture that was illegal but morally justifiable?

In this paper I will argue that torture is morally justified in some extreme emergencies. However, I will also argue that notwithstanding the moral permissibility of torture in some extreme emergencies, torture ought not to be legalised or otherwise institutionalised.

Torture

Before proceeding to the question of the moral justifiability of torture we need some understanding of what torture is. We also need some account of what is morally wrong with torture. As a preliminary working definition sufficient for my purposes here, I suggest that *torture is the intentional infliction of extreme physical suffering on some non-consenting, defenceless, other person for the purpose of breaking their will.* I note that a person might have been tortured, even if in fact their will has not been broken; the purpose of the practice of torture is to break the victim's will, but this purpose does not have to be realised for a process to be an instance of torture. . .

I have suggested that the defining purpose of torture is to break the victim's will. Naturally, different kinds of torture will have different additional purposes, such as to gain information, to terrorise some political group, or to gratify a desire on the part of the torturer to inflict suffering and to exercise power. However, breaking the victim's will is a purpose that is internal to torture, and it is also the means by which these other external purposes are achieved. Here, breaking a person's will can be understood in a minimalist or a maximalist sense. I do not mean to imply that the boundaries between these two senses can be sharply drawn.

Understood in its minimal sense, breaking a person's will is causing them to abandon autonomous decision-making in relation to some narrowly circumscribed area of their life for a limited period. Consider, for example, a thief deciding to disclose or not disclose to the police torturing him where he has hidden the goods he has stolen. Suppose further that he knows that he can only be legally held in custody for a twenty-four-hour period, and that the police are not able to infringe this particular law. By torturing the thief the police might break his will and, against his will, cause him to disclose the whereabouts of the stolen goods.

Understood in its maximal sense, breaking a person's will is seriously undermining a person's capacity for autonomous decision-making for an indefinitely long period of their life. For example, some victims of prolonged torture in prisons in authoritarian states are so psychologically damaged that even when released they are unable to function as normal adult persons, i.e., as rational choosers pursuing their projects in a variety of standard interpersonal contexts such as work and family environments.

It is not simply that the person is coerced into saying or doing what they don't want to do. For this is consistent with the person retaining control over their actions and making a rational decision to, say, hand over their wallet when told to do so by a knife-wielding robber. No doubt the threat of torture, and torture in its preliminary stages, simply functions as a form of coercion in this sense. However, torture proper has as its starting point the failure of coercion, or that coercion is not even going to be attempted. *Torture proper targets autonomy itself,* and seeks to overwhelm the capacity of the victim to exercise rational control over their decisions—at least in relation to certain matters for a limited period of time—by literally terrorising the victim into submission.

Roughly speaking, the elements of torture are as follows. The torturer has physical control over the victim's body, e.g., the victim is strapped to a chair. The victim is then terrorised by means of the controlled use of extreme physical suffering, e.g., the torturer crushes lighted cigarettes into the victim's private parts. *The purpose of this process of terrorising the victim is to cause the victim to cease to act in accordance with his or her own will and act in accordance with the will of the torturer, even if only temporarily. At the point at which the victim does so, the victim's will has been broken.*

The difference between minimalist and maximalist torture is that in the former case the victim's will is broken only temporarily and in a contained manner, and their consequent humiliation is limited, i.e., they survive the trauma and are able to get on with their lives. However, in the maximalist case the victim's autonomy and self-identity are damaged irretrievably. Accordingly, the victim—even if alive and physically well—has not survived intact qua autonomous self.

I will now turn directly to the question of the moral justification for torture. Here I distinguish between one-off cases of torture, on the one hand, and legalised or otherwise institutionalised torture, on the other. I begin with the former.

The Moral Justification for One-off Acts of Torture

In this section I consider one-off, non-institutionalised acts of torture performed by state actors in emergency situations. *I argue that there are, or could well be, one-off acts of torture in extreme emergencies that are, all things considered, morally justifiable.* Accordingly, I am assuming that the *routine* use of torture is not morally justified; so if it turned out that the routine use of torture was necessary to, say, win the war on terrorism, then some of what I say here would not be to the point. However, liberal democratic governments and security agencies have not even begun to exhaust the political strategies, and the military/police tactics short of the routine use of torture, available to them to combat terrorism.

Let us consider some putative examples of the justified use of torture. The first is a policing example, the second a terrorist example. In my view both examples are realistic.

Case Study 1—Beating
Height of the antipodean summer, Mercury at the century-mark; the noonday sun softened the bitumen beneath the tyres of her little Hyundai sedan to the consistency of putty. Her three-year-old son, quiet at last, snuffled in his sleep on the back seat. He had a summer cold and wailed like a banshee in the supermarket, forcing her to cut short her shopping. Her car needed petrol. Her tot was asleep on the back seat. She poured twenty litres into the tank; thumbing notes from her purse, harried and distracted, her keys dangled from the ignition.

Whilst she was in the service station a man drove off in her car. Police wound back the servo's CCTV, saw a heavy-set Pacific Islander with a blonde-streaked Afro entering her car. "Don't panic," a constable advised the mother, "as soon as he sees your little boy in the back he will abandon the car." He did; police arrived at the railway station before

the car thief did and arrested him after a struggle when he vaulted over the station barrier.

In the P.D. on the way to the police station: "Where did you leave the Laser?" Denial instead of dissimulation: "It wasn't me." It was—property stolen from the car was found in his pockets. In the detectives' office: "Its been twenty minutes since you took the car—little tin box like that car—It will heat up like an oven under this sun. Another twenty minutes and the child's dead or brain damaged. Where did you dump the car?" Again: "It wasn't me."

Appeals to decency, to reason, to self-interest: "It's not too late; tell us where you left the car and you will only be charged with Take-and-Use. That's just a six-month extension of your recognizance." Threats: "If the child dies I will charge you with Manslaughter!" Sneering, defiant and belligerent; he made no secret of his contempt for the police. Part-way through his umpteenth, "It wasn't me," a questioner clipped him across the ear as if he were a child, an insult calculated to bring the Islander to his feet to fight, there a body-punch elicited a roar of pain, but he fought back until he lapsed into semi-consciousness under a rain of blows. He quite enjoyed handing out a bit of biffo, but now, kneeling on hands and knees in his own urine, in pain he had never known, he finally realised the beating would go on until he told the police where he had abandoned the child and the car.

The police officers' statements in the prosecution brief made no mention of the beating; the location of the stolen vehicle and the infant inside it was portrayed as having been volunteered by the defendant. The defendant's counsel availed himself of this falsehood in his plea in mitigation. When found, the stolen child was dehydrated, too weak to cry; there were ice packs and dehydration in the casualty ward but no long-time prognosis on brain damage.

(Case study provided by John Blackler, a former New South Wales police officer.)

The classic, indeed cliched, example used to justify torture is that of the so-called 'ticking bomb.' Consider the following case study.

Case Study 2—Terrorist
A terrorist group has planted a small nuclear device with a timing mechanism in London and it is about to go off. If it does it will kill thousands

and make a large part of the city uninhabitable for decades. One of the terrorists has been captured by the police, and if he can be made to disclose the location of the device then the police can probably disarm it and thereby save the lives of thousands. The police know the terrorist in question. They know he has orchestrated terrorist attacks, albeit non-nuclear ones, in the past. Moreover, on the basis of intercepted mobile phone calls and e-mails the police know that this attack is under way in some location in London and that he is the leader of the group. Unfortunately, the terrorist is refusing to talk and time is slipping away. However, police know that there is a reasonable chance that he will talk, if tortured. Moreover, all their other sources of information have dried up. Further, there is no other way to avoid catastrophe; evacuation of the city, for example, cannot be undertaken in the limited time available. Torture is not normally used by the police, and indeed it is unlawful to use it.

In my view, in both these case studies torture is morally justifiable. I draw attention to the following considerations present in both cases. (1) The police reasonably believe that torturing the car thief/terrorist will probably save an innocent life (case study 1) or thousands of innocent lives (case study 2); (2) the police know that there is no other way to save the life (lives); (3) the threat to life is imminent; (4) the baby in case study 1, and the thousands about to be murdered in case study 2, are innocent—the terrorist has no good, let alone decisive, justificatory moral reason for murdering them; (6) the car thief is known not to be an innocent—his action is known to have caused the threat to the baby, and he is refusing to allow the baby's life to be saved; the terrorist is known not to be an innocent person—rather he is known to be (jointly with the other terrorists) morally responsible for planning, transporting, and arming the nuclear device and, if it explodes, he will be (jointly with the other terrorists) morally responsible for the murder of thousands.

If in the light of the above set of moral considerations you are, nevertheless, not inclined to believe that torture is justified I draw your attention to the following in respect of case study 2. The terrorist is culpable on two counts. First, the terrorist

is forcing the police to choose between two evils, namely torturing the terrorist or allowing thousands of lives to be lost. Were the terrorist to do what he ought to do, namely disclose the location of the ticking bomb, the police could refrain from torturing him. This would be true of the terrorist, even if he was not actively participating in planting the bomb. (The same point can be made in respect of the car thief.) Second, the terrorist is in the process of completing his (jointly undertaken) action of murdering thousands of innocent people. He has already undertaken his individual actions of, say, transporting and arming the nuclear device; he has performed these individual actions (in the context of other individual actions performed by the other members of the terrorist cell) in order to realise the end (shared by the other members of the cell) of murdering thousands of Londoners. In refusing to disclose the location of the device the terrorist is preventing the police from preventing him from completing his (joint) action of murdering thousands of innocent people. To this extent the terrorist is in a different situation from a bystander who happens to know where the bomb is planted but will not reveal its whereabouts, and in a different situation from the car thief who inadvertently put the baby's life at risk; rather the terrorist is more akin to someone in the process of murdering an innocent person, and refusing to refrain from doing so.

In both case studies in the institutional environment described, torture is both unlawful and highly unusual. Accordingly, the police, if it is discovered that they have tortured the terrorist, would be tried for a serious crime and if found guilty, sentenced. I will return to this issue in the final section. Here I simply note that the bare illegality of their act of torture does not render it morally impermissible, given it was otherwise morally permissible. Here it is the bare fact that it is illegal that is in question. So the relevant moral considerations comprise whatever moral weight attaches to compliance to the law just for the sake of compliance with the law, as distinct from compliance for the sake of the public benefits the law brings or compliance because of the moral weight that attaches to the moral principles that particular laws might embody. That is, no additional moral considerations are being added to the ledger, such as a significant weakening of the tendency to comply with the law against torture. *I conclude that if torturing the terrorist is morally permissible absent questions of legality, the bare fact of torture being illegal does not render it morally impermissible. . . .*

Two Objections

Some commentators on these kinds of scenario are reluctant to concede that the police are morally entitled—let alone morally obliged—to torture the offender. How could these commentators justify their position?

[1] Perhaps they implicitly assimilate the example to one in which police use of torture is routine, indeed legalised and institutionalised, and there are a host of depravities, injustices and horrific consequences not taken into account in the above-described scenario. However, in our scenarios torture is not institutionalised and/or lawful in the state in question. Moreover, in our scenario police use of torture, far from being routine, is relatively unknown. This kind of emergency situation has only ever happened once before—decades ago—and, let us assume, will not happen again for many years. Accordingly, if the police torture the terrorist then they will be breaking the law, but on the other hand—the issue of saving the city and presumably its institutions aside—their act will not make any significant difference, institutionally speaking. For example, their one-off use of torture is not going to lead to torture being legalised or used more frequently. Indeed, let us further assume that their one-off use of torture will never be discovered—especially since after the event the terrorist, as was the case with the car-thief, will claim at his trial that he had a change of heart and freely decided to assist the police.

[2] Let us now turn to another consideration that might be moving those who hold that the police ought not to torture the offenders. The consideration in question is that torture is an *absolute* moral wrong. On this view there simply are no real or imaginable circumstances in which torture could be morally justified.

This is a hard view to sustain, not the least because being tortured is not necessarily less preferable than being killed, and torturing someone not necessarily morally worse than killing them. Naturally, someone might hold that killing is an absolute moral wrong, i.e., killing anyone—however guilty they might be—is never morally justified. This view is consistent with holding that torture is an absolute moral wrong, i.e., torturing anyone—however guilty they might be—is never morally justified. However, the price of consistency is very high. The view that killing is an absolute moral wrong is a very implausible one. It would rule out, for example, killing in self-defense. Let us, therefore, set it aside and continue with the view that torture, but not killing, is an absolute moral wrong.

For those who hold that killing is not an absolute moral wrong, it is very difficult to see how torture could be an absolute moral wrong, given that killing is sometimes morally worse than torture. In particular, in case study 2 and like cases, it is difficult to see how torturing (but not killing) the guilty terrorist and saving the lives of thousands could be morally worse than refraining from torturing him and allowing him to murder thousands. Here I also note that while torturing the terrorist is a temporary infringement of his autonomy, his detonating of the nuclear device is a permanent violation of the autonomy of thousands. I also note that the doing/allowing distinction has little if any moral purchase here, given the enormity of the evil about to be perpetrated, and given that, by virtue of their institutional role, the police have a moral duty to save the lives of the citizens and therefore, other things being equal, they are morally culpable if they stand by and do nothing.

I conclude that the view that it is, all things considered, morally wrong to torture the terrorist should be rejected. In short, there are some imaginable circumstances in which it is morally permissible to torture someone. . . .

I have argued that torture is not the morally worst act that anyone could, or indeed has or will, perform. If I am right, then it is plausible that there will be at least some scenarios in which one will be forced to choose between two evils, the lesser one of which is torture. Indeed, the above ticking bomb scenario is one such instance, as is the beating of the car thief.

The Moral Justification for Legalised and Institutionalised Torture

I have already argued that torture might be, all things considered, the morally best action to perform in *some* one-off emergency situations. To conclude this paper, all I need to do is demonstrate that *it would be a very bad idea to legalise and institutionalise torture. . .*

First, my argument rests in part on the claim that the view that torture is morally justified in some extreme emergencies is compatible with the view that torture ought not to be legalized or otherwise institutionalized. *It is just a mistake to assume that what morality requires or permits in a given situation must be identical with what the law requires or permits in that situation.* Let me explain.

The law in particular, and social institutions more generally, are blunt instruments. They are designed to deal with recurring situations confronted by numerous institutional actors over relatively long periods of time. Laws abstract away from differences between situations across space and time, and differences between institutional actors across space and time. The law, therefore, consists of a set of generalisations to which the particular situation must be made to fit. Hence, if you exceed the speed limit you are liable for a fine, even though you were only 10 m.p.h. above the speed limit, you have a superior car, you are a superior driver, there was no other traffic on the road, the road conditions were perfect, and therefore the chances of you having an accident were actually less than would be the case for most other people most of the time driving at or under the speed limit.

By contrast with the law, morality is a sharp instrument. Morality can be, and typically ought to be, made to apply to a given situation in all its particularity. Accordingly, what might be, all things considered, the morally best action for an agent to perform in some one-off, i.e, non-recurring, situation might not be an action that should be made lawful. . .

A second residual issue concerns the proposition that, absent legalised/institutional torture, *unlawful* endemic torture in the security agencies of contemporary liberal democracies confronting terrorism is inevitable. The implication here is that unless legalised, torture will become endemic in these agencies. Granting that legalisation/institutionalisation of torture would be profoundly damaging to liberal democratic institutions, it does not follow from this that a torture culture will not come to exist in those agencies in the context of torture being unlawful. Nor does it follow that an unlawful torture culture, indeed an unlawful sub-institution of torture, is inevitable. Here there is a tendency to use the kind of argument that is plausible in relation to, say, the prohibition of alcohol. It is better to legalise alcohol, because then it can be contained and controlled. This form of argument used in relation to torture is spurious. Consuming alcohol to excess is not morally equivalent to torture, and we do not legalise the use of alcohol in emergency situations only. Legalising the use of torture in extreme emergencies would be much more akin to legalising perjury in extreme situations. As with torture—and unlike alcohol—perjury is only morally justified in some extreme one-off situations. However, no-one is seriously considering legalising perjury in one-off extreme situations (at least to my knowledge); and with good reason—to do so would strike at the very heart of the legal system.

The fact is that the recent history of police, military and other organisations in liberal democracies has demonstrated that torture cultures and sub-institutions of torture can be more or less eliminated. However, this can only be achieved if torture is unlawful, the community and the political and organisational leadership are strongly opposed to it, police officers, military personnel and other relevant institutional actors are appropriately educated and trained, and stringent accountability mechanisms, e.g., video-recording of interviews, closed-circuit TV cameras in cells, external oversight bodies, are put in place. It is surely obvious that to re-introduce, and indeed protect the practice of torture, by legalising and institutionalising it, would be to catapult the security agencies of liberal democracies back into the dark ages from whence they came….

One final matter. What should be done to the military officers, police officers or other public officials who torture the terrorist if—after saving the city—their crime is discovered? Quite clearly the public official in question must be tried, convicted, and, if found guilty, sentenced for committing the crime of torture. Naturally, the defence of necessity is available to them. I am not a lawyer, but arguably in the case of the terrorist, the police were defending their own lives and the lives of thousands against an attack that was under way; so the defence of necessity is available. But even if it is not available, as perhaps in the case of the beating of the car thief, nevertheless, there are (to say the least) mitigating circumstances, and the sentence should be commuted to, say, one day in prison. Moreover, he (or she) should resign or be dismissed from their position; public institutions cannot suffer among their ranks those who commit serious crimes. Would public officials be prepared to act to save thousands of innocent lives, if they knew they might lose their job and/or suffer some minor punishment? I believe many would. But if not, then do we really want to set up a legalised torture chamber and put these people in charge of it?

DISCUSSION QUESTIONS:

1. Miller describes torture as the intentional infliction of pain for the purpose of breaking a person's will. Suppose it were possible to break a person's will without causing pain (e.g., we hook someone up to a computer and undermine their rational autonomy in this way). Would that procedure be an instance of torture? Would it ever be morally permissible to break another person's will in that fashion?

2. Do you agree with Professor Miller that it would be morally justifiable to torture the accused in both case 1 and case 2? If you think that it would be justifiable to torture in one but not the other, what is the difference? If you think that it would not be justifiable to torture in either case, suppose the situation had been different and that killing the accused was guaranteed to save the life of the innocent (the child in case 1 or the inhabitants of London in case 2). Would it be morally justifiable to kill the accused to save the people? If you think it would be morally justifiable to kill the accused but not morally justifiable to torture the accused, does this imply that torture is morally worse than death?

3. Do you think that torture should be legalized or institutionalized as long as it were done by the proper authorities? Perhaps we set up a system

where judges could issue warrants for torture just as they issue warrants that allow police officers to violate other rights (e.g., search and seizure, phone taps, etc.)? Would this work to eliminate the potential abuses that worry Miller?

Argument Reconstruction Exercises:

I. Many of Miller's arguments for the moral permissibility of torture rely on suppressed premises that he assumes many of his readers will share. One of these assumptions is that it is morally justifiable to use force against someone who is in the process of murdering an innocent victim. Using that assumption as a premise, identify the argument for the conclusion that it is morally permissible for the authorities to use force against the captured terrorist in the following excerpt:

> Second, the terrorist is in the process of completing his (jointly undertaken) action of murdering thousands of innocent people. . . . To this extent the terrorist is in a different situation from a bystander who happens to know where the bomb is planted but will not reveal its whereabouts. . . rather, the terrorist is more akin to someone in the process of murdering an innocent person, and refusing to refrain from doing so. (page 550)

II. Some people might object to Miller's conclusion about torture because they think that there are at least some morally absolute prohibitions. An absolute moral principle is one that may not be permissibly broken no matter what the consequences. But Miller points out that this objection comes with a price: if torture is an absolute wrong, then certainly anything worse than torture would also be an absolute wrong. The following passage contains an implicit argument for the conclusion that torture is not an absolute wrong:

> Let us now turn to another consideration that might be moving those who hold that the police ought not to torture the offenders. The consideration in question is that torture is an absolute moral wrong. On this view, there simply are no real or imaginable circumstances in which torture could be morally justified. This is a hard view to sustain, not the least because being tortured is not necessarily less preferable than being killed, and torturing someone

not necessarily morally worse than killing them. Naturally, someone might hold that killing is an absolute moral wrong. . . . [but] the view that killing is an absolute moral wrong is a very implausible one. It would rule out, for example, killing in self-defense. Let us, therefore, set it aside. . . (page 551)

III. In essence, Miller's argument for the moral permissibility of torture in rare, one-off cases depends on showing both that there are morally worse acts than torture and that it is always morally permissible to do the lesser of two evils. Identify the premises and conclusion in the following excerpt. The conclusion should read "Therefore, it is possible that an act of torture is morally permissible".

I have argued that torture is not the morally worst act that anyone could, or indeed has or will, perform. If I am right, then it is plausible that there will be at least some scenarios in which one will be forced to choose between two evils, the lesser one of which is torture. (pages 551-552)

IV. Miller makes the point that an absolute prohibition on human killing commits us to radical pacifism. Identify the premises and conlusion in this paraphrased argument.

For those who hold that killing is not an absolute moral wrong, it is very difficult to see how torture could be an absolute moral wrong, given that killing is sometimes morally worse than torture. Since many of us assume that killing is not an absolute moral wrong, therefore, I conclude that torture is not an absolute moral wrong. And if an action is not absolutely wrong, then there are at least some cases in which it is morally permissible. Hence, torture is at least sometimes morally permissible.

19.2 TICKING BOMBS, TORTURE, AND THE ANALOGY WITH SELF-DEFENSE

DANIEL J. HILL (2007)

Daniel Hill is a lecturer in philosophy at the University of Liverpool. His professional interests include philosophy of religion and applied ethics. In this article, Hill argues for the truth of a general moral principle and shows that if this principle is true, it follows that torture is always morally impermissible. Hill considers a variety of different "thought experiments" that purport to show when the use of force against a terrorist would be justified. He concludes that the use of force is sometimes permissible to get people to conform to their **negative duties** but that it is never permissible to use force to get people to conform to their **positive duties**.

Reading Questions:

1. According to moral principle (P), what are the four moral justifications for intentionally inflicting pain on an unwilling person?

2. What is the difference between the Defense Case and the Interrogation Case?

3. What is the difference between the Interrogation Case and the Holding Case?

4. What is the difference between the Holding Case and the Withholding Case?

5. What makes a moral obligation a positive duty?

6. What makes a moral obligation a negative duty?

7. What is the point of the Expert Case?

1. Introduction

One reads in the press that the agents of many countries, and, indeed, many private individuals, engage in torture to coerce others into performing certain actions, frequently the divulging of information ("interrogational torture"). Sometimes this is undertaken for a good end, such as the saving of lives by the disarming of a ticking time-bomb, or the rescue of a kidnap victim. *It will be argued in this paper that such torture and, more generally, interrogational coercion are never morally permissible.* This will be a specific application of a general moral principle that will be proposed:

(P) It is never permissible intentionally to inflict severe pain or severe harm on someone unwilling, unless the pain/harm is intended (i) for their benefit, or (ii) as a punishment, or (iii) as part of the pursuit of a legitimate war, or (iv) to prevent the individual from causing severe pain or severe harm to innocents.[1]

Disagreement with this absolute rejection of interrogational torture could come from several directions. Act utilitarians would assert that it is fairly easy to imagine circumstances in which the ends would justify the means of torture: if it were known that many would be killed or suffer extreme pain as a result of a bomb's exploding it would surely be for the greatest happiness of the greatest number that one inflict some not-too-extreme pain on a single individual with the knowledge of the whereabouts of the bomb. . . .

On the other hand, some deontologists may object that principle (P) does not, despite its intended purpose, rule out interrogational torture, for interrogational torture is indeed intended to "prevent the individual from causing severe pain or severe harm to innocents." More generally, some deontologists argue that it is permissible to inflict severe pain or severe harm in self-defense or in defense of another, and that cases of interrogational torture are analogous to these in the relevant moral respects. The bulk of this paper will be devoted to resisting these objections and arguments and, therefore, to arguing that (P) does indeed absolutely prohibit interrogational torture. . . .

2. The Intention to Cause Pain

Let us consider a couple of examples that might be cited to support the analogy between self-defense and interrogational torture.

> Defense Case: A police officer spots a known terrorist about to detonate a bomb, which, if it goes off, will illicitly inflict serious harm and serious pain on many innocents. The officer fires a Taser at the terrorist, intending to cause no serious lasting harm but so much pain that the terrorist will be paralyzed and unable to detonate the bomb.[2]

Most **deontologists** and **consequentialists** would agree here that it is morally permissible for the police officer to Taser the terrorist in self-defense or defense of others. So far so good, but let us now consider the supposedly analogous case from the world of interrogation.

> Interrogation Case: A known terrorist is in the captivity of the security services of a certain country. He is known to have planted somewhere a ticking bomb, which, if it goes off, will illicitly inflict serious harm and serious pain on many innocents. The security services know that he knows where the bomb is, but he is refusing to divulge its whereabouts. In order to get him to talk they give him electric shocks, intending to cause no serious lasting harm but so much pain that he will say where the bomb is.

The contention of this paper will be that the analogy between Defense and Interrogation is superficial. In fact, it will be contended that there is a fundamental difference between the two. There is a way, admittedly, in which they are similar: each case is a case of intent that pain/harm will be caused—in Defense the terrorist is trying there and then to cause severe pain and severe harm, and in Interrogation the terrorist is deliberately not cooperating in order that the earlier causal chain that he set in motion may reach the terminus he desires. There is also, however, a way in which they are different: *Interrogation is not a case of aggression, unlike Defense.* In Defense the terrorist is *doing* something—he is attempting to inflict severe pain or severe harm—and force is being used to prevent him from causing a tragedy to happen.

In Interrogation, by contrast, the terrorist is power-less, in the custody of the security services, and is not doing anything—he has *already* set in motion a causal chain threatening a tragedy, and force is being used to cause him to perform the positive action of causing a tragedy not to happen. It will be argued that this distinction is of crucial moral significance...

3. Causing a Conscious Action

A possible objection to be considered states that the difference between Defense and Interrogation is merely that in Defense the terrorist is not being caused to perform any action, whereas in Interrogation he is. To show that this is too simple, an example of a *permissible* case in which one *does cause* the terrorist to perform an action will now be presented. This case is a slight variation on Defense above. . .

> Holding Case: A police officer spots a known terrorist about to detonate a bomb, which, if it goes off, will illicitly inflict serious harm and serious pain on many innocents. The detonator button needs to be held down for ten seconds for the bomb to go off. The only way the terrorist can be prevented from holding down the detonator button for ten seconds is if he is caused such pain that he will choose to take his finger off the detonator button in order to get the pain to stop. The officer shoots the terrorist in the foot, intending to cause no serious lasting harm but so much pain that he will make a conscious decision to stop priming the bomb and turn his attention to nursing his foot.[3]

Intuitively, in Holding the police officer is justified in inflicting pain on the terrorist in order to cause him to choose not to detonate the bomb by choosing to take his finger off the detonation button.

Compare this with the following case:

> Withholding Case: A police officer spots a known terrorist about to detonate a bomb, which, if it goes off, will illicitly inflict serious harm and serious pain on many innocents. The detonator button needs to be in the down position for ten seconds for the bomb to go off. The device works in such a way, however, that once pressed the button will remain depressed unless

pulled up by someone with the terrorist's fingerprint. The only way the detonator button can be prevented from remaining depressed for ten seconds is if the terrorist is caused such pain that he will choose to pull the detonator button up in order to get the pain to stop. The officer shoots the terrorist in the foot, telling the terrorist that he can expect more pain in the other foot unless he pulls up the detonator button.[4]

Withholding and Holding are superficially very sim-ilar, but there is one crucial difference: in Holding the terrorist is prevented from performing an action (holding the button down) and in Withholding the terrorist is not prevented from doing anything—instead he is (just) caused to perform an action, the action of pulling the button up. It would seem that this makes a moral difference. Intuitively, it is not permissible to inflict pain in Withholding in order to compel the terrorist to pull the button up, but intuitively it is permissible (as previously stated) for pain to be inflicted in Holding in order that the terrorist might be prevented from pushing the button down.

4. A Possible Reply: Loss of Human Rights

It might be replied that it is permissible for pain to be inflicted on the terrorist in Withholding and sim-ilar cases because the terrorist is guilty of attempting a terrorist atrocity and, as a result of this, has lost his right not to have pain inflicted on him, just as those guilty of crimes lose their right to freedom for a cer-tain time.[5] This means, so the objection goes, that it is morally permissible for pain to be inflicted on him in order that he might be compelled to pull up the detonator button.

It is curious that, while most of those that advance this argument believe that the removal of freedom is a standard punishment for the guilty, relatively few of them believe that the infliction of pain is a standard punishment for the guilty. Yet the removal of freedom is inflicted as a punishment precisely because (at least on a deontological understand-ing) it is judged that the guilty party has lost the right to freedom; why then do not the proponents of the objection suggest the infliction of pain as a routine punishment? Furthermore, even the propo-nents of this objection would still think it morally unacceptable if terrorists were tortured for fun, or if the torturers continued to torture even after the terrorists had aborted the ticking bomb. . . .

5. Another Possible Reply: Still Causing the Atrocity

It might be responded that the terrorist in Interrogation and Withholding and similar cases *is* still performing an evil action, viz., the causation of the terrorist atrocity, and that, therefore, the torturer *is* preventing the terrorist from performing an action, and so there is, after all, a similarity with Defense and Holding and similar cases. Miller (2006) puts it thus:

> [T]he terrorist is in the process of completing his (jointly undertaken) action of murdering thousands of innocent people. He has already undertaken his individual actions of, say, transporting and arming the nuclear device; he has performed these individual actions (in the context of other individual actions performed by the other members of the terrorist cell) in order to realise the end (shared by the other members of the cell) of murdering thousands of Londoners. In refusing to disclose the location of the device the terrorist is preventing the police from preventing him from completing his (joint) action of murdering thousands of innocent people.

Sussman (2005, p. 16) also defends this line:

> Consider again the captured terrorist who we know to have planted a powerful bomb in some crowded civilian area. Although the terrorist is in our power, he refuses to reveal the bomb's location, hoping to strike one last blow against us by allowing a train of events that he has set in motion to come to its intended conclusion. In one sense, the terrorist is indeed defenseless. We can do anything we like to him, and there is nothing he can do to resist or shield himself against us. But such helplessness means neither that the terrorist has ceased to engage in hostilities against us, nor that he is no longer an active military threat. His placing of the bomb was the beginning of an attack on us; his silence, although not any kind of further overt act, is nevertheless voluntary behavior undertaken for the sake of bringing that act to completion. His continued silence thus might well be considered

a part of his attack, understood as a temporally extended action.

This raises the big metaphysical question of when one completes an action, (a) when its effects come about, or (b) when one finishes the *basic* actions (i.e., the bodily movements[6]) that ultimately lead to the effects. Intuitively, only (b) is tenable, as if (a) were correct one would continue performing lots of actions long after one's death. Admittedly, (b) does have the counter-intuitive consequence that a killer kills the victim before the victim dies, but this is less counter-intuitive than the view that one might kill someone after one's death...

6. Positive and Negative Duties

What is the basis of this moral difference between preventing someone from performing an action that will cause a tragedy and causing someone to cause a tragedy not to occur? *It is an instance of the distinction between our duties to perform certain acts of causation on the one hand, our "positive" duties, and our duties not to perform certain different acts of causation on the other hand, our "negative" duties.* Although both the distinction itself and its moral significance have been much attacked in the literature, they do seem to have intuitive support:[7]

> Drowning Case: Suppose *A*'s father and spouse have been deliberately pushed by *B* into a lake and are drowning: *A* can rescue one, but only one, of them. *A* chooses to swim past his father to save his spouse.

Intuitively, in Drowning, *A* has not caused the death of his father; that was caused by *B*. And intuitively there is a moral difference between *A*'s choosing to refrain from saving his father in order to save his spouse on the one hand, and the deliberate pushing in by *B* of *A*'s father on the other hand. Even if *A*'s action of refraining from saving his father is morally bad, it surely isn't as morally bad as that of *B*. Finally, intuitively there is a distinction between the negative duty not deliberately to push the unwilling non-swimmer into a lake— a duty flouted by *B*—and the positive duty to save one's father from drowning if one can—a duty not satisfied by *A*, who could have saved his father, but saved his spouse instead.

It seems permissible, then, in some circumstances to inflict pain to force people to comply with their negative duties, but it does not seem permissible to inflict pain in order to force people to comply with their positive duties, even extremely important positive duties, such as the duty to avert an atrocity that the people in question have set in motion. In this sense negative duties are more important than positive duties, and the infliction of pain to force someone to comply with a positive duty would *itself* be a breach of a negative duty. On the other hand, failure to inflict pain to enforce a positive duty would not itself be a breach of a positive duty, though failure to inflict pain to enforce a negative duty in certain circumstances *would* be a breach of a positive duty: if a police officer refuses to shoot a terrorist in the foot when that is the only way to prevent him from detonating a devastating bomb then he or she is in breach of his or her duty to defend innocent citizens. On the other hand, as has been argued, the officer's duty to defend innocent citizens does not extend to a duty to shoot a captured terrorist in the foot to force him to divulge the whereabouts of a ticking bomb, as this would be a breach of a negative duty.

One can see that it is not the case that positive duties should be enforced by the infliction of pain by considering the following case:

> Expert Case: A ticking bomb has been located, and the only person that can defuse it is a retired bomb-disposal expert. He, however, doesn't want to come to defuse the bomb because he doesn't want to leave the bedside of his dying wife.

It would clearly be wrong on the deontological scheme to torture the bomb-disposal expert in Expert to get him to defuse the bomb, even if he has a duty to help. Moreover, intuitively it would still be wrong to torture him even if he was "on duty" and not retired, but was being insubordinate.

7. Conclusion

It appears that what underlies the cases that have been discussed in this paper is the principle mentioned earlier:

> (P) It is never permissible intentionally to inflict severe pain or severe harm on someone unwilling, unless the pain/harm is intended (i) for their benefit,

or (ii) as a punishment, or (iii) as part of the pursuit of a legitimate war, or (iv) to prevent the individual from causing severe pain or severe harm to innocents.

(P) implies that it is impermissible to act in standard torture cases (such as Interrogation). It does not imply that it is impermissible to act in standard cases of self-defense and defense of others (such as Defense). This is as it should be, for it is intuitively permissible to inflict severe pain or severe harm in Defense and similar cases to prevent the aggressor from causing severe pain or severe harm to innocents, but intuitively impermissible to inflict severe pain or severe harm in cases such as Interrogation and standard torture cases. . .

An attempt has been made to identify the relevant difference in these cases: the fact that in Defense and similar cases pain is being inflicted in order to enforce a negative duty, i.e., to prevent the individual from causing severe pain or severe harm to innocents, whereas in Interrogation and similar cases it is not. . .[8]

NOTES

1. Cf. Kershnar 2005, pp. 228–234.
2. A Taser is a kind of gun that fires projectiles that administer an electric shock.
3. The case is analogous to the case of the fat man's sitting on an innocent discussed in Sussman 2005 (pp. 16–17).
4. This case was suggested by Dr James Heather. Dr Heather intended this example as a *reductio ad absurdum* of the view of this paper, however. The reader may judge for him- or herself whether he was right.
5. Cf. Kershnar 2005, pp. 228–234.
6. The terms "basic action" and "non-basic action" are due to Danto 1963. Davidson 1971 identifies these with bodily movements.
7. The distinction seems first to have been brought to prominence in contemporary moral philosophy by Foot 1967. It is criticized in, e.g., Glover 1977 (p. 97).
8. The author is extremely grateful for helpful discussion to Jamie Dow, James Heather, Harry Lesser, Jonas Olson, and Helen Watt, and also to an anonymous reviewer for *American Philosophical Quarterly* for some very helpful and acute comments.

REFERENCES

Danto, Arthur. 1963. "What We Can Do," *Journal of Philosophy*, vol. 60, pp. 434–445.
Davidson, Donald. 1971. "Agency," in *Agent, Action, and Reason*, ed. R. Binkley, R. Bronaugh, and A. Marras. Toronto: University of Toronto Press.

Davis, Michael. 2005. "The Moral Justification of Torture and Other Cruel, Inhuman, or Degrading Treatment," *International Journal of Applied Philosophy*, vol. 19, no. 2, pp. 161–178; http://www .pdcnet.org/pdf/ijapl92-Davis. pdf, accessed on 19 June 2007.

Foot, Philippa. 1967. "The Problem of Abortion and the Doctrine of Double Effect," *Oxford Review*, vol. 5, pp. 5–15.

Glover, Jonathan. 1977. *Causing Death and Saving Lives.* London: Penguin.

Hill, Daniel J.. 2005. *Divinity and Maximal Greatness.* London: Routledge.

Kershnar, Stephen. 2005. "For Interrogational Torture," *International Journal of Applied Philosophy*, vol. 19, no. 2, pp. 223–241; http://www.pdcnet.org/pdf/ijapl92-Kershnar. pdf, accessed on 16 June 2007.

Miller, Seumas. 2006. 'Torture," in *The Stanford Encyclopedia of Philosophy* (Spring 2006 Edition), ed. Edward N. Zalta; http://plato.stanford.edu/archives/spr2006/entries/ torture/, accessed on 15 July 2006.

Pike, Nelson. 1966. "Of God and Freedom: A Rejoinder," *The Philosophical Review*, vol. 74, pp. 27–46.

Shue, Henry. 1978. 'Torture," P*hilosophy & Public Affairs*, vol. 7, pp. 124–143.

Sussman, David. 2005. "What"s Wrong with Torture?" *Philosophy & Public Affairs*, vol. 33, no. 1, pp. 1–33.

DISCUSSION QUESTIONS:

1. Hill opens his essay with a statement of a moral principle that he calls (P). This principle says that there are only four possible justifications for intentionally causing someone pain without their consent, and doing so to guilty parties to save the lives of innocents is not listed among the four. Given that, doesn't this principle simply beg the question against the person who thinks that torture is sometimes morally permissible? To "beg the question" is to assume from the outset the very claim that is under contention. For example, if you and I were having a debate over the moral permissibility of abortion, and I offer you an argument that begins with the premise that the only possible justification for killing another human is that the other human is guilty of something, I've begged the question against you (since it's obvious that fetuses can't be guilty!). So Hill has to argue for (P) in order to avoid begging the question. Is there an argument for this claim in the essay? Do the thought experiments he cites provide evidence for (P), or are these cases compatible with other moral principles that are slightly different from (P)?

2. Consider the differences between the Holding Case and the Withholding Case. In the former, Hill claims that it is morally permissible to shoot the terrorist in the foot to cause him to release the button. In the latter, Hill claims that it is morally wrong to shoot the terrorist in the foot to cause him to pull the button. Is that really plausible? How could the mere difference of a release versus a pull make the moral difference between whether it is morally permissible to shoot someone or not?

3. One justification for the use of torture in some cases is that the person under torture is still, in some sense, "doing" the action (see Chapter 19.1). And if the terrorist is still "doing" the action, then torture starts to look an awful lot like self-defense. Hill denies that captured persons are still completing the action, and he offers two criteria for deciding when an action is complete: (A) when the bodily movements cease or (B) when the effects of the movements finally come about. He settles for (A) because he thinks that (B) implies that we complete actions after our deaths (since at least some of the effects of our actions will not occur until after we're dead).

   But, as Hill notes, (A) has the counterintuitive result that John Wilkes Booth (the man who assassinated President Lincoln) killed Lincoln the moment Booth pulled the trigger, before the bullet entered Lincoln's body. Given that both options have implausible consequences, why shouldn't we accept a third view about actions? Can you think of one that might be useful in defending the view that terrorists are, in some sense, still engaged in the act of terror even when captured by the authorities?

4. Hill concludes that "it seems permissible, then, in some circumstances to inflict pain to force people to comply with their negative duties, but it does not seem permissible to inflict pain in order to force people to comply with their positive duties" (page 558). Do you think this is right? Can you think of cases where it might be permissible to use force against people to meet their positive duties? How about when governments force people to pay taxes or when we punish people for not feeding their children?

Argument Reconstruction Exercises:

I. Hill's ultimate conclusion is that it is never morally permissible intentionally to inflict pain on an unwilling victim, and this obviously includes torture. His argument for this relies on the moral principle that he states at the outset of the article. See if you can reconstruct his central argument for the conclusion that it is never morally permissible to torture by using his moral principle as an opening premise:

> It will be argued in this paper that torture, and more generally, interrogational coercion are never morally permissible. This will be a specific application of a general moral principle that will be proposed:
>
> (P) It is never permissible intentionally to inflict severe pain or severe harm on someone unwilling, unless the pain/harm is intended (i) for their benefit, or (ii) as a punishment, or (iii) as part of the pursuit of a legitimate war, or (iv) to prevent the individual from causing severe pain or severe harm to innocents. (page 555)

II. Hill's defense of moral principle (P) and ultimately his defense of the wrongness of torture both depend on drawing a distinction between action and inaction. He uses the Holding Case and the Withholding Case to argue for this conclusion. See if you can construct an inference to the best explanation for his conclusion that there is a moral difference between preventing someone from doing something and causing someone to do something:

> Withholding and Holding are superficially very similar, but there is one crucial difference: in Holding the terrorist is prevented from performing an action (holding the button down) and in Withholding the terrorist is not prevented from doing anything—instead he is (just) caused to perform an action, the action of pulling the button up. It would seem that this makes a moral difference. Intuitively, it is not permissible to inflict pain in Withholding in order to compel the terrorist to pull the button up, but intuitively it is permissible for pain to be inflicted in Holding in order that the terrorist might be prevented from pushing the button down. (page 556)

III. One objection that Hill considers attempts to justify torture on grounds that terrorists and others have lost their rights not to have pain inflicted on them. Use the following excerpt to construct an argument for the conclusion that it is morally permissible to inflict pain on a terrorist:

> It might be replied that it is permissible for pain to be inflicted on the terrorist in Withholding and similar cases because the terrorist is guilty of attempting a terrorist atrocity and, as a result of this, has lost his right not to have pain inflicted on him, just as those guilty of crimes lose their right to freedom for a certain time. This means, so the objection goes, that it is morally permissible for pain to be inflicted on him in order that he might be compelled to pull up the detonator button. (page 556)

IV. A second objection that Hill considers attempts to justify torture on grounds that terrorists are still in the process of performing an evil action. And since Hill's own moral principle (P) claims that it is morally permissible intentionally to cause pain to an individual in order to prevent him from causing harm to others, it would follow that at least some acts of torture are morally permissible. Use the following excerpt to construct an argument for the conclusion that it is morally permissible to inflict pain on a terrorist:

> It might be responded that the terrorist in Interrogation and Withholding and similar cases is still performing an evil action, viz., the causation of the terrorist atrocity, and that, therefore, the torturer is preventing an action. (page 557)

CHAPTER 20

Euthanasia

I'm not afraid of being dead. I'm just afraid of what you might have to go through to get there.

—PAMELA BONE, JOURNALIST AND CANCER VICTIM

INTRODUCTION

Until quite recently, Jenny was a happily married mother of two boys. She lived in a small town and worked as a math teacher at the local high school. She spent her summers with her children, aged 10 and 12, and she spent time visiting her aging parents. However, last year after undergoing a routine doctor's examination, she was diagnosed with Lou Gehrig's disease (ALS). She was only 43 years old. This disease affects the brain and central nervous system, impairing the body's ability to communicate with muscle tissue. The disease is also progressive. While symptoms are almost unnoticeable at first (slight twitches, numbness of limbs), the disease gradually paralyzes its victim culminating in death by suffocation or choking. And what is perhaps worse, the disease does not affect either the five senses or one's ability to reason, remember, etc.

Like most ALS patients, Jenny's symptoms were slight at first. The summer after her diagnosis, she took a vacation to the Caribbean with her family, where they swam, snorkeled, and played on the beach. But this year, things are different. She was long ago asked to leave her job as a teacher. Her days are spent at home now. She is restricted to a wheelchair. She cannot comb her hair. She cannot control her bladder and thus must wear a catheter. She cannot defecate on her own. She cannot eat tough foods, for her jaw muscles are severely weakened, and she chokes easily. Jenny's husband cannot care for her

since he must work to pay for the terribly expensive treatments and required homecare.

On her most recent visit to the hospital, the attending doctors gave Jenny one to two months to live. She will likely be hospitalized for most of that time. In addition to requiring a second mortgage on their home, paying for her care these last two months will exhaust all of the money Jenny and her husband have saved to send their boys to college. Furthermore, ALS is uncurable—Jenny is sure to die relatively soon. And aside from the emotional suffering, Jenny will suffer physically as well. So will her husband. So will her children.

What can be done for Jenny and her family? What, morally speaking, is *permissible* for us to do to alleviate their suffering? What, morally speaking, are we *required* to do to alleviate their suffering? The various moral issues surrounding these questions are lumped under the topic of **euthanasia**. Euthanasia is Greek for happy (*eu*) death (*thanatos*). Euthanasia is thus an easy or happy death. What is morally permissible for us to do in order to secure an easy death for ourselves or our loved ones?

As with any issue in applied ethics, making careful distinctions among various cases is often helpful in deciding how we ought to behave. Here are two different distinctions that are crucial for thinking carefully about the euthanasia debate. **Active euthanasia** is any *action* that brings about an easy death for someone who is suffering. Active euthanasia is an instance of killing someone. For example, if one of Jenny's doctors

561

used an injection to stop her heart from beating, he would have performed an instance of active euthanasia. **Passive euthanasia**, on the other hand, is any *omission* that results in an easy death for someone who is suffering. Passive euthanasia is an instance of letting someone die. For example, if someone who is dying from cancer refuses chemotherapy so that she might die more quickly, this is an instance of passive euthanasia. Notice that the distinction between the two is not as clear-cut as it might seem at first. For example, consider the family that turns off the life-support machine that is keeping their aged grandfather alive. Did the family kill him or merely let him die? Or what about a case of withholding food or water from a patient? Is that a case of killing him or merely letting him die?

The second distinction concerns the voluntary nature of the easy death. In an instance of **voluntary euthanasia**, the person who dies has been fully informed and has consented to the euthanasia. For example, if Jenny and her husband talk over the situation and decide that one more month of suffering is not worth the cost of their children missing out on college and she opts to forgo treatment and dies as a result, this is a case of voluntary euthanasia. Jenny chose the option of forgoing treatment voluntarily. However, in an instance of **involuntary euthanasia**, the person who dies has been fully informed and has NOT consented to the euthanasia. This would happen if a doctor purposefully killed a patient who was determined to continue treatments of his condition no matter how bleak the situation appeared. Finally, not all cases of euthanasia are voluntary or involuntary. There is a middle ground. **Nonvoluntary euthanasia** occurs when the person who dies has not given informed consent one way or the other. For example, sometimes doctors allow newborn infants with severe congenital defects to die. Or consider the case of a person injured in a car accident and in a coma at the local hospital. These patients obviously cannot give informed consent to be killed, but neither have they insisted on care. They just don't have the mental resources to do either.

With these distinctions in hand, we can think more carefully about the euthanasia issue. One might think, for example, that voluntary, passive euthanasia is always morally permissible. These are cases in which informed individuals refuse treatment that might prolong their lives at too high a cost (in suffering or dollars or whatever). These people have a right to do what they want with their bodies, and they are not actually killing themselves or being killed. They are merely allowing themselves to die.

However, one might think that nonvoluntary, active euthanasia is always morally wrong. These are cases in which individuals who are incapable of giving informed consent are actively killed to ensure an easy death. This occurs when doctors kill newborns or when a family member kills a mentally disabled and suffering youth. Other cases might be harder to classify. What should we think about voluntary, active euthanasia? If Jenny were to decide that the suffering is simply not worth the pain, is it morally permissible for her husband or a doctor to give her a lethal dose of morphine?

Furthermore, the question of moral *permissibility* is only half of the equation. Many times we ask ourselves whether it would be morally wrong to allow someone to die or to kill someone to save them from a painful life. In these cases, we're trying to figure out what the bounds of morality *allow* us to do. But we might ask what the bounds of morality *require* us to do as well. Could we ever have moral obligations to allow others to die or to kill others who are suffering? If so, then sometimes it is morally wrong for us to force aid on others and—even more shockingly—sometimes it is morally wrong for us to refuse to kill others in need. Could the correct moral principles ever require such a thing of us?

These are questions worth thinking through carefully. With the medical advances of the 20th and 21st centuries, humans are living longer and longer lives. Most adults in the industrialized West will spend some time at the end of their lives in hospitals. And most of us will have to deal with aging parents who suffer from a wide range of debilitating diseases such as Alzheimer's. How we treat such people in these situations matters a great deal to many of us. As you read the following chapters, ask yourself what you would want done for you in the situations described. If you think that an instance of euthanasia is wrong, ask yourself why. And above all, carefully distinguish the cases under consideration to ensure that your view of euthanasia is both accurate and sufficiently fine-grained to capture the morally relevant differences from case to case.

SUGGESTIONS FOR FURTHER READING

Battin, Margaret. "Euthanasia: The Way We Do It, The Way They Do It." *Journal of Pain and Symptom Management*, 1991; 6:5, pp. 298–305.

Biggar, N., *Aiming to Kill: The Ethics of Suicide and Euthanasia.* (London: Darton, Longman and Todd, 2004)

Brock, Dan. "Voluntary Active Euthanasia." In *The Hastings Center Report*, 1992; Vol. 22, No. 2. (Mar.-Apr.), pp. 10–22.

Callahan. Daniel "When Self-Determination Runs Amok." *The Hastings Center Report*, 1992; Vol. 22, No. 2. (Mar.-Apr.), pp. 52–55.

Foley, K. and H. Hendin (eds.). *The Case Against Assisted Suicide: For the Right to End-of-Life Care.* (Baltimore: The Johns Hopkins University Press, 2002)

Kamm, Francis *Myrna Morality. Mortality: Volume I.* (London: Oxford University Press, 1993)

_____. *Morality, Mortality: Volume II.* (London: Oxford University Press, 2001)

Keown, J. *Euthanasia, Ethics and Public Policy: an Argument Against Legalization.* (New York: Cambridge University Press, 2002)

Lo, Ping-Cheung. "Confucian Views on Suicide and Their Implications for Euthanasia." In *Confucian Ethics*, ed. by Ruiping Fan. (Springer, 1999; pp. 69–102).

McMahan, Jeff. *The Ethics of Killing.* (London: Oxford University Press, 2002)

Rachels, James. *The End of Life: Euthanasia and Morality.* (Oxford: Oxford University Press, 1986)

Steinbock, Bonnie. "The Intentional Termination of Life." *Social Science and Medicine 1979*; 1, pp. 69–94.

Weisbard, Alan, & Siegler, Mark. "On Killing Patients with Kindness: An Appeal for Caution." In *By No Extraordinary Means*, ed. by Joanne Lynn. (Bloomington: Indiana Univ. Press, 1986, 108–116)

20.1 ACTIVE AND PASSIVE EUTHANASIA

JAMES RACHELS (1975)

James Rachels grew up in Georgia and spent most of his professional career at the University of Alabama-Birmingham. Dr. Rachels specialized in ethics, and he made many important contributions to the field of applied ethics, especially in issues of non-human animal welfare, euthanasia, and other bioethical issues. This article was written not for philosophers but for practicing medical doctors and was originally published in one of the most influential medical journals in the United States, *The New England Journal of Medicine*. Rachels argues that the longstanding practice of distinguishing between **active euthanasia** and **passive euthanasia** is morally arbitrary. This distinction hinges on the difference between killing a patient and letting a patient die, but Rachels argues that this is a distinction without a moral difference. If so, then the major argument for the claim that it is always wrong to kill a patient via active euthanasia but sometimes permissible to allow a patient to die via passive euthanasia is unsound.

Reading Questions:

1. What is the difference between active and passive euthanasia?
2. Is withholding necessary medical treatment a form of active or passive euthanasia?
3. What is the argument from suffering?
4. Why are some children born with Down syndrome allowed to die?
5. What is the argument from irrelevancy?

6. What thought experiment does Rachels use to show that there is no moral difference between killing and letting die?

The distinction between **active** and **passive euthanasia** is thought to be crucial for medical ethics. The idea is that it is permissible, at least in some cases, to withhold treatment and allow a patient to die, but it is never permissible to take any direct action designed to kill the patient. This doctrine seems to be accepted by most doctors, and is endorsed in a statement adopted by the House of Delegates of the American Medical Association on December 4, 1973:

> The intentional termination of the life of one human being by another—mercy killing—is contrary to that for which the medical profession stands and is contrary to the policy of the American Medical Association.
>
> The cessation of the employment of extraordinary means to prolong the life of the body when there is irrefutable evidence that biological death is imminent is the decision of the patient and or his immediate family. The advice and judgment of the physician should be freely available to the patient and/or his immediate family.

However, a strong case can be made against this doctrine. In what follows I will set out some of the relevant arguments, and urge doctors to reconsider their views on this matter.

The Argument from Suffering

To begin with a familiar type of situation, a patient who is dying of incurable cancer of the throat is in terrible pain, which can no longer be satisfactorily alleviated. He is certain to die within a few days, even if present treatment is continued, but he does not want to go on living for those days since the pain is unbearable. So he asks the doctor for an end to it, and his family joins in the request.

Suppose the doctor agrees to withhold treatment, as the conventional doctrine says he may. The justification for his doing so is that the patient is in terrible agony, and since he is going to die anyway, it would be wrong to prolong his suffering needlessly. But now notice this. *If one simply withholds treatment, it may take the patient longer to die, and so he may suffer more than he would if more direct action were taken and a lethal injection given.* This fact provides strong reason for thinking that, once the initial decision not to prolong his agony has been made, *active euthanasia is actually preferable to passive euthanasia*, rather than the reverse. To say otherwise is to endorse the option that leads to more suffering rather than less, and is contrary to the humanitarian impulse that prompts the decision not to prolong his life in the first place.

Part of my point is that the process of being "allowed to die" can be relatively slow and painful, whereas being given a lethal injection is relatively quick and painless. Let me give a different sort of example. In the United States about one in 600 babies is born with Down syndrome. Most of these babies are otherwise healthy—that is, with only the usual pediatric care, they will proceed to an otherwise normal infancy. Some, however, are born with congenital defects such as intestinal obstructions that require operations if they are to live. Sometimes, the parents and the doctor will decide not to operate, and let the infant die. Anthony Shaw describes what happens then.

> . . . When surgery is denied [the doctor] must try to keep the infant from suffering while natural forces sap the baby's life away. As a surgeon whose natural inclination is to use the scalpel to fight off death, standing by and watching a salvageable baby die is the most emotionally exhausting experience I know. It is easy at a conference, in a theoretical discussion, to decide that such infants should be allowed to die. It is altogether different to stand by in the nursery and watch dehydration and infection wither a tiny being over hours and days. This is a terrible ordeal for me and the hospital staff—much more so than for the parents who never set foot in the nursery.[1]

I can understand why some people are opposed to all euthanasia, and insist that such infants must be allowed to live. I think I can also understand why other people favor destroying these babies quickly and painlessly. But why should anyone favor letting "dehydration and infection wither a tiny being over hours and days?" The doctrine that says that a baby may be allowed to dehydrate and wither, but may not be given an injection that would end its life without suffering, seems so patently cruel as to require no further refutation. The strong language is not intended to offend, but only to put the point in the clearest possible way.

The Argument from Irrelevancy

My second argument is that the conventional doctrine leads to decisions concerning life and death made on irrelevant ground.

Consider again the case of the infants with Down syndrome who need operations for congenital defects unrelated to the syndrome to live. Sometimes, there is no operation, and the baby dies, but when there is no such defect, the baby lives on. Now, an operation such as that to remove an intestinal obstruction is not prohibitively difficult. The reason why such operations are not performed in these cases is, clearly, that the child has Down syndrome and the parents and doctor judge that because of that fact it is better for the child to die.

But notice that this situation is absurd, no matter what view one takes of lives and potentials of such babies. If the life of such an infant is worth preserving, what does it matter if it needs a simple operation? Or, if one thinks it better that such a baby should not live on, what difference does it make that it happens to have an unobstructed intestinal tract? In either case, the matter of life and death is being decided an irrelevant grounds. It is the Down syndrome, and not the intestines, that is the issue. The matter should be decided, if at all, on the basis, and not be allowed to depend on the essentially irrelevant question of whether the intestinal tract is blocked.

What makes this situation possible, of course, is the idea that when there is an intestinal blockage, one can "let the baby die," but when there is no such defect there is nothing that can be done, for

one must not "kill" it. The fact that this idea leads to such results as deciding life or death on irrelevant grounds is another good reason why the doctrine should be rejected.

Killing vs. Letting Die

One reason why so many people think that there is an important moral difference between active and passive euthanasia is that they think killing someone is morally worse than letting someone die. But is it? Is killing, in itself, worse than letting someone die? To investigate this issue, two cases may be considered that are exactly alike except that one involves killing whereas the other involves letting someone die. Then, it can be asked whether this difference makes any difference to the moral assessment. It is important that the cases be exactly alike, except for this one difference, since otherwise one cannot be confident that it is this difference and not some other that accounts for any variation in the assessments of the two cases. So, let us consider this pair of cases:

In the first, Smith stands to gain a large inheritance if anything should happen to his six-year-old cousin. One evening while the child is taking his bath, Smith sneaks into the bathroom and drowns the child, and then arranges things so that it will look like an accident.

In the second, Jones also stands to gain if anything should happen to his six-year-old cousin. Like Smith, Jones sneaks in planning to drown the child in his bath. However, just as he enters the bathroom Jones sees the child slip and hit his head, and fall down in the water. Jones is delighted; he stands by, ready to push the child's head back under if it is necessary, but it is not necessary. With only a little thrashing about, the child drowns all by himself, "accidentally," as Jones watches and does nothing.

Now Smith killed the child, whereas Jones "merely" let the child die. That is the only difference between them. Did either man behave better, from a moral point of view? *If the difference between killing and letting die were in itself a morally important matter, one should say that Jones's behavior was less reprehensible than Smith's.* But does one really want to say that? I think not. In the first place, both men acted from the same motive, personal gain, and both had exactly the same end in view when they acted. It may be inferred from Smith's conduct that he is a bad man, although that judgment may be withdrawn or modified if certain further facts are learned about him—for example, that he is mentally deranged. But would not the very same thing be inferred about Jones from his conduct? And would not the same further considerations also be relevant to any modification of this judgment? Moreover, suppose Jones pleaded, in his own defense, "After all, I didn't do anything except just stand there and watch the child drown. I didn't kill him; I only let him die." Again, if letting die were in itself less bad than killing, this defense should have at least some weight. But it does not. Such a "defense" can only be regarded as grotesque perversion of moral reasoning. Morally speaking, it is no defense at all.

Now it may be pointed out, quite properly, that the cases of euthanasia with which doctors are concerned are not like this at all. They do not involve personal gain or the destruction of normal healthy children. Doctors are concerned only with cases in which the patient's life is of no further use to him, or in which the patient's life has become or will soon become a terrible burden. However, the point is the same in these cases: *the bare difference between killing and letting die does not, in itself, make a moral difference.* If a doctor lets a patient die, for humane reasons, he is in the same moral position as if he had given the patient a lethal injection for humane reasons. If his decision was wrong—if, for example, the patient's illness was in fact curable—the decision would be equally regrettable no matter which method was used to carry it out. And if the doctor's decision was the right one, the method used is not in itself important.

The AMA policy statement isolates the crucial issue very well; the crucial issue is "the intentional termination of the life of one human being by another." But after identifying this issue, and forbidding "mercy killing," the statement goes on to deny that the cessation of treatment is the intentional termination of a life. This is where the mistake comes in, for what is the cessation of treatment, in these circumstances, if it is not "the intentional termination of the life of one human being by another?" Of course it is exactly that, and if it were not, there would be no point to it.

Many people will find this judgment hard to accept. One reason, I think, is that it is very easy to conflate the question of whether killing is, in itself, worse than letting die, with the very different question of whether most actual cases of killing are more reprehensible than most actual cases of letting die. Most actual cases of killing are clearly terrible (think, for example, of all the murders reported in the newspapers), and one hears of such cases every day. On the other hand, one hardly ever hears of a case of letting die, except for the actions of doctors who are motivated by humanitarian reasons. So one learns to think of killing in a much worse light than of letting die. But this does not mean that there is something about killing that makes it in itself worse than letting die, for it is not the bare difference between killing and letting die that makes the difference in these cases. Rather, the other factors—the murderer's motive of personal gain, for example, contrasted with the doctor's humanitarian motivation—account for different reactions to the different cases.

I have argued that killing is not in itself any worse than letting die; if my contention is right, if follows that active euthanasia is not any worse than passive euthanasia. What arguments can be given on the other side? The most common, I believe is the following.

"The important difference between active and passive euthanasia is that, in passive euthanasia, the doctor does not do anything to bring about the patient's death. The doctor does nothing, and the patient dies of whatever ills already afflict him. In active euthanasia, however, the doctor does something to bring about the patient's death; he kills him. The doctor who gives the patient with cancer a lethal injection has himself caused his patient's death; whereas if he merely ceases treatment, the cancer is the cause of the death."

A number of points need to be made here. The first is that it is not exactly correct to say that in passive euthanasia the doctor does nothing, for he does do one thing that is very important: he lets the patient die. "Letting someone die" is certainly different, in some respects, from other types of action—mainly in that it is a kind of action that one may perform by way of not performing certain other actions. For example, one may let a patient die by way of not giving medication, just as one may insult someone by way of not shaking his hand. But for any purpose of moral assessment, it is a type of action nonetheless. The decision to let a patient die is subject to moral appraisal in the same way that a decision to kill him would be subject to moral appraisal: It may be assessed as wise or unwise, compassionate or sadistic, right or wrong. If a doctor deliberately let a patient die who was suffering from a routinely curable illness, the doctor would certainly be to blame for what he had done, just as he would be to blame if he had needlessly killed the patient. Charges against him would then be appropriate. If so, it would be no defense at all for him to insist that he didn't "do anything." He would have done something very serious indeed, for he let his patient die.

Fixing the cause of death may be very important from a legal point of view, for it may determine whether criminal charges are brought against the doctor. But I do not think that this notion can be used to show a *moral* difference between active and passive euthanasia. The reason why it is considered bad to be the cause of someone's death is that death is regarded as a great evil—and so it is. However, if it has been decided that euthanasia—even passive euthanasia—is desirable in a given case, it has also been decided that in this instance death is no greater an evil than their patient's continued existence. And if this is true, the usual reason for not wanting to be the cause of someone's death simply does not apply.

Finally, doctors may think that all of this is only of academic interest—the sort of thing that philosophers may worry about but that has no practical bearing on their own work. After all, doctors must be concerned about the legal consequences of what they do, and active euthanasia is clearly forbidden by law. But even so, doctors should also be concerned with the fact that the law is forcing upon them a moral doctrine that may well be indefensible, and has a considerable effect on their practices. Of course, most doctors are not now in the position of

being coerced in this matter, for they do not regard themselves as merely going along with what the law requires. Rather, in statements such as the AMA policy statement that I have quoted, they are endorsing this doctrine as a central point of medical ethics. In that statement, active euthanasia is condemned not merely as illegal but as "contrary to that for which the medical profession stands," whereas passive euthanasia is approved. However, the preceding considerations suggest that there is really no moral difference between the two, considered in themselves (there may be important moral differences in some cases in their *consequences*, but, as I pointed out, these differences may make active euthanasia, and not passive euthanasia, the morally preferable option). So, whereas doctors may have to discriminate between active and passive euthanasia to satisfy the law, they should not do any more than that. In particular, they should not give the distinction any added authority and weight by writing it into official statements of medical ethics.

NOTE

1. A. Shaw, "Doctor, Do We Have a Choice?" *The New York Times Magazine,* Jan. 30, 1972, p. 54.

DISCUSSION QUESTIONS:

1. Suppose you were suffering from an incurable disease that caused you terrible pain. The doctors unanimously agree that without treatment you'll die within days, but a new medical treatment might extend your life (and your suffering) as much as a month. Do you think that it is morally permissible for you to forgo the treatment even if it cuts your life short by a month? If so, what moral principle explains why it is morally permissible for you to take this course of action? Does the same moral principle also show that it would be morally permissible for you to kill yourself via lethal injection? Why or why not?

2. Consider again Rachels' thought experiment with Smith and Jones. He claims that our moral appraisal of the action/omission of the two men should be the same. Is he right about this? After all, remember that Smith is a child-killer whereas Jones merely

allowed the child to die. While it's true that legal matters are not moral matters, it is interesting that Smith would be found guilty of a heinous crime under our current legal system whereas Jones couldn't even be charged. If the two actions are on a moral par, why does the legal system make a distinction?

3. Given life-prolonging treatments that will very likely be available in the coming decades, it is reasonable to think that many readers of this book will have to make decisions about passive and active euthanasia for people that they love. Suppose you become convinced that active euthanasia is sometimes morally permissible—or more strongly, sometimes morally required. Would you have the courage to follow this moral conviction even if it were illegal to do so? How can we balance the demands of the law with the demands of morality?

Argument Reconstruction Exercises:

I. According to the argument from suffering, it is sometimes morally permissible to deny a patient treatment (i.e., engage in passive euthanasia) when the patient is both suffering and terminal. Use the following excerpt to reconstruct the argument for that conclusion:

> Suppose the doctor agrees to withhold treatment, as the conventional doctrine says he may. The justification for his doing so is that the patient is in terrible agony, and since he is going to die anyway, it would be wrong to prolong his suffering needlessly. (page 564)

II. Rachels thinks that the argument considered above—the argument from suffering—can actually be turned on its head to show that in some cases active euthanasia is permissible whereas passive euthanasia is wrong (he calls the former "preferable" to the latter). See if you can use the same principle used in Exercise I to show that in at least some cases, it is active euthanasia that is morally permissible and passive euthanasia that is morally wrong:

> Suppose the doctor agrees to withhold treatment, as the conventional doctrine says he may. The

justification for his doing so is that the patient is in terrible agony, and since he is going to die anyway, it would be wrong to prolong his suffering needlessly. But now notice this. If one simply withholds treatment, it may take the patient longer to die, and so he may suffer more than he would if more direct action were taken and a lethal injection given. This fact provides strong reason for thinking that, once the initial decision not to prolong his agony has been made, active euthanasia is actually preferable to passive euthanasia, rather than the reverse. (page 564)

III. Remember that if any claim whatsoever entails a statement that is false, this is a reason to think that the first claim is false as well. To show this in an argument is to construct an argument by false implication or a *modus tollens* argument. Furthermore, one of the bedrock principles in ethics is that like cases should be treated alike—arbitrary results are a sure sign of a false moral principle. Knowing this, use Rachels' examples of babies with Down syndrome to construct an argument that concludes that the doctrine that passive euthanasia is morally permissible whereas active euthanasia is not is mistaken:

> What makes this situation possible, of course, is the idea that when there is an intestinal blockage, one can "let the baby die," but when there is no such defect there is nothing that can be done, for one must not "kill" it. The fact that this idea [the idea that passive euthanasia is permissible but active euthanasia is not] leads to such results as deciding life or death on irrelevant grounds is another good reason why the doctrine should be rejected. (page 565)

IV. Rachels' central argument for the moral permissibility of active euthanasia hinges on his defense of the claim that there is no moral distinction to be made between killing and letting die. He states the argument simply in the following excerpt:

> I have argued that killing is not in itself any worse than letting die; if my contention is right, it follows that active euthanasia is not any worse than passive euthanasia. (page 565)

20.2 ACTIVE AND PASSIVE EUTHANASIA: AN IMPERTINENT DISTINCTION?

THOMAS D. SULLIVAN (1977)

Thomas D. Sullivan is Professor of Philosophy and Aquinas Chair in Philosophy & Theology at the University of Saint Thomas in Saint Paul, Minnesota. His work focuses on crucial issues in the Catholic tradition, including issues in the philosophy of religion and medieval philosophy, but he has published important work in applied ethics as well. In this essay, Sullivan responds to James Rachels' arguments that the distinction between passive and active euthanasia is morally irrelevant. In effect, Sullivan agrees with Rachels that this distinction is irrelevant but insists that the traditional opposition to euthanasia does not hinge on this distinction. Instead, he appeals to the **Doctrine of Double Effect** to show that since all cases of euthanasia are ones in which one agent intends to bring about the death of another human, all such actions or omissions are morally wrong.

Reading Questions:

1. According to Sullivan, what is the "traditional" view of the physician's role with regard to a dying patient?

2. What are the two moral principles that Sullivan finds in the prose of the AMA statement from 1973?

3. What does Sullivan think morally ought to be done with the children Rachels describes as suffering from Down syndrome?

4. What is the distinction between ordinary and extraordinary means of preserving life?

5. According to Sullivan, what makes some instances of euthanasia morally wrong?

6. What is the difference between intending and foreseeing a consequence?

Because of recent advances in medical technology, it is today possible to save or prolong the lives of many persons who in an earlier era would have quickly perished. Unhappily, however, it often is impossible to do so without committing the patient and his or her family to a future filled with sorrows. Modern methods of neurosurgery can successfully close the opening at the base of the spine of a baby born with severe myelomeningocoele, but do nothing to relieve the paralysis that afflicts it from the waist down or to remedy the patient's the in continence of stool and urine. Antibiotics and skin grafts can spare the life of a victim of severe and massive burns, but fail to eliminate the immobilizing contractions of arms and legs, the extreme pain, and the hideous disfigurement of the face. It is not surprising, therefore, that physicians and moralists in increasing number recommend that assistance should not be given to such patients, and that some have even begun to advocate the deliberate hastening of death by medical means, provided informed consent has been given by the appropriate parties.

The latter recommendation consciously and directly conflicts with what might be called the "traditional" view of the physician's role. The traditional view, as articulated, for example, by the House of Delegates of the American Medical Association in 1973 declared:

> The intentional termination of the life of one human being by another—mercy killing—is contrary to that for which the medical profession stands and is contrary to the policy of the American Medical Association.
>
> The cessation of the employment of extraordinary means to prolong the life of the body when there is irrefutable evidence that biological death is imminent is the decision of the patient and/or his immediate family. The advice and judgment of the physician should be freely available to the patient and /or his immediate family.

Basically this view involves two points: (1) *that it is impermissible for the doctor or anyone else to terminate intentionally the life of a patient, but (2) that it is permissible in some cases to cease the employment of "extraordinary means" of preserving life, even though the death of the patient is a foreseeable consequence.*

Rachels' Critique of the Traditional View

Does this position really make sense? Recent criticism charges that it does not. The heart of the complaint is that the traditional view arbitrarily rules out all cases of intentionally acting to terminate life, but permits what is in fact the moral equivalent, letting patients die. This accusation has been clearly articulated by James Rachels in a widely read article that appeared in a recent issue of the *New, England Journal of Medicine*, entitled "Active and Passive Euthanasia."[1] By "active euthanasia" Rachels seems to mean *doing something* to bring about a patient's death, and by "passive euthanasia," not doing anything, i.e., just letting the patient die. Referring to the AMA statement, *Rachels sees the traditional position as always forbidding active euthanasia, but permitting passive euthanasia.* Yet, he argues, passive euthanasia may be in some cases morally indistinguishable from active euthanasia, and in other cases even worse. To make his point he asks his readers to consider the case of a Down's syndrome baby with an intestinal obstruction that could easily be remedied through routine surgery. Rachels comments:

> I can understand why some people are opposed to all euthanasia and insist that such infants must be allowed to live. I think I can also understand why other people favor destroying these babies quickly and painlessly. But why should anyone favor letting "dehydration and infection wither a tiny being over hours and days"? The doctrine that says that a baby may be allowed to dehydrate and wither, but may not be given an injection that would end its life without suffering, seems so patently cruel as to require no further refutation.[2]

Rachels's point is that decisions such as the one he describes as "patently cruel" arise out of a misconceived moral distinction between active and passive euthanasia, which in turn rests upon a distinction between killing and letting die that itself has no moral importance.

> One reason why so many people think that there is an important difference between active and passive euthanasia is that they think killing someone is morally worse than letting someone die. But is it? . . . To investigate this issue two cases may be considered that are exactly alike except that one involves killing whereas the other involves letting someone die. Then, it can be asked whether this difference makes any difference to the moral assessments. . . .
>
> In the first, Smith stands to gain a large inheritance if anything should happen to his six-year-old cousin. One evening while the child is taking his bath, Smith sneaks into the bathroom and drowns the child, and then arranges things so that it will look like an accident.
>
> In the second, Jones also stands to gain if anything should happen to his six-year-old cousin. Like Smith, Jones sneaks in planning to drown the child in his bath. However, just as he enters the bathroom Jones sees the child slip and hit his head, and fall

face down in the water. Jones is delighted; he stands by, ready to push the child's head back under if necessary, but it is not necessary. With only a little thrashing about, the child drowns all by himself, "accidentally," as Jones watches and does nothing.[3]

Rachels observes that Smith killed the child, whereas Jones "merely" let the child die. If there's an important moral distinction between killing and letting die, then, we should say that Jones's behavior from a moral point of view is less reprehensible than Smith's. But while the law might draw some distinctions here, it seems clear that the acts of Jones and Smith are not different in any important way, or if there is a difference, Jones's action is even worse.

In essence, then, *the objection to the position adopted by the AMA of Rachels and those who argue like him is that it endorses a highly questionable moral distinction between killing and letting die, which, if accepted, leads to indefensible medical decisions.* Nowhere does Rachels quite come out and say that he favors active euthanasia in some cases, but the implication is clear. Nearly everyone holds that it is sometimes pointless to prolong the process of dying and that in those cases it is morally permissible to let a patient die even though a few hours or days could be salvaged by procedures that would also increase the agonies of the dying. But if it is impossible to defend a general distinction between letting people die and acting, to terminate their lives directly, then it would seem that active euthanasia also may be morally permissible.

A Defense of the Traditional View

Now what shall we make of all this? It *is* cruel to stand by and watch a Down's [syndrome] baby die an agonizing death when a simple operation would remove the intestinal obstruction, but to offer the excuse that in failing to operate we didn't *do* anything to bring about death is an example of moral evasiveness comparable to the excuse Jones would offer for his action of "merely" letting his cousin die. Furthermore, it is true that if someone is trying to bring about the death of another human being, then it makes little difference from the moral point of view if his purpose is achieved by action or by malevolent omission, as in the cases of Jones and Smith.

But if we acknowledge this, are we obliged to give up the traditional view expressed by the AMA statement? Of course not. To begin with, we are hardly obliged to assume the Jones-like role Rachels assigns the defender of the traditional view. We have the option of operating on the Down's baby and saving its life. Rachels mentions that possibility only to hurry past it as if that is not what his opposition would do. But, of course, that is precisely the course of action most defenders of the traditional position would choose.

Secondly, while it may be that the reason some rather confused people give for upholding the traditional view is that they think *killing someone is always worse than letting them die, nobody who gives the matter much thought puts it that way. Rather they say that killing someone is clearly morally worse than not killing them, and killing them can be done by acting to bring about their death or by refusing ordinary means to keep them alive in order to bring about the same goal.*

What I am suggesting is that Rachels's objections leave the position he sets out to criticize untouched. It is worth noting that the jargon of active and passive euthanasia—and it is jargon—does not appear in the resolution. Nor does the resolution state or imply the distinction Rachels attacks, a distinction that puts a moral premium on overt behavior—moving or not moving one's parts—while totally ignoring the intentions of the agent. That no such distinction is being drawn seems clear from the fact that the AMA resolution speaks approvingly of ceasing to use extraordinary means in certain cases, and such withdrawals might easily involve bodily movement, for example unplugging an oxygen machine.

In addition to saddling his opposition with an indefensible distinction it doesn't make, Rachels proceeds to ignore one that it does make—one that is crucial to a just interpretation of the view. Recall the AMA allows the withdrawal of what it calls *extraordinary* means of preserving life; clearly the contrast here is with *ordinary* means. Though in its short statement those expressions are not defined, the definition Paul Ramsey refers to as standard in his book, *The Patient as Person*, seems to fit.

Ordinary means of preserving life are all medicines, treatments, and operations, which offer a reasonable hope of benefit for the patient and which can be obtained and used without excessive expense, pain, and other inconveniences.

Extraordinary means of preserving life are all those medicines, treatments, and operations which cannot be obtained without excessive expense, pain, or other inconvenience, or which, if used, would not offer a reasonable hope of benefit.[4]

Now with this distinction in mind, we can see how the traditional view differs from the position Rachels mistakes for it. *The traditional view is that the intentional termination of human life is impermissible, irrespective of whether this goal is brought about by action or inaction.* Is the action or refraining *aimed* at producing a death? Is the termination of life *sought, chosen or planned?* Is the intention deadly? If so, the act or omission is wrong.

But we all know it is entirely possible that the unwillingness of a physician to use extraordinary means for preserving life may be prompted not by a determination to bring about death, but by other motives. For example, he may realize that further treatment may offer little hope of reversing the dying process and/or be excruciating, as in the case when a massively necrotic bowel condition in a neonate is out of control. The doctor who does what he can to comfort the infant but does not submit it to further treatment or surgery may *foresee* that the decision will hasten death, but it certainly doesn't follow from that fact that he *intends* to bring about its death. It is, after all, entirely possible to foresee that something will come about as a result of one's conduct without intending the consequence or side effect. If I drive downtown, I can foresee that I'll wear out my tires a little, but I don't drive downtown with the intention of wearing out my tires. And if I choose to forego my exercises for a few days, I may think that as a result my physical condition will deteriorate a little, but I don't omit my exercise with a view to running myself down. And if you have to fill a position and select Green, who is better qualified for the post than her rival Brown, you needn't appoint Mrs. Green with the intention of hurting Mr. Brown, though you may foresee that Mr. Brown will feel hurt. And if a

country extends its general education programs to its illiterate masses, it is predictable the suicide rate will go up, but even if the public officials are aware of this fact, it doesn't follow that they initiate the program with a view to making the suicide rate go up. *In general, then, it is not the case that all foreseeable consequences and side effects of our conduct are necessarily intended.* And it is because the physician's withdrawal of extraordinary means can be otherwise motivated than by a desire to bring about the predictable death of the patient that such action cannot categorically be ruled out as wrong.

But the refusal to use ordinary means is an altogether different matter. After all, what is the point of refusing assistance which offers reasonable hope of benefit to the patient without involving excessive pain or other inconvenience? How could it be plausibly maintained that the refusal is not motivated by a desire to bring about the death of the patient? The traditional position, therefore, rules out not only direct actions to bring about death, such as giving a patient a lethal injection, but malevolent omissions as well, such as not providing minimum care for the newborn.

The reason the AMA position sounds so silly when one listens to arguments such as Rachels's is that he slights the distinction between ordinary and extraordinary means and then drums on cases where *ordinary* means are refused. The impression is thereby conveyed that the traditional doctrine sanctions omissions that are morally indistinguishable in a substantive way from direct killings, but then incomprehensibly refuses to permit quick and painless termination of life. If the traditional doctrine would approve of Jones's standing by with a grin on his face while his young cousin drowned in a tub, or letting a Down's baby wither and die when ordinary means are available to preserve its life, it would indeed be difficult to see how anyone could defend it. But so to conceive the traditional doctrine is simply to misunderstand it. It is not a doctrine that rests on some supposed distinction between "active" and "passive euthanasia," whatever those words are supposed to mean, nor on a distinction between moving and not moving our bodies. *It is simply a prohibition against intentional killing, which includes both direct actions and malevolent omissions.*

To summarize—the traditional position represented by the AMA statement is not incoherent. It acknowledges, or more accurately, insists upon the fact that withholding ordinary means to sustain life may be tantamount to killing. The traditional position can be made to appear incoherent only by imposing upon it a crude idea of killing held by none of its more articulate advocates.

Thus the criticism of Rachels and other reformers, misapprehending its target, leaves the traditional position untouched. That position is simply a prohibition of murder. And it is good to remember, as C. S. Lewis once pointed out:

> No man, perhaps, ever at first described to himself the act he was about to do as Murder, or Adultery, or Fraud, or Treachery. . . . And when he hears it so described by other men he is (in a way) sincerely shocked and surprised. Those others "don't understand." If they knew what it had really been like for him, they would not use those crude "stock" names. With a wink or a titter, or a cloud of muddy emotion, the thing has slipped into his will as something not very extraordinary, something of which, rightly understood in all of his peculiar circumstances, he may even feel proud.[5]

I fully realize that there are times when those who have the noble duty to tend the sick and the dying are deeply moved by the sufferings of their patients, especially of the very young and the very old, and desperately wish they could do more than comfort and companion them. Then, perhaps, it seems that universal moral principles are mere abstractions having little to do with the agony of the dying. But of course we do not see best when our eyes are filled with tears.

NOTES

1. *The New England Journal of Medicine*, 292 (January 9, 1975): 78–80.
2. Ibid., pp. 78–79.
3. Ibid., p. 79.
4. Paul Ramsey, *The Patient as Person* (New Haven and London: Yale University Press, 1970), p. 122. Ramsey abbreviates the definition first given by Gerald Kelly, S.J., *Medico-Moral Problems* (St. Louis, Missouri: The Catholic Hospital Association, 1958), p. 126.
5. C. S. Lewis, *A Preface to Paradise Lost* (London and New York: Oxford University Press, 1970), p. 126.

DISCUSSION QUESTIONS:

1. Sullivan accuses Rachels of misunderstanding the AMA policy and the traditional view. Whereas Rachels sees the policy as endorsing a distinction between killing and letting die, Sullivan sees the policy as endorsing a distinction between intentionally killing (or letting die) and non-intentionally killing (or letting die). Which of the two is correct?

2. Sullivan claims that "The traditional view is that the intentional termination of human life is impermissible, irrespective of whether this goal is brought about by action or inaction" (page 572). This principle appears to imply a complete pacifism: it is never morally permissible to intentionally kill or let someone die. Do you think this is correct or do you think that there are some scenarios under which it is morally permissible to intentionally kill or let someone die? What about cases of self-defense, war, abortion, etc.?

3. Sullivan insists that there is a morally relevant difference between doing something to *intentionally* bring about the death of another human being and doing something that you merely *foresee* will bring about the death of another human being (a variation on the Doctrine of Double Effect). For example, it is morally permissible to give a cancer patient a dose of morphine even if you *foresee* that this will shorten her life, but it is morally wrong to give a cancer patient a dose of morphine if you intend to shorten her life. Do you think that there is a morally relevant difference here? If so, can you articulate an argument for this principle?

Argument Reconstruction Exercises:

I. Sullivan spends much of the article reproducing Rachels' reasoning only to show where he thinks it is mistaken. Use the excerpt below to reconstruct Rachels' conclusion for the claim that in some cases active euthanasia is morally permissible.

> Nearly everyone holds that it is sometimes pointless to prolong the process of dying and that in those cases it is morally permissible to let a patient die even though a few hours or days could be salvaged by procedures that would also increase the agonies

of the dying. But if it is impossible to defend a general distinction between letting people die and acting to terminate their lives directly, then it would seem that active euthanasia also may be morally permissible. (page 571)

II. Sullivan ultimately argues that euthanasia—either passive or active—is morally wrong. His argument for this claim relies on a principle about intentions and is stated with the use of rhetorical questions. Under the assumption that all forms of euthanasia are acts or omissions undertaken with the intention of securing the death of the patient, use the following excerpt to construct an argument for the conclusion that euthanasia is morally wrong:

> The traditional view is that the intentional termination of human life is impermissible, irrespective of whether this goal is brought about by action or inaction. Is the action aimed at producing a death? Is the termination of life sought, chosen, or planned? Is the intention deadly? If so, the act or omission is wrong. (page 572)

III. Sullivan seems to appeal to the distinction between ordinary and extraordinary means of preserving life to make a point about the moral permissibility of withdrawing treatment. The catch seems to be that withholding the latter is not indicative of intending the death of a patient whereas withholding the former is. Use the following excerpt to reconstruct an argument for the claim that it is morally wrong to withhold ordinary means of preserving life:

> But we all know it is entirely possible that the unwillingness of a physician to use extraordinary means for preserving life may be prompted not by a determination to bring about death, but by other motives….But the refusal to use ordinary means is an altogether different matter. After all, what is the point of refusing assistance which offers reasonable hope of benefit to the patient without involving excessive pain or other inconvenience? How could it be plausibly maintained that the refusal is not motivated by a desire to bring about the death of the patient? The traditional position, therefore, rules out not only direct actions that bring about death, such as giving a patient a lethal injection, but malevolent omissions as well, such as not providing minimum care for a newborn. (page 572)

IV. Sullivan closes his article by equating euthanasia with murder. He writes that "the criticism of Rachels and other reformers, misapprehending its target, leaves the traditional position untouched. That position is simply a prohibition of murder," (page 573). Can you come up with a simple argument that concludes that all euthanasia is murder?

20.3 SELF-REGARDING SUICIDE: A MODIFIED KANTIAN VIEW

THOMAS E. HILL, JR. (1991)

Thomas E. Hill, Jr. is Kenan Professor of Philosophy at the University of North Carolina-Chapel Hill. He is one of the country's foremost Kant scholars, and his published work includes work in the history of philosophy, social/political philosophy, and applied ethics. In this essay, Hill sidesteps the question of whether or not euthanasia or suicide is ever morally permissible. Instead, he starts with the idea that we often think of suicide as a morally unfortunate event. But why are such cases unfortunate? Hill surveys a number of different types of suicide that we find troubling and claims that each of them can be explained by the following moral principle: the morally ideal person will value life as a rational, autonomous agent for its own sake. Hill develops this principle by appealing to a Kantian moral framework (see Chapter 12.3) that emphasizes the moral importance of autonomy and rationality.

Reading Questions:

1. What is an impulsive suicide?

2. What is an apathetic suicide?

3. What is a self-abasing suicide?

4. What is a hedonistic calculated suicide?

5. What conclusions did Kant draw about the moral permissibility of suicide? Why?

6. What principle does Hill suggest is both in "the spirit of Kant's theory" and helpful in explaining why we find some suicides morally unfortunate?

7. What does it take for a being to be rationally autonomous?

Moral debates about suicide typically focus on the questions of whether suicide and whether we should interfere with suicide attempts. These quest attention to matters such as conflicting rights, social congious belief, and the difficulty of drawing a sharp line between offering in complex cases. My concern will be somewhat different. I want to consider what ideals of attitude toward human life and death may lie behind the common intuition that some suicides are morally objectionable, to some degree, even though not harmful to others and not a violation of anyone's rights.

The puzzling cases arise when the suicide is not failing in his obligations to others, but lacks any overriding moral reason to take his life. He is within his rights and yet his decision still seems morally significant. The issue is not whether suicide is strictly immoral, still less how a sharp line can be drawn between the permissible and the impermissible. The question, rather, is how an ideal person would view such choices. Or, in other words, *what sort of attitudes toward life and death do we, from a moral point of view, want to encourage and see present in those who are moved to consider suicide?*

My suggestion will be that to explain certain common intuitive beliefs on this question we need to move beyond consideration of rights and utility to a qualified Kantian principle about the value of life as a rational autonomous agent. Though I find Kant's rigoristic opposition to suicide untenable, the spirit of his idea of humanity as an end in itself, I think, leads to a more tenable position. This idea, appropriately qualified, opposes attitudes which sometimes

motivate suicide, but does not condemn, in fact it encourages, suicide from other motives in special circumstances. The Kantian idea accords with a view which I believe is widely held in popular thought, though currently unfashionable in philosophy, namely, that moral considerations are not all other-regarding. Though Kant went too far in saying that suicide is always a violation of a duty to oneself, *there is more that a moral person considering suicide needs to think about than his other people.*

My discussion will be divided as follows. First, I state some intuitive beliefs about the sort of cases in which suicide falls short of the morally ideal. These are the intuitions which need to be explained and which prompt us to look beyond rights and utility. Second, I sketch some main points pertinent to suicide in Kant's ethics. Third, I propose a qualified Kantian principle. Fourth, I consider the application of the principle to suicide, indicating how it would support the initial intuitive beliefs about when suicide is objectionable and when it is not.

I. Instances of Morally Unfortunate Suicide

Real life is admittedly more complex than any of our philosophical categories, but to further discussion, I want to focus attention on four specially defined types of suicide. Pure instances are at lease conceivable, though real cases doubtless contain a mixture of elements.

In each case, *we are to imagine that the persons contemplating suicide are free from obligations to others which would be violated or neglected if they choose suicide.* For example, there are no outstanding promises to be kept, no children to care for, no institutional obligations to be met, and so on. Moreover, unlike most actual cases, there are none who will grieve or feel guilt-ridden when they learn of the suicide. As far as anyone can, the persons who choose suicide have already paid their debt of gratitude to the individuals and society who have benefited them, and they have made constructive contributions to charity and other good causes. Perhaps some will say that no one ever discharges his obligation to others, but for present purposes let us suppose that this is not so. The point of setting aside obligations to others in this way is not, of course, to deny their importance in real, typical cases, but simply to isolate other moral considerations which may be relevant.

To further simplify, let us imagine that in the cases we shall consider, there is an absence of the sort of altruistic motives which are often thought to make suicide morally commendable. For example, suicide is not a necessary means to save one's family from disastrous financial costs involved in lingering illness; it is not the only way a spy can keep from betraying his country under torture; it is not a dramatic protest against an unjust war; and so on. *So far as others are concerned, there is no reason for, or against, suicide.*

[1] *Impulsive suicide.* A suicide might be called impulsive if it is prompted by a temporarily intense, yet passing desire or emotion out of keeping with the more permanent character, preferences, and emotional state of the agent. We need not suppose that the agent is "driven" or "blinded" or momentarily insane, but his act is not the sort that coheres with what he most wants and values over time. In calmer, more deliberative moments he would have wished that he would not respond as he did. If he had survived, he would have come to regret his decision. Examples might include cases of lovers who take their lives in moments of intense grief, wealthy businessmen who experience sudden financial disaster and are frightened of facing the world without money, and active, life-loving hedonists enraged at fate when first learning that they have contracted a crippling disease. Some suicides in these circumstances might be rational, but when I refer to suicides as impulsive, I have in mind only those which would have been avoided if the agent had been in full rational control of himself.

[2] *Apathetic suicide.* Sometimes a suicide might result not so much from intense desire or emotion as from apathy. The problem is not overwhelming passion, but absence of passion, lack of interest in what might be done or experienced in a continued life. One can imagine, for example, an extremely depressed person who simply does not care about the future. The causes of his emotional state may lie in personal failure, rejected love, and so on. But what he experiences is not intense shame, anger, fear, etc., but rather emptiness. He may acknowledge that after time, perhaps with psychotherapy and antidepressive drugs, he would again take joy in living. But the thought arouses no current desire to continue living. If his suicide is irrational, it is not because his mind is unclear or his reason swayed by intense emotion.

[3] *Self-abasing suicide.* I call a suicide self-abasing if it results from a sense of worthlessness or unworthiness, which expresses itself not in apathy, but rather in a desire to manifest self-contempt, to reject oneself, to "put oneself down." The motivating attitude is more than an intellectual judgment about one's merits, relative to others or absolutely, according to various standards of morality, social utility, intelligence, etc., though such judgments may be among the causes of the attitude. Particular rejections, failures, and violations of conscience might contribute to the attitude, but it need not be a merely momentary or passing feeling. One's life is seen as having a negative value, not just devoid of things to enjoy, like an empty cupboard, but contemptible, like a despised insect one wants to swat or turn away from in disgust. Such suicide carries a symbolic message, even if only expressed to oneself: "this creature is worth less than nothing." The agent does not irrationally miscalculate whether continued life will bring more joy than misery, for he is not involved in any such calculation. In effect, he denies that he deserves such consideration, even from himself. This is more than self-punishment, which can be a way of acknowledging oneself as a responsible agent and alleviating particular guilt feelings. The self-abasing attitude, on the contrary, says "punishment is too good for me—I should be discarded."

[4] *Hedonistic calculated suicide.* By this I mean suicide that is decided upon as the result of a certain sort of cost/benefit calculation. Seeing that others

will be unaffected by his decision (our simplifying hypothesis), the hedonistic calculator regards his choice as determined by his best estimate of the balance of pleasures and pain he expects to receive under each option. Immediate suicide by a painless method will result in a short, fairly predictable list of pleasures and pains. Continued life will produce a more complex series of experiences more difficult to calculate. Uncertainties cloud the picture and disparate pleasures and pains are hard to weigh against one another with anything like mathematical precision. But, in theory, the problem is seen as simple. One chooses the course that results in the best balance of expected pain and pleasure, taking into account intensity, duration, certainty, etc. More sophisticated calculators may think in terms of preferences and ordinal comparisons, rather than cardinal rankings of sensations, but the central point remains that the value of continued life is seen as a function of the joys and miseries, delights and discomforts, etc., that one is likely to experience. Long life *per se* has no value. But, as long as the pleasure/pain balance is above a certain threshold, the more life the better. When, in one's best estimate, the balance falls irretrievably below the threshold, it is time to end the game. The reason for ending it, like the reason for continuing to live, is to obtain the best balance, over time, of pleasure over pain.

Although these four types of suicide are significantly different, I think that they all reflect an attitude towards life that is less than ideal. This is not to say that suicides of these sorts are wrong or immoral. However, it is meant to imply more than that they are "unfortunate" or that benevolent people would wish that they not occur. My sense is that, though condemnation and blame seem inappropriate, a *person's life story would be morally better if it did not end in one of these ways*. One would not select for emulation a biography which concluded with impulsive, apathetic, self-abasing, or hedonistic calculating suicide. Insofar as one wanted to admire the principal character, one would want to rewrite the ending. . . .

Although I do not want to base any argument on controversial religious premises, it is worth noting that Western religion has often opposed suicide, not simply as against God's commands, but as a failure to treasure the gift of life. Many who come to reject the theological belief that life is literally a "gift" from God, or that we are mere trustees of God's property, still retain a secular analogue of this view. The spirit of thanksgiving, for example, is felt by many who no longer believe in any superhuman person to whom they can literally express gratitude. Doubtless some will attribute this to traces of prior belief, like residual guilt feelings for blasphemy in those who no longer believe in God. Yet this may not be the whole story. Often when moral feelings, seemingly unsupported otherwise, are attributed to religion as the source, I suspect that the reverse may be so. That is, deeply rooted moral beliefs whose grounds are hard to articulate lend support to the religions that offer a story to explain them. Theology is not so much the cause as the outcome. Be that as it may, the main point for present purposes is that it is not a remote and unfamiliar thought that suicide is morally significant because of the attitude it reflects about life, independently of its social consequences and its impact on rights. . . .

II. Kant and Suicide

Taking these intuitive reflections for now as given, let us consider what general moral principle, or principles, might underlie them, accounting for our objections to the first four sorts of cases. Principles regarding human rights are unlikely candidates to account for these cases, because the intuitions we wish to explain concern attitudes falling short of an ideal, not wrongs done to others. Utilitarian considerations might be cited in several cases (for example, impulsive and apathetic suicide), but seem not to be the whole story. The self-abaser, for example, seems to have a less than ideal attitude, quite aside from whether he or others would be happier if he changed. The calculated suicide seems to miss something, just because he considers nothing but utility. Even if (as seems doubtful) utilitarian reflection would always oppose the objectionable attitudes in (1)—(4), I think it is implausible that this adequately reflects our *reasons* for opposing those attitudes, for I suspect we sense the defects in the attitudes while still uncertain about the consequences (for example, whether the depressed person will really be happier if he continues to live). Sophisticated utilitarians may yet come up with explanations,[1] but my doubts are sufficient to lead me to explore in another direction.

An obvious alternative is Kant's moral theory.[2] *My suggestion will be that, though inadequate as it stands, Kant's theory points towards a principle which could ground the intuitive beliefs about suicide which we have just considered.*

The tenets of Kant's moral theory which I think are particularly important to the topic of suicide can be summarized as follows:

[1] In trying to decide whether one should do something, it is extremely important to determine what one's intentions and policies would be in doing it. These, together with one's underlying motive for having those intentions and policies, are what determine the kind of moral worth one's action will have.

[2] An essential feature of our humanity is that we are rational agents with autonomy of the will. This does not mean that we always act rationally or that we always manifest our autonomy, but it does imply that we have certain capacities and predispositions. These include the following: (a) practical reason applied to the satisfaction of our desires: that is, a capacity and disposition to pursue our ends in accord with "hypothetical imperatives," to set ourselves goals and follow informed policies about the best means to achieve them; (b) negative freedom: that is, the ability to act in accord with principles or policies without being fully determined to do so by desires or any external causal factors; (c) positive freedom or autonomy: that is, setting oneself principles and values which stem purely from one's nature as a rational being uncaused and unmotivated by one's desires or any external factors; (d) a predisposition to value one's humanity, or one's nature as a rational and free being, as an "end in itself": that is, to value the preservation, development, exercise, and honoring of one's rational nature independently of benefits and costs measured in terms of pleasure and pain or desire-satisfaction.

[3] All moral considerations are ultimately grounded in our nature as rational beings with autonomy. For example, we are unconditionally obligated to follow the principles and values which we set ourselves as rational and positively free (see (2) c); and nothing else, such as tradition, religious or secular authority, natural instinct, etc., can be the ultimate ground of obligation.

[4] A fundamental moral principle, one to which any rational being with autonomy would commit himself, is: always act so that you treat humanity (that is, autonomy and rationality) never simply as a means, but always as an end in itself (that is, as something with "unconditional and incomparable worth").[3] This applies to "humanity" in oneself as well as in others. The arguments for this are several, but none appeals to the ideas of social utility or maximum satisfaction for the agent.

On the basis of these claims, Kant draws a double conclusion concerning the moral character of suicide.

[5] Suicide (at least suicide for the reasons Kant imagined) is opposed to the principle of humanity as an end in itself stated in (4) above because it "throws away" and degrades humanity in oneself. Thus, suicide expresses an attitude that one's nature as a rational, autonomous person is not of "incomparable worth" and "above all price." Suicide to end pain, for example, places cessation of pain, which is a mere "relative" and "conditioned" value, above rationality and autonomy, which (Kant says) have worth that "admits no equivalent."

[6] *Suicide, therefore, is always, or nearly always, wrong.* In fact, it is contrary to a "perfect ethical duty to oneself." This duty is a stringent prohibition, concerned with motives acts attitudes and not merely intentional "external acts," which is grounded in the value of one's own humanity rather than in regard for others.[4]

These views of Kant's—both the tenets of his moral theory and the conclusions he draws concerning suicide—have provoked much controversy. . .

Re the conclusions concerning suicide, (5) and (6): Kant's view that suicide is always, or nearly always, contrary to a perfect duty to oneself provokes objections on at least two counts. First, that suicide is often justified (for example, to end gross irremediable pain) Second, that, because a person cannot violate his own rights, duties *to* oneself, in a strict sense, are impossible. Both objections, however, would be met if we accepted a qualified position, which remains in line with (5) above yet is consonant with previous modifications of Kant's view. One might hold, for example, that suicide *from certain attitudes* is always, or nearly always, objectionable, at least a falling short of a moral ideal, and that this is not solely because it is contrary to the welfare or rights of others. This would allow that some suicides are justified and even commendable, but suicides rooted in certain attitudes (for example, undervaluation of rational, autonomous human life) would be opposed. They would be opposed, not strictly condemned as immoral; and they would be opposed as out of line with an ideal moral attitude toward one's life, not as a violation of a strict duty to oneself.

III. Kant and the Value of Life

Suppose, then, that we accepted the spirit of Kant's theory but adopted the qualifications mentioned above. What sort of principle might remain, and how would it apply to important choices aside from matters of life and death?

The principle I propose to consider is this: *A morally ideal person will value life as a rational, autonomous agent for its own sake, at least provided that the life does not fall below a certain threshold of gross, irremediable, and uncompensated pain and suffering.*

The main task in explaining the principle is to give some sense to the idea of "life as a rational, autonomous agent," but first some preliminary comments are in order.

First, the principle expresses an ideal rather than a duty. Thus questions of blame, censure, and enforcement associated with violations of duty are not at issue here. Also the principle is not meant to be absolute or unconditional. Other moral considerations, even other ideals, might override it in some circumstances. It is intended as at least one consideration in a pluralistic ethics which admits the need for judgment in weighing considerations of quite different sorts.

In the same spirit the "certain threshold" of pain and suffering is admittedly left indeterminate. At extreme points, one hopes, there will be agreement, but no precise guidelines can be given to settle borderline cases. This indeterminacy, however, should not be confused with vacuousness. Nor should it be supposed that this qualification regarding extreme circumstances implies that in normal circumstances rational, autonomous living should be valued for the sake of pleasure (or a favorable pleasure/pain ratio). The qualification is meant to reflect the idea that although the value of rational, autonomous living is not a function of the pleasure and pain it brings, a sufficiently gross level of suffering can undermine that value, making the sufferer incapable of finding that life meaningful or even tolerable.

The principle is not meant to suggest more than it says. In particular, it does not imply that life has value *only* when rational and autonomous. Nor does the qualification strictly imply that life has *no* value when consumed with gross, irremediable, and uncompensated pain. These matters are left open.

To say that rational, autonomous living is ideally valued for its own sake is to say that, ideally, it is seen as valuable independently of various ends to which it might serve as a means or necessary condition: for example, the general welfare, the greater enjoyment of the agent, the development of culture, or the maintenance of democratic institutions. What is not implied, once again, is that rational, autonomous living is the only good, the complete good, or an unconditional good.

The principle holds that one should value all rational, autonomous life, not simply one's own. Typically, perhaps, a person comes to value his own rational, autonomous life first and foremost, but ideally identification with others and the spirit of a moral point of view will in time lead him to value for others what he has come to prize for himself. Whether an ideal person is completely impartial, valuing the lives of all rational autonomous agents to exactly the same degree, is not determined, one way of the other, by our principle. The point is that all such lives are to be valued independently of various consequences, not that they are always to be prized equally. . . .

These preliminaries aside, the more difficult task is to say what is meant by "life as a rational, autonomous agent." Here I can only sketch the beginnings of an account that obviously needs further development.

First, following Kant, I think of rationality and autonomy as capacities and dispositions which belong to virtually all adult and nearly adult, human beings. Though they may be developed and exercised to greater or lesser degrees, basic rationality and autonomy are not special characteristics of an educated elite. They are features which distinguish virtually all human beings from lower animals.

Second, rational autonomy includes some minimum capacity and disposition to see causal connections (for example, to understand what will happen if one does this or that); to be aware of a variety of wants, for both future states of affairs as well as present ones; to set oneself ends and adopt policies and plans to achieve them; to revise ends and policies in the light of new information; to form and alter goals and policies in response to one's own deepest wants and values, to some extent independent of blind adherence to tradition, authority, and the opinions of others; and to resist immediate temptation in the pursuit of adopted ends, values, and policies.

Third, in saying that an agent is autonomous, I mean in part that he can, within a wide area of life, choose what to value and what not to value without contravening any fixed, objective, preset order of values in the world. As Kant, Sartre, and others have maintained, an autonomous person is a "creator of values," not merely a discoverer of values, at least within a wide range of morally permissible choice.[5] Within that range, we may choose to value some things, and to disvalue others, for their own sakes. Contrary to Moorean intuitionists, intrinsic values do not exist as properties in the world. They are not so much perceived as chosen.

Fourth, an autonomous agent is not restricted to pleasure and pain in what he can value. This is not a point about the causes of valuing, but rather about its scope. That is, human beings, so far as they are autonomous, have the capacity and disposition to care for things other than pleasant and painful experiences. This is not simply a denial of psychological egoism, as traditionally conceived. It is also a denial of psychological hedonism, that is, the view that human beings, whether egoistic or altruistic, can attribute intrinsic value only to pleasure and intrinsic disvalue only to pain. This idea of autonomy, which is found in such diverse thinkers as Kant, Sartre, and Nietzsche, is not so much an assertion of the high-mindedness of human beings as their wide-ranging capacity to form values. It is illustrated not merely in moral commitment and single-minded pursuit of truth, but also in more mundane concerns about what others are saying behind our backs and what is happening to our favorite forest flowers when no one is there to see them. To care about such matters is not the same as caring about their possible consequences or even about the pleasure or pain we may get in contemplating them.

Finally, it should be noted that rational autonomy, as conceived here, is not possession of rights to control one's life, not Sartrean freedom from all objective moral constraints, and not a pure Kantian will independent of all causation and desire. What is intended is a more modest set of capacities, which contrast not with causally explainable moral choices or objective moral constraints, but rather with being governed completely by instinct, being a creature of impulse without goals or policies, having an utterly incoherent set of goals and policies, being unable to follow through on one's own policies and principles, being blindly obedient to the commands or expectations of others, being rigidly bound to unrevisable self-commands, being bound in all one's choices to values one sees as fixed apart from oneself, and being unable to care about anything for its own sake except pleasure and pain. . . .

IV. Applying the Kantian Principle

The modified Kantian principle we have been considering has obvious implications regarding issues in everyday life quite aside from suicide. For example, it tends to oppose drug use which seriously impairs a healthy person's capacities to think and take charge of his life. It commends the development of one's capacities for rational self-control, not simply for the results, but because this is a natural expression of valuing for their own sake one's capacities as a rational autonomous agent.[6] The principle would urge self-respect in the sense of keeping our day-to-day choices in line with the personal standards we set for ourselves,[7] for we are not fully self-governing when our actions fail to match the values we profess to ourselves. In dealing with others, we would be urged to respect their own choices within a range of morally permissible conduct. To place their comfort or happiness above their own declared values (as is often done in benevolent lies) would not be to value them as autonomous agents. There would be a strong presumption against killing human beings in most circumstances. But euthanasia for those who have lost the capacity for even minimally rational, autonomous living would not be ruled out.

Regarding suicide, the Kantian principle, I think, distinguishes cases in just the way I initially proposed. The impulsive suicide, for example, falls short of the ideal in two ways. He places comparatively little value on his continued existence as an autonomous agent, as shown by his willingness to give this up to satisfy a momentary impulse. Further, he makes his choice in an irrational manner, being guided by a passing feeling out of keeping with the more enduring features of his character and personality. He both loses self-control and destroys his potentially controlling self. The apathetic suicide may not reach his decision in an irrational manner, but he chooses to treat his continuing potential to make a life as if it were virtually worthless —he throws it away even in the absence of strong impulses and concerns about his future. The deficiency is not in his feelings (lack of a felt wish to live), but in his policies. His act says, "Others aside, I stand for nothing. My potential to author a life means nothing to me, given that I see no future states that I now feel a desire for."

The self-abasing suicide even more dramatically undervalues his capacities for rational, autonomous living, for he views his life as worth less than nothing. He takes the perspective that the worth of life is measured entirely by one's record and, even more, he denies the possibility that he can make the whole story meaningful by future action; he attributes no value to living as the author of his life. Given his value assumptions, his decision may be rational; but it is not a decision that counts his being rational and autonomous as valuable. For him, all personal worth must be earned, and this attitude is incompatible with valuing life as an autonomous agent for its own sake.

Finally, the hedonistic, calculating suicide is opposed to our Kantian principle because he treats life as a rational, autonomous agent as a derivative value, good only because and so long as it is needed to achieve the ultimate end of maximum pleasure/pain balance. The ultimate values are fixed, not chosen. The prospective content of continued life entirely determines whether it is worthwhile. The pertinent question is, "What will I get?" not "What can I make of it?"

Contrast these cases with suicides that are intuitively unobjectionable. Suicides to avoid living in a subhuman condition do not contravene our principle, because the life that is ended lacks the potential for rational, autonomous agency. Troublesome questions may arise about what exact point in a gradual decline marks the end of "human" life, but, though practically difficult, these present no objections to the main point of the Kantian principle, which is that ideally what is valued is life with certain human potential, not merely being alive. Suicides to end gross, irremediable pain are not opposed to the principle, if the pain is such that it renders a person incapable of making any significant use of his human capacities. To end one's life in these conditions need not express the attitude that rational, autonomous living has no value in itself. It may simply show that one does not hold this value unconditionally and above all else.

Finally, suicide as the only way to avoid a life seen as demeaning and contrary to one's personal standards does not express an attitude inconsistent with the Kantian principle. To be sure, one cuts short the time one could live as a rational, autonomous agent; but doing so can be a manifestation of autonomy, an ultimate decision of the author of a life story to conclude it with a powerful expression of ideals he autonomously chose to live by. The principle affirms a presumption in favor of continued life as long as one's capacities are intact. But we cannot consistently maintain the value of autonomous living without admitting that, under some conditions, autonomously chosen values require one to make the choice that excludes all further choices. If you value being an author and have just one story to write, you should not hurry to conclude it. But sometimes, to give it the meaning you intend, you must end it before you spoil it. . . .

NOTES

1. Modifications in classic utilitarianism include G. E. Moore's "ideal utilitarianism" in *Principia Ethica* (1960) and *Ethics* (1967), Mill's introduction of "qualities" of pleasure in *Utilitarianism*, and rule-utilitarianism of several types.

2. Here I draw from several of Kant's works, especially the *Groundwork of the Metaphysic of Morals* (tr. H. J. Paton, Harper & Row, 1909, pp. 80–116) and *The Metaphysical Principles of Virtue: Part II of the Metaphysic of Morals* (tr. James Ellington, Bobbs Merrill, 1981, pp. 82–85). Suicide is also discussed in Kant's *Lectures on Ethics* (tr. Louis Infield, Harper & Row, 1930, pp. 147–159). My summary concerns less the details of his remarks about suicide than the aspects of his general theory that have important implications regarding suicide. I intentionally omit Kant's unpersuasive argument from the first formula of the Categorical Imperative, *Groundwork*, p. 89.

3. My understanding of this principle is explained in "Humanity as an End in Itself," *Ethics* 91 (October 1980), pp. 84–99.

4. In the *Metaphysics of Morals*, *Kant* leaves open "casuistical questions" about whether taking one's life is wrong in certain extreme cases (for example, anticipation of an unjust death sentence or of madness and death from the bite of a rabid dog). In the *Lectures on Ethics* (tr. Louis Infield, Harper & Row, 1930), he says only Cato's heroic suicide has given the world opportunity to defend suicide. But even that was a violation of himself and so not really noble (pp. 149, 153). In the *Lectures*, Kant also remarks that "life is not to be highly regarded for its own sake" (p. 150), which seems paradoxical. But a close reading, I think, shows that the point is that mere life (including life contrary to duty, life as a beast, etc.) is not what one should value highly. It is rather life as a rational, autonomous, and moral agent.

5. Sartre and Kane differ, of course, on the sense in which we "create values." Kane held that moral principles are self-imposed by our nature as free rational beings, while the value of nonmoral "relative ends," within the limits of these principles, stems from the personal preferences of individuals. Sartre sees all values as created by individual choices, free from all objective rational constraints.

6. Sometimes we value a capacity solely because its employment produces results we like. But sometimes the results of employing a capacity are valued simply as manifestations of an admired capacity. Kant's view of rational autonomy in persons is more nearly the latter attitude, I think. We honor the capacity in all, even those who neglect it. We want all to use it, not to achieve some independently valued result, but because it is too splendid a thing to leave unused (or to misuse or abuse).

7. A fuller account of this sort of self-respect is attempted in my "Self-Respect Reconsidered".

DISCUSSION QUESTIONS:

1. Do you know anyone in your own life who has committed suicide? How did this person's death make you feel? Do you think that his or her death was deficient or unfortunate from a moral point of view? If so, how do you explain this fact? On the one hand, you may think that the person acted wrongly by committing suicide. If so, what moral duty did he or she violate? On the other hand, you may not think that it's a matter of acting wrongly but instead agree with Hill that it was a case in which the person's life story would have been morally better. If so, how?

2. Hill attempts to craft a fine distinction in this article. He doesn't want to say that the sorts of suicides that he's concerned with are morally wrong, but he thinks that they are morally deficient or unfortunate nonetheless. Does this make any sense? If it is morally permissible for an agent to do something, then how could it be morally unfortunate if he does it? How could an action be morally deficient without being morally wrong? What kind of normative ethical frameworks (e.g., Kantian, utilitarian, virtue-based) can make sense out of this distinction?

3. The moral principle that Hill uses to explain the troubling cases of suicide rests on the notion that a morally ideal person will value a rational, autonomous life. Why, though, is autonomy so valuable? One answer is that it allows us to set our own rules and goals in life (*auto* = self, *nomos* = laws/rules). But suppose a rational agent adopted the goal of killing herself. Wouldn't taking her autonomy seriously rationally require that she carry through with this goal? And if so, how could her action be morally deficient?

Argument Reconstruction Exercises:

I. The work of Immanuel Kant is Hill's inspiration for his principle showing how some suicides are morally deficient. Using Hill's analysis, recreate Kant's reasoning for the conclusion that suicide is always, or nearly always, morally wrong:

> A fundamental moral principle, one to which any rational being with autonomy would commit himself, is: always act so that you treat humanity

(that is, autonomy and rationality), never simply as a means, but always as an end in itself (that is, as something with "unconditional and incomparable worth"). This applies to "humanity" in oneself as well as in others. . . . Suicide (at least for the reasons Kant imagined), is opposed to the principle of humanity as an end in itself . . . because it "throws away" and degrades humanity in oneself . . . Suicide, therefore, is always, or nearly always, wrong. (page 578)

II. One common objection to Kant that is briefly mentioned by Hill relies on the idea that it makes no sense to say that we have duties to ourselves because we cannot violate our own rights. See if you can take the following objection and turn it into an argument that concludes first that no one has a duty to himself not to commit suicide and ultimately that it is not the case that suicide is always, or nearly always, wrong.

> Regarding the conclusions concerning suicide... Kant's view that suicide is always, or nearly always, contrary to a perfect duty to oneself provokes objections on at least two counts...Second, that, because a person cannot violate his own rights, duties to oneself, in a strict sense, are impossible. (page 578)

III. The thesis of Hill's essay is a moral principle that he thinks explains some otherwise puzzling moral appraisals of certain suicide cases. He doesn't argue for this principle directly. Instead, he argues for it by inference to the best explanation. See if you can construct the overall argumentative structure of his paper using the following excerpts as guidelines:

> The puzzling cases [of suicide] arise when the suicide is not failing in his obligations to others, but lacks any overriding moral reason to take his life. . . what sort of attitudes toward life and death do we, from a moral point of view, want to encourage and see present in those who are moved to consider suicide? My suggestion will be that to explain certain common intuitive beliefs on this question, we need to move beyond considerations of rights and utility to a qualified Kantian principle about the value of life as a rational autonomous agent. (page 575)

> The principle I propose to consider is this: A morally ideal person will value life as a rational, autonomous agent for its own sake, at least provided that the life does not fall below a certain threshold of gross, irremediable, and uncompensated pain and suffering. (page 579)

IV. Hill sets aside cases in which suicides are morally wrong because of a failure in our obligations to others. Reconstruct the argument below.

> To have an obligation to someone else means that you ought to do something for that person. If you did something wrong, it's because you didn't do what you ought to have done for others. But what about people who have no obligations to others? In that case, suicide can't be morally wrong.

20.4 BUDDHIST VIEWS OF SUICIDE AND EUTHANASIA

CARL B. BECKER (1990)

Carl Becker is a professor in the Graduate School of Human and Environmental Studies at Kyoto University, Japan. His work focuses on unique Japanese or Buddhist responses to philosophical problems, including issues in contemporary ethics and bioethics. In this article, Becker surveys contemporary Japanese attitudes toward death, suicide, and euthanasia and shows that some, but not all, of these attitudes are consistent with a Buddhist ethic. He recounts relevant features in the corpus of Buddhist and samurai teaching to sketch an account of when suicide is morally permissible and when it is wrong. According to this tradition, the moral permissibility of suicides often turned on features such as the inability to avoid suffering or the state of mind of the person considering suicide.

Reading Questions:

1. According to Becker, why do many Japanese reject the brain-death criteria?

2. According to Buddhist tradition, why is the manner of dying at the moment of death important?

3. Why doesn't Buddhism see death as the end of one's existence?

4. According to Becker's interpretation of the Buddhist tradition, what does the moral acceptability of a suicide depend on?

5. What is the Pure Land?

6. What is *seppuku*?

7. Why does Becker think that samurai suicides are similar to contemporary instances of euthanasia?

8. How might a case of painkilling drugs that blur the mind cause a moral dilemma for Buddhist teaching on the moral permissibility of euthanasia?

Bioethics and Brain Death: The Recent Discussion In Japan

Japanese scholars of ethics and religions have been slow to come to grips with issues of bioethics, suicide, and death with dignity. Although the practical problems are frequently addressed in the popular press, and scattered citizen groups are beginning to draw attention to the issues, few people outside of the medical community have seriously addressed these issues.[1] As one recent representative example of this situation, consider the 39th annual meeting of the Japan Ethics Association (the academic association of ethicists from the entire country) held at Waseda University in October of 1988. . . .

The majority of the participants agreed with Anzai Kazuhiro's early presentation that brain death should not be equated with human death.[2] Anzai's reasoning runs as follows: If brain death implies human death, then, by contraposition, human life must imply conscious (brain) life. Now there are clearly segments of our lives in which we are alive but not always conscious. Therefore it is wrong to conclude that a human is dead because he or she lacks consciousness. Of course, this argument can be faulted for collapsing conscious life and brain life, and for failing to distinguish periods of unconsciousness with the expectation of future revival

(like deep sleep) from periods of unconsciousness with no expectation of future revival (like irreversible coma). But it is representative of a widely seen Japanese rejection of brain-death criteria.

This rejection comes partly from the Japanese association of brain-death criteria with organ transplantation. Many Japanese continue to manifest a distaste for organ transplantation, a distaste which dates back to Confucian teachings that the body, a gift from heaven and from one's parents, must be buried whole, and never cut. For this reason, dissections and autopsies were late in coming to Japan, not widely permitted until the nineteenth century.

The modern Japanese practices of universal cremation, of surgical operations, and of flying to other countries to have organ transplants all have superseded the old Confucian prejudice against body-cutting. However, there remains a fear that if brain-death criteria were widely accepted, less conservative elements of society might abuse it for the sake of the "distasteful" practice of organ transplantation.

In his keynote address about Buddhist ethics, Tsukuba Professor Shinjō Kawasaki implied that this rejection of brain-death criteria may also be grounded in a Buddhist view of life and death.[3] He cited the *Visuddhimagga*, which indicates that life energy (*ayus*) is supported by body warmth and conscious faculties (broadly interpretable to include reflexes).[4] If either body heat or reflexes remain, then a person cannot be considered dead. Now Buddhism admits situations (such as meditative trances or hypothermia) in which neither body warmth nor reflexes are externally detectable, but the subject is not yet dead. So lack of warmth and reflexes is a necessary but not sufficient indicator of death; if either persists, it can be said that the body is not yet dead. In other words, Buddhism does not equate life with warmth and reflexes, but holds that body heat and reflexes are the "supports" of life, and therefore life cannot be empirically measurable except through such variables. Kawasaki also reaffirms the widespread Japanese Buddhist view that death is not the end of life, but merely a brief transition to another state, commonly thought to last for forty-nine days, intermediate between life in this body and life in the next. The reluctance to dismiss a body as "dead" prior to its loss of warmth and reflexes is not based on a fear of personal extinction or annihilation, but rather on a Buddhist view of the basic components of the life system.[5]

Chiba's Iida Tsunesuke expands this view by arguing that "persons are not merely the meaningless 'subjects of rights,' but personalities, 'faces' embodying the possibilities of fulfilling the dreams of their parents or loved ones . . . recipients of love, and therefore worthy of honoring."[6] This argument begs the question of "possibilities," since in the case of brain-dead victims, it is precisely such possibilities which are missing. Logically speaking, the "possibilities" argument has long ago been laid to rest by philosophers like Mary Anne Warren, who have demonstrated that we need not treat potential presidents as presidents, potential criminals as criminals, or potential humans as humans.[7] (Japanese society might differ in this respect; until recently, suspicion of crime or likelihood of committing crime were sufficient grounds for arrest, and children of nobles (potential lords) were often honored or killed as real lords.)[8]

However, Iida's argument is important less for its logical persuasion than for its revelation of the Japanese attitude: that *persons are not subjects with rights and individual free wills, but rather objects of the attentions of others.* (Japanese treatment of infants and children reinforces this view that

Japanese children are seen not as persons but as possessions of their parents; this was the legal as well as philosophical status of women and servants as well as children prior to the twentieth century.)

This position is further developed by Ohara Nobuos, who argues that "although a body may be treated as a 'thing' or a corpse by physicians, it remains a body of value and meaning, and in that sense, a *person*, to members of its family. . . . In this sense, even vegetative humans and brain-dead corpses can give joy to other people."[9] Of course this point of view is pregnant with problems which Ohara himself seems loath to acknowledge. Only in the most metaphorical of senses can a corpse "give" anything to anyone; rather, it is the family who may *derive* some sense of joy by beholding the face of one dear to them, even though that person is incapable of ever being conscious in that body again.

This attitude is akin to the Japanese reverence for pictures, sculptures, and myths; it provides no useful guidelines whatsoever to the medical faculty as to when to continue or desist from what kinds of treatment for the patient. To the question "When does a body stop being a person?" the Oharan answer, "It never stops being a person to those who love it," may be psychologically correct for some people, but is a dead end in medical ethics, for it fails to answer the question, "When should a body be treated not as a living person but as a dead body?"

Moreover, even if it were thought to have some utility in the case where relatives or "significant others" remain alive and concerned with the fate of the deceased, it values the person (or corpse) entirely in terms of his value *to others*. In cases where old people die alone and uncared for, the absence of concerned others leaves the medical practitioner utterly without guidelines. (This is consistent with the frequently noted proposition that Japanese without social contexts seem morally at a loss.)[10]

This position also presumes a wishful naïveté on the part of the parent or family, a failure to distinguish between a living human with a potential for interaction and a dead body with only the resemblance of a loved one. This may not bother many Japanese parents, for whom children are indeed "objects." In fact, there are "rehabilitation hospitals" in Japan in which anencephalic infants are cared for and raised for as many years as their parents' finances and interest dictate; they are propped up and made to "greet" their parents whenever the parents desire to visit.[11]

Such unwillingness to admit the finality of death or the fundamental suffering of the human condition runs counter to the basic tenets of Buddhism. We are reminded of the famous story of the woman who asked the Buddha to revive her baby. In response, the Buddha instructed her to ask for food from any house in which no one had died. In the process of asking around the entire village, the woman came to realize that all humans must die and deal with death. In this way she gained enlightenment, stopped grieving for her dead child, and became a follower of the Buddha. The relatives who refuse to pronounce dead a relative as long as he has a "face," or the parents who insist on artificially prolonging the appearance of life of an anencephalic infant, cannot claim to understand Buddhism.

A much larger misunderstanding lurks behind the whole discussion between "brain-death advocates" and "brain-death opposers" in Japan. The real issue is not whether or not every body should immediately be scavenged for spare parts as soon as its brain is iso-electric, as some opponents would purport. Rather, the question is whether it is ever acceptable to desist from treatment after brain death (turning the hospital's valuable and limited resources to other waiting patients). In the absence of brain-death criteria, many otherwise hopeless bodies remain on artificial support systems almost indefinitely. Even if brain-death criteria were accepted, nothing would prevent families from finding hospitals which would preserve the bodies of their beloved on artificial support systems indefinitely, nor would anything require organ donation if the patient and family did not desire it. *Thus the issue, like that of suicide and euthanasia, is not "Should everyone be forced to follow these criteria?" but rather "May people who desire it be allowed to follow these criteria?"* Groundless fears of widespread organ sales or piracy have made this issue into a much greater hobgoblin than it ever needed to become.

This is not merely to criticize the recently voiced positions of Japanese ethicists. Rather, I introduce this body of evidence to demonstrate the slow growth of Japanese thought in bioethics, and particularly their concerns with *bodies of value to others* rather than with *subjects of value to themselves.* This concern finds no support either in Japanese Buddhism nor in samurai teaching, but on the level of popular belief, it may have serious ramifications for Japanese bioethics for many generations to come. . . .

Buddhists have a big contribution to make to the humanization and naturalization of medicine and bioethics. I may not speak for all of Japanese Buddhism, but I shall be happy if this article inspires further dialogue and contributions from the Japanese Buddhist side.

Early Buddhist Views of Death, Suicide, and Euthanasia

Japan has long been more aware of and sensitive to the dying process than modern Western cultures. Moreover, Japan already has its own good philosophical and experiential background to deal effectively with "new" issues of bioethics, such as euthanasia. *Japanese Buddhists have long recognized what Westerners are only recently rediscovering: that the manner of dying at the moment of death is very important.* This fundamental premise probably predates Buddhism itself, but is made very explicit in the teachings of the Buddha.[12] In his meditations, the Buddha noticed that even people with good karma were sometimes born into bad situations, and even those with bad karma sometimes found inordinately pleasant rebirths. Buddha declared that *the crucial variable governing rebirth was the nature of the consciousness at the moment of death.* Thereafter, Buddhists placed high importance on holding the proper thoughts at the moment of death. Many examples of this idea can be found in two works of the Theravada canon, the *Petavatthu* and the *Vimānavatthu* ("Stories of the Departed"). Indeed, in many sutras, monks visit laymen on their deathbeds to ensure that their dying thoughts are wholesome,[13] and the Buddha recommends that lay followers similarly encourage each other on such occasions.[14]

Buddhism sees death as not the end of life, but simply a transition; suicide is therefore no escape from anything. Thus, in the early *saṅgha* (community of followers of the Buddha), suicide was in principle condemned as an inappropriate action.[15]

But the early Buddhist texts include many cases of suicide which the Buddha himself accepted or condoned. For example, the suicides of Vakkali[16] and of Channa[17] were committed in the face of painful and irreversible sickness. It is significant, however, that the Buddha's praise of the suicides is *not* based on the fact that they were in terminal states, but rather that their minds were selfless, desireless, and enlightened at the moments of their passing.

This theme is more dramatically visible in the example of Godhika. This disciple repeatedly achieved an advanced level of *samādhi*, bordering on *parinitvāna*, and then slipped out of the state of enlightenment into normal consciousness again. After this happened six times, Godhika at last vowed to pass on to the next realm while enlightened, and quietly committed suicide during his next period of enlightenment. While cautioning his other disciples against suicide, the Buddha nonetheless blessed and praised Godhika's steadiness of mind and purpose, and declared that he had passed on to *nirvāna*. In short, *the acceptability of suicide, even in the early Buddhist community, depended not on terminal illness alone, but upon the state of selfless equanimity with which one was able to pass away.* It is interesting in passing that all these suicides were committed by the subject knifing himself, a technique which came to be standardized in later Japanese ritual suicide. . . .

In summary, Buddhism realizes that death is not the end of anything, but a transition. *Buddhism has long recognized persons' rights to determine when they should move on from this existence to the next. The important consideration here is not whether the body lives or dies, but whether the mind can remain at peace and in harmony with itself.* The Jōdo (Pure Land) tradition tends to stress the continuity of life, while the Zen tradition tends to stress the importance of the time and manner of dying. Both of these ideas are deeply rooted in the Japanese consciousness.

Religious Suicide and Death with Dignity in Japan

Japanese Buddhists demonstrated an unconcern with death even more than their neighbors. Japanese valued peace of mind and honor of life over length of life. While the samurai often committed suicide on the battlefield or in court to preserve their dignity in death, countless commoners chose to commit suicide in order to obtain a better future life in the Pure Land. On some occasions, whole masses of people committed suicide at the same time. In others, as in the situation depicted in Kurosawa's famous film "Red Beard," a poverty-stricken family would commit suicide in order to escape unbearable suffering in this life and find a better life in the world to come. Often parents would kill their children first, and then kill themselves; this kind of *shinjū* can still be seen in Japan today. The issue for us today is: how does Buddhism appraise such suicide in order to gain heavenly rebirth?

On a popular level, the desire to "leave this dirty world and approach the Pure Land" (*Enri edo, gongu jōdo*) was fostered by wandering itinerant monks such as Kuya in the Heian period, and Ippen[1] in the Kamakura period. The tradition of committing suicide by entering a river or west-facing seashore apparently began in the Kumano area, but rapidly spread throughout the nation along with the Pure Land faith upon which it was based. The common tradition was to enter the water with a rope tied around one's waist, held by one's retainers or horse.[18] If one's nerve and single-minded resolution failed, then one would not achieve rebirth in the Pure Land as desired. In such an instance, either the suicide himself, or his retainers (judging from his countenance), might pull him out of the water and save him from dying with inappropriate thoughts. However, if the suicide retained a peaceful and unperturbed mind and countenance throughout the drowning, the retainers were to let him die in peace, and simply retain the body for funeral purposes. Such situations clearly demonstrate that what is at stake here is not the individual's right to die, but rather his ability to die with peace of mind. If death with a calm mind is possible, then it is not condemned.

A paradigmatic example of this situation can be found in the records of Saint Ippen.[19] Ajisaka Nyūdō, a Pure Land aspirant possibly of noble descent, gave up his home and family to follow the teachings of Saint Ippen. For unclear reasons, Ippen refused him admission to his band of itinerant mendicants, but advised him that the only way to enter the Pure Land was to die holding the Nembutsu (name and figure of Amida) in mind. Nyūdō then committed suicide by drowning himself in the Fuji River.

The scene is vividly depicted in the scroll paintings.[20] Here, Ajisaka is seen with a rope around his waist. His attendants on the shore hold one end of the rope. As he bobs above the current, he is seen perfectly preserving the *gasshō* position, at peace and in prayer. Music is heard from the purple clouds above him, a common sign of Ōjō, or rebirth in the Pure Land.

When Ippen heard of this suicide, he praised Ajisaka's faith, interpreting the purple clouds and Ajisaka's unruffled demeanor as proof of his attainment of rebirth in the Pure Land. At the same time, he warned his other disciples, repeating Ajisaka's last words (*nagori o oshimuna*), not to grieve over their master's passing.[21]

When Ippen himself died, six of his disciples also committed suicide in sympathy, hoping to accompany their master to the Pure Land. This occasioned some debate about the propriety of "sympathy suicide." Shinkyō, Ippen's disciple and second patriarch of the Ji School, declared that the disciples had failed to obtain rebirth in the Pure Land, for their action was seen as "self-willed," and Pure Land faith relies entirely on the power and will of Amida Buddha's. Assertion of self-will is seen as running counter to the reliance on other power demanded by the Amida faith.[22]

Several important points can be learned from these examples. First, *suicide is never condemned per se. Rather it is the state of mind which determines the rightness or wrongness of the suicide situation.* The dividing line between choosing one's own time and place of death with perfectly assured peace of mind, and self-willing one's own death at the time of one's master's death is perhaps a thin grey one, but this should not obscure the criteria involved: death with desire leads not to rebirth in the Pure Land, but death with calm assurance does. Even the method of water suicide, using a rope as a preventive backup, stresses the importance of the state of mind in this action.

Secondly, Ajisaka's famous phrase, "Nagori o oshimuna," means that *Buddhists are not to kill themselves in "sympathy" when others die.* A literal translation would be that we are not to cling to what remains of the name or person, but to let the deceased go freely

on to the next world. In other words, when someone dies with an assured state of mind, it is not for those who remain either to criticize or to wish that he had not died in this situation. Those who are left behind are to respect and not resent, reject, or grieve for a death which might seem to them untimely. . . .

Samurai, *Seppuku*, and Euthanasia

Among the warrior elite, who usually followed Zen Buddhism, suicide was considered an honorable alternative to being killed by others or continuing a life in shame or misery. Beginning with the famous *seppuku* of Minamoto no Tametomox and Minamoto no Yorimasa in 1170, *seppuku* became known as the way that a vanquished but proud Buddhist warrior would end his life.[23] Soon thereafter, headed by Taira Noritsune and Tomomori, hundreds of Taira warriors and their families committed suicide in the battle of Dannoura of 1185. Famous suicides included that of Kusunoki Masashige in 1336, in the battle between Nitta and Hosokawa, and that of Hideyori Toyotomi, under siege by Tokugawa Ieyasu in 1615. In the Tokugawa period, love suicides were dramatized in a dozen plays by Chikamatsu Monzaemon, including *Sonezaki shinjū*, *Shinjū ten no Amijima*, and *Shinjū mannensō*.[24] The forty-seven Akō rônin, who committed suicide after avenging their master's death, was another famous true story, dramatized in the *Chūshingura* plays and films.[25] The samurai's creed, to be willing to die at any moment, was dramatically spelled out by the *Hagakure*.[26] According to the *Hagakure*, the important concern was not whether one lived or died, but (1) being pure, simple, single-minded, (2) taking full responsibility for doing one's duty, and (3) unconditionally serving one's master, without concern for oneself.

Although *seppuku* may seem like a violent death to the observer, it was designed to enable the samurai to die with the greatest dignity and peace.

It is particularly noteworthy that the samurai's code of suicide included a provision for euthanasia: the *kaishakunin* (attendant). Cutting of the *hara* alone was very painful, and would not lead to a swift death. After cutting their *hara*, few samurai had enough strength to cut their own necks or spines. Yet without cutting their necks, the pain of the opened hara would continue for minutes or even hours prior to death. Therefore, the samurai would make arrangements with one or more kaishakunin to assist his suicide. While the samurai steadied his mind and prepared to die in peace, the kaishakunin would wait by his side. If the samurai spoke to the kaishakunin before or during the *seppuku* ceremony, the standard response was *"go anshin"* (set your mind at peace). All of the interactions and conversations surrounding an officially ordered seppuku were also fixed by tradition, so that the suicide might die with the least tension and greatest peace of mind. After the samurai had finished cutting to the prearranged point, or gave some other signal, it was the duty of the *kaishakunin* to cut the neck of the samurai to terminate his pain by administering the coup de grâce.[27]

Many samurai suicides were in fact the moral equivalent of euthanasia. The reasons for a samurai's suicide were either (1) to avoid an inevitable death at the hands of others, or (2) to escape a longer period of unbearable pain or psychological misery, without being an active, fruitful member of society. These are exactly the sorts of situations when euthanasia is desired today: (1) to avoid an inevitable death at the hands of others (including disease, cancer, or bacteria), (2) to escape a longer period of pain or misery without being a fruitful, active member of society.

In regard to (1), most Japanese are now cut down in their seventies by the enemies of cancer and other diseases, rather than in their youth on a battlefield. Regardless of whether the person is hopelessly surrounded by enemies on a battlefield, or hopelessly defeated by enemy organisms within his body, the morality of the situation is the same. In regard to (2), it might be argued that there is a difference between the pain or misery of the permanent incapacitation of a samurai, and the pain or misery of the permanent incapacitation of a hospital patient. But if anything, the hospital patient is in even less of a position to contribute to society or feel valued than is the samurai, so he has even more reason to be granted the option of leaving this arena (world) when he chooses. *The samurai tradition shows that the important issue is not the level of physical pain, but the prospect for meaningful and productive interaction with other members of society.* If there are no prospects for such interactions, then samurai society claimed no right to prevent the person from seeking more meaningful experiences in another world. . . .

Suicide vs. Euthanasia

One important question for Buddhists today remains: what, if any, are the differences between suicide and euthanasia? Obviously one important difference is in the case where the person receiving euthanasia is unconscious. In this case, we have no way of knowing whether the patient genuinely desires euthanasia, unless he or she has previously made a declaration of wishes in a living will. On the other hand, once the consciousness has permanently dissociated itself from the body, there is no reason in Buddhism to continue to nourish or stimulate the body, for the body deprived of its *skandhas* is not a person. The Japan Songenshi Kyōkai (Association for Death with Dignity) has done much to improve the ability of the individual Japanese to choose his time and manner of death.

Another issue is the relation of pain-killing to prolonging life and hastening death itself. The Japan Songenshi Kyōkai proposes the administering of painkilling drugs even if they hasten the death of the patient. Buddhists would agree that relief of pain is desirable, and whether the death is hastened or not is not the primary issue. However, consider a case where the pain is extreme and only very strong drugs will stop the pain. Here there may be a choice between: (a) no treatment at all, (b) pain-killing which only blurs or confuses the mind of the patient, and (c) treatment which hastens the end while keeping the mind clear. In such a situation, the Buddhist would first prefer the most natural way of (a) no treatment at all. But if his mind were unable to focus or be at peace because of the great pain, the Buddhist would choose (c) over (b), because clarity of consciousness at the moment of death is so important in Buddhism.

Doctors who do not like the idea of shortening a person's life would prefer to prolong the material life-processes, regardless of the mental quality of that life. This is where Buddhists disagree with materialistic Western medicine. But there need be no conflict between Buddhism and medicine. There is no reason to assign the doctor the "responsibility" for the death of the patient. Following the guidelines of the Nagoya court, patients potentially eligible for euthanasia are going to die soon anyway, so that is not the fault of the doctor. And the patient has the right to determine his own death. The fact that he is too weak to hold a sword or to cut short his own life is not morally significant. *If his mind is clear, calm, and ready for death, then the one who understands and compassionately assists that person is also following Buddhist morality.* In summary, the important issue for Buddhists here is whether or not the person will be allowed responsibility for his own life and fate. The entire Buddhist tradition, and particularly that of suicide within Japan, argues that personal choice in time and manner of death is of extreme importance, and anything done by others to dim the mind or deprive the dying person of such choice is a violation of Buddhist principles. Japanese Buddhists may respect this decision more than Western cultures, and lead humanitarian bioethics in a different perspective towards dignified death.

NOTES

1. Morioka Masahiro, "Nōshi to wa nan de atta ka" (What was brain death?), in *Nihon Rinri Gakkoi kenkyū happyō yoshi* (Japan Ethics Association outline of presentations) (Japan Ethics Association 39th Annual Conference, Waseda University, October 14–15, 1988), p. 7.
2. Anzai Kazuhiro, "Nō to sono ishiki" (Brain and its consciousness), in *Nihon Rinri Gakkai*, p. 6.
3. Kawasaki Shinjō, "Tōyō kodai no seimei juyō" (The accepted understanding of life in the ancient Orient), in *Nihon Rinri Gakkai*, p. 26.
4. *Visuddhimagga*, pp. 299ff.
5. Kawasaki, "Tōyō kodai no seimei juyō," p. 27.
6. Iida Tsunesuke, "Bioethics wa nani o nasu no ka" (What does bioethics accomplish?), in *Nihon Rinri Gakkai*, pp. 40ff.
7. Mary Anne Warren, "Do Potential People Have Moral Rights?" *Canadian Journal of Philosophy* 7, no. 2 (1978): 275–289.
8. Carl Becker, "Old and New: Japan's Mechanisms for Crime Control and Social Justice," *Howard Journal of Criminal Justice* 27, no. 4 (November 1988): 284–285.
9. Ohara Nobuo, "Sei to shi no rinrigaku" (The ethics of life and death), in *Nihon Rinri Gakkai*, pp. 54–55.
10. Carl Becker, "Religion and Politics in Japan," chap. 13 of *Movements and Issues in World Religions*, ed. C. W-H. Fu and G. S. Spiegler (New York: Greenwood Press, 1987), p. 278.
11. Among the author's students are nurses at such hospitals.
12. Cf. *Hastings Encyclopedia of Religion*, vol. 4, p. 448.
13. *Majhima Nikāya* II, 91; III, 258.
14. *Samyutta Nikāya* V, 408.
15. Tamaki Koshiro, "Shi no oboegaki" (Memoranda on death), in *Bukkyō shisō*, vol. 10, ed. Bukkyō Shisō Kenkyūkai, Tokyo (September 1988), pp. 465–475.
16. *Sūtta Vibhaṅga, Vinaya* III, 74; cf. *Samyutta Nikāya* III, 119–124.
17. *Majhima Nikaya* III, 263–266 (*Channovada-sūtta*) *Samyutta Nikāya* IV, 55–60 (*Channa-vaga*).
18. Kurita Isamu, *Ippen Shōnin, tabi no shisakusha* (Saint Ippen, the meditalive wayfarer) (Tokyo: Shinchosha, 1977), pp. 165–169.
19. Ōhashi Shunnō, *Ippen* (Tokyo; Yoshikawa Kobunkan, 1983), pp. 105ff.
20. *Ippen goroku*, scroll 6, stage 2 (*maki 6, dan 2*).
21. Kurita, *Ippen Shōnin.*
22. Ōhashi, *Ippen*, pp. 107ff.
23. Jack Seward, *Hara-Kiri: Japanese Ritual Suicide* (Tokyo: Charles E. Tuttle, 1968). Seward describes these and many other significant suicides in detail.
24. Donald Keene, trans., *Major Plays of Chikamatsu* (New York: Columbia University Press, 1961).
25. Fujino Yoshiō, ed., *Kanatehon Chūshingura: Kaishakū to kenkyu* (Chūshingura) (Tokyo: Ofūsha, 1975).
26. Watsuji Tetsurō, ed., *Hagakure* (Tokyo: Iwanami Bunko, 1970).
27. All condensed from Seward, *Hara-Kiri*.

DISCUSSION QUESTIONS:

1. Are you comfortable with the idea that doctors might use your brain-dead corpse for particular medical purposes (e.g., organ transplants)? Do you think that brain death is a good criterion for determining the end of a person's life? If so, why is brain activity relevant for who you are as a person? If not, what criterion should we use to determine when a person is no longer in existence on this earth?

2. Becker's account of the moral permissibility of suicide seems to turn on the existence of karma and the assurance of reincarnation. For example, he writes that "Buddha declared that the crucial variable governing rebirth was the nature of the consciousness at the moment of death" (page 586). Is the Buddhist understanding of the moral permissibility of suicide reduced to nonsense if one doesn't already believe in karma and reincarnation? Is there any evidence of the latter?

3. If all that mattered about one's suicide is that it was done in the right frame of mind, it seems that suicides of the young and healthy would be on a moral par with suicides of the old and dying. Do you think that's true? What elements of the Buddhist worldview might you appeal to in order to offer a Buddhist condemnation for the suicides of the young and healthy?

Argument Reconstruction Exercises:

I. Becker recounts a common argument for the conclusion that human death is tantamount to brain death. See if you can find the premises and conclusion in the following excerpt:

> If brain death implies human death, then, by contraposition, human life must imply conscious (brain) life. Now there are clearly segments of our lives in which we are alive but not always conscious. Therefore it is wrong to conclude that a human is dead because he or she lacks consciousness. (page 584)

II. If the brain death view of human life is not correct, what is the alternative? One suggestion recounted by Becker is that it is our possibilities that define us as persons. Using the following excerpt, assume the possibility view of personhood and show that it implies that brain-dead humans are not alive in the relevant sense:

> Iida Tsunesuke expands this view by arguing that "persons are not merely the meaningless 'subjects of rights,' but personalities, 'faces' embodying the possibilities of fulfilling the dreams of their parents or loved ones. . . This argument begs the question

of "possibilities," since in the case of brain-dead victims, it is precisely such possibilities which are missing. (page 585)

III. Another view of personhood explored by Becker is the idea that our personhood is somehow person-relative. This view presents a number of problems mentioned by Becker, but here is another: it appears to imply a contradiction. Recall that anytime a view implies a contradiction, this is a reason to think that the view is false (by *modus tollens*). Use the excerpt below to show that the person-relative view of personhood implies a contradiction:

> This position is further developed by Ohara Nobuo, who argues that "although a body may be treated as a 'thing' or a corpse by physicians, it remains a body of value and meaning, and in that sense, a *person*, to members of its family. . . (page 585)

IV. Ultimately, Becker argues that the manner of dying at the moment of death is the morally important feature of a suicide. Using the following excerpt, construct an argument for the conclusion that the manner of dying at the moment of death is of great moral importance:

> Japanese Buddhists have long recognized what Westerners are only recently rediscovering: that the manner of dying at the moment of death is important. . . In his meditations, the Buddha noticed that even people with good karma were sometimes born into bad situations, and even those with bad karma sometimes found inordinately pleasant rebirths. Buddha declared that the crucial variable governing rebirth was the nature of the consciousness at the moment of death. (page 586)

CHAPTER 21

Capital Punishment

The moral problem that a legal institution of punishment presents can be stated in one sentence. It involves the deliberate and intentional infliction of suffering.
—RICHARD BURGH, "DO THE GUILTY DESERVE PUNISHMENT?"

INTRODUCTION

When we punish people within our system of criminal law, we deliberately use the power of the state to make them suffer. It is wrong to deliberately make others suffer, in the absence of some overriding moral justification. What, then, morally justifies punishment? What, in particular, justifies punishment in what many see as its most severe form, the death penalty?

The question of punishment's justification can be raised in different ways. Focusing our attention on a particular act of punishment, we can ask what justifies the state in punishing a particular person in a particular way for a particular crime. What justifies us in executing this particular person for that crime? Focusing our attention on types of punishment, we can ask what justifies us in making that type of punishment a part of our legal system. What justifies us in having death as the punishment for some crimes?

The question of punishment's justification has traditionally been debated from two perspectives: **Utilitarianism** and **Retributivism**. Utilitarian theories of punishment, like Utilitarian theories generally, look for an act's moral justification in its consequences. Justified punishment involves deliberately making someone suffer, but, in terms of its consequences, it also amounts to making the best of the otherwise bad situation

in which someone has committed a crime. **Act Utilitarian** theories take particular acts of punishment to be justified insofar as they produce at least as much net good as any alternative. **Rule Utilitarian** theories consider general practices or types of punishment to be justified insofar as their adoption produces at least as much net good as any alternative; particular acts of punishment are then justified as instances of a justified practice or type of punishment. Utilitarian theories thus direct our attention to the likely social costs and benefits of various punishments. What benefits will society gain, perhaps in terms of crime deterrence, from including death among the punishments for certain crimes? What will it cost society to administer an effective practice of capital punishment?

Retributivist theories take the justification of punishment to be a matter of justice. Criminals break the law of their own free will and thereby earn a penalty for themselves. Justice demands that they be given what they deserve. Punishment involves deliberately making someone suffer, but, when justified, it is done to meet the demands of justice. Retributivists direct our attention to the issue of what punishments fit what crimes. With regard to a particular application of the death penalty, the issue becomes one of whether the crime involved was grave enough to merit the criminal's execution. With regard to various sorts of crimes, the issue is one of what sorts of crimes are generally so bad as to merit that penalty.

It is important to distinguish Retributivism from the simple-minded view that justice requires us to punish the criminal with the very same sort of suffering inflicted on the victim. We are to execute the murderer, rape the rapist, torture the torturer, and so on. Retributivists are not committed to the view that the only punishment that fits a crime is a punishment that duplicates the crime. Indeed, it is common among Retributivists to claim that some punishments are so barbaric, so cruel in themselves, as to never be morally unjustified, even if they would give criminals what they deserve. We are not justified in torturing the torturer, for example. Retributivism thus directs our attention to the question of whether the death penalty, in itself, or in any of its various forms, from stoning to beheading to hanging to lethal injection, is too cruel to be acceptable.

While Utilitarianism and Retributivism are generally viewed as two opposed approaches to the justification of punishment, discussions of the death penalty often take both into account. This is true of both essays in this chapter. In his selection, Primoratz briefly considers and rejects a Utilitarian attempt to justify the death penalty on the basis of its effectiveness in deterring crime. He instead offers a Retributivist defense of capital punishment as the only penalty that fits the crime of murder. He finds that death, unlike torture, is not so cruel as to be morally unacceptable as a punishment.

In his essay, Bedau argues that the death penalty is never justified. From a Utilitarian perspective, he argues that capital punishment is an ineffective deterrent and much costlier than long-term imprisonment to implement in accord with our moral principles. From a Retributivist perspective, he argues that the death penalty is not supported by the principle that the punishment must fit the crime, and he claims that capital punishment is comparable to torture in being so cruel as to never be morally acceptable.

SUGGESTIONS FOR FURTHER READING

Bedau, Hugo, ed. *The Death Penalty in America: Current Controversies.* (Oxford: Oxford University Press, 1996)

Duff, R.A., & Garland, D, eds. *A Reader on Punishment.* (Oxford: Oxford University Press, 1994)

Gross, Samuel, and Mauro, Robert, eds. *Death and Discrimination.* (Boston: Northeastern University Press, 1989)

Honderich, T. *Punishment: The Supposed Justifications Revisited.* (London: Pluto Publishing, 2005)

Nathanson, Stephen, *An Eye for an Eye? The Immorality of Punishing by Death,* 2nd ed. (Lanham, Maryland: Rowman and Littlefield, 2001)

Primoratz, Igor. *Justifying Legal Punishment,* 2nd ed. (New Jersey: Humanities Press, 1999)

Shafer-Landau, R. "The Failure of Retributivism." *Philosophical Studies* 82, 1996, pp. 289–316.

Ten, C. L. *Crime, Guilt and Punishment.* (Oxford: Oxford University Press, 1987)

Van den Haag, Ernest. "The Death Penalty Once More." 29 *U. C. Davis Law Review* 957 (1965)

Van den Haag, Ernest, and Conrad, John. *The Death Penalty: A Debate.* (New York: Basic Books, 1983)

21.1 JUSTIFYING CAPITAL PUNISHMENT

IGOR PRIMORATZ (1989)

Igor Primoratz, Emeritus Professor at the Hebrew University of Jerusalem, is a specialist in political and legal philosophy. In this essay from his book *Justifying Legal Punishment*, he considers the justification of the death penalty from the perspective of the two classic theories of punishment, **Utilitarianism** and **Retributivism**. He argues that although the death penalty does not meet the Utilitarian standard, it does, however, meet the Retributivist standard. He concludes that death is the only just punishment for the crime of murder, since it alone inflicts on murderers a loss commensurate to the good they have taken, a human life.

Reading Questions:

1. What is the Utilitarian standard for the justification of punishment? Why, according to Primoratz, does the death penalty not meet that standard?

2. What is the Retributivist standard for the justification of punishment? Why, according to Primoratz, does the death penalty meet that standard as a punishment for the crime of murder? Does the death penalty meet that standard as a punishment for any other crimes, according to Primoratz?

3. What are the six objections to the death penalty that Primoratz considers, and what is his response to each?

4. How, according to Primoratz, might Retributivists claim, without contradiction, that the death penalty is a just punishment for murder but not a justified punishment for that crime?

5. Primoratz claims that some punishments (e.g., torture) are cruel in the absolute sense but that capital punishment is not. What does it mean for something to be cruel in the absolute sense?

The Ultimate Deterrent

The issue of capital punishment has been discussed for centuries by philosophers, theologians, legal scholars, social scientists, and reformers of all kinds. These discussions have involved a variety of types of reasoning: some are purely theoretical, some are highly technical statistical or, at a further remove, methodological analyses. But the crucial question, "For or against?" is a moral one. Since it has to do with moral considerations of a rather general nature for abolishing or retaining a legal institution, it also presents a problem for moral and legal philosophy. The best way to avoid the confusion which sometimes results from the great variety of arguments used both in favor of and against capital punishment is to keep the discussion within its proper philosophical context—the debate on the moral justification of punishment in general. For the nature of the arguments we see as relevant for deciding the issue of capital punishment depends on whether we subscribe to the utilitarian or the retributive rationale of punishment.

If we accept the utilitarian theory of punishment—that is, if we hold that the sole justification of punishment is in its good consequences—the issue of capital punishment boils down to the following question: Does this punishment really have those far-reaching desirable consequences its advocates have claimed for it? Is it true that through the threat of this punishment, and this punishment only, the most serious of crimes can be prevented?. . .

Empirical research, conducted by application of scientific methods, has shown that there is no significant correlation between the presence or absence of capital punishment and the rates of those crimes for which it is prescribed and meted out. . . .

Thus, whoever subscribes. . . to a purely utilitarian view of punishment cannot in all consistency defend the death penalty any longer. This kind of punishment simply does not have consequences good enough to justify its infliction, and therefore ought to be abolished.

A Life for a Life

The conclusion of the preceding section is not in the least binding on those retentionists who approach the problem of the moral basis of punishment in general from the retributive standpoint. According to the retributive theory, consequences of punishment, however important from the practical point of view, are irrelevant when it comes to its justification; *The* moral consideration is its justice. Punishment is morally justified insofar as it is meted out as retribution for the offense committed. When someone has committed an offense, he deserves to be punished: it is just, and consequently justified, that he be punished. The offense is the sole ground of the state's right and duty to punish. It is also the measure of legitimate punishment: the two ought to be proportionate. So the issue of capital punishment within the retributive approach comes down to the question, "Is this punishment ever proportionate retribution for the offense committed, and thus deserved, just, and justified?". . . .

In other cases, the demand for proportionality between offense and punishment can be satisfied by fines or prison terms; the crime of murder, however, is an exception in this respect, and calls for the literal interpretation of the **lex talionis.** The uniqueness of this crime has to do with the uniqueness of the value which has been deliberately or recklessly destroyed. . . .

This view that the value of human life is not commensurable with other values, and that consequently there is only one truly equivalent punishment for murder, namely death, does not necessarily presuppose a theistic outlook. It can be claimed that, simply because we have to be alive if we are to experience and realize any other value at all, there is nothing equivalent to the murderous destruction of a human life except the destruction of the life of the murderer. Any other retribution, no matter how severe, would still be less than what is proportionate, deserved, and just. As long as the murderer is alive, no matter how bad the conditions of his life may be, there are always at least some values he can experience and realize. . . .

It seems to me that this is essentially correct. With respect to the larger question of the justification of punishment in general, it is the retributive theory that gives the right answer. *Accordingly, capital punishment ought to be retained where it obtains, and reintroduced in those jurisdictions that have abolished it, although we have no reason to believe that, as* *a means of deterrence, it is any better than a very long prison term. It ought to be retained, or reintroduced, for one simple reason: that justice be done in cases of murder, that murderers be punished according to their deserts.*

Objections to Retribuativism and Replies

There are a number of arguments that have been advanced against this rationale of capital punishment. . . .

One abolitionist argument. . . simply says that capital punishment is illegitimate because it violates the right to life, which is a fundamental, absolute, sacred right belonging to each and every human being, and therefore ought to be respected even in a murderer.

If any rights are fundamental, the right to life is certainly one of them; but to claim that it is absolute, inviolable under any circumstances and for any reason, is a different matter. If an abolitionist wants to argue his case by asserting an absolute right to life, she will also have to deny moral legitimacy to taking human life in war, revolution, and self-defense. This kind of pacifism is a consistent but farfetched and hence implausible position.

I do not believe that the right to life (nor, for that matter, any other right) is absolute. I have no general theory of rights to fall back upon here; instead, let me pose a question. Would we take seriously the claim to an absolute, sacred, inviolable right to life—coming from the mouth of a *confessed murderer*? I submit that we would not, for the obvious reason that it is being put forward by the person who confessedly denied another human being this very right. But if the murderer cannot plausibly claim such a right for himself, neither can *anyone else* do that in his behalf. This suggests that there is an element of reciprocity in our general rights, such as the right to life or property. I can convincingly claim these rights only so long as I acknowledge and respect the same rights of others. If I violate the rights of others, I thereby lose the same rights. If I am a murderer, I have no *right* to live.

Some opponents of capital punishment claim that a criminal law system which includes this punishment is contradictory, in that it prohibits murder and at the same time provides for its perpetration. . . .

This seems to be one of the more popular arguments against the death penalty, but it is not a good one. If it were valid, it would prove too much. Exactly the same might be claimed of other kinds of punishment: of prison terms, that they are "contradictory" to the legal protection of liberty; of fines, that they are "contradictory" to the legal protection of property. Fortunately enough, it is not valid, for it begs the question at issue. In order to be able to talk of the state as "murdering" the person it executes, and to claim that there is "an abnormal and immoral logic" at work here, which thrives on a "contradiction," one has to use the word "murder" in the very same sense—that is, in the usual sense, which implies the idea of the *wrongful* taking the life of another—both when speaking of what the murderer has done to the victim and of what the state is doing to him by way of punishment. But this is precisely the question at issue: whether capital punishment *is* "murder," whether it is wrongful or morally justified and right.

The next two arguments attack the retributive rationale of capital punishment by questioning the claim that it is only this punishment that satisfies the demand for proportion between offense and punishment in the case of murder. The first points out that any two human lives are different in many important respects, such as age, health, physical and mental capability, so that it does not make much sense to consider them equally valuable. What if the murdered person was very old, practically at the very end of her natural life, while the murderer is young, with most of his life still ahead of him, for instance? Or if the victim was gravely and incurably ill, and thus doomed to live her life in suffering and hopelessness, without being able to experience almost anything that makes a human life worth living, while the murderer is in every respect capable of experiencing and enjoying things life has to offer? Or the other way round? Would not the death penalty in such cases amount either to taking a more valuable life as a punishment for destroying a less valuable one, or vice versa? Would it not be either too much, or too little, and in both cases disproportionate, and thus unjust and wrong, from the standpoint of the retributive theory itself?

Any plausibility this argument might appear to have is the result of a conflation of differences between, and value of, human lives. No doubt, any two human lives are *different* in innumerable ways, but this does not entail that they are not *equally valuable.* I have no worked-out general; theory of equality to refer to here, but I do not think that one is necessary in order to do away with this argument. The modern humanistic and democratic tradition in ethical, social, and political thought is based on the idea that all human beings are equal. This finds its legal expression in the principle of equality of people under the law. If we are not willing to give up this principle, we have to stick to the assumption that, all differences notwithstanding, any two human lives, *qua* human lives, are equally valuable. If, on the other hand, we allow that, on the basis of such criteria as age, health, or mental or physical ability, it can be claimed that the life of one person is more or less valuable than the life of another, and we admit such claims in the sphere of law, including criminal law, we shall thereby give up the principle of equality of people under the law. In all consistency, we shall not be able to demand that property, physical and personal integrity, and all other rights and interests of individuals be given equal consideration in courts of law either—that is, we shall have to accept systematic discrimination between individuals on the basis of the same criteria across the whole field. I do not think anyone would seriously contemplate an overhaul of the whole legal system along these lines.

The second argument having to do with the issue of proportionality between murder and capital punishment draws our attention to the fact that the law normally provides for a certain period of time to elapse between the passing of a death sentence and its execution. It is a period of several weeks or months; in some cases it extends to years. This period is bound to be one of constant mental anguish for the condemned. And thus, all things considered, what is inflicted on him is disproportionately hard and hence unjust. . . The argument actually does not hit at capital punishment itself, although it is presented with that aim in view. It hits at something else: a particular way of carrying out this punishment, which is widely adopted in our time. Some hundred years ago and more, in the Wild West, they frequently hanged the man convicted to die almost immediately after pronouncing the sentence. I am not arguing here that we should follow this example today; I mention this piece of historical fact only in order to show that the interval between sentencing someone to death and carrying out the sentence is not a *part* of capital punishment itself. However unpalatable we might find those Wild West hangings, whatever objections we might want to voice against the speed with which they followed the sentencing, surely we shall not deny them the *description* of "executions." So the implication of the argument is not that we ought to do away with capital punishment altogether, nor that we ought to restrict it to those cases of murder where the murderer had warned the victim weeks or months in advance of what he was going to do to her, but that we ought to reexamine the procedure of carrying out this kind of punishment. We ought to weigh the reasons for having this interval between the sentencing and executing, against the moral and human significance of the repercussions such an interval inevitably carries with it.

These reasons, in part, have to do with the possibility of miscarriages of justice and the need to rectify them. Thus we come to the argument against capital punishment which, historically, has been the most effective of all: many advances of the abolitionist movement have been connected with discoveries of cases of judicial errors. Judges and jurors are only human, and consequently some of their beliefs and decisions are bound to be mistaken. Some of their mistakes can be corrected upon discovery; but precisely those with most disastrous repercussions—those which result in innocent people being executed—can never be rectified. In all other cases, of mistaken sentencing we can revoke the punishment, either completely or in part, or at least extend compensation. In addition, by exonerating the accused we give moral satisfaction. None of this is possible after an innocent person has been executed; capital punishment is essentially different from all other penalties by being completely irrevocable and irreparable. Therefore, it ought to be abolished.

A part of my reply to this argument goes along the same lines as what I had to say on the previous one. It is not so far-reaching as abolitionists assume; for it would be quite implausible, even fanciful, to claim that there have *never* been cases of murder which left no room whatever for reasonable doubt

as to the guilt and full responsibility of the accused. Such cases may not be more frequent than those others, but they do happen. Why not retain the death penalty at least for them?

Actually, this argument, just as the preceding one, does not speak out against capital punishment itself, but against the existing procedures for trying capital cases. Miscarriages of justice result in innocent people being sentenced to death and executed, even in the criminal-law systems in which greatest care is taken to ensure that it never comes to that. But this does not stem from the intrinsic nature of the institution of capital punishment; it results from deficiencies, limitations, and imperfections of the criminal law procedures in which this punishment is meted out. Errors of justice do not demonstrate the need to do away with capital punishment; they simply make it incumbent on us to do everything possible to improve even further procedures of meting it out. . . .

The demand to do away with capital punishment altogether, so as to eliminate even the smallest chance of an error of justice—the chance which, admittedly, would remain even after everything humanly possible has been done to perfect the procedure, although then it would be very slight indeed—is actually a demand to give a privileged position to murderers as against all other offenders, big and small. For if we acted on this demand, we would bring about a situation in which proportionate penalties would be meted out for all offenses, *except* for murder. Murderers would not be receiving the only punishment truly proportionate to their crimes, the punishment of death, but some other, lighter, and thus disproportionate penalty. All other offenders would be punished according to their deserts; only murderers would be receiving less than *they* deserve. In all other cases justice would be done in full; only in cases of the gravest of offenses, the crime of murder, justice would not be carried out in full measure. It is a great and tragic miscarriage of justice when an innocent person is mistakenly sentenced to death and executed, but systematically giving murderers advantage over all other offenders would also be a grave injustice. Is the fact that, as long as capital punishment is retained, there is a possibility that over a number of years, or even decades, an injustice of the first kind may be committed, unintentionally and unconsciously, reason enough to abolish it altogether, and thus end up with a system of punishments in which injustices of the second kind are perpetrated daily, consciously, and inevitably?

There is still another abolitionist argument that actually does not hit out against capital punishment itself, but against something else. *Figures are sometimes quoted which show that this punishment is much more often meted out to the uneducated and poor than to the educated, rich, and influential people*; in the United States, much more often to blacks than to whites. These figures are adduced as a proof of the inherent injustice of this kind of punishment. On account of them, it is claimed that capital punishment is not a way of doing justice by meting out deserved punishment to murderers, but rather, a means of social discrimination and perpetuation of social injustice.

I shall not question these findings, which are quite convincing, and anyway, there is no need to do that in order to defend the institution of capital punishment. For there seems to be a certain amount of discrimination and injustice not only in sentencing people to death and executing them, but also in meting out other penalties. The social structure of the death rows in American prisons, for instance, does not seem to be basically different from the general social structure of American penitentiaries. If this argument were valid, it would call not only for abolition of the penalty of death, but for doing away with other penalties as well. . . .

Retributivism without Capital Punishment?

Everything I have said in the preceding section has had a pronounced defensive ring to it. I have attempted to show that none of the standard arguments against the death penalty, which would be relevant within the retributive approach to punishment in general, are really convincing. But I shall end on a conciliatory note. I can envisage a way for a retributive to take an abolitionist stand, without thereby being inconsistent. Let me explain this in just a few words.

The Eighth Amendment to the Constitution of the United States says that "excessive bail shall not be required, nor excessive fines imposed, nor cruel and unusual punishments inflicted." I do not find the idea of a "usual" or "unusual" punishment very helpful. But I do think that punishments ought not to be *cruel*. They ought not to be cruel in the rèlative sense, by being considerably more severe than what is proportionate to the offense committed, what is deserved and just; but they also ought not to be cruel in an absolute sense—that is, severe beyond a certain threshold.

Admittedly, it would be very difficult to determine that threshold precisely, but it is not necessary for my purpose here. It will be enough to provide a paradigmatic case of something that is surely beyond that threshold: torture. I do not believe that a torturer has a *right* not to be tortured. If we could bring ourselves to torture him, as a punishment for what he has done to the victim, I do not think that it could be plausibly claimed that what we were doing to him was something undeserved and unjust. But I also do not think that we should try to bring ourselves to do that, in pursuit of proportion between offense and punishment and in striving to execute justice. Justice is one of the most important moral principles—perhaps the most important one—but it is not *absolute*. On the other hand, I feel that torture is something *absolutely wrong* from the moral point of view: something indecent and inhuman, something immensely and unredeemably degrading both to the man tortured and to the torturer himself, something that is morally "beyond the pale." So to sentence a torturer to be tortured would not mean to give him a punishment which is undeserved and unjust, and hence cruel in the relative sense of the word; but it *would* mean to punish him in a way that is cruel in this second, absolute sense. On account of this, I would say that, when punishing a torturer, we ought to desist from giving him the full measure of what he has deserved by his deed, that we ought to settle for less than what in his case would be the full measure of justice. *One of the moral principles limiting the striving to do justice is this prohibition of cruelty in the absolute sense of the word. We ought not to execute justice to the full, if that means that we shall have to be cruel.*

I do not feel about executing a person in a swift and relatively painless manner the same way I feel about torturing him. But a person, or a society, could come to feel the same way about both. *A person or society that adhered to the retributive view of punishment, but at the same time felt this way about executing a human being, could decide that capital punishment is cruel and therefore unacceptable without being in any way inconsistent.*

DISCUSSION QUESTIONS:

1. Primoratz claims that the good to be produced by our adoption of the death penalty is not sufficiently greater than that associated with other alternative punishments to justify it on Utilitarian grounds. Suppose it were the case that the death penalty produced significantly more net good than any other alternatives as a punishment for various crimes; would the death penalty then be morally justified for those crimes? Would its justification depend on the nature of the crimes?

2. Primoratz defends the death penalty on Retributivist grounds, but is Retributivism correct: Are punishments justified by virtue of giving criminals the penalty that fits their crime? If so, what determines whether a particular punishment fits a particular crime?

3. Is Primoratz correct in his claim that "there is nothing equivalent to the murderous destruction of a human life except the destruction of the life of the murderer"? Is the death penalty a fitting punishment for any crimes besides murder?

4. Is Primoratz correct in his claim that if we "violate the rights of others, [we] thereby lose the same rights"? Does the torturer lose the right not to be tortured, the rapist the right not to be raped? Do we have any rights that define our human dignity in such a way that we can never forfeit them?

5. The greater the penalty, the greater the injustice we do if we apply it incorrectly. Does our application of the death penalty need to meet higher standards of accuracy in order to be justified than our application of other, lesser penalties? How accurate must our application be?

6. Suppose some who commit murder receive the death penalty while others guilty of the same crime receive lesser penalties due to irrelevant considerations such as financial wealth. Are the criminals who receive the death penalty treated

justly in the sense that they get the penalty they deserve? Are they treated unjustly in that they are treated differently than others when there is no relevant difference between them? Is their receipt of the death penalty justified?

7. Primoratz claims that even just penalties are unjustified if they are cruel in the absolute sense, and he offers torture as an example of such a punishment. Is torture too cruel to ever be a justified punishment? What makes it so? Is the death penalty significantly different?

Argument Reconstruction Exercises:

I. Primoratz presents the following argument for the claim that the death penalty is the only fitting punishment for the crime of murder. Identify its premises and conclusion:

> It can be claimed that, simply because we have to be alive if we are to experience and realize any other value at all, there is nothing equivalent to the murderous destruction of a human life except the destruction of the life of the murderer. . . . As long as the murderer is alive, no matter how bad the conditions of his life may be, there are always at least some values he can experience and realize. (page 595)

II. Primoratz offers the following argument in response to the concern that a murderer's life may not be of equal value to that of his or her victim. Identify its premises and conclusion.

> The modern humanistic and democratic tradition in ethical, social and political thought is based on the idea that all human beings are equal. This finds its legal expression in the principle of equality under the law. If we are not willing to give up this principle, we have to stick to the assumption that, all differences notwithstanding, any two human lives, *qua* human lives, are equally valuable. (page 596)

III. Primoratz considers the following objection to capital punishment. Identify its premises and conclusion:

> [In cases of mistaken punishment other than the death penalty,] we can revoke the punishment, either completely or in part, or at least extend

compensation. In addition, by exonerating the accused we give moral satisfaction. None of this is possible after an innocent person has been executed; capital punishment is essentially different from all other penalties by being completely irrevocable and irreparable. Therefore, it ought to be abolished. (page 597)

IV. Primoratz distinguishes two ways in which a punishment can be cruel: it can be cruel in the relative sense of being more severe than the crime merits; it can be cruel in the absolute sense of being beyond a certain acceptable threshold. He then argues that we are not justified in torturing torturers as a punishment for their crime. Identify the premises and conclusion of his argument:

I feel that torture is something *absolutely wrong* from the moral point of view: something indecent and inhuman, something immensely and unredeemably degrading both to the man tortured and to the torturer himself, something that is morally "beyond the pale." . . . On account of this, I would say that, when punishing a torturer, we ought to desist from giving him the full measure of what he has deserved for his deed, that we ought to settle for less than what in his case would be the full measure of justice. (page 598)

21.2 The Case Against The Death Penalty

HUGO BEDAU (1992)

Hugo Bedau was Emeritus Professor of Philosophy at Tufts University and a long-time activist against capital punishment. In this essay, he rejects the moral permissibility of the death penalty on multiple grounds. Relative to **utilitarian** considerations, he argues that it does not deter crime and is more costly than incarceration. Relative to **retributivist** considerations of justice, he argues that it is not required for retribution and is unfair and inequitable in practice; it also carries too great a risk of a grave and irreversible injustice in the execution of the innocent. Bedau also claims that the death penalty is too barbaric to a justified penalty for any crime.

Reading Questions:

1. What are Bedau's three reasons to support his claim that capital punishment is not an effective deterrent?

2. What evidence does Bedau offer to support his claim that our justice system "essentially reserves the death penalty for murderers (regardless of their race) who kill white victims"?

3. What are two factors, other than race, that Bedau claims result in the arbitrary application of the death penalty?

4. What is Bedau's response to the claim that the death penalty is the only punishment that is capable of giving murderers what they deserve?

5. Why, according to Bedau, does the death penalty cost more than long-term incarceration?

Introduction

In 1972, the Supreme Court declared that under then-existing laws "the imposition and carrying out of the death penalty. . . constitutes cruel and unusual punishment in violation of the Eighth and Fourteenth Amendments." (*Furman v. Georgia*, 408 U.S. 238) The Court, concentrating its objections on the manner in which death penalty laws had been applied, found the result so "harsh, freakish, and arbitrary" as to be constitutionally unacceptable. Making the nationwide impact of its decision unmistakable, the Court summarily reversed death sentences in the many cases then before it, which involved a wide range of state statutes, crimes and factual situations.

But within four years after the *Furman* decision, several hundred persons had been sentenced to death under new capital punishment statutes written to provide guidance to juries in sentencing. These statutes typically require a two-stage trial procedure, in which the jury first determines guilt or innocence and then chooses imprisonment or death in the light of aggravating or mitigating circumstances.

In 1976, the Supreme Court moved away from abolition, holding that "the punishment of death does not invariably violate the Constitution." The Court ruled that the new death penalty statutes contained "objective standards to guide, regularize, and make rationally reviewable the process for imposing the sentence of death." (*Gregg v. Georgia*, 428 U.S. 153). Subsequently 38 state legislatures and the Federal government have enacted death penalty statutes patterned after those the Court upheld in *Gregg*. In recent years, Congress has enacted death penalty statutes for peacetime espionage by military personnel and for drug-related murders.

Executions resumed in 1977, and as of May 1997, over 3,200 men and women were under a death sentence and more than 360 had been executed. . . .

Two conclusions are inescapable: Capital punishment does not deter crime, and the death penalty is uncivilized in theory and unfair and inequitable in practice.

Capital Punishment Is Not a Deterrent to Capital Crimes

Deterrence is a function not only of a punishment's severity, but also of its certainty and frequency. The argument most often cited in support of capital punishment is that the threat of execution influences criminal behavior more effectively than imprisonment does. As plausible as this claim may sound, in actuality *the death penalty fails as a deterrent for several reasons.*

1) A punishment can be an effective deterrent only if it is consistently and promptly employed. Capital punishment cannot be administered to meet these conditions.

- The proportion of first-degree murderers who are sentenced to death is small, and of this group, an even smaller proportion of people are executed. Although death sentences in the mid-1990s have increased to about 300 per year,[1] this is still only about one percent of all homicides known to the police.[2] Of all those convicted on a charge of criminal homicide, only 3 percent—about 1 in 33—are eventually sentenced to death.[3]
- Mandatory death row sentencing is unconstitutional. The possibility of increasing the number of convicted murderers sentenced to death and executed by enacting mandatory death penalty laws was ruled unconstitutional in 1976 (*Woodson v. North Carolina*, 428 U.S. 280).
- A considerable time between the imposition of the death sentence and the actual execution is unavoidable, given the procedural safeguards required by the courts in capital cases. Starting with selecting the trial jury, murder trials take far longer when the ultimate penalty is involved. Furthermore, post-conviction appeals in death-penalty cases are far more frequent than in other cases. These factors increase the time and cost of administering criminal justice.

We can reduce delay and costs only by abandoning the procedural safeguards and constitutional rights of suspects, defendants, and convicts—with the attendant high risk of convicting the wrong person and executing the innocent.

2) Persons who commit murder and other crimes of personal violence either may or may not premeditate their crimes.

- When crime is planned, the criminal ordinarily concentrates on escaping detection, arrest, and conviction. The threat of even the severest punishment will not discourage those who expect to escape detection and arrest. It is impossible to imagine how the threat of any punishment could prevent a crime that is not premeditated. Gangland killings, air piracy, drive-by shootings, and kidnapping for ransom are among the graver felonies that continue to be committed because some individuals think they are too clever to get caught.
- Most capital crimes are committed in the heat of the moment. Most capital crimes are committed during moments of great emotional stress or under the influence of drugs or alcohol, when logical thinking has been suspended. In such cases, violence is inflicted by persons heedless of the consequences to themselves as well as to others. Furthermore, the death penalty is a futile threat for political terrorists because they usually act in the name of an ideology that honors its martyrs.
- Capital punishment doesn't solve our society's crime problem. Threatening capital punishment leaves the underlying causes of crime unaddressed, and ignores the many political and diplomatic sanctions (such as treaties against asylum for international terrorists) that could appreciably lower the incidence of terrorism.
- Capital punishment is a useless weapon in the so-called "war on drugs." The attempt to reduce murders in the drug trade by threat of severe punishment ignores the fact that anyone trafficking in illegal drugs is already risking his life in violent competition with other dealers. It is irrational to think that the death penalty—a remote threat at best—will avert murders committed in drug turf wars or by street-level dealers.

3) If, however, severe punishment can deter crime, then long-term imprisonment is severe enough to deter any rational person from committing a violent crime.

- The vast preponderance of the evidence shows that the death penalty is no more effective than imprisonment in deterring murder and that it may even be an incitement to criminal violence. Death-penalty states as a group do not have lower rates of criminal homicide than non-death-penalty states. During the early 1970's death-penalty states averaged an annual rate of 7.9 criminal homicides per 100,000 population; abolitionist states averaged a rate of 5.1.[4]
- Use of the death penalty in a given state may actually increase the subsequent rate of criminal homicide. In Oklahoma, for example, reintroduction of executions in 1990 may have produced "an abrupt and lasting increase in the level of stranger homicides" in the form of "one additional stranger-homicide incident per month." Why? Perhaps because "a return to the exercise of the death penalty weakens socially based inhibitions against the use of lethal force to settle disputes. . . ."[5]
- In adjacent states—one with the death penalty and the other without it—the state that practices the death penalty does not always show a consistently lower rate of criminal homicide. For example, between 1990 and 1994, the homicide rates in Wisconsin and Iowa (non-death-penalty states) were half the rates of their neighbor, Illinois—which restored the death penalty in 1973, and by 1994 had sentenced 223 persons to death and carried out two executions.[6]
- On-duty police officers do not suffer a higher rate of criminal assault and homicide in abolitionist states than they do in death-penalty states. Between 1973 and 1984, for example, lethal assaults against police were not significantly more, or less, frequent in abolitionist states than in death-penalty

states. There is "no support for the view that the death penalty provides a more effective deterrent to police homicides than alternative sanctions. Not for a single year was evidence found that police are safer in jurisdictions that provide for capital punishment."[7]

- Prisoners and prison personnel do not suffer a higher rate of criminal assault and homicide from life-term prisoners in abolition states than they do in death-penalty states. Between 1992 and 1995,176 inmates were murdered by other prisoners; the vast majority (84%) were killed in death-penalty jurisdictions. During the same period about 2% of all assaults on prison staff were committed by inmates in abolition jurisdictions.[8] Evidently, the threat of the death penalty "does not even exert an incremental deterrent effect over the threat of a lesser punishment in the abolitionist states."[9]

Actual experience thus establishes beyond a reasonable doubt that the death penalty does not deter murder. No comparable body of evidence contradicts that conclusion.

Using methods pioneered by economists, three investigators concluded that capital punishment does deter murderers.[10] Subsequently, however, several qualified investigators independently examined these claims—and all rejected them.[11] In its thorough report on the effects of criminal sanctions on crime rates, the National Academy of Sciences concluded: "It seems unthinkable to us to base decisions on the use of the death penalty" on such "fragile" and "uncertain" results. "We see too many plausible explanations for [these] findings. . . other than the theory that capital punishment deters murder."[12]

Furthermore, there are clinically documented cases in which the death penalty actually incited the capital crimes it was supposed to deter. These include instances of the so-called suicide-by-execution syndrome—persons who wanted to die but feared taking their own lives, and committed murder so that the state would kill them.[13]

Although inflicting the death penalty guarantees that the condemned person will commit no further crimes, it does not have a demonstrable deterrent effect on other individuals. Further, it is a high price to pay when studies show that few convicted murderers commit further crimes of violence.[14] Researchers examined the prison and post-release records of 533 prisoners on death row in 1972 whose sentences were reduced to incarceration for life by the Supreme Court's ruling in *Furman*. This research showed that seven had committed another murder. But the same study showed that in four other cases, an innocent man had been sentenced to death.[15]

Recidivism among murderers does occasionally happen, but it occurs less frequently than most people believe; the media rarely distinguish between a convicted offender who murders while on parole, and a paroled murderer who murders again. Government data show that about one in twelve death row prisoners had a prior homicide conviction.[16] But as there is no way to predict reliably which convicted murderers will try to kill again, the only way to prevent all such recidivism is to execute every convicted murderer—a policy no one seriously advocates. Equally effective but far less inhumane is a policy of life imprisonment without the possibility of parole.

Capital Punishment Is Unfair

Constitutional due process and elementary justice both require that the judicial functions of trial and sentencing be conducted with fundamental fairness, especially where the irreversible sanction of the death penalty is involved. In murder cases (since 1930, 88 percent of all executions have been for this crime), *there has been substantial evidence to show that courts have sentenced some persons to prison while putting others to death in a manner that has been arbitrary, racially biased, and unfair.*

Racial discrimination was one of the grounds on which the Supreme Court ruled the death penalty unconstitutional in *Furman*. Half a century ago, in his classic *American Dilemma* (1944), Gunnar Myrdal reported that "the South makes the widest application of the death penalty, and Negro criminals come in for much more than their share of the executions." A recent study of the death penalty in Texas shows that the current capital punishment system is an outgrowth of the racist "legacy of slavery."[17] Between 1930 and the end of 1996, 4,220 prisoners were executed in the United States; more than half (53%) were black.[18]

Our nation's death rows have always held a disproportionately large population of African Americans, relative to their percentage of the total population. Comparing black and white offenders over the past century, the former were often executed for what were considered less-than-capital offenses for whites, such as rape and burglary. (Between 1930 and 1976, 455 men were executed for rape, of whom 405—90 percent—were black.) A higher percentage of the blacks who were executed were juveniles; and the rate of execution without having one's conviction reviewed by any higher court was higher blacks.[19]

In recent years, it has been widely believed that such flagrant racial discrimination is a thing of the past. However, since the revival of the death penalty in the mid-1970s, about half of those on death row at any given time have been black.[20] Of the 3,200 prisoners on death row in 1996, 40% were black. This rate is not so obviously unfair if one considers that roughly 50 percent of all those arrested for murder were also black.[21] Nevertheless, when those under death sentence are examined more closely, it turns out that race is a decisive factor after all.

An exhaustive statistical study of racial discrimination in capital cases in Georgia, for example, showed that "the average odds of receiving a death sentence among all indicted cases were 4.3 times higher in cases with white victims."[22] In 1987 these data were placed before the Supreme Court in *McCleskey v. Kemp* and while the Court did not dispute the statistical evidence, it held that evidence of an overall pattern of racial bias was not sufficient. Mr. McCleskey would have to prove racial bias in his own case—an impossible task. The Court also held that the evidence failed to show that there was "a constitutionally significant risk of racial bias. . . ."(481 U.S. 279) Although the Supreme Court declared that the remedy sought by the plaintiff was "best presented to the legislative bodies," subsequent efforts to persuade Congress to remedy the problem by enacting the Racial Justice Act were not successful.[23]

In 1990, the U.S. General Accounting Office reported to the Congress the results of its review of empirical studies on racism and the death penalty. The GAO concluded: "Our synthesis of the 28 studies shows a pattern of evidence indicating racial disparities in the charging, sentencing, and imposition of the death penalty after the *Furman* decision" and that "race of victim influence was found at all stages of the criminal justice system process. . . ."[24]

These results cannot be explained away by relevant non-racial factors, such as prior criminal record or type of crime. Furthermore, they lead to a very unsavory conclusion: In the trial courts of this nation, even at the present time, the killing of a white person is treated much more severely than the killing of a black person. Of the 313 persons executed between January 1977 and the end of 1995, 36 had been convicted of killing a black person while 249 (80%) had killed a white person. Of the 178 white defendants executed, only three had been convicted of murdering people of color.[25] Our criminal justice system essentially reserves the death penalty for murderers (regardless of their race) who kill white victims.

Both gender and socio-economic class also determine who receives a death sentence and who is executed. During the 1980s and early 1990s, only about one percent of all those on death row were women[26] even though women commit about 15 percent of all criminal homicides.[27] A third or more of the women under death sentence were guilty of killing men who had victimized them with years of violent abuse.[28] Since 1930, only 33 women (12 of them black) have been executed in the United States.[29]

Discrimination against the poor (and in our society, racial minorities are disproportionately poor) is also well established.

Fairness in capital cases requires, above all, competent counsel for the defendant. Yet "approximately 90 percent of those on death row could not afford to hire a lawyer when they were tried."[30] Common characteristics of death-row defendants are poverty, the lack of firm social roots in the community, and inadequate legal representation at trial or on appeal. As Justice William O. Douglas noted in *Furman*, "One searches our chronicles in vain for the execution of any member of the affluent strata in this society"(408 US 238).

The demonstrated inequities in the actual administration of capital punishment should tip the balance against it in the judgment of fair-minded and impartial observers. "Whatever else might be said for the use of death as a punishment, one lesson is clear from experience: this is a power that we cannot exercise fairly and without discrimination."[31]

Justice John Marshall Harlan, writing for the Court, noted:

". . . the history of capital punishment for homicides. . . reveals continual efforts, uniformly unsuccessful, to identify before the fact those homicides for which the slayer should die. . . . Those who have come to grips with the hard task of actually attempting to draft means of channeling capital sentencing discretion have confirmed the lesson taught by history. . . . To identify before the fact those characteristics of criminal homicides and their perpetrators which call for the death penalty, and to express these characteristics in language which can be fairly understood and applied by the sentencing authority, appear to be tasks which are beyond present human ability." (402 U.S. 183 (1971))

Yet in the *Gregg* decision, the majority of the Supreme Court abandoned the wisdom of Justice Harlan and ruled as though the new guided-discretion statutes could accomplish the impossible. The truth is that death statutes approved by the Court "do not effectively restrict the discretion of juries by any real standards, and they never will. No society is going to kill everybody who meets certain preset verbal requirements, put on the statute books without awareness of coverage of the infinity of special factors the real world can produce."[32]

Evidence recently obtained by the Capital Jury Project has shown that jurors in capital trials generally do not understand the judge's instructions about the laws that govern the choice between imposing the death penalty and a life sentence. Even when they do comprehend, jurors often refuse to be guided by the law. "Juror comprehension of the law. . . is mediocre. The effect. . . is to reduce the likelihood that capital defendants will benefit from the safeguards against arbitrariness built into the... law."[33]

Even if the jury's sentencing decision were strictly governed by the relevant legal criteria, there remains a vast reservoir of unfettered discretion: the prosecutor's decision to prosecute for a capital or lesser crime, the court's willingness to accept or reject a guilty plea, the jury's decision to convict for second-degree murder or manslaughter rather than capital murder, the determination of the defendant's sanity, and the governor's final clemency decision, among others.

Discretion in the criminal-justice system is unavoidable. The history of capital punishment in America clearly demonstrates the social desire to mitigate the harshness of the death penalty by narrowing the scope of its application. Whether or not explicitly authorized by statutes, sentencing discretion has been the main vehicle to this end. But when sentencing discretion is used—as it too often has been—to doom the poor, the friendless, the uneducated, racial minorities, and the despised, it becomes injustice.

Mindful of such facts, the House of Delegates of the American Bar Association (including 20 out of 24 former presidents of the ABA) called for a moratorium on all executions by a vote of 280 to 119 in February 1997. The House judged the current system to be "a haphazard maze of unfair practices."[34]

Thoughtful citizens, who might possibly support the abstract notion of capital punishment, are obliged to condemn it in actual practice. In its 1996 survey of the death penalty in the United States, the International Commission of Jurists reinforced this point. Despite the efforts made over the past two decades since *Gregg* to protect the administration of the death penalty from abuses, the actual "constitutional errors committed in state courts have gravely undermined the legitimacy of the death penalty as a punishment for crime."[35]

Capital Punishment Is Irreversible

Unlike all other criminal punishments, the death penalty is irrevocable. . . . Although some proponents of capital punishment would argue that its merits are worth the occasional execution of innocent people, most would hasten to insist that there is little likelihood of the innocent being executed. However, *a large body of evidence from the 1980's and 1990's shows that innocent people are often convicted of crimes—including capital crimes—and that some have been executed.*

Since 1900, in this country, there have been on the average more than four cases each year in which an entirely innocent person was convicted of murder. Scores of these individuals were sentenced to death. In many cases, a reprieve or commutation arrived just hours, or even minutes, before the scheduled execution. These erroneous convictions have occurred in virtually every jurisdiction from one end of the nation to the other. Nor have they declined in recent years, despite the new death penalty statutes approved by the Supreme Court.[36]

Consider this handful of representative cases:

- In 1985, in Maryland, Kirk Bloodsworth was sentenced to death for rape and murder, despite the testimony of alibi witnesses. In 1986 his conviction was reversed on grounds of withheld evidence pointing to another suspect; he was retried, re-convicted, and sentenced to life in prison. In 1993, newly available DNA evidence proved he was not the rapist-killer, and he was released after the prosecution dismissed the case. A year later he was awarded $300,000 for wrongful punishment.

- In Mississippi, in 1990, Sabrina Butler was sentenced to death for killing her baby boy. She claimed the child died after attempts at resuscitation failed. On technical grounds her conviction was reversed in 1992. At retrial, she was acquitted when a neighbor corroborated Butler's explanation of the child's cause of death and the physician who performed the autopsy admitted his work had not been thorough.

- In 1985, in Illinois, Rolando Cruz and Alejandro Hernandez were convicted of abduction, rape, and murder of a young girl and were sentenced to death. Shortly after, another man serving a life term in prison for similar crimes confessed that he alone was guilty; but his confession was inadmissible because he refused to repeat it in court unless the state waived the death penalty. Awarded a new trial in 1988, Cruz was again convicted and sentenced to death; Hernandez was also re-convicted, and sentenced to 80 years in prison. In 1992 the assistant attorney general assigned to prosecute the case on appeal

resigned after becoming convinced of the defendants' innocence. The convictions were again overturned on appeal after DNA tests exonerated Cruz and implicated the prisoner who had earlier confessed. In 1995 the court ordered a directed verdict of acquittal, and sharply criticized the police for their unprofessional handling of the case. Hernandez was released on bail and the prosecution dropped all charges.

- In Alabama, Walter McMillian was convicted of murdering a white woman in 1988. Despite the jury's recommendation of a life sentence, the judge sentenced him to death. The sole evidence leading the police to arrest McMillian was testimony of an ex-convict seeking favor with the prosecution. A dozen alibi witnesses (all African Americans, like McMillian) testified on McMillian's behalf, to no avail. On appeal, after tireless efforts by his attorney Bryan Stevenson, McMillian's conviction was reversed by the Alabama Court of Appeals. Stevenson uncovered prosecutorial suppression of exculpatory evidence and perjury by prosecution witnesses, and the new district attorney joined the defense in seeking dismissal of the charges.

- Another 1980s Texas case tells an even more sordid story. In 1980 a black high school janitor, Clarence Brandley, and his white co-worker found the body of a missing 16-year-old white schoolgirl. Interrogated by the police, they were told, "One of you two is going to hang for this." Looking at Brandley, the officer said, "Since you're the nigger, you're elected." In a classic case of rush to judgment, Brandley was tried, convicted, and sentenced to death. The circumstantial evidence against him was thin, other leads were ignored by the police, and the courtroom atmosphere reeked of racism. In 1986, Centurion Ministries—a volunteer group devoted to freeing wrongly convicted prisoners—came to Brandley's aid. Evidence had meanwhile emerged that another man had committed the murder for which Brandley was awaiting execution. Brandley was not released until 1990.[37]

Each of these cases has a reassuring ending: The innocent prisoner is saved from execution and released. But other cases are more troubling.

- In 1992, Roger Keith Coleman was executed in Virginia despite widely publicized doubts surrounding his guilt and evidence that pointed to another person as the murderer— evidence that was never submitted at his trial. Not until late in the appeal process did anyone take seriously the possibility that the state was about to kill an innocent man, and then efforts to delay or nullify his execution failed.[38] Coleman's case was marked with many of the circumstances found in other cases where the defendant was eventually cleared. Were Coleman still incarcerated, his friends and attorneys would have a strong incentive to resolve these questions. But because Coleman is dead, further inquiry into the crime for which he was convicted is extremely unlikely.
- In 1990, Jesse Tafero was executed in Florida. He had been convicted in 1976 along with his wife, Sonia Jacobs, for murdering a state trooper. In 1981 Jacobs' death sentence was reduced on appeal to life imprisonment, and 11 years later her conviction was vacated by a federal court. The evidence on which Tafero and Jacobs had been convicted and sentenced was identical; it consisted mainly of the perjured testimony of ex-convict who turned state's witness in order to avoid a death sentence. Had Tafero been alive in 1992, he no doubt would have been released along with Jacobs.[39] Tafero's death is probably the clearest case in recent years of the execution of an innocent person.

Several factors help explain why the judicial system cannot guarantee that justice will never miscarry: overzealous prosecution, mistaken or perjured testimony, faulty police work, coerced confessions, the defendant's previous criminal record, inept defense counsel, seemingly conclusive circumstantial evidence, and community pressure for a conviction, among others. And when the system does go wrong, it is volunteers outside the criminal justice system—journalists, for example—who rectify the errors, not the police or prosecutors. To retain the death penalty in the face of the demonstrable failures of the system is unacceptable, especially since there are no strong overriding reasons to favor the death penalty.

Capital Punishment Is Barbarous

Prisoners are executed in the United States by any one of five methods; in a few jurisdictions the prisoner is allowed to choose which one he or she prefers. These are the methods of capital punishment in use in mid-1997.

The traditional mode of execution, hanging, is an option still available in Delaware, New Hampshire and Washington. Death on the gallows is easily bungled: If the drop is too short, there will be a slow and agonizing death by strangulation. If the drop is too long, the head will be torn off.

Two states, Idaho and Utah, still authorize the firing squad. The prisoner is strapped into a chair and hooded. A target is pinned to the chest. Five marksmen, one with blanks, take aim and fire.

Throughout the twentieth century, electrocution has been the most widely used form of execution in this country, and is still utilized in eleven states. The condemned prisoner is led—or dragged—into the death chamber, strapped into the chair, and electrodes are fastened to head and legs. When the switch is thrown the body strains, jolting as the voltage is raised and lowered. Often smoke rises from the head. There is the awful odor of burning flesh. No one knows how long electrocuted individuals retain consciousness.

In 1983, the electrocution of John Evans in Alabama was described by an eyewitness as follows:

> "At 8:30 p.m. the first jolt of 1900 volts of electricity passed through Mr. Evans' body. It lasted thirty seconds. Sparks and flames erupted. . . from the electrode tied to Mr. Evans' left leg. His body slammed against the straps holding him in the electric chair and his fist clenched permanently. The electrode apparently burst from the strap holding it in place. A large puff of grayish smoke and sparks poured out from under the hood that covered Mr. Evans' face. An overpowering stench of burnt flesh

and clothing began pervading the witness room. Two doctors examined Mr. Evans and declared that he was not dead.

"The electrode on the left leg was re-fastened. . . .Mr. Evans was administered a second thirty second jolt of electricity. The stench of burning flesh was nauseating. More smoke emanated from his leg and head. Again, the doctors examined Mr. Evans. [They] reported that his heart was still beating, and that he was still alive. At that time, I asked the prison commissioner, who was communicating on an open telephone line to Governor George Wallace, to grant clemency on the grounds that Mr. Evans was being subjected to cruel and unusual punishment. The request . . .was denied.

"At 8:40 p.m., a third charge of electricity, thirty seconds in duration, was passed through Mr. Evans' body. At 8:44, the doctors pronounced him dead. The execution of John Evans took fourteen minutes."[40] Afterwards, officials were embarrassed by what one observer called the "barbaric ritual." The prison spokesman remarked, "This was supposed to be a very clean manner of administering death."[41]

The introduction of the gas chamber was an attempt to improve on electrocution. In this method of execution the prisoner is strapped into a chair with a container of sulfuric acid underneath. The chamber is sealed, and cyanide is dropped into the acid to form a lethal gas. Here is an account of the 1992 execution in Arizona of Don Harding, as reported in the dissent by U.S. Supreme Court Justice John Paul Stevens:

"When the fumes enveloped Don's head he took a quick breath. A few seconds later he again looked in my direction. His face was red and contorted as if he were attempting to fight through tremendous pain. His mouth was pursed shut and his jaw was clenched tight. Don then took several more quick gulps of the fumes.

"At this point Don's body started convulsing violently. . . . His face and body turned a deep red and the veins in his temple and neck began to bulge until I thought they might explode. After about a minute Don's face leaned partially forward, but he was still conscious. Every few seconds he continued to gulp in. He was shuddering uncontrollably and his body was racked with spasms. His head continued to snap back. His hands were clenched.

"After several more minutes, the most violent of the convulsions subsided. At this time the muscles along Don's left arm and back began twitching in a wavelike motion under his skin. Spittle drooled from his mouth.

"Don did not stop moving for approximately eight minutes, and after that he continued to twitch and jerk for another minute. Approximately two minutes later, we were told by a prison official that the execution was complete.

Don Harding took ten minutes and thirty one seconds to die." (*Gomez v. U.S. District Court,* 112 S.Ct. 1652)

Execution by suffocation in the lethal gas chamber may soon be abolished. In 1996 a panel of judges on the 9th Circuit Court of Appeals in California (where the gas chamber has been used since 1933) ruled that this method is a "cruel and unusual punishment."[42]

The latest mode of inflicting the death penalty, enacted into law by more than 30 states, is lethal injection, first used in 1982 in Texas. It is easy to overstate the humaneness and I efficacy of this method; one cannot know whether lethal injection is really painless. As the U.S. Court of Appeals observed, there is "substantial and uncontroverted evidence. . . that execution by lethal injection poses a serious risk of cruel, protracted death. . . . Even a slight error in dosage or administration can leave a prisoner conscious but paralyzed while dying, a sentient witness of his or her own asphyxiation." (*Chaney v. Heckler,* 718 F.2d 1174,1983).

Nor does execution by lethal injection always proceed smoothly as planned. In 1985 "the authorities repeatedly jabbed needles into. . . Stephen Morin, when they had trouble finding a usable vein because he had been a drug abuser.[43] In 1988, during the execution of Raymond Landry, "a tube attached to a needle inside the inmate's right arm began leaking, sending the lethal mixture shooting across the death chamber toward witnesses.[44]

Its veneer of decency and subtle analogy with life-saving medical practice no doubt makes killing by lethal injection more acceptable to the public.

Journalist Susan Blaustein, reacting to having witnessed an execution in Texas, comments:

> "The lethal injection method... has turned dying into a still life, thereby enabling the state to kill without anyone involved feeling anything. . . . Any remaining glimmers of doubt—about whether the man received due process, about his guilt, about our right to take life—cause us to rationalize these deaths with such catchwords as "heinous," "deserved," "deterrent," "justice," and "painless." We have perfected the art of institutional killing to the degree that it has deadened our natural, quintessentially human response to death.[45]

Most people observing an execution are horrified and disgusted. "I was ashamed," writes sociologist Richard Moran, who witnessed an execution in Texas in 1985. "I was an intruder, the only member of the public who had trespassed on [the condemned man's] private moment of anguish. In my face he could see the horror of his own death.[46]

Revulsion at the duty to supervise and witness executions is one reason why so many prison wardens—however unsentimental they are about crime and criminals—are opponents of capital punishment. Don Cabana, who supervised several executions in Missouri and Mississippi reflects on his mood just prior to witnessing an execution in the gas chamber:

> "If [the condemned prisoner] was some awful monster deemed worthy of extermination, why did I feel so bad about it, I wondered. It has been said that men on death row are inhuman, cold-blooded killers. But as I stood and watched a grieving mother leave her son for the last time, I questioned how the sordid business of executions was supposed to be the great equalizer. . . . The 'last mile' seemed an eternity, every step a painful reminder of what waited at the end of the walk. Where was the cold-blooded murderer, I wondered, as we approached the door to the last-night cell. I had looked for that man before. . . and I still had not found him—I saw, in my grasp, only a frightened child. [Minutes after

the execution and before] heading for the conference room and a waiting press corps, I. . . shook my head. 'No more. I don't want to do this anymore.'"[47]

For some individuals, however, executions seem to appeal to strange, aberrant impulses and provide an outlet for sadistic urges. Warden Lewis Lawes of Sing Sing Prison in New York wrote of the many requests he received to watch electrocutions, and told that when the job of executioner became vacant. "I received more than seven hundred applications for the position, many of them offering cut-rate prices."[48]

Public executions were common in this country during the 19th and early 20th centuries. One of the last ones occurred in 1936 in Kentucky, when 20,000 people gathered to watch the hanging of a young African American male.[49]

Delight in brutality, pain, violence and death may always be with us. But surely we must conclude that it is best for the law not to encourage such impulses. When the government sanctions, commands, and ceremoniously carries out the execution of a prisoner, it lends support to this destructive side of human nature.

More than two centuries ago the Italian jurist Cesare Beccaria, in his highly influential treatise *On Crimes and Punishment* (1764), asserted: "The death penalty cannot be useful, because of the example of barbarity it gives men." Beccaria's words still ring true—even if the death penalty were a "useful" deterrent, it would still be an "example of barbarity." *No society can safely entrust the enforcement of its laws to torture, brutality, or killing. Such methods are inherently cruel and will always mock the attempt to cloak them in justice.* As Supreme Court Justice Arthur J. Goldberg wrote, "The deliberate institutionalized taking of human life by the state is the greatest conceivable degradation to the dignity of the human personality."[50]

Capital Punishment Is Unjustified Retribution

Justice, it is often insisted, requires the death penalty as the only suitable retribution for heinous crimes. This claim does not bear scrutiny, however. By its nature, all punishment is retributive. Therefore, *whatever legitimacy is to be found in punishment as just retribution can, in principle, be satisfied without recourse to executions.*

Moreover, the death penalty could be defended on narrowly retributive grounds only for the crime of murder, and not for any of the many other crimes that have frequently been made subject to this mode of punishment (rape, kidnapping, espionage, treason, drug trafficking). Few defenders of the death penalty are willing to confine themselves consistently to the narrow scope afforded by retribution. In any case, execution is more than a punishment exacted in retribution for the taking of a life. As Nobel Laureate Albert Camus wrote, "For there to be equivalence, the death penalty would have to punish a criminal who had warned his victim of the date at which he would inflict a horrible death on him and who, from that moment onward, had confined him at his mercy for months. Such a monster is not encountered in private life.[51]

It is also often argued that death is what murderers deserve, and that those who oppose the death penalty violate the fundamental principle that criminals should be punished according to their just desserts—"making the punishment fit the crime." If this rule means punishments are unjust unless they are like the crime itself, then the principle is unacceptable: It would require us to rape rapists, torture torturers, and inflict other horrible and degrading punishments on offenders. It would require us to betray traitors and kill multiple murderers again and again—punishments that are, of course, impossible to inflict. Since we cannot reasonably aim to punish all crimes according to this principle, it is arbitrary to invoke it as a requirement of justice in the punishment of murder.

If, however, the principle of just deserts means the severity of punishments must be proportional to the gravity of the crime—and since murder is the gravest crime, it deserves the severest punishment—then the principle is no doubt sound. Nevertheless, this premise does not compel support for the death penalty; what it does require is that other crimes be punished with terms of imprisonment or other deprivations less severe than those used in the punishment of murder.

Criminals no doubt deserve to be punished, and the severity of the punishment should be appropriate to their culpability and the harm they have caused the innocent. But severity of punishment has its limits—imposed by both justice and our common human dignity. Governments that respect these limits do not use premeditated, violent homicide as an instrument of social policy.

Some people who have lost a loved one to murder believe that they cannot rest until the murderer is executed. But this sentiment is by no means universal. Coretta Scott King has observed, "As one whose husband and mother-in-law have died the victims of murder and assassination, I stand firmly and unequivocally opposed to the death penalty for those convicted of capital offenses. An evil deed is not redeemed by an evil deed of retaliation. Justice is never advanced in the taking of a human life. Morality is never upheld by a legalized murder."[52]

Kerry Kennedy Cuomo, daughter of the slain Senator Robert Kennedy, has written:

> "I was eight years old when my father was murdered. It is almost impossible to describe the pain of losing a parent to a senseless murder. . . .But even as a child one thing was clear to me: I didn't want the killer, in turn, to be killed. I remember lying in bed and praying, 'Please, God. Please don't take his life too.' I saw nothing that could be accomplished in the loss of one life being answered with the loss of another. And I knew, far too vividly, the anguish that would spread through another family—another set of parents, children, brothers, and sisters thrown into grief.[53]

Across the nation, many who have survived the murder of a loved one have joined Murder Victims' Families for Reconciliation (headquartered in Virginia), in the effort to replace anger and hate toward the criminal with a restorative approach to both the offender and the bereaved survivors.

Capital Punishment Costs More Than Incarceration

It is sometimes suggested that abolishing capital punishment is unfair to the taxpayer, on the assumption that life imprisonment is more expensive than execution. If one takes into account all the relevant costs, however, just the reverse is true. "The death penalty is not now, nor has it ever been, a more economical alternative to life imprisonment."[54] A murder trial normally takes much longer when the death penalty is at issue than when it is not. Litigation costs—including the time of judges, prosecutors, public defenders, and court reporters, and the high costs of briefs—are mostly borne by the taxpayer. A 1982 study showed that were the death penalty to be reintroduced in New York, the cost of the capital trial alone would be more than double the cost of a life term in prison.[55]

In Maryland, a comparison of capital trial costs with and without the death penalty for the years 1979–1984 concluded that a death-penalty case costs "approximately 42 percent more than a case resulting in a non-death sentence."[56] In 1988 and 1989 the Kansas legislature voted against reinstating the death penalty after it was informed that reintroduction would involve a first-year cost of "more than $11 million."[57] Florida, with one of the nation's most populous death rows, has estimated that the true cost of each execution is approximately $3.2 million, or approximately *six times the cost* of a life-imprisonment sentence."[58]

A 1993 study of the costs of North Carolina's capital punishment system revealed that litigating a murder case from start to finish adds an extra $163,000 to what it would cost the state to keep the convicted offender in prison for 20 years. The extra cost goes up to $216,000 per case when all first-degree murder trials and their appeals are considered, many of which do not end with a death sentence and an execution.[59]

From one end of the country to the other public officials decry the additional cost of capital cases even when they support the death penalty system. "Wherever the death penalty is in place, it siphons off resources which could be going to the front line in the war against crime. . . . Politicians could address this crisis, but, for the most part they either endorse executions or remain silent."[60] *The only way to make the death penalty more "cost effective" than imprisonment is to weaken due process and curtail appellate review, which are the defendant's (and society's) only protection against the most aberrant miscarriages of justice.* Any savings in dollars would, of course, be at the cost of justice: In nearly half of the death-penalty cases given review under federal habeas corpus provisions, the murder conviction or death sentence was overturned.[61]

In 1996, in response to public clamor for accelerating executions, Congress imposed severe restrictions on access to federal habeas corpus[62] and also ended all funding of the regional death penalty "resource centers" charged with providing counsel on appeal in the federal courts.[63] These restrictions virtually guarantee that the number and variety of wrongful murder convictions and death sentences will increase. The savings in time and money will prove to be illusory.

Capital Punishment Is Less Popular Than the Alternatives

It is commonly reported that the American public overwhelmingly approves of the death penalty. More careful analysis of public attitudes, however, reveals that most Americans prefer an alternative; they would oppose the death penalty if convicted murderers were sentenced to life without parole and were required to make some form of financial restitution. A 1993 nationwide survey revealed that although 77% of the public approves of the death penalty, support drops to 56% if the alternative is punishment with no parole eligibility until 25 years in prison. Support drops even further, to 49%, if the alternative is no parole under any conditions. And if the alternative is no parole plus restitution, it drops still further, to 41%.[64] Only a minority of the American public would favor the death penalty if offered such alternatives.

Internationally, Capital Punishment Is Widely Viewed as Inhumane and Anachronistic

An international perspective on the death penalty helps us understand the peculiarity of its use in the United States. As long ago as 1962, it was reported to the Council of Europe that "the facts clearly show that the death penalty is regarded in Europe as something of an anachronism. . . ."[65]

Today, either by law or in practice, all of Western Europe has abolished the death penalty. In Great Britain, it was abolished (except for cases of treason) in 1971; France abolished it in 1981. Canada abolished it in 1976. The United Nations General Assembly affirmed in a formal resolution that throughout the world, it is desirable to "progressively restrict the number of offenses for which the death penalty might be imposed, with a view to the desirability of abolishing this punishment."[66] By mid-1995, eighteen countries had ratified the Sixth Protocol to the European Convention on Human Rights, outlawing the death penalty in peacetime.[67]

Underscoring worldwide support for abolition was the action of the South African constitutional court in 1995, barring the death penalty as an "inhumane" punishment. Between 1989 and 1995, two dozen other countries abolished the death penalty for all crimes. More than half of all nations have abolished it either by law or in practice.[68]

Once in use everywhere and for a wide variety of crimes, the death penalty today is generally forbidden by law and widely abandoned in practice, in most countries outside the United States. Indeed, the unmistakable worldwide trend is toward the complete abolition of capital punishment. In the United States, opposition to the death penalty is widespread and diverse. Catholic, Jewish, and Protestant religious groups are among the more than 50 national organizations that constitute the National Coalition to Abolish the Death Penalty.

NOTES

1. See U.S. Dept, of Justice, "Capital Punishment," annually, 1990 et seq.
2. See *Uniform Crime Reports*, annually, 1990 et seq.
3. See *Uniform Crime Reports*, 1993, and note 2 et seq.
4. See *Uniform Crime Reports*, annually, 1990 et seq.
5. Cochran, Chamlin and Seth. "Deterrence, or Brutalization?" in *Criminology* (1994).
6. U.S. Bureau of Justice Statistics, "Capital Punishment 1994," p. 14; "Death Row U.S.A.", Summer 1996, pp. 7–8.
7. Bailey and Peterson, *Criminology* (1987), p. 22. See also their general discussion of death penalty deterrence in Bedau, ed. *The Death Penalty in America: Current Controversies* (1997).
8. *Sourcebook of Criminal Justice Statistics*, 1994, p. 587, and *Sourcebook* 1995, p. 603.
9. Wolfson, in Bedau, ed., *The Death Penalty in America*, 3rd ed. (1982), p. 167.
10. Ehrlich, in American Economic Review (1974); Phillips, in *American Journal of Sociology* (1980); and Layson, in *Southern Economic Journal* (1985).
11. Lempert, in *Crime & Delinquency* (1983); Peterson and Bailey, in Chambliss, ed., *Criminal Law in Action*, 2nd ed. (1984); Bowers, in Hasse and Inciardi, eds., *Challenging Capital Punishment* (1988); Peterson and Bailey, in *Social Forces* (1988), and Fox and Radelet, in *Loyola of Los Angeles Law Review* (1989).
12. Blumstein, Cohen and Nagin, eds., *Deterrence and Incapacitation* (1975), p.358.
13. West, Solomon, and Diamond, in Bedau and Pierce, eds., *Capital Punishment in the United States* (1976).
14. Bedau, "Recidivism, Parole, and Deterrence," in Bedau, ed., *Death Penalty in America*, 3rd ed.
15. Marquart and Sorensen, in *Loyola of Los Angeles Law Review* (1989).
16. Bureau of Justice Statistics, "Capital Punishment 1994."
17. Marquart, Ekland-Olson, and Sorensen, *The Rope, the Chair, and the Needle: Capital Punishment in Texas, 1923–1990* (1994).
18. Bureau of Justice Statistics, "Capital Punishment 1977"; "Death Row USA," Summer 1996.
19. Bowers, *Legal Homicide* (1984); Streib, *Death Penalty for Juveniles* (1987); "Death Row USA," Summer 1996.
20. "Death Row USA," 1976 et seq. Bureau of Justice Statistics, "Capital Punishment, 1995."
21. *Uniform Crime Reports*, 1972–1995.
22. Baldus, Woodworth, and Pulaski, *Equal Justice and the Death Penalty* (1990), p. 401.
23. See Edwards and Conyers, in *University of Dayton Law Review* (1995).
24. U.S. General Accounting Office, *Death Penalty Sentencing* (1990), pp. 5,6.
25. "Death Row USA," Summer 1996 and *Sourcebook of Criminal Justice Statistics—1995.*
26. U.S. Bureau of Justice Statistics, "Capital Punishment," 1980–1994.
27. *Uniform Crime Reports*, 1980–1994.
28. Memorandum, National Coalition to Abolish the Death Penalty, January 1991.
29. U.S. Bureau of Justice Statistics, "Capital Punishment, 1979"; "Death Row USA," Summer 1995.
30. Tabak, in *Loyola of Los Angeles Law Review* (1984).
31. Gross and Mauro, *Death and Discrimination* (1989), p. 224.
32. Black, *Capital Punishment: The Inevitability of Caprice and Mistake*, 2nd ed. (1982).
33. Symposium on the Capital Jury Project, *Indiana Law Journal* (1995), p. 1181.
34. "Bar Association Leaders Urge Moratorium on Death Penalty," *The New York Times*, Feb. 4, 1997, p. A 20.
35. International Commission of Jurists, *Administration of the Death Penalty In The United States* (1996), p. 69
36. Radelet, Lofquist, and Bedau, in *Thomas M. Cooley Law Review* (1977); Radelet, Bedau, and Putnam, *In Spite of*

Innocence (1992); Bedau and Radelet, "Miscarriages of Justice in Potentially Capital Cases," in *Stanford Law Review* (1987).

37. Davies, *White Lies* (1991).

38. David Kaplan, "Hung on Technicality," *Newsweek*, April 6,1992; Jill Smolow, "Must This Man Die?", *Time*, May 18, 1992, p. 40.

39. Radelet, Lofquist, and Bedau, in *Thomas M. Cooley Law Review* (1997).

40. *Glass v. Louisiana*, 471 U.S. 1080 (1985).

41. *Boston Globe*, April 24,1983. p. 24.

42. Eric Brazi, "State Prepares for Switch to Lethal Injection," *San Francisco Examiner*, Jan. 14,1996.

43. "Murderer Executed After a Leaky Lethal Injection," *The New York Times*, December 14, 1988, p. A29.

44. *Ibid.*

45. Blaustein, "Witness to Another Execution," *Harpers Magazine*, May 1994, p. 53

46. *Los Angeles Times*, March 24, 1985, Pt IV, p. 5.

47. Cabana, *Death at Midnight: The Confession of an Executioner* (1996), p. 177, 186, 190.

48. Lawes, *Life and Death in Sing Sing* (1928).

49. Teeters, in *Journal of the Lancaster County Historical Society* (1960).

50. *The Boston Globe*, August 16, 1976, p. 17.

51. Camus, "Reflections on the Guillotine," in *Resistance, Rebellion, and Death* (1960).

52. Coretta Scott King, Speech to National Coalition to Abolish the Death Penalty, Washington, D.C., September 26, 1981.

53. Kerry Kennedy, Foreword to Gray and Stanley, *A Punishment in Search of A Crime* (1989).

54. Spangenberg and Walsh, in *Loyola of Los Angeles Law Review* (1989), p. 47.

55. N.Y. State Defenders Assn., "Capital Losses" (1982).

56. U.S. Govt. Accounting Office, *Limited Data Available in Costs of Death Sentences* (1989), p. 50.

57. Cited in Spangenberg and Walsh, note 56.

58. David von Drehle, "Capital Punishment in Paralysis," *Miami Herald*, July 10, 1988.

59. Cook and Lawson, *The Costs of Processing Murder Cases in North Carolina* (1993), pp. 97–98.

60. Dieter, *Millions Misspent: What Politicians Don't Say About the High Costs of the Death Penalty* (1992), p. 9.

61. Greenhouse, "Judicial Panel Urges Limits on Appeals by Death Row Inmates," *The New York Times*, Sept. 22, 1989.

62. See Tabak, in *Seton Hall Law Review* (1996); Yackel, in *Buffalo Law Review* (1996); Coyle, in *National Law Journal* (May 20 1996); and the Panel Discussion in *Loyola University Chicago Law Journal* (1996).

63. Carol Castenada, "Death Penalty Centers Losing Support Funds," *USA Today*, Oct. 24, 1995, p. 38; Coyle, in *National Law Journal* (Sept. 18, 1995 and Jan. 15, 1996).

64. Dieter, *Sentencing For Life: Americans Embrace Alternatives to the Death Penalty* (1993).

65. Ancel, *The Death Penalty in European Countries* (1962), p. 55.

66. UN, Ecosoc, Official Records 58th Sess. (1971), Suppl. 1, p. 36.

67. Hood, *The Death Penalty: A Worldwide Perspective*, rev. ed. (1996).

68. Hood, *The Death Penalty* (1996); Amnesty International, press release, Oct. 1996.

DISCUSSION QUESTIONS:

1. Consider Bedau's three reasons to think that the death penalty fails as a deterrent. Are they correct? Are they adequate to show that the death penalty is not a more effective deterrent than long-term incarceration?

2. Is the death penalty currently administered in a way that is arbitrary, racially biased, and unfair? If so, is this a reason to eliminate the death penalty or to modify our administration of it? What changes in the administration of the death penalty would be required to address Bedau's concerns? Would they increase the financial cost of administering the penalty?

3. Bedau presents several cases in which persons initially sentenced to death were later acquitted. Are such cases a good reason to think that there is a substantial risk that we will execute the innocent or a good reason to think that our current safeguards against doing so are working?

4. Are Bedau's eyewitness reactions to executions a good reason to think that the death penalty is, as he writes, "inherently cruel" and too barbarous to be justified? What distinguishes those penalties that are too barbarous to ever be justified from those that are not?

5. Does Bedau give a successful response to the argument that, since justice demands that the punishment fit the crime and death is the only punishment that fits the crime of murder, the death penalty is at least a justified penalty for murder?

6. Bedau notes that we can reduce the financial costs associated with the death penalty and speed up its application by reducing the safeguards we have introduced to increase the fairness and accuracy of its application. What determines the appropriate balance between reducing financial costs and providing prompt justice, on the one hand, and ensuring accuracy and fairness, on the other?

7. Bedau claims that only a minority of Americans favors the death penalty over other alternatives and that the death penalty is widely viewed internationally as inhumane and anachronistic. How, if at all, are the results of such opinion polls relevant to the issue of whether the death penalty is justified?

Argument Reconstruction Exercises:

I. In arguing that the death penalty is not an effective deterrent to violent crime, Bedau appeals to several considerations. Identify the premises and conclusion of the following restatement of his argument:

> A punishment can be an effective deterrent only if it is consistently and promptly applied and only if those likely to commit the crimes for which it is provided are likely to consider seriously the threat of punishment in their deliberations. The death penalty cannot be consistently or promptly applied given current safeguards. Violent criminals often act without premeditation, and those who premeditate often believe they won't get caught. Therefore, the death penalty cannot be an effective deterrent. (pages 601–603)

II. Bedau presents evidence that the death penalty is currently applied in an arbitrary, racially biased, and unfair manner. Is this a good reason to reject the death penalty or to improve our administration of it? Can the same complaint be made with regard to other penalties as well? Identify the premises and conclusion of the following argument:

> We are not justified in adopting the death penalty. We might be justified in adopting it if we could administer it with an appropriate degree of accuracy and fairness, but we cannot. The required degree of accuracy and fairness increases with a penalty's severity and our inability to rectify mistakes in its application. The severity of the death penalty and our inability to rectify mistakes in its application distinguish it from imprisonment and require for its justified application a degree of accuracy and fairness that is beyond us.

III. Bedau considers attempts to defend the death penalty by appealing to the principle of just desserts. Identify the premises and conclusion in this restatement of his argument:

> If the principle—"making the punishment fit the crime"—means making the punishment like the crime itself, then the principle is unacceptable: It would require us to rape rapists and torture torturers. If it means the severity of a punishment must be proportional to the gravity of the crime, it is sound but does not support the death penalty for murder; it only requires that other crimes be punished less severely than murder. (page 610)

IV. Bedau argues that the death penalty cannot be both just and less costly than imprisonment. Identify the premises and conclusion of his argument:

> The only way to make the death penalty more "cost effective" than imprisonment is to weaken due process and curtail appellate review, which are the defendant's (and society's) only protection against the most aberrant miscarriages of justice. Any savings in dollars would, of course, be at the cost of justice: In nearly half of the death-penalty cases given review under federal habeas corpus provisions, the murder conviction or death sentence was overturned. (page 611)

CHAPTER 22

Morality and the Law

Whatever we once were, we're no longer just a Christian nation; we are also a Jewish nation, a Muslim nation, a Buddhist nation, a Hindu nation, and a nation of nonbelievers. We should acknowledge this and realize that when we're formulating policies from the state house to the Senate floor to the White House, we've got to work to translate our reasoning into values that are accessible to every one of our citizens, not just members of our own faith community.

—BARACK OBAMA (CNN NEWS, JULY 2007)

INTRODUCTION

What is the proper relation between our legal system and our moral values? Our morality clearly informs our law. A good bit of what we take to be seriously immoral (e.g. acts of murder and rape), we also make illegal. We use legal measures, such as tax deductions, to encourage activities that we take to be morally virtuous, like charitable giving. Yet, we also think that there are limits to the legal enforcement of moral values. We use the law to encourage charitable giving but not to require it. We don't provide every promise with legal protection. And there are a number of things that we think are seriously morally wrong that we decline to make illegal (e.g., cheating on one's spouse). To what extent, then, should a society's morality be carried over into its legal system?

This question is, in itself, a moral one. It concerns how each society should, from a moral point of view, design its legal system. It is complicated by the fact that societies often contain a great diversity people with a great diversity of moral beliefs. It won't do to simply say that each society should use its legal system to enforce its fundamental or most important moral values, for, given a diversity of moral values in a society, we still face the question of exactly what counts as "the society's moral values." The question is also complicated by the quite plausible assumption that some objectively correct moral values should guide any society in its construction of a legal system, even if they are not part of the society's current moral code. As an objective fact, each society's legal system should meet the appropriate demands of individual liberty, providing for such things as freedom of expression and freedom of association, whether the society recognizes that value or not. No legal system should enforce a practice of human slavery, even if a society's morality may view slavery as permissible.

One approach to the question of the proper relation between a society's law and its morality is **Liberalism**. Its fundamental principle is the **Harm Principle**, aptly stated by John Stuart Mill, in the first essay in this chapter:

> [T]he sole end for which mankind are warranted, individually or collectively in interfering with the liberty of action of any of their number, is self-protection.

People may act in ways that others find morally inappropriate, offensive, and insulting. Their conduct may be unwise or even self-destructive. Yet, so long as they are mentally competent adults, their conduct should not be legally restricted, unless their actions pose a threat of harm to non-consenting others. According to Mill, if an individual's conduct does not pose a threat to non-consenting others, it falls in a private realm of activity that is beyond social regulation. If it does pose such a threat, it is in the public realm and whether and how to regulate it depends on society's interests.

An alternative approach is offered by **Legal Moralism**, according to which societies may properly enforce moral standards beyond those that prohibit harm to non-consenting others. Patrick Devlin develops one form of this view in his essay. According to Devlin, each society must have a public morality, a set of widely accepted moral beliefs that help define its character as a society. Without this shared agreement on matters of morals, a society cannot exist. Each society has a right to use its legal system to protect and preserve those institutions, including its public morality, that are necessary to its existence. It does not matter whether the public morality is correct or incorrect. The society has a right to legally enforce the shared moral values it contains. In properly exercising this right, a society may legally regulate, indeed prohibit, activities that fall in Mill's private realm.

Liberalism and Legal Moralism are best appreciated in terms of their implications for particular issues. These are explored in the essays by Sarah Roberts-Cady, Helen Longino, and Joel Feinberg, as they consider the appropriate boundaries of legal regulation with regard to particular forms of conduct. In her essay, Roberts-Cady considers the French law, enacted in 2010, banning citizens from wearing veils over their faces in public. French legislators have acknowledged that the law is aimed at conservative Muslim traditions in which women are expected to wear a full-face veil in public (the *burqa* or the *niqab*). Roberts-Cady considers the propriety of the law from the perspectives of both Mill's and Devlin's positions and argues that it is a morally impermissible restriction on individual liberty.

Longino and Feinberg both consider the extent to which society is justified in seriously restricting the production, distribution, and consumption of pornography, especially pornography that depicts violence against women. Longino finds a justification for doing so in Mill's theory, on the ground that pornography harms women in multiple ways. She examines and rejects three arguments to the effect that the suppression of pornography violates the liberty of those who create, distribute, and consume it. Feinberg thinks otherwise: pornography, he argues, is not harmful to women in a way that warrants its legal regulation. Feinberg also considers and rejects the claim that pornography is offensive to a large segment of society in a way that justifies its legal suppression. While we might legally suppress violent pornography on the ground that it is contrary to our society's public morality, that position involves a commitment to Devlin's legal moralism, which he finds implausible. The claim that pornography should be legally suppressed because it is in itself objectively wrong relies on the doubtful premise that an activity that does not significantly and directly harm others is nonetheless immoral.

SUGGESTIONS FOR FURTHER READING

Dworkin, Andrea. *Pornography: Men Possessing Women*. (London: The Women's Press, 1981)

Dworkin, Gerald. "Equal Respect and the Enforcement of Morality." *Crime, Culpability and Remedy*, ed. Paul, Ellen Frankel, Miller, Fred D., and Paul, Jeffrey. (Oxford: Oxford University Press, 1990)

———. "Devlin was Right: Law and the Enforcement of Morality." *William and Mary Law Review*, 40, 927, 1999.

Dworkin, Ronald. *A Matter of Principle*. (Cambridge: Cambridge University Press, 1985)

_____. "Pornography and Hate." *Freedom's Law: The Moral Reading of the American Constitution.* (Oxford: Oxford University Press, 1996, pp. 214–226)

Feinberg, Joel. *Harm to Others: The Moral Limits of the Criminal Law.* (Oxford: Oxford University Press, 1984)

_____. *Offense to Others.* (Oxford: Oxford University Press, 1985)

Hart, H. L. A. *Law, Liberty and Morality* (Oxford: Oxford University Press, 1963)

_____. "Social Solidarity and the Enforcement of Morality. In *Essays in Jurisprudence and Philosophy.* (Oxford: Oxford University Press, 1983)

MacKinnon, C. *Only Words.* (London: Harper Collins, 1995)

Raz, J. *The Morality of Freedom.* (Clarendon: Oxford University Press, 1986)

Ten, C. L. *Mill on Liberty.* (Oxford: Oxford University Press, 1980)

22.1 THE HARM PRINCIPLE

JOHN STUART MILL (1869)

John Stuart Mill was a British philosopher, economist, and social theorist. He made major contributions to logic, social philosophy, and ethics. In these selections from his book *On Liberty*, he considers the appropriate limits of societal regulation of individual conduct and argues for what has come to be called the **Harm Principle**: An individual's conduct may be subjected to social regulation, with the compulsion that that involves, only if the conduct is likely to harm others without their consent. Mill notes that his principle applies only to rational adults, and he particularly emphasizes that societies are not justified in compelling people to act in certain ways simply because it is judged to be for their benefit that they do so.

Reading Questions:

1. What sorts of attempts by a society to influence the conduct of its members are governed by the Harm Principle?

2. To what sorts of societies does Mill think his Harm Principle applies? What is his basis for exempting some societies from the principle?

3. How does Mill understand the concept of harm? What are some examples of harmful conduct and of non-harmful conduct?

4. Suppose an activity is likely to harm others without their consent; what, according to Mill, determines whether those engaged in the activity should be compelled to act otherwise?

5 Complete the following to give your own statement of Mill's view: An individual's conduct may be subjected to social regulation if and only if

_____.

6. What considerations does Mill offer in support of the Harm Principle?

7. What four reasons does Mill give to support his claim that freedom of thought and expression is necessary for human well-being?

8. What does Mill offer as the strongest reason against the social regulation of purely personal conduct?

Introduction

The object of this Essay is to assert one very simple principle, as entitled to govern absolutely the dealings of society with the individual in the way of compulsion and control, whether the means used be physical force in the form of legal penalties, or the moral coercion of public opinion. That principle is, that *the sole end for which mankind are warranted, individually or collectively, in interfering with the liberty of action of any of their number is self-protection.* That the only purpose for which power can be rightfully exercised over any member of a civilized community, against his will, is to prevent harm to others. His own good, either physical or moral, is not a sufficient warrant. He cannot rightfully be compelled to do or forbear because it will be better for him to do so, because it will make him happier, because, in the opinions of others, to do so would be wise, or even right. These are good reasons for remonstrating with him, or reasoning with him, or persuading him, or entreating him, but not for compelling him, or visiting him with any evil, in case he do otherwise. To justify that, the conduct from which it is desired to deter him must be calculated to produce evil to some one else. The only part of the conduct of any one, for which he is amenable to society, is that which concerns others. In the part which merely concerns himself, his independence is, of right, absolute. Over himself, over his own body and mind, the individual is sovereign.

It is, perhaps, hardly necessary to say that this doctrine is meant to apply only to human beings in the maturity of their faculties. We are not speaking of children, or of young persons below the age which the law may fix as that of manhood or womanhood. Those who are still in a state to require being taken care of by others, must be protected against their own actions as well as against external injury. For the same reason, we may leave out of consideration those backward states of society in which the race itself may be considered as in its nonage. The early difficulties in the way of spontaneous progress are so great, that there is seldom any choice of means for overcoming them; and a ruler full of the spirit of improvement is warranted in the use of any expedients that will attain an end, perhaps otherwise unattainable. Despotism is a legitimate mode of government in dealing with barbarians, provided the end be their improvement, and the means justified by actually effecting that end. Liberty, as a principle, has no application to any state of things anterior to the time when mankind have become capable of being improved by free and equal discussion. Until then, there is nothing for them but implicit obedience to an Akbar or a Charlemagne, if they are so fortunate as to find one. But as soon as mankind have attained the capacity of being guided to their own improvement by conviction or persuasion (a period long since reached in all nations with whom we need here concern ourselves), compulsion, either in the direct form or in that of pains and penalties for noncompliance, is no longer admissible as a means to their own good, and justifiable only for the security of others.

It is proper to state that I forego any advantage which could be derived to my argument from the idea of abstract right as a thing independent of utility. I regard utility as the ultimate appeal on all ethical questions; but it must be utility in the largest sense, grounded on the permanent interests of man as a progressive being. Those interests, I contend, authorize the subjection of individual spontaneity to external control, only in respect to those actions of each, which concern the interest of other people. If any one does an act hurtful to others, there is a prima facie case for punishing him, by law, or, where legal penalties are not safely applicable, by general disapprobation. There are also many positive acts for the benefit of others, which he may rightfully be compelled to perform; such as, to give evidence in a court of justice; to bear his fair share in the common defence, or in any other joint work necessary to the interest of the society of which he enjoys the protection; and to perform certain acts of individual beneficence, such as saving a fellow-creature's life, or interposing to protect the defenseless against ill-usage, things which whenever it is obviously a man's duty to do, he may rightfully be made responsible to society for not doing. A person may cause evil to others not only by his actions but by his inaction, and in either case he is justly accountable to them for the injury. The latter case, it is true, requires a much more cautious exercise of compulsion than the former. To make any one answerable for doing evil to others, is the rule; to make him answerable for not preventing evil, is, comparatively speaking, the exception. Yet there are many cases clear enough and grave enough to justify that exception. In all things which regard the external relations of the individual, he is de jure amenable to those whose interests are concerned, and if need be, to society as their protector. There are often good reasons for not holding him to the responsibility; but these reasons must arise from the special expediencies of the case: either because it is a kind of case in which he is on the whole likely to act better, when left to his own discretion, than when controlled in any way in which society have it in their power to control him; or because the attempt to exercise control would produce other evils, greater than those which it would prevent. When such reasons as these preclude the enforcement of responsibility, the conscience of the agent himself should step into the vacant judgment-seat, and protect those interests of others which have no external protection; judging himself all the more rigidly, because the case does not admit of his being made accountable to the judgment of his fellow creatures.

But there is a sphere of action in which society, as distinguished from the individual, has, if any, only an indirect interest; comprehending all that portion of a person's life and conduct which affects only himself, or, if it also affects others, only with their free, voluntary, and undeceived consent and participation. When I say only himself, I mean directly, and in the first instance: for whatever affects himself, may affect others through himself; and the objection which may be grounded on this contingency, will receive consideration in the sequel. This, then, is the appropriate region of human liberty. It comprises, first, the inward domain of consciousness; demanding liberty of conscience, in the most comprehensive sense; liberty of thought and feeling; absolute freedom of opinion and sentiment on all subjects, practical or speculative, scientific, moral, or theological. The liberty of expressing and publishing opinions may seem to fall under a different principle, since it belongs to that part of the conduct of an individual which concerns other people; but, being almost of as much importance as the liberty of thought itself, and resting in great part on the same reasons, is practically inseparable from it. Secondly, the principle requires liberty of tastes and pursuits; of framing the plan of our life to suit our own character; of doing as we like, subject to such consequences as may follow; without impediment from our fellow-creatures, so long as what we do does not harm them even though they should think our conduct foolish, perverse, or wrong. Thirdly, from this liberty of each individual, follows the liberty, within the same limits, of combination among individuals; freedom to unite, for any purpose not involving harm to others: the persons combining being supposed to be of full age, and not forced or deceived.

No society in which these liberties are not, on the whole, respected, is free, whatever may be its form of government; and none is completely free in which they do not exist absolute and unqualified. The only freedom which deserves the name, is that of pursuing our own good in our own way, so long as we do not attempt to deprive others of theirs, or impede their efforts to obtain it. Each is the proper guardian of his own health, whether bodily, or mental or spiritual. Mankind are greater gainers by suffering each other to live as seems good to themselves, than by compelling each to live as seems good to the rest. . . .

It will be convenient for the argument, if, instead of at once entering upon the general thesis, we confine ourselves in the first instance to a single branch of it, on which the principle here stated is, if not fully, yet to a certain point, recognized by the current opinions. This one branch is the Liberty of Thought: from which it is impossible to separate the cognate liberty of speaking and of writing. Although these liberties, to some considerable amount, form part of the political morality of all countries which profess religious toleration and free institutions, the grounds, both philosophical and practical, on which they rest, are perhaps not so familiar to the general mind, nor so thoroughly appreciated by many even of the leaders of opinion, as might have been expected.

Of the Liberty of Thought and Discussion

. . . We have now recognized the necessity to the mental well-being of mankind (on which all their other well-being depends) of freedom of opinion, and freedom of the expression of opinion, on four distinct grounds; which we will now briefly recapitulate.

First, if any opinion is compelled to silence, that opinion may, for aught we can certainly know, be true. To deny this is to assume our own infallibility.

Secondly, though the silenced opinion be an error, it may, and very commonly does, contain a portion of truth; and since the general or prevailing opinion on any object is rarely or never the whole truth, it is only by the collision of adverse opinions that the remainder of the truth has any chance of being supplied.

Thirdly, even if the received opinion be not only true, but the whole truth; unless it is suffered to be, and actually is, vigorously and earnestly contested, it will, by most of those who receive it, be held in the manner of a prejudice, with little comprehension or feeling of its rational grounds. And not only this, but, fourthly, the meaning of the doctrine itself will be in danger of being lost, or enfeebled, and deprived of its vital effect on the character and conduct: the dogma becoming a mere formal profession, inefficacious for good, but cumbering the ground, and preventing the growth of any real and heartfelt conviction, from reason or personal experience.

Of the Limits of the Authority of Society Over the Individual

What, then, is the rightful limit to the sovereignty of the individual over himself? Where does the authority of society begin? How much of human life should be assigned to individuality, and how much to society?

Each will receive its proper share, if each has that which more particularly concerns it. To individuality should belong the part of life in which it is chiefly the individual that is interested; to society, the part which chiefly interests society.

Though society is not founded on a contract, and though no good purpose is answered by inventing a contract in order to deduce social obligations from it, every one who receives the protection of society owes a return for the benefit, and the fact of living in society renders it indispensable that each should be bound to observe a certain line of conduct towards the rest. This conduct consists first, in not injuring the interests of one another; or rather certain interests, which, either by express legal provision or by tacit understanding, ought to be considered as rights; and secondly, in each person's bearing his share (to be fixed on some equitable principle) of the labors and sacrifices incurred for defending the society or its members from injury and molestation. These conditions society is justified in enforcing at all costs to those who endeavor to withhold fulfillment. Nor is this all that society may do. The acts of an individual may be hurtful to others, or wanting in due consideration for their welfare, without going the length of violating any of their constituted rights. The offender may then be justly punished by opinion, though not by law. *As soon as any part of a person's conduct affects prejudicially the interests of others, society has jurisdiction over it and the question whether the general welfare will or will not be promoted by interfering with it becomes open to discussion. But there is no room for entertaining any such question when a person's conduct affects the interests of no persons besides himself, or needs not affect them unless they like (all the persons concerned being of full age, and the ordinary amount of understanding).* In all such cases there should be perfect freedom, legal and social, to do the action and stand the consequences.

It would be a great misunderstanding of this doctrine to suppose that it is one of selfish indifference, which pretends that human beings have no business with each other's conduct in life, and that they should not concern themselves about the well-doing or well-being of one another, unless their own interest is involved. Instead of any diminution, there is need of a great increase of disinterested exertion to promote the good of others. But disinterested benevolence can find other instruments to persuade people to their good, than whips and scourges, either of the literal or the metaphorical sort. I am the last person to undervalue the self-regarding virtues; they are only second in importance, if even second, to the social. It is equally the business of education to cultivate both. But even education works by conviction and persuasion as well as by compulsion, and it is by the former only that, when the period of education is past, the self-regarding virtues should be inculcated. Human beings owe to each other help to distinguish the better from the worse, and encouragement to choose the former and avoid the latter. They should be forever stimulating each other to increased exercise of their higher faculties, and increased direction of their feelings and aims towards wise instead of foolish, elevating instead of degrading, objects and contemplations. But neither one person, nor any number of persons, is warranted in saying to another human creature of ripe years, that he shall not do with his life for his own benefit what he chooses to do with it. He is the person most interested in his own well-being: the interest which any other person, except in cases of strong personal attachment, can have in it, is trifling, compared with that which he himself has; the interest which society has in him individually (except as to his conduct to others) is fractional, and altogether indirect: while, with respect to his own feelings and circumstances, the most ordinary man or woman has means of knowledge immeasurably surpassing those that can be possessed by any one else. The interference of society to overrule his judgment and purposes in what only regards himself, must be grounded on general presumptions; which may be altogether wrong, and even if right, are as likely as not to be misapplied to individual cases, by persons no better acquainted with the circumstances of such cases than those are who look at them merely from without. In this department, therefore, of human affairs, individuality has its proper field of action. In the conduct of human beings towards one another, it is necessary that general rules should for the most part be observed, in order that people may know what they have to expect; but in each person's own concerns, his individual spontaneity is entitled to free exercise. Considerations to aid his judgment, exhortations to strengthen his will, may be offered to him, even obtruded on him, by others; but he himself is the final judge. *All errors which he is likely to commit against advice and warning are far outweighed by the evil of allowing others to constrain him to what they deem his good.*

I do not mean that the feelings with which a person is regarded by others, ought not to be in any way affected by his self-regarding qualities or deficiencies. This is neither possible nor desirable. If he is eminent in any of the qualities which conduce to his own good, he is, so far, a proper object of admiration. He is so much the nearer to the ideal perfection of human nature. If he is grossly deficient in those qualities, a sentiment the opposite of admiration will follow.

There is a degree of folly, and a degree of what may be called (though the phrase is not unobjectionable) lowness or depravation of taste, which, though it cannot justify doing harm to the person who manifests it, renders him necessarily and properly a subject of distaste, or, in extreme cases, even of contempt: a person could not have the opposite qualities in due strength without entertaining these feelings. Though doing no wrong to any one, a person may so act as to compel us to judge him, and feel to him, as a fool, or as a being of an inferior order: and since this judgment and feeling are a fact which he would prefer to avoid, it is doing him a service to warn him of it beforehand, as of any other disagreeable consequence to which he exposes himself. It would be well, indeed, if this good office were much more freely rendered than the common notions of politeness at present permit, and if one person could honestly point out to another that he thinks him in fault, without being considered unmannerly or presuming. We have a right, also, in various ways, to act upon our unfavourable opinion of any one, not to the oppression of his individuality, but in the exercise of ours. We are not bound, for example, to seek his society; we have a right to avoid it (though not to parade the avoidance), for we have a right to choose the society most acceptable to us. We have a right, and it may be our duty, to caution others against him, if we think his example or conversation likely to have a pernicious effect on those with whom he associates. We may give others a preference over him in optional good offices, except those which tend to his improvement. In these various modes a person may suffer very severe penalties at the hands of others, for faults which directly concern only himself; but he suffers these penalties only in so far as they are the natural, and, as it were, the spontaneous consequences of the faults themselves, not because they are purposely inflicted on him for the sake of punishment. A person who shows rashness, obstinacy, self-conceit—who cannot live within moderate means—who cannot restrain himself from hurtful indulgences—who pursues animal pleasures at the expense of those of feeling and intellect—must expect to be lowered in the opinion of others, and to have a less share of their favourable sentiments; but of this he has no right to complain, unless he has merited their favour by special excellence in his social relations, and has thus established a title to their good offices, which is not affected by his demerits towards himself.

What I contend for is, that the inconveniences which are strictly inseparable from the unfavourable judgment of others, are the only ones to which a person should ever be subjected for that portion of his conduct and character which concerns his own good, but which does not affect the interests of others in their relations with him. Acts injurious to others require a totally different treatment. Encroachment on their rights; infliction on them of any loss or damage not justified by his own rights; falsehood or duplicity in dealing with them; unfair or ungenerous use of advantages over them; even selfish abstinence from defending them against injury—these are fit objects of moral reprobation, and, in grave cases, of moral retribution and punishment. And not only these acts, but the dispositions which lead to them, are properly immoral, and fit subjects of disapprobation which may rise to abhorrence. Cruelty of disposition; malice and ill-nature; that most anti-social and odious of all passions, envy; dissimulation and insincerity, irascibility on insufficient cause, and resentment disproportioned to the provocation; the love of domineering over others; the desire to engross more than one's share of advantages (the πλεονεξια of the Greeks); the pride which derives gratification from the abasement of others; the egotism which thinks self and its concerns more important than everything else, and decides all doubtful questions in its own favour;— these are moral vices, and constitute a bad and odious moral character: unlike the self-regarding faults previously mentioned, which are not properly immoralities, and to whatever pitch they may be carried, do not constitute wickedness. They may be proofs of any amount of folly, or want of personal dignity and self-respect; but they are only a subject of moral reprobation when they involve a breach of duty to others, for whose sake the individual is bound to have care for himself. What are called duties to ourselves are not socially obligatory, unless circumstances render them at the same time duties to others. The term duty to oneself, when it means anything more than prudence, means self-respect or self-development; and for none of these is any one accountable to his fellow creatures, because for none of them is it for the good of mankind that he be held accountable to them.

The distinction between the loss of consideration which a person may rightly incur by defect of prudence or of personal dignity, and the reprobation which is due to him for an offence against the rights of others, is not a merely nominal distinction. It makes a vast difference both in our feelings and in our conduct towards him, whether he displeases us in things in which we think we have a right to control him, or in things in which we know that we have not. If he displeases us, we may express our distaste, and we may stand aloof from a person as well as from a thing that displeases us; but we shall not therefore feel called on to make his life uncomfortable. We shall reflect that he already bears, or will bear, the whole penalty of his error; if he spoils his life by mismanagement, we shall not, for that reason, desire to spoil it still further: instead of wishing to punish him, we shall rather endeavour to alleviate his punishment, by showing him how he may avoid or cure the evils his conduct tends to bring upon him. He may be to us an object of pity, perhaps of dislike, but not of anger or resentment; we shall not treat him like an enemy of society: the worst we shall think ourselves justified in doing is leaving him to himself, if we do not interfere benevolently by showing interest or concern for him. It is far otherwise if he has infringed the rules necessary for the protection of his fellow-creatures, individually or collectively. The evil consequences of his acts do not then fall on himself, but on others; and society, as the protector of all its members, must retaliate on him; must inflict pain on him for the express purpose of punishment, and must take care that it be sufficiently severe. In the one case, he is an offender at our bar, and we are called on not only to sit in judgment on him, but, in one shape or another, to execute our own sentence: in the other case, it is not our part to inflict any suffering on him, except what may incidentally follow from our using the same liberty in the regulation of our own affairs, which we allow to him in his.

The distinction here pointed out between the part of a person's life which concerns only himself, and that which concerns others, many persons will refuse to admit. How (it may be asked) can any part of the conduct of a member of society be a matter of indifference to the other members? No person is an entirely isolated being; it is impossible for a person to do anything seriously or permanently hurtful to himself, without mischief reaching at least to his near connexions, and often far beyond them. If he injures his property, he does harm to those who directly or indirectly derived support from it, and usually diminishes, by a greater or less amount, the general resources of the community. If he deteriorates his bodily or mental faculties, he not only brings evil upon all who depended on him for any portion of their happiness, but disqualifies himself for rendering the services which he owes to his fellow-creatures generally; perhaps becomes a burthen on their affection or benevolence; and if such conduct were very frequent, hardly any offence that is committed would detract more from the general sum of good. Finally, if by his vices or follies a person does no direct harm to others, he is nevertheless (it may be said) injurious by his example; and ought to be compelled to control himself, for the sake of those whom the sight or knowledge of his conduct might corrupt or mislead.

And even (it will be added) if the consequences of misconduct could be confined to the vicious or thoughtless individual, ought society to abandon to their own guidance those who are manifestly unfit for it? If protection against themselves is confessedly due to children and persons under age, is not society equally bound to afford it to persons of mature years who are equally incapable of self-government? If gambling, or drunkenness, or incontinence, or idleness, or uncleanliness, are as injurious to happiness, and as great a hindrance to improvement, as many or most of the acts prohibited by law, why (it may be asked) should not law, so far as is consistent with practicability and social convenience, endeavour to repress these also? And as a supplement to the unavoidable imperfections of law, ought not opinion at least to organize a powerful police against these vices, and visit rigidly with social penalties those who are known to practise them? There is no question here (it may be said) about restricting individuality, or impeding the trial of new and original experiments in living. The only things it is sought to prevent are things which have been tried and condemned from the beginning of the world until now; things which experience has shown not to be useful or suitable to any person's individuality. There must be some length of time and amount of experience, after which

a moral or prudential truth may be regarded as established: and it is merely desired to prevent generation after generation from falling over the same precipice which has been fatal to their predecessors.

I fully admit that the mischief which a person does to himself may seriously affect, both through their sympathies and their interests, those nearly connected with him, and in a minor degree, society at large. When, by conduct of this sort, a person is led to violate a distinct and assignable obligation to any other person or persons, the case is taken out of the self-regarding class, and becomes amenable to moral disapprobation in the proper sense of the term. If, for example, a man, through intemperance or extravagance, becomes unable to pay his debts, or, having undertaken the moral responsibility of a family, becomes from the same cause incapable of supporting or educating them, he is deservedly reprobated, and might be justly punished; but it is for the breach of duty to his family or creditors, not for the extravagance. If the resources which ought to have been devoted to them, had been diverted from them for the most prudent investment, the moral culpability would have been the same. George Barnwell murdered his uncle to get money for his mistress, but if he had done it to set himself up in business, he would equally have been hanged. Again, in the frequent case of a man who causes grief to his family by addiction to bad habits, he deserves reproach for his unkindness or ingratitude; but so he may for cultivating habits not in themselves vicious, if they are painful to those with whom he passes his life, or who from personal ties are dependent on him for their comfort. Whoever fails in the consideration generally due to the interests and feelings of others, not being compelled by some more imperative duty, or justified by allowable self-preference, is a subject of moral disapprobation for that failure, but not for the cause of it, nor for the errors, merely personal to himself, which may have remotely led to it. In like manner, when a person disables himself, by conduct purely self-regarding, from the performance of some definite duty incumbent on him to the public, he is guilty of a social offence. No person ought to be punished simply for being drunk; but a soldier or a policeman should be punished for being drunk on duty. Whenever, in short, there is a definite damage, or a definite risk of damage, either to an individual or to the public, the case is taken out of the province of liberty, and placed in that of morality or law.

But with regard to the merely contingent, or, as it may be called, constructive injury which a person causes to society, by conduct which neither violates any specific duty to the public, nor occasions perceptible hurt to any assignable individual except himself; the inconvenience is one which society can afford to bear, for the sake of the greater good of human freedom. If grown persons are to be punished for not taking proper care of themselves, I would rather it were for their own sake, than under pretence of preventing them from impairing their capacity of rendering to society benefits which society does not pretend it has a right to exact. But I cannot consent to argue the point as if society had no means of bringing its weaker members up to its ordinary standard of rational conduct, except waiting till they do something irrational, and then punishing them, legally or morally, for it. Society has had absolute power over them during all the early portion of their existence: it has had the whole period of childhood and nonage in which to try whether it could make them capable of rational conduct in life. The existing generation is master both of the training and the entire circumstances of the generation to come; it cannot indeed make them perfectly wise and good, because it is itself so lamentably deficient in goodness and wisdom; and its best efforts are not always, in individual cases, its most successful ones; but it is perfectly well able to make the rising generation, as a whole, as good as, and a little better than, itself. If society lets any considerable number of its members grow up mere children, incapable of being acted on by rational consideration of distant motives, society has itself to blame for the consequences. Armed not only with all the powers of education, but with the ascendancy which the authority of a received opinion always exercises over the minds who are least fitted to judge for themselves; and aided by the natural penalties which cannot be prevented from falling on those who incur the distaste or the contempt of those who know them; let not society pretend that it needs, besides all this, the power to issue commands and enforce obedience in the personal concerns of individuals, in which, on all principles of justice and policy, the decision ought to rest with those who are to abide the consequences. Nor is there anything which tends more to discredit and frustrate the better means of influencing conduct, than a resort to the worse. If there be among those whom it is attempted to coerce into prudence or temperance, any of the material of which vigorous and independent characters are made, they will infallibly rebel against the yoke. No such person will ever feel that others have a right to control him in his concerns, such as they have to prevent him from injuring them in theirs; and it easily comes to be considered a mark of spirit and courage to fly in the face of such usurped authority, and do with ostentation the exact opposite of what it enjoins; as in the fashion of grossness which succeeded, in the time of Charles II, to the fanatical moral intolerance of the Puritans. With respect to what is said of the necessity of protecting society from the bad example set to others by the vicious or the self-indulgent; it is true that bad example may have a pernicious effect, especially the example of doing wrong to others with impunity to the wrong-doer. But we are now speaking of conduct which, while it does no wrong to others, is supposed to do great harm to the agent himself: and I do not see how those who believe this, can think otherwise than that the example, on the whole, must be more salutary than hurtful, since, if it displays the misconduct, it displays also the painful or degrading consequences which, if the conduct is justly censured, must be supposed to be in all or most cases attendant on it.

But the strongest of all the arguments against the interference of the public with purely personal conduct, is that when it does interfere, the odds are that it interferes wrongly, and in the wrong place. On questions of social morality, of duty to others, the opinion of the public, that is, of an overruling majority, though often wrong, is likely to be still oftener right; because on such questions they are only required to judge of their own interests; of the manner in which some mode of conduct, if allowed to be practised, would affect themselves. But the opinion of a similar majority, imposed as a law on the minority, on questions of self-regarding conduct, is quite as likely to be wrong as right; for in these cases public opinion means, at the best, some people's opinion of what is good or bad for other people; while very often it does not even mean that; the public, with the most perfect indifference, passing over the pleasure or convenience of those whose conduct they censure, and considering only their own preference. There are many who consider as an injury to themselves any conduct which they have a distaste for, and resent it as an outrage to their feelings; as a religious bigot, when charged with disregarding the religious feelings of others, has been known to retort that they disregard his feelings, by persisting in their abominable worship or creed. But there is no parity between the feeling of a person for his own opinion, and the feeling of another who is offended at his holding it; no more than between the desire of a thief to take a purse, and the desire of the right owner to keep it. And a person's taste is as much his own peculiar concern as his opinion or his purse. It is easy for any one to imagine an ideal public, which leaves the freedom and choice of individuals in all uncertain matters undisturbed, and only requires them to abstain from modes of conduct which universal experience has condemned. But where has there been seen a public which set any such limit to its censorship? or when does the public trouble itself about universal experience? In its interferences with personal conduct it is seldom thinking of anything but the enormity of acting or feeling differently from itself; and this standard of judgment, thinly disguised, is held up to mankind as the dictate of religion and philosophy, by nine-tenths of all moralists and speculative writers. These teach that things are right because they are right; because we feel them to be so. They tell us to search in our own minds and hearts for laws of conduct binding on ourselves and on all others. What can the poor public do but apply these instructions, and make their own personal feelings of good and evil, if they are tolerably unanimous in them, obligatory on all the world?

DISCUSSION QUESTIONS:

1. Our actions can negatively affect others in a variety of ways. We can harm others, but we can also offend them, hurt their feelings or cause them other forms of displeasure. What distinguishes harm from such other negative effects? Is harm the only negative effect on non-consenting others that is an appropriate basis for social regulation?

2. Harm comes in degrees, and the causal relation between one person's conduct and another person's harm can be very direct or very indirect. How substantial must the harm to others be and how direct must the causal relation be to justify the social regulation of the some conduct?

3. To what extent is the Harm Principle defensible on Utilitarian grounds? Under what sort of conditions will a society's adoption of the principle be in the society's best interest?

4. Is Mill correct in his claim that societies best serve their interest in knowing the truth by having freedom of thought and expression? Might the exercise of free expression sometimes make it more difficult for us to know the truth?

5. Mill acknowledges that the Harm Principle is not properly applied to children, but he claims that it is applicable to rational adults who foolishly cause themselves harm. Are there any cases in which we currently regulate individual behavior to protect rational adults from their own bad choices? Are we justified in doing so?

6. Is Mill correct in his claim that if society interferes with purely personal conduct, it is likely to interfere wrongly and in the wrong place? What are some examples of such misguided social regulation?

Argument Reconstruction Exercises:

I. Identify the premises and conclusion of this restatement of Mill's argument for freedom of expression.

If we prohibit the expression of an opinion that challenges our own view and that opinion is true or even partly true, we deprive ourselves of the chance to gain knowledge. If the opinion is false, we deprive ourselves of the chance to strengthen our own belief by learning how it is superior to the alternative view and we risk reducing our belief to a mere formal profession without rational basis. In either case, it is in our interest to allow the expression of views contrary to our own. (page 620)

II. Mill gives the following argument for not regulating conduct in the private realm. Identify its premises and conclusion.

The interference of society to overrule [an individual's] judgment and purposes in what only regards himself, must be grounded on general presumptions; which may be altogether wrong, and even if right, are as likely as not to be misapplied to individual cases . . . All errors which [an individual] is likely to commit against advice and warning, are far outweighed by the evil of allowing others to constrain him to what they deem his good . (page 621)

III. Consider the following objection to Mill's view that activities in the private realm are not to be socially regulated:

> There is no question here . . . about restricting individuality, or impeding the trial of new and original experiments in living. The only things it is sought to prevent are things which have been tried and condemned from the beginning of the world until now; things which experience has shown not to be useful to any person's individuality. . . . [I]t is merely

desired to prevent generation after generation from falling over the same precipice which has been fatal to their predecessors. (page 623)

IV. Mill offers the following reply to the preceding argument. Identify its premises and conclusion.

> It is easy for anyone to imagine an ideal public, which leaves the freedom and choice of individuals in all uncertain matters undisturbed, and only requires them to abstain from modes of conduct which universal experience has condemned. But where has there been seen a public which set any such limit to its censorship? Or when does the public trouble itself about universal experience? In its interferences with personal conduct it is seldom thinking of anything but the enormity of acting or feeling differently from itself. (page 625)

22.2 MORALS AND THE CRIMINAL LAW

PATRICK DEVLIN (1959)

Patrick Devlin was a British lord and jurist and the author of *The Enforcement of Morals,* from which this selection is taken. Devlin argues that each society must have a public morality, a set of widely accepted moral beliefs that help define its character. However, such a public morality may not be defended by appeal to religion but instead by appeal to that which is required to protect and preserve a particular society. A society must balance its exercise of this right against other moral considerations, including each individual's right to privacy, by limiting its legal enforcement of the public morality to cases in which a moral principle is a well-established part of society's definition of minimally acceptable conduct.

Reading Questions:

1. Devlin claims that while some laws are justified as necessary to the smooth functioning of society, others are only justified as necessary to enforce some moral principle. What is his basis for this claim?

2. What is Devlin's *a priori* argument for the claim that each society requires a shared agreement on matters of morality for its existence?

3. What is Devlin's definition of a society's public morality?

4. What is Devlin's argument for his claim that each society has a right to legally enforce its public morality?

5. What are Devlin's guidelines for determining when and how a society may exercise its right to legally enforce its public morality?

Law, Morals and Religion

Morals and religion are inextricably joined—the moral standards generally accepted in Western civilization being those belonging to Christianity. Outside Christendom other standards derive from other religions. None of these moral codes can claim any validity except by virtue of the religion on which it is based. Old Testament morals differ in some respects from New Testament morals. Even within Christianity there are differences. Some hold that contraception is an immoral practice and that a man who has carnal knowledge of another woman while his wife is alive is in all circumstances a fornicator; others, including most of the English-speaking world, deny both these propositions. Between the great religions of the world, of which Christianity is only one, there are much wider differences. It may or may not be right for the State to adopt one of these religions as the truth, to found itself upon its doctrines, and to deny to any of its citizens the liberty to practise any other. If it does, it is logical that it should use the secular law wherever it thinks it necessary to enforce the divine. If it does not, it is illogical that it should concern itself with morals as such. But if it leaves matters of religion to private judgement, it should logically leave matters of morals also. A State which refuses to enforce Christian beliefs has lost the right to enforce Christian morals.

If this view is sound, it means that the criminal law cannot justify any of its provisions by reference to the moral law. It cannot say, for example, that murder and theft are prohibited because they are immoral or sinful. The State must justify in some other way the punishments which it imposes on wrong-doers and a function for the criminal law independent of morals must be found. This is not difficult to do. The smooth functioning of society and the preservation of order require that a number of activities should be regulated. The rules that are made for that purpose and are enforced by the criminal law are often designed simply to achieve uniformity and convenience and rarely involve any choice between good and evil. Rules that impose a speed limit or prevent obstruction on the highway have nothing to do with morals. Since so much of the criminal law is composed of rules of this sort, why bring morals into it

at all? Why not define the function of the criminal law in simple terms as the preservation of order and decency and the protection of the lives and property of citizens. . . ? The criminal law in carrying out these objects will undoubtedly overlap the moral law. Crimes of violence are morally wrong and they are also offences against good order; therefore they offend against both laws. But this is simply because the two laws in pursuit of different objectives happen to cover the same area. Such is the argument.

Is the argument consistent or inconsistent with the fundamental principles of English criminal law as it exists today? That is the first way of testing it, though by no means a conclusive one. In the field of jurisprudence one is at liberty to overturn even fundamental conceptions if they are theoretically unsound. But to see how the argument fares under the existing law is a good starting-point.

It is true that for many centuries the criminal law was much concerned with keeping the peace and little, if at all, with sexual morals. But it would be wrong to infer from that that it had no moral content or that it would ever have tolerated the idea of a man being left to judge for himself in matters of morals. The criminal law of England has from the very first concerned itself with moral principles. A simple way of testing this point is to consider the attitude which the criminal law adopts towards consent.

Subject to certain exceptions inherent in the nature of particular crimes, the criminal law has never permitted consent of the victim to be used as a defence. In rape, for example, consent negatives an essential element. But consent of the victim is no defence to a charge of murder. It is not a defence to any form of assault that the victim thought his punishment well deserved and submitted to it; to make a good defence the accused must prove that the law gave him the right to chastise and that he exercised it reasonably. Likewise, the victim may not forgive the aggressor and require the prosecution to desist; the right to enter a *nolle prosequi* belongs to the Attorney-General alone.

Now, if the law existed for the protection of the individual, there would be no reason why he should avail himself of it if he did not want it. The reason why a man may not consent to the commission of an offence against himself beforehand or forgive it afterwards is because it is an offence against society. It is not that society is physically injured; that would be impossible. Nor need any individual be shocked, corrupted, or exploited; everything may be done in private. Nor can it be explained on the practical ground that a violent man is a potential danger to others in the community who have therefore a direct interest in his apprehension and punishment as being necessary to their own protection. That would be true of a man whom the victim is prepared to forgive but not of one who gets his consent first; a murderer who acts only upon the consent, and maybe the request, of his victim is no menace to others, but he does threaten one of the great moral principles upon which society is based, that is, the sanctity of human life. There is only one explanation of what has hitherto been accepted as the basis of the criminal law and that's that there are certain standards of behaviour or moral principles which society requires to be observed; and the breach of them is an offence not merely against the person who is injured but against society as a whole.

Thus, if the criminal law were to be reformed so as to eliminate from it everything that was not designed to preserve order and decency or to protect citizens (including the protection of youth from corruption), it would overturn a fundamental principle. It would also end a number of specific crimes. Euthanasia or the killing of another at his own request, suicide, attempted suicide and suicide pacts, duelling, abortion, incest between brother and sister, are all acts which can be done in private and without offence to others and need not involve the corruption or exploitation of others. Many people think that the law on some of these subjects is in need of reform, but no one hitherto has gone so far as to suggest that they should all be left outside the criminal law as matters of private morality. They can be brought within it only as a matter of moral principle. It must be remembered also that although there is much immorality that is not punished by the law, there is none that is condoned by the law. The law will not allow its processes to be used by those engaged in immorality of any sort. For example, a house may not be let for immoral purposes; the lease is invalid and would not be enforced. But if what goes on inside there is a matter of private morality and not the law's business, why does the law inquire into it at all?

I think it is clear that the criminal law as we know it is based upon moral principle. In a number of crimes its function is simply to enforce a moral principle and nothing else. The law, both criminal and civil, claims to be able to speak about morality and immorality generally. Where does it get its authority to do this and how does it settle the moral principles which it enforces? Undoubtedly, as a matter of history, it derived both from Christian teaching. But I think that the strict logician is right when he says that the law can no longer rely on doctrines in which citizens are entitled to disbelieve. It is necessary therefore to look for some other source.

Law and the Public Morality

In jurisprudence, as I have said, everything is thrown open to discussion and, in the belief that they cover the whole field, I have framed three interrogatories addressed to myself to answer:

1. *Has society the right to pass judgement at all on matters of morals? Ought there, in other words, to be a public morality, or are morals always a matter for private judgement?*
2. *If society has the right to pass judgement, has it also the right to use the weapon of the law to enforce it?*
3. *It so, ought it to use that weapon in all cases or only in some; and if only in some, on what principles should it distinguish?*

I shall begin with the first interrogatory and consider what is meant by the right of society to pass a moral judgement, that is, a judgement about what is good and what is evil. The fact that a majority of people may disapprove of a practice does not of itself make it a matter for society as a whole. Nine men out of ten may disapprove of what the tenth man is doing and still say that it is not their business. There is a case for a collective judgement (as distinct from a large number of individual opinions which sensible people may even refrain from pronouncing at all if it is upon somebody else's private affairs) only if society is affected. Without a collective judgement there can be no case at all for intervention. Let me take as an illustration the Englishman's attitude to religion as it is now and as it has been in the past. His attitude now is that a man's religion is his private affair; he may think of another man's religion that it is right or wrong, true or untrue, but not that it is good or bad. In earlier times that was not so; a man was denied the right to practise what was thought of as heresy, and heresy was thought of as destructive of society. . . .

This view—that there is such a thing as public morality—can also be justified by *a priori* argument. What makes a society of any sort is community of ideas, not only political ideas but also ideas about the way its members should behave and govern their lives; these latter ideas are its morals. Every society has a moral structure as well as a political one: or rather, since that might suggest two independent systems, I should say that the structure of every society is made up both of politics and morals. Take, for example, the institution of marriage. Whether a man should be allowed to take more than one wife is something about which every society has to make up its mind one way or the other. In England we believe in the Christian idea of marriage and therefore adopt monogamy as a moral principle. Consequently the Christian institution of marriage has become the basis of family life and so part of the structure of our society. It is there not because it is Christian. It has got there because it is Christian, but it remains there because it is built into the house in which we live and could not be removed without bringing it down. The great majority of those who live in this country accept it because it is the Christian idea of marriage and for them the only true one. But a non-Christian is bound by it, not because it is part of Christianity but because, rightly or wrongly, it has been adopted by the society in which he lives. It would be useless for him to stage a debate designed to prove that polygamy was theologically more correct and socially preferable; if he wants to live in the house, he must accept it as built in the way in which it is.

We see this more clearly if we think of ideas or institutions that are purely political. Society cannot tolerate rebellion; it will not allow argument about the rightness of the cause. Historians a century later may say that the rebels were right and the Government was wrong and a percipient and conscientious subject of the State may think so at the time. But it is not a matter which can be left to individual judgement.

The institution of marriage is a good example for my purpose because it bridges the division, if

there is one, between politics and morals. Marriage is part of the structure of our society and it is also the basis of a moral code which condemns fornication and adultery. The institution of marriage would be gravely threatened if individual judgements were permitted about the morality of adultery; on these points there must be a public morality. But public morality is not to be confined to those moral principles which support institutions such as marriage. People do not think of monogamy as something which has to be supported because our society has chosen to organize itself upon it; they think of it as something that is good in itself and offering a good way of life and that it is for that reason that our society has adopted it. I return to the statement that I have already made, that society means a community of ideas; without shared ideas on politics, morals, and ethics no society can exist. Each one of us has ideas about what is good and what is evil; they cannot be kept private from the society in which we live. *If men and women try to create a society in which there is no fundamental agreement about good and evil they will fail; if, having based it on common agreement, the agreement goes, the society will disintegrate.* For society is not something that is kept together physically; it is held by the invisible bonds of common thought. If the bonds were too far relaxed the members would drift apart. A common morality is part of the bondage. The bondage is part of the price of society; and mankind, which needs society, must pay its price. . . .

Society's Enforcement Right

You may think that I have taken far too long in contending that there is such a thing as public morality, a proposition which most people would readily accept, and may have left myself too little time to discuss the next question which to many minds may cause greater difficulty: to what extent should society use the law to enforce its moral judgements? But I believe that the answer to the first question determines the way in which the second should be approached and may indeed very nearly dictate the answer to the second question. If society has no right to make judgements on morals, the law must find some special justification for entering the field of morality: if homosexuality and prostitution are not in themselves wrong, then the onus is very clearly on the lawgiver who wants to frame a law against certain aspects of them to justify the exceptional treatment. *But if society has the right to make a judgement and has it on the basis that a recognized morality is as necessary to society as, say, a recognized government. then society may use the law to preserve morality in the same way as it uses it to safeguard anything else that is essential to its existence.* If therefore the first proposition is securely established with all its implications, society has a prima facie right to legislate against immorality as such. . . .

I think, therefore, that it is not possible to set theoretical limits to the power of the State to legislate against immorality. It is not possible to settle in advance exceptions to the general rule or to define inflexibly areas of morality into which the law is in no circumstances to be allowed to enter. Society is entitled by means of its laws to protect itself from dangers, whether from within or without. Here again I think that the political parallel is legitimate. The law of treason is directed against aiding the king's enemies and against sedition from within. The justification for this is that established government is necessary for the existence of society and therefore its safety against violent overthrow must be secured. But an established morality is as necessary as good government to the welfare of society. Societies disintegrate from within more frequently than they are broken up by external pressures. There is disintegration when no common morality is observed and history shows that the loosening of moral bonds is often the first stage of disintegration, so that society is justified in taking the same steps to preserve its moral code as it does to preserve its government and other essential institutions.[1] The suppression of vice is as much the law's business as the suppression of subversive activities; it is no more possible to define a sphere of private morality than it is to define one of private subversive activity. It is wrong to talk of private morality or of the law not being concerned with immorality as such or to try to set rigid bounds to the part which the law may play in the suppression of vice. There are no theoretical limits to the power of the State to legislate against treason and sedition, and likewise I think there can be no theoretical limits to legislation against immorality. You may argue

that if a man's sins affect only himself it cannot be the concern of society. If he chooses to get drunk every night in the privacy of his own home, is any one except himself the worse for it? But suppose a quarter or a half of the population got drunk every night, what sort of society would it be? You cannot set a theoretical limit to the number of people who can get drunk before society is entitled to legislate against drunkenness. The same may be said of gambling. The Royal Commission on Betting, Lotteries, and Gaming took as their test the character of the citizen as a member of society. They said: 'Our concern with the ethical significance of gambling is confined to the effect which it may have on the character of the gambler as a member of society. If we were convinced that whatever the degree of gambling this effect must be harmful we should be inclined to think that it was the duty of the state to restrict gambling to the greatest extent practicable.'[2]

Guidelines for Enforcement

In what circumstances the State should exercise its power is the third of the interrogatories I have framed. But before I get to it I must raise a point which might have been brought up in any one of the three. How are the moral judgements of society to be ascertained? By leaving it until now, I can ask it in the more limited form that is now sufficient for my purpose. How is the law-maker to ascertain the moral judgements of society? It is surely not enough that they should be reached by the opinion of the majority; it would be too much to require the individual assent of every citizen. English law has evolved and regularly uses a standard which does not depend on the counting of heads. It is that of the reasonable man. He is not to be confused with the rational man. He is not expected to reason about anything and his judgement may be largely a matter of feeling. It is the viewpoint of the man in the street—or to use an archaism familiar to all lawyers—the man in the Clapham omnibus. He might also be called the right-minded man. For my purpose I should like to call him the man In the jury box, for *the moral judgement of society must be something about which any twelve men or women drawn at random might after discussion be expected to be unanimous.* This was the standard the judges applied in the days before Parliament was as active as it is now and when they laid down rules of public policy. They did not think of themselves as making law but simply as stating principles which every right-minded person would accept as valid. It is what Pollock called 'practical morality', which is based not on theological or philosophical foundations but 'in the mass of continuous experience half-consciously or unconsciously accumulated and embodied in the morality of common sense.' He called it also 'a certain way of thinking on question of morality which we expect to find in a reasonable civilized man or a reasonable Englishman, taken at random.'[3]

Immorality then, for the purpose of the law, is what every right-minded person is presumed to consider to be immoral. Any immorality is capable of affecting society injuriously and in effect to a greater or lesser extent it usually does; this is what gives the law its *locus standi*. It cannot be shut out. But—and this brings me to the third question—the individual has a *locus standi* too; he cannot be expected to surrender to the judgement of society the whole conduct of his life. It is the old and familiar question of striking a balance between the rights and interests of society and those of the individual. This is something which the law is constantly doing in matters large and small. . . .

I do not think that one can talk sensibly or a public and private morality any more than one can of a public or private highway. Morality is a sphere in which there is a public interest and a private interest, often in conflict, and the problem is to reconcile the two. This does not mean that it is impossible to put forward any general statements about how in our society the balance ought to be struck. Such statements cannot of their nature be rigid or precise; they would not be designed to circumscribe the operation of the law-making power but to guide those who have to apply it. While every decision which a court of law makes when it balances the public against the private interest is an *ad hoc* decision, the cases contain statements of principle to which the court should have regard when it reaches its decision. In the same way it's possible to make general statements of principle which it may be thought the legislature should bear in mind when it is considering the enactment of laws enforcing morals.

I believe that most people would agree upon the chief of these elastic principles. There must be toleration of the maximum individual freedom that is consistent with the integrity of society. It cannot be said that this is a principle that runs all through the criminal law. Much of the criminal law that is regulatory in character—the part of it that deals with *malum prohibitum* rather than *malum in se*—is based upon the opposite principle, that is, that the choice of the individual must give way to the convenience of the many. But in all matters of conscience the principle I have stated is generally held to prevail. It is not confined to thought and speech; it extends to action, as is shown by the recognition of the right to conscientious objection in war-time; this example shows also that conscience will be respected even in times of national danger. The principle appears to me to be peculiarly appropriate to all questions of morals. *Nothing should be punished by the law that does not lie beyond the limits of tolerance.* It is not nearly enough to say that a majority dislike a practice; there must be a real feeling of reprobation. Those who are dissatisfied with the present law on homosexuality often say that the opponents of reform are swayed simply by disgust. If that were so it would be wrong, but I do not think one can ignore disgust if it is deeply felt and not manufactured. Its presence is a good indication that the bounds of toleration are being reached. Not everything is to be tolerated. No society can do without intolerance, indignation, and disgust; they are the forces behind the moral law, and indeed it can be argued that if they or something like them are not present, the feelings of society cannot be weighty enough to deprive the individual of freedom of choice. I suppose that there is hardly anyone nowadays who would not be disgusted by the thought of deliberate cruelty to animals. No one proposes to relegate that or any other form of sadism to the realm of private morality or to allow it to be practised in public or in private. It would be possible no doubt to point out that until a comparatively short while ago nobody thought very much of cruelty to animals and also that pity and kindliness and the unwillingness to inflict pain are virtues more generally esteemed now than they have ever been in the past. But matters of this sort are not determined by rational argument. Every moral judgement, unless it claims a divine source, is simply a feeling that no right-minded man could behave in any other way without admitting that he was doing wrong. It is the power of a common sense and not the power of reason that is behind the judgements of society. But before a society can put a practice beyond the limits of tolerance there must be a deliberate judgement that the practice is injurious to society. . . .

The limits of tolerance shift. This is supplementary to what I have been saying but of sufficient importance in itself to deserve statement as a separate principle which law-makers have to bear in mind. I suppose that moral standards do not shift; so far as they come from divine revelation they do not, and I am willing to assume that the moral judgements made by a society always remain good for that society. But the extent to which society will tolerate—I mean tolerate, not approve—departures from moral standards varies from generation to generation. It may be that over-all tolerance is always increasing. The pressure of the human mind, always seeking greater freedom of thought, is outwards against the bonds of society forcing their gradual relaxation. It may be that history is a tale of contraction and expansion and that all developed societies are on their way to dissolution. I must not speak of things I do not know; and anyway as a practical matter no society is willing to make provision for its own decay. I return therefore to the simple and observable fact that in matters of morals the limits of tolerance shift. Laws, especially those which are based on morals, are less easily moved. *It follows as another good working principle that in any new matter of morals the law should be slow to act.* By the next generation the swell of indignation may have abated and the law be left without the strong backing which it needs.

A third elastic principle must be advanced more tentatively. It is that as far as possible privacy should be respected. This is not an idea that has ever been made explicit in the criminal law. Acts or words done or said in public or in private are all brought within its scope without distinction in principle. But there goes with this a strong reluctance on the part of judges and legislators to sanction invasions of privacy in the detection of crime. The police have no more right to trespass than the ordinary citizen has; there is no general right of search; to this extent an Englishman's home is still his castle. . . .

The last and the biggest thing to be remembered is that the law is concerned with the minimum and not with the maximum; there is much in the Sermon on the Mount that would be out of place in the Ten Commandments. We all recognize the gap between the moral law and the law of the land. No man is worth much who regulates his conduct with the sole object of escaping punishment, and every worthy society sets for its members standards which are above those of the law. We recognize the existence of such higher standards when we use expressions such as 'moral obligation' and 'morally bound.' . . .

It can only be because this point is so obvious that it is so frequently ignored. Discussion among law-makers, both professional and amateur, is too often limited to what is right or wrong and good or bad for society. There is a failure to keep separate the two questions I have earlier posed—the question of society's right to pass a moral judgement and the question of whether the arm of the law should be used to enforce the judgement. The criminal law is not a statement of how people ought to behave; it is a statement of what will happen to them if they do not behave; good citizens are not expected to come within reach of it or to set their sights by it, and every enactment should be framed accordingly. . . .

This then is how I believe my third interrogatory should be answered—not by the formation of hard and fast rules, but by a judgement in each case taking into account the sort of factors I have been mentioning. The line that divides the criminal law from the moral is not determinable by the application of any clear-cut principle. It is like a line that divides land and sea, a coastline of irregularities and indentations. . . .

But the true principle is that the law exists for the protection of society. It does not discharge its function by protecting the individual from injury, annoyance, corruption, and exploitation; the law must protect also the institutions and the community of ideas, political and moral, without which people cannot live together. Society cannot ignore the morality of the individual any more than it can his loyalty; it flourishes on both and without either it dies.

NOTES

1. It is somewhere about this point in the argument that Professor Hart in *Law, Liberty, and Morality* discerns a proposition which he describes as central to my thought. He states the position and his objection to it as follows (p. 51). 'He appears to move the acceptable proposition that some shared morality is essential to the existence any society [this I take to be the proposition on p. 12] to the unacceptable proposition that a society is identical with its morality as that is at any given moment of its history so that a change in its morality is tantamount to the destruction of a society. The former proposition might be even accepted as a necessary rather than an empirical truth depending on a quite plausible definition of society as a body of men who hold certain moral views in common. But the latter proposition is absurd. Taken strictly, it would prevent us saying that the morality of a given society had changed, and would compel us instead to say that one society had disappeared and another one taken its place. But it is only on this absurd criterlon of what it is for the same society to continue to exist that it could be asserted without evidence that any deviation from a society's shared morality threatens its existence.' In conclusion (p. 82) Professor Hart condemns the whole thesis in the lecture as based on 'a confused definition of what a society is.'

I do not assert that any deviation from a society's shared morality threatens its existence any more than I assert that any subversive activity threatens its existence. I assert that they are both activities which are capable in their nature of threatening the existence of society so that neither can be put beyond the law.

For the rest, the objection appears to me to be all a matter of words. I would venture to assert, for example, that you cannot have a game without rules end that if there were no rules there would be no game. If I am asked whether that means that the game is 'identical' with the rules, I would be willing for the question to be answered either way In the belief that the answer would lead to nowhere. If I am asked whether a change in the rules means that one game has disappeared and another has taken its place, I would reply probably not, but that it would depend on the extent of the change.

Likewise I should venture to assert that there cannot be a contract without terms. Does this mean that an 'emended' contract is a 'new' contract in the eyes of the law? I once listened to an argument by an ingenious counsel that a contract, because of the substitution of one clause for another, had 'ceased to have effect' within the meaning of a statutory provision. The judge did not accept the argument; but if most of the fundamental terms had been changed, I daresay he would have done.

The proposition that I make in the text is that if (as I understand Professor Hart to agree, at any rate for the purposes of the argument) you cannot have a society without morality, the law can be used to enforce morality as something that is essential to a society. I cannot see why this proposition (whether it is right or wrong) should mean that morality can never be changed without the destruction of society. If morality is changed, the law can be changed. Professor Hart refers (p. 72) to the proposition as 'the use of legal punishment to freeze into immobility the morality dominant at a particular time in a society's existence.' One might as well say that the inclusion of a penal section into a statute prohibiting certain acts freezes the whole statute into immobility and prevents the prohibitions from ever being modified.

2. (1951) Cmd. 8190, para. 159.

3. *Essay in Jurisprudence and Ethics* (1862), Macmillan, pp. 278 and 353.

DISCUSSION QUESTIONS:

1. Devlin offers several examples of laws whose "function is simply to enforce a moral principle and nothing else," ranging from laws regarding euthanasia to ones regarding dueling. Are we justified in having these laws? If so, does Devlin's theory give the best explanation of why we are justified? Can any of them be justified on grounds other than society's right to enforce the public morality?

2. Devlin offers his justification for legally enforcing certain moral principles (that they are part of our public morality) as an alternative to the justification that they are based in correct religious beliefs. Are any other justifications available? Might we be justified in legally enforcing certain moral principles simply because they are objectively correct?

3. Devlin claims that society has a right to legally prohibit violations of its public morality just as it has a right to legally prohibit acts of treason. Each activity threatens something society needs to exist:

a shared morality, an effective government. How analogous are the two cases?

4. As Devlin notes, some critics have charged that he is committed to the implausible view that a society ceases to exist whenever its public morality changes. He claims that his theory lacks this implication. Is he committed to this implausible view or not?

5. Many people think that moral codes that support slavery or the denial of fundamental rights are mistaken. What are the implications of Devlin's theory for a society that has such a code for its public morality? Do these implications pose a problem for Devlin's theory? If so, how might he best respond to it?

6. Devlin makes some moral claims about each society's moral right to legally enforce its public morality. How should we understand his moral claims? Do they have any status other than as parts of the public morality?

Argument Reconstruction Exercises:

I. Devlin supports his theory with several examples of laws that he thinks have no purpose other than to enforce a principle of the public morality. Identify the premises and conclusion of his argument.

> Euthanasia or the killing of another at his own request, suicide, attempted suicide and suicide pacts, duelling, abortion, incest between brother and sister, are all acts which can be done in private and without offence to others and need not involve the corruption or exploitation of others. . . . [N]o one hitherto has gone so far as to suggest that they should all be left outside the criminal law as matters of private morality. They can be brought within it only as a matter of moral principle. (page 628)

II. Devlin argues for his theory by an analogy between society's need for good government and its need for a public morality. Identify the premises and conclusion of his argument.

> [A]n established morality is as necessary as good government to the welfare of society. Societies disintegrate from within more frequently than they are broken up by external pressures. There is disintegration when no common morality is observed and history shows that the loosening of moral bonds is often the first stage of disintegration, so that society is justified in taking the same steps to preserve its moral code as it does to preserve its government and other essential institutions. (page 630)

III. Devlin points out that "people don't think of monogamy as something which has to be supported because our society has chosen to organize itself upon it; they think of it as something that is good in itself and offering a good way of life and that it is for this reason that our society has adopted it" (page 629). Identify the premises and conclusion of the following objection to his view.

> Insofar as we use the legal system to enforce moral principles, we do so because we take the moral principles to be correct, not because they are part of our public morality. According to Devlin's theory, our justification, if any, for legally enforcing moral principles is not that they are correct, but that they are part of our public morality. Devlin's justification for our legally enforcing morality contradicts what we take to be our justification for doing so.

IV. Some critics object that Devlin does not give enough consideration to the negative effect that a society's enforcement of its public morality can have on individuals whose liberty is limited by the enforcement. Identify the premises and conclusion of the following argument.

> There are numerous examples of unjust laws that were enacted to legally enforce a fundamental part of a society's public morality (e.g., legal prohibitions on interracial marriage). Devlin's theory mistakenly implies that these laws were morally justified.

22.3 FRANCE AND THE BAN ON THE FULL-FACE VEIL: A PHILOSOPHICAL ANALYSIS OF THE ARGUMENTS

SARAH ROBERTS-CADY (2012)

Sarah Roberts-Cady is a professor of philosophy and of gender and women's studies at Fort Lewis College and has published in ethics and social and political philosophy. She here considers a specific issue regarding the appropriate limits of legal regulation: Is the recent (2010) French law banning the wearing of full-face veils in public morally permissible? She examines the issue from the perspective of both John Stuart Mill's **Harm Principle** and Patrick Devlin's version of **Legal Moralism**. Roberts-Cady argues that neither position provides a convincing justification for the French law.

Reading Questions:

1. What do President Sarkozy and President Obama think about the legitimacy of a ban on the full-face veil?

2. What is the difference between what Roberts-Cady calls a negative view of liberty versus a positive view of liberty?

3. What is political liberalism?

4. According to Mill, how does the harm principle protect and promote happiness?

5. Why, according to Roberts-Cady, is the veil not merely a symbol of female oppression?

6. Roberts-Cady offers two reasons for thinking that a more specific law that targeted only *forced* veiling would be unlikely to effectively prevent harm. What are they?

7. What is legal moralism?

8. What, according to Roberts-Cady, is Devlin's argument for the conclusion that each state has a right to enact laws to protect its shared moral values?

9. What is Roberts-Cady's objection to Devlin's argument for legal moralism?

10. Roberts-Cady thinks that even if we accept the assumption of legal moralism, it won't follow that the uncovered faces law is legitimate. Why?

In 2010, the French legislature passed a law that bans people from wearing veils over their faces in public. This law is sometimes known as the *visage découvert* or uncovered faces law. While the law doesn't specifically mention the Islamic religion, lawmakers publicly acknowledge that the law is aimed at conservative Muslim traditions in which women are expected to wear a full-face veil in public. The law imposes a fine of €150 (about $215) or a course in citizenship for women who wear a full-face veil in public. It imposes a fine of €30,000 (about $43,000) and a one-year jail term for anyone who forces a woman to wear a full-face veil.

The uncovered faces law has created substantial public debate. Initially, there was a legal debate about whether or not the law was consistent with the constitution of France. That question has been answered for now; it was deemed constitutional by France's Constitutional Council in July of 2010. That wasn't the end of the controversy, of course. Many people hold that even if it is deemed appropriate by the French legislature and the courts, there is something wrong with this law. People argue that government shouldn't dictate what people can or cannot wear, especially when clothing choices are an expression of religious views. This objection raises a different kind of issue. It is a philosophical issue: What *ought* to be the limit of governmental authority? Philosophers have been debating this question for a long time. *This paper will explore two influential and opposing positions in that debate. One position holds that government should be limited to protecting individual liberty. Another position holds that government may rightly enforce any cultural values that are central to the state. Both positions have been used to defend France's uncovered faces law. A careful examination of both positions will make clear that neither provides a convincing argument for the French ban on the full-face veil.*

Political Liberalism and the Uncovered Faces Law

There are a number of different arguments that people have offered in defense of the uncovered faces law, but the most common is an appeal to women's liberties. The French President at the time, Nicolas Sarkozy, stated, "The problem of the *burqa* is not a religious problem; it's a problem of liberty and women's dignity. It's not a religious symbol, but a sign of subservience and debasement. I want to say solemnly, the *burqa* is not welcome in France. In our country, we can't accept women prisoners behind a screen, cut off from all social life, deprived of all identity. That's not our idea of freedom."[1] His argument seems to be that the full-face veil limits women's freedom; the ban is justified as way of restoring women's liberty.

On the other hand, one of the most common objections to the uncovered faces law is based on the claim that it is a violation of the individual right to freedom of religion. In a speech given in Cairo, Egypt on June 4, 2009, U.S. President Barack Obama argued, "It is important for Western countries to avoid impeding Muslim citizens from practicing religion as they see fit, for instance, by dictating what clothes a Muslim woman should wear. We cannot disguise hostility towards any religion behind the pretence of liberalism." He added, "I reject the view of some in the West that a woman who chooses to cover her hair is somehow less equal."[2] President Obama is rejecting Sarkozy's argument for the ban, arguing instead that the uncovered faces law violates women's liberties by violating their freedom of religion.

The two arguments may be reconstructed this way:

President Sarkozy for the law:

1. *A government should protect the equal liberty of every citizen.*
2. *Banning the full-face veil will protect the equal liberty of women.*
3. *Therefore, a government should ban the full-face veil.*

President Obama against the law:

1. *A government should protect the equal liberty of every citizen.*
2. *Protecting the equal liberty of every citizen requires protecting freedom of religion.*
3. *The ban on the full-face veil is a violation of citizens' freedom of religion.*
4. *Therefore, government ought not ban the full-face veil.*

When framed this way, the issue appears to be a debate about the best way to protect liberty: Does the uncovered faces law violate or protect women's liberties? Note the common philosophical starting point: both of these arguments attempt to justify government intervention by appeal to the importance of government protection of liberty. In other words, both arguments appeal to **political liberalism**. In this context, the word "liberal" does not mean liberal democrat as opposed to conservative republican; it means "liberal" as in political liberalism—the political philosophies that have historically influenced the formation of both the governments of the U.S. and France.

The Philosophical Roots of Political Liberalism

While there are many versions of liberalism and much disagreement among liberal philosophers, *one of the common assumptions of liberalism seems to be that the primary function of government is to protect the liberty of citizens.* This is such a widely accepted premise that even American Democrats and Republicans seem to agree about this. They just disagree with each other about how to do that. Republicans have a largely negative view of liberty as the absence of interference from others. Thus, they tend to think that the protection of liberty requires minimizing government interference in our lives— deregulation, lower taxes, etc. On the other hand, Democrats tend to take a positive view of liberty as self-determination or autonomy. As a result, they argue that liberty for all can only come about if government protects equality of opportunity. For example, many people argue that public education and public healthcare programs, while interfering with individual liberty through taxation, also increase positive liberty by ensuring that every citizen, regardless of income, has an opportunity to develop into a thoughtful, healthy and autonomous adult. The point is that regardless of where one stands on these debates, one is likely standing on the backs of the philosophers of liberalism—Locke, Rousseau, and Mill. Thus, the appeal to liberal principles can have a powerful impact on public debate.

Why think that the primary function of government is to protect liberty? It turns out this is a more difficult question to answer than one might think. One of the first liberal thinkers, John Locke, based his argument on the concept of "natural rights." He simply argued that we are all born with certain natural rights to liberty. This seems like a very plausible claim to those who agree with him. In fact, it is so plausible that Thomas Jefferson borrowed Locke's natural rights language in writing the Declaration of Independence. The problem is that the appeal to natural rights is NOT very convincing to those who disagree. In fact, it's not much of an argument

at all. If someone challenges the idea that all humans have a right to freedom of religion (and people do) responding that *we just do, because it is natural* will not change that person's mind. Philosophers recognize this. One needs a better argument. In the centuries following Locke, many philosophers offered up different theoretical arguments in favor of natural rights, most of them not very successful.

In the 19th century, John Stuart Mill adopted a different tactic for defending liberalism. Rather than appealing to a mysterious concept of "natural rights," he appealed to **utilitarianism**. Utilitarianism is a theory that begins with the assumption that all human beings are interested in being happy. It follows from this that we approve of actions or policies that will increase happiness and disapprove of actions or policies that decrease happiness. Mill argues that protecting individual liberties is the best way to create a happy world.

Mill's guiding liberal principle for understanding the limits of government is called the **harm principle**. He expresses it this way:

> [T]he sole end for which mankind are warranted, individually or collectively, in interfering with the liberty of action of any of their number is self-protection. That the only purpose for which power can be rightfully exercised over any member of civilized community, against his will, is to prevent harm to others. His own good, either physical or moral is not sufficient warrant.[3]

Mill's presumption is that each person should be in control of his or her own life. *To the extent that one's actions only affect oneself, no one else should interfere with those actions. On the other hand, to the extent that one's actions affect others, the actions are permissible only if they are conducted with the free and informed consent of those affected.* Each person ought to respect every other person's liberty. The role of the government is to protect individual liberty, and to intervene only to prevent one person from violating another person's liberty. Notice that this gives government a very limited role in the lives of the citizens. This excludes governmental interference for the sake of protecting a person from harming him or herself. If a person wants to harm him or herself, Mill contends that he or she should be free to do so. For example,

Mill does not approve of the government enacting laws against drunkenness if the laws are aimed entirely at protecting one from harming oneself. On the other hand, it would be permissible to enact laws against drinking and driving, since that is aimed at preventing one person from harming another.[4]

Mill uses utilitarianism to defend the harm principle.[5] According to Mill, the harm principle's strict protection of individual liberty promotes happiness in many ways. One of his primary arguments is that each person is the best judge of what will make him or her happy. So maximizing each individual's freedom to pursue happiness in his or her own way will most likely increase total happiness.[6] Mill also argues that society benefits from protecting the liberty of individuals to express diverse opinions and adopt diverse lifestyles. He argues that protecting the freedom of speech of diverse individuals will encourage the kind of public debate that will result in careful, rigorous thinking.[7] Happiness is more likely to be achieved in a society which subjects beliefs to that kind of thoughtful examination. What's more, Mill argues that individuals ought to be able to act on their individual consciences, as long as they don't interfere with a similar liberty in others. He argues that this is important because the development of individuality is essential to human well-being. Mill writes,

> . . . it is the privilege and proper condition of a human being, arrived at the maturity of his faculties, to use and interpret experience in his own way. It is for him to find out what part of recorded experience is properly applicable to his own circumstances and character. The traditions and customs of other people are, to a certain extent, evidence of what their experience has taught *them*; presumptive evidence, and as such, have a claim to his deference: but in the first place, their experience may be too narrow; or they may not have interpreted it rightly. Secondly, their interpretations of experience may be correct but unsuitable to him. Customs are made for customary circumstances, and customary characters; and his circumstances or his character may be uncustomary. Thirdly, though the customs be both good as customs, and suitable to him, yet to conform to custom, merely as custom, does not educate or

develop in him any of the qualities which are the distinctive endowment of a human being. The human faculties of perception, judgment, discriminative feeling, mental activity and even more preference, are exercised only in making a choice. He who does anything because it is custom, makes no choice. He gains no practice either in discerning or in desiring what is best. The mental and the moral, like the muscular powers, are improved only by being used.[8]

Mill argues that allowing individuals the freedom to pursue different lifestyles and customs nurtures a kind of self-realization that is good for both the individual and society.

In addition to noting the benefits of individual liberty, Mill also points out the dangers of government control. He argues that there is no reason to believe that what might be imposed by a government on its people is correct or good. Every government is fallible. Worse, Mill thinks it is likely that government will get things wrong. He writes, ". . . the strongest of all arguments against interference of the public with purely personal conduct, is that when it does interfere, the odds are that it interferes wrongly, and in the wrong place."[9] He concludes that the policy that will promote the most happiness is one in which government may only interfere with the liberty of individual citizens for the sake of preventing them from harming others.

Does the Uncovered Faces Law Protect Liberty?

One can see how liberalism has influenced the debate over the veil. As noted above, it is liberalism that has led some people to oppose the uncovered faces law. One could use the harm principle to argue for the importance of protecting the liberty of individual women to choose to wear a full-face veil without interference from others. One could appeal to Mill's argument that individuals are much better suited than the state to determine what religious beliefs and practices are best for them. *Since Mill favors the strong protection of individual liberty, for him the only possible justification for government interference with wearing a full-face veil would be if banning the full-face veil was necessary to prevent people from harming each other.* For many people, this gets to the heart of the matter. As noted above, some people use liberalism to defend the ban on the basis of the claim that it will protect Muslim women from the harm of an oppressive tradition. The Urban Affairs Minister, Fadela Amara, in an interview with *Le Parisien*, stated, "The burqa is a prison; it's a straitjacket. . . It is not a religious insignia but the insignia of a totalitarian political project that advocates inequality between the sexes and which is totally devoid of democracy."[10] In short, people claim that this ban is justified because it will protect the liberty of women. How plausible is this claim?

Does the veil limit women's freedom? It's important to distinguish between the impact of the veil and other restrictions on women's liberties that are imposed in conservative Muslim communities. It is certainly the case that some of the same fundamentalist Muslims who believe women should wear a full-face veil in public also believe it appropriate to greatly restrict women's participation in society. They often restrict women's social interactions, and prevent women from gaining the benefits of education and employment. In addition, in some conservative Muslim communities, some forms of violence against women are condoned as morally appropriate. A principle focused on liberty would support intervening to protect women from violence, or to protect women's liberty to get an education or apply for a job. However, these practices are *not* what are at issue in this law. The issue in this law is specific to wearing a full-face veil. Is wearing the full-face veil itself harmful?

It is clear that covering one's face is not always or inherently harmful. Most people don't worry about the indignity of full-face motorcycle helmets or ski masks. People aren't concerned for the welfare of children in masks at costume parties. But perhaps these other cases are not analogous, in that they are all temporary face-coverings, rather than permanent features of a person's public persona. Some advocates of the French law claim that the full-face veil relegates women to less-than-full participation in society. Michele Alliot-Marie, the French Justice Minister, justified the ban by arguing that the full-face veil "dissolves the identity of a person in that of a community."[11] The argument seems to be that covering one's face hides one's identity, which prevents one from establishing relationships in one's community. Certainly, to the extent that we identify people by their faces, full-face veiling does create an impediment to identifying a person. However, facial identification is only one of many ways in which people can establish their identities in a community. Further, it is not clear that having one's face regularly covered in public will automatically or inevitably exclude one from participation in society. In this age of email, text messaging, Twitter, and Facebook (despite its name), it is clear that people are quite capable of identification and social interaction without face-to-face visual connection. People's discomfort with the full-face veil is a discomfort with only a particular way of identifying and relating without facial view. This is no doubt a culturally-influenced discomfort, rather than an objective impediment to full social interaction. If this is the case, then *it seems the problem is with those who exclude women wearing veils, not with the women who are wearing veils.* The veil is not what is doing the harm.

It is hard not to suspect that the banning of the full-face veil is less about the harms caused by the veil itself and more about what the veil symbolizes. For many French people, the full-face veil is the visible symbol of the female subordination that is associated with certain fundamentalist Muslim communities. Of course, most liberals would not sanction interfering with liberty to prevent symbols of harm; philosophers like Mill only advocated interfering with liberty to prevent *actual* harm. Perhaps more importantly, this narrow view of the veil as the symbol of female subordination is problematic. There is tremendous diversity among Muslim communities and Muslim traditions. Some Muslim women do not wear veils at all. Among those who do wear a veil, the veil has different meanings. Some Muslims justify the veil by pointing to passages in the *Qur'an* that suggest a woman should cover herself as a way of expressing modesty, "Say to the believing women that they should lower their gaze and guard their modesty. They should draw their veils over their bosoms and not display their ornaments." Other Islamic traditions suggest that the veil is about regulating social contact between men and women; it is a way of preventing inappropriate male attention to women's bodies. Other Islamic women claim it protects them from the kind of social pressures to which Western women are subjected. Western women's bodies are the object of the social gaze, which inevitably judges them inadequate, pressuring women to modify the body with make-up, razors, high heels, push-up bras and plastic surgery. The veil protects Muslim women from that kind of judgment and pressure. In the words of one Muslim feminist, Haleh Afshar (a professor of Politics and Women's Studies at University of York, and the first Iranian woman in the British House of Lords),

> Islamist women are particularly defensive of the veil. The actual imposition of the veil and the form that it has taken is a contested domain. Nevertheless many Muslim women have chosen the veil as the symbol of Islamification and have accepted it as the public face of their revivalist position. For them, the veil is liberating, and not an oppressive force. They maintain that the veil enables them to become the observers and not the observed; that it liberates them from the dictates of the fashion industry and the demands of the beauty myth. In the context of the patriarchal structures that shape women's lives the veil is a means of bypassing sexual harassment and gaining respect.[12]

Admittedly, some feminists worry that this justification is wrongly placing the entire responsibility for avoiding sexual objectification and sexual harassment on women rather than men. The debate about this among feminists is ongoing. The important point is that the veil should not be reduced to a symbol of female oppression. The veil has different meanings for different people. For some women, the full-face veil is a means of liberation from the oppression other women experience in the Western world. In other words, for some women, it may be helpful rather than harmful.

Interestingly, it may turn out that establishing that the veil itself does or does not harm women will not resolve the issue for Mill. *Even if one could establish some harm caused by the veil, Mill would only justify intervention if that was harm caused by one person to another.* As noted above, Mill doesn't think government is justified in interfering with liberty in order to prevent someone from harming him or herself.

Thus, Mill would be in favor of allowing women the freedom to choose to wear a full-face veil, even if it were harmful. On the other hand, even if one could establish that the full-face veil is not *inherently* harmful to women, Mill would disapprove of anyone who forced a woman to wear the full-face veil, since this causes harm by restricting her liberties. Things that are not inherently harmful can become harmful when they are forced on another person. Consider a scene (however unlikely) in which someone is holding a gun to another person's head and ordering that person to dance. Dancing is not inherently harmful. However, forcing someone to dance at gunpoint certainly is. It is harmful in the sense that it is limiting that person's liberty. It seems clear that forcing women to wear a full-face veil in public is harmful in the same way that forcing someone to dance is harmful. The harm done is in violating individual liberty.

It is no doubt for this reason that much of the concern in France is not about women's choices to wear veils, but the pressures placed on women to wear veils. Notice the penalties reflect this; by far the strongest penalties do not go to women in full-face veils, but to people who force them to wear the full-face veil. It appears to be consistent with Mill's harm principle to try to prevent people from forcing women to wear full-face veils. This would be the law intervening to prevent one person from interfering with another's liberty. If that's all the law did, and it did so effectively, then it would be less controversial. The problem is that it also punishes women who wear these veils, regardless of whether or not anyone forced them to do so. In that way, the law limits women's liberty to choose to wear a full-face veil. This would clearly *not* be acceptable under the harm principle. It's a violation of Mill's harm principle in that it interferes with women's freedom to choose to wear a full-face veil, even when that choice is purely self-regarding. Rather than being about the protection of women's liberty, this appears to be paternalistic. The government presumes it is better able to decide how women should dress than the women themselves. This should be troubling to anyone who subscribes to liberalism.

Perhaps more significantly, the French legislators seem to be making the discriminatory assumption that all veil-wearing Muslim women are victims in need of saving. They are utterly ignoring the possibility of strong Muslim women freely choosing to veil as a means to their own liberation.

It is worth adding that, even if the law only prohibited forced veiling, it is unlikely that it could effectively prevent harm. First, it would be very difficult to differentiate forced from voluntary veiling. If a woman is in a situation in which she is being forced to veil, it is likely she is also in a situation in which she would not be free to express her objections to it. Second, if a woman is being forced to veil it is not clear that this will protect her. It is likely that many conservative families, rather than allowing women in their family to go out in public unveiled, will simply choose not to allow women to go out in public. This would make it even more difficult to protect these women from harm.

On the other hand, perhaps the banning of the veil is not about preventing harm to women who wear the veil. Another way people have defended the claim that banning the veil prevents harm to others is by claiming that the full-face veil is a threat to the safety of the general public. The assumption seems to be that public security requires people to show their faces. Some people argue that identification at airports and other security checkpoints is best accomplished with photo ID and facial identification. This is a questionable assumption. There is evidence that facial identification is actually not very effective or accurate. Indeed, identification by fingerprint is vastly superior, and can be done when a person is wearing a full-face veil. Further, even if facial identification was crucial to security, this line of argument would only justify requiring the removal of veils at security checkpoints. To justify mandated unveiling in all public places, one would have to claim that doing so is crucial to preventing crime in a different way. It is hard to see how banning the veil in all public places will actually prevent harm to the public. Someone who wants to harm others in a public place will do so, with or without a face-covering. One can place a bomb in a backpack or open fire on a crowd with or without a veil.

Perhaps a more significant problem is that it would be difficult to apply this policy in a consistent way: Why not ban full-face motorcycle helmets and carnival masks in public places? To apply this law consistently may cause more harm than it prevents. That is, it would cause more restrictions on people's freedoms than it would prevent violent acts. That seems like a clear violation of Mill's principle of utility on which the harm principle is grounded.

In summary, *the uncovered faces law appears to limit liberties more than it protects liberties.* Obama was right; it appears that political liberalism cannot be used to support the ban on the veil.

Legal Moralism and the Uncovered Faces Law

Thus far, I have assumed that this is a debate about the protection of liberty; but the protection of individual liberty is not the only way to frame the debate about the French ban on the full-face veil. Indeed, much of the public discussion of the full-face veil in France has not centered around the protection of individual liberty. Instead, it has focused on the protection of French values and culture. "This is not about security or religion, but respecting our republican principles," declared Justice Minister Michele Alliot-Marie.[13] This emphasis on the way the veil challenges or violates French cultural identity is clearly expressed in the penalty for women who wear the veil; the penalty is a course in citizenship. The assumption seems to be that if a woman wears a veil, she doesn't really understand what it means to be French. Given the growing numbers of Muslims in France, it's hard not to speculate that the French are trying to preserve their French culture by forcing immigrants to assimilate. Is this a philosophically defensible position? It is certainly at odds with liberalism. In fact, its philosophical defense is perhaps better traced to a kind of conservatism called "legal moralism."

One philosophical defense of legal moralism in the twentieth century is offered by the English judge and legal writer, Lord Patrick Devlin, who argues that society is justified in legally enforcing its moral standards. He argues that the heart of a community of people is shared ideas, including shared values. In fact, Devlin holds that these shared values are an essential component of society. He writes,

...an established morality is as necessary as good government to the welfare of society. Societies disintegrate from within more frequently than they are broken up by external pressures. There is disintegration when no common morality is observed and history shows that the loosening of moral bonds is often the first stage of disintegration, so that society is justified in taking the same steps to preserve its moral code as it does to preserve its government and other essential institutions.[14]

Devlin holds that the state has the right to do whatever it must to "safeguard" the morality that is "essential to its existence."[15] Indeed, Devlin compares laws enforcing morality with laws against treason—both are designed for the preservation of the state.[16]

Notice that Devlin's position is that the state may enforce morality, not because the moral standards are known to be true and correct, but because enforcing a culture's moral standards is instrumentally valuable as a means to preserving the state. Thus, in determining which values to enforce, one need not seek out philosophical arguments to support the truth of the moral standards. Indeed, Devlin seems to be skeptical that such arguments exist. He writes,

> But matters of this sort are not determined by rational argument. Every moral judgment, unless it claims a divine source, is simply a feeling that no right-minded man could behave in any other way without admitting that he was doing wrong. It is the power of common sense and not the power of reason that is behind the judgments of society.[17]

Perhaps it is precisely because he doubted that philosophers could offer a rational argument for any claims about universal human rights that Devlin advocated that each society must be held together by its own unique cultural and moral traditions. Rather than attempting to establish what moral standards are appropriate with philosophical argument, Devlin focuses on establishing what moral norms are essential to the preservation of the state. Devlin suggests that the core values of a community for any given society should be determined by the standards of the "reasonable man" in that society. More specifically,

he defines this standard as one of a jury; it is any standard to which twelve randomly-chosen citizens would agree unanimously.[18]

In the case of the uncovered faces law, it appears that legal moralism could be used to justify it in the following way. If one begins with the assumption that it is permissible for governments to enact laws that will preserve their central culture and values, and one further adds the premise that the full-face veil is an affront to French culture and values, then one can clearly conclude that the uncovered faces law is permissible.

Formally, the full arguments could be stated as follows:

Devlin's Argument for Legal Moralism

1. A state has a right to enact laws necessary for preserving itself.
2. A necessary component of preserving any state is maintaining shared values.
3. Therefore, a state has a right to enact laws to maintain shared values.19

The Legal Moralist Argument for the Uncovered Faces Law

1. A state has a right to enact laws to maintain shared values.
2. The uncovered faces law is necessary for maintaining shared French values.
3. Therefore, France has a right to enact the Uncovered Faces Law.

There are many ways to criticize these arguments. First, one may challenge Devlin's argument for legal moralism by challenging the premise which claims that maintaining shared values is necessary for maintaining a state. While having some core moral standards which support the laws of a society is no doubt useful to maintaining a state, it does not follow from this that maintaining a state requires a uniform and unchanging set of values. There is ample empirical evidence (in countries like the U.S.) that significant diversity of moral beliefs and changes in moral standards are consistent with the maintenance of a state.

In fact, one may argue that a state is better served by maintaining mechanisms for critically evaluating a society's shared values. Devlin suggests that a state is morally justified in taking steps to preserve any values central to that state, no matter their merits. This is certainly an assumption worth questioning. It seems clear that uncritical deference to dominant values is dangerous. When the U.S. Constitution was first written, the common assumption was that only the liberty and rights of white males were worth protecting. Appropriately, many people later challenged that assumption, resulting in significant (positive) changes to cultural values and laws. I would argue that the U.S. not only survived this cultural shift, but is stronger and more stable because of it. This seems to point to the fact that critical reflection on cultural values is not only consistent with the preservation of a state; it is perhaps crucial to it.

The uncritical deference to dominant values is clear in the case of the French ban. The French do not ban everything that oppresses women; it seems the French are fine with practices that place women at a disadvantage as long as it is a French way of doing so and therefore doesn't challenge France's identity. For example, the French seem to be blind to the ways in which European women are harmed by their "free" choices to dress in ankle-breaking high heels, and to alter their bodies with make-up and plastic surgery in order to try to live up to socially-constructed standards of beauty. The legal moralist argument suggests that the government ought to allow French citizens to oppress women as long as they do it in a distinctly French way (upholding French values), rather than a Muslim way (which is at odds with their French identity). Surely this reasoning is mistaken.

One might also challenge the premise that banning the full-face veil is necessary for the preservation of the French values. There are actually very few women in France who wear the full-face veil. According to French authorities, although there are about five million Muslims living in France, less than two thousand of them wear a full-face veil.[21] It seems highly unlikely that two thousand women wearing full-face veils will result in any significant impact on the French state. It is even more unlikely that these two thousand women's clothing choices threaten the state's survival by challenging its

values. Thus, it seems likely that the second premise of the argument for the uncovered faces law is also false.

For all of these reasons, *appeals to justify the uncovered faces law for the sake of the preservation of French values are unconvincing.* There is reason to doubt that disagreements about values threaten a state's existence. Also, there is reason to doubt that all values that are essential to a state are worth preserving; some entrenched community assumptions ought to be challenged. Further, the uncovered faces law does not appear to be necessary for the preservation of the state and its values.

In summary, this paper explored two common arguments for the French ban on the veil—one focused on the protection of individual liberty, the other on the protection of state and culture. The French ban on the full-face veil cannot be justified by either approach. In other words, *the most common arguments made in favor of the uncovered faces law are unconvincing.*

NOTES

1. Chrisafis, Angelique. "Nicholas Sarkozy says Islamic veils are not welcome in France." *The Guardian*. Monday, June 22, 2009.
2. http://www.whitehouse.gov/the-press-office/remarks-president-cairo-university-6-04-09
3. Mill, John Stuart. *On Liberty and The Subjection of Woman* (London: Penguin Classics, 2006), 15–16.
4. Mill seemed to take a fairly broad view of harm. Some later thinkers limited it to the interference with liberty. As such, they interpreted the harm principle as stating that the purpose of government would be to keep one person from interfering with the liberties of others. This more restricted principle is sometimes called the "liberty principle." This led to other debates about interpretation of the principle: What counts as "liberty"? Some thinkers, Mill included, seemed to take a largely negative view of liberty as the absence of interference from others. Thus, he argued for restricting government intervention to protecting people from unwanted interference from other people (e.g. enforcing laws against theft, assault, murder). Other thinkers take a positive view of liberty as self-determination or autonomy. As a result, they argue the government should also protect equality of opportunity. For example, many people argue that public education and public healthcare programs, while interfering with individual liberty through taxation, also increase positive liberty by ensuring that every citizen, regardless of

income, has an opportunity to develop into a thoughtful, healthy and autonomous adult. These debates aside, there is general agreement among thinkers in this tradition that the purpose of government intervention is the protection of liberty.

5. In addition to using it to defend the harm principle. Mill also advocates using it to determine how to implement the harm principle. The utilitarian moral principle should determine how to regulate and penalize individual conduct that harms others.

6. Mill, *On Liberty*, 86–87.

7. Ibid. 23.

8. Ibid. 66–67

9. Ibid. 94.

10. "French minister denounces burka." *BBC News*, Wednesday, 16 July 2008.

11. "Face-Veil Ban Under Vote in France." *Al Jazeera*, Sept. 14, 2010.

12. Afshar, Haleh. "Women and the Politics of Fundamentalism in Iran." *Feminism & Race*. Ed. Kum-Kum Bhavnani (Oxford: Oxford University Press, 2001), 351.

13. "French Parliament Adopts Ban on the Full-Face Veil." *France 24*. September 15, 2010.

14. Devlin, Lord Patrick. "Morals and the Criminal Law," Chapter 22.2 this volume.

15. Ibid. 34.

16. To be fair, while Devlin argues that the state has a right to enforce moral norms, he didn't think this was an absolute right, outweighing all other moral considerations. Like Mill, Devlin recognizes the value of respecting individual liberty and privacy. He argues these must be weighed against the government's interest in intervention. Devlin suggests four "elastic" principles which ought to guide and limit the enforcement of moral standards by a government. First, he suggests that the law ought to "tolerate" the maximum liberty "consistent with the integrity of society." Thus, government shouldn't punish a person for a behavior (and thereby interfere with individual liberty) unless it lies "beyond the limits of tolerance." Of course, one cannot set a clear standard for what counts as being beyond the limits of tolerance. He offers the vague suggestion that the limit of tolerance is whatever practices are judged to be "injurious to society." Second, Devlin argues that the standard for what is intolerable must be well-established over time. He recognizes that the limits of tolerance change over time. Some standards last longer than others. Before one can enforce a norm, one must be sure that it is an enduring norm and not merely a passing whim. Third, he writes that the law must be balanced against respect for privacy. He writes, "as far as possible privacy should be respected." Fourth, he argues that "the law is concerned with the minimum and not the maximum." That is, he does not claim laws should enforce every moral standard. Rather, he argues laws should only

enforce the minimum moral standard, below which it would be unacceptable for a citizen to go.

There are two concerns about Devlin's addendums. First, Devlin offers no philosophical defense of the "elastic principles" that provide moral limits to the government enforcement of moral standards. This is probably because he thinks none is possible besides divine command or common sense. The problem is that will hardly be convincing to those rational people who disagree with him. Second, Devlin leaves vague his answer to the most controversial question: When exactly is a society's moral norm so important that it justifies violating individual liberty and privacy? He only vaguely tells his readers that it is when the behavior is long-standing and "injurious to society." This is not a clear line.

What is clear is that Devlin believes that it is morally permissible for the government to go far beyond Mill's harm principle in interfering with the liberty of citizens. He writes, ". . . the law exists for the protection of society. It does not discharge its function by protecting the individual from injury, annoyance, corruption and exploitation; the law must protect also the institutions and the community of ideas, political and moral, without which people cannot live together. Society cannot ignore the morality of the individual any more than it can his loyalty; it flourishes on both and without either it dies."

17. Devlin, "Morals and the Criminal Law," 40.

18. Ibid. 38.

19. H.L.A. Hart calls this the "moderate thesis" of legal moralism. It recommends preserving morality as a means to preserving the state. He contrasts this with the extreme legal moralist thesis, which holds that legal enforcement of morality is good in itself, quite apart from instrumental value to preserving the state (Hart 48–49).

21. "What's hiding behind France's proposed burqa ban?" *The Christian Science Monitor*. January 27, 2010.

BIBLIOGRAPHY

Afshar, Haleh. "Women and the Politics of Fundamentalism in Iran." *Feminism & Race*. Ed. Kum-Kum Bhavnani (Oxford: Oxford University Press, 2001), 348–365.

Berlin, Isaiah. "Two Concepts of Liberty", in *Four Essays on Liberty* (London: Oxford University Press, 2002).

Chrisafis, Angelique. "Nicholas Sarkozy says Islamic veils are not welcome in France." *The Guardian*. Monday, June 22, 2009.

Devlin, Lord Patrick. "Morals and the Criminal Law." Chapter 22.2 this volume.

Erlanger, Steven. "Parliament Moves France Closer to a Ban on Facial Veils." *New York Times*. July 13, 2010.

"Face-Veil Ban Under Vote in France." *Al Jazeera*, Sept. 14, 2010.

"French minister denounces burka." *BBC News*, Wednesday, 16 July 2008.

"French Parliament Adopts Ban on the Full-Face Veil."
France 24, September 15, 2010.

Hart, H.L.A. *Law, Liberty, and Morality* (Stanford: Stanford
University Press, 1963).

Mill, John Stuart. *On Liberty and The Subjection of Women*
(London: Penguin Classics, 2006).

Obama, Barack. White House Press Release. June 4,
2009. http://www.whitehouse.gov/the-press-office/
remarks-president-cairo-university-6-04-09

"What's hiding behind France's proposed burqa ban?"
The Christian Science Monitor, January 27, 2010.

DISCUSSION QUESTIONS:

1. Roberts-Cady is dismissive of the claim that human rights are natural rights. What does it mean for a right to be natural? If Mill is right in his defense of rights, wouldn't all rights turn out to be natural rights? If Mill's argument for human rights fails, how else might we defend the idea that all humans have rights?

2. Mill takes his Utilitarianism to support his Harm Principle. Is the argument from the former to the latter sound? Must a utilitarian accept the harm principle?

3. Some philosophers have argued that legal regulations can be justified on paternalistic grounds, as necessary to protect individuals from harms even when they choose them. For example, many countries have banned the use of harmful drugs, fatty foods, and—most recently, in New York City—large sodas. Might the French ban on full-face veils be justified in this way: The law protects women who wear the veil from a social practice that is actually harmful to them, even though they have consented to it?

4. Many of the women who wear veils were likely raised within homes where an ultra-conservative form of Islam was taught. As adults they freely wear the veil because of the strong indoctrination that they received as children. Some might even compare it to the kind of social engineering that happens in the novel *Brave New World* in which each caste of society is raised to be happy with their predefined place in society. The result is women who really want to wear the veil regardless of whether it is bad for them. Given that our view of the world and ourselves is strongly shaped by our upbringing, what kind of laws might France be

justified in passing to protect young girls growing up in such homes?

5. Roberts-Cady questions whether the French law is effective in protecting French values of gender equality and secularism. But perhaps the motivation for the law is not so much to protect these values as simply to express them. Does each society have a right to use its legal system to express those values that it takes to be fundamental? If so, might this be an appropriate basis for the French law?

Argument Reconstruction Exercises:

I. Roberts-Cady explains how John Stuart Mill appeals to the normative theory known as utilitarianism in order to defend the harm principle. Reconstruct the argument for the harm principle in the following passage.

> Utilitarianism is a theory that begins with the assumption that all human beings are interested in being happy. It follows from this that we approve of actions or policies that will increase happiness and disapprove of actions or policies that decrease happiness. Mill argues that protecting individual liberties is the best way to create a happy world. (page 637)

II. According to Roberts-Cady, the harm principle might actually be used to *defend* a policy that allows women to wear the veil if they so choose even if it's true that doing so is inherently harmful. Reconstruct the argument for this conclusion.

> Since Mill favors the strong protection of individual liberty, for him the only possible justification for government interference with wearing a full-face veil would be if banning the full-face veil was necessary to prevent people from harming each other. As noted above, Mill doesn't think government is justified in interfering with liberty in order to prevent someone from harming him or herself. Thus, Mill would be in favor of allowing women the freedom to choose to wear a full-face veil, even if it were harmful. (page 638)

III. Roberts-Cady objects to legal moralism on the ground that in at least some cases, societies are strengthened by a critical evaluation and even rejection of historical values. Thus, even on the assumption that a state is justified in enacting laws that are necessary for self-preservation, this might be consistent with enacting policies that subvert historical values. Reconstruct her argument for this conclusion.

> In fact, one may argue that a state is better served by maintaining mechanisms for critically evaluating a society's shared values. Devlin suggests that a state is morally justified in taking steps to preserve any values central to that state, no matter their merits. This is certainly an assumption worth questioning… When the U.S. Constitution was first written, the common assumption was that only the liberty and rights of white males were worth protecting. Appropriately, many people later challenged that assumption, resulting in significant (positive) changes to cultural values and laws. I would argue that the U.S. not only survived this cultural shift, but is stronger and more stable because of it. This seems to point to the fact that critical reflection on cultural values is not only consistent with the preservation of a state; it is perhaps crucial to it. (page 643)

IV. Remember the form of an argument by false implication. Such an argument starts with an assumption, shows that the assumption leads to a conclusion that is mistaken, and as a result rejects the assumption. Roberts-Cady uses the example of the uncovered faces law in France to argue that legal moralism has unacceptable consequences. Reconstruct her argument from the following passage.

> The French do not ban everything that oppresses women; it seems the French are fine with practices that place women at a disadvantage as long as it is a French way of doing so and therefore doesn't challenge France's identity. For example, the French seem to be blind to the ways in which European women are harmed by their "free" choices to dress in ankle-breaking high heels, and to alter their bodies with make-up and plastic surgery in order to try to live up to socially-constructed standards of beauty. The legal moralist argument suggests that the government ought to allow French citizens to oppress women as long as they do it in a distinctly French way (upholding French values), rather than a Muslim way (which is at odds with their French identity). Surely this reasoning is mistaken. (page 643)

22.4 PORNOGRAPHY, OPPRESSION, AND FREEDOM

HELEN E. LONGINO (1979)

Helen E. Longino is Professor of Philosophy at Stanford University and has published extensively in the philosophy of science, social epistemology and feminist philosophy. In this essay, she defines pornography and argues that its production, distribution, and enjoyment are injurious to women in three ways that warrant its legal suppression. She also rebuts three attempts to show that efforts to socially and legally control pornography violate a constitutionally protected right to liberty.

Reading Questions:

1. What, according to Longino, distinguishes pornography from erotic literature and art in general?

2. How, according to Longino, is pornography implicated in violent crimes against women?

3. How, according to Longino, does pornography defame and libel women; what vicious lies does it present about them?

4. How, according to Longino, does pornography present a distorted view of women's nature and reinforce the social oppression and exploitation of women?

5. Longino employs a distinction between liberty as license and liberty as independence to respond to the claim that the social and legal regulation of pornography violates the right to liberty. What is the difference between liberty as license and liberty as independence? How does Longino use this difference to argue that restrictions on pornography are not violations of the right to liberty?

Introduction

One of the beneficial results of the sexual revolution has been a growing acceptance of the distinction between questions of sexual mores and questions of morality. This distinction underlies the old slogan, "Make love, not war," and takes harm to others as the defining characteristic of immorality. What is immoral is behavior which causes injury to or violation of another person or people. Such injury may be physical or it may be psychological. To cause pain to another, to lie to another, to hinder another in the exercise of her or his rights, to exploit another, to degrade another, to misrepresent and slander another are instances of immoral behavior. Masturbation or engaging voluntarily in sexual intercourse with another consenting adult of the same or the other sex, as long as neither injury nor violation of either individual or another is involved, are not immoral. Some sexual behavior is morally objectionable, but not because of its sexual character. Thus, adultery is immoral not because it involves sexual intercourse with someone to whom one is not legally married, but because it involves breaking a promise (of sexual and emotional fidelity to one's spouse). Sadistic, abusive, or forced sex is immoral because it injures and violates another.

The detachment of sexual chastity from moral virtue implies that we cannot condemn forms of sexual behavior merely because they strike us as distasteful or subversive of the Protestant work ethic, or because they depart from standards of behavior we have individually adopted. It has thus seemed to imply that no matter how offensive we might find pornography, we must tolerate it in the name of freedom from illegitimate repression. I wish to argue that this is not so, that *pornography is immoral because it is harmful to people.*

What Is Pornography?

I define pornography as *verbal or pictorial explicit representations of sexual behavior that, in the words of the Commission on Obscenity and Pornography, have as a distinguishing characteristic "the degrading and demeaning portrayal of the role and status of the human female. . . as a mere sexual object to be exploited and manipulated sexually."*[1] In pornographic books, magazines, and films, women are represented as passive and as slavishly dependent upon men. The role of female characters is limited to the provision of sexual services to men. To the extent that women's sexual pleasure is represented at all, it is subordinated to that of men and is never an end in itself as is the sexual pleasure of men. What pleases women is the use of their bodies to satisfy male desires. While the sexual objectification of women is common to all pornography, women are the recipients of even worse treatment in violent pornography, in which women characters are killed, tortured, gang-raped, mutilated, bound, and otherwise abused, as a means of providing sexual stimulation or pleasure to the male characters. It is this development which has attracted the attention of feminists and been the stimulus to an analysis of pornography in general.[2]

Not all sexually explicit material is pornography, nor is all material which contains representations of sexual abuse and degradation pornography.

A representation of a sexual encounter between adult persons which is characterized by mutual respect is, once we have disentangled sexuality and morality, not morally objectionable. Such a representation would be one in which the desires and experiences of each participant were regarded by the other participants as having a validity and a subjective importance equal to those of the individual's own desire and experiences. In such an encounter, each participant acknowledges the other participant's basic human dignity and personhood. Similarly, a representation of a nude human body (in whole or in part) in such a manner that the person shown maintains self-respect—e.g., is not portrayed in a degrading position—would not be morally objectionable. The educational films of the National Sex Forum, as well as a certain amount of erotic literature and art, fall into this category. While some erotic materials are beyond the standards of modesty held by some individuals, they are not for this reason immoral.

A representation of a sexual encounter which is not characterized by mutual respect, in which at least one of the parties is treated in a manner beneath her or his dignity as a human being, is no longer simple erotica. That a representation is of degrading behavior does not in itself, however, make it pornographic. Whether or not it is pornographic is a function of contextual features. Books and films may contain descriptions or representations of a rape in order to explore the consequences of such an assault upon its victim. What is being shown is abusive or degrading behavior which attempts to deny the humanity and dignity of the person assaulted, yet the context surrounding the representation, through its exploration of the consequences of the act, acknowledges and reaffirms her dignity. Such books and films, far from being pornographic, are (or can be) highly moral, and fall into the category of moral realism.

What makes a work a work of pornography, then, is not simply its representation of degrading and abusive sexual encounters, but its implicit, if not explicit, approval and recommendation of sexual behavior that is immoral, i.e., that physically or psychologically violates the personhood of one of the participants. Pornography, then, is verbal or pictorial material which represents or describes sexual behavior that is degrading or abusive to one or more of the participants *in such a way as to endorse the degradation*. The participants so treated in virtually all heterosexual pornography are women or children,

so heterosexual pornography is, as a matter of fact, material which endorses sexual behavior that is degrading and/or abusive to women and children. As I use the term "sexual behavior," this includes sexual encounters between persons, behavior which produces sexual stimulation or pleasure for one of the participants, and behavior which is preparatory to or invites sexual activity. Behavior that is degrading or abusive includes physical harm or abuse, and physical or psychological coercion. In addition, behavior which ignores or devalues the real interests, desires, and experiences of one or more participants in any way is degrading. Finally, that a person has chosen or consented to be harmed, abused, or subjected to coercion does not alter the degrading character of such behavior.

Pornography communicates its endorsement of the behavior it represents by various features of the pornographic context: the degradation of the female characters is represented as providing pleasure to the participant males and, even worse, to the participant females, and there is no suggestion that this sort of treatment of others is inappropriate to their status as human beings. These two features are together sufficient to constitute endorsement of the represented behavior. The contextual features which make material pornographic are intrinsic to the material. In addition to these, extrinsic features, such as the purpose for which the material is presented—i.e., the sexual arousal/pleasure/satisfaction of its (mostly) male consumers—or an accompanying text, may reinforce or make explicit the endorsement. Representations which in and of themselves do not show or endorse degrading behavior may be put into a pornographic context by juxtaposition with others that are degrading, or by a text which invites or recommends degrading behavior toward the subject represented. In such a case the whole complex—the series of representations or representations with text—is pornographic.

The distinction I have sketched is one that applies most clearly to sequential material—a verbal or pictorial (filmed) story—which represents an action and provides a temporal context for it. In showing the before and after, a narrator or film-maker has plenty of opportunity to acknowledge the dignity of the person violated or clearly to refuse to do so. It is somewhat more difficult to apply the distinction to single still representations. The contextual features cited above, however, are clearly present in still photographs or pictures that glamorize degradation and sexual violence. Phonograph album covers and advertisements offer some prime examples of such glamorization. Their representations of women in chains (the Ohio Players), or bound by ropes and black and blue (the Rolling Stones) are considered high-quality commercial "art" and glossily prettify the violence they represent. Since the standard function of prettification and glamorization is the communication of desirability, these albums and ads are communicating the desirability of violence against women. Representations of women bound or chained, particularly those of women bound in such a way as to make their breasts, or genital or anal areas vulnerable to any passerby, endorse the scene they represent by the absence of any indication that this treatment of women is in any way inappropriate.

To summarize: *Pornography is not just the explicit representation or description of sexual behavior, nor even the explicit representation or description of sexual behavior which is degrading and/or abusive to women. Rather, it is material that explicitly represents or describes degrading and abusive sexual behavior so as to endorse and/or recommend the behavior as described.* The contextual features, moreover, which communicate such endorsement are intrinsic to the material; that is, they are features whose removal or alteration would change the representation or description.

This account of pornography is underlined by the etymology and original meaning of the word "pornography." *The Oxford English Dictionary* defines pornography as "Description of the life, manners, etc. of prostitutes and their patrons [from πόρνη (porne) meaning "harlot" and γράφειν (graphein) meaning "to write"]; hence the expression or suggestion of obscene or unchaste subjects in literature or art."[3]

Let us consider the first part of the definition for a moment. In the transactions between prostitutes and their clients, prostitutes are paid, directly or indirectly, for the use of their bodies by the client for sexual pleasure.[*] Traditionally males have obtained from female prostitutes what they could not or did not wish to get from their wives or women friends, who, because of the character of their relation to the male, must be accorded some measure of human respect. While there are limits to what treatment is seen as appropriate toward women as wives or women friends, the prostitute as prostitute exists to provide sexual pleasure to males. The female characters of contemporary pornography also exist to provide pleasure to males, but in the pornographic context no pretense is made to regard them as parties to a contractual arrangement. Rather, the anonymity of these characters makes each one Everywoman, thus suggesting not only that all women are appropriate subjects for the enactment of the most bizarre and demeaning male sexual fantasies, but also that this is their primary purpose. The recent escalation of violence in pornography—the presentation of scenes of bondage, rape, and torture of women for the sexual stimulation of the male characters or male viewers—while shocking in itself, is from this point of view merely a more vicious extension of a genre whose success depends on treating women in a manner beneath their dignity as human beings.

Pornography: Lies and Violence Against Women

What is wrong with pornography, then, is its degrading and dehumanizing portrayal of women (and not its sexual content). Pornography, by its very nature, requires that women be subordinate to men and mere instruments for the fulfillment of male fantasies. To accomplish this, pornography must lie. Pornography lies when it says that our sexual life is or ought to be subordinate to the service of men, that our pleasure consists in pleasing men and not ourselves, that we are depraved, that we are fit subjects for rape, bondage, torture, and murder. Pornography lies explicitly about women's sexuality, and through such lies fosters more lies about our humanity, our dignity, and our personhood.

Moreover, since nothing is alleged to justify the treatment of the female characters of pornography save their womanhood, pornography depicts all

---

[*]In talking of prostitution here, I refer to the concept of, rather than the reality of, prostitution. The same is true of my remarks about relationships between women and their husbands or men friends.

women as fit objects of violence by virtue of their sex alone. Because it is simply being female that, in the pornographic vision, justifies being violated, the lies of pornography are lies about all women. Each work of pornography is on its own libelous and defamatory, yet gains power through being reinforced by every other pornographic work. The sheer number of pornographic productions expands the moral issue to include not only assessing the morality or immorality of individual works, but also the meaning and force of the mass production of pornography.

The pornographic view of women is thoroughly entrenched in a booming portion of the publishing, film, and recording industries, reaching and affecting not only all who look to such sources for sexual stimulation, but also those of us who are forced into an awareness of it as we peruse magazines at newsstands and record albums in record stores, as we check the entertainment sections of city newspapers, or even as we approach a counter to pay for groceries. It is not necessary to spend a great deal of time reading or viewing pornographic material to absorb its male-centered definition of women. No longer confined within plain brown wrappers, it jumps out from billboards that proclaim "Live X-rated Girls!" or "Angels in Pain" or "Hot and Wild," and from magazine covers displaying a woman's genital area being spread open to the viewer by her own fingers.* Thus, even men who do not frequent pornographic shops and movie houses are supported in the sexist objectification of women by their environment. Women, too, are crippled by internalizing as self-images those that are presented to us by pornographers. Isolated from one another and with no source of support for an alternative view of female sexuality, we may not always find the strength to resist a message that dominates the common cultural media.

The entrenchment of pornography in our culture also gives it a significance quite beyond its explicit sexual messages. To suggest, as pornography does, that the primary purpose of women is to provide sexual pleasure to men is to deny that women are independently human or have a status equal to that of men. It is, moreover, to deny our equality at one

of the most intimate levels of human experience. This denial is especially powerful in a hierarchical, class society such as ours, in which individuals feel good about themselves by feeling superior to others. Men in our society have a vested interest in maintaining their belief in the inferiority of the female sex, so that no matter how oppressed and exploited by the society in which they live and work, they can feel that they are at least superior to someone or some category of individuals—a woman or women. Pornography, by presenting women as wanton, depraved, and made for the sexual use of men, caters directly to that interest.* The very intimate nature of sexuality which makes pornography so corrosive also protects it from explicit public discussion. The consequent lack of any explicit social disavowal of the pornographic image of women enables this image to continue fostering sexist attitudes even as the society publicly proclaims its (as yet timid) commitment to sexual equality.

In addition to finding a connection between the pornographic view of women and the denial to us of our full human rights, women are beginning to connect the consumption of pornography with committing rape and other acts of sexual violence against women. Contrary to the findings of the Commission on Obscenity and Pornography a growing body of research is documenting (1) a correlation between exposure to representations of violence and the committing of violent acts generally, and (2) a correlation between exposure to pornographic materials and the committing of sexually abusive or violent acts against women.[4] While more study is needed to establish precisely what the causal relations are, clearly so-called hard-core pornography is not innocent.

From "snuff" films and miserable magazines in pornographic stores to *Hustler*, to phonograph album covers and advertisements, to *Vogue*, pornography

---

*This was a full-color magazine cover seen in a rack at the check-out counter of a corner delicatessen.

*Pornography thus becomes another tool of capitalism. One feature of some contemporary pornography—the use of Black and Asian women in both still photographs and films—exploits the racism as well as the sexism of its white consumers. For a discussion of the interplay between racism and sexism under capitalism as it relates to violent crimes against women, see Angela Y. Davis, "Rape, Racism, and the Capitalist Setting," *The Black Scholar*, Vol. 9, No. 7, April 1978.

has come to occupy its own niche in the communications and entertainment media and to acquire a quasi-institutional character (signaled by the use of diminutives such as "porn" or "porno" to refer to pornographic material, as though such familiar naming could take the hurt out). Its acceptance by the mass media, whatever the motivation, means a cultural endorsement of its message. As much as the materials themselves, the social tolerance of these degrading and distorted images of women in such quantities is harmful to us, since it indicates a general willingness to see women in ways incompatible with our fundamental human dignity and thus to justify treating us in those ways.* The tolerance of pornographic representations of the rape, bondage, and torture of women helps to create and maintain a climate more tolerant of the actual physical abuse of women.† The tendency on the part of the legal system to view the victim of a rape as responsible for the crime against her is but one manifestation of this.

In sum, pornography is injurious to women in at least three distinct ways:

1. *Pornography, especially violent pornography, is implicated in the committing of crimes of violence against women.*
2. *Pornography is the vehicle for the dissemination of a deep and vicious lie about women. It is defamatory and libelous.*
3. *The diffusion of such a distorted view of women's nature in our society as it exists today supports sexist*

---

*This tolerance has a linguistic parallel in the growing acceptance and use of nonhuman nouns such as "chick," "bird," "filly," "fox," "doll," "babe," "skirt," etc., to refer to women, and of verbs of harm such as "fuck," "screw," "bang" to refer to sexual intercourse. See Robert Baker and Frederick Elliston, " 'Pricks' and 'Chicks': A Plea for Persons." *Philosophy and Sex* (Buffalo, N.Y.: Prometheus Books, 1975).
†This is supported by the fact that in Denmark the number of rapes committed has increased while the number of rapes reported to the authorities has decreased over the past twelve years. See *WAVPM Newspage*, Vol. II, No. 5, June, 1978, quoting M. Harry, "Denmark Today—The Causes and Effects of Sexual Liberty" (paper presented to The Responsible Society, London, England, 1976). See also Eysenck and Nias, *Sex, Violence and the Media* (New York: St. Martin's Press, 1978), pp. 120–124.

(i.e., male-centered) attitudes, and thus reinforces the oppression and exploitation of women.

Society's tolerance of pornography, especially pornography on the contemporary massive scale, reinforces each of these modes of injury: By not disavowing the lie, it supports the male-centered myth that women are inferior and subordinate creatures. Thus, it contributes to the maintenance of a climate tolerant of both psychological and physical violence against women.

Pornography and the Law

Congress shall make no law respecting the establishment of religion, or prohibiting the free exercise thereof; or abridging the freedom of speech, or of the press; or the right of the people peaceably to assemble, and to petition the Government for a redress of grievances.

—First Amendment, Bill of Rights of the United States Constitution

Pornography is clearly a threat to women. Each of the modes of injury cited above offers sufficient reason at least to consider proposals for the social and legal control of pornography. The almost universal response from progressives to such proposals is that constitutional guarantees of freedom of speech and privacy preclude recourse to law[5]. . . .

There are three ways of arguing that control of pornography is incompatible with adherence to constitutional rights. The first argument claims that regulating pornography involves an unjustifiable interference in the private lives of individuals. The second argument takes the First Amendment as a basic principle constitutive of our form of government, and claims that the production and distribution of pornographic material, as a form of speech, is an activity protected by that amendment. The third argument claims not that the pornographer's rights are violated, but that others' rights will be if controls against pornography are instituted.

The privacy argument is the easiest to dispose of. Since the open commerce in pornographic materials is an activity carried out in the public sphere, the publication and distribution of such materials, unlike their use by individuals, is not protected by rights to

privacy. The distinction between the private consumption of pornographic material and the production and distribution of, or open commerce in, it is sometimes blurred by defenders of pornography. But I may entertain, in the privacy of my mind, defamatory opinions about another person, even though I may not broadcast them. So one might create without restraint—as long as no one were harmed in the course of preparing them—pornographic materials for one's personal use, but be restrained from reproducing and distributing them. In both cases what one is doing—in the privacy of one's mind or basement—may indeed be deplorable, but immune from legal proscription. Once the activity becomes public, however—i.e., once it involves others—it is no longer protected by the same rights that protect activities in the private sphere.*

In considering the second argument (that control of pornography, private or public, is wrong in principle), it seems important to determine whether we consider the right to freedom of speech to be absolute and unqualified. If it is, then obviously all speech, including pornography, is entitled to protection. But the right is, in the first place, not an unqualified right: There are several kinds of speech not protected by the First Amendment, including the incitement to violence in volatile circumstances, the solicitation of crimes, perjury and misrepresentation, slander, libel, and false advertising.† That there are forms of proscribed speech shows that we accept limitations on the right to freedom of speech if such speech, as do the forms listed, impinges on other rights. The manufacture and distribution of material which defames and threatens all members of a class by its recommendation of abusive and degrading behavior toward some members of that class simply in virtue of their membership in it

seems a clear candidate for inclusion on the list. The right is therefore not an unqualified one.

Nor is it an absolute or fundamental right, underived from any other right: If it were there would not be exceptions or limitations. The first ten amendments were added to the Constitution as a way of guaranteeing the "blessings of liberty" mentioned in its preamble, to protect citizens against the unreasonable usurpation of power by the state. The specific rights mentioned in the First Amendment—those of religion, speech, assembly, press, petition—reflect the recent experiences of the makers of the Constitution under colonial government as well as a sense of what was and is required generally to secure liberty.

It may be objected that the right to freedom of speech is fundamental in that it is part of what we mean by liberty and not a right that is derivative from a right to liberty. In order to meet this objection, it is useful to consider a distinction explained by Ronald Dworkin in his book *Taking Rights Seriously.*⁶ As Dworkin points out, the word "liberty" is used in two distinct, if related, senses: as "license," i.e., the freedom from legal constraints to do as one pleases, in some contexts; and as "independence," i.e., "the status of a person as independent and equal rather than subservient," in others. Failure to distinguish between these senses in discussions of rights and freedoms is fatal to clarity and understanding.

If the right to free speech is understood as a partial explanation of what is meant by liberty, then liberty is perceived as license: The right to do as one pleases includes a right to speak as one pleases. But license is surely n   ot a condition the First Amendment is designed to protect. We not only tolerate but require legal constraints on liberty as license when we enact laws against rape, murder, assault, theft, etc. If everyone did exactly as she or he pleased at any given time, we would have chaos if not lives, as Hobbes put it, that are "nasty, brutish, and short." We accept government to escape, not to protect, this condition.

If, on the other hand, by liberty is meant independence, then freedom of speech is not necessarily a part of liberty; rather, it is a means to it. The right to freedom of speech is not a fundamental, absolute right, but one derivative from, possessed in virtue of,

---

*Thus, the right to use such materials in the privacy of one's home, which has been upheld by the United States Supreme Court (*Stanley v. Georgia*, 394 U.S. 557), does not include the right to purchase them or to have them available in the commercial market. See also *Paris Adult Theater I v. Slaton*, 431 U.S. 49.

†The Supreme Court has also traditionally included obscenity in this category. As not everyone agrees it should be included, since as defined by statutes, it is a highly vague concept, and since the grounds accepted by the Court for including it miss the point, I prefer to omit it from this list.

the more basic right to independence. Taking this view of liberty requires providing arguments showing that the more specific rights we claim are necessary to guarantee our status as persons "independent and equal rather than subservient." In the context of government, we understand independence to be the freedom of each individual to participate as an equal among equals in the determination of how she or he is to be governed. Freedom of speech in this context means that an individual may not only entertain beliefs concerning government privately, but may express them publicly. We express our opinions about taxes, disarmament, wars, social-welfare programs, the function of the police, civil rights, and so on. Our right to freedom of speech includes the right to criticize the government and to protest against various forms of injustice and the abuse of power. What we wish to protect is the free expression of ideas even when they are unpopular. What we do not always remember is that speech has functions other than the expression of ideas.

Regarding the relationship between a right to freedom of speech and the publication and distribution of pornographic materials, there are two points to be made. In the first place, the latter activity is hardly an exercise of the right to the free expression of ideas as understood above. In the second place, to the degree that the tolerance of material degrading to women supports and reinforces the attitude that women are not fit to participate as equals among equals in the political life of their communities, and that the prevalence of such an attitude effectively prevents women from so participating, the absolute and fundamental right of women to liberty (political independence) is violated.

This second argument against the suppression of pornographic material, then, rests on a premise that must be rejected, namely, that the right to freedom of speech is a right to utter anything one wants. It thus fails to show that the production and distribution of such material is an activity protected by the First Amendment. Furthermore, an examination of the issues involved leads to the conclusion that tolerance of this activity violates the rights of women to political independence.

The third argument (which expresses concern that curbs on pornography are the first step toward political censorship) runs into the same ambiguity that besets the arguments based on principle. These arguments generally have as an underlying assumption that the maximization of freedom is a worthy social goal. Control of pornography diminishes freedom—directly the freedom of pornographers, indirectly that of all of us. But again, what is meant by "freedom"? It cannot be that what is to be maximized is license—as the goal of a social group whose members probably have at least some incompatible interests, such a goal would be internally inconsistent. If, on the other hand, the maximization of political independence is the goal, then that is in no way enhanced by, and may be endangered by, the tolerance of pornography. To argue that the control of pornography would create a precedent for suppressing political speech is thus to confuse license with political independence. In addition, it ignores a crucial basis for the control of pornography, i.e., its character as libelous speech. The prohibition of such speech is justified by the need for protection from the injury (psychological as well as physical or economic) that results from libel. A very different kind of argument would be required to justify curtailing the right to speak our minds about the institutions which govern us. As long as such distinctions are insisted upon, there is little danger of the government's using the control of pornography as precedent for curtailing political speech.

In summary, neither as a matter of principle nor in the interests of maximizing liberty can it be supposed that there is an intrinsic right to manufacture and distribute pornographic material.

The only other conceivable source of protection for pornography would be a general right to do what we please as long as the rights of others are respected. Since the production and distribution of pornography violates the rights of women—to respect and to freedom from defamation, among others—this protection is not available.

Conclusion

I have defined pornography in such a way as to distinguish it from erotica and from moral realism, and have argued that it is defamatory and libelous toward women, that it condones crimes against women, and that it invites tolerance of the social, economic, and cultural oppression of women. The production and distribution of pornographic material is thus a social and moral wrong. Contrasting both the current volume of pornographic production and its growing infiltration of the communications media with the status of women in this culture makes clear the necessity for its control. Since the goal of controlling pornography does not conflict with constitutional rights, a common obstacle to action is removed.

Appeals for action against pornography are sometimes brushed aside with the claim that such action is a diversion from the primary task of feminists—the elimination of sexism and of sexual inequality. This approach focuses on the enjoyment rather than the manufacture of pornography, and sees it as merely a product of sexism which will disappear when the latter has been overcome and the sexes are socially and economically equal. Pornography cannot be separated from sexism in this way: Sexism is not just a set of attitudes regarding the inferiority of women but the behaviors and social and economic rules that manifest such attitudes. Both the manufacture and distribution of pornography and the enjoyment of it are instances of sexist behavior. The enjoyment of pornography on the part of individuals will presumably decline as such individuals begin to accord women their status as fully human. A cultural climate which tolerates the degrading representation of women is not a climate which facilitates the development of respect for women. Furthermore, the demand for pornography is

stimulated not just by the sexism of individuals but by the pornography industry itself. Thus, both as a social phenomenon and in its effect on individuals, pornography, far from being a mere product, nourishes sexism. The campaign against it is an essential component of women's struggle for legal, economic, and social equality, one which requires the support of all feminists.*

NOTES

1. *Report of the Commission on Obscenity and Pornography* (New York: Bantam Books, 1979), p. 239. The Commission, of course, concluded that the demeaning content of pornography did not adversely affect male attitudes toward women.
2. Among recent feminist discussions are Diana Russell, "Pornography: A Feminist Perspective" and Susan Griffin, "On Pornography," *Chrysalis*, vol. I, no. 4, 1978; and Ann Garry, "Pornography and Respect for Women," *Social Theory and Practice*, vol. 4, Spring 1978, pp. 395–421.
3. *The Oxford English Dictionary*, Compact Edition (London: Oxford University Press, 1971), p. 2242.
4. Urie Bronfenbrenner, *Two Worlds of Childhood* (New York: Russell Sage Foundation, 1970); H.J. Eysenck and D. K. B. Nias, *Sex, Violence and the Media* (New York: St. Martin's Press, 1978); and Michael Goldstein, Harold Kant, and John Hartman, *Pornography and Sexual Deviance* (Berkeley: University of California Press, 1973).
5. Cf. Marshall Cohen, "The Case Against Censorship," *The Public Interests*, no. 22, Winter 1971, reprinted in John R. Burr and Milton Goldinger, *Philosophy and Contemporary Issues* (New York: Macmillian, 1976), and Justice William Brennan's dissenting opinion in *Paris Adult Theater I v. Slaton*, 431 U.S. 49.
6. Ronald Dworkin, *Taking Rights Seriously* (Cambridge, MA: Harvard University Press, 1977), p. 262.

*Many women helped me to develop and crystallize the ideas presented in this paper. I would especially like to thank Michele Farrell, Laura Lederer, Pamela Miller, and Dianne Romain for their comments in conversation and on the first written draft. Portions of this material were presented orally to members of the Society for Women in Philosophy and to participants in the workshops on "What Is Pornography?" at the Conference on Feminist Perspectives on Pornography, San Francisco, November 17, 18, and 19, 1978. Their discussion was invaluable in helping me to see problems and to clarify the ideas presented here.

DISCUSSION QUESTIONS:

1. Consider what you take to be some standard examples of pornography. To what extent does Longino's definition of pornography apply to them? In particular, do they all present behavior that is degrading or abusive to women? Do they all endorse and/or recommend such behavior?
2. Longino claims that pornography is injurious to women because it is "implicated" in crimes of violence against them. What is the relation between the dissemination and viewing of

pornography and violence against women? Is there a causal relation between the two? What sort of relation has to hold between an activity and violent crimes to justify regulating the activity?

3. Does pornography, as Longino claims, defame and libel women (present a lie about women that causes them to be unjustifiably viewed in an unfavorable way)? What is the lie? How does it cause those who view pornography to view women in an unfavorable way? Are other representations of women (e.g., in contemporary advertising), equally defamatory?

4. Longino's response to the claim that the production and distribution of pornography is an exercise of the right to freedom of speech is based on a distinction between liberty as license and liberty as independence. Is there such a distinction, and does it support her argument?

5. How would Mill and Devlin (Chapters 22.1 and 22.2) respond to Longino's claim that the social and legal regulation of pornography is justified? Insofar as either of them would disagree with Longino's position, which view is correct?

Argument Reconstruction Exercises:

I. Given her definition of pornography, Longino argues that pornography, by its very nature, libels women (creates an unjustly unfavorable impression of them) through vicious lies about them. Identify the premises and conclusion of her argument:

> Pornography, by its very nature, requires that women be subordinate to men and mere instruments of the fulfillment of male fantasies. To accomplish this, pornography must lie. Pornography lies when it says that our sexual life is or ought to be subordinate to the service of men, that our pleasure consists in pleasing men and not ourselves, that we are depraved, that we are fit subjects for rape, bondage, torture and murder. Pornography lies explicitly about women's sexuality, and through such lies fosters more lies about our humanity, our dignity and our personhood. (page 649)

II. Longino argues that society's tolerance of pornography adds to the injuries that it causes women. Identify the premises and conclusion of her argument:

> Society's tolerance of pornography, especially pornography on the contemporary massive scale, reinforces each of these modes of injury: By not disavowing the lie, it supports the male-centered myth that women are inferior and subordinate creatures. Thus, it contributes to the maintenance of a climate tolerant of both psychological and physical violence against women. (page 651)

III. Longino argues that the right to free speech does not protect pornography from legal regulation, given its libelous nature. Identify the premises and conclusion of her argument:

> There are several kinds of speech not protected by the First Amendment, including the incitement to violence in volatile circumstances, the solicitation of crimes, perjury and misrepresentation, slander, libel, and false advertising. . . . The manufacture and distribution of material which defames and threatens all members of a class by its recommendation of abusive and degrading behavior toward some members of that class simply in virtue of their membership in it seems a clear candidate for inclusion on the list. The right is therefore not an unqualified one. (page 652)

IV. Longino describes our right to liberty as a right to "the status of a person as independent and equal rather than subservient" (page 652). She then argues that the tolerance of pornography violates women's right to liberty. Identify the premises and conclusion of her argument:

> To the degree that the tolerance of material degrading to women supports and reinforces the attitude that women are not fit to participate as equals among equals in the political life of their communities, and the prevalence of such an attitude effectively prevents women from so participating, the absolute and fundamental right of women to liberty (political independence) is violated. . . . [A]n examination of the issues involved leads to the conclusion that tolerance of this activity violates the rights of women to political independence. (page 653)

22.5 THE FEMINIST CASE AGAINST PORNOGRAPHY

JOEL FEINBERG (1985)

Joel Feinberg was Emeritus Professor of Philosophy at the University of Arizona and an expert in moral, social, and legal philosophy. He is best known for his four-volume work *The Moral Limits of the Criminal Law*, exploring the limits of justified political coercion. Feinberg here considers two lines of argument for the legal regulation of violent pornography. One line of argument is based on the **Harm Principle**: we are justified in using the law to suppress activities that threaten harm to others without their consent. The other line of argument is based on the **Offense Principle**: we are justified in using the law to suppress activities that profoundly offend others without their consent. Feinberg carefully explores each line of argument and finds neither to be persuasive.

Reading Questions:

1. What is Feinberg's definition of pornography? If you have read Longino's essay (Chapter 22.4) on this topic, how does his definition differ from hers?

2. What is Feinberg's basis for claiming that pornography, as he defines it, need not be degrading to women?

3. What is the harm principle and what two ways of applying it to violent pornography does Feinberg consider?

4. What is the offense principle? What basis does it offer for legally suppressing violent pornography?

5. What must be the case, according to Feinberg, for violent pornography to defame women? What are his reasons for claiming that it does not do so?

6. What is "the cult of the macho" and how does Feinberg think it is related to violent pornography and to violence against women?

7. What is Feinberg's distinction between bare-knowledge offense and personal offense?

8. Why does Feinberg think that the offense principle does not justify the legal suppression of violent pornography?

9. What is legal moralism, how is it related to the offense principle, and why, according to Feinberg, doesn't it provide a basis for legally suppressing violent pornography?

In recent years a powerful attack on pornography has been made from a different quarter and on different, but often shifting grounds. Until 1970 or so, the demand for legal restraints on pornography came mainly from "sexual conservatives," those who regarded the pursuit of erotic pleasure for its own sake to be immoral or degrading, and its public depiction obscene. The new attack, however, comes not from prudes and bluenoses, but from women who have been in the forefront of the sexual revolution. We do not hear any of the traditional complaints about pornography from this group—that erotic states in themselves are immoral, that sexual titillation corrupts character, and that the spectacle of "appeals to prurience" is repugnant to moral sensibility. The new charge is rather that pornography degrades, abuses, and defames women, and contributes to a general climate of attitudes toward women that makes violent sex crimes more frequent. Pornography, they claim, has come to pose a threat to public safety, and its legal restraint can find justification either under the harm principle, or, by analogy with Nazi parades in Skokie and K.K.K. rallies, on some theory of profound (and personal) offense.

It is somewhat misleading to characterize the feminist onslaught as a new argument, or new emphasis in argument, against the same old thing. By the 1960s pornography itself had become in large measure a new and uglier kind of phenomenon. There had always been sado-masochistic elements in much pornography, and a small minority taste to be served with concentrated doses of it. There had also been more or less prominent expressions of contemptuous attitudes toward abject female "sex objects," even in much relatively innocent pornography. But now a great wave of violent pornography appears to have swept over the land, as even the mass circulation porno magazines moved beyond the customary nude cheesecake and formula stories, to explicit expressions of hostility to women, and to covers and photographs showing "women and children abused, beaten, bound, and tortured" apparently "for the sexual titillation of consumers."[1] When the circulation of the monthly porn magazines comes to 16 million and the porno industry as a whole does $4 billion a year in business, the new trend , cannot help but be alarming.

There is no necessity, however, that pornography as such be degrading to women. First of all, we can imagine easily enough an ideal pornography in which men and women are depicted enjoying their joint sexual pleasures in ways that show not a trace of dominance or humiliation of either party by the other. The materials in question might clearly satisfy *my previous definition of "pornography" as materials designed entirely and effectively to induce erotic excitement in observers without containing any of the extraneous sexist elements. Even if we confine our attention to actual specimens of pornography—and quite typical ones—we find many examples where male dominance and female humiliation are not present at all.* Those of us who were budding teenagers in the 1930s and 40s will tend to take as our model of pornography the comic strip pamphlets in wide circulation among teenagers during that period. The characters were all drawn from the popular legitimate comic strips—The Gumps, Moon Mullins, Maggie and Jiggs, etc.—and were portrayed in cartoons that were exact imitations of the originals. In the pornographic strips, however, the adventures were all erotic. Like all pornography, the cartoons greatly exaggerated the size of organs and appetites, and the "plot lines" were entirely predictable. But the episodes were portrayed with great good humor, a kind of joyous feast of erotica in which the blessedly unrepressed cartoon figures shared with perfect equality. Rather than being humiliated or dominated, the women characters equalled the men in their sheer earthy gusto. (That feature especially appealed to teenage boys who could only dream of unrestrained female gusto.) The episodes had no butt at all except prudes and hypocrites. Most of us consumers managed to survive with our moral characters intact.

In still other samples of actual pornography, there is indeed the appearance of male dominance and female humiliation, but even in many of these, explanations of a more innocent character are available. It is in the nature of fantasies, especially adolescent fantasies, whether erotic or otherwise, to glorify imaginatively, in excessive and unrealistic ways, the person who does the fantasizing. When that person is a woman and the fantasy is romantic, she may dream of herself surrounded by handsome lovesick suitors, or in love with an (otherwise) magnificent man who is prepared to throw himself at her feet, worship the ground she walks on, go through hell for her if necessary—the clichés pile up endlessly. If the fantasizing person is a man and his reverie is erotic, he may dream of women who worship the ground *he* walks on, etc., and would do anything for the honor of making love with him, and who having sampled his unrivaled sexual talents would grovel at his feet for more, etc., etc.

The point of the fantasy is self-adulation, not "hostility" toward the other sex.

Still other explanations may be available. "Lust," wrote Norman Mailer, "is a world of bewildering dimensions . . ."[2] When its consuming fire takes hold of the imagination, it is likely to be accompanied by almost any images suggestive of limitlessness, any natural accompaniments of explosive unrestrained passion. Not only men but women too have been known to scratch or bite (like house cats) during sexual excitement, and the phrase "I could hug you to pieces"—a typical expression of felt "limitlessness"—is normally taken as an expression of endearment, not of homicidal fury. Sexual passion in the male animal (there is as yet little but conjecture on this subject) may be associated at deep instinctive or hormonal levels with the states that capture the body and mind during aggressive combat. Some such account may be true of a given man, and explain why a certain kind of pornography may arouse him, without implying anything at all about his settled attitudes toward women, or his general mode of behavior toward them. Then, of course, it is a commonplace that many "normal" people, both men and women, enjoy sado-masochistic fantasies from time to time, without effect on character or conduct. Moreover, there are pornographic materials intended for men, that appeal to their masochistic side exclusively, in which they are "ravished" and humiliated by some grim-faced amazon of fearsome dimensions. Great art these materials are not, but neither are they peculiarly degrading to women. . . .

At least one other important distinction must be made among the miscellany of materials in the category of degrading pornography. Some degrading pornography is also violent, glorifying in physical mistreatment of the woman,and featuring "weapons of torture or bondage, wounds and bruises."[3] "One frightening spread from *Chic Magazine* showed a series of pictures of a woman covered with blood, masturbating with a knife. The title was 'Columbine Cuts Up.'"[4] A movie called "Snuff" in which female characters (and, it is alleged, the actresses who portrayed them) are tortured to death for the sexual entertainment of the audiences, was shown briefly in a commercial New York theatre. The widely circulated monthly magazine *Hustler* once had a cover

picture of a nude woman being pushed head first into a meat grinder, her shapely thighs and legs poised above the opening to the grinder in a sexually receptive posture, while the rest comes out of the bottom as ground meat. The exaggeration of numbers in Kathleen Barry's chilling description hardly blunts its horror: "In movie after movie women are raped, ejaculated on, urinated on, anally penetrated, beaten, and with the advent of snuff films, murdered in an orgy of sexual pleasure."[5] The examples, alas, are abundant and depressing.

There are other examples, however, of pornography that is degrading to women but does not involve violence. Gloria Steinem speaks of more subtle forms of coercion: "a physical attitude of conqueror and victim, the use of race or class difference to imply the same thing, perhaps a very unequal nudity with one person exposed and vulnerable while the other is clothed."[6] As the suggested forms of coercion become more and more subtle, obviously there will be very difficult line-drawing problems for any legislature brave enough to enter this area.

Yet the most violent cases at one end of the spectrum are as clear as they can be. They all glory in wanton and painful violence against helpless victims and do this with the extraordinary intention (sometimes even successful) of causing sexual arousal in male viewers. One could give every other form of pornography, degrading or not, the benefit of the doubt, and still identify with confidence all members of the violent extreme category. If there is a strong enough argument against pornography to limit the liberty of pornographers, it is probably restricted to this class of materials. Some feminist writers speak as if that would not be much if any restriction, but that may be a consequence of their *defining* pornography in terms of its most revolting specimens. A pornographic story or film may be degrading in Steinem's subtle sense, in that it shows an intelligent man with a stupid woman, or a wealthy man with a chambermaid, and intentionally exploits the inequality for the sake of the special sexual tastes of the presumed male consumer, but if that were the *only* way in which the work degraded women, it would fall well outside the extreme (violent) category. All the more so, stories in which the male and female are equals—and these materials too can count as pornographic—would fall outside the objectionable category.

May the law legitimately be used to restrict the liberty of pornographers to produce and distribute, and their customers to purchase and use, erotic materials that are violently abusive of women? (I am assuming that no strong case can be made for the proscription of materials that are merely degrading in one of the relatively subtle and nonviolent ways.) Many feminists answer, often with reluctance, in the affirmative. Their arguments can be divided into two general classes. *Some simply invoke the harm principle.* Violent pornography wrongs and harms women, according to these arguments, either by defaming them as a group, or (more importantly) by inciting males to violent crimes against them or creating a cultural climate in which such crimes are likely to become more frequent. The two traditional legal categories involved in these harm-principle arguments, then, are *defamation* and *incitement. The other class of arguments invoke the offense principle* not in order to prevent mere "nuisances," but to prevent profound offense analogous to that of the Jews in Skokie or the blacks in a town where the K.K.K. rallies.

Violent Pornography, the Cult of Macho, and Harm to Women

I shall not spend much time on the claim that violent and other extremely degrading pornography should be banned on the ground that it *defames* women. In a skeptical spirit, I can begin by pointing out that there are immense difficulties in applying the civil law of libel and slander as it is presently constituted in such a way as not to violate freedom of expression. Problems with *criminal* libel and slander would be even more unmanageable, and *group* defamation, whether civil or criminal, would multiply the problems still further. The argument on the other side is that pornography is essentially propaganda—propaganda against women. It does not slander women in the technical legal sense by asserting damaging falsehoods about them, because it *asserts* nothing at all. But it spreads an image of women as mindless playthings or "objects," inferior beings fit only to be used and abused for the pleasure of men, whether they like it or not, but often to their own secret pleasure. This picture lowers the esteem men have for women, and for that reason (if defamation is the basis of the argument) is sufficient ground for proscription even in the absence of any evidence of tangible harm to women caused by the behavior of misled and deluded men.

If degrading pornography defames (libels or slanders) women, it must be in virtue of some beliefs about women—false beliefs—that it conveys, so that in virtue of those newly acquired or reenforced false beliefs, consumers lower their esteem for women in general. If a work of pornography, for example, shows a woman (or group of women) in exclusively subservient or domestic roles, that may lead the consumer to *believe* that women, in virtue of some inherent female characteristics, are only fit for such roles. *There is no doubt that much pornography does portray women in subservient positions, but if that is defamatory to women in anything like the legal sense, then so are soap commercials on TV. So are many novels, even some good ones.* (A good novel may yet be about some degraded characters.) That some groups are portrayed in unflattering roles has not hitherto been a ground for the censorship of fiction or advertising. Besides, it is not clearly the group that is portrayed at all in such works, but only one individual (or small set of individuals) and fictitious ones at that. Are fat men defamed by Shakespeare's picture of Falstaff? Are Jews defamed by the characterization of Shylock? Could any writer today even hope to write a novel partly about a fawning corrupted black, under group defamation laws, without risking censorship or worse? The chilling effect on the practice of fiction-writing would amount to a near freeze.

Moreover, as Fred Berger points out,[7] the degrading images and defamatory beliefs pornographic works are alleged to cause are not produced in the consumer by explicit statements asserted with the intent to convince the reader or auditor of their truth. Rather they are caused by the stimulus of the work, in the context, on the expectations, attitudes, and beliefs the viewer brings with him to the work. That is quite other than believing an assertion on the authority or argument of the party making the assertion, or understanding the assertion in the first place in virtue of fixed conventions of language use and meaning. Without those fixed conventions of language, the work has to be interpreted in order for any message to be extracted from it, and the process of interpretation, as Berger illustrates abundantly, is "always a matter of judgment and subject to great variation among persons."[8] What looks like sexual subservience to some looks like liberation from sexual repression to others. It is hard to imagine how a court could provide a workable, much less fair, test of whether a given work has sufficiently damaged male esteem toward women for it to be judged criminally defamatory, when so much of the viewer's reaction he brings on himself, and viewer reactions are so widely variable.

It is not easy for a single work to defame successfully a group as large as 51% of the whole human race. (Could a misanthrope "defame" the whole human race by a false statement about "the nature of man"? Would every human being then be his "victim"?) Perhaps an unanswered barrage of thousands of tracts, backed by the prestige of powerful and learned persons without dissent might successfully defame any group no matter how large, but those conditions would be difficult to satisfy so long as there is freedom to speak back on the other side. In any case, defamation is not the true gravamen of the wrong that women in general suffer from extremely degrading pornography. When a magazine cover portrays a woman in a meat grinder, all women are insulted, degraded, even perhaps endangered, but few would naturally complain that they were *libelled* or *slandered*. Those terms conceal the point of what has happened. If women are harmed by pornography, the harm is surely more direct and tangible than harm to "the interest in reputation."

The major argument for repression of violent pornography under the harm principle is that it promotes rape and physical violence. In the United States there is a plenitude both of sexual violence against women and of violent pornography. According to the F.B.I. Uniform Crime Statistics (as of 1980), a 12-year-old girl in the United States has one chance in three of being raped in her lifetime; studies only a few years earlier showed that the number of violent scenes in hard-core pornographic books was as high as 20% of the total, and the number of violent cartoons and pictorials in leading pornographic magazines was

as much as 10% of the total. This has suggested to some writers that there must be a direct causal link between violent pornography and sexual violence against women; but causal relationships between pornography and rape, if they exist, must be more complicated than that. . . .

A violent episode in a pornographic work may indeed be a causally necessary condition for the commission of some specific crime by a specific perpetrator on a specific victim at some specific time and place. But for his reading or viewing that episode, the perpetrator may not have done precisely what he did in just the time, place, and manner that he did it. But so large a part of the full causal explanation of his act concerns his own psychological character and predispositions, that it is likely that some similar crime would have suggested itself to him in due time. It is not likely that non-rapists are converted into rapists *simply* by reading and viewing pornography. If pornography has a serious causal bearing on the occurence of rape (as opposed to the trivial copy-cat effect) it must be in virtue of its role (still to be established) in implanting the appropriate cruel dispositions in the first place.

Rape is such a complex social phenomenon that there is probably no one simple generalization to account for it. Some rapes are no doubt ineliminable, no matter how we design our institutions. Many of these are the product of deep individual psychological problems, transferred rages, and the like. But for others, perhaps the preponderant number, the major part of the explanation is sociological, not psychological. In these cases the rapist is a psychologically normal person well adjusted to his particular subculture, acting calmly and deliberately rather than in a rage, and doing what he thinks is expected of him by his peers, what he must do to acquire or preserve standing in his group. His otherwise inexplicable violence is best explained as a consequence of the peculiar form of his socialization among his peers, his pursuit of a prevailing ideal of manliness, what the Mexicans have long called *machismo*, but which exists to some degree or other among men in most countries, certainly in our own.

The macho male wins the esteem of his associates by being tough, fearless, reckless, wild, unsentimental, hard-boiled, hard drinking, disrespectful, profane, willing to fight whenever his honor is impugned, and fight without fear of consequences no matter how extreme. He is a sexual athlete who must be utterly dominant over "his" females, who are expected to be slavishly devoted to him even though he lacks gentleness with them and shows his regard only by displaying them like trophies; yet he is a hearty and loyal companion to his "teammates" (he is always on a "team" of some sort). Given the manifest harm the cult of macho has done to men, to women, and to relations between men and women, it is difficult to account for its survival in otherwise civilized nations. Perhaps it is useful in time of war, and war has been a preoccupation of most generations of young men, in most nations, up to the present. If so, then the persistence of *machismo* is one of the stronger arguments we have (among many others) for the obsolescence of war.

The extreme character of macho values must be understood before any sense can be made of the appeal of violent pornography. The violent porn does not appeal to prurience or lust as such. Indeed, it does not appeal at all to a psychologically normal male who is not in the grip of the macho cult. In fact these pictures, stories, and films have no other function but to express and reenforce the macho ideology. "Get your sexual kicks," they seem to say, "but make sure you get them by humiliating the woman, and showing her who's boss. Make sure at all costs not to develop any tender feelings toward her that might give her a subtle form of control over you and thus destroy your standing with the group. Remember to act in the truly manly manner of a 'wild and crazy guy.'"

In her brilliant article on this subject, Sarah J. McCarthy cites some horrible examples from *Penthouse* Magazine of the macho personality structure which is peculiarly receptive to, and a necessary condition for, the appeal of violent porn:

"There's still something to be said for bashing a woman over the head, dragging her off behind a rock, and having her," said one of the guys in the February 1980 *Penthouse*. . . "Women Who Flirt With Pain" was the cover hype for a *Penthouse* interview with an assortment of resident Neanderthals (a name that would swell them with pride).

"We're basically rapists because we're created that way," proclaims Dale. "We're irrational, sexually completely crazy. Our sexuality is more promiscuous, more immediate, and more fleeting, possibly less deep. We're like stud bulls that want to mount everything in sight. . ."

The letters-to-the-editor in the February *Penthouse* contains an ugly letter from someone who claims to be a sophomore at a large midwestern university and is "into throat-fucking". He writes of Kathy and how he was "ramming his huge eleven-inch tool down her throat." [Sexual bragging, pornography style.] Kathy "was nearly unconscious from coming." [Deceit and self-deception, pornography style.] Gloria Steinem writes in the May 1980 *Ms.*: "Since *Deep Throat*, a whole new genre of pornography has developed. Added to the familiar varieties of rape, there is now an ambition to rape the throat. . ."

Another issue of *Penthouse* contains an article about what they have cleverly called "tossing." A college student from Albuquerque, who drives a 1974 Cadillac and who is "attracted to anything in a skirt," tells how it's done. "How did you get into tossing?," the *Penthouse* interviewer asks. "It just happened," says Daryl. "I was doing it in high school two years ago and didn't know what it was. I'd date a chick once, fuck her in my car, and just dump her out. Literally."[9]

These repugnant specimens are not examples of make-believe violent pornography. Rather, they are examples of the attitudes and practices of persons who are antecedently prone to be appreciative consumers of violent pornography. These grisly sentiments are perhaps found more commonly among working class youths in military barracks and factories but they are only slightly more familiar than similar bravado heard by middle class Americans in fraternity houses and dormitories. These remarks are usually taken as meant to impress their male auditors; they are uttered with a kind of aggressive pride. The quotations from *Penthouse* capture the tone exactly. These utterly outrageous things are said publicly and casually, not in passion, not in hate, not in lust. They seem to say "That's just the way we machos are—for better or worse."

Would it significantly reduce sexual violence if violent pornography were effectively banned? No one can know for sure, but if the cult of macho is the main source of such violence, as I suspect, then repression of violent pornography, whose function is to pander to the macho values already deeply rooted in society, may have little effect. Pornography does not cause normal decent chaps, through a single exposure, to metamorphoze into rapists. Pornography-reading machos commit rape, but that is because they already have macho values, not because they read the violent pornography that panders to them. Perhaps then *constant* exposure to violent porn might turn a decent person into a violence-prone macho. But that does not seem likely either, since the repugnant violence of the materials could not have any appeal in the first place to one who did not already have some strong macho predispositions, so "constant exposure" could not begin to become established. Clearly, other causes, and more foundational ones, must be at work, if violent porn is to have any initial purchase. Violent pornography is more a symptom of *machismo* than a cause of it, and treating symptoms merely is not a way to offer protection to potential victims of rapists. At most, I think there may be a small spill-over effect of violent porn on actual violence. Sometimes a bizarre new sadistic trick (like "throat-fucking"?) is suggested by a work of violent pornography and taken up by those prone to cruel violence to begin with. More often, perhaps, the response to an inventive violent porno scene may be like that of the college *Penthouse* reader to "tossing": "I was doing it in high school two years ago, and I didn't know what it was." He read *Penthouse* and learned "what it was," but his conduct, presumably, was not significantly changed.

If my surmise about causal connections is correct they are roughly as indicated in the following diagram:

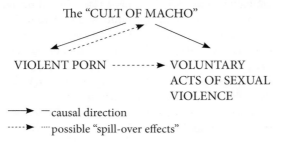

The "CULT OF MACHO"

VIOLENT PORN ---------► VOLUNTARY ACTS OF SEXUAL VIOLENCE

——► ⌐causal direction

-----► ⌐possible "spill-over effects"

The primary causal direction is not from violent pornography to violent real-life episodes. Neither is it from violent pornography to the establishment and reenforcement of macho values. Rather, the cult of macho expectations is itself the primary cause both of the existence of violent porn (it provides the appreciative audience) and of the real-life sexual violence (it provides the motive). The dotted arrows express my acknowledgement of the point that there might be some small spill-over effect from violent pornography back on the macho values that spawn it, in one direction, and on real-life violence in the other, but the pornography cannot be the primary causal generator. Sexual violence will continue to fester so long as the cult of macho flourishes, whether or not we eliminate legal violent pornography.

How then can we hope to weaken and then extirpate the cultish values at the root of our problem? The criminal law is a singularly ill-adapted tool for that kind of job. We might just as well legislate against entrepreneurship on the grounds that capitalism engenders "acquisitive personalities," or against the military on the grounds that it produces "authoritarian personalities," or against certain religious sects on the ground that they foster puritanism, as criminalize practices and institutions on the grounds that they contribute to *machismo*. But macho values are culturally, not instinctively, transmitted, and the behavior that expresses them is learned, not inherited, behavior. What is learned can be unlearned. Schools should play a role. Surely, learning to see through *machismo* and avoid its traps should be as important a part of a child's preparation for citizenship as the acquisition of patriotism and piety. To be effective, such teaching should be frank and direct, not totally reliant on general moral platitudes. It should talk about the genesis of children's attitudes toward the other sex, and invite discussion of male insecurity, resentment of women, cruelty, and even specific odious examples. Advertising firms and film companies should be asked (at first), then pressured (if necessary) to cooperate, as they did in the successful campaign to deglamorize cigarette smoking. Fewer exploitation films should be made that provide attractive models of youths flashing knives, playing chicken or Russian roulette, or "tossing" girls. Materials (especially films) should be made available to clergymen as well as teachers, youth counselors, and parole officers. A strong part of the emphasis of these materials should be on the harm that bondage to the cult of macho does to men too, and how treacherous a trap *machismo* can be. The new moral education must be careful, of course, not to preach dull prudence as a preferred style for youthful living. A zest for excitement, adventure, even danger, cannot be artificially removed from adolescent nature. Moreover, teamwork, camaraderie, and toughness of character need not be denigrated. But the cult of macho corrupts and distorts these values in ways that can be made clear to youths. The mistreatment of women, when its motivation is clearly revealed and understood, should be a sure way of eliciting the contempt of the group, not a means to greater prestige within it.

Rape is a harm and a severe one. Harm prevention is definitely a legitimate use of the criminal law. Therefore, if there is a clear enough causal connection to rape, a statute that prohibits violent pornography would be a morally legitimate restriction of liberty. But it is not enough to warrant suppression that pornography as a whole might have some harmful consequences to third parties, even through most specific instances of it do not. . . .

Those instances of sexual violence which may be harmful side-effects of violent pornography are directly produced by criminals (rapists) acting voluntarily on their own. We already have on the statute books a firm prohibition of rape and sexual assault. If, in addition, the harm principle permits the criminalization of actions only indirectly related to the primary harm, such as producing, displaying or selling violent pornography, then there is a danger that the law will be infected with unfairness; for unless certain further conditions are fulfilled, the law will be committed to punishing some parties for the entirely voluntary criminal conduct of other parties. . . . Suppose that *A* wrongfully harms (e.g. rapes) *B* in circumstances such that (i) *A* acts fully voluntarily on his own initiative, and (2) nonetheless, but for what *C* has communicated to him, he would not have done what he did to *B*. Under what further conditions, we must ask, can *C* be rightfully held criminally responsible along with *A* for the harm to *B*? Clearly *C* can be held responsible if the information he communicated was helpful assistance to *A* and intended to be such. In that case

C becomes a kind of collaborator. Under traditional law, *C* can also incur liability if what he communicated to *A* was some kind of encouragement to commit a crime against *B*. The clearest cases are those in which *C* solicits *A*'s commission of the criminal act by offering inducements to him. "Encouragement" is also criminal when it takes the form of active urging. Sometimes mere advice to commit the act counts as an appropriate sort of encouragement. When the encouragement takes a general form, and the harmful crime is recommended to "the general reader" or an indefinite audience, then the term "advocacy" is often used. Advocating criminal conduct is arguably a way of producing such conduct, and is thus often itself a crime. An article in a pornographic magazine advocating the practice of rape (as opposed to advocating a legislative change of the rape laws) would presumably be a crime if its intent were serious and its audience presumed to be impressionable to an appropriately dangerous degree.

Violent pornography, however, does not seem to fit any of these models. Its authors and vendors do not solicit rapes; nor do they urge or advise rapes; nor do they advocate rape. If some of their customers, some of the time, might yet "find encouragement" in their works to commit rapes because rape has been portrayed in a way that happens to be alluring to them, that is their own affair, the pornographer might insist, and their own responsibility.

Violent Pornography and Profound Offense

The harm principle grounds for legally banning pornography do not appear sufficient. Does the offense principle do any better? Pornographic displays can be public nuisances, of course, and when the balancing tests tip in the nuisance direction, the offending activities may fairly be prohibited, or redirected to less offensive channels. The manner in which degrading and violent pornography offends women (and men who support women's rights) is substantially different from that in which erotica as such offend the prudish. The shame, embarrassment, shock, disgust, and irritation of the latter group can be effectively avoided if the erotic displays are concealed from their view. The offense to a woman's sensibilities when her whole sex is treated as grist for the meat grinder, however, is deeply repugnant to her moral sensibilities whether out of view or not. Feminist writers often make this point by means of analogies to racist literature and films.

Suppose some unscrupulous promoters decide that they can make large profits by pandering to the latent hatred against blacks which they suppose to be endemic in a substantial minority of the white community. Since explicitly racist remarks and overt racist behavior are no longer widely acceptable in American society, many secret black-haters might enjoy an occasional night at the movies where they can enjoy to their heart's content specially made films that lampoon minstrel-style "darkies" "with wide eyes as white as moons, hair shot straight in the air like Buckwheat's, afraid of everything—spiders, [their] own shadows, ghosts."¹⁰ So much for comic openers. The main features could be stories of uppity blacks put in their place by righteous whites, taunted and hounded, tarred and feathered, tortured and castrated, and in the climactic scenes, hung up on gallows to the general rejoicing of their betters. The aim of the films would be to provide a delicious catharsis of pent-up hatred. It would be prudent, on business grounds, to keep advertisements discreet, and to use euphemistic descriptions like "folk films" (analogous to "adult films").

I don't imagine that many blacks would be placated by the liberal lawmaker who argues in support of his refusal to enact prohibitive legislation that there is little evidence of actual harm done to blacks by the films, that they do not advocate violence to blacks or incite mobs to fury, and that for all we know they will make the racists less dangerous by providing a harmless outlet for their anti-social impulses. Neither would many blacks be assuaged by the liberal assurance that we should all be wary of possible harmful effects anyway, continue to look for evidence thereof, and use educational campaigns as a more effective means of exposing the evils of racism. "That is all well and good," the blacks might reply, "but first we must lance this painful boil on our sensibilities. The 'folk films,' whether we are in the audience or not, are morally abominable affronts to us. Their very existence in our midst is a perpetual laceration of our feelings. We aren't present to be

humiliated, but they degrade the very atmosphere in which we breathe and move."

The analogy to violent pornographic films is close though not perfect. (It is an interesting fact to ponder that although there undoubtedly is a large racist underground in this country, no promoter has yet found a way of exploiting it in the manner of our example.) The pornographic films do serve an erotic interest of their customers, and that gives them, *ceteris paribus*, a personal value greater perhaps than that of the "folk films." The racist films, on the other hand, may be easier to disguise as genuine works of drama, thus making it much more difficult for a line to be drawn between them and genuine attempts at dramas about odious people and their victims. The bare-knowledge offense in the two cases seems almost equally profound, going well beyond anything called "mere nuisance," to touch the chord of moral sensibility.

It does not express an unsympathetic attitude toward the offended parties, however, to deny a basis in either the harm or offense principles for the use of legal force to "lance the boil." Profound offense, as I have argued . . ., is either an impersonal and disinterested moral outrage or else an aggrieved response on one's own behalf because of the unpleasant mental states one has been forced to experience. If it is an impersonal response, then it can warrant legal force against its cause only on the basis of the principle of **legal moralism** which is unacceptable to liberals. We would have to argue in that case that the very showing of violent films to appreciative audiences is an evil in itself and one of such magnitude that it can be rightly prevented by legal force if necessary, even though it is not the kind of evil that *wrongs* any one. . . If, on the other hand, the profound offense is a felt personal wrong voiced on one's own behalf as its "victim," then the complaint is that the offending materials cause one to suffer unpleasant states that are a nuisance to avoid. But that offense will not have much weight on the scales if one is not forced to witness the showings, or lurid announcements of the showings, and is not forced to take irritating and inconveniencing detours to avoid them. *The offense principle, in short, will not warrant legal prohibition of the films unless the offense they cause is not reasonably avoidable. and bare-knowledge offense, insofar as* *it is mere offensive nuisance, is reasonably avoidable.* It is only in its character as disinterested moral outrage that it is not reasonably avoidable, but we cannot ban everything that is thought to be outrageous, whether right-violating or not, without recourse to legal moralism.

Racist and porno films do not directly insult specific individuals, but rather large groups, thus diluting the impact of the insult, or at least its directed personal character, proportionately. The "folk films" might be more serious affronts in this respect than the porno films since their target is a much smaller group than half of the human race, and one which has historically been brutalized by slavery and cruel repression. A black man might be more likely to feel a *personal* grievance at the folk film he does not witness than a woman would to a porno film she does not witness, for these reasons. This personal aspect of his offense would overlay the more general disinterested moral indignation he shares with the women who are offended by their bare knowledge of the existence of violent pornographic displays. Nonetheless, understandable as the black's felt grievance may be, the insulting film shown to a willing audience in a private or commercial theatre is in the same boat as the insulting conversations among willing friends in a private home or club. In both cases the conduct is morally execrable, but in neither case do liberal principles warrant state intervention to punish the mischief.

NOTES

1. Lisa Lehrman, Preface to the Colloquium on Violent Pornography: "Degradation of Women Versus Right of Free Speech," *New York University Review of Law and Social Change* 8 (1978–9), p. 181.
2. Norman Mailer, *The Prisoner of Sex* (New York: New American Library, 1971), p. 82.
3. Gloria Steinem, "Erotica and Pornography, A Clear and Present Difference," *Ms*, November, 1978, p. 54.
4. Lisa Lehrman, *op. cit.* (footnote 1) pp. 181-82.
5. Kathleen Barry, *Female Sexual Slavery* (New York: Avon Books, 1979), p. 206.
6. Steinem, *op. cit.* (footnote 3), p. 54.
7. Fred R. Berger, "Pornography, Feminism and Censorship," (Unpublished paper, Philosophy Department, University of California-Davis), pp. 17ff. I am greatly indebted to this scholarly and well-argued essay.
8. Ibid., p. 18.
9. Sarah J. McCarthy, "Pornography, Rape an the Culture of the Macho," *The Humanist*, Sept./Oct., 1980, p. 15.
10. Ibid., p. 11.

DISCUSSION QUESTIONS:

1. Compare Feinberg's definition of pornography with that given by Longino (Chapter 22.4). How do they differ? Is one definition superior to the other?

2. Feinberg claims that if violent pornography defames women, then so do several other representations of women as subservient to men that we are not justified in legally suppressing, from soap commercials to many good novels. Are there relevant differences between the representation of women in violent pornography, on the one hand, and in these other works, on the other, that justify legal regulation only in the case of pornography?

3. While Feinberg acknowledges that a work of pornography or art can defame particular individuals, he questions whether one can defame women as a group. Can violent pornography defame women as a group?

4. Feinberg claims that if violent pornography harms women, the harm is "much more direct and tangible" than defamation. Does violent pornography harm women? If so, what is the nature of the harm, if it is not defamation?

5. Is Feinberg's explanation of the relation between the cult of the macho, violent pornography, and violence against women correct?

6. Feinberg acknowledges that some acts of sexual violence may be harmful side effects of violent pornography, but he argues that, even in these cases, the authors and vendors of pornography do not share any responsibility for the crimes. Is he correct? What would the relationship between pornography and sexual violence have to be in order for pornographers to have some responsibility for the violence?

7. Consider Feinberg's examples of "folk films" and violent pornographic films. Is he correct that the offense principle does not support the legal suppression of either? Should either be legally suppressed? If so, on what basis?

8. How would Devlin (Chapter 22.2) respond to Feinberg's rejection of legal moralism as a basis for

legally suppressing violent pornography? Would Devlin be correct?

Argument Reconstruction Exercises:

I. Feinberg acknowledges that violent pornography portrays women negatively, but claims that it does not defame them in a way that justifies legally repressing it. Here is one of his arguments; identify his premises and conclusion:

> There is no doubt that much pornography does portray women in subservient positions, but if that is defamatory to women in anything like the legal sense, then so are soap commercials on TV. So are many novels, even some good ones. . . . That some groups are portrayed in unflattering roles has not hitherto been a ground for censorship of fiction or advertising. (page 659)

II. Feinberg argues that since a certain set of attitudes (the cult of the macho) is the cause of sexual violence against women, the legal repression of pornography is unlikely to decrease such violence. Identify the premises and conclusion of his argument:

> [I]f the cult of the macho is main source of such violence, as I suspect, then repression of violent pornography, whose function is to pander to the macho values already deeply rooted in society, may have little effect. . . . Pornography-reading machos commit rape, but that is because they already have macho values, not because they read the violent pornography that panders to them. (page 662)

III. Feinberg argues that if the offensive nature of violent pornography takes the form of personal offense, its legal repression is not justified by the offense principle. Identify the premises and conclusion of his argument:

> If . . . the profound offense is a felt personal wrong voiced on one's own behalf as its "victim," then the complaint is that the offending materials cause one to suffer unpleasant states that are a nuisance to avoid. But that offense will not have much weight on the scales if one is not forced to witness the showings, or lurid announcements of the showings, and is not forced to take irritating and inconveniencing detours to avoid them. (page 664)

IV. Feinberg argues that if the offensive nature of violent pornography is an impersonal disinterested moral outrage (bare-knowledge offense), then its offensive nature can justify its legal repression only through an appeal to legal moralism, which is unlikely to succeed. Identify the premises and conclusion of his argument:

> If [the offensiveness of violent pornography] is an impersonal response, then it can warrant legal force against its cause only on the basis of the principle of legal moralism . . . We would have to argue in that case that the very showing of violent films to appreciative audiences is an evil in itself and one of such magnitude that it can be rightly prevented by legal force if necessary, even though it is not the kind of evil that *wrongs* any one. (page 664)

A priori knowable independently of experience but by reason alone. What is known a priori is contrasted with what is known a posteriori, or on the basis of experience.

Abortion the successful and intentional action of terminating a pregnancy by killing the fetus.

Absolute Moral Principles see **Absolutism**.

Absolutism the claim that there are some correct moral principles that we are required to obey, and so some acts that are morally obligatory, no matter what the circumstances. This view is also known as **Moral Conservatism**.

Act-Utilitarianism the view that an act is morally right (permissible) if and only if it will produce at least as much net **intrinsic good** as any other alternative.

Active Euthanasia any action that brings about an easy death for someone who is suffering and is done with that intention.

Ad Hominem Latin for "to the man"; an *ad hominem* is a fallacious argument or response in which one attacks the person making the argument instead of the position itself.

Altruism concern for the welfare of others; Rand characterizes altruism as the view that actions taken for self-benefit are evil and actions taken for the benefit of others are good.

Analysis a description of a concept in terms of its constituent concepts. For example, to analyze the concept of a dog, one would have to be able to produce the necessary and sufficient conditions for being a dog.

Antecedent the "if" portion of a conditional statement; for example, in the statement "if I am in Paris, then I am in France," the statement "I am in Paris" is the antecedent.

Atheistic Existentialism the view that God does not exist, and, given God's non-existence, no human nature, no predetermined set of traits, determines how we shall be and no objective moral values exist to guide our choices. We determine how we are by our free choices. We are nothing other than the sum of our actions. Our existence precedes our essence.

Anthropocentrism any moral view that places humans (Greek: *anthropos*) as the center of moral value or the most morally important element of the universe in virtue of their humanity.

Autonomy the property of being self-ruled (*auto*: self; *nomos*: law).

Biocentrism any moral view that places living things in general (Greek: *bios*) as the center of moral value or the most morally important element of the universe in virtue of being alive (also known as **Life-Centered Views**).

Care as used by Cates and others, care is an attitude marked by a union of both respect and compassion.

Categorical Imperative an imperative that directs us to perform an action, independently of any end we may have (e.g., "Do Y"). See **Hypothetical imperative**.

Charity an act of charity is an act of kindness toward others that is morally good but not morally required (see **Supererogatory**).

Cogency every good inductive argument is cogent; an argument is cogent if and only if it is strong and has all true premises.

Compassion reacting to other beings out of a recognition of their vulnerability and worth.

Compatibilism the view that it is possible for an action to be both free and determined; in other words, freedom and determinism are compatible.

Composite View theories of well-being that state that a good life requires both certain things that are objectively good but also a subjective desire for and appreciation of those good things.

Confirmation test the view that a claim or statement is true only if it is scientifically confirmable.

Consequent the "then" portion of a conditional statement; for example, in the statement "if I am in Paris, then I am in France," the statement "I am in France" is the consequent.

Consequentialism the view that the moral status of actions is determined solely by their consequences.

Counterexample any example that proves an exception to a rule. For example, in logic a counterexample is an instance of an argument form in which all of the premises are true but the conclusion is false (hence the argument is invalid).

Courage one of the virtues; according to Aristotle, it is located in between the vices of fear and confidence.

Cultural Relativism the view that there are moral facts but that the standards that determine the moral facts are culture-relative.

Deductive Argument an argument is deductive if and only if it is impossible for the premises to be true and the conclusion false.

Deontic Theories theories about what makes something morally right or wrong.

Deontological Theories normative ethical theories that deny that the moral status of actions is determined solely by their consequences but instead by duties (see **Nonconsequentialism**).

Descriptive Relativism the non-moral view that as a matter of fact, different cultures (or individuals) often hold different moral standards.

Desert a just entitlement. For example, a worker deserves his paycheck.

Desire-Fulfillment Theories theories of well-being that state that a good life is one in which a person's desires are fulfilled.

Divine Command Theory the view that the moral facts are determined by the commands of God; for example, what makes it wrong to harm others is merely the fact that God has commanded that we not do so.

Divine Moral Voluntarism see **Divine Command Theory**.

Doctrine of Double Effect see **Principle of Double Effect**.

Duty a duty is an obligation; it is not permissible to fail to do one's duty.

Entitlement something to which someone has a right or a just claim. For example, all humans are entitled to speak freely.

Epicureanism a philosophical theory based on the teachings of the Greek philosopher, Epicurus (341 BCE–270 BCE), who took pleasure to the highest good.

Epistemic Facts facts in epistemology (e.g., facts about what is known, reasonable to believe, etc.).

Ethical Egoism the view that an act is morally right (permissible) if and only if it will produce at least as much net **intrinsic good** for the agent as any other alternative. Self-interest is the ultimate standard for moral conduct.

Ethical Universalism the view that the standards for morality are not relative; see **Moral Objectivism**.

Eudaimonia a Greek concept that translates roughly as well-being or flourishing or deep happiness.

Euthanasia Greek for happy (*eu*) death (*thanatos*). Euthanasia is the intentional killing of another from a motivation to relieve suffering, etc.

Existentialism the view that human existence precedes human essence; in other words, humans were not created with built-in goals and values and that the meaning of our lives is up to us, hence we all bear a great moral responsibility.

Extrinsic Goods things that are good by virtue of producing other goods; same as instrumental goods.

Extrinsic Evils things that are evil by virtue of producing other evils; same as instrumental evils.

Future-Like-Ours (FLO) a concept denoting any living being whose future is phenomenologically and objectively similar to that of the average human being (from Don Marquis).

Generosity one of the virtues; according to Aristotle, it is located in between the vices of prodigality and meanness.

Golden Rule a rule of thumb in normative ethics that sanctions an action as morally permissible only if one would be willing to have others act in the same way as well; colloquially put: "do unto others as you would have done unto you."

Good Temper one of the virtues; according to Aristotle, it is located in between the vices of irascibility and unirascibility.

Greater Moral Evil Principle if it is in our power to prevent something bad from happening, without thereby sacrificing anything of comparable moral importance, we ought, morally, to do it.

Greatest Happiness Principle actions are right in proportion as they tend to promote happiness, wrong as they tend to produce the reverse of happiness.

Hard Determinism the view that since every event, including all of our choices and actions, has a cause, we never act freely and, as a result, are never morally responsible for our actions.

Harm Principle the claim that the actions of competent adults may be justly regulated only insofar as they are likely to directly cause significant harm to others without their consent.

Hedonism the view that pleasure is the only **intrinsic good** and pain is the only **intrinsic evil**.

Hobbes, Thomas a British political philosopher (1588–1679) from the early modern period best known as the author of *Leviathan,* in which he presents and defends a primitive version of social contract theory.

Honesty one of the virtues; according to Aristotle, it is located in between the vices of deceiptfulness and brashness.

Human in the **genetic sense**, this is a term that denotes any member of the species *Homo sapiens* (from Mary Anne Warren); in the **moral sense**, this is a term that denotes any full-fledged member of the moral community (i.e., a being with full moral standing).

Hypothetical imperative an imperative that directs us to perform an action relative to achieving a particular end (e.g., "If you want X, then do Y"). See **Categorical Imperative**.

Ideal Observer a person who is best suited to make a moral judgment; such a person has only true beliefs, knows all of the relevant nonmoral information, has no personal interest in the matter at hand, and is impartial in his concern for others.

Immanent Causation the causation of an event by an agent (as opposed to an event).

Incompatibilism the view that no action can be both free and determined; in other words, freedom and determinism are incompatible.

Individual Relativism the view that there are moral facts but that the standards that determine the moral facts are person-relative.

Inductive Argument an argument is inductive if and only if it is possible, but unlikely, for the premises to be true and the conclusion false.

Informed Consent also referred to as **Valid Consent**, this is when a moral agent properly understands a transaction and autonomously agrees to it.

Inherent Worth see **Intrinsic Goods**.

Instrumental Goods those things that are good because of what they can provide and not good for their own sake.

Intergenerational Justice the principles of justice that regulate behavior between members of different generations (e.g., a principle that requires currently existing people to behave a particular way for the benefit of future-existing people).

Intrinsic Goods those things that are good in and of themselves, for their own sake.

Intrinsic Evils those things that are evil in and of themselves for their own sake.

Involuntary Euthanasia the killing or letting die of someone who is suffering and who has refused to give consent to die or who has expressed a desire to remain alive.

Just Deserts see **Desert**.

Justice the subset of morality that is concerned with rights, deserts, or enforceable duties.

Kantian Ethics an approach to ethics informed by the insights of Kant's ethics, especially as presented in his formulations of his Categorical Imperative, such as that right actions must be rationally universalizable and never treat anyone solely as a means but also as an end.

Kantian Universalizability Requirement a requirement for morally right action based on Kant's Categorical Imperative: if an act is morally permissible for one person to perform is one set of circumstances, then it is morally permissible for anyone to perform in the same set of circumstances.

Killing where one agent performs an action that results in the death of another being (contrast with **Letting Die**).

Legal Moralism the view that the immoral character of some conduct, on some versions relative to the society's moral code and on others relative to objective moral standards, is a good reason in support of its legal regulation.

Letting Die where one agent refuses to perform an action that would save the life of another being (contrast with **Killing**).

Lex Talionis the principle that a person who has injured another person ought to be punished in a similar fashion (e.g., an eye for an eye).

Liberality see **Generosity**.

Liberalism in the context of the debate over the proper limits of legal regulation, the view defined by the **Harm Principle** that the actions of competent adults may be legally regulated only insofar as they are likely to directly cause significant harm to others without their consent.

Libertarianism the view that some of our choices are indetermined in a way that enables them to be free in the way required for moral responsibility.

Life-Centered Views see **Biocentrism**.

Loving Saint see **Moral Saint**.

Malthusian Theory theories that take their central position as similar to that of Thomas Malthus, a 19th-century British scholar who argued that population growth will ultimately be checked by limitations in the natural world such as food shortages or disease.

Marginal Utility the point at which doing an action would result in the same value of total consequences as not doing the action. For example, giving your last piece of bread to a hungry person would be an act of marginal utility: in either case, someone goes hungry.

Master Morality Nietzsche's term for tradition-based morality as it is defined by those in power.

Mens rea Latin for "guilty mind;" the mens rea requirements in a legal system are mental requirements that someone must meet to be legally responsible for his or her conduct.

Metaethics the study of the concepts and background assumptions made in ethical theorizing.

Modus Ponens a deductively valid inference pattern that proceeds as follows: if P, then Q. P. Therefore, Q.

Modus Tollens a deductively valid inference pattern that proceeds as follows: if P, then Q. It is not the case that Q. Therefore, it is not the case that P.

Moral Absolutism this is an ambiguous term. One sense of the term simply asserts that there is one, objectively true set of moral claims (see **Moral Objectivism**). The other sense of the term asserts that there are at least some exceptionless moral rules or principles.

Moral Agent any being that can have moral obligations and grant valid consent.

Moral Conservatism see **Absolutism**.

Moral Knowledge knowledge about some moral fact or other.

Moral Nihilism the view that there are no moral facts.

Moral Objectivism the view that there are at least some objective moral facts; these are facts that hold independently of what any person or group of persons believes, feels, etc. and so are just as "real" as scientific facts.

Moral Patient any being whose welfare counts when it comes to morality.

Moral Relativism the view that there are moral facts but that the standards that establish moral facts are relative either to persons or cultures.

Moral Saint Susan Wolf's term for a person who is maximally morally good. If this person is motivated by love, he is a **Loving Saint**; if he is motivated by duty, he is a **Rational Saint**.

Natural Law Theory a normative ethical theory that claims that what is good for living things is the fulfillment of their nature and that there are various natural principles related to these goals that govern how we ought to behave.

Necessary Condition a condition that is required for some further condition to be met; for example, being a mammal is a necessary condition for being a dog.

Negative Duties duties to refrain from doing something to another. For example, the duty not to kill is a negative duty.

Negative Rights rights against others that they not interfere. For example, the right to own a gun is a negative right that others not try to prevent one from doing so.

Nonconsequentialism the view that the moral status of actions is not determined solely by their consequences.

Nonvoluntary Euthanasia the killing or letting die of someone who is suffering but who is unable to give informed consent to die.

Normative Ethical Relativism see **Moral Relativism**.

Objective List Theories theories of well-being according to which certain things are good or bad for people whether or not those people want them or even know about them. Certain things are just objectively good.

Occam's Razor an epistemic principle taken from a philosopher known as William of Occam (c. 1280/5–c. 1347/9); a contemporary version of the principle says that for any two theories that explain a set of data *equally* well, it is more reasonable to adopt the theory with the fewest assumptions. Hence, the principle is a razor that "shaves off" unnecessary entities or commitments.

Offense Principle the view that the offensive nature of conduct is a good reason in support of its legal regulation.

Ontology the study of what exists.

Passive Euthanasia any omission of care that brings about an easy death for someone who is suffering and is done with that intention.

Person a concept that can be used to denote a moral feature of a being (e.g., moral agency) or a psychological feature of a being (e.g., having beliefs, desires, intentions, etc.)

Philosophes intellectual figures of the 18th-century Enlightenment in France.

Political Liberalism the primary function of a just government is the protection and cultivation of liberty.

Positive Duties duties to do something for another. For example, the duty to feed one's children is a positive duty.

Positive Rights rights against others that they provide some benefit. For example, the right to healthcare is a positive right.

Prima Facie Duty an action we have at least one good moral reason to perform.

Principle of Double Effect the view that we may sometimes pursue a good end through means we foresee to have evil effects, so long as the evil effects are unintended and proportionate to the goodness of our goal and we have no better way to achieve the goal.

Principle of Intrinsic Value the view that the realization of any living thing's good is intrinsically valuable (from Paul Taylor).

Principle of Moral Consideration the view that all wild living things are moral patients and hence worthy of moral consideration (from Paul Taylor).

Principle of Utility the principle that acts are morally permissible insofar as they produce at least as much net **intrinsic good** as any alternative.

Proper Pride one of the virtues; according to Aristotle, it is located in between the vices of empty vanity and undue humility.

Psychological Egoism the view that whenever anyone acts, his or her ultimate motivation is self-interest.

Rational Saint see **Moral Saint**.

Reconciliation Project any attempt to reconcile the demands of morality with the demands of self-interest.

Reflective Equilibrium the view that reasonable moral beliefs are those that survive a process of reflecting on all of one's beliefs and balancing beliefs about moral theory against beliefs about moral particulars.

Respect to treat another being as having significant moral value or being worthy of moral consideration.

Retributivism the view that acts of punishment are justified insofar as they achieve justice by giving someone who is guilty the penalty he or she deserves based on the nature of the crime.

Right a moral protection or boundary against unjustified trespass by another moral agent.

Righteous Indignation one of the virtues; according to Aristotle, it is located in between the vices of envy and spite.

Rule-Utilitarianism the view that a moral rule, or set of moral rules, is correct if and only it its adoption will produce at least as much net **intrinsic good** as the adoption of any alternative moral rule or set of moral rules.

Sentience the capacity to suffer or experience enjoyment.

Skepticism the view that a certain range of content is unknown.

Slave Morality Nietzsche's term for a utility-based morality as it is defined by those without power.

Social Contract Theory as a theory about the difference between what is morally right and morally wrong; the view that the difference is specified by those moral rules free, equal and rational self-interested individuals either did or would agree upon under appropriate conditions.

Soft Determinism the view that even though every event, including all of our choices and actions, has a cause, we nevertheless can act freely and, as a result, be morally responsible for our actions.

Soundness every good deductive argument is sound; an argument is sound if and only if it is valid and has all true premises.

Species Egalitarianism the view that a member of one species is just as morally valuable as a member of any other species or that all living things have equal moral standing.

Speciesism the view that species membership is a morally relevant factor and that some species are morally superior to others.

Strong Argument an inductive argument in which the truth of the premises makes the conclusion more likely than not but without guaranteeing it.

Sufficient Condition a condition that, if met, is enough to guarantee that some further condition is met; for example, being a dog is a sufficient condition for being a mammal.

Supererogatory an act that is morally good but not morally required; going beyond one's moral duty in the sense that the act is good to do but not wrong not to do.

Surrealism an artistic and literary movement that began in the 1920s and emphasized unconscious thought; it major figures included René Magritte and Salvador Dalí.

Theories of Well-Being theories that offer an explanation for what makes a life go well or what makes a life a good one.

Transeunt Causation the causation of one event by another.

Truthfulness one of the virtues; according to Aristotle, it is located in between the vices of boastfulness and mock-modesty.

Utilitarianism the view that our moral duties are acts that will produce the most net **intrinsic good**, not only for ourselves, but for everyone. See **Act-Utilitarianism** and **Rule-Utilitarianism**.

Validity a logical relation that holds between the premises and conclusion of an argument; an argument is valid if and only if it is impossible for the premises to be true and the conclusion false.

Value Theories theories about what makes something morally good or bad.

Vice a trained disposition or habit that produces morally bad results; examples of vices include dishonesty, cowardice, avarice, etc.

Virtue a trained disposition or habit that produces morally good results; examples of virtues include honesty, courage, conscientiousness, etc.

Virtue Ethics an approach to ethics that focuses on the traits that define a morally good person.

Voluntary Euthanasia the killing or letting die of someone who is suffering and who has given informed consent to die.

Weak Argument an inductive argument in which the truth of the premises makes the conclusion more likely (but not more likely than not) and without guaranteeing it.

Zero-Sum Game a situation in which one person's gain always precisely matches another person's loss. In a zero-sum game, it's not possible for both players to win.

ARGUMENT RECONSTRUCTION EXERCISE SOLUTIONS

Chapter 6.1:

I. The text from Harman:

> In other words, in both science and ethics, general principles are invoked to explain particular cases and, therefore, in both science and ethics, the general principles you accept can be tested by appealing to particular judgments that certain things are right or wrong, just or unjust, and so forth. . . (page 38)

Here is one possible reconstruction of the argument:

1. In both science and ethics, general principles can explain why we make particular judgments about cases.
2. If a general principle can explain why we make a particular judgment about a case, then the particular judgment can be used to test general principles (suppressed premise).
3. Therefore, in both science and ethics, we can use particular judgments to test general principles.

II. The text from Harman:

> The observation of an event can provide observational evidence for or against a scientific theory in the sense that the truth of that observation can be relevant to a reasonable explanation of why that observation was made. A moral observation does not seem, in the same sense, to be observational evidence for or against any moral theory, since the truth or falsity of the moral observation seems to be completely irrelevant to any reasonable explanation of why that observation was made. (page 39)

Here is one possible reconstruction of the argument:

1. An observation is evidence for a theoretical fact only if the theoretical fact is part of a reasonable explanation for why the observation occurred.
2. But moral facts are theoretical facts that play no part in a reasonable explanation for why we make the moral observations that we do.
3. Therefore, moral observations are not evidence for the truth of moral theories (suppressed conclusion).

Chapter 6.2:

I. The text from Shafer-Landau:

> If we take up an exclusively scientific view of the world, then there is no room for normative principles and normative facts. But such things do exist. There are genuine reasons to believe things, and genuine moral reasons to do things. Science cannot verify the existence of such reasons, duties, or principles. But that only points to the limits of science, rather than the limits of a credible ontology. (page 48)

Here is one possible reconstruction of the argument:

1. If an exclusively scientific view of what exists is correct, then there are no normative principles or normative facts.
2. But there are normative principles and normative facts (e.g., genuine reasons to believe something).
3. Therefore, the exclusively scientific view of what exists is not correct.

II. The text from Shafer-Landau:

> Because reference to the moral quality of the interaction is optional, it isn't required. And Occam's razor tells us that, therefore, we have no reason to believe that it's real. Moral skeptics capitalize on this and allege that either evil is nonexistent, or that evil is a human construct. There is no such thing as evil, really. (page 45)

Here is one possible reconstruction of the argument:

1. Positing the existence of a moral quality is not required to explain a moral observation.
2. We have reason to believe in something only if it is required to explain our observations.
3. Therefore, we have no reason to believe in the existence of moral qualities (like evil).

Chapter 6.3:

I. The text from Shafer-Landau:

Knowledge, it is thought, requires certainty. But certainty is unobtainable in ethics. So moral knowledge itself is impossible. (page 51)

Here is one possible reconstruction of the argument:

1. A person knows a claim only if he is certain of the claim.
2. As a matter of fact, no person is ever certain about any ethical claim.
3. Therefore, no person knows any ethical claim.

II. The text from Shafer-Landau:

Either intractable disagreement among consistent, intelligent parties forces them to suspend judgment about their contested views, or it doesn't. If it does, then we must suspend judgment about *all* of our philosophical views, as well as our belief that there is an external world, that I am an embodied being, that the earth is older than a second, etc. All of these have been challenged by brilliant, consistent, informed skeptics over the millennia. Alternatively, if we are warranted in any of our beliefs, despite the presence of such skepticism, then justified belief is possible, even in the face of persistent disagreement. And so we could retain our moral beliefs, especially those that we have carefully thought through, despite an inability to convince all of our intelligent opponents. (pages 53–54)

Here is one possible reconstruction of the argument:

1. Either intractable disagreement among consistent, intelligent parties rules out knowledge or it doesn't.
2. If it does, then no one knows any philosophical claim, no one knows that there is an external world, etc.

3. If it doesn't, then it is possible to have moral knowledge despite the fact that there is intractable disagreement among consistent, intelligent parties.
4. Therefore, either we accept that no one knows that there is an external world or else the argument from disagreement fails to show that no one has any moral knowledge (suppressed conclusion).

Chapter 7.1:

I. Here is the text from Arthur:

However much people may want to do the right thing, according to this view, we cannot ever know for certain what is right without the guidance of religious teaching. Human understanding is simply inadequate to this difficult and controversial task; morality involves immensely complex problems, and so we must consult religious revelation for help. (page 64)

Here is one possible reconstruction of the argument:

1. Because it is so complex, we can know what is morally right only if we have reliable revelation.
2. The only possible source of reliable revelation is that which comes from God.
3. Therefore, we can know what is morally right only if there is a God.

II. Here is the text from Arthur:

Even if religion is not necessary for moral motivation or guidance, it is often claimed, religion is necessary in another more fundamental sense. According to this view, religion is necessary for morality because without God there could be no right or wrong. God, in other words, provides the foundation or bedrock on which morality is grounded. (page 65)

Here is one possible reconstruction of the argument:

1. There is right and wrong only if there is a foundation on which morality is grounded.
2. If there is a foundation on which morality is grounded, it must be God.
3. Therefore, there is right and wrong only if God exists.

Chapter 7.2:

I. The text from Nielsen:

. . .without God there can be no one overarching purpose, no one basic scheme of human existence in virtue of which we could find a meaning for our grubby lives. It is this overall sense of meaning that man so ardently strives for, but it is not to be found in a purely secular worldview. (page 70)

Here is one possible reconstruction of the argument:

1. Our lives have meaning only if there is an overarching purpose for our lives.
2. There is an overarching purpose for our lives only if God exists.
3. Therefore, our lives have meaning only if God exists.

II. The text from Nielsen:

Human love and companionship are also central to a happy life. We prize them and a life without them is most surely an impoverished life, a life that no man, if he would take the matter to heart, would desire. But I would most emphatically assert that human love and companionship are quite possible in a Godless world. . . (pages 71–72)

Here is one possible reconstruction of the argument:

1. Human love and companionship are sufficient for a happy life.
2. It is possible to have human love and companionship even if God doesn't exist.
3. Therefore, it is possible to have a happy life even if God doesn't exist.

Chapter 7.3:

I. The text from Nietzsche:

It should be noted at once that in this first type of morality [master morality] the antithesis "good" and "bad" means the same thing as "noble" and "despicable" . . . the cowardly, the timid, the petty, and those who think only of narrow utility are despised. (page 78)

Here is one possible reconstruction of the argument:

1. Anything that is despicable is morally bad.
2. Cowardice, timidity, and concern for promoting general utility are despicable.

3. Therefore, cowardice, timidity, and a concern for promoting general utility are morally bad.

II. The paraphrased text:

Those in power think of morality in terms of honor, rights, honesty, tradition, etc. Those without power think of morality in terms of the value of pity, kindness, patience, humility, friendship, etc. How can we explain the differences between these two groups? Easily—each group determines what is morally valuable for themselves. Hence, morality is subjective.

Here is one possible reconstruction of the argument:

1. Those in power think of morality differently from those without power.
2. The best explanation for this difference is that each group of humans determines the moral facts for themselves (i.e., morality is subjective).
3. Therefore, each group of humans determines the moral facts for themselves (i.e., morality is subjective).

Chapter 7.4:

I. The text from Harman:

Now, mere moral diversity is not a disproof of moral absolutism. Where there are differences in custom, there are often differences in circumstance . . . . But, even though the rejection of moral absolutism is not an immediate logical consequence of the existence of moral diversity, it is a reasonable inference from the most plausible explanation of the range of moral diversity that actually exists. (page 84)

Here is one possible reconstruction of the argument:

1. There is a significant range of moral diversity in the actual world.
2. The best explanation for this range of moral diversity is that moral relativism is true.
3. The best explanation of some set of data is likely to be correct.
4. Therefore, it is likely that moral relativism is true.

II. The paraphrased text:

> If moral absolutism is correct, then there is only one, single true morality. But anyone who has ever read a newspaper or traveled abroad knows that people have very different beliefs about what they ought to do. Some people think that it's always wrong to have an abortion, and others think that it's sometimes permissible to have one. So it's obvious that there is no single, true morality. That's why I'm a moral relativist.

Here is one possible reconstruction of the argument:

1. People have very different beliefs about what they ought to do.
2. If people have different beliefs about what they ought to do, then there is no single, true morality.
3. If there is no single, true morality, then moral relativism is true.
4. Therefore, moral relativism is true.

Chapter 7.5:

I. The text from Taylor:

> The argument for descriptive relativism, then, may be summarized as follows. Since every culture varies with respect to its moral rules and standards, and since each individual's moral beliefs—including his inner conviction of their absolute truth—have been learned within the framework of his own culture's moral code, it follows that there are no universal moral norms. (pages 91–92)

Here is one possible reconstruction of the argument:

1. If moral rules and standards vary with cultures and our own moral beliefs are culturally bound, then there are no universal moral norms.
2. If there are no universal moral norms, then descriptive relativism is true.
3. Therefore, descriptive relativism is true.

II. The text from Taylor:

> According to the descriptive relativist there are no moral norms common to all cultures. Each society has its own view of what is morally right and wrong and these views vary from society to society because of the differences in their moral codes. Thus it is a mistake to think there are common norms that bind all mankind in one moral community. (page 90)

Here is one possible reconstruction of the argument:

1. There are no moral norms common to all cultures (i.e., descriptive relativism is true).
2. If there are no moral norms common to all cultures, then there are no moral norms that bind all mankind.
3. If there are no moral norms that bind all mankind, then moral relativism is true.
4. Therefore, moral relativism is true.

Chapter 8.1:

I. The compatibilist objection to Strawson's position is the following:

> [Compatibilists claim] that one may correctly be said to be truly responsible for what one does, when one acts, just so long as one is not caused to act by any of a certain set of contraints [e.g., kleptomanic impulses, obsessional neuroses]. . . . Clearly, this sort of compatibilist responsibility does not require that one should be truly responsible for how one is in any way at all, and so step (2) of the Basic Argument comes out to be false. (pages 106–107)

Here is one possible reconstruction of the argument:

1. We are morally responsible for our actions just so long as we are not caused to act by any of a certain set of constraints (e.g., kleptomanic impulses, obsessional neuroses).
2. We can meet this condition for responsibility even if how we are (our character and motives) is determined in such a way that we are not morally responsible for it.
3. Therefore, we can be morally responsible for some of our actions even if we are determined

II. Strawson's response to the Libertarian reply:

> But how can this indeterminism help with moral responsibility? How can the fact that my effort of will is indeterministic in such a way that its outcome is indeterminate make me truly responsible for it, or even help to make me truly responsible

for it? How can it help in any way at all with moral responsibility? How can it make punishment—or reward—ultimately just? (page 108)

Here is one possible reconstruction of the argument:

1. The fact that our act results from an indeterministic effort of will (one that is not determined by our prior character, motives or other events) does not make it just to reward or punish us for it.
2. If that fact does not make it just to reward or punish us for our act, it does not make us morally responsible for our act.
3. Therefore, even if our will is not determined by our prior character, motives, or other events, that is not sufficient to make us morally responsible for our action.

Chapter 8.2:

I. Ayer offers the following argument:

When I am said to have done something of my own free will it is implied that I could have acted otherwise; and it is only when it is believed that I could have acted otherwise that I am held to be morally responsible for what I have done. For a man is not thought to be morally responsible for an action that it was not in his power to avoid. But if human behavior is entirely governed by causal laws, it is not clear how any action that is done could ever have been avoided. It may be said of the agent that he would have acted otherwise if the causes of his action had been different, but they being what they were, it seems to follow that he was bound to act as he did. (page 112)

Here is one possible reconstruction of the argument:

1. We act freely only if we could have acted otherwise.
2. We are morally responsible for an act only if we could have acted otherwise.
3. We could have acted otherwise than we did only if it was in our power to avoid acting as we did.
4. If human behavior is governed by causal laws, it is never in our power to avoid acting as we do.

5. Therefore, if human behavior is governed by causal laws, we never act freely and we are never morally responsible for our actions.

II. Ayer offers the argument:

Either it is an accident that I choose to act as I do or it is not. If it is an accident, then it is merely a matter of chance that I did not choose otherwise; and if it is merely a matter of chance that I did not choose otherwise, it is surely irrational to hold me morally responsible for choosing as I did. But if it is not an accident that I choose to do one thing rather than another, then presumably there is some causal explanation of my choice: and in that case we are led back to determinism. (page 114)

Here in one possible reconstruction of the argument:

1. Either it is an accident that we choose to act as we do or it is not.
2. If it is an accident that we choose to act as we do, then our choice is merely a matter of chance.
3. If our choice is merely a matter of chance, then we are not responsible for our choice.
4. Therefore, if it is an accident that we choose to act as we do, then we are not responsible for our choice.
5. If it is not an accident that we choose to act as we do, then our choice has a causal explanation.
6. If our choice has a causal explanation, then it is causally determined.
7. Therefore, if it is not an accident that we choose to act as we do, then our choice is causally determined.
8. Therefore, either we are not responsible for our choice or our choice is causally determined.

Chapter 8.3:

I. The reasoning considered and rejected by Chisholm is the following:

Moral responsibility requires free choice in the following way: We are morally responsible for an action only if we could have acted otherwise. But to say that we could have acted otherwise is just to say that we could have done something else, if we had chosen to do something else. So moral responsibility simply requires that we could have done something else if we had chosen to do something else. This sort of hypothetical ability (the ability to do something else if we had chosen to do something else) is consistent with our actual choice being causally determined. Therefore, we can be free in the way required for moral responsibility, even if we are causally determined.

Here is one possible reconstruction of the argument:

1. We are morally responsible for an action only if our act is free in the sense that we could have acted otherwise.
2. To say we could have acted otherwise is to say we could have done something else if we had chosen to do so.
3. Therefore, we are morally responsible for an action only if our act is free in the sense that we could have done something else if we had chosen to do so.
4. We can be free in this sense even if we our choices are causally determined.
5. Therefore, we can be free in the way required for moral responsibility even if our choices are causally determined.

II. The following reasoning attempts to show that the freedom required for moral responsibility involves more than the hypothetical ability to have acted differently if one had chosen to act differently:

> Suppose that Jones murders Smith and cannot help choosing to do so. Someone has gained control of his thoughts and has caused in him an irresistible desire to kill Smith. That desire has caused him to choose to kill Smith and his choice has caused his action. Jones lacks the freedom required to make him morally responsible for his action. Yet, he could have done something else if he had chosen to do something else. Therefore, the freedom required for moral responsibility demands more than the hypothetical ability to have done something else if one had decided to do something else.

Here is one possible reconstruction of the argument:

1. Jones is caused to choose to kill Smith by an irresistible desire that is caused in him by others.
2. If Jones' choice is caused in this way, then Jones is not free in the way necessary to make him morally responsible for killing Smith.
3. Therefore, Jones is not free in the way necessary to make him morally responsible for killing Smith.
4. Jones could have done something else if he had chosen to do something else.
5. Therefore, someone (Jones) can lack the freedom required for moral responsibility even if he could have done something else if he had chosen to do so.

Chapter 8.4:

I. The following argument attempts to show that, in choosing to be a certain way, we are affirming the value for everyone of being that way.

> In fact, in creating the man that we want to be, there is not a single one of our acts which does not at the same time create an image of man as we think he ought to be. To choose to be this or that is to affirm at the same time the value of what we choose, because we can never choose evil. We always choose the good, and nothing can be good for us without being good for all. (page 130)

Here is one possible reconstruction of the argument:

1. To choose to be a certain way is to affirm the goodness for oneself of being that way.
2. To affirm the goodness for oneself of being a certain way is to affirm the goodness for everyone of being that way.
3. Therefore, to choose to be a certain way is to affirm the goodness for everyone of being that way.

II. The following argument concerns the moral implications of God's nonexistence:

> The existentialist, on the contrary, thinks it is very distressing that God does not exist, because all possibility of finding values in a heaven of ideas

disappears along with Him; there can no longer be an *a priori* Good, since there is no infinite and perfect consciousness to think it. Nowhere is it written that the Good exists, that we must be honest, that we must not lie; because the fact is we are on a plane where there are only men. (page 132)

Here is one possible reconstruction of the argument:

1. If God does not exist, there is no infinite and perfect consciousness to conceive an *a priori* Good.
2. An *a priori* Good exists only if some consciousness conceives it.
3. Only an infinite and perfect consciousness can conceive an *a priori* Good.
4. Therefore, if God does not exist, no *a priori* Good exists.

Chapter 9.1:

I. Rand presents the following criticisms of Altruism:

[A]ltruism permits no concept of a self-respecting, self-supporting man—a man who supports his life by his own effort and neither sacrifices himself nor others. It means that altruism permits no view of men except as sacrificial animals and profiteers-on-sacrifice, as victims and parasites—that it permits no concept of a benevolent co-existence among men—that it permits no concept of justice. (page 140)

Here is one possible reconstruction of her intended argument that Altruism is mistaken:

1. If a society were organized according to Altruistic principles, there would not be a benevolent co-existence among individuals.
2. A society in which there is no benevolent co-existence among individuals is a society without justice.
3. Therefore, if a society were organized according to Altruistic principles, it would lack justice.
4. If a society organized according to Altruistic principles would lack justice, then Altruism is mistaken.
5. Therefore, Altruism is mistaken.

II. Rand provides the following objection to Altruism:

Since nature does not provide man with an automatic form of survival, since he has to support his life by his own effort, the doctrine that concern with one's own interests is evil means that man's desire to live is evil—that man's life, as such, is evil. No doctrine could be more evil than that. (page 140)

Here is one possible reconstruction of the argument:

1. If Altruism is true, then it is evil for people to be concerned with their own interests.
2. People have to be concerned with their own interests in order to survive.
3. If it is evil for people to be concerned with their own interests, then it is evil for people to be concerned with their own survival.
4. If Altruism is true, then it is evil for people to be concerned with their own survival [from 1 and 2].
5. It is not evil for people to be concerned with their own survival.
6. Therefore, Altruism is false.

Chapter 9.2:

I. Here is some reasoning in support of Ethical Egoism:

An adequate ethical theory will successfully answer the question, "Why be moral?" To answer that question successfully, a theory must imply that we always have a good reason to do what is right. We only have a good reason to something if it is in our self-interest to do it. Therefore, an adequate ethical theory will imply that what is right is always in our self-interest.

Here's one possible reconstruction of the argument:

1. An adequate ethical theory will successfully answer the question, "Why be moral?"
2. To answer that question successfully, a theory must imply that we always have a good reason to do what is right.
3. We only have a good reason to something if it is in our self-interest to do it.
4. Therefore, an adequate ethical theory will imply that what is right is always is in our self-interest.

II. Here is a response to Rachels' final objection to Ethical Egoism:

> Part of friendship is making a commitment to our friends to give their interests special consideration. This commitment is a factual difference between our friends and strangers that justifies us in assigning greater importance to our friends' interests than to those of others. I have made a similar commitment to myself, a commitment to assign greater interest to my own welfare than to anyone else's. Therefore, there is a factual difference between all others and myself that justifies me in assigning greater importance to my own interests than to anyone else's.

Here is one possible reconstruction of the argument:

1. If, as in friendship, we make a commitment to someone to give their interests special consideration, then that commitment is a factual difference between them and others that justifies us in assigning greater importance to their interests than to those of others.
2. I have made a commitment to myself to give my interests special consideration.
3. Therefore, that commitment is a factual difference between all others and myself that justifies me in assigning greater importance to my interests than to those of others.

Chapter 9.3:

I. Here is one way to understand the argument contained in the rhetorical question, "How would you like it if someone did that to you?"

> Suppose you are about to do something that is wrong because it involves treating someone badly (e.g., stealing his umbrella). Others have a reason not to treat you in that same way (steal your umbrella). Their reason not to treat you in that way is that it is bad for you. Yet, there is nothing special about you or them. So, everyone has this same reason not to treat anyone in this way, that it is bad for the person so treated. In particular, you now have a reason not to treat the person at hand in this way. Your reason is that your behavior is bad for them. That's why you should not do what's wrong in this case.

Here is one possible reconstruction of the argument.

1. Suppose we are about to do something that is wrong because it involves treating someone badly.
2. Others have a reason not to treat us badly.
3. There is no relevant difference between others and us in this case.
4. Therefore, we have a reason not to do what is wrong in this case, namely, that doing so is bad for the other person.
5. Therefore, if a wrong act involves treating someone badly, then we have a reason not to do it.

II. Here is a problem concerning the relation between moral considerations and reasons for action:

> But if something's being wrong is supposed to be a reason against doing it, and if your reasons for doing things depend on your motives and people's motives can very greatly, then it looks as though there won't be a single right and wrong for everybody. There won't be a single right and wrong, because if people's basic motives differ, there won't be one basic standard of behavior that everyone has a reason to follow. (pages 153–154)

Here is one possible reconstruction of the argument:

1. Our reasons for following any basic moral standard of behavior depend on our motives: as our motives vary, so too do the moral standards of behavior that we have a reason to follow.
2. Different people have different motives.
3. Therefore, different people have reasons to follow different moral standards of conduct.
4. If different people have reasons for follow different moral standards of conduct, then there is no single standard of conduct that applies to everyone.
5. Therefore, there is no single standard of conduct that applies to everyone.

Chapter 9.4:

I. Here is an argument for a lack of coincidence between the demands of morality and those of prudence:

> Even in a society in which there are strong external sanctions for immoral behavior, we will maximize our self-interest by following the qualified moral rule: Obey the rules of morality except when a particular violation is likely to maximize your self-interest and you can reliably determine that the chances of detection and punishment are low. If following this rule will maximize our self-interest, then the rationally prudent choice is to follow it. Therefore, even in a society in which there are strong external sanctions for immoral behavior, the unqualified demands of morality and prudence do not coincide.

Here is one possible reconstruction of the argument:

1. Even in a society in which there are strong external sanctions for immoral behavior, we will maximize our self-interest by following the qualified moral rule: Obey the rules of morality except when a particular violation is likely to maximize your self-interest and you can reliably determine that the chances of detection and punishment are low.
2. If following a rule will maximize our self-interest, then the rationally prudent choice for us is to do so.
3. Therefore, even in a society in which there are strong external sanctions for immoral behavior, the rationally prudent rule for us to adopt is the qualified moral rule.
4. Therefore, even in a society in which there are strong external sanctions for immoral behavior, it is not prudent for us to adopt the rules of morality without qualification.

II. Here is an argument to show that dedicated immoralists have no reason to reform:

> Immoralists lack any internal sanctions against immoral behavior, and they can often reliably detect that some immoral behavior to advance their ends is unlikely to result in any external sanction. Since the immoral behavior will advance their ends at no cost in terms of internal or external sanctions,

it is prudentially rational for them. If morality and prudence do not coincide for immoralists, then they have no reason to be reform their immoral behavior. Therefore, immoralists have no reason to reform their behavior in these cases.

Here is one possible reconstruction of the argument:

1. Immoralists are often in a situation in which some immoral behavior to advance their ends carries no internal sanctions for them and is also unlikely to carry any external ones.
2. If some behavior will advance the immoralists' ends and is unlikely to carry any cost for them in internal or external sanctions, then it is prudentially rational for them.
3. If some immoral behavior is prudentially rational for immoralists, then they have no reason to reform their behavior in that case.
4. Therefore, immoralists have no reason to reform some of their immoral behavior.

Chapter 10.1:

I. The following reasoning attempts to show that our lives are as lacking in objective meaning as that of Sisyphus:

> Sisyphus toils after a goal—moving his stone up the hill—of transitory significance; as soon as he achieves it, it disappears and he starts over again. His toils lack any objective meaning. We too toil after goals of transitory significance; none is lasting and, having achieved one, we immediately set forth after the next. Therefore, our toils also lack any objective meaning.

Here is one possible reconstruction of the argument:

1. Sisyphus toils after a goal of transitory significance.
2. Our toils are all directed at goals of transitory significance.
3. Sisyphus' toils are objectively meaningless.
4. Therefore, our toils are objectively meaningless.

II. The following reasoning attempts to show that the meaning that Sisyphus himself gives to his labors is better than any meaning they might gain from being directed toward a goal:

> The meaning that Sisyphus' labors gain from his desiring to engage in them is better than the meaning they might have relative to some external goal.
>
> For suppose that Sisyphus' labors gain meaning by being directed toward a goal (e.g., to build a temple). With the achievement of his goal, Sisyphus has nothing more to do. His existence is marked by the absence of activity. If Sisyphus' labors instead gain meaning by his desiring to engage in them, then Sisyphus never completes his task, and as a result, his existence is always marked by his desired activity. The meaningfulness of an existence that is marked by the achievement of an end followed by inactivity is not as good as the meaningfulness of an existence that is marked by continual, desired, activity.

Here is one possible reconstruction of the argument:

1. In the case where Sisyphus' labors are directed toward some goal, his labors are meaningful but with the achievement of his goal, he has nothing more to do and his existence is marked by the absence of activity.
2. In the case where Sisyphus' labors gain meaning just from his desire to engage in them, his labors are continually meaningful for him and his existence is never marked by the absence of activity.
3. Other things being equal, it is better for a life's meaning to be continual rather than temporary.
4. Therefore, in the case where Sisyphus' labors gain meaning just from his desire to engage in them, his labors are meaningful in a better way than in the case where they gain meaning from being directed toward some goal.

Chapter 10.2:
I. The following argument seeks to show that our well-being is simply a matter of our experiences:

> Nothing adds to or detracts from our well-being unless it effects us in some way, but nothing has an effect on us except insofar as we experience it.

Our well-being is, therefore, entirely defined by our experiences after all.

Here is one possible reconstruction of the argument:
1. Nothing adds to or detracts from our well-being unless it effects us in some way.
2. Nothing effects us unless we experience it.
3. Nothing adds or detracts from our well-being unless we experience it.
4. If nothing adds or detracts from our well-being unless we experience it, then our well-being is defined by our experiences.
5. Therefore, our well-being is defined by our experiences.

II. The following argument concerns what we should conclude from the experience machine thought experiment:

> If we had the option of actually seeing a beautiful painting or instead simply having the experience of seeing it, we would prefer the former. Yet, this does not imply that the beauty of the painting is not just a function of its ability to produce a certain sort of experience in us. So too, the fact that we would prefer actually living a certain life to having the associated experiences does not imply that the value of the life is not just a function of the experiences it contains for those who live it.

Here is one possible reconstruction of the argument:

1. A beautiful painting is such that we would prefer actually seeing it to simply having the experience of seeing it.
2. A good life is such that we would prefer actually living it to simply having the experience of living it.
3. A beautiful painting is nonetheless such that its beauty is a function of its ability to produce a certain sort of experience in us.
4. Therefore, a good life is nonetheless such its goodness is a function of its ability to produce a certain sort of experience in us.

Chapter 10.3:
I. The text from Parfit:

> The simplest [desire-fulfillment theory] is the unrestricted theory. This claims that what is best for

someone is what would best fulfill all of his desires, throughout his life. Suppose that I meet a stranger who has what is believed to be a fatal disease. My sympathy is aroused, and I strongly want this stranger to be cured. We never meet again. Later, unknown to me, this stranger is cured. On the Unrestricted Desire-Fulfillment Theory, this event is good for me, and makes my life go better. This is not plausible. We should reject this theory. (page 188)

Here is one possible reconstruction of the argument:

1. If the Unrestricted Desire-Fulfillment theory is true, then in the case described by Parfit, my life goes better because of the curing of a stranger unbeknownst to me.
2. But it is not plausible to think that my life goes better because of the curing of a stranger unbeknownst to me.
3. Therefore, it is implausible to think that the unrestricted desire-fulfillment theory is true.

II. The text from Parfit:

Some success theorists [deny that something bad can happen to someone after he is dead], since they tell us to ignore the desires of the dead. But suppose that I was asked, "Do you want it to be true, even after you are dead, that you were a successful parent?" I would answer "Yes". It is irrelevant to my desire whether it is fulfilled before or after I am dead. These success theorists count it as bad for me if my attempts fail, even if, because I am in exile, I never know this. How then can it matter whether, when my attempts fail, I am dead? All that my death does is to ensure that I will never know this. If we think it irrelevant that I never know about the non-fulfillment of my desires, we cannot defensibly claim that my death makes a difference. . . (pages 188–189)

Here is one possible reconstruction of the argument:

1. If success theory is true, then the non-fulfillment of my desires is bad for me even when I don't know about it.
2. It is possible for me to have desires that are not fulfilled after I am dead even though I don't know about it.
3. Therefore, if success theory is true, then it is possible for things to be bad for me even after I am dead.

Chapter 11.1:

I. Mill argues as follows for his quality distinction with regard to pleasures and pains:

Of two pleasures, if there be one to which all or almost all who have experience of both give a decided preference, irrespective of any feeling of moral obligation to prefer it, that is the more desirable pleasure. If one of the two is, by those who are competently acquainted with both, placed so far above the other that they prefer it, even though knowing it to be attended with a greater amount of discontent, and would not resign it for any quantity of the other pleasure which their nature is capable of, we are justified in ascribing to the preferred enjoyment a superiority in quality, so far outweighing quantity as to render it, in comparison, of small account. Now it is an unquestionable fact that those who are equally acquainted with, and equally capable of appreciating and enjoying, both, do give a most marked preference to the manner of existence which employs their higher faculties. (pages 195–196)

Here is one possible reconstruction of his argument:

1. If everyone who experiences two different pleasures prefers one over the other, then it is reasonable to judge the one pleasure of higher quality than the other.
2. As a matter of fact, everyone who has experienced pleasures that employ his or her higher faculties prefers those pleasures to those that do not.
3. Therefore, it is reasonable to judge that pleasures that employ our higher faculties are of a higher quality than those that do not.

II. Mill argues that happiness is an intrinsic good:

[T]he sole evidence it is possible to produce that anything is desirable, is that people do actually desire it. If the end which the utilitarian doctrine proposes to itself were not, in theory and in practice, acknowledged to be an end, nothing could ever convince any person that it was so. No reason can be given why the general happiness is desirable, except that each person, so far as he believes it to be attainable, desires his own happiness. This, however, being a fact, we have not only all the proof which the case admits of, but all which it is possible to require, that happiness is a good: that each person's happiness is a good to that person, and the general happiness, therefore, a good to the aggregate of all persons. (pages 200–201)

Here is one possible reconstruction of his argument:

1. If we know that each person desires his or her own happiness for its own sake, we have adequate reason to believe that happiness in general is an intrinsic good.
2. We know that each person desires his or her own happiness for it own sake.
3. Therefore, we have adequate reason to believe that happiness in general is an intrinsic good.

Chapter 11.2:

I. One objection to Moral Conservatism is the following:

> For any act we pick (e.g., killing an innocent child), we can imagine a situation in which we have to do it in order to prevent someone from doing an even worse act of the same kind (killing two innocent children). It is always wrong for us to allow a greater evil when we can prevent it by engaging in a lesser one. No act then is such that it is always wrong for us to do it no matter what the circumstances.

Here is one possible reconstruction of the argument:

1. For any act (e.g., killing an innocent child), there is a situation in which we have to do it in order to prevent someone from doing an even worse act of the same kind (killing two innocent children).
2. It is always wrong for us to allow a greater evil when we can prevent it by engaging in a lesser one.
3. For any act, there is situation in which it would be wrong for us not to do it.
4. Therefore, no act is such that it is always wrong for us to do it, no matter what the circumstances.

II. One argument that it is wrong to kill the fat man in the cave case is the following:

> If those in the cave case kill the fat man to save themselves, they will be acting immorally. They will

be taking the value of their lives to be greater than that of the fat man. No human being has a right to determine that the value of one person's life or the lives of any group of people is greater that than of any other person or group of people. They will be doing what they have no right to do.

Here is one possible reconstruction of the argument:

1. No human being has a right to determine that the value of one person's life or the lives of any group of people is greater that than of any other person or group of people.
2. If those in the cave case kill the fat man to save themselves, they are taking the value of their lives to be greater than that of his.
3. If they take the value of their lives to be greater than that of his, they do what they have no right to do.
4. Therefore, if those in the save case kill the fat man to same themselves, they are acting immorally.

Chapter 11.3:

I. Brandt argues that utilitarian moralities are rational for us to adopt, whether we concerned for others or selfish:

> [If the system of morality is utilitarian, it] can be recommended to a person of broad human sympathies, as an institution that maximizes the expectation of the general welfare; and to a selfish person, as an institution that, in the absence of particular evidence about his own case, may be expected to maximize his own expectation of welfare . . . To put it in other words, a utilitarian morality can be "vindicated" by appeal to either the humanity or to the selfishness of human beings. (page 215)

Here is one possible reconstruction of the argument:

1. If a moral code is utilitarian (its adoption will maximize expected social utility), then persons of broad human sympathies have a reason to adopt it: its general adoption will maximize the general welfare.
2. If a moral code is utilitarian (its adoption will maximize expected social utility), then selfish persons have a reason to adopt it: all else being equal, their individual adoption of

the code is likely to maximize their individual welfare.

3. Therefore, if our moral obligations are defined by a utilitarian moral code, then both those of broad human sympathies and those who are selfish have a reason to be moral.

II. The following argument attempts to show that Rule-Utilitarianism is no better or worse a theory than Act-Utilitarianism:

> Rule-Utilitarianism gives us the same moral guidance as Act-Utilitarianism. Take any type of situation, say one in which we have to decide whether to keep a promise. There are lots of moral rules we might adopt to guide us in such a situation (e.g., if you have made a promise, keep it; if you've made a promise and it's to a friend, keep it; etc). One such rule is: if you've made a promise, then keep it or break it, depending on which alternative will produce the most net good in the circumstances. Our adopting this rule will produce the greatest good, for in following it, we will always, in each case, do what produces the greatest good. This rule is then the one that determines how we should behave, according to Rule-Utilitarianism. Yet, this rule and Act-Utilitarianism tell us to do the same thing: in each case, do the act with the best consequences.

Here is one possible reconstruction of the argument:

1. For any situation, one alternative rule that applies to it is the rule, "If A, then do what will produce the greatest net good," where A is a general kind of situation of which the particular case is an example.
2. Rules of the form, "If A, then do what will produce the greatest net good," are always such that our adopting them will result in at least as much net good as our adopting any alternative rule.
3. According to Rule-Utilitarianism, the moral status of any act is determined by whether it is permitted or prohibited by a rule of the form, "If A, then do what will produce the greatest net good."
4. Therefore, for any situation, Rule-Utilitarianism has the same implication as Act-Utilitarianism.

Chapter 11.4

I. Thomson argues that the bystander who would not sacrifice his own life to save the five people from the oncoming trolley may not sacrifice the life of someone else:

> "What luck," he thinks, "I can't turn the trolley onto myself. So it's perfectly all right for me to choose option (ii) [and turn the trolley onto the one]!" His thought is that since he can't himself pay the cost of his good deed, it is perfectly all right for him to make the workman on the right-hand track pay it—despite the fact that he wouldn't himself pay it if he could. I put it to you that that thought won't do. Since he wouldn't himself pay the cost of his good deed if he could pay it, there is no way in which he can decently regard himself as entitled to make someone else pay it. (page 231)

Here is one possible reconstruction of her argument:

1. The bystander cannot assume the cost of his contemplated good deed (saving the five) by turning the trolley onto himself, and he would not be willing to do so, if he could.
2. If one would not be willing to assume the cost of a contemplated good deed, if one could, then one is not permitted to impose that cost on others, even in a case where one cannot assume it.
3 Therefore, the bystander is not permitted to impose the cost of his good deed on the one workman, even in this case where he can't assume it for himself.
4. Therefore, turning the trolley so as to save the five people at the cost of killing the one workman is not permissible for the bystander.

II. By the following reasoning, the fact that we are selfish can sometimes relieve us from an obligation to help others:

> May we perform a good deed that imposes a cost on others only if we would be willing to pay that cost ourselves if we were in a position to do so? Suppose a bystander can save five people by turning a trolley at the cost of a minor injury to someone else. Suppose too that the bystander is so selfish that he would not be willing to save the five if he were the

one to suffer the minor injury. It is still permissible for the bystander to save the five by turning the trolley at the cost of a minor injury to someone else. We need not, therefore, always be willing to pay the costs of our good deeds in order for them to be permissible.

Here is one possible reconstruction of the argument:

1. Suppose a bystander can save five people by turning a trolley at the cost of a minor injury to someone else.
2. Suppose that the bystander is so selfish that he would not be willing to save the five if he were the one to suffer the minor injury.
3. If we may perform a good deed that imposes a cost on others only if we would be willing to pay that cost ourselves if we were in a position to do so, then it is wrong for the bystander to save the five by turning the trolley at the cost of a minor injury to someone else.
5. It is not wrong for the bystander to do so.
6. Therefore, it is not the case that we may perform a good deed that imposes a cost on others only if we would be willing to pay that cost ourselves if we were in a position to do so.

Chapter 12.1:

I. Aquinas argues that all acts of virtue are prescribed by the natural law:

> [T]here is in every man a natural inclination to act according to reason; and this to act according to virtue. Consequently, considered, thus, all the acts of the virtues are prescribed by the natural law, since each one's reason naturally dictates him to act virtuously. (page 244)

Here is one possible reconstruction of the argument:

1. We have a natural inclination to act according to reason.
2. To act in accord with reason is to act in accord with virtue.
3. Therefore, we have a natural inclination to act in accord with virtue.

II. The following reasoning concerns the connection between morality and the human nature:

> The difference between right and wrong is the difference between what does and does not promote the welfare of human beings. Human beings have a welfare to promote only if they have some natural end or purpose relative to which their welfare is defined. There is, therefore, a difference between right and wrong only if human beings have some natural end or purpose.

Here is one possible reconstruction of the argument:

1. The difference between right and wrong is the difference between what does and does not promote the good of human beings.
2. There is a difference between right and wrong only if human beings have a good.
3. Human beings have a good only if they have some natural end or purpose relative to which that good is defined.
3. Therefore, there is a difference between right and wrong only if human beings have some natural end or purpose.

Chapter 12.2:

I. Gomez-Lobo presents the following argument with regard to the goodness of human life:

> If we have reason to agree that G is intrinsically good and that D, E and F are neither extrinsically nor instrumentally conducive to G but are internal constituents of G, we also have reason to think that they are intrinsically valuable. We all doubtless agree that happiness or the good life is the ultimate worthwhile thing—something that we value not because it will lead to something else but because it is good in itself. Surely life is not external or instrumental to the good life. . . . Life, then—as the key ingredient of the good life (though not the only one)—is worth having for its own sake. (page 250)

Here is one possible reconstruction of the argument:

1. If G is intrinsically good and D is neither extrinsically nor instrumentally conducive to G but an internal constituent of G, then D is intrinsically good.
2. The good life is intrinsically good and life is neither extrinsically nor instrumentally

conducive to the good life but an internal constituent of it.

3. Therefore, life is intrinsically good.

II. To what extent do variations in natural abilities result in variations in how good a life different people can have?

All other things being equal, someone with severe mental disabilities is not as capable of experiencing all the basic human goods as someone without those disabilities. A necessary condition for human flourishing is experiencing basic human goods. Therefore, all other things being equal, someone with severe mental disabilities is not able to have as flourishing a human existence as someone without those disabilities. And since a life is good only to the extent that it is flourishing, all other things being equal, someone with severe mental disabilities will not have as good a life as someone without those disabilities.

Here is one possible reconstruction of the argument:

1. All other things being equal, someone with severe mental disabilities is not as capable of experiencing all the basic human goods as someone without those disabilities.
2. If one person is not as capable of experiencing all the basic human goods as another, then the one is not able to have as flourishing a human existence as the other.
3. Therefore, all other things being equal, someone with severe mental disabilities is not able to have as flourishing a human existence as someone without those disabilities.
4. How good a life someone has is determined by how flourishing a human existence she has.
5. Therefore, all other things being equal, someone with severe mental disabilities is not able to have as good a life as someone without those disabilities.

Chapter 12.3:
I. The following argument concerns how our motives determine the moral worth of our actions:

If we happen to hit the center of a target when actually trying to do something else (e.g., we are instead trying to show how high our arrow can fly), our

hitting the target's center is an accident. We don't deserve any credit as an archer for targets we hit accidentally. Analogously, if we happen to honor our moral obligations when actually trying to do something else, we honor our moral obligation by accident, and we don't deserve any credit as moral agents for obligations we honor by accident. Only acts done with a good will count to our credit as moral agents.

Here is one possible reconstruction of the argument:

1. Archers who hit a target's center while trying to do something else hit the target's center by accident.
2. Those who honor their moral obligations while trying to do something else honor their moral obligations by accident.
3. Archers who hit a target's center by accident do not deserve any credit for hitting the center.
4. Therefore, those who honor their moral obligations by accident do not deserve any credit for honoring them.

II. Kant argues that there is only one categorical imperative:

But if I think of a categorical imperative, I know right away what it contains. For since this imperative contains, besides the law, only the necessity that the maxim conform to this law, while the law, as we have seen, contains no conditions limiting it, there is nothing left over to which the maxim of action should conform except the universality of a law as such; and it is only this conformity that the imperative asserts to be necessary. There is therefore only one categorical imperative and it is this: "Act only on that maxim by which you can at the same time will that it should become a universal law." (page 267)

Here is one possible reconstruction of his argument:

1. If an imperative is categorical, then it requires only that our maxim conform to the universality of law.
2. To require that our maxim conform to the universality of law is to require that we be able to will that it should become a universal law.

3. If an imperative is categorical, then it requires only that we can will that our maxim should become a universal law.

4. Therefore, if an imperative is categorical, it is the imperative, 'Act only on that maxim by which you can at the same time will that it should become a universal law.'

Chapter 12.4:

I. Here is the text from Ross:

> The essential defect of the "ideal utilitarian" theory is that it ignores, or at least does not do full justice to, the highly personal character of duty. If the only duty is to produce the maximum amount of good, the question who is to have the good—whether it is myself, or my benefactor, or a person to whom I have made a promise to confer good on him, or a mere fellow man to whom I stand in no special relationship—should make no difference to my having a duty to produce that good. But we are all in fact sure that it makes a vast difference. (page 273)

Here is one possible reconstruction of the argument:

1. If the "ideal utilitarian" theory is true, then our only moral duty is to produce the maximum amount of good.

2. If our only moral duty is to produce the maximum amount of good, then it never morally matters for whom we produce the good.

3. It sometimes does morally matter for whom we produce some good.

4. Therefore, the "ideal utilitarian" theory is false.

II. Here is the reasoning of one objection to Ross' theory:

> According to the theory of *prima facie* duties what makes a right act right is the fact that it is the most stringent of our various, perhaps competing, *prima facie* duties. But the theory does not go on to explain what makes one *prima facie* duty more stringent than another. Without such an explanation the theory does not fully explain what makes right acts right.

Here is one possible reconstruction of the argument:

1. The theory of *prima facie* duties explains what makes right acts right in terms of one

prima facie duty being more stringent than others.

2. If the theory of *prima facie* duties explains what makes right acts right in terms of one *prima facie* duty being more stringent than others, then it gives a full explanation only if it also explains what makes one *prima facie* duty more stringent than others.

3. The theory of *prima facie* duties does not explain what makes one *prima facie* duty more stringent than others.

4. Therefore, the theory of *prima facie* duties does not fully explain what makes right acts right.

Chapter 12.5:

I. An argument that Rawls' defense of his two principles of justice does not show them to be correct:

> That Rawls' principles of justice characterize our considered judgments of justice in reflective equilibrium indicates that they capture our sense of justice. Analogously, that the members of some culture adopt a particular moral code upon consideration indicates that the moral code captures their general sense of morality. Yet, that that code captures their general sense of morality does not justify them in concluding that it is correct, especially given that other cultures adopt different codes upon consideration. So too, that Rawls' principles capture our sense of justice does not justify us in concluding that they are correct.

Here is one possible reconstruction of the argument:

1. That Rawls' principles of justice characterize our considered judgments of justice in reflective equilibrium indicates that they capture our sense of justice.

2. That the members of a culture adopt a particular moral code upon consideration indicates that the moral code captures their general sense of morality.

3. That the code captures the culture's general sense of morality does not justify those in the culture in concluding that it is correct.

4. Therefore, by analogy, that Rawls' principles of justice capture our sense of justice does not justify us in concluding that they are correct.

II. Rawls responds to the objection that the outcome of the original position choice situation is irrelevant to the justification of principles of justice because the original position is completely hypothetical:

> The answer is that the conditions embodied in the description of the original position are ones we do in fact accept. Or if we do not, then perhaps we can be persuaded to do so by philosophical reflection. . . . These conditions express what we are prepared to regard as limits on fair terms of social cooperation. (page 285)

Here is one possible reconstruction of his argument:

1. The conditions that define the original position are ones we accept or at least would accept upon reflection as fair conditions on the choice of principles of justice by which to organize our society.
2. That particular principles of justice would be chosen by people under conditions we accept or would accept on reflection as fair conditions on the choice of principles of justice by which to organize our society is a relevant consideration in support of those principles.
3. Therefore, that principles of justice would be chosen under the conditions that define the original position is a relevant consideration in support of those principles.

Chapter 12.6:

I. According to the following argument, the contractual model of social relations is clearly unsuitable for understanding the relation between mothering persons and children:

> It stretches credulity even further than most philosophers can tolerate to imagine babies as little rational contractors contracting with their mothers for care. . . [O]ne cannot imagine hypothetical babies contracting either. And mothering persons, in their care of children, demonstrate hardly any of the 'trucking' or trading instinct claimed by Adam Smith to be the *most* characteristic aspect of human nature. (page 297)

Here is one possible reconstruction of the argument:

1. There are no, even hypothetical, conditions in which children are rational contractors.
2. Mothering persons do not relate to their children as traders.
3. If children are not rational contractors, even hypothetically, and mothering persons do not relate to their children as traders, then the contractual model of social relations does not apply to the relation between mothering persons and their children.
4. Therefore, the contractual model does not apply to the relation between mothering persons and their children.

II. The following argument attempts to show that the contractual model of social relations ignores important moral relations between persons:

> Harmony, love, and cooperation cannot be broken down into individual benefits or burdens. They are goals we ought to share and relations *between* persons. And although the degree of their intensity may be different, many and various relations *between* persons are important also at the level of communities and societies. We can consider, of a society, whether the relations between its members are trusting and mutually supportive, or suspicious and hostile. To focus only on contractual relations and the gains and losses of individuals obscures these often more important relational aspects of societies. (pages 298–299)

Here is one possible reconstruction of the argument:

1. Many important relations between individuals in society have moral aspects that are not captured in terms of the gains and losses of individuals, e.g., they involve trust or mutual support.
2. The contract model of social relations obscures these important moral aspects of social relations.
3. If a model obscures important moral features, then it is defective.
4. Therefore, the contract model of morality is defective.

Chapter 13.1:

I. The text from Aristotle:

> . . .the chief good is evidently something final. . . . we call final without qualification that which is

always desirable in itself and never for the sake of something else. Now such a thing happiness, above all else, is held to be; for this we choose always for itself and never for the sake of something else, but honour, pleasure, reason, and every virtue we choose indeed for themselves (for if nothing resulted from them we should still choose each of them), but we choose them also for the sake of happiness, judging that through them we shall be happy. (page 311)

Here is one possible reconstruction of the argument:

1. The chief good of mankind is something final without qualification.
2. If something is always desirable in itself and never for the sake of something else, then it is final without qualification.
3. Only happiness is desirable in itself and never for the sake of something else.
4. Therefore, only happiness is final without qualification.
5. Therefore, happiness is the chief good of mankind.

II. The text from Aristotle:

Presumably, however, to say that happiness is the chief good seems a platitude, and a clearer account of what it is is still desired. This might perhaps be given, if we could first ascertain the function of man. . . .What then can this be? Life seems to belong even to plants, but we are seeking what is peculiar to man. Let us exclude, therefore, the life of nutrition and growth. Next there would be a life of perception, but it also seems to be shared even by the horse, the ox, and every animal. There remains, then, an active life of the element that has rational principle. (page x)

Here is one possible reconstruction of the argument:

1. Humankind's function is either to live or to perceive or to behave rationally.
2. It is not merely to live (for this is shared with plants).
3. It is not merely to perceive (for this is shared with non-human animals).
4. Therefore, humankind's function is to behave rationally.

Chapter 13.2:

I. The text from Hursthouse:

For a start, [Aristotle] tells us that [*eudaimonia*] is what we all want to get in life (or get out of it); what we are all aiming at, ultimately (1094a1-26); the way we all want to be. And we all agree in one sense about what it consists in, namely, living well or faring well. . .What do we say about success and prospering? Well, 'successful' and 'prosperous' have a materialistic sense in which they connote wealth and power; when we use them in this way it is obvious to us (a) that one can be happy and count oneself as fortunate without them and (b) that they do not necessarily bring with them happiness and the good fortune of loyal friends, loving relationships, the joys of art and learning and so on. So many of us will say that (material) success and prosperity is not what we want; that having it doesn't amount to faring well. (page 321)

Here is one possible reconstruction of the argument:

1. Materialistic success is not necessary for living well.
2. Materialistic success is not sufficient for living well.
3. If something is neither necessary nor sufficient for living well, then it is not constitutive of living well.
4. Therefore, materialistic success is not constitutive of living well.
5. *Eudaimonia* consists in living well.
6. Therefore, *eudaimonia* is not constituted by materialistic success.

II. The text from Hursthouse:

But the obstacle may be surmounted by looking carefully at the answer Aristotle gives to this question that apparently has nothing to do with ethics. For his answer is: "If you want to flourish/be happy/successful you should acquire and exercise the virtues—courage, temperance, liberality, patience, truthfulness, friendship, justice. . ." Or, as we might say, be a morally virtuous person. (page 322)

Here is one possible reconstruction of the argument:

1. It is in our best interest to live the good life.

2. If one has an interest in living the good life, one should acquire and cultivate the moral virtues.

3. Therefore, it is in our best interest to acquire and cultivate the moral virtues.

Chapter 13.3:

I. The text from Wolf:

. . .it is generally assumed that one ought to be as morally good as possible and that what limits there are to morality's hold on us are set by features of human nature of which we ought not to be proud. If, as I believe, the ideals that are derivable from common sense and philosophically popular moral theories do not support these assumptions, then something has to change. Either we must change our moral theories in ways that will make them yield more palatable ideals, or, as I shall argue, we must change our conception of what is involved in affirming a moral theory. (pages 330–331)

Here is one possible reconstruction of the argument:

1. One ought to be as morally good as possible.
2. If the ideals from common sense and philosophically popular moral theories are correct, then it is not true that one ought to be as morally good as possible.
3. Therefore, <u>either</u> the ideals from common sense and philosophically popular moral theories are mistaken <u>or</u> else it is not true that one ought to be as morally good as possible.

II. The text from Wolf:

The fact that the moral saint would be without qualities which we have and which, indeed, we like to have, does not in itself provide reason to condemn the ideal of the moral saint. The fact that some of these qualities are good qualities, however, and that they are qualities we ought to like, does provide reason to discourage this ideal and to offer others in its place. In other words, some of the qualities the moral saint necessarily lacks are virtues, albeit nonmoral virtues, in the unsaintly characters who have them. . .Finally, if we think that it is as good, or even better for a person to strive for one of those [non-moral] ideals than it is for him or her

to strive for and realize the ideal of the moral saint, we express a conviction that it is good not to be a moral saint. (page 334)

Here is one possible reconstruction of the argument:

1. If it is ever good to strive for non-moral virtues, then it is good not to be a moral saint.
2. It is often good to strive for non-moral virtues.
3. Therefore, it is good not to be a moral saint.

Chapter 13.4:

I. The text from Friedman:

If Kohlberg's dilemma can indeed be resolved through impartial considerations of justice and rights, then the solution to the dilemma should not depend upon the existence of any special relationship between the person who is dying of cancer and the person who might steal the drug. I suggest, however, that the conviction that many of us have, that Heinz should steal the drug for his nameless wife in the original dilemma, rests at least in part on our notion of responsibilities arising out of the sort of special relationship that marriage is supposed to be. (page 345)

Here is one possible reconstruction of the argument:

1. If Kohlberg's dilemma can be resolved through impartial considerations of justice and rights, then the existence of special relationships between the parties is morally irrelevant.
2. But the existence of special relationships is relevant to resolving the dilemma.
3. Therefore, the dilemma cannot be resolved through impartial considerations of justice and rights.

II. The paraphrased argument:

Morality is based on a prescriptivist conception of judgment (i.e., a system that will generate universalizable ought claims that apply to all moral agents regardless of situational facts). And since justice is the attempt to treat all individuals fairly regardless of situational fact, justice is the primary moral concept.

Here is one possible reconstruction of the argument:

1. The primary goal of morality is to provide rules for treating all individuals fairly regardless of situational fact.
2. Justice is treating all individuals fairly regardless of situational fact.
3. Therefore, justice is the primary goal of morality.

Chapter 13.5:

I. Held claims that dominant moral theories, such as Kantianism and utilitarianism, employ a concept of a person that limits their application:

Dominant moral theories, such as Kantianism and utilitarianism, conceive of persons as rational, autonomous or self-interested individuals. This conception of a person may be suitable for understanding the moral dimensions of legal, political or economic interactions between strangers, but it is not suitable for understanding the moral dimensions of interactions between interconnected persons in the context of the family and friendships. The dominant moral theories are, therefore, unable to give an adequate account of the moral dimensions of interactions between persons in such contexts and are limited in their application.

Here is one possible reconstruction of the argument:

1. Dominant moral theories conceive of persons as rational, autonomous or self-interested individuals.
2. This conception of persons does not capture the moral dimensions of interactions between persons in the context of the family and friendships.
3. If dominant moral theories use a concept of persons that does not capture the moral dimensions of interactions between persons in the context of the family and friendships, then those theories are limited in their application.
4. Therefore, dominant moral theories are limited in their application.

II. As Held notes, the ethics of care is sometimes criticized for not being definitive enough:

While the ethics of care directs our attention to moral considerations that may well be overlooked by such theories as Kantianism and utilitarianism, it does not provide us with any principles that determine the right thing to do when these and other moral considerations conflict. As a result, it does not provide an adequate answer to the primary question of normative ethics: What makes right acts right?

Here is one possible reconstruction of the argument:

1. A correct ethical theory will successfully answer the primary question of normative ethics: What makes right acts right?
2. To answer this question successfully, the ethics of care must include principles that determine the right thing to do when the moral considerations it presents conflict.
3. The ethics of care does not include any such principles.
4. Therefore, the ethics of care is not a correct moral theory.

Chapter 14.1:

I. The text from Singer:

Although humans differ as individuals in various ways, there are no differences between the races and sexes as such. From the mere fact that a person is black, or a woman, we cannot infer anything else about that person. This, it may be said, is what is wrong with racism and sexism. (page 374)

Here is one possible reconstruction of the argument:

1. There are no differences between the races and sexes as such.
2. If there are no differences between the races and sexes as such, then members of all races and sexes should be treated equally.
3. Therefore, members of all races and sexes should be treated equally.

II. The paraphrased text:

No matter what the nature of the being, the principle of equality requires that its interests be given equal consideration. And any being who can suffer will have an interest in not suffering. Therefore, the principle of equality requires that any being who can suffer be given equal consideration.

Here is one possible reconstruction of the argument:

1. If a being has interests, then its interests should be given equal consideration with the interests of all other beings.
2. All beings who can suffer have interests.
3. Therefore, all beings who can suffer should be given equal consideration.

Chapter 14.2:

I. The paraphrased text from Taylor:

To say that something has inherent worth is to say that (a) it deserves the consideration of all moral agents and (b) the realization of its good is intrinsically valuable. And according to the principle of moral consideration, every individual living thing is deserving of moral consideration from all moral agents. And according to the principle of intrinsic value, the realization of the good for every individual living thing is intrinsically valuable. Therefore, all living things have inherent worth.

Here is one possible reconstruction of the argument:

1. If something deserves the consideration of all moral agents AND is such that the realization of its good is intrinsically valuable, then that thing has inherent worth.
2. All living things deserve the consideration of all moral agents.
3. All living things are such that the realization of their respective goods is intrinsically valuable.
4. Therefore, all living things have inherent worth.

II. The text from Taylor:

In what sense are humans alleged to be superior to other animals? We are different from them in having certain capacities that they lack. . . .. Such uniquely human characteristics as rational thought, aesthetic creativity, autonomy and self determination, and moral freedom, it might be held, have a higher value than the capacities found in other species. (page 384)

Here is one possible reconstruction of the argument:

1. If one being has capacities with a higher value than the capacities of some other being, the former is superior to the latter.
2. All humans have capacities with a higher value than the capacities of any non-human.
3. Therefore, all humans are superior to any non-human.

Chapter 14.3:

I. The text from Schmidtz:

French perceives a contradiction between the egalitarian principles Taylor officially endorses and the unofficial principles Taylor offers as the real principles by which we should live. Having proclaimed that we are all equal, French asks, what licenses Taylor to say that, in cases of conflict, nonhuman interests can legitimately be sacrificed to vital human interests? (page 391)

Here is one possible reconstruction of the argument:

1. If species egalitarianism is true, then we cannot legitimately sacrifice nonhuman interests for human interests in cases of conflict.
2. But, Taylor himself allows that we CAN legitimately sacrifice nonhuman interests for human interests in cases of conflict.
3. Therefore, either species egalitarianism is false or else it is not true that we can legitimately sacrifice nonhuman interests for human interests in cases of conflict.

II. The text from Schmidtz:

Species egalitarianism is compatible with our having a limited license to kill. What seems far more problematic for species egalitarianism is that it seems to suggest that it makes no difference what we kill. Vegetarians typically think that it is worse to kill a cow than to kill a carrot. Are they wrong? Yes, according to species egalitarianism. In this respect, species egalitarianism cannot be right. (page 391)

Here is one possible reconstruction of the argument:

1. If species egalitarianism is true, then it is not worse to kill a cow than a carrot.

2. But it IS worse to kill a cow than a carrot.

3. Therefore, species egalitarianism is false.

Chapter 15.1:

I. Here is the text from Marquis:

> The FLO account of the wrongness of killing is correct because it explains why we believe that killing is one of the worst crimes. My being killed deprives me of more than does my being robbed or beaten or harmed in some other way because my being killed deprives me of all of the value of my future, not merely part of it. (page 403)

Here is one possible reconstruction of the argument:

1. The FLO account is the best explanation of the fact that killing another human is among the worst crimes.

2. If some account is the best explanation of some agreed-upon data, then that account is likely to be correct.

3. Therefore, it is likely that the FLO account is correct.

II. Here is the text from Marquis:

> If the FLO account is the correct theory of the wrongness of killing, then because abortion involves killing fetuses and fetuses have FLOs for exactly the same reasons that infants have FLOs, abortion is presumptively seriously immoral. (page 404)

Here is one possible reconstruction of the argument:

1. Abortion involves killing fetuses.

2. Fetuses have FLOs.

3. If the FLO account is the correct, then it is presumptively seriously immoral to kill a being with a FLO.

4. Therefore, if the FLO account is correct, abortion is presumptively seriously immoral.

5. The FLO account IS correct (suppressed assumption argued for elsewhere in the paper).

6. Therefore, abortion is presumptively seriously immoral.

Chapter 15.2:

I. The text from Warren:

> . . .the traditional argument that since (1) it is wrong to kill innocent human beings, and (2) fetuses are innocent human beings, then (3) it is wrong to kill fetuses. (pages 409–410)

Here is one possible reconstruction of the argument:

1. It is wrong to kill innocent human beings.

2. All fetuses are innocent human beings.

3. Therefore, it is wrong to kill any fetus.

4. All abortions kill a fetus (suppressed premise).

5. Therefore, all abortions are wrong (suppressed conclusion).

II. The text from Warren:

> All we need to claim, to demonstrate that a fetus is not a person, is that any being which satisfies none of (1)–(5) is certainly not a person. . . . it seems safe to say that [the fetus] is not fully conscious, in the way that an infant of a few months is, and that it cannot reason, or communicate messages of indefinitely many sorts, does not engage in self-motivated activity, and has no self-awareness. Thus, in the relevant respects, a fetus, even a fully developed one, is considerably less personlike than is the average mature mammal, indeed the average fish. (page 411)

Here is one possible reconstruction of the argument:

1. If a being fails to satisfy ANY of the five central traits of personhood, then that being is not a person.

2. A fetus fails to satisfy ANY of the five central traits of personhood.

3. Therefore, a fetus is not a person.

Chapter 15.3:

I. The text from Thomson:

> Every person has a right to life. So the fetus has a right to life. No doubt the mother has a right to decide what shall happen in and to her body; everyone would grant that. But surely a person's right to life is stronger and more stringent than the mother's right to decide what happens in and to her body, and so outweighs it. So the fetus may not be killed; an abortion may not be performed. (page 418)

Here is one possible reconstruction of the argument:

1. All persons have a right to life.

2. The fetus is a person.

3. Therefore, the fetus has a right to life.
4. In cases of conflict between the right to life and the right to one's body, we ought not violate the right to life.
5. In cases of abortion, the fetus' right to life conflicts with the mother's right to her body.
6. Therefore, we ought not violate the fetus' right to life.

II. The text from Thomson:

> If directly killing an innocent person is murder, and thus is impermissible, then the mother's directly killing the innocent person inside her is murder, and thus is impermissible. (page 419)

Here is one possible reconstruction of the argument:

1. If directly killing an innocent person is murder, then the mother's directly killing the innocent person inside her is murder.
2. Directly killing an innocent person *is* murder.
3. Therefore the mother's directly killing the innocent person inside her is murder.
4. Murder is impermissible.
5. Therefore, it is impermissible for the mother to directly kill the innocent person insider her.

Chapter 15.4:

I. The text from Cates:

> This analysis is governed by a conviction that attempting to be respectful and compassionate is a necessary condition for understanding the moral dimensions of abortion and making appropriate evaluations of particular abortion decisions. (page 429)

Here is one possible reconstruction of the argument:

1. A person can understand the moral dimensions of abortion and make appropriate evaluations of a particular abortion decision only if that person attempts to be respectful and compassionate.
2. Some people do not attempt to be respectful and compassionate when considering the issue of abortion (assumption from argument exercise).

3. Therefore, those people cannot understand the moral dimensions of abortion or make appropriate evaluations of particular abortion decisions.

II. The text from Cates:

> To focus on the matter of informed consent, respect and compassion require that we ponder what it is for a given woman to understand an act of abortion and its possible consequences for her life. Understanding the act may include understanding its moral dimensions, and reaching moral understanding may include feeling and reflecting upon certain emotions like grief and guilt. (page 436)

Here is one possible reconstruction of the argument:

1. An abortion is morally permissible only if the woman has given informed consent.
2. A woman can give informed consent only if she has a reasonable moral understanding of the situation.
3. A woman has a reasonable moral understanding of the situation only if she has felt and reflected on her emotions regarding the situation.
4. Therefore, an abortion is morally permissible only if the woman has felt and reflected on her emotions regarding the situation.

Chapter 16.1:

I. Here is the text from Barry:

> I cannot see that the principle [of equal rights] has any direct intergenerational application. . . . However, the present generation may be able to affect the likelihood that there will be equal rights in the future. Thus, it seems to be a robust generalization that rights suffer at times when large challenges to a system demand rapid and coordinated responses. . . . The more environmental stress we leave our successors to cope with, therefore, the poorer prospects for equal rights. (page 451)

Here is one possible reconstruction of the argument:

1. The environmental stress caused by the current generation makes it likely that

future generations will have make rapid and coordinated responses in order to cope with environmental challenges.

2. It is likely that these rapid and coordinated responses will result in a decreased exercise of individual rights for future generations.

3. Therefore, the environmental stress caused by the current generation makes it likely that future generations will result in a decreased exercise of individual rights for future generations.

4. It is unjust for the current generation to do something that will result in a decreased exercise of individual rights for future generations (this is a version of the equal rights principle).

5. Therefore, it is unjust for the current generation to cause environmental stress.

II. Here is the text from Barry:

> People in the future can scarcely be held responsible for the physical conditions they inherit, so it would seem that it is unjust if people in the future are worse off in this respect than we are. (page 451)

Here is one possible reconstruction of the argument:

1. Future generations are not responsible for the physical conditions they inherit.

2. If future generations are not responsible for the physical conditions they inherit, then justice requires that those who are responsible leave them no worse than they were.

3. Therefore, justice requires that those who are responsible for the physical conditions of future generations leave them no worse than they were.

Chapter 16.2:

I. Here is the text from Hill:

> Some may be tempted to seek an explanation [of our moral discomfort] by appeal to the interests, or even the rights, of plants. . .The temptation to make such a reply is understandable if one assumes that all moral questions are exclusively concerned with whether acts are right or wrong, and this, in turn, is determined entirely by how the acts impinge on the

rights and interests of those directly affected. On this assumption, if there is cause for moral concern, some right or interest has been neglected and if the rights and interests of human beings and animals have already been taken into account, then there must be some other pertinent interests, for example, those of plants. (page 457)

Here is one possible reconstruction of the argument:

1. All moral concerns are about the rightness and wrongness of actions.

2. An action is wrong if and only if it negatively affects the rights and interests of some beings.

3. In the case of destroying nonsentient environments without sentient creatures, the only possible rights and interests affected are those of plants.

4. Therefore, if there is a moral concern about the destruction of nonsentient environments, it must be because of its effects on the interests of plants.

II. Here is the text from Hill:

> . . .the conclusion that plants have rights or morally relevant interests is surely untenable. We do speak of what is "good for" plants, and they can "thrive" and also be "killed." But this does not imply that they have "interests" in any morally relevant sense. Some people apparently believe that plants grow better if we talk to them, but the idea that the plants suffer and enjoy, desire and dislike, etc. is clearly outside of the range of both common sense and scientific belief. (page 457)

Here is one possible reconstruction of the argument:

1. Something has morally relevant interests only if it can suffer, enjoy, desire, dislike, etc. (suppressed assumption).

2. Plants cannot suffer, enjoy, desire, dislike, etc.

3. Therefore, plants do not have morally relevant interests.

Chapter 16.3:

I. The text from Sagoff:

> Do we consume too much? To some, the answer is self-evident. If there is only so much food, timber,

petroleum, and other material to go around, the more we consume, the less must be available for others. The global economy cannot grow indefinitely on a finite planet. As populations increase and economies expand, natural resources must be depleted; prices will rise, and humanity—especially the poor and future generations at all income levels—will suffer. (page 467)

Here is one possible reconstruction of the argument:

1. If the current rate of consumption will cause the poor and future generations to suffer, then we consume too much (i.e. the current level of consumption is morally indefensible).
2. Given the fact that the planet's resources are finite, it is true that the current rate of consumption will cause the poor and future generations to suffer.
3. Therefore, we consume too much (i.e., the current level of consumption is morally indefensible).

II. The text from Sagoff:

Do we consume too much? . . .although we must satisfy basic needs, *a good life is not one devoted to amassing material possessions*; what we own comes to own us, keeping us from fulfilling commitments that give meaning to life, such as those to family, friends, and faith. The appreciation of nature also deepens our lives. As we consume more, however, we are more likely to transform the natural world, so that less of it will remain for us to learn from, communicate with, and appreciate. (page 467)

Here is one possible reconstruction of the argument:

1. If our level of consumption is likely to keep us from fulfilling commitments that give meaning to life and appreciating nature, then we consume too much (i.e., the current level of consumption is morally indefensible).
2. Our level of consumption is likely to keep us from fulfilling commitments that give meaning to life and appreciating nature.
3. Therefore, we consume too much (i.e., the current level of consumption is morally indefensible).

Chapter 16.4:

The text from Milbrath:

A key aspect of my argument, then, is that continuing growth in human population and material consumption is not desirable (we do not want to go there) and very likely not possible. (page 481)

Here is one possible reconstruction of the argument:

1. Continued growth both in population and consumption are neither desirable nor possible.
2. If something is neither desirable nor possible, then it is inimical to a high quality of living.
3. Therefore, continued growth both in population and consumption are inimical to a high quality of living.

II. The text from Milbrath:

I can imagine a biocommunity thriving well without any human members, but I cannot imagine human members thriving without a well-functioning biocommunity. . .Therefore, individuals desiring quality of life must give top priority to protection and preservation of their biocommunity (their ecosystem). (page 482)

Here is one possible reconstruction of the argument:

1. If it is possible for X to thrive without Y but impossible for Y to thrive without X, then—when X and Y's interests conflict—X should be protected and preserved over Y.
2. It is possible for the biocommunity to thrive without humans but impossible for humans to thrive without the biocommunity.
3. Therefore, when the biocommunity and human interests conflict—the biocommunity should be protected and preserved over the interests of humans.

Chapter 17.1:

I. Here is the text from Singer:

. . .if everyone in circumstances like mine gave £5 to the Bengal Relief Fund, there would be enough to provide food, shelter, and medical care for the refugees; there is no reason why I should give more than anyone else in the same circumstances as I am; therefore, I have no obligation to give more than £5. (page 492)

Here is one possible reconstruction of the argument:

1. If everyone in circumstances like mine gave £5 to the Bengal Relief Fund, there would be enough to provide food, shelter, and medical care for the refugees.
2. I am morally obligated to give only enough to provide food, shelter, and medical care for the refugees.
3. Therefore, I am morally obligated to give only £5.
    Singer's criticism: the argument is invalid. The conclusion doesn't follow from the premises. What does follow from the premises is this conclusion: if everyone in circumstances like mine gave £5 to the Bengal Relief Fund, then I am morally obligated to give only £5.

II. Here is the text from Singer:

I could even as far as the application of my argument to the Bengal emergency is concerned, qualify the point so as to make it: if it is in our power to prevent something very bad from happening, without thereby sacrificing anything morally significant, we ought, morally, to do it. An application of this principle is as follows: if I am walking past a shallow pond and see a child drowning in it, I ought to wade in and pull the child out. This will mean getting my clothes muddy, but this is insignificant, while the death of the child would presumably be a very bad thing. (pages 491–492)

Here is one possible reconstruction of the argument:

1. Getting my clothes muddy is morally insignificant.
2. The child's death would be a very bad thing.
3. I morally ought to save the child drowning in the pond.
4. The best explanation of facts 1–3 is that anytime it is in our power to prevent something very bad from happening, without thereby sacrificing anything morally significant, we ought, morally, to do it.
5. Therefore, anytime it is in our power to prevent something very bad from happening, without thereby sacrificing anything morally significant, we ought, morally, to do it.

Chapter 17.2:

I. The text from Arthur:

If it is in our power to prevent something bad from happening, without thereby sacrificing anything of comparable moral importance, we ought, morally, to do it. (page 498)
    One way we can help others is by giving away body parts. While your life may be shortened by the loss of a kidney or less enjoyable if lived with only one eye, those cases are probably not comparable to the loss experienced by a person who will die without a kidney transplant or who is totally blind. . .It seems clear, however, that our code does not require such heroism; you are entitled to your second eye and kidney. (page 499)

Here is one possible reconstruction of the argument:

1. If the Greater Moral Evil Principle is true, then we are sometimes morally required to give away body parts such as eyes or kidneys.
2. But it is not true that we are never morally required to give away our eyes or kidneys.
3. Therefore, the Greater Moral Evil Principle is false.

II. The text from Arthur:

Positive rights, however, are rights to receive some benefit. By contracting to page wages, employers acquire the duty to pay the employees who work for them; if the employer backs out of the deal, the employees' positive right to receive a paycheck is violated. . ...The positive rights you may have are not natural in that sense; they arise because others have promised, agreed, or contracted to do something. (page 499)

Here is one possible reconstruction of the argument:

1. If people who are dying from starvation have a right to assistance from us, then they have a positive right against us.
2. If they have a positive right against us, then we must have promised, agreed, or contracted to do something for them.
3. But we have not promised, agreed, or contracted to do something for those who are dying from starvation (suppressed premise).
4. Therefore, the people who are dying from starvation do not have a right to assistance from us.

Chapter 17.3:

I. The text from Narveson:

> If I lock you in a room with no food and don't let you out, I have murdered you. If group A burns the crops of group B, it has slaughtered the Bs. There is no genuine issue about such cases. It is wrong to kill innocent people, and one way of killing them is as eligible for condemnation as any other. (page 509)

Here is one possible reconstruction of the argument:

1. Any way of killing innocent people is wrong.
2. Actively starving people by eliminating their access to food is one way of killing innocent people.
3. Therefore, actively starving people is wrong.

II. The text from Narveson:

> Rather than insisting, with threats to back it up, that I help someone for whose projects and purposes I have no sympathy whatever, let us all agree to respect each other's pursuits. We'll agree to let each person live as that person sees fit, with only our bumpings into each other being subject to public control. To do this, we need to draw a sort of line around each person and insist that others not cross that line without the permission of the occupant. . .Enforced feeding of the starving, however, does cross the line, invading the farmer or the merchant, forcing him to part with some of his hard-earned produce and give it without compensation to others. That, says the advocate of liberty, is theft, not charity. (page 511)

Here is one possible reconstruction of the argument:

1. Only actions or omissions that "cross the line" into the personal space of others are rightly enforceable.
2. My failure to feed the starving does not "cross the line" into the personal space of others.
3. Therefore, my failure to feed the starving is not rightly enforceable.
4. If an action is not rightly enforceable, then it is not unjust. (suppressed premise from earlier definition of justice)
5. Therefore, my failure to feed the starving is not unjust.

Chapter 18.1:

I. Walzer provides several considerations to show that every act of terrorism is a wrongful act.

> The victims of a terrorist attack are third parties, innocent bystanders; there is no special reason for attacking them; anyone else within a large class of (unrelated) people will do as well. The attack is directed indiscriminately against the entire class . . . [Terrorism is] not only the killing of innocent people but also the intrusion of fear into everyday life, the violation of private purposes, the insecurity of public spaces, the endless coerciveness of precaution. . . . Terrorism is the work of visible hands; it is an organizational project, a strategic choice, a conspiracy to murder and intimidate. . . [T]errorism is random, degrading and frightening. (page 520)

Here is one possible reconstruction of the argument:

1. Acts of terrorism, by their very nature, involve the intentional and indiscriminate killing and injuring of innocent people, the intentional violation of private purposes, the intentional injection of fear and insecurity into everyday life, and the intended result of coercive precautionary measures.
2. Any acts of this sort are *prima facie* morally wrong in a way that no other moral considerations can outweigh.
3. If an act is *prima facie* morally wrong and in a way that no other moral considerations outweigh, then it is morally wrong.

5. Therefore, any acts of terrorism are morally wrong.

II. Here is a consequentialist argument for the conclusion that terrorism is sometimes morally permissible:

> Terrorism is sometimes justified, for it sometimes achieves "the ends of the oppressed" where those ends "could not have been achieved through any other, less wrongful, means."

Here is one possible reconstruction of the argument:

1. If a practice achieves the good of ending substantial political oppression and that good could not have been achieved by any morally preferable practice, then the practice is morally permissible.
2. Terrorism sometimes ends substantial political oppression in situations where that good cannot be achieved by any morally preferable practice.
3. Therefore, terrorism is sometimes morally permissible.

Chapter 18.2:

I. Here is an argument against terrorism based on the proportionality principle:

> A prominent reason for thinking that terrorism is distinctively wrong is that terrorists, unlike combatants who comply with the laws of war, do not acknowledge the moral significance of bearing burdens in order to reduce noncombatant casualties for the sake of the noncombatants themselves. . . Basic respect for the lives of noncombatants seems evidenced . . . by a willingness to bear burdens in order to reduce harm to them. Terrorists . . . do not have this respect for noncombatant lives. (page 530)

Here is one possible interpretation of the argument:

1. Acts of political violence that do not involve basic respect for the lives of noncombatants are morally wrong.
2. Acts of political violence that do not display a willingness to bear burdens in order to reduce harm to noncombatants do not involve basic respect for their lives.

3. Acts of terrorism do not display a willingness to bear burdens in order to reduce harm to noncombatants.
4. Therefore, acts of terrorism are morally wrong.

II. Here is the argument to show that considerations regarding a respect for human lives are insufficient to morally distinguish terrorism from conventional warfare:

> The case of the ANC demonstrates that those who employ terrorism can have and sometimes have had fundamental moral concerns for noncombatants. Such moral concern . . . is overriding neither for terrorists nor for proper combatants. Thus considerations other than proportionality and basic respect for the lives of noncombatants would have to show that terrorism is intrinsically worse than conventional war. (page 531)

Here is one possible interpretation of the argument:

1. Some terrorist groups, such as the ANC, have acted with a fundamental concern for noncombatants.
2. That concern has been no more or less overriding for them than it has been for proper combatants in conventional just warfare.
3. Therefore, with regard to considerations of proportionality and a basic respect for the lives of noncombatants, there need be no difference between terrorists and proper combatants in conventional just warfare.
4. Therefore, such considerations are insufficient to show that terrorism is intrinsically worse than conventional war.

Chapter 18.3:

I. Luban presents an argument in support of the adoption of the hybrid war-law model:

> Terrorists, unlike soldiers in a just war, are neither morally nor politically innocent. . . . They will fight as soldiers when they must, and metamorphose into mass murders when they can. They also aim to kill as many innocent people as possible and cannot be deterred by treats of punishment or the risk of dying in their attack.

They pose a dire threat, and given that threat, it is appropriate to treat them as the hybrid war-law model provides. (page 541)

Here is one possible reconstruction of the argument:

1. Terrorists act as both soldiers and criminals: they fight as soldiers when they must but they aim to kill as many innocent people as they can.
2. The hybrid war-law model recognizes the dual nature of terrorists as both soldiers and criminals.
3. Terrorists also pose a dire threat to our society.
4. Adopting the hybrid war-law model for terrorists is the most effective means by which to meet the dire threat they pose.
5. If the hybrid war-law model recognizes the dual nature of terrorists as soldiers and criminals and is the most effective means by which to meet the dire threat they pose, then we are justified in adopting the hybrid war-law model.
6. Therefore, we are justified in adopting the hybrid war-law model.

II. Luban offers the following objection to the hybrid war-law model:

The model abolishes the rights of potential enemies (and their innocent shields) by fiat—not for reasons of moral or legal principle, but solely because the US does not want them to have rights. The more rights they have, the more risk they pose. But Americans' urgent desire to minimize our risks doesn't make other people's rights disappear. . . . [T]he law model and the war model each comes as a package, with a kind of intellectual integrity. The law model grows out of relationships within states, while the war model arises from relationships between states. Because the law model and war model come as conceptual packages, it is unprincipled to wrench them apart and recombine them simply because it is America's interest to do so. (pages 541–542)

Here is one possible reconstruction of the argument:

1. The provisions in the law model are based on general moral or legal principles concerning

the relations within states; the provisions in the war model are based on general moral or legal principles concerning relations between states.
2. The provisions in the hybrid war-law model are not based on any general moral or legal principles but solely on considerations of national self-interest.
3. Therefore, unlike the law and war models, the hybrid war-law model has no basis in moral or legal principles but only in national self-interest.
4. If the law and war models are each based in moral or legal principles, while the hybrid war-law model has no basis in such principles but only in national self-interest, then we should not adopt the hybrid war-law model in place of the others.
5. Therefore, we should not adopt the hybrid law-war model in place of either the law or war models.

Chapter 19.1:

I. Here is the text from Miller:

Second, the terrorist is in the process of completing his (jointly undertaken) action of murdering thousands of innocent people. . . .To this extent the terrorist is in a different situation from a bystander who happens to know where the bomb is planted but will not reveal its whereabouts. . .rather, the terrorist is more akin to someone in the process of murdering an innocent person, and refusing to refrain from doing so. (page 550)

Here is one possible reconstruction of the argument:

1. It is morally justifiable to use force against someone who is in the process of murdering an innocent victim.
2. In case 2, the captured terrorist is relevantly like someone who is in the process of murdering an innocent victim.
3. Therefore, in case 2, it is morally justifiable to use force against the captured terrorist.

II. Here is the text from Miller:

Let us now turn to another consideration that might be moving those who hold that the police ought not to torture the offenders. The consideration in question is that torture is an absolute moral wrong. On this view, there simply are no real or imaginable circumstances in which torture could be morally justified. This is a hard view to sustain, not the least because being tortured is not necessarily less preferable than being killed, and torturing someone not necessarily morally worse than killing them. Naturally, someone might hold that killing is an absolute moral wrong. . . .[but] the view that killing is an absolute moral wrong is a very implausible one. It would rule out, for example, killing in self-defense. Let us, therefore, set it aside. (page 551)

Here is one possible reconstruction of the argument:

1. If torture is an absolute wrong, then killing is an absolute wrong.
   (Miller defends premise 1 by pointing out that "torturing someone not necessarily morally worse than killing them.")
2. It is implausible that killing is an absolute wrong.
3. Therefore, it is implausible that torture is an absolute wrong.

Chapter 19.2:

I. The text from Hill:

It will be argued in this paper that torture, and more generally, interrogational coercion are never morally permissible. This will be a specific application of a general moral principle that will be proposed:

(P) It is never permissible intentionally to inflict severe pain or severe harm on someone unwilling, unless the pain/harm is intended (i) for their benefit, or (ii) as a punishment, or (iii) as part of the pursuit of a legitimate war, or (iv) to prevent the individual from causing severe pain or severe harm to innocents. (page 555)

Here is one possible reconstruction of the argument:

1. It is never permissible intentionally to torture, unless the pain/harm is intended (i) for their benefit, or (ii) as a punishment, or (iii) as part of the pursuit of a legitimate war, or (iv) to

prevent the individual from causing severe pain or severe harm to innocents.
2. In torture, the pain is not intended for the benefit of the victim.
3. In torture, the pain is not intended as a punishment.
4. In torture, the pain is not part of the pursuit of a legitimate war.
5. In torture, the pain is not intended to prevent the victim from causing sever pain/harm to innocents.
6. Therefore, is never permissible intentionally to torture.

II. The text from Hill:

Withholding and Holding are superficially very similar, but there is one crucial difference: in Holding the terrorist is prevented from performing an action (holding the button down) and in Withholding the terrorist is not prevented from doing anything—instead he is (just) caused to perform an action, the action of pulling the button up. It would seem that this makes a moral difference. Intuitively, it is not permissible to inflict pain in Withholding in order to compel the terrorist to pull the button up, but intuitively it is permissible for pain to be inflicted in Holding in order that the terrorist might be prevented from pushing the button down. (page 556)

Here is one possible reconstruction of the argument:

1. It is not permissible to inflict pain in Withholding.
2. It is permissible to inflict pain in Holding.
3. The only difference between Withholding and Holding is that in the former the actor is causing someone to do something and in the latter the actor is preventing someone from doing something.
4. The best explanation for the data in premises 1–3 is that there is a moral difference between preventing someone from doing something and causing someone to do something.
5. Therefore, there is a moral difference between preventing someone from doing something and causing someone to do something.

Chapter 20.1:

I. Here is the text from Rachels:

> Suppose the doctor agrees to withhold treatment, as the conventional doctrine says he may. The justification for his doing so is that the patient is in terrible agony, and since he is going to die anyway, it would be wrong to prolong his suffering needlessly. (page 564)

Here is one possible reconstruction of the argument:

1. If a patient is in terrible agony and is going to die anyway, it is wrong to prolong his suffering needlessly.
2. In some cases, continuing with medical treatment will prolong the patient's suffering needlessly.
3. Therefore, if a patient is in terrible agony and is going to die anyway, it is permissible to discontinue medical treatment.

II. Here is the text from Rachels:

> Suppose the doctor agrees to withhold treatment, as the conventional doctrine says he may. The justification for his doing so is that the patient is in terrible agony, and since he is going to die anyway, it would be wrong to prolong his suffering needlessly. But now notice this. If one simply withholds treatment, it may take the patient longer to die, and so he may suffer more than he would if more direct action were taken and a lethal injection given. This fact provides strong reason for thinking that, once the initial decision not to prolong his agony has been made, active euthanasia is actually preferable to passive euthanasia, rather than the reverse. (page 564)

Here is one possible reconstruction of the argument:

1. If a patient is in terrible agony and is going to die anyway, it is wrong to prolong his suffering needlessly.
2. In cases where we could end the patient's life directly, withholding medical treatment will prolong a patient's suffering needlessly.
3. Therefore, if a patient is in terrible agony and is going to die anyway, then, in cases where we could end the patient's life directly, merely withholding medical treatment is wrong.

Chapter 20.2:

I. Here is the text from Sullivan:

> Nearly everyone holds that it is sometimes pointless to prolong the process of dying and that in those cases it is morally permissible to let a patient die even though a few hours or days could be salvaged by procedures that would also increase the agonies of the dying. But if it is impossible to defend a general distinction between letting people die and acting to terminate their lives directly, then it would seem that active euthanasia also may be morally permissible. (page 571)

Here is one possible reconstruction of the argument:

1. In some cases, it is morally permissible to let a patient die even when his life could be temporarily prolonged at the cost of his suffering.
2. There is no moral distinction between letting people die and acting to terminate their lives directly.
3. If it is morally permissible to do X, and there is no moral distinction between X and Y, then it is morally permissible to do Y.
4. Therefore, in some cases, it is morally permissible to act to terminate a patient's life directly even when his life could be temporarily prolonged at the cost of his suffering.

II. Here is the text from Sullivan:

> The traditional view is that the intentional termination of human life is impermissible, irrespective of whether this goal is brought about by action or inaction. Is the action aimed at producing a death? Is the termination of life sought, chosen, or planned? Is the intention deadly? If so, the act or omission is wrong. (page 572)

Here is one possible reconstruction of the argument:

1. It is morally wrong to intentionally bring about the death of another human either by action or inaction.

2. Passive euthanasia is intentionally bringing about the death of another human by inaction.
3. Active euthanasia is intentionally bringing about the death of another human by action.
4. Therefore, both passive and active euthanasia are morally wrong.

Chapter 20.3:

I. Here is the text from Hill:

> A fundamental moral principle, one to which any rational being with autonomy would commit himself, is: always act so that you treat humanity (that is, autonomy and rationality), never simply as a means, but always as an end in itself (that is, as something with "unconditional and incomparable worth"). This applies to "humanity" in oneself as well as in others. . . .Suicide (at least for the reasons Kant imagined), is opposed to the principle of humanity as an end in itself. . .because it "throws away" and degrades humanity in oneself. . .Suicide, therefore, is always, or nearly always, wrong. (page 578)

Here is one possible reconstruction of the argument:

1. It is morally wrong to degrade humanity in oneself or others.
2. Suicide always, or nearly always, degrades humanity in oneself.
3. Therefore, suicide is always, or nearly always, morally wrong.

II. Here is the text from Hill:

> Regarding the conclusions concerning suicide. . .Kant's view that suicide is always, or nearly always, contrary to a perfect duty to oneself provokes objections on at least two counts. . .Second, that, because a person cannot violate his own rights, duties *to* oneself, in a strict sense, are impossible. (page 578)

Here is one possible reconstruction of the argument:

1. If suicide is always, or nearly always, wrong, then we must have duties to ourselves not to commit suicide.
2. If we have duties to ourselves not to commit suicide, then it is possible for us to violate our own rights.

3. But it is not possible for us to violate our own rights.
4. Therefore, we do not have duties to ourselves not to commit suicide.
5. Therefore, it is not the case that suicide is always, or nearly always, wrong.

Chapter 20.4:

I. Here is the text from Becker:

> If brain death implies human death, then, by contraposition, human life must imply conscious (brain) life. Now there are clearly segments of our lives in which we are alive but not always conscious. Therefore it is wrong to conclude that a human is dead because he or she lacks consciousness. (page 584)

Here is one possible reconstruction of the argument:

1. If brain death implies human death, then human life implies brain life.
2. But it is not true that human life implies brain life (because some segments of our lives lack consciousness).
3. Therefore, it is not true that brain death implies human death.

II. Here is the text from Becker:

> Iida Tsunesuke expands this view by arguing that "persons are not merely the meaningless 'subjects of rights,' but personalities, 'faces' embodying the possibilities of fulfilling the dreams of their parents or loved ones. . .This argument begs the question of "possibilities," since in the case of brain-dead victims, it is precisely such possibilities which are missing. (page 585)

Here is one possible reconstruction of the argument:

1. A person is alive in the relevant sense as long as it is possible for him to fulfill the dreams of his parents, etc.
2. It is not possible for brain-dead humans to fulfill the dreams of their parents, etc.
3. Therefore, brain-dead humans are not alive in the relevant sense.

Chapter 21.1:

I. Here is Primoratz' argument that death is the only fitting punishment for murder:

> It can be claimed that, simply because we have to be alive if we are to experience and realize any other value at all, there is nothing equivalent to the murderous destruction of a human life except the destruction of the life of the murderer. . . . As long as the murderer is alive, no matter how bad the conditions of his life may be, there are always at least *some* values he can experience and realize. (page 595)

Here is one possible reconstruction of his reasoning:

1. A particular punishment is appropriate for a particular crime only if it inflicts on the criminal a loss that equals the loss the criminal inflicted on his or her victim.
2. In the case of murder, the loss inflicted on the victim includes the inability to ever again experience anything of value.
3. Death is the only penalty that will inflict on the criminal the inability to ever again experience anything of value.
4. Therefore, in the case of murder, death is the only penalty that inflicts on the criminal a loss that equals the loss the criminal inflicted on his or her victim.
5. Therefore, death is the only punishment that is appropriate for the crime of murder.

II. Here is Primoratz's reply to the concern that a murderer's life may not be of equal value to that of his or her victim:

> The modern humanistic and democratic tradition in ethical, social and political thought is based on the idea that all human beings are equal. This finds its legal expression in the principle of equality under the law. If we are not willing to give up this principle, we have to stick to the assumption that, all differences notwithstanding, any two human lives, *qua* human lives, are equally valuable. (page 596)

Here is one possible reconstruction of his reasoning:

1. We should design our legal system so that all human beings are equal under the law.
2. All human beings are equal under the law only if the legal system treats any two human lives, *qua* human lives, as equally valuable.
3. Therefore, we should design our legal system so that it treats any two human lives, *qua* human lives, as equally valuable.

Chapter 21.2:

I. Bedau's considerations against the death penalty include the following:

> A punishment can be an effective deterrent only if it is consistently and promptly applied and only if those likely to commit the crimes for which it is provided are likely to consider seriously the threat of punishment in their deliberations. The death penalty cannot be consistently or promptly applied given current safeguards. Violent criminals often act without premeditation, and those who premeditate often believe they won't get caught. Therefore, the death penalty cannot be an effective deterrent. (pages 601–603)

Here is one possible reconstruction of his argument:

1. The death penalty can be an effective deterrent only if it is consistently and promptly applied.
2. The death penalty cannot be consistently and promptly applied given current safeguards.
3. The death penalty can be an effective deterrent for violent criminals only if they consider it seriously in their deliberations.
4. Violent criminals, who often act without premeditation and in the belief that they won't be caught, don't consider the death penalty seriously in their deliberations.
5. Therefore, given current safeguards, the death penalty cannot be an effective deterrent for violent criminals.

II. Here is an argument concerning the irreparable flaws in the death penalty's application:

> We are not justified in adopting the death penalty. We might be justified in adopting it if we could administer it with an appropriate degree of accuracy and fairness, but we cannot. The required degree of accuracy and fairness increases with a penalty's severity and our inability to rectify mistakes in its

application. The severity of the death penalty and our inability to rectify mistakes in its application distinguish it from imprisonment and require for its justified application a degree of accuracy and fairness that is beyond us.

Here is one possible reconstruction of the argument:

1. We are justified in adopting a penalty only if we can administer it with a degree of accuracy and fairness appropriate to its severity and our ability to rectify mistakes in its application.
2. The severity of the death penalty is so great and our ability to rectify mistakes in its application is so limited as to require a degree of accuracy and fairness it its application that is beyond our ability to achieve.
3. Various forms of imprisonment that are alternatives to the death penalty are moderate enough and our ability to rectify mistakes in their application is great enough that we can apply them with an appropriate degree of accuracy.
4. Therefore, we are not justified in adopting the death penalty for reasons that do not preclude our adopting forms of imprisonment that are alternatives to it.

Chapter 22.1:

I. Here is a restatement of Mill's argument for freedom of expression:

If we prohibit the expression of an opinion that challenges our own view and that opinion is true or even partly true, we deprive ourselves of the chance to gain knowledge. If the opinion is false, we deprive ourselves of the chance to strengthen our own belief by learning how it is superior to the alternative view and we risk reducing our belief to a mere formal profession without rational basis. In either case, it is in our interest to allow the expression of views contrary to our own. (page 620)

Here is one possible reconstruction of the argument:

1. Suppose we prohibit the expression of an opinion that challenges our own view.

2. If the opinion we repress is true or partly true, then we deprive ourselves of the chance to gain knowledge.
3. If the opinion we repress is false, we deprive ourselves of the chance to strengthen our justification of our view and we risk reducing our belief to a formal profession with no rational basis.
4. It is in our interest to extend our knowledge, to strengthen our justification for our beliefs and to avoid reducing our beliefs to mere formal professions with no rational basis.
5. Therefore, if we prohibit the expression of an opinion that challenges our own view, we act contrary to our own interests.

II. Here is an argument of Mill's for not regulating the private realm:

The interference of society to overrule [an individual's] judgment and purposes in what only regards himself, must be grounded on general presumptions; which may be altogether wrong, and even if right, are as likely as not to be misapplied to individual cases . . . . All errors which [an individual] is likely to commit against advice and warning, are far outweighed by the evil of allowing others to constrain him to what they deem his good . . . (page 621)

Here is one possible reconstruction of the argument:

1. If a society regulates that part of our conduct that concerns only ourselves, it will base its regulation on general assumptions that are likely to be wrong or misapplied.
2. The evil that results from regulation of the private realm based on false or misapplied assumptions is likely to be greater than the evil that such regulation is designed to prevent.
3. Therefore, if a society regulates that part of our conduct that concerns only ourselves, it is likely to produce more evil than it prevents.

Chapter 22.2:

I. One argument Devlin presents for his view is the following:

Euthanasia or the killing of another at his own request, suicide, attempted suicide and suicide pacts, dueling, abortion, incest between brother and sister, are all acts which can be done in private and without offence to others and need not involve the corruption or exploitation of others. . . . [N]o one hitherto has suggested that they should all be left outside the criminal law as matters of private morality. They can be brought within it only as a matter of moral principle. (page 7)

Here is one possible reconstruction of his argument in the form of an inference to the best explanation:

1. Our society is justified in regulating the following activities, even though they do not pose a threat of harm or offense to others: euthanasia, suicide, attempted suicide and suicide pacts, dueling, abortion, incest between brother and sister.
2. Our justification in regulating these activities does not stem from a need to protect people from being harmed or offended.
3. The principle that every society has a right to legally enforce its public morality gives the best explanation of why we are justified in regulating these activities.
4. Therefore, the principle that every society has a right to legally enforce its public morality is true.

II. Devlin also argues for his view by an argument from analogy:

[A]n established morality is as necessary as good government to the welfare of society. Societies disintegrate from within more frequently than they are broken up by external pressures. There is disintegration when no common morality is observed and history shows that the loosening of moral bonds is often the first stage of disintegration, so that society is justified in taking the same steps to preserve its moral code as it does to preserve its government and other essential institutions. (page 628)

Here is one possible reconstruction of his argument:

1. Good government is necessary to the welfare of society, and certain activities (e.g., acts of treason) pose a threat to good government.
2. Society is justified in legally regulating those activities.

3. An established morality is necessary to the welfare of society, and certain activities (e.g., violations of the public morality) pose a threat to an established morality.
4. Therefore, society is justified in legally regulating violations of the public morality.

Chapter 22.3:

I. Roberts-Cady explains how John Stuart Mill appealed to the normative theory known as utilitarianism in order to defend the harm principle. Reconstruct the argument for the harm principle in the following passage:

Utilitarianism is a theory that begins with the assumption that all human beings are interested in being happy. It follows from this that we approve of actions or policies that will increase happiness and disapprove of actions or policies that decrease happiness. Mill argues that protecting individual liberties is the best way to create a happy world. (page 637)

Here is one possible reconstruction of her argument:

1. If utilitarianism is true, then we should implement policies that will result in the most happiness overall.
2. A policy protecting individual liberties will result in the most happiness overall.
3. Therefore, if utilitarianism is true, then we should implement the policy of protecting individual liberties.

II. According to Roberts-Cady, the harm principle might actually be used to defend a policy that allows women to wear the veil if they so choose even if it's true that doing so is inherently harmful. Reconstruct the argument for this conclusion:

Since Mill favors the strong protection of individual liberty, for him the only possible justification for government interference with wearing a full-face veil would be if banning the full-face veil was necessary to prevent people from harming each other. As noted above, Mill doesn't think government is justified in interfering with liberty in order to prevent someone from harming him or herself. Thus, Mill would be in favor of allowing women the freedom to choose to wear a full-face veil, even if it were harmful. (pages 638–639)

Here is one possible reconstruction of her argument:

1. The only cases of government interference that are justified are those in which one person harms another.
2. Not all cases of women wearing veils are cases in which one person harms another.
3. Therefore, the government is not justified in interfering in all cases of women wearing veils.

Chapter 22.4:

I. Longino argues that pornography, by its very nature, libels women:

> Pornography, by its very nature, requires that women be subordinate to men and mere instruments of the fulfillment of male fantasies. To accomplish this, pornography must lie. Pornography lies when it says that our sexual life is or ought to be subordinate to the service of men, that our pleasure consists in pleasing men and not ourselves, that we are depraved, that we are fit subjects for rape, bondage, torture and murder. Pornography lies explicitly about women's sexuality, and through such lies fosters more lies about our humanity, our dignity and our personhood. (page 649)

Here is one possible reconstruction of her reasoning:

1. Pornography, by definition, explicitly represents sexual behavior that is degrading or abusive of women so as to endorse such behavior.
2. In doing so, pornography intentionally presents vicious lies about women: that their sexual life is or ought to be subordinate to the service of men, that their pleasure consists in pleasing men and not themselves, that they are depraved and fit subjects for rape, bondage, torture and murder.
3. Through presenting these lies, pornography libels women.
4. Therefore, pornography, by its very nature, libels women.

II. Longino argues that society's tolerance of pornography adds to the injuries that it causes women:

> Society's tolerance of pornography, especially pornography on the contemporary massive scale, reinforces each of these modes of injury: By not disavowing the lie, it supports the male-centered myth that women are inferior and subordinate creatures. Thus, it contributes to the maintenance of a climate tolerant of both psychological and physical violence against women. (page 651)

Here is one possible reconstruction of her argument:

1. Pornography libels women by presenting a false view of them as inferior and subordinate creatures.
2. By tolerating pornography, society supports this false view.
3. By supporting this false view, society supports the toleration of psychological and physical violence against women.
4. Therefore, by tolerating pornography, society supports the toleration of psychological and physical violence against women.

Chapter 22.5

I. Here is one of Feinberg's arguments to show that violent pornography does not defame women in a way that justifies its legal repression:

> There is no doubt that much pornography does portray women in subservient positions, but if that is defamatory to women in anything like the legal sense, then so are soap commercials on TV. So are many novels, even some good ones. . . . That some groups are portrayed in unflattering roles has not hitherto been a ground for censorship of fiction or advertising. (page 659)

Here is one possible reconstruction of his argument:

1. If the portrayal of women as subservient in violent pornography defames them in a way that justifies its legal suppression, then so does the portrayal of women as subservient in advertisements and novels.

2. The portrayal of women as subservient in advertisements and novels does not defame them in a way that justifies its legal suppression.
3. Therefore, the portrayal of women as subservient in violent pornography does not defame them in a way that justifies its legal suppression.

II. Feinberg argues that the legal repression of violent pornography is unlikely to decrease violent crimes against women.

> [I]f the cult of the macho is main source of such violence, as I suspect, then repression of violent pornography, whose function is to pander to the macho values already deeply rooted in society, may have little effect. . . . Pornography-reading machos commit rape, but that is because they already have macho values, not because they read the violent pornography that panders to them. (page 662)

Here is one possible reconstruction of his argument.

1. Pornography-reading machos commit violent crimes against women because they have macho values.
2. Their viewing pornography does not cause them to have those values; their having those values causes them to view pornography.
3. If viewing pornography does not cause men to have the macho values that lead them to commit violent crimes against women, then the legal suppression of violent pornography is unlikely to decrease such crimes.
4. Therefore, the legal suppression of violent pornography is unlikely to decrease violent crimes against women.

READING CREDITS

P. 37: Gilbert Harmon, "Moral Nihilism," selection from *The Nature of Morality: An Introduction to Ethics* (1977), pp. 3-8, 11-16, 21, 23. By permission of Oxford University Press.

P.43: Russ Shafer-Landau, "Values in a Scientific World," selection from *Whatever Happened to Good and Evil?* (2003), pp. 91-101, 140. By permission of Oxford University Press.

P. 50: Russ, Shafer-Landau, "Four Arguments against Moral Knowledge," selection from *Whatever Happened to Good and Evil?* (2003), pp. 102-117. By permission of Oxford University Press.

P. 62: John Arthur, "Does Morality Depend upon Religion?," pp. 257-264, 266. © *John Arthur, 1980, reprinted by permission of Amy Shapiro, Executor, Estate of John Arthur, ashapiro@hhk.com.*

P. 69: Kai Nielsen, "Humanistic Ethics," selection from *Ethics Without God* (Prometheus Press, 1973), pp. 113-127.

P. 78: Friedrich Nietzsche, translated by R. J. Hollingdale, from *Beyond Good and Evil: Prelude to a Philosophy of the Future* (Penguin Classics, 1973). pp. 194-199. Reproduced with the permission of Penguin Books Ltd.

P. 81: Gilbert Harman, "Moral relativism," selection from *Moral Relativism and Moral Objectivity*, by Harman & Thomson (Blackwell, 1996), pp. 3-19.

P. 89: Paul Taylor, "Ethical Relativism and Ethical Absolutism," selection from *Principles of Ethics: An Introduction* (Wadsworth, 1975).

P. 101: Galen Strawson, "The Impossibility of Moral Responsibility," from *Philosophical Studies* 72, 1/2 (August, 1994), pp. 5-24.

P. 112: A. J. Ayer, "Freedom and Necessity," from *Philosophical Essays* (London: Macmillan, 1954), pp. 271-284.

P. 119: Roderick Chisholm, "Human Freedom and the Self," from The Lindley Lecture (1964), pp. 3-15. Copyright Lindley Lecture, University of Kansas, 1964.

P. 128: Jean-Paul Sartre, "Existentialism is a Humanism," selection from *Existentialism*, by Jean-Paul Sartre, translated by Bernard Frechtman (Kensington Publishing Group).

P. 138: Ayn Rand, "The Virtue of Selfishness," from *The Virtues of Selfishness* (NY: The New American Library, 1964), pp. ix-xv. Copyright © Penguin USA.

P. 142: James Rachels, "Three Failed Arguments for Ethical Egoism," from *The Elements of Moral Philosophy* (1999), pp. 84-95. Reproduced with permission of The McGraw-Hill Companies.

P. 149: Thomas Nagel, "Right and Wrong," from *What Does It All Mean? A Very Short Introduction to Philosophy* (1987), pp. 59-71, 73-75. By permission of Oxford University Press.

P. 156: Gregory Kavka, "A Reconciliation Project," from *Morality, Reason and Truth* (1984), ed. D. Copp and D. Zimmerman, pp. 297-319. Reproduced with permission of Rowman and Littlefield Publishers, Inc.

P. 177: Richard Taylor, "The Meaning of Life," from *Good and Evil*, revised edition, by Richard Taylor (NY: Prometheus Books, 2000), pp. 319-334.

P. 184: Robert Nozick, "The Experience Machine," *Anarchy, State, and Utopia* (Basic Books, 1974), pp. 42-45.

P. 187: Derek Parfit, "What Makes Someone's Life Go Best," selection from *Reasons and Persons*.

P. 194: John Stuart Mill, "Utilitarianism," selection from *Utilitarianism* (1863).

P. 204: Kai Nielsen, "Against Moral Conservatism," from *Ethics*, vol. 82, No. 3 (April, 1972), pp. 219-231. Reproduced with permission of Kai Nielsen.

P. 449: Brian Barry, "Sustainability and Intergenerational Justice," from *Theoria* (1997), pp. 43-64.

P. 455: Thomas Hill, "Ideals of Human Excellence and Preserving Natural Environments," from *Environmental* Ethics, vol. 5 (1983), pp. 211-224. Reproduced by permission of the Center for Environmental Philosophy.

P. 466: Mark Sagoff, "Do We Consume Too Much?" revised from *Atlantic Monthly* 279 (1997), pp. 80-96. Reproduced by permission of the author.

P. 480: Lester W. Milbrath, "Redefining the Good Life in a Sustainable Society," from *Environmental Values* 2 (1993), pp. 261-269. Reproduced by permission of The White Horse Press.

P. 490: Peter Singer, "Famine, Affluence and Morality," from *Philosophy and Public Affairs*, vol. 32, 1 (1972), pp. 229-243. Reproduced with permission of Blackwell Publishing Ltd.

P. 497: John Arthur, "Famine Relief and the Ideal Moral Code." © John Arthur, 1996, reprinted by permission of Amy Shapiro, Executor, Estate of John Arthur, ashapiro@hhk.com.

P. 508: Jan Narveson, "Feeding the Hungry," selection from *Moral Madness*, 2e (1999), pp. 143-156. Copyright © 1993 by Jan Narveson. Reprinted by permission of Broadview Press.

P. 519: Michael Walzer, "Terrorism: A Critique of Excuses," from *Arguing About War* (2004), pp. 51-66. Reproduced by permission of Yale University Press.

P. 527: Lionel K. McPherson, "Is Terrorism Distinctively Wrong?" from *Ethics* 117 (2007), pp. 524-526. Reproduced by permission of the author.

P. 538: David Luban, "The War on Terrorism and the End of Human Rights," from *Philosophy and Public Policy Quarterly* 22:3 (Summer, 2002), pp. 9-14.

P. 547: Seumas Miller, "Is Torture Ever Morally Justifiable?" from *International Journal of Applied Philosophy* 19:2 (Fall, 2005), pp. 179-192. Reproduced by permission of the International Journal of Applied Philosophy.

P. 554: David J. Hill, "Ticking Bombs, Torture, and the Analogy with Self-Defense," from *American Philosophical Quarterly* 44:4 (2007), pp. 395-404. Reproduced by permission of North American Philosophical Publications.

P. 563: James Rachels, "Active and Passive Euthanasia," from *New England Journal of Medicine* 292 (1975), pp. 78-80.

P. 569: Thomas D. Sullivan, "Active and Passive Euthanasia: An Impertinent Distinction?" from *Human Life Review* 3:3 (1977), pp. 40-46. Reproduced by permission of the author.

P. 574: Thomas E. Hill, Jr., "Self-Regarding Suicide: A Modified Kantian View," from *Autonomy and Self-Respect* (1991), pp. 85-103. Reprinted with the permission of Cambridge University Press.

P. 583: Carl B. Becker, "Buddhist Views of Suicide and Euthanasia," from *Philosophy East and West* 40:4 (1990), pp. 543-556. Reproduced by permission of the University of Hawai'i Press Journals.

P. 593: Igor Primoratz, "Justifying Capital Punishment," from *Justifying Legal Punishment* (Humanity Books, 1989), pp. 155-159, 161-169.

P. 600: Hugo Adam Bedau, "The Case Against the Death Penalty" (American Civil Liberties Union, 1973; 2012).

P. 617: John Stuart Mill, "The Harm Principle," selection from *On Liberty*, Chapters I and IV.

P. 626: Patrick Devlin, "Morals and the Criminal Law," from *Morals and the Criminal Law*, Maccabean Lecture in Jurisprudence read at the British Academy on March 18, 1959, printed in the Proceedings of the British Academy, vol. XLV (1965), pp. 4-11, 13-18, 20, 22. By permission of Oxford University Press.

P. 635: Sarah Roberts-Cady, "France and the Ban on the Full-Face Veil: A Philosophical Analysis of the Arguments." By permission of the author.

P. 646: Helen E. Longino, "Pornography, Oppression and Freedom: A Closer Look," from *Take Back the Night*, ed. Lederer (William Morrow & Co., 1980), pp. 41-54, © Helen E. Longino, 1979. By permission.

P. 656: Joel Feinberg, "The Feminist Case Against Pornography," from *Offense to Others* (1988), pp. 143-159, 161-162. By permission of Oxford University Press.

INDEX